S0-BCL-753

Introduction to Special Education

Introduction to Special Education

Making a Difference

SIXTH EDITION

Deborah Deutsch Smith
Peabody College
Vanderbilt University

Boston • New York • San Francisco • Mexico City • Montreal • Toronto • London • Madrid
Munich • Paris • Hong Kong • Singapore • Tokyo • Cape Town • Sydney

Executive Editor: *Virginia Lanigan*
Series Editorial Assistant: *Scott Blaszak*
Developmental Editor: *Alicia Reilly*
Marketing Manager: *Kris Ellis-Levy*
Production Manager: *Elaine Ober*
Composition and Prepress Buyer: *Linda Cox*
Manufacturing Buyer: *Megan Cochran*
Cover Administrator: *Linda Knowles*
Photo and Fine Art Researcher: *Helane M. Prottas/Posh Pictures*
Editorial Production Service: *Barbara Gracia*
Interior Design: *Schawk, Inc.*
Electronic Composition: *Schawk, Inc.*

For related titles and support materials, visit our online catalog at www.ablongman.com

Between the time Web site information is gathered and published, some sites may have closed. Also, the transcription of URLs can result in typographical errors. The publisher would appreciate notification where these occur so that they may be corrected in subsequent editions.

Library of Congress Cataloging-in-Publication Data was not available at press time.

ISBN 0-205-47469-1

Printed in the United States of America
10 9 8 7 6 5 4 3 2 1—VHP—10 09 08 07 06

PHOTO CREDITS:
Chapter 1: P. 6, logo and photo courtesy of the Open Doors Organization; p. 7, courtesy of Guide Dogs for the Blind; p. 15, Lydia Gans/World Institute on Disability; p. 16, (left) © Alison Wright/Robert Harding World Imagery; (right) Tim Olis/National Organization on Disability; p. 17, (top) The Kobal Collection; (bottom) PhotoFest; p. 23, logo courtesy of the National Organization on Disability; p. 24, Associated Press, White House; p. 26, Lawrence Jackson/AP/Wide World Photos; p. 30, © James Shaffe/PhotoEdit; p. 31, © Richard Hutchins/PhotoEdit; p. 35 and ix, © Ted Thai/Time Life Pictures/GettyImages.
Chapter 2: P. 43, courtesy of CAST (Center for Applied Special Technology) and used with permission; p. 44, © Christopher Churchill Photography; p. 47, © Tom Lindfors/Lindfors Photography; p. 55, (left, center, right) courtesy of Rick Slaughter; p. 60, © Mary Kate Denny/PhotoEdit; p. 64, © Michael Newman/PhotoEdit; p. 65, © Michael Newman/PhotoEdit; p. 67, © Robin Nelson/PhotoEdit; p. 72 and ix, © Tom Lindfors/Lindfors Photography.
Chapter 3: (top and bottom) courtesy of the Children's Defense Fund; p. 82, (left) Kevork Djansezian/AP/Wide World Photos; (right) © A. Ramey/PhotoEdit; p. 87, © David Grossman/The Image Works; p. 88, © Myrleen Ferguson Cate/PhotoEdit; p. 93, © Tom Lindfors/Lindfors Photography; p. 101, Associated Press, United Cerebral Palsy; p. 109, © Geri Engberg; p. 111 and x, © Michael Mancuso/Omni-Photo Communications, Inc.
Chapter 4: P. 119, Kobal Collection; p. 120, © Tom Lindfors/Lindfors Photography; p. 121, (left) courtesy of Rick Slaughter; (right) courtesy of Lizzz B; p. 128, © Ellen Senisi/The Image Works; p. 136, logo © Operation Smile. Used with permission; p. 137, Marc Ascher, © Operation Smile; p. 139, © Christina Kennedy/PhotoEdit; p. 141, © Nancy Sheehan Photography; p. 151 and x, Daniel Barbier/The Image Bank/Gettylages.
Chapter 5: P. 160 (top) logo courtesy © Schwab Learning; (bottom) Jim Sulley/Medialink. Courtesy of Schwab Learning. Used with permission; p. 163, Photodisk/GettyImages, Inc.; pp. 165 and 452, *Maeve Kaplan-Taylor* and *Kelly/* Illustrated by Pamela Merriam Esty. Copyright © 2005 by B*tween Productions, Inc. Home of the Beach Street Girls. Beacon Street Girls, Kgirl, B*tween Productions, B*Street and the characters Maeve, Kelly, Avery, Charlotte, Isabel, Katani,

Photo credits are continued on page vi and considered an extension of the copyright page.

To all those who have made a difference in my life
and
in the lives of students with disabilities and their families

Photo credits continued

Marty, Nick, Anna, Joline, and Happy Lucky Thingy are registered trademarks and/or copyrights of B*tween Productions, Inc.; p. 167, © Bill Aron/PhotoEdit; p. 172, © Michael Newman/PhotoEdit; p. 178, © Tom Lindfors/Lindfors Photography; p. 183, © Frank Siteman; p. 189, © Jonathan Nouack/PhotoEdit; p. 195 and xi, © David Young-Wolff/PhotoEdit.

Chapter 6: P. 203, © Ellen B. Senisi/The Image Works; p. 204 (left) photo courtesy of David Flink; (right) photo courtesy of Jonathan Mooney; p. 208, Used by permission of HarperCollins Publishers; p. 209, © David Young-Wolff/PhotoEdit; p. 212, Stephen Chernin/© 2003 GettyImages, Inc.; p. 216, © Myrleen Ferguson Cate/PhotoEdit; p. 218, © Spencer Grant/PhotoEdit; p. 227 and xi, Mike Powell/Taxi/GettyImages, Inc.

Chapter 7: P. 237, PhotoFest; p. 241, © Michael Newman/PhotoEdit; p. 252, © Ellen Senisi/The Image Works; p. 255, © Michael Newman/PhotoEdit; p. 257, © Mary Kate Denny/PhotoEdit; p. 259, © Peter Hvizdak/The Image Works; p. 267, © Michelle D. Bridwell/PhotoEdit; p. 269 and xii, Joel Sartore/National Geographic/GettyImages, Inc.

Chapter 8: P. p. 276, Reprinted with permission by Cathy Alexander. Special thanks to her and her daughter, Angie; p. 277, Brian Hamill/GettyImages, Inc.; p. 278, Best Buddies ® logo used with permission of Best Buddies International; (photo, left) Manny Hernandez/Online USA/GettyImages, Inc.; (photo, right) used with permission of Best Buddies International; p. 285, © Paul Conklin/PhotoEdit; p. 287, Paul Kenney/Liaison International; p. 289, PhotoFest; p. 291, (left) cover courtesy of Little, Brown and Company. Used with permission; (right) Rich Pedroncelli/AP/Wide World Photos; p. 293, © Paul Conklin/PhotoEdit; p. 295, courtesy of Downi Creations; p. 296, © Elizabeth Crews/The Image Works; p. 304, *The Tennessean*/Larry McCormack; p. 307 and xii, © Jonathan Nouack/PhotoEdit.

Chapter 9: P. 315, (left) Stephen Shugerman/© 2005 GettyImages, Inc.; (right) HBO/PhotoFest © HBO/Photographer: Bob Greene; p. 316, © Rudi von Briel/PhotoEdit; p. 317, Patricia McDonnell/AP/Wide World Photos; p. 322, AP Photo/*West Hawaii Today*, Michael Darden/AP/Wide World Photos; p. 325, PhotoFest; p. 334, AP Photo/*The Plain Dealer*/Scott Shaw/AP/Wide World Photos; p. 335, BARBIE ®, BECKY ® and associated trademarks are owned by and used with permission of Mattel, Inc. © 2002, Mattel, Inc. All rights reserved; p. 342, Jane Kamin-Oncea/*The Los Angeles Times*; p. 343, courtesy of Rick Slaughter; p. 345 and xiii, Robert Holland/The Image Bank/GettyImages, Inc.

Chapter 10: P. 353, Adam Schafer/Gallaudet University; p. 354, logo courtesy of Gallaudet University; (left) John Consoli/Gallaudet University; (right) Ralph Fernandez/Gallaudet University; p. 358, BARBIE ®, BECKY ® and associated trademarks are owned by and used with permission of Mattel, Inc. All rights reserved; p. 360, Gino Domenico/AP/Wide World Photos; p. 361, Nati Harnik/AP/ Wide World Photos; p. 368, Courtesy of PhonicEar ®, Inc.; p. 370, photo courtesy of the National Captioning Institute; p. 376, From *Dina the Deaf Dinosaur* by Carole Addabbo; illustrated by Valentinue. Stamford, CT: Hannacroix Creek Books. Text copyright © 1998 by Carole Addabbo; Illustrations copyright © 1998 by Patti Zimmer (Valentine). Reprinted with permission; p. 379, © Syracuse Newspapers/Gary Walts/The Image Works; p. 387 and xiii, Larry Steagall/AP/Wide World Photos.

Chapter 11: P. 394, Universal/The Kobal Collection/Nicola Goode; p. 396, (top) photo courtesy of Marsha Miller; (bottom) © ABC Photography Archives. Copyright © 2005 ABC, Inc. All rights reserved; p. 397, (left) © ABC Photo Archives. Photo: Tom Queally. Copyright © 2005 ABC, Inc. All rights reserved; (right) © 2004 ABC, Inc. Photographer: Douglas Ashley/PhotoFest; p. 401, Greg Wahl-Stevens/AP/Wide World Photos; p. 402 (left and right) Joe McNally/Sygma; p. 404, Bill Schaefer/AP/Wide World Photos; p. 406, *The Tennessean*; p. 409 and 411, Photos courtesy of HumanWare™; p. 420, Courtesy of Michael Naranjo and KNME TV of Albuquerque, New Mexico; p. 424 and xiv, © Jamie Bloomquist/Jamie Bloomquist Photography.

Chapter 12: P. 430, Will Hart; p. 435, Photo by Carol Guzy © 1997, *The Washington Post*. Reprinted with permission; p. 442, © Jason Fulford; p. 454 and xiv, Rob Lewine/The Stock Market.

Chapter 13: P. 460, Library of Congress; p. 461, Bruce Allan/AFP/GettyImages, Inc.; p. 462, Photo and poster courtesy of Anthony di Salvo; p. 464, courtesy of Cheryl and Greg Richter; p. 465, photo courtesy of Rick Slaughter; p. 473, Associated Press/Prudential Health Care/Brett Conner; p. 483, courtesy of Easter Seal A.B.L.E. of Tennessee; p. 484, courtesy of Quisenberry Arcari Architects, LLC/Tom Arcari and Winter & Company, LLC/John Dickinson; p. 485, photo courtesy of Rick Slaughter; p. 487 and xv, © Michael Neman/PhotoEdit.

Chapter 14: P. 495, Special Collections, Milbank Memorial Library, Teachers College, Columbia University; p. 496 (left and right) © Chip East/Reuters/Corbis; p. 497, (left) Thos Robinson/© 2004 GettyImages, Inc.; (right) Adamsmith/TAXI/GettyImages, Inc.; p. 503, © Tom Lindfors/Lindfors Photography; p. 506, photo courtesy of Rick Slaughter; p. 508, Keith Srakocic/AP/Wide World Photos; p. 511, © Geri Engbery Photography; p. 517, © David Young-Wolff/PhotoEdit; p. 521, © Fox/PhotoFest; p. 523 and xv, GettyImages, Inc./STONE/Allstock

Brief Contents

Contents

CHAPTER 3

CHAPTER 4

CHAPTER 9

CHAPTER 10

CHAPTER 13

CHAPTER 14

Selected Features

Accommodating for Inclusive Environments

Changing Times

Considering Culture

Disabilities in the News

On the Screen

In the Spotlight

Tips for Classroom Management

Tips for Effective Teaching

Validated Practices

What IDEA '04 Says About

What NCLB Says About

Preface

Henry Adams once said that "a teacher affects eternity; he can never tell where his influence stops." More than ever before, educators have the opportunity and ability to make a real difference in the educational experiences of their students with disabilities, as they help them prepare for happy and productive lives as adults. Today's educators have available to them an increasing number of promising and evidence-based instructional practices that they can implement with confidence in their classrooms. Effective teachers use these tools, which help students of *all* abilities—from the most struggling to the most gifted—master important skills so they may reach their full potential. Advances in technology have remarkable applications for people with disabilities and provide opportunities for greater participation at school, and in life beyond the school setting, than ever before. Contemporary inclusive school practices not only have positively influenced how we think and act but also have changed many outcomes for people with disabilities. More and more adults with disabilities, even those with the most complex problems, live independently, work alongside people without disabilities, and maintain an active and meaningful presence in the community. These inclusive practices also prepare students without disabilities for the more inclusive society that is clearly our future. Social responsibility and activism, philanthropy, and volunteerism provide the framework for all members of society to support individuals with disabilities.

In addition to presenting practical applications of current special education research and promising practices for educating exceptional learners, this edition of *Introduction to Special Education* also reflects a theme of advocacy, examining how each of us can make a difference in the lives of others, whether we are teachers, education professionals, parents, classmates, or neighbors. For those who realize what a difference they can make, all it takes is goodwill and some basic knowledge to see the opportunity, seize the opportunity, and do the right thing.

Since the first edition of this text was published some 15 years ago, life for individuals with disabilities has changed dramatically. The results of 40 years of continuing research and development of effective practices, 30 years of the special education law—the *Individuals with Disabilities Education Act* (IDEA), 15 years of the *Americans with Disabilities Act* (ADA), and many years of social activism have had positive effects on the lives of individuals with disabilities and their families. Normalized participation for people with disabilities—a dream only a few decades ago—is today part of the American scene. Although there is considerable room for improvement, TV, film, advertising, and literature reflect changes that people with disabilities experience and expect today. Sometimes they are central figures in the feature or story, as were Ray Charles in the movie *Ray* and President Franklin Delano Roosevelt in the HBO movie *Warm Springs.* But increasingly, people with disabilities are appearing in supporting roles, such as in the TV shows *Las Vegas, ER,* and *CSI,* where the presence of these individuals is just part of everyday life; each is simply one more person who is involved in the action. In such cases, their inclusion is not portrayed as unusual or out of the ordinary, and their disability is incidental to the story. Such portrayals reflect advances in the rates at which people with disabilities now hold jobs and participate in all aspects of society. In large part, these advances may be attributed to successes achieved at schools where students with disabilities are taught the skills they need to assume their rightful places in the workforce and the community. And yet, even though the presence of people with disabilities is becoming an expectation of normal, daily life, these achievements offer only a glimmer of what's on the horizon.

Organization and Features

In this edition, a *new standard chapter outline* that better reflects current knowledge, validated and promising practices, and IDEA requirements provides the framework for each chapter. I particularly wanted to emphasize the voices of people with disabilities and their successes, along with the power that education professionals have to make a difference in the lives of students with disabilities and of their families. Accordingly,

- Every chapter begins with a *beautiful piece of art* created by a person with a disability.
- Inspiring quotations that should give us all much to think about immediately follow the chapter title.
- Questions raised in the *chapter objectives* of each chapter are answered in the summary section near the end of that chapter.
- Opening sections in each chapter, which are titled *Where We've Been . . . What's on the Horizon?* provide historical context and perspective and hint at what the future may well hold for people with disabilities.
- These opening sections conclude with a section called *Making a Difference,* where you will learn about individuals and organizations that provide examples of social responsibility and effective advocacy.
- Each chapter's *In the Spotlight* feature introduces a person with a disability, a family member, or individuals whose efforts benefit people with disabilities.

1

Disabilities and Special Education: Making a Difference

"So you're saying there is definitely prejudice against [people with disabilities], no doubt about it."

—Larry King

"I think it's an old habit we haven't gotten over yet. I think we will, though, and we need to get that message out, that [people with disabilities] can do much more than [people] think, if we ever give them a chance."

—Christopher Reeve

During this academic term you will study students who don't always learn in typical ways. You will find that students with disabilities require a unique response to their education. You will examine educational systems and services that respond to learners' with very special needs and will see how teachers and education professionals can and do make real differences in the educational outcomes of students with disabilities. Most important, you will come to understand that even those who face the most difficult challenges can and do overcome, compensate, and achieve remarkable outcomes. These results occur when the education they are provided is responsive to the learning situations they bring to the educational system. Before thinking about appropriate educational responses to disabilities—special education—let's consider what disabilities are and the challenges they create.

Chapter Objectives

After studying this chapter, you will be able to:

1. Explain the concepts of "disability" and "handicapped."
2. Describe how the lives of people with disabilities have improved across time.
3. Discuss barriers and challenges that are experienced today by people with disabilities and need to be overcome, and explain how all of us can make a difference.
4. Explain why the federal government provides unique protections for students with disabilities and their families.
5. Explain the key features or fundamental tenets of special education.

Where We've Been . . . What's on the Horizon?

The stories of people with disabilities begin with the earliest record of human history. Throughout time, and even today, these stories are filled with inconsistencies about treatment, acceptance, and success. Although the ancient Greek philosopher Aristotle supported a law that allowed no "deformed" child to live, evidence from ancient Egypt shows that many individuals with disabilities were respected and even given privileged status (Safford & Safford, 1996). Sometimes people with disabilities (particularly individuals with significant visual and hearing problems) were merely considered "odd" or "eccentric" or were accepted as being "just a bit different" (Bragg, 1997). But, both across time and across societies, most people with disabilities were treated terribly. It is important for everyone to know about those awful past events to ensure that such personal tragedies will never happen again. We must all understand how vulnerable people with disabilities are to the harshness of public opinion and the cruelty of others'

3

Where We've Been . . . What's on the Horizon? **317**

vices, such as dialysis
g, boating, sailing, and
g wheelchair basketball,
rs.
se wheelchairs as well as
es seek out travelers
have special seats or
abilities are no longer a
partment buildings with
v provide alternatives to
ch a place in Allentown,
ends who also live in the
droom to the bathroom
for people with limited
and dryer are combined
s from one machine to
another. The water taps and temperature adjustments are controlled with push buttons instead of faucets. And countertops are at the right level for someone who cannot stand. You would think that such living arrangements would be exorbitantly expensive. Not so when you consider that it is almost two and a half times more expensive to live in a nursing home and that, with assistance from the federal government, Judy pays only $500 per month in rent and enjoys the freedom of independent living immensely.

Making a Difference

The Hole in the Wall Camps

For many children, attending camp is a highpoint of their year. They look forward to the outdoor experience where they can meet new friends and participate in activities such as canoeing, telling stories and roasting marshmallows by a fire in the evening, hiking in the woods, swimming in a lake, and learning more about themselves. For children with chronic or life-threatening illnesses, going to summer camp was an impossible dream, because typical camps do not provide the medical attention they needed and because they felt too different from campers without special health care needs. Until 1988, no camps met the needs of these youngsters or their families.

In 1986 Paul Newman had a vision to make camping experiences available to children with chronic medical problems any time of the year and provide their families with a much-needed respite from constantly caring for their sick children. The first Hole in the Wall Camp opened in Connecticut. Revolving around a wild-west theme, it provides campers with a week-long experience where all their medical needs can be met free of cost to the campers and their families.

Staffed by hundreds of volunteers—including doctors, nurses, and camp counselors—more Hole in the Wall Camps followed in New York (Double H Ranch), Florida (Camp Boggie Creek), North Carolina (Victory Junction Gang), and California (Painted Turtle Camp). Camps have also been created in Ireland, France, Africa, and the Middle East. Almost 100,000 seriously ill children from 34 states and 27 countries have participated in these state-of-the-art programs.

To learn more about all of the Hole in the Wall Camps, to see videos of campers enjoying the facilities, to hear Paul Newman describe his joy about making a difference, and to learn how you might become involved, visit www.holeinthewallcamps.org

www.ablongman.com/smith6e

Speech or Language Impairments Defined **121**

Lizzy B in the Spotlight

Lizzy B is a busy middle schooler although her cerebral palsy affects her ability to control her muscles. 11-year-old Lizzy B won the statewide competition and represented Tennessee at the national Young Entrepreneurs annual competition in Minnesota. When people first meet Lizzy B, they often find her speech difficult to understand, but her skills using some pretty complicated speech technology are always expanding. She was recently inducted into the National Junior Honor Society, is active in Girl Scouts, and is learning how to walk in high heels using her walker (not an easy task). Despite her ambitious schedule, after attending the CEO Academy's Fun Shop camp, she decided to start her own business. Amy, Lizzy B's mom, says,

Lizzy B started her card business because she wanted to have greeting cards that showed kids like her, with disability, doing things like regular kids. She never could find any cards that showed children with disabilities. It has been very successful for her, and I think it has really accomplished more than simply showing people with disabilities doing everyday things. It has really opened other people's eyes to the abilities of young people with disabilities.

- Practical applications of classroom techniques are highlighted in recurring features entitled *Accommodating for Inclusive Environments, Validated Practices, Tips for Classroom Management,* and *Tips for Effective Teaching.*

168 Chapter 5 ~ *Learning Disabilities*

tips for Classroom Management

TEACHERS HELPING STUDENTS WITH LEARNING DISABILITIES MAKE FRIENDS

Explicitly Teach

- Rules of playground games
- Comprehension of nonverbal expressions
- Social conventions
- When to terminate a conversation
- How to ask permission to join an ongoing game
- Sharing skills

Pair with a Class-Buddy

- Match students with similar interests
- Create opportunities
- Reward both members of the pair for working and playing together
- Change pairs once a month

Two general reasons account for these students' difficulties developing social competence:

1 Relationships among learning disabilities, language impairments, pragmatics, and social competence
2 The downward spiral of academic failure to positive peer relationships

For some students, impairment in social skills is part of their learning disability (Wiener, 2004). Those students
whose language impairment during t
hindered their developing pragmatics
pages 128 and 142 in Chapter 4) o
understanding others' nonverbal beha
guage effectively in social situations (O
Timler, 2001). These students cannot
bal behaviors, such as facial expression
not comprehend other people's e
(Teglasi, Cohn, & Meshbesher, 2004). R
tionship between social competence a
ments is clear. Poor language skills i
communicate, and communicative com
for social interaction (Elksnin & Elksnin
petence is related, in one way or anot

www.mylabschool.com ~ *Teaching Students with Mental Retardation* 297

Accommodating for Inclusive Environments

Steps for Success in a Modified General Education Curriculum

Specify the Instructional Objectives

- List the objectives in observable terms such that they will communicate to others.
- Focus the objectives on what is directly the instructional target.
- Plan how the objectives will be evaluated to ensure continued student progress.

Sequence Skills

- Be sure prerequisite skills are mastered first.
- Sequence easy skills before more difficult ones.
- Plan to teach confusing concepts separately.

Match Instructional Tactic with Topic or Skill to Be Taught

- Select a tactic that has been proven through rigorous research.
- Monitor its effectiveness continuously.
- Change tactics when it is no longer effective.

Provide Many Opportunities for Practice

- Have students apply their learning in different settings.
- Have students apply their learning with slightly different or expanded tasks or skills.

Be Certain That the Skill Is Truly Mastered

- Have the student demonstrate mastery when performing the skill independently.
- Have the student demonstrate mastery in a variety of settings.

www.mylabschool.com

Validated Practices Effective Teaching Behaviors

What Are Effective Teaching Behaviors?

Effective teaching behaviors are used to increase students' on-task behaviors and academic performance. When effective teaching behaviors are implemented, both you and your students are actively engaged in the learning process.

Why Effective Teaching Behaviors Are Beneficial

When teachers implement effective teaching behaviors, students' engaged learning time is increased; and the more time students are actively engaged in learning, the more they learn. Moreover, when students are engaged in learning, classroom disruption decreases. Several studies have demonstrated that when teachers use praise, call on students often, and engage their students in learning by including questioning and scaffolding in their instruction, not only do problem behaviors lessen, but academic achievement increases as well.

Implementing Effective Teaching Behaviors

The five steps of effective teaching behaviors are (1) planning, (2) starting the lesson, (3) presenting the lesson (4) closing the lesson, and (5) reflecting. Each step is described next.

Planning

- Decide what you want your students to know by the end of the lesson; remember that individual students may have different goals.
- Be sure you feel comfortable teaching the topic and answering questions.
- Determine what resources you will need to carry out the lesson.
- Decide how much time you will spend on the lesson.

Starting the Lesson

- Have all your materials ready and close by before beginning your lesson.
- Begin instruction promptly.
- Get the students' attention (e.g., by turning lights on and off and saying, "It's time for math").
- Provide your students with an advance organizer (e.g., "Today, we are going to . . ., and I expect you to. . . .").
- Begin with a review from a previously taught lesson.
- Assess students' background and knowledge of the lesson's topic.

Presenting the Lesson

- Maintain a brisk pace, but one that isn't so fast that you lose your students.
- Provide a demonstration and guided practice activities before students work independently.
- Allow for independent practice once students have achieved 80 to 90 percent accuracy during the guided practice phase.
- Ask factual questions, one at a time.
- Ask questions that draw on reasoning skills.
- Recognize students' responses by providing praise or corrective feedback.
- Probe students for answers and provide scaffolding.
- Give specific academic praise (e.g., "I like the way you are reading today").
- Be enthusiastic while teaching; show interest (e.g., smile, gesture).
- Orient students to the academic task; refocus unrelated talk.
- Enforce classroom rules; remind students about the classroom rules.
- Be consistent with your consequences (follow through).
- Give specific directives (e.g., "Read page 4").
- Use surface management techniques (e.g., proximity, redirect, "the look," call out student's name, state expected behavior).
- Give specific praise for good behavior (e.g., "Thank you for raising your hand").
- Circulate among your students while they are working independently.

Closing the Lesson

- Review the day's lesson.
- Introduce tomorrow's lesson.

Reflecting

- Ask yourself, "How did the lesson go?" "What went well?" "What should I continue?" "What needs to be changed for next time?"
- Evaluate your instruction and the students' performance.
- Decide what, if anything, needs to be retaught.

This scientifically validated practice is a teaching method proven by systematic research efforts (Englert, Tarrant, & Mariage, 1992; Espin, & Yell, 1994; Rosenshine, 1995; Sutherland, 2000; Sutherland, Wehby, & Copeland, 2000; Wehby, Symons, Canale, & Go, 1998). Full citations are found in the references for this chapter at the end of the book.

—By Kimberly Paulsen, Vanderbilt University

w.mylabschool.com ~ *Collaboration* 385

Collaboration

e essential service needed by many deaf students enrolled in general education
grams is assistance with the translation of spoken English. **Educational inter-
eters** are those related service providers who convert spoken messages into the
dent's preferred communication system, which may be a signed system such as
L or signed English. For many teachers, working with the assistance of an inter-
ter is a novel experience that might occur only once in their teaching career. For
teacher inexperienced in working with students who use sign language, there is
ch to learn, plan for, and coordinate (Williams & Finnegan, 2003). And for many interpreters, working with students in school settings is also a unique experience (Linehan, 2000). A close working relationship is required between this related service provider and teachers, where the interpreter needs to learn academic content and the teacher needs to learn how to work with a translator. Table 10.3 shows the roles and responsibilities of the classroom teacher, the educational interpreter, and the student. Everyone has important issues to consider when students with profound hearing losses and their educational interpreters learn and work together in inclusive educational settings.

The teacher and the interpreter need to coordinate efforts to ensure that they understand each other's roles. *Tips for Effective Teaching* provides some useful

tips for Effective Teaching

WORKING WITH EDUCATIONAL INTERPRETERS

Planning and Organization

- Interpreters and teachers set up standard meeting times.
- They have established clear roles for working together during instruction.
- All meetings regarding the student are scheduled when the student's interpreter can attend.
- Storage and working space are designated for the interpreter.
- Lesson plans and supporting materials are shared days before the instructional activity.
- Teachers and interpreters have time to meet before the instructional activity to clarify vocabulary and content.

Classroom Organization and Management

- The interpreter and the student are able to see the teacher and each other.
- Placement for the interpreter is not distracting to the student's classmates.
- Glare and other visual obstructions are eliminated.

Courtesy and Social Conventions

- Everyone talks directly to the student.
- Eye contact is with the student, not with the interpreter (even when the interpreter is speaking and translating manual communication for the student).
- The interpreter is not an academic tutor or classroom manager who resolves disruption.
- Invite the interpreter to teach the class some sign language or share Deaf literature.

educational interpreters Related service providers for deaf students; translate or convert spoken messages to the deaf person's preferred mode of manual communication

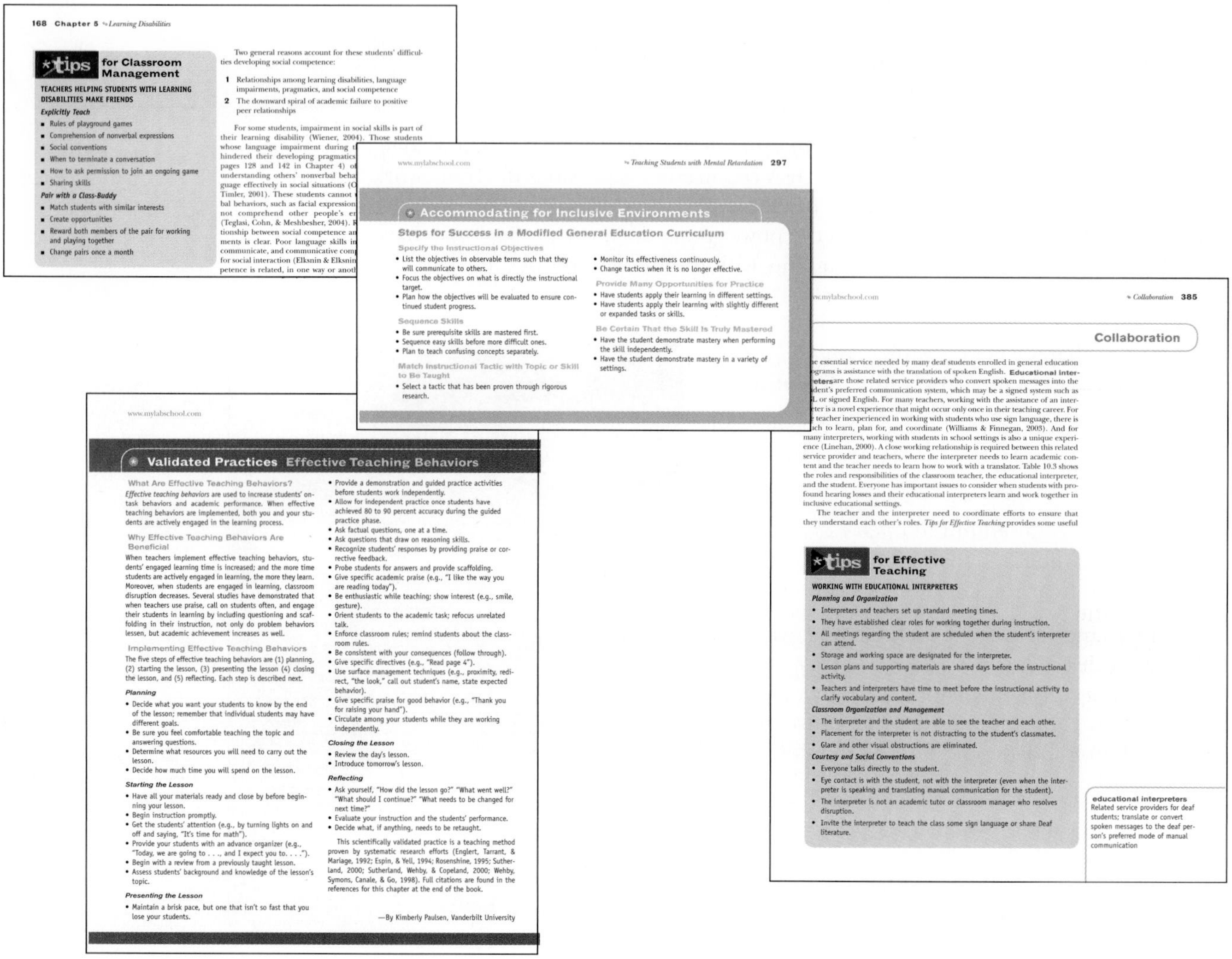

- *Considering Culture* provides mini-cases for educators to ponder that address the diversity of perspectives, background, and experience.

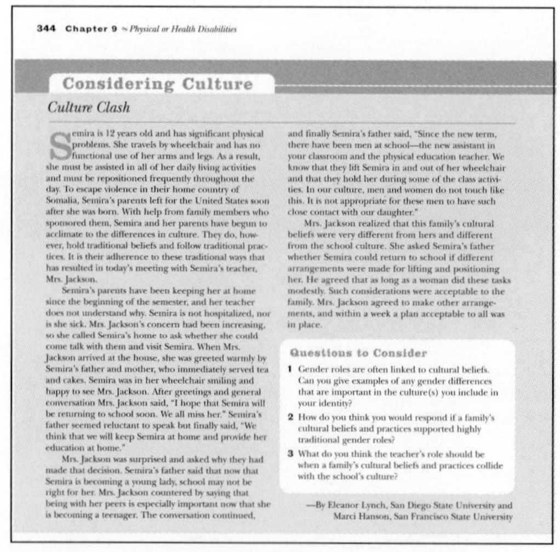

344 Chapter 9 ~ *Physical or Health Disabilities*

Considering Culture

Culture Clash

Semira is 12 years old and has significant physical problems. She travels by wheelchair and has no functional use of her arms and legs. As a result, she must be assisted in all of her daily living activities and must be repositioned frequently throughout the day. To escape violence in their home country of Somalia, Semira's parents left for the United States soon after she was born. With help from family members who sponsored them, Semira and her parents have begun to acclimate to the differences in culture. They do, however, hold traditional beliefs and follow traditional practices. It is their adherence to these traditional ways that has resulted in today's meeting with Semira's teacher, Mrs. Jackson.

Semira's parents have been keeping her at home since the beginning of the semester, and her teacher does not understand why. Semira is not hospitalized, nor is she sick. Mrs. Jackson's concern had been increasing, so she called Semira's home to ask whether she could come talk with them and visit Semira. When Mrs. Jackson arrived at the house, she was greeted warmly by Semira's father and mother, who immediately served tea and cakes. Semira was in her wheelchair smiling and happy to see Mrs. Jackson. After greetings and general conversation Mrs. Jackson said, "I hope that Semira will be returning to school soon. We all miss her." Semira's father seemed reluctant to speak but finally said, "We think that we will keep Semira at home and provide her education at home."

Mrs. Jackson was surprised and asked why they had made that decision. Semira's father said that now that Semira is becoming a young lady, school may not be right for her. Mrs. Jackson countered by saying that being with her peers is especially important now that she is becoming a teenager. The conversation continued, and finally Semira's father said, "Since the new term, there have been men at school—the new assistant in your classroom and the physical education teacher. We know that they lift Semira in and out of her wheelchair and that they hold her during some of the class activities. In our culture, men and women do not touch like this. It is not appropriate for these men to have such close contact with our daughter."

Mrs. Jackson realized that this family's cultural beliefs were very different from hers and different from the school culture. She asked Semira's father whether Semira could return to school if different arrangements were made for lifting and positioning her. He agreed that as long as a woman did these tasks modestly. Such considerations were acceptable to the family. Mrs. Jackson agreed to make other arrangements, and within a week a plan acceptable to all was in place.

Questions to Consider

1 Gender roles are often linked to cultural beliefs. Can you give examples of any gender differences that are important in the culture(s) you include in your identity?
2 How do you think you would respond if a family's cultural beliefs and practices supported highly traditional gender roles?
3 What do you think the teacher's role should be when a family's cultural beliefs and practices collide with the school's culture?

—By Eleanor Lynch, San Diego State University and Marci Hanson, San Francisco State University

- Three new features that appear in selected chapters demonstrate the increased visibility of people with disabilities: *Changing Times, Disability in the News,* and *On the Screen.*

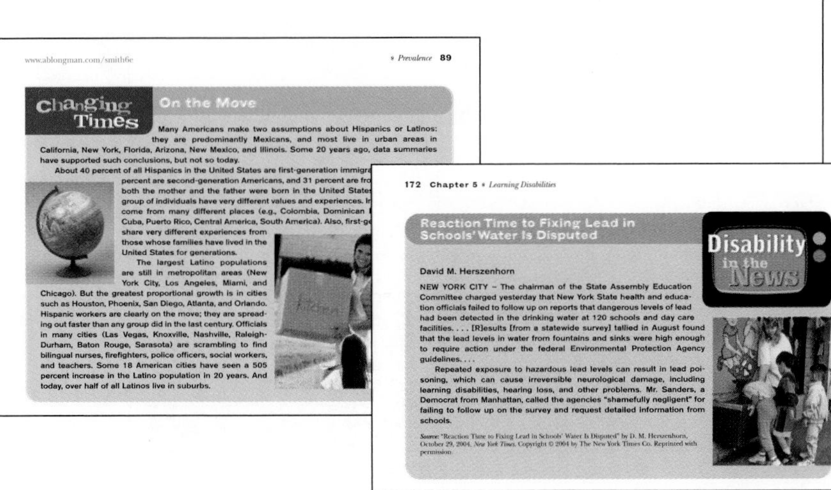

www.ablongman.com/smith6e • *Prevalence* **89**

Changing Times — **On the Move**

Many Americans make two assumptions about Hispanics or Latinos: they are predominantly Mexicans, and most live in urban areas in California, New York, Florida, Arizona, New Mexico, and Illinois. Some 20 years ago, data summaries have supported such conclusions, but not so today.

About 40 percent of all Hispanics in the United States are first-generation immigr[...] percent are second-generation Americans, and 31 percent are fro[...] both the mother and the father were born in the United State[...] group of individuals have very different values and experiences. I[...] come from many different places (e.g., Colombia, Dominican [...] Cuba, Puerto Rico, Central America, South America). Also, first-g[...] share very different experiences from those whose families have lived in the United States for generations.

The largest Latino populations are still in metropolitan areas (New York City, Los Angeles, Miami, and Chicago). But the greatest proportional growth is in cities such as Houston, Phoenix, San Diego, Atlanta, and Orlando. Hispanic workers are clearly on the move; they are spreading out faster than any group did in the last century. Officials in many cities (Las Vegas, Knoxville, Nashville, Raleigh-Durham, Baton Rouge, Sarasota) are scrambling to find bilingual nurses, firefighters, police officers, social workers, and teachers. Some 18 American cities have seen a 505 percent increase in the Latino population in 20 years. And today, over half of all Latinos live in suburbs.

172 Chapter 5 • *Learning Disabilities*

Reaction Time to Fixing Lead in Schools' Water Is Disputed

Disability in the News

David M. Herszenhorn

NEW YORK CITY – The chairman of the State Assembly Education Committee charged yesterday that New York State health and education officials failed to follow up on reports that dangerous levels of lead had been detected in the drinking water at 120 schools and day care facilities. . . . [R]esults [from a statewide survey] tallied in August found that the lead levels in water from fountains and sinks were high enough to require action under the federal Environmental Protection Agency guidelines. . . .

Repeated exposure to hazardous lead levels can result in lead poisoning, which can cause irreversible neurological damage, including learning disabilities, hearing loss, and other problems. Mr. Sanders, a Democrat from Manhattan, called the agencies "shamefully negligent" for failing to follow up on the survey and request detailed information from schools.

Source: "Reaction Time to Fixing Lead in Schools' Water Is Disputed" by D. M. Herszenhorn, October 29, 2004, *New York Times.* Copyright © 2004 by The New York Times Co. Reprinted with permission.

www.ablongman.com/smith6e • *Emotional or Behavioral Disorders Defined* **237**

The Aviator's Tailspin — **ON the screen**

Howard Hughes was almost bigger than life. At age 18, he inherited the family business and used his vast wealth to pioneer the development of commercial aviation and also to fund his passion for making movies. He was an engineering and business genius who designed bombers and spy planes for the U.S. military during World War II; he also led the development of the commercial airline business as CEO of TWA, which flew worldwide. What probably made Hughes most well known, however, was being a flamboyant movie mogul who made epic films and lived the lifestyle of the Hollywood "rich and famous."

In 2004, the acclaimed Hollywood director Martin Scorsese brought to the screen the conflict between Hughes's naturally flashy, public personality and the mental illness that caused Hughes to withdraw from life. Scorsese and Leonardo DiCaprio, who played the part of Hughes, reveal the spiraling tragedy of mental illness and how it often begins in childhood, accelerates, and eventually consumes its victims. Although the condition can be controlled through medication today, Howard Hughes's life was ravaged by obsessive compulsive disorder (OCD), which ultimately resulted in self-imposed isolation and overwhelming fright of infection and human contact. Through *The Aviator,* we can better understand the challenges that emotional or behavioral disorders presents to those affected.

—By Steven Smith

- The theme of what's on the horizon for people with disabilities concludes with a chance for each of us to use our creativity to *Imagine a World* where *all* people have a fair chance to fulfill their dreams of success.

- Whenever appropriate, listings of *supplementary resources* are found after each chapter's summary section. These include popular novels and books, movies (annotated to explain their relevance to the subject of disabilities), and organizations and agencies.

www.ablongman.com/smith6e • *Participation: Inclusive Special Education* **35**

with each specific type of disability who receive more than 80 percent of their education in the general education classroom. You might think that the rates of participation would be similar to the high and low prevalence patterns shown in Figure 1.2 on page 13, which in some respects also reflect the severity of each disability. Note, however, that the data shown in these two charts do not mirror each other. Why is this so? Well, some types of disability impact education differently than others. For example, students with visual disabilities are most likely to receive their education alongside peers without disabilities and to receive specialized instruction in independence, mobility, and braille from special resource personnel either during the summer or part-time during the school year. Students with severe cognitive disabilities or with substantial behavioral problems are more likely to receive their education outside the general education classroom.

Purposes of Special Education

The overarching purpose of special education is to make it possible for all individuals with disabilities to achieve to their fullest potential so that as adults, they can attain full community presence by holding meaningful jobs and living independently. Inclusive education—that is, participating exclusively in the general education classroom using the general education curriculum—is *not* a goal of special education (Kavale & Mostert, 2003). Of course, for most students with a disability, that is the means for them to meet the purposes of special education. For some, however, these purposes can be met only through a different curriculum or through intensive instruction that cannot be offered in the general education program. Regardless of the educational goals set for any individual student with a unique learning need, all students are entitled to a very special education. Imagine an educational system that meets these purposes for each and every individual. The promise of a remarkable future is truly beyond the imaginable!

Imagine a world... free from discrimination and barriers...

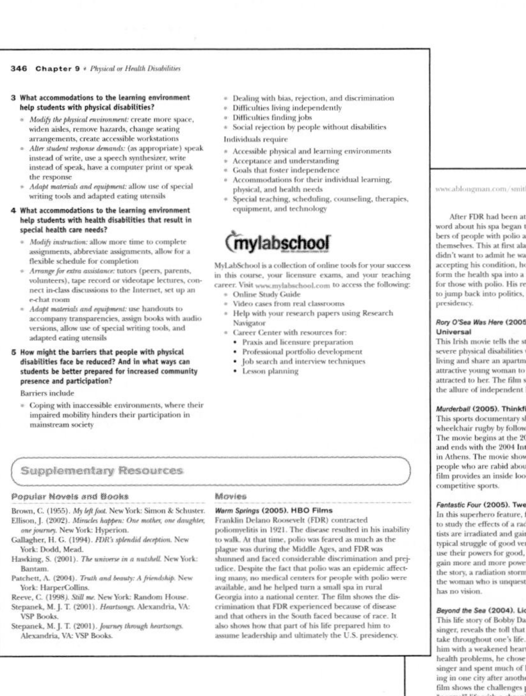

346 Chapter 9 • *Physical or Health Disabilities*

3 What accommodations to the learning environment help students with physical disabilities?

- *Modify the physical environment:* create more space, widen aisles, remove hazards, change seating arrangements, create accessible workstations
- *Alter student response demands:* (as appropriate) speak instead of write, use a speech synthesizer, write instead of speak, have a computer print or speak the response
- *Adapt materials and equipment:* allow use of special writing tools and adapted eating utensils

4 What accommodations to the learning environment help students with health disabilities that result in special health care needs?

- *Modify instruction:* allow more time to complete assignments, abbreviate assignments, allow for a flexible schedule for completion
- *Arrange for extra assistance:* tutors (peers, parents, volunteers), tape record or videotape lectures, connect in-class discussions to the Internet, set up an e-chat room
- *Adapt materials and equipment:* use handouts to accompany transparencies, assign books with audio versions, allow use of special writing tools, and adapted eating utensils

5 How might the barriers that people with physical disabilities face be reduced? And in what ways can students be better prepared for increased community presence and participation?

Barriers include

- Coping with inaccessible environments, where their impaired mobility hinders their participation in mainstream society
- Dealing with bias, rejection, and discrimination
- Difficulties living independently
- Difficulties finding jobs
- Social rejection by people without disabilities

Individuals require

- Accessible physical and learning environments
- Acceptance and understanding
- Goals that foster independence
- Accommodations for their individual learning, physical, and health needs
- Special teaching, scheduling, counseling, therapies, equipment, and technology

mylabschool

MyLabSchool is a collection of online tools for your success in this course, your licensure exams, and your teaching career. Visit www.mylabschool.com to access the following:

- Online Study Guide
- Video cases from real classrooms
- Help with your research papers using Research Navigator
- Career Center with resources for:
  - Praxis and licensure preparation
  - Professional portfolio development
  - Job search and interview techniques
  - Lesson planning

Supplementary Resources

Popular Novels and Books

Brown, C. (1955). *My left foot.* New York: Simon & Schuster.
Ellison, J. (2002). *Miracles happen: One mother, one daughter, one journey.* New York: Hyperion.
Gallagher, H. G. (1994). *FDR's splendid deception.* New York: Dodd, Mead.
Hawking, S. (2001). *The universe in a nutshell.* New York: Bantam.
Patchett, A. (2004). *Truth and beauty: A friendship.* New York: HarperCollins.
Reeve, C. (1998). *Still me.* New York: Random House.
Stepanek, M. J. T. (2001). *Heartsongs.* Alexandria, VA: VSP Books.
Stepanek, M. J. T. (2001). *Journey through heartsongs.* Alexandria, VA: VSP Books.

Movies

***Warm Springs* (2005). HBO Films**

Franklin Delano Roosevelt (FDR) contracted poliomyelitis in 1921. The disease resulted in his inability to walk. At that time, polio was feared as much as the plague was during the Middle Ages, and FDR was shunned and faced considerable discrimination and prejudice. Despite the fact that polio was an epidemic affecting many, no medical centers for people with polio were available, and he helped turn a small spa in rural Georgia into a national center. The film shows the discrimination that FDR experienced because of disease and that others in the South faced because of race. It also shows how that part of his life prepared him to assume leadership and ultimately the U.S. presidency.

www.ablongman.com/smith6e • *Supplementary Resources* **347**

After FDR had been at Warm Springs for some time, word about his spa began to spread, and increasing numbers of people with polio arrived in an effort to help themselves. This at first alarmed Roosevelt, because he didn't want to admit he was like these other people. After accepting his condition, however, he was able to transform the health spa into a full-time rehabilitation clinic for those with polio. His renewed strength allowed him to jump back into politics, where he eventually won the presidency.

***Rory O'Shea Was Here* (2005). W2 Productions and Universal**

This Irish movie tells the story of two young men with severe physical disabilities who emerge from institutional living and share an apartment in the city. They hire an attractive young woman to assist them, and both become attracted to her. The film shows both the challenges and the allure of independent living.

***Murderball* (2005). Thinkfilm and MTV Films**

This sports documentary shows the fierce competition of wheelchair rugby by following one team for two years. The movie begins at the 2002 championships in Sweden and ends with the 2004 International Paralympic Games in Athens. The movie shows the human dramas of real people who are rabid about their sport. The fast-paced film provides an inside look at disabilities along with competitive sports.

***Fantastic Four* (2005). Twentieth Century Fox**

In this superhero feature, five scientists travel into space to study the effects of a radiation storm. All of the scientists are irradiated and gain exceptional powers. In the typical struggle of good versus evil, four of the scientists use their powers for good, while one of them tries to gain more and more powers at all cost. As a subplot of the story, a radiation storm physically alters one scientist; the woman who is unquestioning about his appearance has no vision.

***Beyond the Sea* (2004). Lionsgate**

This life story of Bobby Darin, 1950s and 1960s pop singer, reveals the toll that early childhood illness can take throughout one's life. Darin's rheumatic fever left him with a weakened heart. Despite his continuing health problems, he chose a demanding career as a singer and spent much of his life on the road entertaining in one city after another. Darin died at age 37. This film shows the challenges people face as they try to live a "normal" life with a chronic health condition.

***X-Men* (2000). Twentieth Century Fox**

This film, based on a comic book set in the late sixties, follows "evolved" people called mutants, who are threatened with being rounded up, numbered, and placed in specific centers. A school for mutants, developed by Dr. Xavier and his top mutants (the X-Men), is a safe haven where people and mutants are supposed to live together peacefully. However, a nefarious group of mutants disagree and wage war on "normal" people.

The leader of the X-Men uses a wheelchair, but his leadership is not impaired. The underlying meaning of this film is that people who are different should not be viewed as outcasts or ostracized from society. The comic book on which the movie is based dates back about thirty years and tried to promote tolerance.

***Notting Hill* (1999). Universal Studios**

This romantic comedy about William Thacker, who owns a travel bookshop, takes place in a small section of London. Thacker falls in love with a woman from the United States, Anna Scott. Their relationship is complicated by the fact that she is a world-famous film star. One of William's friends is Bella, who uses a wheelchair. She had fallen down a flight of stairs, which left her paralyzed from the waist down. The film portrays her neither as a victim nor as a person to be pitied. Instead, she is an empowered, pivotal character in the story.

***Mask* (1985). Universal/MCA**

Rocky Dennis is a teenager who is suffering with an incurable disease that has deformed his skull. A gifted youth, he is raised by a caring, loving single mother, who helps her son cope with the painful side effects of his disease. However, she also has a wild side and regularly carouses with bikers, living a hedonistic life. Even though his mother is reckless, her perspective allows Rocky to live for the moment, but in the end he cannot overcome the deadly, incurable disease.

Professional, Parent, and Advocacy Groups

Asthma and Allergy Foundation of America (AAFA) in Washington, DC: www.aafa.org

Council for Exceptional Children, Division for Physical & Health Disabilities (DPHD) in Arlington, Virginia: www.cec.sped.org

National Association of School Nurses (NASN) in Castle Rock, Colorado: www.nasn.org

National Easter Seal Society for Crippled Children and Adults in Landover, Maryland: www.easter-seals.org

Epilepsy Foundation of America in Landover, Maryland: www.efa.org

March of Dimes Birth Defects Foundation in White Plains, New York: www.modimes.com

United Cerebral Palsy Association in Washington, DC: www.ucp.org

- At the end of every chapter is an informative table that ties the *CEC standards, INTASC principles,* and *PRAXIS preparation* to that chapter's content.

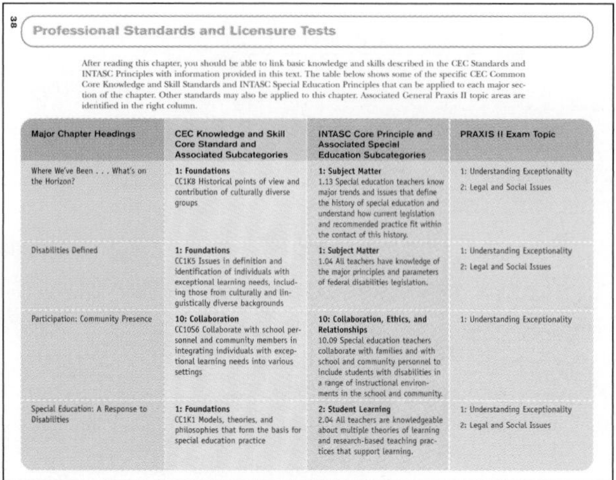

38

Professional Standards and Licensure Tests

After reading this chapter, you should be able to link basic knowledge and skills described in the CEC Standards and INTASC Principles with information provided in this text. The table below shows some of the specific CEC Common Core Knowledge and Skill Standards and INTASC Special Education Principles that can be applied to each major section of the chapter. Other standards may also be applied to this chapter. Associated General Praxis II topic areas are identified in the right column.

Major Chapter Headings	CEC Knowledge and Skill Core Standard and Associated Subcategories	INTASC Core Principle and Associated Special Education Subcategories	PRAXIS II Exam Topic
Where We've Been . . . What's on the Horizon?	**1: Foundations** CC1K8 Historical points of view and contribution of culturally diverse groups	**1: Subject Matter** 1.13 Special education teachers know major trends and issues that define the history of special education and understand how current legislation and recommended practice fit within the contact of this history.	1: Understanding Exceptionality 2: Legal and Social Issues
Disabilities Defined	**1: Foundations** CC1K5 Issues in definition and identification of individuals with exceptional learning needs, including those from culturally and linguistically diverse backgrounds	**1: Subject Matter** 1.04 All teachers have knowledge of the major principles and parameters of federal disabilities legislation.	1: Understanding Exceptionality 2: Legal and Social Issues
Participation: Community Presence	**10: Collaboration** CC10S6 Collaborate with school personnel and community members in integrating individuals with exceptional learning needs into various settings	**10: Collaboration, Ethics, and Relationships** 10.09 Special education teachers collaborate with families and with school and community personnel to include students with disabilities in a range of instructional environments in the school and community.	1: Understanding Exceptionality
Special Education: A Response to Disabilities	**1: Foundations** CC1K1 Models, theories, and philosophies that form the basis for special education practice	**2: Student Learning** 2.04 All teachers are knowledgeable about multiple theories of learning and research-based teaching practices that support learning.	1: Understanding Exceptionality 2: Legal and Social Issues

Up-to-Date Special Education Practices Reflected in IDEA '04

The field of special education is evolving rapidly. The new version of the *Individuals with Disabilities Education Act* (IDEA '04), passed in December 2004 with regulations that went into effect at the beginning of 2006, changed many of the ways in which we deliver a very special education to students with special needs. These innovations and requirements have been comprehensively integrated into this edition in a new chapter (Chapter 6), as well as in new sections and features.

- In this edition a full chapter (Chapter 6) is devoted to ADHD in part because of the large number of students identified with *attention deficit hyperactivity disorder (ADHD)* and in part because ADHD—though not a separate disability—is discussed in IDEA '04.
- The *What IDEA '04 Says About* features explain specific rules and procedures included in the latest version of the special education law, and when appropriate, supporting rules and procedures found in the general education law are outlined in *What NCLB Says About* features.
- Reflecting both new and continuing IDEA '04 regulations, the *Assessment* section of each chapter addresses a specific category of disability. New to this edition, this section highlights *early identification, pre-referral, identification,* and *evaluation* (high stakes testing, alternate assessments, progress monitoring) procedures.
- Because of the emphasis in both the No Child Left Behind Act (NCLB) and IDEA '04, each chapter on a specific category of disability also has a new section called *Access to the General Education Curriculum.* This section provides practical examples of how to accomplish the inclusion of students with disabilities in academic instruction alongside their classmates without disabilities.
- Chapter 5, on learning disabilities, reflects current innovations as well as newly spelled-out IDEA '04 regulations on *early intervening* and *response to intervention.*

A Complete Teaching and Learning Package

Our team has created a complete instructional package for this introduction to the field of special education. The text is central to the course, and its supplements were created to support the text and the learning activities for the academic term. These supplements provide an outstanding array of resources that facilitate learning about students with disabilities and their families.

Resources for Instructors

Instructor's Resource Manual and Test Bank. The Instructor's Resource Manual includes a wealth of interesting ideas and activities designed to help instructors teach the course. Each chapter includes outline and lecture notes, discussion questions, Web activities, handout masters (including case studies), and additional resources. The Test Bank includes hundreds of essay, multiple-choice, and true/false questions.

Computerized Test Bank. The printed Test Bank is also available electronically through the Allyn and Bacon computerized testing system, TestGen EQ. Instructors can use TestGen EQ to create exams in just minutes by selecting from the existing database of questions, editing questions, and/or writing original questions.

PowerPoint™ Presentation. Ideal for use in lectures or student handouts, the PowerPoint™ presentation created for this text provides dozens of ready-to-use graphic and text images.

Videotapes for Lecture Presentation These videos provide a way to bring video into your course for maximized learning.

- **Snapshots: Inclusion Video** (© 1995, 22 minutes in length). This videotape profiles three students of differing ages and with various levels of disability in inclusive class settings. In each case, parents, classroom teachers, special education teachers, and school administrators talk about the steps they have taken to help the student succeed in inclusive settings.
- **Snapshots: LD, MR, EBD; Snapshots: Hearing Impairment, Visual Impairment, Traumatic Brain Injury** (© 1995, closed captioned; each tape 20–25 minutes in length). These tapes are designed specifically for use in college classrooms. The segment for each category of disability profiles three individuals and their families, teachers, and experiences. These programs are of great interest to students; instructors who have used the tapes in their courses have found that they help disabuse students of stereotypical viewpoints and "put a human face" on the course material.
- **Professionals in Action Videotape: Teaching Students with Special Needs** (© 2000, 120 minutes in length). This Professionals in Action video consists of five 15- to 30-minute modules presenting viewpoints and approaches to teaching students with various disabilities in general education classrooms, in separate education settings, and in various combinations of the two. Each module explores its topic via actual classroom footage and includes interviews with general and special education teachers, parents, and students themselves.

Allyn and Bacon Transparencies for Special Education (© 2005). This package includes 100 acetates, over half of which are in full color.

Resources for Students

MyLabSchool with E-Text. The sixth edition of *Introduction to Special Education: Making a Difference* includes access to a text-specific version of Allyn and Bacon's MyLabSchool, a collection of online tools designed to help prepare students for success in this course as well as in their teaching careers. Visit www.mylabschool.com to access the following:

- An E-book of ***Introduction to Special Education: Making a Difference, Sixth Edition***, with integrated pre- and post-tests that generate individualized study plans to identify areas of weakness and strengths and thus help students focus their attention and efforts where they're needed most
- **Video footage of real-life classrooms**, with opportunities for students to reflect on the videos and offer their own thoughts and suggestions for applying theory to practice
- Help with research papers using **Research Navigator**, which provides access to three exclusive databases of credible and reliable source material, including EBSCO's ContentSelect Academic Journal Database, the *New York Times* Search by Subject Archive, and the "Best of the Web" Link Library
- An extensive archive of **text and multimedia cases** that provide valuable perspectives on real classrooms and real teaching challenges
- **Help with lesson planning and building digital portfolios** of professional resources, including study guides for licensure preparation
- An exciting array of **tools and activities** that will help your students study more effectively and can take them beyond the book. These include an electronic version of the Study Guide, Web links, learning activities, chapter summaries, and practice tests.

Study Guide. The Study Guide that accompanies the text contains proven learning strategies such as mnemonics, clustering information into main ideas, and study organizers. It features numerous ways of helping students apply and practice what they have learned in the text, including a timeline, define-the-terms activities, Web activities, alphabet soup, mini-case studies, practice tests, and crossword puzzles.

"What's Best for Matthew?" Interactive CD-ROM Case Study for Learning to Develop IEPs, Version 2.0. This CD-ROM helps pre-service and in-service teachers develop their IEP-writing skills through the case study of Matthew, a nine-year-old boy with autism. It is sold separately and is also available at a reduced price when "value-packaged" with the textbook.

Acknowledgements

It may take a village to raise a child, but it definitely takes many villages and teams of villagers to create and produce an introductory textbook—particularly a major revision like this one. I was able to "pull this one off" because of the incredible support of so many friends and colleagues. Although mere mention in an acknowledgements section is not sufficient, this public recognition of their contributions and personal support represents a sincere expression of my thanks to each of these remarkable individuals.

The Home Team

Thanks must go first of all to Jim Smith. He endured yet another revision effort filling our home, consuming my life, and postponing lots of playtime. He also participated in the development of this edition by helping with some of the "fun stuff," such as selecting artists for the chapter-opening sections and finding interesting stories about people with disabilities. And he assisted with tedious detail work, such as checking reference lists against text. For all this, and for keeping questions like "Aren't you finished with that chapter yet?" and "Why are you doing this?" to a relative minimum—thanks!

Second, I want to thank those wonderful professionals who contributed chapters and major features to this edition. Naomi Chowdhuri Tyler—co-director of the

IRIS Center at Peabody College of Vanderbilt University, friend, and colleague—had a major role in this edition. She contributed the *What IDEA '04 Says About* and *What NCLB Says About* features. She co-authored Chapter 6 on attention deficit hyperactivity disorders. She helped think through how language development, being the foundation for reading, should precede the chapter about learning disabilities and then helped write those sections. And, as with previous editions, she created the Test Bank. Kathleen Lane, of Vanderbilt University, did an outstanding and timely job revising the chapter about students with emotional or behavioral disorders, bringing you absolutely the most current information and practical applications for working with these learners. Craig Kennedy, also of Vanderbilt University, built upon the work of Ann Garfinkle of the University of Montana to create the most up-to-date chapter possible about students with autism spectrum disorders.

This edition includes many new, high-interest, and informative features and boxes. Bringing you techniques that can be implemented with confidence, the *Validated Practices* features, retained from the fifth edition, were written by Kimberly Paulsen, also of Vanderbilt University. New to this edition, the *Considering Culture* features provide provocative stories designed to stimulate you to think creatively about the complexities of culture and diversity. My sincere thanks goes to Ellie Lynch, formerly of San Diego State University, and Marci Hanson of San Francisco State University for providing such innovative features for this edition. The assignment to take several sets of standards, align them with this text, and make them useful for students and instructors was clearly daunting, but Nancy Sileo of the University of Nevada–Las Vegas met the challenge and did the most amazing job and clearly surpassed expectations. And, finally, my thanks goes to Steven Smith, who contributed information about the inclusion of people with disabilities in movies; this information can be found in the occasional *On the Screen* features and in the film annotations at the end of most chapters.

I deeply appreciate the efforts of colleagues here at Vanderbilt University and across the nation who lent their work, expertise, and advice to the creation of many elements included in this edition. Special thanks to (in alphabetical order): Linda Alsop for her help in ensuring that we had accurate information about intervenors and students who are deaf-blind; Stephen Elliott for his generous assistance in sorting out many issues related to IDEA '04 and its requirements for assessing and evaluating students with disabilities; Susan Flippin for her help with the audiograms found in Chapter 10; Kitty Greeley for her contributions to the *Making Accommodations* section of Chapter 14; Lynn and Doug Fuchs for their continuing help surrounding issues related to response to intervention, curriculum based measurement, and educating students with learning disabilities; Amy Harris-Soloman and Lizzy B. for contributing their story to Chapter 4; Chuck Hitchcock of CAST for lending his expertise on issues related to universal design for learning; Gloria Kishi of the Hawaii Department of Education for allowing us to share her data about the participation of diverse students in special education; Sara Moodie for sharing her story and her beautiful art found at the opening of Chapter 12; Kyra Tyler for allowing us to include her school work in Chapter 5; Zina Yzquierdo for her assistance with issues related to speech development and to language acquisition of linguistically diverse youngsters with disabilities. Too many people to mention here helped assemble outstanding photos that illustrate many important innovations in teaching and technology. To each of you I repeat my thanks. One person, however, must be publicly recognized here: Rick Slaughter helped to make this edition even more special by taking wonderful photos of Lizzy B and of Kailyn and her multidisciplinary team members.

The extraordinary team of people at the IRIS Center for Faculty Enhancement at Peabody College at Vanderbilt University helped with a myriad of details and provided me with the support necessary to get this job done. Without them, work at my "real jobs" would have suffered, and life would have been even nuttier than it was. For all their help and support, my deepest thanks are extended to Janice Brown, Janet Church, Pam Dismuke, Erik Dunton, Susan Flippin, Jason Phelan, Georgine Pion, Kim Skow, Judy Smith-Davis, Naomi Chowdhuri Tyler, Debbie Whelan, and Zina Yzquierdo.

Reviewers

I would like to express special appreciation to the following professionals, who assisted with the development of this edition by providing valuable feedback and suggestions for improvement:

J'Anne Affeld, Northern Arizona University
Janet Ambrose, College of Notre Dame of Maryland
Kristin Bewick, Wilkes University
Lessie Cochran, Bowling Green State University
Christina Curran, Central Washington University
Kenneth Derby, Gonzaga University
Josephine Fritts, Ozarks Technical Community College
Mary Jane Hayes, Austin Peay State University
Barbara Hofer, Middlebury College
Patricia McClung, Lee University
Linda McCuen, Anderson College
Jerry Neal, Central Missouri State University
Christine Preisinger, College of St. Rose
Kathleen Puckett, Arizona State University
Brenda Romanoff, University of North Carolina at Charlotte
Mary Sanders, Angelo State University
Bruce Shields, Daemen College
Smita Shukla-Mehta, University of Texas at Tyler
Karen Smith, The University of Texas of the Permian Basin
Jennifer Webb, Walsh University
Barbara Wert, Bloomsburg University.

The Allyn and Bacon Team

Once again, the team at Allyn and Bacon exceeded all reasonable expectations for expertise and support. My thanks to them for allowing me to incorporate some creativity and lots of special features into this edition, even though they knew that some of these "wild" ideas would be fraught with challenges I could never have imagined. In particular, I would like to thank Virginia Lanigan—friend, colleague, and editor (yes, those three words *can* go together)—who paved the way and guided the journey to achievement of the high standards and excellence you find in this text and its supplements. It is an honor and always a learning experience to collaborate with Elaine Ober, production manager at Allyn and Bacon, who treats this effort as though it were "her own" authored work. Elaine immediately caught my vision and infused the project with her creativity and sense of aesthetics. If any of you ever elect to indulge in a personal nightmare and write an introductory text, may you have a developmental editor who is "always there for you," solves problems, contributes great ideas, and is just as wonderful a person as Alicia Reilly.

The devil is indeed in the details, and so many of them surface late in the process when you're bone-weary. Toward the end of a big book project like this one, nothing is more important to an author than to work with a production packager who is professional and efficient, attends to details, is available, is always pleasant, is consistently positive, and finds solutions for impossible deadlines, page-length problems, and layout issues. Barbara Gracia set the highest quality standards and was unfailingly a joy to work with. Finally, I'd like to thank, on your behalf, those talented people who made this edition interesting to look at and easier for you to read and use: Helane Prottas, photo researcher, who kept searching when others would have given up, and Kathy Whittier who did an outstanding job clearing permissions. Connie Day, copy editor, who did an outstanding and thorough job in making this edition clear.

You have in your hands what we all hope is an inviting and contemporary text that provides you with up-to-date content, wherein you hear the voices of the disability community, and through which you will learn what it takes to make a difference in the lives of students with special needs.

D. D. S.

Introduction to Special Education

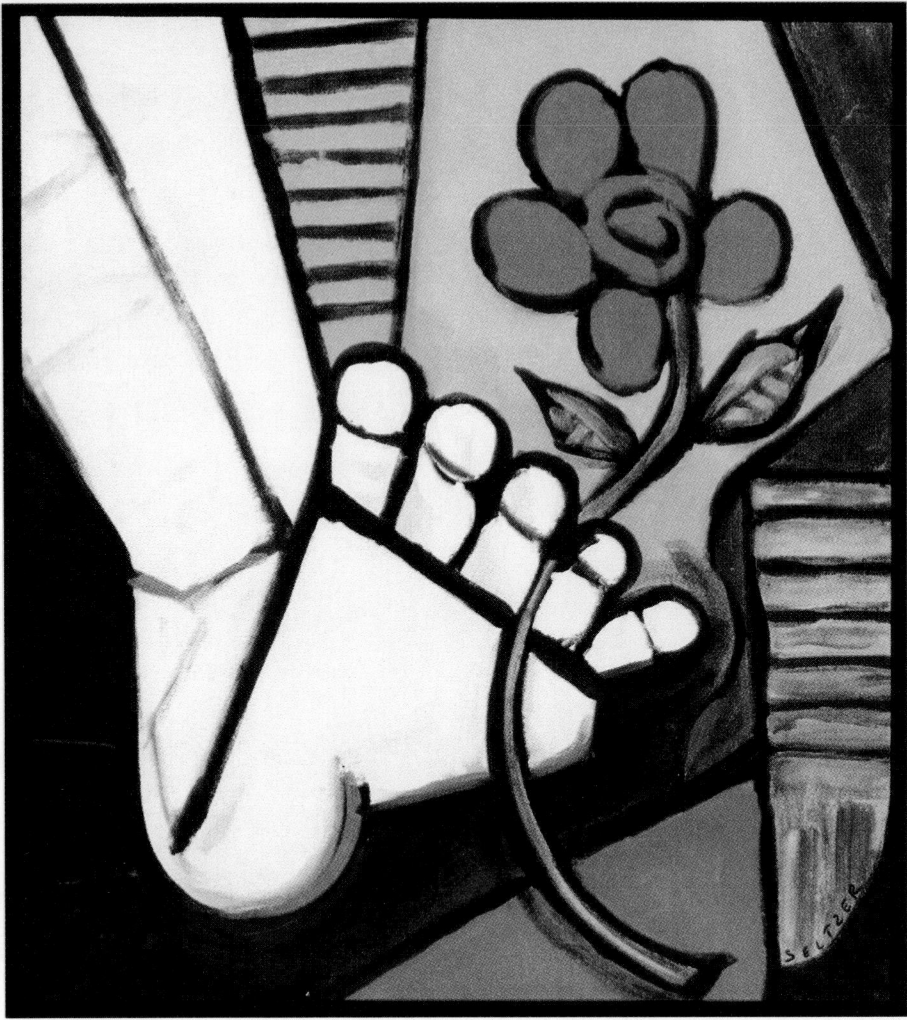

Poster © PhotoFest. Photograph of the artist Christy Brown courtesy of Esras Films Limited and The Radharc Archive.

Christy Brown was born in Ireland in 1932, one of 13 children. His talents were many, as were the challenges his disabilities presented. Robert Collis, the man who taught him how to write commercially successful literature, said that Brown showed us all the "amazing power of the spirit of man to overcome the impossible and, perhaps most of all, the utmost need of the human soul to escape from every sort of prison" (Brown, 1954, pp. 9–10). Christy Brown had cerebral palsy, which left him unable to speak and limited his functional use of most of his body. Although many at first thought he was a "hopeless case," he learned to read, write, paint, and use his toe of his left foot to type out his powerful novel of life in a Dublin slum, *Down All the Days,* and his raw and witty autobiography, which was made into the award-winning film *My Left Foot.* Perhaps more important than his triumphs as a novelist and painter, Christy Brown has become a symbol to those in the disability community of near-limitless possibilities. As Paul Longmore points out, "discrimination is a bigger obstacle than disability. . . . Christy Brown is a hero of our struggle" (Longmore, 2003, p. 130).

1

Disabilities and Special Education: Making a Difference

So you're saying there is definitely prejudice against [people with disabilities], no doubt about it.

—Larry King

I think it's an old habit we haven't gotten over yet. I think we will, though, and we need to get that message out, that [people with disabilities] can do much more than [people] think, if we ever give them a chance.

—Christopher Reeve

During this academic term you will study students who don't always learn in typical ways. You will find that students with disabilities require a unique response to their education. You will examine educational systems and services that respond to learners' with very special needs and will see how teachers and education professionals can and do make real differences in the educational outcomes of students with disabilities. Most important, you will come to understand that even those who face the most difficult challenges can and do overcome, compensate, and achieve remarkable outcomes. These results occur when the education they are provided is responsive to the learning situations they bring to the educational system. Before thinking about appropriate educational responses to disabilities—special education—let's consider what disabilities are and the challenges they create.

Chapter Objectives

After studying this chapter, you will be able to:

1. Explain the concepts of "disability" and "handicapped."
2. Describe how the lives of people with disabilities have improved across time.
3. Discuss barriers and challenges that are experienced today by people with disabilities and need to be overcome, and explain how all of us can make a difference.
4. Explain why the federal government provides unique protections for students with disabilities and their families.
5. Explain the key features or fundamental tenets of special education.

Where We've Been . . . What's on the Horizon?

The stories of people with disabilities begin with the earliest record of human history. Throughout time, and even today, these stories are filled with inconsistencies about treatment, acceptance, and success. Although the ancient Greek philosopher Aristotle supported a law that allowed no "deformed" child to live, evidence from ancient Egypt shows that many individuals with disabilities were respected and even given privileged status (Safford & Safford, 1996). Sometimes people with disabilities (particularly individuals with significant visual and hearing problems) were merely considered "odd" or "eccentric" or were accepted as being "just a bit different" (Bragg, 1997). But, both across time and across societies, most people with disabilities were treated terribly. It is important for everyone to know about those awful past events to ensure that such personal tragedies will never happen again. We must all understand how vulnerable people with disabilities are to the harshness of public opinion and the cruelty of others' actions. Accordingly, in this book, a brief section in every chapter on specific disabilities tells some stories about the discrimination, bias, and challenges faced by those with individual differences. Let's take a few moments to come to a better understanding of the inconsistency of treatment and respect experienced by people with disabilities. Then, you should have a better appreciation of how each of us can make a difference in the lives of people who face many challenges in their lives.

Historical Context: Disabilities

Although across the history of the world many examples of humane treatment and positive inclusion of people with disabilities can be found, it is too easy to find many stories of horrific treatment (Bragg, 1997). Here are a few examples. During ancient Roman times, Balbus Balaesus the Stutterer was caged and displayed along the Appian Way to amuse travelers who thought his speech was "funny." In the Middle Ages and the Renaissance, it was common practice to leave defective babies in the woods or to throw them into rivers to die. Sometimes individuals with disabilities were "protected," even though many of us might consider the circumstances to be unfair. For example, from the 12th to the 18th century, some people with disabilities served as court jesters in palaces and royal courts. Although they lived better than most common people of their times, they were kept for the amusement of royalty and had few freedoms. They were the lucky ones. Most people with disabilities were locked away in asylums or monasteries, and some were thought to be possessed by demons, while others were tried as witches (Bragg, 1997).

Do not be fooled into thinking that such stories are confined to the past, a part of history centuries old. Despite improvements, modern history offers tragic stories as well. For example, around the middle of the last century, Nazi Germany sent millions of Jews, people with disabilities, and members of other targeted groups to their deaths in concentration camps. But that was over 50 years ago; certainly, you might think, such inhumane acts no longer occur. Well, many documented cases of abuse and neglect of children with disabilities *do* occur today. Exposé after exposé, particularly in Third World and developing countries (including members of the former Soviet union) reveals horrible conditions in orphanages and institutions where imperfect children are kept until they die (Bennett, 1997; Powell & Dlugy, 1998). Inhumane treatment of people with disabilities, however, is not a problem that arises just in other countries. Think about adults in the United States with mental illness who are left to wander streets, have few supports to assist them, and remain in jail (not a treatment center) for nuisance crimes.

Sometimes abuses are less obvious, particularly to those who do not experience these challenges directly. Certainly, more and more people with disabilities are included in today's mainstream society, but it is still not easy for them to travel from place to place, find suitable accommodations when they travel, get jobs they are prepared for, or find suitable housing. Although there is considerable room for more progress, more and more people with disabilities can and do assume active roles in today's society.

Challenges That Disabilities Present

Despite the passage of the ADA law in 1990 and the progress people with disabilities have made over the past several decades, much progress remains to be made. Adults with disabilities are chronically underemployed, even when they have the education, training, and desire to hold better jobs (Stapleton & Burkhauser, 2003). Only 29 to 34 percent, a rate that has been consistent for 15 years, are employed. In 2000, only 56 percent of those who say they are able and ready to work found employment. And for those who *are* employed, their income is far less. In 2000, men with disabilities earned an average salary of $20,572, while their counterparts without disabilities made $39,401. Women with disabilities earned $20,762, while their counterparts without disabilities earned $36,774. And, even more disappointing, among people with disabilities only 30 percent of high school graduates and 45 percent with some college education are employed (Van Kuren, 2004). Thus many adults with disabilities remain on the rolls of Social Security Disability Insurance (SSDI) not because they do not want to find employment but because either they cannot find jobs or the jobs they can find do not pay enough.

Source: *Dis"ability" Joke Book,* 5910 77th St. East, Palmetto, FL 34221. Reprinted with permission.

Employers often think of individuals with disabilities as unqualified for their position vacancies. Although in many cases this is an unfounded assumption, this belief is accurate for many, given the high rate of students with disabilities who **drop out** of school and never earn a high school diploma. Whereas almost 80 percent of America's high school students graduate with a diploma, only 56 percent of students with disabilities graduate from high school with a standard diploma (National Center for Educational Statistics [NCES], 2004; U.S. Department of Education, 2002). As adults, students who drop out earn lower wages and experience higher unemployment (Lehr, 2004). Dropout rates are also disproportional: 29 percent as compared to 4 percent (Young, 2004). This situation is improving, however. Across a 10-year period, the number of those with disabilities who do graduate from high school and then attend college has doubled (U.S. Department of Education, 2002). Unfortunately, college completion rates are dismal, with only a quarter finishing.

All students with disabilities are at great risk of dropping out of school, and some are at even greater risk than others. Let's look at some of the details. For example, those with visual disabilities graduate from high school at the highest rate (73 percent), but only 40 percent of those students identified as having emotional or behavioral disorders, and 62 percent of those with learning disabilities, complete high school (U.S. Department of Education, 2002). Through intervention, these data can be altered (Lehr, 2004). Students with disabilities are more likely to dropout when they do not think that school is meaningful or is preparing them for their future (Dunn, Chambers, & Rabren, 2004). When they do not see classes as relevant, cannot get into classes they want, or find their teachers impersonal, they tend not to stay in school. Certainly, the educational system can find ways to change these situations and thereby encourage more students to complete high school. Job training, which is at least part of their school experience, also makes a difference; one year after school completion, special education graduates are more likely than dropouts to hold a job, and they have higher wages (Kohler & Field, 2003). High school graduation is not the only challenge to achieving community and workplace presence.

People with disabilities want to assume their places in modern society (Longmore, 2003). Just as all of us do, they want to make decisions about their lives, chose their friends, hold jobs, and experience life to its fullest. They want to be able to vacation, travel for work, and participate in the benefits that America has to offer. Like Michael Hingson (see *In the Spotlight* for his story), they want these opportunities—even if risks come along with increased participation. What measures can be taken so that more people with disabilities can share in everyday life? In many instances, it takes only simple accommodations or making certain that people know what is available to them. Considerable work remains to ensure that no one with disabilities faces barriers to participation and life satisfaction. The opportunities to make a difference and have a real impact on lives abound.

drop out To leave school before completion

Making a Difference

The Open Doors Organization

Business is always looking for new opportunities, and just like all customers, people with disabilities want to be sought after and have their needs catered to. However, if business executives do not understand the possible profitability of catering to a specialized market, they will not spend their company's money to develop new products or services. And, if potential consumers do not know about a service available for them or how to be discriminating buyers, many will shy away from spending their money even if they desire particular goods or services. Such are the basic economic principles of supply and demand.

Eric Lipp, himself a person with a physical disability, has considerable business experience and understands basic economics very well. Eric sees business opportunities, along with chances to meet the needs of people with disabilities, almost everywhere. In 2000 he founded the Open Doors Organization to achieve two objectives: (1) to enable all persons with disabilities to have the same consumer opportunities as individuals without disabilities and (2) to help businesses succeed in this "niche market."

One of the Open Doors Organization's first major efforts has been to demonstrate to the travel industry that people with disabilities represent a lucrative and relatively untapped consumer group. Partnering with the Harris Poll Group and the Travel Industry Association of America, Open Doors conducted a survey. Here are some of the results that have emerged: Some 54 million people with disabilities in the United States have the financial and physical ability to travel and take vacations. However, only about 11 million (or 20 percent) of these Americans travel annually, and they spend around $13.5 billion on airfare, cruises, hotels, and special-vehicle rentals. The upside potential of tailoring services to challenged travelers is great: an increase of $27 billion dollars annually. The travel industry is responding and expanding travel horizons for people with disabilities. To increase demand, the Open Doors Organization offers these "new" consumers freely available informational resources (e.g., tips for travelers with disabilities). Open Doors is also advocating for more accessible travel and recreation destinations. To learn more about the travel survey and to follow this organization's success, track their activities through the Open Doors Organization's Web site, www.opendoorsnfp.org

Eric Lipp, founder, Open Doors Organization

Disabilities Defined

Think about the question "What is a disability?" Did you think of the concept of **disability** (a condition or impairment) as an absolute—something an individual has or doesn't have? Actually, what at first appears to be a simple question is very complex because there are many different perspectives about what "disability" is and what it is not. The concept of "disability" can mean many different things to each individual and each family involved. You might have included in your answer that the intensity of a disability is the result of different conditions or experiences and that the most effective response to a disability depends on the individual's unique needs. Such answers reflect the idea that individualized accommodations and assistance can reduce the impact of a challenge presented by a disability. A few of you might have answered the question with a comprehensive answer that incorporates all the concepts just mentioned.

Why is understanding how disability is conceptualized important? First, as we have noted, the concept of disability is not as simple as it initially appears. Second, the way people think about what it means to have a disability affects how they interact with indi-

disability Result of conditions or impairments

Michael Hingson and Roselle in the Spotlight

September 11, 2001, changed the lives of most Americans. And the events of that terrible day certainly altered the lives of Michael Hingson and his guide dog, Roselle. On 9/11, Mr. Hingson was working on the 78th floor of North Tower of the World Trade Center in his job as a sales manager for a computer data storage company, and on that day he and Roselle—like so many others—became heroes.

On that morning, Mr. Hingson was hosting a meeting, and Roselle was sleeping under the table at her master's feet. At the sound of a deafening boom, Roselle took her duty station right by Mr. Hingson's feet. David Frank, a coworker of Hingson's, saw debris, burning paper, fire, and smoke out of the office window. They knew they needed to evacuate the building. Roselle and Mr. Hingson guided everyone down the dark and smoky stairways to safety, and once on the ground, they continued to guide people a safe distance from the collapsing buildings. When he was out of harm's way, he called his wife on his cell phone and broke down in tears, "He sobbed tears that seemed connected to hell and yet also to heaven. He hugged Roselle, who was perfectly calm. He hugged and hugged her, unable to find words. Finally, he said, 'Good dog. Good dog.' " (Laskas, 2003, p. 46). He also often recalls that trip down the stairway and "thinks about those firefighters who stopped to pet her on the way up the burning tower. He thinks about how Roselle answered them with dog kisses. He thinks those just may have been the last moments of unconditional love those brave people felt. "Good dog," he says. "Good dog." (Laskas, 2003, p. 48). Ironically, not too many years before 2001, most people with disabilities had not yet taken their places alongside coworkers without disabilities. The normalization movement put Mr. Hingson at risk, but it also placed him in a position to save many lives. Mr. Hingson now works for the California-based Guide Dogs for the Blind.

viduals with disabilities. In turn, those interactions become events that influence individuals' outcomes (Branson & Miller, 2002; Groce, 1985). For example, different perspectives and beliefs of educators result in various responses to disabilities; some—such as low or unreasonably high expectations—can have terrible long-term results (Artiles, 1998, 2003). And finally, understanding what the educational system and its professionals mean when they speak of different disabilities is important for clear communications, is central to the process of identifying those who will benefit from special education, and can impact the selection of appropriate educational interventions. So, let's think together about various ways to conceptualize "disability," consider how attitudes can influence students' lives, and then briefly look at the terms special education uses to describe and classify students with disabilities.

Differing Perspectives

Different disciplines, cultures, and individuals do not agree about what "disabilities" are and how to explain them (Harry, 2002; Lynch & Hanson, 2004; Utley & Obiakor 2001). All education professionals should understand that one's orientation, or way of thinking about "differences," results in distinct responses to disabilities. Three ways of considering disabilities typically guide people's thinking:

- Deficit perspective
- Cultural perspective
- Sociological perspective

Figure 1.1 • A Hypothetical Distribution of Scores Creating a Normal or Bell-Shaped Curve

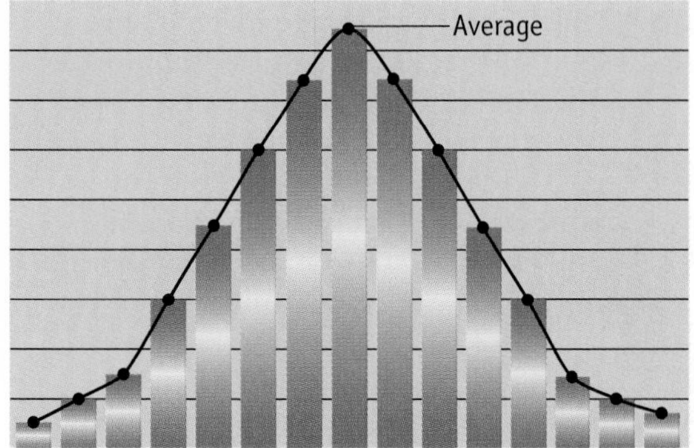

The *deficit perspective* reflects the idea that human behavior and characteristics shared by people are distributed along a continuum. Many psychologists, education professionals, and medical professionals describe children and youth by various characteristics, such as intelligence, visual acuity, academic achievement, or behavior. Actually, scores or measurements received by people tend to create a distribution where the majority of people fall in the middle of the distribution, and that's why they are called "average." The scores from most human characteristics create patterns or form what is called a **normal curve**, like the one shown in Figure 1.1. Because of the way the distribution tends to fall, with the highest number of scores in the middle and proportionally fewer as the distance from the average score increases, the distribution is also referred to as the **bell-shaped curve**.

The expectation, according to this idea, is for the academic achievement of all third graders also to create such a distribution. The number of students obtaining each score would be plotted on the graph. A few students would obtain low scores on the achievement test, and their scores would be plotted at the left-hand side of the graph. The number of students receiving higher scores increases until the average, or mean, score is reached. Somewhere in the middle of the distribution are **typical learners**, those whose behaviors and characteristics represent the average or majority of students. Then, progressively fewer students obtain higher and higher scores on the test, completing the right-hand side of the distribution or curve. The number of characteristics that could be counted in this way is infinite, and each individual student probably falls at a different point on each dimension measured. A tall student may have slightly below average visual acuity but have average scores on the distance he or she can kick a ball. Think about it: The hypothetical average student, or typical learner, probably does not actually exist, or exists *very* rarely because the possible combinations of human characteristics are almost endless.

Regardless, in mainstream America quantifying human performance is the most common method used to describe individuals. Unfortunately, this way of thinking about people puts half of everyone "below average" and forces individuals to be considered in terms of how different they are from the average. For students with disabilities, this approach contributes to the tendency to think about them as deficient, or somehow less than their classmates without disabilities.

A second way to think about disabilities and the people who might be affected does not use a quantitative approach; rather, it reflects a *cultural perspective*. Alfredo Artiles of Arizona State University aptly points out that America today includes many different cultures and that some have values and hold to concepts that differ greatly from mainstream ideas. Nonmajority cultures often hold different perspectives about the concept of disabilities, and many do not think about disabilities in terms of deficits or quantitative judgments about individuals (Artiles, 1998). We believe that this is a very important point for teachers to understand. First, education professionals and the families with whom they work might not share the same understanding of disability. Second, they might not hold a common belief about what causes disabilities.

Knowing that not all cultures share the same concept of disability helps us understand why some families approach education professionals differently when told that their child has a disability. Because disability does not have a single fixed definition, it is not thought about uniformly or universally (Lynch & Hanson, 2004). Families with whom teachers work are likely to have varying understandings about their child from those of school professionals. Also, not all cultures respond the same way to individuals identified as having a disability. In other words, the same individual might be considered "different" or as having a disability in one culture but not in another (Utley & Obiakor, 2001; Jim Green, 2003 October, personal communication). Or the degree of difference might not be considered uniformly.

normal or bell-shaped curve Theoretical construct of the typical distribution of human traits such as intelligence

typical learners Students and individuals without disabilities

Thus disabilities must be viewed within a cultural context. In addition, people from different cultures sometimes view the causes of disabilities in children in various ways. In general, people from the dominant American culture believe in a direct scientific cause-and-effect relationship between a biological problem and the developing baby. Those from other cultures may consider fate, bad luck, sins of a parent, the food the mother ate, or evil spirits to be potential causes of disabilities (Cheng, 1995; Lynch & Hanson, 2004). These alternative views affect the way a child with a disability is viewed within the culture and the types of intervention services that a family may be willing to pursue to address the child's disabilities or special needs. As educators work with families, they should address these issues and reflect sensitivity to the various perspectives family members bring to conversations about individual students.

The *sociological perspective* or orientation presents yet another way to think about individuals with disabilities. Instead of focusing on people's strengths or deficits, it construes differences across people's skills and traits as socially constructed (Danforth & Rhodes, 1997; Longmore, 2002). In this perspective, how a society treats individuals is what makes people different from each other, not a condition or set of traits that are part of the individual's characteristics. The idea is that if people's attitudes and the way society treats groups of individuals change, then the result and impact of being a member of a group changes. In other words, according to this perspective, what makes a disability is how we treat individuals we think of as different. Some scholars and advocates hold a radical view, suggesting that disabilities are a necessity of American society, its structure, and values. Some scholars, such as Herb Grossman, believe that when societies are stratified, variables such as disability, race, and ethnicity become economic and political imperatives (Grossman, 1998). They are necessary to the maintenance of class structure. Classifications result in restricted opportunities that then force some groups of people to fall to the bottom (Erevelles, 1996; Grossman, 1998).

Clearly, debate about this rationale or explanation for disabilities is controversial, but let's see how the sociological perspective might apply to at least one disability. According to this perspective, mental retardation exists because society and people treat these individuals poorly. The logic continues that *all* people have strengths and weaknesses, so if supporting services were available to help *every* individual when problems occur, then people with mental retardation would not be negatively treated and would be successful. In other words, if individuals with significant differences are just treated like everyone else, problems associated with mental retardation will disappear.

Serious issues have been raised regarding sociological perspectives on disabilities. Jim Kauffman, a scholar at the University of Virginia, voices many concerns about this orientation and maintains that disabilities are real, not just sociologically constructed. Despite how people are treated, disabilities significantly affect the people involved (Kauffman, 1997). To him, this perspective arises from a need for "sameness," where everyone is truly alike. This position, Kauffman contends, is dangerous because it (1) minimizes people's disabilities, (2) leads to the conclusion that individuals with disabilities do not need special services, and (3) encourages the attitude that needed services can be discontinued or reduced. All three of these scenarios leave individuals with disabilities vulnerable to diminished outcomes. They also leave students with disabilities at risk of losing their rights to an appropriate education tailored to meet their unique learning needs (Kauffman & Hallahan, 2005). Whether or not you believe that the sociological perspective can be used to explain disabilities, it does explain why many people with disabilities feel they experience bias and discrimination and believe that they belong to a true minority group.

Disability as a Minority Group

Many individuals with disabilities believe that the terms *disability* and **handicap** have very different meanings and interpretations. They are convinced that it is because of their *disabilities* (e.g., conditions and impairments) that society *handicaps* them (e.g.,

handicaps Challenges and barriers imposed by others

presents challenges and barriers). This belief leads many people to think about people with disabilities as belonging to a minority group, much as the concepts of race and ethnicity have resulted in African Americans, Hispanics, Native Americans, and Asian/Pacific Islanders[1] being considered part of historically underrepresented groups (Smart, 2001).

Paul Longmore, a founder of the disabilities studies movement (he is director of the Disability Studies Department at San Francisco State and is himself a person with disabilities), maintains that people with disabilities come together to form a minority group just like other minority groups, whose negative treatment is due to discrimination (Longmore, 2002). Thus the ways in which people are treated by society and by other individuals are what present the real barriers that influence people's outcomes. Difficult situations occur not because of a condition or disability but, rather, because people with disabilities are denied full participation in society as a consequence of their minority status. In fact, federal laws (you will learn more about them later in this chapter) that guarantee adults with disabilities participation in society (the Americans with Disabilities Act [ADA]) and students with disabilities a right to a public education (the Individuals with Disabilities Education Act [IDEA]) are often referred to as civil rights laws. This puts them in the same category as the Voting Rights Act of 1965, which put an end to discriminatory practices that prevented some Americans from exercising their right to vote in state and national elections.

Despite important changes in the ways people with disabilities are protected and included in society, stigma and bias are a long way from being eliminated. Many people with disabilities and observers of societies across the world agree with Rob Kitchin of Queens University of Ireland, who said, "Disabled people are marginalized and excluded from 'mainstream' society. . . . Disabled people represent one of the poorest groups in Western society" (1998, p. 343). We all need to understand that personal attitudes about what a disability is, along with beliefs about the impact of a disability, influence how individuals approach life.

Thomas Hart Benton often spent his summers on Martha's Vineyard where some of his neighbors were the Deaf residents of the island. Two of them appear in this painting.
Thomas Hart Benton, *The Lord Is My Shepherd,* 1926. Tempera on canvas. 33 x 27 3/8 in. (84.46 69.53 cm) Whitney Museum of Art, New York; purchase 31.100. photograph copyright © 1996: R. P. Benton Testamentary Trust/Licensed by VAGA, New York, N. Y. Photo by Robert E. Mates.

Attitudes Matter

Of this there should no longer be doubt: People are treated as a reflection of how they are perceived. Possibly there is no better illustration of this fact in U.S. history than the fascinating story of the settlers of Martha's Vineyard. The 17th Century settlers of Martha's Vineyard came from Kent, England. Apparently, they carried with them both a recessive gene for deafness and the ability to use sign language. The hearing people living on the island were bilingual, developing their oral and sign language skills simultaneously, early in life. Generation after generation, the prevalence of deafness on the island was exceptionally high, being 1:4 in one small community and 1:25 in several others. Probably because deafness occurred at such a high rate and in almost everyone's family, people who could not hear were treated differently from deaf people who lived on the mainland. They were integrated into society and were included in all of the community's work and play situations.

What were the results of such integration and of society's adapting to the needs of people with this disability, rather than requiring them to adapt to the ways of those without it? These individuals were free to marry whomever they wished. Of those

[1]Although regional and personal preferences about specific terms used to refer to ethnic and racial groups vary, these terms are the ones used by the federal government. Throughout this text, we use a variety of terms in an attempt to achieve balance.

born before 1817, 73 percent of the Vineyard Deaf[2] married, whereas only 45 percent of deaf Americans married. Only 35 percent of the Vineyard Deaf married other Deaf people, compared to 79 percent of deaf mainlanders. According to tax records, they generally earned average or above-average incomes, and some Deaf people became quite wealthy. Also, these individuals were active in all aspects of church affairs. Deaf individuals had some advantages over their hearing neighbors and family members. They were better educated than the general population because they received tuition assistance to attend the school for the deaf in Connecticut. According to the reports of their descendants, these people were able to read and write, and there are numerous accounts about hearing people asking their Deaf neighbors to read something to them or write a letter for them.

The story of the English settlers on Martha's Vineyard shows how deafness, a disability historically considered to be extremely serious, did not affect the way of life or achievement of those who lived on the island. For more than two hundred years, life in this relatively restricted and confined environment was much the same for those who had this disability and those who did not. Groce (1985) provides an explanation:

> The most striking fact about these deaf men and women is that they were not handicapped, because no one perceived their deafness as a handicap. As one woman said to me, "You know we didn't think anything special about them. They were just like anyone else. When you think about it, the Island was an awfully nice place to live." Indeed it was. (p. 110)

Disabilities and Students

The federal government, through the Individuals with Disabilities Education Act (IDEA '04)—the national special education law—defines disabilities and reserves special education services for only those students who are eligible. Why would the federal government restrict who is entitled to special education? One reason is that special education is expensive, costing twice as much as the general education offered to typical learners (U.S. Department of Education, 2002). Thus these services need to be delivered judiciously. Nationally, some 11 percent of students between the ages of 6 and 17 are identified as having disabilities and are provided special education services.

Through IDEA '04 and its regulations that are developed by the U.S. Department of Education, the federal government describes 13 disability categories that can be used to qualify infants, toddlers, preschoolers, and students eligible to receive special education services. Within these categories are many conditions, such as stuttering, included as a speech impairment; or attention deficit hyperactivity disorder (ADHD), included under the other health impairment category; and Tourettes syndrome, in the government's emotional disturbance category. Also, in an attempt to avoid either incorrectly labeling young children as having a disability when they do not or identifying them with the "wrong" disability, the federal government provides the option of using a general category (non-disability-specific group) for children under the age of eight (Müller & Markowitz, 2004; U.S. Department of Education, 2005a). Here are the 14 special education categories called out by the federal government:

- Autism spectrum disorders
- Deaf-blindness
- Deafness
- Developmental delay
- Emotional disturbance
- Hearing impairment
- Mental retardation
- Multiple disabilities
- Orthopedic impairment
- Other health impairment
- Specific learning disability
- Speech or language impairment
- Traumatic brain injury
- Visual impairment including blindness

---

[2]A capital D is used here because the Deaf people on Martha's Vineyard represent an important historical group. See Chapter 10 for more information about Deaf culture.

Table 1.1 • Special Education's Disability Categories Ordered by Prevalence

Federal Term	Other Terms	Comments
High Incidence Disabilities		
Specific learning disabilities	learning disabilities (LD)	Includes reading disabilities, mathematics disabilities
Speech or language impairments	speech disorders or language disorders; communication disorders	Speech impairments include problems with articulation, fluency problems, and voice problems
Mental retardation	cognitive disabilities; intellectual disabilities	Ranges from mild to severe, but often overlaps with low incidence disabilities
Emotional disturbance	emotional or behavioral disorders (EBD)	Does not include conduct disorders
Low Incidence Disabilities		
Multiple disabilities	multiple-severe disabilities; developmental disabilities	Does not include all students with more than one disability, varies by states' criteria
Deafness; hearing impairments	hard of hearing and deaf	Includes full range of hearing losses; Deaf is used to signify those who consider themselves part of the Deaf community
Orthopedic impairments	physical impairments (PI); physical disabilities	Category often combined with health impairments because of many overlapping conditions
Other health impairments	health impairments; special health care needs	IDEA '04 includes attention deficit hyperactivity disorder (ADHD) here
Visual impairments	visual disabilities; low vision and blind	Includes full range of visual loss
Autism	autism spectrum disorders (ASD)	ASD is more inclusive; autism is considered as one of five ASD conditions
Deaf-blindness	deafblind	Does not necessarily mean being both deaf and blind
Traumatic brain injury (TBI)		Must be acquired after birth
Developmental delay		Allows for noncategorical identification between the ages of 3 and 9

People view in different ways these **special education categories** or disabilities that require an educational response. First, the names for each of these disability categories differ slightly from state to state and are not necessarily the preferred terminology of parent and professional groups. Second, some categories, such as deafness and hearing impairment, often are combined. Finally, the categories are often ordered and divided by **prevalence** or the size of the category: **high incidence disabilities** (disabilities that occur in greater numbers) and **low incidence disabilities** (disabilities that occur less often). More information about these disabilities and the conditions they include is provided in Chapters 4 through 14 of this text. For now, Table 1.1 offers an overview of the disabilities and the different ways they are referred to in school settings. This table lists the 13 disability-

special education categories System used in IDEA '04 to classify disabilities among students

prevalence Total number of cases at a given time

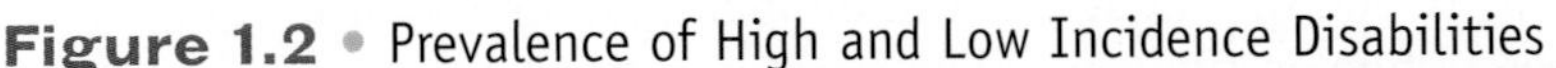

Figure 1.2 • Prevalence of High and Low Incidence Disabilities

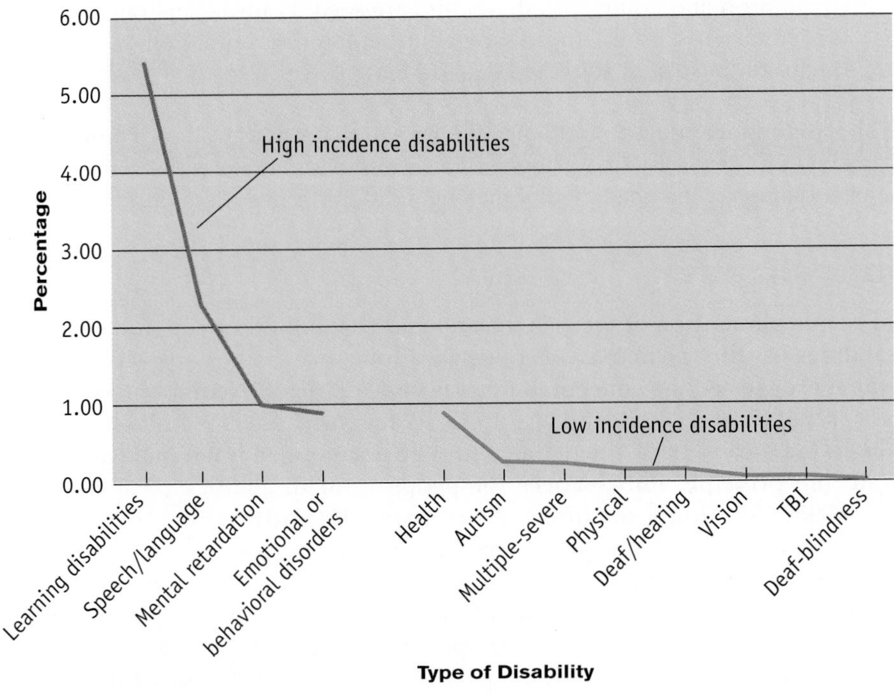

Source: U.S. Department of Education, Percentage (Based on 2003 Population Served Estimates) of Children Ages 6–17 Served Under IDEA, Part B by Disability, Table AA12, www.ideadata.org, 2005b.

specific terms, provides commonly used names for these same disabilities, and indicates whether the government considers them high or low incidence disabilities. In this last regard, Figure 1.2 helps us visualize the prevalence of each disability and clearly shows how students with learning disabilities, for example, far out number those students with other types of problems. Some people tend to think that incidence is related to severity or significance of the disability. In other words, they assume that high incidence disabilities are less severe than low incidence disabilities. Drawing this conclusion is a terrible mistake. All disabilities are serious, and mild to severe cases occur within each type of disability.

Participation: Community Presence

Let's shift our attention now to a more general discussion about all individuals with disabilities, not just those who are of school age. One important marker indicating the success of people with disabilities is their presence in communities as independent adults who assume their places alongside people without disabilities. As we have noted, this accomplishment is not yet fully achieved, but progress has certainly been made. Let's think about what markers or goals we need to measure the successful outcomes of everyone's efforts to ensure that every person with a disability has life satisfaction.

One measure of every community is how it treats and includes each of its members. Here are a few things to consider when thinking about human rights and the treatment of people with disabilities:

- If you do not see children with disabilities, a human rights problem is being hidden.

high incidence disabilities Special education categories with the most students

low incidence disabilities Special education categories with relatively few students

- If you see children or adults with disabilities homeless or begging on the streets, a human rights problem is not being addressed.
- If children and adults with disabilities are served only in separate facilities, programs, or schools, their segregation signals discrimination, lack of inclusion in society, stereotyping, and bias.

We all have opportunities to influence the lives of many and to shape communities. Surprisingly, it is too easy to overlook society's most vulnerable: individuals with disabilities. Taking on the challenge of making a difference for them enriches us all.

Normalization

An essential dimension of special education and a guiding concept for adults with disabilities is the principle of normalization. In 1959, Bank-Mikkelsen of Denmark suggested the concept, but it was Bengt Nirje of Sweden who coined the word *normalization* in 1969 (Biklen, 1985). A few years later, Wolf Wolfensberger brought the idea to the United States, and he encouraged policymakers to incorporate the principle into services for people with disabilities (Wolfensberger, 1972, 1995). According to Nirje (1985), **normalization** means "making available to all persons with disabilities or other handicaps, patterns of life and conditions of everyday living which are as close as possible to or indeed the *same* as the regular circumstances and ways of life of society" (p. 67; emphasis in original). The principle of normalization applies to every aspect of a student's life. Nirje referred to a set of normal life patterns: the normal rhythm of the day, the normal rhythm of the week, the normal rhythm of the year, and the normal development of the life cycle. Until the 1970s, residents with mild and moderate disabilities did much of the day-to-day work in institutions, such as caring for individuals with severe disabilities or performing farm or laundry work. Because of the widely held belief that individuals with disabilities would contaminate the "normal" population, many people spent their entire lives in these institutions, isolated from mainstream society (see Chapter 8 for more information about the reasons why people with mental retardation were institutionalized). Institutional living conflicts with the principle of normalization, and advocacy efforts have resulted in most people, even those with severe disabilities, living in community settings and having a voice in how and where they live (Johnson, 1998). As you think about what the American response to children and adults with disabilities should be, remember the normalization principle. One way to guide us as we think about justice or what is right is to think about normalization. If what we see is not "normal," then perhaps a wrong needs to be righted or someone needs to speak up. These clearly are ways in which we each can make a positive difference in each other's lives.

Advocacy

Today, parents and family members of people with disabilities, special education professionals, and individuals with disabilities commonly insist that the rights of people with disabilities be protected and that needed services be offered. In the early 20th Century, the job of raising America's consciousness about the problems facing people with disabilities rested primarily with professional organizations, and later in the century, parents added their voice to the fight for justice. (Contact information for more such organizations and agencies is provided at the end of this chapter.) It wasn't until the latter part of the century that people with disabilities began to speak on their own behalf. Let's look at a bit of this history to understand an important aspect of the disability advocacy movement in America.

In 1922 the International Council for the Education of Exceptional Children (CEC), the largest special education organization representing all disabilities as

normalization Making available ordinary patterns of life and conditions of everyday living well as gifted students, was founded (Aiello, 1976). CEC's initial members were taking a summer special education class conducted at Teachers College, Columbia University, and they decided to meet annually to continue sharing exciting ideas about special education. Professional organizations such as CEC and the American Speech-Language-Hearing Association (ASHA) have been instrumental in advocating for high-quality special education teachers and other services for every student with disabilities. Many volunteer and parent organizations began to organize after World War II to fight for the provision of educational services in the public schools for students with disabilities (Kirk, 1978). For example, the first parent group, The Arc (formerly the Association for Retarded Citizens of the United States), was founded in 1950 as the National Association of Parents and Friends of Mentally Retarded Children. This group first worked to bring students home from institutions and to have special education services provided to them through the public education system. The power and importance of parent advocacy groups must be recognized and applauded. The strength of the parent movement continues to improve federal laws. Parents argue successfully for funding at the state and national levels, and they serve as "watchdogs" over local educational programs to ensure that each student with a disability has access to a free appropriate public education.

People with disabilities have also formed their own advocacy groups, becoming effectively organized during the late 1980s and 1990s. The first phase was a quest for civil rights; the second phase is focusing on the development of a disability culture (Longmore, 1995; Treanor, 1993). Ed Roberts, founder of the World Institute on Disability and himself a person with disabilities, was a catalyst in organizing people with disabilities to demand access to mainstream U.S. society and the fulfillment of basic civil rights. Justin Dart organized people with disabilities across the nation and used his connections in the business community to ensure the ultimate passage of the civil rights law for people with disabilities, the Americans with Disabilities Act (ADA). Because of all these efforts, the National Council on Disability (NCD), which directly reports to the U.S. president and to Congress, was formed to ensure that the rights of people with disabilities are safeguarded. Today, parents, professionals, and people with disabilities have formed powerful lobbying groups and political action organizations that work to improve the opportunities available to all individuals with disabilities.

Speaking up for the rights of families and children, particularly those with disabilities, is critical to correcting current injustices and ensuring that future generations do not confront insurmountable challenges. Individuals with disabilities, themselves, often are not powerful enough to advocate alone for resolutions to injustices they face. All of us must help. Advocacy doesn't require the actions of a group or organization; each and every one of us can make a difference by speaking up to correct even the smallest injustice. Advocacy has and can make a real difference in the lives of fellow Americans.

Ed Roberts, founder of the World Institute on Disabilities and a leader in the civil rights movement for people with disabilities, was an aggressive advocate for people with disabilities. His legacy is the community participation people with disabilities expect today.

Progress in Participation

Perhaps stimulated by national policies, society now reflects a more sensitive and understanding way of regarding and talking about the minority group that includes children, youth, and adults with disabilities. People with disabilities are visible members of communities, a situation very different from that prevailing some 60 years ago when great efforts were made to hide President Franklin D. Roosevelt's use of crutches and a wheelchair (Gallagher, 1994). (You will learn more about FDR's story in Chapter 9.) The statue of FDR commissioned by the National Organization on Disability was added to his memorial in Washington, DC in 2000. It shows him in a wheelchair much like the one he actually used and is a demonstration of changes in attitudes about disabilities and the people who have them.

Another way to measure and evaluate how any group of people is perceived by a society is to analyze how that group is portrayed in literature and on the screen in

During Franklin D. Roosevelt's presidency, his disability was hidden from the public. Times have changed, however, and the new statue of FDR in Washington, D.C. shows him using a wheelchair.

both film and television (Longmore, 2003; Prater, 2003). Films tend to mirror reality, reflecting the beliefs and attitudes prevalent in a society at the time they were made. They can perpetuate stereotypes, but they also have the potential to influence the way people think and interact with others (Safran, 1998, 2000). Films produced at the beginning of the last century rarely depicted people with disabilities in a positive light. Most such characters were villainous or evil and were often punished by God, through their disabilities, for some sin of theirs or of a family member. Many of those characters were bitter and self-pitying. Thus we have an opportunity to see how beliefs, bias, actions, and stereotypes about people with disabilities have changed across time by analyzing how people with disabilities have been portrayed in cinema. For one such example, see *On the Screen,* which uses the original and remakes of the movie *The Hunchback of Notre Dame* to illustrate how perceptions have changed over time.

Certainly, not all portrayals of people with disabilities have been negative or unfair (e.g., *Shine,* 1996; *Ray,* 2004). Many films made worthy efforts—consider *My Left Foot* (1989), which tells the story of Christy Brown, the artist featured at the opening of this chapter—to represent accurately what life is like for many people with disabilities. More commonly, however, characters with disabilities were developed along these common themes: monsters who have grotesque physical appearances portrayed shallowly to scare and horrify, "crippled" criminals, pitiful war veterans, and amusing cartoon characters that stutter (e.g., Porky Pig), have speech impairments (e.g., Elmer Fudd), have visual disabilities (e.g., Mr. Magoo), or have cognitive problems (e.g., Dopey). Sometimes characters with disabilities were included to elicit pity, as in the tragic victim with mental retardation, Lenny, in Steinbeck's *Of Mice and Men.* Paul Longmore, a disability scholar, insists that disabilities—particularly physical disabilities—are used as a melodramatic device to signal evil or to separate and isolate the key character (Longmore, 2003). He makes his case by highlighting such characters as Captain Ahab, the peg-leg tyrant in *Moby Dick;* Captain Hook in *Peter Pan;* and Darth Vader from the classic trilogy about good and evil, *Star Wars.* According to Longmore, another message frequently embedded in stories that have included characters with disabilities is that social integration is impossible and the "final and only possible solution is often death. In most cases, it is fitting and just punishment. For sympathetic 'monsters,' death is the tragic but inevitable, necessary, and merciful

Disability Across a Century

Victor Hugo's classic 1831 novel, *Notre Dame of Paris,* has been translated often into films typically titled *The Hunchback of Notre Dame.* These movies reveal societal attitudes about people with disabilities at the time each film was made. For example, in the 1923 silent film rendition, Lon Chaney creates Quasimodo, who lives in the bell tower of the Paris cathredral of Notre Dame, as frightening and grotesque. His moving and tragic hero saves the beautiful gypsy, Esmaralda, from the evil judge, but he is brutally killed at the end. In the 1939 version, Charles Laughton's portrayal is the centerpiece of a shocking horror film. Although in this version Quasimodo and Esmaralda survive, at the end Quasimodo speaks to a stone gargoyle on the church and asks, "Why was I not made of stone?" Much more recently, the story was both animated and made into a musical by Disney. In this version, although a cruel crowd rejects and torments Quasimodo, he battles heroically to save the people and city he loves. The film makes the point that people should be seen for who they are, not for how they appear.

—By Steven Smith

outcome" (Longmore, 2003, p. 135). As shown in *On the Screen,* movies can reflect attitudes of the time in which the films were made and how such representations change across time.

People First

People with disabilities express some strong feelings about the words and phrases used to describe them. This issue is very important to people with disabilities, because words send a message to others about our respect for them. Language evolves to reflect changing concepts and beliefs, and some things that people say may have been socially acceptable at one point in history but offensive at another. For example, at the beginning of the 20th Century, such terms as *imbecile, moron,* and *mental retardate* were commonly used, and at the time they were not offensive. Other references, which we think of today as cruel, came and went. In most cases, they were not originally thought of as harmful, but they took on negative connotations. As a result of grassroots advocacy, people with disabilities and their families have influenced the language we use to refer to members of this minority group.

The language preferred by people with disabilities can be confusing because different groups and individuals have very different preferences. Although there are some exceptions (especially for the Deaf), there are two basic rules to follow:

1. Put people first.
2. Do not make the person equal the disability.

Figure 1.3 illustrates the concept of "people first" language. Here is how it is applied: Refer to students with mental retardation, *not* to retarded students; refer to individuals who have learning disabilities, *not* to the learning disabled; refer to children with ADHD, *not* to ADHD kids; and refer to adults with speech impairments, *not* to stutterers.

Figure 1.3 • People First: The Language of Disabilities

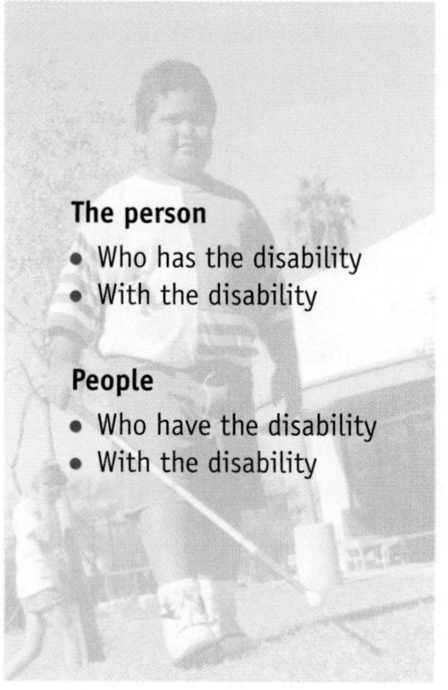

The person
• Who has the disability
• With the disability
People
• Who have the disability
• With the disability

Of course, as with almost everything in life, exceptions to these basic rules about the language of disabilities exist. The exceptions surround two groups of individuals with disabilities, those with substantial visual and hearing problems. They tend to prefer a different descriptive approach. Specifically, for those individuals who use American Sign Language and participate in the heritage and culture of the Deaf (learn more about Deaf culture in Chapter 10), the word *Deaf* is used to signal cultural affiliation. It is capitalized and recognized first, as in this example: "The Deaf girl goes to a boarding school." And it is preferable that the reference to the disability precede the person when an individual associates with the Deaf culture. Otherwise, the "d" is lower case, as in this example: "The boy who is deaf goes to his neighborhood school." A similar preference is commonly held among those with severe visual problems. Thus, even though most people with disabilities would be offended if referred to in other than "people first" language, for many blind and deaf people the "people first" rule does not apply. Remember, however, that not all members of any group agree unanimously on every issue; some people with disabilities might not agree with the rules of language described here. And the rules will certainly change over time. Remember that it is everyone's responsibility to remain sensitive to these issues.

The climate of advocacy, the atmosphere of sensitivity, and the acknowledgement that as a minority group, people with disabilities have had to fight for their places in American society should now be clear. But to achieve the level of participation that people with disabilities deserve and desire requires preparation for these responsibilities, which begins at school with an education. So now let's return to what actually is the focus of this text: the special educational opportunities available to students with disabilities.

Special Education: A Response to Disabilities

Special education is one important way to ensure that the next generation of individuals with disabilities can achieve their dreams of normalization, positive outcomes, independence, and a real community presence. Advances in technology, special education services, educational approaches, and validated practices all should come together to turn the promise of a better future for individuals with disabilities into individual realities. Before we can wisely assess what improvements still need to be made, however, it is important to understand how the education of students with disabilities began and how it has evolved. Let's first turn our attention to the origins of special education.

Origins of Special Education

Although many people believe that special education began in the United States in 1975 with passage of the national law we now call IDEA, special education actually began over 200 years ago. The legend of special education's beginnings is not only famous, it's true! In 1799, farmers in southern France found a young boy in the woods, and they brought that "wild child" to a doctor in Paris. The child was named Victor. Jean-Marc-Gaspard Itard, the doctor who now is recognized as the "father of special education," used many of the principles and procedures of explicit instruction that are implemented today to teach the boy, who probably had mental retardation.

In the early 1800s, Edouard Seguin, one of Itard's students, came to the United States and began efforts in this country to educate students with disabilities. In fact, these early efforts were taking root across Europe as well. For example, in Italy, Maria Montessori worked first with children with cognitive disabilities and showed that children could learn at young ages through concrete experiences offered in environments rich in manipulative materials. Meanwhile, here in the United States, Thomas Hopkins Gallaudet began to develop deaf education, and Samuel Gridley Howe founded the New England Asylum for the Blind (later the Perkins Institute). Elizabeth Farrell initiated public school classes for students with disabilities in 1898.

Inconsistent Opportunities

Although positive attitudes about the benefits of educating students with disabilities emerged centuries ago, the delivery of programs remained inconsistent for almost 200 years. In 1948 only 12 percent of all children with disabilities received special education (Ballard, Ramirez, & Weintraub, 1982). As late as 1962, only 16 states had laws that included students with even mild mental retardation under mandatory school attendance requirements (Roos, 1970). In most states, even those children with the mildest levels of disabilities were not allowed to attend school. Children with more severe disabilities were routinely excluded.

In the early 1970s, Congress studied the problem, and here's what it found (20 U.S.C. section 1400 [b]):

- One million of the children with disabilities in the United States were excluded entirely from the public school system.
- More than half of the eight million children with disabilities in the United States were not receiving appropriate educational services.
- The special educational needs of these children were not being fully met because they were not receiving necessary related services.
- Services within the public school system were inadequate and forced families to find services outside the public school system, often at great distance from their residence and at their own expense.
- If given appropriate funding, state and local educational agencies could provide effective special education and related services to meet the needs of children with disabilities.

Clearly, Congress, when first considering passage of a national special education law, recognized the importance of special education for children with disabilities. It was also concerned about widespread discrimination. It pointed out that many students with disabilities were excluded from education and that frequently those who *did* attend school failed to benefit because their disabilities went undetected or ignored. Congress realized that special education, with proper financial assistance and educational support, could make a positive difference in the lives of these children and their families.

The Backdrop for National Legislation

The end of World War II saw a time of increased opportunities for all Americans, eventually leading to the civil rights movement of the 1960s and to advocacy for people with disabilities during the 1970s. Before then, the courts had been dealing with issues of discrimination and people's civil rights, and concerns about unfair treatment of children and youth with disabilities and their access to education were being brought to the courts and legislatures state by state (Martin, Martin, & Terman, 1996). Table 1.2 summarizes early landmark court cases that paved the way for national special education to be consistently offered to all students with disabilities. After years and years of exclusion, segregation, and denial of basic educational opportunities to students with disabilities and their families, consensus was growing that a national **civil rights** law guaranteeing them access to the educational system was an imperative.

civil rights Rights that all citizens of a society are supposed to have

Table 1.2 • Court Cases That Set the Stage for IDEA

Case	Date	Ruling	Importance
Brown v. Board of Education	1954	Ended White "separate but equal" schools	Basis for future rulings that children with disabilities cannot be excluded from school
Pennsylvania Association for RetardedChildren (PARC) v. Commonwealth of Pennsylvania	1972	Guaranteed special education to children with mental retardation	Court case that signaled a new era for special education
Mills v. Board of Education of the District of Columbia	1972	Extended the right to special education to all children with disabilities	Reinforced the right of all children with disabilities to a free public education

Legal Protections: Civil and Education Rights

The nation's policymakers reacted to injustices revealed in court case after court case by passing laws to protect the civil rights of individuals with disabilities. Because of inconsistencies in the quality of services for students with disabilities, and because of unequal outcomes or results for these individuals, the federal government has taken on an important role in the education and the lives of individuals with disabilities (Hardman & Mulder, 2003; Kirk, 1978). The federal role in these aspects of the lives of people with disabilities has been important historically, and it continues today. Some laws only address children's rights to an education, some focus on individuals' civil rights and access to American society, and some apply to both schools and society. Table 1.3 lists some of the important laws passed by Congress that affect individuals with disabilities. As you study these laws, you should see how some set the stage for others.

Section 504

In 1973 Congress passed **Section 504 of the Rehabilitation Act**. This law requires federal, state, and local governments to improve the access of people with disabilities to society by making accommodations to buildings and other aspects of our physical environment. **Accommodations** are adjustments or alternatives that make it easier to access typical environments. Accommodations to the physical environment include alternatives to stairs (ramps and elevators) and barrier-free sidewalks (via curb-cuts that allow wheelchairs to roll from sidewalk to street to sidewalk without having to make a step up or down). Section 504 guarantees all individuals with disabilities, both adults and children, their civil rights (e.g., the right to vote) and some accommodations to increase their access to society. This provision requires that schools make accommodations for students whose disabilities or conditions require some special attention. For example, students who have restricted access to print (those with limited vision) must be given extended time to complete tests. However, Section 504 proved not to be sufficient. Many adults with disabilities still were being excluded from the community and the workplace. And children and youth with disabilities were being excluded from public schools. Thus, although Section 504 brought to the attention of the public and policymakers that injustices needed to be corrected, it only set the stage for the passage of two other laws: IDEA and the Americans with Disabilities Act. Let's see how these laws guarantee adults a community presence and students an appropriate education.

Section 504 of the Rehabilitation Act of 1973 First law to outline the basic civil rights of people with disabilities

accommodations Supports to compensate for disabilities; adjustments to assignments or tests

Table 1.3 • Landmark Laws (Legislation) Affecting People with Disabilities

Date	Number of Law or Section	Name (and any Abbreviation)	Key Provisions
1973	Section 504	Section 504 of the Rehabilitation Act	• Set the stage for IDEA and ADA • Guaranteed basic civil rights to people with disabilities • Required accommodations in schools and in society
1975	PL 94-142	Education for All Handicapped Children Act (EHA)	• Guaranteed a free appropriate education in the least restrictive environment
1986	PL 99-457	EHA (reauthorized)	• Added infants and toddlers • Provided IFSPs
1990	PL 101-476	Individuals with Disabilities Education Act (IDEA)	• Changed name to IDEA • Added transition plans (ITPs) • Added autism as a special education category • Added traumatic brain injury as a category
1990	PL 101-336	Americans with Disabilities Act (ADA)	• Barred discrimination in employment, transportation, public accommodations, and telecommunications • Implemented the concept of normalization across American life
1997	PL 105-17	IDEA '97 (reauthorized)	• Added ADHD to the "other health impairments" category • Added functional behavioral assessments and behavioral intervention plans • Changed ITPs to become a component of the IEP
2001	PL 107-110	Elementary and Secondary Education (No Child Left Behind) Act of 2001 (ESEA)	• Required that all schoolchildren participate in state and district testing • Called for the 100% proficiency of all students in reading and math by 2012
2004	PL 108-364	Assistive Technology Act of 2004 (ATA) (reauthorized)	• Provided support for school-to-work transition projects • Continued a national Web site on assistive technology (AT) • Assisted states in creating and supporting: device loan programs, financial loans to individuals with disabilities to purchase AT devices, equipment demonstrations
2004	PL 108-446	IDEA '04 (reauthorized)	• Required special education teachers to be highly qualified • Mandated that all students with disabilities participate annually in either state and district testing with accommodations or in alternate assessments • Eliminated IEP short-term objectives and benchmarks, except for those who use alternate assessments • Changed identification procedures for learning disabilities • Allowed any student to be placed in an interim alternative educational setting for involvement in weapons, drugs, or violence

Americans with Disabilities Act (ADA)

After almost 20 years of implementing Section 504 of the Rehabilitation Act of 1973, it became apparent to advocates, many of whom were themselves adults with disabilities, and to Congress that this law was not sufficient and did not end discrimination against adults with disabilities. Stronger measures were called for. On July 26, 1990, the first President Bush signed the **Americans with Disabilities Act (ADA)**, which bars discrimination in employment, transportation, public accommodations, and telecommunications. He said, "Let the shameful walls of exclusion finally come tumbling down." Senator Tom Harkin (D-IA), the chief sponsor of the act, spoke of this law as the "emancipation proclamation" for people with disabilities (West, 1994). Both Section 504 and the ADA are considered civil rights and antidiscrimination laws (de Bettencourt, 2002). The ADA supports and extends Section 504 and provides adults with disabilities greater access to employment and participation in everyday activities that adults without disabilities enjoy. ADA guarantees people with disabilities access to all aspects of life through concepts of **universal design**—where the physical environment is adjusted so that everyone has an easier time navigating it (Center for Universal Design, 2003). ADA also implements the concept of normalization across all aspects of American life. This law requires employers not to discriminate against qualified applicants or employees with disabilities. It requires new public transportation (buses, trains, subways) and new or remodeled public accommodations (hotels, stores, restaurants, banks, theaters) to be accessible to persons with disabilities. It also requires telephone companies to provide relay services so that individuals who are deaf and people with speech impairments can use ordinary telephones. Since passage of the ADA law, great strides have been made. However, injustices remain. Here's an example: People want to participate in the freedoms that life in the United States offers (Longmore, 2003). Many want to vote in local and national elections. The ADA law is supposed to guarantee individuals with disabilities such rights; however, as you will see by reading *Disability in the News* we can't assume that even what appear to be the simplest of barriers to civil participation have been eliminated. Regardless of the work still to be done, this and the next generation of people with disabilities will benefit from improvements that have been made in access and opportunities for participation.

Section 504 and the ADA also affect the educational system, but there are some important differences between them and the education law that guarantees students with disabilities the right to a free appropriate public education. Section 504 and ADA have a broader definition of disabilities. They guarantee the right to accommodations to students who do not need special education services attending public schools and to all those attending postsecondary schools who meet this broader definition. For example, it is under the authority of ADA that college students with special needs are entitled to special testing situations (untimed tests, someone to read the questions to the test taker, braille versions) and that schoolchildren with attention deficit hyperactivity disorder (ADHD) who do not qualify for special education receive needed accommodations.

Americans with Disabilities Act (ADA) Antidiscrimination legislation guaranteeing basic civil rights to people with disabilities

universal design Barrier-free architectural and building designs that meet the needs of everyone, including people with physical challenges

Education for All Handicapped Children Act (EHA) or Public Law, PL 94-142 Originally passed in 1975 to guarantee a free appropriate public education to all students with disabilities

Individuals with Disabilities Education Acts

As you have just learned, in the 1970s when Congress investigated how students with disabilities and their families were welcomed into the educational system, they found widespread patterns of exclusion, denial of services, and discrimination. Consequently, it decided that a universal, national law guaranteeing the rights of students with disabilities to a free appropriate public education was necessary. The first version of the special education law was passed in 1975 and was called **Public Law (PL) 94-142, Education for All Handicapped Children Act (EHA)**. (The first set of numbers refers to the session of Congress in which the law was passed, the second set to the number of the law. Thus EHA was the 142nd law

Barriers Restrict Voting by People with Disabilities

Date: 10/19/2004

WASHINGTON, DC–Twenty-one percent of U.S. adults with disabilities—representing more than eight million potential voters—say they have been unable to vote in presidential or congressional elections due to barriers faced either at, or in getting to, the polls. . . . N.O.D.'s poll, conducted by Harris Interactive®, found that of the roughly one-fifth of U.S. adults with disabilities who said they had wanted to vote, but were not able to:

- **29 percent said they could not get accessible transportation;**
- **22 percent said their eligibility had been challenged;**
- **21 percent reported the polling place was not accessible;**
- **21 percent reported their mental or physical abilities were questioned;**
- **19 percent said they could not understand the voting machine;**
- **18 percent said they were made to feel embarrassed or uncomfortable;**
- **12 percent reported that needed alternative voting formats (large print ballots, computer assisted voting booths, paper ballots, etc.) were not available;**
- **12 percent said needed assistance (e.g., a sign language interpreter) was not available; and**
- **8 percent said they were not allowed to have someone help them with the voting machine.**

passed in the 94th session of Congress.) Congress gave the states two years to get ready to implement this new special education law, so it actually went into effect in 1977. That law was to be in effect for 10 years, and for it to continue, a reauthorization process was required. After the first 10-year period, the law would have to be reauthorized every three years, although it sometimes takes up to five years to actually get the job done. As you read this section, follow along in Table 1.3 on page 21. Notice that each time this education law was reauthorized, more protections and services were added.

EHA was reauthorized the first time in 1986. Congress added services to infants, toddlers, and their families in this version of the special education law. In its next reauthorization (PL 101-476), Congress (retroactively) changed the name of the law to the **Individuals with Disabilities Education Act (IDEA)**. Besides changing the name, Congress called out two conditions (autism and traumatic brain injury) as special education disability categories and strengthened services to help students' transition from high school to postsecondary experiences. IDEA was once again reauthorized in 1997, and issues such as access to the general education curriculum, participation in state- and district-wide testing, and discipline assumed prominence in this version of the law. Two other important laws were passed before the next reauthorization of IDEA in 2004: reauthorization of the Elementary and Secondary Education Act or No Child Left Behind Act of 2001 (NCLB) and the Assistive Technology Act of 2004 (ATA). IDEA '04 took many of its elements (e.g., requirements for all teachers to be highly qualified and for all students to participate in states' and districts' accountability systems) from NCLB—the education law about the education of general students. ATA improves the access of people with disabilities to the community and schools through assistive technology. Let's take a brief look at these laws before returning to a discussion of the IDEA law and the court cases that explain and further define it.

Individuals with Disabilities Education Act (IDEA) The 1990 reauthorization of PL 94-142

Justin Dart, a hero to many in the Disability Advocacy Movement, was instrumental in the passage of the Americans with Disabilities Act (ADA). Many believe that without his political savvy, his persistent advocacy, and his unparalleled commitment to the civil rights of people with disabilities, the law, if passed, would not have had its scope or national impact. Here, in 1998, Dart shakes hands with President Clinton after the signing of an executive memorandum on the ADA.

No Child Left Behind Act (NCLB)

The academic achievement of America's schoolchildren is a national concern (Tollestrup, 2003). Here are a few reasons why this is so:

- Federal discretionary spending on education has more than doubled since 1996.
- Fewer than one-third of fourth graders read proficiently.
- Reading performance has not improved in over 15 years.
- Fewer than 20 percent of high school seniors are proficient in math.

The federal government decided to take action, and the last reauthorization of the Elementary and Secondary Education Act, which is known as the **No Child Left Behind Act of 2001 (NCLB)**, mandates higher standards for teachers, greater expectations for students, and stringent accountability procedures (e.g., high-stakes testing) to improve America's students' standing in world achievement rankings. Unlike previous versions of this law, NCLB did not ignore students with disabilities, even though these students have a separate federal law that guides their education. NCLB requires that 95 percent of all schoolchildren be full participants in state and district testing. It mandates that students with disabilities participate in states' accountability systems and that school districts report their results to state officials (Kyle, Papdopoulou, & McLaughlin, 2004). The main purpose of these requirements is to ensure that all students, including those with disabilities, achieve to higher standards and that educators be held responsible. NCLB also includes as a goal that *all* students demonstrate proficiency in reading and mathematics by 2012 (Ziegler, 2002). One major goal of NCLB is to raise academic achievement for all students, while closing the achievement gap between poor, inner-city schools and middle-class suburban schools. Here are a few of the main features of NCLB as they are related to students with disabilities (National Center for Learning Disabilities, 2004):

- Use of scientifically based programs and interventions
- Access to the general education curriculum
- Insistence on highly qualified teachers
- Evaluation of students' performance with appropriate accommodations

No Child Left Behind Act (NCLB) Reauthorization of the Elementary and Secondary Education Act mandating higher standards for both students and teachers, including an accountability system

Assistive Technology Act of 2004 (ATA)

On October 25 of 2004, President George W. Bush signed PL 108-364, the **Assistive Technology Act of 2004 (ATA)**, into law. This law is of growing importance to people with disabilities because they are convinced that increased accessibility in their future rests, in part, with technology. Like Section 504, ATA addresses both the educational system and community access. Assistive technology (AT) is critical to the participation of people with disabilities in the workplace, in the community, and at school; it removes barriers that restrict people's lives. For example, AT enables people with hearing problems to go to their neighborhood theaters and hear the movie's dialog through assistive listening devices or read it via captions. It allows people with physical disabilities to join friends at a local coffee house by using a variety of mobility options. AT is also spelled out in the law that guides the development of special education for each student with a disability. AT is what provides text-to-audio translations to those who can't access printed passages because they cannot see and immediate audio-to-text translations to those who cannot hear lectures, and so on (Hitchcock & Stahl, 2003). The potential of AT is limited only by our lack of creativity and innovation. However, AT is expensive and far outside of many people's budgets, particularly those who are under- or unemployed. For both students and adults, the ATA law offers, through the states, loan programs, training activities, demonstrations of new devices, and other direct services. This law allows students to test equipment and other AT devices both at school and at home before purchasing them.

Information technology is important and unfettering to all of us, and restrictions on access to it result in barriers with considerable consequences. Here's how NCD advised the president of the United States about this issue:

> For America's 54 million people with disabilities, however, access to such information and technology developments is a double-edged sword that can release opportunities or sever essential connections. On the one hand, such developments can be revolutionary in their ability to empower people with seeing, hearing, manual, or cognitive impairments through alternative means of input to and interaction with the World Wide Web, information transaction machines, and kiosks. On the other hand, electronic information and technological developments can present serious and sometimes insurmountable obstacles when, for example, basic principles of accessibility or universal design are not practiced in their deployment. (NCD, 2001 p. 1)

IDEA '04

On December 3, 2004, President George W. Bush signed into law the reauthorized version of the act protecting the educational rights of students with disabilities. Though still called IDEA, but now referred to as IDEA '04, this law is formally titled the *Individuals with Disabilities Education Improvement Act of 2004* (PL 108-466). When it went into effect in June of 2005, teachers, as well as students with disabilities and their families, saw many changes and refinements, such as required participation in states' accountability systems (e.g., high stakes testing, alternate assessments), reduction in the paperwork burden caused by Individualized Education Programs (IEPs), increased options for communications between home and school, clarification about schools' discipline options, requirements for special education teachers to be highly qualified, and delays in when lawyers can get involved in disputes. Throughout this text, you will find features that explain the requirements of IDEA '04 (see the *What IDEA '04 Says About* feature in each chapter).

Assistive Technology Act (ATA) Law that facilitates increased accessibility through technology

"America's schools educate over 6 million children with disabilities. In the past, those students were too often just shuffled through the system with little expectation that they could make significant progress or succeed like their fellow classmates. Children with disabilities deserve high hopes, high expectations, and extra help." President George W. Bush at the signing of the Individuals with Disabilities Education Improvement Act of 2004 (IDEA '04), December 3, 2004.

Court Decisions Defining IDEA

It is the role of the courts to clarify laws passed by Congress and implemented by the administration (implementation of IDEA is the responsibility of the U.S. Department of Education). Although Congress thought it was clear in its intentions about the educational guarantees it believed were necessary for children with disabilities and their families, no legal language is perfect. Since 1975, when PL 94-142 (IDEA) became law, a very small percentage of all the children who have been served have been involved in formal disputes. Those disputes concern the identification of students with disabilities, evaluations, educational placements, and the provision of a free appropriate public education. Most disputes are resolved in noncourt proceedings or **due process hearings**. Some disputes, however, must be settled in courts of law—a few even in the U.S. Supreme Court. Through such litigation, many different questions about special education have been addressed and clarified. Table 1.4 highlights a few important U.S. Supreme Court decisions related to IDEA.

The issues and complaints the courts deal with are significant, and the ramifications of those decisions can be far-reaching. Here's one example of a Supreme Court decision (*Cedar Rapids School District* v. *Garret F.*) about a student with a disability and whether his school district had the obligation to pay for continuous one-on-one nursing care while he attended school. Garret F. was paralyzed as the result of a motorcycle accident at the age of 4. He requires an electric ventilator (or someone manually pumping an air bag) to continue breathing and to stay alive. When Garret was in middle school, his mother requested that the school pick up the expenses of his physical care while he was in school. The district refused the request. Most school district administrators believed that providing "complex health services" to students was not a related service (and hence not the district's responsibility) but rather a medical service (excluded under IDEA regulations). In other words, across the country, districts had interpreted the IDEA law and its regulations to mean that schools were not responsible for the cost of health services. The Supreme Court, however, disagreed. The justices decided that if a doctor is not necessary to provide the health service, and the service is necessary to keep a student in an educational program, then it is the school's obligation to provide the "related service." The implications of this decision are enormous (Katsiyannis & Yell, 2000): the costs for additional personnel (potentially between $20,000 and $40,000 per school year), but

due process hearing
Noncourt proceeding before an impartial hearing officer, used when parents and school personnel disagree on a special education issue

Table 1.4 • Landmark U.S. Supreme Court Cases Defining IDEA

Case	Date	Issue	Finding/Importance
Rowley v. Hendrick Hudson School District	1984	FAPE	School districts must provide those services that permit a student with disabilities to benefit from instruction.
Irving Independent School District v. Tatro	1984	Defining related services	Clean intermittent catheterization (CIC) is a related service when necessary to allow a student to stay in school.
Smith v. Robinson	1984	Attorney's fees	Parents are reimbursed legal fees when they win a case resulting from special education litigation.
Burlington School Committee v. Department of Education	1984	Private school placement	In some cases, public schools may be required to pay for private school placements when the district does not provide an appropriate education.
Honig v. Doe	1988	Exclusion from school	Students whose misbehavior is related to their disability cannot be denied education.
Timothy W. v. Rochester New Hampshire School District	1989	FAPE	Regardless of the existence or severity of a student's disability, a public education is the right of every child.
Zobrest v. Catalina Foothills School District	1993	Paid interpreter at parochial high school	Paying for a sign language interpreter in a nonpublic school setting does not violate the constitutional separation of church and state.
Carter v. Florence County School District 4	1993	Reimbursement for private school	A court may order reimbursement to parents who withdraw their children from a public school that provides inappropriate education, even though the private placement does not meet all IDEA requirements.
Doe v. Withers	1993	FAPE	Teachers are responsible for the implementation of accommodations specified in individual students' IEPs.
Cedar Rapids School District v. Garret F.	1999	Related services	Health attendants are a related service and a district's expense if the service is necessary to maintain the student in the educational programs.

increased liability for schools, additional considerations for individualized education program (IEP) teams, the administrative costs for increased staff, and the complications of yet another adult in a classroom. Now let's consider more fully special education and the services it provides to students with disabilities and their families.

Special Education Defined

Special education is meant for infants, preschoolers, elementary through high school students with disabilities, and (in some cases) individuals with disabilities up through the age of 21. **Special education** is specially designed instruction to meet these individuals' unique learning needs. This instruction might be delivered in many different types of settings, such as hospitals, separate facilities, and homes; but most commonly it is delivered at the student's local school in the general education class with neighborhood friends. Though nearly all students with disabilities

special education
Individualized education and services for students with disabilities sometimes including gifted and talented students

participate in the general education curriculum and attend class alongside their peers without disabilities, some students receive a different curriculum. Some of these unique instructional targets are braille for students who are blind, manual communication systems for students who are deaf, social skills training for students with emotional or behavioral disorders, and so on. Although general education and special education articulate, these two educational approaches are *not* the same. They differ along some very important dimensions. First and foremost, special education and general education are not designed for students with the same learning styles or needs. Second, some differences are based in law—what is stated in IDEA and its regulations—and result in key components of special education. Third, general education tends to focus on groups of learners, whereas the special education approach focuses on individuals.

One way to gain a better understanding of what special education is might be to study some of its key, or distinguishing, features. No single description of special education can be put forth because these services must be designed for each individual to meet his or her unique learning needs. The following fundamental tenets provide the foundation for the educational services delivered to students with disabilities:

- Free appropriate public education
- Least restrictive environment
- Systematic identification procedures
- Individualized education programs
- Family involvement
- Related services
- Access to the general education curriculum

We'll consider each of these features briefly here and examine them in more detail in Chapter 2.

Free Appropriate Public Education (FAPE)

Remember that when Congress first passed the IDEA law in 1975, it was concerned that many students with disabilities were being denied a public education or were not receiving all the services they needed to profit from the instruction offered to them. (Review the "congressional findings" listed on page 19 that led Congress to write the original IDEA law.) Thus, from the very beginning of IDEA, Congress stipulated that educational services for students with disabilities are to be available to parents at no additional cost to them. These students—no matter what the complexity of their educational needs, the accommodations or additional services they require, or the cost to a school district—are entitled to a **free appropriate public education (FAPE)**. Note that Congress included the word *appropriate* in its language about the public education that these students have a right to receive. FAPE must be individually determined because what is appropriate for one student with a disability might not be appropriate for another.

free appropriate public education (FAPE) Ensures that students with disabilities receive necessary education and services without cost to the family

least restrictive environment (LRE) Educational placement with as much inclusion and integration with typical learners as possible and appropriate

Least Restrictive Environment (LRE)

The second key feature of special education is that students with disabilities receive their education in the **least restrictive environment (LRE)**. In other words, special education services are not automatically delivered in any particular place and should offer as much access as possible to the general education curriculum and the general education classroom. LRE and its relationship to FAPE can be confusing. To compare these two concepts, see *What IDEA Says About FAPE* and *What IDEA Says About LRE*. Today, LRE is often misinterpreted as being equal to general education class placements. However, IDEA '04 does not mandate that students with disabilities receive all of their education in the general education setting. In fact, the U.S. Department of Education, in its 2005 regulations implementing IDEA '04, explains LRE in this way:

> . . . to the maximum extent appropriate, children with disabilities including children in public or private institutions or other care facilities, are educated with children who are nondisabled; and special classes, separate schooling or other removal of children with disabilities from regular educational environment occurs only if the nature or severity of the disability is such that education in regular classes with the use of supplementary aids and services cannot be achieved satisfactorily. (U.S. Department of Education, 2005a, p. 356)

The federal government continues in its explanation of LRE to include a discussion of an array of placements, in addition to the general education classroom, that are appropriate for some students with disabilities. It does so by describing a continuum of alternative placements, including resource rooms, special classes, special schools, home instruction, and instruction in hospital settings. For some students, exclusive exposure to the general education curriculum is not appropriate. For example, a secondary student with significant cognitive disabilities might need to master **functional** or **life skills**—those abilities needed for independent living as an adult. That student might also need to receive concentrated instruction on skills associated with holding a job successfully. To acquire and become proficient in skills necessary to live in the community and to be employed often requires instruction outside of the general education curriculum, outside of the general education classroom, and beyond the actual school site. **Community based instruction**—a well-researched, effective special education approach—uses the community, actual job settings, and real situations when functional and life skills are the target of instruction (Dymond & Orelove, 2001). Clearly, there can be no single or uniform interpretation of LRE. A balance must be achieved between instruction and a curriculum that are appropriate and where that instruction can be delivered.

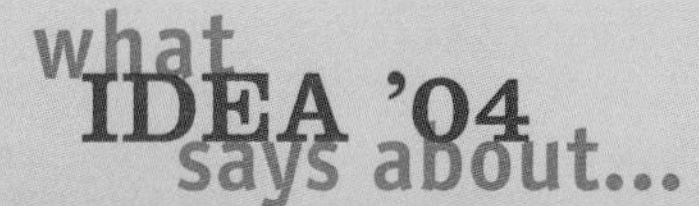

Free Appropriate Public Education (FAPE)

Special education and related services

- Will be provided without charge, although parents of infants and toddlers with disabilities may be charged for some services based on a sliding fee scale
- Must meet state standards and curriculum requirements
- Include appropriate preschool, elementary, or secondary school education in that state
- Must be consistent with the student's Individualized Educational Program (IEP)[3]

Systematic Identification Procedures

To decide which students qualify for special education—those who actually have disabilities—and what that education should consist of requires systematic identification procedures. Educators must be careful not to identify students without disabilities incorrectly. Because current methods tend to overidentify culturally and linguistically diverse students as having disabilities and to underidentify them as being gifted and talented, many professionals conclude that the special education identification process is flawed and needs a major overhaul (MacMillan & Siperstein, 2002). Accordingly, new procedures are being developed to identify students with disabilities and to qualify them for special education. These procedures are discussed in greater detail throughout this book, but for now it is important to know that the roles of general and special education teachers in the identification process are evolving and expanding. Teachers have primary responsibility for what is called the **pre-referral process**. During this phase, general education teachers are responsible for gathering the documentation necessary to begin the special education referral process (Fuchs & Fuchs, 2001). The

functional or life skills Skills used to manage a home, cook, shop, commute, and organize personal living environments with the goal of independent living

community based instruction The teaching of functional skills in real-life situations

pre-referral process Steps taken prior to actual referral to special education

[3]Naomi Chowdhuri Tyler contributed all *What IDEA '04 Says About* features in this book.

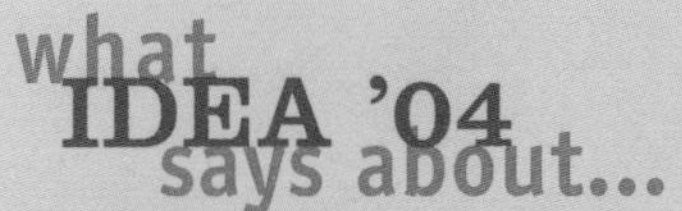

Least Restrictive Environment (LRE)

- Provides that to the maximum extent possible, children with disabilities are to be educated with nondisabled peers
- Ensures a continuum of alternative placements
- Provides for supplementary services (resource room or itinerant instruction) in conjunction with general education
- Is individually determined and is based on evaluations of the student
- Is evaluated at least annually
- Is based on the child's IEP
- Is as close to the child's home as possible, and whenever possible is at that child's neighborhood school

first task is to ensure that difficulties are not attributable to a lack of appropriate academic instruction. The next task is to collect data about the target student's performance, showing that typical classroom procedures do not bring about sufficient improvements in academic or social behavior. Then, for a student who does not make expected gains, further classroom evaluations are conducted (Gresham, 2002). The ensuing informal assessments include comparisons with classmates who are achieving as expected, descriptions of interventions tried, accommodations implemented, types of errors made, and levels of performance achieved (Gregg & Mather, 2002). Students who continue not to profit from instruction in their general education class are referred for formal evaluation and probable provision of special education services.

Individualized Education Programs

The next chapter of this book is devoted to the individualized education plans required by IDEA '04 for all students with a disability who are receiving special education services. For now, it is important to know that at the heart of individualized programs are individualized education plans (IEPs) for schoolchildren ages 3 to 21 and individualized family service plans (IFSPs) for infants and toddlers (birth through age 2) with disabilities and their families. In some states, the guarantee of an individualized education is extended to gifted students as well, but because gifted students' education is not addressed by federal law, this is not a requirement. IEPs and IFSPs are the cornerstone that guarantees an appropriate education to each student with a disability. An appropriate education is tailor-made, individually designed, and complete with supportive (related) services. The IEP is the communication tool, so every teacher working with a special education student should have access to the student's IEP and should become very familiar with its contents because this document includes important information about the accommodations needed, the special services provided, and unique educational needs of the individual.

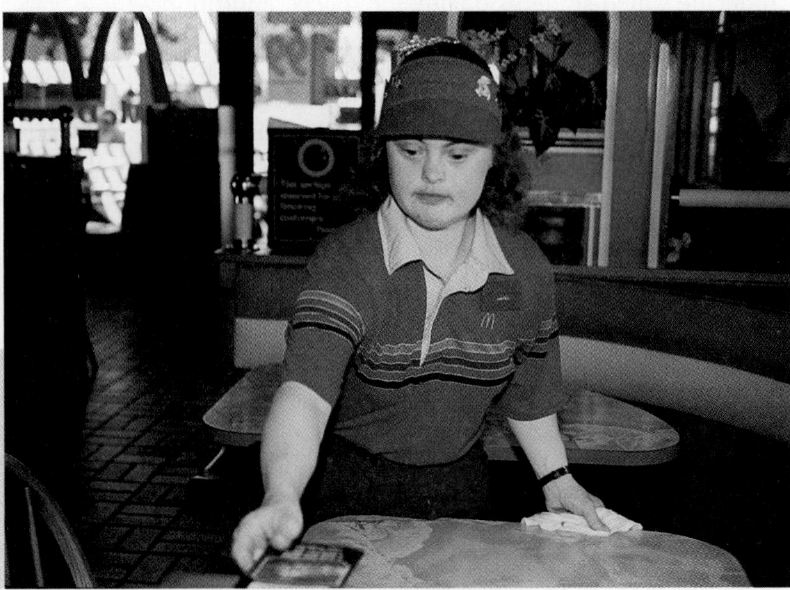

Many businesses are now helping individuals with disabilities find their places in the community and in employment settings. Restaurant work seems to be one of the most popular employment settings for individuals with disabilities.

Partnerships with communities can enrich the curriculum and link home communities and schools together in meaningful ways.

Family Involvement

Expectations for parent and family involvement are greater for students with disabilities than for their peers without disabilities. The importance of family involvement must not be underestimated because the strength of families and their involvement in school can make a real difference in the lives of their children (Garcia, 2001). The parents of students with disabilities have important roles to play. For example, they are expected to participate in the development of their children's IEPs. One idea behind the IEP is for parents to become partners with teachers and schools, so many parents and families participate actively in decision making about their child's education. All parents of children with disabilities enjoy the right to due process, procedures to follow when they do not agree with schools about the education planned for or being delivered to their children. Also, they are entitled to services not usually offered to parents of typical learners. For example, for infants and toddlers with disabilities (ages birth to 2), parents and their children receive intensive instruction through special education.

Related Services

An important difference between special education and general education is the array of services offered to students and their families. Special education provides additional services to help students with disabilities profit from instruction. It includes direct services from special education teachers, as well as instruction and therapy from **related services** professionals—experts from a broad array of disciplines other than education. These multidisciplinary services, in many cases, are what makes inclusion possible for many students with disabilities, because they provide individualized assistance to these students for extended periods of the school day. Three commonly used related services are speech therapy, physical therapy, and assistive technology. Related services are discussed throughout this text, but note here that special education is a comprehensive set of services designed to support the education of students with disabilities. Therefore, special education consists of many different professions and specialty areas. When some or all of these related services are enlisted, the result is **multidisciplinary teams**, which are groups of professionals with different areas of expertise who work together to meet the educational needs of each student with a disability.

related services Special education services from a wide range of disciplines and professions

multidisciplinary teams Individually determined groups of professionals with different areas of expertise

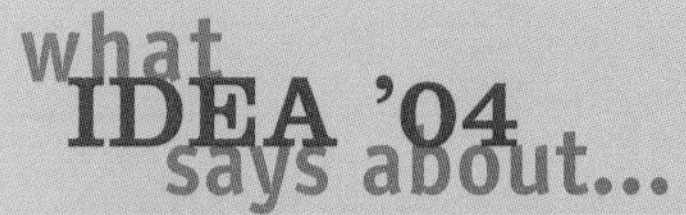

Access to the General Education Curriculum

The IEP of each student with a disability must:

- Indicate how the disability affects involvement and progress in the general education curriculum
- Include annual goals that reflect participation and progress in the general education curriculum
- Describe any program modifications and/or assessment accommodations
- Indicate how the student will participate in extracurricular and nonacademic activities
- Discuss plans for integrating the student with his or her nondisabled peers

The schools must facilitate greater access through:

- Universal design
- Assistive technology
- Accommodations

Access to the General Education Curriculum

Because too few students with disabilities leave school with a standard diploma, parents, policymakers, and advocates insist that these students should participate in the general education curriculum and be part of the accountability measures (e.g., state- and district-wide tests) that monitor all students' progress (U.S. Department of Education, 2002). Increased participation in the general education is expected to lead to increased graduation rates. Therefore, beginning with IDEA '97, extended through NCLB in 2001, and reinforced in IDEA '04, IEPs must address students' access and participation in the general education curriculum and justify any limitations (Wehmeyer, Lattin, Lapp-Rincker, & Agran, 2003). If a student is removed from the typical general education curriculum, the IEP must specifically explain why the student cannot participate at this particular time (U.S. Department of Education, 2005a). *What IDEA '04 Says About Access to the General Education Curriculum* highlights these key points. It is important to remember, however, that the general education curriculum is not appropriate for all students with disabilities. Some require an alternative curriculum, intensive treatment, or supplemental instruction on topics not available or suitable for instruction in the general education classroom. Here are a few examples of such individualized programs that might require removal from the general education setting and reduced access to its curriculum: orientation and mobility training for students who are blind, learning job skills in community placements, learning how to use public transportation or receiving social skills training for a student with mental retardation, physical therapy for a student with cerebral palsy, speech therapy for a student with a stuttering problem, phonics instruction for a third grader with learning disabilities, and so on. Remember that placement issues, LRE, access to the general education curriculum, and alternative curricular options are not mutually exclusive. Each can be in effect for part of the school day, the school week, or the school year.

Validated Practices

With the passage of NCLB in 2001 and IDEA in 2004, emphasis has been placed on teachers applying **validated practices**, which are interventions or teaching tactics proven through systematic and rigorous research, with all students. Sometimes such practices are referred to by different terms, such as *scientifically based practices* or *evidence-based practices.*

Special education can be defined, in part, by its practices. In some ways, these practices distinguish special education from general education. When a student with disabilities needs intensive intervention on a particular topic or skill, that is the time to put a validated practice into action. Although any teacher (general educator, special educator, or paraprofessional) can successfully implement such interventions, many of these methods differ in various ways (such as focusing on the individual instead of the group or targeting mastery of skills rather than understanding process) from the methods generally used with typical learners. Special education methods are more *intensive* and *supportive* than those used for students without learning problems. What you will notice is that many of these proven interventions share six common features (Deshler, 2003; Torgeson, 1996). That is, effective special education can be thought of as

1 Validated (using practices proved effective through research)
2 Individually determined (matching teaching procedures to individuals)

validated practices
Thoroughly researched or evidence-based practices

3 Explicit (directly applying interventions to content and skills)
4 Strategic (helping students apply methods to guide their learning)
5 Sequential (building upon previous mastery)
6 Monitored (evaluating progress frequently and systematically)

It is important to remember that most students with disabilities do not need this intensive instruction for all of their education. But when their learning is not on a par with that of their general education classmates, it is time for action.

Special education comprises a rich, verified, and effective set of interventions (Cook & Schirmer, 2003). However, even well-researched practices must be properly selected and implemented (Hockenbury, Kauffman, & Hallahan, 1999–2000). In other words, all educators need to become knowledgeable consumers of research. In every chapter about a disability, you will learn about validated practices that do make a difference, and one such practice will be highlighted in a special box. Because no single practice is effective with all students with disabilities, assessing the success (or failure) of the interventions used is at the heart of making special education truly special for students with disabilities. As Don Deshler of Kansas University reminds us, when all of these features are put into place, students with disabilities soar (Deshler, 2003)!

Frequent Monitoring of Progress

Even when teachers carefully select validated practices, there is no guarantee that the individual student will respond positively or sufficiently. For this reason, teachers use **progress monitoring**—a set of evaluation procedures that assess the effectiveness of instruction on skills while they are being taught. The four key features of this approach are that students' educational progress is measured (1) directly on skills of concern, (2) systematically, (3) consistently, and (4) frequently.

The areas of most concern are measured directly to check progress made on the curricular tasks, skills, or behaviors where interventions are being directed. Thus, if reading comprehension is being targeted for improvement, then it is this skill that is assessed. If the acquisition of subtraction facts is the focus of instruction, then the number or percentage of those problems that are answered correctly is recorded. Instruction and assessment are linked (Fuchs & Fuchs, 2001). These assessments also occur often (daily or weekly). They are used to provide educators with useful feedback on the basis of which they can quickly modify their instructional approaches (McMasters et al., 2000). Because this approach tailors the special education a student receives (e.g., guiding the selection of practices and monitoring their effectiveness), it is an important element that must not be missed. For this reason, you will learn more about curriculum based measurement (CBM) in Chapter 5, and more about other methods of progress monitoring throughout this text.

Participation: Inclusive Special Education

Students with disabilities are no longer the responsibility of "someone else," like the special education teacher, and they are no longer those students who receive their education "someplace else," like at the special school. Students with disabilities are the shared responsibility of everyone. The developing consensus is that for most such students, inclusion in general education, with required modifications, accommodations, or assistive technology, is the most appropriate. However, for some, participation in separate programs for at least some period of time is more effective (Kauffman et al., 2005; Martin, Martin, & Reed, 2006). Regardless of where they receive their education, it must be effective: The practices and instruction provided

progress monitoring Systematically and frequently assessing students' improvement in the skills being taught must produce results (Heward, 2003). Where, then, do the 5.5 million students with disabilities who attend public schools receive their education? And what should that education comprise? Let's conclude this introduction to special education with a few thoughts on these issues.

Participation in General Education Classes

Every year, increasing numbers of students with disabilities receive more of their education in general education classes, alongside their classmates without disabilities. It is inaccurate to picture the vast majority of children and youth with disabilities arriving at school in a little yellow bus with big letters marking the bus and its riders as belonging to special education. Most students with disabilities do *not* attend special education classes for most of the school day and participate with typical learners only during music, art, physical education classes, recess, and lunch period. Here are the facts: The federal government indicated that in the 2000–2001 school year, 96 percent of all students with disabilities received their education at neighborhood schools (U.S. Department of Education, 2002). These students are not just attending school on general education campuses; they are accessing the general education curriculum in general education classes to the greatest extent possible. Across the nation, 97 percent of elementary and middle school students with disabilities and 95 percent of high school students with disabilities participate in general education classes for at least 40 percent of their school day. Well over half of them participate in general education classes for well over 80 percent of every school day.

Participation rates, however, vary by disability (see each disability-specific chapter in this text for more information). Figure 1.4 shows the percentage of students

Figure 1.4 • Inclusion of High and Low Incidence Disabilities

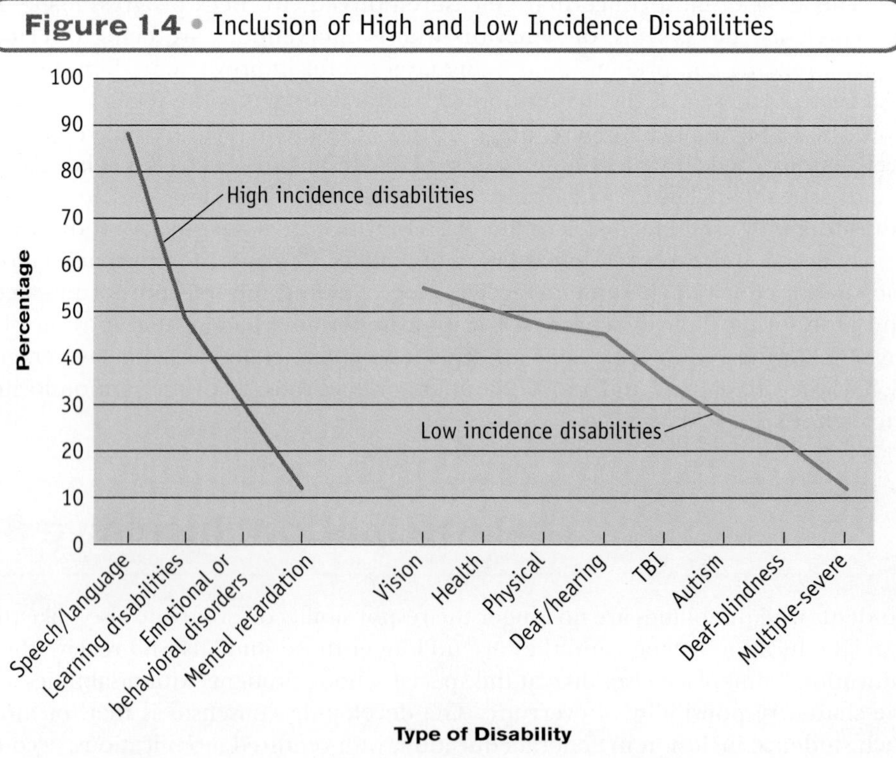

Source: U.S. Department of Education, Percentage of Children Ages 6–21 Served in Different Educational Environments Under IDEA, Part B, by Disability, Table AB2, www.ideadata.org, 2005b.

with each specific type of disability who receive more than 80 percent of their education in the general education classroom. You might think that the rates of participation would be similar to the high and low prevalence patterns shown in Figure 1.2 on page 13, which in some respects also reflect the severity of each disability. Note, however, that the data shown in these two charts do not mirror each other. Why is this so? Well, some types of disability impact education differently than others. For example, students with visual disabilities are most likely to receive their education alongside peers without disabilities and to receive specialized instruction in independence, mobility, and braille from special resource personnel either during the summer or part-time during the school year. Students with severe cognitive disabilities or with substantial behavioral problems are more likely to receive their education outside the general education classroom.

Purposes of Special Education

The overarching purpose of special education is to make it possible for all individuals with disabilities to achieve to their fullest potential so that as adults, they can attain full community presence by holding meaningful jobs and living independently. Inclusive education—that is, participating exclusively in the general education classroom using the general education curriculum—is *not* a goal of special education (Kavale & Mostert, 2003). Of course, for most students with a disability, that is the means for them to meet the purposes of special education. For some, however, these purposes can be met only through a different curriculum or through intensive instruction that cannot be offered in the general education program. Regardless of the educational goals set for any individual student with a unique learning need, all students are entitled to a very special education. Imagine an educational system that meets these purposes for each and every individual. The promise of a remarkable future is truly beyond the imaginable!

Summary

After centuries of neglect, exclusion, inconsistent treatment, and restrictions on their participation at school and in the community, people with disabilities are taking their places alongside classmates, coworkers, teammates, and neighborhood friends. Adults with disabilities are seeing physical and social barriers being reduced, so they have a better chance of having successful careers, choosing from a wide selection of leisure time activities, and living independently. Today's students with disabilities have access to an array of services, instructional techniques, and curricula that supports each and every individual so that all will achieve their potential.

Addressing the Chapter Objectives

1 What do the concepts "disability" and "handicapped" mean?

- The distinction emanates from the basic premise that society handicaps people because of disabilities
  - Disabilities: are conditions, impairments
  - Handicaps: present challenges, barriers
- Reflects the conviction that people with disabilities constitutes a minority group deserving civil rights protections
  - Reduce bias and discrimination in society: the workplace, housing, and community
  - Resulting outcomes: fewer challenges and increased participation

2 In what ways have the lives of people with disabilities improved across time?

- Public opinion has become more enlightened, and society no longer tolerates injustices or cruel and inhumane treatment.
- Individuals with disabilities, both students and adults, have legal protections.
- It is less common for people with disabilities to be rejected, institutionalized, ridiculed, abused, or neglected.
- Adults with disabilities are taking their places in society, having a community presence, and living independently.
- Students with disabilities are guaranteed a free appropriate public education and are to be included in general education settings to the greatest extent possible.

3 How might barriers and challenges experienced today by people with disabilities be overcome? How can all of us make a difference?

- Reduce high school and postsecondary school dropout rates.
  - Raise expectations.
  - Provide greater supports.
  - Target goals: provide greater access to and participation in the general education curriculum and increase graduation rates.
- Improve employment rates.
  - Expect people with disabilities to be among your coworkers.
  - Question when their presence is insufficient.
- Increase community participation.
  - Advocate for the removal of physical and attitudinal barriers.
  - Be alert to the absence of people with disabilities, and support measures designed to improve their participation.

4 Why does the federal government provide unique protections for students with disabilities and their families?

- Without protections, these students and their families were denied public education, had to pay for needed services, and experienced segregation and exclusion.
- A truly special education improves outcomes and results for students with disabilities.

5 What are the key features (fundamental tenets) of special education? Explain each.

- Free appropriate public education (FAPE): at no cost to the family, individually determined, designed to meet the unique needs of each student
- Least restrictive environment (LRE): supports FAPE, maximally inclusive, includes an array of placement options
- Systematic identification procedures: ideal procedure identifies those with disabilities, qualifies those whose disabilities have educational significance, neither over- nor underidentifies individuals in need of special education, includes pre-referral steps and a multistep process
- Individualized education programs: guaranteed through IFSPs and IEPs, might or might not include gifted and talented students (state-determined), tailor-made and complete with all necessary special education and related services
- Family involvement: has higher expectations for parent and family participation, includes more oppor-

tunities for communication between home and school, seeks the development of home/school partnerships, provides requirements for due process
- Related services: multidisciplinary teams of professionals; uniquely formed because of the needs of the infant, toddler, preschooler, or student; provided regardless of cost and at no expense to the family
- Access to the general education curriculum: participation in the standard curriculum (or explanation provided when such participation is not appropriate), included in the state's and district's accountability system
- Validated practices: instructional techniques and methods applied have been verified as effective through systematic research
- Frequent monitoring of progress: students' educational performance is assessed daily, weekly, and/or monthly to ensure continued and sufficient improvement

mylabschool
Where the classroom comes to life!

MyLabSchool is a collection of online tools for your success in this course, your licensure exams, and your teaching career. Visit www.mylabschool.com to access the following:

- Online Study Guide
- Video cases from real classrooms
- Help with your research papers using Research Navigator
- Career Center with resources for:
    - Praxis exams and licensure preparation
    - Professional portfolio development
    - Job search and interview techniques
    - Lesson planning

Supplementary Resources

Popular Novels and Books

Longmore, P. K. (2003). *Why I burned my book and other essays on disability.* Philadelphia: Temple University Press.

Reeve, C. (2002). *Nothing is impossible: Reflections on a new life.* New York: Random House.

Professional, Parent, and Advocacy Groups

American Speech-Language-Hearing Association (ASHA) in Rockville, MD: www.asha.org

Council for Exceptional Children (CEC) in Arlington, Virginia: http://www.cec.sped.org

Epilepsy Foundation of America in Landover, MD: www.epilepsyfoundation.org

Learning Disabilities Association of America (LDA) in Pittsburgh: www.ldanatl.org

Office of Special Education Programs (OSEP) in Washington, DC: www.ed.gov/osers/osep

Open Doors Organization in Chicago: www.opendoorsnfp.org

The Arc in Dallas: www.thearc.org

United Cerebral Palsy (UCP) in Washington, DC: www.ucp.org

Professional Standards and Licensure Tests

After reading this chapter, you should be able to link basic knowledge and skills described in the CEC Standards and INTASC Principles with information provided in this text. The table below shows some of the specific CEC Common Core Knowledge and Skill Standards and INTASC Special Education Principles that can be applied to each major section of the chapter. Other standards may also be applied to this chapter. Associated General Praxis II topic areas are identified in the right column.

Major Chapter Headings	CEC Knowledge and Skill Core Standard and Associated Subcategories	INTASC Core Principle and Associated Special Education Subcategories	PRAXIS II Exam Topic
Where We've Been . . . What's on the Horizon?	**1: Foundations** CC1K8 Historical points of view and contribution of culturally diverse groups	**1: Subject Matter** 1.13 Special education teachers know major trends and issues that define the history of special education and understand how current legislation and recommended practice fit within the contact of this history.	1: Understanding Exceptionality 2: Legal and Social Issues
Disabilities Defined	**1: Foundations** CC1K5 Issues in definition and identification of individuals with exceptional learning needs, including those from culturally and linguistically diverse backgrounds	**1: Subject Matter** 1.04 All teachers have knowledge of the major principles and parameters of federal disabilities legislation.	1: Understanding Exceptionality 2: Legal and Social Issues
Participation: Community Presence	**10: Collaboration** CC10S6 Collaborate with school personnel and community members in integrating individuals with exceptional learning needs into various settings	**10: Collaboration, Ethics, and Relationships** 10.09 Special education teachers collaborate with families and with school and community personnel to include students with disabilities in a range of instructional environments in the school and community.	1: Understanding Exceptionality
Special Education: A Response to Disabilities	**1: Foundations** CC1K1 Models, theories, and philosophies that form the basis for special education practice	**2: Student Learning** 2.04 All teachers are knowledgeable about multiple theories of learning and research-based teaching practices that support learning.	1: Understanding Exceptionality 2: Legal and Social Issues

Legal Protections: Civil and Education Rights	**1: Foundations** CC1K4 Rights and responsibilities of students, parents, teachers and other professionals, and schools related to exceptional learning needs	**1: Subject Matter** 1.11 Special education teachers have knowledge of the requirements and responsibilities involved in developing, implementing, and evaluation IEPs, IFSPs, and IAPs for students with disabilities.	1: Understanding Exceptionality 2: Legal and Social Issues
Special Education Defined	**1: Foundations** CC1K2 Laws, policies, and ethical principles regarding behavior management planning and implementation	**1: Subject Matter** 1.04 All teachers have knowledge of the major principles and parameters of federal disabilities legislation.	1: Understanding Exceptionality 2: Legal and Social Issues 3: Delivery of Services to Students
Participation: Inclusive Special Education	**7: Instructional Planning** CC7S1 Identify and prioritize areas of the general curriculum and accommodations for individuals with exceptional learning needs	**7: Planning Instruction** 7.02 All teachers plan ways to modify instruction, as needed, to facilitate positive learning results within the general curriculum for students with disabilities.	3: Delivery of Services to Students

Note: The following sources apply to all Professional Standards and Licensure Tests tables in this book.

Sources: Council for Exceptional Children (2005). *CEC knowledge and skill based for all beginning special education teachers: Common core cross-listed with INTASC special education (Common core-2001).* Received via email attachment from: S. Morris at CEC April 2005.

Council for Exceptional Children (2005). *CEC knowledge and skill based for all beginning special education teachers.* Retrieved from the worldwide web July 14, 2005: **www.cec.sped.org/ps/perf_based_stds/knowledge_standards.html**

Interstate New Teacher Assessment and Support Consortium INTASC Special Education Subcommittee (May 2001). Model standards for licensing general and special education teachers of students with disabilities: A resource for state dialogue. Retrieved from the worldwide web July 14, 2005: **www.intasc.org**

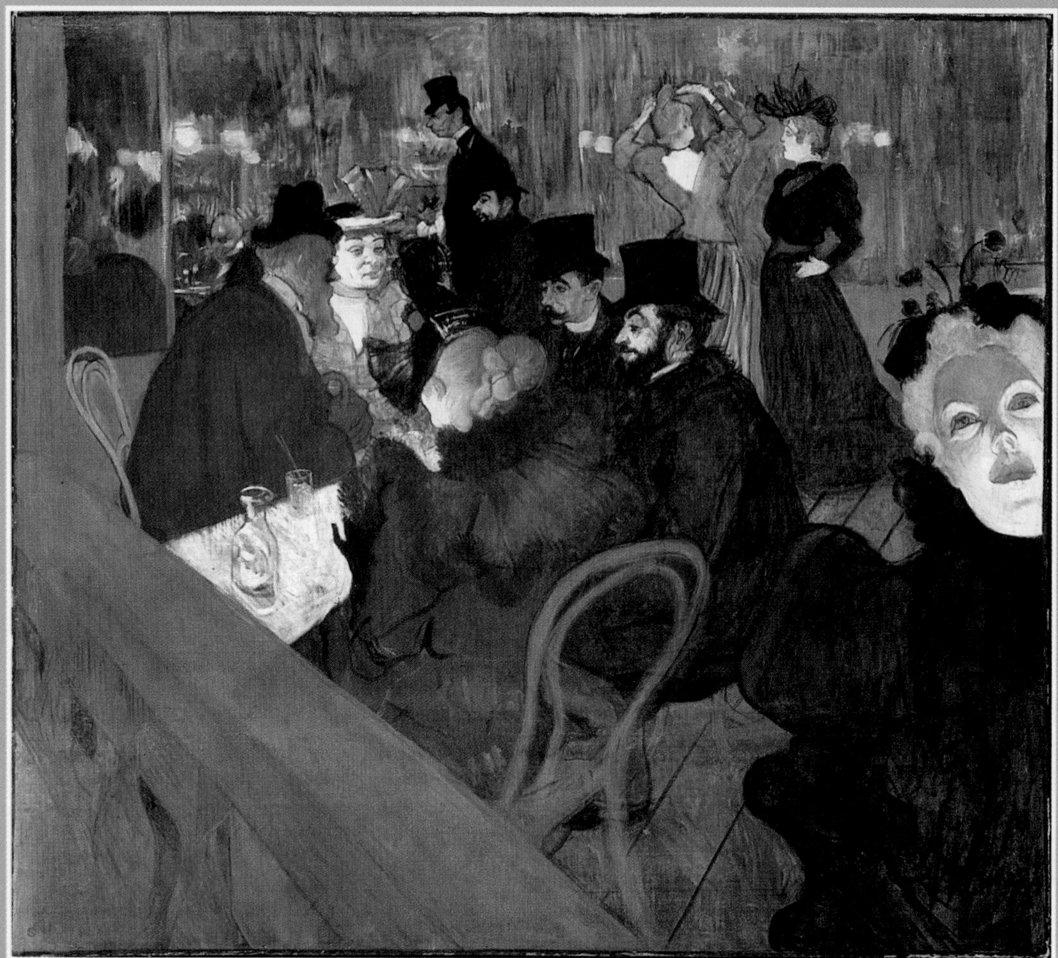

Henri Marie Raymond de Toulouse-Lautrec, *At the Moulin Rouge,* 1892/95. Oil on canvas, 48 7/16 × 55 1/2 inches; 123 × 141 cm. Helen Birch Bartlett Memorial Collection, 1928.610. Photography © The Art Institute of Chicago. Photograph of the artist: Getty Images, Inc./Hulton Archive Photos.

Henri de Toulouse-Lautrec, born into a noble French family, was closely related to the royal families of France and England. His childhood was privileged, but also tragic. Probably due to a hereditary condition, he had a speech impairment and was frail. He was highly intelligent but missed months of school. His bones were weak, and he used a wheelchair for many long periods during his childhood. Early on, Lautec retreated to painting and became highly productive and successful. However, because of his disabilities, his adult life was often in turmoil and plagued by alcoholism. (Art Institute of Chicago, 1999; Denvir, 1991; Perruchot, 1962).

At the Moulin Rouge was painted in 1895 and is now on display at the Art Institute of Chicago. This painting follows a typical theme of Lautrec, who was fascinated by the nightlife of Paris.

Individualized Special Education Programs: Planning and Services

2

"One size does not fit all."

Sharon Borthwick-Duffy
Professor of Special Education,
University of California-Riverside

Individualized education is what can make the real difference in the long-term results of people with disabilities. Goals that reflect high, yet realistic, expectations lead to real community presence and participation, meaningful careers, independence, and maximal achievement. How are these goals tailored to each student's abilities and needs, determined, and attained? The paths taken by educators, individual students with disabilities, and their families are planned and charted through the individualized special education process. Individualized programs are the heart of the process, guaranteeing every infant, toddler, student with a disability, and their families services and supports essential to successful school experiences. Individualized family service plans (IFSPs) for infants and toddlers, individual education programs (IEPs) for schoolchildren, statements of transition services for adolescents, and behavioral intervention plans are cornerstones that guarantee an appropriate education in the least restrictive environment to each student with a disability. All education professionals must know the key components or essential features of special education because the responsibility for these individuals' education belongs to all of us. Here, we will first consider ways to help students with disabilities participate successfully in general education. Then we'll turn our attention to special education's services, settings, and personnel. And finally, we will examine the plans that put special education's services and supports into action.

Chapter Objectives

After studying this chapter, you will be able to:

1. Explain five important approaches used to help students with disabilities access the general education curriculum.
2. Discuss each placement option used to deliver special education to students with disabilities.
3. Describe special education's related services and how multidisciplinary teams are formed.
4. Explain the IEP process.
5. List the different individualized education plans used for individuals with disabilities (birth through age 21).

Access to the General Education Curriculum

Placement in special education is hard to justify when it includes low expectations and locking students into a curriculum that prohibits them from realizing their full potential. In the past, special education was for too many students a "dead end track"—stigmatizing, degrading, and less effective than their previous placements in general education (Obiakor & Ford, 2002). However, special education *is* special when it is individualized to meet the needs of each student with disabilities, and the effort is spurred on and supported by school leaders (Sataline, 2005). (See *In the Spotlight* on page 44 for the story of William Henderson, one such exceptional principal.) The intent is for these services to improve access to and participation in the general education curriculum or to deliver a program that helps the student achieve independence. Under these conditions, few disagree that special education services benefit students with disabilities and their families. Although in recent years, experts have gained considerable knowledge and understanding about how best to educate students with disabilities, questions remain about how to help them achieve to their

Figure 2.1 • Adjusting Access to the Curriculum for All Students, Those with and Those without Disabilities.

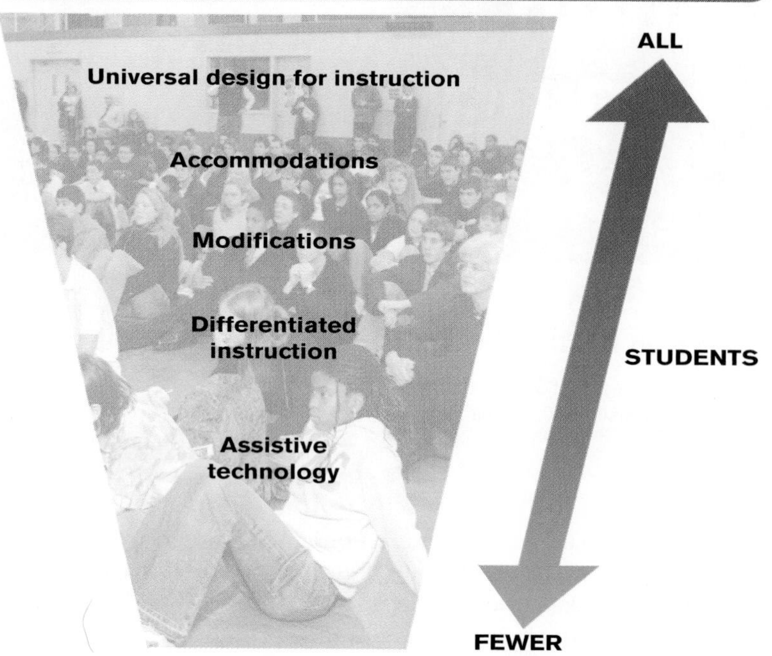

fullest potential. New principles and practices can and do make real differences. Figure 2.1 shows how some concepts (such as universal design for learning) help all students, while other supports (such as assistive technology) are designed for only a few. Let's consider ways in which educators can help students better access the general education curriculum.

Universal Design for Learning

Universal design provides people with disabilities greater access to the community and the workplace by removing or reducing barriers found in the environment. These principles, first outlined in the Americans with Disabilities Act (ADA), are now being applied to instruction through IDEA '04 (Center for Applied Special Technology [CAST], 2004a). (See *What IDEA '04 Says About Universal Design* for an overview of how these principles are applied in the education law.) In the broadest sense, applying principles of universal design to instruction seeks to remove barriers that any individual might face when participating in instructional activities (Hitchcock & Stahl, 2003). **Universal design for learning (UDL)** is a way to help all students, not just those with disabilities, to access the curriculum in nonstandard ways. Most often, UDL has technology at the core of its solution to finding increased ways for students to approach and participate in instruction. UDL varies from typical special education techniques in many ways (Bremer et al., 2002; Whitbread, 2004). Here are a few examples:

1. Unlike accommodations and modifications made for students with disabilities, universal design creates alternatives open to all students.
2. Universal design techniques are not added to the instructional routine but, rather, are part of the standard delivery of instruction.
3. Multiple and flexible methods and options of presentation, expression, and engagement are provided.

The goal of UDL is for more students to be able to access the content of instruction, thereby reducing the number of students who need special accommodations and supports. This goal is accomplished by creating multiple pathways for students to access the curriculum and the learning environment (CAST, 2004b). Let's think again about the ADA law and then see how its ideas can influence how we think about the curriculum. ADA requires that the physical environment be made more accessible. Removing barriers is necessary so that people with disabilities can participate more fully in events and activities of daily life, but many people without disabilities benefit as well. For example, curb-cuts enable people who use wheelchairs to use sidewalks, cross streets, and move independently as they shop or to get from a parking lot to a restaurant to meet friends. But curb cuts also help mothers with strollers walk through neighborhoods and help people with shopping carts get from the grocery store to their cars.

universal design for learning (UDL) Increases access to the curriculum and instruction for all students

e-books Electronic versions of textbooks allowing for the application of universal design

Let's translate this concept about opening access to the community into making the curriculum more accessible and participation in classroom activities easier. Here's an example. Current technology allows publishers to produce **e-books**—

that is, electronic or digital versions of traditionally printed books—easily and inexpensively. Because of these electronic (digital) versions, print does not have to be the only way to access content presented in books. For students with low vision who have difficulty reading standard-size print on a page, the computer can be used to immediately enlarge the print or to change its mode of access from seeing to listening. Thus a social studies text might be "heard" instead of "read." By using the same electronic version of the book, the computer can also convert print to braille. In this case, blind students who use tactile means of accessing print can read the same social studies text and complete the same assignments as their classmates without disabilities. And now, students do not have to wait for a manually produced braille version to come from some centralized resource center. The benefits of making digital versions of textbooks available to students with disabilities should be obvious. IDEA '04 encourages the development of universal design features so that more students can access the general education curriculum. Also, because the burden of supplying digital versions of textbooks is no longer substantial, IDEA '04 requires publishers to make digital versions of their textbooks available to school districts whose states sign up with the National Instructional Materials Access Center (NIMAS Development and Technical Assistance Centers, 2005).

The benefits of e-books and the availability of universal design can be important for students without disabilities as well (Müller & Tschantz, 2003). Think about students learning English, who could profit from being able *both* to see and to hear text passages. UDL allows the broadest spectrum of learners to access the curriculum: students with varying learning style preferences, those with disabilities, and those with other special needs. As you can imagine, the advantages of applying principles of universal design in teaching these students are great. Of course, teachers need to be sure that Web sites utilized to enhance instruction are accessible (Hoffman, Hartley, & Boone, 2005). For some students, barriers that inhibit access to the general education curriculum and participation in instruction with their classmates without disabilities vanish when UDL features are applied to classroom

what IDEA '04 says about...

Universal Design

Products or services developed under the concept of universal design may be used

- By people with the widest possible range of functional capabilities
- With or without assistive technologies
- When developing and administering student assessments
- To maximize access to the general education curriculum

Universal design for learning is the logical extension and application of the concepts of universal design put forth in the Americans with Disabilities Act (ADA). Universal design seeks to improve access to the physical environment and to the community; universal design for learning seeks increased access to instruction.

Principal William Henderson in the Spotlight

Bill Henderson is in constant motion. He is the principal at one of Boston's most sought-after public schools. The Patrick O'Hearn Elementary School is located in a section of Boston that includes people from very diverse ethnic and linguistic backgrounds. Many of the families that the O'Hearn serves are considered low income. Yet, the school's students have excelled at high levels. Bill Henderson expects the best from his teachers, his students, and himself. "We expect more of ourselves than we do of others." But, making the mark isn't necessarily easy for anyone in the O'Hearn educational community. One-third of O'Hearn's students have significant disabilities, many with special health care needs. And, their principal uses

braille to read, a white cane to help him navigate the hallways and playgrounds of his school, a talking watch to know the time, a computer with a screen reader, and a little device to take braille notes. There are 225 students attending the O'Hearn from early childhood through fifth grade. Henderson is excited to have an inclusive school. Parents of children both with and without disabilities recognize the benefits to all children of the kind of collaborative and differentiated instruction that is necessary for children with unique needs. Just like his students, families, and teachers, Henderson is truly special. Special, that is, beyond his unique talent to understand how to inspire students to achieve. Although he cannot see the faces of his students, he recognizes each of them by their voices and knows their names. He tries to involve families at every level possible. But maybe what's most important is that everyone knows that their leader really cares about them.

situations. Use your imagination and see how many applications of universal design you can create to solve challenges associated with access to the curriculum, extracurricular activities, environment, and community. Each new idea can make a world of difference for many more students with disabilities!

Instructional Accommodations

Most students with disabilities require adjustments to standard instructional routines to access the general education curriculum. Some require many adjustments, others only a few, and they differ in the types and extent of adjustments they need made to the learning environment (Whitbread, 2004). Most students require **accommodations**, where they complete the same assignments or tests as their classmates but with simple changes in elements such as timing, formatting, setting, scheduling, response, or presentations. Here are a few examples of accommodations:

- Enlarged text
- Sign language interpreter
- Audio versions of books
- Braille
- Removal of extraneous details from worksheets
- Word processors

accommodations Supports to compensate for disabilities, adjustments to assignments or tests

modifications Adjustments to assignments or tests that reduce the requirements

Instructional Modifications

For some students with disabilities, accommodations are not sufficient. They require more adjustments or **modifications**, where assignments or tests are reduced or altered. Students may be required to master fewer objectives, may be allowed to provide only specific parts of answers, or may be given alternative assignments (e.g., posters or photo essays instead of written reports).

Differentiated Instruction

Many students with disabilities require even more changes to their instructional programs. For some instructional topics, accommodations or modifications are not sufficient for them to access or participate successfully in the general education curriculum. These students require an individualized change in how instruction is delivered (Haager & Klingner, 2005). **Differentiated instruction** is designed to improve access to the general education curriculum by adapting instruction to each student's diverse learning needs (Hoover & Patton, 2004). In other words, instruction is adjusted in response to the individual's readiness, interests, and learning profile, whether the student is struggling or accelerated (Tomlinson et al., 2003). Thus different instructional methods might be employed for members of a class who are all learning the same content.

How might instruction be differentiated? Flexible grouping practices are one simple way to differentiate instruction (Haager & Klingner, 2005). Students with comparable abilities and achievement can be grouped so that the pace of their instruction can be different from that of other groups (Tomlinson et al., 2003). Or students might be assigned to heterogeneous groups where students complement each other's strengths and can help each other as they solve problems or complete assignments. At some point for almost every student with a disability, teachers take a direct approach by providing instruction that is

- Individually determined
- Validated
- Explicit
- Intensive
- Sustained

These key features of differentiated instruction can be critical to students with disabilities being able to master important skills needed to succeed in the general education classroom. Remember, *there is no single answer* to the question "What is an appropriate education for students with disabilities?" For this reason, "One size does not fit all," and different special education services must be available to support each student (Borthwick-Duffy, Palmer, & Lane, 1996).

what IDEA '04 says about...

Assistive Technology

An assistive technology device

- Is an object, piece of equipment, or product system
- Can be purchased commercially, modified, or customized
- Is used to improve, increase, or maintain the skills of a child with a disability
- Does *not* include any surgically implanted medical device or its replacement

Assistive technology services include the provision of

- A functional evaluation of student needs in the school setting
- The assistive technology device for the child
- Support for the use of the device (e.g., selection, fitting, repair, replacement)
- Coordination of other necessary services and use of the assistive technology device
- Training on the device for the child, family members, and education professionals, as appropriate

Assistive Technology

For many students with disabilities, universal design features, together with accommodations and differentiated instruction, still are not sufficient for success. They need even more assistance to successfully participate in learning activities, access the general education curriculum, and interact with their friends freely. Their individual needs are greater; they require more intensive accommodations. Advancements in a variety of technologies range from simple stands designed for those without enough strength to hold books to electronic speech devices that enable those who cannot speak to participate in conversations with friends and join in question-and-answer sessions in class. As you can see from the information found in *What IDEA '04 Says About Assistive Technology*, the term **assistive technology (AT)** refers *both* to equipment and to a special education related service, and AT is guaranteed through IDEA '04. Table 2.1 gives

differentiated instruction Providing an individualized array of instructional interventions

assistive technology (AT) Equipment (devices) or services to help compensate for an individual's disabilities

Table 2.1 • Examples of Assistive Technology

Instructional Area	Example of Assistive Technology Option
Communication	Picture board (communication board)
	Voice output device
Writing	Pencils with a grip
	Spell checker software
Mathematics	Calculator
	Clocks with enlarged numbers
Reading	Audio versions of books
	Print-to-voice outputs via computers
Study Skills	Electronic organizers
	Color-coded files

some examples of instructional areas supported with AT options (Demchak & Greenfield, 2003). When a student's IEP indicates that a student needs a specific type of equipment to benefit from instruction, this device becomes one of the accommodations to the learning situation that the student must receive. However, not every device you can think of is considered assistive technology by IDEA '04. For example, IDEA '04 clarified for school districts and families that costs for the follow-up and maintenance of surgically implanted medical devices, such as cochlear implants, are not the responsibility of the schools (Kravetz, 2005).

Universal design for learning, instructional accommodations, differentiated instruction, and assistive technology are some important components of special education. Together, these supports help create that very special instruction that enables students with disabilities to attain their individualized goals and, more important, to achieve their dreams of independence and success. Although these underpinnings of special education are important, it's the professionals and the services they deliver that make special education truly special for students with disabilities and their families. Let's turn our attention to how students with disabilities are educated.

Settings, Services, and Personnel

Special education is an evolving concept: Its services and interventions continue to expand and develop. Special education includes direct classroom instruction as well as other (related) services that support each program designed for a student with a disability. Together, these services are meant to be flexible and responsive to the unique needs of each student with a disability. The purpose is for all of them to achieve to their potential. This support varies in type, intensity, location, personnel, and duration. One way to think about special education and its related services is to envision a support system that contains a rich array of services consisting of components that are individually determined and applied. The term **array of services** means students do not have to travel, step by step, up and down a ladder of services and placements but, rather, have many services available to them as required. For example, in some cases, with support from a consulting teacher or specialist (e.g., an SLP), the general education classroom can meet the needs of the student. In other cases, these students require more intensive services from many different specialists. For most, intensive services are required for a short period of time, but for some they are needed across their entire educational experience. The models and approaches for providing an appropriate education to each and every infant, toddler, preschooler, and student with a disability are many. Let's consider the major approaches now.

array of services
Constellation of special education services, personnel, and educational placements

Models for Inclusive Special Education

We need to remember that the word *inclusion* has many different meanings. To some, it means receiving a free appropriate education in any setting, whereas to most, inclusion means being able to attend a neighborhood school and participate as much as possible in the general education curriculum and in other activities

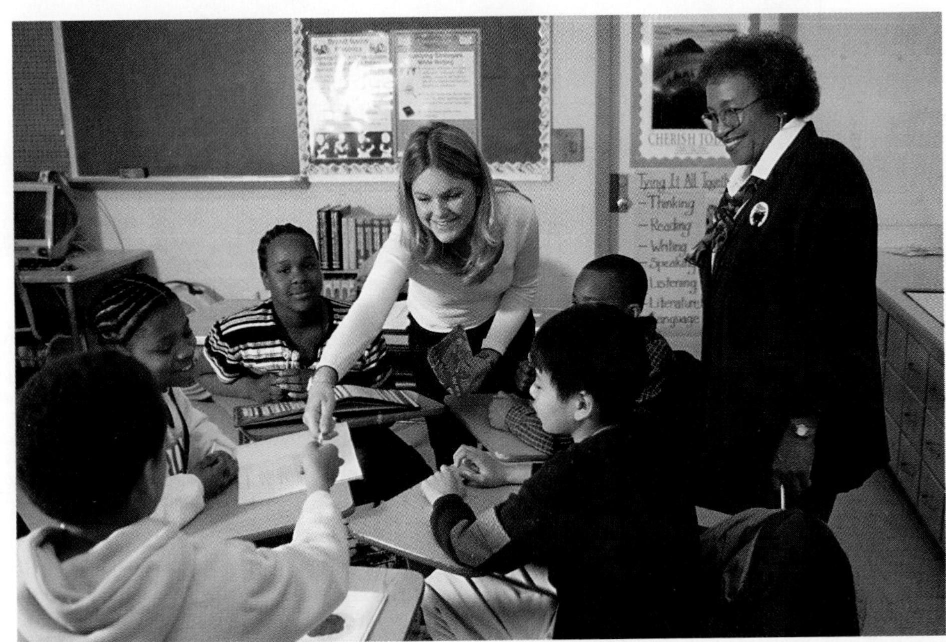

General and special education teachers work side by side in the pull-in service delivery model.

alongside classmates without disabilities. However, it is important to understand that some parents and educators believe that inclusive education must be delivered totally in the general education classroom.

Inclusive education (see Chapter 1 again for the introduction to this concept and its rationale) and the full inclusion model gained momentum toward the end of the last century. Regardless, IDEA '04 reinforces the idea that a **continuum of services**—services of increasing intensity and duration—should be available to support the unique learning needs of students with disabilities. This continuum includes a variety of alternatives and ways to deliver special education services. For example, in **pull-in programming**, special education and services related to it are brought to the student exclusively in the general education classroom. With this concept, services such as speech services are delivered in the student's general education classroom, rather than in another room. **Co-teaching** is another full inclusion model where general education and special education teachers team-teach (Friend, 2000; Magiera et al., 2005). They blend their expertise and work side by side to modify the curriculum, implement a variety of teaching strategies, and help students work with instructional materials (Villa, Thousand, & Nevin, 2004).

Almost *all* students with disabilities attend general education classes for a significant part of their school day, but most receive at least some of their special education services outside of the general education setting. In other words, models other than pull-in programming are more common when intensive services are being delivered. However, while participating in the general education curriculum, most students, even those with mild disabilities, require some accommodations (e.g., extended time on the weekly math test) and possibly additional assistance from a classmate (e.g., peer tutoring). In such instances, the special education teacher works as a **consulting teacher** who helps design services and supports that are implemented by the general educator. Typically, these two educators work as partners in close **collaboration**. Together, they might plan for the student with disabilities to have some help with note taking from a classmate. Whether a student with disabilities attends the general education classroom setting all day long or for a substantial part of the school day, one goal is maximal integration and participation in typical school activities.

continuum of services Each level of special education services is more restrictive, and services come in a lock-stepped sequence

pull-in programming Special education or related services delivered exclusively in the general education classroom

co-teaching General and special education teachers team teaching

consulting teacher Special education teacher serving as a resource to general education teachers

collaboration Professionals working in partnerships to provide educational services

Intensive and Sustained Services and Supports

All disabilities are serious and require unique responses. Although some students need special education services to succeed in only one area of the curriculum (e.g., math), most require intensive special education services across many parts of the curriculum (e.g., math, reading, social studies, and science). And some individuals require services beyond what one specialist or profession can provide. In such cases, a multidisciplinary team must be formed to address all of the students' needs.

Some students' needs bring together many different disciplines (e.g., speech/language pathologists [SLPs], audiologists, interpreters for the deaf, school counselors), whereas others have many different special education teachers (e.g., orientation and mobility teachers, vision experts who teach braille). In some cases a **paraprofessional** (sometimes called a para-educator or aide) supports the special education program (Trautman, 2004). In cases of supporting students with severe disabilities in general education programs, paraprofessionals can be assigned to an individual student. However, in most cases they are assigned to one class or shared across several classes and teachers. Some paraprofessionals provide one-on-one tutoring, assist with health care needs, or help the target student with behavior management activities (Allen & Ashbaker, 2004). Some serve as translators, working with students who are learning English as their second language. They also can provide connections and communications between home and school for families who are not native English speakers and do not understand the jargon of schools. Usually, paraprofessionals are assigned to one teacher across the entire school day, helping with all aspects of the class's academic, social, and extracurricular activities. Paraprofessionals spend about 90 percent of their time participating in instructional activities, gathering data, implementing behavior management plans, preparing materials, and meeting with teachers (The Study of Personnel Needs in Special Education [SPeNSE], 2000).

Special education is often a balance of intensive services that are followed up with sustained supports. Thus a problem area is first resolved through **explicit instruction**, where the skills of concern are directly taught. Then some accommodations or instructional supports (e.g., prompts to use a newly mastered strategy, corrective feedback regarding appropriate behavior) are arranged to ensure continued progress and program continuity. Therefore, IDEA '04 requires that students' progress be carefully monitored to make certain that they continue learning at a sufficient pace. It is very common for students with disabilities to perform sporadically, needing additional intensive services, more accommodations, or new supports from time to time.

paraprofessional An aide who assists and supports the special education program

explicit instruction Directly instructing on the topic of concern

noncategorical or **cross-categorical special education** Special education services delivered in terms of students' needs, not their identified disability

pullout programs Providing special services outside of the general education classroom

Settings or Placement Options

The vast majority of students with disabilities experience the special education continuum or different services and settings across their schooling. Very rarely are they grouped together exclusively by their disability label. Although students receiving special education services who are over the age of nine must be identified as having one of the disabilities listed by IDEA '04, most states and school districts do not group students in terms of these special education categories for delivery of educational services. Instead, services are designed for students who share similar types of problems, regardless of the name attached to their disability. Such mixing of students with different types of disabilities is called **noncategorical** or **cross-categorical special education**. For example, regardless of their disability, students who need to master learning strategies that help them study and remember academic content gleaned from high school science texts may be grouped together. Or students who need specific instruction on beginning reading skills might be grouped together. Considerable support exists for such grouping arrangements (Fisher, Frey, & Thousand, 2003). Therefore, it is unusual today to find public school programs offered exclusively to students with one particular type of disability.

When students with disabilities are not receiving their education in the general education classroom, a number of placement options are available to them. **Pullout programs** are special education services provided outside of the general education setting; they can include resource rooms, partially self-contained special classes, and special therapy settings. For the vast majority of students who receive most of their education in general education classes, the setting for pull-out special education services is the resource room, where they spend part of the school day. Table 2.2 describes the placement options or settings typically used for the delivery of special education services.

Placement should not be dictated by the type of disability the student has. It is supposed to change with the needs of the student. Also, more restrictive placements (e.g., special schools or separate classes) should not necessarily be associated with more severe situations. The assumption that a student with a severe disability is most appropriately served in a full-day special education classroom is just as inaccurate as concluding that another student with a moderate disability will profit maximally in the general education classroom. Make no assumptions about what is "right." For example, a student with a learning disability may not be able to profit from the type of initial reading instruction offered in the general education classroom, so until she or he masters basic reading skills, that student is better served in an intensive special education program.

The student's age is often a factor in placement decisions (Hanson et al., 2001). For example, many students with severe disabilities attend inclusive preschools, and parents are universally positive about those experiences. However, as these students get older and their educational goals become more and more different from those of their peers without disabilities (e.g., life and vocational skills versus preparation for college), specialized and more restrictive programs often become the preferred choice. Smaller classes, more specialized therapies and services, peer acceptance, and specialized teaching skills are available outside the general education setting. Also, maintaining positive peer relationships with classmates without disabilities often becomes more difficult for students with severe disabilities as they progress in age and in school years (Hall & McGregor, 2000). For these reasons, many parents have observed that their children with severe disabilities prefer friendship opportunities with others with similar disabilities—opportunities found more readily in special education settings (Palmer et al., 2001).

LRE and FAPE are complex concepts. Although some parents and professionals believe that LRE equals the general education classroom, others feel that LRE is to be balanced with FAPE (see Figure 2.2). Therefore, debate will continue about where students with disabilities should receive all or part of their education and about what the best models for delivery of services are. Regardless, it is important to recognize that few advocate for only fully inclusive settings or only fully segregated settings for any group of students. Future research findings should guide educators and families as they decide which combination of options is most appropriate for each student's best long-term outcomes. Quite probably, the guiding principle will be based not on placement (where education is delivered) but on how a student can best access the general education curriculum, master academic targets, and develop the life skills needed to succeed as an independent adult.

Let's look at some of the facts about where these students are educated. In the 1999–2000 school year, 96 percent of all students

Figure 2.2 • The Challenge of Balancing FAPE and LRE

Achieving a balance between free appropriate public education and least restrictive environment can be difficult.

Table 2.2 • Service Delivery Options

Type	Description	Government Category	Government Criterion
Pull-in Programming (Full Inclusion)	All special education and related services are brought to the student in the general education classroom setting.	Regular (general education) class	No separate government category exists. Although all services are delivered in the general education category, placement data are reflected in the "less than 21%" category.
Co-Teaching	General education and special education teachers teach together in the same classroom for the entire school day. Students may be "pulled out" for related services.	Regular (general education) class	No separate government category exists. Although all services are delivered in the general education category, placement data are reflected in the "less than 21%" category.
Consultation/ Collaborative Teaching	General education and special education teachers work together to meet the needs of students with special needs. Students are seldom removed from the general education class.	Regular (general education) class	Students receive special education and related services outside the general education class for less than 21% of the school day.
Itinerant or Consultative Services	The teacher and/or student receives assistance from a specialist who may serve many students at many schools.	Regular (general education) class	Students receive special education and related services outside the general education class for less than 21% of the school day.
Resource Room (Pullout Programming)	Student attends a regular class most of the day but goes to a special education class several hours per day or for blocks of time each week.	Resource room	Includes students who receive special education and related services for at least 21% and not more than 60% of their school day.
Special Education Class (Partially Self-Contained)	Student attends a special class but is integrated into regular education classes for a considerable amount of time each day.	Separate class	Students receive special education for more than 60% of their day, outside of the general education classroom.
Special Education Class (Self-Contained)	Student attends a special class most of the school day and is included in regular education activities minimally.	Separate class	Students receive special education for more than 60% of their day, outside of the general education classroom.
Special Education Schools (Center Schools)	Center schools—some private, others supported by the state—typically serve only students with a specific category of disability. Some offer residential services; others do not.	Public separate school facility; private separate school facility; public residential facility; private residential facility	Includes students who receive their education (a) in a separate day school, (b) in a public or private residential facility at public expense, (c) in a hospital setting, or (d) at home.

with disabilities—those with mild to moderate disabilities as well as those with severe disabilities—attended neighborhood schools (U.S. Department of Education, 2002). Also, the rate at which students with disabilities participate in general education classes has increased consistently over the past 10 years, while the number of students attending separate schools has declined by about 15 percent, showing a trend toward inclusive education. These data should help you put placement—that is, where students with disabilities receive their education—into perspective:

- Less than 3 percent of all students with disabilities attend separate facilities or special education (center) schools.
- Over 80 percent attend general education classes for more than 40 percent of every school day.
- Almost 60 percent of elementary and middle school students receive over 80 percent of their education in general education classes.

The data just reported indicate substantial inclusion of students with disabilities. Placement rates are changing, and they do reflect more inclusive practices today. For example, in 1984–85 only about 25 percent of all students with disabilities attended general education classes for more than 80 percent of the school day; in 1988–89 the percentage increased to 31; in 1998–99 it rose to 47; and today, if we include high school students, that proportion is even closer to half (National Center for Education Statistics [NCES], 2002; U.S. Department of Education, 2005). Resource room placements are becoming a less common placement option. Additional data indicate that the average class size of resource rooms is rapidly becoming too great for students to be provided, in that setting, with the special instruction they need. These facts worry some learning disabilities experts, who are concerned an option that many students with disabilities need is disappearing or becoming ineffective (Moody et al., 2000).

Be careful not to make assumptions about data drawn from large groups, such as the data we just presented from the federal government. Placement rates vary considerably across states (U.S. Department of Education, 2005). For example, New York's rate of segregated day and residential placements is almost five times Texas's rate. In Oregon, 72 percent of all students with disabilities receive their education in general education classes for most of the school day, whereas in the District of Columbia, 14 percent do so. Placement rates also vary widely by state and by disability. For example, in North Dakota, 73 percent of all students with visual disabilities receive their education in general education classrooms, whereas in Utah, some 34 percent do. Clearly, it is not only students' characteristics that determine where they receive their special education. Beliefs and stereotypes must also play a role in placement decisions.

Related Services and Providers

Many students with disabilities need additional help to profit from special education. **Related services** are typically beyond what general and special education teachers can provide; they bring to the student the expertise of professionals outside the field of education (Etzel-Wise & Mears, 2004; Neal, Bigby, & Nicholson, 2004). These experts facilitate the attainment of LRE and FAPE (Downing, 2004). Related services professionals could include those who provide assistive technology, audiology, occupational therapy, physical therapy, school health services, speech/language pathology, or other services needed by the student. This unique feature of special education offers a wide range of services and expertise to students and their families (see Table 2.3 for some examples). Unfortunately, particularly for students with high incidence disabilities (e.g., learning disabilities), IEP teams often fail to fully consider students' needs for related services (Mitch Yell, as quoted in Earles-Vollrath, 2004).

related services Special education services from a wide range of disciplines and professions

Table 2.3 • Examples of Related Services and Providers

Related Service	Provider	Explanation
Assistive technology	Assistive technologist	Offers high-tech equipment, low-tech aids, and other devices that help compensate for an individual's disabilities (e.g., speech-to-text translators, holders to keep books open, wheelchairs)
Audiology services	Audiologist	Diagnoses hearing losses and auditory problems
Counseling services	Social workers, psychologists, guidance counselors, school counselors	Provides individual counseling, group counseling, guidance, and consultation
Interpreters for the deaf	Interpreter	Translates auditory communications into sign language for deaf students
Nursing, medical services	School nurse	Provides and assists with special health care needs
Occupational therapy	Occupational therapist (OT)	Directs activities that help improve muscular control and develop self-help skills
Orientation and mobility (O & M)	Orientation mobility specialist	Teaches blind students and students with low vision how to move through environments, traveling safely and efficiently from place to place
Parent counseling and training	School counselor, parent counselor, psychologist	Assists parents in preparation for IEP meetings and in becoming more involved in their child's special education program
Physical therapy	Physical therapist (PT)	Treats physical disabilities and motor problems through many nonmedical means
Psychological services	School psychologist, clinical psychologist, educational diagnostician, psychometrician	Administers psychological and educational tests and interprets results
Speech/language therapy	Speech/language pathologist (SLP)	Diagnoses and treats problems in the area of speech and language development
Therapeutic physical education (therapeutic recreation)	Therapeutic physical therapist, Recreation specialist	Assesses and provides instruction in leisure skills and recreational activities
Transportation	Transportation specialist	Provides travel to and from school, as well as in and around school

school nurse A related service professional who delivers health services that need not be provided by a physician

itinerant Working in different locations

physical therapist (PT) A related service provider who works on motor skills

Three commonly used related services are speech therapy, physical therapy, and assistive technology. These and other related services are discussed in detail throughout this book. For now, it is important to think of special education as a comprehensive set of services consisting of many different professions and specialty areas. IDEA '04 does not provide a precise list of related services because its authors were afraid of being too prescriptive; rather, such services are to be determined by the exact needs of the individual (Downing, 2004). With exceptions for very young children in some states, related services are provided at no cost to the student's family. However, in some cases, related services are paid for by agencies other than schools (e.g., Medicare, private insurance companies). Some medical services are considered related services. Here's a guideline to help determine whether a medical service is also a related service: If a **school nurse** can provide a medical service needed by the student, it is likely to be a related service. However, services that must be performed by a physician are not related services (Bigby, 2004; National Association of School Nurses [NASN], 2004).

Highly Qualified Teachers

NCLB considers teachers to be highly qualified if they

- Hold at least a bachelor's degree
- Are appropriately licensed or certified according to state licensing and certification requirements
- Have not had certification or licensure requirements waived on an emergency, temporary, or provisional basis
- Can demonstrate adequate knowledge in the core academic subjects (English, reading or language arts, mathematics, science, foreign languages, civics and government, economics, arts, history, and geography) that they currently teach by passing a state academic subject test; completing coursework equivalent to an academic major, degree, certification or credentialing; pass a "high objective uniform state standard of evaluation" (HOUSSE)

Scheduling and orchestrating these services are not simple tasks. Success often depends on the teamwork of general and special educators working at the same school. Most related service specialists are **itinerant**, assigned to students attending different schools. Depending on the situation, many of them travel great distances to meet the needs of individual students. For example, a **physical therapist (PT)** might provide physical therapy several times per week with two students who attend one school, with three students at another school, and so on. Schools located in rural settings often have a difficult time arranging for all of the related services that students with disabilities require, and they sometimes contract with specialists who are in private practice and travel long distances to work with students who need their services. Scheduling these professionals' time can be complicated but is important, to ensure that no educational opportunity is missed. Regardless of the remoteness of a school, the distance a specialist might have to travel, or the shortage of related service specialists and resulting difficulty, there is no acceptable excuse for these experts not being made available. Related services are part of the appropriate education guaranteed by IDEA '04.

Highly Qualified Special Educators

A special educator might be a resource specialist, a consultant, an itinerant teacher, a special education classroom teacher, a job coach, a home or hospital teacher, or an administrator. The skills needed by special educators are many. They must have in-depth knowledge about making accommodations, differentiating instruction, implementing practices validated through rigorous research, monitoring students' progress, and ensuring that every student with a disability receives an appropriate education and achieves to the greatest degree possible. As you can see from *What NCLB Says About Highly Qualified Teachers,* NCLB (the No Child Left Behind Act of 2001, which is the reauthorization of the Elementary and Secondary Education Act) requires all general education teachers to be "highly qualified." NCLB expects teachers to hold a credential, have a degree, or demonstrate competency in every content area in which they teach. When IDEA was reauthorized in 2004, language was included affirming that special education teachers also must be highly qualified. *What IDEA '04 Says About Highly Qualified Teachers,* summarizes requirements for special education teachers. Because of these requirements that teachers be highly qualified, co-teaching is gaining in popularity, particularly at the middle and high school levels, where meeting the requirements of every core subject area that special educators teach is not possible. Blending the expertise of general education professionals (e.g., math, science, history, English) and special educators through co-teaching arrangements can make the education that students with disabilities receive truly special (Magiera et al., 2005).

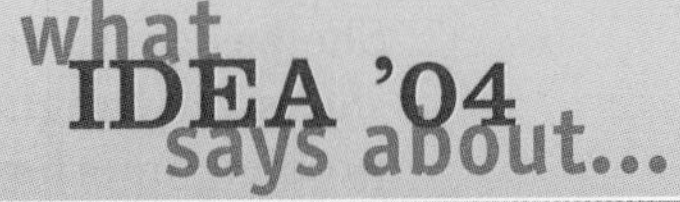

Highly Qualified Teachers

IDEA '04 considers teachers to be highly qualified if they

- Meet all the standards for highly qualified teachers required for NCLB
- Hold state certification or licensure as a special education teacher

Collaborative Multidisciplinary Teams

At the heart of special education are the wonderful professionals who join with families to collaborate and provide multidisciplinary services and supports to students with disabilities. Such teams must include

- At least one general education teacher (if the student is participating in general education)
- At least one special education or (when appropriate) related service provider(s)
- A representative of the school district who is knowledgeable about the general education curriculum and available school resources, and who can provide or supervise the provision of uniquely designed instruction to meet the student's needs
- Someone to interpret the instructional implications of the assessment results
- The parent(s)
- The student (if appropriate)
- Other people whom the school or parents invite

These multidisciplinary teams of experts not only deliver critical services to students with disabilities and their families but also act as valuable resources to teachers as they strive to meet the needs of each student.

Many others also contribute to the appropriate education of students with disabilities. Advocates and lawyers are examples. When everyone works together, they do more than ensure the protection of basic rights guaranteed by IDEA '04: They orchestrate the best education possible. When each individually arranged IEP Team develops partnerships, collaborates, and works together so that students' programs are coordinated, results are remarkable, allowing individuals to overcome challenges posed by disabilities.

Making a Difference

Truly Special Educators

As you have learned, the challenges facing individuals with disabilities and their families are great. But you have also learned that a truly special education, delivered by highly qualified educators and related services professionals, leads to excellent results. When special education is individually tailored to the unique needs of each student with a disability, and when all the services necessary are provided, even the most ambitious goals can be achieved. Across the country, countless teams of professionals are working together to make real differences in the lives of these individuals. Here is an example of such a team.

Kailyn is a nine-year-old student with cerebral palsy, a neuromotor disorder. She has considerable difficulties walking and using her hands to write. Although she is very bright, she has trouble making her speech understandable, and that problem interferes with her communication and her participation in class discussions. The very special professionals who have come together to reduce the impact of Kailyn's disabilities on her participation in the general education classroom and in extracurricular activities are many. Ms. Tyler is the special education teacher who coordinates Kailyn's services and monitors her IEP very carefully. Also part of the team of professionals working with Kailyn is Mrs. Huff, a PT who provides Kailyn with physical therapy designed to help her develop motor skills and strength so that she can use her wheelchair less and her walker more. Ms. Nee, an assistive technologist, is an expert in communication devices, and she has taught Kailyn to press buttons to use equipment that can "speak" for her. She either presses buttons telling the machine to say pre-programmed phrases or types in the words she wants to speak so that she can enter into conversations with people who have not yet learned to understand her speech. Ms. Edmonds, also an assistive technologist, is helping determine which AT devices are best suited for Kailyn's difficulties turning pages in books, holding a pencil, and working with the computer's keyboard. Mrs. Kenneth, a SLP, is also a member of the team. She provides direct speech therapy services to Kailyn twice a week and also consults monthly with both Ms. Tyler and Mr. Peterson, the general education teacher, to answer questions and provide follow-up activities so Kailyn will use and fully master the skills she is learning in therapy sessions. Together, this marvelous team of professionals meets often to monitor Kailyn's progress, plan for upcoming instructional activities, discuss accommodations that need to be implemented (or discontinued), and coordinate their efforts. The team holds high expectations for Kailyn and for themselves, for they are confident they are making a real difference in her life today and for the future. Wouldn't it be wonderful if every student with a disability had available such skilled and dedicated professionals across their entire school careers!

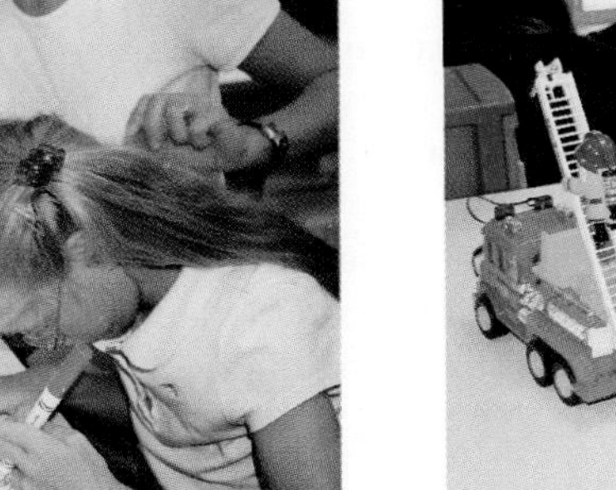

Mrs. Huff and Kailyn

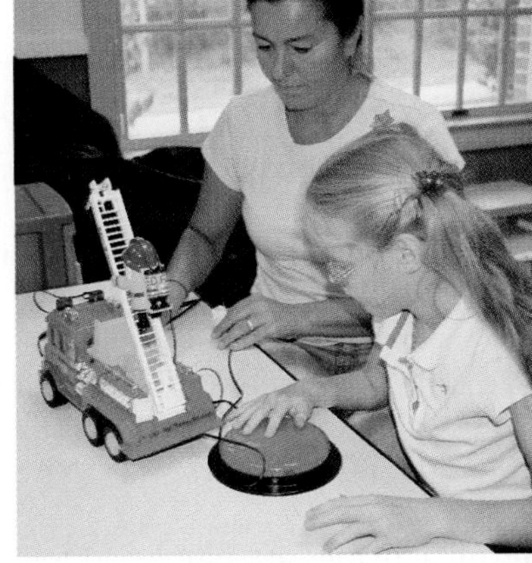

Ms. Tyler and Kailyn

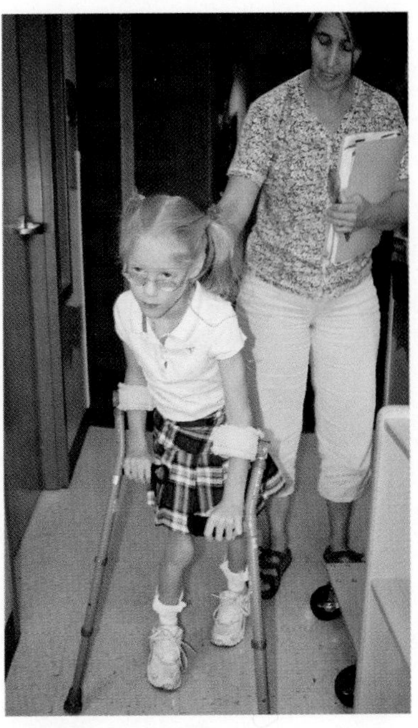

Ms. Nee and Kailyn

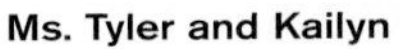

The IEP Process

IDEA '04 mandates that an individualized program be delivered to every infant, toddler, and student who has been identified as having a disability and who is in need of special education. Students' individualized education programs (IEPs) are meant to guide instruction and the delivery of services that are the foundation for an appropriate education (Kamens, 2004). Although some students without disabilities receive accommodations for special conditions through Section 504 of the Rehabilitation Act, only those with disabilities are required to have IEPs. These plans focus on both these students' strengths and their needs and are agreed upon by their parents and the school district's education professionals. IDEA '04 spells out the process or steps that should be used to develop individualized programs offered under the auspices of special education. And although education of the gifted is not included in the federal special education law, many states follow the requirements of IDEA '04 and develop IEPs for gifted students. Thus, in states where educational services are offered to those who demonstrate accelerated academic performance or high levels of creativity, the IEP process is often activated for gifted students, just as it is for students with disabilities.

Steps

The IEP process is meant to be deliberate and equitable, and the individualized program plans that it generates are the means by which the educational concepts outlined in the law are guaranteed to each student and that student's family (Office of Special Education Programs [OSEP], 2000). The formation of an individualized program involves seven steps (see Figure 2.3), beginning with pre-referral and ending with evaluation of a youngster's program. These steps are

1 Pre-referral
2 Referral
3 Identification
4 Eligibility
5 Development of the IEP
6 Implementation of the IEP
7 Evaluation and reviews

Let's look at these seven steps in more detail to get a better understanding of what each means and how they form the IEP process.

Step 1: Pre-Referral

The IEP process is initiated through a series of pre-referral interventions. The interventions implemented vary depending on the kind of problem the student is exhibiting. The major purposes of this stage of the IEP process are to

- Document and explain students' difficulties and challenges
- Test the effectiveness of classroom accommodations and modifications
- Assess the power of various instructional interventions
- Monitor students' progress (NASBSE & ILIAD Project, 2002).

Pre-referral activities are employed to screen students before more formal identification procedures are implemented. In general, before any formal referral to special education is made, teachers and family members work together to see whether educational or behavioral difficulties can be resolved in the general education classroom. The assessments used during this step of the IEP process are intervention-based and are made in the student's general education class using direct measures of performance (McNamara & Hollinger, 2003). The point here is to avoid unnecessary assessments and placements in special education, which

Figure 2.3 • The Seven Steps in the IEP Process

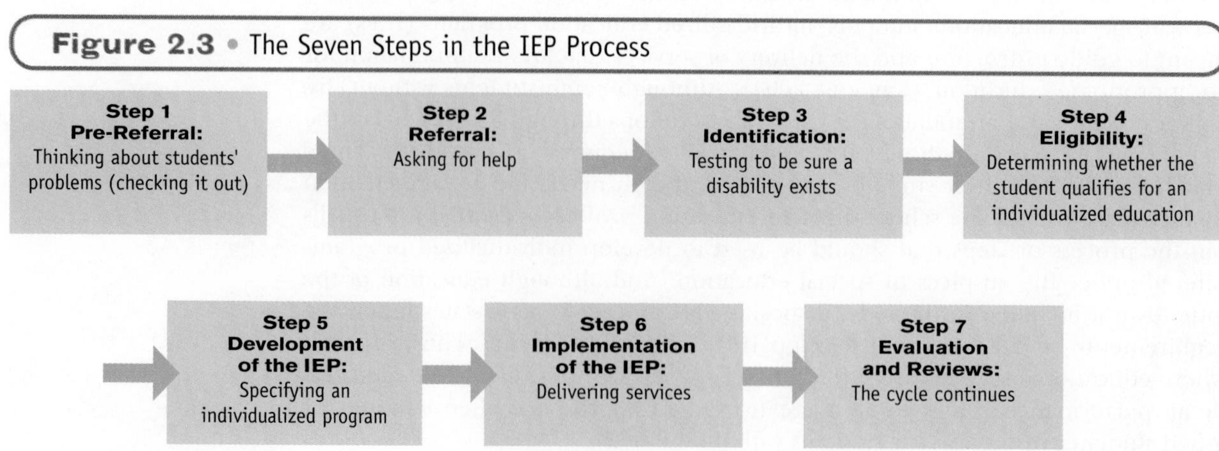

are costly in time, money, and resources. During this pre-referral period, teachers try different validated teaching approaches to determine whether faulty instruction is the source of the problem (Barnett et al., 2004). They also make basic accommodations to the instructional program and systematically differentiate instruction more intensively. General education teachers receive both assistance and consultation from specialists. Students whose learning remains challenged are referred to special education and the next step of the IEP process. Because IDEA '04 stresses the importance of this step, you will find a section about pre-referral in each of the chapters that follow.

Step 2: Referral

If pre-referral interventions are unsuccessful, an individual is referred for special education services. Referrals can come from many different sources. For infants, toddlers, and preschoolers, IDEA '04 stresses the importance of an activity it calls "**child find**," where those with disabilities are actively sought. In these cases, referrals can come from parents, a social service agency, public health nurses, day care professionals, or a doctor. Young children who are **at risk** of having disabilities because of improper prenatal care, low birth weight, accident or trauma during infancy, or child abuse are referred for special services. Also, those with visible indications of a disability (e.g., a missing arm or leg, facial differences resulting from Down syndrome) or other signals of significant developmental delay (e.g., an 18-month-old not walking independently or a three-year-old not talking) are usually identified early and receive early intervention services during infancy or their preschool years. Typically, the referral process begins sooner for children with severe disabilities, because their disabilities are obvious at birth or during infancy. As children grow older, other signs often trigger referrals. For example, a toddler who is not walking by age two and a preschooler not talking by age three are both candidates for early referrals. As children get older, reasons for referrals change as well. Students whose academic performance is significantly behind that of their classmates or who continually misbehave and disrupt the learning environment often draw the attention of their teachers.

Step 3: Identification

Assessment is one foundation of the planning process. The purpose of this step in the IEP process is to determine whether a youngster has a disability, whether special education is required, and what types of services are needed. Evaluations are conducted by multidisciplinary teams made up of professionals who have expertise in each area of concern. Each member helps to evaluate the student's unique strengths and needs. For example, if a language impairment is suspected, an SLP is a member of the team. If there may be a hearing problem, an audiologist participates, and so on. For students who are 16 years old or older, evaluation includes assessments related to the need for transition services.

Information can come from a broad range of sources, including the youngster's parents and family members. The professional who coordinates the identification process varies by state and district. In some states, the assessment team leader is a school psychologist, an educational diagnostician, or a psychometrician. In other states, a teacher from the student's school leads the team's efforts.

At this step, many different types of data are used to inform the team about the student's abilities. Medical history, information about social interactions at school and at home, adaptive behavior in the community, educational performance, and other relevant factors are considered. Evaluations include an array of assessment instruments and procedures. Information should be collected, perhaps from family members, about individuals' major life activities: performance at home, at school, in interpersonal relationships, and during leisure time. Formal tests—tests of intelligence, academic achievement, and acuity (e.g., vision

child find A requirement of IDEA '04 to help refer and identify children and youth with disabilities

at risk Condition or situation making it probable that a child will develop disabilities and hearing)—are part of the information used to make decisions about students and their potential special education status. Tests about a student's learning style are often included to help identify accommodations that may be effective to support the individual's successful access to the general education curriculum. Less formal assessments (school observations of social behavior, examples of academic assignments, direct measurements of academic performance, and portfolio samples of classroom performance) are also important pieces of evidence for this step in the IEP process. One result of the evaluation step of the IEP process can be determination that the individual does not have a disability. In these instances, the IEP process is discontinued. For those individuals who do have disabilities, this phase of the process results in a baseline of performance that guides the development of the individualized program plan and later will help evaluate the program's effectiveness.

Step 4: Eligibility

The information from the assessment step is used to identify students who actually have a disability *and* qualify for special education services. For those students, the IEP committee then determines what components of the full range of special education and related services are needed so that an appropriate education can be planned for and ultimately delivered. The education of those students who do not meet the eligibility requirements remains the responsibility of general educators.

Step 5: Development of the IEP

After thorough completion of the pre-referral, referral, evaluation, and eligibility steps of the IEP process, it is time to develop the actual individualized program plan—an individualized family service plan (IFSP) for infants and toddlers or an IEP for preschoolers and schoolchildren and a transition component of the IEP for those students with disabilities who are 16 years or older. For those students who qualify for special education, the next step requires that parents and the IEP Team make decisions about appropriate education, services, and placement. The assessment results are used to help make these decisions. It is at this point that the IEP Team begins its work to outline the individualized education needed by the student of concern. Collectively, the team members—including parents and the individual (if appropriate)—now use the knowledge they have gained to identify resources needed for that student to access the general education curriculum, determine the appropriate goals for that individual, and then turn all of that knowledge into a good educational program for the student. Of course, goals must reflect having greater success with the general education curriculum or preparing for independence and a community presence later in life. Now is the time when the constellation of services and supports that become part of the student's appropriate education are determined.

Step 6: Implementation of the IEP

Once the IEP is developed, the student's services and individualized program begin. The IEP now lays out what constitutes an appropriate education for the student, the extent to which the student participates in the general education curriculum, the accommodations the student receives both for instruction and for testing, and the array of multidisciplinary services from related service providers that support the student's educational program. For students who are participating in a different curriculum or whose goals differ from those of the general education curriculum, the IEP has specified alternate assessment procedures as well.

Minor adjustments in students' goals or in the benchmarks that indicate their attainment do not signal a need for a new IEP or another IEP meeting. Services continue. However, major changes in goals, services, or placement do require parents to be notified in writing. Some changes, particularly if they involve a more restrictive placement, may necessitate a meeting of the IEP Team and the family. Most often, this situation arises when issues surrounding discipline are the reason for the change in placement or services. Later in this chapter you will learn more about behavioral intervention plans, which must be developed as part of students' IEPs when serious behavioral infractions (e.g., bringing guns or drugs to school, fighting, being "out of control") occur. You will also learn about the rules that must be followed when such infractions cause students' placements to be changed, even for a relatively short period of time. Even under these circumstances, however, educators and students are to persist in their progress toward attainment of the goals specified in the students' IEPs. Special services, as indicated in the IEP developed during Step 5, must continue.

Step 7: Evaluation and Reviews

IDEA '04 requires accountability for each IEP developed. In most states, students' IEPs are reviewed annually. Under an IDEA '04 pilot program, which is attempting to reduce paperwork and administrative burdens on educators, 15 states conduct these reviews every three years. The purpose of the IEP review meetings is to ensure that students are meeting their goals and making educational progress. Because accountability measures determine whether the student is making progress, educators are careful to describe expectations for tasks and skills the student needs to learn in terms that can be evaluated. Whether the IEP process is for an infant or toddler (an IFSP) or a schoolchild (an IEP and possibly a transition component), the expectation is that frequent assessments of the individual's performance will occur, even if major IEP reviews occur once a year or only every three years.

NCLB *and* IDEA '04 require that *all* students participate in annual state- or district-wide testing or in alternate assessments. Alternate assessments are made available to students learning English as their second language and to students with disabilities whose IEP goals focus less on accessing the general education curriculum and more on skills related to independence, life skills, and community presence. Most students with disabilities participate in these high-stakes testing situations with supports from accommodations like those they receive when they are accessing the general education curriculum (Bolt & Thurlow, 2004). For example, students who use enlarged print or braille to read classroom materials receive these accommodations in the testing situation as well. Remember that in addition to annual assessments, students with disabilities frequently receive less formal evaluations of their progress. Sometimes these assessments are even daily or weekly. The purpose of such measurements of progress is to guide instruction and be sure those interventions scheduled are effective.

Roles of Education Professionals

Crucial to positive experiences for students with disabilities are all education professionals working at every school. Surprisingly, after some 30 years of including more and more students with disabilities in general education classes, too many teachers and education professionals still report that they feel ill-prepared to accept responsibilities associated with the education of these students (Fisher, Frey, & Thousand, 2003; Hammond & Ingalls, 2003). Their attitudes, particularly if they are uneasy with and even reject students with disabilities, influence outcomes for these students (Cook, 2001; Cook et al., 2000). Such negative attitudes are often subtly expressed in the ways they talk about students with disabilities and the accommodations needed for their successful participation in the general education curriculum (Smith, Salend, & Ryan, 2001). A key person in the

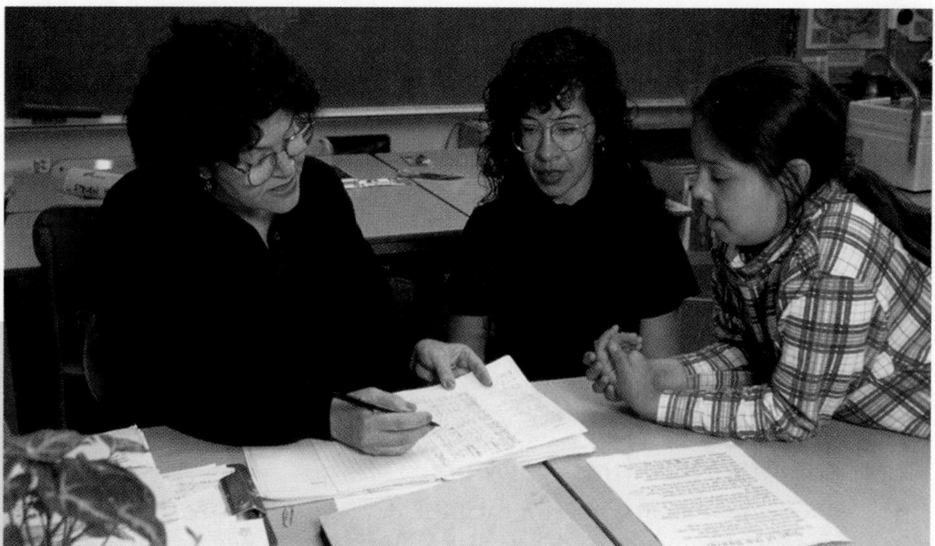

When parents, teachers, and students share the results from IEP team meetings, everyone understands goals, expectations, and the purpose of instruction.

collaborative effort at every school is the school principal (Praisner, 2003). Because principals often coordinate management efforts at their site, they can be most helpful in developing and ensuring the delivery of accommodations and modifications (particularly for large-scale assessments), in monitoring the array of services indicated on every student's IEP, and in ensuring the coordination of services throughout the school and across the district. They, like Bill Henderson (read again *In the Spotlight* on page 44), also set the tone for positive attitudes crucial to all students' success.

The educational system has not established for each profession definitive roles to guide teachers and other professionals as they collaborate to provide an effective education for every student at the school. In other words, no single or uniform answers can be provided to questions about how special education and its related services should be delivered and what the precise roles and responsibilities of each professional are. At one school, the principal and the school team might assign duties differently than a team at another school (Praisner, 2003). For example, at one school the school counselor coordinates the entire schedule, whereas at another a special education teacher schedules related services for the students with disabilities and the principal's assistant develops the other teachers' and students' schedules.

What, then, are the different roles and responsibilities of the education professionals working together in inclusive settings? Who should be responsible for what? Not all these issues have been resolved, perhaps because of the disconnect between general and special education (Finn, Jr. et al, 2001). Another reason may be lack of time for good communication. The IEP process and the widespread inclusion of students with disabilities require true partnerships among those who share responsibility for the education of students with disabilities. Douglas Fisher and his colleagues help us think about how both general and special education teachers contribute to providing an appropriate education to every student with a disability (Fisher, Frey, & Thousand, 2003). See Table 2.4 for some examples.

Roles of Families

IDEA '04 stresses the importance of involving families of students with disabilities in the IEP process. The IEP process itself can help develop partnerships among parents and extended family members, schools, and professionals

Table 2.4 • Roles of General and Special Educators in the Education of Students with Disabilities

Role	Special Educators	General Educators
Pre-referral and Referral	Assist with data collection Test effectiveness of educational modifications and accommodations	Conduct pre-referral assessments Instruction using tactics of varying intensity Instruction under different conditions
Instruction	Individualize instruction (1:1; 1:3) Apply instruction to small groups Adapt materials and instruction Consult with and provide assistance to other educators	Apply instruction to whole class and small groups Ensure maximal access to the general education curriculum by implementing adaptations and accommodations Train and supervise peer tutors
Assessment	Monitor progress frequently Determine appropriate adaptations and accommodations	Develop and maintain portfolios Implement adaptations and accommodations for testing situations
Communication	Foster parent partnerships Communicate with school personnel about needed accommodations	Communicate with parents and families Work in partnership with special education personnel
Leadership	Train and supervise paraprofessionals Advocate for each student with a disability Coordinate students' related services Conduct inservice training sessions about access to the general education curriculum	Work with paraprofessionals Participate in IEP meetings Facilitate the scheduling and delivery of related services
Record Keeping	Develop the IEP Maintain records of accommodations and IEP progress	Maintain ancedotal records Keep records of accommodation use and effectiveness

Source: From "What do special educators need to know and be prepared to do for inclusive school to work?" by D. Fisher, N. Frey, & J. Thousand *Teacher Education and Special Education, 26,* (2003), p. 45. Copyright © 2003 by The Council for Exceptional Children. Partially adapted with permission.

(Sopko, 2003). The importance of these partnerships cannot be overestimated (Dabkowski, 2004).

When parent involvement is high, student alienation is lower and student achievement is enhanced (Brown, Paulsen, & Higgins, 2003; Dworetzky, 2004). Educators need to recognize, however, that many parents believe the schools control the special education process. Too many families feel disenfranchised or confused about rules, regulations, and the purpose of special education (Cartledge, Kea, & Ida, 2000). Most parents want to participate in their children's education, but sometimes they do not understand the educational system. Read *Cultural Considerations* on page 62 to learn how one teacher took some extra steps to build meaningful connections with such a family.

Also, families often need help to participate effectively in IEP meetings and in the resulting individualized programs (Tornatzky, Pachon, & Torres, 2003). Here are some tips teachers can give parents to help them be better prepared for participation in IEP meetings (Buehler, 2004):

- Make a list of important questions to ask IEP team members.
- Outline points to make about your child's strengths.
- Bring records regarding your child's needs.
- Ask for clarification.

Considering Culture

Parents, Involvement, and the IEP Process

Individualized Special Education Programs

Janelle, the Special Education Resource Teacher at Hurston Elementary School, is concerned that so few parents of students she serves participate in their son's or daughter's IEP. She believes that parental input is extremely valuable, and she is a little irritated that so many parents "just don't seem to care." When Janelle expressed her frustration to the school principal, the principal suggested that she get better acquainted with the families whose children are on her caseload by making home visits or meeting parents at a location convenient for them. So Janelle began contacting families. Many agreed to meet with her, and she visited with them at a variety of places, including homes, fast-food restaurants, and malls. Janelle then shared what she had learned with the principal.

"Nhan's mother met me in a small apartment that she, her husband, their three children, two cousins, their wives, and their six children share. Her role in the family is to take care of the children—nine in all—while the other family members are at work. As recent immigrants from Vietnam, they are all adjusting to a new language and to a world with different ways of living, rearing children, and doing business. Each family member works long hours, and Nhan's mother can't leave the children she is watching. Even if she could, she doesn't know how to drive. It was clear that she loves and cares about Nhan and the whole family, but special education is completely new to her. I can certainly see that it can't be her highest priority."

"I thought that I was never going to get to meet Martha's family. Both parents had all kinds of excuses for putting off our meeting. Martha's mother finally agreed to meet me at the park where she takes her toddler to play. When I said that I would like to learn more about her family and their goals for Martha, she became very nervous, so I switched the topic of conversation to her toddler, the park, all kinds of things. She relaxed and seemed more comfortable. I asked again if there was anything that she could tell me that might help me develop a better school program for Martha. She said that Martha is shy and embarrassed that she doesn't do well in school. We talked about ways to help her learn at school and at home, and Martha's mother seemed relieved. When I asked if there was anything else that she would like to tell me, she hesitated then said, 'My husband and I don't have the right documents. I was afraid that you were going to take Martha out of school and turn us in. I am so glad that you are going to teach her instead.' Of course she and her husband don't want to come to a school. They're afraid."

"There were many reasons why parents weren't involved in the IEP process. I was wrong in thinking they didn't care. Every parent I met cared about their child, their family, and me as their child's teacher. They just can't show it in the ways I expected them to. The best part is that each parent and I worked out a way to communicate, share information, and involve them in their child's IEP. This has been one of the best experiences I've ever had."

Questions to Consider

1 How do you define parental involvement? Compare your responses with those of others in the class.
2 What are some strategies you might use with the parents that Janelle talked with?

—By Eleanor Lynch, San Diego State University and Marci Hanson, San Francisco State University

- Be assertive and proactive, but not aggressive or reactive.
- Listen and compromise.
- Remain involved with professionals.
- Know about placement and service options, and explore each with the team.

For families who do not speak English well enough to understand the complicated language used to talk about special education issues, participation may seem impossible (Hughes, Valle-Riestra, & Arguelles, 2002). In such instances, schools must welcome family members and people from the community who are fluent in the family's native language and also knowledgeable about the special education process and procedural safeguards guaranteed them through IDEA '04 (for a summary of those safeguards, see *What IDEA '04 Says About Procedural Safeguards*). The law encourages the family's maximal participation, so it requires schools to find interpreters to the extent possible. Remember, it is the obligation of educators to include parents and students and to inform them about the efforts that will be made on their behalf.

Procedural Safeguards

Parents of each student with a disability have the right to

- Receive a written explanation of the procedural safeguards afforded by law (in their native language unless it is feasibly impossible to do so)
- Be invited to all meetings held about their child's educational program
- Give permission for their child to be evaluated and to obtain independent evaluations
- Access to their child's educational records
- Understand requirements for their child's placement in interim alternate educational settings, private schools, and during due process proceedings
- Resolve complaints through the use of mediation, due process hearings, state-level appeals, and civil actions, within specified time periods and with opportunities for the agency to resolve the complaints
- Collect attorneys' fees if they prevail in court

Roles of Students

IDEA '04 strongly suggests that students be involved in the development of their own IEPs. Surprisingly, many students are unfamiliar with their IEPs, not knowing its contents or the goals established for them (Lovitt & Cushing, 1994). One result is a lack of "ownership" in the school program especially designed for them. Involving students has many benefits (Test et al., 2004). Particularly if they are active participants, they can learn important skills needed in life. Here are two examples. **Self-determination** is the ability to identify and achieve goals for one's self. **Self-advocacy** comprises the skills necessary to stand up and explain what you need to achieve those goals. These two skills are inter-related and can be fostered during the IEP process if students are involved (Wood et al., 2004). Here are some ways for older students to contribute to their IEP meetings:

- Describe their strengths, weaknesses, and needs.
- Evaluate their progress toward accomplishing their goals.
- Bring a list of accommodations, and explain how each is helpful.
- Communicate their preferences and interests.
- Articulate their long-term goals and desires for life, work, and post-secondary schooling.

Tools for Individualized Programs

For an educational program to be appropriate for each young child or student with a disability, it must be individualized. Therefore, it is clear that there is no single answer to the educational needs of all students with disabilities: no standard program, no single service delivery option, no single place where education is received, and no single curriculum. For these reasons, the expression "One size doesn't fit all" has become a mantra of special education (Borthwick-Duffy, Palmer, & Lane, 1996). Four tools, or program plans, serve to coordinate and document the individualized education provided to infants, toddlers, and students with disabilities. The tools that guarantee an appropriate education to those with disabilities are

- The individualized family service plan (IFSP)—for infants and toddlers
- The individualized education program (IEP)—for preschoolers through high school students

self-determination Behaviors needed for independent living, which include making decisions, choosing preferences, and practicing self-advocacy

self-advocacy Expressing one's rights and needs

When families are welcome at school, everyone is enriched.

- An additional statement of transition services—initiated at age 16 for those students who require special education services; designed to help them make successful transitions to independence, community living, and work
- A behavioral intervention plan—for those who commit serious behavioral infractions

Let's look at each of these plans in turn.

Individualized Family Service Plans (IFSPs)

Infants or toddlers (birth through age two) who have disabilities or who are at great risk for disabilities were originally guaranteed the right to early intervention programs through PL 99-457, which was passed in 1986, and that right continues today through IDEA '04. (For a review of IDEA legislation, see Chapter 1 and Table 1.3.) **Individualized family service plans (IFSPs)** are written documents that ensure that special services are delivered to these young children and their families. The IFSP is the management tool that guides professionals as they deliver these children's special education programs. **Service coordinators** are the professionals who provide oversight and coordination of the services outlined in IFSPs. The key components of these early education management plans are

- The child's current functioning levels in all relevant areas (physical development, cognitive development, language and speech development, psychosocial development, and self-help skills)
- The family's strengths and needs in regard to the development of their child
- The major outcomes expected (expressed with procedures, evaluation criteria, and a time line)
- The services necessary and a schedule for their delivery
- Projected dates for initiation of services
- The name of the service coordinator

Individualized family service plan (IFSP) Identifies and organizes services and resources for infants and toddlers (birth to age three) and their families

service coordinator Case manager who oversees the implementation and evaluation of IFSPs

- A biannual review (every six months), with the child's family, of progress made and of any need for modifications in the IFSP
- Indication of methods for transitioning the child to services available for children ages three to five

To many service coordinators and early childhood specialists, the IFSP is a working document for an ongoing process in which parents and specialists work together, continually modifying, expanding, and developing a child's educational program. Children and families who participate in early intervention programs often find these years to be an intense period, with many professionals offering advice, training, guidance, and personalized services, as well as care and concern. Also, the transition to preschool at the age of three can be particularly difficult and frightening. One reason is that services that are delivered primarily at the family's home now will be delivered at a preschool. Thus IFSPs include plans for transition efforts for these youngsters and their families to bridge a time of very intensive and individually delivered intervention to a more traditional classroom situation (CEC, 1999). IDEA '04 allows states to give families the option of delaying entrance into school-based preschool programs by keeping their child in an early intervention program, but when they do so, the family sometimes has to pay for some or all of the services.

Named after Susan Gray, a pioneer in the Head Start movement, the preschool at the John F. Kennedy Center at Vanderbilt University remains an active research center. Here, young children with and without disabilities learn together.

Individualized Education Programs (IEPs)

The documents designed to ensure that students with disabilities who are age 3 to 21 receive special education and related services appropriate to their needs are the **individualized education programs (IEPs)**. These management tools are the cornerstones of every educational program planned for preschoolers (ages 3 to 5) and students with a disability (Office of Special Education Programs [OSEP], 2000). IDEA '04 delineated the minimal contents of the IEP, and it is important that every educator know these key components:

- *Current performance:* The student's present levels of educational performance and indications about how the student's disability influences participation and progress in the general education curriculum
- *Goals:* Statement of measurable goals related to participation in the general education curriculum, as well as meeting other educational needs resulting from the disability
- *Special education and related services:* Specific educational services to be provided, including accommodations, program modifications, or supports that allow participation in the general education curriculum and in extracurricular activities
- *Participation with students without disabilities:* Explanation about the extent to which the student will *not* participate in general education classes and in extracurricular activities alongside peers without disabilities
- *Participation in state- and district-wide testing:* Description of accommodations needed for these assessments (if the student will not be participating, a statement listing reasons for nonparticipation and explaining how the student will be alternately assessed)
- *Dates and places:* Projected dates for initiation of services, where they will be delivered, and expected duration of those services
- *Transition service needs:* Beginning at age 16, for those students whose goals are related to community presence and independence, a transition component is included in the IEP to identify postschool goals and address transition assessments and service needs

individualized education program (IEP) Management tool to identify and organize needed services

Table 2.5 • Differences Between IFSPs and IEPs

Feature	IFSP	IEP
Target of Services	Infants and toddlers with disabilities (birth to two) Families of these children	Preschoolers with disabilities students with disabilities (ages 3 to 21)
Place for Services	Natural environment Homes Day care Clinics	Schools
Costs to Families	Costs for some services may be charged to families (on a sliding scale according to income)	No cost to families (unless they elect other options) (FAPE)
Lead Agency	State designates (considerable variation)	State education agency (schools)

- *Age of majority:* Beginning at least one year before students reach the age of majority, they must be told about those rights that transfer to them
- *Measuring progress:* Statement of how the student's progress will be measured and how parents will be informed about this progress

IEPs should be written for each student with a disability, so each IEP will be different from the next. Some might include the services of a SLP, others might involve a PT, and so on. All the needs of the student should be expressed, not just a selected few. Academic areas may be reflected, but so may areas not typically part of educational programs for students without disabilities (e.g., fine and gross motor skills and functional life skills). Services indicated on the IEP must be provided. Services not being readily available is no reason for omitting them from an IEP: If the student needs the service, it must be delivered. For example, if a student needs the services of an assistive technologist and some special equipment, those services and that equipment need to be made available. Any change in placement, in the related services specified in the IEP, or in major goals necessitates another IEP meeting and mutual approval by the family and the school district.

The contents of IEPs should be available to all educators who work with the student. IEPs are meant to be a communication tool. Surprisingly, teachers often do not even know what services, goals, and objectives the education of their students should include. This situation leads one to ask how an appropriate education can be delivered when the educators who interact with students with disabilities do not understand what the students' education should comprise. The answer is obvious. An appropriate education *can't* be delivered under these circumstances. For easy reference, Table 2.5 lists some important differences between the IFSP for infants and toddlers, and the IEP for schoolchildren.

statement of transition services Component of IEPs for students older than age 16 to assist students moving to adulthood

behavioral intervention plan Includes a functional assessment and procedures to prevent and intervene for behavioral infractions

interim alternative educational setting (IAES) A special education placement to ensure progress toward IEP goals, assigned when a serious behavioral infraction requires removal from current placement

Statement of Transition Services

When IDEA was reauthorized in 1997, plans to help students transition from school to postsecondary experiences became a special education requirement. At that time, it was a separate document—a mini-IEP in its own right—for students age 14 and older and was called an individualized transition plan (ITP). But since then, these plans for assessments and services to prepare for postschool life, or **statements of transition services**, have been made a part of the students' IEPs; they are no longer stand-alone documents. IDEA '04 increased to 16 the age for initiation of the transition component of students' IEPs (for more information, see *What IDEA '04 Says About Transition Services*). Transition planning can be most important for high school students with disabilities. Although more of these students than ever before (some 56 percent) graduate from high school with a standard diploma and the number of them attending college has doubled, their employment statistics are dismal (U.S. Department of Education, 2002; Van Kuren, 2004). Here are a few shocking statistics: Only 30 percent of high school graduates with disabilities and 45 percent with some college education are employed. And only 25 percent of those who go to college graduate. One way to make a difference and improve the outcomes of people with disabilities is through transition planning and services. Helping students set goals for themselves, gain work experience, and develop skills needed for independent living can be critical to the life satisfaction experienced by adults with disabilities (Neubert, 2003).

what IDEA '04 says about...

Transition Services

The IEP in effect when a child turns 16 must

- Include postsecondary goals that are appropriate, measurable, and based on the results of transition evaluations in the areas of training, education, employment, and independent living skills (when appropriate)
- List transition services and coursework required to help the student meet those goals
- Include (at least 1 year prior to the student's reaching the age of majority) a statement that the student has been informed about his or her rights as an adult
- Include (upon the student's exiting high school) a summary of transition needs and accomplishments
- Be reviewed and updated annually thereafter

The transition component supplements and complements the school-based IEP process. Whereas the IEP describes the educational goals and objectives that a student should achieve during a school year, the transition services part of the IEP focuses on the academic and functional achievement of the individual so that the movement from school to postschool activities will be successful (National Center on Secondary Education and Transition [NCSET], 2005). Transition components are designed to facilitate the process of going from high school to any of these postschool options: postsecondary education, vocational education, integrated employment (including supported employment), adult services, or community participation (de Fur, 2003). These last years of school, however, can be critical to these students' achievement of special education outcomes and to their smooth and successful transition to adulthood.

Behavioral Intervention Plans

IDEA '04 requires that when any student with a disability commits serious behavioral infractions, a **behavioral intervention plan**, which is like an IEP but addresses the behavioral infraction, be developed. See *What IDEA '04 Says About Behavioral Intervention Plans* for a summary of what the legislators had in mind when they included these plans in the law. Why did behavioral plans for students who have major behavioral issues become part of students' IEPs? One reason reflects concerns of Congress and the public about violence, discipline, and special education students. Students without disabilities can be expelled for breaking certain school rules (e.g., bringing guns to school, engaging in serious fighting), but some students with disabilities cannot. These students can, however, be removed from their current placement and receive their education away from their assigned classroom(s) in what is called an **interim alternative educational setting (IAES)** for up to 45 school days. Continued progress toward the attainment of IEP

Learning job skills is an important part of the high school curriculum for many students with disabilities.

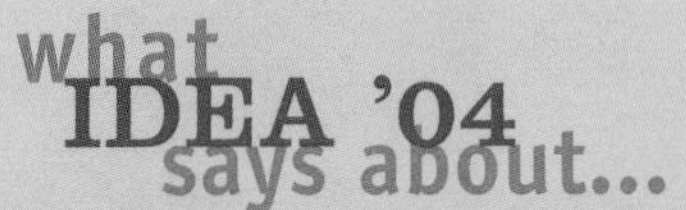

Behavioral Intervention Plans

When considering a situation where student behavior

- *Interferes with learning,* the IEP team should consider the use of positive behavioral interventions and supports, and other strategies.
- *Violates the student conduct code,* a functional behavioral assessment may be administered and behavioral intervention services and modifications (which include a behavioral intervention plan) may be implemented if appropriate.
- *Is determined to be the result of manifestation determination,* the IEP team must:
  - Conduct a functional behavioral assessment and implement a behavioral intervention plan, or
  - For students with a current behavioral intervention plan in place, review previous functional behavioral assessments and modify the existing plan, if necessary.

objectives must be one intention of the IAES placement. Students who cannot be expelled are those whose disruptive behavior was caused by the disability. Under the older versions of IDEA, this protection was called the **stay-put provision**. Through a process called **manifestation determination**, educators figure out whether the disability caused the infraction. All students with disabilities who are violent or "out of control" must have behavioral intervention plans developed for them. These plans focus not only on the control or elimination of future serious behavioral infractions but also on the development of positive social skills.

To develop behavioral plans, educators use a process called **functional behavioral assessment (FBA)**, which clarifies the student's preferences for specific academic tasks and determines when the undesirable behavior is likely to occur (Kern et al., 2001). Originally developed for students with severe disabilities, IDEA '04 suggests the use of FBAs when students with any disability are faced with disciplinary actions. The FBA process leads teachers directly to effective interventions with socially validated outcomes (Barnhill, 2005; Ryan, Halsey, & Matthews, 2003). FBAs help determine the nature of the behavior of concern, the reason or motivation for the behavior, and under what conditions the behavior does and does not occur (Hanley, Iwata, & McCord, 2003).

The goal of the assessment is to determine what activities are associated with problem behaviors and to identify the student's interests and preferences (Shippen, Simpson, & Crites, 2003). Instructional activities are then modified to incorporate the student's "likes" into activities where problems typically occur. Here's how it works: Ethan's behavior during activities that require him to write is highly disruptive. However, he likes to use the computer, so he is allowed to complete written assignments using a word processing program on a computer. The double benefit is that his academic performance is improving and his disruptive behavior has decreased. There is a major caution, however. These assessments often miss behaviors that occur rarely—a real problem because many low frequency infractions (e.g., hitting a teacher, setting a fire, breaking a window) are the most dangerous and serious (Nichols, 2000). Because of the propensity of students with emotional or behavioral disorders to exhibit behavior problems, FBAs are used with most of these students. Therefore, more details about FBA are found in Chapter 7.

Evaluating Progress and Revising Programs

Assessments of students' performance have many different purposes. Four common purposes of evaluation are particularly important in special education:

1. Identify and qualify students for special education.
2. Determine annual gains in performance.
3. Guide instruction.
4. Change a student's services.

Eligibility

Remember, special education is only for students with disabilities that affect their education and learning. Determining eligibility for special education usually includes a "battery of tests" (more than one test or type of assessment) and is conducted by evaluation experts (e.g., school psychologists, diagnosticians, audiologists, ophthalmologists). Such evaluations often include standardized tests that were normed on large groups of people. (Intelligence and achievement tests are examples of standardized instruments.) The use of standardized tests concerns many educators, partly because such tests can contribute to the overrepresentation of culturally and linguistically diverse students in special education (see Chapter 3). In an attempt to resolve or at least monitor this problem, IDEA '04 requires states to collect data and change practices that may be discriminatory. Remember, all evaluation instruments or procedures selected should reflect the purpose or intended outcomes of the evaluation process. Thus, if the purpose is to determine whether a student has a disability and qualifies for special education, standardized tests are typically part of the assessment package. They are used again when students are reevaluated to determine whether special education services are still necessary. Specific identification methods vary somewhat by disability, so a section in each of the chapters about specific disabilities is devoted to this topic.

Statewide and District-Wide Assessments

All teachers, parents, and policymakers are concerned about how well students are learning and mastering the curriculum. Therefore, NCLB requires educational accountability by insisting that all students participate in state- and district-wide assessments (Ziegler, 2002). (See *What NCLB Says About High Stakes Testing* on page 70, for a review of these rules.) Because the overall results from individual schools are used to "grade" a school's effectiveness and sometimes affect the school's funding, these yearly assessments are often referred to as **high stakes testing**. The ultimate expectation is that all children will achieve proficiency in reading and math, and if children's test scores indicate that they do not reach those levels, the schools they attend will experience significant disincentives. All students with disabilities must participate in their school district's accountability system. Students who are participating in the general education curriculum may take tests with accommodations if those are called out in the student's IEP (Shriner & Destefano, 2003). Although many different types of accommodations are used, the five most common are providing the answers orally (dictated response), enlarged print, extended time, braille, and using a sign language interpreter (Bolt & Thurlow, 2004). Students whose curriculum targets life skills and community presence most often participate in **alternate assessments**, which evaluate students' progress toward meeting goals that are not part of the general education curriculum (Thompson et al., 2004). Very few students with disabilities receive alternate assessments because IDEA '04 allows states to give this option to only a very small proportion of students. For more about the participation of students with disabilities in statewide and district-wide accountability systems, see *What IDEA '04 Says About High Stakes Testing* on page 71.

One hope for the NCLB/IDEA '04 accountability and assessment requirements is that teachers will concentrate their efforts on the education of students with disabilities, increasing their participation in the general education curriculum and improving their achievement. Some evidence shows that students' achievement increases when accountability measures are stringent (Fuchs et al., 2000). However, some educators and parents have concerns about high stakes testing. Fears arise on several fronts. Some general educators are afraid that students with disabilities cannot make sufficient progress in the general education curriculum. They are worried

stay-put provision Prohibits students with disabilities from being expelled because of behavior associated with their disabilities

manifestation determination Determines whether a student's disciplinary problems are due to her or his disability

functional behavioral assessment (FBA) Behavioral evaluations to determine the exact nature of problem behaviors

high stakes testing State- and district-wide assessments to ensure all students' progress in the curriculum

alternate assessments Means of measuring the progress of students who do not participate in the general education curriculum what NCLB says about...

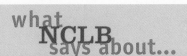

High Stakes Testing

NCLB requires schools to make *adequate yearly progress* (AYP) according to three conditions:

- At least 95 percent of students in every subgroup (e.g., students with disabilities, students who are English language learners) must participate in state assessments.
  - Students with disabilities may participate with or without accommodations.
  - Students with significant cognitive disabilities may take an alternate assessment.
- Students (including each subgroup) must meet or exceed the state's AYP objectives for students scoring at or above the proficient level.
  - If one subgroup fails to make the required progress, the school can still make AYP if that subgroup's "not proficient" percentage has declined by 10 percent and made progress on other indicators.
- Progress must be made on one additional academic indicator.
  - Graduation rate is the high school indicator.
  - States can determine their own elementary and middle level indicators.

Schools that fail to make their goals are subject to improvement, corrective action, or restructuring measures. Schools that meet or exceed their goals are eligible for awards.

that as greater numbers of students with disabilities are included in their classes, the probability will increase that disincentives—reductions in the school's budget, bad reports in the press, and poor public image—will result. In response, special education experts counter that when students with disabilities receive proper accommodations while taking these tests, they perform well and do not negatively affect school performance (Elliott, Kratochwill, & McKevitt, 2001). Some special educators and parents are concerned that if the stakes are too high, the temptation to manipulate school results will actually hinder the progress of students with disabilities. In fact, some evidence supports this concern. Evidently, some educators have decided that students without disabilities have greater "up-side" potential of making gains and improving the overall average of the school. Consequently, they are focusing their instructional time and attention on those students at the expense of students with disabilities (Rubin, 2004). Special educators must remain diligent to ensure that this practice does not become commonplace.

Progress Monitoring

Although it is important to monitor the overall achievement of a school and how well its students are mastering the general education curriculum, yearly tests do not provide teachers with enough information about the progress of individual students to guide instruction. Other types of assessments are better suited to monitoring students' progress and adapting instruction accordingly. Careful and consistent progress monitoring is important so that minimal instructional time will be wasted using tactics that are ineffective or have lost their utility for an individual student. Teachers need to document these students' improvements in academic achievement, in behavior, or in attainment of life skills. They use results from these evaluations both to guide their instruction and to communicate with students, parents, and the IEP Team, as well as with other teachers and education professionals. So let's look in more detail at few of the techniques teachers use to monitor students' progress.

All students experience assessments on their classroom performance. Weekly spelling tests, exams after the completion of social studies units, and history papers are all examples of students' classroom work that is graded. Such evaluations of students' work are **authentic assessments** because they use the work that students generate in classroom settings as the evaluation measurements. Results on students' class assignments (book reports, math tests), anecdotal records, writing samples, or observational data on behavior are examples of authentic assessments. In other words, evaluation is made directly from the curriculum and the students' work. For students with disabilities, teachers often collect more authentic assessments than they do for their students without disabilities (Fuchs et al., 2001). They do so because it is easy for students with disabilities to fall behind more quickly than their classmates.

authentic assessments Performance measures that use work generated by the student

portfolio assessment Authentic assessments where students select their work for evaluation

curriculum based measurement (CBM) Evaluating students' performance by frequently and directly collecting data on academic tasks

Authentic assessments can be comprehensive and include ongoing, systematic evaluations of students' performance. **Portfolio assessment** is an authentic assessment that includes samples of a student's work, over a period of time, to show the student's growth and development. This evaluation process involves students in both instruction and assessment because they select the exhibits of their work (Curran & Harris, 1996; Hébert, 2001). A portfolio may include prizes, certificates of award, pictures, dictated work, photographs, lists of books read, and selections from work done with others. It may also include reports, written by the teacher or by others who work with the child, about challenging situations or patterns of behavior that should be a focus of concern.

Considered both a self-correcting instructional method and an evaluation system, **curriculum based measurement (CBM)** is a detailed data collection system that frequently measures how well a student is learning specific instructional targets. With CBM, teachers quickly know how well their students are learning and whether the chosen instructional methods are effective (Fuchs et al., 2001). For example, a teacher instructing a youngster in math keeps a record of the number or percentage of problems correctly solved across time. Using this system, teachers track the percentage of words spelled correctly, the number of new arithmetic facts memorized, the number of words read correctly per minute (reading fluency), or the number or percentage of topic sentences included in writing assignments. These records help teachers judge whether the instructional methods selected are both efficient and effective (Fuchs & Fuchs, 2001). CBM is often part of the evaluation system used during the pre-referral stage of the IEP process, particularly for students suspected of having learning disabilities (Bradley, Danielson, & Hallahan, 2002; Fuchs, Fuchs, & Powell, 2004). Therefore, more details about the implementation of this measurement technique are found in Chapter 5.

what IDEA '04 says about...

High Stakes Testing

IDEA '04

- Allows funding to be used for technical assistance and direct services to schools identified for improvement under NCLB based on scores of students with disabilities
- Requires all children with disabilities to participate in assessments with the appropriate accommodations or in alternate assessments as delineated in their IEPs
- Stipulates that alternate assessments must be aligned with the state's challenging academic content and student achievement standards or measure student achievement against alternate academic standards, if applicable
- Requires states to report the numbers of students taking assessments with and without accommodations, and the numbers of those taking alternate assessments

Change in Services or Supports

Remember that IDEA '04 guarantees students with disabilities and their families a continuum of services. However, the intention is for these services not to be sequential or lock-stepped. Rather, they are to be a flexible constellation, coming into action when supports need to be increased due to a lack of student progress or phased down when they are no longer necessary. In other words, the needs of individual students are not fixed but, rather, change over time. A student with a reading disability might, for some period of time, need intensive instruction outside the general education classroom. There, intensive instruction would be delivered to a very small group of learners, all struggling with the task of learning how to read. However, when the reading difficulty is resolved, that student may well move immediately back to the general education setting, where continued progress in reading is monitored every several weeks and then every month or so. When changes in placement, to either a more or a less restrictive setting, are considered, the IEP Team and the family (and in some cases the student) must be in communication. In some cases the whole IEP Team, which includes the parents, holds a meeting. However, IDEA '04 requires schools only to notify parents in writing about changes being made to the student's program. Regardless, for correct decisions to be made about whether a student's services need to be more or less intensive, information must be current and precise. Typically, authentic assessments are used for this purpose.

Source: © 1997 John Trevor, *Albuquerque Journal*, Reprinted by permission.

Imagine a world...

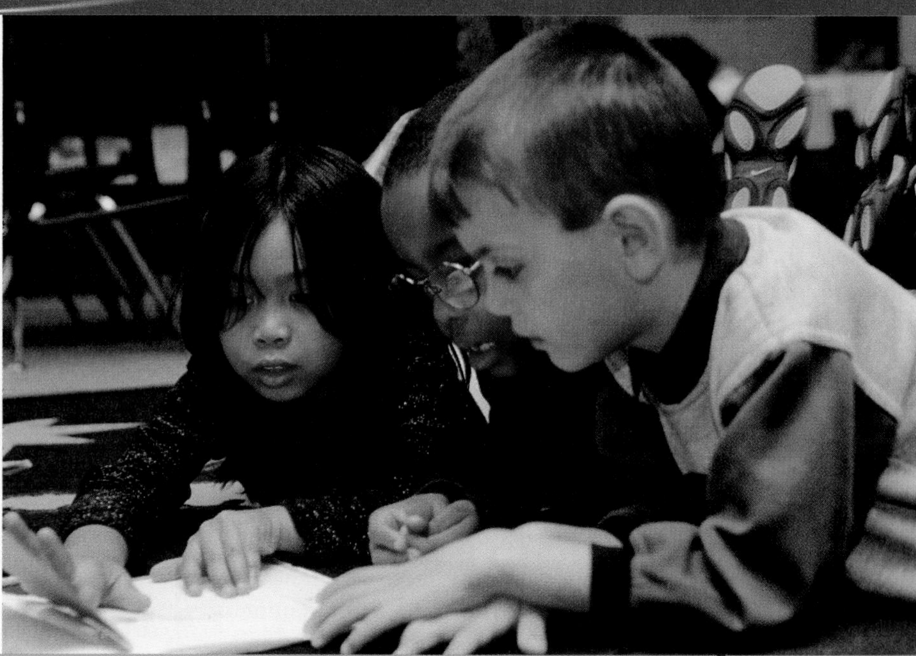

where all children receive an appropriate education ...

Summary

A cornerstone of the federal laws ensuring all infants, toddlers, preschoolers, and students with disabilities a free appropriate education in the least restrictive environment is the individualized education created through the special education process. IDEA '04 guarantees these individuals and their families a tailor-made education program guided by uniquely created planning documents: the individualized family service plan (IFSP) and the individualized education program (IEP). The IEP is further supported, when necessary, by behavioral intervention plans and by statements of transition services. These plans bring together a multidisciplinary team of general educators, special educators, and related service providers for the purpose of assisting each young child and student with a disability reach his or her full potential and achieve community presence and independence as an adult.

Addressing the Chapter Objectives

1 What are the five important approaches used to help students with disabilities access the general education curriculum?

- Universal design for learning
- Instructional accommodations
- Modifications
- Differentiated instruction
- Assistive technology

2 How is each placement option used to deliver special education to students with disabilities?

- *Pull-in programming:* All services are provided in the general education classroom
- *Co-teaching:* General and special education teachers team-teach
- *Consultation/collaborative teaching:* General education and special education teachers work together, but some services are offered outside the general education classroom

- *Itinerant/consultative services:* The special education teacher consults with the general educator, who delivers most of the specialized services
- *Resource room:* Special education is delivered outside the general education classroom for at least 21 percent, but not more than 60 percent, of the school day
- *Self-contained special education class:* Special education is delivered in a separate class for more than 60 percent of the school day
- *Special education (center) schools:* Separate day or residential facilities

3 What are special education related services and how are multidisciplinary teams formed?

- Specialized services that support special education
- Delivered by specialized professionals from different disciplines (e.g., SLPs, PTs, assistive technologists, school nurses)
- Individually determined by the specific needs of the individual with disabilities

4 What is the IEP process?

- Pre-referral
- Referral
- Identification
- Eligibility
- Development of the IEP
- Implementation of the IEP
- Evaluation and reviews

5 What are the different individualized education plans used for individuals with disabilities (birth through age 21)?

- Individualized family service plans (IFSPs)
- Individualized education programs (IEPs)
  - Statement of transitional services
  - Behavioral intervention plan

mylabschool™
Where the classroom comes to life!

MyLabSchool is a collection of online tools for your success in this course, your licensure exams, and your teaching career. Visit www.mylabschool.com to access the following:

- Online Study Guide
- Video cases from real classrooms
- Help with your research papers using Research Navigator
- Career Center with resources for:
  - Praxis exams and licensure preparation
  - Professional portfolio development
  - Job search and interview techniques
  - Lesson planning

Supplementary Resources

Because popular novels, books, and movies do not typically address the individualized education programs, the sections—standard in other chapters of this book that list such resources are not included in this chapter.

Professional, Parent, and Advocacy Groups

Center for Applied Special Technology (CAST) in Wakefield, Massachusetts: www.cast.org

National Association of School Nurses (NASN) in Castle Rock, Colorado: www.nasn.org

National Association of State Directors of Special Education (NASDSE) in Alexandria, Virginia www.nasdse.org

National Center on Secondary Education and Transition (NCSET) at the University of Minnesota in Minneapolis: www.ncset.org

NICHCY in Washington, DC: www.nichcy.org

PACER (Parent Advocacy Coalition for Educational Rights) Center in Minneapolis: www.pacer.org

The Center for Universal Design in Raleigh, North Carolina: www.design.ncsu.edu

Professional Standards and Licensure Tests

After reading this chapter, you should be able to link basic knowledge and skills described in the CEC Standards and INTASC Principles with information provided in this text. The table below shows some of the specific CEC Individualized General Curriculums Knowledge and Skill Standards and INTASC Special Education Principles that can be applied to each major section of the chapter. Other standards may also be applied to this chapter. Associated General Praxis II topic areas are identified in the right column.

Major Chapter Headings	CEC Knowledge and Skill Core Standard and Associated Subcategories	INTASC Core Principle and Associated Special Education Subcategories	PRAXIS II Exam Topic
Access to the General Education Curriculum	**4: Instructional Strategies** GC4K1 Sources of specialized materials, curricula, and resources for individuals with disabilities	**4: Instructional Strategies** 4.11 Special education teachers collaborate with general education teachers to infuse individualized goals and specialized strategies into instruction for students with disabilities.	1: Understanding Exceptionality 2: Legal and Social Issues 3: Delivery of Services to Students
Settings, Services, and Personnel	**1: Foundations** GC1K5 Continuum of placement and services available for individuals with disabilities	**1: Subject Matter** 1.08 Special education teachers have knowledge of when and how to develop, structure, and implement accommodations, modifications, and/or adaptations to provide access to the general curriculum for students with disabilities.	1: Understanding Exceptionality 2: Legal and Social Issues 3: Delivery of Services to Students
The IEP Process	**8: Assessment** GC8K2 Laws and policies regarding referral and placement procedures for individuals with disabilities	**1: Subject Matter** 1.11 Special education teachers have knowledge of the requirements and responsibilities involved in developing, implementing, and evaluation IEPs, IFSPs, and IAPs for students with disabilities.	1: Understanding Exceptionality 2: Legal and Social Issues

Tools for Individualized Programs	**8: Assessment** GC8K3 Types and importance of information concerning individuals with disabilities available from families and public agencies	**8: Assessment** 8.07 Special education teachers plan and conduct assessments in the school, home, and community in order to make eligibility and placement decisions about individual students with disabilities.	1: Understanding Exceptionality 2: Legal and Social Issues 3: Delivery of Services to Students
Evaluating Progress and Revising Programs	**8: Assessment** GC8S3 Select, adapt and modify assessments to accommodate the unique abilities and needs of individuals with disabilities	**8: Assessment** 8.11 Special education teachers ensure that students with disabilities participate in district and statewide assessments and document on the IEP the use of accommodations or an alternate assessment when appropriate.	1: Understanding Exceptionality 3: Delivery of Services to Students

The Gift by Michael A. Naranjo. Reproduced with kind permission of the artist. Photograph of *The Gift* © Mary Fredenberg. Photograph of the artist courtesy of Laurie and Michael Naranjo.

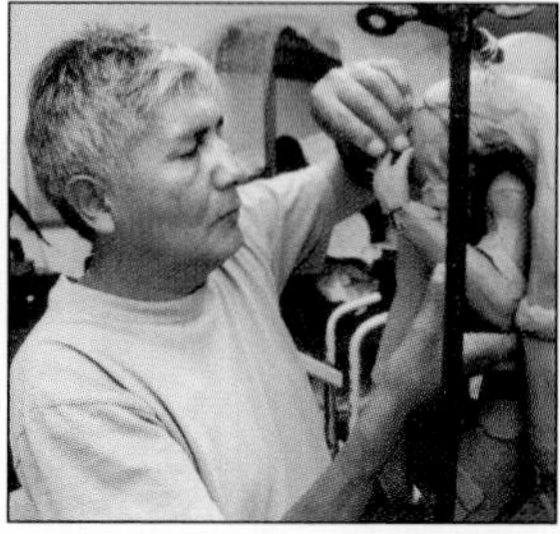

Michael Naranjo lost his sight during the Vietnam War. Although his mother was a well-known potter from Santa Clara Pueblo in northern New Mexico, Naranjo did not dedicate himself to sculpture until he was recovering from the injuries he received in battle. He is now a respected sculptor whose work is included in important collections across the nation. He is truly a very special person who contributes his time and work to Very Special Arts and community programs for young artists, particularly those with disabilities.

3

Cultural and Linguistic Diversity

Lilly Cheng of San Diego State University often tells the following story. Think of the possibilities if each of us stops to save just one starfish!

> An old man was walking on a beach one morning and saw some movements from a distance. He was very curious about the movements and as he walked closer, he saw a young girl picking something from the beach and throwing it into the ocean. When he got very near, he saw that the girl was throwing starfish that had washed up on the beach into the ocean. The old man said to the girl, "The sun is out and there are hundreds of starfish on the beach. You can't save them all. They'll all perish." The young girl picked up one more starfish, and while she was throwing the starfish into the ocean, she said, "This one won't."

Cultural or linguistic diversity is not a disability. For some, however, it can be handicapping and can put children and their families at risk for discrimination, bias, reduced opportunities, and challenging life situations. Concerns about diverse students' educational outcomes and high rate of being identified as having disabilities are widespread. These individuals are at particular risk because a disproportionate number of them are poor and, therefore, are exposed to the ravages of limited access to health care, being homeless, and attending low-quality schools. Government officials are very concerned about special challenges faced by diverse students with disabilities and their families. Therefore, these students' situations are addressed both in IDEA '04 and the annual reports to Congress about the implementation of IDEA. Schools must address and pay attention to the specific learning characteristics and needs of these students. To help, the government provides extra funding to assist schools serving students with and without disabilities who live in poverty (U.S. Department of Education, 2002). When disability is compounded by diversity, it is everyone's responsibility to ensure that the educational system's response is truly special.

Chapter Objectives

After studying this chapter, you will be able to:

1. Explain what is meant by the term *diverse.*
2. Discuss ways in which poverty puts many culturally and linguistically diverse students at risk for low educational results and for having disabilities.
3. Describe key features of multicultural education.
4. Discuss how schools can be more responsive to English language learners.
5. Describe additional considerations that diverse students with disabilities and their families require.

Where We've Been . . . What's on the Horizon?

America is a nation founded in diversity, and it remains a country whose populace reflects great and increasing differences (Goode, 2002). Since the nation's beginning, the face of the United States has been one of perpetual change, and so it remains today. America's schoolchildren are diverse in so many different ways. The languages, beliefs, and traditions they bring to school represent cultures from all over the world. Their heterogeneity is marked along multiple dimensions: language, values, religion, perspectives, priorities, and culture. All schools and teachers face the challenge of creating appropriate educational opportunities where instruction is effective for *every* student. The United States is clearly a multicultural country, so we must judge ourselves in terms of what we do with our diversity, how we treat each other, how we understand each other's similarities and differences, and how we learn from one another. By using this diversity to our advantage, we can make the educational environment richer, and all children will flourish.

Historical Context

Education in the United States has faced issues of bilingualism and multiculturalism throughout the country's history. In the late 19th and early 20th Centuries, families often lived in communities where everyone had the same background, and children attended schools where they were taught in their home language (e.g., Swedish, German, Dutch). Then, during the time of World War I, Americans looked inward and came to foster "Americanization," the idea that the United States should become a "**melting pot**"—a country where individuals were assimilated and abandoned their home languages and cultures as soon as possible. The anticipated result was a new, homogenized American experience. But the melting pot model seemed to fail. Instead of creating a harmonious new culture, it led to racism, segregation, poverty, and aggression toward each new immigrant group. The nation also lost the richness that results when a country welcomes and celebrates its many cultures and languages. By the 1960s, however, a new model emerged. **Cultural pluralism** is the idea that people should not abandon their home culture, but rather maintain their various ethnic languages, cultures, and institutions, while still participating in society as a whole.

Despite what was thought to be a more accepting climate for diversity, the harsh reality was that racial, cultural, and language differences resulted in some students being inappropriately labeled as having mental retardation. Important court cases involving diverse students and their schooling discovered major examples of discrimination. In 1970, the case v. of *Diana* v. *State Board of Education* found that using IQ tests to identify Hispanic students as having mental retardation was discriminatory. In 1971, the case of *Larry P.* v. *Riles* brought to the attention of the courts and schools the overrepresentation of African American children in classes for students with mental retardation and possible discrimination through biased testing. In 1974, the U.S. Supreme Court ruled, in *Lau* v. *Nichols* (a case brought on behalf of students whose native language was Chinese), that schools must offer services to help students overcome language barriers. Since the court's decision in *Lau*, education laws passed by Congress—including IDEA '04—require schools to help students whose home language is not English access the curriculum and participate in instruction at school.

Periodically the right of diverse children to an education comes into question. In 1982, the Supreme Court decided a Texas case about whether children of Mexican nationals residing in Texas without proper documentation had a right to a free public school education (*Phyler* v. *Doe*). The Supreme Court ruled that such children do have this right. Despite the highest court's decision, California voters in 1994 passed Proposition 187, prohibiting undocumented immigrants from receiving public benefits, including education. (This action was later ruled illegal by the federal government.) In many states (e.g., Arizona, California, and Massachusetts), bilingual education has come under attack, but although it might be limited or restricted in some states, bilingual education is not banned anywhere (Pat DiCerbo, NCELA, December 8, 2004, personal communication). What is important to know is this: Schools must take action to rectify the language deficiency of every student whose native language is not English (Antunez, 2001).

In part because of the 1960s civil rights movement, the attention from court cases, and the continuing challenges faced by culturally and linguistically diverse students, education professionals and policymakers are focusing special attention on this group of learners. Because too many of them fail or underachieve, advocacy agencies (e.g., Children's Defense Fund [CDF]), policy institutes (e.g., Tomás

melting pot Concept of a homogenized United States; cultural traditions and home languages are abandoned for the new American culture

cultural pluralism All cultural groups are valued components of the society; language are traditions of each group are maintained

Rivera Center, Pew Hispanic Center), information clearinghouses (e.g., National Clearinghouse for English Language Acquisition and Language Instruction Educational Programs [NCELA]), federal agencies (e.g., U.S. Department of Education), and research centers (e.g., National Center for Culturally Responsive Educational Systems) are diligently working to understand *why* these students' education is so precarious and *how* educators can make a difference in their results.

Challenges That Diversity Presents

Culturally and linguistically diverse children are more likely to find themselves challenged by a multitude of factors that put them at risk for unnecessarily unsatisfactory outcomes. Disproportionately, these students

- Are poor
- Have limited access to health care
- Are homeless
- Live migrant lives
- Attend inferior schools
- Have learning styles and experiences at variance with schools
- Experience school failure
- Are more likely to be identified as having a disability
- Struggle with English language acquisition
- Drop out of school

In this chapter, you will learn that most diverse students do *not* have disabilities, but many do have special needs attributable to their diversity. You will learn about the risk factors listed above, but most important, you will see that when their special needs are attended to correctly, the outcomes for these children can be outstanding. Quality education can and does make a difference.

Making a Difference

The Children's Defense Fund

The public might be surprised to learn that 12 million children live in poverty in the United States and that millions more children and their families live on the margins, just above official federal poverty levels. It is appalling that in the world's wealthiest nation, so many children are at risk for underachievement, disabilities, and illness and have so little chance for an improved life style. Poor children in America are the least protected against disease because they are uninsured and have limited access to health care. Also, poor children tend to attend the least generously funded schools and too often are taught by less experienced (and less qualified) teachers. Whereas parents of more affluent children advocate for their children's welfare, parents who live in poverty often find themselves disenfranchised, without a voice to argue for their rights or for services to meet their needs.

In 1973, Marian Wright Edelman founded the Children's Defense Fund (CDF) to serve as an advocacy agency representing the needs of children and families. A graduate of Spellman College and Yale Law School, Mrs. Edelman became the first Black woman admitted to the Mississippi Bar. Many lucrative career choices were available to her, but she decided to follow Dr. Martin Luther King to Washington, DC and served as legal counsel to the Poor People's Campaign.

CDF performs research and summarizes results in its publication, *The State of America's Children*. It also conducts public education campaigns and builds coalitions to benefit the most vulnerable in American society. Because of Mrs. Edelman's leadership, CDF has been instrumental in helping to reduce teen pregnancy (overall teen birth rates have decreased more than 10% and Black teen birth rates 24%) and child gun deaths, which have fallen by 50% (from 15 to 8 per day). The CDF report *Children Out of School* was critical to the policy development needed for the original passage, in 1975, of what is now called IDEA, the law that guarantees all children and youth with disabilities a right to a free appropriate public education.

To learn more about CDF, go to the Web site: **www.childrensdefense.org**

Cultural and Linguistic Diversity Defined

Source: Reprinted by permission from the *Albuquerque Journal.*

Students who are considered "historically underrepresented" in the United States are those students who fall into one of these federal categories: African American (Black), Hispanic (Latino/a), Asian/Pacific Islander, American Indian/Alaska Native (Native American).[1] Whether in the majority or not, they are often referred to as "minorities." And whether or not they have an Anglo parent or family member, they are not considered White (Caucasian). Generally, three groups of students are thought of as diverse: culturally diverse students, linguistically diverse, and culturally and linguistically diverse students with disabilities.

Cultural Diversity

Students who come from backgrounds different from American mainstream society, which predominantly adheres to Western European cultural traditions are thought of as **culturally diverse**. How many different cultures are represented by America's students has not been determined, but it could be over a thousand. Being from a culture different from the dominant American culture does not directly cause disabilities or poor academic performance. However, because of misunderstandings of culturally accepted and expected behaviors and norms of conduct, being culturally diverse can put students at risk of being identified as having a disability (Baca & Cervantes, 2004; Gollnick & Chinn, 2002; Voltz, 2005).

Linguistic Diversity

Individuals whose home language or native language is other than English are referred to as **linguistically diverse**. Many culturally diverse students, but certainly not all, are also linguistically diverse. Most education professionals use the term **English language learners** (ELLs) to describe these students. The older term, **limited English proficient** (LEP), is the one used in IDEA '04. (See Table 3.1 for the IDEA '04 definition.) In many school districts, including Chicago, Los Angeles, and Fairfax County, Virginia, students and families use over 100 different languages; New York City reports that its students speak over 145 different languages (Gersten & Baker, 2000). Nationally, however, the majority of ELLs speak Spanish (NCES, 2003). They represent the most rapidly growing segment of the U.S. student population (Goode, 2002; Suro & Passel, 2003).

culturally diverse Being from a cultural group that is not Eurocentric or of mainstream America

linguistically diverse Having a home or native language other than English

English language learners (ELLs) or limited English proficient (LEP) Students learning English as their second language

Diversity and Disability

Culturally and linguistically diverse students with disabilities are the third subgroup of diverse learners. The focus of this text is on students with disabilities. Thus, in the remaining chapters you will learn about students with particular disabilities

[1]Many terms are used to refer to different groups of people in the United States. The federal government uses one set (American Indian/Alaska Native, Asian/Pacific Islander, Black, Hispanic, White); people from specific locales use other specific referents (Anglo, African American, Latino/Latina, Chicano/Chicana); and for broad inclusion, other terms are used (Native American for all Native peoples). The terms used in this text reflect a balance of national and local preferences.

Table 3.1 • Definitions of Diverse Learners

Term	Definition
Limited English Proficient (LEP) *English Language Learner (ELL)*	**1.** An individual, aged 3–21, enrolled or preparing to enroll in an elementary school, **a.** who wasn't born in the United States or whose native language isn't English **b.** who is a Native American or Alaska Native, or native resident of the outlying areas and comes from an environment where a language other than English has significantly impacted level of English language proficiency, or **c.** who is migratory, with native language other than English, from an environment where a language other than English is dominant; and **2.** whose difficulties in speaking, reading, writing, or understanding English may be sufficient to deny the child **a.** ability to meet proficient level of achievement on State assessments; **b.** ability to successfully achieve in class where instruction is in English; or **c.** opportunity to participate fully in society
Culturally Diverse	Students who come from backgrounds different from American mainstream society; may or may not be of immigrant status
Linguistically Diverse	Students whose home, primary, or native language is one other than English; are considered LEP or ELL; require language supports in classroom settings
Diverse Students with Disabilities	Culturally and/or linguistically diverse students who also have at least one of the 13 disabilities identified in IDEA '04.

IDEA '04 Sec. 602(18). "Limited English Proficient." ESEA Sec. 9101(25) Authority: 20 U.S.C. 1401(18).

(e.g., learning disabilities, deafness, special health care needs). You will learn about specific causes, characteristics, and how education can make a real difference for students who have disabilities. Diverse students, like all others, can and do have disabilities, and their diversity can affect their disability in many different ways (Potter, 2002). Read *Cheyenne in the Spotlight* to learn about Cheyenne Lone Fox, the way he views his disability, and how his family and Lakota tribal community provide positive influences for him. It is important for all of us to remember that culturally and

Cheyenne in the Spotlight

Cheyenne Lone Fox and his family are members of the Lakota tribal community in North Dakota. This family and their community illustrate how much attitude and determination influence the way people behave. They believe that negative energy gets in the way of achieving important accomplishments and that positive energy makes a major difference. Cheyenne has cerebral palsy. He uses a wheelchair most of the time, and in class he needs the assistance of a note-taker because he doesn't have good control of his arms or hands. At home, Cheyenne uses a voice-activated computer to do much of his homework, but despite these obstacles he is determined to attend college and later law school. He works hard so he can participate in community events; he even exercised 90 minutes a day on a treadmill so he would be strong enough to walk a mile to a stadium where he could attend a professional football game. Why does he set such high goals for himself? Here's what he says:

> If I focused on what was bad about it or what I can't do—then I'd miss out on what was good to enjoy. . . . I've got lots of things to do . . . . I've modeled myself after William Wallace in the *Brave Heart* movie, a film that was an inspiration to me. In that movie he said, "Men don't follow titles—they follow courage," and that's the way I try to live.

Paula, Cheyenne's mother adds, "We don't see it as a difficult situation–we see it as more of a challenge." Some might think that Cheyenne is not being realistic and that his expectations for himself are too high, but his family, culture, and community see disability as a situation that can be overcome.

linguistically diverse students are particularly vulnerable. In this chapter, you will learn that more of their families live in poverty, a condition that limits their access to health care and increases the likelihood of their experiencing other risk factors associated with placement in special education. These students also have reduced opportunities for being identified for gifted education. In short, although their diversity can and should be enriching, it can also result in additional challenges that negatively affect school success.

Characteristics

Culturally and linguistically diverse students are distinctive in many ways. Many of their unique qualities or circumstances are not personality or behavioral traits but, rather, situations in which these learners frequently find themselves because of language or culture that is different from that of America's mainstream. These students are often confusing to educators. Teachers sometimes mistakenly misinterpret a difference as a disability or a problem. Instead, they should understand that differences might best be addressed through a change in teaching approach or an accommodation. Let's look at three areas that often present difficulties to diverse learners and to their teachers:

- Language differences and language disorders
- Clashes between home and school cultures
- Behavioral differences, behavioral disorders, and attention deficit hyperactivity disorders

Language

Both culturally diverse and linguistically diverse children exhibit language and communication differences that often raise educational questions but should not always result in special education (Cheng, 1999). It is not always easy to tell a speech or language impairment from a language difference. Let's first look at characteristics exhibited by many linguistically diverse students and then turn our attention to the language skills of culturally diverse students.

When students can share their talents and achievements, the entire school is enriched.

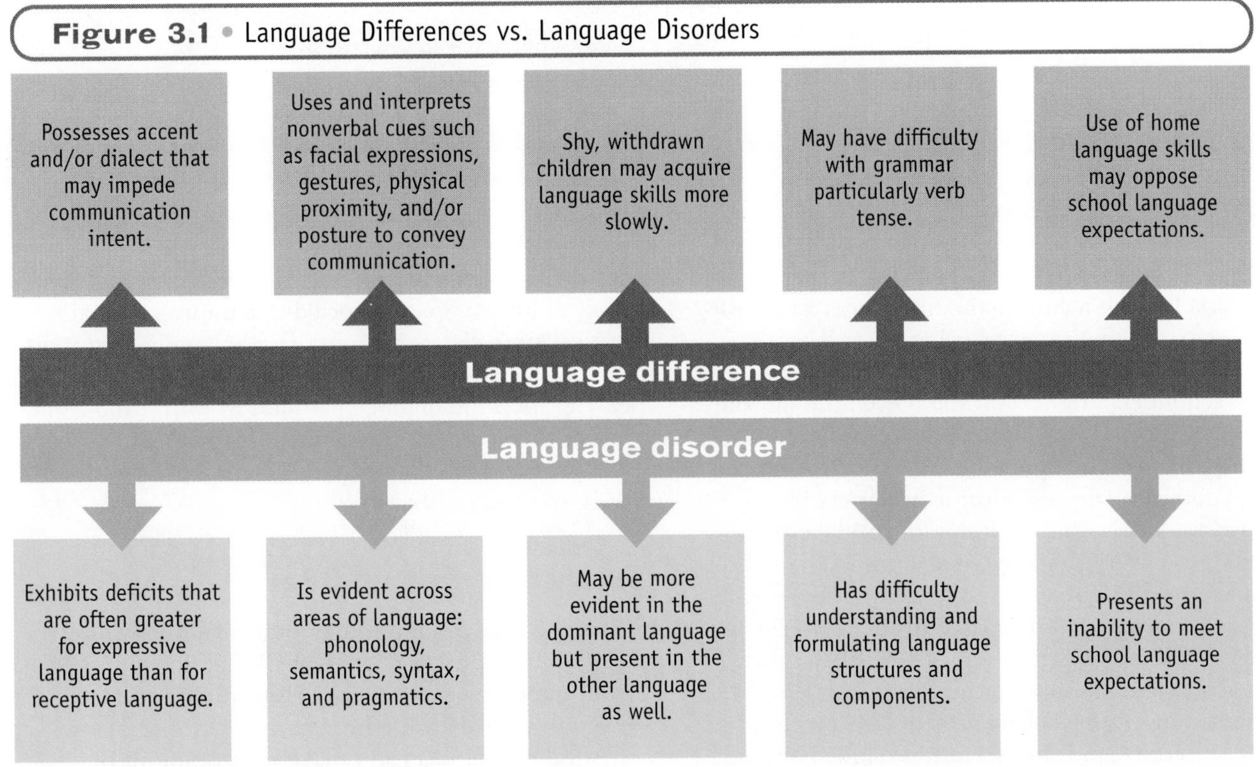

Figure 3.1 • Language Differences vs. Language Disorders

Source: Courtesy of and thanks to Zina Yzquierdo, Department of Special Education, Vanderbilt University, 2005. Reprinted by permission.

Some children may speak forms of a language that vary from its literate or standard form (Cheng, 1999). For example, the spoken Spanish used in South Texas generally varies from the spoken Spanish used in New Mexico, both of which may differ from the standard form of Spanish. These variations are dialects and should not automatically be considered language deficiencies. Some languages do not include certain sounds or grammatical structures found in English. For example, the *f, r, th, v,* and *z* sounds do not exist in Korean. Many English consonant sounds do not exist in Chinese, so a Chinese-speaking child's difficulty with some English sounds may reflect the child's inexperience with the sounds, rather than speech impairments (see Chapter 4). Although many of these children are referred for speech therapy for an articulation problem, their distinctive speech is simply an accent, and therapy probably is not necessary.

Detecting the differences among language impairments, learning disabilities, and language differences can be difficult, even for well-trained professionals (Salend & Salinas, 2003). Sometimes children are wrongly identified and find themselves placed in special education even though they have no language impairment or learning disability (Ruiz, 1995). At other times, children's disabilities are masked by the language difference, and they wait years for the special services they need. One general guideline for determining whether a bilingual student has a language impairment is to discover whether the impairment occurs in *both* English and the child's dominant language. For example, a Spanish-speaking child who converses perfectly in Spanish with his brothers on the playground but who has limited ability to use conversational English has a problem, but it is not a language impairment. Rather, it is due to an inadequately developed second language. Zina Yzquierdo (2005) helps us visualize these differences (see Figure 3.1). However, when an individual faces challenges speaking and interacting with teachers and peers in the classroom and on the playground, very special efforts like the one described in *Considering Culture* must be put into action.

Considering Culture

New World, New Language

Multicultural and Bilingual Special Education

Maria Perea is a cute, petite first grader who shyly plays *near,* but rarely *with,* her peers. Maria's family recently emigrated from Mexico, and this is the first school experience for Maria even though she was identified shortly after birth as having a developmental disorder. The first-grade teacher, Patty, is excited to have a child with Down syndrome in her classroom, and she works closely with the itinerant special education teacher to ensure that the curriculum is adapted to meet Maria's needs. Maria likes to help the teacher care for the classroom's pet guinea pig, and she often sits on the teacher's lap for story time and songs. Patty, however, is worried that Maria never makes a peep! She doesn't talk, join in songs or rhymes, or play much with the other children—and they seem to exclude her from their play. Patty decides to consult the bilingual teacher, Sonia, who works at the other end of the school. Sonia visits Patty's class and observes, then gently engages Maria in play while speaking with her in Spanish. Patty notices that Maria actually speaks to Sonia! Both Patty and Sonia agree that it is essential not only that Maria receive special education services related to her learning and developmental needs but also that she get assistance from a bilingual educator to support her language needs. Patty and Sonia and the special education teacher meet with Mr. and Mrs. Perea and present their concerns about Maria's language supports. Mr. and Mrs. Perea are surprised to learn that they can request services for their daughter, because this would not happen in their country of origin. They indicate that they want Maria to speak! The team, including Maria's parents, decide to explore educational options for Maria that include either transferring Maria to a bilingual (Spanish) class at another school where she would also receive special education services, or working with the district to fund a Spanish-speaking paraprofessional to assist in Patty's classroom and provide language support to Maria as needed. The district also employs a Spanish-speaking speech/language pathologist (SLP); the team requests that a referral be made to have the SLP assess Maria's speech and language skills and that Maria receive services as needed.

Questions to Consider

1. Imagine that you move to another country where you do not speak the language. What do you think your experiences would be? How would you feel? Even in your daily life here at home, are you ever frustrated that you can't make your opinions or needs clearly understood? Are others ever exasperated or impatient with your inability to communicate effectively? Can you imagine being treated as though you were a child or were too inept to understand? What would it be like to be ignored because you can't speak adequately with others?
2. If you know teachers who have linguistically diverse students in their class, ask them: What curricular goals do they have for these students? How do the diverse students differ from those students who are not bilingual? What communication challenges do they face as teachers? What communication challenges do their ELL students face?

—By Eleanor Lynch, San Diego State University and Marci Hanson, San Francisco State University

Some 20 percent of the current school population does not speak English at home (Baca, 1998). Although many Hispanic children come to school speaking Spanish, some come to school speaking a combination of two languages (Sileo, Sileo, & Prater, 1996). Native Americans speak over 187 different languages (Krause, 1992), and people from Southeast Asia and the Pacific speak hundreds of different languages and dialects (Cheng & Chang, 1995). Many of these students use both English and their home language within the same communication. That is, they are **code switching** (Brice & Rosa-Lujo, 2000). Code switching is not a disorder but rather a way for people to achieve mastery of two languages, and it is often a sign that dual language proficiency is developing.

code switching Using two languages in the same conversation; a sign of developing dual language proficiency

Language is a major issue for many students, even those who speak English at home. Many African American children, for example, come to school speaking a **dialect** of English. Another group of learners and their language differences have come to the attention of educators, Congress, and the public. These children speak a variation of standard English often referred to as **Ebonics**. Interestingly, although this form of American English is often considered substandard, it is used to generate millions of dollars in advertisements, music, television, and film. What is the concern? Should Ebonics be discouraged at school? Most schools and mainstream American institutions do not accept this form of English, and many leaders in the Black community believe its use in inappropriate settings has a negative impact on those individuals who cannot "switch codes." They believe strongly that schools must "teach standard English to all of our nation's children yet celebrate their diversity and their ability to communicate effectively in a variety of settings" (Taylor, 1997, p. 3). Educators must continually find effective ways to teach students who come to school without a basic mastery of English. If they do not succeed, the outcomes are serious because, at least in American society, academic achievement is a predictor of future success (Seymour, Abdulkarim, & Johnson, 1999).

Cultural Comprehension

Children come to school with a pretty good understanding of the norms and expectations of their home cultures (Lynch & Hanson, 2004). They typically develop this comprehension of cultural preferences by the time they are five years old. They understand "proper" behavior when interacting with adults, and they know what is "appropriate" when playing with each other. What children do not know, particularly if kindergarten is their first school experience, is that the "rules" of home might not match the rules or conventions of school. Diverse children and their families do not understand that they have a new culture—the one of schooling—to learn. Teachers who are **culturally competent** know the background, heritage, and traditions of their students, and they adjust their teaching and make accommodations accordingly. Culturally competent teachers create learning environments that are **culturally responsive**, where the curriculum includes multiple perspectives and examples (Kozleski, Sobel, & Taylor, 2003).

For teachers, the root of the problem is usually a lack of understanding about the roles that culture and language play in the learning process (Yates, Hill, & Hill, 2002). Some cultural characteristics and students' resulting behaviors and actions can be at odds with the classroom culture. A mismatch of home and school cultures (sometimes referred to as **cross-cultural dissonance**) may explain why many diverse students seem to be constantly in trouble, why their behavior patterns seem offensive to teachers from America's mainstream culture, and why traditional classroom instruction is often ineffective (Harry, 1992).

Competition pervades American classroom culture (Lynch & Hanson, 2004). Spelling bees, behavior games, even earning stars of different colors for excellent performance are forms of competition that some diverse students find peculiar. In many Native, Latino, and Asian cultures, cooperation, not competition, is valued. Hence children who come from cultures that do not value individual competition are often uncomfortable when encouraged to be better than everyone else. Such students might learn more readily when assigned to cooperative learning groups to work together on academic assignments (Fletcher, Bos, & Johnson, 1999). Remembering that competitiveness is not a universally desired attribute, let's think about the clash of cultures between home and school that can result when children try to please their teachers and learn new skills. Hawaiian children, for example, may take their newly developed competitiveness to home and community, where the standard of cooperation is preferred and their sudden taste for competition might even be interpreted as a behavioral disorder. At school, on the other hand, the lack of competitiveness might

dialect Words and pronunciation characteristic of a geographic region or ethnic group and different from those of standard language

Ebonics A learned and rule-governed dialect of nonstandard English, spoken by some African Americans

culturally competent Knowing and understanding the cultural standards from diverse communities

culturally responsive A curriculum that includes multiple perspectives

cross-cultural dissonance Mismatch that occurs when the home and school cultures are in conflict

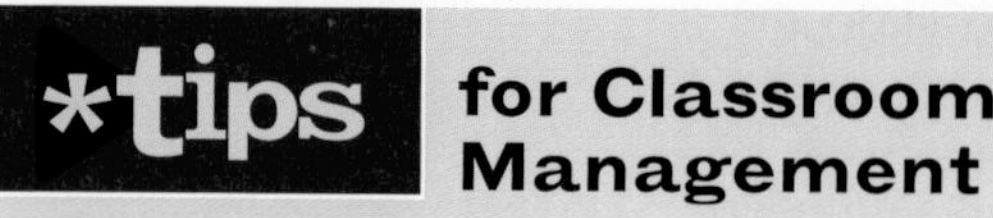

for Classroom Management

BEHAVIOR MANAGEMENT

1 Lay the foundation for a well-managed classroom.
- Understand all students' home cultures and determine whether misunderstandings between home and school cultures are likely.
- Be certain that all students understand the norms of school and classroom behavior.
- Express and expect consistently high standards of conduct.

2 Ensure that all students comprehend classroom rules, procedures, and expectations.
- Have class discussions about acceptable and unacceptable behaviors.
- Have students explain if there are any interaction styles that make them feel uncomfortable and with what types of interaction are they most at ease.
- Discuss home and school differences in degrees of directness, sharing, emotionality, and personal space.
- Hold high expectations of students to respect each other.

3 Develop a comprehensive behavior management plan.
- Develop strategic plans.
- Implement disciplinary actions consistently.
- Be sure the consequences for infractions are clear, fair, thoroughly understood, and consistently applied.

be interpreted as a lack of motivation. When home and school cultures clash, children can become terribly confused and poorly educated (Obiakor, 1994).

"Caught between two cultures" is a phrase frequently used to describe the experience of many Native students who do not attend a tribal school. Native children's communication at home tends to be symbolic and filled with nonverbal nuances. To these children, adults at school talk too much, are overly blunt, seek disturbingly direct eye contact, and ask questions that are inappropriately personal (Garrett et al., 2003). Also, views about what is important often differ between home and school. The result can be disengagement, incorrect referrals to special education, misidentification as having a disability, and eventual dropout (Artiles, 2003).

Behavior

Cultural conflicts may also explain why culturally diverse students find themselves in trouble at school (Harry, 1992; 2002). Much of behavior is based in culture, so children from nondominant cultures are more likely to be at variance with the culture of school (Cartledge & Loe, 2001). And when the cultures of school and home collide, the results can be tragic because inappropriate behavior can trigger the special education referral process (Rivera & Smith, 1997). Boys who "act out," do not comply with expectations at school, and have trouble controlling their anger are more likely than others to be referred for special education services. This reason may partially explain why so many Black males are identified as having emotional or behavioral disorders (Hosp & Reschly, 2002; 2003). Home and school cultural conflicts may also explain why so many Black youngsters (both boys and girls) screen positively for ADHD (see Chapter 6), particularly when tested by White teachers (Reid et al., 2001). What leads to this interpretation for some African American boys may well be their nonverbal behaviors and their movement styles (Neal et al., 2003). Assuming an assertive or defiant posture, arm swinging, and walking with a swagger can all lead to tension between educators and a student. Misunderstandings among students can also lead to management issues (Voltz, 2005). For example, different cultures have different attitudes about sharing. In some families and communities, property, toys, and belongings are communal; everyone shares everything. But the dominant American or Anglo culture tends to teach "what is mine is mine." Such differences in cultural understanding can lead to confusion, arguments, and eventually classroom management problems. Sometimes neither children (nor their teachers) understand that a particular behavior is acceptable in one setting but not another. For example, having fun with a group of friends, "messing around," making spontaneous and clever jokes, striking poses, and kidding around by physically touching a peer might bring positive attention and make the child popular after school. However, during class time or during period changes, such behaviors are troubling to teachers and school administrators. Most children must learn to sort out different behavioral expectations across a variety of settings and situations, but many do not and therefore need help to learn. Of course, these reasons do not explain all behavioral infractions that teachers have to deal with in classroom settings, but understanding the basis for some of the problems experienced in classrooms can lead to more effective solutions. This chapter's *Tips for Classroom Management* (and those in the remaining chapters of this text) suggest some simple ways in which teachers can prevent or address problems that often arise in typical classroom settings.

It is important to keep in mind that other issues can arise when behavior appropriate in one environment, such as the home, is inappropriate in another environment, such as the school. A silent child might be behaving in a desirable way according to standards of his home culture, for example, but be characterized at school as "withdrawn" or "anxious." A good way for educators to assist children in their efforts to sort out the different behavioral expectations at school, at home, and in the community is to patiently help them understand what is appropriate in

Prevalence

Of this there is no question: The demographics of America's students are changing, particularly because they reflect growing numbers of different immigrant groups. At the turn of the 20th Century, Irish, English, Italians, Germans, Swedes were all thought of as belonging to different and unique immigrant groups. At the turn of the 21st Century, however, descendents from all those groups were typically thought of as one group representing "mainstream" America, while Hmongs, Vietnamese, East Indians, Mexicans, and hundreds of others from many different countries are viewed as the "new face" of America. Before considering groups of students and then the number or percentage of them with disabilities, it is important to understand how easy it is to misinterpret national data, particularly when they reflect people's race, ethnicity, and culture.

National data about diversity and students must be interpreted carefully for several reasons. The federal government uses only five categories to describe all Americans along the dimensions of race and ethnicity: White (Caucasian), Black (African American), Hispanic (Latino/a), Asian/Pacific Islander, and American Indian/Alaska Native (Native American). Most Americans do not fit discretely into these five categories. For example, when asked about their backgrounds, many people (for example, the golfer Tiger Woods) think of themselves as best belonging to a group that might be called "multiracial," but the government does not have such a category. At the same time, many of these categories are too inclusive. Consider tribal communities, all with very different values and traditions. Even though these communities speak as many as 187 different languages (Krause, 1992), they are all grouped together as American Indian/Alaska Natives.

Using behavior and dress that is "cool" among friends, but not acceptable by teachers, can send messages to educators that result in significant negative consequences.

Another problem with this classification system is that it makes assumptions that immigrants, first-generation Americans, and multigenerational Americans who are from the same ethnic group hold similar cultural values. Take, for example, two Asian/Pacific Islanders or, even more specifically, two Chinese American students. One student, Peter Chin, is a fifth-generation American whose family has lived in the United States for 150 years. Peter's family does not follow Chinese traditions, and they all speak only English. The other student, Ping Mao, was born in the United States and is a first-generation American. Her family adheres to Chinese traditions and speaks a dialect of Chinese at home. Although the federal government's classification system places these two students in the same category, they bring to school very different backgrounds. And, as the

Pew Hispanic Center makes clear (see *Changing Times*), common assumptions about the backgrounds of diverse individuals and where they live may well be wrong because population **demographics** are not static (Suro, 2002; Suro & Singer, 2002). Generalizing about individuals who belong to a group can lead to some terrible mistakes.

The federal classification system has many additional problems. For example, many people who find themselves "counted" in one of these categories feel no personal connection with it. Regardless, it is the system the federal government uses. Let's now turn our attention back to the racial and ethnic composition, or diversity, of today's students.

Diverse Students

According to the National Center for Educational Statistics (NCES), some 47.7 million students were enrolled in public elementary and secondary schools in the 2001–2002 school year (Young, 2004). Using the 2000 census, the federal government reports that 1.0 percent of these students were American Indian/Alaska Native, 3.8 percent were Asian/Pacific Islander, 17.5 percent were Hispanic, and 14.8 percent were Black. The remaining 62.9 percent were reported in the White category (U.S. Department of Education, 2002). Interestingly, students who are not included in the count of White students are called culturally diverse and are often considered "minority" students, even if they constitute the majority of the school population. National data mask variations seen in specific locales. In many states, the "minority" is the majority. For example, in six states (California, Hawaii, Louisiana, Mississippi, New Mexico, and Texas) and the District of Columbia, White students made up less than half of the student population. In New Mexico, over half of the students attending public school were Hispanic, and in Hawaii, 72.3 percent were Asian/Pacific Islanders (Young, 2004). This trend is certain to continue with the growth of the Hispanic population (Suro & Passel, 2003; Tornatzky, Pachon, & Torres, 2003).

Students whose native or home language is other than English are considered linguistically diverse. Although in many districts students and families use over 100 different languages (a fact that can be daunting to educators), it is important to

The diversity of America's schoolchildren is increasing dramatically. Teachers have wonderful opportunities to enrich their instruction with interesting information and stories from many different cultures and heritages.

Changing Times: On the Move

Many Americans make two assumptions about Hispanics or Latinos: they are predominantly Mexicans, and most live in urban areas in California, New York, Florida, Arizona, New Mexico, and Illinois. Some 20 years ago, data summaries have supported such conclusions, but not so today.

About 40 percent of all Hispanics in the United States are first-generation immigrants, but some 29 percent are second-generation Americans, and 31 percent are from families where both the mother and the father were born in the United States. Hispanics as a group of individuals have very different values and experiences. Immigrant families come from many different places (e.g., Colombia, Dominican Republic, Mexico, Cuba, Puerto Rico, Central America, South America). Also, first-generation families share very different experiences from those whose families have lived in the United States for generations.

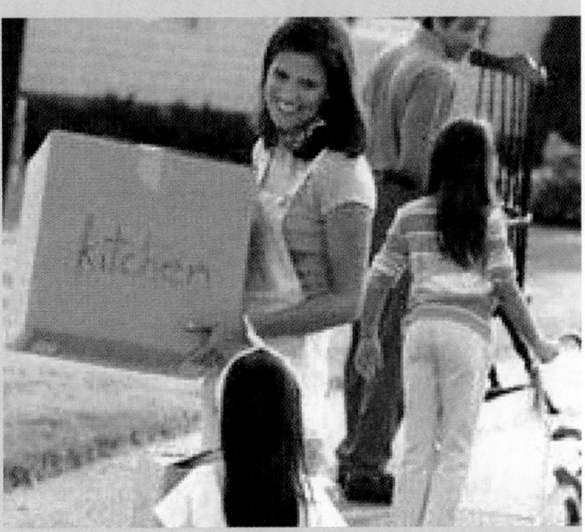

The largest Latino populations are still in metropolitan areas (New York City, Los Angeles, Miami, and Chicago). But the greatest proportional growth is in cities such as Houston, Phoenix, San Diego, Atlanta, and Orlando. Hispanic workers are clearly on the move; they are spreading out faster than any group did in the last century. Officials in many cities (Las Vegas, Knoxville, Nashville, Raleigh-Durham, Baton Rouge, Sarasota) are scrambling to find bilingual nurses, firefighters, police officers, social workers, and teachers. Some 18 American cities have seen a 505 percent increase in the Latino population in 20 years. And today, over half of all Latinos live in suburbs.

understand that ELLs represent a small fraction (only 5 percent) of all schoolchildren and that nationally, the majority of ELLs speak Spanish (NCES, 2003). It is also very important to put diverse students in perspective: The majority of them speak English. Indeed, less than a third of all American Indian/Alaska Native, Asian/Pacific Islander, and Hispanic students are ELLs (Tornatzky, Pachon, & Torres, 2003).

Diverse Students with Disabilities

Although students who are diverse bring special challenges to schools, remember that neither cultural nor linguistic diversity results in a need for special education. Not all White students have disabilities or learning problems, and neither do all diverse students. Likewise, giftedness should not be thought of as belonging to one group more than to another. The federal government requires the states to report data about the race/ethnicity of all students with disabilities. (Because IDEA '04 does not include gifted students, comprehensive data are not available about diverse students' representation in these programs.) Collectively across all categories, 62 percent of those students provided with special education services are White, 20 percent are Black, 15 percent are Hispanic, 2 percent are Asian/Pacific Islanders, and slightly more than 1 percent are American Indian/Alaska Native (U.S. Department of Education, 2005).

demographics Characteristics of a human population

Over- and Underrepresentation of Diverse Students

You just learned about the prevalence, or representation, of all students grouped by race or ethnicity who attend public schools in the United States. You also learned about their prevalence in special education. Let's compare these two sets of data to see why education professionals, policymakers, and parents are concerned about some groups' participation in special education. Here's a very simple way to look at these data: Compare the percentage of a group of students in the general population to their percentage in special education (or in gifted education). If a group's percentage in the general population is lower than its percentage in special education, the situation reflects **overrepresentation** of that group. The reverse situation is called **underrepresentation**: A group's percentage in the general population is higher than it is in special education or in gifted education. Any variance between a group's representation in the general population and in one of these subgroups is called **disproportionate representation**. Now, let's study such comparisons.

Review the data presented in this section again. You will see that the percentage of White students in the general student population is about the same as the percentage of White students receiving special education services (62.9 vs. 62.3 percent). The percentage of American Indian/Alaska Native students in the general population and the percentage of such students in the special education population are quite similar (1.0 vs. 1.5 percent), but the numbers of these students are small when compared to the total group. In this case, then, "a little" overrepresentation is greater than it first appears. Applying this method of comparison to Black students, however, yields different results. Because their percentage of the general population is lower than their percentage in the special education population (14.8 vs. 19.8 percent), many experts believe that these students are overrepresented as students with disabilities (Donovan & Cross, 2002).

As you continue to make comparisons, you will find that both Hispanic and Asian/Pacific Islanders are underrepresented in special education (Zehr, 2004). National data tend to mask those at the local level, however. At the local level, more disturbing data are available about the overrepresentation of diverse students in spe-

Figure 3.2 • Disability by Ethnicity of Students Attending the Public Schools in Hawaii.

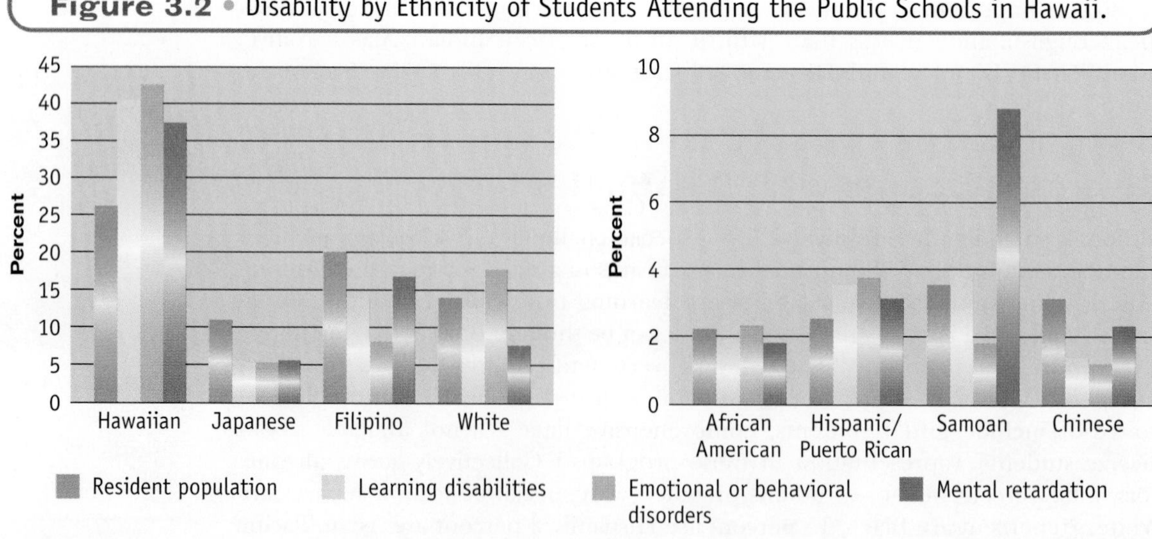

Source: Hawai'i DOE Student Information System, April 2003 and Gloria Kishi, 2004. Reprinted by permission and courtesy of Gloria Kishi.

Table 3.2 • Percentage of Students Ages 6–21 Served, by Disability and Race/Ethnicity, 2003[a, b, c]

Disability	American Indian/ Alaska Native	Asian/ Pacific Islander	Black (non-Hispanic)	Hispanic	White (non-Hispanic)
Specific learning disabilities	1.7	1.7	19.3	20.1	57.2
Speech or language impairments	1.3	2.9	15.3	16.3	63.9
Mental retardation	1.2	1.9	34.2	13.9	48.4
Emotional disturbance	1.5	1.2	28.6	10.2	58.6
Multiple disabilities	1.4	2.5	20.3	14.1	61.8
Hearing impairments	1.3	4.9	16.3	21.0	56.5
Orthopedic impairments	0.9	3.2	14.9	18.0	63.4
Other health impairments	1.1	1.5	16.1	9.2	72.1
Visual impairments	1.2	3.9	17.7	17.8	59.4
Autism	0.7	5.0	15.7	10.4	68.1
Deafblindness	2.3	4.6	13.8	20.7	58.6
Traumatic brain injury	1.4	2.5	17.3	11.9	67.0
Developmental delay	3.5	2.7	22.1	8.7	63.0
All disabilities	1.5	2.1	20.5	16.7	59.4

[a]Due to rounding, rows may not sum up to 100 percent.
[b]Race/ethnicity distributions include outlying areas.
[c]Data based on December 1, 2003 count, updated as of July 31, 2004.

cial education programs. Data from Hawaii's Department of Education offer a good indication why educators are concerned about diverse children's disproportionate participation in special education (Kishi, 2004). In 2003, Hawaiian and part-Hawaiian children represented about 26 percent of the overall student population, but they represented about 37 percent of the special education student population. Look at Figure 3.2. This chart shows how disability was distributed across the major ethnic groups attending the Hawaiian public schools. The first bar for each group shows the overall percentage of students from that ethnic group; the second shows the percentage identified as having learning disabilities; the third, behavioral or emotional disorders; and the fourth, mental retardation. Compare these sets of data. Note that Hawaiian and Samoan students are clearly overrepresented in special education categories, but their Japanese and Filipino peers are underrepresented in special education. The situation of Hawaiian students is not much different from that of Native American students in North and South Dakota and Montana (Harry, 1994).

Another way to consider disporportionality is to examine how students from different groups are represented in specific disability categories. Look at Table 3.2 to see the national data available from the federal government (U.S. Department of Education, 2005). (Remember, when reflecting on these data, that percentage data are distorted for groups with relatively small numbers.) On the table, the number appears in color when the representation in a disability category exceeds that group's representation in the resident or general population. Obviously, some major concerns are the overrepresentation of Black students in the mental retardation category and in the emotional or behavioral disorders category.

overrepresentation Too many students from a diverse group assigned to a special education category, relative to the level expected on the basis of the proportion of that diverse group in the population of students

underrepresentation Insufficient presence of individuals from a diverse group in a special education category; that is, their presence in smaller numbers than would be predicted on the basis of their proportion in the population of students

disproportionate representation Unequal proportion of group membership; either over- or underrepresentation

What about diverse students' representation in gifted education? As we have noted, IDEA does not include gifted education, and states are not required to report data about these students. Regardless, reports from researchers who study these issues overwhelmingly indicate that African American, Hispanic, Hawaiian, and Native American students are underrepresented in education of the gifted (Bernal, 2000; Ford et al., 2000). And here again, because of these students' lower proportion in the general population, their situation is masked when you look at national data. However, when you look at state or district data (as we did for diverse students living in the state of Hawaii), disparities become more obvious. Students from an Asian background are less than half as likely as other diverse students to be identified as having a disability (U.S. Department of Education, 2001). They are more likely to be included in gifted education, but the reverse is true for their Black, Latino/a, and American Indian peers.

Causes and Prevention

Clearly, diversity, poverty, and disabilities in America today are related. But it is very important to understand how they are related, and how they are not:

- Diversity does not cause disabilities.
- Poverty places students at substantial risk for disabilities.
- Not all diverse students are poor, although they are disproportionately likely to be poor. (The majority of poor children are White.)

Terrible mistakes can be made when people assume that all diverse students are poor or that all poor students have disabilities. Unfortunately, the economic conditions of many families from diverse groups did not improve greatly in times of prosperity (CDF, 2004). However, under the right conditions—high-quality preschools, emphasis on literacy development during the school years, and schools with adequate resources and programs—schools can make a real difference in the outcomes for these children (Lee & Burkam, 2002). Issues of cultural and linguistic diversity, along with poverty, are complex and intertwined. It is important not to oversimplify them.

Causes

Regardless of our background, all of us are susceptible to thousands of individual causes of disabilities. Some, such as those stemming from genetics and heredity, are biological causes and are at the root of many disabilities. For example, Down syndrome and fragile X syndrome are genetic causes. Muscular dystrophy is an inherited condition passed on through families. Not all health conditions are inherited, although many are so serious that they result in disabilities. Thus, when a virus causes a severe hearing loss, it is considered a biological cause and results in a disability. In addition to biological reasons for disabilities or special needs, other causes are environmentally based. For example, toxins abound in our environment. All kinds of hazardous wastes are hidden in neighborhoods and communities. Anyone can get sick—and even have a resulting disability—from exposure to environmental toxins. Just think about the nuclear disaster at Chernobyl and the devastating effects this accident had on thousands of people living in the region when the accident at the power plant occurred! Exposure to environmental toxins can happen anywhere, including the United States, where old dump sites hide dangerous wastes out of sight but not so far away that neighbors are safe from harm.

Students who are engaged in learning, using activities that are designed for them, flourish in the learning environment. Here, students are learning how paper is recycled along with the environmental benefits of reducing solid waste.

Some causes of disabilities, however, are unusually common among children and youth who come from diverse backgrounds. Some of these causes are biological, but most are environmental. For example, sickle cell anemia (discussed in Chapter 9 under special health care needs) is hereditary and is disproportionately present in African Americans. One environmental toxin that causes disabilities such as mental retardation and learning disabilities is lead. Most of us do not think of lead poisoning as much of a concern in America today, because its two major sources—lead-based paint and exhaust fumes from leaded gasoline—have been largely eliminated. Leaded gas and lead-based paint are no longer sold in this country. Unfortunately, however, the lead has remained in dirt that children play in, and lead-based paint remains on the walls of older apartments and houses, where children breathe the lead directly from the air and household dust, eat paint chips, or put their fingers in their mouths after touching walls or window sills. The Children's Defense Fund (CDF) reports that some 16 percent of low-income children have lead poisoning, compared to 4 percent of all children in the United States (CDF, 2004). Lead is not the only source of environmental toxins that government officials worry about; other concerns include mercury found in fish, pesticides, and industrial pollution from chemical waste (Schettler et al., 2000).

Social and economic inequities have a significant impact on our nation's children (CDF, 2004; Kozol, 1991, 1995). Many situations can put children at risk for disabilities or conditions that result in special needs. Let's look at two that are of critical concern: poverty and homelessness.

Poverty

The link among childhood poverty, poor school outcomes, and disabilities is now clear and well documented (Lee & Burkam, 2002; U.S. Department of Education, 2002). More than any other factor, including diversity, poverty accounts for poor school performance. Race and ethnicity are related to poverty (e.g., 34 percent of Black children and 29 percent of Hispanic children are poor, compared to only 9 percent of White children). Far more poor students than

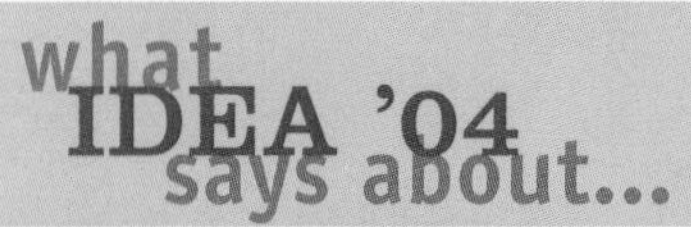

Homeless Students

IDEA '04 defines *homeless children* as children who do not have a regular or adequate nighttime residence. They might be living in a motel, hotel, trailer park, camp ground, or emergency or transitional shelter. They might have been abandoned in a hospital or might be awaiting foster care placement. They could be living in cars, public spaces, abandoned buildings, substandard housing, train depots or bus stations. They could also be mobile, living for a while in any of the above-mentioned situations. Those homeless children with disabilities must

- Receive the special education services specified in their IEPs
- Have those services monitored and evaluated
- Have their IEPs follow them if they move from one school to another or from one district to another

one would expect from their representation in the general population arrive at kindergarten already identified as having a disability (D'Anguilli, Siegel, & Maggi, 2004). CDF gives us some additional and alarming facts to consider when we think about the relationship between the conditions under which children live and the incidence of disabilities in children (CDF, 2004).

Each day in America:

- 390 babies are born to mothers who received late or no prenatal care
- 860 babies are born at low birthweight
- 1,186 babies are born to teen mothers
- 1,707 babies are born without health insurance
- 2,171 babies are born into poverty

There is no denying the lifelong impact of poor nutrition, limited or no access to health care (being uninsured), and not receiving immunizations on time during childhood (CDF, 2004). During the school years, the effects can be seen in learning and behavior problems. Across a lifespan, the effects can be seen in employment and life satisfaction outcomes.

Homelessness

Not all poor children are homeless, but the relationship between homelessness and poverty is obvious. **Homeless** children and those of immigrants and migrant workers often experience disruption and dislocation—circumstances that can adversely affect their physical, mental, and academic abilities (Markowitz, 1999). Children who live in shelters experience daily humiliation at school when peers learn that they have no home (CDF, 2001). These students often change schools every few months, breaking the continuity of their education and leaving gaps in their knowledge that result in reduced academic achievement. Educators must understand that their low academic performance occurs because of many factors, including fragmented education, absenteeism, and high risk for health problems.

Being homeless is difficult for children (Markowitz, 1999; Zima et al., 1998). And unfortunately, the number of homeless families is on the rise: In 1988, 34 percent of the homeless were children; in 2003, 40 percent of them were children (CDF, 2004). In one study, researchers tested children who were living in an urban shelter and found that 46 percent of all the children had a disability. The most common disability, affecting some 30 percent of them, was emotional or behavioral disorders. Because of the lack of social services and shelters, being homeless in rural areas is also challenging (Van Kuren, 2003). Being from a migrant worker's family also places children at risk for poor school performance. Over 80 percent of migrant and seasonal farm workers are U.S. citizens or legal immigrants (Henning-Stout, 1996). These workers earn incomes below the federal poverty level. Most migrant families live in Florida, Texas, or California between November and April and move to find agricultural work the rest of the year. Approximately half a million migrant students live in the United States, and about 75 percent of them are Hispanic. Because of the high percentage of homeless children who also have disabilities, IDEA '04 pays special attention to them and their unique needs (see *What IDEA '04 Says About Homeless Students*).

homeless Not having a permanent home

Prevention

How can disabilities in diverse children be prevented or avoided? According to CDF, the most effective and efficient way to reduce the number of children who actually have disabilities, and thus to make an enormous difference in the outcomes of children, is to remove the risk variables of poverty by

- Improving these youngsters' and their families' access to health care
- Guaranteeing universal vaccinations against disease
- Ensuring safe living environments (CDF, 2004)

Of course, effecting such sweeping social changes is beyond individuals' capabilities, but there are actions that alert educators can take to make a real difference in the lives of children. For example, even without universal health care or guarantees that all workers will be insured, many free services are available to the poor and to people who live in urban centers. Unfortunately, available community health care services are often not accessed because families are afraid or unaware of them (Tornatzky, Pachon, & Torres, 2003). Being knowledgeable about resources in your community and then helping to increase awareness of their availability could help poor parents gain access to medical services that would prevent disabilities from occurring.

Overcoming Challenges

Many positive and effective actions are available to reduce the impact of disabilities that cannot be prevented. Education is one of those important responses. Research findings are beginning to reveal why many diverse students fare so poorly, and we are also coming to understand what to do to improve results for these students. Let's look at three barriers to these students' success:

- Little or no access to high-quality preschool experiences
- Attending inferior schools
- Disengagement, alienation, and dropping out of school

As we think about barriers or challenges, let's also consider how they can be removed or reduced.

First, poor children are handicapped from the start (Thurston & Navarrete, 2003). They come to kindergarten and first grade the least prepared for schooling, with fewer "readiness" skills than more affluent peers, and one and a half times more likely already to have been identified as having a disability and to have had an IEP developed (D'Angiulli, Siegel, & Maggi, 2004). These children's achievement is not on a par with others when they begin elementary school (Lee & Burkam, 2002). Why might this be so? One reason is that fewer diverse children have had a school experience before first grade: 55 percent of White three- and four-year-olds attend preschool, whereas only 35 percent of Latinos/as do (Pew Hispanic Center, 2002). Policy experts at the Tomás Rivera Center at the University of Southern California suggest that all poor children, along with those of working parents living at the margins of poverty, should have access to free, high-quality preschool experiences (Tornatzky, Pachon, & Torres, 2003).

Second, diverse students tend to attend inferior schools. Poor children are exposed to the poorest of schools, a compounding factor in their low achievement (Artiles et al., 2002). Inner city and rural schools tend to have fewer human and financial resources. These schools have the lowest budgets, provide the fewest materials, and offer the least services. They tend not to offer

Figure 3.3 • Dropout Rates by Race and Ethnicity

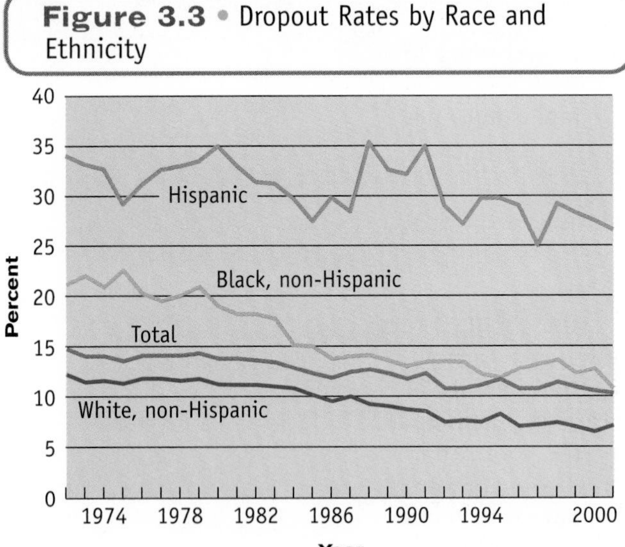

Source: U.S. Department of Education, National Center for Educational Statistics, 2003.

advanced placement (AP) courses or college-prep classes. They have fewer or no after-school enrichment activities, computers, or Internet access (Tornatzky, Pachon, & Torres, 2003). Schools where poor students attend also have the greatest percentage of least-prepared, inexperienced, and uncertified teachers (who also have the highest turnover rates) (Ingersoll, 2001). Diverse students are more likely to attend schools where at least 20 percent of their classmates are also diverse or are on the free-lunch program, a signal of poverty (NCES, 2003). Despite the Supreme Court decision over 50 years ago in *Brown* v. *Board of Education* (Topeka, Kansas) that separate schools are not equal, today White students and students of color remain apart (Rothstein, 2004). All of these factors put many diverse learners at even greater disadvantage and reduce the probability of their having good educational outcomes. But there is good news too: *Diverse students can catch up!* New research findings show that with intensive and sustained education, even those learners who come to school far behind can match the achievement of their more affluent classmates (D'Anguilli, Siegel, & Maggi, 2004). This intensive education must focus on phonics, reading, and literacy. It must be rich in reading experiences and multi-tiered so that those who gain skills quickly can move on, while those who progress more slowly receive intensive instruction. The education must be sustained in order to significantly change the dismal path that so many diverse students find themselves moving along.

Third, diverse students often are disengaged from the learning process, feel alienated, and as a result drop out at a higher rate than their White peers. The message sent by inferior schools and low expectations is clear, so it is not surprising that diverse students often feel alienated from the educational system (Brown et al., 2003). And when students see little value in schooling, they are more likely to have a high absentee rate and eventually to drop out; indeed, the dropout rate for poor Latinos/as is as high as 30 to 40 percent (Tornatzky, Pachon, & Torres, 2003). Look at Figure 3.3 to see the dramatic differences in dropout rates for Black and Hispanic students. The graph shows us that although all students are less likely to leave school before graduating than they were some ten years ago, the differences among racial and ethnic groups remain a problem. Some 91 percent of White students and 96 percent of Asian/Pacific Islanders graduate from high school. However, the percentages for other groups are worrisome: 86 percent of Black students and only 66 percent of Latinos/as (Kaufman, Alt, & Chapman, 2004). When immigrants are factored out of the Hispanic group's data, the high school graduate percentage rises to 73 (Pew Hispanic Center, 2002). Poverty, once again takes its toll. In 2001, students from low-income families were six times more likely than others to leave school without graduating. These statistics can be turned around! Schools that are smaller, offer more personalized instruction, and demand higher performance have better retention rates (Furger, 2004 November). How can we make a difference? Here are a few ideas (D'Anguilli, Siegel, Maggi, 2004; Tornatzky, Pachon, & Torres, 2003):

- Provide diverse students with high-quality early education experiences.
- Give them intensive and sustained instruction during their school years.
- Make education relevant to them.
- Anchor instructional content and activities to students' culture and backgrounds.

advanced placement (AP) courses High school courses that carry college credit

Assessment

Evaluating students' performance, abilities, and achievement has many different purposes. One purpose is to evaluate students' general academic performance. This type of assessment is undertaken to answer the question: How well are students mastering all of the curriculum targets that are part of the state's standards? This question is usually answered by administering an achievement test to a group of learners once a year. A second purpose of assessment is to get an indication of how well a student is learning skills or knowledge being taught. These assessments are taken more frequently than yearly achievement tests and come in many different forms (e.g., weekly spelling tests, a test on a history unit, a portfolio of a semester's writing assignments, curriculum based measurements on oral reading, or summary data taken on a student's classroom behavior). These evaluations of students' performance are more direct because they use students' actual schoolwork or measurements of classroom behavior and answer these questions: How well is the student doing with his or her school work? How effective are the teaching procedures being implemented? A third purpose is to determine whether a student has a disability and whether that disability seriously affects his or her educational performance. This assessment process is conducted to answer the question: Does a student qualify for special education services? We will briefly consider each of these purposes as they affect culturally and linguistically diverse learners with disabilities, but first let's turn our attention to students identified as having disabilities before they start kindergarten.

Early Identification

Whether they are diverse learners or not, children identified as having disabilities during infancy and the preschool years tend to have very serious problems that come to the attention of physicians, day care workers, preschool teachers, and family members. Discussions about the signals of each specific disability that are apparent during early childhood are found in the respective chapters of this text (e.g., physical disabilities or special health care needs in Chapter 9, and low vision and blindness in Chapter 11). What is important to remember is that more culturally and linguistically diverse children come to kindergarten and first grade already identified as having disabilities and already having had an IEP developed for them (D'Angiulli, Siegel, & Maggi, 2004). One likely explanation is poverty and limited access to health care (CDF, 2004).

Pre-Referral

As you learned in Chapter 2, general and special educators are very much involved in the identification process. In fact, they work together long before formal testing actually begins. For children who are of school age, general education teachers are the usual source of referrals to special education. They, along with special education colleagues, typically work together to gather information about a student of concern *before* a formal referral is made. Remember, the prereferral phase is the step in the process that is intended to reduce the number of unnecessary and inappropriate assessments. The hope is that this step will also help avoid misidentifying diverse students as having disabilities (Baca and Cervantes, 2004; Donovan & Cross, 2002). The National Alliance of Black School Educators (NABSE) and the Council for Exceptional Children's ILIAD Project suggest that administrators (e.g., principals) create pre-referral teams, if possible, at every school (NABSE & ILIAD, 2002). These teams of experts work

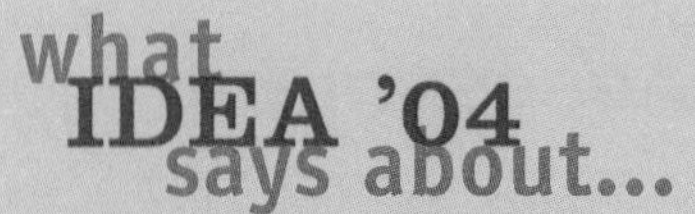

Nondiscriminatory Testing

Tests, assessment procedures, and evaluation materials used to determine eligibility for special education must

- Not be discriminatory on a racial or cultural basis
- Be administered in the language or form most likely to provide accurate information on the child's abilities (unless this is simply not possible)
- Be used in accordance with the original purpose of the measure to ensure reliability and validity
- Include a variety of assessment tools
- Be administered by trained and knowledgeable personnel

together to design and test interventions and modify instruction for specific students to be certain that students who are actually referred to special education have first had many opportunities to learn and improve their performance. Members of these teams should collectively have expertise that includes knowledge and experience in educating diverse learners, individualizing instruction, taking part in the special education identification process, and working collaboratively. The pre-referral process has many benefits, including early intervention for diverse students who are struggling and are having trouble keeping up with their classmates (Grupp, 2004).

Identification

Students from ethnic and racial groups that are not part of the dominant American culture are often at a disadvantage when taking standardized tests. Also, students who have not yet fully mastered English cannot demonstrate their abilities in such testing situations (Thurlow & Liu, 2001; Yzquierdo & Blalock, 2004). Differences in culture and in language contribute to some students being misidentified as having a disability or to their being excluded from education of the gifted (Ochoa et al., 1999). For other students, test results present an incorrect and depressed picture of their abilities. Despite all of the negative attention and charges of discrimination leveled at IQ tests and other standardized tests, and despite court rulings that bias plagues these testing procedures, educators still rely on what appears to be the simplest and most clear-cut form of student evaluation: the standardized test.

How can discrimination in the assessment process occur? There are many reasons for bias, but some of the major ones are worthy of attention and thought. For one thing, the content of the test items might give an advantage to groups with specific experiences and interests. For example, asking a child who has never been fishing to explain how to bait a fishing line might negatively affect the impression others have of that child's expressive language and cognitive abilities. A second reason is that diverse groups are not always represented in the standardization population. Also, opportunities for unfair evaluations are created when an individual untrained in multicultural and bilingual techniques conducts the evaluation. To stress the importance of nonbiased evaluations, IDEA requires that **nondiscriminatory testing** be established in each state. Take a look at *What IDEA '04 Says About Nondiscriminatory Testing* to see how the law and regulations address this important issue.

How might bias be removed? One way might be to rethink and broaden the narrow view of intelligence reflected in standardized tests. A restricted concept of aptitude—that it reflects only students' abilities to achieve academically—may be one reason why disproportionate numbers of students from culturally and linguistically diverse groups continue to be unidentified when they need special education, to be misidentified as needing special education, and to be underrepresented in education of the gifted (Ford et al., 2002). Although this theory is invoked more often when considering gifted children, educators of diverse children have taken a growing interest in Howard Gardner's (1983) theory of **multiple intelligences**. In Gardner's model, intelligence consists of eight different intelligences: verbal linguistic, logical/mathematical, visual/spatial, musical/rythmic, bodily/kinesthetic, naturalistic, interpersonal, and intrapersonal (Kornhaber, Fierros, & Veenema, 2004). To be considered gifted, individuals need to demonstrate talent in only one area. June Maker and her colleagues (Maker, Nielson, & Rogers, 1994) originally applied Gardner's theory to children from

nondiscriminatory testing Assessment that takes into account cultural and linguistic diversity

multiple intelligences Multidimensional approach to intelligence inspired by Howard Gardner's theory; allowing those exceptional in any one of eight areas to be identified as gifted diverse backgrounds, believing that a multiple approach better reflects talent fostered across cultures. They point out that one's culture may influence how ability is expressed. They give as an example the fact that oral storytelling may be a common form of linguistic giftedness in one culture, whereas writing a novel may be a predominant form in another. Students identified as gifted through this process often made gains equal to or greater than those of other gifted students identified through the standard IQ testing process. Applying such innovative concepts to the identification process may well help to reduce the underrepresentation of diverse students in gifted education programs.

Another means of solving the problem may well rest with the use of different assessment procedures. Performance based diagnostic procedures, such as authentic and portfolio assessments, have particular merit for students at risk for over- or underrepresentation in special education (Hébert & Beardsley, 2001). Curriculum based measurement has also been suggested as a means of more fairly evaluating students' abilities, because assessment is based on classroom performance (Donovan & Cross, 2002; Reschly, 2002). And yet another solution may be to incorporate flexible and sensitive identification systems that change depending on the individual's situation: stage of English language acquisition, family, culture, length of time in the United States, economic status, and region (Cuccaro, 1996; Yzquierdo & Blalock, 2004). The identification process could include input from multiple sources, such as parents, extended family members, church and community leaders, and service clubs (Patton & Baytops, 1995; Rogers-Dulan, 1998). Experts agree on one thing: Even minor changes in current practice can make a difference (Ortiz, 1997; Ortiz & Yates, 2001). Here are some of their recommendations:

- Provide early pre-referral intervention.
- Develop assessment portfolios.
- Conduct assessments in the student's dominant language.
- Use qualified personnel competent in their own and the student's language and familiar with the student's culture.
- Use interpreters, if necessary, who are proficient in the child's native language and familiar with the special education system and the assessment process.

Evaluation: High Stakes Testing

NCLB and IDEA '04 require that all students participate in state and district assessments. However, special arrangements can and should be provided for students who have special needs or circumstances. For example, ELLs who have been in the United States less than one year are exempted from taking the tests. ELLs, particularly those with disabilities, are entitled to either alternate assessments or accommodations (see *Accommodating for Inclusive Environments* for some examples). The National Center for Educational Outcomes (NCEO) stresses that the purpose of these accommodations is to give students an opportunity to demonstrate their knowledge and skills, rather than emphasizing their disabilities or lack of English fluency (NCEO, 2005a). How do educators decide which accommodations ELLs with disabilities should be provided in testing situations? One guideline is that the accommodations made for instruction should also be provided during testing (Baca & Cervantes, 2004; Thurlow & Liu, 2001). Thus, if a student is allowed extra time to complete assignments, then allowing extra time would be a proper accommodation during an assessment. How many ELLs with disabilities might warrant special accommodations? Martha Thurlow and Kristin Liu (2001) estimate that the number approaches half a million students.

What are some of the benefits of including diverse students with disabilities in high stakes testing and other reform agenda? Although both the testing movement

Accommodating for Inclusive Environments

English Language Learners with Disabilities Participating in High Stakes Testing

Native Language Accommodations

- Have text passages in both English and native language
- Provide questions in both languages
- Accept answers in either language
- Allow use of bilingual dictionaries
- Translate directions

English Language Accommodations

- Read questions orally in English
- Explain the directions
- Simplify the test's language

Nonlinguistic Accommodations

- Give extra time to take the test
- Administer the test either individually or in a small group
- Allow for short breaks

Alternate Assessments

- Monitor growth in language proficiency
- Use portfolio assessment documentation

and the inclusion of these youngsters is new, some positive outcomes have already been noted (McLaughlin, Pullin, & Artiles, 2001; NCEO, 2005b):

- High-stakes accountability has put pressure on schools to get their ELLs to learn English faster and earlier.
- Accountability measures have now brought diverse students' educational needs to the attention of school district administrators, which in turn will bring additional resources and help to these students and their teachers.
- Learning problems are addressed early and intensively.
- An atmosphere of high expectations is created.

Early Intervention

The early childhood years represent a critical period for cognitive, social, and emotional development. It is during these early years that children develop a readiness for school and for life. The basic building blocks for language, learning, and literacy are formed before children head off to kindergarten and first grade. Poor children tend not to have the same readiness skills as their more affluent peers (Lee & Burkam, 2002). And those youngsters who have poor health, as well, face even greater challenges. High quality preschool experiences include exposure to oral language, reading, and storytelling and to models of standard English, how to work in groups, and how to follow instructions. It is at preschool that many children learn the rules and conventions of the school culture. These skills are the fundamentals to a "good start" on the path toward school success (Tornatzky, Pachon, & Torres, 2003).

Although it is not universally available, many poor children benefit greatly from the federal Head Start program, begun in 1964 as part of the federal initiative called the War on Poverty. Head Start is for children from low-income families. In 1994 the program was expanded to include children from birth to age three through the Early Head Start program. Results from early intervention programs are outstanding, reflected by long-term positive changes for children and families (Malveaux, 2002). Participating preschoolers end up with better academic outcomes when they are in school, lower dropout rates, and fewer referrals to special education. And all of this ends up saving school districts over $11,000 per child, proving that prevention now is a much better option for everyone than remediation later! Early education services definitely make a real difference in the lives of children and their families. Unfortunately, most children eligible for Head Start do not participate in programs designed to reduce the impact of risk factors that contribute to disabilities (Currie & Thomas, 1995). Head Start services include a physical examination and full health assessments (immunization status; assessment of growth, vision, hearing, and speech; and screening for anemia, sickle cell anemia, lead poisoning, tuberculosis, and infections). Remember, access to health care is an important factor in preventing disabilities.

Young children often use toys and dolls to practice and expand language and learn social conventions. They also learn they are valued when dolls reflect their own appearances. Notice the adaptive devices that accompany these toys.

Truly including preschoolers with disabilities, particularly those from diverse backgrounds, in early intervention programs is not always an easy task. The process involves considerable planning and thought, but long-term results clearly justify the effort. Here are a few ideas about how to accomplish good integration in preschool settings (Kraft, 2001):

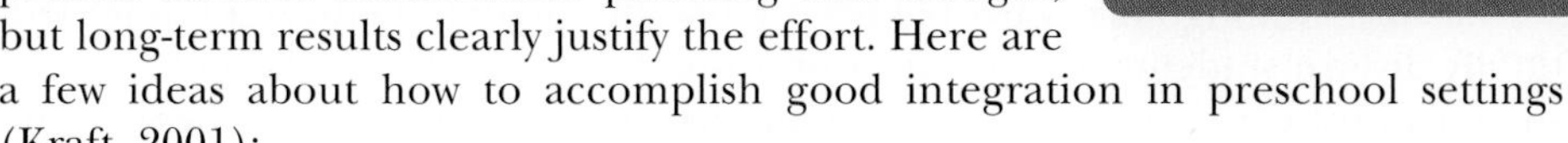

- Incorporate pictures of diverse children with disabilities into the classroom decor along with pictures of typically developing youngsters.
- Monitor the accessibility of the physical environment to be sure all children can move around freely and safely.
- Communicate with families consistently and frequently (not just when there is a problem).
- Include adults with disabilities on the staff to provide role models for young children.
- Encourage typical peers to play and interact with their peers who have disabilities.

Language and literacy development can play a key role in solving the problems of Hispanic educational achievement. Direct efforts focused on developing these skills should begin during the preschool years. Now is the time to anchor instruction by developing literacy through the culture and history of preschoolers' diverse communities (Tornatzky, Pachon, & Torres, 2003). As we have noted, children have an awareness of cultural differences and develop their own cultural identities early in life (Lynch & Hanson, 2004). The opportunities for enriching the curriculum, instruction, and activities are increased when students represent different cultures. Accordingly, rather than a "unit" about each cultural group being presented during a designated week, the history, customs, art, literature, music, and famous people from all cultures should be woven into every curriculum topic presented across the school year. The curriculum can be modified to reflect more culturally appropriate components. For example, it can include activities involving creative arts from different cultures—music, artwork, and drama from students' diverse backgrounds and home experiences (Santos et al., 2000). The curriculum can also incorporate stories from a wide variety of cultural and ethnic traditions.

Teaching Diverse Students with Disabilities

When culturally and linguistically diverse students have disabilities, the response to their education must be truly special. Three critical components must be present. Their education

1. Must be steeped in the practices of multicultural education
2. Must include intensive support for language development
3. Must incorporate the most current evidence-based practices to address each student's particular disabilities

Access to the General Education Curriculum: Multicultural Education

Multicultural education incorporates some important principles and values that help all students find relevance in the general education curriculum, thereby improving their access to academic content. Multiculturalism "supports positive basic commonalities while recognizing and nourishing constructive differences. It takes into account cultural tenacity, ethnic loyalties, and linguistic pride" (Winzer & Mazurek, 1998 p. 27). Who exactly is it that **multicultural education** is for? Although many people believe that multicultural education is for culturally diverse students, the answer to this question definitely is "Everyone!" All students profit from learning more about classmates and their home communities (Banks, 2002). Students whose home cultures are understood, valued, and respected do not feel marginalized, rejected, or isolated. Teachers who use key features of multicultural education (Ford et al., 2002; Lynch & Hanson, 2004; Tiedt & Tiedt, 2002):

- Connect instruction to students' experiences and background by incorporating examples that celebrate diversity
- Understand differences between home and school cultures
- Avoid clashes resulting from differences between the traditions, values, expectations, and view of appropriate behavior typical of the home and those typical of the school
- Provide reading assignments that come from many different sources, where the central characters reflect the ethnic and racial diversity of students in the class and at the school

Teachers do not reflect the diversity of their students (Tyler, Lopez-Reyna, & Yzquierdo, 2004). In fact, only 0.04 percent of U.S. special education teachers in elementary school and 2.2 percent of secondary special education teachers are African American males (Voltz, 1998). And, of course, no one teacher can reflect all of the diversity seen in America's students. Thus all teachers must work hard to become better prepared to work with children from many different backgrounds.

By developing culturally responsible schools and classrooms, teachers demonstrate respect for children's home cultures. **Contextualized instruction** with relevant and interesting content motivates students to do their best (Montgomery, 2001). Teachers can provide contextualized instruction by teaching with examples from many American experiences (Castellano & Díaz, 2002; Kea & Utley, 1998). Although it is important not to become "cultural tourists" by celebrating holidays of countries or traditions of places that these students have never visited, cultures

multicultural education
Education that incorporates the cultures of all students into instruction

contextualized instruction
Instruction that incorporates students' cultures, interests, and backgrounds into course content

can be meaningfully linked to instruction and the classroom experience (Artiles et al., 2002). Some teachers both have students celebrate local holidays and post pictures of events from the local community. Many teachers have found that using magazines (such as *Essence, Ebony, Canales, Latina, Pamir,* or *Indian Country Today*) for supplemental reading activities piques students' interest and can provide them with excellent role models (Christina Amanapour, the journalist; Venus Williams, the tennis star; Zubin Mehta, the musician) to emulate (Jairrels, Brazil, & Patton, 1999; Sileo & Prater, 1998). Schools can also recognize and value different cultures by supporting their clubs and groups (ESL clubs, Movimiento Estudiantil Chicano de Aztlan [MEChA] clubs, chapters of African American sororities and fraternities, and arts, music, dance, and crafts clubs). However, it is important not to stereotype groups of individuals or make assumptions that people hold similar beliefs and traditions. For example, to assume that an American-born child of Japanese heritage maintains the same cultural belief system as a recent Japanese immigrant is just as erroneous as assuming that a child of Cherokee heritage who lives in Denver is completely assimilated into the dominant U.S. culture. These beliefs can be influenced not only by the cultural background of students but also by such factors as the length of time their families have been in America; the geographic region of the country in which they live; the age, gender, and birthplace of each child; the language spoken at home; the religion practiced by the family; the proximity to other extended family members; and the socioeconomic level of the family (Gollnick & Chinn, 2002).

Instructional Accommodations

Making accommodations for students who are not on a par with classmates in the understanding and use of English is an imperative. It is impossible to access learning, profit from instruction, or participate in a learning community if you do not understand the language being spoken or read. Learning to speak English and developing enough proficiency to profit from academic instruction in English is a slow and complex process—and, as Leonard Baca of the University of Colorado's Bueno Center points out, it is not an automatic or natural process for many children (Baca & Cervantes, 2004). ELLs' language patterns can often be confusing to educators, to their families, and even to themselves. Over 20 years ago, Jim Cummins helped us appreciate what mastery of a language means for students, and his theory holds true today (Cummins, 1984). Achieving **conversational English** allows children to communicate well on the playground and interact in English with friends and teachers, but conversing at this level is different from having the language skills necessary for **classroom English**. Conversational skills in a second language can be acquired within 2 to 3 years, but the more complex language abilities needed for academic work require some 5 to 7 years of meaningful exposure and practice (Zelasko & Antunez, 2000). These two abilities do not develop sequentially, nor do they develop independently. Table 3.3 provides some examples of these types of language skills and of ways in which teachers can help students see the connections between them. Teachers also need to understand that the ability to translate one language into another is not sufficient (Cheng, 1996). Mastery of a language also requires appreciation and understanding of idioms and of nuances that express feelings, anecdotes, and nonverbal messages. Truly a lot for students to learn!

For linguistically diverse students to profit from instruction, they must master English. The goal of **bilingual education** is for students to master both their home language and English. Many experts point out that across the world, mastering more than one language is the norm and that it has many social, economic, and personal benefits (Antunez & Zelasko, 2001). However, debate about the use of bilingual education has raged in many states. Why is this so? One explanation is that becoming truly bilingual is a very slow process, and it takes time away from

conversational English Level of English mastery adequate for general communications but not necessarily for academic learning

classroom English Level of English mastery required to access the general education curriculum and profit from instruction

bilingual education Teaching in and seeking mastery of students' native language and English

Table 3.3 • Examples of Different English Skills

Conversational English	Classroom English	Showing Relationships
Want to go to the movie on Saturday?	Read pages 167 to 184 for homework tonight.	Our daily class schedule let's us know what to do when; the table of contents in a book tells us what we've learned and what topics are coming next.
Look at the beautiful flowers.	Photosynthesis is the process whereby plants generate food from sunlight and water.	To make our food it takes a process: for a burrito, you put a cheese and meat into a tortilla and roll it up.

learning content in the standard curriculum. Thus, many experts advocate using methods that help students learn English as quickly as possible (Tornatzky, Pachon, & Torres, 2003). One approach that has rapid mastery of English as its goal is **English as a Second Language (ESL)**. Schools across the country have adopted different ways to help students master English and thereby be able to access the general education curriculum, often combining ESL and bilingual education. Table 3.4 summarizes these methods. One validated method, **sheltered English**, helps students master the elements of the English language that are necessary for success when learning specific academic content (Rossell, 2004/2005; Short & Echevarria, 2004/2005). Teachers help students by explicitly teaching the vocabulary and concepts used in the curriculum after identifying the language demands of the subject to be taught. They also relate these new language skills to students' background knowledge, give them many opportunities for practice, and provide them with feedback to help with comprehension. Students' success increases when teachers use sheltered English, because language learning and content instruction are integrated.

Although the federal government does not mandate that states and districts use any specific accommodation or method, it does have some clear requirements about ELLs and their schooling (Antunez, 2001). The Office of Civil Rights and the U.S. Department of Education mandate that schools provide equal educational opportunities to ELLs, and they must include remediation of deficiencies in using the English language. They also make it clear that federal law is violated if

- Students cannot participate in instruction or access the curriculum because they do not speak or understand English
- They are assigned to special education because of their lack of English skills
- Their educational programs do not teach them English as quickly as possible
- Educational programs are "dead end tracks"
- Parents receive notifications and communications from schools in a language they do not understand

English as a second language (ESL) Instructing students in English until English proficiency is achieved; does not provide support in the student's native or primary language

sheltered English Restating concepts and instructions, explicitly teaching vocabulary, using visuals and concrete examples, and relate new language skills to students' experiences to provide language support to ELLs

Validated Practices

As you learned in Chapters 1 and 2, the special education knowledge base not only is developing but is already rich in validated practices that enhance the learning and performance of students with disabilities. Although many proven interventions are designed to help students with a particular problem (e.g., positive behavior supports for students with behavioral issues, intensive reading

Table 3.4 • Language Approaches Used with English Language Learners

Language(s) of Instruction	Typical Program Names	Native Language of LEP Students	Language of Content Instruction	Language Arts Instruction	Linguistic Goal of Program
English and the native language	• Two-way bilingual education, • Bilingual immersion, or • Dual language immersion	Ideally, class consists of 50% English-speaking and 50% LEP students sharing same native language.	Both English and the native language	English and the native language	Bilingualism
	• Late-exit or • Developmental bilingual education	All students speak the same native language.	Both; at first, mostly the native language is used. Instruction through English increases as students gain proficiency.	English and the native language	Bilingualism
	• Early-exit or • Transitional bilingual education	All students speak the same native language.	Both at the beginning, with quick progression to all or most instruction through English.	English; native language skills are developed only to assist transition to English	English acquisition; rapid transfer into English-only classroom
English	• Sheltered English, • Structured immersion, or • Content-based ESL	Students can share the same native language or be from different language backgrounds.	English adapted to the students' proficiency level and supplemented by gestures and visual aids.	English	English acquisition
	• Pull-out ESL	Students can share the same native language or be from different language backgrounds; students may be grouped with all ages and grade levels.	English adapted to the students' proficiency level and supplemented by gestures and visual aids.	English; students leave their English-only classroom to spend part of their day receiving ESL instruction	English acquisition

Source: "If your child learns in two languages" (pp. 20–22), by N. Zelasko and B. Antunez, 2000. From askncbe@ncbe.gwu.org National Clearinghouse for Bilingual Education, George Washington University. Public domain.

for Effective Teaching

PROVIDING LANGUAGE SUPPORTS FOR ENGLISH LANGUAGE LEARNERS

1 *Build vocabulary as an anchor to curriculum.* Teach seven or fewer new words that convey key concepts of the academic content being learned.
2 *Use visuals to support vocabulary and language acquisition.* Develop visual aids (graphic organizers, concept and story maps, word banks) to help provide a concrete structure for thinking about new information.
3 *Implement cooperative learning and peer tutoring.* Group students and encourage them to question each other and to provide feedback about vocabulary and content comprehension.
4 *Use the native language strategically.* Use levels of English at which students are fluent, and introduce complexity in students' native language.
5 *Adjust demands of expressive language.* Accept varying levels of language output as determined by the cognitive demands of the learning situation.

instruction for those with learning disabilities), others are more generic (e.g., learning strategies, individualizing instruction). In each chapter of this book that focuses on a specific disability, at least one validated practice is featured. Thus, for example, validated practices for deaf and hard of hearing students should be included in the educational programs of diverse students with a significant hearing loss. And so on. Diverse students with disabilities need a dually special program.

ELLs with disabilities must have educational programs that support their development of full English competence and also include strategies that address their specific disability. Russell Gersten and Scott Baker, along with other researchers, are convinced that for these learners to develop the language necessary to profit from academic instruction, some key components (see *Tips for Effective Teaching*) must be integrated into their instructional activities (Gersten & Baker, 2000; Muller & Markowitz, 2004). They are confident that two strategies, in particular, are very useful to teachers who do not themselves speak all of the languages spoken by their students: cooperative learning and peer tutoring. Both approaches have students work together on academic tasks; for **cooperative learning** they work in small groups and for **peer tutoring** they work in pairs (Fletcher, Bos, & Johnson, 1999). These approaches are thought to be powerful in several different ways. Students who come from cultures that do not value individual competition are more comfortable, and peers can help each other learn academic tasks. Of course, merely assigning students to small groups, and telling them to help each other does not guarantee academic improvement. Although classmates can be very helpful to each other, students also need structure and guidance from the teacher. **Reciprocal teaching** is one way to incorporate the principles of cooperative learning and peer tutoring, along with instruction that is rich with demonstration, careful instruction, and feedback (see *Validated Practices* for an example).

And finally, the importance of providing the support of multicultural education to all diverse students with disabilities cannot be understated. It is critical that teachers be sensitive to their students' home cultures and backgrounds and use differences to their advantage as they enrich the curriculum and their teaching routines. As a reminder, when multicultural education is infused into special education, some key features set it apart (Baca & Cervantes, 2004; Gollnick & Chinn, 2002):

- Sensitivity to students' backgrounds and home cultures
- High expectations and opportunities for success
- Family and community involvement
- Respect for "non-mainstream" values and attitudes
- Support and inclusion
- Accommodations
- Individualized instruction
- Documented results

cooperative learning Small groups of students working together to learn the same material

peer tutoring Classmates helping each other in pairs

reciprocal teaching A tactic wherein teachers and students switch roles reading stories and asking questions, focusing on predicting, summarizing, questioning, and clarifying reading passages

Technology

Technology has changed all of our lives. And technology will certainly continue to affect the lives of those with disabilities and their families. It seems the possibilities are endless. Technology can be used as a tool to help teachers enrich the curricu-

Validated Practices Reciprocal Teaching

What Is Reciprocal Teaching?

Reciprocal teaching helps students who can read words but have difficulty with comprehension. Reciprocal teaching includes four components: (1) predicting, (2) questioning, (3) summarizing, and (4) clarifying. At first, the teacher models the method by reading stories and asking questions. Then the student and the teacher switch roles.

Why Reciprocal Teaching Is Beneficial

Bilingual students benefit from scaffolding, an instructional process that gives students temporary support as they learn a new skill. Scaffolded instruction increases bilingual students' comprehension skills by providing them with opportunities to play the teacher's role. Students who effectively assume the teacher's role understand the material they have read.

Implementing Reciprocal Teaching

Reciprocal teaching requires you to be very active with your students as they learn the method. You might need to demonstrate the technique several times to be sure the students know the steps. Once they know the procedure, have them become the teacher as you become the student. Here is how the components work:

Predicting

- Read the title of the book to the students and ask them to predict what they think the story is about.
- Ask students to share their background knowledge of the topic.
- Refer to background knowledge and predictions as you read by anchoring examples in the students' culture.
- As you are reading, stop at headings from the story and make new predictions.

Questioning

- Ask questions such as "Why do you think the boys were scared?"
- Avoid using fill-in-the-blank questions, because you want to encourage higher-level thinking skills.
- If students have difficulty forming questions, they should summarize first.
- Provide prompts as needed when students assume the teacher's role.

Summarizing

- Identify the main idea and supporting details.
- Provide summaries without looking at the passage.
- You may need to remind students of the following guidelines for summarizing.
  - Identify the topic sentence, making one up if needed.
  - Disregard trivial or redundant information.

Clarifying

- Clarify when having difficulty with
  - Referents (such as *she, it, they,* and *you*)
  - Troublesome or novel vocabulary
  - Unorganized text or incomplete information
  - Figurative language

This scientifically validated practice is a teaching method proven by systematic research efforts (Johnson, Fletcher, & Bos, 2002; Klinger & Vaughn, 1996; Palinscar & Brown, 1987). Full citations are found in the references for Chapter 3.

—By Kimberly Paulsen, Vanderbilt University

lum, facilitating opportunities to make instructional activities and learning more relevant to diverse students. It can also become a tool for accommodations in assessment and instruction. However, it is important for educators to understand that some diverse families' access to technology may be restricted. Poor children are less likely to have access to a computer. Whereas 20 percent of poor children have computers at home, 85 percent of middle-class children do (Martella, 2002). What is often called the **digital divide** could well become yet one more handicap for diverse students and their families to overcome, separating them from others who have home-based Internet access and the availability of Web sites in their home languages (Tornatzky, Pachon, & Torres, 2003). Thus teachers must be cautious about assigning homework where computer and Internet access is either required or very useful. One helpful option in such cases is for teachers to schedule time in the school's computer lab so these students can develop important

digital divide Unequal availability of technology as a consequence of differences in socioeconomic status computer literacy skills and also enrich their learning of content presented in the general education curriculum.

One recurrent theme of this chapter centers on anchoring instruction to students' culture, thereby making instruction more relevant to diverse learners. The Internet can help greatly in this regard (Haynes, 2005). Materials and information are available—often even organized into thematic units that enable students to explore and learn about topics of special interest to them. For example, through the Internet, teachers are sharing units they have developed for others to use and adapt for their own instruction (e.g., see everythingESL.net for activities about Martin Luther King, Jr., Teaching About America). Students can also be given the option of searching out specific topics of their own choice (e.g., historical figures from different countries, or cultures from a specific period of time) for reports or independent study.

Technology is becoming an important accommodation for ELL students. For example, **computerized language translators** are able to translate words and phrases into many languages. Seiko, among many other companies, produces not only inexpensive bidirectional dictionaries but also translators that can handle complicated verb conjunctions. Such devices may have a significant impact for ELL special education students. For instance, they may be able to use computers to write assignments in their primary language, check the spelling and punctuation, and then press a button to translate their work into English! Or translators could help students expand their vocabularies. Such devices can also save time for the bilingual teacher or volunteer, who can use them for immediate translations of specific words or explanations of phrases and idioms. They are being used as accommodations in both instructional and assessment situations. And teachers can use language translators to improve communications (both written and oral) between home and school, regardless of the language used at home.

Transition

The relationships among education, wages, and life outcomes are clear: High school graduates are more likely to be employed than high school dropouts, and people with college degrees earn more than people without. High school graduation is one criterion for entrance into a community college, a college, or a university. Unfortunately, data indicate that diverse students are underrepresented in postsecondary education and also have a high rate of not completing college (Slater, 2004; Tornatzky, Pachon, & Torres, 2003). Why might this be so? Remember, poor students often attend poor schools where a rich curriculum is not offered, textbooks are outdated, and teachers are less experienced. In fact, at many inner city schools, advanced placement courses are not even available. Sometimes, diverse students are advised not to take the core subjects required for admission to college (and hence do not get enough science, math, and foreign language courses), and these students' parents are less likely to know which high school courses are necessary for college admission and which courses are not. When disability compounds diversity, the challenges can be even greater. Diverse students with disabilities graduate from high school with a standard diploma at a much lower rate than their White peers with disabilities. Whereas Whites with disabilities have a 62 percent high school graduation rate, diverse students' rates are 56 percent for Asian/Pacific Islanders with disabilities, 52 percent for Hispanics, 48 percent for American Indian/Alaska Natives, and 40 percent for Blacks (U.S. Department of Education, 2002). Although these rates are dismal, they are showing some improvement. Possibly, now, with increased attention to the challenges that diverse students with disabilities face, outcomes will improve even more.

computerized language translators Computers that provide translations of written text from one language to another

Collaboration

In this chapter and each of the following ones, we highlight different collaborative efforts of professionals—teachers and related service providers—who come together to provide an appropriate education to students with disabilities. Here, we emphasize the unique needs and special partnerships that can be formed to benefit linguistically diverse students with disabilities. For them, **collaboration**—school personnel with different areas of expertise working together—often means forming partnerships in nontraditional ways. For diverse students, collaboration might mean seeking expertise from a range of experts who can form a unique multidisciplinary team. Such a team might consist of many special education colleagues, migrant education teachers, teachers who are themselves bilingual and fluent in the language of a particular student with disabilities, SLPs, and ESL teachers (Salend & Salinas, 2003). Sometimes, teachers are provided with the assistance of paraprofessionals who are bilingual and speak students' native language. **Bilingual paraprofessionals** are assistants who help students learn the English required to profit from classroom instruction. They might provide needed testing accommodations (e.g., explaining directions for a test in both English and Spanish) or help these students access the curriculum by explaining, in both the child's native language and in English, concepts being taught or vocabulary that is unfamiliar. Teachers need to work closely with bilingual paraprofessionals, however, to be sure that they know the language accommodation that is supposed to be provided and that they understand their role in helping students learn English as their second language.

The diversity of schoolchildren in the United States is increasing dramatically. Teachers have wonderful opportunities to enrich their instruction with interesting information, stories, and learning opportunities from many different cultures and heritages.

Particularly in urban areas, it is common for classrooms to include linguistically diverse students who speak many different languages. Often the teachers and the bilingual paraprofessional do not speak all of the languages students and their families bring to school (or there are insufficient numbers of bilingual paraprofessionals available). In these situations, educators find it useful to seek help from community partners. The effort to involve families that do not speak English well in their children's school life, might mean finding community members who are very familiar with the special education process and can explain it to people who have no knowledge of the American educational system and do not speak English. It could also mean finding community members willing to volunteer and work in the classroom as interpreters for children just learning English. Students' home communities are often good sources of partnerships, with many individuals who stand ready to help and are waiting to be asked. Remember an important perspective reflected in African American communities: "It takes a whole village to raise a child." Unfortunately, educators do not typically tap these valuable resources, which are important, permanent parts of students' lives.

Partnerships with Families and Communities

The strength of families and their involvement in school can make a real difference in the lives of children (Garcia, 2001). However, the participation of parents of culturally and linguistically diverse students with disabilities is often disappointing (Shapiro et al., 2004). What appears to be lack of interest may instead be unfamiliarity with the process and a result of educators' actions (Davis et al., 2002). Many culturally and linguistically diverse families come to the school situation themselves burdened with alienation, feelings of distrust, and lack of information (Brown et al., 2003). Some Latina and African American mothers say they have received negative treatment and

collaboration School personnel with different areas of expertise working in partnerships

bilingual paraprofessionals Classroom assistants fluent in at least two languages

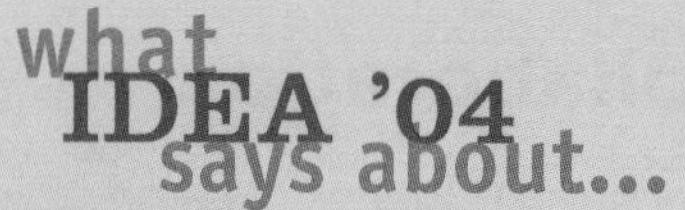

Native Language and Families

Every reasonable effort must be taken to ensure that parents

- Are notified *in a language they understand* about the scheduling of IEP meetings
- Understand and can participate in group discussions at IEP meetings about the placement of their child
- Are provided, if necessary, with explanations of the technical terms used in special education

have been subjected to condescending attitudes and disapproving judgments from school and social service personnel (Harry, 2002; Shapiro et al., 2004). They also report poor and inefficient ways in which educators communicate (Davis et al., 2002). Native parents also object to indifference, inaccurate understanding of their culture and traditions, and inappropriate communication styles (Banks, 2004). Possibly parents misinterpret professionals' communications because the latter are long on jargon and short on explanation.

In many school–home relationships, cross-cultural dissonance (acute misunderstanding of fundamental issues and values about education, disability, and home–school interaction) may undermine special education for students with disabilities (Harry, 1992). Teachers may use language and special education jargon that parents do not understand. Even those who speak English may not be proficient enough in this second language to understand and communicate with educators using technical language or jargon (Holman, 1997). To them, the word *disability* may mean only a physical or sensory disability or only a severe disability—an interpretation very different from educators' view of disability (Thorp, 1997). For those who speak a language other than English, the interpreter selected might not understand the special education process. Most important, educators must develop trust and respect between home and school. IDEA '04 and the Office of Civil Rights (OCR) (see *What IDEA '04 Says About Native Language and Families*) provide guidance about communicating with and involving families of students with disabilities whose first language is not English.

Family members need to be respected and not to be given assignments they are unable to complete. For example, many parents who are not proficient in English are embarrassed that they cannot help their children with homework (Milian, 1999). To avoid humiliation, they might agree to help their children with schoolwork but then be unable to follow through. Likewise, educators should not make promises they cannot keep. Parents are often limited to playing the role of "consent giver" and "educational planner" rather than being accepted as full partners in the special education of their sons and daughters (Harry, 1992). Instead of encouraging parents just to be loyal supporters and passive recipients of information, educators should seek parents' input about how they would like to be involved in their child's educational program. (Thorp, 1997). They need information. In fact, families report that they are more satisfied with the educational system when they receive frequent communications (Hughes, Valle-Riestra, & Arguelles, 2002). They also report that they want more involvement with schools. An overwhelming majority of Hispanic families report that they want their children to go to college, but they do not understand that a few simple choices, such as enrolling in the right courses and signing up correctly for the SAT, will make that option more probable (Tornatzky, Pachon, P., & Torres, 2003). Maybe apparent disengagement is a communication problem rooted in a lack of cultural sensitivity.

Educators tend to assume that "working with parents" means "working with Mom and Dad." In many cultures "family" is a large constellation that many include people who are not actually related. Often, extended family members play a crucial role in the life of the individual with disabilities. For some African American families, church and community leaders lend support and resources to the student with disabilities (Rogers-Dulan, 1998). For that child, the concept of extended family may well include key members of the community. For Native American children, these may be tribal elders whose exclusion would be considered an offense (Vraniak, 1998). Before making any decisions about treatments or educational strategies, it may be necessary to consult with these tribal elders and allow time for their response. Without understanding the cultural demands and expectations of the child's family, educators can inadvertently create unfortunate and unnecessary obstacles to the development of real partnerships.

In part, a child's success in school depends on respect between the school and the family. Children must feel confident that their teachers and schools value diverse cultural heritages and languages. To encourage confidence and cooperation, a teacher can bring the strengths, contributions, culture, and language of the family directly into the school experience. For example, a grandmother who creates pottery following ancient techniques might demonstrate her art. A church leader could explain a religious holiday or event. And a tribal leader might be asked to officiate at a school awards ceremony. Any such family participation in school events helps foster home–school partnerships and promote children's success at school. Here are a few tips about how to foster meaningful partnerships with diverse families (Brown et al., 2003; Kraft, 2001; Milian, 1999; Parette & Petch-Hogan, 2000; Thorp, 1997):

- Develop an atmosphere of trust and respect.
- Make families and communities feel welcome at school.
- Select community leaders to serve as representatives of both school and home, and involve them regularly.
- Identify families' preferred means of communication and use it effectively.
- Communicate on a regular, ongoing basis (not just when there is a problem).
- Use interpreters who are knowledgable about schools, special education, and its programs.
- Incorporate materials and activities that reflect the diversity of the community.
- Seek meaningful ways (such as actively sharing culture, art, music, and recreational activities) to involve families and communities (as they feel comfortable).
- Hold meetings with families at times and places that are manageable for them.

Building the right partnerships often requires working in difficult situations, for many of these families and communities are fighting for their own survival and often feel disenfranchised. It is the crucial job of educators to find real and meaningful ways to involve these families and communities.

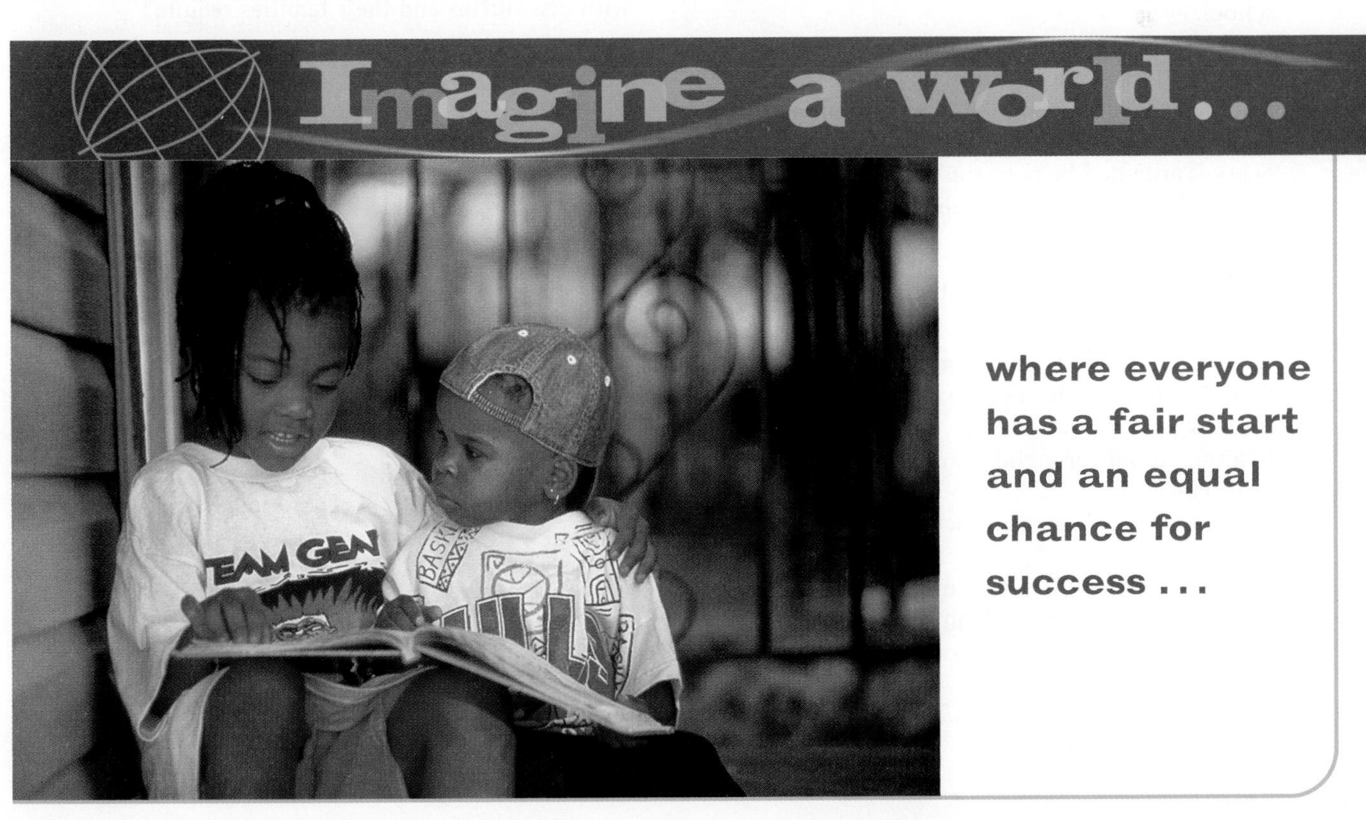

Imagine a world...
where everyone has a fair start and an equal chance for success . . .
TEAM GEN

Summary

Education should reflect the rich diversity of culture and language found in communities across this country, and special education should capitalize on each student's background as an appropriate individualized education program is created. Many exceptional children are bilingual, and many more come from diverse cultural backgrounds. The combinations of disability, giftedness, cultural diversity, and ELL present many challenges to these children, their families, and educators as schools attempt to ensure that special education services are delivered to children who need and are entitled to them.

Addressing the Chapter Objectives

1 What is meant by the term *diverse?*

- Being from one of these groups: African American (Black), Hispanic (Latino/a), Asian/Pacific Islander, American Indian/Alaska Native
- Being from a culture different from "mainstream America"
- Speaking a language at home other than English
- Whether accurate or not, considered a minority

2 How does poverty put many culturally and linguistically diverse students at risk for low educational results and having disabilities?

- Poverty results in reduced access to health care.
- Diverse young children are less likely to attend preschool.
- Poor children are more likely to be homeless or to live a mobile or migrant life.
- Fewer poor children have computers at home (the digital divide).
- Schools attended by poor students have low expectations, few resources, unqualified teachers, and a less demanding curriculum.

3 What are the key features of multicultural education?

- Students' cultural backgrounds and traditions are integrated into the curriculum.
- Students' home cultures are respected and understood.
- Relevant and meaningful examples anchor instruction.
- Clashes between home and school cultures are minimized.
- Culturally diverse family members and communities feel included and welcome.
- All educators are culturally competent.

4 How can schools and teachers be more responsive to English language learners?

- Be sensitive to the different patterns and rates of language acquisition.
- Understand the differences between conversational and classroom English.
- Encourage quick mastery of English through ESL, bilingual, and sheltered instruction.
- Ensure meaningful communications and partnerships with families and communities.
- Provide bilingual paraprofessionals and volunteers.
- Use language accommodations.

5 What additional considerations do diverse students with disabilities and their families require?

- All the components of multicultural education
- Intensive assistance in learning English
- Explicit instruction
- Intensive efforts for family involvement
- Application of validated practices

Supplementary Resources

Popular Novels and Books

Anaya, R. A. (1979). *Tortuga.* Berkeley, CA: Editorial Justa.
Dorris, M. (1989). *The broken cord.* New York: Harper & Row.
Carter, F. (1997). *The education of Little Tree.* Albuquerque: University of New Mexico Press.
Kenzaburo, O. (1994). *The pinch runner memorandum.* London: M. E. Sharpe.
Kozol, J. (1995). *Amazing grace: The lives of children and the conscience of a nation.* New York: Crown.
Ng, F. M. (1993). *Bone: A novel.* New York: Hyperion.
Southgate, D. E. (1996). *The other way to dance.* New York: Laurel-Leaf Books.
Williams-Garcia, R. (1995). *Like sisters on the homefront.* New York: Peguin Books.

Movies

The Education of Little Tree (1997). Paramount
During the depression, Little Tree's parents die, and he goes to live with his grandparents. They teach this eight-year-old boy the Cherokee ways of East Tennessee. However, a complaint is filed against the boy's grandparents because they did not enroll him in school. Authorities place the boy in a boarding school, where he is abused because he is not familiar with the customs of this new world, so his grandfather liberates him.

This film begins with a young boy acclimating to a rural lifestyle where he is taught to live in harmony with nature. Once Little Tree is enrolled in a boarding school, cultural differences become apparent, and the disparity between this setting and his previous environment becomes intolerable. Each culture holds different values sacred, one nature and the other discipline.

Lean on Me (1989). Warner Brothers
An inner city public school has deteriorated and is suffering from overcrowded classrooms, drug addicted students, gang members, and violence, making it impossible to maintain order. A principal is hired to turn the school around, and he begins by expelling all the known troublemakers. He is willing to take any measure, legal or illegal, to ensure that his students are safe and prepared for the state's school evaluation test.

The school in the film represents a realistic portrayal of typical inner city school from the late 1980s and early 1990s. The film shows that school administrators and principals can have a tremendous impact on the lives of students by helping to engage them in both academics and school life. The result is a reduction in school failure and in dropout rates.

Stand and Deliver (1988). Warner Brothers
Based on the true story of one teacher who has high hopes for his students from a low-income neighborhood in East Los Angeles and who challenges them to take the advanced placement test in calculus. So, they have to attend summer school for several extra hours a day. The students actually get the highest score in the state, but they are accused of cheating.

In East Los Angeles, where the majority of residents are Hispanic, the schools are underfunded, and the education the students receive is inferior to that provided by other schools in the same district. Officials from the Board of Education for the State of California challenged the students' results because of their biases about Latino/a students. Without the persistence and strength of their teachers, these students could not have overcome low expectations and would have fulfilled their and others' expectation that they would fail.

Professional, Parent, and Advocacy Groups

Children's Defense Fund (CDF) in Washington, DC
www.cdf.org

Division for Culturally and Linguistically Diverse Exceptional Learners (DDEL) Council for Exceptional Children (CEC) in Arlington, Virginia
www.cec.sped.org or www.cec.sped.org/dv/ddel

National Association for Bilingual Education (NABE) in Washington, DC: www.nabe.org

National Center for Culturally Responsive Educational Systems (NCCRESt) in Denver
nccrest.org

National Clearinghouse for English Language Acquisition & Language Instruction Education Programs (NCELA) at George Washington University in Washington, DC: www.ncbe.gwu.edu

National Association for Multicultural Education (NAME) in Washington, DC: www.nameorg.org

Pew Hispanic Center of the Pew Charitable Trusts in Washington, DC: www.pewhispanic.org

Tomás Rivera Policy Institute at the University of Southern California in Los Angeles: www.trpi.org

Professional Standards and Licensure Tests

After reading this chapter, you should be able to link basic knowledge and skills described in the CEC Standards and INTASC Principles with information provided in this text. The table below shows some of the specific CEC Common Core Knowledge and Skill Standards and INTASC Special Education Principles that can be applied to each major section of the chapter. Other standards may also be applied to this chapter. Associated General Praxis II topic areas are identified in the right column.

Major Chapter Headings CEC Knowledge and Skill	Core Standard and Associated Subcategories	INTASC Core Principle and Associated Special Education Subcategories	PRAXIS II Exam Topic
Where We've Been . . . What's on the Horizon?	**5: Learning Environments and Social Interactions** CC5K9 Ways specific cultures are negatively stereotyped	**3: Diverse Learners** 3.09 Special education teachers actively ask questions, seek information from others, and take actions to guard against inappropriate assessment and identification of students whose cultural, ethnic, gender, and linguistic differences may be confused with manifestations of a disability.	1: Understanding Exceptionality 2: Legal and Social Issues
Cultural and Linguistic Diversity Defined	**1: Foundations** CC1K5 Issues in definition and identification of individuals with exceptional learning needs, including those from culturally and linguistically diverse backgrounds	**3: Diverse Learners** 3.03 All teachers understand that a disability can be perceived differently across families, communities, and cultures based on differing values and belief systems.	1: Understanding Exceptionality 2: Legal and Social Issues
Characteristics	**6: Communication** CC6K2 Characteristics of one's own culture and use of language and the ways in which these can differ from other cultures and uses of languages	**3: Diverse Learners** 3.08 Special education teachers understand that second language learners can also have language-based disabilities.	1: Understanding Exceptionality
Causes and Prevention	**2: Development and Characteristics of Learners** CC2K3 Characteristics and effects of the cultural and environmental milieu of the individual with exceptional learning needs and the family	**2: Student Learning** 2.07 Special education teachers seek to understand the current and evolving development and learning of individual students from a life-span perspective.	1: Understanding Exceptionality

Assessment	**8: Assessment** CC8S2 Administer nonbiased formal and informal assessments	**8: Assessment** 8.09 Special education teachers are aware of and guard against over and under identification of disabilities based on cultural, ethnic, gender, and linguistic diversity.	3: Delivery of Services to Students
Teaching Diverse Students with Disabilities	**3: Individual Learning Differences** CC3K5 Differing ways of learning of individuals with exceptional learning needs including those from culturally diverse backgrounds and strategies for addressing these differences	**4: Instructional Strategies** 4.10 Special education teachers know a range of specialized instructional strategies that have been found through research and best practices to support learning in individual students with disabilities.	1: Understanding Exceptionality 3: Delivery of Services to Students
Transition	**5: Learning Environments and Social interactions** CC5S1 Create a safe, equitable, positive, and supportive learning environment in which diversities are valued	**7: Planning Instruction** 7.07 Special education teachers oversee the development of individualized transition plans to guide learners' transitions from preschool to elementary school, middle school to high school, and high school to postschool opportunities.	3: Delivery of Services to Students
Collaboration	**10: Collaboration** CC10K4 Culturally responsive factors that promote effective communication and collaboration with individuals with exceptional learning needs, families, school personnel, and community members	**10: Collaboration, Ethics, and Relationships** 10.04 All teachers accept families as full partners in planning appropriate instruction and services for students with disabilities and provide meaningful opportunities for them to participate as partners in their children's instructional programs in the life of the school.	2: Legal and Social Issues 3: Delivery of Services to Students
Partnerships with Families and Communities	**10: Collaboration** CC10S10 Communicate effectively with families of individuals with exceptional learning needs from diverse backgrounds	**3: Diverse Learners** 3.06 Special education teachers seek to understand how having a child with disabilities may influence a family's views of themselves as caregivers and as members of their communities.	1: Understanding Exceptionality 3: Delivery of Services to Students

Hagood Mill by Judy Taylor. © Judy Taylor. Used with kind permission of the artist.

Judy Stermer Taylor majored in speech therapy at the University of New Mexico, in part to resolve her own stuttering problems. As a child, she was convinced that she could not draw or paint (or compete with her highly successful and talented sister, who was painting murals by the age of 7) because she was left-handed and had learning disabilities. She discovered her artistic talents when working with a patient at a nursing home who needed help communicating with others. The woman's stroke had left her unable to read printed words. When Taylor could not find suitable pictures to use to help the woman communicate her needs, she sketched images to represent items and actions. Judy Taylor is now an award-winning artist, whose work is collected worldwide.

4

Speech or Language Impairments

Many, many insights into the problem of stuttering are lost . . . when the person who stutters is viewed solely through the lens of stuttering. Placing the part of the person called "stuttering" into the whole of the person who stutters called "the person" is the challenge . . . .

Edward Conture, Vanderbilt University

Language is the foundation for all learning. We use it to clarify what we observe, engage others, express our needs, and interact with friends and family. For most of us, learning to communicate effectively comes naturally. We don't even remember learning our first language. For some of us, however, speaking or acquiring the fundamentals of language and mastering its nuances are challenging. For those individuals, teachers can play an instrumental role in providing the foundation for one of the most important skills everyone needs for a successful life: knowing how to communicate effectively with others.

Our society places a high value on oral communication, and for most of us, it is the primary method of interacting with others. We talk with each other to share knowledge, information, and feelings. Most of us, in fact, prefer talking to other forms of communication. Note the intensity of conversations in college dining halls, in hallways at schools, and on cell phones; think about how often we choose to call someone instead of writing a letter. Clearly, communication with others is a crucial part of life, a fundamental aspect of the human condition.

As you learned in the previous chapter, language instruction is critical for many of America's linguistically diverse students who come to school with so much to learn. Not only do they need to master the academic content presented, but at the same time they need to become fluent in a new language. Although many English language learners (ELLs) need extra help from their teachers so they can master their new language as quickly as possible, the vast majority of these students do *not* have language-related disabilities as well. In this chapter you will learn about students who *do* have speech or language impairments, and you will also discover that these problems are common for many students with disabilities. For example, the co-occurrence of speech or language impairments with learning disabilities is estimated at 96 percent (Sunderland, 2004). So many of these individuals follow the same path: As preschoolers, they don't develop language on time. By third grade their difficulties learning to read have signaled learning disabilities to their teachers, and throughout their schooling they struggle with most academic subjects that require mastery of skills related to the applications of language: reading, writing, and oral communication. As you will learn in this chapter and in the next, which is about learning disabilities, language is the foundation for success at school and in life. You will also learn that many proven ways to help individuals with speech or language impairments are now available; it is our job to know when and how to help.

Chapter Objectives

After studying this chapter, you will be able to:

1. Describe "speech impairments" and "language impairments."
2. Discuss the prevalence of speech or language impairments, and indicate how the prevalence of this type of disability is related to that of learning disabilities.
3. Describe the differences among language delays, language differences, and language impairments.
4. Explain the benefits of augmentative and alternative communication.
5. Discuss how classroom teachers can make a difference in the development of children's language.

Where We've Been . . . What's on the Horizon?

Long before the first passage of IDEA in 1975, **speech/language pathologists (SLPs)**—the professionals who help students maximize their communication skills—worked in schools and provided support services to teachers and direct services to students and their families (American Speech-Hearing-Language Association [ASHA], 2002). After World War II and until the 1970s, the majority of their time was spent with students who had trouble correctly producing speech sounds. After 1975, special education became more developed, and the roles of SLPs changed. More students with complex speech and language problems came the nation's public schools. Because most teachers had little preparation in the area of language development, SLPs came to assume a greater role in providing an appropriate education to students with significant language problems. They provide unique expertise to these students and their families, and the high quality of their services make real differences in the results for these individuals. Enhancing the work of SLPs are advances in technology. Today, technology allows individuals to speak who do not have the motoric abilities to make speech sounds on their own. These students can participate in class discussions, chat with their friends, and take their places in the community with the assistance of communication devices. We can only imagine how future technological developments will provide even more benefits to individuals with speech and language impairments, their teachers, and their families. Let's first learn about how far this field and the individuals affected have come.

Historical Context

Records dating before 1000 B.C. reveal that at that time, many individuals with disabilities were considered fools, buffoons, and sources of entertainment, often because of their speech or language problems. For example, as we noted in Chapter 1, in the time of the Roman Empire, people with disabilities were exhibited in cages along the Appian Way—the main road into and out of Rome—for the amusement of those passing by. People even planned special family outings to see Balbus Balaesus the Stutterer, who would attempt to talk whenever a coin was thrown into his cage (Van Riper & Erickson, 1996).

Speech or language impairments have been documented throughout the centuries, and so have treatment programs. The foundation for today's special education services for students with these disabilities was laid at the beginning of the last century. At that time, what was called speech correction was offered in clinics, not at schools. The first school-based programs were offered in 1910 when the Chicago public schools hired an itinerant teacher to help children who "stammered" (Moore & Kester, 1953). In 1913, the superintendent of the New York City schools began a program of speech training for children with speech impairments. A year later, Smiley Blanton opened the first university speech clinic at the University of Wisconsin. In 1925, a small group of professionals created the American Academy for Speech Correction (later called the American Speech and Hearing Association, and now called the American Speech-Language-Hearing Association but typically referred to as just ASHA) to share their ideas and research. By 2004, ASHA had grown to over 118,000 speech, language, and hearing professional members (ASHA, 2005).

During the late 1950s and 1960s, SLPs—then called speech therapists or speech clinicians (notice the emphasis on the word *speech*)—each worked with more than 200 children per week primarily in small groups and for as little as 30 minutes a day. Most of these children could not produce speech sounds correctly; nearly all had articulation problems. Students with significant language and cognitive problems typically did not receive services from SLPs because the general belief of that day was that they were not developmentally able to profit from therapy. All of that

speech/language pathologist (SLP) A professional who diagnoses and treats speech or language impairments; a related services provider

A Hero Arrives on the Scene

People with disabilities do need heroes, not uncomplaining overcomers, but real disabled heroes who fight bias and battle for control of their lives and insist that they will make their mark in the world. Christy Brown, difficult and dangerous as he is, is such a hero. Paul Longmore, 2003, p. 130

Sometimes, a film becomes a landmark portrayal representing an issue larger than the film itself. To many people with disabilities, the film *My Left Foot,* depicting the life of Christy Brown, is such a movie. The movie and its expression of rage—not due to his disabilities, but rather to the way he is treated because of them—combined with humor made Christy Brown a "hero" or symbol of the disability movement.

Christy Brown, a man born with cerebral palsy to a poor Irish family, was able to develop control of only his left foot, which he used as his means of communication because his speech was difficult to understand. His mother's strength and love, along with individual attention from a qualified instructor, helped Christy find his voice both literally and creatively, becoming an acclaimed artist, poet, and author. This documentary-like film offers insight into the emotional psyche of someone with disabilities. We empathize with him not just because of his physical limitations or difficulty communicating, but also because of those universal problems that everyone experiences, such as heartache and grief. Also portrayed is the importance of integrating people with disabilities into mainstream society and receiving special and individualized instruction. Oscars for Best Actor and Best Supporting Actress, respectively, rewarded Daniel Day-Lewis and Brenda Fricker for their performances in this film, which presented the lives of real people with dignity and respect.

—By Steven Smith

changed in 1975 with the passage of IDEA. SLPs began providing more and more individual services to a broader range, but fewer, students with disabilities; accordingly, ASHA coined the term *speech/language pathologist (SLP)* to reflect the wider range of the services these specialists now provide to students with many more types of conditions and disabilities.

Challenges That Speech or Language Impairments Present

Speech impairments can affect how a person interacts with others in all kinds of settings and can influence an individual's success in school, social situations, and employment. Stuttering, for example, can result in emotional problems because listeners—and often the individuals themselves—react to nonfluent speech with embarrassment, guilt, frustration, or anger (Conture, 2001; Ramig & Shames, 2006). The condition can lead to confusion, feelings of helplessness, and diminished self-concept. The long-term effects can be quite serious. Some individuals respond by acting overly aggressive, denying their disability, and projecting their own negative reactions onto their listeners. Others withdraw socially, seeking to avoid all situations in which they have to talk, and ultimately they become isolates. Some spend considerable effort avoiding words that contain sounds that are difficult for them not to repeat over and over again.

Many individuals with disabilities deal with multiple problems, and this sometimes leads people to draw inaccurate conclusions about the individuals involved. For example, Christy Brown, whose life story, *My Left Foot*, was both a book and a movie, had a condition called cerebral palsy (CP). CP, which usually results from brain damage that occurred at or before birth, affects individuals' abilities to control their muscles. (You will learn more about CP in Chapter 9.) CP can hinder a person's ability to control muscles for walking, writing, or forming speech sounds. But because the condition sometimes causes labored and slow speech, some people wrongly assume that other signs of CP go hand in hand with reduced mental abilities. The result, as clearly depicted in the movie about Brown's life (see *On the Screen* found on page 119), is often discrimination and bias (Longmore, 2003). Like Christy Brown, Lizzy B (see *In the Spotlight* on page 121) has CP, and both of them are proof that we should never make hasty assumptions about people's possibilities!

Effective language is the foundation for school success. Problems with acquiring and developing language during early childhood are strong predictors of problems not only in communicating with others, but also in learning to read, write, and succeed in most academic areas (Ely, 2005). Language impairments have the potential of being even more serious than speech impairments, because they can affect all aspects of a student's classroom experiences (Wetherby, 2002). Thus, when preschool teachers see signs of language problems, immediate advice and help should be sought from SLPs to determine whether intervention is warranted. Early intervention is powerful, and classroom teachers can help to alter the path that these early predictors of academic problems signal.

Speech or Language Impairments Defined

To understand speech or language impairments, you must first understand the communication process people use to interact with others. At least two people are needed: a sender and a receiver. The process also requires a message. First, the sender has a thought or idea, which then is translated into a code the receiver can understand. Communication occurs only when the receiver understands the message as the sender intended it to be understood. The sender can impair effective communication in two ways. One way is by producing speech that is not understandable because speech sounds are not produced correctly. The other way is for the sender to be unable to produce the intended message because of difficulties using language. At the root of the first communication problem are speech impairments, and the bases for the second problem are language impairments. Before thinking about these two overarching communication problems, let's learn about how effective communications happen.

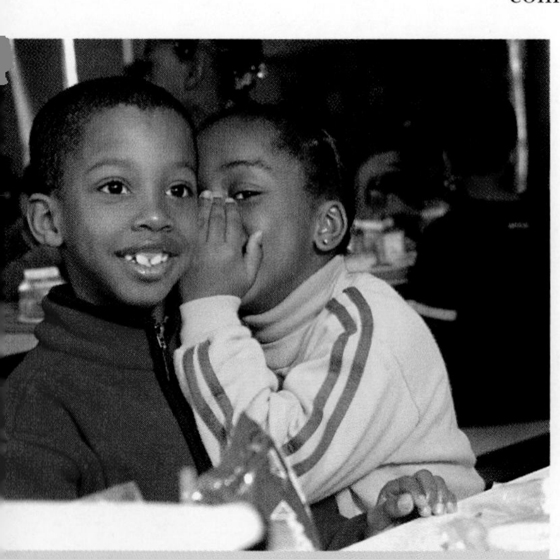

These children are engaged in the communication process by taking turns sending and receiving messages.

The Communication Process

Coding thoughts into symbols or signals is an important part of communication. **Communication symbols**—such as speech sounds, written words, or hand gestures (e.g., waving hello or pointing a finger)—relay messages. Communication symbols are used in combination with each other and are governed by rules that constitute language and allow language to have meaning. They can refer to something: a past, present, or future event; a person or object; an action; a concept or emotion. They are needed to exchange knowledge and information. **Communication signals** are nonverbal expressions of a social formality or convention and usually announce some immediate event, person, action, or emotion. For example, the U.S. Marine Band playing "Hail to the Chief" signals the appearance of the president of the United States. A teacher rapping on a desk announces the need to pay attention or to be quieter.

Lizzy B in the Spotlight

Lizzy B is a busy middle schooler although her cerebral palsy affects her ability to control her muscles. 11-year-old Lizzy B won the statewide competition and represented Tennessee at the national Young Entrepreneurs annual competition in Minnesota. When people first meet Lizzy B, they often find her speech difficult to understand, but her skills using some pretty complicated speech technology are always expanding. She was recently inducted into the National Junior Honor Society, is active in Girl Scouts, and is learning how to walk in high heels using her walker (not an easy task). Despite her ambitious schedule, after attending the CEO Academy's Fun Shop camp, she decided to start her own business. Amy, Lizzy B's mom, says,

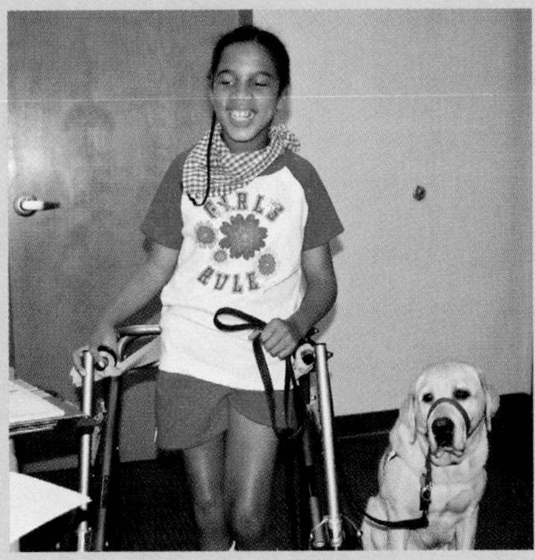

Lizzy B started her card business because she wanted to have greeting cards that showed kids like her, with disability, doing things like regular kids. She never could find any cards that showed children with disabilities. It has been very successful for her, and I think it has really accomplished more than simply showing people with disabilities doing everyday things. It has really opened other people's eyes to the abilities of young people with disabilities.

Once thought is coded, the sender must select a mechanism for delivering the message. The sender chooses from a number of mechanisms: voice, sign language, gestures, writing tools. The delivery system must be useful to the receiver. For example, selecting voice via telephone to transmit a message to a deaf person is useless (unless that person has a voice-decoding telephone device). Sending a written message to someone who cannot read also results in ineffective communication.

Communication requires the receiver to use the eyes, the ears, or even the tactile (touch) sense (as do those who use Braille) to convey the message to the brain where it is understood. Receivers must understand the code the sender uses and must be able to interpret the code so that it has meaning. Communication is unsuccessful if the sender or receiver cannot use the signals or symbols adequately. And if either person has a defective mechanism for sending or receiving the information, the communication process is ineffective. Figure 4.1 illustrates the communication process via an example from a fast-food restaurant.

At this point, it might be helpful to distinguish among three important and related terms: speech, language, and communication.

- **Speech** is the vocal production of language (e.g., the speaker says the word *ball*).
- **Language** is a rule-based method of communication involving the comprehension and use of the signs and symbols by which ideas are represented (e.g., the speaker says the word *ball* to mean the object).
- **Communication** is the process of exchanging knowledge, ideas, opinions, and feelings through the use of verbal or nonverbal (e.g., a gesture) language (e.g., the speaker uses the word for a purpose: "The ball is red." "Give me the red ball").

communication symbols Voice, letters of the alphabet, or gestures used to send communication messages

communication signals A variety of nonverbal cues that announce some immediate event, person, action, or emotion

speech Vocal production of language

language Rule-based method used for communication

communication Transfer of knowledge, ideas, opinions, or feelings

Figure 4.1 • The Communication Process

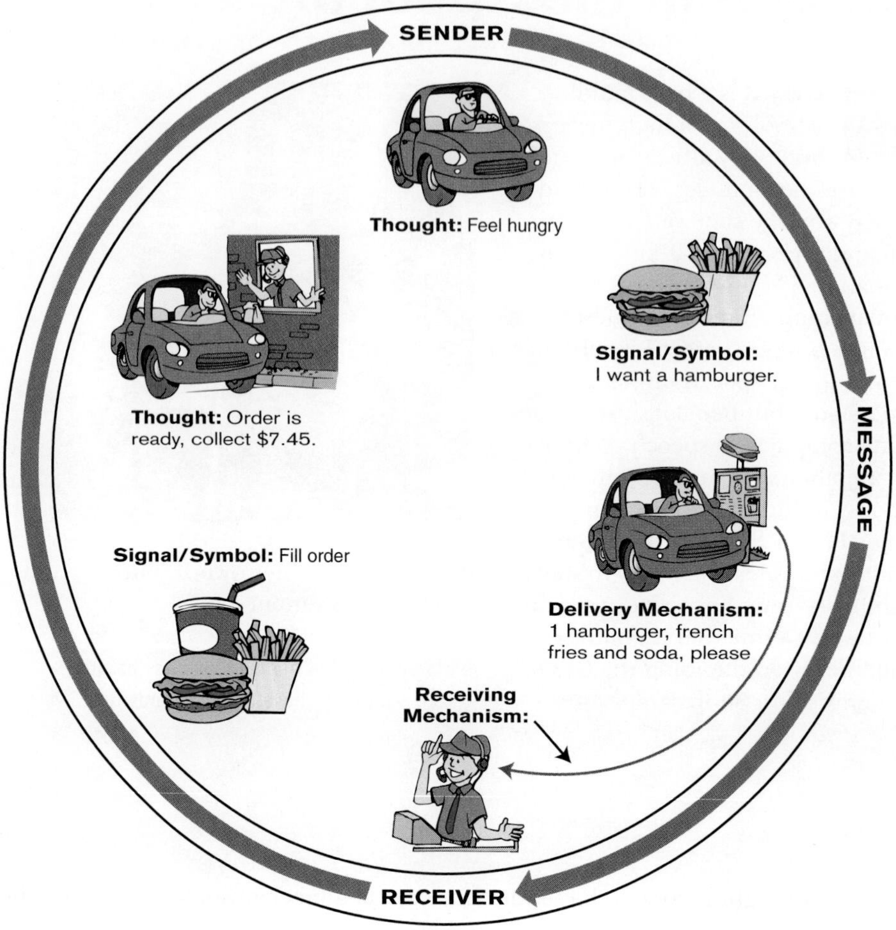

respiratory system The system of organs whose primary function is to take in oxygen and expel carbon dioxide

vibrating system The larynx and vocal folds, which vibrate and produce the sounds and pitch of speech

resonating system Oral and nasal cavities where speech sounds are formed

speech mechanisms The various parts of the body (tongue, lips, teeth, mandible, and palate) required for oral speech

communication disorders Disorders in speech, language, or hearing that impair communication

Understanding how our bodies work to produce speech and language is helpful in understanding what happens when a breakdown in the system results in speech or language impairments. Refer to the diagram of the head and chest cavity shown in Figure 4.2 as you read the following description of the process of generating speech. When we want to speak, the brain sends messages that activate other mechanisms. The **respiratory system** is the group of muscles and organs (diaphragm, chest muscles, lungs, throat) that take in oxygen and expel gases from our bodies. Its secondary function is to provide the air and pressure necessary to produce speech sounds. The **vibrating system** includes the larynx and the vocal folds, and together they produce the voice. The larynx sits on top of the trachea, which houses the vocal folds. As air is expelled from the lungs, the flow of air causes the vocal folds to vibrate and produce sounds; the vocal folds lengthen or shorten to cause changes in pitch. As the sounds travel through the throat, mouth, and nasal cavities—the **resonating system**— the voice is shaped into speech sounds by the **speech mechanisms**, sometimes called the articulation mechanisms, which include the tongue, soft and hard palates, teeth, lips, and jaw.

Next, let's turn our attention to impairments in communication.When an individual has a problem producing speech or using language to communicate, the individual has a disability. **Communication disorders** is a broad, umbrella-term often used by speech and language professionals to include all disabilities that result in difficulties with speech, language, and hearing. IDEA '04, however, con-

Figure 4.2 • The Body's Systems for Generating Voice and Speech

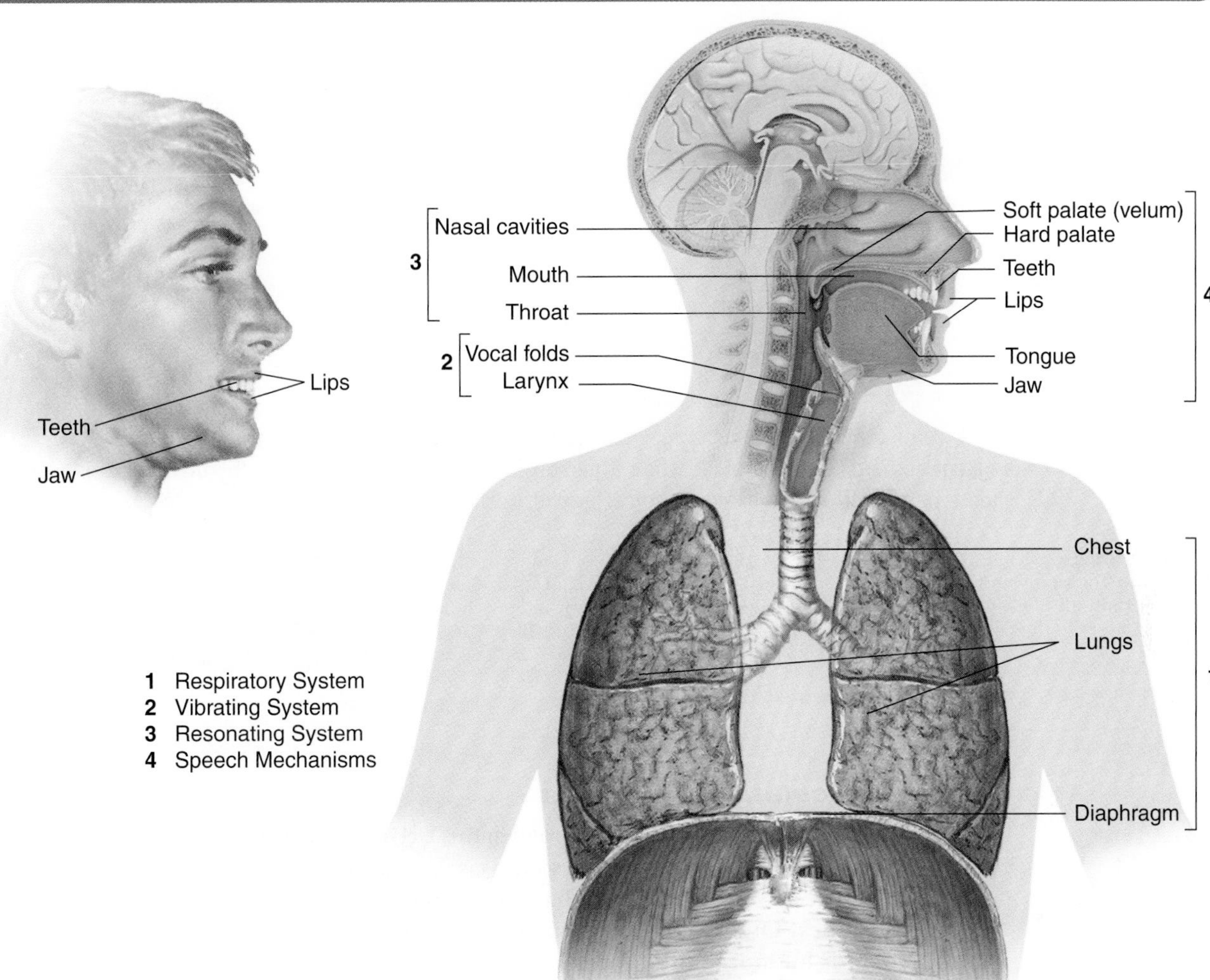

siders speech or language impairments as one disability and hearing impairments (hard of hearing and deafness) as two others. That's the organizational system used in this book. IDEA'04 considers speech impairments and language impairments to be one special education category, but as you will learn, they are truly distinct (see Table 4.1, page 124, for official definitions of this disability). Let's look at each type to better understand how the problem areas associated with these impairments influence the effectiveness of individuals' communications.

Speech Impairments

The receiver of communication must understand the sounds of the words spoken to understand the full message. If speech sounds are incorrectly produced, one sound might be confused with another, either changing the meaning of the message or yielding no meaning. When speech is abnormal, it is unintelligible, is unpleasant, or interferes with communication (Bernthal & Bankson, 2004; Hall, Oyer, & Haas, 2001). **Speech impairments** include three major types of problems: difficulties with articulation, fluency, and voice. Problems with any one of these speech impairments are distracting to the listener and can negatively affect or interrupt the communication process.

speech impairments Abnormal speech that is unintelligible, is unpleasant, or interferes with communication

Table 4.1 • Definitions of Speech or Language Impairments

Source	Definition
Federal Government[1]	Speech or language impairment: A communication disorder, such as: • *stuttering,* • *impaired articulation,* • *a language impairment,* • *or a voice impairment,* that adversely affects a child's educational performance.
American Speech-Language-Hearing Association[2]	Speech and language disorder: A speech and language disorder may be present when a person's speech or language is different from that of others of the same age, sex, or ethnic group; when a person's speech and/or language is hard to understand; when a person is overly concerned about his or her speech; or when a person often avoids communicating with others.

Sources: [1]34 CFR Parts 300 and 303, Assistance to States for the Education of Children with Disabilities and the Early Intervention Program for Infants and Toddlers with Disabilities; Proposed Regulations (p. 313), U.S. Department of Education, 2005a, *Federal Register,* Washington, DC; and [2]"Definitions of Communication Disorders and Variations" by American Speech-Language-Hearing Association Ad Hoc Committee on Service Delivery in the Schools, 1993, *Asha, 35,* (Suppl. 10), pp. 40–41. Rockville, MD: ASHA. Reprinted by permission.

Articulation Problems

The most common speech impairment, **articulation problems**, exists when the process of producing speech sounds is flawed, and the resulting speech sounds are incorrect. Some individuals have no physiological reason for their articulation difficulties. Others correctly articulate a sound when it occurs in one position in words but not in other positions. They may be able to pronounce a sound consistently without errors when it occurs at the beginning of a word but cannot do so when the sound occurs in the middle or at the end of a word. Table 4.2 describes the four kinds of articulation errors, but as you read about them, remember that articulation is related to the speaker's age, culture, and environment. For example, a young child's errors may be developmentally correct, whereas the same speech product made by an older child may well reflect an articulation problem. The difference could also be due to regional speech patterns, foreign language accents, or cultural speech preferences, but none of these speech differences reflects a speech impairment. Regional differences in speech—dialects—do *not* need attention from an SLP.

articulation problems Abnormal production of speech sounds

fluency problems Hesitations or repetitions of sounds or words that interrupt a person's flow of speech; stuttering is an example; a speech impairment

dysfluencies Aspects of speech that interrupt the pattern of speech; also known as fluency problems

stuttering The lack of fluency in an individual's speech pattern, often characterized by hesitations or repetitions of sounds or words; a speech impairment

Fluency Problems

When the rate and flow pattern of a person's speech is of concern, it is most likely that the individual is experiencing a **fluency problem**. Fluency problems, or **dysfluencies**, usually involve hesitations or repetitions of parts of words that interrupt the flow of speech (Conture, 2001). **Stuttering** is one type of fluency problem where sounds or parts of words are repeated. Some young children (ages 3 to 5) demonstrate dysfluencies in the course of normal speech development, and these are not usually indicative of a fluency problem in need of therapy. With older individuals, the repetition of words or phrases (e.g., "The the boy boy went to the a a show") is typically *not* a sign of stuttering, but frequently repeating sounds or parts of words (e.g., The b-b-boy wha-wha-ent to the sha-sha-show.") *is* a signal of this speech impairment (Ratner, 2005).

Table 4.2 • Four Kinds of Articulation Errors

Error Type	Definition	Example
Omission	A sound or group of sounds is left out of a word. Small children often leave off the ending of a word (sounds in the final position).	Intended: *I want a banana.* Omission: *I wanna nana.*
Substitution	A common misarticulation among small children; one sound is used for another.	Intended: *I see the rabbit.* Substitution: *I tee the wabbit.*
Distortion	A variation of the intended sound is produced in an unfamiliar manner.	Intended: *Give the pencil to Sally.* Distortion: *Give the pencil to Sally* (the /p/ is nasalized).
Addition	An extra sound is inserted or added to one already correctly produced.	Intended: *I miss her.* Addition: *I missid her.*

Voice Problems

The third type of speech impairment, a **voice problem**, is not very common in students, but if a child's voice is unusual given the age and sex of the individual (e.g., too husky for a young girl or two high for an older teenage boy), immediate attention from a professional should be arranged. Two qualities of voice are important. **Pitch** is the perceived high or low quality of voice. **Loudness** is the other main aspect of voice.

Age is a critical variable for all three types of speech impairments (Bernthal & Bankson, 2004). Correct production does not develop at the same time for all speech sounds (Small, 2005). Thus, articulation behavior that is developmentally normal at one age is not acceptable at another. The chart in Figure 4.3 gives examples of the ages when various speech sounds develop (Sander, 1972). By age 8½, most children have mastered the last sound (*z*, as in *was*) at 90 percent accuracy. In the case of stuttering, age is also important; it is normal for very young children (between the ages of 3 and 5) to be dysfluent—their speech includes many hesitations and repetitions—as they master oral communication and language. Young children (below age 6) often exhibit high rates of dysfluencies and may even fit a definition of stuttering. Dysfluencies are likely to occur in exciting, stressful, or uncommon situations (Conture, 2001; Gregory et al., 2003). However, more than half of those preschoolers who stutter recover by the age of seven (Ratner, 2005). And in the case of voice, pitch changes during puberty, particularly for boys. Of course, this pitch change is a normal part of development and disappears as the boy's body grows and voice pitch becomes stabilized. It is important that adults not become alarmed or pay too much attention to speech errors during the normal developmental period.

Language Impairments

Language is the complex system we use to communicate our thoughts to others. Oral language is expressed through the use of speech sounds that are combined to produce words and sentences. The use of sounds, letters (symbols), and words is governed by the rules of language. What we know about speech sounds, letters, words (or vocabulary), and rules of language influences the way we speak, read, write, and spell. Not all language systems—consider manual communication or sign language—use speech sounds, but they all follow rules that guide communication and conversations. When an individual has **language impairments**, there is a

voice problem An abnormal spoken language production, characterized by unusual pitch, loudness, or quality of sounds

pitch An aspect of voice; its perceived high or low sound quality

loudness An aspect of voice, referring to the intensity of the sound produced while speaking

language impairments Difficulty or inability to master the various systems of rules in language, which then interferes with communication

Figure 4.3 • Sander's Chart, Indicating When 90% of All Children Typically Produce a Specific Sound Correctly

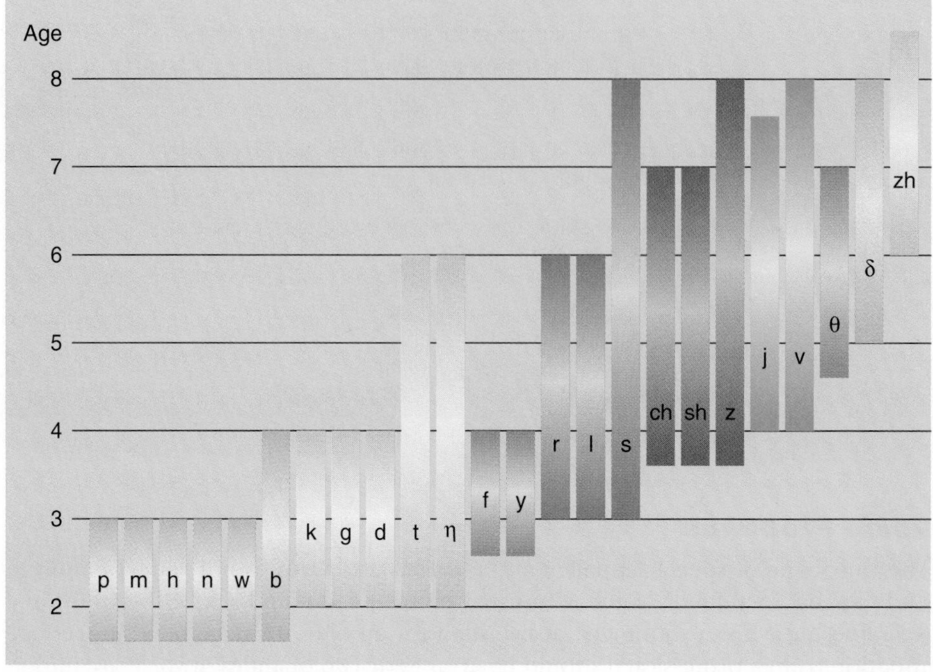

Notes: Average-age estimates and upper-age limits of customary consonant production. The solid bar corresponding to each sound starts at the median age of customary articulation; it stops at the age level at which 90% of all children are customarily producing the sound.

The θ symbol stands for the breathed "th" sound, as in the word *bathroom.* The δ symbol stands for the voiced "th" sound, as in the word *feather.* The η symbol stands for the "ing" sound, as in the word *singing.* The zh symbol indicates the sound of the medial consonant in *measure* or *vision.*

Source: "When Are Speech Sounds Learned?" by E. K. Sander, 1972, *Journal of Speech and Hearing Disorders, 37,* p. 62. © American Speech-Language-Hearing Association. Reprinted by permission.

breakdown in one of the three aspects of language (see below), and effective communication is hindered. It is helpful to understand how these components are all supposed to come together in order to recognize when it is not functioning properly. As you read this section, follow along using the language scheme depicted in Figure 4.4. Now, let's think about the three aspects of language:

- Form
- Content
- Use

The rule system used in all language (oral, written, and sign) is the **form** of language. Oral language uses sounds or sound combinations; written language uses letters and letter combinations to produce the words and word combinations (sentences) of language; and manual communication uses hand and finger movements. In oral language, form has three components: phonology, morphology, and syntax.

The sound system of language, **phonology**, includes rules that govern various sound combinations (Small, 2005). The phonology of language varies with the language. For example, the speech sounds of Hawaiian are different from those of English. The English language uses 45 different speech sound combinations; the Hawaiian language uses only half that number. Swahili and some Native American languages use "clicking" sounds not found in European languages. Rules in each language govern how vowels, consonants, their combinations, and words are used. Awareness of the relationship between sounds in words and sound symbol is called **phonological awareness**. These skills develop during the preschool years and appear to be prerequisite to reading (Jenkins & O'Connor, 2002; Norris & Hoffman, 2002). Phonological awareness and the development of reading are discussed in the Early Intervention section of this and the next chapter, which is about learning disabilities. For now, remember that the foundation for language is also the foundation for reading and that phonological awareness is one key element of this foundation.

form The rule system of language; includes phonology, morphology, and syntax

phonology The rules within a language used to govern the combination of speech sounds to form words and sentences

phonological awareness Understanding, identifying, and applying sound–symbol relationships (letter sounds, rhyming)

Figure 4.4 • Scheme of Language

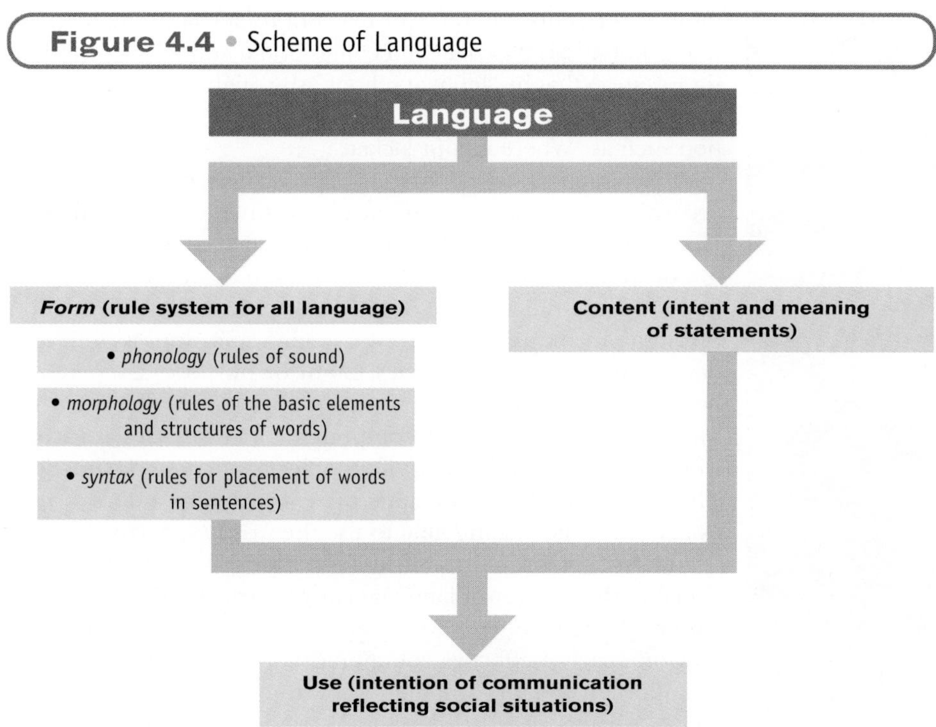

Morphology consists of the rules that govern the parts of words that form the basic elements of their meanings and structures. For example, prefixes and suffixes change the meanings of the roots of specific words: An *-ed* at the end of a verb changes the tense to past; a *un-* at the beginning of a word signals negation (that is, it means that something is not). Note the difference in the meanings of the following words: cover, uncover, covered, uncovered, covers, discovered, discovering, discover, discovery, recover. The rules governing the structure of words enable us to understand the words' meanings.

Words are placed in sentences in accordance with the rules of **syntax**. Like phonology rules, syntax rules vary in different languages. Compare how a sentence is made into a question in the English language ("I want to eat." "Do you want to eat?") to the way statements and questions are formed in Spanish ("Quiero comer." "?Quiere comer?"). Note that in English, the placement of the verb and the subject change when the question is formed. But in Spanish they do not; rather, the person's intonation indicates that a question is being asked. The rules within a language determine the meaning of the communication. In English, nouns and pronouns generally precede verbs in a sentence, and when they do not, the construction might be a question: "It is one o'clock." "Is it one o'clock?" The placement of the words in sentences can change their meaning. For example, "The car hit the boy" has a meaning very different from "The boy hit the car." Rules also structure our placement of adverbs and other parts of speech. Knowing the difference between "I hardly studied this chapter" and "I studied this chapter hard" requires an understanding of how the elements of the English language are put together. For some youngsters these subtleties can be difficult to master.

The second aspect of language, **content**, reflects the intent and meaning of spoken or written statements. The rules and form of language are important, but for communication to be effective, words must be meaningful. **Semantics** is the system where the intent and meanings of words and sentences make up the content of the communication. The key words in a statement, the direct (e.g., *Susan, the dog, that car*) and implied referents (e.g., *she, this, that*) to these words, and the order of the words used all affect the meaning of the message. When senders of messages use indirect or

morphology Rules that govern the parts of words that form the basic elements of their meanings and structures

syntax Rules that govern word endings and the order of words in phrases and sentences

content An aspect of language that governs the intent and meaning of the message delivered in a communication

semantics The system within a language that governs the content, intent, and meanings of spoken and written language

Children with speech or language impairments need many opportunities to practice their newly acquired skills with their peers.

implied referents, the receiver may not understand the message that is intended. When a child comes home and tells his mother, for instance, that he "left it at school," she might be unclear about what the child left at school, unless he is answering a direct question such as "Where is your jacket?"

The application of language in various communications according to the social context of the situation is called **use**. How the words are used within the social context of the communication produces "intent." For example, an individual may make a request, give an order, or supply some information through a communication; the communication is different depending on the individual's intent or purpose. Use extends beyond just vocabulary—beyond simply knowing the word for something. An important component of use is **pragmatics**, which is the understanding of an object's purpose or function. Thus, knowing that a key starts the car or opens a door is necessary to a child's being able to use the word *key* correctly.

Mastery of form, content, and use combine and lead the individual to the mastery of language, or **communicative competence**. Being able to produce speech and language correctly is only one part of effective communication (Ruiz, 1995). It is just as important to know when and how to communicate appropriately. Learners need to develop an understanding about what may be said and what should not be said across a variety of situations. To achieve competence in communication, a person must be able to use language correctly in a social context. Being able to communicate effectively is an essential component of being socially able (Olswang, Coggins, & Timler, 2001). Social competence and communicative competence are related. Social conventions or rules are used to initiate conversations and to communicate with others. Individuals who have problems with pragmatics and communicative competence often do not know how to tell peers that they would like to join in a ball game at recess or do not understand when a conversation is finished. Students who have not developed communicative competence also face challenges when interacting with adults and people in authority. For example, the student might know that it's fine to say, "Hey, dude" or "Like, duh" to a peer but not understand that using such expressions with the principal (instead of "Good morning, Mrs. Rodgers" or "Yes, of course") may lead to trouble. Teachers can make a difference by helping students truly master communication skills. They can provide many opportunities for students to practice using language correctly and appropriately every school day.

Characteristics

Children with speech or language impairments are a large and diverse group of learners. Some have speech impairments, many have language impairments, some have both speech and language impairments, and still others have coexisting disabilities (e.g., learning disabilities and language impairments). In this chapter, we focus on speech and language impairments. In later chapters, we will concentrate on other primary disabilities.

Individuals with different speech impairments have different characteristics and learning needs. For example, a child with a voice problem has a different remediation program than a child who has difficulty articulating speech sounds correctly. Certainly, students with speech impairments have entirely different characteristics and remediation programs than those with language difficulties. Use Table 4.3 to compare characteristics across different types of speech or language problems.

use An aspect of language; applying language appropriately

pragmatics The understanding of an object's purpose or function

communicative competence Proficiency in all aspects of communication in social and learning situations

Speech

Most students whose primary disability is speech impairments (articulation, fluency, or voice problems) attend general education classes and function well academically with their peers. Usually their disability does not influence their academic learning. If their speech impairment is severe and sustained, however, they may have difficulties with peers in social interactions. Depending on how the peer group reacts to an individual's disability, many people with severe speech impairments have long-term difficulties with self-concept and independence (Anderson & Shames, 2006).

Table 4.3 • Signs or Characteristics of Speech or Language Impairments

Speech

- Makes consistent and age-inappropriate articulation errors
- Exhibits dysfluencies (repetitions, prolongations, interruptions) in the flow or rhythm of speech
- Has poor voice quality, such as distracting pitch
- Is excessively loud or soft

Language

- Is unable to follow oral directions
- Is unable to match letters with sounds
- Cannot create rhymes
- Cannot break words into syllables
- Has an inadequate vocabulary
- Demonstrates poor concept formation
- Does not understand nuances, nonverbal messages, or humor
- Has difficulty conveying messages or conversing with others
- Has difficulty expressing personal needs

Social difficulties are particularly common for those who stutter (Ramig & Shames, 2006). Stuttering can negatively affect a person's sense of adequacy and confidence. To avoid embarrassment, many people who stutter avoid situations in which they have to talk; some lash out and vent their frustration and anger on others. Consequently, their disability can influence the types of jobs they seek, the friends they make, their relationships with others, and their overall quality of life. Think about how you react to people with severe speech impairments. Do you look away from them? Do you try to be helpful to the stutterer by finishing his or her sentence? Do you try to avoid the person? Now think about how young children treat their peers who use different speech sounds, who stutter, or who have a different voice quality. Facing these reactions is an everyday reality for individuals with speech impairments. It is understandable that some would like to withdraw from a society that treats them as different. Teachers and peers can be most helpful; their actions can make a real difference in the way students with speech impairments feel about themselves and others (Gregory et al., 2003; Salend, 2005). For example, teachers can make a difference by

- Creating classroom environments where all peers are supportive of each other
- Maintaining eye contact with the student with speech or language impairments throughout the duration of every conversation
- Not finishing sentences or filling in words for individuals who stutter

Classmates' reaction to students with speech or language impairments can be insensitive and, in some cases, even worsen the individual's problems. When reactions are intense, the result can be disruptions to the learning environment or even conflicts during recess or after school. Teachers can turn such situations around by involving peers in positive ways, such as teaching them how to respond constructively and encouraging them not to laugh or tease their classmate with the disability. *Tips for Classroom Management* gives more ideas about how peers can become positive elements in the lives of individuals who face challenges caused by speech or language impairments.

Language

Young children with language impairments develop language late: While their peers without disabilities are talking by the age of three, they are not. And problems continue to mount as they progress through school: As their classmates without disabilities are beginning to read independently by third grade, they are not. Then their problems with reading inhibit their achievement in all academic

DEVELOPING SENSITIVITY

Focus on the Classmates

1 Help classmates understand how they can help a peer with speech or language impairments, such as giving simple instructions about how to play a game or showing how to complete the last steps in a long set of directions.
2 Have class discussions about how feelings, attitudes, and reactions matter.
3 Hold classmates responsible for any teasing and laughing when they hear speech impairments.
4 Instruct classmates not to avoid eye contact when a person with speech or language impairments is having a problem communicating.
5 Teach classmates not to fill in remaining parts of words or sentences for a person who is stuttering.

Focus on the Individual

1 Think with the student with the speech or language problem about constructive and positive ways to deal with awkward or confronting situations.
2 Practice ways to seek assistance from classmates.
3 Create opportunities to practice new speech and language skills in a "safe" environment before practicing these skills with the entire class.

A teacher needs to be a good role model!

areas where speaking and writing are the foundations. In addition, like their peers with speech impairments, many of these individuals have problems making friends and developing positive social relationships (ASHA, 2002). Language abilities influence the development of social skills. Let's think a little more about these issues.

Reading and Academic Performance

Mounting research evidence shows that children identified with language impairments during the preschool years are very likely to be identified as having learning disabilities by third or fourth grade (Ely, 2005; Falk-Ross, 2002; Fuchs & Fuchs, 2005). Preschoolers with language impairments who later have problems learning to read have great difficulty identifying or understanding the relationships between the sounds in words and the symbols that represent those sounds in print (Fletcher et al., 2002). In other words, what initially is a problem with oral language later manifests itself in challenges with what is seen and read on the printed page. The co-occurrence of language impairments with learning disabilities is estimated at well over 90 percent (Sutherland, 2004). You will learn in the next section of this chapter that data from the federal government about the prevalence of these two disabilities support the strong connection between language impairments diagnosed in preschoolers and a diagnosis of learning disabilities during the school years. Because reading skills lead to literacy and are the basis of nearly every academic assignment given in high school, students with language impairments are vulnerable to school failure. But early intervention—teaching preschoolers the skills of phonemic awareness and the sounds that letters of the alphabet represent—can reduce the number of elementary students who have problems learning how to read (Jenkins & O'Connor, 2002; Lyon et al., 2001).

Receptive Language

Being able to understand communication well is important to all interactions, including those in the classroom. Students must comprehend instructions for completing their assignments, following classroom and school rules, and understanding lectures. Problems with receptive language can have disastrous results academically and socially. For example, the student who can remember only one part of directions with many components might experience considerable confusion and embarrassment. When the teacher says to the class, "Put away your pencils and paper, get your coats, and line up at the door for recess," students with receptive language difficulties might "hear" only the last thing they heard. Thus they might line up at the door without having either put their work away or put their coats on. The teacher may think that the individual is defiant, rather than experiencing problems with receptive language. To help, the teacher could restate the three-part instructions slowly and simply or have a peer help the student who continually has such difficulties.

Social Competence

Language plays a key role in developing and maintaining social relationships; social communication requires linguistic and communicative competence (Olswang, Coggins, Timler, 2001). Being able to understand messages and to communicate well is important in interactions with peers and adults. Here are a few reasons why this is so: Effective communication is required to resolve conflicts and disagreements, solve problems, negotiate solutions, share, and develop friendships. Being able to apply complex language skills is a key to understanding others' points of view and to clearly presenting one's feelings. Being adept in the pragmatics of language contributes to successful conflict resolution, comprehension of social situations, and understanding of communications that are ambiguous (Salend, 2005). Students with language impairments are at a higher risk of having difficulties developing positive peer relationships (Ratner, 2005). The characteristics of students who need help developing effective communication skills provide signals that perceptive teachers use to know which of their students may need explicit language instruction (Anderson & Shames, 2006). Here are a few signals that should trigger intervention. Look for students who

- Initiate conversations less
- Rely heavily on adults for their verbal interactions
- Have low social status
- Are often ignored, rejected, and treated harshly by their peers
- Do not have friends or seem extremely lonely

Language Differences, Delays, and Impairments

In the previous chapter about culturally and linguistically diverse students, you learned that many students attending U.S. public schools are at great risk for being incorrectly identified as having disabilities. You learned that students' differences in language are often the root of their misidentification as having a disability, particularly a speech or language impairment. In fact, considerable confusion surrounds these students, and it often takes an expert in normal language development—such as an SLP—to sort out those students with from those without disabilities. Some issues and situations particularly contribute to this confusion: language differences, acquisition of a second language, and language delays. Let's think a bit about these issues.

Many times, **language differences**—regional speech patterns, foreign accents, or second language acquisition—are confused with language impairments (Salend, 2005). Language differences, which result from historical, social, regional, and cultural influences and are sometimes perceived by educators as inferior or nonstandard may take the form of **dialects**, (Payne & Taylor, 2006). Children from diverse backgrounds who use dialects, whether they are from Appalachia or from a predominantly Black inner city community, are often misidentified as having language impairments. Another type of language difference occurs when individuals are learning English and have not yet fully mastered their second language (Salend & Salinas, 2003). Professionals who are able to discriminate between language differences and language impairments are proficient in the rules of the particular student's dialect, in those of the individual's first language, and also in nondiscriminatory testing procedures. It is important that identification procedures be applied to diverse groups of learners carefully.

English language learners (ELLs) may or may not have language impairments. Again, as you learned in Chapter 3, truly mastering a second language takes a long time. It is not easy to determine whether a child who is not a native speaker of English is merely learning a new language or also has language impairments (Baca & Cervantes, 2004; Salend, 2005). ELLs may appear to be fluent in English because they converse with their classmates on the playground and express their basic needs in the classroom, but even so, they may not yet have developed sufficient fluency in their second language to participate fully in academic instruction. These abilities, however, are only some of the language skills

language differences Emerging second language acquisition or nonstandard English

dialects Words and pronunciation from a geographic region or ethnic group, different from those of standard language

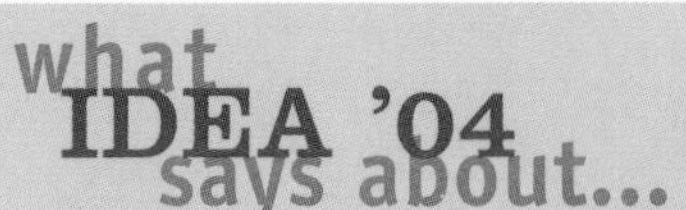

Developmental Delays

In addition to the specific disability categories listed in IDEA '04, a child within the ages of 3 to 9 may be considered as having a disability if:

- He or she meets their state's definition of having a developmental delay.
- The developmental delay was identified through the use of appropriate diagnostic instruments and procedures.
- The child shows delays in any one or more of five specified areas (physical development, cognitive development, communication development, social or emotional development, adaptive development).
- The delay is significant enough to warrant special education and related services.

acquired on the way to communicative competence. Cultural differences and family values also influence how individual children learn language skills, and it is important to understand that different interaction styles result in different paths to communicative competence. English being a second language does not result in a disability. However, because of the impact of poverty, many ELLs face risk factors for many different disabilities, including language impairments (Children's Defense Fund (CDF), 2004; Utley & Obiakor, 2001). Someone proficient in the student's native language can be most helpful. That person can assist in determining whether mastery of English is not yet complete or whether, because the student has similar problems in both languages, she or he may have a language impairment that requires intervention.

Delays in development—be they delays in physical, motor and coordination, or language development—are often signs that a young child may have disabilities. **Language delays**, signaled by the child not developing language skills at the same age as most children do, are a common indication of disabilities in very young children. But language delays are not a characteristic of disabilities for every child; some children are just slower to develop language than other children. They are "late bloomers" or "late talkers." How do you tell the difference between those who will catch up and those who will struggle? At the present time, research does not provide clear predictors to help us decide who needs intervention and who does not (Dale et al., 2003). But research does reveal that up to 40 percent of those who are not beginning to talk by the age of two continue to have problems and are at great risk for school failure (Ratner, 2005). Thus all children with delayed language acquisition should be referred for help, but now they do not have to be identified as having a specific disability. IDEA '04 specifically addresses the issues of developmental delays, allowing children younger than age eight to qualify for special education services without being labeled—or mislabeled—with a one disability or another. *What IDEA '04 Says About Developmental Delays* explains more about what the law requires.

Children with typical language development gain skills in an orderly fashion, in roughly the same sequence across the first 18 months of life (Owens, Jr., 2006). Look first at the profile of the normally developing child; the typical ages when they achieve major language milestones are shown in the left column of Table 4.4. Note that most children after age 3 (40 months) use some fairly sophisticated language, but the three-year-old with language problems is only beginning to use two-word combinations. The gaps between these two children widen quickly. For many individuals with mental retardation, delays continue. They develop language in the correct sequence but never complete the acquisition of complex language; their language development remains below that of their peers without disabilities (Wetherby, 2002). For many students with language impairments, however, it is not just at what rate (how slowly) a child develops language, but also how it develops differently, that signals a problem. Often, both lateness and an uncharacteristic pattern of language development signal language impairments. Children with language impairments make mistakes at an age when their peers don't. They might omit the verb, put the wrong ending on a word, or have incomplete vocabulary development for their age (Plante & Beeson, 2004). So, the kindergartener with language impairments might say, "I go store." or "This green clay" (omitting *is*) or "The paint guy (instead of *the painter*) get (instead of *gets*) more big one (instead of *bigger brushes*)."

language delays Slowed development of language skills; may or may not result in language impairments

Table 4.4 • Comparison of Language Acquisition Skills

Age in Months			
Typical	**Delayed**	**Attainment**	**Examples**
13	17	First words	mamma, here, doggie, bye bye, this
17	38	50-word vocabulary	more juice, here ball, here kitty
18	40	First 2-word combinations	
22	48	Later 2-word combinations	Mommy purse, cup floor, keys chair
24	52	Mean sentence length of 2 words	Andy sleeping
27	55	First appearance of *-ing*	
30	63	Mean sentence length of 3.1 words	
	66	First appearance of *is*	My car's gone!
37	73	Mean sentence length of 4.1 words	
38	76	Mean sentence length of 4.5 words	
40	79	First appearance of indirect requests	Can I get the ball?

Source: Adapted from Shames, Wiis, & Secord (1994).

Prevalence

Official reports show that learning disabilities (see Chapter 5) make up the largest single category of exceptional learners and that speech or language impairments make up the second-largest category, containing 19 percent of all students with disabilities (U.S. Department of Education, 2002). However, more students actually have speech or language impairments than have learning disabilities. How could this be? Well, the federal government "counts" students in only one category, the category reflecting the student's primary disability. However, many students have more than one disability. When both primary and secondary disabilities are considered, speech or language impairments emerge as the largest special education category (ASHA, 2002). Parents of all students with disabilities confirm this fact (Blackorby et al., 2002). They report students in every special education category as having difficulties communicating. Although the majority (57 percent) of them can speak clearly enough to be understood, the remainder experience considerable difficulties speaking, conversing, or understanding others' communications.

Data from the federal government confirm the relationship between early identification of speech or language impairments and later identification of learning disabilities (U.S. Department of Education, 2005b). Figure 4.5 shows the number of individuals diagnosed with speech or language impairments across age groups, compared to those identified with learning disabilities. Note that many more young children are found to have speech or language impairments, but as they get older their diagnosis changes to learning disabilities, most often because language difficulties impact their ability to stay on a par with others academically, particularly in subjects that require reading mastery. For example, at age three—when children who are not developing oral language are first identified—the speech or language impairments category is almost nine times larger than the learning disabilities category. However, at third grade (age eight)—when reading problems become first apparent—the learning disabilities category becomes

Figure 4.5 • Number of Individuals Served Through IDEA '04 by Age

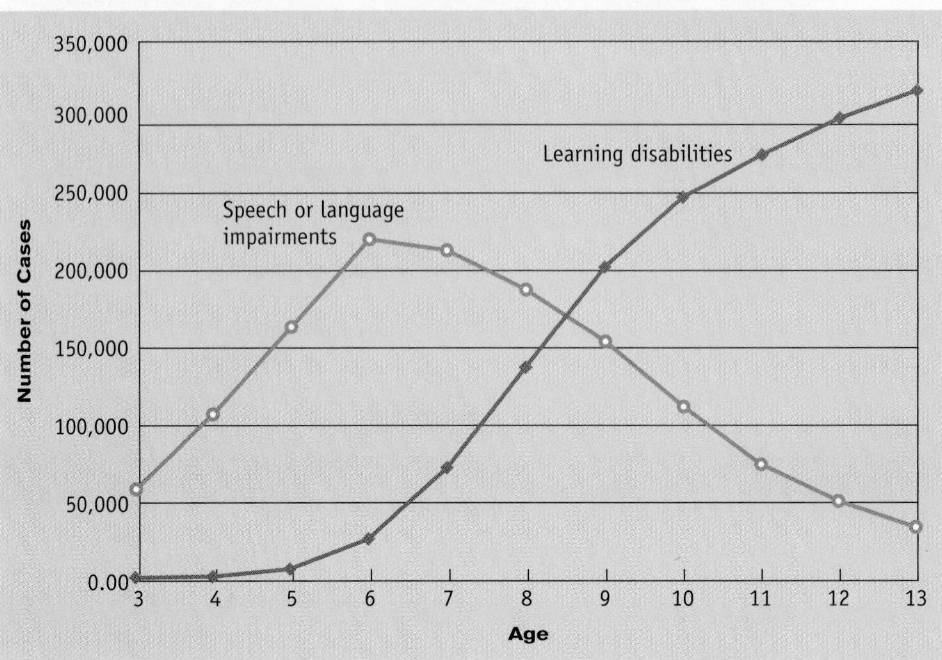

almost the same size as the speech or language impairments category. From that point on, as reading becomes a more integral part of all schoolwork, the numbers of students assigned to the learning disabilities category grows dramatically, while those assigned to the speech or language impairments category decreases. These data certainly support the premise that as the expectations and demands of the curriculum increase, the impact of language impairments becomes more and more apparent.

Causes and Prevention

Researchers work hard to find factors that cause specific disabilities because finding a cause often makes it possible to take preventive measures. Unfortunately, as with so many disability areas, the causes for most cases of speech or language impairments are unknown. Consequently, ways to prevent them from occurring in the first place have not yet been identified. The causes of certain conditions, however, are well known. For some of those conditions, impairments are preventable or can be treated to reduce or eliminate the challenges they present. The known causes of speech impairments tend to differ from the known causes of language impairments. We will first consider speech impairments and then turn our attention to language impairments.

Causes

Speech impairments can result from many different conditions, including brain damage, malfunction of the respiratory or speech mechanisms, and malformation of the articulators. Some children make articulation errors because they do not use the right motor responses to form sounds correctly. They make errors because of the way they use the speech mechanisms—tongue, lips, teeth, mandible (jaw), and/or palate—to form the speech sounds. For others, the cause may be a physical or organic problem, such as a **cleft palate**, where an opening exists in the roof of the mouth, or a **cleft lip**, where the upper lip isn't connected, resulting in an inability to form some speech sounds.

A cleft lip or palate affects the ability to produce speech. Its incidence varies by race/ethnicity: about 1 of every 500 live births for Asian Americans, about 1 of 750 for Whites, and about 1 of 2,000 for African Americans (McWilliams & Witzel, 1998). The proportions of cleft lips and palates tend to be consistent; about 25 percent involve only the lip, 50 percent involve the lip and the palate, and the remaining 25 percent involve the palate alone. Most cleft lips can be repaired through plastic surgery and do not have a long-term effect on articulation. A cleft palate, however, can present continual problems because the opening of the palate (the roof of the mouth) allows excessive air and sound waves to flow through the nasal cavities. The result is a very nasal-sounding voice and difficulty in producing some speech sounds, such as *s* and *z*. A cleft palate is one physical cause of a speech impairment that requires the intensive work of many specialists. Plastic surgeons (such as the specialists highlighted in *Making a Difference*) on page 136 orthodontists, and SLPs often join forces to help individuals overcome the speech disability that results from cleft lips and palates.

Although professionals can describe stuttering, they are unable to pinpoint or agree on a single cause for the problem (Ratner, 2005). Experts do believe, however, that stuttering episodes are related to stress, particularly when the conversational situation is very complex or unpredictable (Hall, Oyer, & Haas, 2001). Dysfluencies are more likely to occur and reoccur when the situation is challenging or confusing.

Voice problems, which are less common in schoolchildren, can be symptomatic of a medical problem. For example, conditions that interfere with muscular activity, such as juvenile arthritis, can result in a vocal disturbance. Voice problems also can be caused by the way the voice is used: Undue abuse of the voice by screaming, shouting, and straining can damage the vocal folds and result in a voice disorder. Rock singers frequently strain their voices so much that they develop nodules (calluses) on the vocal folds, become chronically hoarse, and must stop singing or have the nodules removed surgically. Teachers who notice changes in children's voices that are not associated with puberty should refer the student to an SLP.

Language impairments have many causes. Brain injury can result in conditions such as aphasia, which interferes with language production. Genetic causes are implicated when members of both the immediate family and the extended family exhibit language impairments (Owens, Metz, & Haas, 2003). The environment, especially the lack of experiences that stimulate language development, is also a major factor contributing to language impairments.

Clearly, then, heredity does not explain all language impairments. The quality and quantity of early language input has a definite effect on vocabulary development and language development (Harwood, Warren, & Yoder, 2002). Inability to benefit from language models can also contribute to inefficient or delayed language acquisition. For example, chronic **otitis media**, or middle ear infection, can cause children to miss hearing and imitating others' language during key developmental periods and may result in difficulties with language development (Roberts & Zeisel, 2002). Poor language development can be caused by environmental factors, including lack of stimulation and of the proper experiences for cognitive development and learning language. Some children do not develop language because they have no appropriate role models. Some are left alone too often; others are not spoken to frequently. Some are punished for speaking or are ignored when they try to communicate. Many of these children have no reason to speak; they have nothing to talk about and few experiences to share. Such youngsters are definitely at risk for developing significant language impairments.

cleft palate An opening in the roof of the mouth causing too much air to pass through the nasal cavity, resulting in a speech impairment

cleft lip A congenital condition where the upper lip is not formed or connected properly to allow for correct articulation of sounds, resulting in a speech impairment

otitis media Middle ear infection that can interrupt normal language development

Prevention

Many measures can be taken to prevent speech or language impairments. Many preventive measures have a medical basis and are implemented prior to the birth of a baby. For example, polio and rubella can have devastating effects on an unborn baby; proper immunization protects adults and children from these and other diseases. A nutritional supplement of folic acid during pregnancy can reduce the risk of cleft palates and lips by 25 to 50 percent (Maugh, 1995). Proper prenatal care is important to the health of babies. Good nutrition influences the strength and early development of very young children.

You will remember from Chapter 3 that the link between poverty and disabilities is clear (CDF, 2004). Those who are poor are less likely to have access to information and medical programs, which puts them at risk for diseases that result in disabilities (Utley & Obiakor, 2001). The availability of proper medical care before and after birth is crucial. Access to health care during childhood is important so that diseases in early childhood, such as measles and otitis media, can be avoided or treated early. Better public education programs available to the entire population inform people of the necessity of good prenatal care, nutrition, and medical care. Innovative approaches to the dissemination of information about the importance of protecting children from disease can make real differences in reducing the numbers of individuals who have language problems because they did not receive immunizations or early treatment for illness. For example, TV or radio advertisements may reach some families; different approaches might be more effective when informing other families. Health fairs sponsored by churches, sororities, fraternities, and other community organizations may prove to be more effective than traditional means in communicating important information to the African American community (CDF, 2004).

Overcoming Challenges

Not all disabilities and conditions are permanent. In many cases therapy, effective instruction, and lots of hard work can restore effective speech or language functioning (ASHA, 2002). In others, strategic actions can help individuals compensate for the problems presented by disabilities. What is critical to facilitate outstanding results is intervention provided early enough to reduce or prevent the residual problems created by the disability or condition.

In addition to therapy and instruction, many individuals with speech or language impairments benefit greatly from technology, and the range of applications is considerable. Some applications correct speech mechanisms that are faulty or damaged. For example, an **obturator** forms a closure between the oral and nasal cavities when the soft palate is missing or has been damaged by a congenital cleft. An artificial larynx can be implanted in cases where the vocal folds have become paralyzed or have been removed because of a disease. This and other applications of medicine and technology can help many individuals with speech or language impairments communicate more effectively so they can participate fully at school and in the community.

Making a Difference

Operation Smile

Operation Smile
Changing Lives One Smile at a Time

In a January 2004 article in *Us Weekly* magazine, singer/actress Jessica Simpson aptly pointed out, "A smile is the best gift you can give someone. It changes a life." How true, particularly for children born with a cleft lip that further compounds the speech challenges of a cleft palate, all of which makes the formation of correct speech sounds difficult. Children with cosmetic differences, especially deformities in the facial area, usually experience rejection and ridicule. Around the world, people's reaction to these individuals is harsh, as they are shunned and denied personal interactions. In recent years, techniques in reconstructive surgery have improved greatly, making it possible for surgeons to change people's appearance and repair cleft lips so that the birth defect is almost unnoticeable and to repair cleft palates, making intelligible speech a reality. However, the costs of such procedures put surgery out of the reach of most families; making the possible impossible for many children around the world.

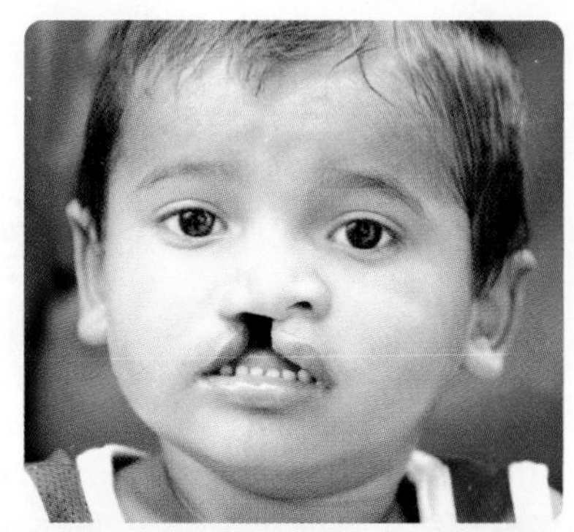

In 1982 Dr. William Magee, a plastic surgeon, and Kathleen Magee, Dr. Magee's wife, a nurse and clinical social worker, traveled to the Philippines with a group of medical volunteers. The purpose of their trip was to repair children's cleft lips and cleft palates. They had no idea how many children were in need, but there were far more than those volunteers could help on their first trip. The Magees saw a need and so Operation Smile was founded to provide free reconstructive surgery to children and young adults.

Today, thousands of volunteers join together to serve tens of thousands of children. They offer medical training and continuing education to health care professionals who assist children and their families in their home countries and communities, provide surgery in over 20 countries, and bring sponsored patients with the most complicated and intensive needs to the United States. Today, according to *Forbes* magazine's annual survey of U.S. charities, Operation Smile is one of the 200 largest in the United States.

To learn more about Operation Smile, go to the organization's Web site: **www.operationsmile.org**

Assessment

SLPs provide direct services, both therapy and instruction. They do so for students whose speech or language impairments are their primary disabilities, as well as for those students whose primary challenges stem from other disabilities, such as mental retardation or autism. They also consult and collaborate with teachers and families about many students who have problems with their speech or language development. Another important role these experts play is during the assessment process. SLPs have major responsibilities for initial diagnosis, determination of the types and intensity of services required, and evaluation of students' progress (ASHA, 2002). They perform these duties across age groups—from the preschool years through high school—and use many different methods to determine which students have speech or language impairments.

Even for preschoolers, parents and educators can request that the local school district help arrange a speech or language evaluation for those who are not developing those skills on par with their peers. Bringing services to the individual as quickly as possible after it is clear that a problem exists makes a big difference in long-term results. But before treatment can begin, the problem must be diagnosed. Let's see how SLPs come into action when speech or language impairments are suspected in preschoolers or students.

Early Identification

As you saw in Figure 4.5 on page 134, the relationship between early identification of language problems and later identification of learning disabilities is clear. This situation reflects differences in curricular demands across the grades: In preschool and kindergarten language development is the focus, but across the elementary years the focus shifts to reading and the more complex demands of the academic curriculum. Because this association between language impairments in early childhood and learning disabilities during the school years is strong and has been widely accepted, the

obturator A device that creates a closure between the oral and nasal cavities when the soft palate is missing or damaged; helps compensate for a cleft palate

Considering Culture

Speech Disorders or Linguistic Differences?

Amazu and Jaja seem to enjoy their Head Start class. They actively play with the other children on the playground, sit and listen during story time, and love playing in the blocks area. Trina, the twin's teacher, is pleased that the boys have made such a good transition to preschool after moving with their family from Nigeria. Many children in her class are English language learners, and Trina tries especially hard to support their learning English as quickly as possible. However, she has noticed that Amazu is not learning English as rapidly as his brother, Jaja. In fact, he does not appear to use speech when communicating with his brother or others, and Trina worries that he might have developmental difficulties. Further, the program's screening tests revealed that he is not functioning at age level in his language development. Trina approached the boys' parents, Mr. and Mrs. Madubuike, and suggested that Amazu be referred for further testing. Although the parents were not particularly worried about their son, they agreed. Indeed, subsequent testing revealed that Amazu shows marked delays in speech and language skills. Thus, both an early childhood special educator and a speech/language pathologist who work with the Head Start program were asked to assist in developing appropriate learning strategies for Amazu. Like Amazu's teacher, these professionals are uncertain about the reasons for the boy's delays in speech and language skills. They might be a result of a developmental disorder or might be attributed to his family speaking a primary language other than English. After all, exposure to the English language at preschool is a new experience. On the one hand, they want to ensure that Amazu receives early support, but on the other hand, they don't want to jump to conclusions that may be inaccurate. Everyone meets and shares their observations honestly. Trina, Amazu's parents, the early childhood special educator, and the SLP agree on a strategy. The specialists will consult with Trina and Amazu's parents, suggesting activities to encourage Amazu to use speech—in either his native language or English. They will help Trina develop language enrichment experiences at school that can also be used at home. All agree to monitor Amazu's development and meet again in a few months to review their findings.

Questions to Consider

1. If possible, observe a teacher or speech/language pathologist (SLP) working with English language learners (ELLs) in a classroom or assessment situation. Can you sort out which behaviors result from cultural or language differences and which might be the result of language impairments?
2. What are your experiences working with children whose language is different from your own? What resources will you seek out when you have concerns about a linguistically diverse student in your classroom?

—By Eleanor Lynch, San Diego State University, and Marci Hanson, San Francisco State University

importance of identifying these children as soon as possible is also now universally recognized (Bakken & Whedon, 2002). Review Table 4.4 on page 133, and use it as a guide to when preschoolers should be referred for a speech and language evaluation. The story in *Cultural Considerations* demonstrates how vigilant preschool teachers can help get services to students and their families as quickly as possible. Remember, early identification and treatment make a real difference in students' long-term results.

Pre-Referral

As you are learning, the pre-referral stage in the special education identification process is important to ensure that students are not incorrectly identified as having a disability they do not have. Pre-referral activities are conducted primarily by the general education classroom teacher, with the help and consultation of special educators and related service providers. When the speech or language abilities of a student present concerns, SLPs play a vital role in helping teachers schedule different interventions and instructional procedures to determine whether alterations to the learning environment result in improved performance or whether intensive special education services are required (ASHA, 2002).

As experts in language development, SLPs can help determine whether students actually have language impairments or might instead either be experiencing some delays in language acquisition that can be remediated through instruction or be in the natural process of learning English as their second language. Remember discussions in the previous chapter about the dangers of misidentifying culturally and linguistically diverse students as having disabilities. Remember also the dangers of not identifying those students who *do* have language impairments quickly enough to avoid those problems compounding. Neither general nor special education teachers typically have the expertise to make these distinctions. That is the specialty of SLPs (ASHA, 2002). During this prereferral assessment phase, SPLs

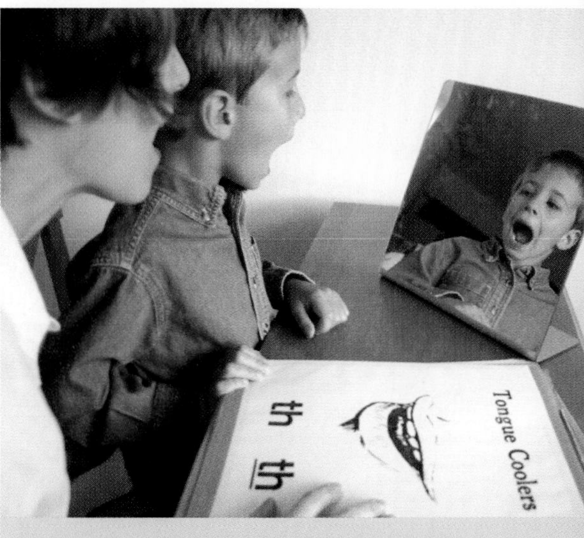

SLPs make a real difference because therapy can reduce or correct speech and language impairments.

- Analyze the student's school records
- Conduct evaluations in the classroom
- Suggest alternative instructional procedures and evaluate their effectiveness
- Collaborate with the student's family
- Consult with the school-based team and help determine whether the IEP process needs to continue

Identification

For those individuals whose performance improves with teacher-implemented instruction or whose speech or language problems do not reflect disabilities (that is, they are attributable to dialects or typical second language acquisition), the assessment/identification process is discontinued. In those cases where multiple classroom interventions have been unsuccessful, the next step usually involves a variety of instruments and procedures, such as

- Checklists of developmental milestones
- Informal hearing assessments
- Standardized interview protocols
- Questionnaires for family members
- Formal observations in natural settings

All of this information helps to determine which professionals need to be involved for more formal assessment procedures.

In most states and school districts, when the problem is suspected to be based in either speech or language skills, the SLP is a member of the assessment team and often coordinates the entire assessment and identification process. The SLP brings together a multidisciplinary team of experts that reflects the initial understanding of the individual student's abilities, as well as her or his needs. Team membership reflects information that was gathered during earlier steps in the IEP process. Thus, if a hearing problem is suspected, an audiologist is a member of the team. This specialist conducts formal hearing assessments and also interprets the results to the individual's family and teachers. If the student's primary or native language is not English, an expert in second language acquisition is brought into the assessment effort to determine whether problems are rooted in the process of learning a new language or are compounded by language impairments.

When language impairments are suspected, much valuable information is gathered that not only can be used in the identification process, but also can help teachers as they plan instruction. It is important for educators to know what facts are available—even if gathered for another purpose—to guide instruction. Let's take at what constitutes a balanced assessment, often coordinated by the SLP.

Evaluation: Diagnosis of Language Impairments

Determining whether a student has language impairments, identifying the exact nature of the problem, making specific intervention plans for both direct services and follow-through activities, and developing accountability systems to ensure progress is being made—it all adds up to no simple task. SLPs use multiple methods, combined in such a way as to provide balanced assessments. Typically, these evaluations include standardized tests and descriptive assessment methods. Because data are collected to provide information about the individual's functional communication abilities, testing often occurs both in the clinic and in the student's natural environments (home, classroom, playground) and situations (with teachers, family members, friends). Balanced assessments may include some or all of the following evaluation measures (ASHA, 2002).

- *Parent/staff/student interviews:* People who interact frequently with the individual of concern have considerable insight and information to contribute during the assessment process. Particularly for students with severe disabilities, relatives know how well the individuals can express their needs and desires, how well they understand others' communications, and the extent of their ability to play and socialize with others.
- *Student history:* Creating a comprehensive record of the student's medical, family, and school history is most helpful in complicated situations. Gathering information from all possible sources can reveal much about the causes of the difficulties, the nature of the problems, and what interventions might be most effective.
- *Checklists and developmental scales:* Collecting information that is organized or categorized to indicate where individuals are having difficulties and where they are not having problems is important for several reasons. First, it provides profiles and patterns that help direct the SLP toward potentially effective methods, and second, it begins the process of creating a baseline of performance to use when evaluating the effectiveness of the treatment program.
- *Progress monitoring:* By using direct measurements of students' performance on academic and other classroom activities, SLPs determine where and how language impairments manifest themselves in students' educational performance. Learning that an individual's language impairments are the root of a learning problem not only helps the SLP determine where to target therapy but also helps the teacher schedule appropriate instructional remediation.
- *Dynamic assessment:* The evaluation process used to "test out" different language interventions is referred to by SLPs as **dynamic assessment**. The purpose is to guide learning to determine the student's potential for learning. Experts in learning disabilities use a similar process to determine whether the student is **resistant to treatment** and, therefore, in need of more intensive and sustained explicit instruction. Through this process of multilevel intervention, successively more (and more intensive) procedures are used until the severity of the individual's problem is clear.
- *Portfolio assessment:* As described in Chapter 2, creating a collection of the student's work is called portfolio assessment. For the purpose of language evaluations, the following items might be included:
  - Samples of written assignments
  - Video and/or recordings of communications with the SLP, family members, teachers, and classmates
  - Transcriptions of oral communications
- *Observational and anecdotal records:* Notes about how well students communicate in a variety of natural settings helps the SLP to develop a descriptive record of their abilities and challenges.

dynamic assessment Assessment process used by SLPs to determine the potential effectiveness of different language interventions

resistant to treatment Not learning through validated methods typically applied in general education settings and therefore in need of more intensive and sustained explicit instruction

- *Standardized tests:* Finally, as one would expect, SLPs administer nationally normed tests and interpret those results as they plan treatment programs and later evaluate the effectiveness of these programs.

Early Intervention

For most very young children identified as having disabilities, it is their late language development patterns that set them apart from their normally developing peers. So when young children do not develop language at the expected rate, intervention both at home and at preschool (or day care) is needed. In every community, early intervention programs are available to provide therapy and instruction to children and to assist parents in helping their children develop language skills. With training and guidance from SLPs, parents can be excellent language teachers for their children with language impairments. In fact, when home-based intervention is provided by parents, children's language scores improve more than when only clinic-based instruction is provided by professionals (Cleminshaw et al., 1996; Hall, Oyer, & Haas, 2001).

Preschool programs make a significant, positive, and long-term difference for young children and their families (Bailey et al., 1999). For example, low birth weight infants who received a customized day care program averaged 15 IQ points higher than the control group (Education of the Handicapped, 1992). Only two percent of these youngsters—at risk (because of their low birth weight) for speech or language impairments, mental retardation, and learning disabilities—were identified as having a disability later on; the control group was nine times more likely to have a disability. During a child's developmental period, the acquisition of good communication and language skills is crucial to the child's later development of academic and social skills. However, it is important to remember that preschool programs must be of high quality, with an appropriate child-to-adult ratio. Evidence now exists that when child-to-staff ratios follow the guidelines set by the American Public Health Association and the American Academy of Pediatrics (3:1 for infants, 4:1 for 2-year-olds, and 7:1 for 3-year-olds), children's readiness for school, particularly in the area of language, is above

The language development of preschool children can be fostered through exciting activities that provide many opportunities to share, explore, play, and learn.

for Effective Teaching

PROMOTING PRESCHOOLERS' LANGUAGE

1. Encourage literacy by connecting oral, written, and print language experiences through telling, reading, enacting, and creating stories.
2. Create enthusiasm by making trips to the public library.
3. Arrange classrooms with interesting materials and provide high-interest activities.
4. Provide reasons for oral communication by placing materials within view of the children but out of their reach.
5. Arrange the environment to encourage more communication from children, such as by providing insufficient materials (e.g., paper, paints, or crayons), thus requiring them to request more.
6. Create situations in which children do not have all the materials they need to perform an activity (painting without brushes, sandbox pails but no shovels) so that they have to make verbal requests for the supplies they need.
7. Make children make choices and request their preferred activity or the materials they want.
8. Develop situations in which children are likely to need help and must communicate their needs to each other or an adult.
9. Create absurd and surprising situations (giving them clay instead of crackers at snack time).
10. Allow children to talk frequently and develop elaborative vocabulary using "make believe" situations that they generate.

average (Lombardo, 1999). What tactics are included in effective preschool programs? First, the preschool experiences should be in "language-rich" environments where young children have opportunities to explore, exchange ideas, interact with familiar and novel toys and objects, and engage in interesting activities that motivate children to talk (Justice, 2004). Second, language development should be integrated into every lesson throughout the day, not be allocated to a specific unit or time of the day. Some of those procedures are found in *Tips for Effective Teaching*. Also, two specific areas for instruction should be included in the preschool curriculum:

- Pragmatics
- Phonological awareness

Professionals first recognized the importance of pragmatics over a quarter of a century ago (Blank, Rose, & Berlin, 1978). Young children must develop a rich and deep vocabulary early in life so that they have the words to communicate with others. But for vocabulary to be useful, the child must understand the *function* of the object the word represents. That is, children must know what an object is before they can label it meaningfully, describe it, or refer to it when communicating. For example, a child must know what a cup is—an object that holds liquid, is picked up, and is used to drink from—before that child can develop a concept about cups or use the word meaningfully in conversation. Teachers and family members can help children expand their abilities in the area of language use and pragmatics by including explanations about the purpose or function of specific objects during the natural course of events across the day. As a child is getting ready to draw a picture, the adult might say, "Let's find the *green* crayon, so you can draw a picture of the grass. Where is the *yellow* crayon so you can draw the sun? What *color* will the flowers be? Find those crayons so you can color the flowers those colors."

As you have learned, and will learn more about in Chapter 5, developing phonological awareness seems to be either a prerequisite to or a great help in learning to read (Norris & Hoffman, 2002). Skills that are part of phonological awareness include being able to:

- Detect sound segments
- Match beginning sounds
- Identify sound segments in words and phrases
- Rhyme

Children who do not develop these skills appear to be at great risk for reading failure during the elementary years. Fortunately, research findings also show that this situation can be corrected for many individuals (Jenkins & O'Connor, 2002; Lyon et al., 2001). These findings explain why the federal government strongly encourages the early teaching of phonics, sound segmentation, sound–symbol relationships, and the use of books that incorporate rhymes (e.g., *Cat in the Hat* and other Dr. Suess books). In this regard, SLPs can be most helpful to teachers who may not feel proficient with these complex language models and related remediation strategies.

Teaching Students with Speech or Language Impairments

Look again at Figure 4.5 on page 134. Notice that at ages 5, 6, and 7—Kindergarten, first, and second grade—the students identified as having speech or language impairments far outnumber those identified as having learning disabilities. But as children reach third grade the picture changes, with dramatic increases in the number of students with learning disabilities. As you have learned, the phenomenon occurs because as the demands of the curriculum increase, being able to read well and independently becomes a necessity. How can more students be helped so that fewer face these difficulties? Let's see if we can figure out some ways.

Access to the General Education Curriculum

The ways to enrich classroom environments and help all students develop better language skills are many. Let's focus on three general methods that benefit all students now, and then we'll turn our attention to methods that are of even greater benefit to those with language impairments. We will first consider

- Instructional supports
- Explicit language instruction
- Language-sensitive environments

One way in which teachers can help students develop language skills is to modify their standard instructional procedures by adding instructional supports that foster a language-rich instructional environment and help more students profit from typical instruction. Here are a few key elements that effective teachers consider when creating such supportive classrooms (Culatta & Wiig, 2006; McCormick, 2003; Wetherby, 2002).

- Match language with the comprehension abilities of the students.
- Be responsive to students' language needs by adjusting, modifying, and supplementing instruction.
- Supply examples relevant to students' experiences and cultures.
- Provide multiple examples to illustrate a point or explain a concept.
- Use specific referents (e.g., instead of "Open your book," say, "Open the red geography book to page 105").
- Avoid indirect expressions (e.g., instead of "Do you get it?" say, "Do you understand how to complete your homework assignment?").

A second way to help all students is to give **explicit instruction**—that is, to teach the specific skills desired, whether the instructional targets are oral language or reading. Language development should be part of the curriculum. The benefits of direct language instruction are many for students both with and without disabilities. Just as time is devoted to teaching mathematics, reading, spelling, and social studies, time should be allocated to teaching the language skills that underlie these subjects. During these sessions, students should be encouraged to listen, expand their vocabularies, and extend their communication skills. All students can profit from explicit instruction in particular language areas. For example, using and understanding metaphors and analogies is challenging for most students, even the most able (Pan, 2005). Figures of speech are difficult for many students to comprehend, for they are not literal or direct translations of the words used in such phrases. "The president is the head of state." "The eyes are windows to the soul." "He's between a rock and a hard place." "My heart goes out to you." "Time flies." Students whose abstract thinking skills are not well developed, and those who are learning English as a second language, frequently find it difficult to grasp the

explicit instruction Direct teaching of the specific skills that make up the instructional target meaning of common metaphors and analogies used in texts and in oral presentations. Teachers should not assume that children understand nonliteral language and should help their students develop the flexible thinking skills needed to solve the problems that such language use presents. Mere exposure to analogies and metaphors is not enough. Teachers need to include direct instruction about the use of figurative language; when they do, students' facility with language expands into a new dimension. They know they have discovered something exciting—and they feel proud. As with most language skills, instruction about these conceptually difficult aspects of language use should be integrated into content lessons.

Instructional Accommodations

Even slight modifications in teaching style and instructional activities can be most helpful and can have great benefits for all students, particularly those who are struggling with the foundational language skills needed for academic success (McCormick, 2003). Providing opportunities for language use and for expanding comprehension of receptive language, and incorporating these opportunities into standard classroom routines are just the support that many students with language impairments, as well as linguistically diverse students, urgently need. Making such adjustments or accommodations is not difficult. The first step in making a difference for these students is being aware that they have some special needs (Salend, 2005). The second step is recognizing that many of these students benefit greatly even when some simple methods—creating more opportunities for students to talk about academic content, reviewing difficult vocabulary before and after each day's lesson, restating instructions for class and homework assignments—are implemented. And the final step is creating **language-sensitive environments**, classrooms where language development is fostered and all students' language needs are supported. Some easy and helpful suggestions about how to create classrooms where all students' language development is enriched can be found in *Accommodating for Inclusive Environments.*

Validated Practices

Effective teachers help students with language difficulties in other ways as well. **Content enhancement strategies** are designed to help them organize their learning and remember complex content presented either in lectures or in textbooks. Content enhancement strategies come in many different forms. They are designed to help students see relationships among concepts and vocabulary (Rock, 2004; Vaughn, Bos, & Schumm, 2003). One type of these strategies is **graphic organizers**, which help students structure their learning, visualize the way information is presented in lectures and organized in texts, map out stories to improve comprehension, and see the relationships among vocabulary and concepts (Boulineau et al., 2004; Ives & Hoy, 2003). Graphic organizers come in many different forms. See *Validated Practices* on page 146 for an example of one version of a graphic organizer, which was designed to distill and organize complicated content from a social studies textbook.

The benefits of content enhancement strategies and instructional supports are many. These instructional techniques improve children's written and oral language skills and their ability to remember information (Hudson & Gillam, 1997; Mastropieri, Scruggs, & Graetz, 2003). Why do they work so well for students with disabilities, particularly those with cognitive or language disabilities? First, they provide structure for learning concepts; they impose organization on what might initially appear to the students to be overwhelming and confusing. Second, they give learners a strategy for approaching the learning task and addressing its elements sequentially. Third, content enhancement strategies allow students to use simpler vocabulary or to make connections with their own experiences. And finally, they allow students to visualize content being learned, which helps many students remember key points and concepts.

language-sensitive environments Classrooms that encourage, foster, and support language development

content enhancement strategies Methods to help students organize and remember important concepts

graphic organizers Visual aids used to help students organize, understand, and remember academic content

Accommodating for Inclusive Environments

Creating Language-Sensitive Classrooms

For Expressive Language

- Ask for clarification when student uses nonspecific vocabulary. Explain why their initial verbalization was unclear.
- Create opportunities for students to use new vocabulary and talk about concepts being learned.
- Give students reasons to talk.
- Encourage students to use new vocabulary words learned in class in other situations.
- When a student uses incorrect grammar or vocabulary, model the correct language.

For Receptive Language

- Rephrase directions (if student appears unresponsive) and instruction (if student appears confused).
- Repeat instructions, if necessary.
- Start with one-step instructions and gradually build to multistep instructions.
- Provide physical cues when giving instructions (e.g., holding up the book they should be opening, pointing to the line-up area).
- Rather than ask students if they understand something (to which a "yes" response is usually given), ask them to:
  - Repeat the instructions back to you.
  - Restate content in their own words.
  - Show you what they are supposed to be doing.
  - Work one or two problems and then check with you to be sure they are doing them correctly.
- Have each student partner with another student to provide support and enhance comprehension during activities
- Teach students to recognize when they do not understand something and how to verbalize that.
- Allow students to ask questions if they are confused.

For Pragmatics

- Teach and practice how to interpret facial expressions and body language.
- Teach scripted responses for certain social conventions.
- Teach the importance of different registers and when and how to use them.
- Avoid using sarcasm, which can be interpreted literally.

Attribute webs are popular graphic organizers. Here's how they work:

- Identify important aspects of a word.
- Position the key word in the center of the web.
- Place characteristics of the key word on extensions of the web.
- Group attributes by similarities.

Some software programs, including *Kidspiration®* (for young children in kindergarten through fifth grade) and *Inspiration®* (for students in grades 6 through 12), can assist students with the creation of graphic organizers, such as attribute webs. In Figure 4.6, *Inspiration®* was used to organize and visualize Shakespeare's play *Macbeth.* The software can also transform the content of the web into an outline to help students study for tests or write reports.

Another popular graphic organizer uses Venn diagrams to help students categorize or group information. Here are the key features of such diagrams:

- They compare and contrast meanings and characteristics of two concepts.
- They identify attributes of the two concepts.
- They place attributes in appropriate circles.
- They move similarities between the two concepts to the overlapping segments of the circles.

Figure 4.7 provides examples of diagrams developed by a second grader to organize science concepts. Graphic organizers, along with the software that makes them

Validated Practices Graphic Organizers

What Are Graphic Organizers?

Graphic organizers are visual aids used to assist students in organizing and comprehending large amounts of information from expository text. These visual-spatial arrangements connect important words or statements to diagrams. Graphic organizers include maps, pictures, graphs, charts, diagrams, and photographs.

Why Graphic Organizers Are Beneficial

Students often have difficulty reading and comprehending information presented in content area textbooks (e.g., science, social studies, health). In addition, many books are poorly organized, confusing students even more. Graphic organizers help students by including only the crucial information, making what is important clear and precise. Graphic organizers may illustrate relationships among concepts, show a process, or present a sequence. When students generate their own graphic organizers, they are demonstrating their comprehension of the course content. An additional benefit of graphic organizers is that they force you, the teacher, to focus on the specific information you are presenting.

Implementing Graphic Organizers

When you begin to use graphic organizers with your class, *you* should develop them. Students can follow along and use your visual aid as a guide to the lecture and an aid to comprehending the content. As students become comfortable using graphic organizers, they should generate their own. Here are four guidelines to follow when constructing graphic organizers:

Select and Divide the Chapters

- Select material that is difficult for students to understand or that is poorly organized.
- Divide the chapter into sections. (Typically, textbooks are organized by sections. If this is true, develop a graphic organizer for each section. If there are no sections, develop a graphic organizer for every 1,500 words.)

Construct an Outline

- Select main ideas from the reading material.

Select the Graphic Organizer's Format

- Formats must match the structure of information and can include diagrams that sequence, that compare and contrast, or that classify.
- Graphic organizers must be clear, must be easy to follow, and must fit on one page.

Prepare the Graphic Organizer

- Your version should include all of the information and serve as an answer key.

Figure A •

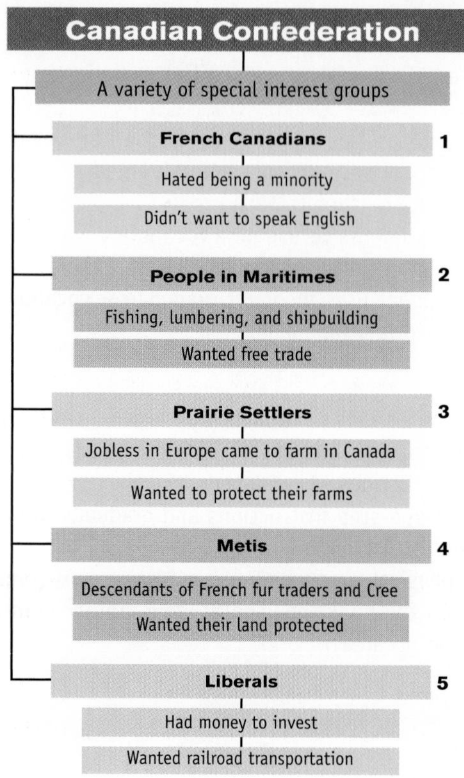

Source: "The Effectiveness of Graphic Organizers for Three Classifications of Secondary Students in Content Area Classes" by S. V. Horton, T. C. Lovitt, and D. Bergerud, 1990, *Journal of Learning Disabilities, 23,* pp. 12–22, 29. Copyright 1990 by Pro-Ed, Inc. Reprinted by permission.

- The version prepared for students should have some information missing: the important facts you want them to focus on.

Graphic organizers can be used either when presenting new material or when reviewing content. If students are working on multiple graphic organizers independently, it may be helpful to have them number their pages. Graphic organizers work well when students are assigned to cooperative learning groups. Once graphic organizers have been completed, discuss and correct them. Graphic organizers with accurate information can serve as great study guides. Figure A shows a completed graphic organizer used in a middle school social studies course.

This scientifically validated practice is a teaching method the efficacy of which proved by systematic research efforts (Boyle, 1996; Horton, Lovitt, & Bergerud, 1990; Lovitt, & Horton, 1994; Scanlon, Deshler, & Schumaker, 1996). Full citations are found in the references for this chapter.

By Kimberly Paulsen, Vanderbilt University

Figure 4.6 • An Example of a Computer-Generated Graphic Organizer for the Shakespeare's Play *Macbeth*

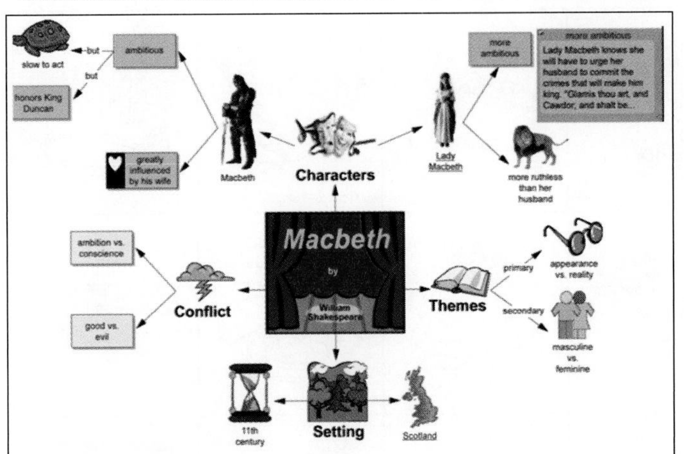

Macbeth **by William Shakespeare**

I. Themes

A. appearance vs. reality

By showing the characters' struggles to understand strange visions and discover the difference between truth and deceit, the play seems to tell the audience that nothing is ever what it seems to be. Every time the characters think they understand another character's words or actions, they find out they were wrong. This keeps them nervous and off-balance. In this way, Shakespeare uses the symbolism of appearance vs. reality not only to inform the audience, but to build suspense.

"Fair is foul, and foul is fair..."
Witches, Act 1, Scene 1

B. masculine vs. feminine

The characters' words portray one view of gender roles, while their actions clearly demonstrate another. This results in another layer of ambiguity that underscores the appearance vs. reality theme. The reader (or audience member) must really consider what is being said and done in the play, and wonder themselves what is true and what is not.

II. Setting

A. Scotland

B. 11th century

Macbeth was written 400 hundred years after the actual event, so for Elizabethans it was ancient history, too.

III. Conflict

A. ambition vs. conscience

Both Macbeth and his wife are ambitious, but their consciences prove to be much stronger. Ambition drives them to commit terrible crimes, but guilty consciences punish them both with insanity, dishonor

Source: © 2005 Inspiration Software®, Inc. Diagram created in Inspiration® by Inspiration Software®, Inc. Used with permission.

easier to produce, benefit students with a broad range of learning challenges. Now let's turn our attention to applications of technology that were specifically designed for individuals with speech or language impairments.

Technology

Advances in assistive technology have made a tremendous difference in the lives of individuals with speech or language impairments, and no doubt the future holds unimaginable breakthroughs that will change their lives even further. Software such as that shown in Figures 4.6 and 4.7 assists a broad range of students. Other technologically advanced equipment is designed specifically for those with communication challenges. **Augmentative and alternative communication (AAC) devices** provide different means for individuals with speech or language impairments to interact and communicate with others (Kangas & Lloyd, 2006). AAC includes both **low-tech devices** (such as communication boards) and **high-tech devices** (such as speech talkers). AAC devices can be electronic or nonelectronic, they can be constructed for a certain individual, and they can be simple or complex. What all AAC systems have in common is that they are used to augment oral or written language production. A variety of low-tech AAC devices have been in use for many years (Reichle, Beukelman, & Light, 2002). For example, **communication boards** are like placemats where pictures and words are available for the individual who cannot speak or cannot speak clearly and communicates

Figure 4.7 • A Second Grader's Content Enhancements: Venn Diagram of the Differences and Similarities Between Two Plants

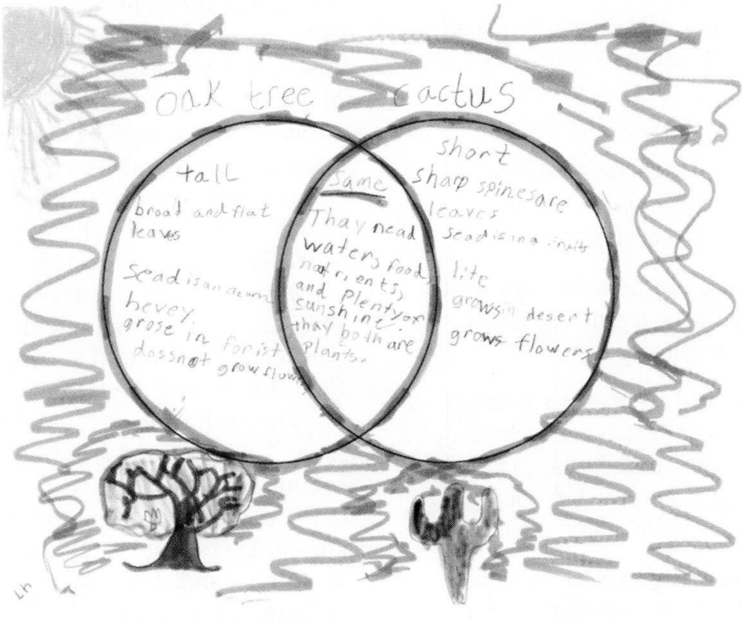

Reprinted by permission of Kyra Tyler.

Figure 4.8 • Communication Board

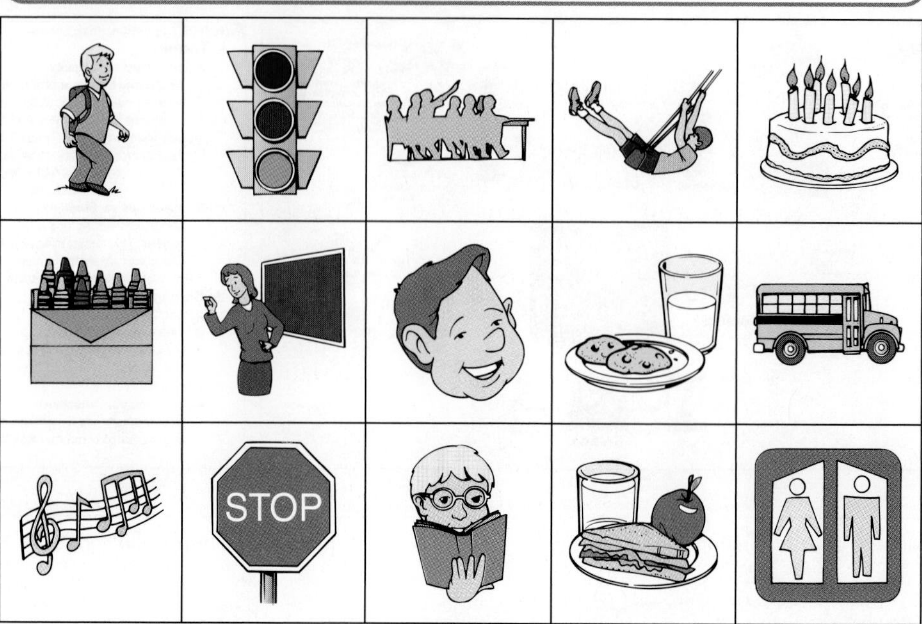

by pointing to pictures or words that have been placed on the board. (A communication board is shown in Figure 4. 8.)

Advances in computer technology, particularly speech synthesizers, have changed the mode of communication for many of these individuals. With a computer, a person can type in a message and have it converted into voice or print. Some computers allow the individual to select the voice qualities the machine uses! Some computerized communication devices are even small enough to be worn on a person's wrist. Many machines that generate speech and language use an icon system that can be accessed by touch or, for those with limited motor abilities, by switches. However, for some individuals, learning the graphic symbols used with the more sophisticated equipment can be daunting, requiring considerable effort and instruction (Wilkinson & McIlvane, 2002). Communicating via a **speech synthesizer**, which produces speech through a computer or high-tech device, can take years to master and is best learned in natural environments found at school and home (Harwood, Warren, & Yoder, 2002). For those who master the complicated process, like Lizzy B (read again *In the Spotlight* on page 121, the results are fantastic, allowing them to communicate with people who might not otherwise understand them. The current capabilities of electronic AAC systems are amazing, and the devices continue to improve and to get more affordable. They are even becoming culturally sensitive by allowing for the inclusion of symbols related to cultural events, such as Navajo ceremonies and traditional customs (Stuart & Parette, 2001).

The demonstrated benefits of AAC are remarkable (Reichle, Beukelman, & Light, 2002). Students with little or no speech or language abilities are now able to communicate with others because of AAC devices. Many of these youngsters have developed language abilities that they had not been expected to achieve. The benefits of AAC are still unfolding, but it is clear that they have been underestimated. Most users and their families report great satisfaction with AAC. They believe the child not only develops competence in communication but also gains self-esteem and independence.

augmentative and alternative communication (AAC) devices Assistive technology that helps individuals communicate, including devices that actually produce speech

low-tech devices Simple assistive technology devices such as communication boards

high-tech devices Complex assistive technology devices that use computers

communication boards Low-tech assistive technology devices that display pictures or words that the individual can point to in order to communicate

speech synthesizers Assistive technology devices that create "voice"

Transition

Adults with speech or language impairments comprise several different subgroups. Some have only speech impairments, others have only language impairments, and some have both impairments. Age of onset and causation, however, are what make these subgroups different from one another. Despite having great difficulties as children, the vast majority of these individuals, when adults, experience a lifetime of using normal communication (Owens, Metz, & Haas, 2003). Typically, the problems experienced by adults who were not identified as having speech or language impairments when they were children are caused by disease, accidents, or aging. Those who had some kind of speech or language impairment during childhood represent a small percentage of this adult group. Relatively little is known about how these children fare when they are adults.

In one of the few, completed comprehensive follow-up studies of youth with disabilities, students with learning disabilities and speech impairments appeared to have better outcomes than other youth with disabilities (Wagner et al., 1992). They seem to function fairly well some 5 years after graduation. Few are socially isolated. By this time they are beginning to move away from home; 40 percent live independently. They also are employed at about the same rate as their peers without disabilities. Their long-term prospects, however, may not be as good. Although some 95 percent are taught almost exclusively in general education classes, only 65 percent of students with speech impairments graduate with a diploma (U.S. Department of Education, 2002, 2005b). Serious concerns about their success as adults can be raised. Changing this situation will require offering more services while these students are in high school and expanding the roles of SLPs to provide assistance with the development of literacy by linking therapy to the high school curriculum (AHSA, 2002). Also, to remain in academic content courses, these students may require more access to tutoring, more services from guidance counselors, more accommodations and special services, and increased instruction in listening and speaking skills.

Collaboration

SLPs are an important resource to general and special education teachers. Almost every school in the United States has an SLP working there at least once a week, usually more often. At some schools, an SLP is a permanent faculty member. In most cases, however, SLPs' time is shared across several schools. SLPs are typically itinerant related services providers who travel from one school to another providing services to students and to teachers. SLPs are experts in the areas of speech, language, and communication. Whenever teachers have concerns or questions about these abilities in their students, they should seek out the advice of their school's speech/language professional. Remember, "early screening, assessment, and treatment of an impairment—typically considered special education or related services—may actually prevent further disability or handicapping conditions" (ASHA, 2002, pp. III–260). There is so much to be gained! Teachers should not hesitate in seeking help from SLPs when they think that a student has a communication problem.

The roles played by SLPs working in today's schools are many. Most SLPs are members of ASHA, the professional organization representing most professionals working in the areas of speech, language, and hearing (audiologists). This organization helps us understand the many responsibilities assumed, and duties performed,

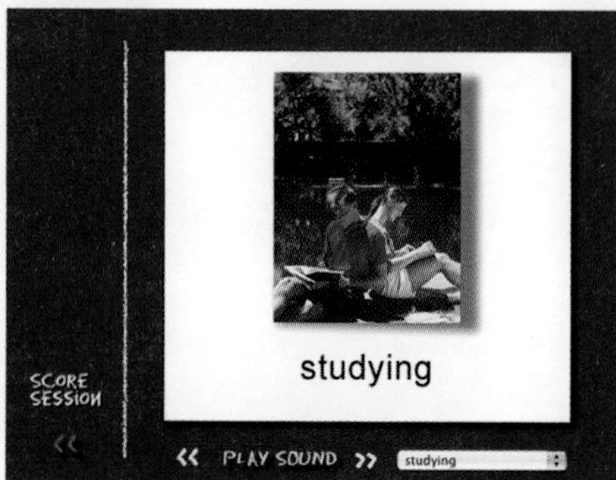

Software program like *FAST-SORT: Articulation* and *FAST-SORT: Vocabulary* are used in individual and small-group therapy sessions. They are also used to facilitate follow through both in the classroom and at home.

by SLPs as they work with teachers to serve students (ASHA, 2002). Here are a few examples of the major areas where these professionals apply their knowledge and skills:

- *Pre-referral:* assist teachers with the selection and application of intervention strategies, accommodations, or supports that might address a student's learning needs and eliminate the need for special education services.
- *Screening:* use commercially available or informal procedures (e.g., checklists, classroom observations, interviews) to distinguish students with language differences and delays from those needing formal evaluation for suspected language impairments.
- *Referral:* request implementation of the full, formal assessment process.
- *Identification:* conduct assessments to determine special education eligibility for speech or language impairments.
- *IEP Team:* work with other professionals to identify student's abilities and need for special education serves and develop the individualized plan (the IFSP or IEP).
- *Therapy:* deliver direct services to treat speech or language impairments.
- *Consultation:* provide advice and assistance to teachers to guide classroom-based instruction and follow-through activities.
- *Evaluation:* contribute to judgments about the effectiveness of the interventions and programs implemented.

Approximately 95 percent of students with speech or language impairments receive their education almost exclusively in general education classrooms (U.S. Department of Education, 2002, 2005b). And for most of these students, the services they receive from SLPs are indirect. In other words, classroom teachers are guided by SLPs in the selection and application of interventions through a consulting model (Sutherland, 2004). They can help teachers with all language-based academic instruction (e.g., reading, spelling, writing). In addition to collaborating with teachers, SLPs often work in collaboration with families, particularly with families of those with disabilities. We will conclude this chapter by examining how families make a difference in the speech and language development of students with disabilities.

Partnerships with Families and Communities

The quality of their home's language environment has significant and long-term effects on young children (Robinson, 2003). Some families need guidance as they attempt to develop nurturing environments for their children. For these reasons, most preschool programs include a strong family component, where professionals assist parents in implementing language-learning lessons at home and in helping their children transfer (or generalize) their learning from school to home.

Children (and adults) spend less time at home with family than ever before, so involving parents in their children's preschool programs can be challenging. For example, about 7 million children of working parents, as early as 11 weeks old, spend 30 hours per week in child care (Children's Defense Fund, 2004). Parents and children spend less time together today than they did 20 years ago. Regardless, the child's parents and the home environment provide the foundation for these skills. Even for those children who spend most of their days away from home, those whose home environment is rich in language—where parents talk to their children, where children are given the opportunity to explore the use of language, and where experiences are broad—usually develop fine speech and language skills. When children do not have appropriate language models—when they do not hear language used often, when they do not have experiences to share or a reason to talk—it is not uncommon for their language to be delayed and even to become impaired (Robinson, 2003).

What kinds of strategies can parents use at home to improve their child's language skills? Specialists suggest that family members specifically label or name objects in the home (Gleason, 2005). They also suggest that simple words be used more often to describe the objects the child is playing with: "This ball is red. It is round. It is soft." They can encourage repetitions of correct productions of sounds and can repeat the child's error to help the child make a comparison. They can play a game of "fill in the blank" sentences. They can ask the child questions that require expanded answers. The family should include the child in activities outside the home, too, such as visits to the zoo, the market, or a shopping center, so that the child has more to talk about. Practicing good language skills can be incorporated into everyday events. Family members should model language and have the child imitate good language models. Parents can encourage children to engage in "storytelling." Through these stories, children should describe, explain, and interpret their experiences or the stories they have read. Children need a reason to talk, and the home environment can foster children's oral expression by providing many rich and diverse experiences for children to talk about and good language models for children to imitate.

Imagine a world...
where communication has no boundaries . . .

Summary

Communication requires at least two parties and a message. Communication is impaired when either the sender or the receiver of the message cannot use the signs, symbols, or rules of language effectively. Communication occurs only when the message is understood by the receiver as intended by the sender. The sender may have an idea or thought to share with someone else, but the sender's idea needs to be translated from thought into some code that the other person can understand—that is, into some form of language. For most of us, oral language is the primary mode of socializing, learning, and performing on the job. Therefore, communicative competence—what speakers need to know about language to express their thoughts—is the most important goal for students with speech or language impairments. Because oral communication (or sign language for those who are deaf) occurs in a social context, this ability directly affects an individual's social competence as well.

Addressing the Chapter's Objectives

1 What are speech impairments and language impairments?

- *Speech impairments* are present when the sender's speech impairs the communication. They include problems with articulation, fluency, and voice (pitch or loudness).
- *Language impairments* exist when the sender of the message cannot effectively employ the signs, symbols, or rules that govern the form, content, or use (pragmatics) of language.
- The child's age and the stressfulness of the situation must be considered when determining whether a child should be referred to an SLP for assessment.

2 What is the prevalence of speech or language impairments? How is the prevalence of this type of disability related to that of learning disabilities?

- Speech or language impairments category:
  - Is second largest (when only primary disability is counted)
  - Is largest (when both primary and secondary disabilities are counted)
  - Includes 19 percent of all students with disabilities
- Speech or language impairments:
  - Can coexist with every disability
  - Coexist with 96 percent of cases of learning disabilities
- The prevalence of language impairments is related to age and to increased demands of the curriculum as students get older:
  - More preschoolers identified as having language impairments
  - More students above third grade identified as having learning disabilities

3 How do language delays, language differences, and language impairments differ?

- In *language delays*, language acquisition follows the normal developmental sequence but proceeds more slowly than in the typical learner; may be a signal of disabilities.
- In *language differences*, English is being learned as a second language, or a regional dialect is involved.
- In *language impairments*, language is acquired in an abnormal or atypical developmental sequence; this hinders communication and the transfer of knowledge and information.

4 What is augmentative and alternative communication (AAC), and how do these devices benefit to this population of learners?

- AAC is assistive technology.
- AAC devices use technology to help people with speech or language impairments communicate.
  - *Low-tech devices:* nonelectronic, simple devices such as communication boards
  - *High-tech devices:* electronic devices utilizing computers, such as speech synthesizers

5 How can teachers enhance language development and help to remediate language impairments?

- *Instructional supports:* match language to students'; adjust, modify, and supplement instruction; relate instruction to students' experiences and culture; use specific (concrete) referents; give multiple examples.
- *Explicit instruction:* directly teach language skills, and include language development as a curricular target.
- *Content enhancements:* graphic organizers, such as attribute webs and Venn diagrams, visually impose structure on content and assist with learning and remembering.
- *Language-sensitive classrooms:* provide opportunities to use language, motivation and reasons to talk, multiple language experiences, support for different levels of language skills; includes evaluation.
- Teachers collaborate with SLPs about all students whose language or communication abilities are of concern and provide classroom follow-through on targets mastered in therapy.

MyLabSchool is a collection of online tools for your success in this course, your licensure exams, and your teaching career. Visit www.mylabschool.com to access the following:

- Online Study Guide
- Video cases from real classrooms
- Help with your research papers using Research Navigator
- Career Center with resources for:
  - Praxis exams and licensure preparation
  - Professional portfolio development
  - Job search and interview techniques
  - Lesson planning

Supplementary Resources

Popular Novels and Books

Butler, S. (1936). *The way of all flesh.* New York: Limited Editions Club.

Caldwell, E. (1948). *Tobacco road.* New York: Grosset and Dunlap.

Johnson, W. (1930). *Because I stutter.* New York: Appleton.

Melville, H. (1962). *Billy Budd.* Chicago: University of Chicago.

Sedaris, D. (2000). *Me talk pretty one day.* New York: Little, Brown.

Movies

A Fish Called Wanda (1987). Thames

Four thieves steal diamonds, but two members of the gang, Wanda and Otto, are in a plot to double-cross the others. They rat on George, the leader of the gang, to the police. However, George has already double-crossed the others by moving the diamonds without anyone knowing. Wanda tries to get the location of the diamonds out of George's lawyer; they fall in love and make off with the diamonds. One member of the gang, Ken, has a nervous stutter. Although this film takes comedic advantage of a person's disability, which could be offensive to some, his stuttering does provide some of the funniest scenes. No one really treats Ken differently, other than Otto who is mean to everyone. Revenge, however, is Ken's at the end of the movie.

Professional, Parent, and Advocacy Groups

American Speech-Language-Hearing Association in Rockville, Maryland: www.asha.org

National Institute on Deafness and Other Communication Disorders (NIDCD), National Institutes of Health (NIH) in Bethesda, Maryland www.nidcd.nih.gov

Division for Communication Disabilities & Deafness (DCDD), Council for Exceptional Children (CEC) in Arlington, Virginia www.cec.sped.org *or* education.gsu.edu/dcdd

Stuttering Foundation of America in Memphis, Tennessee: stuttersfa.org/

Professional Standards and Licensure Tests

After reading this chapter, you should be able to link basic knowledge and skills described in the CEC Standards and INTASC Principles with information provided in this text. The table below shows some of the specific CEC Common Core Knowledge and Skill Standards and INTASC Special Education Principles that can be applied to each major section of the chapter. Other standards may also be applied to this chapter. Associated General Praxis II topic areas are identified in the right column.

Major Chapter Headings	CEC Knowledge and Skill Core Standard and Associated Subcategories	INTASC Core Principle and Associated Special Education Subcategories	PRAXIS II Exam Topic
Where We've Been ... What's on the Horizon?	**1: Foundations** CC1K8 Historical points of view and contribution of culturally diverse groups	**6: Communication** 6.03 All teachers understand that linguistic background has an impact on language acquisition as well as communication content and style.	1: Understanding Exceptionality 2: Legal and Social Issues
Speech or Language Impairments Defined	**1: Foundations** CC1K5 Issues in definition and identification of individuals with exceptional learning needs, including those from culturally and linguistically diverse backgrounds	**6: Communication** 6.02 All teachers collaborate with speech/language pathologists and other language specialists to identify the language and communications skills that need to be developed in students with disabilities and to work cooperatively to teach those skills.	1: Understanding Exceptionality 2: Legal and Social Issues
Characteristics	**6: Language** CC6K2 Characteristics of one's own culture and use of language and the ways in which these can differ from other cultures and uses of languages	**2: Student Learning** 2.05 All special education teachers have knowledge of a wide array of disabilities and are cognizant of the range and types of individual variation that exist within disability categories.	1: Understanding Exceptionality
Causes and Prevention	**6: Language** CC6K1 Effects of cultural and linguistic differences on growth and development	**2: Student Learning** 2.06 Special education teachers understand how disabilities in one area can impact learning and development in other areas.	1: Understanding Exceptionality

Assessment	**8: Assessment** CC8K4 Use and limitations of assessment instruments	**8: Assessment** 8.08 Special education teachers initiate, contact, and collaborate with other professionals throughout the identification and initial planning process.	3: Delivery of Services to Students
Teaching Students with Speech or Language Impairments	**6: Language** CC6K4 Augmentative and assistive communication strategies	**6: Communication** 6.06 Special education teachers know how to assess, design, and implement strategies that foster the language and communication development of students with disabilities, including nonverbal and verbal communication.	3: Delivery of Services to Students
Transition	**7: Instructional Planning** CC7S14 Prepare individuals to exhibit self-enhancing behavior in response to societal attitudes and actions	**7: Planning Instruction** 7.09 Special education teachers take the primary responsibility for planning and developing an expanded curriculum, such as the development of functional life skills and communication skills, when needed.	3: Delivery of Services to Students
Collaboration	**10: Collaboration** CC10S9 Communicate with school personnel about the characteristics and needs of individuals with exceptional learning needs	**10: Collaboration, Ethics, and Relationships** 10.07 Special education teachers work with related services professionals to design, implement, and evaluate instructional plans for students with disabilities.	3: Delivery of Services to Students
Partnerships with Families and Communities	**10: Collaboration** CC10K3 Concerns of families of individuals with exceptional learning needs and strategies to help address these concerns	**10: Collaboration, Ethics, and Relationships** 10.09 Special education teachers collaborate with families and with school and community personnel to include students with disabilities in a range of instructional environments in the school and community.	3: Delivery of Services to Students

Edouard Manet, *Claude Monet with his wife in his floating studio.* 1874. Scala/Art Resource, NY. Photograph of the artist: Felix Nadar, Musée d'Orsay, Paris, France. © Reunion des Musees Nationaux/Art Resource, NY.

Edouard Manet was born in Paris in 1832. His father's ambitions for him were to carry on the family tradition and become a lawyer. Despite outraged protests, Manet became one of the most famous impressionist painters of his day. Possibly he turned to art because of his difficulties at school. One headmaster considered him to be "feeble" another referred to him as "distracted," not "very studious," and "mediocre" (Schneider, 1968). If his father had not been a highly respected community leader, Manet would have been dismissed from school. To keep him from a career as an artist, his father got him a commission in the navy, but Manet failed the naval examination (Bolton, 1989) and turned to art. In the 1800s, the special education category of learning disabilities had not been identified. Whether Manet actually had learning disability or not cannot be verified. Regardless, from all accounts, academic learning was clearly a challenge for him.

5

Learning Disabilities

It's not a lot of fun to talk about your handicaps, except in golf.

Charles Schwab

We have all had the experience: No matter how hard we try, we have trouble understanding the information presented. In school we may sit through lectures and not understand the messages the instructor is trying to deliver. We may not understand the reading material for a particular class. We find it impossible to organize our thoughts to write a coherent essay or report. Sometimes we stumble over words and are unable to convey our thoughts, feelings, or knowledge. And occasionally we are uneasy and uncomfortable with other people. For most of us, these situations are infrequent. For people with learning disabilities (LD), however, one or more of these situations are commonplace. **Learning disabilities** is a condition that, despite the lack of other problems, such as mental retardation or emotional or behavioral disorders, causes significant learning problems, most often in areas related to reading and writing (Fuchs, Fuchs, Mathes et al., 2001). As you learned in the previous chapter, what often begins as a language problem in the preschool years becomes a reading problem by third grade and evolves into a pervasive academic problem as the demands of the curriculum increase through middle school and high school. In part because of the characteristics of this disability and in part as a result of academic failure, many of these individuals have difficulty achieving social competence as well (Bryan, Burstein, & Ergul, 2004). Despite all of these challenges, many individuals overcome their learning disabilities. Such success happens more often when they receive highly specialized, intensive, individualized instructional programs as early as possible. Even so, the impact of a learning disability usually lasts a lifetime (Goldberg et al., 2003).

Chapter Objectives

After studying this chapter, you will be able to:

1. List the key features of the IDEA '04 definition of learning disabilities.
2. Discuss the different types of learning disabilities.
3. Explain how an individual's response to intervention (RTI) is assessed.
4. Explain what is meant by the practice of "early intervening," and explain why it holds great promise.
5. Describe two validated practices that make a difference in the learning outcomes of students with disabilities.

Where We've Been . . . What's on the Horizon?

Debate and controversy have surrounded the field of learning disabilities from its inception and continue today (Hammill, 1990; Kirk, 1977; Vaughn & Fuchs, 2003). Parents, professionals, and policymakers continue to ask questions: What is the best way to identify and meet the learning needs of students with learning disabilities? How many students truly have this condition? How can services be delivered as early as possible? All of these questions lead to an overriding one: How should this disability be defined? These questions cannot be answered in this chapter because they are not yet resolved. However, we can come to an understanding of those issues that are the basis for them. Before learning about current thinking on these topics, let's see how the field of learning disabilities began and explore the path it has taken to the present.

Historical Context

On April 6, 1963, Professor Sam Kirk and others coined the term *learning disabilities* at a meeting of parents and professionals in Chicago. The nation's public schools have since experienced an explosion in the numbers of students identified, special teachers hired, and services offered. The effort began in elementary schools and was later extended to high schools. It continues to expand today, as more special programs for postsecondary students and adults with disabilities are developed.

The study of learning disabilities, however, put down roots long before 1963 (Hammill, 1990; Wiederholt, 1974). During the 1920s and 1930s, Samuel Orton, a specialist in neurology, developed theories and remedial reading techniques for children with severe reading problems, whom he called "dyslexic" and believed to be brain-damaged. In the 1930s, Helen Davidson studied letter "reversals"—writing some letters (such as b, d, q, and g) backwards—a problem consistently observed in many students with learning disabilities (Davidson, 1934, 1935). In the 1930s and 40s, Sam Kirk, who worked at the Wayne County School (you will learn more about this school in Chapter 6), helped to develop a set of word drills and other teaching procedures he referred to throughout his career. In 1961 he and his colleagues published the *Illinois Test of Psycholinguistic Abilities (ITPA),* which sought to identify individuals' strengths, weaknesses, learning styles, and learning preferences (whether they learned better by seeing or by hearing information presented). This test was used for many years to identify students with learning disabilities. Also in the 1960s, Marianne Frostig developed materials designed to improve students' visual perception, which is the ability to understand information that is seen. Her notion was that if visual perceptual skills were enhanced, reading abilities would also show improvement (Frostig, 1978).

The 1970s saw the field of learning disabilities embroiled in heated debate, and at the heart of the controversy was what approach for treatment of learning disabilities was most effective. In what was called the **process/product debate**, one group promoted instruction directed at improving students' perceptual abilities to improve their academic performance (e.g., reading). The other group argued that directly teaching academic skills (e.g., explicitly teaching students to read) is the best approach. The dispute was resolved when Don Hammill and Steve Larsen's research analysis showed that perceptual approaches were seldom effective in teaching academic skills but that direct-instruction techniques do make a difference (Hammill & Larsen, 1974).

Possibly more than any other disability, fads and invalidated practices are promoted, often through the press, to solve problems associated with learning disabilities. For example, one fad suggested having students with learning disabilities, regardless of their ages, use crawling exercises to "re-pattern" or re-train their brains. Others have claimed that special diets or plants on students' desks improve academic and behavioral performances. Still others blamed fluorescent lighting for learning disabilities. Most of these claims were backed up by very little scientific evidence of effectiveness (Keogh, 1974). Such promotion of invalidated practices is the major reasons for today's emphasis on the use of scientifically validated or evidence-based practices; proposed interventions must be thoroughly tested through rigorous research (Soltes, 2002).

learning disabilities (LD) A condition that causes significant learning problems, most often related to reading and writing; a disability of unexpected under-achievement that is typically resistant to treatment

process/product debate Argument about whether perceptual training or direct (explicit) instruction is the more effective way to teach reading

Challenges That Learning Disabilities Present

Individuals with learning disabilities whose learning problems do not receive early attention can have serious, life-long challenges to face (National Institutes of Health, 2005). Early, intensive intervention makes a difference, and it is imperative that young children and their families get services as early as possible. Just like other individuals with disabilities, those with learning disabilities range widely in abilities. Some students have a mild learning disability. With direct assistance, they access the general education curriculum successfully and take advantage of postsecondary

Candace Cordiella in the Spotlight

Today **Candace Cordiella** is a well-known advocate for and expert on the educational rights of children with learning disabilities, but this important career wasn't Candace's first. She was a successful executive in the fashion industry when her daughter, then a second grader, was diagnosed with learning disabilities and related language impairments. It was at this point that Candace decided that she should "find out what this whole special education thing was about." And, boy, did she!

It all started when her daughter's school district decided to serve all students with learning disabilities in general education classes and close their separate special education classrooms for these students. But the district made the switch without informing or consulting with parents. Needless to say, many parents banned together, learning a lot about advocacy and also becoming a powerful network. Because she lives in the Washington, DC, area, the next step for Candace was almost predictable. She recalls her early days of being mentored by other mom's of kids with disabilities: "One day we were talking about my little kid in my little school, and the next day they were saying, okay, we're all going to Congress tomorrow and you're coming along." Candace was suddenly directing her talents and understanding of the business world to the business of educating students with disabilities. Convinced that parents need to be informed—armed with knowledge—she was instrumental in creating the award-winning Web site ldonline. Supported by public television in the Washington, DC, area, ldonline was the first (and is by far the most visited) site about learning disabilities on the Internet. She serves on many national boards, mentors the next generation of parent-advocates, and has recently started a new organization and Web site, The Advocacy Institute. And, oh yes, when IDEA '04 was being written by Congress, Candace was on the Hill safeguarding the hard-won rights of students with disabilities. Candace and parents like her make a real difference not only for their own children, but for everyone else's too.

educational opportunities. Those with severe learning disabilities require intensive, sustained remediation and support throughout their school years and often into adulthood. All students with learning disabilities learn differently from their classmates without disabilities, and in many cases these students learn differently from each other. Some have questioned whether they are simply **low achievers**—students without disabilities whose academic performance is below that of their classmates. But it is now clear: These students' reading achievement differs dramatically from students without disabilities as well as from those who might be considered low achievers (Fuchs et al., 2002). Achieving reading fluency (being able to read quickly and correctly) and developing reading proficiency (reading efficiently with understanding) are particularly difficult for these individuals. Problems learning to read compound as students progress through school and independent reading becomes not just an academic goal but an expectation of the curriculum. Once this cycle is established, all aspects of academic performance are affected, and then school failure contributes to feelings of inadequacy and lack of self-confidence. All of this underscores the importance of early intervention, new ways to identify and bring services to those individuals as quickly as possible. How to accomplish this response is the greatest challenge facing professionals, families, and the individuals involved. Advocates for students with learning disabilities help ensure that the services these students require are available. Candace Cordiella is one of those special people who make things happen. The story of her path from professional, to mom, to advocate (see *Candace Cordiella in the Spotlight*) is fascinating and illustrates that each of us is capable of making a difference in the lives of many.

low achievers All students who experience school failure and poor academic achievement

Making a Difference

Charles Schwab and the Charles and Helen Schwab Foundation

Most highly successful businessmen don't reveal what might be construed as vulnerability. Clearly, it just isn't considered good business sense. In highly competitive marketplaces, any sign of weakness could be a signal for a takeover or a "hostile action." At the same time, most Americans are not comfortable openly talking about disabilities, particularly their own. And learning disabilities are not readily "visible"—not immediately signaled by a cane, wheelchair, glasses, or hearing aid. Such disabilities are not even understood by many of the individuals affected or by their families. The result is that too often, individuals with learning disabilities have to struggle on their own and figure it out by themselves, with little opportunity to profit from the guidance of people who have successfully compensated for or overcome the effects of their learning disabilities.

One highly successful businessman decided to break with tradition and speak out about the challenges he faced in school, and others are now joining him, serving as role models for individuals with learning disabilities and providing assistance to parents, teachers, and kids. Charles Schwab, the billionaire who founded the discount stock brokerage house, has faced the challenges of learning disabilities his whole life. His academic strengths were math and science, but he struggled with reading and all of its related subjects. Charles Schwab demonstrated his resilience and innovative thinking from a young age when he discovered that classic comic books, such as *Moby Dick*, provided an easier way to read "novels" assigned in English classes (Askman, 2005). Despite his reading problems, Charles Schwab persevered through college and graduate school, earning a BS and an MBA from Stanford University by focusing on his strengths—subjects related to numbers, such as economics. Two years after graduating from Stanford, he started an investment advisory newsletter, and a few years later, he founded his own brokerage house in San Francisco. Because he thought that the stock market should be accessible to everyone, he initiated the concept of the discount brokerage firm (Jones, 2003).

After discovering that his son had a learning disability, Charles Schwab and his wife, Helen, decided to help other families who struggled with this invisible disability. They started Schwab Learning, which operates two Web sites—one for parents (**www.SchwabLearning.org**) and one for kids (**www.SparkTop.org™**). SchwabLearning.org gives parents the answers to the million-and-one questions they have when their child has learning disabilities. The site addresses a parent's practical needs with information about IEPS, behavior issues, and the like; it also provides emotional support so parents know they are not alone in this journey. SparkTop.org is a place where kids with learning disabilities can learn about how their brains work, feel good about themselves, get answers to their questions, and enjoy the company of other kids just like them. The site reassures kids with LD that they're just as smart as other kids. They may struggle with reading or writing or math, but there are lots of things they're good at.

Charles Schwab took an invisible disability and made it okay to be visible.

To see how these two Web sites make a difference in the lives of teenagers with learning disabilities and parents of children with learning disabilities of all ages, check out: **www.schwablearning.org**, and **www.sparktop.org**

Learning Disabilities Defined

Professionals and parents use the term *learning disabilities* to describe a condition of **unexpected underachievement**—academic performance significantly below what would be predicted from the individual's talents and potential shown in other areas. This category includes 5.4 percent of all students and almost half of those identified by the schools as having a disability (U.S. Department of Education, 2005a). The federal government and almost every state use the term *specific learning disabilities,* and a similar definition (see Table 5.1), to describe this condition (Müller & Markowitz, 2004).

Regardless of the definition used, there always seems to be dissatisfaction (Elksnin et al., 2001; Kirk, 1977). Although some of the disagreement is due to differing philosophies and theories about the nature of the condition, most concerns stem from more practical problems:

- Delay in delivering needed services to students
- Overwhelming number of students identified with learning disabilities
- Inconsistency of characteristics observed in those identified

Before turning our attention to the types of learning disabilities, let's briefly consider these concerns. First, before the passage of IDEA '04, nearly all states insisted that students identified as having learning disabilities demonstrate a discrepancy between their potential (score on an intelligence test) and their performance (academic achievement) and that this discrepancy be significant (at least two years behind their expected grade level). So students waited—sometimes for years—to get help, even though their teachers knew they had a problem. The discrepancy requirement is one reason why so many students are identified in third grade: By then their struggles with school work are demonstrated by scores on achievement tests indicating first-grade performance. The second concern stems from the size of this special education category; over half of all students receiving special education services are identified as having learning disabilities. Third, students with learning disabilities express unique learning patterns. Some have problems in every academic area, some have problems only in reading or in math, and some have additional problems with social skills. In other words, this disability represents a **heterogeneous** group of learners; that is, individuals identified with this disability exhibit a wide range of strengthens and abilities, approach learning in a variety of ways, and respond to interventions inconsistently. The result is that no single treatment, explanation, or accommodation is uniformly effective. Regardless, let's think about some types, or common patterns, of problem areas that often define learning disabilities for the individuals involved.

General Unexpected Underachievement

Some students experience difficulties with all academic performance; they are behind the academic achievement of their classmates in every subject. Low educational performance not only describes students with learning disabilities, of course. It can also include low-achieving students who may or may not have disabilities. But many experts are certain that learning disabilities are different from low achievement (Kavale & Forness, 2000). Whereas mental retardation, poor motivation, or poor teaching might explain low achievement, learning disabilities probably reflect deficits in the ability to process information or remember it (Torgeson, 2002).

unexpected underachievement A defining characteristic of learning disabilities; poor school performance cannot be explained by other disabilities or limited potential

heterogeneous Exhibiting great variety, such as a wide range of strengths and abilities in a group

Table 5.1 • Definitions of Learning Disabilities

Source	Definition
Federal Government[1]	Specific learning disability means a disorder in one or more of the basic psychological processes involved in understanding or in using language, spoken or written, that may manifest itself in an imperfect ability to listen, think, speak, read, write, spell, or to do mathematical calculations, including such conditions as perceptual disabilities, brain injury, minimal brain dysfunction, dyslexia, and developmental aphasia. The term does not include learning problems that are primarily the result of visual, hearing, or motor disabilities, mental retardation, emotional disturbance, or environmental, cultural, or economic disadvantages.
National Institutes of Health (NIH)[2]	Learning disabilities are disorders that affect the ability to understand or use spoken or written language, do mathematical calculations, coordinate movements, or direct attention. Although learning disabilities occur in very young children, the disorders are usually not recognized until the child reaches school age.

Sources: [1]From 34 CFR Parts 300 and 303, Assistance to States for the Education of Children with Disabilities and the Early Intervention Program for Infants and Toddlers with Disabilities; Proposed Regulations (pp 312–313), U.S. Department of Education, 2005b, *Federal Register*, Washington, DC; and [2]"What is learning disabilities?" NINDS Learning Disabilities Information Page by National Institutes of Health, National Institute of Neurological Disorders and Stroke, 2005, retrieved from www.ninds.nih.gov

Reading/Learning Disabilities

Most commonly, students identified as having learning disabilities have much lower reading abilities than all other students (Fuchs, Fuchs, Mathes et al., 2002). The term **reading/learning disabilities** is used when the student's reading abilities are significantly below those of classmates without disabilities *and* significantly below what is expected on the basis of the student's other abilities. Reading difficulty is the most common reason for these students' referrals to special education. Because reading and writing are intimately related, most of these students also have problems with written communication (Troia & Graham, 2004). Obviously, reading and writing are important skills; in school, students must be able to read information from a variety of texts and write using varying formats. As the complexity of academic tasks increases, students who are not proficient in reading and writing cannot keep pace with the increasing academic expectations of school settings.

Reading/learning disabilities can cause pervasive academic problems because reading skills are increasingly important as the curriculum becomes more advanced. To understand printed text requires proficiency in a number of skills: reading words, comprehending language, and accessing background language (Jenkins & O'Connor, 2002). Students must be able to decode words and read with enough fluency to gain information at a rate close to that of their classmates. These students are slow in acquiring the necessary skills, and they acquire these skills differently than students without reading disabilities (Compton, 2002).

reading/learning disabilities Condition where a student's learning disability is most significant in reading

mathematics/learning disabilities Condition where a student's learning disability is most significant in areas related to mathematics

Mathematics/Learning Disabilities

More than 50 percent of students with learning disabilities also have difficulties with mathematics (Fuchs & Fuchs, 2001). **Mathematics/learning disabilities** are indicated when performance in mathematics is substantially below what is expected on the basis of the student's other abilities. Relatively few students identified as having learning disabilities have only mathematics disabilities; for most, this difficulty is part of their overwhelming and pervasive underachievement (Jordon & Hanich, 2003). Students with mathematics disabilities have problems that stem from their difficulties retrieving information from long-term memory; they have trouble remembering basic number facts (Robinson, Menchetti, & Torgeson,

2002). Other students' mathematics disabilities result from their inability to solve multistep problems, such as borrowing in subtraction, computing long division, and solving word problems (Bryant, Bryant, & Hammill, 2000; Bryant, Hartman, & Kim, 2003). Because math problem solving places demands on both reading and information processing skills, this area of the mathematics curriculum can be challenging for both teachers and students.

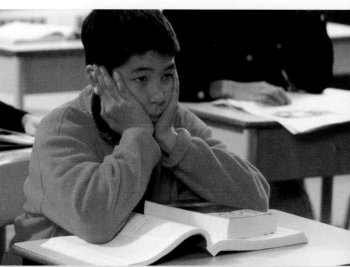

Many students with learning disabilities experience considerable challenges keeping up with their classmates. With explicit and sustained intervention, the results for these students can be outstanding.

Resistant to Treatment

Consensus is growing about some important differences among individuals with and without learning disabilities: Those with learning disabilities are **resistant to treatment**; they do not profit from the instruction typically used in general education classes (Gresham, 2002; Vaughn & Fuchs, 2003). The evidence is mounting that these students do not learn at the same rate or in the same ways as their classmates (Fuchs, Fuchs, Thompson et al., 2002). These students require intensive, individualized instruction. The premise is that if a student receives instruction or intervention typically used in general education programs and does not respond or improve sufficiently, then more intensive intervention explicitly directed toward the skill to be learned is necessary. As you will learn in the Assessment section of this chapter, the concept that learning disabilities are resistant to treatment is being incorporated into new identification procedures for learning disabilities outlined by IDEA '04.

Characteristics

Unexpected underachievement and being resistant to treatment are coming to be thought of as defining characteristics of learning disabilities (Kavale & Forness, 1996; Vaughn & Fuchs, 2003). Even so, the feature cited most often across these students is probably their heterogeneity—their remarkable individuality (Bradley, Danielson, & Hallahan, 2002). And yet, despite their unique traits, some characteristics are commonly seen with learning disabilities; these are listed in Table 5.2. In addition, more general characteristics seem to be at the root of the problems these individuals face. In order to consider how we can make a difference and improve these students' results, let's explore each of these commonly observed characteristics:

- Holding negative attributions
- Being nonstrategic
- Being unable to generalize or transfer learning
- Processing information inefficiently or incorrectly
- Possessing poor social skills

Negative Attributions

Motivation and attribution are related. Motivation is the inner drive that causes individuals to be energized and directed in their behavior. Motivation can be explained as a trait (a need to succeed, a need not to fail, a sustained interest in a topic) or as a temporary state of mind (preoccupation with a test or class presentation tomorrow, a passing interest in a topic). **Attributions** are self-explanations about the reasons for one's success or failure. Differences in motivation and attributions may account for differences in the way people approach tasks and for differences in their success with those tasks (Ring & Reetz, 2000). Assuming

resistant to treatment A defining characteristic of learning disabilities; validated methods typically applied in general education settings are not adequate to bring about sufficient learning

attributions Explanations that individuals give themselves for their successes or failures

Table 5.2 • Characteristics of Learning Disabilities

Academic	Social	Behavioral Style
Unexpected underachievement	Immature	Inattentive
Resistant to treatment	Socially unacceptable	Distractible
Difficult to teach	Misinterprets social and nonverbal cues	Hyperactive
Inability to solve problems	Makes poor decisions	Impulsive
Uneven academic abilities	Victimized	Poorly coordinated
Inactive learning style	Unable to predict social consequences	Disorganized
Poor basic language skills	Unable to follow social conventions (manners)	Unmotivated
Poor basic reading and decoding skills	Rejected	Dependent
Inefficient information processing abilities	Naïve	
Inability to generalize	Shy, withdrawn, insecure	
	Dependent	

responsibility for success is an internal attribution in which individuals understand the relationships among effort, task persistence, ability, and interest.

By contrast, year after year of frustration and failure at school can negatively affect students' motivation and convince them that there is nothing they can do to be successful. Students can develop a negative attitude and come to believe that their failure is a result of lack of ability, rather than a signal to work harder or ask for help. This cycle can even lead students to believe that external factors—luck, extra help, the teacher giving them a break, or a classmate doing them a favor—are the reasons for whatever successes they do have (Carlson et al., 2002). When people expect to fail, they can also become too dependent on others—and all too ready to just give up. This **learned helplessness** increases the likelihood of poor performance. Students who expect failure are less likely to be motivated to learn or to expend the effort it takes to learn (Pearl, 1982; Switzky & Schultz, 1988). They can appear to others as "passive" or not actively involved in their learning. They do not ask questions, seek help, or read related material to learn more. These characteristics compound their disabilities.

By comparing low-achieving students' motivation and attributions with those of high-achieving students, we can better understand the concepts of attribution and learned helplessness. Let's look at a classroom situation, such as writing a social studies term paper, to see how students' motivation affects the way they approach the task. High achievers, when given the assignment of writing a term paper on, say, the Revolutionary War, approach the task with confidence, knowing that they are capable of producing a thorough and well-written paper. They realize that if they read their textbook and other materials available at the library, they will know enough about the topic to prepare the paper. Because of past successes, they know that making an effort results in success. Therefore, these students will proofread their term papers and even add extras (such as maps and diagrams) to the final product. Low-achieving students with and without disabilities, in contrast, do not approach this assignment with much vigor. They seem overwhelmed by the assignment and complain that it is too difficult. These children believe that it is useless to ask for assistance, spend time in the library, or read extra materials.

learned helplessness
Usually a result of repeated failure or excessive control by others; individuals become less willing to attempt tasks and less able to believe that their actions can result in success

Instead, they write a short and incomplete term paper that is probably not developed with care or proofread. Teachers can turn this situation around! They can help students overcome these problems by involving them in the learning process, responding positively, praising them, promoting mastery, and creating a challenging and stimulating instructional environment (Sexton, Harris, & Graham, 1998). Teachers can point out the relationship between effort and accomplishment and thereby change students' negative attributions into positive ones that lead to success. A new series of books about the adventures of a group of middle school girls can help teachers in this effort. One of those upbeat *Beacon Street Girls*, Meave, has reading/learning disabilities.

In the innovative new book series *Beacon Street Girls*, B*tween Productions targets girls between the ages of 9 to 13. The stories focus on the adventures of five teenage girls. Maeve, a main character, said "I like school but sometimes it's hard because I have dyslexia. That's ok, soon enough I'll be pursuing the stage." She and her friends provide great role models.

Being Nonstrategic

Approaching learning in an organized manner leads to efficient and effective learning. Not paying attention to the important features of a learning task or not structuring one's learning is a problem observed among many students with learning disabilities (Deshler, 2005). Applying strategies for organizing information (such as the graphic organizers and content enhancements described on pages 144–146 in Chapter 4) can help them remember content and study more efficiently (Boulineau et al., 2004; Masterpieri et al., 2003). Being proficient in the use of thinking skills—classifying, associating, and sequencing—also helps students become more strategic learners. **Classifying** enables the learner to categorize and group items together in terms of the characteristics they have in common. Usually, people remember more items in a list if they approach the task by **chunking**, or organizing information by groups. For example, if you forget your grocery list and are already at the store, you might try to remember what items you need by thinking about groups of items. You might recall that potatoes and corn were on the list when you think of vegetables and that ice cream, pizza, and TV dinners were on the list when you think of frozen foods. **Associating** means seeing the relationships that exist among and between different knowledge bases. By associating facts or ideas, the mind is able to find the "common denominators" (for example, softness or hardness, style of painting) and connections that link units of information. **Sequencing** information puts units of information in order along some dimension. For example, physical items can be sorted and sequenced by size, weight, or volume. Facts, events, and ideas can be sequenced by time, importance, or complexity. With instruction and practice, these thinking skills can be learned and developed into useful tools for learning that help students approach learning tasks more purposefully.

Inability to Generalize

Most students with learning disabilities are unable to **generalize**—that is, to transfer their learning to novel situations or extend their learning of one skill to similar skills (Rivera & Smith, 1997). For example, they might apply a newly learned study skill in history class but not in English class. Or a child might master borrowing in subtraction when a zero appears in the units column but not apply that rule when there is a zero in the tens column as well. Long-standing research has shown that some teaching methods can actually interfere with students learning the concept of generalization (Ellis, 1986). For example, the overuse of feedback on performance (knowledge of results) can reinforce dependency, learned helplessness, and learning inactivity. One way to encourage generalization is explicitly to make connections between familiar problems and those that are new or novel (Fuchs, Fuchs, Mathes et al., 2002). And when teachers carefully broaden the categories—either the skill or the situation—and point out similar features, students extend their learning more readily. Thus, if a student knows how to solve subtraction problems

classifying A thinking skill; the ability to categorize items or concepts by their common characteristics

chunking A thinking skill to aid memory; organizing information by groups or topics

associating A thinking skill; the ability to see relationships among different concepts or knowledge bases

sequencing A thinking skill; categorizing and putting items, facts, or ideas in order along various dimensions

generalizing Transferring learning from particular instances to other environments, people, times, or events that require borrowing without zeros in the numerator, teachers should carefully point out the similarities between problems that include zeros (500 − 354 = ?) and those that do not (467 − 189 = ?).

Faulty Information Processing

Many people with learning disabilities have difficulty learning to read and write, understanding things they are told, and even expressing themselves through oral communication. To explain why, researchers are studying theories of learning and then applying them to the way students with learning disabilities actually learn. Many years ago, Janet Lerner created a scheme to help us understand the information processing theory by comparing the human brain to a computer (Lerner, 1993). In her concept (see Figure 5.1), the flow of information that occurs when people are learning new skills begins with the input of information, continues with the processing of that information, and ends with its output. Like the computer, the human brain takes in information, processes that information (makes associations, stores information, calls it up, acts upon it), and generates responses from it.

Figure 5.1 • Information Processing Theory and Its Similarities to the Computer System

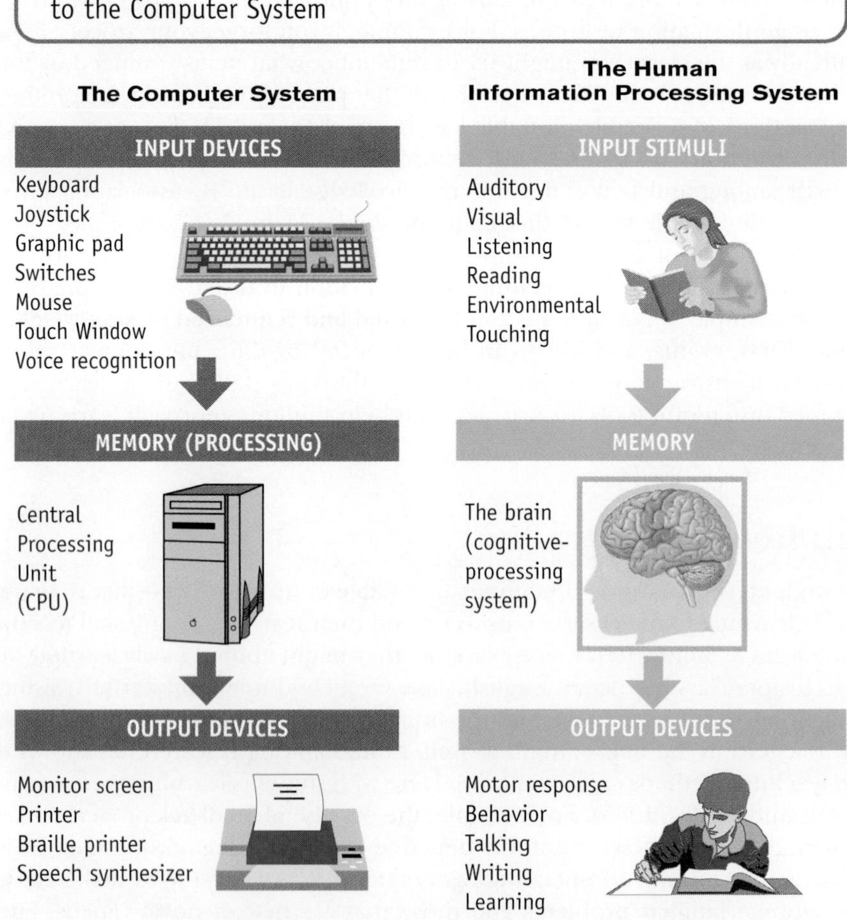

Source: Janet Lerner, *Learning Disabilities: Theories, Diagnosis, and Teaching Strategies,* Sixth Edition. Copyright © 1993 by Houghton Mifflin Company. Adapted with permission.

Learning to understand the "rules of the game" comes with lots of practice and experience. Teachers can help students with learning disabilities develop the complex skills needed in social situations by arranging opportunities for them to play and learn.

How can teachers help students process information? Some simple actions can make a difference in how well students understand the task and can thereby improve their academic performance:

- *Repeat important information in different ways:* "Remember to study for this week's exam. On Friday, you will have a test over Chapter 6 of your history book."
- *Organize content systematically:* Put information into sequential order ("First the English raised taxes on the colonists. Then the Americans protested. In Boston, they dumped the tea being delivered by boat into the harbor.")
- *Provide students with relevant information:* "Fish have gills, scales, and fins. Horses have _____, _____, and _____."
- *Anchor content and assignments to students' experiences and interests:* On the list for book reports, include books representing a variety of sports, hobbies, adventures, biographies, mysteries, and characters from different cultures and backgrounds

Poor Social Skills

Over 30 years ago, Tanis Bryan brought the challenges that many students with learning disabilities face with social skills to the nation's attention and expanded our understanding of this disability beyond its effects on academic skills (Bryan, 1974). Deficits in social skills are now considered a common and defining characteristic of learning disabilities (Kavale & Mostert, 2004). Though not all individuals with learning disabilities have problems with social skills, the great majority do (Gresham, Sugai, & Horner, 2001; Vaughn, Elbaum, & Boardman, 2001). Specifically, about a quarter of them are average or above average in social skills and social competence. For the other 75 percent of these individuals, problems with social skills negatively influence their self-concept, their ability to make friends, their interactions with others, and even the way they approach schoolwork (Bryan, Burstein, & Ergul, 2004).

*tips for Classroom Management

TEACHERS HELPING STUDENTS WITH LEARNING DISABILITIES MAKE FRIENDS

Explicitly Teach

- Rules of playground games
- Comprehension of nonverbal expressions
- Social conventions
- When to terminate a conversation
- How to ask permission to join an ongoing game
- Sharing skills

Pair with a Class-Buddy

- Match students with similar interests
- Create opportunities
- Reward both members of the pair for working and playing together
- Change pairs once a month

Two general reasons account for these students' difficulties developing social competence:

1. Relationships among learning disabilities, language impairments, pragmatics, and social competence
2. The downward spiral of academic failure to positive peer relationships

For some students, impairment in social skills is part of their learning disability (Wiener, 2004). Those students whose language impairment during the preschool years hindered their developing pragmatics (for a review, see pages 128 and 142 in Chapter 4) often have difficulty understanding others' nonverbal behavior and using language effectively in social situations (Olswang, Coggins, & Timler, 2001). These students cannot understand nonverbal behaviors, such as facial expressions, and therefore do not comprehend other people's emotional messages (Teglasi, Cohn, & Meshbesher, 2004). Remember, the relationship between social competence and language impairments is clear. Poor language skills impair the ability to communicate, and communicative competence is necessary for social interaction (Elksnin & Elksnin, 2004). Social competence is related, in one way or another, to almost every action and skill that people perform. **Social competence** is the ability to perceive and interpret social situations, generate appropriate social responses, and interact with others. Thus the very nature of learning disabilities explains, in part, why many students with learning disabilities have problems developing satisfactory social skills.

The second reason is directly related to these students' academic failure. Poor educational performance lowers self-esteem and self-confidence, which in turn undermines the ability to make friends with classmates who are high achievers. And so it continues: Poor social skills contribute to poor academic performance, and experiencing school failure compounds the social issues the individual must confront (Elliott, Malecki & Demaray, 2001). Difficulty with social skills, coupled with low achievement and distracting classroom behavior, influences the social status of those with learning disabilities. Their peers see them as overly dependent, less cooperative, and less socially adept (Kuhne & Wiener, 2000). They are rejected by fellow students and are not included in games on the playground or in groups in the classroom (Le Mare & de la Ronde, 2000; Norwicki, 2003). It is not surprising that some students with learning disabilities prefer pull-out programs and do not like inclusive classroom situations (Vaughn, Elbaum, & Boardman, 2001). Teachers can make a real difference and help students with learning disabilities who also experience social problems. Some ideas about how to take direct action are listed in *Tips for Classroom Management.*

Signs of these problems begin early, during the preschool years, as these children experience strong feelings of loneliness and lack of friends (Bryan, Burstien, & Ergul, 2004). Rejection and inadequate social skills persist through adolescence (Le Mare & de La Ronde, 2000). During the later school years, these students do not seek the support of peers or friends as do their classmates without disabilities, so feelings of loneliness, rejection, and isolation persist. Of even more concern is their tendency to be victimized—threatened, physically assaulted, or subjected to theft of their belongings—more than their peers.

The use of social skills training programs, even though they sometimes have limited results, is strongly encouraged by researchers (Kavale & Mostert, 2004).

social competence Being able to understand social situations and respond appropriately in them

Experts recommend implementing programs that match the intervention to the individual's unique problem areas. For example, if a student has not acquired a social skill, then modeling, coaching, practice, and specific feedback can make development of the missing skill possible. Peer tutoring, reinforcement, and contingencies that reward the entire class (those with and those without disabilities) can help to extend or generalize initial learning. Also, teachers can play an instrumental role in reducing peer rejection by pairing classmates in areas of mutual interest. For example, teachers might plan activities so that students with and without learning disabilities who share common interests (sports, music, hobbies) are assigned to work together on an academic task such as a social studies report.

Prevalence

Across the nation, policymakers and parents express great concern about the number of children identified by school personnel as having a learning disability (Finn, Rotherham, & Hokanson, 2001; Vaughn & Fuchs, 2003). Three major issues are the basis for concerns about the prevalence of learning disabilities.

1. *Size:* Nearly half of all students with disabilities are identified as having learning disabilities, and the number increases each year.
2. *Cost:* Special education costs almost twice as much as general education.
3. *Misidentification:* Diverse learners are disproportionately represented in special education.

This special education category is by far the largest, including 5.4 percent of all schoolchildren and almost half of all students identified as having a disability (U.S. Department of Education, 2005a). When IDEA was first passed and was being implemented in 1976–77, only about one-quarter of all students with disabilities were served through the learning disabilities category. In the 10-year period from the 1990–91 to the 1999–2000 school year, the learning disabilities category grew by 34 percent (U.S. Department of Education, 2002). The rate at which assignment to the learning disabilities category has increased far surpasses that for students with speech or language impairments or emotional or behavioral disorders, and the prevalence of mental retardation among students has decreased slightly over the years. These relationships are shown in Figure 5.2.

Why is there such concern about the size of the learning disabilities category? One reason is cost (Vaughn & Fuchs, 2003). Although variation exists across the nation and even district by district, every student with a disability costs more to educate than their classmates without disabilities (Chambers, Parrish, & Harr, 2002). It costs about twice as much to educate a student with disabilities as to educate a student without disabilities. Because the federal government does not fully cover these costs, the public and the media make the case that students with disabilities are being educated at the expense of their classmates without disabilities. This situation has caused many to believe that the special education rolls should be reduced, and partly because of its size, the learning disabilities category is the one they target (Finn et al., 2001; Lyon et al., 2001).

The third concern is whether students are being correctly identified. Some experts have called the category of learning disabilities a "dumping ground" where any student unsuccessful in the general education curriculum can be

Figure 5.2 • Comparison of Prevalence Rates of Students with High Incidence Disabilities

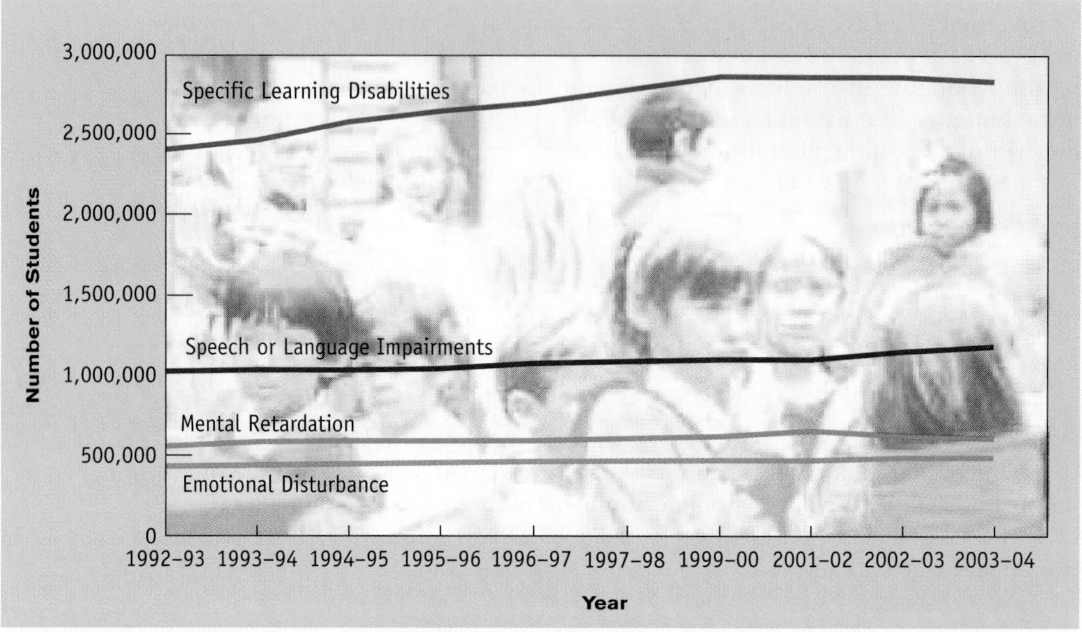

The numbers of children with learning disabilities, mental retardation, emotional disturbance, and speech or language impairments served under IDEA are shown for ages 6 to 21 and school years 1992–93 through 2003–2004.

Source: From the *Twenty-Second and Twenty-Third Annual Reports to Congress on the Implementation of the Individuals with Disabilities Education Act,* U.S. Department of Education, 2000, 2001. Washington, DC: Government Printing Office, and U.S. Department of Education, Number of Children Served Under IDEA by Disability and Age Group, 1994 through 2003, Table AA9, Age Group 6–21, 2005c, www.ideadata.org

placed (Reschly, 2002). Thus it is possible that some of these students do not have a disability but simply are failing in the general education curriculum and were given the label so they could get extra attention and special assistance. Which students are being included in this category? One very carefully conducted study gives us a hint (MacMillan, Gresham, & Bocian, 1998). These researchers matched the state's guidelines for learning disabilities with 61 actual students who were identified by school districts. Their results indicated that 10 did not meet the criterion for any special education category, 19 had IQ scores below 76 (which should have qualified them for services in the mental retardation category), and 9 also met the criteria for ADHD (see Chapter 6 for more information about this condition).

Despite these three serious concerns, experts do not foresee the number of students classified with learning disabilities decreasing in the years to come. Even if identification procedures and the definition of learning disabilities are changed to reflect newer ideas, such as unexpected underachievement and resistance to treatment, it is doubtful that fewer students will be identified with learning disabilities. In fact, estimates are that as many as 6 percent of all children have unexpected underachievement and also experience resistance to treatment (Learning Disability Summit, 2001). Clearly, these students require very special attention.

Causes and Prevention

Just as there are numerous manifestations of learning disabilities, there are multiple causes, levels of severity, and preventive measures. Unfortunately, researchers do not have much concrete information about the causes of learning disabilities (Bender, 2004). Without definitive causes or explanations for the problem, effective prevention will remain illusive.

Causes

Surprisingly little is actually known about the causes of learning disabilities. One assumption embedded in definitions of learning disabilities is that the origin of many of these individuals' problems is neurological—that there may be brain damage. For the vast majority of students with disabilities, there is *no* documentation of neurological impairment, but for those who do have brain damage, there are many specific causes. For example, lack of oxygen before, during, or after birth can result in neurological difficulties that affect the individual's ability to learn.

Heredity may make a more significant contribution to learning disabilities than was previously understood. Many individuals with learning disabilities report they have relatives who have similar problems, but a genetic link to learning disabilities has proven difficult to document (Decker & Defries, 1980, 1981). Today, because of modern scientific techniques, researchers are discovering some genetic causes of learning disabilities. For example, Turner syndrome has a definite link to mathematics disabilities in girls (Rovet, 2004). Some experts are searching for an interactive relationship among several genes hoping to identify risk factors for reading disabilities (Wood & Grigorenko, 2001).

Finally, a strong relationship exists between learning disabilities and low socioeconomic status (SES) (Blair & Scott, 2002). Whether factors associated with poverty (such as limited access to health care, living in dangerous environments filled with toxins, or the lack of a supportive environment) puts these children at great risk for learning disabilities is not known, but the relationship is clear. Certainly, cases of learning disabilities attributable to poverty could be prevented.

Prevention

Without knowing a specific cause of learning disabilities, it is impossible to develop a set of preventive procedures or strategies. But, when we *do* know a cause of a disability, we should take action. For example, as we have noted, environmental toxins can cause neurological damage, which in turn can result in a learning disability. Clearly, society at large and local communities should do everything they can to eliminate toxins from children's lives. As reported in *Disability in the News*, such dangers are even found at the nation's schools (Herszenhorn, 2004, October 29). We can all make a difference in the lives of all children by not tolerating situations that place America's children at risk for such harm. Until such time as specific causes for learning disabilities are discovered, definitive prevention strategies cannot be developed. However, the impact of the disability can be lessened, and in some cases the condition remediated or compensated for, through education.

Overcoming Challenges

Although poor teaching can cause school failure and may be a factor in the identification of some students, it is not an actual cause of learning disabilities. Good teaching, on the other hand, can prevent school failure and can also help students compensate for their learning challenges (Fuchs & Fuchs, 2001; Graham, Harris, &

Reaction Time to Fixing Lead in Schools' Water Is Disputed

David M. Herszenhorn

NEW YORK CITY – The chairman of the State Assembly Education Committee charged yesterday that New York State health and education officials failed to follow up on reports that dangerous levels of lead had been detected in the drinking water at 120 schools and day care facilities. . . . [R]esults [from a statewide survey] tallied in August found that the lead levels in water from fountains and sinks were high enough to require action under the federal Environmental Protection Agency guidelines. . . .

Repeated exposure to hazardous lead levels can result in lead poisoning, which can cause irreversible neurological damage, including learning disabilities, hearing loss, and other problems. Mr. Sanders, a Democrat from Manhattan, called the agencies "shamefully negligent" for failing to follow up on the survey and request detailed information from schools.

Source: "Reaction Time to Fixing Lead in Schools' Water Is Disputed" by D. M. Herszenhorn, October 29, 2004, *New York Times*.

Larsen, 2001). Obviously, poor teaching should be eliminated as a reason for school failure! When educators target the right skills, set goals and expectations high, use validated instructional procedures, and support students as they stretch to meet their goals, education makes a real difference in the results of these students.

How can teaching be considered a preventive measure? Evidence is mounting that one way to reduce the number of school-age students who struggle with academic learning is to teach the foundations of reading during the preschool years. The notion is "catch them before they fail" (Torgeson & Wagner, 1998). For instance, systematic instruction before first grade to develop skills prerequisite to reading, such as sound–symbol awareness, has great benefits. This early instruction may reduce the degree of a reading disability or even help some students avoid reading challenges altogether (Compton, 2002). This knowledge has caused educators to modify the ways in which students with learning disabilities are identified, by merging assessment with instruction. Let's now turn our attention to these new systems.

Assessment

Each Assessment section of this text highlights different features of the evaluation process. Each begins by discussing identification during the preschool years, continues through the pre-referral and identification stages, and concludes with at least one aspect of evaluating students' progress. Although IDEA '04 does not require states to change the way they identify students with learning disabilities, it does allow them to adopt a new method (see *What IDEA '04 Says About Eligibility for Learning Disabilities*. This new approach gives general education teachers more of the responsibility and also sets the stage for drastic changes in the identification process for students with learning disabilities. In this chapter, we first talk about the preschool situation and then focus on features of the new way to identify students with learning disabilities.

what IDEA '04 says about...

Eligibility for Learning Disabilities

When determining eligibility for the category of learning disability, a local educational agency (e.g., school district):

- Is *not* required to consider whether a child shows a discrepancy between school achievement and intellectual ability
- May include documentation on the child's response to scientific, research-based intervention as part of the formal evaluation procedures

Early Identification

Preschoolers typically are *not* identified as having learning disabilities. Look again at Figure 4.5, on page 134 in the previous chapter. During the preschool years, more youngsters are identified with language impairments, but then, in third grade, learning disabilities becomes the prevailing label. At present, most students with reading/learning disabilities are not identified or given special services during the preschool years; their first identification is later during their school years. Some of them are not even identified until college.

With the importance of early intervention so well understood, why are individuals with learning disabilities typically not identified earlier? For one thing, professionals have been reluctant to identify or label children as having a learning or reading disability in the preschool years, or even by first grade, for fear of making a diagnostic mistake. Young children do not develop at exactly the same rate. Some children who do not develop as quickly as their peers do not have a disability; they will catch up. Still others are the youngest in their class and are thus not, and should not be, developmentally equal to their classmates. Another reason lies in the concept of "significant discrepancy" between achievement and potential. When children are very young, such discrepancies are impossible to detect.

Might there be a way to identify those preschoolers who would profit from intensive early intervention that might prevent later reading problems? One way might be to identify young children at risk. Another way might be to find those showing early warning signs. Who might be likely candidates? Preschoolers at risk are those who were not talking by age 3, had low birth weights, were premature babies, or come from poverty (Anderson & Shames, 2006; Blair & Scott, 2002). Those displaying early warning signs are not developing the precursors to reading, such as phonemic awareness (sound–symbol relationships) and knowing the letters and sounds of the alphabet (Bursuck et al., 2004). Researchers are now confident that these precursors are reliable predictors of reading success; that is, those preschoolers who possess these skills become good readers (Bishop, 2003; Speece et al., 2003; Torgesen & Wagner, 1998). In the section *Early Intervention*, on page 178, you will learn more about delivery of services to preschoolers who might be at risk for later learning disabilities. But now let's turn our attention to the new prereferral and identification process just approved in IDEA '04 for schoolchildren.

Pre-Referral: Response to Intervention

Until the reauthorization of IDEA in 2004, a few places in the nation were piloting and implementing a new identification process for learning disabilities. This new process is not mandated by IDEA '04, but it is encouraged in the law and most likely will become widely adopted (OSEP, 2005). To better understand these changes, it may be helpful first to review the traditional method for identifying students with learning disabilities. The standard procedure uses **discrepancy formulas** to determine whether the gap between a student's achievement and her or his potential is significant and accounts for that student's learning failures. Although many different types are applied across the nation, such formulas have been the common way to identify students as having learning disabilities (Schrag, 2000). Two test results are needed to apply every discrepancy formula: an IQ score and the score from a standardized achievement test. Considerable dissatisfaction

discrepancy formulas Calculations used to determine the gap between a student's achievement and her or his potential; used to identify students with learning disabilities with discrepancy formulas exists (Bradley, Danielson, & Hallahan, 2002). Here are just a few criticisms:

- IQ tests are not reliable and are unfair to many groups of children.
- Results have little utility in planning a student's educational program.
- The process does not help determine which interventions might be successful.
- Outcomes are not related to performance in the classroom, in the general education curriculum, or on state- or district-wide assessments.
- Children must fail before they can qualify for needed services. Thus early intervention is delayed until the gap becomes great enough for children to meet this criterion.

With such concerns, why were discrepancy formulas used for so long? One important reason is that they give the identification process some appearance of objectivity. Another reason is that the results are easy for parents and teachers to understand (Ahearn, 2003). Diagnosticians or school psychologists give a child an IQ test and an achievement test and then apply the formula. Whether the child is included in the learning disabilities category thus becomes a cut-and-dried, "yes or no" answer. Another reason is that the discrepancy system is fairly easy to apply. The teacher refers the student, the diagnostician gives some tests, and the identification process moves along.

IDEA '04 now allows states and school districts to use the pre-referral step in the IEP process for at least initial identification of students with learning disabilities, and even for full identification. The purpose is to find those students who are "resistant to treatment" through a process that determines their **response to intervention (RTI)**. The RTI system "filters" children through many stages of learning opportunities to determine whether they are resistant to instructional intervention (Fuchs, Fuchs, & Compton, 2004). The system does this evaluation by systematically providing students with more and more intensive instruction (Fuchs & Fuchs, 2005).

How does this pre-referral process work? Although it can be applied for any academic area, RTI is receiving most attention for its application to reading—the most common problem among students with learning disabilities. Lynn and Doug Fuchs and Sharon Vaughn are some of the innovators who have researched this concept and developed one approach to its implementation. Here's what they suggest should happen in the general education setting (Fuchs & Fuchs, 2005; Vaughn, 2005):

1. All students in kindergarten or in first, second, third, or fourth grade experience universal screening and are tested once in the fall.
2. Students demonstrating skills that put them at risk for reading failure are identified for intervention.
3. Validated procedures (e.g., direct instruction on reading skills such as sight word vocabulary and phonics) are implemented, and students' progress is monitored throughout and after intervention.
4. Students who do not learn after receiving three increasingly intensive levels of instruction are either identified as having learning disabilities or sent on for further assessments by a multidisciplinary team, depending on the district's rules for identification.

response to intervention (RTI) A multitiered pre-referral method of increasingly intensive interventions; used to identify "nonresponders," or students with learning disabilities

Which students are they looking for? This process is intended to identify students who are resistant to treatment—those who fail to make adequate progress (Fuchs, 2003; Speece, Case, & Molloy, 2003). These are the students who do not profit from instruction in the general education classroom and are in need of special education (Fuchs & Fuchs, 2005; Vaughn, 2005). Figure 5.3 indicates how this

Figure 5.3 • Comparison of CBM Data for Three Students

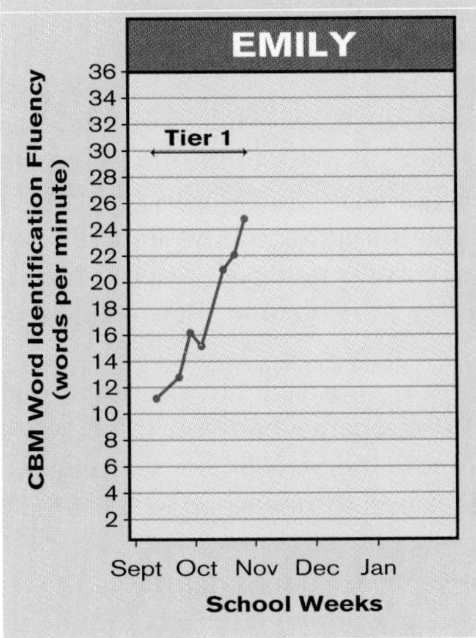

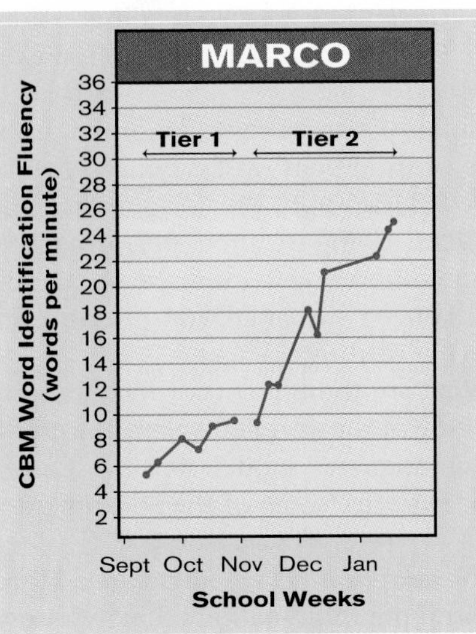

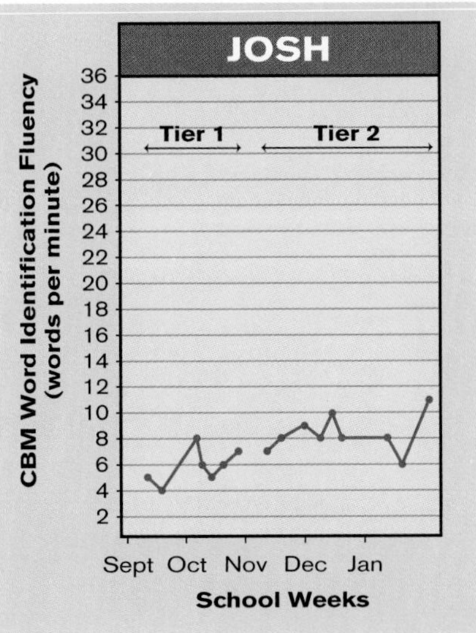

Emily and Marco, general education students who responded to intervention, and Josh, is resistant to treatment and needs sustained, intensive, and explicit intervention.

process might be implemented. During *Step 1, Screening*, each first grader in a class read a list of words aloud, and the number of correctly read words in a one-minute sample was recorded. The data from each student scoring below criterion (Marco, Emily, and Josh) were graphed. These three first graders remained in the general education class but moved on to *Step 2, Tier 1 Assessment*. Their performance on the word identification task was assessed each week to determine whether peer tutoring, extra attention, and modified textbooks resolved their reading problems. Marco, clearly at risk for reading failure, as indicated by the score he received on the initial screening assessment, responded satisfactorily to intervention at this level and returned to the general education program. Emily and Josh's progress was insufficient, however, so they moved on to *Step 3, Tier 2 Assessment*. They both remained in the general education program but received more intensive instruction from a paraprofessional under the supervision of a reading specialist who carefully matched the types of instruction chosen for them (such as active responding, cues, prompts, and/or direct instruction on phonics) to their skill levels. As you can see from Emily's chart in Figure 5.3, she responded to this level of instruction, so she returned to the general education program. But Josh's performance indicated that he is "resistant to treatment," and he entered *Step 4, Disability Classification/Special Education Placement*. At this step, a multidisciplinary team will determine the exact nature of Josh's disability, his strengths, and his needs for supports and sustained, intensive intervention.

Lynn and Doug Fuchs report that over 60 percent of students in a pilot program testing this new identification process could not sustain the improvement made in their first intensive experience and had to return to special education to resume academic growth (Fuchs & Fuchs, 2001). Others report that referrals to special education declined by 74 percent (McNamara & Hollinger, 2003). Progress-monitoring systems (see Chapter 2 for a review), such as curriculum based measurement (CBM), that do not rely on infrequently administered standardized achievement tests are embedded in the RTI approach. You will learn more about CBM later in this chapter (see page 177).

What skills for reading are being tested through the RTI system? Different abilities are assessed in different grades (Fuchs, 2003; Fuchs & Fuchs, 2005).

- *Kindergarten:* letter–sound fluency; say the sound represented by a letter
- *Grade 1:* word identification fluency; word recognition on a timed test
- *Grades 2–3:* passage reading; read a paragraph aloud
- *Grade 4:* maze fluency; fill in missing words when reading a passage

Examples of targets for each grade are shown in Figure 5.4. There you find segments of the Fuchs' assessments. Now review again the sample graphs shown in Figure 5.3 for Emily, the "responder," and for Josh, the student who is resistant to treatment. Compare their performances, and you should see how students can respond differently to intensive interventions. Such assessments tell teachers which students need sustained and intensive intervention to overcome their challenges mastering reading.

What are the benefits of RTI? Proponents of this approach are confident that RTI resolves the problems with the traditional "discrepancy between intelligence and achievement" model (Speece, Case, & Molloy, 2003; McNamara & Hollinger, 2003). Here are some of the advantages that RTI is usually described as offering:

1. *No delay in receiving intervention.* More intensive instruction is delivered promptly, eliminating a long waiting period of continued failure before help is received.
2. *Reduces inappropriate referrals.* RTI provides teachers with better guidance in determining which students are in need of special education.
3. *Poor teaching not a reason.* Inefficient instruction is eliminated as a reason for learning disabilities.
4. *Assessment leads to intervention.* RTI combines assessment with intervention.

Figure 5.4 • Response to Intervention Assessment Samples: Kindergarten Through Fourth Grade

Kindergarten
Letter-Sound Fluency

Teacher: *Say the sound that goes with each letter.*

Time: 1 minute

p U z u y
i t R e w
O a s d f
v g j S b
k m n b V
Y E i c x
É

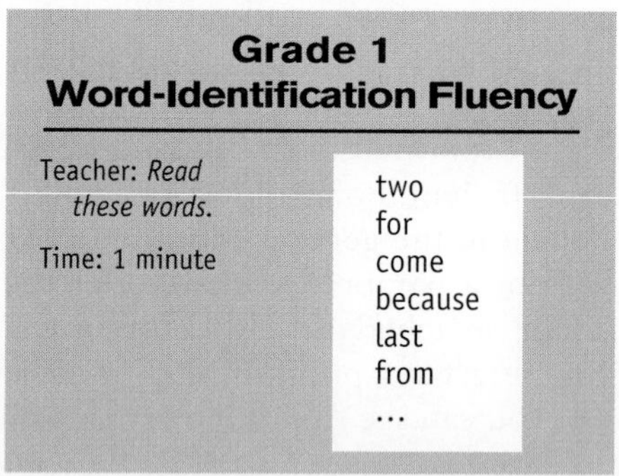

Grade 1
Word-Identification Fluency

Teacher: *Read these words.*

Time: 1 minute

two
for
come
because
last
from
...

Grades 2–3
Passage Reading Fluency

- Number of words read aloud correctly in 1 minute on end-of-year passages

Grades 4–6
Maze Fluency

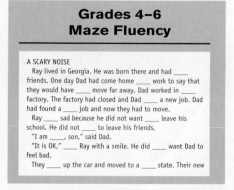

A SCARY NOISE
Ray lived in Georgia. He was born there and had ____ friends. One day Dad had come home ____ work to say that they would have ____ move far away. Dad worked in ____ factory. The factory had closed and Dad ____ a new job. Dad had found a ____ job and now they had to move.
Ray ____ sad because he did not want ____ leave his school. He did not ____ to leave his friends.
"I am ____, son," said Dad.
"It is OK," ____ Ray with a smile. He did ____ want Dad to feel bad.
They ____ up the car and moved to a ____ state. Their new

Source: Adapted with permission. Courtesy of Lynn Fuchs and Doug Fuchs.

5 *No stigma:* All students enter the process.

6 *Low achievement is distinguished from learning disabilities.* Low performance improves but growth remains insufficient, thereby separating these two groups of students.

The support for RTI is growing, although some professionals adhere to the traditional discrepancy model (Kavale, Holdnack, & Mostert, 2005). Others remain concerned about what it will take to implement this new model (Ahearn, 2003). What will it take to make the RTI system work in schools across the country? Clearly, changing to this new system will require considerably more support for general education teachers who are adding assessment to their instructional duties (Denton, Vaughn, & Fletcher, 2003). General and special education teachers will need to collaborate more than ever before by helping each other tie assessment to intervention. Although making these changes takes considerable effort, this new system has the potential to make real differences in the education of students with learning disabilities.

Identification

As more and more states adopt RTI, the pre-referral process may replace the identification step in the IEP process for learning disabilities (Fuchs, Mock et al., 2003). In many states, however, traditional diagnostic procedures will follow the pre-referral stage. Information about the student's academic performance gathered during the pre-referral stage is used in the final identification step. In other words, pre-referral does not replace, but rather supports, formal referrals to special education for all students who do not succeed with more intensive instruction (Speece, Case, & Molloy, 2003). Then, just as under the guidelines of IDEA before the 2004 version was passed, a multidisciplinary team administers a comprehensive assessment battery of tests that might include standardized tests of intelligence, achievement, hearing, and vision. The purposes of this step in the assessment process are to specifically determine the cause of the student's problems and to ensure that a student with mental retardation or another disability is not misidentified as having a learning disability.

Evaluation: Curriculum Based Measurement (CBM)

As you learned in Chapter 2, *progress monitoring* is an important component of an effective education for students with disabilities. **Curriculum based measurement (CBM)** is a form of progress monitoring that uses direct and frequent measurements of students' actual performance, such as oral reading rate, percentage of correct answers to mathematics problems, and number of homework assignments produced correctly and turned in on time. CBM enables elementary, middle school, and high school teachers to evaluate individual students' progress and also to assess the effectiveness of the instructional methods they are using (Espin, Weissenburger, & Benson, 2004; IRIS Center, 2005). It can also be used to compare one student's daily achievements with those of classmates and to track trends across time.

Six steps are used in the CBM system (Fuchs, Fuchs, & Powell, 2004).

1 *Create or select appropriate tests (probes).* Probes are matched to the student's grade, and they sample skills to be mastered across the school year. Thus, as time progresses, students should get more items correct.

2 *Administer and score probes.* Probes are presented frequently (e.g., weekly or monthly) to ensure that students' data are valid (reflect performance of the same skills being taught) and reliable (consistently represent the students' abilities on the targeted skills).

curriculum based measurement (CBM) A system of progress monitoring; evaluates performance frequently (daily or weekly) by collecting data directly on mastery of academic subjects being taught

3. *Graph the scores.* Visual representations of student's performance enable students to see their progress and teachers to make instructional decisions (see Figure 5.3 again for some sample charts).
4. *Set goals.* Targets, which sometimes are called benchmarks, help students and teachers understand how much growth is expected or required.
5. *Make instructional decisions.* The student's performance is used to evaluate the instructional program in order to retain effective strategies and discontinue ineffective ones.
6. *Communicate progress:* CBM data and graphs facilitate communication with parents, other teachers, and students.

CBM has many benefits, besides being an integral part of the new RTI system for pre-referral and identification of students with learning disabilities. Teachers who use CBM find that it facilitates communication with parents and students because it focuses everyone's attention on instructional targets and the student's performance (Hosp & Hosp, 2003). CBM also helps teachers plan more effective instruction, helps students see that they are responsible for their learning and resulting performance, and reflects progress on learning the curriculum content.

Early Intervention

The importance of the preschool years, when the foundations for learning are developing and become established, cannot be overstated. This is true for all children. Early childhood is a critical period, in which many developmental milestones—the basis for school achievement and life success—occur. Most youngsters learn these basic skills naturally, but for others they need to be taught directly. Although very few preschoolers are identified as having learning disabilities, those who do have such disabilities, along with some peers without disabilities, begin their struggle learning to read during these early years. For many of them, early action by teachers can divert their path away from reading and school failure toward success. Let's first look at these foundation skills and then learn about some ways in which teachers can make a difference in the results of these preschoolers.

Learning basic reading skills like sound-to-symbol relationships is essential for reading success. Students who do not learn these skills naturally must receive direct instruction aimed at achieving mastery. The preschoolers are listening to a story about Willy the gorilla and his adventures.

Core Skills of Reading

Reading is crucial to school success, and it is a skill that is difficult for most students with learning disabilities to master. Researchers are now confident that the essential, foundation, or core skills that make for good readers are developed much early than was originally thought (Jenkins & O'Connor, 2002). In particular, three skills that begin to develop during the preschool years are important for later success with reading. They are

- Phonological awareness
- Rapid naming of alphabetic sounds and letters
- Beginning phonics

Mastering language is a prerequisite for reading. As you learned in the previous chapter, the importance of facility with language explains why so many preschoolers who are identified with language impairments during the preschool years are identified with learning disabilities during their school years. One important set of skills both for language development and for later reading success is **phonological awareness**—identifying, separating, and manipulating the sound units of spoken language (Vaughn & Linan-Thompson, 2004). Indicators of phonological awareness include hearing and identifying sounds in words, breaking or segmenting words and phrases into their smallest units, and rhyming. Although some experts believe that skills such as actual letter and word identification and decoding are superior to phonological awareness as predictors of which students will later have trouble mastering reading, it is clear that this core skill develops early (Hammill, 2004; Ehri et al., 2001; Nelson, Benner, & Gonzalez, 2003). The second skill that seems to predict later success with reading is **letter fluency**, which is indicated by calling out quickly the letters of the alphabet upon seeing them in any order (Speece et al., 2003). The third set of skills that begins to develop during these early years is **phonics**—the ability to decipher printed words or identify the sounds that are represented by individual letters and groups of letters. A good start on learning phonics and on learning how to decode printed words is also an indication that the individual will become a good reader (Bursuck et al., 2004). These three skills, along with others (such as vocabulary and sight word development), form the early foundations for the good start students need as they begin the process of mastering reading. For those who do not develop these skills on their own, teachers can make a real difference through instruction. It is also important to understand that teaching isolated skills, such as phonological awareness or rapid naming of letters and their sounds, might not be sufficient for many students with reading/learning disabilities. They are more likely to need intensive instruction to put those and other core skills together to become proficient readers (Hammill, 2004; Swanson et al., 2003).

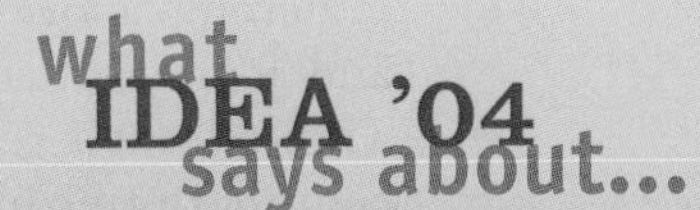

Early Intervening Services

In order to provide early intervening services, a local educational agency (e.g., school district) may

- Use a specified portion of IDEA funds for students in kindergarten through grade 12 who need additional academic and behavioral support to succeed in the general education classroom but have not yet been identified as needing special education or related services
- Emphasize services for students in kindergarten through grade 3

The services and activities provided may include

- Professional development for teachers and other school staff that will enable them to deliver scientifically based academic instruction and behavioral interventions
- Instruction for teachers and school staff on the use of adaptive and instructional software
- Educational and behavioral evaluations, services, and supports (which may include scientifically based literacy instruction

Early Reading Instruction

Thus the origins of literacy take shape during early childhood, long before children actually begin to read (Dickinson & McCabe, 2001). Early instruction in phonological awareness (e.g., *cat* has three sounds, *fall* and *wall* rhyme), letter naming, and decoding is helpful for all preschoolers (Pullen & Justice, 2003). Whether they are English language learners with learning disabilities or native English speakers, for preschoolers and kindergarteners who do not learn these precursors to reading on their own, instruction in these very important skills can avoid later reading problems (Leafstedt, Richards, & Gerber, 2004). For some, direct instruction in the general preschool or general education setting is sufficient; for others, intensive intervention is necessary. In either case, a long-term, positive impact on youngsters' reading abilities can be the outcome (Fuchs, Fuchs, & Thompson, 2002). Unfortunately, success is not universal, and some 30 percent of these youngsters remain resistant to treatment (Jenkins & O'Connor, 2002).

In addition to explicit instruction on skills that form the foundation for reading, preschool and kindergarten teachers should not lose sight of the importance of developing language- and literacy-rich environments (Katims, 1994). Literacy is not just decoding or even comprehending the printed work; it is a reflection of a greater set of skills and abilities that include reflective thinking. Children need

phonological awareness Identifying, separating, or manipulating sound units of spoken language

letter fluency Quickly reading and naming letters of the alphabet

phonics The sounds represented by letters and letter-groups to develop a love for reading, to gain skills and attitudes that favor future literacy, and to recognize both that reading is important to them and that it is fun. Through their retelling and reenacting their favorite stories, the important concept that print has meaning is understood early and becomes a basis for future instruction.

Teaching Students with Learning Disabilities

Again, one defining characteristic of individuals with learning disabilities is their unexpected underachievement—performance that demands a unique, individualized, and intensive reaction. These students' low achievement separates them more each school year from their classmates without disabilities (Deshler, 2005), as is illustrated in Figure 5.5.

Access to the General Education Curriculum: Early Intervening

In this chapter we have stressed the importance of preschoolers and students in the elementary grades developing the foundation skills for reading. In the early grades, reading is an academic target for instruction, but quickly it becomes a skill needed for overall academic success. Reading is one important way in which students access the content presented in the basic general education curriculum. Whether students are at risk for school failure, are diverse learners facing the challenges of learning English as a second language, or are on the way to being identified as having learning disabilities, it is critical that they receive extra help and learn the core skills of reading (see Table 5.3) as early as possible. The exciting news is that explicit instruction in these core skills makes a genuine difference and can turn many struggling readers into confident readers (Bishop, 2003; Bursuck et al., 2004).

What makes educators so certain about the power and importance of providing explicit instruction in the core skills of reading as soon as students show signs of strug-

Figure 5.5 • The Widening Performance Gap Between Students with and without Learning Disabilities as They Get Older

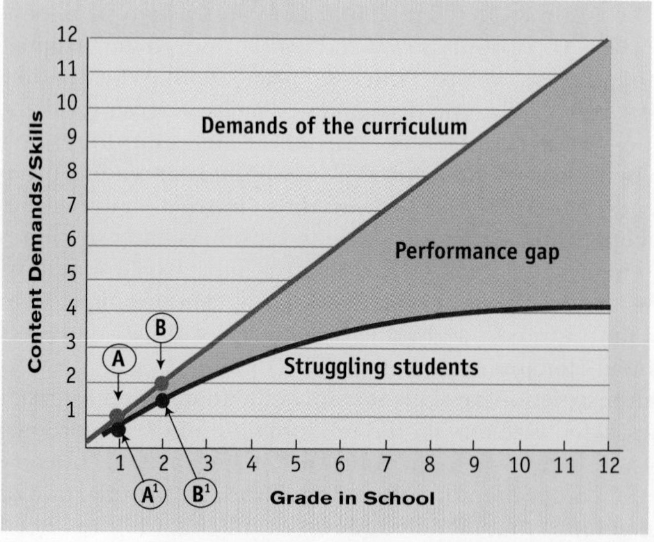

NOTE: First grade student (A) and second grade student (B) is meeting the demands of the curriculum, showing grade-level achievement. Struggling first grade student (A^1) and second grade student (B^1) begin the path of under achievement.

Source: "A closer look: Closing the performance gap" by D. D. Deshler, *StrateNotes, 13* (January 2005), page 1. Reprinted by permission.

Table 5.3 • Core Skills of Reading

Domain	Explanation	Example
Phonological awareness	Includes identifying smallest units of sound, segmenting words (breaking words into sound units), manipulating sounds in words	Knowing *cat* has three sound units, c-a-t Saying each sound (phoneme) in the word *cat* Rhyming *cat* and *mat*
Letter–sound correspondence	Knowing the sound each letter or combinations of letters represents	Identifying the names and sounds of letters presented in random order
Phonics	Sound–symbol relationships for reading and spelling	The letter *s* indicates both the sounds *s* and the sound *z* as in *saw* and *was*
Word identification fluency	Reads individual words quickly	Reads words from lists accurately and at a satisfactory rate
Fluency	Reads passages orally correctly and quickly	Reads sentences and paragraphs accurately and at a satisfactory rate
Comprehension	Comprehends reading passages	Understands content of a paragraph

gling? Here are some key findings that support this conclusion (Dion et al., 2004; Ehri et al., 2001; Fuchs, Fuchs, & Compton, 2004):

- Students who fail to acquire the core skills of reading soon after entering school become poor readers.
- Students who complete first grade without having mastered phonological awareness tend to be poor readers in fourth grade.
- Readers who are struggling at third grade tend to be poor readers at ninth grade.
- Struggling readers do not catch up on their own.
- Intensive and explicit instruction on the core skills of reading (such as sound–symbol relationships), delivered early, often helps such students become better readers.

Armed with the knowledge that intervening early can be critical to the success of so many students, federal, state, and school district officials have been trying to figure out how to get additional services to all students who need them. Of course, students with reading/learning disabilities qualify for special education. For them, intensive and explicit instruction is part of their IEPs and their guarantee for an appropriate education. However, for those who do not have disabilities (or have not yet qualified for special education), the challenge is to get services to them quickly. IDEA '04 allows restricted funding for a new process to deliver prevention services to struggling learners. **Early intervening** brings intensive instruction to all struggling learners in the hope of preventing learning problems that will only compound as time passes. See *What IDEA '04 Says About Early Intervening Services* on page 179 to learn what the law allows.

Instructional Accommodations

Universal design for learning, which we discussed in Chapter 2 on pages 42–43, provides multiple ways for all students to access the general education curriculum. You may recall that universal design for learning uses the computer to provide greater access to printed material for those students who profit more by listening to

early intervening Providing explicit and intensive instruction to all struggling students to prevent the compounding of learning problems

Accommodating for Inclusive Environments

Adjusting Content and Providing Instructional Supports

Provide Structure and a Standard Set of Expectations

- Help students develop organizational skills.
- Establish sets of rules for academic and social activities and tasks.
- Adhere to a well-planned schedule.
- Match your language to the comprehension level of the student.
- Be consistent.

Adjust Instructional Materials and Activities

- Individualize instruction; be sure the reading level is appropriate.
- Break tasks down into smaller pieces (or chunks).
- Begin lessons with advance organizers.
- Supplement oral and written assignments with learning aids (computers).
- Assign a peer tutor.
- Modify tests, allowing the student to take more time or complete the test in a different way (listen to a tape of the test).
- Evaluate the effectiveness of your instructional interventions, and when they are not effective, change them.

Give Students Feedback and Reinforcement for Success

- Tell students when they are behaving properly.
- Reward students for improvement.
- Praise students when they have done well or accomplished a goal.
- Inform students when they are not meeting expectations.
- Encourage students to develop partnerships among themselves, and reinforce those who do so.

Make Tasks Interesting

- Develop attention by making assignments interesting and novel.
- Vary the format of instruction and activities.
- Use high-interest curriculum materials.
- Encourage students to work together during extracurricular activities.

print-to-speech translations of texts or by being able to refer to definitions or examples of difficult words and concepts. Clearly, classroom computers can be used to make excellent accommodations. On the horizon is a special typeface for use in textbooks. For the benefit of students with reading/learning disabilities, the typeface was designed specifically to avoid letters that can be inverted or mirrored (Curtis, 2005). Read Regular® (see Figure 5.6 to see examples of this new typeface) helps clarify specific letters that are often confusing by making them more clearly unique (Frensch, 2005). Also, teachers who adjust the content and presentation of

Figure 5.6 • Example of Read Regular® and Times Roman Typefaces

abcde	abcde
nopqr	nopqr
Read Regular®	Times Roman

Source: Read Regular typeface copyright © 2001–2005 by Natascha Frensch. Reprinted by permission.

their instruction improve outcomes of students with disabilities. Some techniques are useful for students with many different disabilities but are critically important to the success of students with learning disabilities. For example, the link between learning disabilities and language impairments is now clear. Therefore, teachers who adjust their language to the level of listening comprehension of their students or break learning tasks into smaller segments help many students with many different types of learning needs. *Accommodating for Inclusive Environments* provides several ideas about adjusting content and providing instructional supports to students.

When peers tutor each other, the academic performance for each member of the pair of students improves, and teachers are free to work with other students.

Validated Practices

Over 30 years of research findings have demonstrated that students with learning disabilities learn well when taught with validated practices (Swanson & Sachse-Lee, 2000; Vaughn, Gersten, & Chard, 2000). Teachers must deliberately select instructional materials and procedures that have been systematically evaluated, even though they will not be uniformly powerful. Remember that students with learning disabilities have great individual differences. Because of their heterogeneity, teachers cannot assume that a tactic effective with one student will be effective with every other. Let's consider two practices that have broad applications:

- Peer tutoring
- Learning strategies

Having students teach each other—**peer tutoring**—is one practice that is consistently effective across all grades and subjects (e.g., early ready skills, reading comprehension, mastery of high school world history). It also benefits different types of learners, such as those at risk, English language learners, and students with learning disabilities (Fuchs, Fuchs, Al Otaiba et al., 2001; Mastropieri et al., 2003; Sáenz, Fuchs, & Fuchs, 2005). Teachers are most excited about one particular application of peer tutoring, **Peer-Assisted Learning Strategies (PALS)**. PALS is an instructional tactic utilizing classmates as academic peer tutors. It works with students often referred to as difficult to teach, can be implemented with entire classes of general education students, and frees teachers to work more intensively with students who need more help (Dion et al, 2004; Mathes & Babyak, 2001). Many general education teachers use PALS during the pre-referral and RTI process described in the Assessment section of this chapter. This one-on-one tutoring system is considered to be of low intensity and seems powerful enough to help about 80 percent of low-achieving students (Mathes, Torgesen, & Allor, 2001). The remaining students require more intensive one-on-one instruction. See *Validated Practices* to learn how PALS is put into action.

Another set of validated practices developed for middle school and high school students with learning disabilities helps them become more strategic learners. Don Deshler, Jean Schumaker, and their colleagues at the University of Kansas Center for Research on Learning began developing the learning strategies approach some 25 years ago. Their work has grown from one strategy into a powerful and effective curriculum (Deshler et al., 2001; Swanson & Sachse-Lee, 2000). Its purpose is to give these students a plan and methods for success. The **Learning Strategies Curriculum** comprises many individual learning strategies that help students learn and remember information more efficiently. These powerful interventions help students compensate for their learning disabilities (Deshler, 2005; Deshler & Roth, 2002).

The learning strategies concept caused the nation to change its thinking about the purpose of high school special education. Formerly, secondary special education teachers practiced "crisis teaching"—that is, tutoring students with learning disabilities so that they might have a better chance of receiving a passing grade on tomorrow's test or the term paper due next week. The Learning Strategies

peer tutoring Students teaching each other

Peer-Assisted Learning Strategies (PALS) A validated method wherein students coach each other to improve academic learning; peer tutoring for reading and mathematics

Learning Strategies Curriculum Instructional methods to help students read, comprehend, and study better by helping them organize and collect information strategically; a supplemental high school curriculum designed for students with learning disabilities; developed at the University of Kansas Center for Research on Learning

Validated Practices Peer-Assisted Learning Strategies (PAL

What Is PALS?

Peer-Assisted Learning Strategies (PALS) is an instructional approach that uses classmates as tutors who exchange the roles of coaches and players. PALS is used across a wide range of grade levels—from kindergarten through high school—to teach students many different skills. For example, kindergarteners have helped each other learn the core or foundations skills of reading (e.g., sound–symbol relationships, sight words). English language learners (ELLs) with learning disabilities have improved their reading comprehension, and middle school students have improved their skill in charting and graphing data.

Why PALS Is beneficial

The PALS instructional approach multiplies the opportunities for individualized instruction and the implementation of validated instructional tactics across entire classes of students. Using classmates as teachers frees the teacher to provide more intensive supports to students who need them the most. The procedures also actively involve students in learning. When students are trained in how to tutor and are taught the instructional tactic they are applying, peer tutoring has consistently proved effective, boosting gains in learning. Also, students report that they enjoy tutoring each other, which adds a motivating element to the classroom routine.

Implementing PALS

PALS is designed to supplement, not replace, regular instructional routines or elements of the standards-based curriculum. Before classmates work together, the teacher instructs the class about the application of the tactic, the roles each pair will exchange, when to take turns, and how to provide corrective feedback. The teacher practices the instructional routines with the entire class until they demonstrate understanding of their roles and responsibilities. Student pairs work together on a specific academic task (e.g., letter–sound recognition in reading, sight word vocabulary, math facts, story comprehension) for four weeks and then switch partners. Here's a general example of how PALS is applied:

Frequency

- PALS is usually scheduled three or four times per week.
- Sessions last between 20 and 35 minutes.
- Each session is divided into 10-minute segments so each peer has a turn as coach and player.
- Sessions may be divided in half so that more than one skill can be the target of instruction.
- Sessions continue for a semester or half of the school year.

Partners

- Rank-order students in a class from the strongest to the weakest on the targeted skill.
- Divide the class in half.
- Pair the top-ranked student in the high-performing group with the top-ranked student in the low-performing group.
- Continue the process until every student has a partner.
- Each member of the pair, during every session, takes a turn at being the "coach," or tutor, and being the "player," or student being tutored.

Curriculum includes many different strategies and addresses a variety of skills that students with learning disabilities need to access the general education curriculum successfully and perform well on state- and district-wide assessments. Some strategies help students write multiparagraph themes, personal narratives, reports, letters, and even essays (Isaacson, 2004; Schumaker & Deshler, 2003). Many strategies assist students in gaining meaning from complicated social studies and science texts, and others help them remember information.

Each learning strategy typically includes these key features:

- Advance organizers
- Step-by-step procedures for application of the strategy
- Mnemonics
- Built-in systems for progress monitoring

advance organizers A tactic that previews lectures and provides organizing structures to acquaint students with the content, its organization, and its importance before the lesson

At the beginning of a lesson or unit, students are given a rationale, or reason, to learn and apply a strategy ("This strategy will help you remember history better"). Accordingly, each unit begins with an **advance organizer** that explains to students why the content is important ("This information will be on the state's achievement test") and mentions some features of the content on which to focus their

- Student pairs work together for about a month and then are assigned new partners.

Roles

- The coach asks the player to do the task (e.g., read a passage, compute subtraction problems).
- The player performs the task (e.g., reads out loud, solves the problems).
- The coach listens or watches and provides corrective feedback.
- Pairs change roles every 10 minutes.

Figure A is a sample worksheet for use by a pair of kindergarten students learning sight words. Special worksheets or materials do not have to be prepared to implement peer tutoring. Texts and workbooks used for standard instruction can be utilized for PALS lessons.

What Word?

Students learn to recognize common words (sight words) that cannot be easily sounded out.

The coach points to the sight word on a lesson page and asks,

- "What word?"
- The Player responds.

The coach follows with praise or correction, as in the "What Sound" activity.

- Students take turns identifying the words.
- Lessons build cumulatively across lessons.

Figure A • "What word?" Activity from Lesson 30.

				What word?
and	on	was	is	
the	and	is	was	
☺	☺	☺	☺	

This scientifically validated practice is a teaching method that has been proved effective by many systematic research efforts. A complete annotated reference list can be found on the PALS Web site: **http://kc.vanderbilt.edu/kennedy/pals**. Interactive modules demonstrating K-PALS (for kindergarteners) and PALS (for elementary-age students learning to read) are available on the IRIS Web site: **http://iris.peabody.vanderbilt.edu**

Source: Copyright © IRIS Center for Faculty Enhancement, Vanderbilt University and the John F. Kennedy Center, PALS Project. **http://iris.peabody.vanderbilt.edu** Reprinted by permission.

—By Kimberly Paulsen, Vanderbilt University

attention ("Notice that the American soldiers in the Revolutionary War used nonconventional fighting tactics, while the British soldiers lined up in rows, shooting their rifles in the traditional way across a field"). Each strategy is organized systematically and follows a definite sequence. To help students remember the strategy, the first letters of the steps spell out an easy word to remember. Try this simple paraphrasing strategy as you study this chapter; it has helped thousands of high school students remember information from general education texts. The strategy is called RAP:

Read the paragraph.

Ask yourself the Main Idea and Details in the paragraph.

Put the Main Idea and Details in your own words.

Notice that RAP is a mnemonic. **Mnemonics** are memory aids that help people remember items that go together. These simple "word tricks" are useful when preparing for tests (even the SAT), learning vocabulary needed to access the general education curriculum, or studying complex information (Jitendra et al., 2004; Mastropieri & Scruggs, 1997; Terrill, Scruggs, & Mastropieri, 2004). Here's another

mnemonics A learning strategy that promotes remembering information by associating the first letters of items in a list with a word, sentence, or picture (e.g., HOMES for the Great Lakes)

Figure 5.7 • The Great Lakes Mnemonic: HOMES

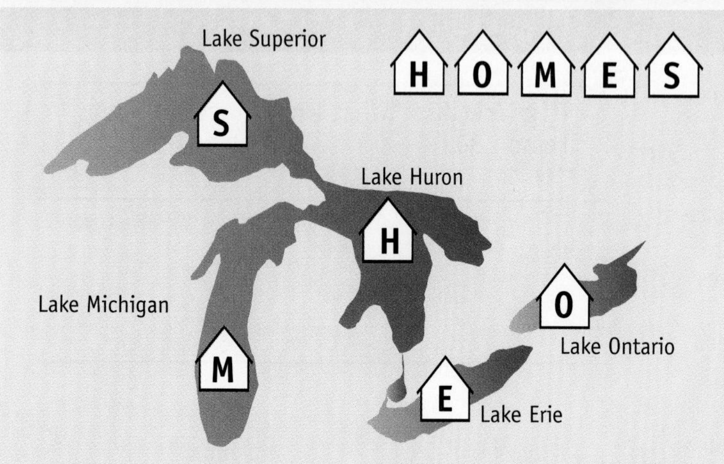

example, one that is also shown in Figure 5.7: The word HOMES helps us remember the names of the Great Lakes (Huron, Ontario, Michigan, Erie, and Superior).

Technology

Today, computers are common in schools and at home. The 1990s saw expanded capabilities of computers as well as substantial price reductions, making access to technology available to all students in most school settings. The benefits to students with disabilities are many, and the possibilities opened up by technology continue to be discovered. Some educators are suggesting that technology be viewed as a "cognitive prosthesis" for students with learning disabilities (Lewis, 1998). Rapid advances have changed the way educators design instructional opportunities. Let's look at a few of those advances and see how they benefit students with learning disabilities. For example, technology can

- Augment an individual's strengths
- Compensate for the effects of disabilities
- Provide alternative modes of performing tasks

Much of the technology that benefits everyone is particularly useful to students with learning disabilities by helping them become more efficient and effective learners (Bryant & Bryant, 2003; Raskind & Higgins, 1998). Table 5.4 highlights some of these benefits and suggests how assistive technology can reduce the barriers to success that these individuals face at home, at school, and in daily life. Special devices dedicated to one function, such as the Quicktionary Reading Pen from Seiko Instruments, which actually rolls over a printed word and both provides a definition and "says" the word for the user, can help students compensate for a particular problem. In Chapter 4 you learned about graphic organizers, such as story maps and about special software, such as *Kidspiration*® and *Inspiration*®, that help students of all ages to take notes or create visual displays of the content being learned. (See again *Validated Practices* on page 146.) Graphic organizers have application across academic subjects and ages and are especially useful when the student is organizing the content being studied for social studies or science. Their effectiveness in helping students comprehend even difficult reading passages in basal readers or high school science texts has been demonstrated again and again (Boulineau et al., 2004; Masterpieri et al., 2003). Translating content into visual displays is also helpful to students with mathematics/learning disabilities studying algebra—one subject that is a "gatekeeper" to a standard high school diploma (Ives & Hoy, 2003).

As you learned earlier in this chapter, one characteristic that most students with learning disabilities share is their poor motivation for learning. Many teachers describe students with learning disabilities as "inactive learners." We also noted that teachers can make a difference by assigning work that is interesting and interactive. Incorporating technology with instruction serves two purposes: It can help students with learning disabilities participate more fully in the general education curriculum, and it creates active learning environments (Bryant & Bryant, 2003). The Internet and related telecommunications applications (such as e-mail) have great benefits for us all, but particularly for students with learning disabilities. Here are some examples: Instead of just reading about art and history in textbooks, students can visit virtual museums and libraries all around the world to experience the content of their teacher's lessons. And students who are studying World War II in Holland can find information about Anne Frank to use in class

Table 5.4 • Assistive Technology Options for Students with Learning Disabilities

Barriers	Difficulties	Assistive Technology Solution
Print	Reading	Audiotaped books "Talking" computers Captioned film and videos Semantic mapping software (story mapping) Web-based texts Hypermedia and hypertext
	Writing	Word processing programs (including grammar assistance) Desktop publishing Computer-based thesauruses Editing aids Planning aids Word prediction software
	Spelling	Spellcheckers Voice input devices
Communication	Organization	Manipulating graphics Presentation packages (e.g., Powerpoint, Persuasion) Semantic mapping software
	Speech	E-mail Voice output systems Sythesized speech
Solving problems	Calculating	Handheld calculators Spreadsheets Graphics programs
Being organized	Daily life	Personal organizers Electronic calendars Computer "stickies" Electronic address books
	Study skills	Organizing software (outlines, graphic organizers) Timing devices
Learning	Researching topics	CD-ROM-based reference books Internet databases Computer-based instruction (hypermedia, hypertext)
	Remembering	Outlining systems (main ideas from details)

reports and term papers (Mulholland, 2005). The Web offers excitement and enrichment that might otherwise be missing from the curriculum. It also might provide the motivation necessary to elicit the extra effort that students with learning disabilities must invest.

Word processing technology is also a boon to students with learning disabilities who need to improve their writing abilities or who find writing assignments aversive (Graham, Harris, & Larsen, 2001; MacArthur, 2000). The task of writing a term paper and other major assignments can be daunting for students with learning disabilities. Many give up before completing all of the steps necessary to produce a final version: select a topic, generate and organize the content of their paper, create drafts of the text, revise it, proofread it, edit it, and so on. However, print on a computer screen is easier to see and read than print on paper. The spellchecker, thesaurus, and grammar correction functions available on most word processing programs are a big help to those struggling to get a term paper written. A written paper produced on a computer is more attractive than the often-messy product of students with poor handwriting and visual organizational skills. Many features of word processing programs (e.g., table features, tracking for editing, word predictions) help students improve both the quality and the quantity of their writing (Bryant & Bryant, 2003). The computer can also facilitate collaboration between students, making it easier for two or more students to work together on a writing task. Advances in software and hardware can help students with learning disabilities compensate for their learning challenges. However, teachers and parents must beware: Not all software is equally useful, and not all of it has been carefully evaluated (Higgins, Boone, & Williams, 2000).

Transition

Many adults with learning disabilities have productive careers and are highly successful, but too often people with this disability struggle to realize their potential. Clearly, the experiences of adults with learning disabilities are as varied as the population itself. What we know is that despite individual success stories, there is room for a lot of improvement. One key to positive results is postsecondary education. Let's first consider the outcomes of adults and then turn our attention to how postsecondary educational experiences can make a real difference in the lives of these individuals.

Adult Outcomes

Remember the story you read in this chapter's "Making a Difference" section about Charles Schwab, the founder of the discount stock brokerage firm. He is not the only billionaire with learning disabilities (Jones, 2003). Richard Branson, a British entrepreneur whose first business was a mail-order record sales company and whose second business was Virgin Music (a highly successful recording studio), is probably best known in the United States as the founder of the Virgin Atlantic Air, the discount airline. Less well known is that Branson had a reading disability and reports that he continues to struggle with spelling (Branson, 1998). Another billionaire with reading disabilities is Craig McCaw, who is often credited with pioneering the nation's wireless (cell phone) communications systems (Academy of Achievement, 2005). These highly successful businessmen are not the only individuals who have been able to overcome or compensate for their problems. For example, several present-day celebrities—Cher, Magic Johnson, Brook Theiss, Bruce Jenner, and Greg Louganis, among others—have acknowledged having a learning disability. And Stephen Cannell, a prolific TV writer and producer (*The Rockford Files, The A-Team, Hunter*) and author, has learning disabilities (Cannell, 1999). Success stories also are told about individuals from previous times presumed by many to have had learning disabilities. Debate continues, for example, about whether Hans Christian Andersen and Albert Einstein had the condition (Aaron, Phillips, & Larsen, 1988; Kihl, Gregersen, & Sterum, 2000; Thomas, 2000). And many are convinced that Leonardo da Vinci, Thomas Edison, Nelson Rockefeller, and President Woodrow Wilson had learning disabilities.

For most adults with learning disabilities, being rich or famous is not in their futures, but being happy and productive should be a goal for each of them. For many adults with learning disabilities, life is complicated by problems that began in early childhood. Even those individuals who compete well in college often report persistent problems with reading and writing (Wilson & Lesaux, 2001). Many explain that they have difficulty understanding what they read, retaining information, and reading quickly enough to feel effective in daily life (Shessel & Reiff, 1999). As you have learned throughout this book so far, validated practices used today bring about great improvements in performance. In fact, the use of these effective teaching tactics may well be one reason why high school graduation rates and college attendance rates have increased for these individuals. More and more adults with learning disabilities are college graduates, earn the same wages as their coworkers without disabilities, and report high satisfaction with their jobs (Madaus et al., 2003).

Attending college is becoming a reality for more and more students with learning disabilities, and what a difference this experience can make in their lives.

It is important for teachers to recognize that improved academic performance is not the only answer to better outcomes for these individuals. Teachers can help students master additional sets of important life skills, such as self-advocacy and self-regulation. For example, **self-advocacy**—being able to explain what accommodations help improve performance and to ask for them—can make a real difference at school, in the workplace, and for life in general (Gerber & Price, 2003). Learning how to advocate effectively for oneself is not always easy. It requires the individual to truly understand the problem that needs to be addressed, what accommodation helps to overcome the challenge, and how and when that accommodation should be put into effect. And the individual needs to be able to discuss the problem and potential solutions in a positive, nonthreatening manner. Employers, particularly in this age of the Americans with Disabilities Act (ADA), report that they would like to know how to help their employees with disabilities perform optimally, but too often they don't even know that they have hired a person with a learning disability. The reason for this is that many workers with learning disabilities believe they face discrimination on the job, and they fear that revealing their disability to their employers will result in negative consequences (Dickinson & Verbeek, 2002). These beliefs may stem from their insecurities, negative self-concepts, and internalized assumptions about being "dumb" because they were unable to compete successfully during their school years. Teachers can help replace this negative thinking with the pride that comes from setting and attaining goals. They can also help their students understand and explain, to employers and others, the challenges their learning disabilities present and which accommodations actually reduce their impact.

Workers with learning disabilities who have college degrees earn substantially more than those who did not receive postsecondary degrees (Madaus et al., 2003). Among these college graduates, two important factors lead to success and job satisfaction. First, those workers who use accommodations at work have high job satisfaction. Second, college graduates with learning disabilities who like their jobs indicate that they use **self-regulation** techniques—strategies that help them be independent, such as setting goals for themselves and using time effectively. This information should help teachers decide which additional curriculum targets are important for middle school and high school students with learning disabilities. Helping more of these individuals transition to postsecondary education is clearly a promising way to improve their quality of life and success as adults. Let's consider these issues next.

Postsecondary Options

Although the number of college students and graduates with learning disabilities is increasing, the number could be far greater (Sitlington, 2003). Many individuals with learning disabilities believe that **postsecondary education**—educational opportunities beyond high school—is not an option for them because they did not complete high school. Whereas the high school graduation rate for all of America's students is 72 percent, it is 62 percent for those with learning disabilities; the other

self-advocacy Capacity to understand, ask for, and explain one's need for accommodations

self-regulation Managing one's own behaviors through goal setting, time management, self-reinforcement, and other self-management techniques

postsecondary education Educational opportunities beyond high school; two-year or four-year colleges and universities

Cartoon by Mike Lynch. Reprinted by permission.

28 percent drop out of high school (National Center for Educational Statistics [NCES], 2003; U.S. Department of Education, 2002). However, for both those who are high school graduates and those who are not, college attendance is now more of a possibility. Although entrance requirements vary greatly from college to college, many community colleges do not require their students to have a high school diploma or even a graduation equivalence diploma or certificate (GED) (Savukinas, 2002). And some colleges even have a separate admissions route for students with disabilities (Madaus, 2005). Today the ADA also helps students with disabilities once they are admitted. The law makes it quite clear: Students with disabilities must have access to postsecondary education, and colleges and universities must make reasonable accommodations to ensure such access (Simon, 2001). However, supports and services vary greatly. The offices of disability services at some colleges and universities have large staffs that offer many different services (e.g., tutoring, study groups, instruction about time management, coordination of testing accommodations), but other such offices may have only one staff member who provides help in locating interpreters for the deaf, in obtaining e-textbooks, or arranging for testing accommodations (Block, 2005).

More and more people with disabilities are taking advantage of 2-year and 4-year postsecondary educational opportunities. In 1978 only 3 percent of college first-year students reported having a disability, whereas in 1998 some 9 percent of all undergraduates reported that they have a disability. Of those, 11 percent indicated that they had learning disabilities (the largest group—29 percent—of college students with disabilities were those with physical impairments). However, over half (51 percent) of all college students with disabilities who asked for accommodations were students with learning disabilities (NCES, 2003). Clearly, learning self-regulation and self-advocacy skills in high school are generalizing to the postsecondary experience and yielding success that is seen later in the workplace!

What supports and accommodations are becoming more widely available to assist students during their college experience? Here are some recommended by parents and professionals in this area (Mull, Sitlington, & Alper, 2001; Ofiesh, Hughes, & Scott, 2004):

- Alternative exam formats
- Extended time
- Electronic versions of textbooks
- Tutors
- Readers, classroom notetakers, or scribes
- Registration assistance, priority class registration, course substitutions
- Adaptive equipment and technology (phonetic spellcheckers, hand-held organizers)
- Flexible course schedules

Some college graduates with learning disabilities have some additional recommendations to help others succeed (Mooney & Cole, 2000). One important tip is to get organized: Every notebook should have a return address, backpacks and notebooks need a consistent "home" or place to be stored, notes and notebooks should be reorganized weekly, and mental checklists should be completed at the end of every class ("Do I have all of my stuff?" "Did I leave anything under the seat?" Middle school and high school teachers can help students master these self-management skills before they enter college. Because attending college is often a family decision, we continue this conversation about students with learning disabilities and postsecondary experiences in the section Partnerships with Families and Communities.

Collaboration

More than ever before, the importance of general education professionals working closely with specialists in learning disabilities is self-evident. Two major shifts in practice make real partnerships a necessity:

- The inclusion of more and more students with learning disabilities in the general education classroom
- The increased role of general education teachers in the pre-referral process and the multilevel, RTI identification system for students with learning disabilities (review this chapter's Assessment section)

Before considering these growing realities in today's classrooms, let's examine the concept of collaboration and what it takes to make it work. Collaboration—educators with different areas of expertise working in partnerships—is one key to the development of successful educational experiences for students who are difficult to teach (Friend & Bursuck, 2006). "True" collaboration blooms when certain important conditions exist:

- Communication is open and ongoing.
- Participation is voluntary.
- Parity exists in the relationship.
- Goals are shared.
- Evaluation of student performance is continual.
- Decision making is done as a team.
- Resources are pooled.
- Trust and respect are the basis of the partnership.
- Planning time is scheduled.

In such collaborative settings, all students profit. General education students benefit from the unique expertise of the special educator, and students with disabilities find the general education classroom responsive to their learning needs.

Are there many opportunities for collaboration among special and general education professionals? The answer is "yes!" It is particularly true for students with learning disabilities. As you will recall, they represent nearly half of all students identified by the schools as having a disability and thus qualifying for special education services. And, almost all of them spend almost 80 percent of their school day in the general education classroom, accessing the general education curriculum. In fact, fewer resource rooms are in operation today than some 15 years ago. In 1988–89, 58 percent of students with learning disabilities received special education services through resource room arrangements; in 1999–2000, that figure had dropped to 37 percent (U.S. Department of Education, 1991, 2005a). As the number of resource rooms is declining, however, the size of these classes is increasing to levels that sometimes exceed the general education class size (Moody et al., 2000). Therefore, special and general education teachers must forge effective partnerships to deliver an appropriate education to these students.

Even with the best collaborative efforts, however, some students with learning disabilities need more intensive instruction than can be offered in the general education setting (Deshler et al., 2001). Sometimes, to actually master a learning strategy, these students need many opportunities for individualized instruction, repeated practice, feedback from the instructor, and extra time to become independent in the learning strategy's use. Often, this instruction needs to be delivered

Considering Culture

Service Challenges in College Learning Disabilities

All eyes in the family are on Alan. He is to be the first member of the family to go to college. His parents have worked hard all of their lives for this moment, and they are so proud that Alan was admitted to the *premier* university in the state. Their words of advice as he trundled off to his new experience were to "always work hard and make your family proud!" But his first semester at college has been a learning experience in more ways than one! Alan has alternately been thrilled to be in college, and totally disheartened and determined to drop out of college and get a job. He often laments, "Why does this have to be so hard! Why is it happening to me now? How can I face my family? I can't tell them that I need 'special help' in *college*!"

Alan reflects on the support he had in high school. There his teachers did so much to help him, because he was identified as having learning disabilities and he had an IEP. He typically was allowed more time on tests, his teachers reviewed notes with him and worked with him individually, and at times they gave him optional assignments. He also received individualized coaching on study skills. His grades were excellent. In fact, in his senior year when he told a friend that he had learning disabilities, she exclaimed, "How can that be? You're so smart!"

But college was a whole different ballgame. No one seemed to care. He was truly on his own. At the advice of classmates in his dorm, he signed up for a linguistics class that freshmen often took. He floundered. Learning the phonetic alphabet was not his cup of tea! His academic world seemed to be falling apart. But then his life turned around when one of his professors suggested that he work with the campus Office for Students with Disabilities. What a difference that made! The staff there helped him find notetakers for classes, encouraged him to use computers in class as needed, and helped him get approval to have more time for tests. They even worked with him to find an alternative to fulfill the university's foreign language requirement. He also learned to screen classes and then select those that best suited his learning style.

Questions to Consider

1 Think about your family's expectations for your development and your future. What cultural values, beliefs, and events in your family's history have you internalized and have probably played a role in your goal setting? (Some of these may be so subtle that they are difficult to identify.)

2 We often think that cultural issues apply only to people who speak a language other than English or who were not born in this country. What are some primary values inherent in the majority culture? How are these enacted in our educational systems?

— By Eleanor Lynch, San Diego State University, and Marci Hanson, San Francisco State University

by a specialist. Once the skill or strategy is mastered, the student can apply it in the general education classroom. Here again, the general education and special education teachers must work closely together to be sure the student actually uses this new information appropriately within the general education content and curriculum. Students who have difficulty transferring knowledge and information to other settings and situations require extra supports from their teachers working as a team. Here's how teachers can help students generalize the application of a study strategy, such as RAP, to a general education science class—and also help students take more responsibility for managing their own instructional programs: The special education teacher explains the RAP strategy to the science teacher and asks the science teacher (1) to remind the student to apply the strategy while studying and (2) to check to be sure that the student is using RAP correctly. The special education teacher then teaches the student to keep a record of the times he or she used the strategy. Finally, the teacher rewards the student for improved performance in science class.

Partnerships with Families and Communities

So many issues are important to families of individuals with disabilities. Throughout this book we highlight many concerns unique to these parents and families. In this chapter, we briefly discuss two issues that on the surface do not seem to be uniquely pertinent to individuals with learning disabilities. But recently they have taken on greater importance to such students. As you have just learned, more and more students with learning disabilities are continuing their educational careers on through the postsecondary years. College selection decisions are a major event for most of us, but if you have learning disabilities, picking the right college is often the key to becoming a graduate. Also, with the ever-increasing inclusion of students with disabilities in general education programs, and with more and more expectations for students with learning disabilities to access the general education curriculum, homework has taken on greater meaning for these students. We will examine both of these issues, first turning our attention to the developing (and changing) partnership between parents and their children with learning disabilities in selecting the "right" college and then turning our attention to homework.

College Selection

Leaving high school can be a troubling time for both the individual with learning disabilities and her or his family (Madaus, 2005). In high school, students have IEPs to guide the delivery of their educational programs and supportive services. There is no IEP for college. In high school, students' teachers often seek them out; such is not the case in the typical college experience. Flexibility and freedom of choice can be almost overwhelming, and as you will read in *Considering Culture*, they can be significant issues for many families of these students.

For all students, picking the right college is one key to a successful outcome. College can be a more positive experience for students with learning disabilities if they plan ahead while in high school and choose a college carefully (Shaw, 2005). Many students with learning disabilities elect to attend community colleges close to their homes, where they can continue to receive support from their families, test out their success with college coursework, attend smaller classes, and shift to either a technical program or a bachelor's degree program later (Brinckerhoff, 2005).

Any individual who wants to enter a 4-year college as a first-year student should visit different college campuses, investigate what support services are offered, and meet with college staff. Attending special summer programs or taking a college class can help sharpen study skills and time management skills—a problem that plagues most first-year students, not just those with learning disabilities. Issues related to selecting the "right" college are not the exclusive concern of those with learning disabilities, but such individuals do have more factors to weigh (Lissner, 2005).

Like everyone thinking about attending college, these questions must be considered:

- Does the school have the right academic programs?
- Where is the school located?
- What are its admissions standards?
- How big is the overall student body, and how large are the typical introductory courses?
- Does the school have extracurricular programs? The right ones?
- How much are tuition and fees, along with other costs?

for Effective Teaching

ASSIGNING AND ADAPTING HOMEWORK

1. Make sure students can complete the home-work assignment.
2. Write the assignment on the board.
3. Explain the assignment carefully.
4. Remind students of the due date periodically.
5. Coordinate with other teachers to avoid homework overload.
6. Establish with parents and other teachers a standard policy about late and missed assignments.
7. Provide additional one-on-one assistance.
8. Allow for alternative formats (audio taping rather than written assignments) or the use of learning tools (calculators, word processing, diagrams and charts).
9. Adjust assignment length.
10. Provide access to a peer tutor.

Source: Adapted from "Homework Practices That Support Students with Disabilities" by B. Bursuck, M. Montague, and S. Vaughn, 2001 Spring, *Research Connections in Special Education, 8,* pp. 2–3 (ERIC/CEC).

For students with learning disabilities, these additional questions should be considered:

- How comprehensive is the school's office of disabilities?
- What types of supports and services are offered?
- What supports and services do I need for success?

As we mentioned in the Transition section of this chapter, the range of services available through the office of disability services at different colleges varies greatly. One way for potential applicants to find out what services are available is to analyze each school of interest. Many different software programs and college directories are available to help with this task. Once decisions are made about the types of supports needed, possible academic majors or career training programs, and location, many more issues need to be discussed. For example, costs are always important to families as they make decisions about which college is right for their child. Few scholarships are available for students with disabilities, and sometimes college costs are higher (Brinckerhoff, 2005). But many colleges and universities—including Stanford, the University of Connecticut, the University of North Carolina–Chapel Hill, and the University of Georgia—now offer comprehensive supports and services particularly designed for their students with learning disabilities. Such services might include faculty who have received special training about accommodations, tutoring, learning strategy instruction, frequent monitoring of student progress, and summer transition programs (the summer before the first year begins). However, there are usually a limited number of slots for such special programs, so they require special application and also come at extra cost. For many students with learning disabilities, it is the partnership they create with the staff at their college's office of disability services that makes success in postsecondary education more easily achieved.

Many variables need to be considered, but one thing is clear: Preparation to go to college must begin early in students' academic careers. In elementary school they learn the fundamentals on which future learning will be based. In middle school they begin being independent learners, and in high school they learn the basic content and skills they will need to succeed when they experience the freedom and challenges of college. One mechanism used to help students learn to study on their own is homework. So let's consider this important component of the general education curriculum.

Homework

Homework is a time-honored component of the general education program. It is intended to help students become independent learners. Homework also serves as one communication tool to keep parents informed both about the work being done at school and about their child's progress in the curriculum (Bursuck, Montague, & Vaughn, 2001). However, the word *homework* can strike terror into the parents of students with learning disabilities—and probably into the children as well. The mere mention of the word may revive memories of long, unpleasant nights spent cajoling a student with learning disabilities into completing unfinished assignments. Such nights often end in shouting matches between parent and child, sometimes with one or both in tears.

Homework is a reality of school life, and teachers can make homework a more positive experience by making certain that students know how to do the assignment. *Tips for Effective Teaching* provides some guidelines that teachers can follow to get more benefits from assigning homework and even use it to forge an improved partnership with families. When homework assignments are considered carefully, with planning and instruction, the benefits can be many.

Despite the negative situations that homework can create for the family, it accounts for about 20 percent of the time most children spend on academic tasks (Bryan & Sullivan-Burstein, 1998). Although many students and their parents would like to see homework "just go away," it is unlikely that homework will be discontinued. General education teachers place great importance on homework. They consider homework to be a serious part of the instructional program and also to provide opportunities for home–school communication. Many teachers believe that when homework is not completed, parents have not met their expectations (Epstein et al., 1997). How might communication between teachers and parents about homework improve? Research has yielded some guidelines (Jayanthi et al., 1997):

- Parents and teachers need to communicate more about homework, with both parties feeling free to initiate the conversation.
- Parents need to tell teachers about homework difficulties.
- Teachers need to tell parents about the quality and completion of homework assignments.
- Parents need to implement consequences when homework is not completed or is unsatisfactory.
- Parents need to know whom to contact at school about homework issues.
- Teachers need to find ways to communicate with parents who do not speak English.
- Teachers need to determine alternative ways for children to get assistance with homework assignments that their parents do not know how to help them complete.

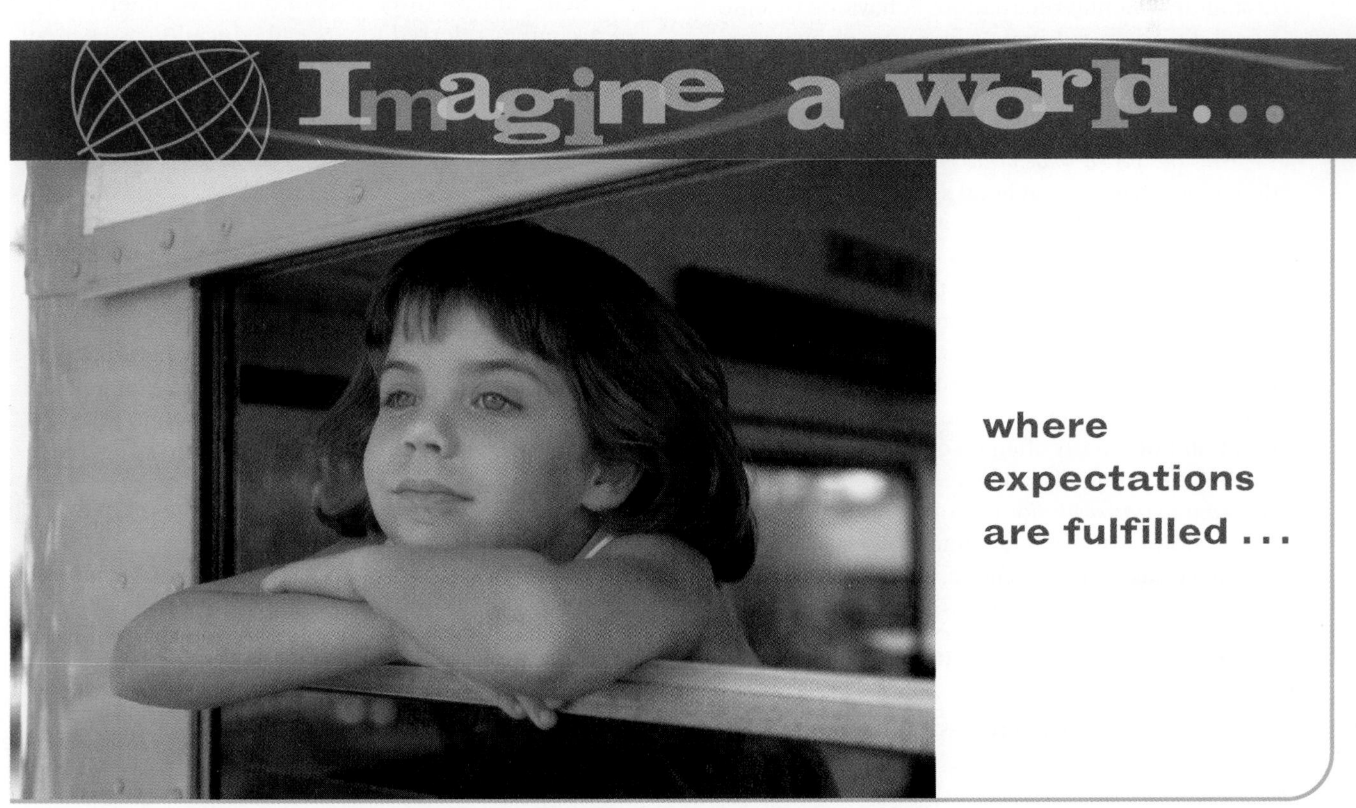
Imagine a world...
where expectations are fulfilled . . .

Summary

Individuals with learning disabilities do not learn in the same way or at the same pace as their classmates without disabilities. These students are resistant to treatment, and they often do not learn along with their classmates through validated instructional practices used in general education classes. They require sustained, intensive, and explicit instruction to succeed. Students with learning disabilities are often characterized as having unexpected underachievement because their academic performance does not match their potential or what their other abilities would lead one to expect. Reading/learning disabilities are the most common type of this disability. These students are very different from each other in characteristics, learning preferences, and the accommodations they require to access the general education curriculum and to acquire basic skills needed for content instruction. New methods for pre-referral assessments and multitiered interventions are being implemented to avoid the long periods of instructional inaction that resulted from traditional identification procedures. When taught by highly qualified teachers who can effectively apply interventions validated by research, these students make substantial progress, and many overcome their learning challenges.

Addressing the Chapter Objectives

1 What are the key features of the current federal definition of learning disabilities?

- Involves one or more of the psychological processes needed to understand or use spoken or written language
- May result from central nervous system dysfunctions
- Can result in problems listening, thinking, speaking, reading, writing, spelling, or computing
- Excludes students whose primary problems are due to visual disabilities, hearing impairments, physical disabilities, mental retardation, behavioral or emotional disorders, cultural or linguistic diversity, or poverty

2 What are the different types of learning disabilities?

- *General unexpected underachievement:* overall low academic performance, general school failure
- *Reading/learning disabilities:* reading performance is both below that of classmates *and* below what is expected on the basis of the student's other abilities; most common type of learning disabilities
- *Mathematics/learning disabilities:* mathematics performance is both below that of classmates *and* below what is expected on the basis of the student's other abilities; most often co-occurs with reading/learning disabilities
- *Resistant to treatment:* nonresponsive to standard instruction in the general education classroom; requiring sustained, intensive, explicit instruction that is monitored for progress frequently

3 How is an individual's response to intervention (RTI) assessed?

Through the pre-referral process, four general steps are followed:

- All students experience universal screen in the fall of every school year.
- Those students exhibiting a level of skills that puts them at risk for school failure are identified for intervention.
- General educators, peer tutors, or paraprofessionals deliver increasing levels of intensive and individualized instruction to those students who continue to perform unsatisfactorily.
- Students who do not learn sufficiently after experiencing at least three tiers of multilevel intervention are either referred for special education assessment or identified as having learning disabilities (depending on each state's regulations).

4 What is the practice of "early intervening," and why does it hold great promise?

Early intervening:

- Is allowed by IDEA '04, but funds meant to provide services to students with disabilities cannot be used for these activities
- Provides more intensive instruction to all students who are not profiting from instruction being provided in the general education classroom, whether they have disabilities, are at risk, or are struggling learners

Benefits of early intervening and RTI:

- No delay in receiving intervention
- Reduced inappropriate referrals to special education
- Eliminates poor teaching as a reason for disabilities
- Assessment directly leads to instruction
- No stigma in being referred to special education because all students are universally screened
- Low achievement is distinguished by learning disabilities

5 What are two validated practices that are effective with students with learning disabilities, and how do they work?

Two of the many validated practices that have proved effective with students with learning disabilities are Peer-Assisted Learning Strategies (PALS) and the Kansas Learning Strategies Curriculum.

The key features of PALS:

- Peer tutoring
- Coaches and players exchange turns during each session
- Students are trained in the method of instruction, their roles, and how to provide corrective feedback
- Pairs are exchanged every month
- Pairs work together on specific assignments (e.g., sight words, math facts)

The key features of the Learning Strategies Curriculum:

- Developed for middle school and high school students with disabilities
- Goes beyond crisis teaching
- Helps students become strategic learners
- Incorporates mnemonics, advance organizers, and structured materials with measures for monitoring progress

mylabschool
Where the classroom comes to life!

MyLabSchool is a collection of online tools for your success in this course, your licensure exams, and your teaching career. Visit www.mylabschool.com to access the following:

- Online Study Guide
- Video cases from real classrooms
- Help with your research papers using Research Navigator
- Career Center with resources for:
  - Praxis exams and licensure preparation
  - Professional portfolio development
  - Job search and interview techniques
  - Lesson planning

Supplementary Resources

Popular Novels and Books

Branson, R. (1998). *Losing my virginity.* New York: Three Rivers Press, Random House.

Brown, C. (1965). *Manchild in the promised land.* New York: Macmillan.

Louganis, G., & Marcus, E. (1996). *Breaking the surface.* New York: Random House.

Mooney, J., & Cole, D. (2000). *Learning outside the lines.* New York: Simon & Schuster.

Moss, P. B. (1989). *An autobiography: P. Buckley Moss: The people's artist.* Waynesboro, VA: Shenandoah Heritage.

Sacks, O. (1985). *The man who mistook his wife for a hat.* New York: Summit Books.

Movies

***Summer School* (1987). Paramount**

This light-hearted comedy is about a number of students forced to attend summer school as a consequence of their poor academic performance during the school year. After wasting much of the summer term, in fear of failure and of costing their teacher his job, the students make a tremendous effort on their final exam.

One student in the class has reading disabilities, and even though this film is a comedy, it provides an example of how a student with a significant learning disability can slip through the cracks of the educational system. The film shows how not receiving specialized services can affect such students' confidence and why they fall further behind. The film also shows that once a learning disability is recognized, individualized instruction can aid students.

Professional, Parent, and Advocacy Groups

Council for Learning Disabilities (CLD) in Overland Park, Kansas
www.cldinternational.org

Division for Learning Disabilities (DLD) Council for Exceptional Children in Arlington, Virginia
www.cec.sped.org *or* www.teachingld.org

Learning Disability Association of America (LDA) (formerly the Association for Children with Learning Disabilities [ACLD]) in Pittsburgh, Pennsylvania
www.ldanatl.org

National Center for LD (NCLD) in New York City
www.ncld.org

LD OnLine in Washington, DC
www.ldonline.org

Charles and Helen Schwab Foundation in San Mateo, California
www.schwablearning.org and www.sparktop.org

Professional Standards and Licensure Tests

After reading this chapter, you should be able to link basic knowledge and skills described in the CEC Standards and INTASC Principles with information provided in this text. The table below shows some of the specific CEC Learning Disabilities Knowledge and Skill Standards and INTASC Special Education Principles that can be applied to each major section of the chapter. Other standards may also be applied to this chapter. Associated General Praxis II topic areas are identified in the right column.

Major Chapter Headings	CEC Knowledge and Skill Core Standard and Associated Subcategories	INTASC Core Principle and Associated Special Education Subcategories	PRAXIS II Exam Topic
Where We've Been ... What's on the Horizon?	**1: Foundations** LD1K1 Historical foundations, classical studies, and major contributors in the field of learning disabilities	**1: Subject Matter** 1.13 Special education teachers know major trends and issues that define the history of special education and understand how current legislation and recommended practice fit within the contact of this history.	1: Understanding Exceptionality 2: Legal and Social Issues
Learning Disabilities Defined	**1: Foundations** LD1K5 Current definitions and issues related to the identification of individuals with learning disabilities	**1: Subject Matter** 1.12 Special education teachers serve as a resource to others by providing information about the laws and policies that support students with disabilities and how to access additional information when needed.	1: Understanding Exceptionality 2: Legal and Social Issues
Characteristics	**2: Development and Characteristics of Learners** LD2K3 Psychological, social, and emotional characteristics of individuals with learning disabilities	**2: Student Learning** 2.07 Special education teachers seek to understand the current and evolving development and learning of individual students from a life-span perspective.	1: Understanding Exceptionality
Causes and Prevention	**2: Development and Characteristics of Learners** LD2K1 Etiologies of learning disabilities	**2: Student Learning** 2.08 Special education teachers seek a holistic understanding of each student's current learning and development, based on knowledge of the student's performance within a variety of settings.	1: Understanding Exceptionality 2: Legal and Social Issues

Assessment	**8: Assessment** LD8S1 Choose and administer assessment instruments appropriate to the individual with learning disabilities	**8: Assessment** 8.06 All special education teachers understand how to administer, score, interpret, and report on formal and informal assessments related to their areas of specialization.	1: Understanding Exceptionality 3: Delivery of Services to Students
Teaching Students with Learning Disabilities	**4: Instructional Strategies** LD4S9 Implement systematic instruction in teaching reading comprehension and monitoring strategies	**4: Instructional Strategies** 4.11 Special education teachers collaborate with general education teachers to infuse individualized goals and specialized strategies into instruction for students with disabilities.	3: Delivery of Services to Students
Transition	**5: Learning Environments and Social Interactions** LD5S1 Plan instruction for independent functional life skills relevant to the community, personal living, sexuality, and employment	**7: Planning Instruction** 7.07 Special education teachers oversee the development of individualized transition plans to guide learners' transitions from preschool to elementary school, middle school to high school, and high school to postschool opportunities.	3: Delivery of Services to Students
Collaboration	**10: Collaboration** LD10K1 Co-planning and co-teaching methods to strengthen content acquisition of individuals with learning disabilities	**10: Collaboration, Ethics, and Relationships** 10.05 All special education teachers provide leadership that enables teams to accomplish their purposes.	2: Legal and Social Issues 3: Delivery of Services to Students
Partnerships with Families and Communities	**10: Collaboration** LD10K2 Services, networks, and organizations that provide support across the life span for individuals with learning disabilities	**10: Collaboration, Ethics, and Relationships** 10.06 Special education teachers take a life span view of students with disabilities and use their knowledge of disabilities, legislation, special education services, and instructional strategies to ensure implementation of each student's individual education program.	1: Understanding Exceptionality 2: Legal and Social Issues 3: Delivery of Services to Students

Carousel Horse 2 by Robert Toth. © Robert Toth. Used with kind permission of the artist.

Robert Toth is a renowned sculptor and painter whose work is represented in the National Portrait Gallery, Lincoln Center, and the Vatican Museum. Toth was not successful at school. His learning disabilities, along with his coexisting attention deficit hyperactivity disorder, created challenges for him at school that seemed almost insurmountable. (He says he can't even recall how many times he had to repeat fourth grade.) His mother, herself a well-known artist, created opportunities for success for her son by helping him develop his skills with clay and paint. His creativity and artistic talents have become the means through which he demonstrates his giftedness, as well as being the path he has followed in overcoming his disabilities.

6

Attention Deficit Hyperactivity Disorder

"*When I approach a child, he inspires in me two sentiments: tenderness for what he is and respect for what he may become.*"

Louis Pasteur

In recent years, educators, parents, policy makers, and the press have expressed concerns about a large group of today's students. Teachers report that many of their students have great difficulty paying attention. Parents are confused by some of their children's behavior, reporting that these children are disorganized, distracted, or even defiant. Both teachers and parents describe a group of students as in "constant motion." And periodically on the front page of magazines and sections of newspapers, the press brings to the public's attention that many of America's students are prescribed drugs to control their behavior. A good portion of these students has difficulty meeting the expectations of the general education curriculum; their educational performance is negatively influenced. In response, Congress called out the condition, **attention deficit hyperactivity disorder (ADHD)**, in the IDEA law.

IDEA '04 does *not* list attention deficit hyperactivity disorder (ADHD) as a separate disability category but instead includes it under the category of "other health impairments." However, teachers and parents consistently note that it is a condition frequently seen among students in America's schools. They report that these students are substantially different from their peers and cause concern because of their inability to focus their attention or control their behavior. Although ADHD is not a distinct IDEA '04 disability category, most teachers are likely to encounter many students who exhibit these characteristics; thus an entire chapter of this book is devoted to ADHD.

Chapter Objectives

As you read this chapter, ponder these students' needs, the supports they require, and the outcomes they should achieve. After studying this chapter, you will be able to:

1. Recognize the characteristics of students with ADHD.
2. Understand the relationship of ADHD to other, coexisting disabilities.
3. Understand medical treatment of ADHD.
4. Identify various accommodations and classroom interventions used with students with ADHD.
5. Discuss the importance of collaborating and developing partnerships with families and with other professionals.

Where We've Been . . . What's on the Horizon?

Considerable controversy has surrounded ADHD for decades. Some cite scientific evidence for the existence of the disorder and effective treatment options for children with ADHD characteristics, others counter that the condition is a fabrication to justify the increasingly high rates of medical treatment for what might otherwise be considered typical, energetic behaviors of childhood (Barkley, 1998, 2002; Kendall et al., 2003). Possibly because of such controversy, the 1997 reauthorization of IDEA was the first instance of ADHD receiving federal government attention. Until then, ADHD was considered a symptom of other conditions

This chapter was coauthored by Deborah Deutsch Smith and Naomi Chowdhuri Tyler of Vanderbilt University.

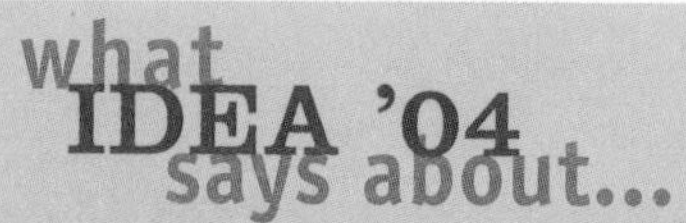

Attention Deficit Hyperactivity Disorder (ADHD)

Children with ADHD are not automatically protected by IDEA. Specifically, students with ADHD

- Are not guaranteed eligibility for special education or related services, even with medical diagnoses and medication prescriptions
- Are specifically called out only under the "other health impairments" category, which does not list every disability and condition
- May also be eligible for services under other categories, such as learning disabilities and emotional or behavioral disorders
- May receive special education services if the condition adversely affects educational performance

(such as learning disabilities, traumatic brain injury, or emotional or behavioral disorders), and officials were confident that students with ADHD who required special education services were receiving them through the various IDEA disability categories (U.S. Department of Education, 2005). Subsequently, during the 1997 IDEA reauthorization, ADHD was included within the category of "other health impairments" but was not identified as a distinct category of its own. (See *What IDEA '04 Says About ADHD* for more information about this condition and the law.) Thus, although ADHD might be one of the "newest" conditions recognized by IDEA, it is neither newly discovered nor only recently studied.

Historical Context

Dr. George Still, a British physician, is generally considered to have been the first to document characteristics in children that we now associate with ADHD (Gephart, 2003). In his classic 1902 article "Some Abnormal Psychical Conditions in Children," he described children who had problems with inattention and impulsivity, which he attributed to an "abnormal defect of moral control" (Still, 1902, p. 1008). The first systematic study of what we now call ADHD began in 1919, after World War I, when Kurt Goldstein, a psychiatrist in Frankfurt, Germany, was working with soldiers who had returned from the war with brain injuries. Dr. Goldstein found many of his patients distractible, unable to attend to relevant cues, confused, and hyperactive. They also had difficulties with reading and writing that they had not experienced before going to battle. Goldstein brought his carefully recorded observations with him when he immigrated to America, and others used them as a foundation for work done with children. Alfred Strauss and Heinz Werner, around 1937, worked together at the Wayne County Training Center in Michigan, a residential special education school. All the students who attended the center were thought to have mental retardation (this was a long time before the development of many different special education categories, refined diagnostic procedures, and inclusive schooling). A group of these children caught the attention of Dr. Strauss and Dr. Werner, who thought them different from the others living at the center. These children had symptoms very similar to the group of veterans that Goldstein had described years earlier. One big difference was that the children, whose brain injury was only suspected, had never developed strong skills in reading, writing, and speaking, whereas the veterans' lost abilities could be attributed to documented brain injury. Regardless, researchers at the center felt that these children did not have mental retardation but did have minimal brain damage, a condition that came to be called "Strauss Syndrome" (Stevens & Birch, 1957).

The Wayne County Center must have been a very special place. Even a cursory study of the history of special education brings one back to this center and the pioneering work done there during the middle of the last century. During the late 1930s, many special education pioneers worked at the center, most under the direction or influence of Dr. Strauss. These innovators, whose work is the foundation for many present-day special education practices, became convinced that not all the children at the center had the same type of disability. They concluded that one reason for some children's disabilities could be brain damage. Newell Kephart, one of these pioneers, who later spent most of his career at Northern Colorado State University, studied under Strauss's direction at the center. He tried to find ways to remediate these children's problems through repeated motor activities (Kephart, 1960). Laura Lehtinen also worked with Strauss at the center and later at a private school in Michigan that they started for students with brain injury—the Cove School. There, she developed highly structured teaching routines similar to many

attention deficit hyperactivity disorder (ADHD) A condition characterized by hyperactivity, impulsivity, and inattention; included in the "other health impairments" category of those applied today through direct and explicit instruction (Strauss & Lehtinen, 1947). Interest in these children continued, even though they weren't studied as a distinct group of learners with disabilities. For example, William Cruikshank and his colleagues devoted their careers to students who behaved as if they had brain damage, even though it couldn't be documented (Cruikshank et al., 1961), and Cruikshank was one of the first to develop educational programs for children with characteristics similar to those of children with ADHD. Barbara Keogh also thought that in the case of one group of students with learning disabilities—those with hyperactivity—there might be a biological reason why they had difficulty acquiring information and making decisions (Keogh, 1971). These pioneers all laid the foundation for work being done today in both learning disabilities and ADHD.

Challenges That Attention Deficit Hyperactivity Disorder Presents

Many students, not just those diagnosed with ADHD, experience inattentiveness, hyperactivity, or impulsivity. However, students and adults diagnosed with ADHD face many additional challenges in their lives. For example, these students are particularly at risk for failing in school, being suspended, abusing substances, dropping out of school, and having a very high rate of conflicts with their families over doing chores and their homework assignments (Salend & Rohena, 2003). Many of these students believe that they can never meet their parent's expectations. ADHD can also negatively influence these students' relationships with their classmates. Because of their hyperactivity and poor social skills, many students with ADHD are rejected by their peers and disliked by their teachers (Bryan, 1997; Olmeda, Thomas, & Davis, 2003). Rejection by classmates can leave these students lonely and without friends. *The Story of Joey Pigza* on page 208 provides a portrait of one child with ADHD and the effect of his behavior on his classroom and teacher.

Although many years ago most professionals believed that children and youth with ADHD would "grow out of their problems," we now know that for most such individuals, the symptoms continue throughout their lives (Barkley, 1998; Weyandt et al., 2003). The characteristics associated with ADHD can affect adult life in many ways. For example, Kessler and colleagues (2005) found that ADHD was associated with an average of 35 lost days of work per year, totaling more than $19 billion in lost human capital nationally. Adults with ADHD can have very successful lives, but they often require accurate identification and effective services (CHADD, 2005).

Several of these students may have ADHD; the exact numbers are difficult to determine.

Making a Difference

Project Eye-To-Eye

ADHD symptoms of inattention and hyperactivity-impulsivity are self-reported among many college students, including those who have not been diagnosed with the disorder, but professionals estimate that 2 to 4 percent of college students may have ADHD (Dupaul et al., 2001). These students often struggle individually and do not have the support of knowing others with similar experiences.

Three young men who have first-hand knowledge about these frustrations decided to help others and give young students the assistance that they themselves didn't have. Jonathan Mooney and David Cole, two Ivy League graduates (of Brown University) wrote *Learning Outside the Lines,* a handbook for college students with LD/ADHD. They then founded Project Eye-To-Eye, a mentoring program at Brown University in which college students with LD/ADHD work with public school students with LD/ADHD. David Flink, another Brown alum with a learning disability, helped found the national Project Eye-To-Eye organization and is managing director of the program, which is currently based in New York City.

The project's mission is to develop a nationwide coalition of partnerships with local community organizations to provide mentors for students with LD/ADHD. The overriding principle is that of empowerment through building self-esteem. The program seeks to facilitate academic achievement through self-advocacy, the development of meta-cognitive skills, and the use of learning strategies and academic accommodations. A key component of the project is the use of art, through which students are encouraged to express themselves, empowered to develop strengths, and validated as having unique gifts. An additional project goal is that of parental networking, which connects parents to information and support and enables them to advocate better for their children. Finally, the project provides its members with opportunities for professional development.

David Flink

Project Eye-To-Eye currently has 12 chapters nationwide, with each site serving an average of 12 mentor–student pairs, 12 parents, and 70 university/school professionals. The mentors spend at least two hours per week with their mentees, one hour engaged in artistic endeavors and one hour outside the art classroom. The project also uses a cohort of speakers, Mouth-to-Mouth, who (along with Mooney, the executive director), speaks to thousands of interested people per year, increasing the information dissemination component of the project.

For more information on this project, contact David Flink; Project Eye-To-Eye; 180 West End Ave. #16E; New York, NY 10023; (917) 755-8865; info@projecteyetoeye.org.

Jonathan Mooney

Attention Deficit Hyperactivity Disorder Defined

Although many people refer to ADHD as attention deficit disorder (ADD), the medically correct term is attention deficit hyperactivity disorder (ADHD) (Fowler, 2004). Possibly because ADHD is not a separate disability category under IDEA '04, the condition is not uniformly understood. The federal government provides little guidance to states and school districts about the definition to use when identifying students with this condition and qualifying them as eligible for special education services under the "other health impairment" category. In the

United States, the most widely accepted and used definition of ADHD is the one developed by the American Psychiatric Association (APA) in its *Diagnostic and Statistical Manual of Mental Disorders* (DSM-IV-TR) which has a stronger medical theme for diagnosis than the federal criteria. Table6.1 provides both the IDEA and the DSM-IV-TR definitions.

To help clarify its definition, the APA further explains ADHD by stating that it "is a persistent pattern of inattention and/or hyperactivity-impulsivity that is more frequent and severe than is typically observed in individuals at a comparable level of development" (APA, 2000, p. 85). Symptoms of the condition must occur in more than one setting. Possibly one of the most important things to consider is that nearly everyone, both children and adults, can exhibit inattention, excessive activity, or impulsivity (DuPaul et al., 2001). These characteristics signal ADHD only when they become excessive and cause "significant impairment in social, academic, or occupational functioning" (APA, 2000, p. 93).

General Education Students with ADHD

Like some students with other health impairments whose conditions do not affect their educational performance (see Chapter 9 for more information about these students), not all students with ADHD qualify for special education services. If the condition does not cause school failure, students may receive accommodations (such as extended time on tests or to complete assignments) through Section 504 of the Rehabilitation Act, instead of direct special education services to address their unique learning needs.

Special Education Students with ADHD

To qualify for special education services through the IDEA '04 "other health impairments" category because of ADHD, individuals must "experience heightened alertness to environmental stimuli, which results in limited alertness to their educational environment," which adversely affects educational performance (U.S. Department of Education, 2005). The challenges and obstacles these individuals face are often greater than those that confront many students with other disabilities, because it is most likely that ADHD coexists with another disability, compounding the problems to overcome.

Coexisting Disabilities

For most of these students, ADHD coexists with another disability (Pierce, 2003), a situation commonly referred to as **comorbidity**, and they are identified and served in special education categories such as the learning disabilities category or the emotional or behavioral disorders category (U.S. Department of Education, 1999). The reason for this is that the characteristics of ADHD overlap with those of some other disabilities. Let's look at its overlap with two other conditions.

Comorbidity with Learning Disabilities

Some studies have shown that 70 percent of children with ADHD also have a learning disability (Mayes, Calhoun, & Crowell, 2000; Pierce, 2003). Many students with ADHD do score higher on tests of intelligence than other students, including those individuals with learning disabilities and significant reading problems (Kaplan et al., 2000). However, they do tend to score lower on standardized achievement tests than their classmates without disabilities (Barkley, 1998). Studies on whether these students are more likely to have more problems with written communication, reading, math, or spelling have yielded conflicting results (Mayes, Calhoun, & Cromwell, 2000; Willcutt & Pennington, 2000). Some experts believe that these students fall into separate cognitive, biological, and

comorbidity Coexisting disabilities

Table 6.1 • Definitions of ADHD

Source	Definition
Federal Government[1]	Defined as one condition included under the "Other Health Impairments" category having limited strength, vitality or alertness, including heightened alertness to environmental stimuli, that results in limited alertness with respect to the educational environment. . . . adversely affects a child's educational performance
DSM-IV-TR[2]	**A.** Either (1) or (2) **1.** six (or more) of the following symptoms of *inattention* have persisted for at least 6 months to a degree that is maladaptive and inconsistent with developmental level: *Inattention* **a.** often fails to give close attention to details or makes careless mistakes in schoolwork, work, or other activities **b.** often has difficulty sustaining attention in tasks or play activities **c.** often does not seem to listen when spoken to directly **d.** often does not follow through on instructions and fails to finish schoolwork, chores, or duties in the workplace (not due to oppositional behavior or failure to understand instructions) **e.** often has difficulty organizing tasks and activities **f.** often avoids, dislikes, or is reluctant to engage in tasks that require sustained mental effort (such as schoolwork or homework) **g.** often loses things necessary for tasks or activities (e.g., toys, school assignments, pencils, books, or tools) **h.** is often easily distracted by extraneous stimuli **i.** is often forgetful in daily activities **2.** six (or more) of the following symptoms of *hyperactivity-impulsivity* have persisted for at least 6 months to a degree that is maladaptive and inconsistent with developmental level: *Hyperactivity* **a.** often fidgets with hands or feet or squirms in seat **b.** often leaves seat in classroom or in other situations in which remaining seated is expected **c.** often runs about or climbs excessively in situations in which it is inappropriate (in adolescents or adults, may be limited to subjective feelings of restlessness) **d.** often has difficulty playing or engaging in leisure activities quietly **e.** is often "on the go" or often acts as if "driven by a motor" **f.** often talks excessively *Impulsivity* **g.** often blurts out answers before questions have been completed **h.** often has difficulty awaiting turn **i.** often interrupts or intrudes on others (e.g., butts into conversations or games) **B.** Some hyperactive-impulsive or inattentive symptoms that caused impairment were present before age 7 years. **C.** Some impairment from the symptoms is present in two or more settings (e.g., at school, work, or home). **D.** There must be clear evidence of clinically significant impairment in social, academic, or occupational functioning. **E.** The symptoms do not occur exclusively during the course of a Pervasive Developmental Disorder, Schizophrenia, or other Psychotic Disorder and are not better accounted for by another mental disorder (e.g., Mood Disorder, Anxiety Disorder, Dissociative Disorder, or a Personality Disorder).

NOTE: *Code* based on type:
Attention Deficit Hyperactivity Disorder, Combined Type: If both Criteria A1 and A2 are met for the past 6 months; *Attention-Deficit Hyperactivity Disorder, Predominantly Inattentive Type:* If Criterion A1 is met but Criterion A2 is not met for the past 6 months; or *Attention-Deficit Hyperactivity Disorder, Predominantly Hyperactive-Impulsive Type:* If Criterion A2 is met but Criterion A1 is not met for the past 6 months.

Sources: [1]From 34 CFR Parts 300 and 303, Assistance to States for the Education of Children with Disabilities and the Early Intervention Program for Infants and Toddlers with Disabilities; Proposed Regulations, U.S. Department of Education, 2005, *Federal Register,* Washington, DC, and [2]Reprinted with permission from the *Diagnostic and Statistical Manual of Mental Disorders, fourth edition, Text Revision* (pp. 92–93).

behavioral subgroups (Bonafina et al., 2000). Whether subgrouping has any usefulness to teachers at the moment is unclear. What each of these students requires is an individualized educational program to meet his or her specific learning needs.

Comorbidity with Emotional or Behavioral Disorders

ADHD often occurs in students with emotional or behavioral disorders (Pierce, 2003). These students usually receive special education services under the category of emotional or behavioral disorders. In one study, approximately 42 percent of students with ADHD received special education services under the EBD category (Bussing et al., 1998). Sadly, of that group, one-fourth received no mental health services, such as counseling. ADHD is more likely to be identified in boys, particularly boys with acting out behaviors (Merrell & Boelter, 2001; Reid et al., 2001). When ADHD coexists with emotional or behavioral disorders, students urgently need help to avoid serious, dangerous, or violent situations (Bussing et al., 1998; Gresham, Lane, & Lambros, 2000).

Characteristics

Students with ADHD often exhibit characteristics that undermine success in school (Carlson et al., 2002). Students with ADHD rely, more than others, on external factors to explain their accomplishments, and therefore they are less persistent, expend less effort, prefer easier work, and take less enjoyment in learning.

Learning Characteristics

At the root of many problems experienced by students with ADHD are problems with at least one of these three learning characteristics:

- Inattention
- Hyperactivity
- Impulsivity

These learning characteristics explain why these students seem not to pay attention, miss the little (but important) details about assignments, and seem to submit perpetually incomplete schoolwork (Salend, Elhoweris, & van Garderen, 2003). Look again at Table 6.1 and the DSM-IV-TR types of ADHD. The key characteristics are discussed in more detail below.

Inattention

Inattention is a characteristic commonly observed by parents, teachers, and researchers (Fowler, 2002, 2004). The inability to pay attention has serious consequences. This problem explains why many of these individuals have difficulty following teachers' directions and seem to be confused about where they are supposed to be and what they are suppose to do. Students who cannot focus on the task to be learned or who pay attention to the wrong features of the task are also said to be distractible. Problems with attention make it challenging for students to shift from one task to another, making transitions from one activity to another difficult. Inattention also contributes to an inability to focus on details or to approach learning in an organized or efficient fashion. In all of these situations, teachers can be most helpful by using directions that are clear and concise, giving students plenty of notice about upcoming changes in activities, and using predictable and standard schedules.

inattention Inability to pay attention or focus

The Story of Joey Pigza

Joey Pigza Swallowed the Key is the story of a young boy's experiences with ADHD. Hysterically funny at some points, heart-wrenchingly painful at others, this wonderful book gives readers an inside look into the mind of a child with ADHD.

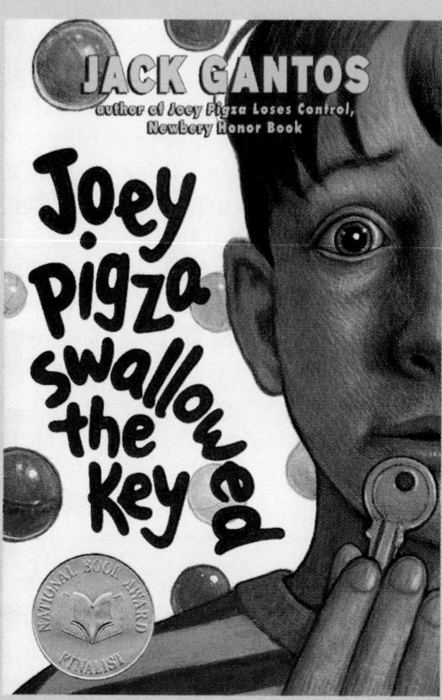

At school they say I'm wired bad, or wired mad, or wired sad, or wired glad, depending on my mood and what teacher has ended up with me. But there is no doubt about it, I'm wired.

This year was no different. When I started out, all the days there looked about the same. In the morning I'd be okay and follow along in class. But after lunch, when my meds had worn down, it was nothing but trouble for me.

One day, we were doing math drills in class and every time Mrs. Maxy asked a question, like "What's nine times nine?" I'd raise my hand because I'm really quick at math. But each time she called on me, even though I knew the answer, I'd just blurt out, "Can I get back to you on that?" Then I'd nearly fall out of my chair from laughing. And she'd give me that whitelipped look which meant, "Settle down." But I didn't and kept raising my hand each time she asked a question until finally no other kid would raise their hand because they knew what was coming between me and Mrs. Maxy.

"Okay, Joey," she'd say, calling on me and staring hard at my face as if her eyes were long fingers that could grip me by the chin. I'd stare right back and hesitate a second as if I was planning to answer the question and then I'd holler out really loud, "Can I get back to you on that?" Finally, after a bunch of times of me doing that in a row, she jerked her thumb toward the door. "Out in the hall," she said. And the class cracked up.

So I went and stood in the hall for about a second until I remembered the mini-Superball in my pocket and started to bounce it off the lockers and ceiling and after Mrs. Deebs in the next class stuck her head out her door and yelled, "Hey, cut the racket," like she was yelling at a stray cat, I remembered something I wanted to try. I had seen the Tasmanian Devil on TV whirling around like a top so I unbuckled my belt and pulled on the end really hard, as if I was trying to start a lawn mower. But that didn't get me spinning very fast. So I took out my high-top shoelaces and tied them together and then to the belt and wrapped it all around my waist. Then I grabbed one end and yanked on it and sort of got myself spinning. I kept doing it until I got better and better and before long I was bouncing off the lockers because I was dizzy too. Then I gave myself one more really good pull on the belt and because I was already dizzy I got going really fast and began to snort and grunt like the Tasmanian Devil until Mrs. Maxy came out and clamped her hands down on my shoulders. She stopped me so fast I spun right out of my shoes and they went shooting up the hall.

"You glue your feet to the floor for five whole minutes or you can just spin yourself down to the principal's office," she said. "Now, what is your choice going to be?"

"Can I get back to you on that?" I asked.

Source: From *Joey Pigza Swallowed the Key* (pp. 3–6) by Jack Gantos, 1998, New York: Farrar, Straus, & Giroux.

Hyperactivity

Hyperactivity is another defining symptom of ADHD. **Hyperactivity** is often difficult to define because the judgment about whether a certain level of a specific activity is too much, or "hyper," is subjective. If, for example, the activity is admired, the child might be described as energetic or enthusiastic rather than hyperactive. If the activity is annoying, teachers often describe the individual as "fidgety," "squirming in the chair," or continually "off task" (Fowler, 2002). The DSM-IV-TR also gives some good examples about which there is considerable consensus (APA, 2000). Look again at Table 6.1, re-read the DSM-IV-TR description of hyperactivity, and think about former classmates who fit the image you form of students with this type of ADHD.

hyperactivity Impaired ability to sit or concentrate for long periods of time

Inattention—a characteristic of ADHD—is often misunderstood as daydreaming or simply not paying attention to the important task of the moment such as studying.

Some research indicates that hyperactivity diminishes with age (Biederman, Mick, & Faraone, 2000). However, adolescents and adults with ADHD may have continued trouble with distractions due to daydreaming, or an ongoing stream of thoughts and ideas flowing through their minds at times when concentration is necessary, such as during a college course or business meeting (Shaw & Giambra, 1993). Still others report that although excessive activity is reduced, it is replaced with feelings of internal restlessness (Weyandt et al., 2003).

Impulsivity

One characteristic associated with ADHD, **impulsivity**, is commonly observed among students with learning disabilities (APA, 2000). This trait may explain why these children are unable to focus on the relevant components of problems that need to be solved or of tasks that need to be accomplished, and why they may disrupt the learning environment for an entire class (Duhaney, 2003). These students tend to blurt out a quick response before thinking the question through (remember Joey Pigza?). They tend to redirect the topic of class discussion, talk out of turn, or "butt into conversations" (APA, 2000; Fowler, 2002, 2004). All of these actions add up to poor responses from their classmates and decreased social acceptance (Merrell & Boelter, 2001).

Academic Performance

Many students with ADHD experience considerable difficulty with academic performance. Because of their distractibility and inability to focus, they spend less time engaging in academic tasks than their classmates without ADHD (Duhaney, 2003). The result is often lower grades and increased risk for school failure. These students have trouble studying for long periods of time. They tend to be disorganized and forgetful. These are the students who can't find their homework, forgot when an assignment was due, or meant to get the permission form for the field trip signed by a parent . . . but didn't. Many teachers comment that these students' handwriting is messy, their work is sloppy and careless, their assignments are often incomplete, and the work they turn in is not logical or presented in an organized way (Fowler, 2002).

impulsivity Impaired ability to control one's own behavior

for Effective Teaching

PUTTING STRUCTURE TO LEARNING

Promote Effective Completion of Assignments

1. Define goals clearly, and provide concrete examples.
2. Offer a rationale for completing the assignment.
3. Provide clear, concise, and step-by-step directions for all assignments, both orally and in print.
4. Have students first review the assignment.
5. List all materials needed.
6. State specifically how much time is allowed.
7. Help students gauge and manage their time.
8. Explain how assignments will be evaluated. Provide a checklist of items to be included.

Provide Structures for On-Task Behavior

1. Assign a classmate to help students stay on task.
2. Tailor pace of instruction to student's needs.
3. Arrange more frequent, yet shorter, study periods.

Support Self-Management Skills

1. Have students evaluate their own work, helping to correct their mistakes.
2. Teach and have students practice study skills such as skimming, previewing, and highlighting.
3. Teach techniques such as learning strategies and the use of content organizers.
4. Teach self-regulation strategies.

Utilize Effective Teaching Techniques

1. Use methods that reflect the student's cultural style.
2. Monitor student learning and modify or supplement instruction if students appear to be struggling.

These students, possibly more than others, need structure to support their learning and social performance (Salend, Elhoweris, & Garderen, 2003). There are many ways teachers can help. First—and this benefits *all* students in class—they should make assignments interesting, individualized when possible, and relevant to students' backgrounds and interests. Content enhancements and the use of learning strategies are also of great benefit. Graphic organizers (see *Validated Practices* on page 146 in Chapter 4 for an example) and study guides help students organize their thinking and their work. Such aids, as well as those tactics listed in *Tips for Effective Teaching* provide ways to help students with ADHD approach tasks and complete their work.

Social Behavior

As ADHD characteristics (inattention, hyperactivity, impulsivity) intensify, antisocial behaviors increase and positive social interactions decrease (Merrell & Boelter, 2001). This situation might explain why, surprisingly, students who identify themselves as having ADHD also describe themselves as having more internalizing behaviors and are more introspective about their problems (Volpe et al., 1999). They come to judge themselves as social failures and tend to engage in solitary activities (playing computer games, watching television). Their hyperactivity and poor social skills are reasons why many students with ADHD are rejected by their peers and disliked by their teachers (Bryan, 1997; Olmeda, Thomas, & Davis, 2003). These facts can contribute to a cycle of increasing alienation and withdrawal. Fortunately, teachers can make a difference by helping students with ADHD engage more often in behaviors that their classmates find desirable (turn-taking in conversations, asking to join a game rather than barging in and grabbing equipment). In this regard, direct instruction on how to interact with others and behave in a more socially appropriate manner is often very effective. Interventions such as functional behavioral assessments (discussed in Chapter 7) are often conducted to help professionals reduce or eliminate inappropriate behaviors, or substitute more appropriate behaviors in their place. Also, self-management (e.g., self-monitoring behavior, self-instruction) strategies (discussed later in this chapter) that include rewards for conforming to classroom rules are very helpful with these students (Reid & Lienemen, 2006; Reid, Trout, & Schartz, 2005). For students with ADHD who do not qualify for special education services, general educators must make accommodations to the learning environment so that academic performance is not negatively affected and instruction meets their individual needs.

Remember, ADHD is marked by a specific set of behaviors that many people exhibit occasionally; it is the excessive degree to which these distracting behaviors occur that undermines functioning to the point where ADHD is identified. Most visitors to a general education classroom can pick out the students with ADHD. They are the students who need to sharpen their pencils more often than their classmates, to look for something on the bookshelf several times during quiet time, or to play with pencils on the desk during the teacher's lecture (Duhaney, 2003). The temptation of talking with the students at neighboring desks is overwhelming. Although these students' are seemingly always in trouble, most of their infractions are relatively minor. But when they are totaled up for an entire school day, the excessiveness of the disturbance they cause becomes readily apparent. Teachers can help these students manage their disruptive and distracting behaviors by planning ahead and implementing some simple procedures, such as those listed in *Tips for Classroom Management* (Carbone, 2001; Duhaney, 2003).

Although parents and teachers may tend to focus on the negative aspects of ADHD, there are positive characteristics as well. For example, intense creativity, intuitiveness, emotional awareness, and exuberance are all positive traits associated with ADHD (Honos-Webb, 2005). Individuals with ADHD may take an unusual or nonstandard approach to problem solving, look at situations from a different perspective, and exhibit an ability to "think outside the box" (Hallowell & Ratey, 2005). See *In the Spotlight* to learn how JetBlue CEO David Neeleman attributes his success as an entrepreneur to these positive ADHD traits.

PUTTING STRUCTURE TO BEHAVIOR

Managing the Physical Environment

1 Keep loud noise and distractions to a minimum.
2 Arrange desks for efficent traffic flow.
3 Dismiss students in small groups.

Preventing Problem Behaviors

1 Have a comprehensive behavior management plan.
2 Remind students of classroom rules.
3 Provide frequent feedback.
4 Deliver positive consequences immediately and frequently.
5 Introduce new activities and schedules incrementally.

Supporting Student Independence

1 Teach and support time management skills.
2 Teach students self-regulation strategies.
3 Warn students of approaching transitions (e.g., time for a new activity).

Intervening for Problem Behaviors

1 Stand close to the student (proximity control).
2 Avoid drawing attention to the student's behavior.
3 Conceal your frustration and redirect behavior.
4 Explain clearly why the behavior is inappropriate.
5 Provide alternatives (e.g., teach students to count to 5 before raising their hand).

Prevalence

Little consensus exists about how many students actually have ADHD. For example, the National Institutes of Mental Health (NIMH) report that an estimated 4 percent of all individuals between the ages of 9 and 17 have ADHD, boys being about two to three times more likely to have the condition than girls (NIMH, 2005). The American Psychiatric Association (APA) and CHADD both indicate that between 3 and 7 percent of all schoolchildren have ADHD (APA, 2000; CHADD, 2005). The U.S. Department of Education cites a prevalence rate of some 3 to 5 percent of the school population, boys being some four to nine times more likely than girls to have ADHD (Office of Special Education Programs, 2003, 2004).

The data just reported provide three different answers to the question "How many students have ADHD?" This is because the percentages reported by government and private agencies are only estimates of the overall proportion of America's students who have ADHD. No national registry or required reporting system exists for ADHD.

There is also no answer to the question "How many students receive special education services?" You are probably thinking that even though the number of students in America with ADHD is unknown, the government must know how many students with ADHD the nation serves through special education. But it's just not that simple. As you have learned in previous chapters, IDEA '04 requires states to report each year the number of students with disabilities, by disability category (e.g., learning disabilities, mental retardation), that they serve. However, states report the number of students served only by their *primary* disability. Because ADHD is only one condition of many included in the "other health impairments" category (see Chapter 9 for discussions about these students), these students are reported as falling in *that* category and so cannot be counted separately as having ADHD. Further complicating the problem is the fact that ADHD coexists with many other disabilities. Thus many students with ADHD are counted in the learning disabilities category, others in the emotional or behavioral disorders category, some in the mental retardation category, and a few with their peers who have traumatic brain injury. This is why the number of students with ADHD who receive special education services is unknown, just as is the overall number of these students attending public school.

Is ADHD increasing? Because (for the reasons listed above) a historical record of the prevalence of ADHD does not exist, it is impossible to know with any confidence whether the number of students with ADHD is increasing more rapidly than

David Neeleman in the Spotlight

David Neeleman lives with ADHD and maybe his condition has proved to benefit his fast-paced lifestyle and success. "Even as he talks about his passion—the airline he founded—David Neeleman fidgets. He fingers the airport identity pass he wears around his neck. He plucks a model airplane off the tabletop and scans its underbelly. Sometimes when you talk to him, his head seems elsewhere. 'Out in space,' he readily admits" (Woodyard, 2002).

These words could easily have been written about many children with ADHD. Yet they come from a *USA Today* article on JetBlue CEO and airline entrepreneur David Neeleman, an adult who exhibits the classic distractibility and impulsivity characteristics of ADHD. Neeleman, who discovered that he had ADHD during his late thirties, considers it an asset. Where a magazine reporter might describe him as a pacing, BlackBerry-monitoring, cell-phone-talking interviewee, he sees his behavior as multitasking at its best (Mount, 2004). Neeleman regards his creativity (which helped him invent the e-ticket), energy, and ability to multitask as positive reflections of his ADHD. However, he also uses specific strategies to counter the more frustrating aspects of the disorder. For example, to keep himself organized, he develops routines, always puts important things such as wallets and watches in the same place, and surrounds himself with highly organized people.

the student population in general. Nevertheless, some say that the number of students identified with ADHD is increasing (Future of Children, 2005). Others believe that the proportion is not getting greater but only appears to be, because of the way these students are being counted (Salend & Rohena, 2003).

Are more schoolchildren identified with ADHD in the United States than in other countries? Here we can give you a definitive answer: Yes. ADHD is not found only in the United States, but its prevalence is higher here. Part of the reason is the definition. Although the DSM-IV-TR definition is widely accepted in the United States, it is not the definition used worldwide. In Europe, particularly in Britain, the definition employed by the World Health Organization (WHO) is more commonly accepted, which results in fewer students being identified with ADHD (Reason, 1999). This definition requires that the individual have both significant inattention and hyperactivity (WHO, 2005). When *both* characteristics are required, the prevalence falls to between 0.5 and 1 percent of the student population, compared to the range of 2 to 7 percent identified in the United States. A key difference between these two definitions is the emphasis on problems associated with impulsivity, and British psychologists believe that their more stringent view of ADHD reduces the risk of including children from different cultural backgrounds who come from homes where behaviors expected in school are not instilled from early childhood. In fact, U.S. experts are beginning to understand the danger of misinterpreting the behaviors of students from diverse cultures as signaling a disability, rather than a mismatch between the culture of the school and teachers and that of the student (Gay, 2002). No studies have specifically looked only at the performance and effects of interventions specifically for diverse learners (Olmeda, Thomas, & Davis, 2003). Regardless, experts tend to agree that culture may be an important factor to consider; not only in understanding behavior patterns that don't match those of classmates, but also in selecting the best interventions to help students improve. *Considering Culture* describes a scenario in which school personnel and family members work together to improve the educational outcomes for a student with ADHD.

Causes and Prevention

Scientists are working diligently to identify the causes of ADHD, for without understanding the direct causes of any disability, it is nearly impossible to figure out how to prevent or correct the problem. New information is changing the ways in which investigators are interpreting ADHD and its origins (OSEP, 2003). For example, the problem was once thought to be associated mainly with difficulties related to attention, but today more emphasis is being placed on impulsivity—not being able to inhibit or control one's behavior.

Causes

The exact causes of ADHD are not known, but many experts believe the condition is due to inherent differences in the way the brains of individuals with ADHD function (Barkley, 1998, 2002; Fowler, 2002). Researchers are beginning to believe that a biological predisposition (e.g., temperament and neurological development) for ADHD places some individuals more at risk for developing the condition. Such beliefs support the growing consensus that ADHD has a neurological basis (Salend & Rohena, 2003). A body of research is now focused on the **executive functions** of children with ADHD (Barkley, 1998)—the cognitive abilities that enable us to plan, self-regulate, inhibit inappropriate behaviors, and engage in goal-directed activities (Weyandt, 2005). These executive functions, though associated primarily with the frontal lobes and prefrontal cortex of the brain, involve detailed connections between various other brain regions as well (Weyandt, 2005). It also appears that genetics may contribute to ADHD; the condition is often observed in many members of the same family (Barkley, 1998, 2002; National Institute of Mental Health [NIMH], 2005). Of course, one must never discount the interplay between biology and the environment, and most experts are convinced that parenting and teaching styles, as well as individuals' unique experiences, can make the situation better or worse (CHADD, 2005).

Many studies have attempted to pinpoint precise neurological conditions related to ADHD. The results of these studies are interesting, but not definitive. For example, researchers have found that subjects with ADHD show

- Decreased blood flow and electrical activity in the frontal lobes of the brain (areas that are responsible for executive functions)
- Anatomical differences, in various regions of the brains, from their peers without ADHD
- Differences in neurotransmitter levels (chemicals responsible for the transfer of messages from one part of the brain to another)
- Differences in abilities to track objects visually (e.g., trouble staying on one line of printed text when reading) (Austin, 2003; Barkley 1998, 2002; Ward & Guyer, 2000; Weyandt, 2001, 2005)

These studies indicate clear physiological differences between individuals with and without ADHD, but they provide no definitive answer to the question of the source of these differences. In other words, it is not known whether the structural differences identified are responsible for the ADHD characteristics; whether they result in learning disabilities and emotional or behavioral disorders, which manifest themselves in characteristics shared with ADHD; or whether the physiological attributes are completely unrelated to the ADHD. Further research is needed in this area (Weyandt, 2001).

Considering Culture

High Energy, Low Performance

Derek's transition from elementary school to middle school has been a disaster so far. He is late to classes because he has trouble remembering where the next room is. His homework is usually late, if it is turned in at all, and it always looks as if it has been retrieved from a garbage can. When teachers call on him in class, he doesn't know what they have been talking about or where they are in the lesson. In gym class and on the school campus, he seems to have boundless energy, but he never applies it to accomplish what needs to be done. Concerned about Derek's performance, his teacher, Mr. Neumann, calls Derek's home. Derek's grandmother answers and says, "I'm glad you called. I don't know what to do with that boy. His mother is gone, his father works two jobs, and I'm in charge. Trouble is, I'm 77 and not doing so well myself. I know that Derek wants to do well in school, but he just can't seem to get himself together, and you know how hard it is for African American kids growing up. I'm afraid that if he's not successful at school, he may fall in with the wrong crowd."

Mr. Neumann gets Derek's father's permission for some assessments and permission to talk with his former teachers and the special education resource teacher at the middle school. Mrs. McDonald, his 5th grade teacher, says, "Derek's always had trouble staying organized, but he's smart and a really cool kid. I helped him find ways to stay organized with different-color pocket folders, notebooks, and labels. We also developed a quiet signal in class to help Derek pay attention. Of course middle school presents more challenges, but I'm sure he'll do well with some help."

The assessment results showed that Derek is smart; in some areas, he even scored above grade level. But the results also showed that he has difficulty staying on task, following through with assignments and activities, and focusing on solving problems. When the information was shared with the IEP team, they decided that Derek does have ADHD but that he should remain in Mr. Neumann's class, with consultation from the special education teacher. Now Derek has a special place to keep his school books, notebooks, and papers at home and at school. His notebooks include sections for assignments, homework, and notes from each class. He has a list of things to do each day and when to do them. He also has a group of friends who walk with him from class to class. To help Derek direct some of his boundless energy, Mr. Neumann has arranged for him to try out for some after-school sports teams, where he is an enthusiastic and developing player. The after-school sports have even given Derek's grandmother support in the form of adult supervision, and the grade requirement for athletes has motivated Derek to do well in school. Now that he is doing so much better in school, his father and grandmother worry much less about his future.

Questions to Consider

1 What do you think your first response might be to a student who doesn't pay attention in class, is very active, and is completely disorganized?

2 What do you think might have happened in Derek's life if his teachers, his grandmother, his father, and other members of the IEP team had simply seen him as a "difficult" student?

—By Eleanor Lynch, San Diego State University and Marci Hanson, San Francisco State University

Prevention

Until more is understood about the exact causes of ADHD and the factors that contribute to it; the development of effective ways to prevent the condition will continue to elude researchers. If indeed there is a biological predisposition to ADHD, there are many ways to lessen its impact on both the individual involved and the family. The behavioral accommodations and interventions discussed later in this chapter can reduce or eliminate the periods when ADHD characteristics tend to manifest themselves (e.g., transition times), thus reducing the effects of the condition and preventing problems at home and in the classroom. Similarly, the instructional techniques and suggestions provided can help students continue to make academic gains, thus avoiding many of the negative school outcomes associated with this disorder.

executive functions Higher-order cognitive functions that influence the ability to plan, self-regulate, and engage in goal-directed behavior

Overcoming Challenges

Behavioral techniques, direct and systematic instruction that is evaluated on a frequent basis, and highly motivating instructional materials have proved successful with many children currently identified as having ADHD. In fact, most education and medical experts agree that teaching should be the first step in helping students with ADHD (Guyer, 2000; OSEP, 2003, 2004). However, before teachers even have the opportunity to work with them, many of these students need additional help—for example, in the form of medication. The American Academy of Pediatrics explains it this way: Just as some students need glasses to see better, some students need medication to help them pay better attention and control their behavior (American Academy of Pediatrics, 2005). Possibly more than any other group of students with disabilities, students with ADHD are prescribed medication to assist them with their school-related problems. In fact, over 2 million students with ADHD take prescriptions such as Ritalin, Concerta, Adderall, or Dexadrine to help them control their behavior (Austin, 2003). These stimulant medications sometimes increase the arousal level of the central nervous system, possibly enhancing blood flow to the frontal lobes or increasing electrical activity in the brain and subsequently improving functions such as attention, planning, and self-regulation attributed to these sections (DuPaul, Barkley, & Connor, 1998). Another possibility is that these stimulants (but not other stimulants, such as caffeine in coffee) increase the levels of certain neurotransmitters that enhance brain functioning (Ward & Guyer, 2000). However, the exact processes through which stimulant medications work is not thoroughly understood at this time (Weyandt, 2001).

Many physicians prescribe Ritalin, Dexedrine, or Concerta to help children with ADHD focus their attention on assigned tasks, and the medication is effective for some (Forness & Kavale, 2001). However, controversy surrounds the use of behavior control drugs for these youngsters and the appropriateness of educators recommending their use to parents (Gotsch, 2002). Of particular concern is the rapid increase in prescriptions for these drugs—an increase of some 35 percent over a recent 5-year period, to raise the number to some 20 million prescriptions written in 12 months. Other concerns stem from the side effects (e.g, reduction in appetite, problems sleeping, jitteriness, dizziness) experienced by many youngsters and the need to monitor these students' health and performance carefully (Academy of Pediatrics, 2005; NIMH, 2005). Worry about safety and use make some health care providers reluctant to prescribe these drugs.

In general, medical treatment appears to alleviate the symptoms of ADHD but does not necessarily directly improve academic functioning. The National Institutes of Health (NIH) now indicate that these medications are more effective than behavior therapy alone in controlling the underlying characteristics of ADHD (NIH Consensus Development Conference Statement, 2000). However, they do not seem to have a positive effect on academic performance. To gain improvement in both academics and behavior requires a combination of behavioral and medical interventions (Jensen, 2000; Pappadopulos & Jensen, 2001).

When students use such medication, educators need to work with the family closely. First, these medications are not uniformly effective. Some drugs work better with particular individuals than with others. Second, it may take several adjustments to get the appropriate dosage for optimum performance; teachers need to communicate with families regarding their classroom observations after a dosage change. Also, many of these drugs have negative side effects (American Academy of Pediatrics, 2005). Because students attend school for a large portion of their day, teachers need to monitor the effects of these medications on their students who take them. In addition, it is recommended that, for these students, a school nurse be part of the IEP team.

Medicating Young Minds

Time magazine, November 3, 2003, investigated the increased use of drugs to treat children with mood and behavior problems. The drugs provide obvious positive outcomes for many children, with parents, teachers, and doctors touting their effectiveness in maintaining emotional stability, allowing the children to remain focused and successful in school, and improving interpersonal and social interactions. However, other professionals have voiced serious apprehensions. Here are some of the issues raised in this cover story:

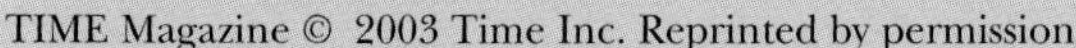

- Only a few of the newest drugs were developed specifically for children. The majority of these medications are approved for adults but are being used in smaller doses with children, a potentially risky practice when childhood metabolisms are taken into account.
- Children without disorders could be receiving medication. Without careful evaluation, the rush to medicate could result in drug treatment for children exhibiting normal variations in behavior.
- Scientists do not know enough about the long-term effects of many of the medications. For example, the frontal lobes of the brain, often a target for drugs to treat ADHD, depression, and obsessive-compulsive disorder, do not fully mature until age 30. Very little is known about the impact of these drugs on still-developing young brains.
- Many of the medications include negative side effects. Headaches, lack of appetite, insomnia, stomach pain, irritability, and nervousness are all common side effects of drugs used to treat ADHD.

Assessment

As we have seen in previous chapters, the assessment of students with disabilities occurs across several settings. In some cases, a disorder is suspected early in a child's life, and appropriate evaluations are conducted before the elementary school years in order for the child to qualify for early intervention services. In other cases, classroom teachers suspect the existence of a disorder and use a variety of pre-referral strategies and assessments to determine whether a full evaluation and referral to special education are necessary. If a full evaluation is warranted, a variety of assessment instruments are used to evaluate the child's abilities. Although many experts in ADHD advocate for comprehensive psychological and even medical evaluations, IDEA '04 does not require such costly medical or psychiatric diagnoses for these individuals (Weyandt, 2001; U.S. Department of Education, 2005). Finally, unless otherwise noted in an IEP, all students must participate in state- and district-wide standardized testing; in these cases, assessment accommodations may be warranted for a child with a disability. All of these situations, and applications for students with ADHD, are discussed next.

Early Identification

The symptoms of ADHD do arise during early childhood, but the acknowledgement of their presence is often retrospective. In other words, few preschoolers are identified as having ADHD because of (1) the fear of misidentifying children as having disabilities when their problems may be due to developmental lags or immaturity and (2) the fact that the characteristics of ADHD (e.g., short attention span, being in constant motion) are typical of many young children without ADHD. Thus, unless doctors and education professionals can document some incident that caused brain damage, identification during the early childhood years is not likely (NIMH, 2005). Nevertheless, the federal government requires that for students to receive special education services for ADHD, the symptoms must have been present before the age of seven (OSEP, 2003).

Pre-Referral

The primary purpose of pre-referral is to avoid unnecessary referrals to special education by implementing research-validated practices in the general education classroom. If the implemented practices work—that is, if the behaviors of concern decrease significantly or disappear—then a referral is not needed. For students who may have ADHD, the pre-referral process should contain multiple steps, and the efficacy of each attempt should be documented.

In the pre-referral phase for students with ADHD, a teacher's actions should focus on preventing problem behaviors. For children with a predisposition toward inattention or hyperactivity, the physical and instructional structure of the classroom must be considered. Students with self-regulation difficulties do better in structured settings, so teachers need to have a well-planned behavior management system in place, complete with rules, procedures, and consistently delivered consequences. Maintenance of a regular classroom routine is very important, as are clearly articulated instructions and expectations for academic and social tasks. Well-planned transition times can decrease the opportunities for "problem" behaviors.

Other colleagues, such as teachers or a school nurse, can be helpful resources. At an initial level, a **school nurse** can be consulted to rule out other conditions (e.g., hearing loss) through general screening procedures. If other conditions might be the source of behavioral problems, then the evaluation process involves professionals with expertise in those areas of concern (e.g., an audiologist). When the school nurse suspects the presence of ADHD characteristics, the direction of the evaluation efforts is adjusted accordingly. Other teachers can conduct classroom observations to help the general educator find additional ways to improve the classroom structure and educational environment. Parents and family members are a critical resource at this stage, both for feedback regarding interventions that have been successful in the past and to maintain consistency between the home and school environments. If a variety of methods have been employed to increase attention or reduce hyperactivity, with little or no success, then a formal referral to special education is warranted.

Identification

Experts strongly suggest that the identification process for ADHD include multidimensional evaluations (Barkley & Edwards, 1998; Gordon & Barkley, 1998; Weyandt, 2001). Such comprehensive assessments would include many different types of procedures such as

- Diagnostic interviews
- Medical examinations
- Behavior rating scales
- Standardized tests
- Observations

school nurse Related service professional providing medical services at school

Parents and school personnel should work together for behavioral and medical management of ADHD.

Because prescription medicines are widely used to assist in the management of hyperactivity, many parents of children with ADHD seek help from their doctors first. Thus the medical profession often is involved in these students' diagnosis, even though only three states require diagnosis by either a physician or a mental health professional as part of the eligibility determination for ADHD (Müller & Markowitz, 2004). (Only five states call out special guidelines for qualifying these students for special education services.)

Even if the student's pediatrician or family doctor makes a diagnosis of ADHD, school personnel must also make a determination about whether the student qualifies for accommodations though Section 504 or for special education services. They use a multilevel approach to gather all the information they need to understand the nature of the individual's problems and the types of supports and services needed (Merrell & Boelter, 2001; Salend & Rohena, 2003). These education professionals collect data about the student's academic performance, behavioral patterns, social interactions, and medical history. They compare this information with the DSM-IV-TR definition of ADHD to determine both needs and eligibility. The subjectivity of some of the assessment procedures (e.g., a parent's perception of hyperactivity compared to a teacher's) requires that caution be exercised. Cooperation among the many people involved in this process is vital. Remember that for a student to receive special education services, the characteristics of ADHD must be significant, must be observed across several settings, must be documented (even if retrospectively) as having existed before the age of seven, and must seriously affect educational performance.

Once a child is identified as having ADHD, the school's multidisciplinary team goes into high gear to develop the student's IEP and determine what accommodations and services are required. A broad array of professionals from a wide variety of disciplines, including a school nurse and a physician, should work with that student's parents throughout the IEP development and implementation process (Austin, 2003). Each professional uses a variety of assessment tools and techniques to monitor the student's academic and behavioral progress. For those students who are receiving medication, it is important that teachers work closely with the family and health professionals to monitor the effectiveness of the medications and ensure that the student doesn't experience negative side effects (American Academy of Pediatrics, 2005; OSEP, 2003).

Evaluation: Testing Accommodations

Just as for students with other disabilities, many types of accommodations are available to students with ADHD; however, one accommodation seems to be the most commonly offered. Whether the students special needs are addressed through IDEA '04 or through Section 504, the most common accommodation to testing situations for students with ADHD is extended time (Elliott & Marquart, 2004). When offered this accommodation, students with disabilities typically take only 8 or 12 minutes longer to answer test items. But does having longer to complete a test make a difference in results? Surprisingly, whether for students with disabilities or without disabilities, extended time does not significantly improve students' scores. What is interesting, however, is that students who are offered extended time feel better about the testing situation, claim they were more motivated to complete the test, felt less frustrated, and thought they performed better. Outcome measures—measures of how well the students actually did on the test—did not support students' feelings about their performance (Elliott & Marquart, 2004).

Early Intervention

Once again, remember that the federal government does not consider ADHD a separate disability or special education category. Therefore, states are not required to report how many students are being provided services through IDEA, so we do not know how many preschoolers (or students) have ADHD or how many of them actually receive special education services. Identification of ADHD in preschoolers is very difficult. The markers of ADHD are hard to discern during the early childhood years, because the differences between a very busy, typical two-year old and a two-year old with this condition are difficult to distinguish (OSEP, 2003). Therefore, it is likely that very few toddlers or preschoolers will ever be served through IDEA because of ADHD. Regardless, the federal government requires special education students with ADHD to have demonstrated signs or symptoms of the condition before they reached the age of seven.

Teaching Students with ADHD

Because identification as having ADHD does not guarantee that a student will qualify for special education services, most students with this disorder—both those with and those without IEPs detailing special education services—are educated in the general education classroom. A variety of instructional accommodations and interventions have proved useful for enhancing instruction and the long-term academic success of these students.

Access to the General Education Curriculum

ADHD has been referred to as an "educational performance problem" (Fowler, 2002, 2004). Over time, the consequence of not providing assistance to those students affected is poor academic achievement. To the extent that students with ADHD miss blocks of information and experience interruptions in the learning process, their access to the general education curriculum is inconsistent. The cumulative effects of missing instruction can be disastrous. Mary Fowler and the U.S. Department of Education's Office of Special Education Programs help us understand what these educational performance problems are and how teachers can help (Fowler, 2002, 2004; OSEP, 2003). Table 6.2 highlights some of these performance areas and how they might be addressed. Being able to pinpoint where

Table 6.2 • Possible Solutions to Educational Performance Problems

Educational Performance Problems	Potential Solutions
Initiating work	• Gain student's attention. • Use clear, one-step instructions. • Provide directions orally and in writing.
Remaining on task	• Seat student away from distractions (e.g., door, window, computer stations). • Use hands-on activities. • Assign highly motivating activities.
Making transitions from one activity to another	• Give a five-minute warning before changing from one activity to another. • Use a standard, predictable schedule. • Remind student about requirements for shift (e.g., clear desk, keep pen and paper on top of desk, line up in small groups).
Completing assignments	• Set a standard for acceptable work. • Provide a rationale for completion. • Assign a peer assistant.

individual students' problems occur increases the likelihood of selecting effective accommodations and interventions sooner. Remember, even though two students might have the same condition (e.g., ADHD or learning disabilities with ADHD), their performance problems and the solutions to them could well be different.

Instructional Accommodations

Accommodations to the classroom's physical environment can help students with ADHD by reducing distracting stimuli. The location of a student's workspace should be considered. For example, a desk or work area in a quiet, relatively distraction-free area, of the classroom is more conducive to concentration than a desk next to high-traffic areas, such as those near the pencil sharpener, hallway door, or trashcan. Placing the student near the teacher allows for easier monitoring and reinforcement, and seating next to a peer who models staying "on task" behavior can positively influence a student's behavior (OSEP, 2004). Other physical accommodations can include pointers or bookmarks to help a student track words visually during reading exercises, timers to remind students how much time is left before an assignment must be finished, visual cues as prompts to change behavior (e.g., turning the classroom lights off to indicate that the noise level is too high) (OSEP, 2004).

Aspects of the learning environment can also be structured to enhance educational outcomes for students with ADHD. As you can see from the suggestions below, many of these accommodations reflect the concepts of universal design. In other words, these accommodations provide benefits for *all* students but are particularly helpful for students with ADHD. Many students learn better when more difficult subjects such as reading and math are taught early in the day; when instruction is exciting, engaging, and culturally relevant to the student; and when the pace of the presentation varies. Students show improved academic results when teachers carefully monitor their understanding of key concepts and adjust the lesson accordingly. Such adjustments can be accomplished easily through teacher questioning and the use of physical responses by the students (e.g., the students each hold up one finger to indicate that the answer to a teacher's question is "yes" or two fingers

Accommodating for Inclusive Environments

Instructional and Testing Accommodations

Instructional Accommodations

- Allow extended time for completion of assignments.
- Break instructional sequences or academic tasks into smaller segments to help maintain attention.
- Arrange more frequent, yet shorter, study periods.
- Set timers for specific tasks to help students stay focused.
- Teach and practice organizational skills (e.g., give guided practice, designate places where students are expected to store instructional materials, and reinforce their doing so).
- Read directions to students to help them refocus.
- Use computer word processing programs to assist with writing activities.
- Allow the use of pointers and tracking devices (e.g., a ruler) to help students track text on a page.

Testing Accommodations

- Testing accommodations should match instructional accommodations whenever possible.
- Select evaluation measures that match the students' preferences.
- Make sure the utility of evaluation measures is not undermined by the impact of ADHD characteristics (e.g., inability to complete lengthy tests due to inattention or impulsivity).
- Allow extended time for test taking.

to indicate a "no" response). Furthermore, all classrooms run more smoothly when directions are clear, concise, and thorough (even better when they are presented both visually and orally) so that students understand what they are supposed to be doing (Salend, Elhoweris, & van Garderen, 2003). See *Accommodating for Inclusive Environments* for additional accommodations to use with students with ADHD.

Validated Practices

How does a teacher help the student with ADHD? As for their counterparts who have emotional or behavioral disorders, functional behavioral assessments (FBAs) are useful in determining the reasons why students with ADHD engage in certain behaviors. (We first introduced FBAs on page 68 in Chapter 2, and you'll learn more about their application for students with emotional or behavioral disorders in Chapter 7.) For example, if FBA results indicate that a student engages in acting-out behaviors to avoid seatwork, the teacher can do several things, such as analyze the work to see whether it is too difficult for the student and/or implement behavioral techniques to eliminate the inappropriate student behavior.

Like their counterparts who have only learning disabilities, students with ADHD respond well to highly structured learning environments where topics are taught directly. Many students with ADHD struggle with motivation and lack the persistence to make the extra effort to learn when it is difficult for them (Carlson et al., 2002). Professionals suggest that carefully planned educational procedures, such as giving rewards, making assignments more interesting, letting students chose their academic assignments from a group of alternatives selected by the teacher, shortening the task, and giving clear and precise instructions, can lead to academic improvement (Powell & Nelson, 1997). Peer tutoring has proved to be very effective for students with ADHD, as well as for those with learning disabilities (DuPaul et al., 1998; Fuchs & Fuchs, 1998). Over 50 percent improvement in academic tasks has been achieved by involving peers in the instructional program. Although it is important for teachers and parents to pay attention to these students' academic problems, it is also imperative to help them develop social skills that are acceptable to their peers.

Self-management tactics (see *Validated Practices* on pages 224–225 for one example) help students learn to control their own behavior and to be responsible for many aspects of their school programs. Typically, experts group **self-management strategies**, also referred to as **self-regulation strategies**, into four categories (Reid & Lienemen, 2006):

- Self-monitoring
- Self-instructions
- Self-reinforcement
- Goal setting

Here's one way that self-management (self-regulation) works. Hayden is unable to stay on task, and she frequently daydreams instead of completing independent work. The teacher and Hayden meet. The teacher explains to Hayden that she is now going to be responsible for monitoring her own behavior. By using **self-monitoring**, Hayden keeps track of her performance (being on task) by collecting data. Through this process, Hayden learns to evaluate her own behavior: to determine whether it is appropriate (on task) or not (off task) and record this information by marking either a smiley face or a sad face on a chart. She uses this process each time she hears a beep on the CD that her teacher prerecorded. Every time she hears the beep, she asks herself, "Was I paying attention? Was I doing what the teacher asked us to do?" Students can also benefit from **self-instruction**, or **self-talk**, in which they use self-induced statements to guide their actions. Hayden reminds herself, "Double-check my answers. Did I answer all of the questions? Just a little bit longer. Stay focused and I can finish this whole worksheet." **Goal setting** is helpful to both teachers and students as they determine the level of expected performance for a task. Hayden and her teacher decide that her goal is to maintain on-task behavior for an entire 30-minute period. **Self-reinforcement** is a powerful self-regulation strategy that allows students to earn rewards for accomplishments. Thus, Hayden earns a sticker for every 10 smiley faces on her chart.

Self-monitoring is particularly helpful both to teachers and to students with ADHD because it does not take much teacher time to implement and it helps students focus on controlling their own behaviors (Daly & Ranalli, 2003). One fun interpretation of the techniques has come to be called "countoons." This simple way for students to keep a record of their own behaviors was first developed and researched by Marilyn Cohen in the early 1970s at the University of Washington's Experimental Education Unit (Kunzelmann et al., 1970). An example of a countoon is shown in Figure 6.1. This technique provides a clear picture—a visual—of the target behavior and its occurrence; provides immediate feedback; is an active way to involve students; and facilitates communication among the student, the teacher, and the family.

self-management or **self-regulation strategies** Includes many techniques that the individual uses, individually or in combination, to modify her or his own behavior or academic performance

self-monitoring Keeping a record (data) of one's own performance

self-instruction or **self-talk** Self-induced statements to assist in self-regulation

goal setting Determining desired behavior and the criteria that will mark its attainment

self-reinforcement Awarding self-selected reinforcers or rewards to oneself contingent on meeting self-selected criteria

For students with ADHD, organizers to help them focus their learning can be very beneficial (Salend, Elhoweris, & van Garderen, 2003). Graphic organizers, discussed on pages XX in Chapter 4, can help students identify the important elements of the material being learned. For students whose inattentiveness and distractibility interfere with their ability to see a writing task through to completion, graphic organizers help them break a writing assignment into smaller components. An example is shown in Chapter 4's *Validated Practices* (see on page 146).

Technology

Advances in technology have improved all of our lives, and for individuals with disabilities, particularly those with ADHD, technology offers many possibilities. Because both those with and those without disabilities use many of these helpful technological devices, they do not call attention to the individual with the problem. Also, because of the increase in the number of devices and software, the rel-

Figure 6.1 • Examples of a Countoon for Self-Recording of Wandering Around

What I do			My count	What happens
Read my book F1	Wander around F2	Read my book F3	1 2 3 4 5 6 7 8 9 10 11 12 F4	I get to play F5

Source: From "Using countoons to teach self-monitoring skills" by P. M. Daly and P. Ranalli. *Teaching Exceptional Children, 35,* (2003) p. 33. Copyright © 2003 by The Council for Exceptional Children. Reprinted by permission.

atively low cost of many of them, and the fact that their use is commonly accepted, the distinction between instructional and assistive technologies is increasingly blurred (Van Kuren, 2003). Computers help everyone turn in more readable and pleasing papers. For those students who cannot write legibly or produce a neat report, word processing makes the individual's disability less visible and is one avenue to better grades. Electronic personal organizers and personal digital assistants (PDAs) such as those manufactured by Palm™ are very "in." Everyone seems to have or want such a device to help manage time, remember appointments, and give reminders of important due dates. For many students with ADHD, personal organizers provide the structure necessary to reduce the number of incomplete homework assignments or skipped meetings with a tutor. Even the new Apple iPods™ have a calendar function and other applications that can help students organize their lives.

Some software programs provide special benefits to individuals whose thinking skills seem disorganized. For example, *Report Writer Interactive*® provides the user with structure during the writing process. This software, like other, similar programs, help students organize their thoughts, place them in a logical sequence, and then produce a written document that is formatted and pleasing in appearance. As we noted in Chapter 4, other programs, such as *Kidspiration*® and *Inspiration*®, help students by facilitating their creation of graphic organizers for studying and writing reports.

Some aspects of technologically based learning activities appear to be particularly suited to students with ADHD. Web pages that provide interesting text and stimulating pictures combined with movies or audio clips allow students to change activities frequently, rather than being engaged in a reading activity for a prolonged period of time. Similarly, the ability to click on hyperlinks to access more information or engage in interactive learning activities provides further opportunities to shift attention frequently.

When teachers include technology in instruction, they do need to be sure that it is accessible (Hoffman, Hartley, & Boone, 2005). Computer usage does not always equate to the ability to obtain information. For example, some software programs are not intuitive to students, who cannot figure out how to open files or access or retrieve information. Teachers should not assume that even simple PDF files or Powerpoint® slides are accessible to every student. Similarly, not all on-line learning activities are equally accessible. Determining how useful any type of technology might be should be done carefully, perhaps with help from a specialist in assistive technology.

Validated Practices Self-Management

What Is Self-Management?

Self-management techniques are a systematic process used to teach students with severe disabilities to manage their own behavior. The three types of self-management are self-monitoring, self-evaluation and self-reinforcement. When teaching self-management skills to students, teachers first model the process of self-management and then provide students with ample opportunities to learn and practice the strategy on their own. Many students require positive and corrective feedback during the learning process in order to master the technique.

Why Self-Management Is Beneficial

It is important for students to take responsibility for their learning and actions. Students who are able to "control" their behavior become independent and are able to generalize this ability to other aspects of their lives. In addition, when students are able to use self-management techniques, you will be able to spend more time teaching instead of managing student behavior.

Implementing Self-Management

A brief description of some self-management procedures follows, and Figure A shows an example of a data collection system for a student to use.

Figure A • Sample Self-Monitoring Form for On-Task Behavior

Sample Self-Monitoring Form for On-Task Behavior

Student's name: *Erik* Date: *11–6*

Ask yourself: **"Was I working?"**
Check yes or no when you hear the beep.

	1	2	3	4	5	6	7	8	9	10
☺ YES	✓		✓	✓	✓		✓		✓	✓
☹ NO		✓				✓		✓		

Variations:

Was I **paying attention?**
Was I **on time?**
Was I **listening?**

Did I **turn in my homework?**
Did I **raise my hand?**
Did I **wait to be called on?**
Did I **bring my materials?**

I had **a positive attitude.**
I had **appropriate adult interaction.**
I am **on-task.**

Select the Behavior for Self-Management

Identify and define the behavior.

- Select behaviors you can easily describe, define, count, and evaluate.
- Identify functional behaviors with social-value important to the student (e.g., staying on task, completing homework).

Transition

Few youngsters "grow out of" their disabilities. For most, disabilities last a lifetime. Of course, with effective education, positive experiences, and a great deal of hard work, people with disabilities are able to compensate for their problems and to participate fully in the community and the workplace. In this respect, individuals with ADHD share experiences with their counterparts who have other disabilities. A combination of medical intervention and counseling—including individual, family/marriage, and/or vocational counseling—can be effective in promoting positive outcomes for adults with ADHD (Murphy, 1998).

As you learned in Chapter 1, more and more students with disabilities are attending postsecondary schools, but these individuals' success rates are disappointing (U.S. Department of Education, 2002). The transition to college can be difficult for many students, and for those with disabilities, the move away from family and the loss of supports from a school-based IEP team can be devastating. Many colleges and universities have centers on campus designed to help students with disabilities cope with the increased demands of college courses. Some centers offer intensive supports, and evidence now indicates that they make a real difference in

- Select behaviors the student has ample opportunities to use.
- Select behaviors manageable for the student to perform and record.

Determine mastery criteria.

- Consider the student's current level of task performance (e.g., on task 50 percent of the time).
- Compare that level of performance with that of peers to set goals and criteria (e.g., on task 90 percent of the time).

Measure current performance levels.

- Conduct 4 or 5 observations to determine the student's current level.

Choose self-management component.

- Self-monitoring (e.g., "Am I on task?")
- Self-evaluation (e.g., "Did I reach my goal today?")
- Self-reinforcement (e.g., "I did a good job today.")

Develop the Self-Management Component

- Finalize and describe behaviors.
- Be sure others can consistently observe those behaviors.
- Determine when and how data will be collected.
- Develop a simple data-recording system.

Teach Students to Use Self-Management

Introduce the procedure.

- State the behavior and provide both examples of effective use of the procedure and examples of its ineffective use.
- Explain the importance of the behavior.
- Provide ample opportunities for supervised practice using the recording system.
- Discuss criteria for mastery.
- Teach self-recording procedure.

Provide practice and assess mastery.

- Provide guided practice and role playing.
- Assess mastery during role playing.
- Discuss when self-management will be implemented.
- Provide independent practice.
- Assess mastery and independence.

Evaluate the Student's Performance

- Assess performance against criteria.
- Assess maintenance.
- Assess generalization.

This scientifically validated practice is a teaching method proved effective by systematic research efforts. (Connell, Carta, & Baer, 1993; Dunlap et al., 1991; Hall, McClannahan, & Krantz, 1995; Hughes & Boyle, 1991; King-Sears & Carpenter, 1997; Prater, Hogan, & Miller, 1992.) Full citations are found in the references for this chapter at the end of the book.

Source: From *Innovations: Teaching self-management to elementary students with development disabilities* (p. 21) by M. E. King-Sears and S. L. Carpenter, 1997, Washington, DC: American Association on Mental Retardation. Reprinted with permission of the American Association on Mental Retardation via Copyright Clearance Center.

the outcomes of college students with ADHD (Getzel, McManus, & Briel, 2004). The supports offered at Virginia Commonwealth University provide a model for the types of services that should be available if the dream of college graduation is to become a reality for more students with ADHD (and learning disabilities). Here are some of the important components of such effective programs:

- Each student has an Individualized Academic Support Plan (similar to an IEP but used for postsecondary students).
- Individual students have frequent communications (through e-mail, telephone, or in-person meetings) with the academic specialist.
- The center provides help and instruction about study skills (e.g., writing strategies, test-taking strategies, time management, organizers).
- Students learn what accommodations are effective for them and advocate for the use of these accommodations in all relevant courses.
- Assistance is provided to help students understand their disabilities and manage stress associated with the challenges the disability brings.
- Career development activities (e.g., internships, resumé development, practice with interviewing) are provided.
- Assistive technology is available and supported.

Collaboration

When medical treatment of ADHD symptoms is used, the school nurse is frequently the individual responsible for dispensing medication at school. Prescription drugs are considered controlled substances, so school nurses must deal with issues related to safe administration of medications, adherence to state guidelines regarding the administration of controlled substances, monitoring the impact of the medication on student performance (including potential side effects), and maintenance of proper documentation (NASN, 2002a). The school nurse is also an important part of the IEP team for students who take stimulant medications, and he or she acts as a liaison between members of the school, home, and medical communities (NASN, 2002b). Even if a school nurse is not assigned specifically to an individual school, one should be available through the district office.

Students on any medication program should be monitored closely to maximize benefits as well as spot any potentially harmful side effects. The teacher is often the adult who spends the most time with a child during the school day and, accordingly, has the potential to provide the most information regarding the impact of the medication. According to Ward and Guyer (2000), a teacher has the opportunity to

- Observe the child in a typical academic setting and note responses to the environment
- Observe the child once medication has been prescribed to note the effect on the child
- Note the effects of dosage changes
- Observe the length of time that positive effects from medication last
- Identify possible side-effects
- Note changes in behavior and academic performance

Collaboration with the school nurse is important to ensure that medically related information is shared with the appropriate partners. As a medical liaison, the school nurse can communicate with the doctor who prescribed the drugs and give feedback that will help determine the appropriate dosage levels for a student. Furthermore, the school nurse may be able to answer questions from both teachers and parents regarding drug-related issues, such as long-term impact and potential side-effects.

Partnerships with Families and Communities

The challenges faced by families of students with ADHD are great. Students with this condition receive considerable negative feedback, and they often bring this hostility home (Fowler, 2002). Reports about arguments regarding chores, following families' rules, disobeying, and being "impossible to count on" are common. In addition to these problems, many families struggle with challenges related to cost. Many insurance companies will not pay for behavior control medications or for treatment of mental illness, which ADHD is often considered (NIMH, 2005). While some families are frustrated that their health insurance policies do not cover the medical costs related to their children's ADHD, many other families have no health insurance at all, so they must either pay for medication and treatment themselves or not avail themselves of these services.

Having information empowers all of us. This fact is particularly true for parents of children who have different learning styles, are not typical learners, or behave erratically. Children with ADHD bring many challenges to their families, and their inconsistent behaviors often result in confusion: Maybe Juan isn't trying hard enough, Evan is just forgetful and scattered, Connor doesn't seem to care, or Lyra has an attitude problem. Teachers can help parents of students with ADHD better understand the issues and challenges this condition presents, and, as a by-product, help themselves and their other students as well (Mathur & Smith, 2003). How can teachers help? One way is to assist parents in finding accurate information about this condition through the Internet and community agencies. Teachers can help parents assess the accuracy of the information they find, and they can help families determine the effectiveness of some of the strategies suggested. Another way to help is to put families in touch with professionals or with other parents who have formed support groups. And yet another is to directly help design programs that build partnerships between home and school.

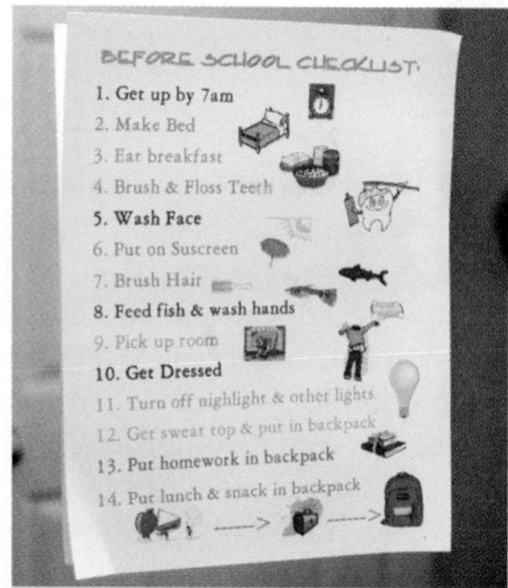

The student, the family, and teacher are all helped by providing organizational supports.

Teachers can help families as they design ways to organize and structure schoolwork. Through effective home and school communications, teachers can share what they find helps students organize their work and manage their time at school. For families that have Internet technology available at home, educators can capitalize on this means of quick and easy communication either through e-mail or via the Web (Salend et al, 2004). Teachers can also assist families in home implementation of those techniques that have proved effective at school (Mathur & Smith 2003; OSEP, 2003). Here are a few examples of ways to help these students at both school and home:

- Post a schedule for the week (*school:* on the corner of the student's desk; *home:* on the refrigerator).
- Set a time to discard out-of-date materials (*school:* clean out desk and locker every Friday afternoon; *home:* sort out the contents of the backpack every Saturday morning).
- Put things in the same place (*school:* worksheets to be completed in a stacking tray; *home:* homework and assignments in progress in a bin by the kitchen door).
- Use specific rewards and consequences for both appropriate and inappropriate behaviors (*school:* reward improved academic performance, lose points or privileges for breaking classroom rules; *home:* movie night for a good week at school, suspension of television privileges for an evening for skipped chores).

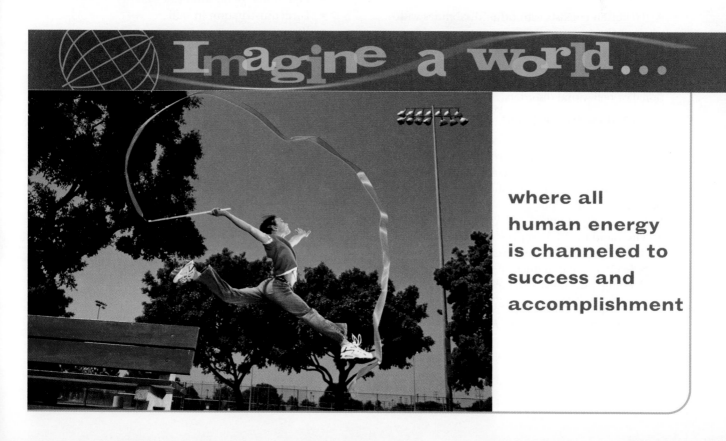

Imagine a world...

where all human energy is channeled to success and accomplishment

Summary

In 1997, when the government called out ADHD as a separate condition, it was confident that this designation would cause very few additional students to be included in special education. The government came to this conclusion because it believed that most students with ADHD who qualified for special education services were already being served through existing special education categories. The characteristics that define ADHD—inattention, hyperactivity, and impulsivity—tend to overlap with other disabilities. ADHD is still not a separate special education category; rather, it is a condition specifically addressed in the special education category IDEA '04 calls "other health impairments." Students with ADHD receive special education services *only* if the disorder significantly affects their school performance. A variety of accommodations and academic interventions are available to enhance the school success of students with ADHD, many of which have been proved effective for students with learning disabilities and emotional or behavioral disorders. Because of the prevalence of medical intervention for students with ADHD, collaboration with the school nurse is important. Finally, outcomes for students with ADHD are improved when there is strong collaboration and consistency between the home and school environments.

Addressing the Chapter Objectives

1 What are the common characteristics of students with ADHD?

- Inattention
- Hyperactivity
- Impulsivity
- Academic difficulties
- Social difficultires

2 What is the relationship of ADHD to other, coexisting disabilities?

- ADHD often coexists with other disabilities with which it shares various characteristics.
- 70 percent of children with ADHD also have a learning disability.
- 42 percent of children with ADHD also have emotional or behavioral disorders.

3 How is ADHD treated medically?

- Stimulant medications, such as Ritalin, Dexadrine, and Concerta, are typically prescribed to increase attention and reduce hyperactivity.
- Medical therapy has proved more effective than behavior therapy alone.
- Concerns exist about
  - The rapid increase in prescriptions for these drugs (35 percent over a recent 5-year period)
  - Side effects (e.g, reduction in appetite, problems sleeping, jitteriness, dizziness)

4 What are various accommodations and classroom interventions used for students with ADHD?

- Accommodations
  - Reducing distractions
  - Preferential seating near the teacher
  - Pointers to help with visual tracking
  - Extended time
  - Timers
  - Visual cues and prompts
  - Breaking activities and assignments into smaller segments
- Instructional techniques
  - Highly structured setting
  - Functional behavioral assessments
  - Direct instruction in skills
  - Peer tutoring
  - Self-regulation strategies
  - Learning strategies
  - Content organizers

5 Why are collaboration and partnerships with families and other professionals important?

- Collaboration with the school nurse provides
  - Medical liaison between family and medical community
  - Professional knowledge regarding medications
- Collaboration with families
  - Provides teachers with key information about the student
  - Provides families with professional information from teachers
  - Allows for consistency between behavioral interventions at home and at school

mylabschool
Where the classroom comes to life!

MyLabSchool is a collection of online tools for your success in this course, your licensure exams, and your teaching career. Visit www.mylabschool.com to access the following:

- Online Study Guide
- Video cases from real classrooms
- Help with your research papers using Research Navigator
- Career Center with resources for:
  - Praxis exams and licensure preparation
  - Professional portfolio development
  - Job search and interview techniques
  - Lesson planning

Supplementary Resources

Popular Novels, Children's Books, and Adolescents' Books

Gantos, J. (1998). *Joey Pigza swallowed the key.* New York: Farrar, Straus and Giroux.

Kraus, J., & Martin, W. (2005). *Cory stories: A kid's book about living with ADHD.* Washinton, DC: Magination Press.

Quinn, P. O., & Stern, J. M. (2001). *Putting on the brakes: Young people's guide to understanding attention deficit hyperactivity disorder* (rev. ed.). Washington, DC: Magination Press, An Educational Publishing Foundation Book, American Psychological Association.

Professional, Parent, and Advocacy Groups

Attention Deficit Information Network (AD-IN) in Needham, Massachusetts: www.addinfonetwork.com

Children and Adults with Attention-Deficit/Hyperactivity Disorder (CHADD) in Landover, Maryland: www.chadd.org

National Institute of Mental Health, National Institutes of Health in Bethesda, Maryland www.nimh.nih.gov

World Health Organization in Geneva, Switzerland www.who.int/en/

Professional Standards and Licensure Tests

After reading this chapter, you should be able to link basic knowledge and skills described in the CEC Standards and INTASC Principles with information provided in this text. The table below shows some of the specific CEC Individualized General Curriculums Knowledge and Skill Standards and INTASC Special Education Principles that can be applied to each major section of the chapter. Other standards may also be applied to this chapter. Associated General Praxis II topic areas are identified in the right column.

Major Chapter Headings	CEC Knowledge and Skill Core Standard and Associated Subcategories	INTASC Core Principle and Associated Special Education Subcategories	PRAXIS II Exam Topic
Where We've Been . . . What's on the Horizon?	**1: Foundations** GC1K3 Historical foundations, classic studies, major contributors, major legislation, and current issues related to knowledge and practice	**1: Subject Matter** 1.12 Special education teachers serve as a resource to others by providing information about the laws and policies that support students with disabilities and how to access additional information when needed.	1: Understanding Exceptionality 2: Legal and Social Issues
Attention Deficit Hyperactivity Disorder Defined	**1: Foundations** GC1K1 Definitions and issues related to the identification of individuals with disabilities	**1: Subject Matter** 1.02 All teachers know which key concepts, ideas, facts, and processes in their content area students should understand at different grades and developmental levels and can appropriately structure activities that reflect the scope and sequence of the content area.	1: Understanding Exceptionality 2: Legal and Social Issues
Characteristics	**2: Development and Characteristics of Learners** GC2K4 Psychological and social-emotional characteristics of individuals with disabilities	**2: Student Learning** 2.08 Special education teachers seek a holistic understanding of each student's current learning and development, based on knowledge of the student's performance within a variety of settings.	1: Understanding Exceptionality 2: Legal and Social Issues
Causes and Prevention	**2: Development and Characteristics of Learners** GC2K1 Etiology and diagnosis related to various theoretical approaches	**2: Student Learning** 2.04 All teachers are knowledgeable about multiple theories of learning and research-based teaching practices that support learning.	1: Understanding Exceptionality 2: Legal and Social Issues

Assessment	**8: Assessment** GC8S1 Implement procedures for assessing and reporting both appropriate and problematic social behaviors of individuals with disabilities	**8: Assessment** 8.08 Special education teachers initiate, contact, and collaborate with other professionals throughout the identification and initial planning process.	1: Understanding Exceptionality 2: Legal and Social Issues 3: Delivery of Services to Students
Teaching Students with ADHD	**4: Instructional Strategies** GC4S3 Teach learning strategies and study skills to acquire academic content	**4: Instructional Strategies** 4.13 Special education teachers identify instructional strategies that have been successful in different learning environments and work to embed these strategies across environments for individual students with disabilities.	2: Legal and Social Issues 3: Delivery of Services to Students
Transition	**7: Instructional Planning** GC7K2 Model career, vocational, and transition programs for individuals with disabilities	**7: Planning Instruction** 7.05 All teachers monitor student progress and incorporate knowledge of student performance across settings into the instructional planning process, using information provided by parents and others in those settings.	2: Legal and Social Issues 3: Delivery of Services to Students
Collaboration	**10: Collaboration** GC10S2 Select, plan, and coordinate activities of related services personnel to maximize direct instruction for individuals with disabilities	**10: Collaboration, Ethics, and Relationships** 10.05 All special education teachers provide leadership that enables teams to accomplish their purposes.	2: Legal and Social Issues 3: Delivery of Services to Students
Partnerships with Families and Communities	**10: Collaboration** GC10K1 Parent education programs and behavior management guides that address severe behavior problems and facilitate communication for individuals with disabilities	**10: Collaboration, Ethics, and Relationships** 10.09 Special education teachers collaborate with families and with school and community personnel to include students with disabilities in a range of instructional environments in the school and community.	1: Understanding Exceptionality 2: Legal and Social Issues

Pink Flags by Shirley Mason (Sybil). Courtesy of White House Gallery and used with kind permission of James Ballard.

Shirley Mason became famous not because of her paintings but, rather, through a best-selling book and the Emmy-winning TV movie about her life, in which actress Sally Field appeared as Mason, who was also known as Sybil. In today's terminology, Sybil's disability would probably fall in the category of emotional or behavioral disorders. Described at the time as exhibiting "multiple personality disorder," Sybil played host to 16 different personalities, two of whom were male. She received psychiatric treatment for some 11 years, beginning when she was a graduate student at Columbia University in New York City. She lived the last 20 years of her life quietly in Lexington, Kentucky, where she produced some of her finest paintings and ran a successful art gallery.

Emotional or Behavioral Disorders

7

“Just as we cannot fiscally afford a health care system in which a family's first contact with medical services is an emergency room, . . . we similarly cannot afford to wait until youth develop antisocial behavior patterns, fail school, and begin committing delinquent acts before intervening.”

Hill Walker and Herb Severson
University of Oregon

Where We've Been . . . What's on the Horizon?

Over the course of history, people have recognized emotional or behavioral disorders, particularly in adults. Yet opinions about how to identify and respond to these individuals have shifted dramatically over time. As you will see, some of the historical treatment of people with emotional or behavioral disorders is shocking.

Chapter Objectives

After studying this chapter, you will be able to:

1 Explain how an unclear definition can influence how we identify and support students with emotional or behavioral disorders.

2 Identify academic and social characteristics of these students.

3 Describe the causes of emotional or behavioral disorders.

4 Identify strategies for improving learning outcomes for these students.

5 List strategies for improving postsecondary outcomes for these students.

Historical Context

It was probably Leo Kanner's 1957 book *Child Psychiatry* that sparked the development of services for children in America. In ancient times, people believed that those with emotional or behavioral disorders were possessed by the devil. During some periods, such as in ancient Egypt, treatment was enlightened and humane (Deutsch, 1949). However, the mystery surrounding mental illness often fostered negative assumptions about its causes and resulted in horrible treatment. Some societies believed that these disorders were contagious, and affected people were removed from the community to protect others. Treatments in the middle ages and later reflected such beliefs and commonly included imprisonment, placement in poorhouses, beatings, chainings, straitjacketing, and other cruel actions. The first institution for people with mental disorders was established in London in 1547. Officially named St. Mary of Bethlehem, it became known as Bedlam, a term that now means a place of noise and uproar. Those in the institution were chained, starved, and beaten. A popular form of entertainment in London was to take the family for an outing to view the “lunatics” at Bedlam.

By the 18th Century, changes began. Philippe Pinel, a French psychiatrist, in 1792 ordered humanitarian reform, including unchaining, for mental patients at the Saltpêtrière, a Paris asylum for the “insane” (Brigham, 1847). In the United States, major reform in the identification and treatment of people with emotional

This chapter was contributed by Deborah Deutsch Smith and Kathleen Lane, Vanderbilt University.

or behavioral disorders began with the efforts of reformers in the 1800s. Benjamin Rush, the father of American psychiatry and a signer of the Declaration of Independence, proposed more humane methods of caring for these children. Dorothea Dix influenced the founding of state institutions for people with mental disorders. By 1844 many states had institutions for people with mental disorders, and the Association of Medical Superintendents of American Institutions for the Insane (now the American Psychiatric Association) was founded. But the hope associated with early institutions soon gave way to pessimism as institutions became more custodial.

Before the late 1800s and the onset of public school for children with emotional or behavioral disorders, most of these children received no services at all. The passage of compulsory education laws at the end of that century prompted educational services for these students, even though many attended ungraded classes along with other students who struggled in the general education settings. The early public school classes provided many noneducational services to these students, including mental and health care, much like today's wraparound services. Thus a "safety net" of school, community, and social services existed to help children and their families (Duckworth et al., 2001).

The 1960s and 1970s saw numerous advances for children with emotional or behavioral disorders, as researchers, scholars, and educational developers created new ways to teach these students. In 1962 Norris Haring and Lakin Phillips published *Educating Emotionally Disturbed Children,* a book that described their experimental work in the Arlington, Virginia, public schools. Their approach stressed behavioral principles, a structured environment, and interactions between the child's home and school environments. Meanwhile, Eli Bower developed a definition of behavioral disorders that is the basis for the federal definition and the definitions used in many states today (Bower & Lambert, 1962). In the 1960s, Nicholas Hobbs initiated Project Re-Ed. This landmark effort clearly showed the effectiveness of an ecological approach, where the child's home and community environments are considered. Through this approach, children attended residential schools for short periods of time and returned to restructured community and family environments. Frank Hewett's Santa Monica Project developed the engineered classroom, demonstrating the positive impact of a highly structured classroom environment using behavior management principles.

In 1964 the classic applied behavioral analysis study about the effects of teacher attention on a preschooler's social interactions with his peers during playtime was published (Allen et al., 1964). This study sparked a new interest in the important effects of the environment on people's actions. The development of applied behavioral analysis techniques with children, initiated by Montrose Wolf, Don Baer, and Todd Risley, was instrumental in the application of token economies in classroom settings nationwide. Montrose Wolf is also credited with developing the Teaching-Family Model, which was begun at the University of Kansas and was later extended to a well-known program at Boys Town in Nebraska. These pioneering efforts have been replicated across the nation, both at schools and in residential settings. They have also evolved and been further developed into the validated practices advocated through IDEA '04 and the professional literature. These practices make it possible to alter what might otherwise be a tragic path for many students with emotional or behavioral disorders. Be sure to read *Chris Hughes in the Spotlight.* Learn how this teacher helped develop a very successful positive behavior support program at his middle school, and think about how each one of us can make a difference for so many.

Challenges That Emotional or Behavioral Disorders Present

Students with emotional or behavioral disorders are among some of the most difficult to teach. Yet it is imperative that all teachers understand not only the characteristics of these students but also how to meet their educational, social, and

Chris Hughes in the Spotlight

Chris Hughes goes the extra mile to make a difference in the lives of his students. He is a middle school teacher in Middle Tennessee who, in conjunction with the school site positive behavior support team, has helped to design, implement, and evaluate a strong positive behavior support (PBS) program. As part of the primary intervention plan, Chris works with students to develop PBS videos. Each video is 4 to 5 minutes in length and features students introducing the schoolwide expectations through the use of clever examples of appropriate and inappropriate behavior. These videos, which are often set to music, are played at the beginning of the school day to remind students what is expected of them.

Any adult who sees a student meeting these expectations may give that student a PBS ticket to reinforce the behavior. Students save these PBS tickets for a special assembly held at the end of each month. During this assembly, students listen to music, dance, play basketball, and participate in drawings using the remaining PBS tickets. Mr. Hughes has worked with parent volunteers and other members of the PBS team to obtain a range of reinforcers, including t-shirts, restaurant certificates, music, bikes, CD players, and even a computer! Each month the number of tickets required for entry increases. When students enter the gym they count out the requisite number of tickets and place them (along with any other PBS tickets) into a large, clean trashcan. Every 10 minutes, random drawings occur to distribute the reinforcers.

Schoolwide data indicate that this program is lowering levels of student risk. The PBS team has also used the schoolwide data to identify students who need more support. Chris Hughes, along with three other teachers, teaches a special elective class for those students. These classes include curriculum designed to improve study skills and conflict resolution skills. Chris Hughes is a dynamic teacher who has taken prevention seriously. As Mr. Hughes would say, "PBS—That's the Ticket!"

behavioral needs, given that these students struggle both within and beyond the school setting. When compared to general education students and students in other disabilities categories, students with emotional or behavioral disorders have the most negative outcomes. For example, students with emotional or behavioral disorders lag behind other students in key academic areas such as reading and math skills, with approximately 50 percent performing in the bottom quartile (SEELS, 1999). The academic deficits show up in low grade point averages, with a disproportionate percentage of students earning Ds and Fs (Wagner, Marder et al., 2003). They also tend to have academic deficits in many areas (e.g., reading, math, writing, social studies, and science), and these deficits don't appear to get better over time. These academic problems either remain the same (Mattison, Hooper, & Glassberg, 2002) or worsen (Greenbaum et al., 1996; Nelson et al., 2004) as these students move into their secondary years.

Not only do students with emotional or behavior disorders experience less positive outcomes while in school than other students with and without disabilities (e.g., earning lower grades, missing more school, higher number of suspensions; SEELS, 1999), but they also continue to struggle when they leave school. These students are much more likely than other students with disabilities to

- Struggle to find jobs and remain employed
- Have problems with criminality
- Abuse drugs and alcohol
- Require mental health services

In short, life beyond school doesn't seem to improve for students with emotional or behavioral disorders (Walker, Ramsey, & Gresham, 2004). In fact, as shown in the film *The Aviator* and discussed in *On the Screen,* mental illness often begins in childhood and accelerates through adulthood. Given that these individuals do not perform well during and after their school years, we must learn better methods of serving them effectively and early (Lee, Sugai, & Horner, 1999). We need to figure out how to make a difference.

Making a Difference

Chicago Youth Centers

Making success possible for students with emotional or behavioral disorders demands the concerted efforts of many. The systematic intervention required to make a difference means that educators must collaborate with each other and also work in partnership with community agencies. Resources available in communities can help children and youth stay out of trouble and succeed at school (Sinclair et al., 1998; Tobin & Sugai, 1999). Although there are many community-based programs in place to support these youngsters, we'd like to look at one program that is making just such a difference.

The Chicago Youth Centers (CYC) is a large independent youth service center that provides an array of programs to over 11,000 youngsters every year (CYC, 2005). CYC was founded in 1956 with the goal of serving some of Chicago's most challenging neighborhoods by offering a range of after-school programs in academics, athletics, arts, and counseling. Specifically, the program offers six content areas—nature and environment, math and science; health, social and physical development; academic support and enhancement; the arts; career exploration, business and community outreach; and leadership development. CYC offers after-school programs in some of the poorest inner city areas of Chicago, most in partnership with the local schools. One of CYC's programs, Girl Power, helps young girls by focusing on promoting education and prevention of teenage pregnancy and drug use. Success stories abound. Thousands of former participants have gone on to college and become civic and business leaders. And many have returned to volunteer at CYC. Unfortunately, not enough of these wonderful programs exist. To learn more about CYC, it's very special programs, and how to get involved, visit its website at **www.chicagoyouthcenters.org**

Emotional or Behavioral Disorders Defined

emotional disturbance The term used in IDEA '04 for emotional or behavioral disorders

emotional or behavioral disorders A disability characterized by behavioral or emotional responses that are very different from all norms and referent groups and have adverse effects on educational performance

Emotional or behavioral disorders (EBD) are difficult to define. In fact, some think that people are identified as having this disability when adults in authority say so (Hallahan & Kauffman, 2006). In other words, in many cases the application of the definition is subjective. Definitions of this disability, including the one used in IDEA '04, are based on the one developed by Eli Bower (1960, 1982). Let's first look at the federal definition. IDEA '04 uses the term **emotional disturbance** to describe students with **emotional or behavioral disorders**, which is the special education category under which students whose behavioral or emotional responses are not typical are served (see Table 7.1).

Old versions of IDEA used the term *serious emotional disturbance* to describe this disability area, but *serious* was dropped in 1999 when the U.S. Department of Education created the regulations for the 1997 version of IDEA. The government did not, however, change the substance of the definition when it changed the term. Here's what it said about the deletion: "[It] is intended to have no substantive or legal significance. It is intended strictly to eliminate the pejorative connotation of

The Aviator's Tailspin

Howard Hughes was almost bigger than life. At age 18, he inherited the family business and used his vast wealth to pioneer the development of commercial aviation and also to fund his passion for making movies. He was an engineering and business genius who designed bombers and spy planes for the U.S. military during World War II; he also led the development of the commercial airline business as CEO of TWA, which flew worldwide. What probably made Hughes most well known, however, was being a flamboyant movie mogul who made epic films and lived the lifestyle of the Hollywood "rich and famous."

In 2004, the acclaimed Hollywood director Martin Scorsese brought to the screen the conflict between Hughes's naturally flashy, public personality and the mental illness that caused Hughes to withdraw from life. Scorsese and Leonardo DiCaprio, who played the part of Hughes, reveal the spiraling tragedy of mental illness and how it often begins in childhood, accelerates, and eventually consumes its victims. Although the condition can be controlled through medication today, Howard Hughes's life was ravaged by obsessive compulsive disorder (OCD), which ultimately resulted in self-imposed isolation and overwhelming fright of infection and human contact. Through *The Aviator,* we can better understand the challenges that emotional or behavioral disorders presents to those affected.

—By Steven Smith

the term 'serious'" (U.S. Department of Education, 1999, p. 12542). In addition, some implied parts of the federal definition are important to understand. For example, although only one characteristic listed in the IDEA '04 definition need be present for the student to qualify for special education, whatever the characteristics, the child's educational performance must be adversely affected. Because nearly all of us experience some mild maladjustment for short periods of our lives, the definition also requires that the child exhibit the characteristic for a long time and to a marked degree, or significant level of intensity.

The IDEA '04 term and definition have been criticized by many professionals (Kauffman, 2005). To them, using only the word *emotional* excludes students whose disability is only behavioral. The exclusion of students who are "socially maladjusted" contributes to this misunderstanding because the term is not actually defined in IDEA '04. Many educators interpret the term *social maladjustment* as referring to students with **conduct disorders** or those youth who have been adjudicated for rule violations (American Psychiatric Association, 2000). And the reference to "educational performance" has been narrowly interpreted to mean only academic performance and not behavioral or social performance, life skills, or vocational skills.

Responding to these criticisms, a coalition of 17 organizations, which calls itself the National Mental Health and Special Education Coalition, drafted another definition (see again Table 7.1) and continues to lobby federal and state governments to adopt it (Forness & Knitzer, 1992). It is unlikely, however, that this definition will gain universal acceptance, because some people are concerned that it would be a more inclusive definition; it might identify too many children (Kauffman, 2002 July 14, personal communication). Regardless, it is useful to see this disability from another perspective.

conduct disorders A psychiatric term describing externalizing, "acting-out" behaviors

Table 7.1 • Definitions of Emotional or Behavioral Disorders

Source	Definition
Federal Government[1]	Emotional Disturbance: The term means a condition exhibiting one or more of the following characteristics over a long period of time and to a marked degree that adversely affects a child's educational performance: • An inability to learn that cannot be explained by intellectual, sensory, or health factors • An inability to build or maintain satisfactory interpersonal relationships with peers and teachers • Inappropriate types of behavior or feelings under normal circumstances • A general pervasive mood of unhappiness or depression • A tendency to develop physical symptoms related to fears associated with personal or school problems Emotional disturbance includes schizophrenia. The term does not apply to children who are socially maladjusted, unless it is determined that they have an emotional disturbance.
National Mental Health and Special Education Coalition[2]	Emotional or Behavioral Disorders: The term emotional or behavioral disorder means a disability characterized by behavioral or emotional responses in school so different from appropriate age, cultural, or ethnic norms that they adversely affect educational performance. Educational performance includes academic, social, vocational, and personal skills. Such a disability: • Is more than a temporary, expected response to stressful events in the environment • Is consistently exhibited in two different settings, at least one of which is school-related • Is unresponsive to direct intervention in general education, or the child's condition is such that general education interventions would be insufficient Emotional or behavioral disorders can coexist with other disabilities. This category may include children or youths with schizophrenic disorders, affective disorders, anxiety disorder, or other sustained disorders of conduct or adjustment when they adversely affect educational performance in accordance with [the opening part of the definition].
DSM-IV-TR[3]	Oppositional Defiant Disorder: A recurrent pattern of negativistic, defiant, disobedient, and hostile behavior toward authority figures . . . characterized by the frequent occurrence of at least four of the following behaviors: • Losing temper (Criterion A1) • Arguing with adults (Criterion A2) • Actively defying or refusing to comply with the requests or rules of adults (Criterion A3) • Deliberately doing things that will annoy other people (Criterion A4) • Blaming others for his or her mistakes or misbehavior (Criterion A5) • Being touchy or easily annoyed by others (Criterion A6) • Being angry and resentful (Criterion A7) • Being spiteful or vindictive (Criterion A8)

Sources: [1]From 34 CFR Parts 300 and 303, Assistance to States for the Education of Children with Disabilities and the Early Intervention Program for Infants and Toddlers with Disabilities; Proposed Regulations, U.S. Department of Education, 2005, *Federal Register,* Washington, DC.

[2]"A new proposed definition and terminology to replace 'serious emotional disturbance' in IDEA" by S. R. Forness and J. Knitzer, 1992, *School Psychology Review, 21,* p. 13.

[3]From *Diagnostic and Statistical Manual of Mental Disorders Text Revision, Fourth Edition, (DSM-IV-TR)* (p. 102), by the American Psychiatric Association (APA), 2000, Arlington, VA: APA. Reprinted with permission.

Emotional or behavioral disorders can be divided into three groups that are characterized by:

1 Externalizing behaviors
2 Internalizing behaviors
3 Low incidence disorders

Some emotional or behavioral disorders manifest themselves outwardly. **Externalizing behaviors** constitute an acting-out style that could be described as aggressive, impulsive, coercive, and noncompliant. Other disorders are more accurately described as "inward." **Internalizing behaviors** are typical of an inhibited style that could be described as withdrawn, lonely, depressed, and anxious (Gresham et al., 1999). Students who exhibit externalizing and internalizing behaviors, respectively, are the two main groups of students with emotional or behavioral disorders, but they do not account for all of the conditions that result in placement in this special education category. The 4th edition of the *Diagnostic and Statistical Manual* (DSM-IV-TR) published by the American Psychiatric Association (APA, 2000) also describes disorders usually first diagnosed in children, but not all of these are considered disabilities by the federal government (tic disorders, mood disorder, and conduct disorders). Table 7.2 defines and explains some of the common externalizing and internalizing behaviors seen in special education students. Remember that conditions disturbing to other people are identified more often and earlier. Teachers must be alert to internalizing behaviors, which are equally serious but are not always identified, leaving children without appropriate special education services. It may be that teachers are less likely to notice internalizing behaviors because they are less likely than externalizing behaviors to interfere with instruction (Lane, 2003). Also, of course, emotional or behavioral disorders can coexist with other disabilities. Let's look at each of these types in turn.

Table 7.2 • Examples of Externalizing and Internalizing Behavior Problems

Externalizing Behaviors	Internalizing Behaviors
Violates basic rights of others	Exhibits painful shyness
Violates societal norms or rules	Is teased by peers
Has tantrums	Is neglected by peers
Steals; causes property loss or damage	Is depressed
Is hostile or defiant; argues	Is anorexic
Ignores teachers' reprimands	Is bulimic
Demonstrates obsessive/compulsive behaviors	Is socially withdrawn
Causes or threatens physical harm to people or animals	Tends to be suicidal
Uses lewd or obscene gestures	Has unfounded fears and phobias
Is hyperactive	Tends to have low self-esteem
	Has excessive worries
	Panics

externalizing behaviors Behaviors directed toward others (e.g., aggressive)

internalizing behaviors Behaviors directed inward (e.g., withdrawn, anxious, depressed)

Externalizing Behaviors

When we think about emotional or behavioral disorders, we probably first think of behaviors that are "out of control"—aggressive behaviors expressed outwardly, usually toward other persons. Some typical examples are hyperactivity, a high level of irritating behavior that is impulsive and distractible, and persistent aggression. Young children who have serious challenging behaviors that persist are the most likely to be referred for psychiatric services (Maag, 2000). Three common problems associated with externalizing behavior are hyperactivity, aggression, and delinquency. Hyperactivity was discussed in Chapter 6 because it is a common characteristic of ADHD. Remember that ADHD and emotional or behavioral disorders often occur in combination. So it shouldn't be surprising to find that hyperactivity is a common problem among these children as well.

Aggression may be turned toward objects, toward the self, or toward others. The DSM-IV-TR does not directly define aggression, but it does include elements of aggression in two of the disorders it describes: conduct disorders and oppositional defiant disorder (see again Table 7.1). Aggressive behavior, particularly when it is observed in very young children, is worrisome. This is not just because of the behavior itself—though its hazards should not be minimized—but also because of its strong correlation with long-term problems (dropping out of school, delinquency, violence). A pattern of early aggressive acts beginning with annoying and bullying, followed by physical fighting, is a clear pathway, especially for boys, to violence in late adolescence (Talbott & Thiede, 1999).

Some 30 to 50 percent of youth in correctional facilities are individuals with disabilities (IDEA Practices, 2002). In this group, learning disabilities and emotional or behavioral disorders are about equally represented (45 and 42 percent, respectively). Delinquency, or juvenile delinquency, is defined by the criminal justice system rather than by the medical or educational establishments. Delinquency consists of the commission by juveniles of illegal acts, which could include crimes such as theft or assault. Remember that although some children who are delinquent have emotional or behavioral disorders, many do not—just as some children with emotional or behavioral disorders are delinquent but many are not. However, it is very important to understand that many of these children are at great risk for being involved with the criminal justice system (Edens & Otto, 1997). Their rates of contact with the authorities are disproportionately high. While still in high school, students with emotional or behavioral disorders are 13 times more likely to be arrested than other students with disabilities (U.S. Department of Education, 2001).

Internalizing Behaviors

Internalizing behaviors are typically expressed by being socially withdrawn. Examples of internalizing behaviors include

- Anorexia or bulimia
- Depression
- Anxiety

anorexia Intense fear of gaining weight, disturbed body image, chronic absence or refusal of appetite for food, causing severe weight loss (25 percent of body weight)

bulimia Chronically causing oneself to vomit or otherwise remove food to limit weight gain

Serious eating disorders that usually occur during students' teenage years are **anorexia** and **bulimia** (Manley, Rickson, & Standeven, 2000). These disorders occur because of individuals' (typically girls') preoccupation with weight and body image, their drive for thinness, and their fear of becoming fat. Many causes for these problems have been suggested; they include the media's projection of extreme thinness as the image of beauty and health, competition among peers, perfectionism, personal insecurity, and family crisis. Regardless of the cause, teachers can help by spotting these preoccupations early and seeking assistance from the school's support team or school nurse.

It is often difficult to recognize depression in children. Among the components of **depression** are guilt, self-blame, feelings of rejection, lethargy, low self-esteem, and negative self-image. These tendencies are often overlooked or may be expressed in behaviors that appear to signal a different problem entirely. Because children's behavior when they are depressed often appears so different from the depressed behavior of adults, teachers and parents may have difficulty recognizing the depression. For example, a severely depressed child might attempt to harm himself by running into a busy street or hurling himself off a ledge. Adults might assume that this behavior was normal because many children accidentally do those things, or they might minimize its seriousness. In addition, children usually do not have the vocabulary, personal insight, or experience to recognize and label feelings of depression.

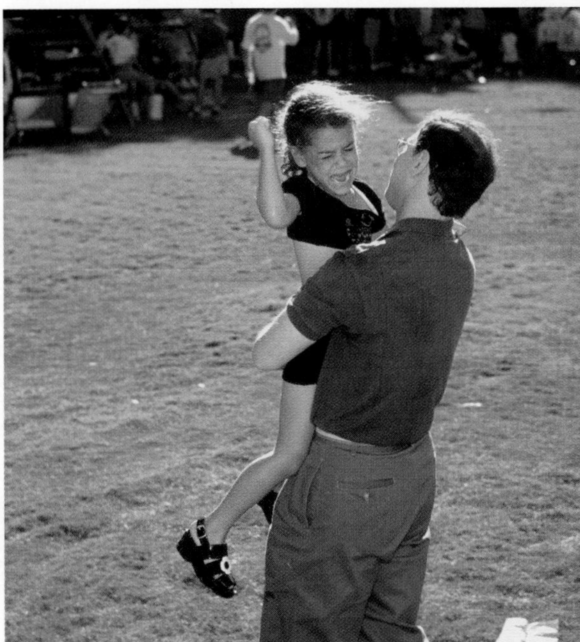

Tantrums and behaviors considered as "out of control" can be clear signals for the need for early intervention.

Finally, **anxiety disorders** may be demonstrated as intense anxiety upon separation from family, friends, or a familiar environment; as excessive shrinking from contact with strangers; or as unfocused, excessive worry and fear. Anxiety disorders are difficult to recognize in children. Because withdrawn children engage in very low levels of positive interactions with their peers, peer rating scales may help educators identify these disorders. Children with internalizing behavior problems, regardless of the type, tend to be underidentified, and this leaves many of them at risk of remaining untreated or receiving needed services later than they should. For those who do receive intervention support, medications such as antidepressants and antianxiety agents may be a component of a more comprehensive intervention plan. If these youngsters are taking medications, it is important for teachers and parents to work collaboratively to ensure that medication is delivered as prescribed, particularly if medication is to be taken during the school day.

Low Incidence Disorders

Some disorders occur very infrequently but are quite serious when they do occur. Consider schizophrenia, which can have tragic consequences for the individuals involved and their families. **Schizophrenia**, sometimes considered a form of psychosis or a type of pervasive developmental disability (APA, 2000), is an extremely rare disorder in children, although approximately 1 percent of the general population over the age of 18 has been diagnosed as having schizophrenia. When it occurs, it places great demands on service systems. It usually involves bizarre delusions (such as believing one's thoughts are controlled by the police), hallucinations (such as voices telling one what to think), "loosening" of associations (disconnected thoughts), and incoherence. Schizophrenia is most prevalent between the ages of 15 and 45, and experts agree that the earlier the onset, the more severe the disturbance in adulthood (Newcomer, 1993). Children with schizophrenia have serious difficulties with schoolwork and often must live in special hospital and educational settings during part of their childhood. Their IEPs are complex and require the collaboration of members from a multidisciplinary team.

Excluded Behavior Problems

Two groups of children—the **socially maladjusted** and those with conduct disorders—are not eligible for special education services (unless they have another qualifying condition as well). Neither group is included in the IDEA '04 definition. Although social maladjustment is widely discussed, particularly when politicians and educators talk about discipline and violence in schools, IDEA '04 does not call it out as a special education category or as a subcategory of emotional or behavioral disorders (see Table 7.3 for recommended programs to prevent bullying). In the DSM-IV-TR, the APA defines conduct disorders as "a repetitive and persistent

depression A state of despair and dejected mood

anxiety disorders Conditions causing painful uneasiness, emotional tension, or emotional confusion

schizophrenia A disorder, rare in children, that includes bizarre delusions and dissociation from reality

socially maladjusted A term applied to students who do not act within society's norms but are not considered to have emotional or behavioral disorders

Table 7.3 • Recommended Programs to Prevent Bullying

Bullying Prevention Program	Steps to Respect	Bully-Proofing Your School
• Description: This empirically validated program is considered to be the "gold standard" of programs designed to reduce and prevent bullying in schools. The program focuses on restructuring the school environment both to decrease the opportunities to engage in bullying and to reduce the negative social consequences of bullying.	• Description: This program was designed by the Committee for Children and is based on social learning principles. Steps to Respect is intended to reduce bullying and to develop prosocial relationships with peers within the context of a school-based program.	• Description: This program is a highly used, research-validated program that involves three domains: (1) increasing awareness of bullying problems, (2) providing explicit instruction in how to protect yourself, and (3) developing a positive school climate.
• Age Groups: Elementary, middle school, and junior high students	• Age Groups: Elementary students	• Age Groups: Elementary and middle school students
• Contact Information: Center for the Study and Prevention of Violence Institute of Behavioral Science University of Colorado at Boulder Box 442 Boulder, CO 80309-0442 FAX 303 443 3297	• Contact Information: Committee for Children 568 First Avenue South, Suite 600 Seattle, WA 98104-2804 FAX 206 438 6765	• Contact Information: Sopris West Educational Services 4093 Specialty Place Longmont, CO 80504-5400 FAX 888 819 7767

Source: Adapted from Walker, Ramsey, & Gresham (2004), pp. 272–274.

pattern of behavior in which the basic rights of others or major age-appropriate societal norms or rules are violated" (2000, p. 93). Section 504 and ADA do not have exclusions for social maladjustment, so the educational system is required to make accommodations for these students even though they do not qualify for special education services (Zirkel, 1999).

The law is clear that social maladjustment and conduct disorders are not subsets of emotional or behavioral disorders, but how to help such students, in practice, is much less clear (Costenbader & Buntaine, 1999). Why is there confusion about the educational needs of children who are socially maladjusted or who have conduct disorders? Some explanations are related to definitional issues; others are related to what people think is best for the students involved (Kauffman, 1999; Walker et al., 2001). Here are five reasons:

1 No generally agreed-upon definition of social maladjustment exists.
2 It is very difficult to distinguish students with externalizing emotional or behavioral disorders from students with conduct disorders.
3 A more inclusive definition will increase special education enrollment to levels beyond tolerance and acceptability.
4 Because the needs of students with conduct disorders are best met by specialists prepared to deal with their problems, they should be identified as special education students, even if technically they do not qualify as students with disabilities.
5 Many people believe these students are just choosing to misbehave and do not have disabilities.

Characteristics

Students with emotional or behavioral disorders display some common characteristics, which teachers can use to identify them early enough for intervention to make a difference. Table 7.4 lists typical signs and characteristics that these children often exhibit.

Social Skills

Typically, these students are less socially skilled than their peers. Their antisocial behaviors (impulsivity, poor interpersonal skills with both peers and adults) are prime reasons for their referral to special education (U.S. Department of Education, 2001). Social skills are the foundation for practically all human activities in all contexts (academic, personal, vocational, and community). Examples of social skills include being able to resolve conflicts with peers and adults, join a group, and make your need for assistance known. We use social skills to interact with others and perform most daily tasks. Possibly more than any other group of children with disabilities, students with emotional or behavioral disorders present problems with social skills to themselves, their families, their peers, and their teachers (Gresham, 2002; Gresham, Lane, MacMillan, & Boscian, 1999; U.S. Department of Education, 2001).

These students' behavior patterns can be self-defeating, impairing their interactions with others in many negative ways. Some students with externalizing problems are prone to what Hill Walker, Frank Gresham, and their colleagues call *behavioral earthquakes*—behaviors that occur rarely but are extreme, such as setting fires, being cruel to others, abusing animals, and assaulting adults. Students with externalizing behavioral disorders exhibit at least some of the following behaviors in excess:

- Tantrums
- Aggression
- Noncompliance
- Coercive behaviors
- Poor academic performance

Table 7.4 • Possible Signs or Characteristics of Emotional or Behavioral Disorders

Experiences	Demonstrates	
Problems with authority figures	Hyperactivity	Agression
Peer rejection	Impulsivity	Hostility
Anorexia or bulimia	Distractibility	Noncompliance
Disruption in family life	Anxiety	Tantrums
Loneliness	Withdrawal	Coercive behaviors
Academic failure	Depression	Suicidal tendencies

In this regard, teachers can make a real difference through the instructional procedures they select. By using effective teaching procedures and actively engaging students with emotional or behavioral disorders in learning, teachers can bring about improvements in their classroom behaviors as well as their academic performance. (See the *Validated Practices* box for examples.) In contrast, students with internalizing patterns tend to exhibit behaviors that reflect depression, withdrawal, and anxiety.

Instruction in social skills can positively influence the development of social competence (Bullis, Walker, & Sprague, 2001). Effective social skills training programs teach, in natural settings such as classrooms and home, specific skills (e.g., how to interact with others) that address individual students' needs, rather than teaching global skills (e.g., self-concept, self-esteem) to groups. Skills that are not in the students' behavioral repertoire—"can't do" problems (acquisition deficits) rather than "won't do" problems (performance deficits) are taught (Gresham, 2002). Key components of effective programs make the difference. For example, instruction in social skills is initiated as early as possible. Teachers and parents are trained in the use of positive discipline techniques. The instruction is embedded within the general education curriculum and includes considerable demonstration and practice, as well as attention to generalization and maintenance of the acquired skills. Peers learn to help and provide support for each other. The outcomes of such a program are outstanding, but it must begin early (Frey, Hirschstein, & Guzzo, 2000; Hawkins et al., 1999). Individuals who participated in social skills training programs as first graders were, at age 18

- 20 percent less likely to commit violent crimes
- 38 percent less likely to drink heavily
- 35 percent less likely to become pregnant or contribute to a pregnancy

Academic Performance

"School failure is the common link between delinquency and disability" (U.S. Department of Education, 2001, p. II-3). Regardless of intellectual potential, students with emotional or behavioral disorders typically do not perform well academically (Lane & Wehby, 2002). They could be referred to as underachievers, and they lack basic reading and math skills. Of course, the more severe the disability, the greater overall performance is affected, and the greater the likelihood of the child's becoming delinquent and having recurrent problems with the law (Archwamety & Katsiyannis, 2000). Clearly, being in personal turmoil affects one's ability to attend to school tasks and to learning in general. Failure at academic tasks compounds the difficulties these children face, not only at school but also in life. Their frustration with the educational system (and its frustration with them) results in these students having the highest dropout rates of all students (National Center for Educational Statistics [NCES], 2005). The outcomes of school-leavers are not good. It is important for teachers to know that when students' academic deficits, particularly in the area of reading, are remediated, their disruptive behaviors decrease (Lane, 1999; Lane, O'Shaughnessy et al., 2001; Lane, Wehby et al., 2002). Thus educators can make a real difference in the lives of these individuals by targeting *both* social behaviors and academic skills. Instruction should be delivered in a systematic and predictable manner. See *Tips for Effective Teaching* on page 247 to learn some guidelines for giving instructions or commands to students.

Delinquency

Clearly, students served through the emotional or behavioral disorders category have a greater probability than others of running afoul of the law and winding up in the juvenile justice system (Walker & Sprague, 2000). Once they are in the

Validated Practices Effective Teaching Behaviors

What Are Effective Teaching Behaviors?

Effective teaching behaviors are used to increase students' on-task behaviors and academic performance. When effective teaching behaviors are implemented, both you and your students are actively engaged in the learning process.

Why Effective Teaching Behaviors Are Beneficial

When teachers implement effective teaching behaviors, students' engaged learning time is increased; and the more time students are actively engaged in learning, the more they learn. Moreover, when students are engaged in learning, classroom disruption decreases. Several studies have demonstrated that when teachers use praise, call on students often, and engage their students in learning by including questioning and scaffolding in their instruction, not only do problem behaviors lessen, but academic achievement increases as well.

Implementing Effective Teaching Behaviors

The five steps of effective teaching behaviors are (1) planning, (2) starting the lesson, (3) presenting the lesson (4) closing the lesson, and (5) reflecting. Each step is described next.

Planning

- Decide what you want your students to know by the end of the lesson; remember that individual students may have different goals.
- Be sure you feel comfortable teaching the topic and answering questions.
- Determine what resources you will need to carry out the lesson.
- Decide how much time you will spend on the lesson.

Starting the Lesson

- Have all your materials ready and close by before beginning your lesson.
- Begin instruction promptly.
- Get the students' attention (e.g., by turning lights on and off and saying, "It's time for math").
- Provide your students with an advance organizer (e.g., "Today, we are going to . . ., and I expect you to. . . .").
- Begin with a review from a previously taught lesson.
- Assess students' background and knowledge of the lesson's topic.

Presenting the Lesson

- Maintain a brisk pace, but one that isn't so fast that you lose your students.
- Provide a demonstration and guided practice activities before students work independently.
- Allow for independent practice once students have achieved 80 to 90 percent accuracy during the guided practice phase.
- Ask factual questions, one at a time.
- Ask questions that draw on reasoning skills.
- Recognize students' responses by providing praise or corrective feedback.
- Probe students for answers and provide scaffolding.
- Give specific academic praise (e.g., "I like the way you are reading today").
- Be enthusiastic while teaching; show interest (e.g., smile, gesture).
- Orient students to the academic task; refocus unrelated talk.
- Enforce classroom rules; remind students about the classroom rules.
- Be consistent with your consequences (follow through).
- Give specific directives (e.g., "Read page 4").
- Use surface management techniques (e.g., proximity, redirect, "the look," call out student's name, state expected behavior).
- Give specific praise for good behavior (e.g., "Thank you for raising your hand").
- Circulate among your students while they are working independently.

Closing the Lesson

- Review the day's lesson.
- Introduce tomorrow's lesson.

Reflecting

- Ask yourself, "How did the lesson go?" "What went well?" "What should I continue?" "What needs to be changed for next time?"
- Evaluate your instruction and the students' performance.
- Decide what, if anything, needs to be retaught.

This scientifically validated practice is a teaching method proven by systematic research efforts (Englert, Tarrant, & Mariage, 1992; Espin, & Yell, 1994; Rosenshine, 1995; Sutherland, 2000; Sutherland, Wehby, & Copeland, 2000; Wehby, Symons, Canale, & Go, 1998). Full citations are found in the references for this chapter at the end of the book.

—By Kimberly Paulsen, Vanderbilt University

criminal justice system, they are less likely to receive services, supports, and intensive IEPs (National Center on Education, Delinquency and Juvenile Justice [NCJJ], 2002). Their paths to long-term negative outcomes are taking shape (Walker and Sprague 1999). Look at Figure 7.1, which highlights some of the major markers or signals for quick and early intervention in an effort to alter predictable patterns of negative results.

In recent years, students' behaviors at school have become increasingly challenging, hostile, and even violent (Bender, Shubert, & McLaughlin, 2001; Maag, 2001). Certainly, acute alarm over school violence is a recent phenomenon; 10 years ago it was not a concern (Furlong & Morrison, 2000). Even today, 95 percent of students attending public school are well behaved and respond to positive reinforcement or simple classroom management interventions. However, some 5 percent—those with the most challenging behaviors—do not respond to traditional tactics.

Despite all the media attention and parents' perceptions that schools are out of control, school violence is actually on the decline, and schools are the safest

Figure 7.1 • The Path to Long-Term Negative Outcomes for At-Risk Children and Youth

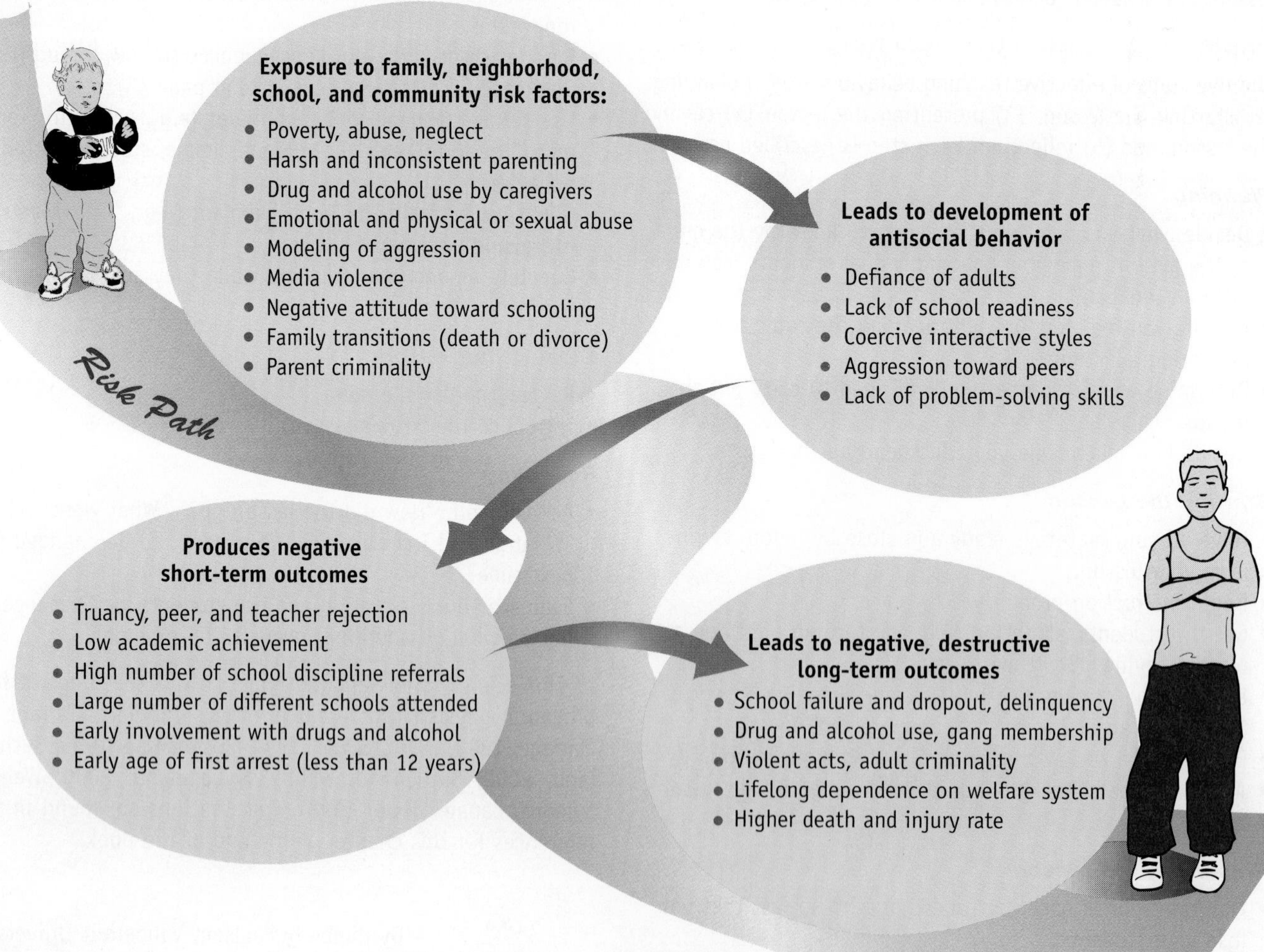

Exposure to family, neighborhood, school, and community risk factors:
• Poverty, abuse, neglect
• Harsh and inconsistent parenting
• Drug and alcohol use by caregivers
• Emotional and physical or sexual abuse
• Modeling of aggression
• Media violence
• Negative attitude toward schooling
• Family transitions (death or divorce)
• Parent criminality
Risk Path
Leads to development of antisocial behavior
• Defiance of adults
• Lack of school readiness
• Coercive interactive styles
• Aggression toward peers
• Lack of problem-solving skills
Produces negative short-term outcomes
• Truancy, peer, and teacher rejection
• Low academic achievement
• High number of school discipline referrals
• Large number of different schools attended
• Early involvement with drugs and alcohol
• Early age of first arrest (less than 12 years)
Leads to negative, destructive long-term outcomes
• School failure and dropout, delinquency
• Drug and alcohol use, gang membership
• Violent acts, adult criminality
• Lifelong dependence on welfare system
• Higher death and injury rate

Source: Walker, H. M. & Sprague, J. (1999). The path to school failure, delinquency, and violence: Causal factors and potential solutions. *Intervention in School and Clinic, 35,* 67–73. Copyright 1999 by Pro-Ed, Inc. Reprinted by permission.

place where children can spend their days (CDF, 2004). Violent incidents, such as the 1999 murders at Columbine High School in Colorado and the 2005 murders at Red Lake, Minnesota, raise concern, but it is the increase in more frequent and small acts of defiance that has educators worried. Aggression—both verbal and physical—is on the increase. Some scholars and social observers have speculated about why this is so (Begley, 1999; Bender, Shubert, & McLaughlin, 2001):

1 Aggression, violence, and alienation observed in schools simply mirror their presence in society at large.
2 Individuals who see high rates of violence become desensitized, devaluing life.
3 Fewer hospital and center school placements are available, limiting supports for these students.
4 General education teachers are not trained to deal with violence and aggression.

GIVING INSTRUCTIONS

1 Use as few commands as possible to teach and manage behavior.
2 When giving commands, focus on initiating commands rather than terminating commands.
3 Give one command at a time.
4 Be clear and direct.
5 Allow at least 10 seconds for students to respond.
6 Repeat the command one time only.
7 Be relatively close to the student when delivering a command.

Source: Adapted from *Antisocial behavior in school: Evidence-based practices,* 2nd ed., (p. 171), by H. M. Walker, E. Ramsey, and F. M. Gresham, 2004, Belmont, CA: Wadsworth.

As Americans puzzle about the "whys" of school violence, educators must ponder predictors and prevention. Violence is comparatively rare, but the prospect of even a single case in five years demands that schools be prepared. Thus researchers are turning their attention to the problem and are providing teachers and administrators with information about how to prevent school violence and what actions to take if it does occur (Bender & McLaughlin, 1997; CDF, 2001, 2004; Myles & Simpson, 1998). Let's take a look at some of the circumstances surrounding school violence, including how to prevent it and also support instruction, in *Accommodating for Inclusive Environments* on page 248.

Prevalence

For two major reasons, it is difficult to estimate accurately the prevalence of emotional or behavioral disorders. First, the definition remains unclear and subjective. Second, because the label is viewed as stigmatizing, many educators and school districts are reluctant to identify many children. About 1 percent of all schoolchildren are identified as having this disability (U.S. Department of Education, 2005b). Some believe that the actual prevalence should be approximately 3 to 6 percent of all students (Kauffman, 2005).

Important factors in prevalence are gender and race. Clear differences show up in the identification of this exceptionality. Males are far more likely than females to be identified as having an emotional disturbance. The reason for this gender difference is not clear, but it is probably linked to boys' higher propensity to be troublesome and violate school rules, coupled with girls' tendency toward less disruptive, internalizing behaviors that are less likely to result in referral. Whereas Asian American and Hispanic students tend to be underrepresented in this special education category, African Americans are overrepresented (Kauffman, 2005). In fact, African American students are approximately 1.5 times more likely than Caucasian students to be identified as having emotional or behavioral disorders (National Research Council, 2002). Read *Considering Culture* on page 250 to see how parents and teachers may have conflicting viewpoints about how to best help these students—and to approach resolving such conflicts.

Accommodating for Inclusive Environments

Being Prepared for School Violence

Develop Schoolwide Positive Behavior Support Programs to

- Establish common rules and expectations for all students in all school settings (e.g., classroom, hallways, cafeterias, etc.).
- Teach these rules and expectations to all students.
- Reinforce students who follow the rules and meet these expectations.
- Provide more intensive levels of support (secondary and tertiary interventions) to meet the behavioral, social, and academic needs of students who are not responding to the schoolwide (primary) intervention efforts.

Be Alert to

- Whispers and talk of potential confrontation
- Unattended book bags and backpacks
- Students with a history of violence
- Closed classroom doors

Make Plans for

- Teacher buddy systems
- Responding to the sounds of gunshots
- Hostage crises
- All-clear signals

Practice for a Crisis by Knowing

- Where students should go during an incident
- Whom to notify
- Roles for every staff member

Train and Inform All School Staff Members About

- General methods used to resolve conflict
- Standard procedures to follow
- The contents of every behavioral intervention plan

Be Prepared to

- Develop trust and positive relationships with all students.
- Consistently apply behavioral techniques and consequences.
- Dress appropriately (comfortable shoes, loose clothing).
- Put valuables and fragile items out of reach.

Apply These Principles if a Crisis Occurs

- Remain calm and in control.
- Keep tone of voice steady and firm.
- Seek assistance.
- Ignore accusations.

Prepare for Emergencies

- Obtain a copy of your school's emergency plans.
- Review emergency procedures.

Causes and Prevention

As is true of most disabilities, the specific causes of emotional or behavioral disorders remain elusive. However, relationships between some causal factors and this disability are becoming clearer. For example, children who experience physical abuse have a higher probability of being identified with emotional or behavioral disorders (Cauce et al., 2000). A link between the factors of poverty and this disability is apparent as well (Children's Defense Fund [CDF], 2004; Hosp & Reschly, 2002). And it is likely that for some children, a biological explanation will emerge (Forness & Kavale, 2001).

Causes

The reasons why such problems arise in a particular child are usually difficult to identify precisely, and the disability is likely to be the result of multiple and overlapping factors (Walker & Sprague, 2000). At least three general areas can contribute to emotional or behavioral disorders: biology, home and community, and school. Let's look at each in turn.

Biology

Just as for many other disabilities, more and more biological and genetic causes for emotional or behavioral disorders are being identified (Forness & Kavale, 2001). For example, research now tells us that a definite relationship exists between prenatal drug exposure and childhood emotional or behavioral disorders: 53 percent of drug-exposed participants in Headstart preschool programs are identified as having these disabilities as early as kindergarten (Sinclair, 1998). Mood disorders, depression, and schizophrenia may have a genetic foundation (APA, 2000). Knowing whether biological reasons are part of the cause of a disorder can play a role in treatment. For example, knowing that depression has a biological cause allows for the development and use of medications prescribed to target this condition (Forness & Kavale, 2001). Antidepressants are now an important component in many treatment programs for depression (Pappadopulos & Jensen, 2001). As researchers continue to find biological causes, more medical treatments will become available.

Home and Community

Environment and culture are the context in which behavior unfolds (Maag, 2000). No one lives in a social vacuum. Everyone is a member of an immediate family, an extended family, or a community network (neighborhood, church, clubs). All of these environments shape and influence each individual's growth and development, whether positively or negatively. Rarely does a single negative experience lead to or aggravate emotional problems, but combinations of poverty, abuse, neglect, parental stress, inconsistent expectations and rules, confusion, and turmoil over long periods of time can do so. Being poor is a contributing factor (CDF, 2004; Hosp & Reschly, 2002). So are lack of supervision, erratic and punitive discipline, low rate of positive interactions, high rate of negative interactions, lack of interest and concern, and poor adult role models (Reid & Patterson, 1991). For example, children whose parents are violent and have arrest records also tend to become violent and to find themselves in trouble with the law (Hallahan & Kauffman, 2006; Rudo, Powell, & Dunlap, 1998). Another link with poverty is clear: Students whose family incomes are in the bottom 20 percent of American families are five times more likely to drop out of school than their peers whose family incomes are in the top 20 percent of American families (NCES, 2001).

School

Teachers and schools can have a tremendous influence on students (Tolan, Gorman-Smith, & Henry, 2001). Teachers' expectations affect the questions they ask students, the feedback they give, and the number and character of their interactions with students. Problems can get better because of teachers' actions—and they can get worse for the same reason. In other words, what educators do makes a difference. For example, a teacher who is unskilled in managing the classroom or insensitive to students' individual differences may create an environment wherein aggression, frustration, and withdrawal are common responses to the environment or the teacher. But, teachers skilled at managing classroom behavior can systematically select interventions that match the students' behavior and apply them consistently. When effective teaching and behavior management methods are in place, students' outcomes improve (Rivera & Smith, 1997; Smith & Rivera, 1993). Good teachers are able to analyze their relationships with their students and the learning environment, and they keep close watch on problems and potential problems. Here are some key components of safe and effective schools (McLane, 1997; Walker & Gresham, 1997; Walker, Ramsey, & Gresham, 2004; Walker & Sprague, 2000):

- Consistency of rules, expectations, and consequences across the school
- Positive school climate
- Schoolwide strategies for resolving conflict
- High level of supervision in all school settings

Considering Culture

Nearly at an Impasse!

Donalene Lewis and her son's teacher, Melinda, begin at an impasse! Jamal is a fifth grader in Melinda's class, and Melinda thinks he should be referred for special education testing because of his behavior in the classroom. Jamal is not paying attention in class, frequently disrupts his classmates, and is prone to inappropriate and abusive verbal outbursts. Melinda feels that he has behavioral disorders and she wants help managing his behavior. Melinda knows that Jamal's mother is struggling to support her family and that she works several part-time jobs to keep their apartment and provide basic needs. Recently, Melinda asked Mrs. Lewis to meet with her, and during their conference, Melinda raised the possibility that Jamal might need some extra services. Donalene hit the roof! She recounted her struggle raising Jamal—his prematurity and long stay in the hospital, his repeated subsequent hospitalizations, and her tireless attempts to get him the medical care that he needed. She emphatically stated, "And now he is at Drew Elementary School with other kids in his neighborhood. He's doing fine in school and he likes playing basketball on the playground. There's no way he's going to be put in special education just because that's what they do with Black kids! Now I know we can't talk about everything wrong with society. But why is it always the Black kids that are diagnosed? Jamal is just a little more rambunctious than others, and the school should help him to get along. That's what a school is supposed to do."

Melinda feels herself begin to get defensive and even angry that she should have to cope with this. She finds herself just wanting to get Jamal out of the classroom! But she also remembers how great Jamal is at science projects; he is always eager and creative. And it is obvious how much this mother cares about her youngster and wants what is best for him. Melinda invites Mrs. Lewis to review Jamal's schoolwork. She points out the areas in which he is falling behind, but she also points out all the strengths Jamal shows, particularly in science. She invites Mrs. Lewis to visit the classroom and observe how the other children react when Jamal has an outburst and how marginalized he is becoming; his classmates are avoiding him during free time and many don't want to be partnered with him for group projects. She has noticed Jamal walking with some older kids after school—kids who often get into trouble in the neighborhood. Melinda asks Mrs. Lewis to review this information, visit the class, and then meet with her again in several weeks to discuss the observations they both have made.

Questions to Consider

1 Can you understand Mrs. Lewis's perspective? Can you understand why she feels that Jamal will be better served by not being labeled and isolated?

2 Did you know that children of color are overrepresented in the population of children in special education? Why do you think that is the case?

3 As a teacher, what can you do to bridge this communication divide and get Jamal the help that he may need, while acknowledging and honoring Mrs. Lewis's concerns?

—By Eleanor Lynch, San Diego State University and Marci Hanson, San Francisco State University

- Cultural sensitivity
- Strong feelings of identification and involvement on the part of students
- High levels of parent and community involvement
- Well-utilized space and lack of overcrowding

Prevention

One of the first steps in preventing the development of emotional or behavioral disorders is determining which children exhibit behaviors that are often predictive of later problems. Astute adults almost universally and immediately identify even very young children with emotional or behavioral disorders, particularly in cases of individuals with externalizing behavior patterns. Why might this be so? Standards for normal behavior change as children grow up and move through the stages of their lives. When children behave quite differently from what is expected for their age group, it becomes a cause for concern. For example, the behavior of an 8-year-old who suddenly begins to wet the bed, clings to his mother, and stops talking creates great concern. Even though almost identical behavior would be totally acceptable for a toddler, an 8-year-old who acts in this way is perceived as having a problem. Think of examples of behavior that provoke concerns about children of one age but, when demonstrated by a child of a different age, raise no questions at all.

The fact that behavior inappropriate for an individual's age draws attention and can result in the individual's being identified as having an emotional or behavioral disorder makes some experts worry about subjectivity in the assessment process. Also, students with internalizing behaviors are often missed when only teacher referrals are used. Experts recommend that standardized tests or procedures be used in the identification process (Gresham et al., 1999). Some such methods are available. For example, the *Student Risk Screening Scale* and the *Systematic Screening for Behavior Disorders* are assessment instruments that take some of the subjectivity out of the identification process.

Some concerns about this category of special education focus on the disproportionate number of African American males, particularly children who are disruptive, identified as having emotional or behavioral disorders (Townsend, 2000; U.S. Department of Education, 2005b). Whereas these boys are overrepresented, other groups, such as Asian Americans and girls, are underrepresented. The possible explanations for this disproportionate representation include a lack of reliable methods for identifying these children, particularly those with internalizing behaviors. Current knowledge can guide educators' actions until more accurate assessment procedures are available:

- Evaluation measures should come from at least two different settings.
- Performance in both academics and social skills should be considered.
- Information should come from a range people in the child's life.
- Many methods to assess students' behavior should be used (behavior rating scales, ecological assessments, interviews, standardized tests, social work evaluations, psychiatric analyses, functional assessments).

Overcoming Challenges

Prevention and treatment of emotional or behavioral disorders can be accomplished in many different ways, but the implementation of three different approaches could cause a substantial reduction in the prevalence of this disability:

1. Medical management
2. Reducing overrepresentation
3. School-based interventions

Medical management can attack issues of prevention on at least two different fronts. For example, the behavioral effects of fetal alcohol syndrome can be prevented if pregnant women do not drink. In other cases, prevention consists of eliminating or ameliorating the symptoms of the disability at its initial onset. And in yet other cases, the condition can be treated through medication. Considerable controversy exists about the use of prescription drugs to reduce hyperactivity and the disruption that the condition causes (Zametkin & Earnst, 1999). Read again *Disability in the News* on page 216 in Chapter 6. Considering the fact that American children are being prescribed and taking drugs such as Ritalin at a rate some five times higher than children elsewhere in the world, many educators have been calling for a greater use of classroom management interventions and interventions based on the reason why problem behaviors occur (functional assessment-based interventions) to reduce both inappropriate behavior and the use of medication (Pancheri & Prater, 1999; Umbreit, Lane, & Dejud, 2004). Some experts who have studied this issue believe that medication is effective

(Forness & Kavale, 2001). However, they have also concluded that medication is even more powerful when used in combination with behavior management techniques. In the same study, Steve Forness and Ken Kavale found that the majority of children with school behavior problems have treatable psychiatric disorders, such as mood disorders, anxiety disorders, or schizophrenia. Antidepressants are effective in some of these cases.

The overrepresentation of African American boys in special education concerns educators, policymakers, and parents (National Alliance of Black School Educators [NABSE] & ILIAD Project, 2002). More so than any other group, these youngsters are clearly overrepresented in the emotional or behavioral disorders category (U.S. Department of Education, 2005b). Although the number of youths held in the juvenile justice system is small—less then 1 percent of all youths—more than half of them—58 percent—are diverse (CDF, 2004). In particular, the following data are most alarming: Although Black youths represent some 15 percent of all youths under age 18, they represent 26 percent of juvenile arrests, 31 percent of referrals to the court system, and 40 percent of those in residential placements. One reason for their disproportionate representation is that these students are three times more likely to be suspended from school (Townsend, 2000). Being suspended is part of a vicious cycle that compounds students' problems at school. Specifically, students who are suspended cannot participate in the academic learning opportunities at school. They also miss learning more about the norms of the school culture and the behavior expected there, because they are "on the streets" engaging in unsupervised activities. This situation then leads to lower academic achievement and higher probability of future misbehavior. All of these factors contribute to special education referrals. It is important that educators become more culturally sensitive and help students understand rules of conduct and what is considered appropriate behavior at school, in the neighborhood, and with authority figures (Cartledge, Kea, & Ida, 2000).

In recent years, school-based interventions have focused on building three-tiered models of **positive behavior support** (PBS) containing primary (schoolwide), secondary (more focused, often small groups), and tertiary (highly focused, individualized) levels of support. The goal of PBS is to meet all students' needs by providing progressively more intensive levels of support to ensure that all students know and are recognized for meeting the given expectations (Lewis & Sugai, 1999). PBS programs

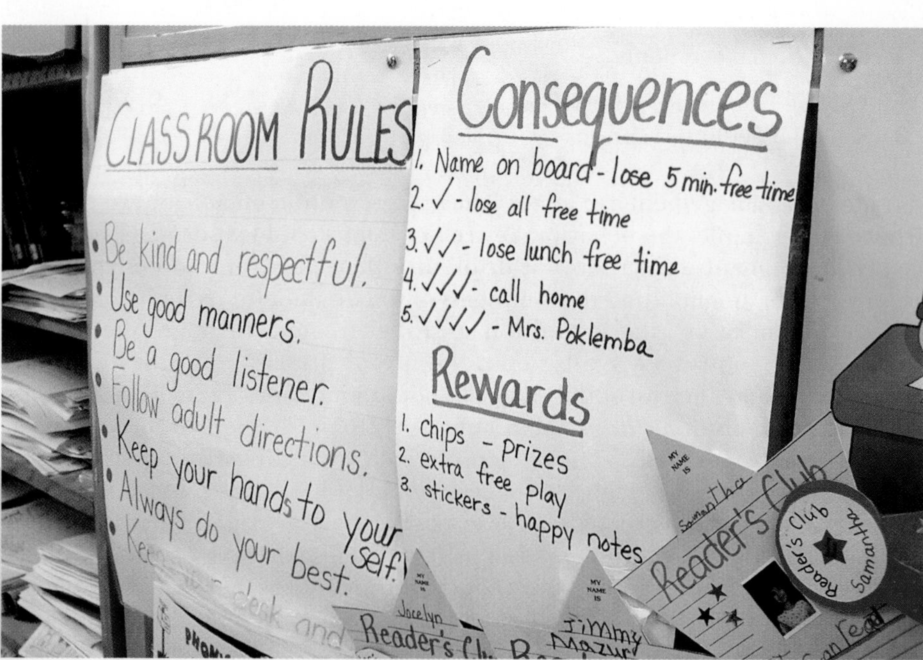

Many behavior problems can be prevented when all students understand and follow consistent, positive rules in the classroom.

have been associated with decreases in office referrals, improved social interactions, and improved academic outcomes (Hunter & Chopra, 2001; Tolan, Gorman-Smith, & Henry, 2001). One important premise of such programs is prevention (Horner et al., 2001). The aim is to create a school culture where positive behavioral support, social skills instruction, and consistency serve as the foundation for direct intervention when it actually needs to be applied. All students are taught what behaviors teachers and the school community expect. They are also taught what they should expect from each other. Expectations are clear, concise, and simple (e.g., follow directions, be responsible, be safe, be prepared). For those who cannot meet these expectations, more focused intervention (e.g., secondary and tertiary levels) is provided (Lane, Wehby, Menzies, et al., 2003). In some cases, successful programs include intense and individualized consequences. Such programs apply **functional behavioral assessments** to determine the cause of the behavior and to help identify actions that will effectively remediate extreme patterns of behavior. Some educators add a mentorship element, where successful secondary students with emotional or behavioral disorders help elementary students understand classroom expectations and how to act appropriately (Burrell et al., 2001).

It is well documented that early intervention can change patterns of behavior that eventually develop into long-term problems for both the individual and society (Bullis, Walker, & Sprague, 2001; Feil, Walker, & Severson, 1995; Strain & Timm, 1998; Walker & Sprague, 2000). Very young children who exhibit antisocial behavior, set fires, are cruel to animals, and are highly aggressive are most at risk for having serious externalizing behavioral disorders, and they are identified by elementary or middle school. The predictors of this outcome are now known, and structured and intensive preschool programs can in most cases provide the early intervention necessary to prevent disastrous results and reduce the need for disciplinary actions in the school setting (see *What IDEA '04 Says About Discipline and Students with Disabilities*).

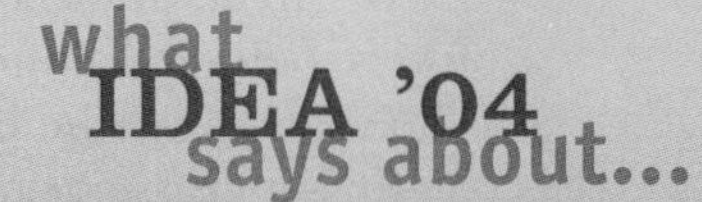

Discipline and Students with Disabilities

- Students who violate student conduct code will be individually considered for changes in placement, with consideration given to unique circumstances.
- Conduct code violations can result in removal to Interim Alternative Educational Settings (IAES), another setting, or suspension for up to 10 school days to the extent that such alternatives are applied to students without disabilities (SWD).
- Students removed from current placements continue to receive educational services in order to progress toward IEP goals.
- Within 10 school days of a change-of-placement decision, IEP team must determine whether the behavior was the result of either (a) the disability or (b) poor implementation of the IEP.
- If either of these applies (manifestation determination), the team must (a) conduct a behavioral assessment, (b) implement a behavioral intervention, and (c) return the child to the original placement.
- When behavioral intervention plans are already in existence, the team will review and modify them as necessary.
- Regardless of manifestation determination, students may be removed to IAES for up to 45 school days for violations involving weapons, drugs, or infliction of serious bodily injury.

However, even though knowledge exists about how to reduce or prevent some problems associated with emotional or behavioral disorders, the necessary actions are usually not taken. In a provocative commentary, Jim Kauffman (1999) points out that despite discussions about the importance of prevention efforts, actions in the last decade of the 20th Century did not keep pace. Possibly for fear of misidentifying children, public systems tend to provide intervention services too late, when the chance of success is reduced. Intervention must begin early and proceed deliberately. Clearly, for most children, particularly those at low risk, classroom interventions can be successful. However, Kauffman estimates that some 5 to 10 percent of students in general education may require intensive, intrusive, individualized help. But the way the education system is set up "prevents prevention." Here is how Jim Kauffman thinks it should work:

- Reward desirable behavior.
- Punish, through nonviolent means, undesirable behavior.
- Provide direct instruction for both social and academic skills.
- Correct the environmental conditions that foster deviant behavior.
- Give students clear expectations.
- Standardize responses to children across the entire school setting.
- Monitor students' behavior closely.

positive behavior support A three-tiered model of support offering progressively more intensive levels of intervention

functional behavioral assessments A process in which interviews, observations, and environmental manipulations are conducted to determine "why" certain behaviors occur

In addition to Kauffman's suggestions, other methods can prevent inappropriate behavior. Functional behavioral assessments can help teachers determine what events cause the behavior to occur and what other events contribute to the behavior's increase or maintenance (Tobin, Sugai, & Colvin, 1996). Many teachers use a less complicated system that employs the antecedent, behavior, and consequence events to target behavior for specific interventions. *Tips for Classroom Management* offers guidelines for another approach to classroom management—the Good Behavior Game, originally developed by Barrish, Sanders, and Wolf in 1969.

What teachers do in school and classroom settings can make a real difference in reducing and preventing behavior problems for both those at risk for emotional or behavioral disorders and those already so identified (Kamps et al., 1999). Here's what works:

- *Behavior Management.* Include a point system for appropriate behavior and task completion, wherein good behavior is charted and students earn rewards.
- *Systematic Intervention Plans.* Use a hierarchy of tactics, depending on students' behavior.
- *Home–School Communication.* Include notes to the home and home-based reward systems.
- *Peer Involvement.* Have classmates remind each other of classroom expectations.
- *Classroom Structure.* Employ guided practice and well-organized transitions from activity to activity.
- *Supervised Free Periods.* Have adults monitor unstructured parts of the school day (recess, hall changes, lunch).
- *Consistent Standards.* Be sure all school staff members use the same standards for acceptable behavior and hold high expectations for academic performance.

Assessment

Many different types of assessments must be employed to better serve students with emotional or behavioral disorders (Walker, Ramsey, & Gresham, 2004). Specifically, we need reliable, valid, precise, and cost-effective instruments that will allow educators to

- Screen large numbers of students
- Identify and place students who have, or are at risk for, emotional or behavioral disorders
- Monitor student progress
- Provide necessary and sufficient intervention and instruction
- Document the effectiveness of various intervention efforts

In each case, the purpose of the assessment is to generate information that will contribute to the best possible decisions for the student (Witt et al., 1988).

Early Identification: Screening

The main reason for using screening tools is to identify students who show "soft signs" that are associated with emotional or behavioral disorders. What are soft signs? As you'll recall, not all students with emotional or behavioral disorders have acting-out problems. Some students have internalizing behavior disorders, which means that they are often painfully shy, anxious, or depressed. These students may struggle in their interactions with peers and teachers. Still other students have externalizing behavioral disorders, which means that they exhibit verbal and physical aggression and challenge their teachers by refusing to follow directions or comply with their requests. Given this wide range of students with emotional or behavioral disorders, it is important to use screening tools that are able to detect both types of behavioral concerns.

Fortunately, some excellent screening tools and procedures are available. One example is an empirically validated, cost-effective screening instrument called *Systematic Screening for Behavior Disorders,* developed by Hill Walker. It is used to identify elementary-age students with internalizing and externalizing behaviors. This three-stage process begins with teacher nominations and rankings, is followed by teacher rating scales, and concludes with direct observations.

for Classroom Management

PLAYING THE GOOD BEHAVIOR GAME

1. Class (teacher and students) determines specific behaviors of concern.
2. Class suggests privileges or prizes to win (end of day, end of week).
3. Teacher determines criterion level for winning (cut-off scores, where more than one team can win or all teams can lose).
4. Teacher divides class into teams.
5. Be sure all students understand the rules.
6. Inform parents, principal, and fellow teachers about the game being played.
7. Keep scores as a source of data to evaluate the game's effectiveness.

By using screenings across the grades, it is possible to identify students who, without the necessary supports, may otherwise go on to develop behavior problems that might ultimately require special education services. The goal of screening is to catch students early and provide the support necessary to prevent the development of more serious problems (Lane, 2004). Yet many schools do not use systematic screening. Why? Some schools are concerned about having to provide extra supports to students who are identified during the screening process. Limited resources complicate the implementation of early screening; however, it may be less costly than intervening later when the behavior problems have become more extreme. Other schools are concerned that students identified via screening might eventually go on to require special education services under the IDEA '04 label of emotionally disturbed. As mentioned earlier, this label can be aversive to

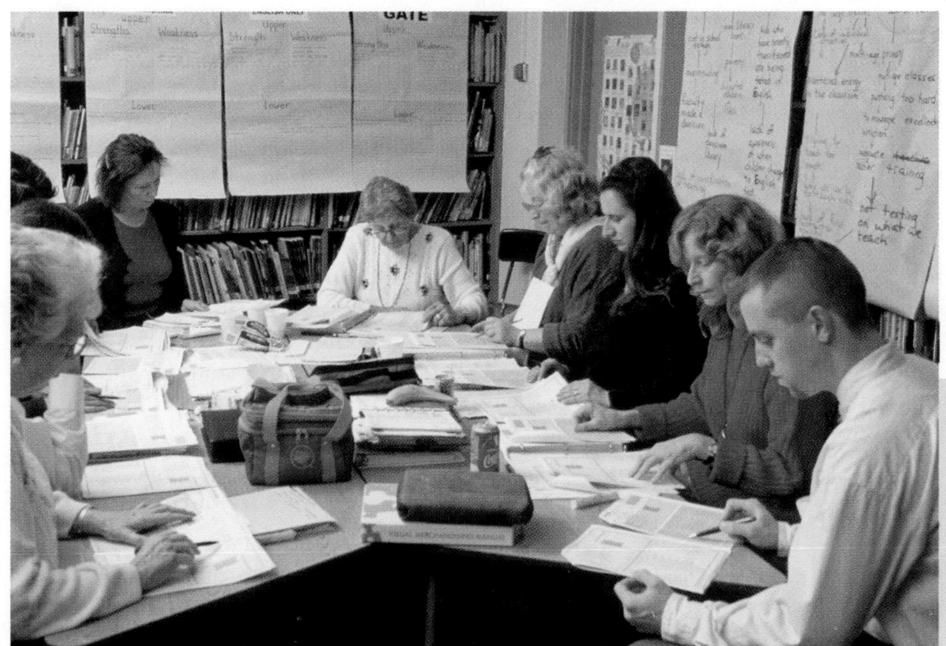

When schools screen all students for potential problems and when teachers and administrators share their observations, supports and interventions can be delivered quickly and serious problems avoided.

parents and has implications regarding how these students can be disciplined (Kauffman, 2001). Therefore, screening instruments are available but are not always used.

Pre-Referral: Early Intervention

General education teachers use their knowledge and skills to support students with emotional or behavioral problems. Teachers often develop group-based classroom management plans to support good behavior, work with parents to help these students develop the skills necessary to be successful in the classroom, and modify assignments and expectations. Yet, when behavioral excesses and deficits become so extreme that they undermine all the teacher's efforts to provide instruction, or when the students' academic performance is far below grade level and below realistic expectations, the teacher will refer the student to the pre-referral intervention team (Lane, Mahdavi, & Borthwick-Duffy, 2003).

The pre-referral intervention is a general education process in which professionals work together with parents to design interventions to be conducted in the general education classroom. The goal of the pre-referral process is to reduce the number of inappropriate referrals to special education and to help students perform more successfully in the general education setting. The interventions generated by the team of professionals are put into place by the classroom team with the support of the broader team. It is recommended that data be collected to

- Ensure that people agree with the goals, procedures, and outcomes
- Make sure the intervention is put in place as designed
- Monitor student progress
- Determine when to fade or modify the plan

If the interventions proposed by the pre-referral intervention team embody the above recommendations (Lane & Beebe-Frankenberger, 2004) but do not produce the desired outcomes, the next step is to formally refer the student to be assessed for special education eligibility.

Identification

If the pre-referral interventions fall short of meeting the intended objectives, teachers are likely to seek parent permission to begin a more formal process of assessing the student to determine whether he or she qualifies for special education services. This process involves a range of assessments, among them measures of cognitive ability, achievement in various skill areas, social competence, and behavioral performance, that include student-administered tests, behavior rating scales, and direct observations.

If the results of these assessments, which are interpreted by the multidisciplinary team, indicate that special education services under the federal label of emotional disturbance are warranted, and if the parent agrees, the student will be placed into special education. It is important to remember that students who qualify for special education services are not necessarily placed in a self-contained classroom. As discussed in Chapter 2, the provision of least restrictive environment (LRE) must be met.

Evaluation

Once a student is placed in special education, her or his performance will be evaluated in a variety of ways. First, the goals and objectives specified in the IEP, which include social, behavioral, and academic areas, are evaluated via curriculum based and other performance based measures. For example, aggressive acts may be measured using direct observation or office referral data. Oral reading fluency may be assessed using curriculum based probes designed for a given grade level. It is important that each objective be monitored frequently, on an ongoing basis, with assessment tools that are sensitive enough to detect change.

Second, students will take the same statewide achievement tests as other students who are not receiving special education services and students who are receiving special education services under other high incidence disability categories. Depending on the nature of the student's disability, it is possible that modifications such as additional time may be specified in the IEP. These assessment results will guide decisions about how to shape a student's program and when to recommend changes in placement. It is important that all assessments be reliable, valid, and feasible in a school setting (Walker, Ramsey, & Gresham, 2004).

Early Intervention

Most students with emotional or behavioral disorders have poor educational outcomes. The blame for such dismal results rests, in part, with the educational system and its inability to meet the complex needs of these children—needs that must be met beginning when the children are very young. Severe disabilities, such as a psychosis, sometimes manifest themselves during the early developmental period, but some types of emotional or behavioral disorders are difficult to identify in young children. For example, internalizing behavior problems are not usually identified until children are of school age. However, extreme externalizing behaviors are often obvious by age 3. Although most preschoolers behave well and learn social rules quickly, some do not (Little, 2002). Indeed, 15 percent of preschoolers engage daily in three or more acts of overt aggressive behavior (e.g., hitting and kicking, pushing), and 10 percent exhibit daily episodes of serious antisocial behavior (e.g., calling names, playing mean tricks). Early intervention is important, because it can help prevent the children who display soft signs of emotional or behavioral problems from experiencing some negative outcomes.

Benefits

The early identification and management of young children with this disability has many benefits (Bullis, Walker, & Sprague, 2001; Feil, Walker, & Severson, 1995; Walker & Sprague, 1999, 2000). First, problem behaviors seen in preschoolers tend to be very stable over time. In other words, they do not go away without intervention, and they may even worsen. The behavior problems seem to follow a progression similar to the following: disobedient at home, having temper tantrums, teacher reports of fighting or stealing. Second, behavior problems are predictive of future learning problems and delinquency. Third, children with early onset of antisocial behavior (e.g., aggression) are only 3 to 5 percent of this population, but they account for 50 percent of all crimes committed by children and youth. Fourth, if children's disorders can be identified early, professionals may be able to intervene with the child and family promptly and avoid predictable negative outcomes. Figure 7.1 on page 246 highlights those markers that are now becoming reliable predictors of long-term negative outcomes for these individuals. Fortunately, quick, direct, and intensive early intervention can alter the path to negative outcomes for many of these individuals.

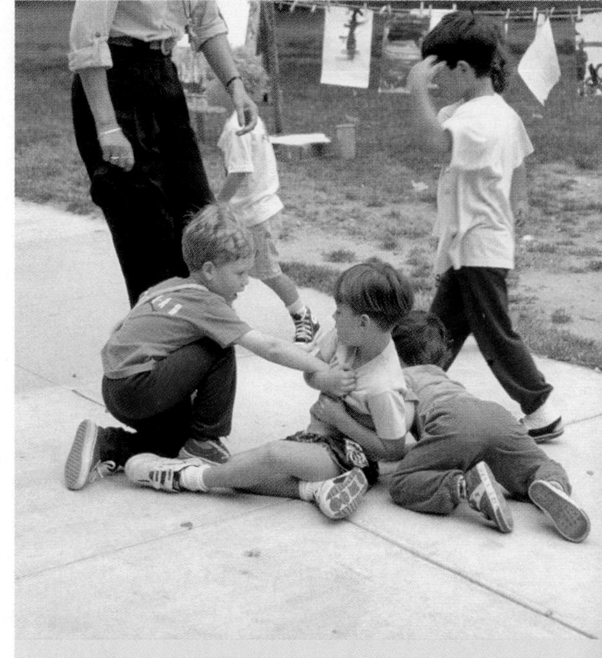

Many preschoolers need direct intervention to learn early that aggressive and antisocial behaviors are not acceptable.

Early intervention can rectify problems before they grow more serious or become firmly entrenched patterns, can help avoid a later need for psychotropic medication to control behavior, can reduce stress in the family, and can effect changes in the young child's behavior when the possibility for change is strongest. In a developing strand of longitudinal research, Phil Strain, Matt Timm, and their colleagues are demonstrating the power of early intervention (Strain et al., 1982; Strain & Timm, 1998, 1999). They have followed up 40 individuals, now in their late twenties and early thirties, who participated in the Regional Intervention Project (RIP), a behavioral intervention preschool program for children at risk for emotional or behavioral disorders. Their results are amazing and very unlike what would be expected for young children displaying serious aggressive and antisocial behaviors. Two of their subjects are enrolled in doctoral programs, three have earned master's degrees, three have received bachelor's degrees, five others are enrolled in college, three are high school graduates, and the remaining three are high school dropouts. Compare these results with those typically seen for students with emotional or behavioral disorders who have a 55 percent high school dropout rate! Other studies of early intervention have also shown the power of such programs. For example, the one developed by Hill Walker and colleagues, *First Step to Success,* shows that early intervention programs can make a real difference (Walker et al., 1998). This is particularly true when the programs have the following components:

- Parent involvement
- Teaching, through examples, about the relationship between behavior and its consequences
- Instruction on appropriate behaviors for different settings (setting demands)
- Showing how to make and keep friendships

Signals of Risk

The relationships among emotional or behavioral disorders, serious juvenile problems, and poor adult outcomes are clear. Signals of later problems in young boys and girls include the following five characteristics (Day & Hunt, 1996; Miller-Johnson et al., 1999; Strain & Timm, 1998; Walker & Sylvester, 1994).

1. Problem behaviors are identifiable by age 3 and often stable by age 8.
2. Overt (e.g., bullying) and covert (e.g., stealing) antisocial activities are becoming behavior patterns.
3. Problems happen across settings (at home, at school, and in the community).
4. The child is both overactive and inattentive.
5. Extreme aggression is frequent.

Of these five characteristics of young children prone to later problems, the single best predictor is aggression. And without intervention, problems tend to persist. For example, sixth graders referred for special services because of both violent and nonviolent inappropriate social behaviors are likely to present chronic discipline problems during their remaining school years and also to drop out of school (Tobin & Sugai, 1999). Individuals who exhibit these five characteristics are likely candidates for other negative outcomes: substance abuse, teen pregnancy, suicide, AIDS, poor marital relations, chronic unemployment, and psychiatric disorders (depression and personality disorders). Long-term follow-up studies have established the effectiveness of early intervention for these individuals, so it is critical that action be taken when they are preschoolers (Strain & Timm, 1998).

Teaching Students with Emotional or Behavioral Disorders

Students with emotional or behavioral disorders receive their education in a variety of settings: general classrooms, separate special education classrooms, special schools, the juvenile justice system, institutions, and hospitals. They live in a variety of settings as well: in family homes, in community-based residential group homes, in halfway houses, and with foster families. These students are included less in general education classrooms than their peers with disabilities. Despite the movement toward inclusion and more integration of special education students into general education classes, the placement rates of students with emotional or behavioral disorders has changed little over the past 10 years. Consider the following placement rates reported by the federal government and others (Edens & Otto, 1997; NCJJ, 2002; U.S. Department of Education, 2005b).

- More than 17 percent of students with emotional or behavioral disorders (compared to less than 4 percent of their peers with disabilities) attend school in segregated settings, either separate schools or separate facilities.
- About 30 percent attend general education classes at least 79 percent of the school day (compared to 50 percent of all students with disabilities).
- About 50 percent of all students with disabilities in residential programs are identified as having this disability.
- Some 60 percent of students in the juvenile justice system are identified by schools as having emotional or behavioral disorders.
- Separate special education classes are the educational placement option most commonly used.

Teaching students with emotional or behavioral disorders is challenging for many reasons. One key challenge is providing an educational program that meets their behavioral, social, and academic needs. Historically, educational programs for these students have focused predominantly on their behavioral and social needs, with little emphasis on academic skills. Fortunately, great progress has been made in the last 25 years on how to support these youngsters academically (Lane, 2004; Lane, Gresham, & O'Shaughnessy, 2002).

While these students are in school, their educational programs are also different from those of their peers with and without disabilities. Possibly because of the excessive number of externalizing behaviors they present, their educational programs have traditionally focused almost exclusively on behavior management and social adjustment. Unfortunately, a balance of these features with either academic or vocational components is not often achieved. Ironically, research shows that when these students are engaged in academic learning, their disruptive behavior improves as well (Lane, 1999; Lane et al., 2001). The field of emotional or behavioral disorders has begun to explore the effectiveness of various instructional approaches to improving the academic skills of students with and at risk for emotional or behavioral disorders (Lane, 2004).

Obviously, emotional or behavioral disorders have grave effects on the life of the individual, whether child or adult. Without intervention, the person is likely to live with emotional pain and isolation and may even engage in ever-increasing antisocial activity. Once students with behavioral or emotional problems are identified and receive appropriate services, they generally have an opportunity to improve their academic skills, enhance their personal relations, and enjoy more satisfying interactions with other people.

Behavior problems may be reduced when students are actively engaged in learning.

However, academic deficits have been known to remain the same or even worsen over time, even with the support of special education services (Greenbaum et al., 1996; Lane et al., 2005a & b; Mattison, Hooper, & Glassberg, 2002; Nelson, Benner, Lane, & Smith, 2004). This disability also affects their relationships with family members, adults, their peers, and their teachers—who have the highest turnover rates in the field of education (U.S. Department of Education, 2001).

Access to the General Education Curriculum

In recent years, we have identified validated methods (Babyak, Koorland, & Mathes, 2000; Cocharan et al., 1993; Dawson, Venn, & Gunter, 2000; Falk & Wehby, 2001; Scott & Shearer-Lingo, 2002) and curricula (e.g., *Phonological Awareness Training for Reading;* Lane, 1999; Lane et al., 2001; Lane et al., 2002) to improve the reading skills of students with or at risk for emotional or behavioral disorders. Some of the validated methods include

- Peer tutoring
- Story mapping
- Modeling
- Repeated readings

Less attention has been devoted to teaching writing and math skills. However, personalized instruction has resulted in improved spelling skills for these students (McLaughlin, 1992). Tutoring and direct instruction techniques have also been proved to boost performance in basic math skills (Franca et al., 1990; Harper et al., 1995; Nelson, Johnson, & Marchand-Martella, 1996). Mnemonic strategies, such as those described on page 185 in Chapter 5, have helped these students learn important math skills (Cade & Gunter, 2002). Although it is encouraging to find specific instructional techniques that promote basic skills in reading, writing, and math skills, few validated practices guide us on how best to teach students with emotional or behavioral disorders more complex, higher-level skills.

Instructional Accommodations

Hill Walker and his colleagues offer the following guidelines for implementing evidenced-based interventions with these students (Walker, Ramsey, & Gresham, 2004):

- Set the stage for educating and supporting these students by establishing a positive relationship grounded in trust, safety, and predictability.
- Begin with proactive approaches to clarify expectations and rules for academic and social performance.
- Teach relevant skills (e.g., hand raising) that are likely to produce even better results than the undesirable behaviors (e.g., talking out or yelling).
- Identify students who might be at risk for emotional or behavioral problems as early as possible so that early intervention can begin.
- Teach empathy, social skills, and problem solving strategies as part of the regular school program.
- Realize that even basic academic demands could be frustrating or aversive to these youngsters.

Students with emotional or behavioral disorders often come from chaotic family environments and tend to view school as an aversive, unpredictable place. Beginning with a proactive, positive plan that explicitly teaches expected behaviors in all settings (e.g., classroom, playground, hallways, lunch time) essentially levels the playing field for these students. If they do not respond to these primary intervention efforts, more intensive intervention can attempted. Refer to *Accommodating for Inclusive Environments* on page 248.

Functional Behavioral Assessments and Behavioral Intervention Plans

Behavioral intervention plans became a requirement of IDEA when it was reauthorized in 1997. Most students with emotional or behavioral disorders, particularly those with externalizing behavior problems, have a behavioral intervention plan as part of their IEP. Although these plans focus on functional behavioral assessments, they should also stress the development of positive social skills (Deveres, 1999a, 1999b). Let's take a look at the current requirements in *What IDEA '04 Says About Functional Behavioral Assessments.*

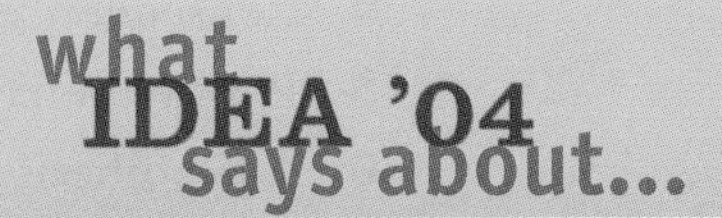

Functional Behavioral Assessments

Students who violate the student conduct code may receive a functional behavioral assessment and behavioral intervention services and modifications (including a behavioral intervention plan), if appropriate.

In cases of manifestation determination, the IEP team must

- Either conduct a functional behavioral assessment and implement a behavioral intervention plan
- Or, for students with a current behavioral intervention plan in place, review previous functional behavioral assessments and modify the existing plan, if necessary

The process used to develop behavioral intervention plans can be most helpful when educators are designing individualized instruction for students. The functional behavioral assessment phase helps to clarify the student's preferences for specific academic tasks, determine when undesirable behavior is likely to occur, and identify the reason why the problem behavior is occurring (Kern et al., 2001). Here's how it works: The goal of the functional behavioral assessment is to determine what activities are associated with problem behaviors and to identify the student's interests and preferences. Instructional activities are then modified to incorporate the student's "likes" into activities where problems typically occur. In other words, circumstances and events in the classroom that occur before the behavior (antecedents) and after it (consequences) are modified so that students learn a new, more adaptive behavior that works better than the former behavior to "get" or "avoid" something. For example, James's behavior during activities that require him to write is highly disruptive. However, he likes to use the computer, so he is allowed to complete written assignments using a word processing program on a computer. The double benefit is that his academic performance is improving and his disruptive behavior has decreased. In this example, James's disruptive behavior was accurately interpreted by the teacher to indicate that he was trying to avoid a task too difficult for him (writing). One caution, however: Functional assessments often miss behaviors that occur rarely (Nichols, 2000). This can be a real problem, because many low-frequency infractions (e.g., hitting a teacher, setting a fire, breaking a window) are the most dangerous and serious.

Why did behavioral intervention plans become adopted as part of IDEA '04? The law reflects concerns of Congress and the public about violence, discipline, and special education students. In the early versions of IDEA, students with disabilities could not be expelled if their disruptive behavior was caused by the disability. Students with emotional or behavioral disorders were typically protected by what was called the "stay put provision." Under that provision, educational services could not be stopped, and these students could not be expelled from school. The 1997 version of IDEA changed that protection. Students with disabilities who violate school rules, particularly in the areas of weapons violence and drugs, are subject to disciplinary actions just like their peers without disabilities. But there are limits, and the end result is that students with disabilities who are violent or "out of control" have behavioral intervention plans. These plans seek to eliminate undesirable behaviors and replace them with appropriate ones. The behavioral intervention plan becomes part of the student's IEP. Here are some guidelines about these plans (Hartwig & Ruesch, 1998). Functional behavioral assessments and behavioral intervention plans should include descriptions of

1. The problem behavior(s)
2. Events preceding the problem behavior
3. Classroom rules

4 Consequences for infractions
5 Positive behaviors incompatible with the problem behavior
6 A hypothesis about why the problem behavior is occurring
7 An intervention to either (a) teach the student a desired behavior to replace the problem behavior or (b) arrange events and circumstances in the classroom to prompt and reinforce the desired behavior

Validated Practices

Many different approaches are used in the education and treatment of students with emotional or behavioral disorders. Which approach is selected depends on what conceptual model the professional uses to teach these children. Table 7.5 lists seven major conceptual models of treatment and education. This overview is meant to illustrate the range of options and orientations available—from clinical to behavioral to holistic to eclectic. Generally, educators integrate some elements of many of these approaches into the educational programs they design for these children, incorporating the behavioral approach along with a direct focus on academic instruction.

Table 7.5 • Conceptual Models of Treatment and Education

Behavioral approach	Based on the work of B. F. Skinner and other behaviorists, this model focuses on providing children with highly structured learning environments and teaching materials. The student's behaviors are precisely measured, interventions are designed to increase or decrease behaviors, and progress toward goals is measured carefully and frequently.
Psychoanalytic (psychodynamic) approach	Based on the work of Sigmund Freud and other psychoanalysts, this model views the problems of the child as having a basis in unconscious conflicts and motivations: based not on the behavior itself, but on the pathology of one's personality. Treatment is generally long-term individual psychotherapy designed to uncover and resolve these deep-seated problems.
Psychoeducational approach	The psychoanalytic view is combined with principles of teaching, and treatment is measured primarily in terms of learning. Meeting the individual needs of the youngster is emphasized, often through projects and creative arts, through everyday functioning at school and home.
Ecological approach	The problems of the child are seen as a result of interactions with the family, the school, and the community. The child or youth is not the sole focus of treatment; the family, school, neighborhood, and community also are changed in order to improve the interactions.
Social-cognitive approach	The interactions between the effects of the environment and the youngster's behavior are taught to the child. This approach seeks to integrate and reconceptualize behavioral and cognitive psychology. The result is a view that takes into account the interactions among the individual's physical and social environments, personal factors (thoughts, feelings, and perceptions), and the behavior itself.
Humanistic education approach	Love and trust, in teaching and learning, are emphasized, and children are encouraged to be open and free individuals. The approach emphasizes self-direction, self-fulfillment, and self-evaluation. A nonauthoritarian atmosphere in a nontraditional educational setting is developed.
Biogenic approach	Physiological interventions such as diet, medications, and biofeedback are used, based on biological theories of causation and treatment.

Source: Schema is borrowed from *Characteristics of Behavioral Disorders of Children and Youth* (8th ed., pp. 71–89) by J. M. Kauffman, 2001, Columbus, OH: Merrill.

Although many different methods, programs, and curricula exist for students with emotional or behavioral disorders, some features are common to most. These include direct evaluation of success using CBM (see Chapter 5 for a review), functional assessments and behavioral intervention plans (above) and other strategies for reducing inappropriate behaviors and increasing positive ones.

When thinking about strategies for altering behavior, it is important to recognize that discipline is not equivalent to punishment (Maag, 2001). Rather, discipline is training that results in improvement of performance, whereas punishment is supposed to result in decreases in behavior. A systematic discipline strategy, in which a hierarchy of interventions is systematically applied, helps to create safe schools where violence and abuse are eliminated and academic achievement is increased (Myles & Simpson, 1998).

Effective and efficient instruction cannot occur in chaos or in a repressive environment. What is required is a positive learning climate where children can learn, create, discover, explore, expand their knowledge, and apply new skills. When disruption is high, causing educators to spend time and energy addressing conduct problems, students do not learn effectively or efficiently. Disruption—whether it arises from several individuals or from most of the class—can be held to a minimum without destroying the climate needed for learning. To accomplish this goal, teachers must be familiar with an array of proven interventions and must know when these are most appropriately applied. Interventions applied systematically through a progression—a hierarchy—can lead to effective discipline.

The **Intervention Ladder** (see Figure 7.2) was developed to help teachers better understand how to match interventions with the level and severity of disruptive behavior (Smith, 1984; Smith & Rivera, 1993). The foundation upon which the ladder stands includes basic preventive measures that good teachers incorporate into all of their instruction. For example, educators are encouraged to make school challenging and exciting so that all students are actively engaged in learning and thus are less likely to be disruptive (Nelson et al., 2004). Also, all members of the school must be aware of the basic rules or standards of behavior, and everyone must consistently apply the same consequences when the standards are violated (Rosenberg & Jackman, 1997, 2002). The Intervention Ladder organizes interventions from the simplest and least intrusive to the most complex and punitive. Only after evaluation procedures indicate that a mild intervention is not successful are more intensive procedures implemented. Some interventions shown on the ladder are simple to apply and can positively influence most incidents that occur in classroom settings. Let's look at three of these tactics: behavior-specific praise, positive reinforcement delivered in the form of points, and a group contingency. Then we will discuss the use of punishment.

It is well documented that behavior-specific praise increases the appropriate behavior of disruptive students as well as the time students spend working on class assignments (Brophy, 1981; Hall, Lund, & Jackson, 1968; O'Leary & Becker, 1969). Remarkably, praise is underutilized in both general education and special education classrooms, and sometimes students with disabilities receive less than one praise statement per hour (Gable et al., 1983; Wehby, Symons, & Shores, 1995). Moreover, as few as 5 percent of teachers' praise statements are behavior-specific. When used consistently and directly, praise has powerful results, as in the following example: "Jemma, congratulations on studying and staying focused. You earned 90 percent on your fractions test!" (Sutherland, Wehby, & Yoder, 2001). For some reason, it seems difficult for teachers to change their actions and incorporate more specific praise into their instructional routines (Sutherland & Wehby, 2001). Considering this tactic's simplicity and power, behavior-specific praise should become part of every teacher's repertoire.

Positive reinforcement is a mainstay of behavior management programs. Just like the benefits of praise, this intervention's positive effects are well known and substantially researched (Maag, 2001). Many different versions of positive reinforcement programs have been developed over the years, since their initiation in the 1960s. Many include a system that allows students to earn points for good

Intervention Ladder A hierarchy of disciplinary tactics organized from the least intrusive and complex to the most intrusive and complicated

Figure 7.2 • The Intervention Ladder

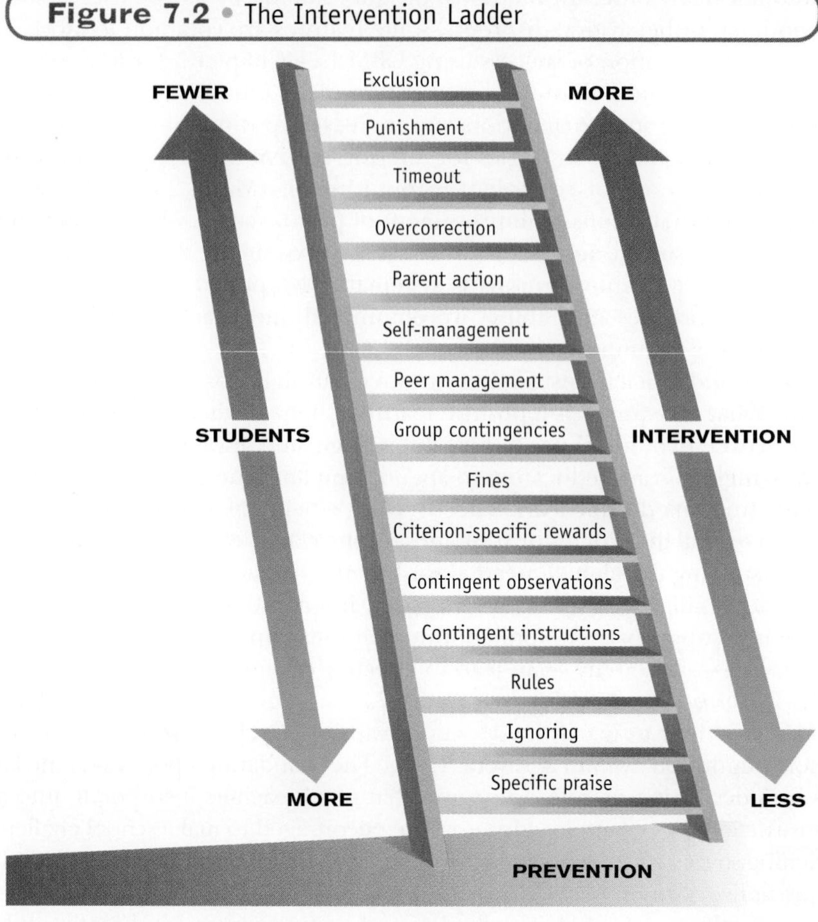

Source: From *Effective Discipline* (2nd ed., p. 17) by D. D. Smith and D. P. Rivera, 1993, Austin, TX: Pro-Ed. Reprinted by permission.

behavior and then trade in those points for prizes or privileges. Reinforcement systems can be as simple or as complicated as teachers want to make them (Cruz & Cullinan, 2001). In some systems, students earn proportionately more points for behaviors that are more complex or important (completing assignments) than for behaviors deemed easier or less important (speaking nicely to classmates). Privileges (breakfast in the classroom, quiet free reading time) can be purchased with points, and points are deducted for serious offenses (aggression, destruction of property).

Group contingencies are reinforcement systems that involve the entire class and have numerous applications for general education classroom settings. One version of a group contingency is the Good Behavior Game originally developed by Barrish, Sanders, and Wolf in 1969. The technique uses class competition to reduce disruption. The class is divided into teams. In some versions of the game, a tally of infractions is kept to record violations of classroom rules. At the end of the day, the teams with the fewest infractions—and therefore the fewest points—wins (all teams can win or lose). Students have indicated that they like this approach because of the game-like features, student involvement, and fun (Babyak, Luze, & Kamps, 2000).

Another practice is punishment. Punishment is technically defined as any consequence that reduces the rate or strength of the behavior being punished. Thus, if the behavior does not decrease, then technically the strategy (e.g., raising your voice) isn't punishment. Punishment has many different forms (Maag, 2001). Punishment has been administered in the form of fines, restitutional activities (e.g., cleaning the classroom for defacing a wall), suspension, and even corporal punishment. Note that punishment is placed high on the Intervention Ladder because most classroom infractions do not warrant such a serious intervention, which can have an overall negative impact on students and the school environment. Unlike positive approaches to managing classroom behaviors, punishment tends to produce an immediate result. Its effects are often short-term, however, and the unwanted behavior may return soon (Axelrod & Hall, 1999).

Taken to its highest level, punishment is very serious and negative. Many states still allow the application of corporal punishment (paddling, spanking, rapping hands). All educators should be aware of the potentially devastating effects that corporal punishment can have on children. But despite all its negative effects and the lack of research to support its use, corporal punishment persists (Lohrmann-O'Rourke & Zirkel, 1998). Those most vulnerable to its application are students with disabilities, students from poverty, and culturally and linguistically diverse boys (Townsend, 2000).

Many people mistakenly believe that punishment must involve physical hitting, screaming, or embarrassment for the child, which means that many different tactics—including corporal punishment—fall within this category. But not all punishment is counter productive. Some teachers find that certain forms of punishment can be an important part of an effective teaching plan to change unwanted behaviors. For example, mild reprimands, temporary withdrawal of attention, and the loss of certain privileges are all punishing tactics (they are intended to reduce the frequency of the target behavior) but do not have the negative long-term effects of corporal punishment (Smith & Rivera, 1993). Corporal punishment should be avoided in school settings, because it

- Only temporarily halts undesired behaviors
- Does not teach new skills or knowledge
- Causes teachers to become engaged in power struggles with students
- Leads to an unhealthy and negative interaction with students
- Is initiated and dictated by the student
- Can change the classroom into a battleground where the focus is on power and coercion
- Models a negative style of interaction with others

Reprinted with special permission of King Features Syndicate.

Remember, too, that any form of punishment should always be accompanied by teaching a new behavior. All classrooms must be safe and orderly environments where students can feel secure as they attempt the difficult tasks of learning and where they can trust the educators charged with this important responsibility.

Technology

The computer can be especially helpful to students with emotional or behavioral disorders (Bryant & Bryant, 2003; Rivera & Smith, 1997). It can serve as an emotionally neutral system with which to interact, have fun, achieve success, and engage actively in learning (Lucent Technologies, 1999). Computers facilitate learning without imposing the pressure of subjective judgments; a computer does not criticize the student using it. Answers are simply right or wrong. Thus a computer serves as a safe environment in which to practice and improve skills. When a teacher incorporates computer-assisted instruction as an individualized learning activity for a child, the computer mirrors many of the attributes of a good teacher. Specifically, it

- Provides immediate attention and feedback
- Customizes (to varying degrees) instruction to the skill level of the child
- Allows students to work at their own pace
- Makes corrections quickly
- Produces a professional-looking product
- Keeps accurate records of correct response and error rates
- Ignores inappropriate behavior
- Focuses on the particular response
- Is nonjudgmental

However, using a computer is not a substitute for learning to interact appropriately with other people, and a teacher should not rely solely on computer interactions with children who have emotional or behavioral disorders. In arithmetic, for example, a teacher might introduce the instruction, allow drill and practice on the computer, and then return periodically to check the student's progress. In reading, computer-proved modeling can be used to increase the number of words read correctly and the percentage of words read correctly (Dawson, Venn, & Gunter, 2000). Many computer-learning programs are available at different levels. By consulting with computer specialists, teachers can ensure that their judgments about the learning needs of the students are translated into the appropriate computer materials.

Transition

Students with disabilities face daunting obstacles when they enter mainstream society and feel the pressures of independent adult life (Wehmeyer et al., 2000). These obstacles are even more significant for students with emotional or behavioral disorders, whose outcomes are dismal. In most cases, only through timely interventions can the path to adulthood at the margin be altered and avoided.

Results for students with this disability are not good (U.S. Department of Education, 2001). In fact, some think that outcomes are worse for individuals with emotional or behavioral disorders than for any other group of students with disabilities (Chesapeake Institute, 1994; Jolivette et al., 2000; NCES, 2002; Wagner, Cameto, & Newman, 2003). A review of the data reveals that these students

- Have lower grades than any other groups of students with disabilities
- Fail more courses than other students with disabilities

- Fail minimal competence tests more than other students with disabilities
- Are retained more often
- Do not graduate from high school with a diploma at an expected rate (42 percent, compared to 50 percent for all students with disabilities and 76 percent for all students in the general population)
- Miss more days (18 per year) of school because of absenteeism than their peers with disabilities
- Have a high dropout rate (51 percent) compared to other students with disabilities (29 percent) and to peers without disabilities (5 percent)
- Are 13 times more likely to be arrested while in high school than their peers with disabilities and 4 times more likely to be arrested than their classmates without disabilities
- Are very likely (58 percent of them) to be arrested within 5 years of leaving school (compared to 30 percent for all students with disabilities)

Turning around the dismal outcomes experienced by many individuals with emotional or behavioral disorders can be achieved, but it takes sustained efforts and supports from professionals across the school years.

How might these dismal outcomes be changed? Treatment and intervention are part of the answer. Students in the criminal justice system do not receive services, supports, or the delivery of intensive IEPs (NCJJ, 2002). Also, their transition back to their communities and home schools is problematic (Griller-Clark, 2001). That is, these students do not receive support services (such as pre-placement planning and counseling), their IEPs frequently include no detailed transition plan, and often, these students' educational records are not even transferred to their receiving schools. Clearly, such lack of attention to smoothing transitions is not helpful.

Individuals with emotional or behavioral disorders who receive counseling experience some improved outcomes (Hunter, 2001; Schoenwald & Hoagwood, 2001). Social skills training (discussed earlier in this chapter), instruction in self-determination (discussed in detail on page 298 of Chapter 8), and stable home environments also contribute to better results as adults (McConaughy & Wadsworth, 2000; Test et al., 2000; Wehmeyer et al., 2000).

Collaboration

One compounding problem for students with emotional or behavioral disorders is school failure, and school failure compounds other problems these individuals face. As we have noted, educational and life-long outcomes can be improved. However, improvement requires the concerted efforts of all partners (school, community, and social services) to assist both families and children (Eber et al., 2002). This is particularly true when the goal is to provide these students an education in the most inclusive environment possible.

Issues about inclusion spark controversy in special education (Fuchs & Fuchs, 1994). For students with emotional or behavioral disorders, it is no different. As you have learned, these students' rates of inclusion are low (U.S. Department of Education, 2005b). One reason is general educators' concerns about including students with aggressive behaviors: They feel that they are neither trained nor equipped to handle these students. They also believe that general education settings are not equipped to control these students' behaviors or to provide necessary therapeutic instruction (Cheney & Barringer, 1995). In addition, some experts question whether placement in general education classrooms benefits these students (Kauffman,

2005). Although many educators and parents of students with disabilities assume that students benefit from being exposed to socially appropriate peer role models, this may not hold true for students with emotional or behavioral disorders. It is only through intensive direct instruction that these individuals learn correct social behaviors (Walker & Sprague, 1999, 2000).

Thus it may be that inclusion is not desirable in some cases and not possible in others. Students detained by the criminal justice system, for example, are unable to participate in inclusion classes. During the time of their incarceration, it is especially important that their educational needs not be neglected. Students have a right to receive appropriate and individualized special education even if they are in correctional settings such as halfway houses, jails, or prisons. Unfortunately, students in these settings often do not receive the intensive education they need, either in social skills or in academics (Lane, Gresham, & O'Shaughnessy, 2002).

Partnerships with Families and Communities

Parenting a child with emotional or behavioral disorders is usually quite difficult. These families are most likely to be blamed for their children's problems and are also more likely than others to make significant financial sacrifices to secure services for their children (Ahearn, 1995). Increasingly, though, teachers are paying more attention to both the contributions and the needs of family members and are listening more carefully to parents' concerns. Let's look at two issues that often arise in the family lives of these children: negotiating the mental health care system and foster home placement.

Mental Health Care

Accessing America's mental health care system can be a daunting experience even for the most capable and most affluent. For those who have limited resources or who distrust the social services system, the barriers can be so great that needed services are not sought or received (CDF, 2004). These barriers may include lack of transportation, lack of child care for other children, lack of information about what services are available and where they can be received, and lack of emotional support. In January of 2001, the Surgeon General's National Action Agenda for Children's Mental Health stressed the importance of coordinating services across many agencies to ensure that children in need of mental health services receive them (Hoagwood, 2001a). Advocating for **wraparound services** reflects recognition of the importance of supporting children and families in trouble and the knowledge that comprehensive early intervention can prevent a terrible future.

Parent involvement is critical in achieving child mental health and positive outcomes. Parents attending school events, volunteering to help in their child's classroom, and providing follow-up to behavioral intervention programs initiated at school are all necessary to the development of good child mental health. Engaging families, particularly those from diverse cultures, takes considerable effort and skill (Cartledge, Kea, & Ida, 2000). Communication is one key to developing the trust and respect necessary to make families want to become actively involved at school. Also, children whose families are involved at school have greater academic success. For some children, however, parental efforts alone are not sufficient. Mental health care services make a difference in the lives of these students and their families. Unfortunately, the mental health needs, particularly of students with emotional or behavioral disorders who live in poverty, are not addressed because of fragmented services and gaps in treatment (CDF, 2004). Educators can assist parents in getting the professional help they need if families are connected to schools. As you have learned, parent–school partnerships emerge when educators are culturally competent, respect family members, increase communication, and keep their promises.

wraparound services A service delivery model in which needs are met through collaboration of many agencies and systems (education, mental health, social services, community)

Foster Care

The U.S. Department of Health and Human Services estimates that some 588,000 children are in the foster care system in this nation (Adoption and Foster Care Analysis and Reporting System, 2002). Although this number represents a 5 percent reduction from the previous year (between 2000 and 2001), it is alarming, especially because social service agencies are reluctant to take children from their families and place them in an alternative home environment.

The numbers of children living in foster care are troubling, but even more so is the percentage of those children who have emotional or behavioral disorders (Armsden et al., 2000). Estimates range from 35 to 60 percent, almost five times higher than in the general student population. Also, a higher number of these youngsters than would be expected have internalizing problems (anxiety, depression, and poor school performance). Of course, it is not known whether these emotional or behavioral problems are one reason for the children's placement in foster homes or whether the placements and histories of disrupted attachments contribute to—or even cause—these problems.

On another note, the plight of these individuals is compounded by the lack of continuity of services. For example, some 20,000 young people "age out" of foster care programs each year on their 18th birthdays (Ama & Caplan, 2001). Many of them are still in high school, trying to graduate with a high school diploma. However, because few transition programs are available, they end up homeless, facing one more serious challenge in their young lives.

What can be done to improve these individuals' situations? Educators can create positive and consistent classroom environments, can be sure students understand the consequences of their actions, and can teach them the skills they need to avoid negative outcomes (O'Dell et al., 2001). It also is important (though not the responsibility of the school) to ensure that these children have access to the mental health services they need to resolve their confusion about family life (Hoagwood, 2001b).

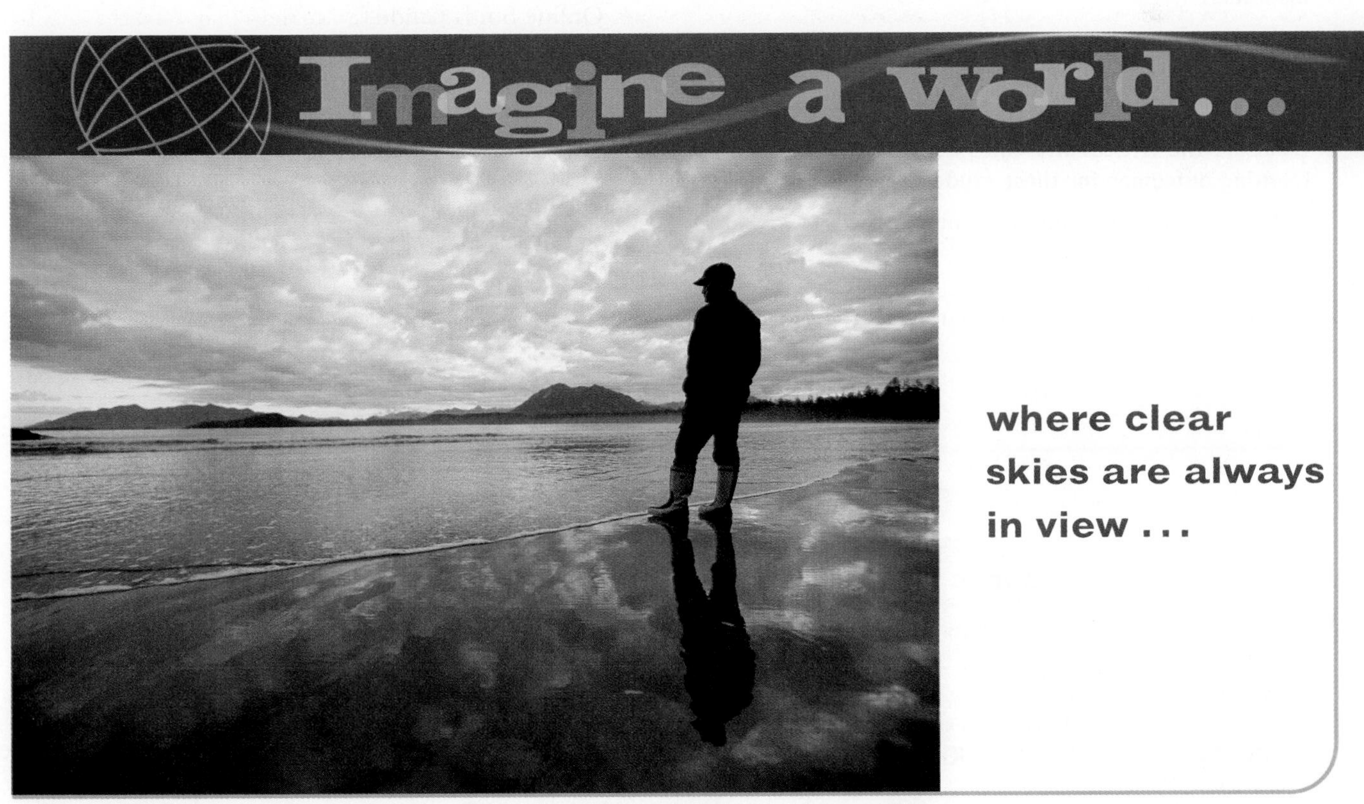

Imagine a world . . .
where clear skies are always in view . . .

Summary

Exactly what constitutes emotional or behavioral disorders reflects, in part, societal standards for behavior and expectations about the development of children. Many behaviors that our society labels as disordered in a particular individual might be acceptable if that person were a different age, lived in a different society, came from a different culture, or exhibited the behaviors under different circumstances. Of course some conditions are considered disturbed no matter the age or the social context. Early screening and evidenced-based interventions with children with emotional or behavioral disorders is critical to avoid the negative outcomes often awaiting these students in the absence of effective instruction and mental heath supports.

Addressing the Chapter Objectives

1 How does an unclear definition influence how we identify and support students with emotional or behavioral disorders?

- Makes it difficult to coordinate services with mental health providers
- Makes it difficult to determine eligibility

2 What are the academic and social characteristics of these students?

- Poor social skills
- Acquisition and performance deficits in academic and social areas
- Poor academic performance that doesn't improve over time

3 What are the main causes of emotional or behavioral disorders?

- Biology
- Home and community
- School

4 What are the critical strategies needed to improve learning outcomes for these students?

- Implement screening instruments.
- Use validated practices.
- Provide early intervention.
- Provide sound instruction that meets their academic and behavioral needs.

5 What strategies improve postsecondary outcomes for these students?

- Provide engaging instruction to keep students in school.
- Address their academic, social, and behavioral needs.
- Work collaboratively with families, foster care, and mental health services.

mylabschool
Where the classroom comes to life!

MyLabSchool is a collection of online tools for your success in this course, your licensure exams, and your teaching career. Visit www.mylabschool.com to access the following:

- Online Study Guide
- Video cases from real classrooms
- Help with your research papers using Research Navigator
- Career Center with resources for:
  - Praxis and licensure preparation
  - Professional portfolio development
  - Job search and interview techniques
  - Lesson planning

Supplementary Resources

Popular Novels and Books

Atwood, M. (1996). *Alias Grace.* New York: Doubleday.

Duke, P. (1987). *Call me Anna: The autobiography of Patty Duke.* New York: Bantam.

Jamison, K. R. (1995). *An unquiet mind: A memoir of moods and madness.* New York: Knopf.

Karr-Morse, R., & Wiley, M. S. (1997). *Ghosts from the nursery: Tracing the roots of violence.* New York: Atlantic Monthly Press.

Kesey, K. (1977). *One flew over the cuckoo's nest.* New York: Penguin.

Nasar, S. (1998). *A beautiful mind: The life of mathematical genius and Nobel laureate John Nash.* New York: Touchstone.

Pelzer, D. (1995). *A child called "It": One child's courage to survive.* Deerfield Beach, FL: Health Communications.

Plath, S. (1971). *The bell jar.* New York: Harper & Row.

Sedaris, D. (1997). *Naked.* Boston: Little, Brown.

Movies

Secret Window (2004). Columbia

Right after his divorce, a successful and prolific author moves into what was his vacation home. He wants the isolation that the secluded location offers so he can get over both the unfaithfulness of his ex-wife and writer's block. The stress of the situation causes his mind to create another personality—a stalker who accuses the writer of stealing a story that became a successful novel. The stalker threatens the writer and his children. The tragic results include arson, murder, and insanity.

Identity (2003). Columbia

A therapist hypnotizes a prisoner with multiple personality disorder in an attempt to find his murderous personality. The result is that all of the prisoner's personalities meet at a small motel similar to the one where he was abandoned as a child. His personalities are very different from each other and include a police officer, a criminal, a child and his parents, a prostitute, a young couple, and several others. Because of a torrential rainstorm, all the personalities are trapped together at the motel. One by one, each is murdered, eventually leaving one surviving character.

This violent film uses an unlikely method of therapy and an extreme case of schizophrenia to weave a thrilling story. It does little, however, to provide any understanding of mental illness.

***A Beautiful Mind (2001).* Universal**

Based loosely on the life of John Forbes Nash, Jr., a genius in mathematics, who develops a revolutionary economic theory. As Nash is working, he begins to do top-secret code breaking for the FBI, but his wife becomes suspicious of his secretive behavior. She discovers that he is actually schizophrenic and that the FBI agent, along with other people in Nash's life, are all figments of John's imagination.

This story depicts the fine line between genius and insanity, taking a close look at the schizophrenia that affected Nash for his entire life. Nash confronted his illness and spent time in an institution. Through medication, along with the love and support of his wife, he was able to cope with his illness, and in the twilight of his life he was awarded the Nobel Prize. This film won the Oscar for best picture, and Jennifer Connolly won an Oscar for best supporting actress as Nash's wife.

Girl, Interrupted (1999). Columbia Pictures

After graduation from school, Susanna attempts suicide, so her parents check her into a mental hospital where she is diagnosed with borderline personality disorder. She is put on a floor for young women who have different emotional or behavioral disorders. Susanna's friendship with the other patients helps her develop a strong sense of self.

This film is based on the memoirs of Susanna Kaysen, who actually spent over a year in an institution during the 1960s. It tells the story of the depersonalization that adolescent treatment centers often inflict and reveals their relatively poor outcomes. Angelina Jolie won the Oscar as best supporting actress for her role as a sociopath and Susanna's closest friend.

One Flew Over the Cuckoo's Nest (1979). United Artists

When McMurphy is convicted of a petty crime, he convinces everyone that he is insane in order to avoid doing time in jail. Accordingly, he is sent to a mental institution to serve out his sentence. McMurphy's presence gives the other patients a new lease on life, but all this activity disrupts the hospital routine. Consequently, the head nurse becomes his enemy. She ends up riding him to the breaking point, and she makes certain that this is the last time he challenges the system.

The film implies that the characters in the institution are not as crazy as the world outside and that when someone does not conform, the system forces the person to obey the rules. This movie shows the horror of institutions and illustrates how much those who are committed and their caretakers have in common. This film won five Academy Awards in 1976.

Professional, Parent, and Advocacy Groups

American Psychiatric Association in Washington, DC
www.psych.org

American Psychological Association (APA) in Washington, DC: www.apa.org

Council for Children with Behavioral Disorders (CCBD), CEC in Arlington, Virginia
www.cec.sped.org or www.ccbd.net

National Alliance for the Mentally Ill (NAMI) in Arlington, Virginia 22201-3042: www.nami.org

National Mental Health Association in Alexandria, Virginia 22314-2971: www.nmha.org

The Center for Mental Health Services Knowledge Exchange Network in Washington, DC
www.mentalhealth.org

Professional Standards and Licensure Tests

After reading this chapter, you should be able to link basic knowledge and skills described in the CEC Standards and INTASC Principles with information provided in this text. The table below shows some of the specific CEC Emotional or Behavioral Disorders Knowledge and Skill Standards and INTASC Special Education Principles that can be applied to each major section of the chapter. Other standards may also be applied to this chapter. Associated General Praxis II topic areas are identified in the right column.

Major Chapter Headings	CEC Knowledge and Skill Core Standard and Associated Subcategories	INTASC Core Principle and Associated Special Education Subcategories	PRAXIS II Exam Topic
Where We've Been . . . What's on the Horizon?	**1: Foundations** BD1K3 Foundations and issues related to knowledge and practice in emotional or behavioral disorders	**1: Subject Matter** 1.13 Special education teachers know major trends and issues that define the history of special education and understand how current legislation and recommended practice fit within the contact of this history.	1: Understanding Exceptionality 2: Legal and Social Issues
Emotional and Behavior Disorders Defined	**1: Foundations** BD1K1 Educational terminology and definitions of individuals with emotional or behavioral disorders	**1: Subject Matter** 1.12 Special education teachers serve as a resource to others by providing information about the laws and policies that support students with disabilities and how to access additional information when needed.	1: Understanding Exceptionality 2: Legal and Social Issues
Characteristics	**2: Development and Characteristics of Learners** BD2K3 Social characteristics of individuals with emotional or behavioral disorders	**2: Student Learning** 2.06 Special education teachers understand how disabilities in one area can impact learning and development in other areas.	1: Understanding Exceptionality
Causes and Prevention	**2: Development and Characteristics of Learners** BD2K1 Etiology and diagnosis related to various theoretical approaches in the field of emotional or behavioral disorders	**2: Student Learning** 2.02 All teachers continually examine their assumptions about the learning and development of individual students with disabilities.	1: Understanding Exceptionality

Assessment	**8: Assessment** BD8S2 Assess appropriate and problematic social behaviors of individuals with emotional or behavioral disorders	**8: Assessment** 8.04 All teachers engage all students, including students with disabilities, in assessing and understanding their own learning and behavior.	1: Understanding Exceptionality 3: Delivery of Services to Students
Teaching Students with Emotional or Behavioral Disorders	**4: Instructional Strategies** BD4S1 Use strategies from multiple theoretical approaches for individuals with emotional or behavioral disorders	**4: Instructional Strategies** 4.07 All teachers use strategies that promote the independence, self-control and self-advocacy of students with disabilities.	1: Understanding Exceptionality 3: Delivery of Services to Students
Transition	**4: Instructional Strategies** BD4K3 Resources and techniques used to transition individuals with emotional or behavioral disorders into and out of school and post-school environments	**7: Planning Instruction** 7.07 Special education teachers oversee the development of individualized transition plans to guide learners' transitions from preschool to elementary school, middle school to high school, and high school to postschool opportunities.	2: Legal and Social Issues 3: Delivery of Services to Students
Collaboration	**10: Collaboration** BD10K4 Role of professional groups and referral agencies in identifying, assessing, and providing services to individuals with emotional or behavioral disorders	**10: Collaboration, Ethics, and Relationships** 10.09 Special education teachers collaborate with families and with school and community personnel to include students with disabilities in a range of instructional environments in the school and community.	2: Legal and Social Issues 3: Delivery of Services to Students
Partnerships with Families and Communities	**10: Collaboration** BD10K2 Parent education programs and behavior management guides that address severe behavioral problems and facilitate communication for individuals with emotional or behavioral disorders	**10: Collaboration, Ethics, and Relationships** 10.10 Special education teachers understand the impact that having a child with a disability may have on family roles and functioning at different points in the life cycle of a family.	1: Understanding Exceptionality 2: Legal and Social Issues 3: Delivery of Services to Students

Cats and Kittens (watercolor). No date. Courtesy of the Courthald Institute Gallery, Somerset House London.

Gottfried Mind, sometimes called the "Raphael of Cats," depicted cats almost exclusively and was known to have an obsession with the focus of his work and life. When Mind was not painting or drawing cats, he was carving them out of chestnuts (Foucart-Walter & Rosenberg, 1987). His modest apartment was filled with cats and kittens, and when he worked, cats were in his lap and on his shoulders. Mind (1768–1814) was born and lived all his life in Bern, Switzerland. He was known all over Europe, and his work was popular with cat lovers. Most of his work remains in private collections today and is rarely seen in public. He is probably one of the few artistic masters of the 18th and 19th Centuries with documented mental retardation. He died of a stroke at age 46.

8

Mental Retardation

> *What people really need are choices—the proverbial array of options we have talked about for years. There are no panaceas, no perfect worlds, no nirvana. This is just life as we know it, support it, and nurture it. People with disabilities just want to live it.*
>
> **Diane McComb**
>
> Executive Director, Maryland Association of Community Services

All disabilities are serious. The compounding effects of impaired intellectual functioning and the stigma associated with this situation make mental retardation most challenging for the individuals involved and their families. **Mental retardation** is the disability that results in impaired cognitive abilities and the need for assistance to achieve independence and participation in the community. Mental retardation is sometimes called **cognitive** or **intellectual disabilities**. Differences in abilities experienced by people with mental retardation, and the way society reacts to those differences, can create obstacles or opportunities for these individuals and their families. People with this disability and those who teach them and provide them with supports often must make very special efforts to ensure that they learn all the skills they will need in adult life. Although many of them may require considerable special assistance and support from teachers and others, it is important always to remember that individuals with mental retardation are people first. They are members of families, they have relationships with friends and neighbors, and they have personalities shaped by their innate characteristics as well as by their life experiences. Students with mental retardation go to school, plan for the future, hope for a good job, wonder whom they will marry, and anticipate adulthood. They have hopes and dreams like everyone else. Like Angie, whose story the *In the Spotlight* feature tells, these individuals live and work in the community and are taking their places in society. They experience joy, sadness, disappointment, pride, love, and all the other emotions that are a part of living.

Chapter Objectives

After studying this chapter, you will be able to:

1. Discuss the key components of the 2002 AAMR definition of mental retardation.
2. Explain the levels of severity and outcomes of people with mental retardation.
3. Explain the four levels of supports and how they make a difference in the lives of people with mental retardation.
4. Describe two ways in which causes of disabilities can be organized, and list three major known causes of mental retardation.
5. Describe two validated approaches that make a difference in the outcomes of students with mental retardation who are not fully accessing the general education curriculum.

Where We've Been . . . What's on the Horizon?

Mental retardation has always been a part of human history. Systematic efforts in education and treatment did not begin until the late 1700s when farmers from the countryside of southern France brought a young boy they had found in the woods to a doctor in Paris. On that landmark day in 1798, when Jean-Marc-Gaspard Itard started working with Victor, "the wild boy of Averyon," special education began (Itard, 1806).

Angie in the Spotlight

Angie loves people, and she loves working outside. That's why her stockman job at Wal-Mart suited her just fine! Her main responsibilities were to bring in carts from the cart corrals and to help customers with carry-outs. In the seven years since a job coach from The Arc helped her get her first job at Wal-Mart (as a cotton candy maker) she became an important member of the store's team. Angie received an exemplary service award. She was a regular participant in staff meetings and made suggestions for store improvements.

Angie's mom said, "I feel that she was a shining example of a willing spirit, determination and the power of working hard at whatever she does."

But, like most young people, Angie figured out that she had different career aspirations and wanted to work helping animals in need. So, [after] leaving Wal-Mart on great terms, Angie is now pursuing a career helping animals at the county humane society.

Source: Reprinted with permission by Cathy Alexander. Special thanks to her and to her daughter, Angie.

Historical Context

By the mid-19th Century, residential institutions had appeared throughout Europe and Great Britain. In 1848 Samuel Gridley Howe, the first director of the Perkins Institute for the Blind in Boston, expanded the center to include individuals with mental retardation. Later it became a separate institution, the Walter E. Fernald State School. Ironically, Howe clearly predicted the hazards of residential institutions: Isolating people with disabilities both geographically and socially from mainstream society leads not only to separation but also to fear, mistrust, and abuse. Despite warnings to keep their numbers down and their size small, institutions spread over the United States. By 1917 all but four states had institutions for people with mental retardation, and many of them were large.

This rise in the number and size of institutions for people with mental retardation was based on unjustified fear of these people and their supposed negative effect on society (Winzer, 1993). In 1877 Richard Dugdale, a member of the New York Prison Association, made up a story about the Jukes family to illustrate that people with mental retardation were a danger to society. Dugdale believed that mental retardation was a hereditary condition and that people with it were the source of the crime, poverty, and other social ills plaguing the country at that time. The logic worked this way: The Jukes, and families like them, were the source of poverty, immorality, crime, and more "feeblemindedness" (through high rates of reproduction). They were a menace to society, and good people should be protected from them. Members of such families therefore should be cast away, put in institutions, and not allowed to have more offspring. Dugdale was not the only propagator of such theories. In 1912 Henry Goddard released the story of Deborah Kallikak, who came from a family of "feebleminded" people, who were prone to becoming criminals. Goddard maintained that because mental retardation was passed on by heredity, nothing could be done to correct the situation. Goddard's conclusion was that people with mental retardation should be removed from society and their population controlled (Elks, 2005; Gelf, 1995). Such negative attitudes contributed to the terrible conditions that prevailed in institutions for people with mental retardation—conditions that were hidden from the public until 1965 when Burton Blatt published a horrific photographic essay, "Christmas in Purgatory."

mental retardation or **cognitive** or **intellectual disabilities** A disability characterized by impaired intellectual functioning, limited adaptive behavior, need for supports, and initial occurrence before age 18

The oldest U.S. organization in the history of special education dates from 1876. It was first called the Association of Medical Officers of American Institutions and is now named the American Association on Mental Retardation (AAMR). In 1919 the AAMR formed a committee to develop a classification system for mental retardation, and its first definition was published in 1921 (Bryant, Taylor, & Rivera, 1996). AAMR continues to refine the definition of mental retardation as new knowledge becomes available. Another important organization, The Arc (formerly the Association for Retarded Citizens), was founded in 1954 by parents. People First, the first self-advocacy group, an organization of people with mental retardation, formed in the 1970s. It helps people with mental retardation learn about and gain access to their rights as U.S. citizens.

Television news commentator Geraldo Rivera launched his career in the early 1970s when he exposed the terrible conditions that people with mental retardation endured at Willowbrook State School in New York.

During the 1960s and 1970s, researchers developed and refined new systems of instruction. Behavioral approaches that included token economies, positive reinforcement, direct instruction, and task analysis (breaking tasks down into small, teachable units) proved highly effective, and through them, students with mental retardation learned skills they had never mastered with instructional procedures used previously (Ayllon & Azrin, 1964, 1968; Birnbrauer et al., 1965). Jim Lent and his colleagues at the Mimosa Cottage Project demonstrated that children with mental retardation could learn many complex tasks and skills used in daily life and on the job (Lent & McLean, 1976). Procedures developed at this research center in Parsons, Kansas, have since come to be widely applied in special education programs.

Benjt Nirje in Sweden, also in the 1960s, inspired a new philosophy—a new movement—called normalization, which took hold worldwide (Nirje, 1969). **Normalization** is the concept that people with mental retardation should have available to them "patterns of life and conditions of everyday living which are as close as possible to the regular circumstances and ways of life of society" (Nirje, 1976). At about the same time, Bob Perske formulated the concept of **dignity of risk**, which is a practice based on the premise that people with mental retardation should experience life's challenges and adventures but not be overprotected (Perske, 1972). Wolf Wolfensberger used the principle of normalization to call for the closing of all U.S. institutions for people with mental retardation (Wolfensberger, 1972).

Television exposés, court actions, and eventually the rise of the advocacy movement subsequently led to widespread deinstitutionalization of people with mental retardation. But toward the beginning of the effort to improve living conditions for people with mental retardation, it took investigative reporting to shock the American public into insisting that the care and treatment of people with mental retardation at state residential schools and institutions be improved. In 1972, one such youthful and daring reporter, Heraldo Rivera, launched his career by using a stolen key to enter Willowbrook State School on Staten Island in New York. He showed the world the brutal and terrible conditions in which adults and children with mental retardation were forced to live at the time. The conditions were not isolated to Willowbrook; they were commonplace. Today, besides living with a family member, most people with mental retardation (some 400,000) live in the community with supports, and few live in large institutions, locked away, away from public scrutiny (Lakin, Braddock, & Smith, 2004a).

Challenges That Mental Retardation Presents

Across time, people with mental retardation have been referred to in different ways, including some that now seem cruel. When the first special class was begun in Providence, Rhode Island, in 1896, it was established for "defective children." Since the development of the intelligence (IQ) test, around the turn of the century, people have been grouped, classified, and served on the basis of the score they received on one of these tests. These groupings, or classifications, led to other terms. One

normalization Making available ordinary patterns of life and conditions of everyday living

dignity of risk The principle that taking ordinary risks is part of the human experience classification method, popular among educators in the 1960s and 1970s, distinguished educable mental retardation (EMR)—the category for those with IQ scores from 50 to 80—from trainable mental retardation (TMR)—the category for those with IQ scores between 25 and 50. These subgroups were linked solely to IQ scores. The use of EMR and TMR fell into disfavor, possibly because educators knew that all people can learn and that education and training should not be separated. Perhaps they also realized that suggesting that certain human beings were merely "trainable" sounded like comparing them to animals. Clearly the discrimination and bias associated with cognitive disabilities and the terms used for this disability are real and personally hurtful to the individuals involved. Labels, name calling, and stigma are frequently experienced by people with mental retardation, whether at school or in the community (Finlay & Lyons, 2005). Clearly, we can each make a real difference in the acceptance of all individuals by not condoning—let alone making—negative assumptions and statements. In one state, Minnesota, members of the legislature understand the importance of language and what individuals with disabilities are called. They have banned derogatory language and referents. *Disability in the News* tells how this state is taking action and making a difference in the lives of many people.

Making a Difference

Best Buddies

Across the United States, the dream of families and of their sons, daughters, brothers, and sisters with mental retardation is to be a part of everyday communities. Unfortunately, successful integration of individuals with intellectual disabilities in schools, workplaces, and mainstream society remains elusive for many. Sufficient opportunities for socialization and job coaching are not available for people with mental retardation to become independent and to be fully included in their communities. The necessary supports are not yet in place for an inclusive America to be a reality.

Probably because of his family's long history of advocacy and volunteerism on behalf of people with mental retardation, Anthony Shriver—nephew of John F. and Ted Kennedy, son of Eunice Shriver, and brother of Maria Shriver—saw a need to create opportunities for people to reach out to other people. Shriver also understood that students without disabilities, from middle school through college, needed a vehicle to create friendships and supports for others faced with cognitive challenges. As a response, in 1989 while at Georgetown University, he initiated the first chapter of **Best Buddies** and encouraged his college friends to work with him to expand the program.

Today, Best Buddies comprises six divisions that involve over 250,000 participants every year. All 50 states have active chapters, as do 15 countries worldwide. The middle school, high school, and college divisions match students with peers with intellectual disabilities to foster one-on-one friendships structured around social activities. Through the citizens' division, people from corporate and civic communities are paired with individuals with mental retardation so they can share time together; the jobs' division is a supported employment program. The newest program, e-Buddies® creates e-mail friendships.

To become a Best Buddies volunteer, to establish a campus chapter, or to learn more about any of the six divisions, go to **www.bestbuddies.org**

Anthony Shriver

Minnesota to Consider Changes in Terms Used for the Disabled

Associated Press
January 30, 2005

Minnesota legislators have proposed a bill to erase terms like "mental retardation," "handicapped" and "idiot" from state statutes.

Disabled people, who say they are sick of being called names like "retard" and worse, welcomed the proposal, which was announced Thursday.

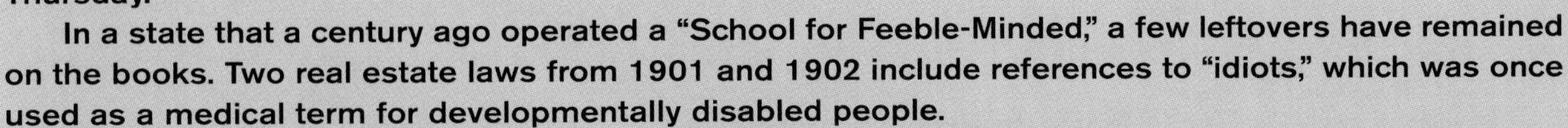

In a state that a century ago operated a "School for Feeble-Minded," a few leftovers have remained on the books. Two real estate laws from 1901 and 1902 include references to "idiots," which was once used as a medical term for developmentally disabled people.

"Words do hurt and they do have meaning," [State Senator Sheila M. Kiscaden] said. "When you start using that language differently, it changes your thinking about people."

Some disabled people and their advocates said that they supported the bill. Karen Loven, of Oakdale, who has developmental disabilities, said, "People have been calling me names no matter where you go. I have a disability. I'm not retarded. You can't even walk down the street without people calling you names."

Mental Retardation Defined

Two different definitions of mental retardation are used in the United States today. Most states follow IDEA '04, the federal definition (Müller & Markowitz, 2004). However, many professionals prefer the one adopted in 2002 by the American Association on Mental Retardation (AAMR) because it is more detailed and allows for a clearer understanding of the supports the individual needs at school, at home, and in the community. Both basic definitions are shown in Table 8.1. Accompanying the AAMR definition (the tenth definition this professional organization has developed and supported since 1921), and expanding on how it should be applied, are five assumptions:

1. Limitations in present functioning must be considered within the context of community environments typical of the individual's age peers and culture.
2. Valid assessment considers cultural and linguistic diversity as well as differences in communication and in sensory, motor, and behavioral factors.
3. Within an individual, limitations often coexist with strengths.
4. An important purpose of describing limitations is to develop a profile of needed supports.
5. With appropriate personalized supports over a sustained period, the life functioning of the person with mental retardation generally will improve. (Luckasson et al., 2002, p. 1)

Both the current AAMR definition and its predecessor, which was in effect between 1992 and 2002, have a positive orientation. Before then, definitions used a *deficit perspective* and described only the limitations of the individual. The more modern view conceptualizes mental retardation in terms of the levels of supports needed for the individual to function in the community as independently as possible (Polloway, 1997). Definitions following the deficit perspective used expressions

Best Buddies A program that pairs college students with people with mental retardation to build relationships, friendships, and opportunities for supports

Table 8.1 • Definitions of Mental Retardation

Source	Definition
Federal Government[1]	Mental retardation means significant subaverage general intellectual functioning, existing concurrently with deficits in adaptive behavior and manifested during the developmental period, that adversely affects a child's educational performance.
American Association of Mental Retardation[2]	Mental retardation is a disability characterized by significant limitations both in intellectual functioning and in adaptive behavior as expressed in conceptual, social, and practical adaptive skills. This disability originates before age 18.

Sources: [1]From 34 CFR Parts 300 and 303, Assistance to States for the Education of Children with Disabilities and the Early Intervention Program for Infants and Toddlers with Disabilities; Proposed Regulations (p. 311), U.S. Department of Education, 2005a, *Federal Register*, Washington, DC.

[2]From *Definition of mental retardation* (p. 1) by R. Luckasson, S. Borthwick-Duffy, W. H. E. Buntinx, D. L. Coulter, E. M. Craig, A. Reeve, R. L. Schalock, M. E. Snell, D. M. Spitalnik, S. Spreat, & M. J. Tassé, 2002, Washington, DC: American Association on Mental Retardation (AAMR). Reprinted with permission.

such as: "significantly subaverage general intellectual functioning," "deficits in adaptive behavior," and "deficits in intellectual functioning." The two recent AAMR definitions—the 1992 and the 2002 definitions—changed to a positive orientation that addresses the interplay among capabilities of individuals; the environments in which they live, learn, and work; and how well each person functions with various levels of support. The needs of people are planned for by thinking about the intensity of supports (intermittent, limited, extensive, or pervasive) that they need in specific areas to function. The 2002 AAMR definition includes a cautious use of IQ scores but stresses concepts of adaptive behavior and systems of supports.

The condition of mental retardation is described and defined by AAMR in terms of three major components:

1. Intellectual functioning
2. Adaptive behavior
3. Systems of supports

Across each of these components, mental retardation varies along a continuum. Most individuals with mental retardation have mild cognitive disabilities, have adequate adaptive behavior to live and work independently in the community, and usually require few supports. Typically, individuals with moderate to severe mental retardation require considerable supports. Let's examine each of these components in turn.

Intellectual Functioning

In its explanation of the 2002 AAMR definition, the organization stresses that individuals with mental retardation have intellectual functioning "significantly below average," or below levels attained by 97 percent of the general population. This level of functioning may be determined by clinical judgment or by a score on a test of intelligence. If a standardized test is used, the individual must score at least two standard deviations below the mean for the test. On IQ tests, intelligence is regarded as a trait that is distributed among people in a predictable manner. This statistical distribution can be represented as a bell-shaped curve, called the normal curve. In this curve the majority of a population falls in the middle of the bell, at or around an intelligence quotient (IQ) score of 100, and fewer and fewer people fall to either end of the distribution, having very low or very high intelligence. IQ level is then determined by the distance a score is from

Figure 8.1 • The Normal Curve, IQ, and Mental Retardation

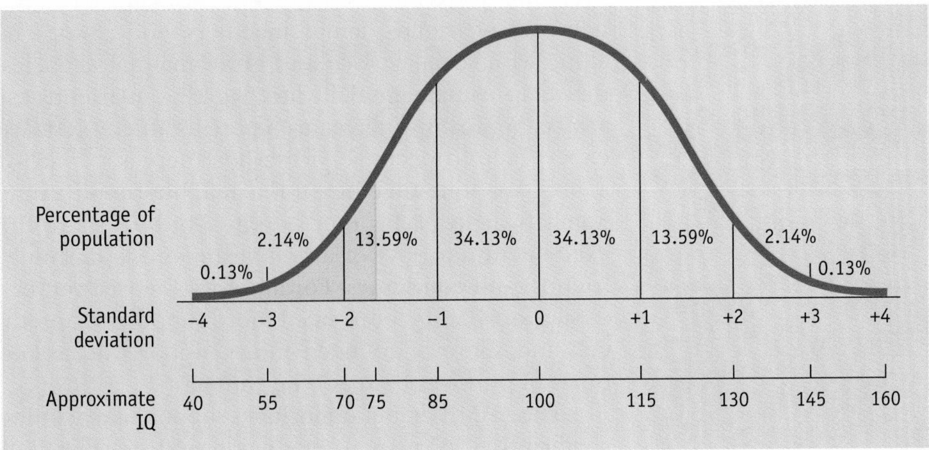

the mean, or average, score. You can visualize the theoretical construct of the normal distributions or bell-shaped curves by studying Figure 8.1. This figure shows how IQ scores are supposed to be distributed, as well as illustrating what is meant by two standard deviations below the mean or typical score.

The 2002 AAMR definition uses IQ scores to partially explain mental retardation by using a cutoff score of about 70 and below. This definition also codes intellectual abilities to express levels of severity in the following ways:

- Mild mental retardation: IQ range of 50 to 69
  Outcomes: Has learning difficulties, is able to work, can maintain good social relationships, contributes to society
- Moderate mental retardation: IQ range of 35 to 49
  Outcomes: Exhibits marked developmental delays during childhood, has some degree of independence in self-care, possesses adequate communication and academic skills, requires varying degrees of support to live and work in the community
- Severe mental retardation: IQ range of 20 to 34
  Outcomes: Has continuous need for supports
- Profound mental retardation: IQ under 20
  Outcomes: Demonstrates severe limitations in self-care, continence, communication, and mobility; requires continuous and intensive supports

Adaptive Behavior

"**Adaptive behavior** is the collection of conceptual, social, and practical skills that people have learned in order to function in their everyday lives" (AAMR, 2002, p. 73). Adaptive behavior is what everyone uses to function in daily life. People with mental retardation, as well as many people without disabilities, can have difficulty because they do not have the skill needed in specific situations or because they do not know what skill is needed in a particular situation. Or maybe they just do not want to perform the appropriate adaptive behavior when the situation calls for it. Regardless, lacking proficiency in the execution of a wide variety of adaptive skills can impair one's abilities to function independently. What, then, are these "conceptual, social, and practical skills?" Practical skills include such activities of daily life as eating, dressing, toileting, mobility, preparing meals, using the telephone, managing money, taking medication, and housekeeping. Take a look at Figure 8.2 for more examples of these three major areas of adaptive skills.

adaptive behavior
Performance of everyday life skills expected of adults

Figure 8.2 • Adaptive Skill Areas

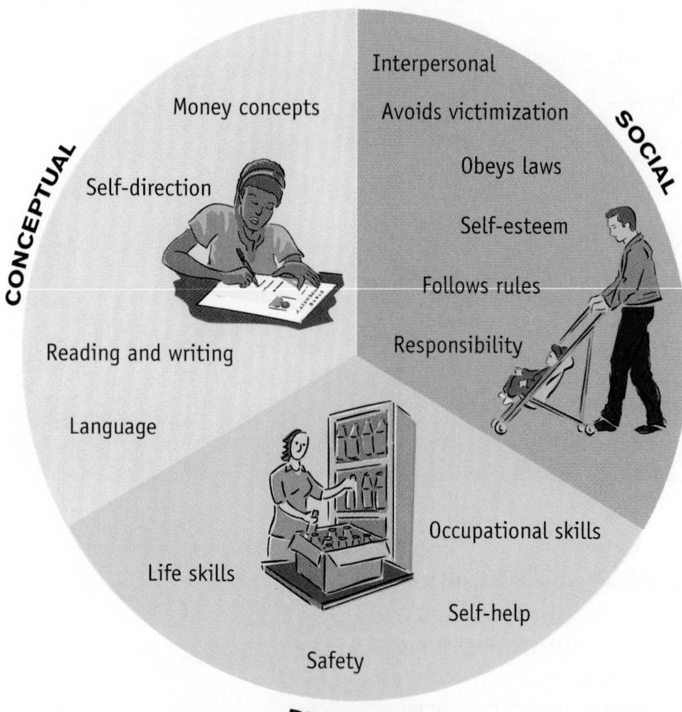

Systems of Supports

Everyone needs and uses **systems of supports**: the networks of friends, family members, and coworkers, along with social service and governmental agencies, that help us manage daily life. We ask our friends for advice. We form study teams before a difficult test. We expect help from city services when there is a crime or a fire. We join together for a neighborhood crime watch to help each other be safe. And we share the excitement and joys of accomplishments with family, friends, and colleagues. For all of us, life is a network of supports. Some of us need more supports than others, and some of us need more supports at certain times of our lives than at other times.

The AAMR definition includes support as a defining characteristic of mental retardation and specifies four levels of intensity across different types of support needed by people with mental retardation (Luckasson et al., 1992, 2002). Figure 8.3 is a diagram of the supports that people with mental retardation need. It shows areas where supports can be provided and how that support might be delivered. Supports can be offered at any one of four levels of intensity: intermittent, limited, extensive, pervasive. Some people with mental retardation require supports in every area; others might need supports for only one area; and the level of support can vary from one area to another. Finally, Figure 8.3 includes the outcomes (or goals) of this systems approach.

Characteristics

Although every person is an individual, and stereotypes can be unfair and inaccurate when applied to individual people, it is helpful to understand some characteristics that educators frequently encounter when working with students with mental retardation. The three defining characteristics of mental retardation are

1. Problems with cognition
2. Problems with adaptive behavior
3. Need for supports to sustain independence

Some specific conditions compound these main effects. For example, **fragile X syndrome** is the most common inherited type of mental retardation, and the severity of characteristics associated with the syndrome vary greatly. One reason may be that nearly half of the individuals affected also have autism (see Chapter 12 for more information about this disability) (Demark, Feldman, & Holden, 2003). Regardless of the severity of their retardation or coexisting conditions, most individuals with fragile X syndrome have difficulties in social communications, in understanding nonverbal behaviors, in using expressive language, and in being engaged in academic learning (Philofsky et al., 2004; Roberts et al., 2005; Sudhalter & Belser, 2001). They avoid eye contact, turn away from face-to-face contacts during conversations, and have stylized and ritualistic greetings. However, when teachers make specific efforts to involve youngsters with fragile X syndrome in ongoing academic activities, these students' engagement levels approximate those of their classmates. Many educators and

systems of supports Network of supports everyone develops to function optimally in life

fragile X syndrome The most common inherited reason for mental retardation

Figure 8.3 • Systems of Supports

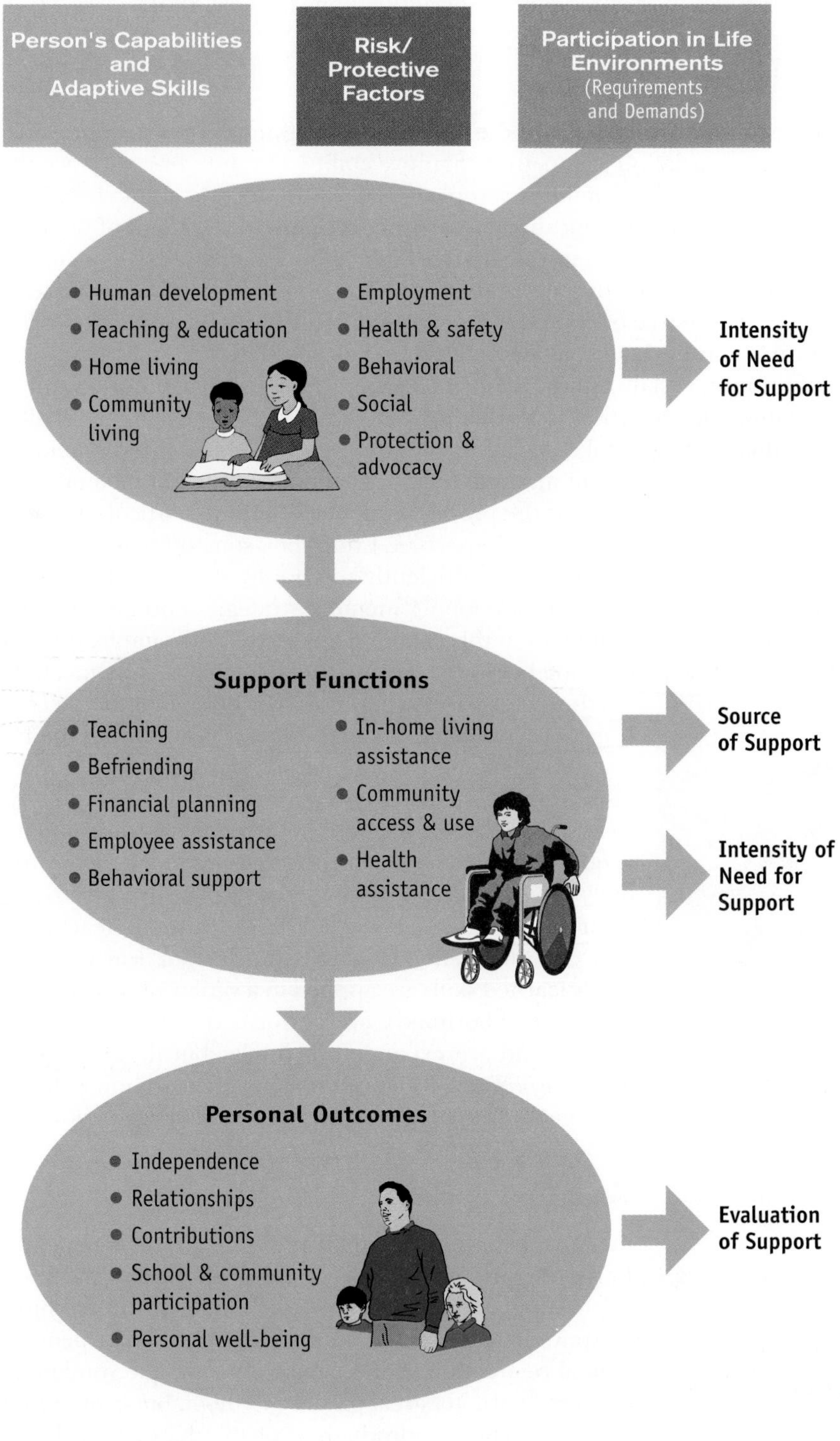

Person's Capabilities and Adaptive Skills

Risk/ Protective Factors

Participation in Life Environments (Requirements and Demands)

- Human development
- Teaching & education
- Home living
- Community living
- Employment
- Health & safety
- Behavioral
- Social
- Protection & advocacy

→ Intensity of Need for Support

Support Functions

- Teaching
- Befriending
- Financial planning
- Employee assistance
- Behavioral support
- In-home living assistance
- Community access & use
- Health assistance

→ Source of Support

→ Intensity of Need for Support

Personal Outcomes

- Independence
- Relationships
- Contributions
- School & community participation
- Personal well-being

→ Evaluation of Support

Source: From *Mental Retardation, Definition, Classification, and Systems of Support,* 10th Edition, by A.A.M.R. Copyright 2002 by American Association on Mental Retardation. Reprinted by permission of American Association on Mental Retardation via Copyright Clearance Center.

researchers have noted that individuals with mental retardation, regardless of the reason for the disability, have difficulty recognizing emotions, which might explain some of the challenges they experience in social situations (Moore, 2001).

Cognition

The most common, and perhaps the most acutely defining, characteristic of people with mental retardation is impaired cognitive ability. This trait has pervasive effects, whether the disability is mild or severe. It makes simple tasks difficult to learn. It can interfere with communicative competence, because the content of the message is harder to deliver and comprehend. It influences how well one can remember and how flexible one is in the application of knowledge and skills already learned. Ultimately, the degree of cognitive impairment determines the types of curriculum content these individuals are taught: academic or life skills.

Learning new skills, storing and retrieving information (memory), and transferring knowledge to either new situations or slightly different skills are challenges for individuals with mental retardation. Memory—especially short-term memory—is often impaired. The student may also have trouble with long-term memory, finding it hard to remember events or the proper sequence of events, particularly when the events are not clearly identified as important. Even when something is remembered, it may be remembered incorrectly, inefficiently, too slowly, or not in adequate detail. Teachers can assist students in developing memory strategies and help them compensate for their lack of abilities in this area in many ways. For example, the student can learn to create picture notebooks that lay out the sequence of steps in a task that needs to be performed, the elements of a job that need to be done, or a checklist of things to do before leaving the house.

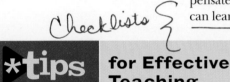

One characteristic of mental retardation is that individuals with this disability are frequently less able than their peers to acquire knowledge through incidental learning—that is, to acquire learning as an unplanned result of their ordinary daily experiences. For some, it seems that direct instruction is required for almost every task to be learned. Teachers must plan for the generalization (transfer) of learning so that newly learned skills are applied in a variety of settings (school, home, neighborhood), are performed with and for different people, and are expanded to similar but different contexts. *Tips for Effective Teaching* offers some ideas on how to help children generalize their learning of new skills and knowledge.

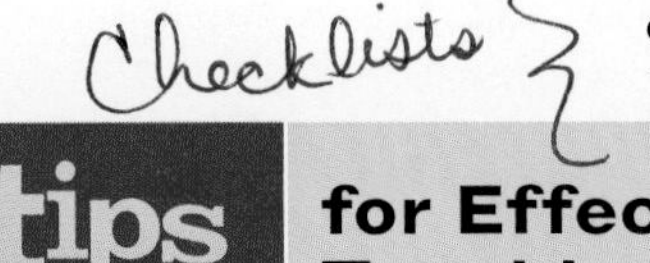

PROMOTING GENERALIZATION

Across Skills

1. Select learning objectives that are specific to the skill being taught.
2. Gain students' attention before beginning instruction.
3. Actively involve the students in the lesson.
4. Teach with real materials (rather than symbols or abstractions) or provide concrete examples.
5. Ensure that the first skill taught is mastered.
6. Point our similarities among different skills.
7. Provide many opportunities for practice.
8. Reward instances of generalization from one skill to another.

Across Settings

1. Be sure the skill is mastered in at least one setting.
2. Vary instructors.
3. Vary materials and examples.
4. Explain that the skill to be applied is the same and only the setting differs.
5. Vary settings, being sure to include environments where the skill is to be applied.
6. Provide plenty of opportunities for practice in different settings.

Adaptive Behavior

Adaptive behaviors are skills one uses to live independently. Review Figure 8.2 again, and think about each skill and its importance to independent functioning in the community. Adaptive behavior is not a problem area only for people with mental retardation. Think about some people you know who are very smart, get great grades in school, but cannot manage daily life. These individuals probably have difficulties with some adaptive skills. Now think about people you know who are highly successful on the job but have no social skills. Or think of those who have great personal hygiene and grooming skills but are unable to balance their personal budgets. All of these people have problems in at least one adaptive skill area. Adaptive skills are not behaviors that people, regardless of ability or disability, always master without instruction. Many IEP goals for adaptive behaviors stress independence. However, Craig Kennedy wisely cautions that this direction may be somewhat misguided: "Simply put, people with severe disabilities have to depend on other people" (2001, p. 123). He suggests that goals should be thought of in terms of interdependence, where at least two peers work together, providing each other with assistance and support.

Learning a life skill such as washing clothes in an actual laundry room can improve the likelihood that a student will master the skill and be able to use it in a number of real settings.

Need for Supports

Four sources of supports can be made available to people with mental retardation. They are

- Natural supports
- Nonpaid supports
- Generic supports
- Specialized supports

Supportive relationships exist among people in almost every setting and in almost every aspect of life. People help each other in simple and complex day-to-day tasks. **Natural supports** are the individual's own resources, family, friends, and neighbors. Natural supports can also come from coworkers on the job or peers at school (Chadsey & Beyer, 2001; Kennedy, 2001). **Nonpaid supports** are ordinary neighborhood and community supports. Examples of these kinds of supports include clubs, recreational leagues and groups, and private organizations. Everyone has access to **generic supports**, which are such services as public transportation and states' human services systems. **Specialized supports** are disability-specific, such as human services delivered to families of children with disabilities, special education, special early intervention services, and vocational rehabilitation services. The amount of support needed can vary for each individual and can change over time. Think of support as a fluid concept that is responsive by providing only as much assistance as needed, when it is necessary. Remember the *Making a Difference* section in this chapter. Best Buddies was designed to create more natural supports for individuals with mental retardation by connecting them with college students. With more and more of such programs available, supports needed for a greater community presence for more individuals with mental retardation will become a reality.

Prevalence

The cognitive abilities of students with mental retardation are below those of 97 percent of their peers (AAMR, 2002). Regardless, the prevalence of mental retardation is much less than 3 percent of the student population. According to the federal government, slightly more than 1 percent (that is, 1 out of every 100) of our nation's schoolchildren between the ages of 6 and 17 are identified and served as having mental retardation as their primary handicapping condition (U.S. Department of Education, 2005b). During the 1999–2000 school year, some 546,429 children with mental retardation were served across the country. Most students with mental retardation function at high levels and need few supports. In other words, most fall into the mild range.

Why is the prevalence for this special education category much lower than the 3 percent suggested by using the statistical calculation of two standard deviations from the mean of an IQ test? One reason is that school districts prefer to use other special education categories for students who meet the criteria for mental retardation (MacMillan, Gresham, & Bocian, 1998). Another reason is concern about representation of diverse students in special education and in this category. In particular, African American students are overrepresented and Hispanics underrepresented

natural supports Supports that occur as a natural result of family and community living

nonpaid supports Ordinary assistance given by friends and neighbors

generic supports Public benefits to which everyone has access

specialized supports Disability-specific benefits to help people with disabilities participate in the community in the mental retardation category. Although Black students represent 14.5 percent of the student population, they represent 34.2 percent of students with mental retardation (U.S. Department of Education, 2001). Could this placement rate reflect a relationship between poverty and disabilities? Possibly so. But why, then, are Hispanics not overrepresented as well? Although Latinos/Latinas represent 16.2 percent of the general student population, they represent only 9.1 percent of those served through the mental retardation category.

Causes and Prevention

Mental retardation is caused by many factors; many of these are known, but others remain unidentified (The Arc, 2005). The link between the identification of specific causes of mental retardation and the development and implementation of preventive measures is clear. When a cause is identified, ways to prevent the debilitating effects of cognitive disabilities have often followed soon after. But it takes action for solutions actually to prevent or reduce the impact of the condition.

Causes

According to The Arc, a parent organization advocating for individuals with mental retardation, several hundred causes of mental retardation have been discovered, but for about one-third of those affected the cause is unknown (The Arc, 2005). Of those known causes, three conditions—explained later in this section—are the most common reasons for mental retardation:

1. Down syndrome
2. Fragile X syndrome
3. Fetal alcohol syndrome

Many different systems for organizing the causes of mental retardation can be applied. Sometimes they are divided into four groups: socioeconomic and environmental factors, injuries, infections and toxins, and biological causes. AAMR divides them instead into three groups by time of onset—that is, by when the event or cause first occurred (AAMR, 2002):

1. *Prenatal:* causes that occur before birth
2. *Perinatal:* causes that occur during the birth process
3. *Postnatal:* causes that happen after birth or during childhood

Prenatal causes exert their effects before birth. Examples include genetics and heredity, toxins taken by the pregnant mother, disease, and neural tube defects. Genetics and heredity include conditions such as fragile X syndrome and Down syndrome, as well as phenylketonuria (PKU). Prenatal toxins include alcohol, tobacco, and drug exposure resulting from the behavior of the mother during pregnancy. Diseases and infection, such as HIV/AIDS, can devastate an unborn baby. Neural tube disorders, such as anencephaly (where most of the child's brain is missing at birth) and spina bifida (incomplete closure of the spinal column), are also prenatal causes of mental retardation.

Perinatal causes occur during the birthing process. They include birth injuries due to oxygen deprivation (anoxia or asphyxia), umbilical cord accidents, obstetrical trauma, and head trauma. They also include low birth weight.

Postnatal causes occur after birth. The environment is a major factor in many of these situations. Child abuse and neglect, environmental toxins, and accidents

prenatal Before birth

perinatal During birth

postnatal After birth

are examples of postnatal causes. An additional reason for being identified as having mental retardation is societal biases, particularly toward diverse students.

Now let's turn our attention to some major causes of mental retardation across the three periods of onset. In particular, let's think about some genetic causes, both prenatal and postnatal toxins, low birth weight, and child abuse. Finally, we will briefly return to the situation of Black youngsters and their risk for being identified as having mental retardation.

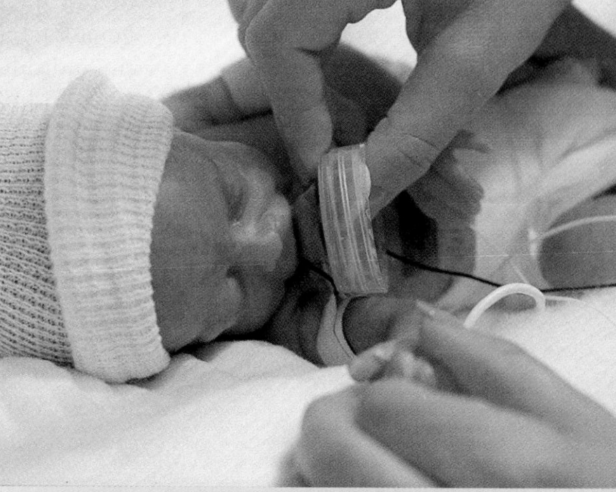

Advances in medical technology can save the lives of infants who previously might not have survived. They can prevent or lessen the impact of disabilities. Medical advances, however, can also result in disabilities.

Genetic Causes

Today, more than 500 genetic causes associated with mental retardation, many of them rare biological conditions, have been identified (The Arc, 2001). For example, fragile X syndrome is an inherited disability caused by a mutation on the X chromosome, and it was identified in 1991. It is now recognized as the most commonly known inherited cause of mental retardation, affecting about 1 in 4,000 males and 1 in 8,000 females (Crawford, Acuna, & Sherman, 2001). A common associated condition is recurrent otitis media (middle ear infection) with resulting hearing and language problems. Cognitive disabilities can be severe. Many of these individuals are challenged by limited attention span, hyperactivity, stereotypic behaviors (such as hand flapping or hand biting), and an inability to relate to others in typical ways. It is believed that almost half of individuals with fragile X syndrome have coexisting autism (Abbeduto et al., 2004; Demark, Feldman, & Holden, 2003). Many of these individuals also have repetitive speech patterns (Belser & Sudhalter, 2001).

Another example of a genetic cause for mental retardation due to a chromosomal abnormality is **Down syndrome** (a chromosomal disorder wherein the individual has too few or too many chromosomes). The nucleus of each human cell normally contains 23 pairs of chromosomes (a total of 46). In the most common type of Down syndrome, trisomy 21, the 21st set of chromosomes contains three chromosomes rather than the normal pair. Certain identifiable physical characteristics, such as an extra flap of skin over the innermost corner of the eye (an epicanthic fold), are usually present in cases of Down syndrome. The degree of mental retardation varies, depending in part on how soon the disability is identified, the adequacy of the supporting medical care, and the timing of the early intervention. The great majority of people with Down syndrome have a high incidence of medical problems (National Down Syndrome Society [NDSS], 2005). For example, about half have congenital heart problems, and these individuals have a 15 to 20 times greater risk of developing leukemia. Although people with Down syndrome have intellectual disabilities, they have fewer adaptive behavior challenges than many of their peers with mental retardation (Chapman & Hesketh, 2000). These individuals do, however, have a higher prevalence of obesity, despite typically consuming fewer calories (Roizen, 2001). Possibly their reduced food consumption explains why individuals with Down syndrome are less active and less likely to spend time outdoors than their brothers and sisters. Teachers should help increase these students' opportunities for recreation and social outlets by creating exciting reasons to exercise and play with friends.

Some genetic causes of disabilities are not so definite but rather result from interplay between genes and the environment. **Phenylketonuria (PKU)**, also hereditary, occurs when a person is unable to metabolize phenylalanine, which builds up in the body to toxic levels that damage the brain. If untreated, PKU eventually causes mental retardation. Changes in diet (eliminating certain foods that contain this amino acid, such as milk) can control PKU and prevent mental retardation, although cognitive disabilities can be seen in both treated and untreated individuals with this condition. Because of the devastating effects of PKU, it is critical that the

Down syndrome
Chromosomal disorder with identifiable physical characteristics, resulting in delays in physical and intellectual development

phenylketonuria (PKU)
Inherited condition that results in mental retardation from a build-up of toxins from foods (such as milk) containing amino acids

diet of these individuals be strictly controlled. Here, then, is a condition rooted in genetics, but it is an environmental factor (a protein in milk) that becomes toxic to the individuals affected and causes the mental retardation. And both prompt diagnosis and parental vigilance are crucial to minimizing retardation. Now let's look at some toxins that do not have a hereditary link.

Toxins

Poisons that lurk in the environment, **toxins**, are both prenatal and postnatal causes of mental retardation, as well as of other disabilities. Many believe that the increased rates of attention deficit hyperactivity disorder, learning disabilities, and even autism are due to some interplay of genetics, environmental factors, and social factors (Office of Special Education Programs, 2000; Schettler et al., 2000). Clearly, exposures to toxins harm children and are a real source of disabilities. Here are two reasons why toxins deserve special attention:

1. Toxic exposures are preventable.
2. Toxins abound in our environment.

Let's think about how toxins can harm children. Mothers who drink, smoke, or take drugs place their unborn children at serious risk for premature birth, low birth weight, and mental retardation (The Arc, 2001). One well-recognized cause of birth defects is **fetal alcohol syndrome (FAS)**, which is strongly linked to mental retardation and results from the mother's drinking alcohol during pregnancy. FAS is recognized by Congress as the most common known cause of mental retardation. It costs the U.S. taxpayers 5.4 billion dollars in 2003 alone, and the costs in quality of life to the individuals affected and their families are immeasurable (U.S. Senate Appropriations Committee, 2004). The average IQ of people with FAS is 79, very close to the cutoff score for mental retardation (Bauer, 1999). This means that almost half of those with FAS qualify for special education because of cognitive disabilities. This group's average adaptive behavior score is 61, indicating a strong need for supports. These data explain why some 58 percent of individuals with FAS have mental retardation and why some 94 percent require supplemental assistance at school. Unfortunately, most of these people are not free of other problems in the areas of attention, verbal learning, and self-control (Centers for Disease Control [CDC], 2004a). Estimates are that some 5,000 babies with FAS are born each year. An additional 50,000 show fewer symptoms and have what is considered the less serious condition **fetal alcohol effects (FAE)**, which, like FAS, is caused by mothers drinking alcohol during pregnancy (Davis & Davis, 2003).

Toxins abound in our environment. All kinds of hazardous wastes are hidden in neighborhoods and communities. One toxin that causes mental retardation is lead. Two major sources of lead poisoning can be pinpointed. One is exhaust fumes from leaded gasoline, which is no longer sold in the United States. The other source is lead-based paint, which is no longer manufactured. Unfortunately, however, it remains on the walls of older apartments and houses. Children can get lead poisoning from a paint source by breathing lead directly from the air or by eating paint chips. For example, if children touch paint chips or household dust that contains lead particles and then put their fingers in their mouths or touch their food with their hands, they ingest the lead. And lead is not the only source of environmental toxins that government officials should be worried about; other concerns include mercury found in fish, pesticides, and industrial pollution from chemical waste (Schettler et al., 2000).

toxins Poisonous substances that can cause immediate or long-term harm

fetal alcohol syndrome (FAS) and **fetal alcohol effects (FAE)** Congenital conditions caused by the mother's drinking alcohol during pregnancy and resulting in reduced intellectual functioning, behavior problems, and sometimes physical differences

Low Birth Weight

Low birth weight is a major risk factor for disabilities and is definitely associated with poverty and with little or no access to prenatal care (Children's Defense Fund [CDF], 2004). Medical advances of the 1980s have greatly increased the likelihood that infants born weighing less than 2 pounds will survive. These premature, very small infants make up less than 1.4 percent of all newborns and are at great risk for disabilities, including mental retardation (Allen, 2002). However, babies born between 3 and 5 pounds also are at greater risk for disabilities than many doctors and parents believe. Babies with moderately low birth weight represent 5 to 7 percent of all births, but they represent 18 to 37 percent of children with cerebral palsy and 7 to 12 percent of children with cerebral palsy who also have mental retardation. Whereas about 5 percent of White babies have moderately low birth weight, between 10 and 12 percent of African American babies are born early and have low birth weight.

Although politically incorrect, Jimmy, a character with mental retardation from Southpark, is included in this cartoon series.

Child Abuse and Neglect

Abused children have lower IQs and reduced response rates to cognitive stimuli (CDF, 2001, 2004). In one of the few studies of its kind, Canadian researchers compared abused children with those not abused, and the results of abuse became clear (Youth Record, 1995). The verbal IQ scores were very different between the two groups of otherwise matched peers: The abused children had an average total IQ score of 88, whereas the average overall IQ of their nonabused peers was 101; and the more abuse, the lower the IQ score. The link between child abuse and impaired intellectual functioning is now definite, but the reasons for the damage are not known. Rather than resulting from brain damage, the disruption in language development caused by the abusive situation may be the source of permanent and profound effects on language ability and cognition. Or the abuse may itself be a result of the frustration often associated with raising children with disabilities. Remember, the connection between neglect and mental retardation has long been recognized and is part of the early history and documentation of this field.

Discrimination and Bias

It is important to remember that many subjective reasons account for students' placement in special education. There is little doubt that poverty and its risk factors are clearly linked to disabilities (CDF, 2004; National Research Council, 2002). It is also true that culturally and linguistically diverse children are overrepresented in some categories of special education (Hosp & Reschly, 2002, 2003; U.S. Department of Education, 2005a). This situation is particularly true for Black students, who are almost three times more likely to be identified as having mental retardation than their White peers (National Alliance of Black School Educators & ILIAD Project, 2002). Specifically, a definite relationship exists between poverty and three other factors: ethnicity, gender, and mental retardation (Oswald et al., 2001). However, this relationship may be somewhat different from what one might initially suspect: The risk factors of poverty (limited access to health care, poor living conditions) do not entirely explain this disproportionate representation (Ford et al., 2002; Neal et al., 2003). Rather, "the increased rate of identification among students of color may be attributable to systemic bias" (Oswald et al., 2001, p. 361). Black students who live in a predominantly White neighborhood are more likely to be identified as having mental retardation than those who live in a neighborhood with more diversity. One conclusion is that students are more vulnerable to discrimination when they represent a minority. Many strategies can be undertaken to reduce mistakes in the identification process, including pre-referral intervention, appropriate and meaningful curricula, and instruction anchored in culturally relevant examples.

Prevention

Many cases of mental retardation can be prevented by directly addressing the cause. According to The Arc, because of advances in research over the last 30 years, many cases of mental retardation are prevented (The Arc, 2005). For example, each year 9,000 cases of mental retardation are prevented via the measles and Hib vaccines,

1,250 cases via newborn screening for phenylketonuria (PKU) and congential hypothyroidism, and 1,000 cases via the anti-RH immune globulin. Even more cases are preventable. Most of these strategies (see Table 8.2) are simple and obvious, but the effects can be significant. For example, in the case of child abuse, teachers now have a legal (and, many believe, a moral) responsibility to report suspected cases so that further damage to the child might be avoided.

Education and access are at the heart of many prevention measures. For example, education about the prevention of HIV/AIDS can be effective with all adolescents, including those with mental retardation (Johnson, Johnson, & Jefferson-Aker, 2001). Public education programs can also help pregnant women understand the importance of staying healthy. Other prevention strategies involve testing the expectant mother, analyzing the risk factors of the family (genetic history of disabilities or various conditions), and taking action when necessary; screening infants; protecting children from disease through vaccinations; creating positive, nurturing, and rich home and school environments; and implementing safety measures. Note that not all of these strategies are biological or medical. It is important to look at *all* aspects of the child and the environment.

The importance of immunization programs to protect children and their mothers from disease cannot be overemphasized (The Arc, 2005; CDF, 2004). The incidence of disabilities, including mental retardation, has been greatly reduced by immunization against viruses such as rubella, meningitis, and measles. However, immunization is still not provided universally. Despite more federal and state programs to assist families in protecting their children, only some 78 percent of two-year-olds had received all recommended immunizations in 2002. Why is this so? Some families do not have access to immunizations because a health care facility is unavailable or is too far from home, or because the immunizations are too expensive. Some families ignore or are uninformed about the risks of skipping vaccinations, and other families avoid immunizations for religious reasons or believe that

Table 8.2 • Prevention of Mental Retardation

For Pregnant Women	For Children	For Society
Obtain early prenatal medical care.	Guarantee universal infant screening.	Eliminate the risks of child poverty.
Seek genetic counseling.	Ensure proper nutrition.	Make early intervention programs universally available.
Maintain good health.	Place household chemicals out of reach.	Provide parent education and support.
Avoid alcohol, drugs, and tobacco.	Use automobile seatbelts, safety seats, and cycle helmets.	Protect children from abuse and neglect.
Obtain good nutrition.	Provide immunizations.	Remove environmental toxins.
Prevent premature births.	Prevent or treat infections.	Provide family planning services.
Take precautions against injuries and accidents.	Have quick and easy access to health care.	Provide public education about prevention techniques.
Prevent or immediately treat infections.	Prevent lead poisoning.	Have universal access to health care.
Avoid sexually transmitted diseases.	Guarantee proper medical care for all children.	Vaccinate all children.
	Provide early intervention programs.	
	Eliminate child abuse and neglect.	

Maria Shriver, author of *What's Wrong with Timmy,* brother of Anthony Kennedy Shriver who founded Best Buddies, and niece of John F. Kennedy, follows in her family's footsteps by showing us all how we can through our actions make a difference in the lives of people with disabilities.

the risk of getting the disease from the vaccination itself is greater than the risk of being unprotected. As a result, easily preventable cases of mental retardation due to infection still occur.

People must not underestimate the importance of prenatal care. For example, FAS and FAE are 100 percent preventable (CDC, 2004b; Davis & Davis, 2003). Pregnant mothers who do not drink alcohol prevent this condition in their children! Staying healthy also means taking proper vitamins and eating well, and there are good examples of why this is essential. For example, folic acid reduces the incidence of neural tube defects. By eating citrus fruits and dark, leafy vegetables (or taking vitamin supplements), one receives the benefits of folic acid—a trace B vitamin that contributes to the prevention of conditions such as spina bifida and anencephaly. Here's proof that such prevention measures make a difference: In 1992 the U.S. Public Health Service recommended that all women thinking about becoming pregnant take folic acid daily, either through diet or supplements, and mandated that cereal be fortified with folic acid. Since then, the prevalence of spina bifida has dropped by 31 percent and that of anencephaly by 16 percent (CDC, 2004b). Think of the difference yet to be made if all potential moms ate well and planned ahead!

We also noted that prematurity (being born before 37 weeks of pregnancy) and low birth weight are risk factors for mental retardation and other disabilities. Unfortunately, relatively little is known about how to prevent many of these cases (Alexander & Slay, 2002). It is known that it is important for as many unborn babies as possible to reach full-term and that good prenatal care is an important part of making that happen.

Couples can take certain actions before the woman becomes pregnant to reduce the risk of biologically caused mental retardation. For example, gene therapy may become universally available to families who know they are at risk for having offspring with PKU (Eisensmith, Kuzmin, & Krougliak, 1999). Some couples have medical tests before deciding to conceive a child. These tests, combined with genetic counseling, help couples determine whether future children are at risk for certain causes of mental retardation. In one study, the majority of women who received genetic counseling either because of their age or because of an abnormal blood test indicated that they would avoid or terminate the pregnancy if a test was positive for a disability (Roberts, Stough, & Parrish, 2002). Tay-Sachs disease, for example, is a cause of mental retardation that can be predicted through genetic testing. Other couples take tests for defects after they find out that the woman is pregnant. These tests can determine, in utero, the presence of approximately 270 defects. It is possible that prenatal gene therapy, now in experimental phases, will one day correct such abnormalities before babies are born (Ye et al., 2001).

Overcoming Challenges

Although some conditions or causes of mental retardation cannot be prevented, at least at the present time, the impact of the condition can be reduced substantially. For example, we saw in this chapter that PKU is a genetic reason for mental retardation but that it takes factors in the individual's environment for damage to be devastating. Infant screening can detect the problem. Here's how it works: In a procedure developed by Robert Guthrie in 1957, a few drops of the newborn's blood are taken from the heel to determine whether the infant has the inherited genetic disorder that prevents metabolizing phenylalanine, a naturally occurring amino acid found in milk. This test, which costs 3 cents, makes it possible to change any affected baby's diet before the disastrous effects of PKU can begin to mount. Guthrie developed the test because his son and his niece had PKU, and he wanted to prevent the condition from affecting others. In the past, PKU was responsible for 1 percent of all severe cases of mental retardation, nearly all of which are now identified and the severity of the problem substantially reduced (Schettler et al., 2000).

Assessment

Students with mental retardation are identified by assessing their intellectual functioning and their adaptive skills. Once an individual is identified as having mental retardation, an assessment of that individual's need for supports is conducted to determine the interventions and the intensity of services required.

The use of standardized tests of intelligence has been criticized for years in the courts, among professionals, and by parents. Tests of intelligence alone do not reliably predict an individual's abilities, they discriminate against culturally and linguistically diverse students, and they do not lead to educationally useable results (Artiles et al., 2002; National Research Council, 2002). As you have learned, the use of IQ tests with culturally and linguistically diverse students has led to lawsuits, which motivated the state of California to ban their use when diverse students are being identified for mental retardation. Despite the problems they are subject to, IQ tests continue to be used, probably because they are relatively simple to administer and provide a definitive answer—a score for people to use (AAMR, 2002). New ways of determining students' eligibility for special education are being implemented (National Research Council, 2002). For example, Iowa permits the use of curriculum based measurements (CBM) and other direct measures of student performance (portfolios) to identify students eligible for special education. But for now, IQ tests remain a common means of assessing intellectual functioning.

Although "mental age" is an outdated and ambiguous concept, it is still used by some professionals to describe the intellectual functioning of an individual. Mental age (MA) is used to describe the developmental level—or level of acquired ability or knowledge—compared with the age of the individual. Mental age is calculated as the chronological age (CA) of children *without* mental retardation whose average IQ test performance is equivalent to that of the individual *with* intellectual disabilities. For example, a man of 35 who has an IQ of 57 might be said to have a mental age of 9 years, 5 months. Such a comparison is imprecise and inaccurate, because adults have the physical attributes, interests, and experiences of their adult peers without disabilities. Describing them in terms of mental age ignores or underestimates these characteristics. At the same time, the mental age comparison can overestimate certain intellectual skills, such as the use of logic and foresight in solving problems.

Early Identification

Assessing young students' abilities in natural settings leads to meaningful plans for instruction.

Many students with mental retardation, particularly those with moderate to severe cognitive disabilities, come to school already identified as having disabilities. Such individuals tend to face challenges during their school years and in their adult lives (Keogh, Bernheimer, & Guthrie, 2004). For those with biological reasons for their mental retardation, families and doctors recognize the problem early in life, sometimes during infancy or while they are toddlers. Children identified with disabilities early in life receive special early intervention programs specified in their IFSPs (see Chapter 2 for a review). Other children with cognitive disabilities are identified during the preschool years because they are not developing speech, language, or motor skills at the same rate as their classmates without disabilities. In such cases, it is often the alert preschool teacher who initiates the referral process by working with professionals in the local Child Find Office.

Pre-Referral

Individuals who are not identified with cognitive disabilities until their school years typically have mild mental retardation. Their challenges with adaptive behavior and learning the academic skills taught in kindergarten, first grade, and second grade signal their disability. Typically, their learning patterns indicate an overall delay, making it impossible for them to stay on a par with their classmates without disabilities across *all* skill areas. Thus, whereas a student with learning disabilities may have challenges with only one academic skill area, such as reading, the student with mental retardation has problems keeping up in every area. African American and Native American students are the most at risk of being misidentified as having mental retardation (see Chapter 3 for a review). These two groups of students are overrepresented in special education and too often identified as having mental retardation (U.S. Department of Education, 2005b). Remember that Black students, who make up some 14 percent of all schoolchildren, represent 34 percent of students identified as having mental retardation. The national percentages for Native American students are too low for their overrepresentation to be obvious, but their situation is similar to that of their Black peers. One state's data tell the story. In Alaska, Native students account for 21 percent of the school population, but 38 percent of students in that state who are served in the mental retardation category are Alaska Natives.

The pre-referral step in the school identification process for special education can be particularly important to diverse students for two reasons. First, it is important to get special services to those who need them. Second, it is equally important not to make a mistake and place students in the mental retardation category if they do *not* have cognitive disabilities. Thus teachers need all the information they can gather about students' classroom performance, must use scientifically validated instructional practices for every skill area of concern, and must monitor students' performance to determine under what conditions they learn the best. The team conducting the evaluation for the purpose of identification will then have the information they need to determine which diagnostic tests they should employ for the next step in the IEP process (again, see Chapter 2 for a review).

Identification

Assessment of individuals' adaptive behavior remains a hallmark of the identification of mental retardation. Since 1959, professionals have agreed that IQ scores alone are not enough to qualify individuals for services, to predict their outcomes, or to assist in the development of appropriate educational programs (Kennedy, 2001). Adaptive behavior must also be considered (look again at Figure 8.2). Measures of adaptive skill areas are used to determine whether the individual actually performs the everyday skills expected of an individual of that age in a typical environment.

Assessment of adaptive skills is typically done through interviews and observation. Because parents and teachers are the source of information and may be biased in their assessments, some practitioners express concern about the accuracy of these evaluation methods. The tendency to overestimate an individual's skills or to assess them inaccurately against a nonspecified age-relevant standard is great. Nevertheless, researchers are becoming more confident about using adaptive skill assessments (Hatton et al., 2003). They believe that indicators of adaptive skills provide a more accurate picture of individuals' strengths and needs for support than scores on tests of intelligence. Today, more standardized assessment instruments are available to help assess adaptive behavior. For example, *Assessment of Adaptive Areas (AAA)* is a test that enables the examiner to convert scores to age equivalents across adaptive skill areas. This highly useful instrument brings more objectivity to the determination of individuals' abilities, helps professionals determine what supports are needed, and allows for better communication with families about these important areas. The *Supports Intensity Scale (SIS),* developed by AAMR in 2005, measures the intensities of supports that each person needs to participate fully in community life. The test helps make these determinations through at least two interviews, which could include the person with the disability, a parent or sibling, or a staff member who has worked with the individual.

Evaluation: Alternate Assessments

Over 40 percent of students with mental retardation receive a substantial part of their education in the general education classroom accessing the general education curriculum (U.S. Department of Education, 2005b). Most of these students participate in state- and district-wide assessments with accommodations or modifications. However, many of their peers with mental retardation are monitored for yearly progress through other means. IDEA '04 and the No Child Left Behind Act (NCLB) allow states to employ a different system to assess the progress of a small percentage of students who cannot participate in the required annual state- and district-wide assessments (U.S. Department of Education, 2005a). When NCLB was originally passed, it allowed 1 percent of all students to receive their annual evaluation of progress through **alternate assessments**—evaluations of yearly progress made for those students whose IEP goals do not reflect the general education curriculum (Briggs, 2005). Many students whose progress is measured through alternate means (e.g., portfolios) have restricted access to the general education curriculum. These students are not working toward a regular high school diploma, are participating in a functional or life skills curriculum, and have IEPs that clearly identify both the alternate curriculum and the alternate assessment. For these students, most of whom have severe cognitive disabilities, the real life skills that they are being taught are used as part of the measure of their achievement (Browder et al., 2003). In other words, alternate assessments are used to evaluate students' achievement of authentic skills in real-life environments as well as their learning of content (e.g., reading and math) that reflects the general education curriculum (Briggs, 2005; Browder et al., 2004). In 2005, the Secretary of Education increased the number of students whose progress could be documented through alternate assessments. Now individual states can be granted permission to test an additional 2 percent of all their students through alternative means.

alternate assessments Individualized means of measuring the progress of students who do not participate in the general education curriculum

Different systems are used to document progress (Browder et al., 2003; National Center for Educational Outcomes, 2005). Many states use portfolios, anecdotal notes, work samples, and video tapes to illustrate the progress students are making toward achieving their IEP goals, such as using public transportation independently or getting to work on time. Some states use checklists of performance tasks along with selected grade-level content standards or benchmarks. Still others use direct measurements or data collected on specific instructional targets, such as sight word vocabulary or consumer mathematics. Because many students with mental retardation are learning to read and calculate, their assessments may include standardized tests that measure gains in these academic areas (Tindal et al., 2003).

Early Intervention

Early identification and intervention are important to children with mental retardation and their families. Early intervention can limit the severity of mental retardation or even prevent it (Guralnick, 1998; U.S. Department of Education, 2001). Preschool experiences provide the foundation for the development of important skills later in school and in life, and they occur at a time when the family is beginning its long involvement in the education of their child with a disability.

The power of early intervention is remarkable, and early childhood education programs are essential for young children with disabilities and young children who are at risk for developmental delay or school failure. The data prove this point indisputably. A well-controlled and randomized study followed up two groups of low-income African American three- and four-year olds at age 40 (Schweinhart, 2005). One group attended preschool and the other did not. Those who received preschool experiences outperformed those who did not on all measures: IQ scores, high school graduation, income, home and car ownership, and citizenship. The study also showed that return to taxpayers was great: Every tax dollar spent on the preschool experience provided an economic return of $17 from education savings, taxes on earnings, welfare savings, and savings of some of the costs that crime inflicts on society. And of course, these calculations do not fully reflect the human benefits. The longitudinal effects of high-quality preschool experiences show how early intervention makes real differences in the lives of people—*all* people.

It is quite probable that inclusive education is more of a reality at preschools across the nation than at elementary, middle, and high schools. The preschool curriculum lends itself to inclusive practices, and worries about achieving high scores on state and district achievement tests are not a concern with this age group. Findings from the long-standing program at the University of North Carolina-Chapel Hill clearly show benefits from high-quality inclusive preschools (Manuel & Little, 2002):

1. Children with and those without disabilities play together.
2. Children with disabilities show higher rates of social interactions.
3. Typically developing children have no negative consequences.
4. Typically developing children show a greater appreciation and respect for individual differences.

Jessie *Elizabeth*
Down syndrome Originals © dolls like *Jessie* and *Elizabeth* that are made by Downi Creations provide children with lovely toys with which they can identify. Such dolls can lessen the stigma of this disability on the children and their families.

However, not all preschool programs achieve equally. What are some of the features of effective preschool settings? Here is a list of some of their key features:

- Full day program
- Accredited standing

- Well-prepared teachers
- About a third of the student population has disabilities
- Positive interactions with children
- Family partnerships
- Multidisciplinary team approach (including SLPs, special educators, PTs, behavior analysts)
- Fun

Policymakers, parents, and educators recognize the importance of comprehensive and sustained services for these children while they are toddlers and preschoolers. They also understand that students participating in early intervention programs are very diverse in their types of disabilities and in the severity of their disabilities. These factors influence students' short- and long-term results.

Teaching Students with Mental Retardation

Most students with mental retardation have mild disabilities. Increasingly, these students are included in general education classes. Their learning goals are often similar or identical to those of their peers without disabilities. Of course, in these situations teachers have to adapt their techniques and adjust the curriculum somewhat to accommodate these students' special learning needs. Some teachers modify worksheets, provide more detailed instructions about how assignments are to be completed, include students in setting goals, and have students participate in the evaluation of their own work (Copeland et al., 2002).

Many students with intellectual disabilities, however, have very complex learning needs. They might require intensive, specialized instruction from a variety of professionals in settings away from the traditional school building—for example, learning how to ride a bus by using public transportation. Merely making accommodations to the general education curriculum is not sufficient. Many students with mental retardation require a different curriculum that includes daily living skills, so that their long-term goal of independent living can be met (Johnson, 2005). Others need more direct and concrete instruction. Let's examine some of these issues.

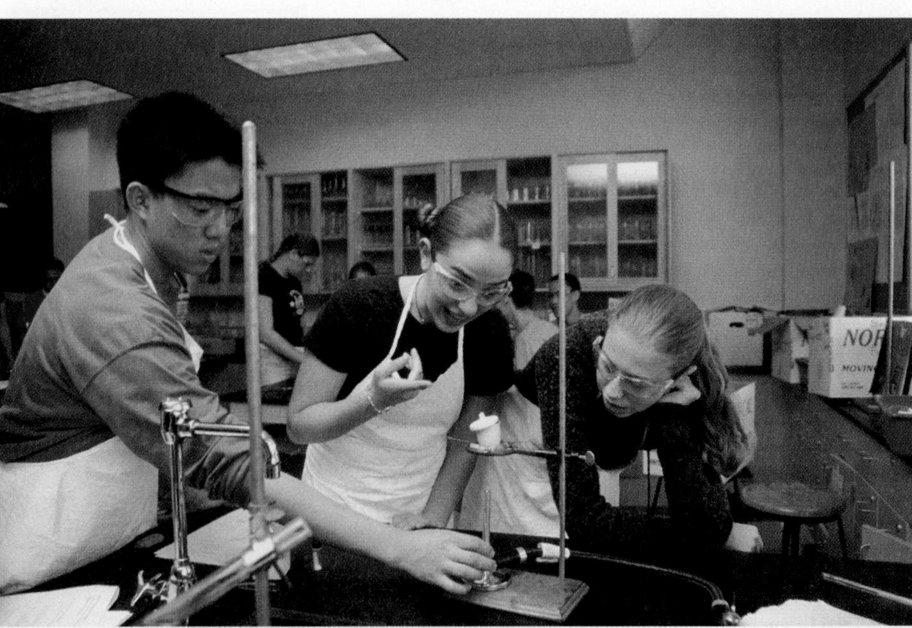

For students who have difficulty reading high school science textbooks, having opportunities to access the general education curriculum in a variety of ways can lead to the successful mastery of difficult material.

Accommodating for Inclusive Environments

Steps for Success in a Modified General Education Curriculum

Specify the Instructional Objectives

- List the objectives in observable terms such that they will communicate to others.
- Focus the objectives on what is directly the instructional target.
- Plan how the objectives will be evaluated to ensure continued student progress.

Sequence Skills

- Be sure prerequisite skills are mastered first.
- Sequence easy skills before more difficult ones.
- Plan to teach confusing concepts separately.

Match Instructional Tactic with Topic or Skill to Be Taught

- Select a tactic that has been proven through rigorous research.
- Monitor its effectiveness continuously.
- Change tactics when it is no longer effective.

Provide Many Opportunities for Practice

- Have students apply their learning in different settings.
- Have students apply their learning with slightly different or expanded tasks or skills.

Be Certain That the Skill Is Truly Mastered

- Have the student demonstrate mastery when performing the skill independently.
- Have the student demonstrate mastery in a variety of settings.

Access to the General Education Curriculum

Many students with mental retardation access the general education curriculum and attend general education classes along with their neighborhood friends. In fact, almost 15 percent of elementary school students with cognitive disabilities receive about 80 percent of their education in the general education classroom (U.S. Department of Education, 2005b). An additional 30 percent of these students spend close to half of their time learning alongside their peers without disabilities. The percentages change somewhat during the high school years as the demands of the curriculum increase, but what is important to understand is that students with mental retardation are successfully learning to read, write, and calculate (Tindal et al., 2003).

Some teachers are helping all students to more easily access difficult academic content. For example, Geoff Ruth takes an "outside the book" approach to chemistry. He says, "Without a textbook, I can create curriculum that engages students by relating science to their everyday lives. Lessons become clearer when I link the topic to an issue that affects them personally" (Ruth, 2005, p. 22). He believes that *all* of his students are more engaged in learning and that they are mastering, in groups, concepts that they would be unlikely to understand through a traditionally written textbook. Even when they do not discard textbooks altogether, teachers can help students learn difficult content by linking the content to experiences or situations they all experience.

Instructional Accommodations

For many students with mental retardation, accommodations (e.g., extended time to complete assignments, notetakers to help them write down important points from lectures) are not sufficient. For some assignments, they may need only

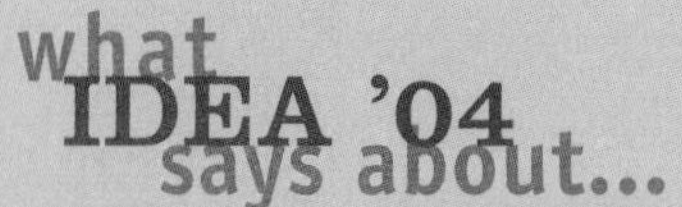

Transition and Functional Skills

The transition process should focus on improving a student's achievement to facilitate development of skills necessary to function in postschool activities that include

- Postsecondary education
- Vocational education
- Integrated employment (including supported employment)
- Continuing and adult education, adult services
- Independent living
- Community participation

In addition to instruction and related services provided for younger students, the individually determined process may include

- Community experiences
- Employment objectives
- Other postschool adult living objectives
- Acquisition of daily living skills
- Functional vocational evaluation

accommodations, but for some content in the general education curriculum they need further help. They require more adjustments, or **modifications**, where assignments or tests are reduced or altered. Students may be allowed to master fewer objectives or to provide only specific parts of answers, or they may be given alternative assignments (e.g., photo essays instead of written reports). *Accommodating for Inclusive Environments* on page 297 provides some ways to ensure students' learning through modifications in the content contained in the general education curriculum.

Validated Practices

Some students with mental retardation need access to a different or additional curriculum to achieve full participation in the community after graduation from high school. These students require a **functional curriculum**, one that focuses on life skills. Why might some students require a different curriculum or need special instruction in adaptive behavior? Carolyn Hughes answers this question for us: "Unfortunately, the traditional secondary school curriculum does not address the needs many students have in order to achieve adult outcomes that many of us take for granted such as maintaining personal relationships, having a job, or owning a car" (Hughes, 2001, p. 85). Learn what the federal government has to say in *What IDEA '04 Says About Transition and Functional Skills.*

A functional curriculum teaches skills that are used in everyday life or that prepare students for life after graduation (Brolin, 2002). These should include the skills required for personal maintenance and development, homemaking and community life, work and career, recreational activities, and travel within the community (Repetto, 2003). Students' reading, writing, and mathematics instruction often focuses on practical skills. The reading program would include reading for protection and information. Here, survival words (street signs: *walk, don't walk, stop;* safety words: *danger, poison, keep out*) might be the topics of instruction. Such sight words can be taught by using a procedure called time delay, where students are instructed by means of a technique often applied in the teaching of a foreign language. In the case of language instruction, the word is said, and then the student is given a short period of time to provide the correct answer. If the answer is not provided quickly enough, the instructor provides it as a model. The *Validated Practices* feature offers an example of time delay used to teach sight words.

Writing instruction might center on taking phone messages, writing directions for getting to a restaurant, or taking notes on how to do a job. Mathematics instruction includes such topics as telling time, making change, money skills, and cooking measures. All instruction using this system is practical. For example, counting is taught by taking inventory of books in the library rather than by absentmindedly reciting numbers from 1 to 20. A unit on measurement becomes an opportunity to teach cooking, rather than an exercise in solving problems in a workbook.

One validated approach that is often included in a functional curriculum is teaching **self-determination**—how to make choices and advocate for oneself (Kohler & Field, 2003; McComb, 2003). People with mental retardation are allowed fewer choices than other people with disabilities and their peers without disabilities (Wehmeyer & Metzler, 1995). Every day, people make choices for themselves. They decide where to sit, where to eat, what to eat, how long to stay, where to go, and with whom to interact. For people with mental retardation, particularly those who were allowed to make few choices while they were growing up, the need to make

modifications Adjustments to assignments or tests, reducing the requirements

functional curriculum A curriculum made up of skills needed for daily living

self-determination The decision making, choosing of preferences, and self-advocacy needed for independent living

Validated Practices Progressive Time Delay

What Is Progressive Time Delay?

Progressive Time Delay (PTD) is an instructional procedure that systematically increases the number of seconds between a stimulus (e.g., "What's this word?") that cues a student to perform a task (e.g., reading the word). Prompts are faded by systematically inserting a fixed amount of time between the target stimulus and the prompt.

Students will give one of five types of responses: (1) Unprompted correct: the student gives the correct answer *before* the controlling prompt is presented. (2) Prompted correct: the student gives the correct answer *after* the controlling prompt is given. (3) Unprompted error: the student provides an incorrect response *before* the controlling stimuli is presented. (4) Prompted error: the student gives an incorrect answer *after* the controlling prompt is presented. (5) No response error: the student does not respond *after* the controlling prompt.

Why Progressive Time Delay Is Beneficial

PTD has been shown to be effective in teaching students tasks such as reading words, setting tables, doing laundry, and completing job applications. PTD requires you to interact with your student on a constant basis. This, coupled with an effective data collection system, will ensure that you are providing your students with consistent feedback. Because of this high level of student-teacher interaction and immediate feedback, students learn quickly with few errors.

Implementing Progressive Time Delay

Wolery, Ault, and Doyle (1992) provide a detailed description of the nine components of PTD. Below is a brief description of applying the nine steps to teach counting dollar bills. Figure A is an example of a completed data collection chart.

Identify the stimulus that cues the student to respond.

- You say "Jeff, count these dollar bills."

Identify the controlling prompt.

- Jeff says, "Three dollars."

Determine the student's ability to wait for the prompt.

- Identify a task your student *does not* know how to do.
- Provide the student with a prompt to complete the unfamiliar task.
- Determine how long the student can wait before doing the task.

Identify the number of 0-second-delay trials needed.

During this stage, you will present the word and say it simultaneously, so there is no time for errors.

- "Jeff, how many dollar bills are here? (*Pause*) Three."

There is no set number of times that this needs to occur. Use your judgment.

Determine the length of the prompt delay interval.

- Because it is easy to remember, increase the length of the prompt by 1 second.

Determine the schedule for increasing the prompt delay interval.

- Because it is easy to remember, increase the prompt delay at each session.

Determine the consequences for each student response.

- For each prompted and unprompted correct response, the student will receive a reward.
- For each unprompted incorrect response, say, "Wrong, there are one, two, three dollar bills."
- For each prompted error or no response, say, "Jeff, count one, two, three dollars."

Select a data collection system.

- Select a system you can use to record the five types of responses (see Figure A).

Figure A • Sample Data Collection Sheet

Student Joe Instructor S. L. Date 6/1 Session 3

Start time 2:00 Stop time 2:10 Total time 10 min.

Task Counting dollar bills

Trial/ Step	Stimulus/Task Analysis	Delay	Unprompted Correct	Prompted Correct	Unprompted Error	Prompted Error	No Response
1	$5	4"		✓			
2	$3	4"		✓			
3	$4	4"		✓			
4	$1	4"	✓				
5	$2	4"	✓				
Number of Each Response Type			2	3	0	0	0
Percent of Each Response Type			40	60	0	0	0

Key: ✓ = occurrence

Implement, monitor, and adjust the program based on student patterns.

- Use the data you have collected to adjust your teaching and the intervention you are using.

This scientifically validated practice is a teaching method that has been proved by systematic research efforts (Browder & Xin, 1998; Colins & Stinson, 1994–1995; Mechling, Gast, & Langone, 2002; Wolery, Ault, & Doyle, 1992). Full citations can be found in the references for this chapter.

—By Kimberly Paulsen, Vanderbilt University

Table 8.3 • Task Analysis for Zipping a Jacket

1. Engage zipper
   a. Student stands with unzipped coat on.
   b. Left fingers grasp bottom of jacket on left side near zipper.
   c. Right hand (thumb and first finger) grasps talon, with talon pointing down.
   d. Right hand pulls down firmly.
   e. Left hand lifts slider and slides it into the zipper stop.
2. Pull up zipper
   a. Left hand maintains downward pull.
   b. Right hand pulls up on talon to top of jacket.
3. Set zipper
   a. Bend talon down.

decisions is unfamiliar. Other people make even the simplest decisions for them. Self-determination must be part of the curriculum, particularly for high school students, because it is now clear that these skills are highly related to success in all aspects of adult life (Repetto, 2003).

When teaching functional or life skills, teachers often find that they need to create their own instructional programs because few are available from commercial publishing houses. In these circumstances, teachers find that **task analysis**—breaking skills down into teachable units—is helpful because the results of the process provide a guide to sequence instruction. Simple, linear tasks are easily approached in this manner. For example, buttoning a shirt, zipping a jacket, tying shoes, cooking, using public transportation, making change, and telling time are all skills that are often part of these students' IEPs and that are easily subjected to task analysis. Teachers can select two different sequences for chaining. In *forward chaining*, students are taught to perform the first step in the chain first. In the task of zipping a jacket, for example, students would be taught to engage the tab first. Each step up the chain of steps is taught and mastered before the next step in the chain is introduced. In some cases, however, the teacher might elect to teach the steps in reverse order, which is called *backward chaining* or reverse chaining. (In tying shoes, for example, it may be best for the student to learn first to complete the bow.) Table 8.3 offers an example of a skill (zipping a jacket,) that was task-analyzed and taught to a young child with mental retardation through direct instruction techniques. To complete their instruction, teachers make certain that their students can apply their newly learned skills in real-life situations. For example, the teacher would ensure that the student zips up the jacket when going outside to play on a cold day. In some cases, these practical applications should also occur away from the school setting, and this is why the concept of community based instruction was developed.

Community based instruction (CBI), which is used to teach functional skills, self-determination, and adaptive behaviors, occurs in the environments in which the need for these skills arises naturally. Remember that generalization is difficult for many students with a disability, and CBI is designed to help students learn to apply skills in all appropriate settings. Like task analysis, CBI is a crucial teaching tool for many students with mental retardation. Let's look at some examples. Learning how to make change is more natural when using real coins at the neighborhood store than when using paper cutouts of coins in the classroom. Learning how to use public transportation to get from home to work is more effec-

task analysis Breaking down problems and tasks into smaller, sequenced components

community based instruction (CBI) Teaching functional skills in the environments in which they are needed tive when actually making such trips on a city bus than when pretending to do so at school. Also, rather than addressing a specific curriculum area (such as self-help or language skills) in artificial settings, CBI allows for these skills to be taught in at least four important situations: vocational environments, community settings, recreation and leisure activities, and home and family. For many students with mental retardation, learning those skills required for independence and community presence needs to begin during the school years, with formal and guided instruction to ensure that they learn the skills they need. For example, learning important job skills is part of their curriculum, and the best place to learn those skills is in the community at actual job sites. However, the story in *Cultural Considerations* shows that educators must consider many issues before planning these educational experiences.

CBI is very effective with students who need to learn adaptive behaviors and have difficulties with generalization. However, CBI poses a dilemma for some educators because it is not compatible with inclusive education in age-appropriate general education placements. When a student is learning in the community while other students of the same age are learning in the school building, the student with mental retardation is deprived of inclusion opportunities with peers. How can the benefits of CBI be weighed against the benefits of inclusive settings? How should this dilemma be resolved? Read again Diane McComb's wise words at the opening of this chapter. Possibly the best answer lies in having many options available so that people with mental retardation and their families can choose what's best for each of them.

Technology

Many of us spend increasing portions of our day on the computer, where papers are prepared, budgets maintained, information sought, and friends kept close. People now correspond via e-mail at a relatively high rate, and until recently students with mental retardation were often excluded from this exchange. But thanks to a Best Buddies program called **e-Buddies**, e-mail is now an important part of school and daily life for students with mental retardation (e-Buddies, 2005). This program has helped students with mental retardation connect with each other across the nation, and it also facilitates the development of friendships between people with and people without disabilities. Other examples of how technology can help students with mental retardation are as simple as the use of a calculator to perform arithmetic tasks. This enables such students to compensate successfully for the difficulties they often face when they have to solve mathematical problems used in important life skills such as balancing a checkbook. Computer-based video instruction is being used to teach words found on grocery aisles (Mechling, Gast, & Langone, 2002). The result can be better access to and participation in the community.

Communication between school and home is a major issue for some families. Technology can facilitate such communication. For example, some teachers have created Web sites to post homework assignments, and others e-mail the assignments to families (Salend et al., 2004). The purpose is to ensure that families can help their children complete assignments and to provide guidelines for evaluating the progress students are making in developing independent study skills. The use of the Internet can help those students who have difficulty copying and remembering homework assignments and those who are often absent because of illness. Despite the digital divide (problems associated with poor families not having access to computers), many educators find that frequent e-mail notes are an excellent means of communicating to the family information about the progress of a student with disabilities (Davern, 2004). Whether the notes be handwritten or e-mailed (now allowed by IDEA '04), it is important for teachers to find ways to interact with students' families consistently and often.

e-Buddies A program that creates e-mail friendships between people with and without mental retardation

Considering Culture

Finding the Right Vocational Opportunity

Martin has taught the "Transition to Work" class for students with mental retardation at Jefferson High School for seven years. He has won awards from the local Chamber of Commerce and The Arc for his skill in finding "real-world" placements that often become full-time jobs for his students when they complete school. This year he has encountered a situation that is new to him. After he worked diligently to get a training placement in a popular coffee shop for Amira Abdullah, a 16-year-old with intellectual disabilities, her parents have refused to allow her to participate. In a meeting with Amira and her parents, her father said, "Amira may not work at this place. We would not allow any of our girls to serve the public or be unsupervised in such a setting. It is immodest and asking for trouble and embarrassment. To imagine Amira, with her special problems, in such a situation does not make sense."

Martin knew that Mr. Abdullah's background and faith caused him to hold very traditional views of women, but he also knew the value of vocational skills for Amira. As the meeting continued, he talked with Mr. and Mrs. Abdullah about all the things that Amira would learn: money management, self-fulfillment, personal independence. Mr. Abdullah listened politely and then explained that all of those things would be handled within the family—that there was no need for outsiders to teach such things. At this point Amira said quietly, "Papa, my friends are going to work. I want to work, too." Mr. Abdullah seemed surprised, but his wife smiled slightly as she looked fondly at Amira. Martin was also surprised to hear Amira speak out, and it gave him an idea. He knew that Mr. Abdullah had a very successful business, so he wondered aloud if it would be possible to respect Mr. Abdullah's concerns *and* honor Amira's request. He asked Mr. Abdullah to think about creating a training opportunity within his business where Amira could continue to learn under family supervision with the help of a job coach. They talked about possibilities, and then Mr. Abdullah asked if they could meet with Martin again the next week.

When they met again, Mr. Abdullah said that the whole family had talked and that Amira's brothers and sisters had been very persuasive. They had all had small jobs in the business and thought that Amira should, too. Mrs. Abdullah said that Amira knows everyone in the building and everyone knows her. Perhaps she could deliver the mail and be a courier within the building. She said that she thought Amira would do well but that they did not know how to teach her the job and its responsibilities. Martin happily stepped in, complimenting them on the idea and assuring them that he and a job coach would teach Amira how to do the job. Within a few months, Amira was going to work, earning her own money, and feeling very proud that, like her friends, she had a job.

Questions to Consider

1 If you had been in Martin's position, what do you think your first reaction to Mr. Abdullah's concerns might have been?

2 Sometimes teachers become frustrated with students' parents because they think the parents are being overprotective. Did you ever feel that your parents were overprotective? In what circumstance? Do you think their behavior was based on cultural or religious traditions and beliefs or on concern for your well-being?

3 What are examples of a cultural or religious values that may affect individuals with disabilities differently than those without disabilities?

—By Eleanor Lynch, San Diego State University and Marci Hanson, San Francisco State University

Transition

Individuals with mental retardation do lead satisfying lives as adults. They work, establish close relationships with friends and family, live in their home communities, and pursue desired activities. Some may require assistance only from time to time during their lives, whereas others with more significant cognitive disabilities may always need assistance and supports. What should be the general goals for people with moderate to severe mental retardation? Parents and professionals have been grappling with this important question, because its answer could provide a framework for the curriculum, instruction, and experiences offered to students with mental retardation. This question has stimulated an important discussion about quality of life and people with mental retardation. Before talking about employment and community adjustment (the topics more traditionally related to transition issues), let's briefly consider quality of life and how this concept could guide instruction and decisions about adult living arrangements.

Quality of Life

Quality of life is a person's satisfaction with life, which includes a sense of contentment that results in part from feelings of dignity, value, worth, and respect (Wolfensberger, 2002). An assessment of quality of life helps to determine how well the individual's needs and desires are being met and reflects outcomes such as empowerment, independence, social belonging, community presence, and life satisfaction (Kraemer, McIntyre, & Blacher, 2003). Quality of life is a complex and elusive concept. Judgments about quality of life must be made by each individual, for what one person perceives as good may not be perceived as good by another. In other words, no single standard can be applied to all people (Edgerton, 1996).

Young adults who live and work in the community express greater satisfaction with their lives than those who do not (Kraemer, McIntyre, & Blacher, 2003). Those people with mental retardation who work in the community have higher satisfaction scores than those who work in sheltered workshops, who work in day/activity centers, or who do not work. These findings are important because they inform educators about many of the goals that should be included in the IEPs of students still attending school. For all of us, success after school is related to how well prepared we are for adulthood. But for individuals who face more challenges than most others, preparation for work, independence, and a real community presence can be the key to satisfaction with life. For these goals to be achieved requires substantial instruction, which must be part of the curriculum for these students (Repetto, 2003). Transition education does make a difference: Graduates of special education programs are more likely to be employed and to have higher earnings, particularly if they had received vocational education, paid work experience, strong parental involvement, and interagency collaboration during their high school years (Kohler & Field, 2003). In preparation for the transition from school to adult life, parents believe that their children should have instruction related to self-determination while in high school (Grigal et al., 2003). (For a review, see the *Validated Practices* feature on page 299.)

Supported Employment

Just as it is for most everyone, having a good job is important to people with mental retardation. Jobs give them an opportunity to earn money, to form friendships, to engage in the social activities of the community, and to develop a sense of self-satisfaction about making a contribution. Achieving success on the job can be challenging for many people with intellectual disabilities. A traditional means of helping these individuals after the high school years and in the workplace is through vocational rehabilitation services, which are provided by every state. **Vocational rehabilitation** is a government service that provides training, counseling, and job placement services; it has been effective with clients who avail themselves of these services and who have mild mental retardation (Moor, Harley, & Gamble, 2004). Those with moderate to severe mental retardation often need more assistance to gain paid work in the community. **Supported employment** is funded by governmental agencies and assists individuals who could not otherwise hold a competitive job by helping them locate a job, learn the skills needed to be successful in that position, and keep the job. Supported employment began over 20 years ago, has evolved over the years, and pays off daily. This system has proved that people with disabilities, previously considered unable to work in the community,

quality of life A subjective and individual-specific concept reflecting social relationships, personal satisfaction, employment, choice, leisure, independence, and community presence

vocational rehabilitation A government service that provides training, career counseling, and job placement services

supported employment A government program to help individuals with disabilities be successful in competitive employment situations can be productive workers (Conley, 2003). Supported employment not only provides work experience but also results in improved wages for people with mental retardation (Mank, Cioffi, & Yovanoff, 2003).

Through supported employment, a job developer finds or even designs work that an individual with mental retardation or other severe disabilities can accomplish. A job coach might work alongside the individual, helping her or him to learn all parts of the job. Coworkers are trained to assist their coworkers with disabilities as they work alongside them (Butterworth et al., 2000). And employers are becoming more involved in the lives of their employees with disabilities (Mank, Cioffi, & Yovanoff, 2003). An additional result often is the development of friendships that exist at work and after hours—something important to everyone (Chadsey & Beyer, 2001). Improvements also occur in hourly wages, types of jobs held, and the number of them available. It is now clear that high expectations are achievable!

Independent Living

Most people with mental retardation do not have severe disabilities, and living independently in the community is a realistic goal. Historically, those with moderate, severe, and profound disabilities found themselves confined to residential institutions. During the last half of the 20th Century, the deinstitutionalization movement sought to close all institutions and bring all people with mental retardation to community settings. Today, more people with cognitive disabilities are living in the community outside of their family homes. This progress has been relatively recent. Since 1993, 30 percent more of these individuals have come to live in community placements, and more than twice as many now live in small residential arrangements (anywhere from 1 to 6 people) as did ten years earlier (Lakin, Braddock, & Smith, 2004b). Despite these improvements, the rate of reducing the size and number of large, congregate institutions for persons with mental retardation has slowed, in part because community based alternatives are insufficient (Lakin, Braddock, & Smith, 2004a). Bringing about a further increase in community living for people with high needs for support involves considerable effort, person-centered planning, and individualized instruction (Holburn & Vietze, 2002). But when that effort is invested, more individuals leave institutional life and successfully live in the community (Holburn et al., 2004).

Because living independently in the community is related to being satisfied with life, it is an important goal for most individuals with mental retardation (Cummins, 2001). For many adults with mental retardation, community living has positively replaced less satisfactory experiences with residential institutional life. However, merely living in a community setting, such as a group home or some other supportive housing arrangement, does not guarantee life satisfaction (Perry & Felce, 2005). In some cases, support from staff is the critical variable for success. In other cases, it is the number of people living in the setting that makes a difference in the members' quality of life. Interestingly, the optimal number appears to be around six; people come to develop natural supports and friendships with each other when there are neither too few nor too many to develop a talent network (Emerson et al., 2001).

What people become is limited only by their dreams and imaginations. The Court Jesters are a group of entertainers with mental retardation. This troupe of magicians performs illusion tricks for audiences across the country.

Instruction to help individuals with mental retardation prepare for adult life should include learning self-determination skills: making choices and decisions for themselves. One facet of assuming control of one's life is being able to make choices; making decisions is also associated with higher levels of adaptive behavior (Kennedy & Lewin, 2002; Stancliff, 2001). For these reasons, self-determination has become a target of instruction for many students with mental retardation. Self-determination comprises the attitudes and abilities required to act on one's own behalf, to make decisions for oneself, and to make choices. Such a curriculum embodies four basic principles: freedom, authority, support, and responsibility (Moseley & Nerney, 2000). These principles are applied across all adaptive areas and are taught through meaningful and real experiences. Although the normalization movement is well established, people with mental retardation typically do not have many experiences or opportunities to make their own decisions, be independent, or assume the role of self-advocate (Cone, 2001). They often do not get a chance to make simple decisions (what movie to see, at what restaurant to eat, whether to go to church, or whom to visit), even when the person making the decision was hired to help the person with mental retardation accomplish his or her goals. Parents, in particular, express concern about their children's need to learn how to make choices and good decisions (PACER, 2002). Like everyone else, individuals with mental retardation become adults and need to be prepared to assume their rights, responsibilities, and obligations.

Collaboration

Successful integration of people with mental retardation at school and in society requires considerable teamwork and effort. Teachers of students with moderate to severe cognitive disabilities, from preschools to high schools, work with a wide variety of professionals. For example, collaboration with SLPs to develop and expand these individuals' speech and language abilities is a major component of many instructional programs. To develop effective partnerships with professionals from an array of disciplines requires teachers to understand the vocabulary and concepts used by multidisciplinary team members so that each student's instructional program is both balanced and appropriate.

Teaching and including students with cognitive disabilities does not always come naturally. Unfortunately, in mixed-ability classes, teachers often ignore students with disabilities and call on more able students for class discussion. However, students can be taught to facilitate their own participation in the instructional setting. In novel studies, researchers taught students with disabilities to solicit attention from their teachers by prompting their teachers to provide them with feedback (Alber & Heward, 1997; Craft, Alber, & Heward 1998). The students were taught to ask their teachers questions like "How am I doing?" and to make statements such as "Look, I'm finished." The result was better academic performance and a substantial increase in teachers' rates of praising students with disabilities. This direct approach can also help reduce behavior problems that arise because the curriculum, instruction, or materials are too challenging for included students. Some smart teachers work together, each prompting students with cognitive disabilities to keep them actively involved in the instructional program. They, as in the examples found in *Tips for Classroom Management,* on page 306 use specific instructions and positive feedback to avoid behavior problems and maintain students' interest in class activities.

Partnerships with Families and Communities

The families of individuals with mental retardation—especially the mothers of those with conditions such as Down syndrome and fragile X syndrome—face special challenges (Abbeduto et al., 2004). Clearly, life becomes more complicated when one must coordinate the supports needed by a son or daughter with mental retardation

for Classroom Management

GUIDING STUDENTS THROUGH INSTRUCTION AND FEEDBACK

Instruction

1 Ensure that students understand classroom rules and expectations.
2 Use simple instructions and directions about expected classroom behaviors.
3 Actively involve the students in the lesson.
4 Prompt students about how they are supposed to behave during each type of lesson.
5 Explain the consequences of misbehaving or disturbing the lesson.

Feedback

1 Use simple, clear, and direct feedback regarding the exact behaviors required.
2 Remind students about how they are supposed to behave during each type of lesson.
3 Praise students during the lesson for meeting the classroom expectations.
4 Deliver consequences for misbehaving or disturbing the lesson.
5 Reward students for meeting expectations over an entire period.

and also balance the needs of all other family members. Therefore, it is not uncommon for all family members—dads, brothers, and sisters—to take an active role in the life of their family member with mental retardation. Most of these families require additional services and supports at some time, especially during periods of transition. These supports might include personal care, family support, respite care, financial allowances, subsidies, counseling and guidance, and in-home assistance. Many families also gain strength and information from organizations such as The Arc and other parent support and advocacy groups. However, it is the families themselves who provide the vital day-to-day supports for each other and for their family member with the disability. Educators should remember that when the school year ends, their work is done, but the family's work is not. Although issues change across time, it often seems that families simply move from one challenge to another.

Support from Dads

Fathers are very important in the lives of their children, and this is no less true for children with disabilities. Fathers of children with disabilities are as involved and spend about the same amount of time with their children as fathers whose children do not have disabilities (Beach Center, 2002a&b). They just do things differently. These fathers spend more time doing child care. They watch more TV and spend more time at home than other fathers. Those fathers who do take part in the rearing of their children with disabilities also tend to have higher levels of satisfaction with their marriages.

Fathers of these children, however, have a serious complaint about service providers, and this is a message that educators should listen to carefully: They believe they are treated like second-class citizens (Beach Center, 1995a&b). They get the clear impression that mothers are assumed to be the "experts" about their children. One father even reported that a social worker thanked him for his cooperation but said she would check the accuracy of his answers with his wife. Some fathers believe that the professionals, predominantly female, are not sensitive to their emotional perspectives about their children. It is important to remember that fathers are a real part of the family's support team. They need to be involved and included.

Support from Brothers and Sisters

Siblings of people with disabilities also tend not to be thought of as part of the overall system of supports critical to the independence and success of their family member with disabilities. Although they often assume responsibility for their siblings with mental retardation when their parents are no longer able, brothers and sisters seldom receive much attention from social service agencies, educators, researchers, or policymakers (Seltzer & Krauss, 2001). They often maintain regular and personal contacts with their less able brothers or sisters and stand ready to assume the role of caregiver (Hannah & Midlarksy, 1999, 2005). Many—36 percent in one study—even intend to reside with their sibling when their parents' health or age prevents their continuing to care for their son or daughter with disabilities. This is particularly true when the adult with mental retardation is in poor health. Policymakers and community service providers must come to understand and better appreciate the roles that siblings intend to play in the care of their brothers and sisters with disabilities.

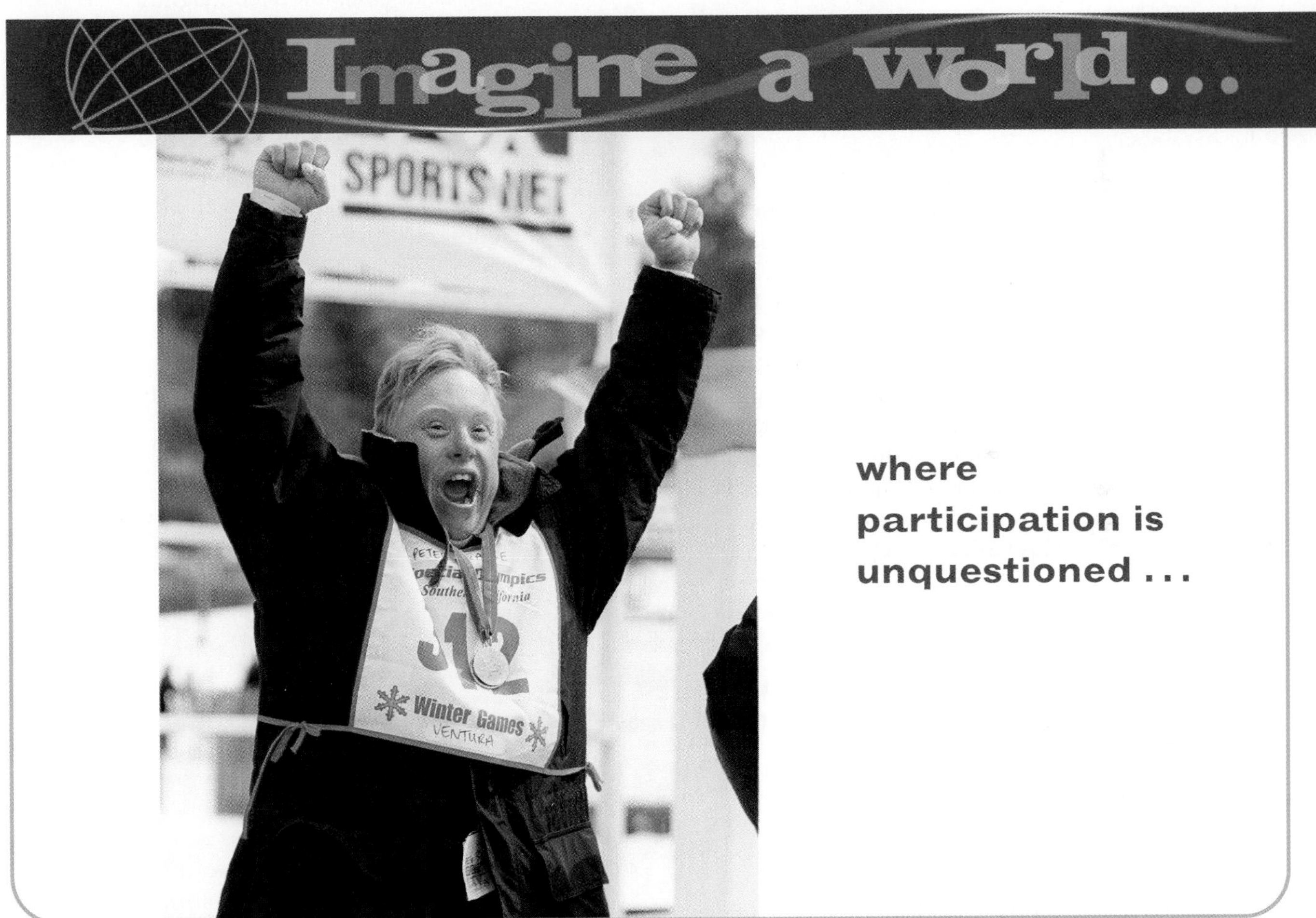
Imagine a world...
where participation is unquestioned...
Winter Games
VENTURA

Summary

People with mental retardation (intellectual or cognitive disabilities) have significantly impaired intellectual functioning and problems with adaptive skills. They require a variety of supports that may vary in intensity and duration. Some individuals require all four types of supports—natural, nonpaid, generic, specialized—at an intense level across their lifetimes to achieve community presence, be independent, and attain a high quality of life. Other individuals require few supports to take their rightful places in society. Mental retardation emerges during the developmental period, between birth and age 18.

Addressing the Chapter Objectives

1 What are the key components of the 2002 AAMR definition of mental retardation?

- *Intellectual functioning:* difficulties learning and remembering
- *Adaptive behavior:* problems with skills needed in daily life
- *Systems of supports:* networks of friends, family members, coworkers social service and govermental agencies

2 How are the levels of severity and outcomes of people with mental retardation categorized?

The 2002 AAMR definition uses IQ scores to partially explain mental retardation by applying a cutoff score of about 70 and below. This definition also codes intellectual abilities to express levels of severity in the following ways:

- Mild mental retardation: IQ range of 50 to 69
  Outcomes: Has learning difficulties, is able to work, can maintain good social relationships, contributes to society
- Moderate mental retardation: IQ range of 35 to 49
  Outcomes: Exhibits marked developmental delays during childhood, has some degree of independence in self-care, possesses adequate communication and academic skills, requires varying degrees of support to live and work in the community
- Severe mental retardation: IQ range of 20 to 34
  Outcomes: Has continuous need for supports
- Profound mental retardation: IQ under 20
  Outcomes: Demonstrates severe limitations in self-care, continence, communication, and mobility; requires continuous and intensive supports

3 What are the four levels of supports and how they make a difference in the lives of people with mental retardation?

- Natural supports (the individual's own resources, family, friends, neighbors, coworkers, classmates)
- Nonpaid supports (clubs, recreational leagues, private organizations)
- Generic public supports (transportation, state's human services)
- Specialized supports (special education, early intervention preschools, transition and vocational rehabilitation services)

Systems of supports help individuals achieve community presence, attain quality of life, live independently, and hold competitive jobs.

4 What are two ways to organize causes of disabilities, and what are the major known reasons for mental retardation?

- Causes can be grouped by
  - *Time of onset:* prenatal, perinatal, or postnatal
  - *Reason:* heredity, environment, and/or society
- Major types or reasons
  - *Genes and heredity:* fragile X syndrome, Down syndrome, phenylketonuria (PKU)
  - *Environment:* toxins, child abuse and neglect, discrimination and bias
  - *Conditions:* disease, low birth weight

5 What are two validated practices that make a difference in the outcomes of students with mental retardation who are not fully accessing the general education curriculum?

- Self-determination
  - Teaches how to make choices and decisions
  - Includes self-advocacy
  - Provides skills necessary for adult life, independent living, work, and community presence
- Community based instruction
  - Teaches skills in natural environments
  - Uses real materials and settings for instruction
  - Provides opportunities to learn, practice, and generalize self-determination, functional skills, and adaptive behaviors
  - Removes students from the general educational setting for instruction

Supplementary Resources

Popular Novels and Books

Meyers, R. (1978). *Like normal people.* New York: McGraw-Hill.

Perske, R. (1986). *Don't stop the music.* Nashville, TN: Abingdon Press.

Sachs, O. (1987). *The man who mistook his wife for a hat and other clinical tales.* New York: Harper & Row.

Shriver, M. (2001). *What's wrong with Timmy?* Boston: Warner Books and Little, Brown, and Company, AOL Time Warner Companies.

Simon, R. (2002). *Riding the bus with my sister.* Boston: Houghton Mifflin.

Steinbeck, J. (1937). *Of mice and men.* New York: Viking Press.

Movies

I Am Sam (2001). New Line Cinema

Sam, who has significant cognitive disabilities, is raising his young daughter independently. However, some social workers believe that Sam will not be capable of raising an adolescent. This film is contrived but raises interesting questions about people with mental retardation and their ability to assume adult responsibilities. Sam and his daughter have a loving relationship, but the question is whether that alone is enough for the court of law to award him custody.

The Other Sister (1999). Touchtone.

Because of her mental retardation and challenging behaviors, Carla attended a special boarding school. After graduation, Carla's overprotective mother still treats her like a young girl, but Carla wins her fight to live in her own apartment. At the local community college she meets her future husband, Daniel, who also has mental retardation. He lives independently through a community based living arrangement because a close friend who lives upstairs checks up on him. Although some of the acting and language artificially represents characters with mental retardation, the film does present people with developmental or cognitive disabilities in a modern perspective.

Sling Blade (1996). Miramax

Karl, an adult with mental retardation, was placed in an institution for killing his mother and her lover. He is released after serving 20 years and returns to the town where he grew up. He gets a job that draws on his talent of fixing things such as lawnmowers. Karl, who was a suitable father figure, befriends a young boy named Frank, whose mother is dating a mean, abusive drunk. Karl protects Frank by killing the mother's boy friend. He is returned to the same institution where he had spent most of his life. This film deals with the bias experienced by someone who looks and behaves differently. Billy Bob Thorton won an Oscar for his performance as Karl in this film, which he also directed.

Forrest Gump (1994). Paramount

This epic tale follows the life of the fictional Forrest Gump, a person with cognitive disabilities. Forrest performs extraordinary feats throughout his life. His disability does not prevent him from becoming an All-American football player, the recipient of a medal of honor in the Vietnam War, a successful shrimp boat captain, and a father. This uplifting story depicts the unpredictability of life and gives everyone hope of achieving the unimaginable. The film offers a positive portrayal of a person with disabilities. It won six Oscars, including Best Picture. Tom Hanks won the Oscar for Best Actor in the title role.

What's Eating Gilbert Grape (1993). Paramount

Gilbert lives in a small town with his younger sister, his extremely obese mother, and his brother, who has mental retardation. Gilbert is forced to be the patriarch, providing for his dysfunctional family and acting as the primary caretaker of his brother. However, Gilbert falls in love with Becky, who is passing through town with her grandmother. Gilbert readjusts his priorities and deals with the guilt of putting himself before the needs of his family.

This film attempts to depict the level of supports, care, and attention that teenagers with mental retardation require. The feelings that Gilbert experiences are similar to those felt by many brothers and sisters of individuals with disabilities—responsibility, love, resentment, guilt, and dedication. Leonardo DiCaprio gives an incredible performance as the younger brother.

Professional, Parent, and Advocacy Groups

American Association on Mental Retardation (AAMR) in Washington, DC: www.aamr.org

The Arc (formerly the Association for Retarded Citizens of the United States, ARC-US) in Silver Spring, Maryland: www.thearc.org

Division on Mental Retardation & Developmental Disabilities (MRDD), Council for Exceptional Children in Arlington, Virginia www.cec.sped.org or www.mrddcec.org

The National Down Syndrome Society in New York City: www.ndss.org

People First in London, England www.peoplefirstltd.com

Professional Standards and Licensure Tests

After reading this chapter, you should be able to link basic knowledge and skills described in the CEC Standards and INTASC Principles with information provided in this text. The table below shows some of the specific CEC Mental Retardation Knowledge and Skill Standards and INTASC Special Education Principles that can be applied to each major section of the chapter. Other standards may also be applied to this chapter. Associated General Praxis II topic areas are identified in the right column.

Major Chapter Headings	CEC Knowledge and Skill Core Standard and Associated Subcategories	INTASC Core Principle and Associated Special Education Subcategories	PRAXIS II Exam Topic
Where We've Been . . . What's on the Horizon	**1: Foundations** MR1K4 Historical foundations and classic studies of mental retardation/developmental disabilities	**1: Subject Matter** 1.01 Special education teachers have a solid understanding of the major concepts, assumptions, issues, and processes of inquiry in the subject matter that they teach.	1: Understanding Exceptionality 2: Legal and Social Issues
Mental Retardation Defined	**1: Foundations** MR1K1 Definitions and issues related to the identification of individuals with mental retardation/developmental disabilities	**1: Subject Matter** 1.12 Special education teachers serve as a resource to others by providing information about the laws and policies that support students with disabilities and how to access additional information when needed.	1: Understanding Exceptionality 2: Legal and Social Issues
Characteristics	**2: Development and Characteristics of Learners** MR2K3 Psychological, social/emotional, and motor characteristics of individuals with mental retardation/developmental disabilities	**2: Student Learning** 2.05 All special education teachers have knowledge of a wide array of disabilities and are cognizant of the range and types of individual variation that exist within disability categories.	1: Understanding Exceptionality

Causes and Prevention	**2: Development and Characteristics of Learners** MR2K1 Causes and theories of intellectual disabilities and implications for prevention	**2: Student Learning** 2.01 All general and special education teachers have a sound understanding of physical, social, emotional and cognitive development from birth through adulthood and are familiar with the general characteristics of most disabilities.	1: Understanding Exceptionality
Assessment	**8: Assessment** MR8S1 Select adapt and use instructional assessment tools and methods to accommodate the abilities and needs of individuals with mental retardation and developmental disabilities	**8: Assessment** 8.11 Special education teachers ensure that students with disabilities participate in district and statewide assessments and document on the IEP the use of accommodations or an alternate assessment when appropriate.	3: Delivery of Services to Students
Teaching Students with Mental Retardation	**4: Instructional Strategies** MR4K1 Specialized materials for individuals with mental retardation/ developmental disabilities	**4: Instructional Strategies** 4.10 Special education teachers know a range of specialized instructional strategies that have been found through research and best practices to support learning in individual students with disabilities.	3: Delivery of Services to Students
Transition	**7: Instructional Planning** MR7S3 Plan instruction for independent functional life skills relevant to the community, personal living, sexuality, and employment	**7: Planning Instruction** 7.07 Special education teachers oversee the development of individualized transition plans to guide learners' transitions from preschool to elementary school, middle school to high school, and high school to postschool opportunities.	3: Delivery of Services to Students
Collaboration	**10: Collaboration** MR10S1 Collaborate with team members to plan transition to adulthood that encourages full community participation	**10: Collaboration, Ethics, and Relationships** 10.09 Special education teachers collaborate with families and with school and community personnel to include students with disabilities in a range of instructional environments in the school and community.	2: Legal and Social Issues 3: Delivery of Services to Students

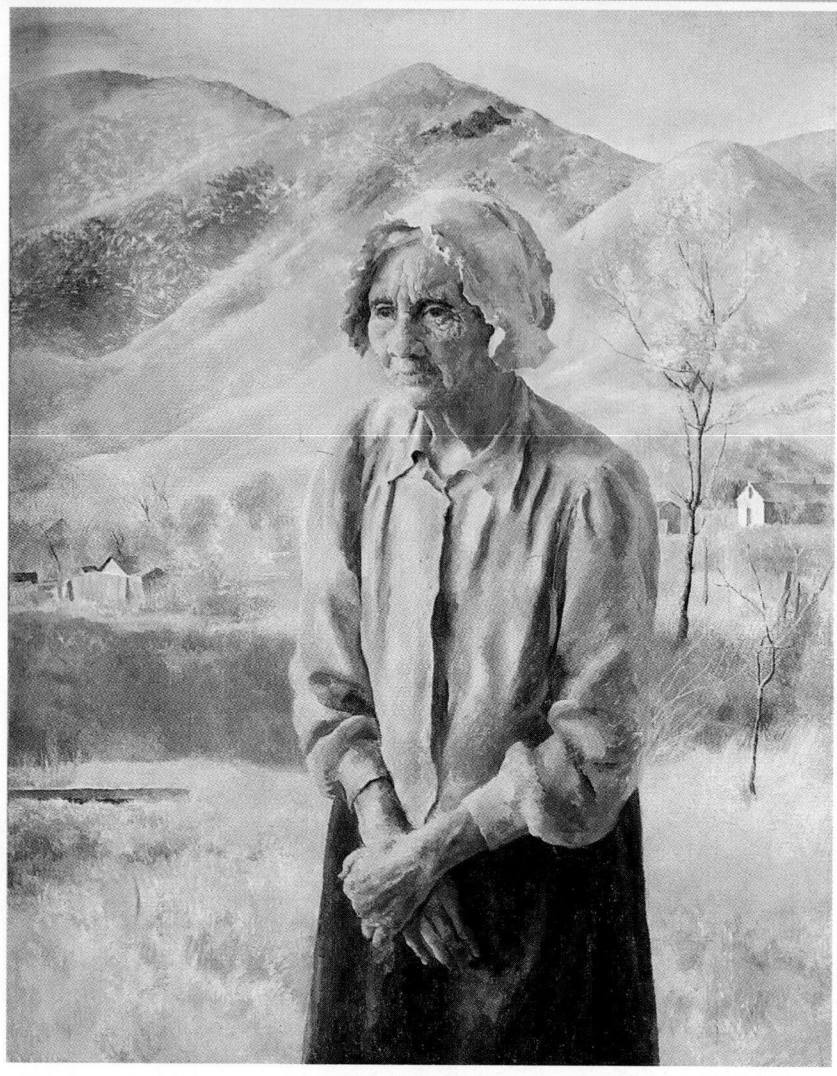

Henriette Wyeth, *Doña Nestorita*. Oil on canvas, 1940. Gift of Mr. and Mrs. Donald Winston. Collection of the Roswell Museum and Art Center.

Henriette Wyeth, an extremely prominent artist in her own right, came from a family of successful and well-known artists. Her father was the famous artist and illustrator N. C. Wyeth, her brother Andrew and her sister Carolyn also were well-known artists, and her husband was Peter Hurd, the renowned Western painter. Henriette Wyeth faced many challenges during her youth. She grew up in a high-achieving family that had exceptional expectations for her. She often spoke of the path that she took to find the right outlet for her creativity and talents and how her physical challenge helped to shaper her future: "I wanted to be a singer. Due to polio at three, I couldn't play the piano. I wanted to be an actress, too. By the age of sixteen, I was hooked on painting. I thought everyone drew—like having salt and pepper on the table" (Horgan, 1994, p. 30).

In 1940, Wyeth painted Doña Nestorita, a blind Mexican woman of 90 years who had lived most of her simple life in the rural Southwest. Wyeth described her as "charming, of great dignity, in a pitiful, tiny, blind person" (Horgan, 1994, p. 58).

9

Physical or Health Disabilities

We have nothing to fear but fear itself.

Franklin Delano Roosevelt

President of the United States and founder of the March of Dimes

Youth, beauty, and physical fitness are obsessions of modern American society. Through singers, dancers, and actors, the entertainment industry projects ideals of beauty not within the reach of most adolescents. The advertising industry urges us to purchase certain styles of clothes, special cosmetics and hair products, new exercise equipment, and even cars to make ourselves more attractive. Have you noticed messages about physical perfection in television shows, commercials, music videos, and movies? Have you or your friends assigned popularity ratings to others (such as ranking them on a scale of 1 to 10) on the basis of physical appearance? Sometimes, American society equates physical perfection with virtue or goodness, imperfection and deformities with evil (Longmore, 2003). Think, for example, of the deformed Darth Vader, always dressed in black in the Star Wars films. This symbolism has been repeated in many books and movies, including *The Hunchback of Notre Dame* (see page 17 in Chapter 1), *Dark Crystal, The Lion King,* and *The Wizard of Oz.*

Students with **health disabilities** or **special health care needs** are those individuals whose health situations are precarious and therefore whose ability to learn is compromised. Students with **physical disabilities** are those individuals who face physical challenges because their bodies are impaired. These two groups of students do not conform to the standards of beauty, strength, or energy emphasized by the fashion, advertising, sports, and entertainment industries so influential in our society. Unfortunately, the prejudices of society frequently are reflected in schools as well. These students—whose appearance is unusual because of deformities or muscle problems, or whose very walking ability, to say nothing of their athletic prowess, is challenged by wheelchairs or braces—may also suffer prejudice in school. All of us can participate in eliminating discrimination and harsh circumstances, but educators are in a very special position because they can create appropriate and supportive learning environments.

One way to remove many of the challenges people face is by revealing them and thus making us all aware of the difficulties and unfair situations we impose on others. Writers, media professionals, and filmmakers have unique opportunities to bring abuses—both historical and current—to the public's attention. Margaret Nagel, screenwriter and sister of a person with disabilities, used her position and created an opportunity to tell an important story, a part of American history, about a president who had to hide his disability from the public. *In the Spotlight* gives us an example of how everyone can make a difference by watching for opportunities to raise public awareness about people with disabilities and their experiences.

Chapter Objectives

After studying this chapter, you will be able to:

1. Explain how physical or health disabilities are organized.
2. Discuss the steps teachers should take to assist a student who is having a seizure.
3. Describe accommodations to the learning environment that help students with physical disabilities.
4. Describe accommodations to the learning environment that help students with health disabilities that result in special health care needs.
5. Explain how barriers that people with physical disabilities experience can be reduced and how students can be better prepared for increased community presence and participation.

Where We've Been . . . What's on the Horizon?

Not long ago, students with physical or health disabilities were isolated and educated in separate schools, and people with these challenges found it almost impossible to participate in daily life because of barriers everywhere (curbs, stairs, doors too heavy to open, and a lack of accessible recreational opportunities). They were also shunned because they looked different or were thought of as sick. Although much room for improvement remains, life in general and schools in particular are more accessible and accepting today. Also, advances in both medical and assistive technology amaze us all and dramatically improve the ability of people with physical disabilities and special health care needs to participate more fully in more aspects of daily life.

Historical Context

The history of physical disabilities can be traced back to 11,000-year-old gravesites (Frayer et al., 1987). Evidence of treatment for spinal cord injuries goes back to prehistoric times, the earliest documented treatment being the application of meat and honey to the neck (Maddox, 1987). Beginning with Hippocrates (400 B.C.), treatment usually included traction or even a stretching rack in an attempt to straighten the back or push in a deformity. Even though it was usually not successful, spinal surgery was performed as long ago as A.D. 600, but it was not until the mid-1800s that anesthesia became available and sterile techniques were used.

Hippocrates recognized that epilepsy originated in the brain but believed that it was caused by problems with the normal passage of "phlegm" from the brain or from sitting too long in the sun (Scheerenberger, 1983). Descriptions of conditions such as hemophilia, cerebral palsy, and epilepsy can be found in written records as early as 200 B.C. Hemophilia, the most common bleeding disorder, has long been recognized as a hereditary condition; rabbis noted that its transmission was from mothers to sons and was traced through royal and noble families in Spain, Germany, Russia, and England (Heller et al., 2000). William J. Little, an English surgeon, described the condition now known as cerebral palsy in well-researched case studies in 1861.

Perspectives on the best ways to educate students with physical or health disabilities have changed across the years. The first U.S. educational institution for students with physical disabilities was established in Boston in 1893: the Industrial School for Crippled and Deformed Children (Eberle, 1922). The first public school classes for "crippled children" were established in Chicago at the turn of the century (La Vor, 1976). But separate schools were the most common service delivery option. One reason was that such regional facilities provided centralized places where expensive equipment (e.g., therapeutic swimming pools) and highly skilled professionals could be made available to all students with very special physical or health care needs living nearby. Although such centers allowed for treatment, education, and facilities not feasible when these youngsters attend schools spread across a wide geographic region, the result was isolation and segregation. Today most of these students attend local schools with their brothers, sisters, and neighborhood friends.

Advances in medicine have eliminated some diseases and conditions and reduced the impact of others. For a look at "then versus now," compare this introductory text's topics with those found in one published in 1948, *Helping Handicapped Children in School* (Dolch, 1948). It included separate chapters titled "Crippled Children" and "Health Handicaps." The chapter on "crippled children" focused primarily on heart trouble caused by rheumatic fever, measles, scarlet fever, and diphtheria. These diseases, once common, are now rare. The chapter on "crippled children" included a section about infected and decayed teeth.

We reviewed the history of legislation and advocacy for people with disabilities in Chapter 1. It is important to recognize that people with physical disabilities took the lead in advocating for improved access to society and removal of barriers in the physi-

health disabilities or **special health care needs** Chronic or acute health problems resulting in limited strength, vitality, or alertness

physical disabilities Conditions related to a physical deformity or disability of the skeletal system and associated motor function

Margaret Nagel in the Spotlight

Margaret Nagel, screenwriter and former actress, has a unique perspective on and understanding of disabilities. When she was a child, her older brother was critically injured in a car accident, and after coming out of a coma, he had speech impairments and physical disabilities. Nagel recalls that growing up in the same room with her brother was like growing up in a rehabilitation center, but because she didn't know her brother before his accident, she didn't share the grief of other family members. "I just took him at face value for who he was." But she also learned that people are afraid of disability. She reports that even today when she goes somewhere with her brother, she sees people who are clearly uncomfortable.

Margaret learned only recently that Franklin Delano Roosevelt (known to many as FDR), the U.S. president who brought America out of the Depression and through World War II, had physical disabilities. Because of her personal background, she became fascinated by the man and his story. FDR was from a very wealthy family. At age 39 he contracted polio, which left him unable to walk. He found himself an outcast with a disease that all feared, and although he had considerable resources, no rehabilitation center was available to help people who had polio overcome the physical challenges that were the tragic legacy of this disease. Consequently, FDR started his own center—Warm Springs—in rural Georgia. In her first screenplay, which she called *Warm Springs,* Nagel brings to the screen FDR's experiences with the stigma of disability and poverty in the South in the early part of the last century. Nagel unveiled FDR's well-guarded secret (of the 35,000 pictures of Roosevelt that exist today, only two show him in a wheelchair). Nagel took the opportunity and created a film (HBO Films) more about disability awareness than about the biography of an American president. She created a painstakingly researched and compelling story that probes discrimination on the basis of class, race, and disability in the 20th Century and helps us better understand our present.

FDR as played by Kenneth Branagh.

cal environment. Like many underrepresented groups, the disability community needed a catalyst to begin an organized civil rights movement. In the view of many, Ed Roberts (also mentioned in Chapter 1) was just that catalyst (Shaw, 1995; Stone, 1995). Although Section 504 of the Rehabilitation Act (prohibiting discrimination) was passed in 1973, it took a wheelchair sit-in, orchestrated by Ed Roberts, to bring about implementation of the Section 504 regulations. The irony of some of these early personal stories is great. Here's a wonderful example. At the age of 14, Ed Roberts almost died from polio. After considerable struggle and persistence, in the early 1960s he was ready to attend college, but the University of California (UC) at Berkeley declared that he was "too disabled" for the campus to accommodate. Also, the California Department of Vocational Rehabilitation would not pay for his education because he was "too handicapped." Despite this rejection, he paid for the personal care attendants he needed to attend UC, and he became known as one of the "Rolling Quads" on campus. After receiving his bachelor's and master's degrees, he became the director of the agency that had previously refused to support his education. In 1984, with the monetary award he received from being honored as a MacArthur fellow, Roberts co-founded the World Institute on Disability, an event that many mark as the formal beginning of the civil rights movement for people with disabilities. Roberts died in 1995 at the age of 56, but his movement is thriving, and the voices of people with disabilities are heard across the nation, still demanding acceptance, access, and inclusion.

Changing Times: Moving Around Town

Travel is second nature to many Americans. We travel to far-away destinations for entertainment, on vacations, and to visit friends and families. For some of us, travel is an expectation of work. Not being able to attend conferences, participate in national sales meetings, and meet with clients presents a barrier faced by many people with disabilities. Although airline travel has become easier for people with disabilities, once they arrive at their destination, they are often unable to rent suitable cars or ride in taxicabs to get around in cities away from home. Such restrictions limit employment opportunities as well as chances for just plain fun.

At least one major city, New York, already noted for its vast fleet of taxis, is making a commitment to accessible cabs. According to the *New York Times* (October 16, 2004), the fleet has been expanded from 3 to 30 accessible cabs. That is, 30 out of the 12,487 taxis on the streets of Manhattan are now wheelchair accessible. All of this happened through a complicated bidding process with both winning and losing companies indicating that "(w)e really thought we were [making] a socially responsible investment."

These cabs will be joining the already accessible city bus system, which now has every bus outfitted with lifts, along with alternative vehicles for those individuals who cannot use other MTA transportation options.

Challenges That Physical or Health Disabilities Present

Think about how you have reacted in the past to people you have met who look different. The reactions of others have been and continue to be a major problem for individuals with physical and health problems and only compound the challenges they face because of their disabilities (Smart, 2001). Many physical and health differences are obvious, even at first meeting. As a consequence, individuals with these disabilities are forced often to deal with the negative reactions of others. Educators can play an important role in helping students without disabilities understand how their words and actions affect others. They can also help students with these disabilities prepare to enter a changing society that has greater opportunities for participation.

Has life improved for people with health and physical disabilities across the last 20 years? The answer to this question is a resounding "Yes!" Of course, these challenges should never be minimized, but society and schools have become more responsive. Since the initial passage in 1990 of the Americans with Disabilities Act (ADA), physical barriers (e.g., curbs and stairs) and discrimination have been reduced but certainly not eliminated. Unfortunately, physical barriers—such as doors too heavy to open, school entrances too steep to negotiate, and unsuitable bathrooms—still exist in many schools and public buildings. Even though not all problems are yet resolved, important changes signal a better future of access and inclusion in mainstream society.

Wouldn't it be wonderful if one challenge of physical or health disabilities was that people have too many choices for participation in inclusive and normalized experiences? Considering that only a relatively few opportunities existed some 20 years ago, it is important to note how quickly situations can change. Some improvements are highlighted in *Changing Times.* Here are a few other examples:

- The U.S. National Parks Service maintains accessible trails for outdoor adventures.
- Car rental agencies now have specially adapted vehicles for drivers with disabilities, allowing travelers with special needs to rent cars just like everyone else.

- Special cruise ships now offer passengers health services, such as dialysis for kidney patients.
- Special programs for children and youth offer skiing, boating, sailing, and camping adventures.
- Children who use wheelchairs grow up today playing wheelchair basketball, cheered on by cheerleaders who also use wheelchairs.
- Marathon races have special events for those who use wheelchairs as well as those who run using bionic limbs.
- Resorts and vacation planners and city tourism offices seek out travelers with disabilities by offering free rides in boats that have special seats or advertising accessible monorails.

Smart living arrangements for people with physical disabilities are no longer a dream for the future. Although not yet commonplace, apartment buildings with every accommodation and adaptive device imaginable now provide alternatives to nursing homes (Schwartz, 2005). Judy Bowman lives in such a place in Allentown, Pennsylvania. She uses her motorized wheelchair to visit friends who also live in the building, has a motorized lift that takes her from her bedroom to the bathroom (and even into the shower), and has appliances designed for people with limited motor functioning. Here are a few examples: Her washer and dryer are combined in one unit so she doesn't have to move heavy, wet clothes from one machine to another. The water taps and temperature adjustments are controlled with push buttons instead of faucets. And countertops are at the right level for someone who cannot stand. You would think that such living arrangements would be exorbitantly expensive. Not so when you consider that it is almost two and a half times more expensive to live in a nursing home and that, with assistance from the federal government, Judy pays only $500 per month in rent and enjoys the freedom of independent living immensely.

Making a Difference

The Hole in the Wall Camps

For many children, attending camp is a highpoint of their year. They look forward to the outdoor experience where they can meet new friends and participate in activities such as canoeing, telling stories and roasting marshmallows by a fire in the evening, hiking in the woods, swimming in a lake, and learning more about themselves. For children with chronic or life-threatening illnesses, going to summer camp was an impossible dream, because typical camps do not provide the medical attention they needed and because they felt too different from campers without special health care needs. Until 1988, no camps met the needs of these youngsters or their families.

In 1986 Paul Newman had a vision to make camping experiences available to children with chronic medical problems any time of the year and provide their families with a much-needed respite from constantly caring for their sick children. The first Hole in the Wall Camp opened in Connecticut. Revolving around a wild-west theme, it provides campers with a week-long experience where all their medical needs can be met free of cost to the campers and their families.

Staffed by hundreds of volunteers—including doctors, nurses, and camp counselors—more Hole in the Wall Camps followed in New York (Double H Ranch), Florida (Camp Boggie Creek), North Carolina (Victory Junction Gang), and California (Painted Turtle Camp). Camps have also been created in Ireland, France, Africa, and the Middle East. Almost 100,000 seriously ill children from 34 states and 27 countries have participated in these state-of-the-art programs.

To learn more about all of the Hole in the Wall Camps, to see videos of campers enjoying the facilities, to hear Paul Newman describe his joy about making a difference, and to learn how you might become involved, visit **www.holeinthewallcamps.org**

Physical or Health Disabilities Defined

The federal government considers physical disabilities and health disabilities as separate special education categories. Figure 9.1 illustrates a widely used organizational scheme for these two disabilities and shows how each category includes many different conditions. IDEA '04 uses the term **orthopedic impairments** to refer to conditions that in this text we call physical disabilities. Students with physical disabilities have problems with the structure or the functioning of their bodies. The federal government, through IDEA '04, uses the term **other health impairments** to describe, collectively, conditions and diseases that create special health care needs or health disabilities for students. The IDEA '04 definitions for these disabilities are found in Table 9.1. These two special education categories are not as separate or discrete as their definitions make them seem. For example, some conditions typically grouped under physical disabilities or orthopedic impairments also result in long-term health problems. One student with cerebral palsy may face physical challenges and need considerable assistance from a physical therapist (PT) to learn how to control movement, and yet have no special health care needs. Another student also with cerebral palsy may have both physical limitations and serious health care needs. Many children with health-related disabilities also have limitations to their physical well-being and require ongoing medical attention. And some combine major health issues with speech or language impairments (Owens, Metz, & Haas, 2003). Many of them present special needs at school. However, possibly more than is true of any other group, many students with physical or health problems require accommodations to participate in general education environments but do *not* require special education services.

Figure 9.1 • An Organizational Scheme.

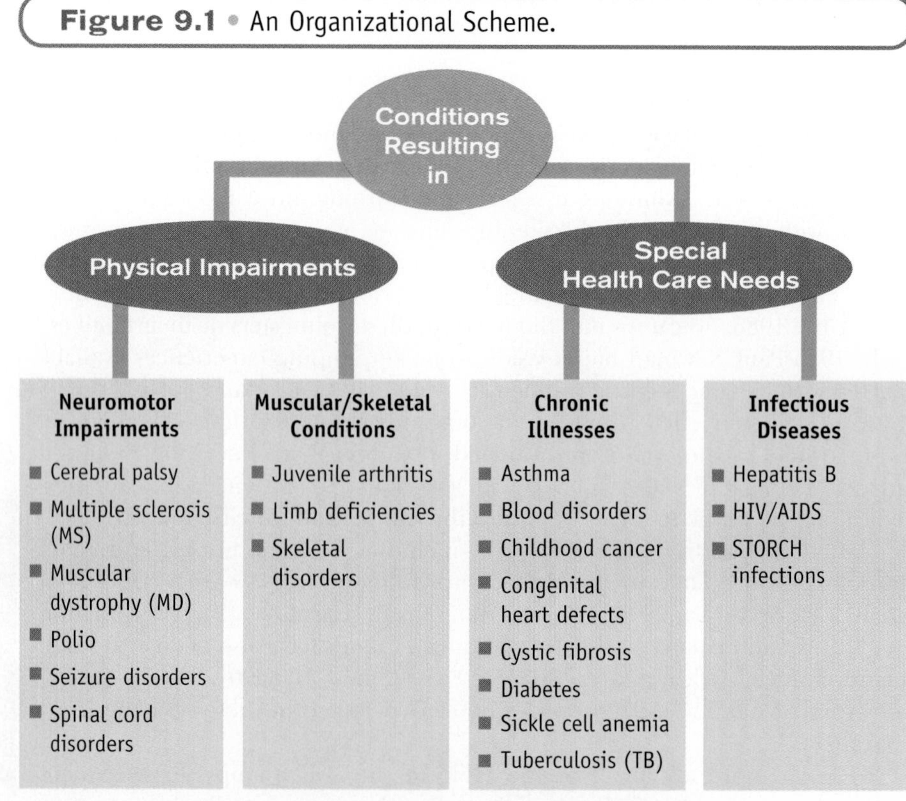

This diagram lists and categorizes the conditions, disorders, impairments, illnesses, and diseases that can result in physical challenges or special health care needs in children.

orthopedic impairments The term used in IDEA '04 for physical disabilities

other health impairments The term used in IDEA '04 for health disabilities

Table 9.1 • Definitions of Physical and Health Disabilities

Source	Physical Disabilities (Orthopedic Impairments)
Federal Government	Orthopedic impairment means a severe orthopedic impairment that adversely affects a child's educational performance. The term includes impairments caused by a congenital anomaly, impairments caused by disease (e.g., poliomyelitis, bone tuberculosis, etc.), and impairments from other causes (e.g., cerebral palsy, amputations, and fractures or burns that cause contractures).
	Health Disabilities (Other Health Impairments)
Federal Government	Other health impairment means having limited strength, vitality, or alertness, including a heightened alertness to environmental stimuli, that results in limited alertness with respect to the educational environment, that— 1. Is due to chronic or acute health problems such as asthma, attention deficit disorder or attention deficit hyperactivity disorder, diabetes, epilepsy, a heart condition, hemophilia, lead poisoning, leukemia, nephritis, rheumatic fever, and sickle cell anemia; and 2. Adversely affects a child's educational performance.

Sources: From 34 CFR Parts 300 and 303, Assistance to States for the Education of Children with Disabilities and the Early Intervention Program for Infants and Toddlers with Disabilities; Proposed Regulations (pp. 311–312), U.S. Department of Education, 2005a, *Federal Register*, Washington, DC.

Although we discussed attention deficit hyperactivity disorder (ADHD) in a separate chapter (see Chapter 6), note that IDEA '04 includes this condition as part of the "other health disabilities" category. In this chapter, we present information about conditions more traditionally considered physical or health disabilities.

Physical Disabilities

The two major groups of physical disabilities are

1 Neuromotor impairments
2 Muscular/skeletal conditions

Explanations for many conditions that lead to a physical disability are found in Table 9.2. Some diseases, such as polio, are now prevented in the United States. Others, such as multiple sclerosis, are found in adults but seldom seen in children; and some, such as muscular dystrophy and spina bifida, have extremely low prevalence rates. Other conditions, such as epilepsy and cerebral palsy, are more prevalent, and teachers should have knowledge about these conditions because they might teach students who have special needs as a consequence of them. **Neuromotor impairments** are conditions caused by damage to the central nervous system (the brain and the spinal cord). The resulting neurological impairment limits muscular control and movement. **Muscular/skeletal conditions** are impairments that affect the limbs or muscles. Individuals with these conditions usually have trouble controlling their movements, but the cause is not neurological. Some need to use special devices and technology even to do simple tasks—such as walking, eating, or writing—that most of us take for granted. And, because physical disabilities are often so obvious, it is easy to overlook the associated difficulties many of these individuals have with social skills (Coster & Haltiwanger, 2004).

When responsible educators encounter diseases and conditions they know little about, they seek out all the information they need to provide an appropriate education to students involved. Educators also understand that these disabilities

neuromotor impairments Conditions involving the nerves, muscles, and motor functioning

muscular/skeletal conditions Conditions affecting muscles or bones and resulting in limited functioning

Table 9.2 • Types of Physical Conditions

Condition	Description
Neuromotor Impairments	
Seizure disorders	*Epilepsy*, the most common type of neuromotor impairment in children, is a condition of recurrent convulsions or seizures caused by abnormal brain electrical activity. It is treated with medications and frequently is well controlled without any effect on learning or motor skills.
Cerebral palsy (CP)	*Cerebral palsy* is an incurable and nonprogressive condition caused by brain injury that sometimes limits the individual's ability to control muscle groups or motor functioning in specific areas of the body or, infrequently, the entire body. It may be associated with multiple disabilities. Physical therapy offers benefits.
Spinal cord disorders	*Spina bifida*, a neural tube birth defect, is the improper closure of the protective tissue surrounding the spinal cord. It results in limited neurological control for organs and muscles controlled by nerves that originate below the level of the lesion. Increasing numbers of children have suffered traumatic head or spinal cord injuries resulting in permanent disabilities. *Spinal cord injuries*, typically the result of injuries from accidents or abuse, can cause severe motor impairments and even paralysis. Health care needs for both groups include good skin care, management of bladder and bowel care, and physical therapy.
Polio	*Polio*, caused by a viral infection, almost totally prevented in children immunized in the United States, attacks the spinal cord and can result in paralysis and motor disabilities. Health care needs parallel those for spinal cord disorders.
Muscular dystrophy (MD)	*Muscular dystrophy*, an exceptionally rare, incurable, and progressive disease, weakens and then destroys the affected individual's muscles. Health care needs center on lung function support, prevention of pneumonia, and physical therapy.
Multiple sclerosis (MS)	*Multiple sclerosis*, a chronic disease typically occurring in adults, causes the myelin covering the nerve fibers of the brain and spinal cord to deteriorate, impeding the transmission of electrical signals from the brain to other parts of the body. Health care needs parallel those for MD.
Muscular/Skeletal Conditions	
Juvenile arthritis	*Juvenile arthritis* is a disease caused by an autoimmune process resulting in swelling, immobility, and pain in joints. Health care needs include medication to suppress the process and orthopedic and physical therapy to maintain function in small and large joints.
Limb deficiencies	*Skeletal problems* in which the individual's limb(s) is shortened, absent, or malformed. They may occur from congenital conditions or from injuries. Health care needs focus on adaptive interventions to support or improve functioning of the affected limb(s).
Skeletal disorders	*Dwarfism*, a condition caused by abnormal development of long bones, may result in varying degrees of motor disabilities. Health care needs may include human growth hormone to improve height.
	Osteogenesis imperfecta, sometimes known as brittle bone disease, is a condition in which normal calcification of the bones does not occur, leading to breakage and abnormal healing of bones with accompanying loss of height. Health care interventions include physical therapy and medical care.
	Scoliosis, a curvature of the spine that occurs in children during puberty and may, in severe form, limit mobility of the trunk. Health care needs include monitoring of the amount of curvature of the spine and appropriate interventions to arrest the process.

range in severity from mild to severe. And, in many cases, they are only one of multiple conditions an individual must face (Kennedy & Horn, 2004; McDonnell, Hardman, & McDonnell, 2003). For example, epilepsy is frequently found in children with mental retardation. But remember never to make the terrible error of associating health or physical disabilities with a cognitive disability. They do not always go hand in hand. Now, let's focus on some specific physical disabilities.

Neuromotor Impairments

Estimates are that some 315,000 students between age 6 through 14 have epilepsy; many of these students have other disabilities or conditions (e.g., mental retardation, cerebral palsy) as well (Epilepsy Foundation of America [EFA], 2005a). **Epilepsy**, also called **seizure disorders** or convulsive disorders, is a condition where the individual has recurrent seizures resulting from sudden, excessive, spontaneous, and abnormal discharge of neurons in the brain. Seizures can be accompanied by changes in the person's motor or sensory functioning and can also result in loss of consciousness. Today, medication helps control and even "cure" seizure disorders (EFA, 2005b). For some 70 percent of those affected, medication ends the occurrence of seizures. For those with other coexisting conditions, such as mental retardation and cerebral palsy, the rate of successful treatment through medication is much lower.

Another neuromotor impairment encountered in schools is cerebral palsy: **Cerebral palsy** is not a disease but, rather, a nonprogressive and noninfectious condition that affects body movement and muscle coordination. It is a result of damage, usually because of insufficient oxygen getting to the brain. Cerebral palsy that occurs before or during the birth process is called *congenital cerebral palsy* and accounts for some 70 percent of cases (United Cerebral Palsy Association [UCP], 2001). *Acquired cerebral palsy* occurs after birth but during early childhood and is usually caused by brain damage resulting from accidents, brain infections, or child abuse. Regrettably, once it is acquired, it cannot be cured (at least today).

Muscular/Skeletal Conditions

One of the muscular/skeletal conditions most commonly seen in children is limb deficiencies. **Limb deficiencies** can be the result of a missing or nonfunctioning arm or leg and can be either acquired or congenital. Regardless of when the impairment occurred, the result is a major impediment to normal physical activity and functioning. Although the root of the disability is physical, many individuals with a limb deficiency have difficulty adjusting to their situation. The attitudes of teachers and classmates, and of course the support given by family members, can be major contributors to their psychological health. **Robotics**—the science and technology that develop computer-controlled mechanical devices, including artificial arms and legs—now provides much assistance to those with missing limbs. A good example is the prosthetic arm designed by Hanger Prosthetics and Orthothics for surfer Bethany Hamilton who lost her arm to a shark attack. The way her new arm works is shown in Figure 9.2. And artificial legs (such as the C-leg developed by Otto Boch and the Boston Digital Arm developed by Liberating Technologies) also use microprocessors, hydraulics, and electronic sensors to allow a freedom of movement thought to be impossible only a few years ago (except, of course, by screenwriters who created characters like Robo-cop).

A relatively common muscular/skeletal condition affecting joints and the function of muscles is **juvenile arthritis**. Some 300,000 students have juvenile arthritis (Arthritis Foundation of America [AFA], 2005). Just over one-fourth of students with juvenile arthritis qualify for special education services; most of the others receive accommodations through Section 504. Although there are many different forms of this disease, it is typically chronic and painful. Juvenile arthritis usually develops in early childhood and can cause many absences from school. These children often need help keeping up with their classmates because they miss so much

epilepsy or **seizure disorders** A tendency to experience recurrent seizures resulting in convulsions; caused by abnormal discharges of neurons in the brain

cerebral palsy A neuromotor impairment; a nonprogressive disease resulting in motor difficulties associated with communication problems and mobility problems

limb deficiencies Missing or nonfunctioning arms or legs resulting in mobility problems

robotics Use of high-tech devices to perform motor skills

juvenile arthritis A chronic and painful muscular condition seen in children

Figure 9.2 • Prosthetic Arm

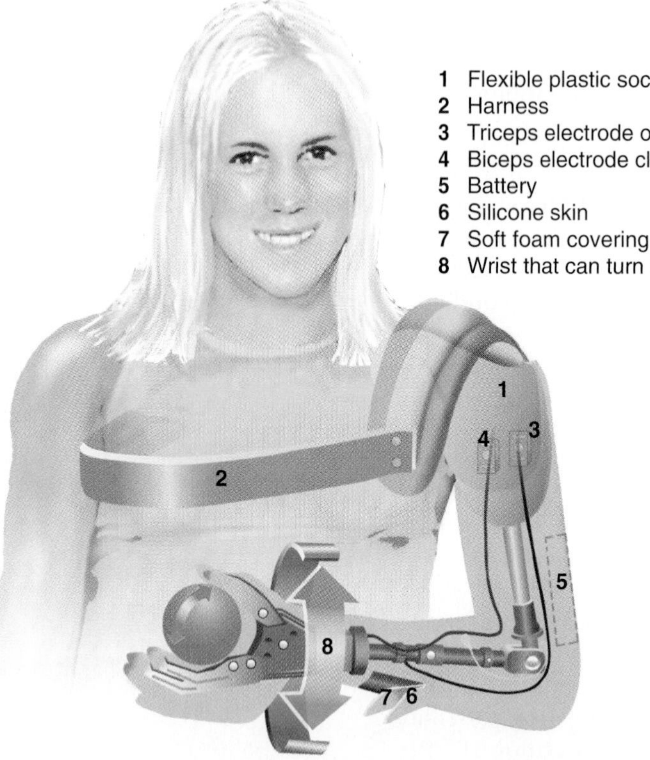

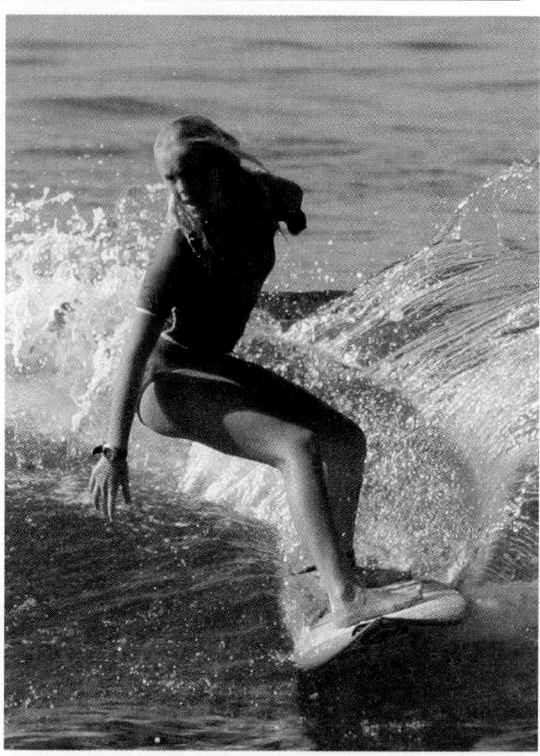

This prosthetic arm was developed for Bethany Hamilton after she lost her arm to a shark attack in March of 2004. She is shown competing in her first surfing tournament since losing her left arm in a shark attack.

Source: Hanger Prosthetics and Orthothics Inc. Redrawn by permission.

class instruction. Teachers must understand that their ability to move may be inconsistent (better at different times of the day) and that sitting for extended periods of time can cause them to become stiff and to experience considerable pain. These children need to be allowed to move around a lot. Those who have a high rate of absences probably need tutoring and extra help to keep up with their peers (AFA, 2005). Some promising medical treatments can reduce the amount of disability from the disease. However, such medications can have side effects that alter some aspect of personality and physical appearance.

Health Disabilities

The two types of health disabilities are

1 Chronic illnesses

2 Infectious diseases

Study Table 9.3. It includes definitions of illnesses and diseases seen in children. Of course, some general principles apply to all children who are sick, whatever the cause. All children have episodes of illness during childhood, but most of these are of short duration and not very serious. For a small number, however, their illnesses are chronic, lasting for years or even a lifetime. Students with chronic illnesses often do not feel well enough to consistently focus their attention on the instruction or may not be at school when important content is presented.

medically fragile A term used to describe the status of individuals with health disabilities

For many years the term *medically fragile* was used to describe all children with special health care needs, but it is now more selectively applied. **Medically fragile** is a status; it is not assigned to any specific condition but, rather, reflects the individual's

Table 9.3 • Types of Health Conditions

Condition	Description
Chronic Illnesses	
Asthma	*Asthma*, a condition caused by narrowing of airways accompanied by inflammatory changes in the lining of the airways, may result in severe difficulty in breathing with chronic coughing. Health care needs include appropriate medications, environmental modifications, and monitoring and frequently result in no limitation of activities.
Cystic fibrosis	*Cystic fibrosis* is a genetic birth defect that results in chronic lung infections and digestive difficulties. Health care interventions include aggressive care of lung infections and function and replacement of required enzymes for aiding digestion.
Diabetes	*Diabetes* is the loss of the ability of the pancreas to produce enough insulin, resulting in problems with sugar metabolism. Health care needs include the monitoring of blood sugar levels, appropriate diet and exercise regimens, and knowledgeable response for insulin reactions.
Congenital heart defects	*Congenital heart conditions* can result in high rates of school absences for specialized health care. Most have had surgical intervention and medical monitoring by specialists. Health care needs include taking medications during the school day.
Tuberculosis (TB)	*Tuberculosis*, a disease caused by bacterial infection, rarely causes severe disease in children older than infancy. Most often the bacteria remain sequestered and harmless until late adulthood or when the body's immune system fails. The rates of infection are on the rise in many parts of the United States.
Childhood cancer	*Cancer*, the abnormal growth of cells, can affect any organ. The most common types of cancer in children are leukemia and lymphomas. While going through treatment, children may feel too ill to profit from classroom instruction. *Leukemia* causes an abnormal increase in the white blood cells, which are important in the body's defenses against infection. It often results in anemia and enlargement of the lymph glands, spleen, and liver. *Lymphomas* are malignant and cause enlargement of the lymph nodes.
Blood disorders	*Hemophilia*, a genetic condition typically linked with males, is characterized by poor blood clotting, which can result in massive bleeding from cuts and internal hemorrhaging from bruises. *Sickle cell anemia*, a hereditary disorder, causes a distortion in the red blood cells that restricts their passage through the blood vessels.
Infectious Diseases	
HIV and AIDS	*Human immunodeficiency virus (HIV)*, a potentially fatal viral infection that in school-aged children results from transmission from a mother infected with the virus to her newborn child or from transfusion with blood or blood products carrying the virus, causes *acquired immunodeficiency syndrome (AIDS)*. Health care needs include careful monitoring of general health, specialists to care for potentially overwhelming lung infections, and medications that slow or cure infections. The infection is acquired primarily through the exchange of body fluids in older children, through sexual abuse in younger children, through sexual activity in adolescents, and through intravenous drug use. Health care needs include sources of confidential care, counseling, and health education.
STORCH	*STORCH* is the acronym for a group of congenital infections that have the potential of causing severe, multiple impairments. It stands for syphilis, toxoplasmosis, other, rubella, cytomegalovirus, and herpes.
Hepatitis B	*Hepatitis B*, a viral disease, is infectious and causes inflammation of the liver. It is characterized by jaundice and fever. Cases of this dangerous virus are on the increase.

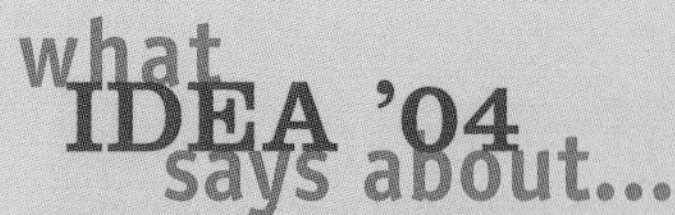

Eligibility and Educational Significance

The impact of the disability on a child's education is a key consideration. In order to qualify for services under the category of "orthopedic impairment," a student must meet two criteria:

1. The student must have a severe orthopedic impairment.
2. The impairment must adversely affect educational performance.

Similarly, to qualify under the "other health impairment" category, the student's condition must

- Result in limited strength, vitality, or alertness (this can include a heightened alertness to environmental stimuli that subsequently reduces the student's alertness to the educational environment)
- Be due to chronic or acute health problems
- Adversely affect educational performance

health situation. Students can move in and out of fragile status. It is important to understand that because of medical technology, a greater number of medically fragile children now survive health crises. In the past, many of these youngsters would not have lived long enough to go to school. Others would have been too sick to attend their neighborhood schools and would have received most of their schooling through hospital-based or home-based instruction. Even though many are now stable enough to attend school, they require ongoing medical management. For most, it is necessary for teachers to be familiar with procedures that must be followed if an emergency occurs. The "if, thens" must be carefully outlined and planned in collaboration with doctors and the medical profession (Emory University Medical School, 2003; Heller et al., 2000). Although the contingencies for the "worst case scenarios" must be arranged, in most cases the accommodations required for these students are not terribly dramatic. (However, not having backup power for a student's ventilator could have disastrous results.)

Chronic Illnesses

The most common chronic illness among children is **asthma**, a pulmonary disease causing labored breathing that is sometimes accompanied by shortness of breath, wheezing, and a cough. It is the leading cause of school absences and hospitalizations of children (Asthma Foundation, 2005; National Institute of Environmental Health Sciences [NIEHS], 2005). A combination of three events causes the wheezing: (1) tightening of the muscles around the bronchial tubes, (2) swelling of the tissues in these tubes, and (3) an increase of secretions in these tubes. Years ago, many people believed asthma to be a psychological disorder. It is not; its origin is physical. Many factors (such as chalk dust, dirt in the environment, dust mites, and pollen) can trigger an asthma attack, as can physical activity or exertion. Many students who have asthma are unable to participate in sports or even in physical education activities. As IDEA '04 points out, few of these students actually need special education (see *What IDEA '04 Says About Eligibility and Educational Significance*), but they might need special accommodations so that their illness does not hinder their learning.

Infectious Diseases

In part because they are so frightening and in part because they are so dangerous, infectious diseases catch our attention. However, in many instances, occurrence is rare and the public reaction to those who contract the disease is irrational. Here's an example. The **human immunodeficiency virus (HIV)** is a very serious disease and a potentially fatal viral infection that is transmitted primarily through the exchange of bodily fluids in unprotected sex or by contaminated needles. Before blood-screening procedures were instituted, the virus was also transmitted in blood transfusions. HIV is the virus responsible for **acquired immunodeficiency syndrome (AIDS)**, a deadly disease that destroys the immune system and can be communicated to an unborn child by an infected mother. From the beginning of the epidemic through 2002, a total of 9,300 American children were infected with HIV/AIDS (National Institute of Allergy and Infectious Disease, 2004). Because of its very low prevalence among children, few teachers have a student with AIDS; we mention the disease here because of the significant media attention devoted to it. The effects of the infection in children include central nervous system damage, additional infections, developmental delay, motor problems, psychosocial stresses, and death. HIV/AIDS is an infectious disease, but unlike most others, such as flu

asthma The most common, chronic health condition resulting in difficulty breathing

human immunodeficiency virus (HIV) A microorganism that infects the immune system, impairing the body's ability to fight infections

acquired immunodeficiency syndrome (AIDS) A usually fatal medical syndrome caused by infection from the human immunodeficiency virus (HIV) and the common cold, it is serious and life-threatening. For many years, parents and educators were concerned that noninfected children could catch the disease from a classmate. It is now clear that this is highly unlikely. With proper precautions (the use of gloves when bandaging a child's cut finger and normal sanitary procedures such as frequently washing your hands), everyone at school is safe and will not catch this disease.

Characteristics

The characteristics of students with physical or health disabilities are as unique to the individuals as the conditions that created their special needs. The health care needs of some children are so consuming that everything else becomes secondary. Other students, such as some with physical disabilities, require substantial alterations to the physical environment, so that learning is accessible to them, but are quite similar to their typical classmates in many learning characteristics. For still others, their health situation requires intense special accommodations at some points in time, but less so at other times.

The education professionals who make a real difference in the academic lives of these students are first and foremost responsive to the individual learning needs they bring to school. Thus, instead of making generalizations about these students, here we will discuss three of the more common conditions seen at schools. (Remember, however, that both physical and health disabilities are low incidence special education categories.) We will look more closely, then, at

- Epilepsy
- Cerebral palsy
- Sickle cell anemia

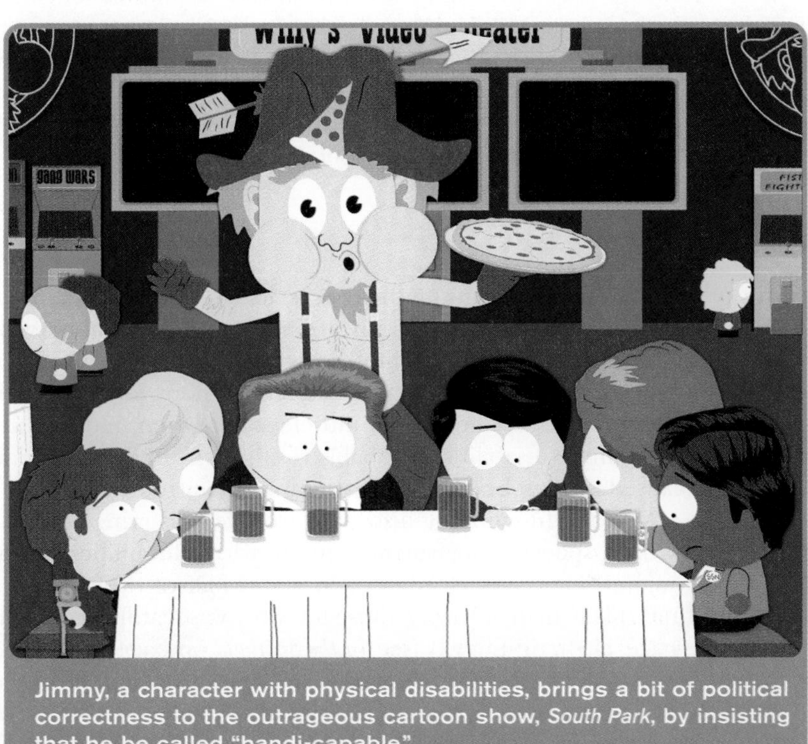

Jimmy, a character with physical disabilities, brings a bit of political correctness to the outrageous cartoon show, *South Park*, by insisting that he be called "handi-capable."

Epilepsy

Seizures may involve the entire brain (**generalized seizures**) or only a portion of the brain (**partial seizures**). The frequency of seizures may vary from a single isolated incident to hundreds in a day. Some individuals actually anticipate their seizures because they experience a **preictal stage**, or an **aura**, and have heightened sensory signals of an impending seizure, such as a peculiar smell, taste, vision, sound, or action. Others might experience a change in their behavior. Knowing about an aura pattern is helpful, because it enables the person to assume a safe position or warn the teacher and companions before a seizure begins.

The Epilepsy Foundation of America (2005a) identifies four main types of seizures:

1 Absence seizures
2 Simple partial seizures
3 Complex partial (psychomotor) seizures
4 Generalized tonic–clonic seizures

Some seizures are difficult for the individual involved and others to recognize. For example, **absence seizures** or **petit mal seizures** are characterized by short lapses in consciousness. Because absence seizures are not dramatic, a teacher might wrongly assume that the child is merely daydreaming or not paying attention. **Simple partial seizures**, which cause people affected to think that their environments are distorted and strange and that inexplicable events and feelings have occurred, can also be difficult to identify. With these seizures, teachers might incorrectly believe that the student is acting out or exhibiting bizarre behavior patterns. **Complex partial seizures** (also called psychomotor or focal seizures) are short in duration, and the individual returns to normal activities quickly. Sometimes, teachers interpret the child's behavior during this type of seizure as misbehavior or clowning. This situation can be confusing to the child, who is unaware of the episode. **Generalized tonic–clonic seizures** (formerly referred to as grand mal seizures) are the most serious type of seizure and result in convulsions and loss of consciousness. The dramatic behaviors exhibited during a tonic-clonic seizure may at first be frightening to the teacher and to other students in the class. The student may fall to the floor and experience a stiff (tonic) phase, in which the muscles become rigid, followed by a clonic phase, in which the individual's arms and legs jerk. *Tips for Classroom Management* describes how to manage each type of seizure at school.

generalized seizures Seizures involving the entire brain

partial seizures Seizures involving only part of the brain

preictal stage or **aura** Warning of an imminent seizure in the form of heightened sensory awareness

absence seizures or **petit mal seizures** Seizures characterized by a short lapse in consciousness

simple partial seizures Seizures that cause people affected to think their environments are distorted or strange

complex partial seizures A type of epilepsy causing a lapse in consciousness

generalized tonic–clonic seizures Grand mal seizures; the most serious type of epilepsy, resulting in convulsions and loss of consciousness

Cerebral Palsy

The severity of the condition depends on the precise location of brain damage, the degree of brain damage, and the extent of involvement of the central nervous system (UCP, 2001). Individuals with cerebral palsy whose motor functioning is affected show these characteristics alone or in combination: jerky movements, spasms, involuntary movements, and lack of muscle tone. Often, individuals with cerebral palsy have multiple disabilities, probably resulting from the same damage to the brain that caused the cerebral palsy. For example, many individuals who have severe difficulties in motor functioning also have trouble mastering oral speech. These individuals have speech impairments and physical disabilities. Although some degree of mental retardation is present in about half of the children with cerebral palsy, others, like Christy Brown (whose life story was featured in the movie *My Left Foot*—see page 119) and Lizzy B (see *In the Spotlight* on page 121), are intellectually gifted. It is a tragic mistake to assume that cerebral palsy and mental retardation always occur in combination. Figure 9.3 on page 328 illustrates four ways in which areas of the body can be affected by cerebral palsy: monoplegia, paraplegia, hemiplegia, and quadriplegia.

*tips for Classroom Management

MANAGING SEIZURES AT SCHOOL

1 *Absence seizure:* Momentary loss of awareness, sometimes accompanied by blinking or movements of the face or arms; may be frequent; fully aware after an episode
- Be sure key parts of the lesson are not missed

2 *Simple partial seizure:* Consciousness not lost; unable to control body movements; experiences feelings, visions, sounds, and smells that are not real
- Comfort and reassure if the child is frightened

3 *Complex partial seizure:* Consciousness clouded, unresponsive to instructions, inappropriate and undirected behaviors, sleepwalking appearance, of short duration (a minute or two); prolonged confusion after an episode, no recall of seizure
- Gently guide child back to seat
- Speak softly
- Insure child's safety
- Ignore uncontrollable behaviors
- Ensure full consciousness before changing locations
- Help child sort out confusions

4 *Generalized tonic clonic seizure:* Body stiffens and jerks; may fall, lose consciousness, lose bladder control, have erratic breathing; lasts several minutes; can be confused, weary, or belligerent afterwards
- Remain calm
- Reassure classmates
- Ease child to floor
- Clear area
- Rest head on a pillow
- Turn on side
- Do not put anything in child's mouth
- Do not restrain
- Let rest after jerking ceases
- Re-engage in class participation

Source: Adapted from *Managing Seizures at School,* Epilepsy Foundation Answerplace (2005a). Available from: **www.epilepsyfoundation.org/answerplace/social/education/k12/managing.cfm**

Another way in which cerebral palsy is classified is in terms of how the individual's movement is affected:

- **Spastic cerebral palsy**: Movements are very stiff.
- **Athetoid cerebral palsy**: Involuntary movements are purposeless or uncontrolled, and purposeful movements are contorted.
- **Ataxia cerebral palsy**: Movements such as walking are disrupted by impairments of balance and depth perception.

Many individuals with cerebral palsy have impaired mobility and poor muscle development. Even if they can walk, their efforts may require such exertion and be so inefficient that they need canes, crutches, or a wheelchair to get around. Students with

spastic cerebral palsy
Characterized by uncontrolled tightening or pulling of muscles

athetoid cerebral palsy
Characterized by purposeless and uncontrolled involuntary movements

ataxia cerebral palsy
Characterized by movement disrupted by impaired balance and depth perception

Figure 9.3 • Areas of the Body Affected by Cerebral Palsy

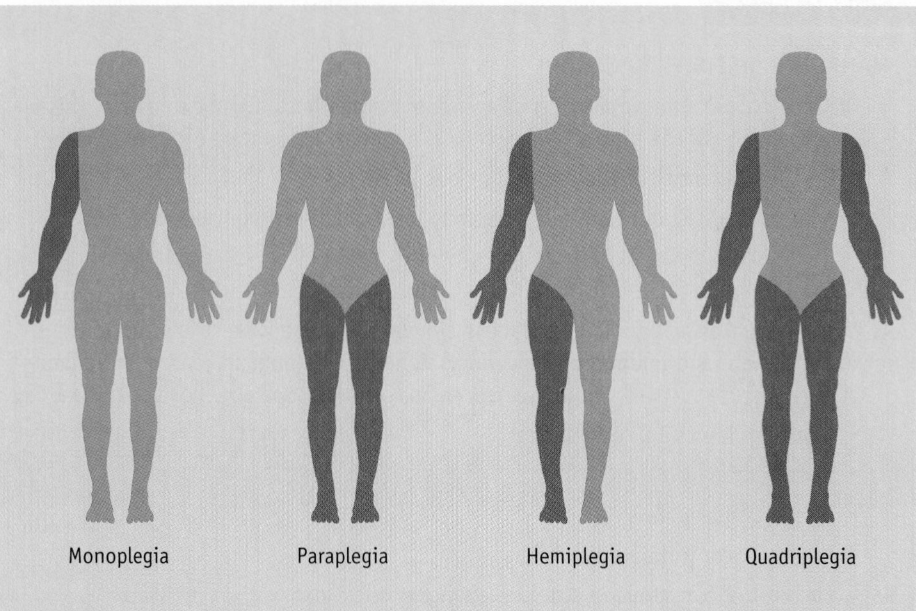

cerebral palsy may also need braces to help support the affected limbs and make them more functional or to prevent contractures that would eventually lead to bone deformities and further mobility limitations. Proper positioning of the body also must be considered. Many children need wedges, pillows, and individually designed chairs and worktables so that they can be comfortable; breathe easier; avoid injuries, contractures, and deformities; and participate in group activities.

Sickle Cell Anemia

Some diseases strike one group of students more than another. For example, **sickle cell anemia** is a hereditary, life-threatening blood disorder, and 95 percent of all cases occur among African Americans (Guthrie, 2001). This condition causes the red blood cells to become rigid and take on a crescent, or sickle, shape. During what is called a "sickling crisis," this rigidity and the crescent shape of the cells do not allow blood to flow through the vessels, depriving some tissues of oxygen and resulting in extreme pain, swollen joints, high fever, and even strokes. *Tips for Effective Teaching* provides important information about appropriate responses to characteristics of sickle cell anemia and how best to help students who have special health care needs because of this condition (Emory School of Medicine, 2005).

Prevalence

sickle cell anemia A hereditary blood disorder that inhibits blood flow; African Americans are most at risk for this health impairment

Physical or health disabilities in children are low incidence disabilities (see Figure 1.2 on page 13 for a review of the prevalence rates among students in special education categories). Despite the overall low prevalence rates for these two disabilities, to the individuals and families that are affected, even one case is too many. In the 2003–2004 school year, 0.88 percent of all students were served through the federal government's "other health disabilities" category. This percentage includes those students identified with ADHD as their primary disability and explains why this category is the biggest of the low incidence disabilities. The physical disabilities category includes some 0.13 percent of all students. Together, then, these two categories represent about 1 percent of all American students (U.S. Department of Education, 2005b). Within this 1 percent, there is considerable variability and many different diseases and conditions. To get a better understanding of this diversity, let's consider a few specific prevalence rates (Asthma Foundation, 2005; EFA, 2005b; Centers for Disease Control, 2005a, 2005b; National Human Genome Research Institute, National Institutes of Health, 2005; National Institute of Allergy and Infectious Disease, 2004; National Institute of Environmental Health Sciences [NIEHS], 2005; UCP, 2001).

- Asthma, the leading cause of school absenteeism is on the rise and affects over 5 million children, some 8 to 12 percent of all students.
- About 1 percent of the general population has epilepsy, but substantially less than 1 percent of students do. Medication controls about 80 percent of all cases.
- About 0.03 percent of all children have cerebral palsy, and some of them do not require special education services.
- Pediatric AIDS is on the decline. In 1998 a total of 382 cases of pediatric AIDS occurred in the United States; in 2003 that number had dropped to 92. However, although still low (less than 5 percent of all cases), the rate of youth between the ages of 13 and 24 with HIV/AIDS increased between 1999 and 2003. More than 95 percent of all people infected with HIV live in developing nations.
- A startling 8 percent of African Americans have inherited sickle cell anemia.
- The last case of polio (a viral infection that attacks the nerve cells in the spinal cord that control muscle function) in the United States was reported in 1979, and it is almost eradicated worldwide. A total of 748 confirmed cases in 2003 occurred in only six countries.

TEACHING STUDENTS WITH SICKLE CELL ANEMIA

1. Emotional stress or strenuous exercise can trigger a sickling crisis. Monitor the student carefully.
2. Work closely with the student and family. Develop plans for peers to bring assignments home and explain them when the student has to be absent.
3. Frequent hospitalizations are common. Provide students with "make-up" work so they can stay current with assignments when hospitalized or absent from school.
4. Pain episodes are prevented by drinking more water. Let the student keep a water bottle at hand and allow for frequent bathroom breaks.
5. Pain episodes are prevented by avoiding extreme temperatures. Do not let the student either get overheated or be exposed to excessive cold.
6. Anemia causes people to tire easily. Encourage rest periods, and let the individual quietly step out of sports and recreational activities.
7. Sickle cell anemia places the individual at risk for other infections. Keep safe and sterile classroom and school environments.
8. Be alert for instances of fever, headache, chest pain, abdominal pain, numbness, or weakness. If you observe one of these symptoms, call a doctor or the school nurse.
9. Children are sensitive. Avoid calling undue attention to the child.

Source: Adapted from the Georgia Comprehensive Sickle Cell Center, www.SCinfo/teacher.htm, The Sickle Cell Foundation of Georgia, Emory University School of Medicine, Department of Pediatrics, Morehouse School of Medicine, www.emory.edu/PEDS/SICKLE/teacher.htm. Retrieved July 4, 2005.

Causes and Prevention

There are almost as many different causes, preventions, and treatments as there are different illnesses, diseases, and conditions that result in disabilities. Instead of discussing these specifically for each condition, we will cite some common themes and conditions as examples. Individual students' programs must reflect the impact of the disability on them, their own and their family's priorities, and the skills that must be mastered to achieve independent living as an adult. The summary in Table 9.4 was designed to broaden your understanding of these children's conditions, what caused them, and how they might have been prevented.

Table 9.4 • Causes and Prevention of Physical or Health Disabilities

Physical Disabilities		Health Disabilities	
Causes	**Prevention**	**Causes**	**Prevention**
Motor vehicle accidents	Child restraints Safety belts Auto air bags Motorcycle helmets	Poisoning/toxins	Knowledge of resources in emergencies Safe storage of poisons
Water and diving accidents	Diving safety Swimming safety	Diseases (polio, measles; colds, flu)	Vaccinations Good hygiene
Gunshot wounds	Gun control Weapons training Locked storage of ammunition	Premature birth	Prenatal care Access to health care
Sports injuries	Headgear and protective equipment Safe playing fields Conditioning/training	Asthma	Removal of allergens
Child abuse	Family support services Parent training Alert teachers	HIV infection	Use of gloves around blood Abstinence or safe sex Avoidance of drugs Screening of blood and plasma

Causes

The many causes that result in physical and health disabilities can be grouped into some general areas:

- Infections and allergies
- Heredity
- Accidents and injuries
- Multiple factors
- "Unknown"

Infections cause many different kinds of special health care needs. Hepatitis B, HIV/AIDS, CMV, and STORCH are some examples. In children under age 13, the cause of HIV infection can be traced primarily to the risk behaviors of their parents. In contrast, the HIV infections of adolescents are caused primarily by their own risk behaviors. Asthma is most often the result of an allergic reaction to certain substances (allergens) found in the environment. A variety of substances can trigger reactions, and they vary with the individual; for some people it may be foods, for others plants, environmental pollutants, chemicals, cigarette smoke, dust mites, cockroaches, pets, or viruses.

Genetic profiles are the cause of many disabilities. For many disabilities, where only a few years ago the cause was unknown, a genetic link is now being documented. The most common inherited blood disorder in the United States is sickle cell anemia (National Human Genome Research Institute, 2005). Hemophilia, which occurs in only 1 in every 10,000 births, seems to be linked to the X chromosome because it is carried by the mother and passed on to the son. Muscular dystrophy, a relatively rare neuromotor disease (with an incidence of about 2 in every 10,000 people) is another hereditary condition.

Injuries, both from accidents and from child abuse, can lead to cerebral palsy, seizure disorders, spinal cord injuries, brain damage, and even death. For example, spinal cord injury in young children, which is often caused by automobile accidents, can also result from child abuse. In older children, the most common causes of spinal cord injury are car accidents, falls and jumps, gunshot wounds, and diving accidents. These cases underscore the importance of safety equipment (e.g., seat belts, helmets, protective gear) and of caution.

Some conditions have multiple causes. In congenital cerebral palsy, a developing infant may have been deprived of enough oxygen when something went wrong during birth. Cerebral palsy may also result from the effects of premature birth, very low birth weight, blood type (Rh) incompatibility, a pregnant mother's infection, or attacks on the fetus or newborn by dangerous microorganisms (UCP, 2001). Acquired cerebral palsy can be caused by vehicle accidents, brain infections such as meningitis, poisoning through toxins such as lead (ingested in paint chips from walls), serious falls, or injuries from child abuse.

Prevention

It is important to remember that many disabilities occur through no one's fault and cannot be avoided. For most conditions that cannot be prevented, the effects can be lessened through treatment. Other physical and health conditions are relatively easy to prevent. You have learned about many of the keys to preventing disabilities. These perennial themes cannot be overemphasized:

- Good prenatal care
- Universal immunization programs
- Avoidance of injuries
- Hygiene

Access to health care for pregnant women and later for young children can prevent many disabilities and reduce the impact of those that cannot be avoided (Children's Defense Fund [CDF], 2004). Prenatal care can ensure access to intensive medical care for the mother and infant if problems occur; provide diagnosis and treatment for diseases in the mother that can damage the developing infant; and help prevent exposure of the fetus to infections, viruses, drugs, alcohol, and other toxins.

Vaccinations (immunizations) safeguard children from infectious diseases and avoid millions of dollars in health care costs and the complication of millions of lives by disabilities. Vaccines have almost eradicated some diseases in the United States and have thus reduced the rate of disabilities caused by such diseases. Remarkably, however, only 78 percent of America's children are protected (CDF, 2004). One reason is restricted access to health care for those families living in poverty or without health insurance. Another reason is faulty information about the risk of disabilities caused by vaccines. The Institute of Medicine's Immunization Safety Review Committee and the Centers for Disease Control have found *no link* between vaccines and conditions such

TOLES © 2004 *The Washington Post.* Reprinted with permission of Universal Press Syndicate. All rights reserved.

Table 9.5 • Preventing Disease

- Refer sick children to the school nurse and to the parents.
- Keep play areas, toys, and other objects in the classroom disinfected (clean) so they will not transmit diseases.
- Have all students wash their hands frequently.
- Use some commonsense hygienic precautions at school.
- Use fresh pairs of disposable gloves when helping a bleeding child or cleaning up an accident, and safely dispose of the soiled gloves.

as autism, ADHD, language delays, sudden infant death syndrome, multiple sclerosis, sleep disorders, emotional or behavior disorders, tics, and asthma.

Protection from injuries is another way to prevent many physical disabilities. The use of seat belts, car seats, helmets, and other protective devices (e.g., knee and elbow protectors) can reduce injuries from motor vehicle and sports-related accidents. Proper storage of poisons and household chemical and supervision of their use also prevents physical and health disabilities. Finally, family support services and training in effective parenting avoid harm in two ways: by preventing child abuse and by making parents aware of the dangers of physical punishment.

Using commonsense precautionary measures, school personnel can help reduce—though not eliminate—the spread of infection (Edens, Murdick, & Gartin, 2003). Students usually become infected outside of the school, infect others, and then get sick themselves. Regardless, good hygiene does prevent some instances of disease. Table 9.5 lists some important, yet simple, measures that teachers can employ to protect themselves and their students from contagious diseases present in many classroom environments.

Overcoming Challenges

Remember that some conditions, even when the cause is known, can't be prevented. Also, treatment doesn't guarantee a "cure," but the impact of the condition, its severity, or the frequency of its occurrence might be reduced. Here are a few examples.

Medical advances have helped many individuals who would otherwise have faced overwhelming challenges. For example, although surgery is not a complete cure for all spinal column (neural tube) defects, its use in infants born with these conditions (to repair their backs and prevent infections such as meningitis) generally avoids mental retardation. Some children with spina bifida have hydrocephaly, a buildup of excess fluid in the brain. For them, a shunt surgically implanted to drain excess spinal fluid from the brain reduces the degree of or eliminates associated mental retardation. On the horizon are more medical advances, such as marrow and cord blood stem cell transplants to eliminate or reduce the impact of sickle cell anemia (Emory University School of Medicine, 2003).

Prevention and treatment are not just in the hands of those in the medical profession. Although teachers can't cure diseases, they can and do make a real difference in reducing the frequency of episodes of some illnesses by carefully considering the classroom environments they foster. As you have learned, asthma is often triggered by exposure to specific allergens, many of which can be eliminated. This reduces the chance of asthma attacks and cuts down on the resulting illnesses and absences from school (NIEHS, 2005; National Association of School Nurses, 2002). Teachers also play a very special role by helping these individuals find activities that reduce unsafe physical exertion. For all students with health disabilities, consultation with the student, the parents, the school nurse, and perhaps the student's physician leads to the development of plans that reduce the probability of health-related episodes or can be put into action when a crisis occurs.

Advances in assistive devices or equipment—wheelchairs, prosthetic devices, computers—help individuals with physical or health disabilities overcome some challenges. Such technology improves access and participation at school, in the community, and in all aspects of daily life. For example, special wheelchairs have been designed for marathon races, basketball, and skiing. Some chairs have electronic switches to enable persons with only partial head or neck control or finger or foot control to move about independently. Prosthetic devices with computer chips and hydraulic features provide freedom of movement never thought possible only a few years ago. Computer technology also helps those who face challenges from restricted movement. For example, computers can be operated by voice, the gaze of an eye, a mouthstick, a sip-and-puff breath stick, a single finger, a toe, a headstick, or other creative method suitable to an individual's abilities. Special keyboards are available for people with limited dexterity or hand strength, and others are wireless so they can be used at some distance from the actual computer. Keyboards can appear on the screen, to be touched with a stylus. And voice recognition software lets people who cannot use their hands work on a computer. Finally, unlike students with physical disabilities who use equipment and special devices to gain fuller participation in daily life, **technology-dependent students** use medical equipment—such as ventilators that help them breathe—to survive.

Assessment

Astute educators carefully monitor and evaluate the physical and health status of their students with special physical or health care needs. Such needs are often inconsistent, requiring frequent changes in accommodations and considerations. Some situations are directly related to medications and treatment, and others are a function of the disease, illness, or condition. For example, children who receive cancer treatment go through periods of feeling too sick to profit from much of the instructional day. Sometimes these periods may last only several hours, and at other times they may result in frequent or long-term absences. Some may even require periods of home instruction. The right courses of action must be individually determined and uniquely responsive.

Early Identification

Family doctors or pediatricians typically diagnose physical or health disabilities in infants and toddlers. Some conditions are identified at birth or soon afterwards because symptoms or risk variables for the conditions either are immediately apparent or are discovered through **universal screening**—testing of all newborns—mandated by the state in which the infant lives. In Chapter 8 on mental retardation, you learned that PKU is now identified through universal screening of newborns, preventing severe mental retardation through early identification and treatment. The medical profession increasingly has the ability to identify more conditions early. For example, sickle cell anemia can now be identified through newborn screenings (Emory University School of Medicine, 2005). Early identification of these disabilities also happens through alert preschool teachers, the services of states' Child Find offices (see page 57 in Chapter 2), and a multidisciplinary array of professionals (e.g., physical therapists [PTs], occupational therapists [OTs], and school nurses).

Pre-Referral

Because most students with physical or health disabilities are identified outside of the educational community, pre-referral is not a typical option. However, as individual IEPs are being developed or reevaluated, teachers collaborating with health

technology-dependent students Individuals who probably could not survive without high-tech devices (such as ventilators)

universal screening Testing of everyone, particularly newborns, to determine existence or risk of disability professionals, PTs, OTs, and the family provide valuable information that contributes to the development of effective programs for these students. For students whose health conditions or physical disabilities originate after they have entered school, the pre-referral process helps determine what accommodations and services students require to meet specific needs. Because pre-referral activities occur in the classroom and are directly related to instructional tasks, opportunities to assess the power of specific validated practices abound, thus reducing the time involved in finding out which interventions are effective and which are not.

Identification

Although teachers rarely participate in the initial diagnosis of disease or physical conditions, they are in a unique position to help these students and their families. Because students spend a considerable portion of their day at school, educators are often the first to notice a change in the health or physical status of their students. In some cases, they are quickly able to determine whether the intensity of an accommodation needs to be altered. They notice that one student may now be able to work more independently or that another student needs additional supports. The more rapidly adjustments are made, the more effective the instructional program will be. In other cases, alert teachers notify parents of changes in students' health or physical status so that referrals to health care professionals can be made without loss of precious time.

Evaluation: Testing Accommodations

As you have learned through *What NCLB* and *IDEA '04 Say About High Stakes Testing* on pages 70 and 71 in Chapter 2, test taking is an important area in which teachers should make adjustments for students with disabilities. Such accommodations or modifications should be individually determined and should reflect the specific problems the student faces (Thurlow et al., 2000). Assessment and evaluation should reflect what the student knows and should not present an inaccurate picture of the student's abilities by focusing more on the disability than on what the student has learned. The risk is that without accommodations, the test will merely measure the degree of physical difficulty experienced by the individual, rather than her or his actual intellectual or academic abilities. (Imagine trying to take a timed test while your body goes through uncontrollable jerky movements.)

Think about how unfair and what a missed opportunity it would be for all people if Stephen Hawking, one of the preeminent physicists of our times, were not allowed to use assistive technologies. If he was not allowed to take a high school physics test using a computer, he would fail it. And, so would we!

What accommodations do teachers usually select for students with disabilities? Findings are consistent. Teachers most often use the following accommodations in testing situations (Gibson et al., 2005; Shriner & DeStefano, 2003):

- *Scheduling accommodations:* providing extra time to take the test
- *Setting accommodations:* allowing the student to take the test in a distraction-free setting or in another place
- *Accommodations regarding directions:* reading the directions to the student, simplifying the direction statements
- *Accommodations by assisting during testing:* reading the items to the student

Testing accommodations are usually offered as a group or set of adjustments, not provided one at a time (Niebling & Elliott, 2005). In other words, several accommodations are delivered together, whether or not each individual one is needed. This is not the best practice. Because of the unique needs of each student with disabilities, it is important that teachers select accommodations on an individual basis. One rule of thumb is to use, in testing situations, the same accommodations that the student has used effectively during instruction.

Early Intervention

Whether disabilities are physical or health-related, early intervention programs provide a strong foundation for the child and family. To ensure the success of children's intervention programs, the early intervention team must support parents' efforts and reinforce their enthusiasm. Motor development and positioning and the development of communication skills are often target areas for young children with physical or health disabilities.

For some children, particularly those with physical disabilities, early intervention programs focus primarily on motor development (Barnes & Whitney, 2002). For example, children born with cerebral palsy may have reflex patterns that interfere with the typical motor development that sets the stage for maximum independence, including body schema, body awareness, purposeful motor use, and mobility. Proper positioning and handling, as well as lifting and assisting with movement, often require skill and knowledge about the condition and its individual effects on the young child. So before teachers or parents begin working with the infant, toddler, or preschooler, they must be trained and supervised to be sure that they do not put the child at risk for injury (Heller et al., 2000). Enlisting multidisciplinary team members such as the OT, PT, and school nurse can ensure the development of an effective program delivered by the right people. The student's program usually includes a regimen of special exercises to develop motor skills. The purpose may be to strengthen weak muscle groups through the use of weights or to adapt to and use artificial limbs or orthopedic devices. Once teachers and family members know how to assist the child with the exercises, they should not hesitate and should encourage the youngster to move, play, and interact with the environment.

Because this is a time of tremendous physical and sensorimotor growth, normal motor patterns must be established as early as possible. For those children who already have abnormal motor patterns, repeating those patterns should not be encouraged. The child should always, both at school and at home, be positioned properly so that alignment, muscle tone, and stability are correct during all activities. Specific equipment, such as foam rubber wedges, Velcro™ straps, and comfortable mats are used to properly position children with physical disabilities. Although some of this equipment is costly, other items can be made rather inexpensively. Parents and teachers need to keep in touch with therapists to be certain that they are working properly with their children. Teachers must also remember that children should not remain in the same position for too long. They should be repositioned every twenty minutes or so.

Barbie® now has a friend, Share a Smile Becky®, who provides a role model for girls with disabilities in a fashion similar to the one Barbie® provides for girls without disabilities.

Communication is difficult for some of these young children (Owens, Metz, & Haas, 2003). Parents and professionals should acknowledge and reinforce every attempt at communication. Although determining how a child with severe disabilities is attempting to communicate can be difficult, an observant person can learn a great deal about the child's communication abilities, even when others believe that the child cannot communicate at all. A good observer will be able to answer questions like these: In what specific ways does the child react to sounds? How does the child respond to certain smells? Does the child have different facial movements when different people enter the room? Does the child gaze at certain objects more than others? How is anger expressed to the family? Through careful observation and experience, parents, teachers, and family members can recognize meaningful communication even when others believe there is none. Parents and professionals should also remember that communication is a two-way street. Children learn to communicate with others by being communicated with. Talk to the child, express feelings with face and body, play games together, and encourage the child to listen to tapes and the radio.

Teaching Students with Physical or Health Disabilities

Recall that each student with physical or health disabilities has individualized needs, even those whose diagnoses seem to be the same. Although many of their special needs seem similar to those of students with other types of disabilities, each student has a unique combination of challenges that must be addressed. For example, many students with disabilities need flexible schedules, more time to learn academic tasks, and extra assistance. This may also be the case for some students with physical or health disabilities. However, one area of particular concern to students with physical disabilities is having a learning environment free from physical barriers that inhibit their movement and their interactions with the curriculum and with classmates. Students with health disabilities may require different approaches, each reflecting their health status and each flexibly applied across a short period of time. We begin our discussion with more general ideas about how to help these students better access the general education curriculum. Then we will continue the conversation about their education with suggestions on how to enhance the physical environment.

Access to the General Education Curriculum

Many students with physical or health disabilities spend a substantial portion of their day learning the general education curriculum alongside classmates without disabilities. Many are on the path to a standard diploma. Even so, there is room for considerable improvement. Let's consider what proportions of these students spend at least 79 percent of their day in the general education program (U.S. Department of Education, 2005b):

- Students with physical disabilities
  - Elementary students, 53 percent
  - High school students, 43 percent
- Students with health disabilities
  - Elementary students, 52 percent
  - High school students, 50 percent

The result of these participation rates is that 63 percent of students with physical disabilities and 67 percent of those with health disabilities graduated with a standard diploma in 2000 (U.S. Department of Education, 2002). These are some of the highest graduation rates among students with disabilities, but even more of these students dream of graduating from high school and going on to college. How can we make more of those dreams a reality?

One way may be to enable students to approach learning with the positive attitudes and skills they needed in order to learn. Although the idea was not developed or validated specifically with students with physical or health disabilities, promoting fundamental skills for learning is one important way to help more of them be successful in the general education curriculum. Steve Elliott helps us understand what

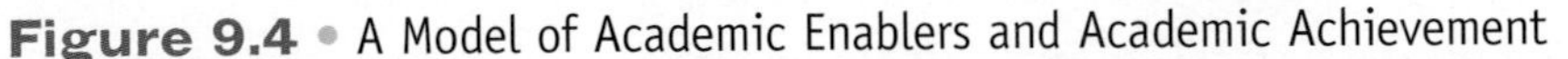
Figure 9.4 • A Model of Academic Enablers and Academic Achievement

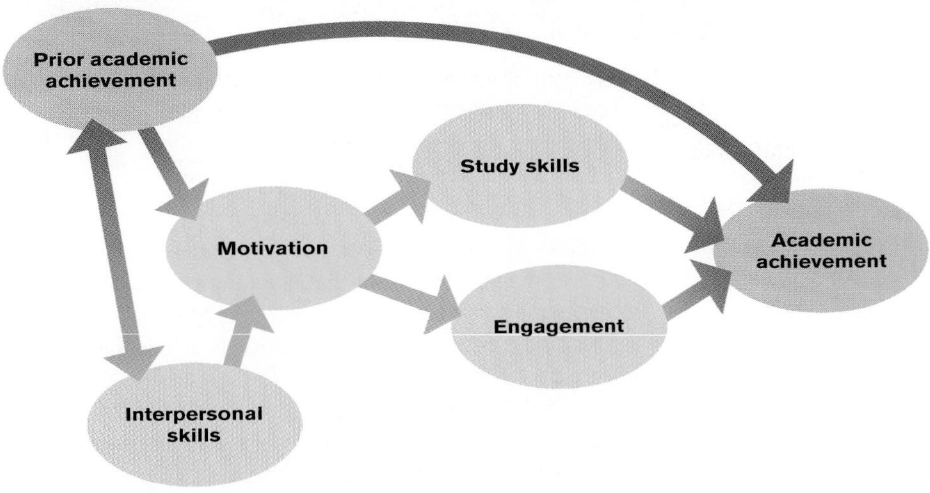

Source: From: DiPerna, J. C., Volpe, R., & Elliott, S. N. (2002). A model of academic enablers and elementary reading/language arts achievement. *School Psychology Review, 31*(3), 301. Copyright © 2002 by the National Association of School Psychologists, Bethesda, MD. Adapted with permission of the publisher. www.nasponline.org

it takes for students to benefit from classroom instruction (Elliott, 2003; Elliott et al., 2004). **Academic enablers** are skills and behaviors that influence successful academic performance. These skills include

- *Interpersonal skills:* social skills necessary to work with others in cooperative learning situations
- *Motivation:* approach to the learning task, persistence, and level of interest
- *Study skills:* strategies that facilitate learning
- *Engagement:* attention, active learning, and full participation in instruction

An assessment instrument known as *ACES: The Academic Competence Evaluation Scales* can help determine whether students possess these foundation skills or need additional instruction to develop them. Figure 9.4 helps us visualize Elliott's validated scheme, which illustrates the interplay among four important skills or behaviors and academic achievement. What does this conceptual framework tell us? First, it proves again that motivation is central to learning. Second, it verifies that students need to be active learners who are "engaged" in the curriculum. Third, it confirms the idea that students need ways and structures to help them approach and organize their learning. And fourth, we are reminded that students learn best when they are excited about learning and actively involved in instructional activities.

Teachers make a real difference by planning activities that are relevant to students, helping students learn how to work together, and teaching them strategies to use in approaching difficult content. For students who are distracted because of their health situations or have frequent absences, arming them with strategies that help them be more efficient learners may well be the key to improving their success and graduation rates. Many such strategies have been proved effective. *Validated Practices* explains one such teaching technique, **story maps**, that helps students organize and remember information.

academic enablers Skills and behaviors (interpersonal skills, motivation, study skills, engagement) that influence successful academic performance

story maps Simple diagrams that help students organize and recall important elements and features of stories they have heard or read

Instructional Accommodations

Adjustments to the learning environment are often easy to make but still critical to success. Sometimes, simple schedule flexibility is all that is needed. At other times, extending dues dates so that the student with a health condition has more time to

Validated Practices Story Maps

What Are Story Maps?

Story maps are simple diagrams used to assist students, at any grade level, in organizing and recalling elements from stories they have listened to or read. Even first-graders can use simple "who, what, where, when, why" maps, or "first, next, last" sequence maps. More complex maps that incorporate setting, characters, trouble, action, sequence, and outcomes can be used with older students.

Why Story Maps Are Beneficial

Mapping techniques help students remember what they have read by requiring them to paraphrase the information. When students are able to put text into their own words, they are more likely to remember the information.

Implementing Story Maps

Story mapping requires that you provide students with a blank map to complete. Two common story map techniques are the Model-Lead-Test method (Idol, 1987) and Story Frames (Fowler, 1982). The Model-Lead-Test method requires students to be actively engaged in learning and gives students frequent opportunities to practice a new skill while you directly supervise and provide continuous feedback. Here is how the Model-Lead-Test method works:

Model Phase

- Read a story or passage aloud to your students.
- Stop reading when you come to a key element of the story (e.g., character, setting).
- Ask students to identify the key element. You may need to prompt them ("This says Sally woke up one morning. So, Sally must be one of our _________?")
- Model what to do next by writing the information on your map.
- Have students fill in the information on their maps.

Lead Phase

- Students read the story independently.
- Students complete their maps, with your assistance if necessary.
- Review completed maps with your class, adding missed information.

Test Phase

- Students read the story independently.
- Students complete their maps independently.
- Ask your students the following questions: "Who were the main characters?" "Where did the story take place?" "What was the main idea of the story?"

You can use or adapt the story map shown in Figure A to help students organize and comprehend reading passages. Regardless of the format you use, remember to review completed story maps to ensure that the information presented is accurate and complete. Provide corrective feedback as needed.

This scientifically validated practice is a teaching method proven by systematic research efforts (Carnine, Silbert, & Kameenui, 1997; Fowler, 1982; Idol, 1987; Williams, 1998; Williams et al., 1994). Full citations are found in the references for Chapter 9 at the end of this text.

Figure A • Components of the Story Map

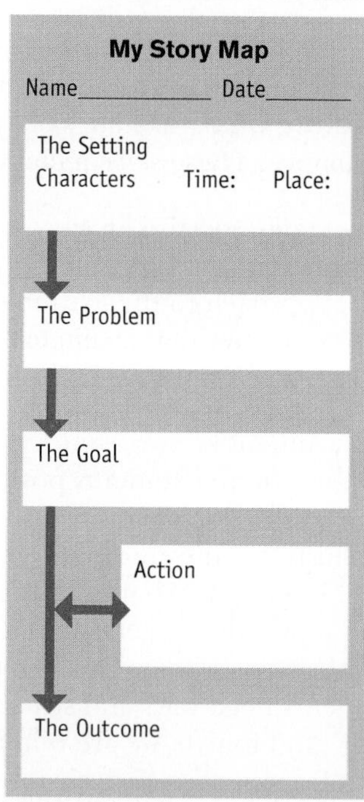

Source: From "Group story mapping: A comprehension strategy for both skilled and unskilled readers" by L. Idol, 1987, *Journal of Learning Disabilities, 20,* p. 199. Copyright 1987 by Pro-Ed, Inc. Reprinted with permission.

—By Kimberly Paulsen, Vanderbilt University

complete complex assignments is sufficient. However, if students become too sick or fragile to attend school, more complicated measures may be necessary to help them keep up and be on track when they return. Here are just a few ideas that have been successful:

- Ensure that the district provides a home or hospital teacher for long periods of illness.
- Use Internet video conferencing or telephone hookups so that important lessons aren't missed and that class participation can happen from home.
- Videotape special activities.
- Have classmates take turns acting as a neighborhood peer tutor after school.
- Incorporate the Web into instruction and assignments so that students who must be absent can engage in learning away from school.

Students with physical disabilities may need other kinds of accommodations. Teachers often look for complex answers when only simple solutions are required. Here are a few easy ways to create accommodations for students who cannot write as fast and efficiently as others (Thompson et al., 2001; Elliott et al., 2000):

- Allow students extra time to complete written assignments.
- Let students use computers for their written work so they can increase their speed and produce pleasing documents.
- Ask a classmate of a student who cannot write to make that student an extra copy of her or his own notes by using carbon paper or photocopying them.
- Tape children's work papers to their desks.
- Provide extra-thick pencils.
- Have students tape-record instead of write their assignments.

These simple adjustments send a threefold message: (1) You are willing to give the student a chance. (2) The student is important to you. And (3) You have high expectations for the student to produce acceptable schoolwork. *Accommodating for Inclusive Environments* provides some more tips about adapting instructional settings.

Validated Practices: Universal Design

Although the ADA law is over 25 years old, the challenges and barriers that students with physical disabilities face are great. Of course, all schools must meet the special architectural codes and implement the concept of universal design (see Chapter 1 for a review of this important principle) required by this law, and schools must be "barrier-free." Thus many of us are surprised when we learn that Anjali Forber-Pratt, on her first day of high school, found that some of her classes where scheduled on the second floor although no elevator was available for her to use, the bathrooms were not accessible, and many of the passageways were too narrow for her to pass through (Helman, 2002). Why might such barriers create challenges for people with physical disabilities? Some public buildings are so old that they are exempt from ADA codes until they are remodeled. Also, some individuals need greater accommodations than those specified by the law. And, many times unknowingly, we create unnecessary obstacles for each other.

How can educators help students with physical problems access the educational environment? First, they can determine where barriers exist by critically observing all of the places the child needs to go: the bathroom, the lunchroom, the playground, the gymnasium, the music room, the library, the bus, and so on. Although administrators and teachers cannot always change the height of bathroom sinks, mirrors, towel dispensers, and door handles, they can advocate for improvements. They should also remember that barriers are not only physical.

* Accommodating for Inclusive Environments

Adapting All Aspects of the Classroom

Adapt the Physical Environment

- Remove hazards
- Create more workspace
- Provide storage space for equipment
- Make furniture accessible
- Widen aisles
- Use positioning devices
- Change seating arrangements
- Rearrange furniture

Change Student Response Mode

- Allow speaking instead of writing
- Use a speech synthesizer
- Allow writing instead of speaking
- Allow computer-print output

Alter Materials and Equipment

- Give handouts
- Adapt writing tools
- Use special eating utensils
- Explore assistive and adaptive technology

Modify the Activity

- Allow more time to complete the assignments
- Abbreviate assignments
- Create a flexible schedule

Provide Extra Assistance

- Arrange peer tutors
- Have parents or family members help
- Find volunteers to assist
- Tape record or videotape lessons
- Use e-mail for help sessions

Inclusion necessitates accommodations beyond curb cuts, ramps, elevators, and bathroom alterations required by law. It also necessitates the spirit of belonging, being part of the school community.

Second, teachers should assess their classroom's room arrangement to be sure that space and design don't restrict access to learning. Making any necessary improvements can become an excellent learning opportunity for the entire class. Although teachers and students cannot alter the structure of the school building, they can redesign the space within a classroom. Students can collect data by using simple frequency counts to study the traffic patterns in the classroom. They can redesign the organization of desks, tables, work areas, storage space, and learning centers. Through drawings and models, they can generate visual design alternatives to the way their environment is currently structured. They can work together as a class to evaluate the functionality of these potential re-creations of their learning environment and, as a unit, can decide how best to use the space allocated to them in what is referred to as a classroom. This activity can create a more exciting and useful learning environment for every class member and can be particularly helpful to students who face physical challenges.

As the entire class works to create a better learning environment, everyone's learning styles and needs must be considered. Students with physical problems provide a special opportunity for creativity. The class must become sensitive to the physical environment and to how it can create unnecessary barriers to learning and social interaction. Students with physical problems may require specially fitted chairs, desks, and worktables, and perhaps extra space for maneuvering bulky equipment such as crutches or wheelchairs. These factors need to be considered when redesigning physical space. Many students with severe physical impairments require bulky language boards or computers for communication, and these may present challenges not only during instruction and small-group work activities but also for storage and security. Space must be allocated so that everybody can interact with students using assistive technology. The benefits of students participating in the creation of a fully accessible learning environment can be great. In addition to designing room arrangements appropriate to each class member's learning style and physical requirements, the activity itself is a wonderful learning experience that draws on many different types of thinking skills, as well as integrating many academic areas (e.g., math, reading, and even history).

Technology

Computers allow access to other environments and people. This technology can be turned into a great advantage for students who must stay at home for any length of time. Whether an illness requires one day at home or a month, students can use the Internet and e-mail to talk to classmates, get tomorrow's homework assignments, or work with their science group on its project. They can also conduct library research by connecting to an information system and can even communicate with students around the country about information they are gathering from a central database.

Assistive technology (discussed in Chapter 2) includes a wide array of devices and tools that enable individuals to interact with others, benefit from school, and participate in mainstream society (Bryant & Bryant, 2003). The 1990 reauthorization of IDEA and the courts have clarified the role of assistive technology in the schools: It is a related service that is provided so that a student with disabilities can profit from special education. Assistive technology does not, however, include medical services provided by physicians. The adaptations that technology provides for individuals with special physical and health considerations include **high-tech devices**, such as computers that control the environment, ventilators, or hardware and software allowing for voice output of printed text. **Low-tech devices** assist persons with simple adjustments, such as holders to keep books at the correct level to see print on a page, built-up spoons, or rubber bands wrapped around pencils to make them easier to hold. Not all technology is expensive or even sophisticated. In many cases, creativity and individualization are the keys to solving problems (Bryant & Bryant, 2003).

Transition

About 63 percent of students with physical disabilities and 68 percent of students with health disabilities complete high school and earn a standard diploma (U.S. Department of Education, 2002). This rate should be higher! Without a high school diploma, the chance of attending college is small, and a college degree may be the ticket to a high-paying job. Many individuals with physical or health disabilities do attend college. In fact, 15 percent of college freshmen attending four-year institutions of higher education report that they have a health-related disability (Henderson, 2001). They report having many different diseases and conditions, including severe allergies, cystic fibrosis, cancer, lupus, and multiple sclerosis. The vast majority of these individuals hold positive attitudes about their college experiences, and some 79 percent of them predict that they will earn a bachelor's degree. Although the rate of college attendance has been stable for students with health disabilities, it has dropped dramatically for those with physical disabilities. In 1988 some 13 percent of college freshman indicated that they had a physical disability, but that percentage dropped to 7 in 2000. As college campuses have become more accessible, it is surprising that the numbers of students who have physical challenges haven't reflected such improvements. Elementary through high school teachers can help improve these statistics by encouraging these students to set high goals for themselves and making it clear that going to college entails a lot of hard work but is worth the effort.

high-tech devices Complex assistive technology devices that usually involve a computer or computer chips

low-tech devices Simple assistive technology devices such as communication boards, homemade cushions, or a classroom railing

Her specially trained dog, Jumar, helps Christina Kimm, a special education professor at California State University–Los Angeles, negotiate a large urban college campus and remain as independent as possible despite her continuing problems from polio as a child.

Independent living is the goal for many adults with physical or health disabilities. The "independent living movement"—people helping themselves to live on their own—has had great influence on the lives of people with disabilities. Increasingly, these adults take control of their lives and their jobs, establish friendships, have families, and exert political power. Legislation such as ADA has had a tremendous impact on the ability of adults with disabilities to pursue their rights and end discrimination, but they must be prepared to take their places in mainstream society. High school transition programs can be very helpful in this regard, by teaching students how to be responsible for planning their own lives, advocate for themselves, locate the resources they need, and take active roles in their medical management.

As you learned in *Changing Times* on page 316, independence is important to all people but is of vital concern to most people with physical or health disabilities. Earlier in this chapter, you learned about improved access, independence, and participation for many aspects of life: housing, school, work, travel, and leisure activities. Opportunities have been expanded through removal of barriers, specialized activities, and assistive technology. One more service is helping many individuals with physical or health disabilities gain even more independence. When we think of **service** or **assistance animals**—animals individually trained to benefit a person with a disability—we usually think of a guide dog for people with visual disabilities. But more and more animals, particularly dogs and Capuchin monkeys, are assisting people with physical limitations to live independently and participate in society more fully (Delta Society, 2005a). For example, Dr. Christina Kimm, a special education professor at California State University, Los Angeles, has achieved more independence and a more balanced life since Canine Companions of San Diego matched her with Jumar, who can pull her wheelchair, pick things up, open doors, push elevator buttons, turn lights off and on, and bring her a telephone receiver. He is even an able assistant in the classroom, handing out papers to Dr. Kimm's students, for example. And service dogs have performed even more amazing feats: One called 911 (and thus saved the life of his handler) by pressing a special button with his paw (CNN, 2004). All service animals are highly trained; they are not pets (Delta Society, 2005b). Certain important rules should guide our interactions with the working team of dog and person (handler) with a disability:

1. Speak to the person first and do not distract the dog.
2. Ask and receive permission before touching a service dog.
3. Do not offer the animal food.
4. Don't be offended if the handler doesn't want to talk about himself or herself or about the animal.

Collaboration

Over half of students with physical or health disabilities spend over 40 percent of their school day in general education classes (U.S. Department of Education, 2005b). Thus it is likely that general education teachers, as well as special education professionals, will work closely with these students' multidisciplinary teams as everyone collaborates to implement each student's IEP. In particular, physical therapists and occupational therapists play unique roles in the assessment of these students' needs and in the implementation of their IEPs. For example, **physical therapists (PTs)** evaluate the quality of the students' movement and later teach them how to compensate for and change inefficient motor patterns. **Occupational therapists (OTs)** work closely with PTs to assess and later work with upper-body movement, fine motor skills, and daily living activities. Together, PTs and OTs analyze the student's physical characteristics and determine what assistive devices will benefit the individual (Heller et al., 2000). Rehabilitation engineers and assistive technologists also work with many students with physical disabilities and recommend and devise mobility systems and special seating systems. They can create equipment that attaches other devices (e.g., communication devices) to wheelchairs.

Multidisciplinary teams specially composed to meet the needs of students with health disabilities often include a school nurse. Remember, a **school nurse** is a related service provider described in IDEA '04 as a professional who helps students receive an appropriate education. What is very important is that all educators seek the help of the family and of students' multidisciplinary teams who can assist in designing the best instructional environment possible.

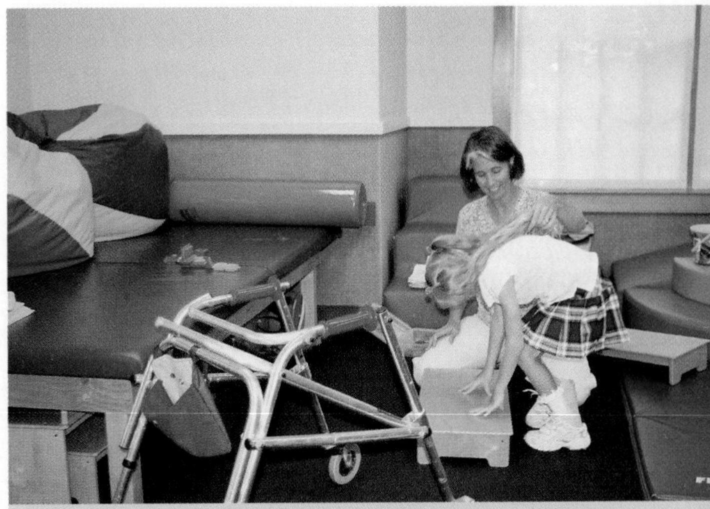

Kailyn works with her physical therapist on balance and walking skills. With a lot of work, Kailyn might soon be leaving her canes and walker behind.

Partnerships with Families and Communities

One real challenge facing families (and teachers) of students with special health care needs is sorting out how to manage and negotiate the "medical maze," or as some might say, identifying resources available in the medical–health care community. At times families are seeking information about conditions and appropriate health care responses for their children. At other times they are trying to locate health or community services to assist them with the care of their child who has either a health or a physical disability. One common theme heard over and over again is how overwhelming life becomes when a child is sick. Today, families frequently turn to the Internet for information, which they discover is "sometimes . . . like being hit by a tidal wave" (Smith, 2005, p.1). So families often turn to schools and teachers for help.

One place to begin the search for information is the National Dissemination Center for Children with Disabilities, which is just called—NICHCY. The Office of Special Education Programs, a division of the U.S. Department of Education, funds this clearinghouse (www.nichcy.org) designed to help those looking for resources and information about students with disabilities. Here are some more useful sites that include specific information about health conditions and the healthcare community (Küpper, 2005):

- www.healthfinder.gov is sponsored as a government service that connects the user with a wide range of health-related resources.
- www.medlinepuls.gov is provided by the U.S. National Library of Medicine and includes an on-line encyclopedia of medical terms and conditions.
- www.familydoctor.org is operated by the American Academy of Family Physicians and provides many useful databases, including one for "searching by symptoms."
- www.chid.nih.gov is a health-related database produced by the National Institutes of Health and provides considerable information even on rare conditions and diseases.
- www.health.gov provides a master set of links to many health clearinghouses and information centers.

service or **assistance animals** Animals (dogs, monkeys) trained to serve the individual needs of people with disabilities

physical therapist (PT) A professional who treats physical disabilities through many nonmedical means; provides a special education related service

occupational therapist (OT) A professional who directs activities that help improve muscular control and develop self-help skills; provides a special education related service

school nurse A professional who assists with medical services at school and designs accommodations for students with special health care needs; provides a special education related service

Considering Culture

Culture Clash

Semira is 12 years old and has significant physical problems. She travels by wheelchair and has no functional use of her arms and legs. As a result, she must be assisted in all of her daily living activities and must be repositioned frequently throughout the day. To escape violence in their home country of Somalia, Semira's parents left for the United States soon after she was born. With help from family members who sponsored them, Semira and her parents have begun to acclimate to the differences in culture. They do, however, hold traditional beliefs and follow traditional practices. It is their adherence to these traditional ways that has resulted in today's meeting with Semira's teacher, Mrs. Jackson.

Semira's parents have been keeping her at home since the beginning of the semester, and her teacher does not understand why. Semira is not hospitalized, nor is she sick. Mrs. Jackson's concern had been increasing, so she called Semira's home to ask whether she could come talk with them and visit Semira. When Mrs. Jackson arrived at the house, she was greeted warmly by Semira's father and mother, who immediately served tea and cakes. Semira was in her wheelchair smiling and happy to see Mrs. Jackson. After greetings and general conversation Mrs. Jackson said, "I hope that Semira will be returning to school soon. We all miss her." Semira's father seemed reluctant to speak but finally said, "We think that we will keep Semira at home and provide her education at home."

Mrs. Jackson was surprised and asked why they had made that decision. Semira's father said that now that Semira is becoming a young lady, school may not be right for her. Mrs. Jackson countered by saying that being with her peers is especially important now that she is becoming a teenager. The conversation continued, and finally Semira's father said, "Since the new term, there have been men at school—the new assistant in your classroom and the physical education teacher. We know that they lift Semira in and out of her wheelchair and that they hold her during some of the class activities. In our culture, men and women do not touch like this. It is not appropriate for these men to have such close contact with our daughter."

Mrs. Jackson realized that this family's cultural beliefs were very different from hers and different from the school culture. She asked Semira's father whether Semira could return to school if different arrangements were made for lifting and positioning her. He agreed that as long as a woman did these tasks modestly. Such considerations were acceptable to the family. Mrs. Jackson agreed to make other arrangements, and within a week a plan acceptable to all was in place.

Questions to Consider

1 Gender roles are often linked to cultural beliefs. Can you give examples of any gender differences that are important in the culture(s) you include in your identity?

2 How do you think you would respond if a family's cultural beliefs and practices supported highly traditional gender roles?

3 What do you think the teacher's role should be when a family's cultural beliefs and practices collide with the school's culture?

—By Eleanor Lynch, San Diego State University and Marci Hanson, San Francisco State University

Providing useful information to family members might be time-consuming and is sometimes not directly linked to instruction, it can be part of building important bonds with parents and extended family members. For many educators, such tasks come naturally, as part of their "helping" orientation. Of course, there are many other important ways in which educators need to partner with families and be sensitive to their concerns. Such sensitivity does not always come spontaneously but, rather, requires careful thought. The story in *Considering Culture* makes the point that educators have many issues to consider—some of them not initially obvious—when providing an appropriate education for students with disabilities.

Imagine a world...

where the promise of the future and joy of the present have no restraints ...

Summary

Students with physical and health disabilities resulting in special health care needs can present unique difficulties to their families and teachers. These students require considerable flexibility, accommodations, and adjustments to both their learning and their physical environments. These categories represent low incidence disabilities that contain many rare diseases and conditions. Even when these two special education categories are combined, the number of students involved is small—less than 2 percent of all students with disabilities. Many of these students access the general education curriculum and graduate from high school, but their graduation rates certainly need improvement. As advances in technology and opportunities for community presence expand, one important challenge facing educators is helping them be well prepared to take advantage of a changing world.

Addressing the Chapter Objectives

1 How are physical or health disabilities classified and organized?

- Physical disabilities
  - *Neuromotor impairments:* seizure disorders, cerebral palsy, spinal cord disorders, polio, muscular dystrophy (MD), multiple sclerosis (MS)
  - *Muscular/skeletal conditions:* juvenile arthritis, limb deficiencies, skeletal disorders
- Health disabilities
  - *Chronic illnesses:* asthma, diabetes, cystic fibrosis, congenital heart defects, tuberculosis (TB), childhood cancer, blood disorders
  - *Infectious diseases:* HIV/AIDS, STORCH infections, hepatitis B

2 What are some steps teachers should take when a child is having a seizure?

- Seek medical assistance.
- Create a safe place free from hazards.
- Loosen clothing, particularly around the neck.
- Protect the head from injury.
- Turn the person sideways to ensure free passage of air.
- For seizures lasting longer than five minutes, call for an ambulance.
- Upon return of consciousness, keep the individual calm and offer further assistance.

3 What accommodations to the learning environment help students with physical disabilities?

- *Modify the physical environment:* create more space, widen aisles, remove hazards, change seating arrangements, create accessible workstations
- *Alter student response demands:* (as appropriate) speak instead of write, use a speech synthesizer, write instead of speak, have a computer print or speak the response
- *Adapt materials and equipment:* allow use of special writing tools and adapted eating utensils

4 What accommodations to the learning environment help students with health disabilities that result in special health care needs?

- *Modify instruction:* allow more time to complete assignments, abbreviate assignments, allow for a flexible schedule for completion
- *Arrange for extra assistance:* tutors (peers, parents, volunteers), tape record or videotape lectures, connect in-class discussions to the Internet, set up an e-chat room
- *Adapt materials and equipment:* use handouts to accompany transparencies, assign books with audio versions, allow use of special writing tools, and adapted eating utensils

5 How might the barriers that people with physical disabilities face be reduced? And in what ways can students be better prepared for increased community presence and participation?

Barriers include

- Coping with inaccessible environments, where their impaired mobility hinders their participation in mainstream society
- Dealing with bias, rejection, and discrimination
- Difficulties living independently
- Difficulties finding jobs
- Social rejection by people without disabilities

Individuals require

- Accessible physical and learning environments
- Acceptance and understanding
- Goals that foster independence
- Accommodations for their individual learning, physical, and health needs
- Special teaching, scheduling, counseling, therapies, equipment, and technology

mylabschool™
Where the classroom comes to life!

MyLabSchool is a collection of online tools for your success in this course, your licensure exams, and your teaching career. Visit www.mylabschool.com to access the following:

- Online Study Guide
- Video cases from real classrooms
- Help with your research papers using Research Navigator
- Career Center with resources for:
  - Praxis and licensure preparation
  - Professional portfolio development
  - Job search and interview techniques
  - Lesson planning

Supplementary Resources

Popular Novels and Books

Brown, C. (1955). *My left foot.* New York: Simon & Schuster.

Ellison, J. (2002). *Miracles happen: One mother, one daughter, one journey.* New York: Hyperion.

Gallagher, H. G. (1994). *FDR's splendid deception.* New York: Dodd, Mead.

Hawking, S. (2001). *The universe in a nutshell.* New York: Bantam.

Patchett, A. (2004). *Truth and beauty: A friendship.* New York: HarperCollins.

Reeve, C. (1998). *Still me.* New York: Random House.

Stepanek, M. J. T. (2001). *Heartsongs.* Alexandria, VA: VSP Books.

Stepanek, M. J. T. (2001). *Journey through heartsongs.* Alexandria, VA: VSP Books.

Movies

***Warm Springs* (2005). HBO Films**

Franklin Delano Roosevelt (FDR) contracted poliomyelitis in 1921. The disease resulted in his inability to walk. At that time, polio was feared as much as the plague was during the Middle Ages, and FDR was shunned and faced considerable discrimination and prejudice. Despite the fact that polio was an epidemic affecting many, no medical centers for people with polio were available, and he helped turn a small spa in rural Georgia into a national center. The film shows the discrimination that FDR experienced because of disease and that others in the South faced because of race. It also shows how that part of his life prepared him to assume leadership and ultimately the U.S. presidency.

After FDR had been at Warm Springs for some time, word about his spa began to spread, and increasing numbers of people with polio arrived in an effort to help themselves. This at first alarmed Roosevelt, because he didn't want to admit he was like these other people. After accepting his condition, however, he was able to transform the health spa into a full-time rehabilitation clinic for those with polio. His renewed strength allowed him to jump back into politics, where he eventually won the presidency.

Rory O'Sea Was Here (2005). W2 Productions and Universal
This Irish movie tells the story of two young men with severe physical disabilities who emerge from institutional living and share an apartment in the city. They hire an attractive young woman to assist them, and both become attracted to her. The film shows both the challenges and the allure of independent living.

Murderball (2005). Thinkfilm and MTV Films
This sports documentary shows the fierce competition of wheelchair rugby by following one team for two years. The movie begins at the 2002 championships in Sweden and ends with the 2004 International Paralympic Games in Athens. The movie shows the human dramas of real people who are rabid about their sport. The fast-paced film provides an inside look at disabilities along with competitive sports.

Fantastic Four (2005). Twentieth Century Fox
In this superhero feature, five scientists travel into space to study the effects of a radiation storm. All of the scientists are irradiated and gain exceptional powers. In the typical struggle of good versus evil, four of the scientists use their powers for good, while one of them tries to gain more and more powers at all cost. As a subplot of the story, a radiation storm physically alters one scientist; the woman who is unquestioning about his appearance has no vision.

Beyond the Sea (2004). Lionsgate
This life story of Bobby Darin, 1950s and 1960s pop singer, reveals the toll that early childhood illness can take throughout one's life. Darin's rheumatic fever left him with a weakened heart. Despite his continuing health problems, he chose a demanding career as a singer and spent much of his life on the road entertaining in one city after another. Darin died at age 37. This film shows the challenges people face as they try to live a "normal" life with a chronic health condition.

X-Men (2000). Twentieth Century Fox
This film, based on a comic book set in the late sixties, follows "evolved" people called mutants, who are threatened with being rounded up, numbered, and placed in specific centers. A school for mutants, developed by Dr. Xavier and his top mutants (the X-Men), is a safe haven where people and mutants are supposed to live together peacefully. However, a nefarious group of mutants disagree and wage war on "normal" people.

The leader of the X-Men uses a wheelchair, but his leadership is not impaired. The underlying meaning of this film is that people who are different should not be viewed as outcasts or ostracized from society. The comic book on which the movie is based dates back about thirty years and tried to promote tolerance.

Notting Hill (1999). Universal Studios
This romantic comedy about William Thacker, who owns a travel bookshop, takes place in a small section of London. Thacker falls in love with a woman from the United States, Anna Scott. Their relationship is complicated by the fact that she is a world-famous film star. One of William's friends is Bella, who uses a wheelchair. She had fallen down a flight of stairs, which left her paralyzed from the waist down. The film portrays her neither as a victim nor as a person to be pitied. Instead, she is an empowered, pivotal character in the story.

Mask (1985). Universal/MCA
Rocky Dennis is a teenager who is suffering with an incurable disease that has deformed his skull. A gifted youth, he is raised by a caring, loving single mother, who helps her son cope with the painful side effects of his disease. However, she also has a wild side and regularly carouses with bikers, living a hedonistic life. Even though his mother is reckless, her perspective allows Rocky to live for the moment, but in the end he cannot overcome the deadly, incurable disease.

Professional, Parent, and Advocacy Groups

Asthma and Allergy Foundation of America (AAFA) in Washington, DC: www.aafa.org

Council for Exceptional Children, Division for Physical & Health Disabilities (DPHD) in Arlington, Virginia: www.cec.sped.org

National Association of School Nurses (NASN) in Castle Rock, Colorado: www.nasn.org

National Easter Seal Society for Crippled Children and Adults in Landover, Maryland: www.easter-seals.org

Epilepsy Foundation of America in Landover, Maryland: www.efa.org

March of Dimes Birth Defects Foundation in White Plains, New York: www.modimes.com

United Cerebral Palsy Association in Washington, DC: www.ucp.org

Professional Standards and Licensure Tests

After reading this chapter, you should be able to link basic knowledge and skills described in the CEC Standards and INTASC Principles with information provided in this text. The table below shows some of the specific CEC Physical and Health Disabilities Knowledge and Skill Standards and INTASC Special Education Principles that can be applied to each major section of the chapter. Other standards may also be applied to this chapter. Associated General Praxis II topic areas are identified in the right column.

Major Chapter Headings	CEC Knowledge and Skill Core Standard and Associated Subcategories	INTASC Core Principle and Associated Special Education Subcategories	PRAXIS II Exam Topic
Where We've Been . . . What's on the Horizon	**1: Foundations** PH1K2 Historical foundations related to knowledge and practices in physical and health disabilities	**1: Subject Matter** 1.13 Special education teachers know major trends and issues that define the history of special education and understand how current legislation and recommended practice fit within the contact of this history.	1: Understanding Exceptionality 2: Legal and Social Issues
Physical or Health Disabilities Defined	**1: Foundations** PH1K1 Issues and educational definitions of individuals with physical and health disabilities	**1: Subject Matter** 1.08 Special education teachers have knowledge of when and how to develop, structure, and implement accommodations, modifications and/or adaptations to provide access to the general curriculum for students with disabilities.	1: Understanding Exceptionality 2: Legal and Social Issues
Characteristics	**2: Development and Characteristics of Learners** PH2K2 Etiology and characteristics of physical and health disabilities across the life span	**2: Student Learning** 2.05 All special education teachers have knowledge of a wide array of disabilities and are cognizant of the range and types of individual variation that exist within disability categories.	1: Understanding Exceptionality
Causes and Prevention	**2: Development and Characteristics of Learners** PH2K3 Secondary health care issues that accompany specific physical and health disabilities	**2: Student Learning** 2.03 All teachers recognize that students with disabilities vary in their approaches to learning depending on factors such as the	1: Understanding Exceptionality 2: Legal and Social Issues

		nature of their disabilities, their level of knowledge and functioning, and life experiences.	
Assessment	**8: Assessment** PH8S3 Use results of specialized evaluations to make instructional decisions for individuals with physical and health disabilities	**8: Assessment** 8.10 Special education teachers regularly use ongoing assessment and student progress monitoring to make instructional decisions and adaptations and modifications in instruction.	2: Legal and Social Issues 3: Delivery of Services to Students
Teaching Students with Physical or Health Disabilities	**5: Learning Environments and Social Interactions** PH5K1 Adaptations of educational environments necessary to accommodate individuals with physical and health disabilities	**4: Instructional Strategies** 4.08 All teachers expect and support the use of assistive and instructional technologies to promote learning and independence of students with disabilities.	1: Understanding Exceptionality 3: Delivery of Services to Students
Transition	**10: Collaboration** PH10S6 Participate in transdisciplinary teams to provide integrated care and transition services	**7: Planning Instruction** 7.07 Special education teachers oversee the development of individualized transition plans to guide learners' transitions from preschool to elementary school, middle school to high school, and high school to postschool opportunities.	3: Delivery of Services to Students
Collaboration	**10: Collaboration** PH10K3 Roles and responsibilities of school and community-based medical and related services personnel	**10: Collaboration, Ethics, and Relationships** 10.07 Special education teachers work with related services professionals to design, implement, and evaluate instructional plans for students with disabilities.	2: Legal and Social Issues 3: Delivery of Services to Students
Partnerships with Families and Communities	**10: Collaboration** PH10S5 Collaborate with families of and service providers to individuals who are chronically or terminally ill	**10: Collaboration, Ethics, and Relationships** 10.09 Special education teachers collaborate with families and with school and community personnel to include students with disabilities in a range of instructional environments in the school and community.	2: Legal and Social Issues 3: Delivery of Services to Students

Dorothy Brett, *Spring*. Private Collection, New Mexico, Courtesy Owings-Dewey Fine Art, Santa Fe, New Mexico. Photograph of the artist from Sean Hignett, *Brett: From Bloomsbury to New Mexico: A Biography*. London and New York: Hodder Stoughton and Franklin Watts. Copyright 1984 by Sean Hignett.

Dorothy Brett was born of a noble British family (Hignett, 1983). Although her childhood was quite sheltered, as a young adult and student at the Slade Art College in London, she became exposed to young artists like Dora Carrington and the liberal thinking of the day. Brett's associations with the Bloomsbury Group—two of its most famous members were writer and publisher Virginia Woolf and economist John Maynard Keynes—broadened her horizons. In 1924, Brett followed D. H. Lawrence to New Mexico to be part of a utopian colony. Lawrence returned to England, but Brett remained in America and became part of an artists' colony often referred to as the Taos Artists. Brett was partially deaf almost her entire life. A self-portrait she completed in 1924 shows her with the hearing aid of the day—an ear trumpet that she named Toby (Hignett, 1983).

10

Deaf and Hard of Hearing

They are facing not a theory but a condition, for they are first, last, and all the time the people of the eye.

George Veditz

President, National Association of the Deaf, 1913

The process of hearing is remarkable. Being able to hear and turn sounds into meaning is an assumption of life—a given—for most of us. It is an ability we often take for granted. The content or associations of sound affect us in different ways. We are warmed by the sound of an old friend's voice, startled by a loud clap of thunder, fascinated by the sound of the wind rushing through trees, lulled by the ocean, excited by the roar of a crowd, consumed by the music of a rock group, and inspired by the uplifting sounds of a symphony. One important way in which most of us learn about the thoughts, ideas, and feelings of others is by listening to people tell us about their experiences. Through this exchange we expand our knowledge, share ideas, express emotions, and function in typical workplaces and social settings. People who are **deaf**—those with profound hearing loss who cannot understand sounds with or without hearing aids—and people who are **hard of hearing**—those with hearing losses that impair their understanding of sounds, including communication—profit from listening devices and other hearing technologies that enable them to comprehend oral speech and communications.

Chapter Objectives

After studying this chapter, you will be able to:

1. Explain variables that must be considered when planning instruction for students with hearing problems.
2. List and explain the major causes of hearing loss.
3. Describe and justify universal hearing screening of newborns.
4. Discuss the concept of Deaf culture, list examples or signs of Deaf culture, and describe its importance to the Deaf.
5. List the major types of assistive technology specifically designed for people with hearing problems, and provide examples for each.

Where We've Been . . . What's on the Horizon?

We know through the writings of Aristotle, Plato, and the emperor Justinian that ancient Greeks and early Romans discussed issues concerning people who were deaf. Over the history of Western civilization, attitudes have varied. Some societies protected such people; others ridiculed and persecuted them and even put them to death (Branson & Miller, 2002). In America, attitudes toward and acceptance of people with profound hearing loss have changed greatly over time. Debates raged from the 1860s to the 1960s about which language system is preferred or even allowed: oral language or manual communication and sign language. Some argument continues today, but for members of the Deaf community, American Sign Language (ASL) has become not only their language but also a symbol of their culture and heritage.

Historical Context

Documents dating back to the 1500s mention physicians in Europe who worked with people who were deaf. Pedro Ponce de Leon (1520–1584), a Spanish monk believed to have been the first teacher of deaf students, had remarkable success teaching his students to read, write, and speak. William Holder and John Wallis, who lived during the 1600s, are credited with instituting educational programs in England for deaf individuals. Like the Spanish before them, they advocated using writing and manual communication to teach speech. By the 1700s, schools for the deaf had been established by Henry Baker in England, Thomas Braidwood in Edinburgh, Abbé Charles Michel de l'Epée in France, and Samuel Heinicke in Germany. The concept of special schools for the deaf then came to America.

Thomas Hopkins Gallaudet, a young divinity student, went to study in England and France so he could start the first special school for the deaf in the United States. At that time, the French at the school begun by l'Epée were experimenting with methods of manual communication, mainly sign language. Gallaudet was greatly influenced by the effectiveness of these methods, and he brought Laurent Clerc, a deaf Frenchman and well-known educator of the deaf, to the United States. Together, in 1817, they began the first American school for deaf students in Hartford, Connecticut. (Many of the Deaf children of Martha's Vineyard, whom you learned about in Chapter 1, attended this residential school.) Laurent Clerc is often credited with being the father of education for the deaf in the United States (Carroll, 2002).

Other Americans interested in education of the deaf also went to Europe and were impressed by the results of oral approaches. And thus began the highly contentious debates about the benefits of oral communication versus manual communication or sign language. Some even refer to this period of time as the "Hundred Years' War" (Drasgow, 1998). The battles were initiated and fueled through the debates of Edward Gallaudet, Thomas Gallaudet's son, and Alexander Graham Bell (Alby, 1962; Adams, 1929). Each of these men had a deaf mother and a highly successful father. Bell invented the telephone and the audiometer and worked on the phonograph. Gallaudet was the president of the nation's college for the deaf and was a renowned legal scholar. These two men clashed. Bell believed that residential schools and the use of sign language fostered segregation. He also felt that communities of deaf people would lead to more deaf people marrying each other and that the result would eventually be a deaf variety of the human race (Campbell, 1999). Therefore, he proposed legislation to prohibit two deaf adults from marrying, eliminate residential schools, ban the use of manual communication, and not allow people who were deaf from becoming teachers. Gallaudet strongly opposed Bell's positions, and he won support from Congress for the manual approach and for separate center schools. But these conflicts were far from settled.

The development of the hearing aid has had a significant impact on the lives of people with hearing loss. Old versions, such as the hearing trumpet used by Dorothy Brett (the artist whose work and picture are shown at the beginning of this chapter), made sounds a little louder. Advances in batteries developed during World War II made battery-operated hearing aids possible. These early devices, however, were bulky and difficult to use. Small hearing aids worn behind the ear were created after the development of the transistor in the 1950s. Today's versions use microchips to tailor sound amplification to the needs of the individual.

Unlike people with other disabilities, many people with profound hearing loss consider themselves *not* people with disabilities but, rather, people who are members of a minority group. They consider themselves "Deaf" (notice the capital D). They are members of the Deaf community and are united by **Deaf culture**, a culture rich in heritage and traditions. In the United States their primary language is **American Sign Language (ASL)**—a language that uses manual communication signs, has all of the elements (grammar, syntax, idioms) of other languages, and is not parallel to English in either structure or word order. ASL is not a mere translation of oral speech or of the English language (as is Signed English); it is a

deaf Having profound hearing loss

hard of hearing Having hearing losses that impair understanding of sounds and communication

Deaf culture Structures of social relationships, language (ASL), dance, theater, literature, and other cultural activities that bind the Deaf community

American Sign Language (ASL) The language of Deaf Americans that uses manual communication; a signal of Deaf culture

James Woodenlegs in the Spotlight

James Woodenlegs is one busy man. He is a member of the Northern Cheyenne Tribe, a spiritual leader, and a graduate of Gallaudet University. He, along with other Native American Gallaudet alumni, represented the Deaf community at the 2005 opening of the new Smithsonian Institution Museum, the National Museum of the American Indian. Both the opening of the museum and their participation gave these Americans great pride and hope about achieving more recognition of their place in American History.

Woodenlegs is an important member of the Intertribal Deaf Council and leads the group in traditional ceremonies. He is a keeper of Indian heritage and a favorite storyteller of elementary students attending Kendall School on Gallaudet's campus. College and university programs seek him out as a guest lecturer on both Deaf and Native American issues. Recently, he blended many of his talents by conducting a Native blessing ceremony for the American Sign Language program at the University of New Mexico.

fully developed language. (In fact, many states allow ASL as an option to meet the high school foreign language requirement, and the same is true of many colleges and universities.) Since the late 1980s, Deaf pride has also united the Deaf community quite publicly. One reason was the "Deaf President Now Movement" that originated in 1988 when a hearing president who did not know ASL was appointed by the school's Board of Trustees to lead Gallaudet University (Gannon, 1989). After protests from Deaf Gallaudet students and the Deaf community, which closed the campus and included a march on Washington, DC, I. King Jordan who announced his retirement in 2006 became the first Deaf college president of Gallaudet University and the first Deaf college president in the nation.

Challenges That Hearing Loss Presents

Most of us communicate with others through a process of telling and listening. This process is one important way in which we learn about the world we live in, subjects at school, and others' perspectives on issues and concerns. Those who cannot hear or speak oral language have a more restricted ability to communicate—a difference that shapes the way these students are taught, the content of their curricula, and the related services they require for an appropriate education.

Issues are very different across groups of students with hearing loss. For example, students with moderate to mild hearing loss profit from hearing aids and may not even qualify for special education. Unfortunately, these students' special needs are often overlooked because the assumption is that their assistive devices fully compensate for their disability (Harrington, 2003). A second group of these learners use oral language as their means of communication and learning. A third group is made up of diverse students who are deaf—individuals such as James Woodenlegs, who is featured in this chapter's *In the Spotlight;* their fascinating and full lives are enriched by multiple cultures. And a fourth group uses sign language often, a practice that separates them from the hearing community. The use of ASL, the language and manual communication system of the Deaf community, has become the focal point of the controversy. Some argue that all young children with profound hearing loss should learn ASL as their native language (and that English become their second language). However, hearing parents are often concerned that their children will become isolated from them and their family members if they learn ASL as their primary language. New medical technologies on the horizon, such as advances in surgically implanted hearing devices, may correct or lessen the effects of hearing loss for even more individuals.

Making a Difference

Gallaudet University and the Laurent Clerc National Deaf Education Center

Again and again we are reminded how one personal connection can change the lives of those involved and affect the lives of many others. But perhaps the connection between Thomas Hopkins Gallaudet and Dr. Mason Cogswell, the father of a daughter who was deaf, has had the greatest long-term impact on later generations (Carroll, 2002).

Gallaudet and Cogswell were neighbors in Hartford, Connecticut. Because there was no school for his daughter, Alice Cogswell, the medical doctor sought the help of Gallaudet, an itinerant preacher. In 1816, Dr. Cogswell sent Gallaudet to Europe to study methods for the "proper" education of such individuals. Gallaudet returned to the United States with Laurent Clerc, a French educator of the deaf who used manual communication systems. Together they began the first American school for the deaf, which remains in Hartford and is still educating students today. In 1856, Amos Kendall donated part of his Washington, DC, estate and helped to begin a school for elementary students who were deaf (Laurent Clerc National Deaf Education Center, 2005). In 1864 Gallaudet's son, Edward, carried on and established what is now called Gallaudet University alongside Kendall Green Elementary School. What these pioneers began has evolved into a movement, a culture, and the Deaf community.

Thomas Gallaudet and Alice Cogswell

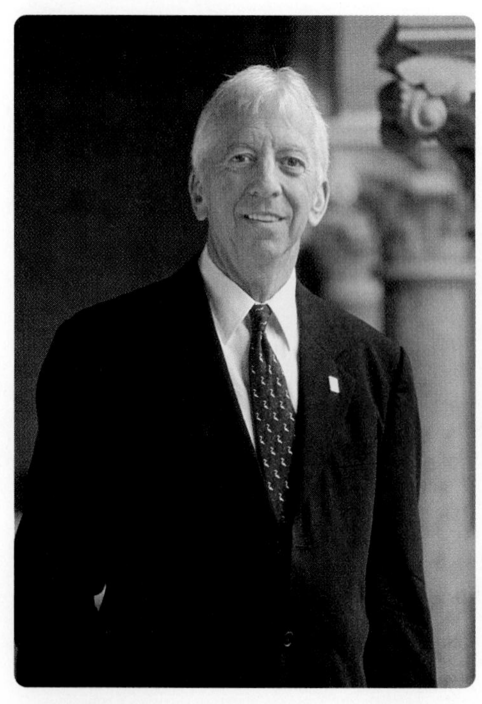

I. King Jordan

Across time the needs of those who are deaf, their family members, and the public in general have become more and more apparent. Today, the umbrella of Gallaudet University and the Laurent Clerc National Deaf Education Center offers a vast range of services. The Kendall Demonstration Elementary School, the Model Secondary School for the Deaf, and Gallaudet University provide education to Deaf students. The Exemplary Programs and Research Division not only conducts research about deafness, academic achievement, and cochlear implants but also facilitates the work conducted at regional centers across the nation. The information unit provides information briefs about all aspects of deafness, publishes several magazines and many popular books, and is responsive to questions from the public. In addition, the center is always hosting social activities, sporting events, and competitions—ranging from beauty pageants to robot-building contests. But most important, Gallaudet and the Clerc Center are at the heart of "family" for thousands of Deaf people living everywhere in America today. To learn more about the comprehensive services that are meeting the needs of so many people or to find more information about deafness or the Deaf culture and its community, visit this Web site **http://clerccenter.gallaudet.edu**

Table 10.1 • Definitions of Deaf and Hard of Hearing

Source	Definition of Deafness
Federal Government[1]	Deafness means a hearing impairment that is so severe that the child is impaired in processing linguistic information through hearing, with or without amplification, that adversely affects a child's educational performance.
	Definition of Hard of Hearing (hearing impairment)
Federal Government[1]	Hearing impairment means an impairment in hearing, whether permanent or fluctuating, that adversely affects a child's educational performance but that is not included under the definition of deafness
Federally Funded Technical Assistance Clearinghouse[2]	A person who is hard of hearing perceives some sound and has sufficient hearing to use auditory-based methods of communication, sometimes with visual supplements. Some people who are severely hard of hearing use oral-aural communication, which combines speech, speech-reading, use of personal hearing aids (including the newer cochlear implant technology), and other augmentative devices.

Sources: [1]From 34 CFR Parts 300 and 303, Assistance to States for the Education of Children with Disabilities and the Early Intervention Program for Infants and Toddlers with Disabilities; Proposed Regulations (pp. 310, 311), U.S. Department of Education, 2005a, *Federal Register*, Washington, DC.

[2]From *Students Who Are Deaf or Hard of Hearing in Postsecondary Education* (p. 2), by American Council on Education, 2005, Washington, DC: HEATH Resource Center.

Deafness and Hard of Hearing Defined

Although the federal government in IDEA '04 describes two groups of students with hearing loss—those who are deaf and those who are hard of hearing—it considers them as belonging to one special education category, which it calls "hearing impairments." The government's definitions for deafness and for hearing impairments are provided in Table 10.1, along with the definitions for students with hearing loss used by a federally sponsored information resource center.

Hearing loss results when the hearing mechanism is damaged or obstructed in such a way that sounds cannot be perceived or understood. The damage can occur either before or after birth. To better understand impaired hearing, it is helpful to know how the process of hearing works when the hearing mechanism is functioning properly. We will discuss that briefly and then study three factors that affect problems associated with hearing loss:

- Degree of loss
- Age when the loss occurs
- Type of hearing loss

The Process of Hearing

Sound waves pass through the air, water, or some other medium. They cause the eardrum to vibrate. These vibrations are carried to the inner ear, where they pass through receptor cells that send impulses to the brain. The brain translates these impulses into meaningful sound. Refer to Figure 10.1, a diagram of the ear, to trace the process of normal hearing as sound moves from the outer ear, through the middle ear, and then to the inner ear and finally is translated into electrochemical signals and transmitted to the brain via the auditory (eighth cranial) nerve.

Figure 10.1 • The Structure of the Human Ear

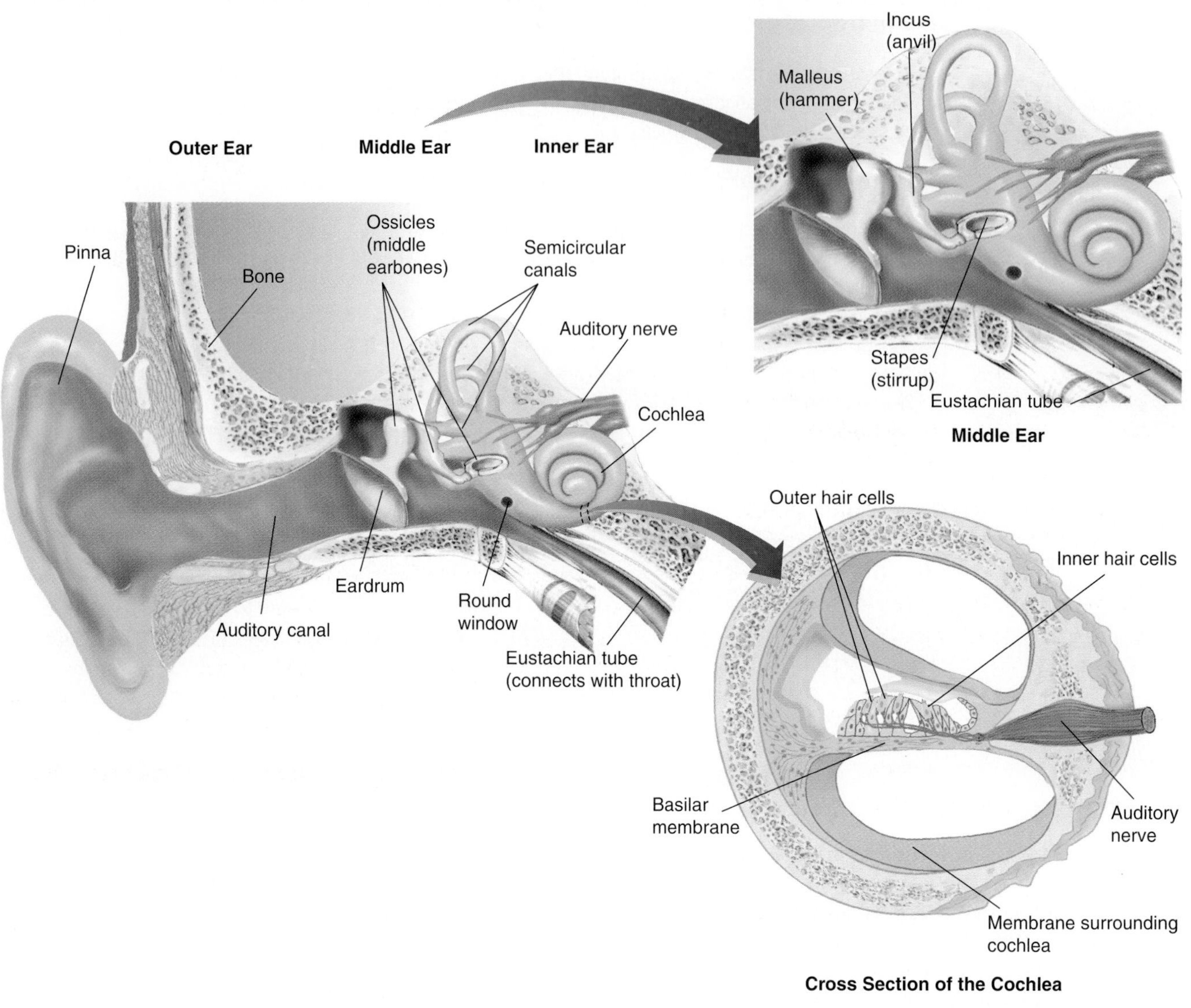

Source: From N. R. Carlson, *Physiology of Behavior,* 8th ed. Published by Allyn and Bacon. © 1998 by Pearson Education. Adapted by permission of the publisher.

pinna Outer structure of the ear

tympanic membrane or **eardrum** Vibrates with the presence of sound waves and stimulates the ossicles of the middle ear

Eustachian tube Equalizes pressure on both sides of the eardrum

In general, here is how it works. A person speaks, and the sound waves that make up the words pass, or propagate, through the air or some other medium. The **pinna** (sometimes called the auricle) is the outer structure that we commonly call the ear. Sound waves are caught by the pinna and funneled down the auditory canal to the middle ear. The middle ear is an air-filled chamber that contains the **tympanic membrane** or **eardrum**. The middle ear also contains the **Eustachian tube**, which equalizes the pressure on the two sides of the eardrum. Sound waves cause the eardrum to vibrate, and those vibrations cause the hammer (malleus) and anvil (incus) to move and the stirrup (stapes) to oscillate. These three tiny bones together are called the **ossicles**. The eardrum converts pressure variations to mechanical vibrations, which are then transmitted to the fluid contained in the compartments of the inner ear: the cochlea and the semicircular canals (which help us keep our balance).

The **cochlea** is a hollow, spiral-shaped bone that actually contains the organs of hearing (see Figure 10.1, Cross Section of the Cochlea). The mechanical vibrations caused by variations in the pressure that the stirrup exerts on the fluid are transmitted to the basilar membrane of the cochlea. This membrane supports the **hair cells**, which respond to different frequencies of sound. Each hair cell has about a hundred tiny, rigid spines, or cilia, at its top. When these hair cells move, they displace the fluid that surrounds them and produce electrochemical signals, which are sent through nerve cells along the **auditory nerve** (the eighth cranial nerve) to the brain, where the signals are perceived as tones. When these hair cells vibrate, they also create very low-level sounds called **otoacoustic emissions (OAEs)**. OAEs are a relatively new discovery. The ability to recognize them with special computer equipment is what makes it possible to diagnose deafness in newborns (Ross & Levitt, 2000).

Obstructions or damage anywhere along this path (from the outer ear, through the middle ear, to the inner ear) can result in hearing loss. The type of loss and how it is treated vary depending on its severity and on where the problem occurs. The impact is also affected by the individual's age at the time of the damage. In summary, the three parts of the hearing mechanism are

- *Outer ear:* the pinna and auditory canal
- *Middle ear:* the eardrum, Eustachian tube, and ossicles (hammer, anvil, and stirrup)
- *Inner ear:* the cochlea, its membranes and hair cells, and the semicircular canals

Types of Hearing Loss

There are two general types of hearing loss:

1. Conductive hearing loss
2. Sensorineural hearing loss

Blockage or damage to the outer or middle ear that prevents sound waves from traveling (being conducted) to the inner ear is called a **conductive hearing loss**. Generally, someone with a conductive hearing loss has a mild to moderate hearing disability. Some conductive hearing losses are temporary; in fact, we have all probably experienced a conductive hearing loss at some point in our lives. For example, you may have experienced a temporary loss of hearing as a consequence of a change in air pressure when flying in an airplane. Riding in a car in the mountains may also cause a temporary hearing loss.

Children often experience head colds and ear infections that result in a temporary loss of conductive hearing. Therefore, it is likely that on any given day, 20 percent of elementary school students have a mild conductive hearing loss, and some 80 percent of all children experience such hearing problems at some time between kindergarten and fifth grade (Gordon-Langbein & Metzinger, 2000). If the hearing loss was caused by a head cold, the hearing difficulties disappear once the ear infection clears up. Many conductive hearing losses that would otherwise *not* be considered "temporary" can usually be corrected with hearing aids or through surgery or other medical techniques.

When damage to the inner ear or the auditory nerve causes the problem, it is referred to as a **sensorineural hearing loss.** Some people refer to this type of hearing loss as nerve deafness. Sensorineural hearing losses are much more difficult to correct than conductive hearing losses. Individuals affected by a sensorineural loss are able to hear different frequencies at different intensity levels; their hearing losses are not flat or even. Sensorineural losses are less common in young children than the conductive types, but teachers need to understand that hearing aids can have mixed results with sensorineural losses.

ossicles Three tiny bones (hammer or malleus, anvil or incus, stirrup or stapes) in the middle ear that pass information to the cochlea

cochlea Structure that contains the organs of hearing

hair cells The part of the cochlea that responds to different frequencies of sound and produces electrochemical signals sent on to the brain

auditory nerve The eighth cranial nerve, which carries messages from the hearing mechanisms to the brain

otoacoustic emissions (OAEs) Low level of sound produced when the hair cells inside the inner ear vibrate

conductive hearing loss Hearing impairment that is due to damage or obstruction to the outer or middle ear and that interferes with transfer of sound to the inner ear

sensorineural hearing loss Hearing impairment due to damage to the inner ear or the auditory nerve

Degree of Hearing Loss

Hearing loss is often categorized as follows (Owens, Metz, and Haas, 2003):

- *Mild hearing loss (21–40 dB):* only speech that is soft or is produced at a distance is difficult to hear or understand
- *Moderate hearing loss (41–55 dB):* typical conversational speech is hard to follow
- *Moderately severe hearing loss (56–70 dB):* only loud speech can be heard
- *Severe hearing loss (71–90 dB):* even loud speech is hard to understand
- *Profound hearing loss (91 dB +):* considered "deaf," assistive listening devices alone enable the individual to understand information presented orally

Children learn and practice many skills through imaginary play. Dolls, like this signing Barbie®, that reflects one's culture and language can send important messages about approval to children.

Classifying hearing loss in these terms is difficult and does not always accurately represent the individual's ability to hear or the type of accommodations needed. Why might this be so? The answer rests partly in the amount and type of **residual hearing**—how much functional hearing—the person has. If the amount of loss is considerable and is predominantly in the sound ranges of speech, using oral communication will be more difficult than if the loss occurs outside of the speech bands (more details about this are provided in the Assessment section of this chapter). If the loss is conductive, the pattern is "flat"—that is, there is about the same amount of loss across the frequencies of different speech sounds; but if the loss is sensorineural, the ability to understand sounds (to hear) is uneven. Regardless, it is important to know that with a mild loss, the individual can still hear nearly all speech sounds and can hear most conversations (Moores, 2001). At the other end of the continuum, most people with profound hearing loss have hearing abilities that provide them with little useful hearing even if they use hearing aids.

Individuals with hearing loss are also grouped by their functional hearing abilities. Here's how to think about a functional organizational system: People who are hard of hearing can process information from sound, usually with the help of a hearing aid. Nearly all people who are deaf perceive some sound, but they cannot use hearing as their primary way to gain information.

Age of Onset

We have seen that the type and degree of hearing loss are important factors in the impact of hearing losses, but possibly most important is the age when the hearing loss occurs. As with most other disabilities, hearing loss can be congenital—occurring at or before birth—or acquired (adventitious)—occurring after birth. But, with hearing losses the more important consideration is whether the hearing loss occurred before or after the individual developed oral language. Individuals who are **prelingually deaf** become deaf before they learn to speak and understand language. They either are born deaf or lose their hearing as infants. Approximately 95 percent of all deaf children and youth are prelingually deaf. Their inability to hear language affects seriously their abilities to communicate with others and to learn academic subjects taught later in school. One in ten of those who are prelingually deaf have at least one deaf parent. Children in this group typically learn to communicate during the normal developmental period. However, instead of learning oral communication skills, many learn through a combination of manual communication (sign language) and oral language. Individuals who are **postlingually deaf** experience profound hearing loss after they have learned to speak and understand language. Many are able to retain their abilities to use speech and to communicate with others orally.

residual hearing The amount of functional hearing a person has

prelingually deaf Having lost the ability to hear before developing language

postlingually deaf Having lost the ability to hear after developing language; having acquired or adventitious deafness

Deaf of Deaf Members of the Deaf community who are prelingually deaf and have at least one parent who is Deaf

CODA A child of a Deaf adult who may or may not have a hearing loss

Characteristics

It's hard to generalize about students who are deaf or hard of hearing. They are all individuals with different learning styles and abilities, but they do share one characteristic: Their ability to hear is limited. As we have noted, the severity of the hearing loss and the age at which the loss occurred determine how well a person will be able to interact with others orally. IDEA '04 stresses the importance of the communication needs and style of students with hearing loss; those important points are summarized in *What IDEA '04 Says About Considering the Communication Needs of Students with Hearing Loss.* Another factor is whether the individual has coexisting disabilities. Estimates are that at least 30 to 40 percent of those who are deaf or hard of hearing have additional disabilities that often result from the same condition, disease, or accident that caused the hearing loss (Johnson & Winter, 2003). For example, trauma before or at birth often results in more than one disability. However, students whose deafness is inherited tend *not* to have multiple disabilities. The needs of students who are deaf differ from the needs of those who are hard of hearing. Also, among those who are deaf, two distinct groups exist: those who are Deaf and those who are deaf. Accordingly, we will discuss the characteristics of members of these two groups separately.

Students Who Are Members of the Deaf Community

In America, Deaf persons are members of the Deaf community, use ASL as their primary language, and typically do not use oral language as their means of communication. In other countries, Deaf communities exist but they use their own sign language as their means of communication. For example, in Britain they use BSL, in Greece GSL, and so on. But Deaf communities around the world report a sense of empowerment, belonging, and optimism (Davey, 2005; Nikolaraizi & Makri, 2004/2005). Furthermore, diverse members of the Deaf community often share determination and a positive outlook; this underscores the truly multicultural nature of deafness from a minority group perspective (Anderson & Miller, 2004/2005). As we consider Deaf people, their culture, and their language, think about how being a member of the Deaf community affects the lives of these individuals.

Deaf Culture

Members of the Deaf community consider the Deaf a minority group much like ethnic and racial minorities in this country (Branson & Miller, 2002; Zazove et al., 2004). To them, *deafness is not a disability* but, rather, one aspect of their lives that binds them together as a minority group rich in culture, history, language, and the arts. The language of the American Deaf community is ASL, which is used in all aspects of their culture. For example, plays are written in ASL and performed by Deaf theater groups around the world. ASL is also the language of a folk literature that has developed over the years. This community unites in many ways by coming together socially and for the purpose of advocacy, such as when they began the Deaf President Now Movement in 1988.

For many Deaf people, being **Deaf of Deaf** (being born Deaf of Deaf parents) or even being a **CODA** (Child of a Deaf Adult) is a source of considerable pride (Soloman, 1994). Although these individuals clearly

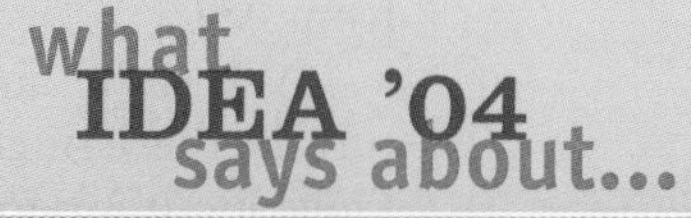

Considering the Communication Needs of Students with Hearing Loss

When developing the IEP for a student who is deaf or hard of hearing, the IEP Team must consider

- The individual's language and communication needs
- Opportunities for direct communication with peers and professional personnel in the student's language and communication mode
- The student's academic level
- The student's full range of needs, including opportunities for direct instruction in her or his language and communication mode

Deaf theater productions are performed using American Sign Language (ASL) and can be enjoyed by everyone at many venues across the country. Here, Tyrone Giofdano and Michael McElroy are signing a scene during a rehearsal of "Big River" in New York.

represent a minority within a minority, life can be substantially easier for them. They learn sign language as their native language, which they develop naturally just as hearing babies develop oral language. These children are not preoccupied by their deafness but, rather, are engaged in childhood and play (Sheridan, 2001). For these individuals, their deafness is a language difference, not a disability (Drasgow, 1998; Lane, 1995). They are much like those you learned about in Chapter 1 who grew up in the Deaf communities that thrived on Martha's Vineyard during the 1800s (Groce, 1985; Kageleiry, 2002). Because everyone on the island of Martha's Vineyard at that time knew sign language (a precursor to ASL), the Deaf there were not handicapped by their inability to hear or communicate orally. Deaf individuals consider themselves part of the Deaf community. Most are active in its activities and clubs, attend Deaf Theater, travel in groups, use ASL as their language, and believe that it is important to learn about their culture. Some of those who became Deaf later in life, and perhaps learned ASL at a school for the Deaf, have grown away from their families because they no longer live in the hearing world. In fact, to the delight of many and the criticism of others, some Deaf families are looking to re-create the separateness of the "old days" on Martha's Vineyard (Szalay, 2005). *Disability in the News* tells how Martin Miller—along with 100 other Deaf families—are creating a Deaf town in South Dakota (Davey, 2005).

ASL: Deaf Language

ASL (American Sign Language) is the fifth most commonly studied foreign language on college campuses across the country (Davey, 2005). It is a complete and complex language and is *not* a translation of the English language (National Institute on Deafness and Other Communication Disorders [NIDCD], 2000). **Signed English** is a manual communication translation of English. ASL has its own rules for grammar, punctuation, and sentence order. Also, as we have noted, ASL is not a universal language. For example, British Sign Language (BSL) is very different from ASL.

ASL is the language of the Deaf community and the focal point for Deaf culture in the United States. To most people who are Deaf, it is a second language. Only about 5 percent of Deaf individuals are born of Deaf parents and learn ASL as their native language. The vast majority of others are assimilated into the culture later in life, often at residential schools for the Deaf (Fletcher, 1994). It is important to remember that Deaf students and their families consider themselves members of a minority group. As is true of other culturally diverse students, the educators who teach them have much to learn about and understand.

Students Who Are Deaf

People who are deaf also have profound hearing loss, but they use oral communication when others are talking and express themselves orally. Instructionally, these two groups are very different from each other. What about the majority of the prelingually deaf? Recall that 95 percent of deaf children are born of hearing parents. Many of these youngsters do not develop language (either oral or manual) at the time when they developmentally should, which can be devastating to

signed English Translation of English into a form of manual communication

Disability in the News

As Town for Deaf Takes Shape, Debate on Isolation Re-Emerges

The New York Times nytimes.com expect the world®

Date: 3/21/2005
Monica Davey

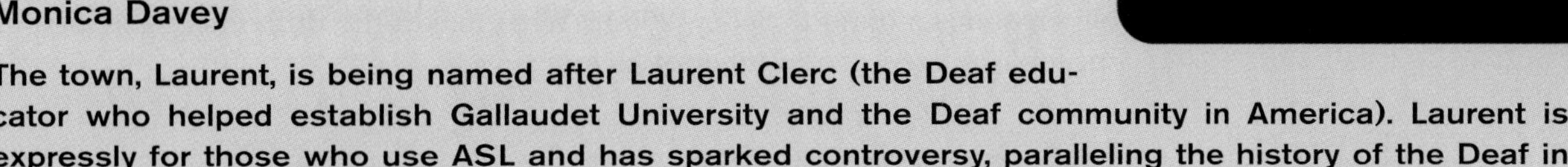

The town, Laurent, is being named after Laurent Clerc (the Deaf educator who helped establish Gallaudet University and the Deaf community in America). Laurent is expressly for those who use ASL and has sparked controversy, paralleling the history of the Deaf in America. To Martin Miller, his wife, and their four children the motivation of living in an exclusively ASL town is simple: to live life where they are fully engaged in all aspects of daily life. Other Deaf people—even those not intending to move to Laurent—applaud Miller's efforts to create a place where life is adapted to meet the needs of the Deaf (fewer sirens and more lights on fire engines and police cars, more unobstructed views) and so full participation in all social situations is possible. However, critics argue that Deaf towns only promote segregation and isolation—themes familiar to the debates about schools for the deaf held in the 1800s.

the individual's development of cognitive and social skills. The challenges for these youngsters and their families are great. Many parents fear that if their children learn ASL as their first language, they will be excluded from mainstream society, seek out the Deaf community, and be lost to their natural family (Goldberg, 1995).

Academic Achievement

A long-term problem for deaf individuals is their academic achievement, particularly in the area of reading (Johnson, 2001–2002; Moores, 2001). Reading skills are important for many reasons. First, being able to profit from captions for television and film requires an ability to read and comprehend. Second, the Internet and e-mail communications depend on reading skills. Third, individuals who are deaf who have higher reading abilities are more likely to graduate from college and to obtain higher-paying jobs when in the workforce (Cuculick & Kelly, 2003). But reading is a challenge for many students who are deaf. For example, by age 20, half of such students tested read below the mid-fourth-grade level, leaving them unable to read most newspapers, which are written at least at the fifth-grade level. Of high school graduates who are deaf, 15 percent of White graduates, 6 percent of Black graduates, and 5 percent of Latinos/as could read above the sixth-grade level (Goldin-Meadow & Mayberry, 2001). These outcomes should show improvement for the next generation of students for several important reasons (Marschark, 2001). First, with earlier identification and intervention, the academic achievement of these students improves greatly. Second, new approaches and validated practices, such as bilingual/bicultural instruction, make substantial differences in the learning outcomes of students with disabilities. Also, more motivation might exist for deaf people to learn to read. Many technological advances that have been developed to benefit people with hearing loss, such as captioned television and films, require an ability to read well.

Speech Abilities

Being able to hear is related to the ability to speak intelligibly. Although there are some remarkable exceptions, as a general rule of thumb, as the degree of hearing loss increases, the intelligibility of speech decreases (Svirsky et al., 2002). When investigators compared two groups of children between the ages of five and ten—those with profound hearing loss and those with mild to severe hearing loss—the evidence was unmistakable. The speech of those with profound losses was not intelligible. For those with mild to severe losses, the speech of 82 percent was intelligible (Yoshinaga-Itano & Sedey, 2000). What makes the difference? Intelligibility of speech is related to a number of factors:

- Degree of hearing loss
- Age of the individual
- Communication mode used by the family
- Presence of another disability

Being able to understand someone's speech is also partly determined by the listener's experience (Most, Weisel, & Lev-Matezky, 1996). The resulting inconsistency in the ability to understand the speaker is one reason why data about the intelligibility of deaf children's speech are confusing. Unfortunately, a relationship also exists between a person's speech ability and how others perceive that person's overall abilities: As ratings of intelligibility go down, ratings of cognitive competence and personality decline. Learning to speak is a difficult and arduous task for children who are deaf, requiring years of effort and systematic instruction. Because it is so easy to misjudge the intentions and actions of students who have difficulty communicating, teachers who are careful not to interpret deaf students' behaviors harshly make a real difference in the outcomes of these students.

Students Who Are Hard of Hearing

Students who are hard of hearing have milder losses than their peers who are deaf. Typically, they have conductive hearing losses, which are more easily helped with a hearing aid. Unfortunately, however, these students are easily overlooked or their disability minimized. It is important for educators to understand that students who are hard of hearing find it more difficult than their classmates without disabilities to learn vocabulary, grammar, word order, and language (National Dissemination Center for Children with Disabilities [NICHCY], 2004). Even a mild hearing loss in one ear can cause a student to struggle academically (Haller & Montgomery, 2004; Tharpe, 2004). One reason may be the extra effort it takes to listen carefully to the teacher, take notes, and process what is being presented. Another reason is that we often don't realize that a little difference in hearing ability makes a big difference in what is understood. For example, in a noisy classroom even a loss of 16 db (just within the range of what is considered normal hearing) results in missing up to 10 percent of what a teacher says a mere three feet away from the student with the hearing loss (Harrington, 2003). Without amplification, those with losses of 35 to 40 db—clearly in the range of a mild loss—may miss 50 percent of what the teacher or classmates say during discussions! Clearly, these students should be supported with many visuals, such as pictures, graphs, charts, and written notes about the topic of discussion, as well as with special seating arrangements so they can see everyone who is taking turns speaking. *Tips for Classroom Management* provides some suggestions about helping students who are hard of hearing to profit more from the general education curriculum.

for Classroom Management

MAKE ADJUSTMENTS FOR EASE OF HEARING AND SEEING SPEAKERS

- Place the student as close to the speaker as possible.
- Instead of a blackboard, use an overhead projector or a computer with a projection system so the speaker can face the class when talking. (Be sure there is no glare obstructing the projection.)
- Reduce background noise as much as possible.
- Do not stand with direct light behind you.
- For class discussions, make certain the student knows who is about to speak and ensure that he or she is able to see each individual who is talking.
- For class discussions, arrange students' chairs in a circle so the student can see everyone's face.

Prevalence

Hearing loss is associated with age. Over half of the people with hearing problems are over the age of 65. In fact, 1 in 3 adults over the age of 65 has hearing loss, though interestingly, only 25 percent of them use a hearing aid (HearingLoss.org, 2005). Although hearing loss in children is the number-one birth defect in the United States, it is still a very low incidence disability, affecting only 0.13 percent of all students (U.S. Department of Education, 2005b). Approximately 1 in every 1,000 babies is born profoundly deaf, and another 2 to 3 have less severe hearing loss.

Obtaining reliable statistics, however, about the number of special education students with hearing problems is difficult because states use different criteria for counting who is deaf, is hard of hearing, and/or has multiple disabilities. In addition, the U.S. Department of Education only reports students by their primary disability. For example, hearing loss is a characteristic of Down syndrome (American Speech-Language-Hearing Association [ASHA], 2005a). However, these students are typically only reported in the mental retardation category, or possibly in the multiple disabilities category, but never in the federal hearing impairments category. Also, the government's counts do not include students with hearing loss but do not need special education because hearing aids allow them to hear well enough to participate in typical classroom activities without additional assistance. Considering these factors, the number of students who are deaf and hard of hearing is probably underestimated.

Causes and Prevention

It is not a surprise to learn that hearing loss can result from illness or injury. For example, sustained loud noise can cause a hearing loss. In addition, some types of deafness are the result of heredity. This was the reason why Alexander Graham Bell, in the late 1800s, proposed legislation to ban marriage between two deaf people; fortunately, he was unsuccessful. For educators, understanding the causes of hearing loss can be useful, because the type of loss can have a bearing on the accommodations necessary for effective instruction. For everyone, knowing how to prevent hearing loss or minimize its effects is important.

Causes

The cause most often associated with hearing loss *in children* is unknown, but it is suspected that 50 percent of newborns who are deaf have genetic reasons for their deafness (ASHA, 2005a). Some causes of childhood deafness or hearing problems are very rare. For example, congenital cytomegalovirus (CMV) infection, a herpes virus, affects about 2 percent of all newborns but in rare cases can cause mild to profound sensorineural hearing losses and other disabilities as well. Other causes—although the incidence is still low—are more common than CMV. The four most common *known* causes for children's deafness and hearing problems, in order of prevalence, are

1. *Heredity and Genetics* The most common known causes of deafness and profound hearing loss in children, documented as being responsible for more than 150 different types of deafness, have a hereditary origin. Genetic causes can be both congenital and sensorineural. Most children whose deafness is inherited are less likely to have multiple disabilities.
2. *Meningitis* The second most common known cause of childhood deafness is a disease that affects the central nervous system (specifically the meninges, the coverings of the brain and spinal cord, and their circulating fluid). Most cases that involve a hearing loss are bacterial infections rather than the more lethal viral meningitis. This disease is the most common cause of students' postnatal deafness and is one major cause of acquired profound sensorineural hearing losses (not present at birth). These hearing losses may occur after the individual has developed some speech and language. Although vaccines do exist to prevent this disease, no national immunization program protects all children from the ravages of meningitis.
3. *Otitis Media* Infections of the middle ear result in an accumulation of fluid behind the eardrum that interrupt the process of hearing. The condition can be corrected and treated with antibiotics and other medical procedures. Depending on the frequency and duration of the infections, the result can be a language impairment that affects future academic learning. Chronic, untreated otitis media can cause a permanent conductive hearing loss by damaging the eardrum and resulting in a mild to moderate hearing loss (Laurent Clerc National Deaf Education Center, 2002). Typically these individuals are classified in the "hard of hearing" group, have conductive hearing losses, and profit from the use of hearing aids.
4. *Noise* Only recently has noise been acknowledged as a major contributor to hearing loss in teenagers and adults. The dangers of noise are now clear: It is a major cause of hearing loss that can be prevented (Haller & Montgomery, 2004). European countries took steps to ensure noise abatement first, but the United States is taking action as well. The U.S. Occupational Safety and Health Administration (OSHA) has set standards indicating that exposure to noise louder than 105 dB for longer than an hour is unsafe. Imagine the damage caused by the sound levels of a rock concert (which often reach 125 dB), a car stereo, or an I-Pod or MP3 player. Indications are that young males are more likely to acquire noise-induced hearing losses because they frequently engage in activities such as mowing the lawn, firing a gun, riding a motorcycle, and fixing a car engine. Even infants and toddlers can sustain irreversible noise-induced hearing losses. Most hearing loss from noise occurs slowly, across years of exposure, without any pain or awareness (NIDCD, 2002a). Figure 10.2 shows what sounds are considered in the danger zone.

Prevention

Many cases of childhood hearing loss are preventable. For example, maternal rubella (German measles) was once a major cause of deafness in newborns; in 1972 it was responsible for almost 11 percent of known causes of deafness, but

Figure 10.2 • Decibel Levels of Noise in American Environments

Hearing Level in Decibels	Examples of Common Sounds
30	Soft whisper, quiet library
40	Leaves rustling
50	Rainfall, refrigerator
60	Normal conversation, air conditioner
70	City or freeway traffic, sewing machine
80	Hair dryer, alarm clock
90*	Lawn mower, motorcycle
100	Garbage truck, snowmobile
110	Shouting at close range, dance club, race car
120	Jet plane taking off, car stereo turned all the way up
130	Live rock music, jackhammer
140	Firecracker, nearby gunshot blast, jet engine

*Levels 85 decibels and above are considered hazardous.

Source: U.S. Congress Select Committee on Children, Youth, and Families.

because of immunizations that rate had dropped to 1 percent in 1998. All cases of noise-induced hearing loss are preventable. Avoiding noises over 85 dB (look again at Figure 10.2) and wearing earplugs in places such as woodworking shops and when mowing the lawn can reduce or eliminate a major reason for hearing loss in adults.

Overcoming Challenges: Technology

Technology and assistive devices can be credited with much of the improved access to mainstream society experienced by people with disabilities, but the promise for tomorrow hints at participation not even dreamed of a generation or two ago. Minda Huebner (2002) helps us see into the future. "In my vision of tomorrow's world, I see many technological advancements that will . . . enable people with

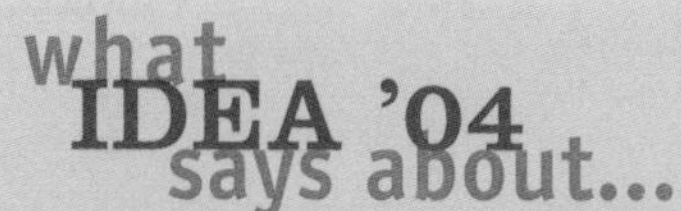

Hearing Aids and Cochlear Implants

Through its assistive technology and related services provisions, IDEA '04 specifically addresses the use of hearing aids, while indirectly addressing cochlear implants. For example, districts must ensure that

- Assistive technology devices and/or services are made available to a child with a hearing disability
- Hearing aids worn in school by children with hearing impairments are functioning properly

Furthermore,

- The term *assistive technology device* does not include a surgically implanted medical device or its replacement
- The term *related services* does not include a surgically implanted medical device, nor does it include optimization of functioning, maintenance, or replacement of the device.

hearing loss to understand things that do not have lips, like televisions, telephones, and intercoms" (p. 9). Here are some of the advances she envisions:

- Special glasses that show movie captions that are invisible to everyone else
- Telephones that show the words of conversations on mini-screens
- Waterproof hearing aids that let everyone participate in water fights, soccer in the rain, and swim meets
- Home computers that make all of the lights in the house flash and alarm clocks vibrate when the smoke alarm goes off
- Lights on all cars' dashboards to indicate when an emergency vehicle is near

Clearly, the possibilities are endless, but barriers can make it impossible for many to experience Huebner's dreams about tomorrow. The costs of assistive devices, although they decrease across time, limit people's access to helpful equipment. As you might imagine, cost is a major issue for people who are deaf or hard of hearing; many are unable to afford improved hearing aids or the wide range of devices that would help them. Government agencies are usually not of much assistance (Trychin, 2001). Assistive devices can be grouped into four categories:

- Assistive listening devices
- Telecommunication devices
- Computerized speech-to-text translations
- Alerting devices

Assistive Listening Devices

Assistive listening devices help people with hearing losses by increasing the amplification of sounds in the environment, including others' speech. Three general types of assistive listening devices are available: hearing aids, cochlear implants, and FM transmission systems. Read *What IDEA '04 Says About Hearing Aids and Cochlear Implants* to learn about some specific federal guidelines for two of these assistive listening devices.

Most conductive losses can be corrected with medicine or surgery, so people who use **hearing aids**—assistive devices that amplify sounds but are not surgically implanted—typically have sensorineural hearing losses. The hearing aid is the most commonly used assistive device for this group of people; it amplifies sound so that the person can hear more easily. These assistive listening devices have improved greatly over the years—look again at the photo of Dorothy Brett, the artist whose work is shown at the beginning of this chapter, and her hearing trumpet, a precursor to today's hearing aids. Today's hearing aids allow many individuals to hear well within the normal range. These devices have eliminated the need for special education for many children who are hard of hearing; with their hearing aids, they can profit from general education classes and participate fully in mainstream society. Four different kinds of hearing aids are available:

- Behind the ear (BTE)
- In the ear (ITE)
- In the canal (ITC)
- Completely in the canal (CIC)

assistive listening devices (ALDs) Equipment (e.g., hearing aids, audio loops, FM transmission devices) that helps improve the use of residual hearing

hearing aids Assistive listening devices that intensify sound

Figure 10.3 • Cochlear Implant

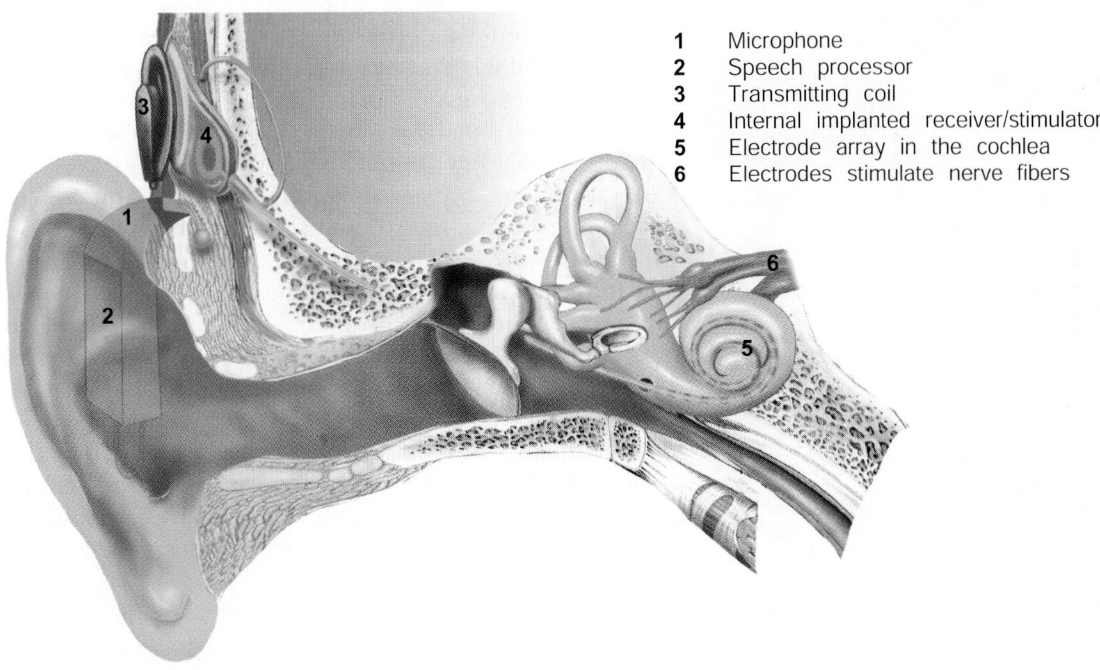

Courtesy Cochlear Ltd.

Because appearance is particularly important to children and teenagers, few select BTEs, even though they tend to be somewhat more effective than those that are hidden in the ear. Many hearing aids are digital and are designed to address each individual's hearing profile. **Digital hearing aids** automatically adjust volume by amplifying sounds only to the degree necessary to compensate for the loss at each frequency of sound. They also significantly reduce background noise. Older analog models amplify all sounds equally, making it impossible to discriminate speech from noise. A new type of hearing aid is gaining in popularity, possibly because of issues related to keeping hearing aids clean and undamaged. The Songbird Disposable Hearing Aid (SDHA), which now also comes in a digital version, costs about $1 per day it is worn (Ross, 2002). Certainly, disposable aids have great advantages for children, who often damage their aids and find it impossible to keep them clean. Teachers and parents must recognize, however, that hearing aids do not solve all problems associated with hearing loss. Even when hearing aids are carefully matched to and programmed for the individual, they do not completely overcome the limitations of an impaired ear (Ross, 2002; Sweetow & Luckett, 2001).

Another type of assistive listening device helps those with sensorineural hearing losses access the world of sounds. **Cochlear implants** are surgically implanted devices that use a small speech processor and microphone to detect sound and then send electrical signals to the implanted receiver/stimulator, which stimulates the occiscles and the the cochlea, passing information on through the auditory nerve to the brain. Figure 10.3 shows a typical cochlear implant, which converts acoustic information to electrical signals that stimulate the individual's remaining auditory nerve fibers. Since the U.S. Federal Food and Drug Administration approved cochlear implants in 1990, great advances have been made (NIDCD, 2002b). Originally thought to hold the promise of "bionic ears," they first were used only with people who experienced severe hearing losses later in life. These individuals have already developed the ability to understand

digital hearing aids Assistive listening devices that amplify sound according to individuals' hearing profiles

cochlear implant A microprocessor, surgically placed in the hearing mechanism, that replaces the cochlea so that people with sensorineural hearing loss can perceive sounds

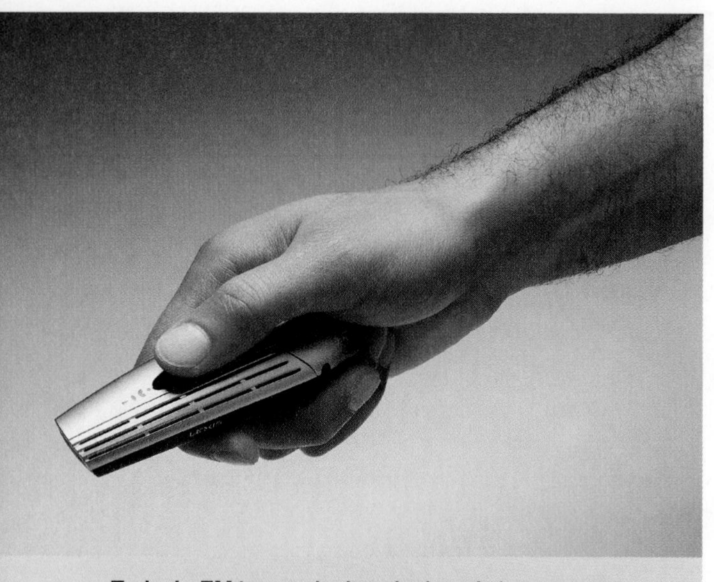

Today's FM transmission devices bring greater freedom to teachers and students. With wireless microphones that can be clipped to a shirt and receivers small enough to attach to hearing aids, teaching and learning is certainly less cumbersome.

speech and language, so their experiences with implants are very different from those of infants and young children with congential deafness who have not yet learned to process and understand sounds. Because research is showing that individuals who received implants before the age of 2 have better expressive language than those who received implants later, infants as young as 1 year now receive implants (Bergeson, Pisoni, & Davis, 2003; Kirk et al., 2002). Even so, the verbal abilities of most "implanted" preschoolers lag behind those of their peers without hearing loss (Chin & Kaiser, 2002). It is important to put these data into perspective: Relatively few infants and toddlers have received implants, and their surgeries were recent. In 1997, a total of 8 children 18 months old or younger had received a cochlear implant (Sorkin, 2002). That number had risen to 90 in 2000 and to 149 in 2001. It can take years before implants actually provide their intended benefits, because the brain has to learn to translate the electronic impulses generated by implants into meaningful messages (Marschark, 2001). Much, therefore, remains to be learned about implants and children.

Background noise is a major problem in many classrooms, lecture halls, theaters, auditoriums, recreational centers, cafeterias, and other large rooms (Smaldino, 2004). **FM (frequency-modulated) transmission devices** overcome the distance and noise problems that nearly always arise in general education classrooms (Halligan, 2003). New versions of this technology use small devices, which provide freedom of movement for both teacher and students. The teacher speaks into a small microphone either clipped to a shirt or worn lavaliere style (as a pendant on a chain). Students receive sound through a small receiver connected directly to their hearing aids. Background noise is reduced, and teachers are free to move around the classroom without worrying about having their faces in full view of all their students. For large rooms such as lecture and concert halls, another solution is the **audio loop**, which routes sound from its source directly to the listener's ear through a specially equipped hearing aid or earphone. Sound may travel through a wire connection or through radio waves. Audio loops are inexpensive and are easy to install in rooms that seat up to 100 persons. Since passage of the ADA law, audio loops are found in most concert halls, theaters, airports, and churches, giving people with hearing loss greater access to events. Of course, such sound systems benefit only those individuals who profit from amplification.

What's on the horizon? Blue Cross Insurance Company now approves, for reimbursement, surgically implanted hearing aids that cause the middle ear bones to vibrate and thereby transmit sound to the inner ear (Blue Cross of California, 2004). For those with moderate to severe sensorineural hearing losses who find that hearing aids are not effective enough, these middle ear implants provide about 85 percent improvement in hearing and do not amplify distracting background noise as they increase the individual's ability to hear speech (Wagner, 2002). Clearly, the use of these devices will become commonplace in the near future. Other research efforts will not yield results that can be applied for pubic benefit for many years to come. Here's an example: Although some animals are able to regenerate hair cells automatically and regain the ability to hear, these cells do not regenerate automatically in humans (Uffen, 2005). About 80 percent of irreversible hearing loss is caused by damage to the hair cells in the inner ear. Researchers have been able to make hair cells regenerate experimentally, but getting the right hair cells to grow in the proper numbers remains challenging (Bauman, 2004). Even so, this potential medical technology holds promise for what may become a way to treat this type of sensorineural hearing loss (Vanderhoff, 2003).

FM (frequency-modulated) transmission devices Assistive listening devices that provide oral transmissions directly from the teacher to students with hearing loss

audio loop A listening device that directs sound from the source directly to the listener's ear through a specially designed hearing aid

Telecommunication Devices

Assistive **telecommunication devices** are designed to improve access to and enjoyment of cinema and television through sight. Many different types of telecommunication devices and systems help people with hearing loss. For example, **captions** are printed words that appear at the bottom of a TV screen (like the subtitles that translate dialog in foreign films or the ticker seen on news shows). "The French Chef with Julia Child" was the first captioned television show, appearing on public television in 1972. It used **open captions**, which are seen by all viewers, but they were unpopular with the general public. In the 1980s another system was developed. **Closed captions** uses a system that allows the viewer to choose whether the captions are seen on the TV screen. All television sets sold since 1993 are equipped with an internal, micro-sized decoder that allows captions to be placed anywhere on the screen (to avoid interfering with on-screen titles or other important information in the program) and to appear in different colors. Nearly all TV programming today includes the option of viewing closed captions. Captioning is an important tool for people who are deaf, because it affords them equal access to public information, emergency broadcasting, and entertainment. Data indicate that deaf people use captions. They spend some 84 percent of their viewing time reading the captions, 14 percent watching the video picture, and only 2 percent not watching the video (Jensema, Danturthi, and Burch, 2000). Captioning has been much slower in coming to the movie theaters, and people with profound hearing losses have had to wait to see films until they are available in captioned DVDs. However, experiments with different captioning systems for movie theaters are moving forward. For example, **rear window captioning (RWC)** projects captions from a message board on the theater's rear wall onto a clear plastic screen that attaches to the moviegoer's seat; the individual looks at a transparent Plexiglas panel to see the captions and forward to see the movie.

Another important assistive device enables those who are deaf to make and receive telephone calls. The **text telephone (TTY)**, formerly referred to as the telecommunication device for the deaf (TDD), prints out the voice message for the person with a hearing loss and can also be used to send messages. Most TTYs have one major drawback: A unit is required at both the sending and the receiving end. There are two solutions to this problem. First, the Federal Communications Commission requires all states to have a **telecommunications relay service (TRS)**, which allows a TTY user to "talk" to a person using a standard phone. An operator at a relay center places the call on a voice line and reads the typed message from the TTY to the non-TTY user. The relay service enables deaf individuals to use the phone, via an 800 phone number, for everything from calling a doctor to ordering a pizza. Most people who are deaf or hard of hearing prefer to use their voice on a phone call, and a new device is now available. The **voice carry over (VCO)** is a TTY that includes the option of using both voice and text. For those who want to use their voices but need to receive telephone communication through print, these phones allow for both voice and text transmissions. A relay operator types what the hearing person says, which is then displayed on the text phone. VCOs have many advantages, particularly for hearing people with deaf family members or friends, for businesses that want both options but do not want to invest in two different phones, and for public places so that everyone has access to the telephone system. For those who want quicker response times and the option for both parties to talk at the same time, a two-phone-line VCO system is now available. And there is even a TTY/voice answering machine that takes messages in either format.

The demand for TTYs is decreasing because of technology designed for use by the general public. For example, more and more people with hearing losses communicate with family, friends, and business associates by using e-mail. Network-enabled **personal data assistants (PDAs)** are devices that allow the user to send text messages, use e-mail, and access the Web via wireless telephone systems. PDAs are reducing the need for TTYs. For all users, PDAs can vibrate with each incoming communication, allow for immediate responses that are typed, and free people from specific locations to send and receive messages.

telecommunication devices Devices that provide oral information in alternative formats (e.g., captions for TV or movies)

captions Subtitles that print words spoken in film or video

open captions Subtitles or tickers that are part of the screen image of a film or video for everyone to see

closed captions Subtitles to a film or video that are available only to those who select the option

rear window captioning (RWC) Closed captions used in movie theaters that projects printed words onto a clear screen on the back of the seat in front of the moviegoer

text telephone (TTY) A device that allows people to make and receive telephone calls by typing information instead of speaking; formerly called the telecommunication device for the deaf (TDD)

telecommunications relay service (TRS) A telephone system, required by federal law to be available in all states, wherein an operator at a relay center converts a print-telephone message into a voice-telephone message

voice carry over (VCO) A text telephone allowing both voice and text

personal data assistants (PDAs) Devices that allow the user to send text messages, use e-mail, and access the Web via wireless telephone systems

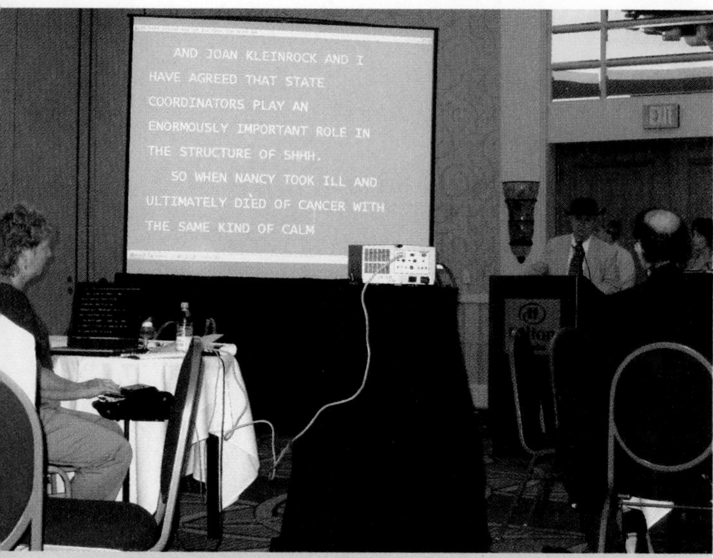
AND JOAN KLEINROCK AND I
HAVE AGREED THAT STATE
COORDINATORS PLAY AN
ENORMOUSLY IMPORTANT ROLE IN
THE STRUCTURE OF SHHH.
SO WHEN NANCY TOOK ILL AND
ULTIMATELY DIED OF CANCER WITH
THE SAME KIND OF CALM
EXIT

Realtime captioning (RTC) allows everyone to read those parts of lectures they missed because they couldn't hear the teacher (or maybe because they were not paying attention and thinking about what to wear to Saturday night's party).

Speech-to-Text Translations

Workers with profound hearing losses attending conferences and meetings often experience the same frustrations as college students during college lectures. It is difficult to take notes and read lips or watch a sign language interpreter simultaneously. **Real-time captioning (RTC)** can help deaf people in such situations. Several systems have been developed. C-Print® can translate up to 300 words a minute and is the fastest translation system currently available. C-Print® uses a laptop computer, a specially developed word abbreviation software program, and a computer visual display. The trained C-Print® captionist listens to the lecture and types codes that represent words into the computer; the transcription is instantly shown on a monitor or on the individual's laptop. It is ideal for lectures (Stinson et al., 2001). Once the lecture is completed, students can also get a printout—a benefit that lots of class members can appreciate. Many students who attend traditional colleges and universities, and who would otherwise have to rely on an interpreter, report that RTC does not make them feel different and even improves social interactions (Kramlinger, 1996).

Another system that might solve problems associated with accessing the general education curriculum, which relies heavily on oral communication (at least for those who have good reading abilities), is technology-based speech-to-text translations. **Automatic speech recognition (ASR)** is technology that enables the computer automatically to convert speech at rates below 160 words per minute into text with error rates of less than 3 to 4 percent (Davis, 2001). ASR was developed for dictation, so the system does not recognize multiple speakers and is not beneficial for group discussion periods. Regardless, the benefits to persons with hearing disabilities are great.

Alerting Devices

Alerting devices make people who are deaf aware of an event or important sound in their environment via a loud noise or the sense of sight or touch. A loud gong, flashing light, or vibration can signal a fire alarm, doorbell, alarm clock, or telephone. Some such devices attach to a lamp that flashes on and off for a signal. Others attach to vibrators (in the bed for an alarm clock or on a person's belt as a personal signaler). Some alerting devices include sound-sensitive monitors that let the deaf person know about a baby who is crying or about an out-of-the-ordinary sound. Some such systems are now wireless, allowing great flexibility in placement of these devices and in the number of them that can be activated at any one time (Vanderhoff & Lakins, 2003).

Assessment

As you have learned, sound is caused by perception of the vibration of molecules propagated through some medium such as air, water, or wires. Two qualities of sound are measured in the assessment process: frequency and intensity. The **frequency of sound** is the number of vibrations per second. High frequencies are perceived through our ears as high pitch or tone; low frequencies are perceived as low pitch or deep sounds. **Hertz (Hz)** is the unit in which frequency is measured. The normal ear hears sounds that range from approximately 20 Hz to 20,000 Hz; speech sounds fall about in the middle of the human hearing range (between 250 Hz and 4,000 Hz). Those of you who have some knowledge of music might find Lowenbraun's (1995) explanation of hertz helpful. The frequency of middle C on the piano is approximately 250 Hz. The next vertical line on the audiogram, 500 Hz, is approximately one octave above middle C; 1,000 is two octaves above middle C; and so on. (See the scale in Figure 10.4 on page 372.) Humans cannot perceive some sounds, whatever their hearing abilities. For example, some dog whistles use high frequencies that are beyond humans' hearing range.

The second sound quality assessed is **sound intensity**, or loudness. **Decibels (dB)** are the units employed to measure the intensity of sounds. Softer, quieter sounds have lower decibel measurements; louder sounds have higher decibel numbers. A decibel level of 125 or greater is painful to the average person. Decibel levels ranging from 0 to 120 dB are used to test how well an individual can hear different frequencies; a child with normal hearing should be able to perceive sounds at 0 dB. The scale used to assess hearing has been adjusted so that 0 indicates no loss and numbers greater than 0 indicate the degree or amount of loss. Small numbers indicate mild losses; large numbers indicate moderate to severe or profound losses.

Early Identification

In 41 states and Washington, DC, **universal newborn hearing screening** is now a reality, and legislation is pending in 3 more states (ASHA, 2005b). In 2003, 87 percent of all newborns were screened for hearing loss, a 17-fold increase from 10 years earlier, when only 5 percent of newborns were tested (Johnson & Winter, 2003). Early detection is cost effective and reliable, providing critical information to families and service agencies early. Young children with profound hearing losses who receive early intervention services have much better outcomes than those who do not (Magnuson, 2000). In fact, those identified before they are 6 months old experience *half* the delays of those identified after they are 18 months old (Yoshinaga-Itano & Apuzzo, 1998). One reason for these improved outcomes is that infants even as young as 3 months old can now be fitted with hearing aids so that they will not miss out on important opportunities to learn at the right developmental ages (Hoover, 2000). A number of different and reliable methods for testing are now available, making it possible to identify children early and bring them needed services so they do not miss out on the early stages of learning language (Cone-Wesson, 2003). One means of finding newborns with hearing loss who need further testing is to determine the presence of the OAEs (low-level sounds) produced by normally working ears when the hair cells in the middle ear vibrate (read again page 357 in this chapter for a review). Ears that are not working normally do not produce OAEs. Before the discovery of OAEs and the implementation of universal infant screening, young children typically were not identified until they are $2\frac{1}{2}$ years old, and intervention did not begin until a year later. The impact of universal screening is tremendous. Whether the option selected is manual communication or a cochlear implant or some combination of hearing aids and signing, early identification and intervention are responsible for higher results for these individuals (Sussman et al, 2004). Who knows what the future holds for babies identified with hearing loss today? All we know for certain is that the improvements possible will be amazing!

Pre-Referral: Hearing Screenings

As you have learned, the pre-referral stage in the special education identification process is important to ensure that students with disabilities are identified correctly and quickly. Students with mild to moderate hearing losses are frequently overlooked and are often incorrectly thought to have an attention or a learning problem. Some states and school districts screen all of their students for both hearing and vision problems, but not all do. Regardless, teachers should be

real-time captioning (RTC) Practically instantaneous translations of speech into print; an accommodation for students who are deaf attending lectures

automatic speech recognition (ASR) Technology that converts speech into text almost instantaneously

alerting devices Assistive devices for people who are deaf to make them aware of events in their environment through a loud sound or other means (e.g., flashing lights, vibrators)

frequency of sound The number of vibrations per second of molecules through some medium such as air, water, or wires causing sound

hertz (Hz) Unit of measure for sound frequency

sound intensity Loudness

decibel (dB) Unit of measure for intensity of sound

universal newborn hearing screening Testing of all newborns for hearing loss

Figure 10.4 • Travis's Audiogram

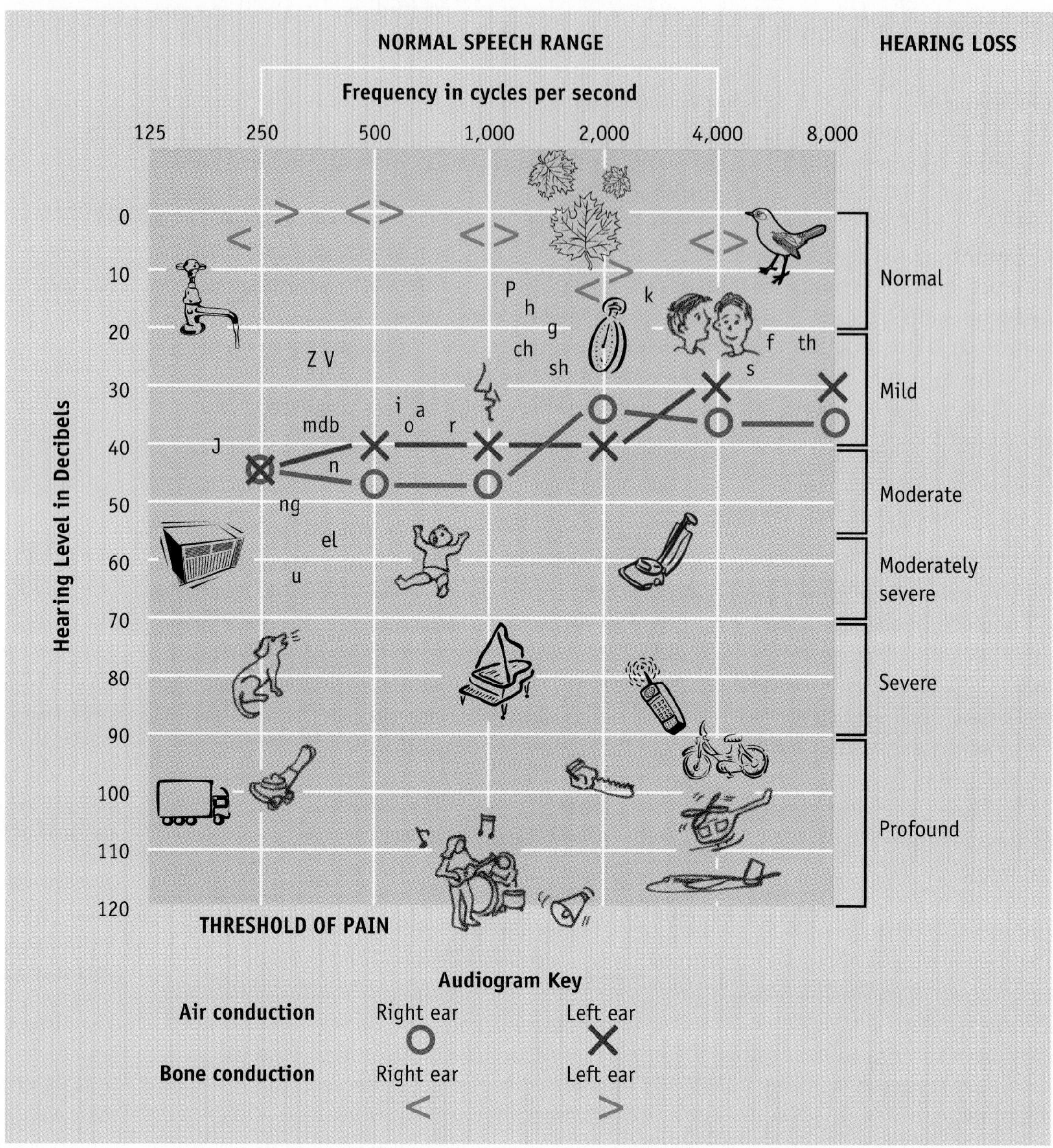

Source: Hearing in Children (p. 7) by J. L. Northern and M. P. Downs, 1984, Baltimore: Williams & Wilkins. Reprinted by permission.

attentive and should refer "questionable" students to an SLP for an initial assessment. If a student needs further diagnosis by an **audiologist**—a specialist in the assessment of hearing abilities—a multidisciplinary team will be put into place. But it is important to remember that many students with mild hearing losses go unnoticed and that the educational (and social) results can be tragic. With quick action, students whose hearing problems can be at least partially solved by the use of a hearing aid can profit from classroom instruction. Those students whose wait for services was long because their hearing loss was not identified early can still profit from the services of SLPs and from therapy for language development. Thus, even high school teachers should be attentive to possible hearing problems among their students.

audiologist Related service provider; diagnoses hearing losses and auditory problems

Identification: Auditory Assessments

Earlier we reviewed how infants' hearing is assessed. Different methods are used for babies and adults. For children and adults, audiologists use **pure sounds**—sound waves of specific frequencies—at various combinations of hertz (Hz) and decibels (dB) and also at various bands of pitch and loudness. These assessments are conducted in soundproof rooms so that distractions such as those found in classrooms are eliminated. They also use special equipment, such as an **audiometer**, an instrument that produces sounds at precise frequencies and intensities. The results of these audiological assessments are plotted on an **audiogram**, which is a grid or graph. Along the top of the graph are hertz levels; the vertical lines represent different levels of sound frequency, in hertz. Each ear is tested separately. A hearing threshold is determined by noting when the person first perceives the softest sound at each frequency level. Sometimes a hearing threshold is reported only for the better ear, and sometimes an average of an individual's scores at three different frequencies (500, 1,000, 2,000 Hz) is used. Any score falling below the 0-dB line on an audiogram represents some degree of hearing loss, because the audiometer is set to indicate that a person has no hearing loss at 0 dB for various hertz levels.

Most children's hearing is assessed by the **air conduction audiometry method**, which uses pure-tone sounds generated by an audiometer. Earphones are placed over the child's ears, and the child raises his or her hand when hearing a sound. Such testing is usually done by a pediatrician at a well-child checkup or by a school nurse. When a hearing loss is suspected, audiologists use an additional procedure to determine whether the loss was due to damage in the outer, middle, or inner ear. The **bone conduction audiometry method** uses a vibrator placed on the forehead so that sound can bypass the outer and middle ear and go directly to the inner ear. When the bone conduction thresholds are normal (near 0 dB) and the air conduction thresholds are abnormal, the hearing loss is conductive. Now let's review the audiograms of two children, Travis and Heather. Because Travis and Heather were suspected of having hearing losses, the audiologist used both the air conduction and the bone conduction methods.

Travis's audiogram, shown in Figure 10.4, indicates that he has a conductive hearing loss. The loss, of about 40 dB, is in the mild range with the amplification of hearing aids. Note how flat the profile is for Travis's air conduction test. However, the bone conduction test reveals that when the middle ear is bypassed, his hearing is much closer to 0 dB. Travis's hearing loss either is temporary or can be corrected through surgery or other medical treatment. Note also that different codes are used for Travis's right and left ears: O for the right ear and X for the left ear. Remember that each ear is tested independently. Travis's hearing threshold for each ear is marked on his audiogram. Most children with normal hearing have auditory thresholds (the points when they first perceive sound) at approximately 0 dB; Travis's thresholds are considerably below 0. Travis's hearing abilities are plotted on an audiogram form designed by Northern and Downs (1984) a long time ago. This form graphically shows where various speech and other sounds occur and helps us visualize how sounds at different frequencies come together to convey meaning. If the individual's hearing threshold falls below the picture, then that person cannot perceive the sound pictured. Without a hearing aid, Travis, for example, can perceive only a few sounds (*ng, el,* and *u*).

Heather has a sensorineural hearing loss, as indicated in her audiogram, which is shown in Figure 10.5. A sensorineural hearing loss is caused by a defect in or damage to the inner ear and can be more serious than conductive hearing losses. Heather has a 30-dB loss. Note the similarity between her scores from the air conduction and bone conduction tests. Heather's hearing was also tested with her hearing aids on. Note that with the use of aids, Heather's hearing loss is no longer so serious; it is now at a mild functional level. The shaded area on this audiogram (sometimes called the "speech banana" because of its shape) marks the area where speech sounds fall. Because Heather's hearing abilities lie above this area on her

pure sounds Pure-tone sound waves; used across specific frequencies to test an individual's hearing ability

audiometer An instrument that audiologists use to measure hearing

audiogram A grid or graph used to display a person's hearing abilities

air conduction audiometry method A method to test hearing that uses pure-tone sounds generated by an audiometer

bone conduction audiometry method A method to test for conductive hearing loss; uses a vibrator placed on a person's forehead so that sound bypasses the outer and middle ear and goes directly to the inner ear

Figure 10.5 • Heather's Audiogram

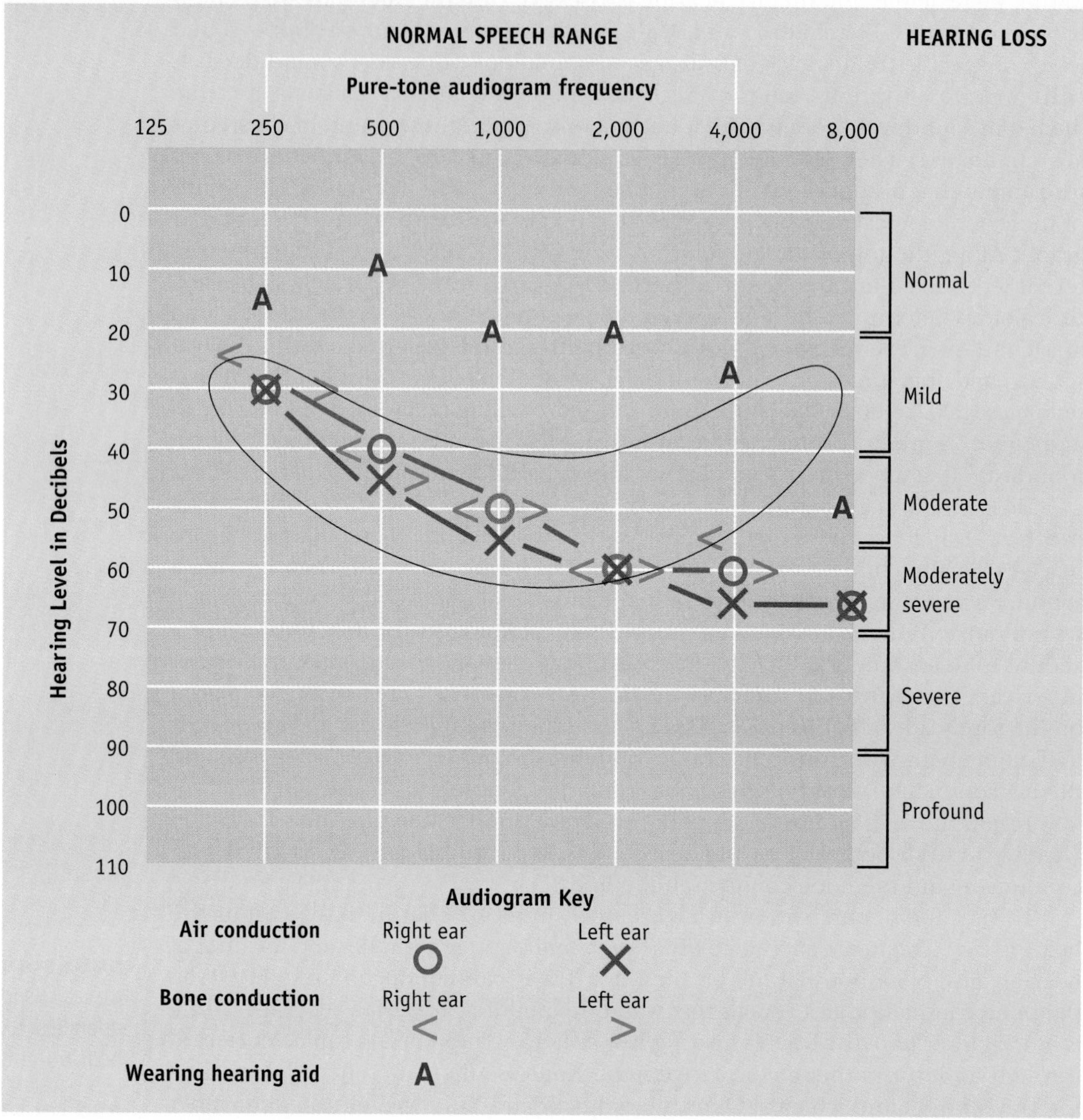

audiogram (see the top of the audiogram), the audiologist knows that Heather can hear the speech sounds at the sound intensities measured during audiological assessment. Along the side of the graph are intensity levels measured in decibels, so horizontal lines represent different levels of loudness.

Evaluation: State- and District-wide Assessments

Like other students with disabilities, the vast majority of those with hearing loss participate in the annual assessment required by NCLB. Students who are hard of hearing join their classmates without disabilities in these evaluations, but they use the accommodations that are specified in their IEPs and are used during instruction in the general education setting. These students, along with their counterparts who are deaf and are also participating in the general education curriculum, may need some additional accommodations during these testing situations. For example, they may need a written set of directions about how to take the test to augment the oral directions given by the teacher. Or they may need to have special instructions about how to take the test delivered to them individually.

These annual achievement tests—and NCLB requirements that by 2014, schools ensure that all students be 100 percent proficient in reading and mathematics—have those working at residential schools for Deaf students concerned (Steffan, 2004). Remember that the academic achievement levels for students who are deaf are low, particularly in reading. As we have discussed, there are many reasons for these disappointing data. Although hope abounds regarding improvement, it is unlikely that overall scores will reach 100 percent. Will these very special schools be accused of not meeting their benchmarks for adequate yearly progress (AYP)? Will these schools be thought of as inferior or their students as not being able to "meet the mark?" We hope not! Rather, these students—possibly 100 percent of students attending a school for the Deaf—will be given alternate assessments each year. These assessments will reflect each student's IEP benchmarks and short-term objectives, which themselves will reflect higher expectations for reading and mathematics achievement levels for each individual student.

Early Intervention

Early intervention positively affects the lifelong outcomes of deaf and hard of hearing children (Nittrouer & Burton, 2003; Marschark, 2001; Yoshinaga-Itano & Sedey, 2000). Obviously, early identification is a prerequisite to early intervention. Now, because more and more states require hearing screening for newborns, the promise of early intervention is a reality for these infants, toddlers, and preschoolers and their families. Why are early identification and the resulting intervention so important?

1. Early identification allows children to be fitted with hearing aids as soon as possible, which can be as early as four weeks old or to be scheduled for cochlear implants during infancy, as early as one year old.
2. Early intervention, before the age of six months, pays off in better reading achievement and speech abilities in later years.
3. Preschool programs allow students with hearing losses to develop language at the right developmental periods of their lives.
4. Early intervention programs help families better understand and meet the very special needs of their family members.

Evidence connecting language development and academic achievement for deaf students is mounting. You just learned that deaf and hard of hearing students have significantly low academic achievement, but these old data may well not hold true for today's preschoolers who receive the benefits of early identification and ensuing early intervention services (Marschark, 2001; Nittrouer & Burton, 2003; Yoshinaga-Itano & Apuzzo, 1998). Deaf children of Deaf parents learn sign language during their infancy. They "babble" with their hands at about the same time that hearing infants make babbling sounds. They produce two-word utterances at about the same time as their peers who do not have hearing losses. These Deaf youngsters learn English as a second language. By the time they reach school age, most of them are reading at two grade levels above deaf children of hearing parents (Marschark, 1993).

One reason for this difference is that Deaf children of Deaf parents learned language during the proper developmental period, whereas (before universal screening) most deaf children of hearing parents were not identified until age 3—an age when language development should be well under way. With this knowledge, many hearing families, once their child's deafness is identified, choose to learn and use some combination of oral language and a manual communication system so that they can communicate more fully with their child. Some professionals recommend a radical approach: They suggest that infants and their families be taught ASL so that these preschoolers can acquire ASL as their "native" language (Drasgow, 1998).

The wonderful and engaging story of Dina, the Deaf dinosaur, teaches the importance and acceptance of ASL to those who use it as their primary language.

However, it is important to recognize that, like mastering any second language, becoming fluent in ASL is no easy task. And of course, learning and using ASL is not the only answer to helping students with hearing losses.

Several issues are very important during these developmental periods. First, it is critically important that parents talk to their children, whether they use manual communication systems, ASL, or speech. Second, they need to get assistance from early intervention specialists who can guide them in how best to interact with their children. Because IDEA '04 provides educational services to infants and toddlers as soon as they are identified as having hearing loss, services are available that are effective and of high quality. Third, professionals and families need to communicate. Professionals must be sensitive to families' experiences and cultures. The story told in this chapter's *Considering Culture* illustrates the importance of forming partnerships with families on the basis of respect and understanding.

Today, with early identification *and* early intervention—the two must go hand in hand—the outcomes for all students with hearing loss will be improved. Researchers are confident that intensive speech and language development during their preschool experience leads to later success during the school years (National Center for Hearing Assessment and Management, 2005; Nittrouer & Burton, 2003). Here are the important messages:

- Early identification and intervention make a difference.
- Infants who receive amplification *and* early intervention by the time they are 6 months old are significantly ahead at first grade.
- Early-identified babies are 1 to 2 years ahead of their later-identified peers with hearing loss.
- Early intervention makes the greatest difference in language, cognition, and social skills.

Teaching Students with Hearing Losses

A full array of educational services and placements should be available to every student who is deaf or hard of hearing. These educational programs typically include the services of audiologists, SLPs, interpreters, teachers of the deaf, and, for those

Considering Culture

"Why Don't They Understand How Important It Is?"

Darlene, a preschool teacher, was at her wits' end! She requested a meeting with her school's consulting teacher for students who are deaf and with an audiologist. She wanted some suggestions about how to help little Ani Fiatoa better. Ani is a bouncy, smiling $3\frac{1}{2}$-year-old who is enrolled in the Lively Oaks Elementary School's preschool program. The Fiatoa family moved to the city two years ago from the South Pacific, where Ani was born. At 18 months of age, Ani was diagnosed with a severe hearing loss, and she now uses hearing aids in both ears. Ani's parents are warm and loving and seem to like Ani's placement in a regular community preschool, where she is learning to socialize with children without hearing loss. She also is learning sign language from Ms. Peek, the itinerant teacher who is a specialist in deaf education. The Fiatoa family attends meetings when requested and *seem* to endorse the program's strategies. However, Darlene was frustrated. It is difficult for her to get Ani to make eye contact—an essential skill for communicating, particularly with sign language. On numerous occasions, Darlene has explained to Ani's family members that eye contact is crucial. She also has encouraged them to take sign language classes. They don't seem concerned. Darlene even observed that Ani rarely makes eye contact with her parents.

Darlene described these issues to a friend who had worked in the South Pacific. The friend explained that it is disrespectful in some cultures for children to make eye contact with elders. This was an "aha" experience for Darlene! Perhaps the Fiatoas weren't merely disregarding her suggestions but rather had trouble integrating these teaching strategies into the ways their family members communicated. Darlene read more about the childrearing practices and customs of the South Pacific and then consulted with Ms. Peek to identify strategies that would be respectful of the family's preferred communication patterns and also support Ani's use of sign language. One idea was to make a videotape of Ani and her teacher signing. Darlene could then talk with the Fiatoas, show the tapes, and ask whether they would be comfortable using more eye contact to help Ani learn sign language. This strategy worked like a charm.

Questions to Consider

1 What are some strategies and resources that you can use to learn more about the customs and preferences of the many cultural groups in the United States? Check out the references listed in this text, search the Internet, and read novels that describe the practices and customs of various groups.

2 Can you identify community resources to contact when you meet a family from a cultural group with which you are not familiar? Ideally, these resources would be individuals who are bicultural and are well acquainted with the practices of the given cultural group as well as with those of the mainstream culture. (They are often referred to as cultural guides in the literature.)

—By Eleanor Lynch, San Diego State University and Marci Hanson, San Francisco State University

with multiple disabilities, OTs and PTs. Across the nation, placement options are also great and include general education classrooms, resource rooms, special classes, special day schools, and residential center schools (e.g., schools for the deaf). When thinking about school placements, the types of accommodations needed by these students, and the professionals who are brought together to form multidisciplinary teams, remember that the educational needs of every student with hearing loss are unique. IDEA '04 mandates that school placements and methods of instruction be individually determined for every student with a disability (U.S. Department of Education, 2005a). Regardless, general principles of good instruction apply to students with hearing loss, just as they do to all other students. *Validated Practices: Just Plain Common Sense* reminds us that too often we make educating students more complicated than we need to; using good judgment is part of the recipe for success.

Validated Practices Just Plain Common Sense

What Are "Just Plain Common Sense" Instructional Practices?

Simple, inexpensive, down-to-earth teaching methods can help deaf or hard of hearing students become successful in the general education curriculum. In other words, complicated or expensive procedures are not always required. Also, you are not expected to be familiar with every possible modification or accommodation. Rather, rely on the assistance of a teacher of the deaf and hard of hearing and/or on a deaf interpreter. Their jobs are to help you make the proper adjustments to the classroom routine, instructional procedures, or curriculum.

Why "Just Plain Common Sense" Instructional Practices Are Beneficial

Deaf or hard of hearing students often need help to learn effectively in the general education setting. Most of these students do not have multiple disabilities and profit greatly from the general education experience when proper, simple modifications are made.

Implementing Classroom Modifications

Hearing loss can range from a mild deficit to complete deafness. Many students have hearing problems that place them at a disadvantage, particularly when participating in group instruction.

Listening

Excessive background noise is often a problem for students with hearing loss. Here are some suggestions for reducing background noise:

- Have a rug in your classroom. If the floors are bare, put tennis balls on the bottom of chair legs.
- Make sure your heating/cooling system and lights are in good working condition so they are as quiet as possible.
- Decrease sound vibration with curtains or blinds on the windows.
- Seat students who are deaf or hard of hearing where they can see everyone who may be speaking.
- Seat students who are deaf or hard of hearing away from air conditioners, pencil sharpeners, computer centers, and any other areas with high noise levels.
- Do not seat students with hearing losses in a "special area" away from their peers.

Instructional Tips

These simple, easy-to-implement strategies can benefit all students:

- Seat all students where they can see everyone who may be speaking.
- Be alert to classroom noise and seek to reduce it.
- Use visual displays (e.g., graphic organizers, story maps, semantic features analyses) in your teaching. Give specific directions, and be sure to ask your students to clarify what you have said.
- Define key vocabulary words slowly and carefully.
- Use manipulatives to explain math concepts.
- Show multimedia presentations with subtitles.
- Have students share their notes.
- Use maps, globes, and charts to demonstrate key concepts.
- Use familiar, concrete objects and examples when presenting abstract concepts.
- Provide students with ample opportunities for discussion.
- Teach and practice using elaboration (e.g., provide analogies, paraphrase material, identify main ideas, summarize key points).

Speaking

- Be aware of your pace, and slow down if students appear to be confused.
- Keep your hands away from your face when speaking.
- Always face students who are deaf and hard of hearing when speaking.
- Keep the use of figurative language to a minimum.

This scientifically validated practice is a teaching method proved via systematic research efforts. (DiSarno, Schowalter, & Grassa, 2002; Kaderavek, & Pakulski, 2002; Luetke-Stahlman, 1999). Full citations are found in the references for this chapter.

—By Kimberly Paulsen, Vanderbilt University

Access to the General Education Curriculum: Deafness and LRE

IDEA mandates that all students with disabilities receive a free appropriate education (FAPE) in the least restrictive environment (LRE). What is the least restrictive environment for deaf children? IDEA '04 makes some specific statements about addressing the communication needs of students with hearing loss. For a reminder, read again *What IDEA '04 Says About Considering the Communication Needs of Student's with Hearing Loss* on page 359. It is necessary to weigh these issues carefully when determining what constitutes an appropriate education and what environment is the least restrictive for these students. Many parents and members of the Deaf community believe that the general education classroom is not the least restrictive setting for deaf children.

> The general education classroom with an interpreter can be a restrictive environment if the student cannot communicate with peers and with staff in the school. The residential school settings where students live in dorms and attend school with peers who are deaf and hard of hearing have a 24-hour communication environment. That educational environment might be the least restrictive environment—one that does not restrict the student as he or she communicates with peers and staff and participates in extracurricular activities without communication barriers. (Fielder, 2001, p. 58)

For students who rely on sign language as their primary means of communication, the general school environment, where administrators, teachers, and classmates are not fluent in sign language, can result in considerable isolation. It is important to recognize that nearly all general education classes use an auditory/oral-only approach to deliver instruction, and this can restrict access to the general education curriculum for those students who are deaf. Also, Deaf students who attend general education classes are often not included in nonacademic activities by their hearing classmates; the major reason for exclusion and rejection is difficulty with communication (Most, Weisel, & Lev-Matezky, 1996). Of course, isolation does not have to be the outcome of general education placements.

The Deaf community advocates strongly for residential schools as a placement option. What is at issue? At the same time that advocacy groups for people with mental retardation fought to close institutions, the Deaf community fought to keep residential center schools for deaf students open and fully funded. Remember that deafness in children is a low incidence disability; in the general school-age population, only a few students have this disability. The result can be that there is only one deaf child at a neighborhood school or even in an entire school district. Without a critical mass of these youngsters, they often feel isolated and rejected because few others use or understand their method of communication. This situation leads the Deaf community, some educators, and many parents to conclude that a separate program best meets the needs of deaf students and is also the least restrictive option (Steffan, 2004).

Particularly during the high school years, some students who are deaf select the educational option of a residential center school. Although they have been declining in enrollment over the last 20 years, the 57 all-deaf schools in America are considered, particularly by members of the Deaf community, an important part of the array of services that should be available to this group of students. Eighty-two percent of students attending residential center schools have severe to profound hearing losses, and they report great satisfaction with their school placements (Byrnes & Sigafoos, 2001).

Determining the LRE for students with disabilities can be difficult, particularly for deaf students. A variety of professionals, possibly the student, and the student's parents come together to create a team that solves this problem. The team makes the decision on the basis of answers to the following questions:

- How severe is the student's hearing loss?
- Is the student able to use speech?
- Can appropriate educational services be made available locally?
- Are the necessary support services available?

Interpreters and classroom teachers work side-by-side in integrated education settings. To have access to information, deaf children who use ASL need interpreters for every instructional activity, whether in a classroom or on a field trip.

Interpreting what *least restrictive environment* (LRE) means is possibly more controversial for students who are deaf than for any other group of students. Table 10.2

Table 10.2 • LRE and Placement Considerations

	Type of Hearing Loss	
Considerations	**Hard of Hearing**	**Deaf**
Severity of loss	Youngsters with mild to moderate hearing loss can remain in the general education curriculum with consultative or supportive services from various experts such as SLPs and audiologists.	Students with severe to profound hearing loss require intensive instruction in communication skills and need assistance from an array of related services.
Potential for using residual hearing	Most of these students profit from hearing aids, thereby allowing them to benefit, with some adaptations, from typical oral methods of instruction.	Most deaf students have little useful residual hearing and require considerable accommodations to benefit from oral instructions.
Academic achievement	The academic achievement levels of deaf and hard of hearing students tend to be lower than levels of their hearing peers. Students with less hearing loss and no multiple disabilities are usually close to grade level but might need some additional academic instruction.	The academic achievement levels of students who are deaf are considerably below those of their hearing peers. These students need considerable instruction in basic language and communication skills, as well as intensive academic remediation.
Communicative needs	Many of these students go undetected for a long time. If the loss occurred before or during the youngsters' development of language, it is likely that they will require SLP services as well as academic assistance.	Total communication is the most commonly used approach with deaf youngsters, but the help of educational assistants is necessary, and in many rural regions this expertise is not available.
Preferred mode of communication	Most of these students should be expected to become proficient using oral language.	Most postlingually students who are deaf learn (or retain) their use of oral language. Intelligible speech and lipreading are typically unattainable goals for most prelingually children who are deaf, so for them manual communication is preferred.
Placement preference	The vast majority of these students attend their neighborhood schools with their hearing peers.	Many deaf students also attend their neighborhood schools. However, a significant number of them prefer center schools where their classmates share their deafness and their mode of communication.

helps us understand the many different issues that parents, teachers, and multidisciplinary team members must consider when determining what is the LRE for individual students with hearing loss. Remember that, as with every student with a disability, placement decisions must be reconsidered at various points across the students' school careers.

Instructional Accommodations

Since the advent of PL 94-142 in 1975, more and more deaf and hard of hearing students have been educated in general education classes with generally positive results, particularly for students who are hard of hearing (Easterbrooks & Baker, 2002).

Accommodating for Inclusive Environments

Modifying the Delivery of Instruction

Teacher's Communications

- Articulate clearly, but do not talk louder than usual unless you have an unusually soft voice.
- Address the student directly.
- Use the student's name first, before asking a question.
- Do not exaggerate your lip movements.
- Do not chew gum or cover your mouth when talking.
- Do not turn your back to the class when speaking.
- Avoid moving around the classroom while speaking.
- Speak somewhat more slowly.
- Repeat information by paraphrasing.

Additional Teacher Assistance

- Use handouts to support important information from lectures, guest speakers, field trips, and instructional media.
- Post key terms (information, vocabulary).
- Restate other students' questions if the speaker cannot be clearly heard or seen by the student who is deaf or hard of hearing.
- Spend time talking with the student with hearing loss so that you can become familiar with each other's speech.
- Bend down to be at the student's eye level when talking to small groups or working individually with the student.
- If the student has an educational interpreter, create times for planning and systems for partnering.
- Keep expectations high.
- Consult with a certified teacher of the deaf.

Assistance from Classmates

- Ask classmates to rotate as notetakers.
- Set up a buddy system: one classmate per class, unit, or topic.

Remember that most students with hearing loss can hear satisfactorily with amplification (that is, a hearing aid) and therefore can attend school and function well with their classmates without disabilities. In most schools, information is presented orally, and students learn through a combination of textbooks, lectures, and class discussions. Teachers can help students with hearing problems gain better access to the general education curriculum and participate in class activities by modifying the delivery of instruction (Williams & Finnegan, 2003). The lists included in *Accommodating for Inclusive Environments* remind us that even small adjustments can make a big difference in how well students with hearing loss are able to access the curriculum and participate in learning activities with their classmates (Yarnell & Schery, 2003). Most students who are hard of hearing require only these simple adjustments, as long as an array of supplemental services, supports, accommodations, and assistance are available when needed. Some students with hearing loss require more supports. For them, just sitting closer to the teacher is not enough. However, technology is often an important part of providing both appropriate and meaningful instruction to these students (Halligan, 2003). Review the Overcoming Challenges: Technology section of this chapter (see pages 365–366) as a reminder of the vast array of assistive devices that make a positive difference for these learners.)

Teachers should seek the help of specialists and others who can provide guidance in making the learning environment as effective as possible for all students in the class. For example, classroom teachers have found that the SLP assigned to their school can offer many good ideas about activities that foster better speech and language. The specialist can also provide suggestions about classroom organizers that will help these students gain more from traditional classroom settings. Parents are another important source of information. The child's parents can help teachers come to a better understanding of their child's preferred learning styles and special needs. For instance, one child might profit from having a classmate serve as a resource to ensure that homework and other assignments are correctly understood. Another child might prefer to tape lectures and listen to them carefully in a quiet setting at home in the evening. Yet another student might benefit from being able to do extra outside reading on specific topics. Teachers must remember that each child is unique and must capitalize on each child's strengths, not just attend to that student's disabilities.

Validated Practices

Best educational practices for students who are deaf are still developing. Overall, deaf students' academic achievement is improving, but more progress must be made. One factor that makes a difference is the communication system used to convey instruction. Generally, four different approaches are used to deliver instruction to students who are deaf.

1 *Oral-Only* The **oral-only approach** teaches and uses speech exclusively and encourages students to use as much of their residual hearing as possible. This method was the most popular for students who are deaf until the 1970s. The system uses amplification to help children learn how to speech-read (lip-read) and how to speak. This approach does *not* allow children to use any form of manual communication such as finger spelling or signing. In fact, even natural signing, such as using gestures, is discouraged. Those who follow the oral approach believe that individuals who are deaf must live and work in a world where most people hear normally and communicate through oral expression and that reliance on signing or manual communication excludes individuals from mainstream society.

2 *Total Communication* The method that combines oral speech and manual communication (signing) is called the **total communication approach**. Total communication allows the child to communicate through whatever mode is easiest and most effective. The philosophy behind this approach is that every child should be able to use whatever channels are available to learn and comprehend messages. About 72 percent of students who are deaf are taught using this method (Moores, 2001), as are about 51 percent of the total of all students who are deaf and hard of hearing (Gallaudet Research Institute, 1998, 2005).

3 *Cued Speech* Another approach, **cued speech** uses hand signals to accompany oral speech. These hand signals help deaf people read lips to determine, for example, whether the word spoken was *pan* or *bat*, which look alike to the person reading lips (Roffé, 2000). Cued speech is popular with hearing parents because it is easy to learn and follows the format and structure of the English language (which ASL does not).

4 *Bilingual-Bicultural* The **bilingual-bicultural approach** is the newest method for teaching Deaf students, and it is gaining in popularity and research verification (Easterbrooks & Baker, 2002; Most, 2003). Research findings indicate that by learning ASL as their first language and written English as their second language, many Deaf students reach achievement levels that approximate those of their peers without hearing problems (Easterbrooks, 1999; Evans, 2004; Marschark, 2001).

Although you might hear a lot about ASL, it is important to recognize that most elementary and secondary school teachers of the deaf do not use ASL. Only about 11 percent of teachers of the deaf use ASL in their school classes (Gallaudet Research Institute, 2005). About 55 percent of students who are deaf and hard of hearing are taught through a combination of sign and speech, but the sign language used is not typically ASL. Often, a type of manual communication that more closely matches the grammatical form and structure of standard English is used.

oral-only approach A method of instruction for students with hearing loss, using only oral means to communicate

total communication approach A method of instruction for students with hearing loss, employing any and all methods of communication (oral speech, manual communication, ASL, gestures)

cued speech Hand signals for "difficult to see" speech sounds; assists with speech reading

bilingual-bicultural approach A method of instruction for students who are deaf, combining practices of ESL and bilingual education; ASL is the native language, and reading and writing in English are taught as a second language

Finger spelling, a form of manual communication different from ASL, assigns each letter of the alphabet a sign. This system is efficient and has been used for centuries; an accomplished person can finger-spell at a rate equivalent to that of typical speech. Signed English uses finger spelling exclusively to translate English: Words are spelled out, but the rules of grammar and language are the same as for English speech. Finger spelling is often used along with ASL when no sign exists for a word or name.

"Shoe" published September 11, 1993. Copyright © 1993, Tribune Media Services. Reprinted with permission.

Technology

In the Overcoming Challenges: Technology section of this chapter (see pages 365–366), we talked about many assistive devices developed specifically for people with hearing loss. In this section, we describe a technology that was designed for distance education but has great applications for students who need assistance taking notes and gaining the most from lectures. *Silicon Chalk* works this way: It posts via the computer the instructor's lecture notes, which may be from a variety of sources such as a PowerPoint presentation or notes written on an electronic whiteboard. Students take notes electronically. These notes can be shared among classmates, which is a boon to students who may need to be sure they captured all of the information presented. *Silicon Chalk* also supports class discussions, which become permanent notes to use when studying. The system encourages students to work together, helping each other extend learning from the classroom setting (Silicon Chalk, 2004). Such advances in technology, designed for other purposes, have great application to students with disabilities. We just need to be creative in their application.

Transition

The purpose of school-to-work transition programs for students who are deaf or hard of hearing is to improve the adult outcomes for these individuals. Of crucial importance are obtaining equitable employment, being able to get and hold a job commensurate with one's abilities, earning a fair wage, and being satisfied with the job. As for many of us, college graduation is an important part of finding a well-paying and satisfying job. But as, we have noted, many students who have hearing loss also have difficulties with reading: As a group, their average reading achievement levels are at the elementary school level (Kelly, Albertini, & Shannon, 2001). Students with higher reading achievement levels are more likely to attend college and to graduate (Cuclick & Kelly, 2003). Thus, the work toward a smooth transition needs to begin during the elementary school years, and reading must take on greater importance for all students, particularly those who are deaf or hard of hearing (Bowe, 2002).

Just like many college students with disabilities and their families, many people who are deaf wonder whether college is worth the effort and expense. The answer is a resounding yes. Data supporting the benefits of a college education are available for Gallaudet alumni, who, in general, could be considered relatively affluent. From the latest data available, which was collected almost 10 years ago (so today's figures are probably much higher), the 1998 median annual income of Gallaudet alumni was $31,700 for those with an associate's degree, $40,000 for those with a bachelor's degree, and $50,000 for those with a master's degree (Schroedel & Geyer, 2000). College graduates were very satisfied with their lives, even though some of them faced challenges to success. For example, one-third fewer women were graduates, and more of them were employed in clerical positions than in the professions.

Table 10.3 • Roles and Responsibilities of Educational Interpreters, Teachers, and Students who are Deaf

The Interpreter	The Teacher	The Deaf Student
Holds long conversations with the student after class	Introduces the interpreter to the class	Makes certain the interpreter uses preferred mode of communication
Asks for clarification when the teacher speaks too fast or was not heard	Talks to the student, not to the interpreter	Notifies the interpreter when there is going to be a change in schedules or when that person will not be needed
Considers teaching hearing students some basic signs	Adjusts pace of speech to allow for the translation	Is clear about whether the interpreter should speak for the student
Only interprets; does not tutor or provide assistance with assignments	Arranges for peers to take notes for their peer who is deaf	Determines desired role with peers
Maintains confidentiality of personal and private information	Seeks assistance of interpreter when working with others (e.g., SLPs)	Meets with the interpreter on a regular basis to provide feedback, resolve problems, and evaluate progress

Students who are deaf or hard of hearing have many college opportunities that provide specialized support, but unfortunately, 71 percent of college students who are deaf drop out, compared to 43 percent of their peers without disabilities (Gallaudet Research Institute, 2005). State and privately funded universities and colleges offer special programs for deaf and hard of hearing students. *College and Career Programs for Deaf Students* lists about 125 postsecondary accredited programs designed specifically for deaf students (King et al., 2001). The federal government also supports a range of such postsecondary schools and programs across the nation. Gallaudet University serves both undergraduate and graduate students, the National Technical Institute for the Deaf (NTID) at the Rochester Institute of Technology in New York offers technical and vocational degrees, and there are four federally funded postsecondary schools (Seattle Community College, California State University-Northridge, St. Paul Technical College, and the University of Tennessee Consortium). Thus the options for postsecondary education are many, but students must be prepared to take advantage of them.

IDEA '04 does not have authority over colleges and universities; however, many of the accommodations that students received during their elementary and high school careers are available to them at two- and four-year institutions of higher education (ACE HEATH, 2005). The academic accommodation most frequently requested by students who are deaf is interpreters. These college students also often request notetakers and tutors. Now that specialized technologies have been developed, students are also requesting that their dorm rooms be equipped with alerting devices and that lectures and classes use real-time captioning. Students who are hard of hearing, however, take less advantage of accommodations that would be provided if they only make the request. Possibly because these students are often "underserved" during their elementary and high school years, they do not realize that assistive listening devices (such as hearing aids and audio loops) would increase their participation in campus life and also make their access to learning easier and more enjoyable. Knowing that special services are often available to college students with hearing loss is important. All of us can make a difference by helping make sure these individuals know what is offered on their campus. Then they can decide whether they want to take advantage of these services.

Collaboration

One essential service needed by many deaf students enrolled in general education programs is assistance with the translation of spoken English. **Educational interpreters** are those related service providers who convert spoken messages into the student's preferred communication system, which may be a signed system such as ASL or signed English. For many teachers, working with the assistance of an interpreter is a novel experience that might occur only once in their teaching career. For the teacher inexperienced in working with students who use sign language, there is much to learn, plan for, and coordinate (Williams & Finnegan, 2003). And for many interpreters, working with students in school settings is also a unique experience (Linehan, 2000). A close working relationship is required between this related service provider and teachers, where the interpreter needs to learn academic content and the teacher needs to learn how to work with a translator. Table 10.3 shows the roles and responsibilities of the classroom teacher, the educational interpreter, and the student. Everyone has important issues to consider when students with profound hearing losses and their educational interpreters learn and work together in inclusive educational settings.

The teacher and the interpreter need to coordinate efforts to ensure that they understand each other's roles. *Tips for Effective Teaching* provides some useful

for Effective Teaching

WORKING WITH EDUCATIONAL INTERPRETERS

Planning and Organization

- Interpreters and teachers set up standard meeting times.
- They have established clear roles for working together during instruction.
- All meetings regarding the student are scheduled when the student's interpreter can attend.
- Storage and working space are designated for the interpreter.
- Lesson plans and supporting materials are shared days before the instructional activity.
- Teachers and interpreters have time to meet before the instructional activity to clarify vocabulary and content.

Classroom Organization and Management

- The interpreter and the student are able to see the teacher and each other.
- Placement for the interpreter is not distracting to the student's classmates.
- Glare and other visual obstructions are eliminated.

Courtesy and Social Conventions

- Everyone talks directly to the student.
- Eye contact is with the student, not with the interpreter (even when the interpreter is speaking and translating manual communication for the student).
- The interpreter is not an academic tutor or classroom manager who resolves disruption.
- Invite the interpreter to teach the class some sign language or share Deaf literature.

educational interpreters Related service providers for deaf students; translate or convert spoken messages to the deaf person's preferred mode of manual communication tips for developing partnerships with these professionals. As responsibilities and duties are defined, it should be clear that the teacher has the primary responsibility and the interpreter plays a supporting role (Antia & Kreimeyer, 2001). In other words, the teacher should deliver instruction and remediation (when necessary), and the interpreter should be present to facilitate communication. Because the interpreter may not be an expert in the content of the curriculum, the teacher should give the interpreter copies of lesson plans, lists of key terms, and textbooks to ensure clear and accurate translation of the teacher's lectures and instructions. The teacher and interpreter must also work together on a number of issues, many of which are minor but quite important. For example, the interpreter should sit in a glare-free, well-lit location that has a solid-color background and does not block anyone's view of the blackboard or of the teacher. Teachers and interpreters also need to agree on and understand each others' roles—how much extra help the teacher provides the student and how much extra help the interpreter offers.

Partnerships with Families and Communities

Although language, social and emotional development, and technology are important to the overall development of children who are deaf and hard of hearing, possibly the most important factor in these children's lives is acceptance and inclusion by their families. Some parents and other family members (grandparents, siblings, extended family members) adjust quickly to the demands presented by a child with hearing loss. This is particularly true for children whose parents are deaf. To Deaf parents, the birth of a Deaf child is typically cause for great celebration—and also a great relief (Blade, 1994). These parents know ASL, use it as their native language, and will teach it to their infant through the normal developmental process. However, the birth of a deaf child to hearing parents can be frightening, even devastating to some (Calderon & Greenberg, 1999). However, with support and services, families typically come to welcome their new member with joy and acceptance.

Today, particularly with the Internet making information almost immediately available, parents have more assistance than ever before. Both private (e.g., the Alexander Graham Bell Association for the Deaf and Hard of Hearing) and public organizations (e.g., NICHCY) make available information briefs and resource pages that are most helpful to parents. Although too much information initially can be overwhelming, the Internet has made services for parents and their children with disabilities more readily available and more accessible. Because of the earlier identification of infants with hearing loss, parents (and their children) receive services more quickly and with less effort on their part than only a few years ago. So once again, what we know from the past may be less relevant than we realize. What *does* matter is that social service agencies are quick to respond with early intervention services soon after early diagnosis.

Although one would imagine that hearing families of children who are deaf and hard of hearing experience substantial stress because of their child's hearing loss, this stress is not overwhelming (Sheridan, 2001). Stress typically arises from concern about their ability to communicate with their children, but these families develop coping strategies fairly quickly. The strategies that they use, however, differ by cultural and ethnic group. In other words, White, African American, and Hispanic families use different coping and problem solving strategies. Regardless, what is most important to all families is developing effective communication modes with their youngsters and receiving effective support services (Moores, Jartho, & Dunn, 2001).

Imagine a world . . .

where friends are always close at hand . . .

Summary

Hearing, like vision, is a "distance sense" that provides us with information from outside our bodies. When hearing is limited, it affects the individual in significant ways, limiting communication, access to orally presented information, and independent living. Advances in technology, including cochlear implants, have changed the lives of people with hearing problems. These advances provide them with devices that both help compensate for challenges in hearing sounds in the environment and in communicating with others, and also actually improve acuity and sound perception. More than any other group of people with disabilities, the Deaf make up a community united by a rich culture and a unique communication system. Deafness and hard of hearing is a low incidence disability for children, affecting about 0.14 percent of all students.

Addressing the Chapter Objectives

1 What variables need to be considered when planning instruction for students with hearing problems?

- *Amount of loss:* the deaf and the hard of hearing
- *Age of onset:* prelingually deaf and postlingually (after the age of 2) deaf
- *Type of loss:* conductive and sensorineural

2 What are the major causes of hearing loss? Provide an explanation for each cause.

- The majority of causes for hearing loss are unknown.
- The four major causes of hearing loss are
    - *Hereditary conditions:* most common cause of prelingual deafness; can be both congenital and sensorineural
    - *Meningitis:* a disease that affects the central nervous system; the most common cause of acquired deafness in children; results in a sensorineural hearing loss; vaccines are available to protect people from this disease
    - *Otitis media:* middle ear infections; chronic, untreated otitis media interrupts normal language development and can result in permanent conductive hearing loss
    - *Noise:* totally preventable cause of hearing loss that is gradual in onset and the result of loud sounds in the environment

3 What is universal hearing screening of newborns and why is it important?

- Universal screening allows for the identification of hearing loss at birth, reducing the (previous) average age of identification from 2½ to 3 years of age.
- Early identification allows for services to children and their families to begin immediately and sets the stage for better language and cognitive development.

4 What is Deaf culture? Give some examples or signs of Deaf culture, and describe its importance to the Deaf.

Deaf culture is

- Beliefs, customs, practices, and social behavior of the Deaf community
- Reflected in art, music, literature, and related intellectual activities

Signs of Deaf Culture are

- American Sign Language (ASL) binding the Deaf community
- Advocacy and political action

Significance is that

- Culture removes the association of deafness with disability and reinterprets deafness as a characteristic of a (historically misunderstood) minority group
- ASL is a bona fide language at the heart of a proud heritage and traditions

5 What are the major types and examples of assistive technology specifically designed for people with hearing problems?

- Assistive listening devices: both digital and analog hearing aids (BTE, ITE, ITC, CIC), FM transmission devices, audio loop
- Telecommunication devices: captioning, text telephone (TTY), telecommunications relay service, voice carry over
- Speech-to-text translations: real-time translations (college lectures, courtroom proceedings, business meetings), real-time captioning, C-Print™, speech recognition
- Alerting devices: special signaling devices for alarms, doorbells, telephone rings

Supplementary Resources

Popular Novels and Books

Davis, L. J. (Ed.). (1999). *Shall I say a kiss? The courtship letters of a Deaf couple, 1936–1938.* Washington, DC: Gallaudet University Press.

Dunai, E. C. (2002). *Surviving in silence: A deaf boy in the Holocaust.* Washington, DC: Gallaudet University Press.

Golan, L. (1995). *Reading between the lips.* Chicago: Bonus Books.

Tiefenbacher, W. (Ed.). (2001). *Deaf girls rule.* Washington, DC: Gallaudet University Press.

Walker, L. A. (1986). *A loss for words: The story of deafness in a family.* New York: Harper & Row.

Whilestone, H., & Hunt, A. E. (1997). *Listening with my heart.* New York: Doubleday.

Wright, M. H. (1999). *Sounds like home: Growing up Black and Deaf in the South.* Washington, DC: Gallaudet University Press.

Movies

***Dear Frankie* (2005). Miramax**

Set on Scotland's coast, this film tells the story of nine-year-old Frankie, who is deaf, his single mom, and a fictitious sea-faring father. Frankie looks forward to letters from his father, actually written by his mother. Frankie excitedly writes to his "dad" about all his adventures and his life at home in Scotland. However, one day a ship comes to port that has the same name Frankie's mother picked for the ship of his "pen-pal" dad. To avoid being revealed, his mother pays a stranger to pretend to be Frankie's dad. Then, complicating matters further, Frankie's biological father wants to reconnect with his son.

This engaging film visits many themes, including loneliness, vulnerability, resilience, and relationships. It also shows the life of a fully included student who is deaf, has friends, functions well academically, and is basically a happy child. The film shows the struggles of a single mother with a child with disabilities. It also suggests the great lengths to which family members often go to create happiness in the lives of their children.

Mr. Holland's Opus (1995). Buena Vista
Mr. Holland is a high school music teacher who connects with his students through music. His greatest challenge occurs when his child is born deaf. His wife enrolls their son in a special school and learns sign language, but Mr. Holland is hesitant and distant. He believes he cannot share his passion for music with his deaf son. Once his son convinces him that he is not so different, Mr. Holland dedicates himself to learning sign language and finding a way to introduce his son to music.

This film sets up a situation in the extreme, where one person's entire life revolves around sound, and the other is completely unable to hear. But even so, it is possible for these two to find common ground. One technique that Mr. Holland employs is to use coordinated lights to help his son gain a sense of how dynamic and electric music can be.

Professional, Parent, and Advocacy Groups

Alexander Graham Bell Association for the Deaf and Hard of Hearing in Washington, DC
www.agbell.org

American Speech-Language-Hearing Association (ASHA) in Rockville, Maryland
www.asha.org

Cochlear Implant Education Center, Laurent Clerc National Deaf Education Center, Kendall School, Gallaudet University in Washington, DC
http://clerccenter.gallaudet.edu

John Tracy Clinic in Los Angeles
www.jtc.org

Self-Help for Hard of Hearing People (SHHH), Inc. in Bethesda, Maryland
www.shhh.org

National Institute on Deafness and Other Communication Disorders (NIDCD) Information Clearinghouse in Bethesda, Maryland
www.nidcd.nih.gov

The National Theater of the Deaf in Hartford, Connecticut
www.ntd.org

Professional Standards and Licensure Tests

After reading this chapter, you should be able to link basic knowledge and skills described in the CEC Standards and INTASC Principles with information provided in this text. The table below shows some of the specific CEC Deaf and Hard of Hearing Knowledge and Skill Standards and INTASC Special Education Principles that can be applied to each major section of the chapter. Other standards may also be applied to this chapter. Associated General Praxis II topic areas are identified in the right column.

Major Chapter Headings	CEC Knowledge and Skill Core Standard and Associated Subcategories	INTASC Core Principle and Associated Special Education Subcategories	PRAXIS II Exam Topic
Where We've Been . . . What's on the Horizon	**1: Foundations** DH1K4 Issues and trends in the field of education of individuals who are deaf or hard of hearing	**1: Subject Matter** 1.12 Special education teachers serve as a resource to others by providing information about the laws and policies that support students with disabilities and how to access additional information when needed.	1: Understanding Exceptionality 2: Legal and Social Issues
Deafness and Hard of Hearing Defined	**1: Foundations** DH1K1 Educational definitions, identification criteria, labeling issues, and incidence and prevalence figures for individuals who are deaf or hard of hearing	**1: Subject Matter** 1.04 All teachers have knowledge of the major principles and parameters of federal disabilities legislation.	1: Understanding Exceptionality 2: Legal and Social Issues
Characteristics	**1: Foundations** DH1K3 Etiologies of hearing loss that can result in additional sensory, motor, and/or learning differences	**2: Student Learning** 2.06 Special education teachers understand how disabilities in one area can impact learning and development in other areas.	1: Understanding Exceptionality 2: Legal and Social Issues
Causes and Prevention	**2: Development and Characteristics of Learners** DH2K2 Impact of the onset of hearing loss, age of identification, and provision of services on the development of the individual who is deaf or hard of hearing	**2: Student Learning** 2.04 All teachers are knowledgeable about multiple theories of learning and research-based teaching practices that support learning.	1: Understanding Exceptionality 2: Legal and Social Issues

Assessment	**8: Assessment** DH8K2 Specialized procedures for evaluation, eligibility, placement, and program planning for individuals who are deaf or hard of hearing	**8: Assessment** 8.08 Special education teachers initiate, contact, and collaborate with other professionals throughout the identification and initial planning process.	2: Legal and Social Issues 3: Delivery of Services to Students
Teaching Students with Hearing Loss	**4: Instructional Strategies** DH4K3 Instructional strategies for teaching individuals who are deaf or hard of hearing	**4: Instructional Strategies** 4.07 All teachers use strategies that promote the independence, self-control, and self-advocacy of students with disabilities.	2: Legal and Social Issues 3: Delivery of Services to Students
Transition	**7: Instructional Planning** DH7K1 Model programs, including career/vocational and transition, for individuals who are deaf or hard of hearing	**7: Planning Instruction** 7.07 Special education teachers oversee the development of individualized transition plans to guide learners' transitions from preschool to elementary school, middle school to high school, and high school to postschool opportunities.	2: Legal and Social Issues 3: Delivery of Services to Students
Collaboration	**10: Collaboration** DH10S1 Coordinate support personnel to meet the diverse communication needs of the individual who is deaf or hard of hearing and the primary caregivers	**6: Communication** 6.02 All teachers collaborate with speech/language pathologists and other language specialists to identify the language and communications skills that need to be developed in students with disabilities, and to work cooperatively to teach those skills across settings.	2: Legal and Social Issues 3: Delivery of Services to Students
Partnerships with Families and Communities	**10: Collaboration** DH10S2 Provide families with knowledge, skills, and support to make choices regarding communication modes/philosophies and educational options across the lifespan	**10: Collaboration, Ethics, and Relationships** 10.10 Special education teachers understand the impact that having a child with a disability may have on family roles and functioning at different points in the life cycle of a family.	2: Legal and Social Issues 3: Delivery of Services to Students

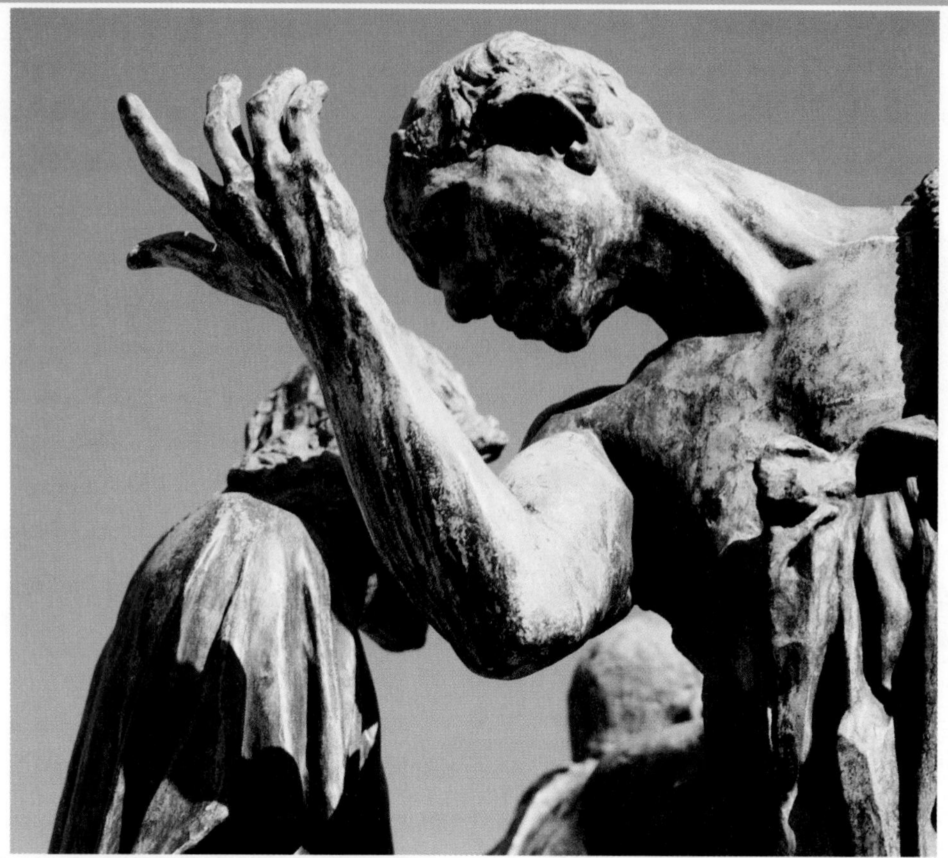

Auguste Rodin, *The Burghers of Calais (detail)*. © SuperStock. Photograph of the artist: GettyImages, Inc./Hulton Archives Photos.

François Auguste René Rodin was born and raised on the Left Bank of Paris. His father was a clerk in the police department. Although the family was not rich, the neighborhood in which they lived was rich in artists, poets, writers, and creative people. He is said to have once remarked that his native Paris gave him "million de pensees"–millions of thoughts (Hale, 1969). Rodin might have been drawn to art because of his lack of success at school. His first school experiences were not positive—after three years he still could not spell, which was a problem that followed him the rest of his life. At age 10 he was sent to a country school but again was unsuccessful. At age 13 he dropped out of school. Some believe that Rodin's frustration and failure at school were the result of a severe vision problem; it was reported that he was so nearsighted that he could not see the blackboard (Hale, 1969). Perhaps for these reasons he chose sculptures as his medium of expression, one that is more tactile than visual. He is considered one of the best sculptors of all time.

The Burghers of Calais (1884-1886) shows the emotions of six city leaders when they surrendered their lives and city to the conquering English. Breaking with tradition, Rodin showed these men with the weight of defeat on their bodies and the fear of death on their faces. These sculptured figures demonstrate Rodin's understanding of the human condition.

11

Low Vision and Blindness

Somewhere along the way, you may lose something you thought was important, but everything you need to fulfill you is inside you or right in front of your eyes. You just have to reach. It won't often be easy, but it will be a great adventure.

Erik Weihenmayer

Although we act on information gained through our sight, we seldom give much thought to the process of seeing. Sometimes we stop to reflect on the beauty of a particular sunset, the stars at night, a flower in bloom, or the landscape after a snowstorm. We use our sense of sight all of our waking hours, yet we do not think about vision and how it functions. Most of us use vision in our work. For example, people use sight when they use the Internet, write memos, look up telephone numbers, or direct people to various offices. We use our vision for recreation when we watch a movie, view television, or read a book. Some of us actually prefer learning by reading or looking at information, rather than listening to a lecture or instructions. Such people are known as visual learners. We also use our vision for self-defense; for example, we look in all directions before crossing a street on foot or entering an intersection when driving a car. Unlike touch and taste, vision and hearing are **distance senses**—senses that provide us with information outside our bodies. These senses developed to alert us to the presence of helpful as well as dangerous elements in the environment.

Clearly, those of us with unimpaired vision profit from this sense. We learn by observing events, we use our vision to move freely in our environment, and we remain alert to danger by using our sight. People with **visual disabilities** have limited use of their sight, but with systematic instruction, advances in technology, and elimination of barriers associated with stereotypes and discrimination, most can lead fully integrated and independent lives.

Chapter Objectives

After studying this chapter, you will be able to:

1. Divide visual disabilities into two functional subgroups.
2. Discuss ways to accommodate the general education setting for students with visual disabilities.
3. Explain why orientation and mobility targets must be an intensive part of the curriculum for many students with visual disabilities.
4. Describe types of assistive technology that benefit people with visual disabilities at school, in the workplace, and in independent living.
5. Discuss issues surrounding braille and reading literacy.

Where We've Been . . . What's on the Horizon?

Records from ancient Egypt confirm that people with visual disabilities were accepted in some societies of the ancient world. Homer, the Greek poet who in the 8th Century B.C. composed the *Odyssey* and the *Iliad,* was blind. The ancient Greeks held Homer and his work in the highest regard, considering him a source of wisdom and a model of heroic conduct. Despite evidence of the acceptance of some individuals who were blind, there is no record of a systematic attempt to educate them or integrate them into society until the 18th Century. And, even with modern efforts to develop educational programs, the bias and discrimination that people who are blind have experienced are not entirely things of the

Ray, the Power of Music

ON the screen

Through Jamie Foxx's 2004 Oscar-awarding winning performance, the life of the talented singer and musician Ray Charles comes to the screen. The film *Ray* provides a sometimes raw but always candid look at America during the 20th Century. Beyond offering fine acting performances and remarkable music, the film teaches lessons of American history. What we see and hear through this film is not just the great talent of a remarkable and self-taught musician who could change his unique style to evolve with the times. We also learn how attitudes evolve across a lifetime. This film not only reveals the truth about growing up poor and Black in the rural South, it also shows us what life was like at residential schools for the blind, *and* it reveals the struggles many individuals face—and overcome—to reach their potential. Ray Charles fought prejudice on two levels: race and disability. *Ray* shows in vivid terms how bias and discrimination can consume individuals, threatening to destroy their talents and depriving us of their gifts. This film is as much about disability as it is about race, genius, the music business, and life's excesses.

By Steven Smith

past. A recently produced film about the life of Ray Charles documents how attitudes and opportunities can change even across one lifetime (read this chapter's *On the Screen: Ray, the Power of Music* for more information). Before thinking more about today, let's trace the development of educational services for students with visual disabilities.

Historical Context

In 1784 Valentin Haüy opened the first school for the blind. At this Parisian school, the Institution for Blind Youth, he conceived a system of raised letters on the printed page. The French Revolution in 1789 ended Haüy's work on this innovative reading system, but by the early 1800s, another Frenchman had developed a tactile system for reading and writing. Louis Braille, who was blind, designed an embossed six-dot cell system, the forerunner of the reading and writing method used today.

In 1821 Samuel Gridley Howe opened the first center school for students who were blind in the United States, the New England Asylum for the Blind (now the Perkins School for the Blind). Around 1832, the New York Institute for the Blind and the Pennsylvania Institution for the Instruction of the Blind were founded. These 19th-Century schools were private boarding schools, usually attended by children from wealthy families.

The first day classes for students with visual disabilities began in Scotland in 1872. The Scottish Education Act required students who were blind to be educated with their sighted classmates and to attend schools in their local communities. Note that our mainstreaming and "inclusion" movements are not new concepts: Their roots are deep in the history of education of students with disabilities. In the United States, the first concentrated attempts to integrate students who are blind into local public schools were made in Chicago. In 1900 Frank Hall, the superintendent for the Illinois School for the Blind, convinced people to allow students who were blind to attend local schools in a region of Chicago near where they lived. These students attended general education classes but also had a special education teacher who taught braille and helped them participate in the general education curriculum. Note that access to the general education curriculum is also not as new a concept as most of us think it is. Frank Hall also developed a mechanical writer—a small,

distance senses Senses—both hearing and vision—used to gain information; developed to guard against danger

visual disabilities Impairments in vision that, even with correction, affect educational performance, access to the community, and independence portable machine for taking notes and completing other written tasks in braille—the precursor to the sophisticated technology available today.

Edward Allen taught the first class for the partially sighted in 1913 in Boston; later that year, Robert Irwin started a class in Cleveland. These programs were modeled after classes in England in which schoolwork was almost exclusively oral. Reading and writing tasks were kept to a minimum, and students attending these classes participated in general education as much as possible. These classes were generally called "sight saving classes." This method was popular for almost 50 years (from about 1915 to 1965), until Natalie Barraga's research on visual efficiency appeared in 1964 (Barraga, 1964; Barraga & Collins, 1979). She proved that people do not have a limited amount of sight that can be used up; rather, vision can become more limited when it is not used.

Although reading and writing are difficult tasks to many individuals with visual disabilities, another major area of difficulty is freedom of movement. Between 1918 and 1925, dog guides were trained to help French and German veterans of World War I. Guide dogs (Seeing Eye dogs) were introduced in the United States in 1928 (Tuttle & Ferrell, 1995). The more popular method of enhancing mobility is the long cane, developed around 1860. Richard Hoover, after whom the Hoover cane is named, is credited with developing a mobility and orientation system in 1944. Before this time, there was no systematic method for teaching individuals with visual disabilities how to move freely in their environments.

During the 1950s, medical advances that helped save the lives of infants born prematurely, by providing them extra oxygen, ironically inflicted the disease **retinopathy of prematurity (ROP)**, formally known as retrolental fibroplasia, which causes visual disabilities ranging from mild visual loss to blindness in surviving infants. During the 1960s, the rubella (German measles) epidemic left many children with multiple disabilities, often including visual disabilities. The dramatic increase in students with visual disabilities strained the capacity of residential schools, which before World War II had served 85 percent of all students with visual disabilities (Sacks & Rosen, 1994). At the same time, parents of such students began to call for their children to attend their local public schools. Today, the majority of students with visual disabilities live at home and attend local public schools. Students with visual disabilities who attend residential schools represent less than 4 percent of all elementary and middle school students with disabilities and about 8 percent of high school students with disabilities (U.S. Department of Education, 2005a).

Advances in technology have significantly influenced the lives of individuals with visual disabilities. Over the past 30 years, improvements in computer capabilities have allowed for efficient and inexpensive print enlargements and immediate translation of print into braille. The first print-to-voice translator, the Kurzweil Reader, was developed in the 1970s. Although crude and expensive when compared to today's optical scanners and everyday computers that translate print-to-voice, they did provide immediate access to printed text not available before. This machine was the breakthrough technology that allowed individuals who were blind immediate access to all printed information, yet it only hinted at the remarkable innovations since developed and still to come.

What might be on the horizon? There is no way to predict what future inventions will make the world more accessible to people with visual disabilities. One thing is clear, though: If the technology is designed for the "mass market" and *everyone* can benefit from it, the costs will go down and availability will increase (Fruchterman, 2003). For, example, over a century ago the radio brought news and entertainment to people wherever they were. While providing service to all, the radio benefited people who could not read the size of print used in newspapers or could not enjoy movies shown in local theaters. The next equally significant breakthrough may well have been cell phone technology (Fruchterman, 2003). Present cell phones can download software, provide access to the Internet, store music, and even help us plan our day. Greater demand will drive down costs. With the addition of voice recognition and braille-device hookups, people with visual disabilities will have even greater access to the world beyond them.

retinopathy of prematurity (ROP) A cause of visual disabilities from prematurity and excess oxygen used to help the infant breathe but damaging to the retina

Second grade teacher Angela Wolf, who is blind, successfully teaches her students reading and other academic subjects.

Challenges That Visual Loss Presents

People with visual disabilities vary widely in their abilities. Because of the growing number of low birth weight babies, there is an increase in multiple disabilities making this a diverse group of individuals as well (Hatton, 2001). **Visual efficiency**—how well a person can use sight—is an important concept. Think about it as you continue to learn more about this disability and how it impacts the people affected by it. Visual efficiency is an interesting factor because it is not perfectly associated with the ability to see; people with the same visual acuity or the same amount of peripheral vision may differ in their visual efficiency (their abilities to use their sight). Visual efficiency influences how individuals learn best (through visual, tactile, or auditory channels) and what accommodations students profit from the most. For example, a student's visual efficiency could affect how the classroom needs to be organized, where the child should sit, whether additional equipment (assistive technology, braillers) is required, and whether adapted materials (texts with enlarged print) are necessary.

Because of advances in technology, the passage of the ADA law, and changing attitudes, more people who are blind or have low vision are assuming their places in the mainstream of society. Remember the story, told in Chapter 1, of Michael Hingson and his guide dog Roselle, who helped coworkers escape one of the collapsing World Trade Center towers. He probably would not have had a job there some 15 years before that terrible event on 9/11. Opportunities are increasing. For example, Angela Wolf recently completed the teacher education program at the University of Texas and earned an elementary general education teaching certificate. An activist, a busy professional, and married to a musician, Angela applies outstanding teaching skills to help her students progress in reading and the rest of their academic subjects. Most amazingly, her second graders don't take advantage of the fact that Angela is blind; rather, they assume more responsibility for their behavior and don't let classmates abuse the situation. Here's what one of her students has to say: "She can teach without seeing, and that's really hard to do. Especially when kids aren't always good. She's special and very smart and knows all of our voices, even from the other side of the room" (Randall, 2005). Angela is not alone in illustrating that expectations for people with disabilities are often based on perceptions rather than on reality (Runyan & Jenkins, 2001). See *In the Spotlight* on page 401 to learn about Marla Runyan, one of many individuals who are blind but whose accomplishments remind us that limitations need not impose insurmountable obstacles.

Making a Difference

"Extreme Makeover: Home Edition"

What we all see on television is to many of us overwhelming, alarming, and sad. Some of the most popular television shows focus on autopsies, murder, and missing persons. The TV news brings horror and terror on the streets of the world into our homes. And "reality television" seems to place people at risk and has viewers squirming while watching contestants touch, swim in, and eat things that nightmares are made of.

Tom Forman, an award-winning news producer before heading up "Extreme Makeover: Home Edition" for Endemol Entertainment, knew American TV viewers wanted a change: "Reality TV was not nice when we put this (show) on the air. We all knew we wanted to do a show about helping people, but we didn't know that it would work." Forman and his team believed that many people would rather watch a real fairy tale—a show with a guaranteed happy ending. And was he right! The show has garnered Emmy nominations and has become exceptionally popular. But entertainment isn't the only key aspect of the show Forman

Tom Forman

and his team of designers, builders, and sponsors have developed. Also important is how they change lives and bring to the public's attention the needs of families, many of them with children with disabilities. They have shown Americans how to put the Americans with Disabilities (ADA) law and the concepts of universal design into practice. In each episode, they show how even the simplest accommodations make homes livable and how little details, such as placing a light switch at a universally appropriate height or including an accessible swing for a child with a disability, brings pleasure to every family member and to television viewers as well.

Although "Extreme Makeover: Home Edition" has many stories from which to select, the Vardon family's strength, character, and devotion to each other are clearly among the reasons why they were selected to participate. Stefan Vardon, then 14-years old, wrote a school essay about his Deaf parents and Lance, his blind, autistic younger brother. Stefan signs to his mom and dad and speaks to his brother. His school essay sparked the Makeover Team to create a home with the latest alerting and communication devices for Stefan's parents and a safe, fascinating, and tactile environment for Lance. As viewers watched the Vardons' home being remodeled, everyone learned about more than accessibility and accommodations for families with disabilities. They all experienced the joy associated with making a difference in the lives of others.

The Vardon family

Remarkably, at the end of two seasons, the show had recreated the living arrangements for 24 families—clearly a daunting pace fueled by the passion of making a difference by improving the lives of people who face great challenges. For an overview of other families touched by this show, go to **http://abc.go.com/primetime/xtremehome/index.html**

Low Vision and Blindness Defined

The federal government in IDEA '04 includes blindness as part of its visual impairments category and does not define low vision or blindness separately. As you will note when you review Table 11.1, the government uses the term *visual impairment* for what we call visual disabilities and *partial sight* for what we refer to as low vision. The government has an additional term and definition for individuals who have severe visual loss. The criteria for *legal blindness,* discussed later in this section, are also found in Table 11.1.

Visual loss results when the body's mechanism for vision is damaged or obstructed in such a way that objects in the environment cannot be perceived or understood. To better understand impaired vision, it is helpful to know how the process of vision works when these mechanisms are functioning properly. Then, as we did for hearing, we'll study three important factors that affect the problems these individuals' face:

1. Degree of loss
2. Age when the loss occurs
3. Type of loss

visual efficiency How well a person can use sight

Table 11.1 • Definitions of Low Vision and Blindness

Source	Definition of Visual Disabilities
Federal Government[1]	Visual impairment including blindness means an impairment in vision that, even with correction, adversely affects a child's educational performance. The term includes both partial sight and blindness.
	Definitions of Low Vision
Education Professionals[2]	A level of vision which, with standard correction, hinders an individual in the planning and/or execution of a task, but which permits enhancement of the functional vision through the use of optical or nonoptical devices, environmental modifications and/or techniques.
United Nations and Centers for Disease Control[3]	Visual acuity between 20/70 and 20/400, with the best possible correction, or a visual field of 20 degrees or less
	Definition of Blindness
United Nations and Centers for Disease Control[3]	Visual acuity worse than 20/400, with the best possible correction, or a visual field of 10 degrees or less
	Definition of Legally Blind
Federal Government[4]	Central visual acuity of 20/200 or less in the better eye, with best correction, or a diameter of visual field that does not subtend an angle greater than 20 degrees at its widest point

Sources: [1]From 34 CFR Parts 300 and 303, Assistance to States for the Education of Children with Disabilities and the Early Intervention Program for Infants and Toddlers with Disabilities; Proposed Regulations (p. 314), U.S. Department of Education, 2005b, *Federal Register*, Washington, DC.

[2]"Instruction in the use of vision for children and adults with low vision: A proposed program model." by A. Corn, 1989, *RE:view, 21,* p. 28.

[3]"Vision Impairment" by Centers for Disease Control (CDC), National Center on Birth Defects and Developmental Disabilities, 2005, p. 1.

[4]"Key Definitions of Statistical Terms, Statistics and Sources for Professionals." American Foundation for the Blind (AFB), 2005, p. 1.

The Process of Vision

When people see normally, four elements must be present and operating:

1. Light
2. Something that reflects light
3. An eye processing the reflected image into electrical impulses
4. A brain receiving and giving meaning to these impulses

As you read the next paragraph, use the picture of the eye in Figure 11.1 to trace how the normal visual process works.

Light rays enter the front of the eye through the cornea. The **cornea** is transparent and curved. The **iris**, the colored part of the eye, expands and contracts in response to the intensity of light it receives. The **pupil** is the opening in the center of the iris. Light rays pass through the pupil to the **lens**, which is behind the iris. The lens brings an object seen into focus by changing its thickness. The process of adjustment by the lens to bring things that are close and those that are far away into focus is called **accommodation**. The lens focuses light rays onto the **retina**, the inside lining at the back of the eye. It is made up of photosensitive cells that react to light rays and send messages along the optic nerve to the visual center of the brain.

cornea Transparent, curved part of the front of the eye

iris Colored part of the eye

pupil Hole in the center of the iris that expands and contracts, admitting light to the eye

lens Part of the eye, located behind the iris, that brings objects seen into focus

accommodation The focusing process of the lens of the eye

retina Inside lining of the eye

Types of Visual Loss

As we have noted, how well people can use their sight is called visual efficiency. Visual efficiency is influenced by many factors, including the person's acuity and peripheral vision, environmental conditions, and psychological variables. **Visual acuity** is how well a person can see at various distances. **Peripheral vision** is the width of a person's field of vision, or the ability to perceive objects outside the direct line of vision. This aspect of vision helps people move freely through their environment. It helps them see large objects and movement. Severe limitation in peripheral vision is sometimes called **tunnel vision** or **restricted central vision**. Some people with visual disabilities have little functional use of sight, but the great majority have substantial use of their vision, particularly with correction (glasses or contact lenses).

Figure 11.1 • The Structure of the Human Eye

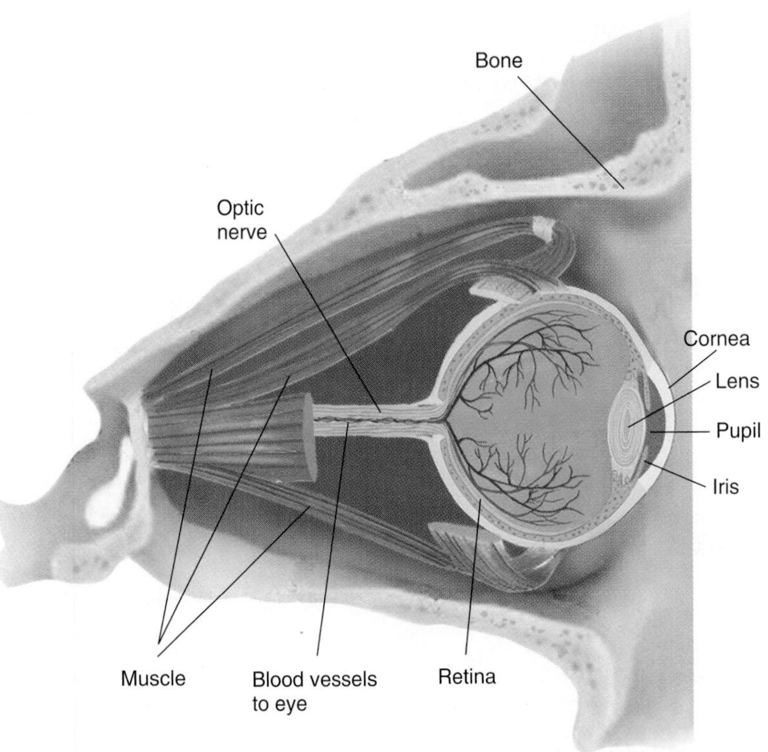

Although many people do not realize it, the vast majority of people with visual disabilities use vision as their primary method of learning. For many their **residual vision**, which is the amount of vision they have left, can be further developed. The vision of some is static, remaining the same from day to day, whereas others find that their ability to see varies by the day, time of day, or setting (Levin, 1996). For some, higher or lower levels of illumination affect how well they can see, but for others, lighting level makes little difference. For some individuals, distance and contrast significantly affect how well they can process information presented through the visual channel. Some are color blind; others are not. For most, optical aids such as glasses have a positive effect.

The eye is a very complicated mechanism. Damage to any part of the eye can result in serious limitations in one's abilities to see and process information through the visual channel. Table 11.2 lists conditions that affect various parts of the eye by using an organizational system originally suggested by Tuttle and Ferrell (1995). These conditions can result in blindness or severe visual disabilities. Many disorders can be corrected or reduced because of advances in medical technology, but not all can be corrected—at least not today.

Degree of Visual Loss

Professionals divide persons with visual disabilities into two subgroups:

1. Low vision
2. Blindness

Individuals with **low vision** use sight to learn, but their visual disabilities interfere with daily functioning. **Blindness** means that the person uses touch and hearing to learn and does not have functional use of sight. Parents and professionals use functional definitions for these two subgroups. Remember, this classification system is based on how well people can use their sight, even if its use is severely limited.

The term *low vision* was coined in the 1950s (Mogk & Goodrich, 2004). But some 30 years ago Anne Corn developed the definition commonly used today.

visual acuity Sharpness of response to visual stimuli

peripheral vision The outer area of a person's visual field

tunnel vision or **restricted central vision** Severe limitation in peripheral vision; limitations in the width of the visual field

residual vision The amount and degree of vision of which a person has functional use despite a visual disability

low vision Degree of visual loss wherein the individual uses sight to learn and to execute tasks, but visual disabilities interfere with daily functioning

blindness Degree of visual loss wherein the individual uses touch and hearing to learn and does not have functional use of sight

Table 11.2 • Types of Visual Loss

Type	Definition
Conditions of the Eye	
Myopia	Nearsightedness; condition allows focus on objects close but not at a distance.
Hyperopia	Farsightedness; condition allows focus on objects at a distance but not close.
Astigmatism	An eye disorder that produces images on the retina that are not equally in focus.
Conditions of the Eye Muscles	
Strabismus	Improper alignment of the two eyes causes two images to be received by the brain, with the possible result of one eye becoming nonfunctional.
Nystagmus	Rapid, involuntary movements of the eye that interfere with bringing objects into focus
Conditions of the Cornea, Iris, and Lens	
Glaucoma	Fluid in the eye is restricted, causing pressure to build up and damage the retina.
Anindia	Undeveloped iris, due to lack of pigment (albinism), results in extreme sensitivity to light.
Cataract (opacity of the crystalline lens)	A cloudy film over the lens of the eye
Conditions of the Retina	
Diabetic retinopathy	Changes in the eye's blood vessels are caused by diabetes.
Macular degeneration	Damage to a small area near the center of the retina results in restricted fine central vision and difficulties in reading and writing.
Retinopathy of prematurity (ROP)	Excess oxygen to infants causes retinal damage; was called retrolental fibroplasia.
Retinal detachment	Detachment of the retina interrupts transmission of visual information to the brain.
Retinitis pigmentosa	Genetic eye disease leads progressively to blindness; night blindness is the first symptom.
Retinoblastoma	Tumor
Condition of the Optic Nerve	
Atrophy	Reduced function of the optic nerve

That definition is found in Table 11.1 on page 398. According to the functional definition, students with low vision use their sight for many school activities, including reading. In contrast, students who are blind do not have functional use of their vision and may perceive only shadows or some movement. These youngsters must be educated through tactile and other sensory channels and are considered functionally blind. Blindness can occur at any age, but its impact varies with age.

There is also an entirely different way to categorize people with visual problems. It is used so that these individuals can receive special tax benefits and mate-

Marla Runyan in the Spotlight

Marla Runyan has this thing about breaking barriers—and breaking records in the process. She was first diagnosed with Stargardt's disease when she was nine years old, and one result was that Marla is blind. She cannot read print, sees only the "big E" on the Snellen chart, and isn't sure whether it's soup when she puts her hand on a Campbell's can. As a kid, not much would stop her. Although she couldn't see, she learned to ride horses and play the violin. And sports became her passion. But many people—teachers, athletic officials, and even some coaches—thought she couldn't succeed, certainly not in the "real" Olympics.

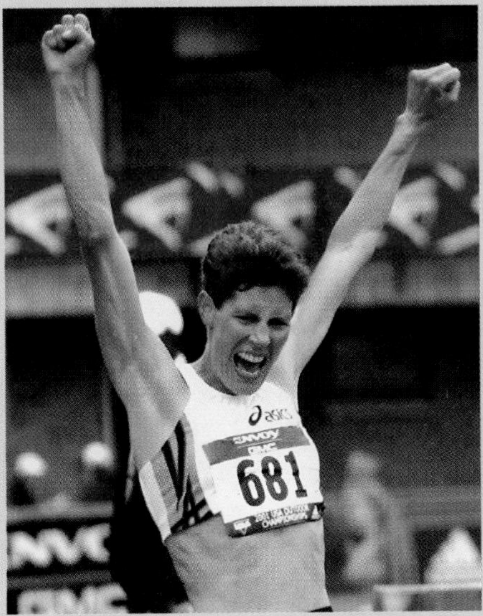

Throughout college, Marla continued to train while studying to become a teacher of students with disabilities. Once again she broke barriers, proving to everyone that she could become a teacher of students with low incidence disabilities. She earned two degrees—a bachelor's degree in the Education of the Deaf and a master's degree in the Education of Deaf-Blind Children—from San Diego State University. At the same time, she was competing in some of the most difficult events for any athlete. For example, she was entering and winning heptathlon events (which consists of seven track and field events: 200-meter dash, high jump, shot put, 100-meter hurdles, long jump, javelin throw, and 800-meter run). In 1996, she amazed the sports world by qualifying for the U.S. Olympic team and broke the American record for the heptathlon. After that she concentrated on running. She represented the United States in both the 2000 and the 2004 Olympic games, breaking U.S. records all the way along her path of victories.

Marla did not compete during the 2005 season. She and her husband and coach, Matt Lonergan, who live and work out in Eugene, Oregon, were expecting their first child. What Marla continues to show everyone is that for her and for others with disabilities, there is "no finish line," only a continuous run toward success, breaking barriers and records along the way.

rials from the federal government and private agencies. **Legally blind** is the term used by the federal government for this purpose. (Its definition and the criteria for qualifying for benefits through this category are also found in Table 11.1.) Despite the long-term movement toward functional definitions of visual disabilities and the fact that many people who meet the criteria for classification as legally blind use print to read and gain information, the designation of legal blindness is still used.

Age of Onset

Just as for deaf or hard of hearing students, another way to group individuals with visual disabilities is in terms of the age of onset (when the disability occurred):

- **Congenital blindness** (existing at birth or during infancy)
- **Adventitious blindness** (occurring after the age of two)

This distinction is important because people who lose their sight after age two remember what some objects look like. The later the disability occurs, the more they remember. Visual memory is an important factor in learning, for it can influence one's development of concepts and other aspects important to learning.

legally blind A category of blindness used to qualify for federal and state benefits

congenital blindness Blindness present at birth or occurring during early infancy

adventitious blindness Blindness occurring after the age of two

The photo on the left shows what a person with a limited visual field, or tunnel vision, might see; the photo on the right shows what a person with restricted visual acuity (see page 399) might see.

Characteristics

Because the needs of students who are blind differ from those who have low vision, we have discussed the characteristics of these two general groups separately. Remember that no one set of characteristics fits all, however, and teachers must adjust their thinking to every particular student's characteristics and needs and to the demands of each situation.

Students with Low Vision

Students with low vision read print and typically access the general education curriculum alongside their peers without disabilities. Most students with low vision *do* require accommodations and some extra assistance from classmates and teachers.

Reading Standard Print

Some 81 percent of students with visual disabilities have sufficient functional vision to read the standard print (12-point type) used in elementary and high school textbooks and to move in their environments independently (Wilkinson, & Trantham, 2004). The vast majority of these students learn to read and write, watch television, and use their vision to function in society. As we just mentioned, most students with visual disabilities can in fact read the same printed books as their classmates without visual problems, though much more slowly (Gompel, van Bon, & Schreuder, 2004). In other words, their reading rate is slower and they are likely to need more time to complete reading assignments. Also, to adjust for varying typeface and print style, they may hold the books closer to their eyes than their peers do (Wilkinson & Trantham, 2004). Many of these students, however, cannot read the smaller print found, for example, in newspapers. Fortunately, most newspapers are now available online, where the size of the print displayed on the computer screen can be adjusted.

Reading Enlarged Print

enlarged print Adjusted size of print so individuals with low vision can read

Enlarged print offers the option of having the print on the page larger than what is typical. Enlarged-print versions of reading materials have been available for many years. Many standard publications (for example, dictionaries, thesauruses, and atlases, as well as Book-of-the-Month Club offerings and Reader's Digest Condensed Books) are available in enlarged type.

Many students with visual disabilities use their vision to read, but they need specially adapted or enlarged-print versions of the books used in their classes. These adapted books are available from each state's materials centers. However, one complaint has been the excessive length of time it often takes to get large-print accommodations (Frank, 2000). Fortunately, this barrier is easily overcome today, thanks to the availability of copiers, scanners, and computers that readily adjust the size of what is printed. Also, as you learned in the section on universal design for learning in Chapter 2, IDEA '04 mandates that publishers provide electronic versions of adopted textbooks. All of these options quickly and easily allow print size and format to be modified to meet the individual needs of each learner.

Students with low vision who use enlarged print and their teachers often need assistance in determining how much text needs to be adjusted. Determining the amount of increase is a complicated process that involves calculating the individual's speed or rate of reading text passages across a range of print sizes (Bailey et al., 2003; Lueck et al., 2003). Teachers of the visually impaired are valuable resources whom general education or special education teachers should consult when they are varying the print size for either instruction or assessments.

A third group of students with low vision cannot profit from print whether it be standard size or enlarged. These individuals have good central vision but a limited visual field. For them, enlargements may actually be a hindrance. However, audio versions of books, **personal readers** (people who read text to them), or computer-generated print-to-voice systems (described earlier in this chapter) may be good alternatives.

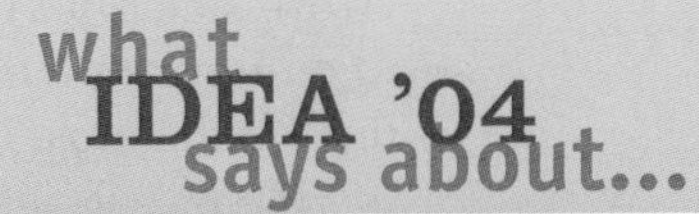

Braille and Its Use

The IEP Team for each student with a visual disability must consider special factors about each child's method of reading:

- All IEPs for children with visual disabilities must address the issue of braille instruction and the use of braille in classroom settings.
- Evaluate the child's reading and writing skills, educational needs, and future need for instruction in braille or use of braille.
- Provide instruction in braille and allow the child to use braille, if that method is deemed appropriate for that student.
- The decision whether to use braille with any student cannot be based on factors such as the availability of alternative reading methods or the availability of braille instruction.
- Once the decision is made, services and materials must be delivered without undue delay.

Students Who Are Blind

Students who are blind differ greatly from students with low vision (HEATH Resource Center, 2001). Many of these individuals do not read print but instead need printed materials that have been translated into nonprint formats: recorded, print-to-speech, or braille. They typically use aids to move around independently. And for some, learning how to socialize and interact easily with others does not come naturally. Let's first turn our attention to a special reading system developed for people who cannot see print.

Reading Braille

Many people who are blind use a tactile system for reading and writing. **Braille** is a coded system of dots embossed on paper so that individuals can feel a page of text. The number of people who use braille is declining. In 1963 over 50 percent of persons with severe visual disabilities used braille; in 1978 less than 20 percent did. Today, even though technology has made braille versions of text more readily available, only about 85,000 of the 1 million people in the United States who are legally blind use braille (Sinatra, 2002). For children the story is much the same. In 1992 only 10 percent of blind students used braille (American Printing House for the Blind, 1992). Today, although there are some 55,200 legally blind students in the United States, only 5,500 use braille—a figure that remains at the same 10 percent level as a decade ago (American Foundation for the Blind [AFB], 2002). Concern about the reading abilities of students with visual disabilities is widespread: Their literacy levels are alarmingly low. Many professionals believe that there should be a renewed effort to teach students who cannot read print this tactile method

personal readers People who read for others

braille A system of reading and writing that uses dot codes embossed on paper; tactile reading; in 1824, Louis Braille created a precursor to the method used today

(Wormsley, 2004). Therefore, Congress addressed the issue of braille instruction when it wrote IDEA '04. Read *What IDEA '04 Says About Braille and Its Use* to learn that braille must be considered when these students' IEPs are being developed.

Many reasons have been suggested to explain why fewer people are using braille as a reading method today. First, for many, reading braille can be very cumbersome and slow. Trent and Truan (1997) report that typical braille readers in high school achieve a rate of only 42 words per minute and that the best reader in their study read 103 words per minute. Adults using braille read 30 percent more slowly (at a rate of about 134 words per minute) than those who read print (Wetzel & Knowlton, 2000). Becoming even minimally proficient at the braille method of reading takes extensive training and practice. Braille also uses different codes for different types of reading, such as math and music, which makes it even more difficult for students with cognitive impairments to master braille completely.

Can you think of some other reasons why braille is less popular today? Here are a few reasons:

- Teachers not knowing how to use or teach the braille method
- Unavailability of teachers who know how to teach braille
- Increasing availability of audio versions of books
- Immediate computerized print-to-voice translations
- Difficulty, in both cost and time, of getting braille versions of books

One barrier to those who use braille has been unavailability of braille versions of texts used in the general education classroom. Availability and cost of books are no longer issues that burden people who use this means of reading. The same technology that makes print-to-voice translations readily available also reduces the costs and increases access to braille versions of books. For example, a scanner, along with special software and printers, now can translate standard print into braille almost instantaneously. Also, electronic versions of textbooks provided to states by textbook publishers allow for easy production of braille versions of all texts used in the schools. Because of the inclusion of braille in IDEA '04, concerns about the literacy rates of this group of learners, and improved availability of braille versions of texts, more experts are thinking about braille instruction and the goal of braille literacy for more students who are blind (Wormsley, 2004). Table 11.3 shows the 12 components of instruction leading to braille literacy, as identified by Koenig and Holbrook (2000), and provides some applications of these instructional targets.

Learning to use a long cane is part of the school curriculum for these students. Orientation and mobility instruction is part of every school day.

Orientation and Mobility

Students with very low visual efficiency need special orientation and mobility training to increase their ability to move around independently. **Orientation** is the mental map that people have of their surroundings (Hill, 1986). Most of us use landmarks and other cues to get from one place to another. Think about how you get from your house to a friend's home or from one class to another on campus. What cues or landmarks do you use? These cues or landmarks make up our mental maps and our orientation to our environments. Remember that these mental landmarks are learned and that students need to know their schools well. For example, they need to know emergency evacuation procedures, exit paths from the school buildings, and how to move through their environment safely both during normal school hours and in times of stress (Cox & Dykes, 2001). **Mobility** is the ability to travel safely and efficiently from one place to another.

Table 11.3 • Braille Literacy Skill Areas

1. Emergent Braille Literacy
Listen to adults read; develop hand-finger skills; observe proficient braille reading.

2. Pre-braille—Early Formal Literacy
Learn hand-finger skills, tactile discrimination, and hand movement; expand conceptual knowledge and vocabulary; develop early reading skills; become motivated.

3. Beginning Braille Literacy
Learn braille decoding and word analysis skills; learn braille writing; build fluency; apply literacy skills throughout day.

4. Begin Dual Media (print and braille)
Learn print and braille reading concurrently; learn print and braille writing concurrently; develop vocabulary, comprehension, and reading for specific purposes; engage in leisure reading.

5. Intermediate Braille Literacy
Use reading as a tool for learning; continue fluency building; incorporate technology into reading experiences.

6. Advanced Braille Literacy
Learn computer braille and foreign language braille; continue using and developing braille for math and science, continue inclusion of technology; balance literacy tools (braille and recorded material).

7. Braille Literacy for Those with Print Literacy
Learn tactile perception, hand movements, and letter or symbol recognition in braille; begin learning contractions; learn braille writing skills; apply literacy skills daily.

8. Listening, Aural-Reading and Live-Reader Skills
Develop auditory skills (e.g., auditory awareness, sound localization); acquire information by listening; learn how to use recorded textbooks; direct activities of live readers.

9. Technology Skills
Gain access to printed information through technology; take notes by using braille: use speech-synthesizing devices; use the Internet to gather information.

10. Keyboarding and Word-Processing
Master touch typing; use word processing software, along with all editing features; apply keyboarding and word processing in daily applications.

11. Slate-and-Stylus Skills
Master a variety of slate and stylus equipment; become proficient in their use; apply these skills in practical situations.

12. Signature-Writing Skills
Learn how to write a signature for legal purposes; practice with many different writing tools (e.g., pens, pencils); understand about when and why signatures are necessary; apply skill appropriately.

Source: Adapted from "Ensuring high-quality instruction for students in braille literacy programs" by A. J. Koenig and M. C. Holbrook, *Journal of Visual Impairment and Blindness, 94,* pp. 689–690. Copyright © 2000 by American Federation for the Blind. Reprinted with permission of the American Federation for the Blind via Copyright Clearance Center.

According to the American Foundation for the Blind (AFB), 109,000 blind adults use the long cane and most of them who do are younger (AFB, 2005). One reason why two-thirds of cane users are under the age of 65 is probably that learning how to be independently mobile by using a long cane is difficult, and proficient use requires many years of instruction and practice. Here's how it works. While a person is walking, the cane is tapped on the ground and makes a sound. It helps the user know when a hallway ends, when stairs begin and end, and when doors are reached. A long cane does not always help the individual avoid many obstacles found in modern society. For example, protruding and overhanging objects are undetectable with the traditional long canes. But there is a new way to avoid such dangerous situations (Eye of the Pacific, 2005). The LaserCane® now allows for safer travel through offices, busy streets, and shopping malls. This innovation resembles a long cane but adds a device that emits three invisible beams. When a beam is not returned to the device (such as when it doesn't bounce back from a sidewalk), a sound alerts the user that he or she is approaching a step down. A vibrator signals that there is an obstruction ahead. Global positioning technology (the technology that provides automobile drivers with maps and directions) has made possible a new navigational device that creates standard routes (from home to work and back), announces points of interest in the surrounding area (including ATM machines), and also provides map cards with the name of the streets to help people be more independent and mobile.

orientation The mental map people use to move through environments; a topic of instruction for students who are blind

mobility The ability to travel safely and efficiently from one place to another; a topic of instruction for students who are blind

Not all people who need assistance with mobility use long canes; guide dogs assist some. The number of guide dog users is relatively small. Of the 1.3 million legally blind people in America, only about 7,000 (less than 4 percent) use guide dogs to help them move about independently (AFB, 2005).

Even when an individual is using a long cane or a guide dog, there are times, such as when she or he is crossing a busy street or entering an unfamiliar building, that assistance from sighted people is helpful. In such a situation, the sighted person must be sensitive to a number of different issues:

1. Be sure the person wants help.
2. Ask the individual in order to be sure whether he or she wants assistance.
3. If the answer is yes, guide the individual by offering your arm, holding it in a relaxed position.
4. The individual usually will gently grasp your arm at or above your elbow and will walk slightly behind you or to your side. (Never push or pull as you walk.)
5. Enjoy a conversation, and walk with ease.

As you can tell, learning to be independently mobile can be a daunting task for many individuals who are blind. Building enough confidence to tackle a city street takes years of practice. And some of those learning experiences should be fun! Sports and recreation programs and activities not only contribute to better orientation and mobility skills but also help students become engaged and active. Special sports programs are available to individuals who are blind or have low vision. Special skiing, sailing, hiking, baseball, bowling, bicycling, and horseback riding are very popular. However, some people with visual disabilities choose not to participate in special programs but, rather, compete with sighted athletes. And, like Marla Runyan (read again *In the Spotlight* on page 401), they excel. Another such athlete who is blind is Erik Weihenmayer, whose passion is climbing (see his photo at the end of this chapter). He was the first blind person to hike the 60-mile-long Inca Trail in Peru. Among the mountains he has conquered are El Capitan in California, Aconcagua in Argentina, Mt. McKinley in Alaska, and Kilimanjaro in Africa (Weihenmayer, 2001). With each success, he has shown everyone that we can all "touch the top of the world." But it is not necessary to climb mountains or run marathons to learn the enjoyment of being active and being outside. Those with visual disabilities are learning every day that they do not have to be super athletes to participate in athletic events. Here's an example. Teams of teenagers with visual disabilities, along with guides, took a 4-day, 139-mile bicycling trip from Nashville to the home of Helen Keller via the Natchez Trace (Associated Press, 2002; Duzak, 2002). In addition to learning the joy of the freedom of mobility and movement, students who participate in sports and recreational opportunities learn important social skills that benefit them at school and later in life (Shapiro et al., 2005).

Social Skills

For all of us, the process of learning social skills begins in infancy and continues to develop throughout childhood. The infant learns to make eye contact, smile, and touch appropriately. For those whose vision is restricted, the process of developing social skills and learning expected ways of interacting with others usually does not happen without instruction and effort. The process begins with the infant and family members (Loots, Devisé, & Sermijn, 2003). It continues as the child learns to interact with playmates during preschool and with teachers and peers during the school years. Children learn how to gain access to play groups, resolve conflicts, attract and direct attention of peers, play, and maintain friendships. Whereas sighted children learn these skills through typical interactions, many children with visual disabilities need explicit instruction to develop these skills (Heller et al., 1996).

Because students with visual disabilities have fewer opportunities or incentive for social interactions, many of these students need help in this area (Shapiro et al., 2005). Consider how sight contributes to social interactions. Being unable to see

A family is instrumental in building the confidence of a blind family member. Without that confidence, these children could not make such trips as this 3-day, 139-mile trek from Nashville, Tennessee, to Tuscumbia, Alabama, the home of Helen Keller.

peers' nonverbal cues, which serve to guide their sighted classmates' social interactions, is a major problem for these youngsters. Next time you are interacting with friends, consider how nonverbal cues (facial expressions, rolling the eyes, a shrug of the shoulders) affect the meaning of a message. Now think about how the literal message of the interaction (without the nonverbal cues) would be understood by someone who could not use sight during the interaction. Receiving incomplete communication messages can have a serious impact on the individual.

In general, students with visual disabilities tend to be less assertive than their sighted peers, which may disturb the necessary balance and equilibrium in social exchanges (Buhrow, Hartshorne, & Bradley-Johnson, 1998). Many lack play skills, ask too many irrelevant questions, and engage in inappropriate acts of affection (Rettig, 1994). Inappropriate or immature social behaviors can inhibit the child's ability to interact positively with others, to be included in small social groups, and to make friends (MacCuspie, 1992). Also, not understanding social situations can lead to unfortunate and disruptive behaviors. One way to improve such situations is to use clear instructions, along with some of the other tactics found in this chapter's *Tips for Classroom Management.*

In all of these instances, teachers, families, and peers can make a positive difference by helping these students develop social competence (Jindal-Snape, 2005). Fortunately for busy teachers, research shows that the application of self-management strategies (read again *Validated Practices* in Chapter 6) and help from classmates can make a real difference. Peers can be taught to model appropriate social skills, to prompt their classmate when these skills

for Classroom Management

USE OF EXPLICIT RULES

- Make all rules clear, even those implied in games and social situations.
- State rules positively and describe the environment to the student with visual loss.
- Discuss rules so that they are well understood.
- Remind students of rules before times of high-probability infractions (group activities, assemblies).
- Review rules periodically, using full descriptions of the environment and the situations.
- Be sure rules are consistently applied.
- Reward students for following the rules.
- Explain the consequences for breaking the rules and apply them systematically.

should be applied, and to provide feedback. Teachers can also help these students understand the explicit and implicit rules of games and social interactions. Meanwhile, parents can organize small play groups at home and provide direct feedback about their youngster's interpersonal interactions.

Another characteristic of some individuals who are blind is not related to reading or to mobility. Many of them develop behaviors, such as rocking or inappropriate hand movements (McHugh & Lieberman, 2003). It is important for teachers to understand such behaviors that are often observed in students who are blind. Here's what we now know today:

- Stereotypic rocking is associated with blindness, particularly in cases of congential blindness (such as ROP).
- These mannerisms are more often seen in individuals who as infants spent long periods hospitalized.
- Stereotypic rocking neither destroys property nor results in injury to others.
- The behavior is often annoying to others and interferes with typical socializations.
- Although the behavior is often persistent, it can be modified, reduced, and eliminated.

Prevalence

According to the American Foundation for the Blind (AFB), approximately 1.3 million Americans are legally blind and there are some 10 million with low vision or blindness (AFB, 2005). However, the vast majority of these people are over the age of 65. Worldwide, only 4 percent of all blind people are children (Hatton, 2001). Visual disabilities are clearly associated with increasing age. The proportion of children with visual disabilities is much smaller than the proportion of people with this disability in the general population. Advances in medicine have had two major effects on the incidence of visual loss: (1) The incidence of visual disabilities has increased with the increasing number of older Americans. (2) The incidence of visual disabilities in children has greatly decreased (Mogk & Goodrich, 2004). Among preschoolers, only 1 in 20 have a visual loss (Prevent Blindness America, 2004a). The number increases to about 1 in 4 during the school years, but most of these children do not need special education because their problems are corrected to the point where their loss does not substantially affect their educational performance. About 5 of every 10,000 students (about 0.05 percent) have visual disabilities and receive special services (U.S. Department of Education, 2005a). Nationally, only 23,973 students between the ages of 6 and 17 receive special education because of low vision or blindness. The vast majority of them are students with low vision. Also, many children with visual disabilities are not counted in this special education category. Nearly two-thirds of children with visual disabilities have more than one disability (Centers for Disease Control [CDC], 2005). In these cases, the more severe the visual loss, the greater the likelihood that the student is included in the multiple disabilities category (Dote-Kwan, Chen, & Hughes, 2001).

Causes and Prevention

Medical technology is helping to identify more specific causes of disabilities, information that may then lead to either cures or preventive measures. For example, two causes of visual disabilities were reduced dramatically during the last part of the 20th Century: retinopathy of prematurity (ROP) and rubella. Today, precautions are being taken to prevent many cases of ROP in low birth weight babies, and when

ROP is not prevented, it often can be corrected with eye surgery. Today, a vaccine protects everyone from rubella, a cause of congenital visual disabilities and also of multiple disabilities.

Causes

Almost half of the children who are blind have the disability because of prenatal factors, mostly hereditary. Researchers are working to identify genes that cause some forms of blindness. The gene that causes retinitis pigmentosa has now been located and isolated, and there is hope for a cure in the near future. Other medical advances—such as laser treatment, surgery, and corneal implants—also help to reduce the incidence of visual disabilities among children or to lessen their severity. Although medical advances have reduced the prevalence of visual disabilities in children, medical technology can cause increases in this disability as well. Today more infants survive premature birth and very low birth weights of even less than two pounds. The result, however, is often the child having multiple disabilities, frequently including visual disabilities (Dote-Kwan, Chen, & Hughes, 2001; Hatton, 2001).

Prevention

In many cases visual disabilities can now be prevented, but a great deal more could be done. For example, the incidence of visual disabilities can be greatly reduced by protecting against eye injuries (Prevent Blindness America, 2005a & b). In many cases, prevention is truly the application of common sense and reasonable safety measures. Each year thousands of children under the age of five have eye injuries (Prevent Blindness America, 2005a). These accidents occur at home, at school, or in the car, and many of them could be prevented. Putting sharp objects (even pencils) out of the reach of children, being certain that toys are safe, and getting help as soon as possible when injuries do happen can make all the difference. Early treatment can avoid a lifetime of visual problems.

For those visual disabilities that cannot be avoided, their impact can be lessened through early and consistent treatment. Unfortunately, not all U.S. children have early access to health care. In fact, poor children are between 1.2 and 1.8 times more likely to have visual disabilities (Sherman, 1994). Considering the long-term costs to society and to these individuals, the problem of access to health care must be addressed.

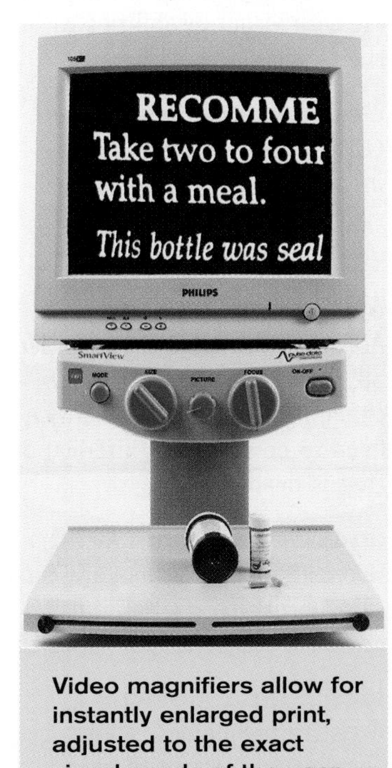

Video magnifiers allow for instantly enlarged print, adjusted to the exact visual needs of the user.

Overcoming Challenges: Technology

The telephone and the phonograph are examples of technological advances that were created for the general population but have special benefits for people with visual disabilities because they offer inexpensive access to both entertainment and information. Large-print books, computerized versions of popular novels, audio versions of books, and computers are other examples of items developed for the general population that have increased the access of people with visual disabilities to mainstream society. Everyone now has greater access to printed information through electronic books and laptop computers that enable the reader to increase the size of print or to switch from print to voice easily.

These exciting technological advances open up a new world for people with visual disabilities. Clearly, these advances facilitate their participation and give them independence in all aspects of modern society. However, three major barriers inhibit their access: cost, complexity, and information. With the average costs of assistive devices ranging from $1,000 to $10,000 and the vast number of options available, careful selection of the right equipment is important. However, as we noted earlier, when equipment is developed for the mass market (cell phones are a good example), people with disabilities also benefit because the devices are both accessible and affordable (Fruchterman, 2003). Assistive devices can be grouped into three categories:

- Visual input devices
- Audio input devices
- Tactile input devices

Visual Input Devices

Visual input devices are equipment or technologies that help people with visual loss access visual information in the environment. Many of these devices are used to enlarge print so that it is easier for a person with visual loss to see and read. For example, **closed-circuit television (CCTV)** technology allows video magnifiers to enlarge the print found in printed texts and books (American Association of Retired Persons [AARP], 2002; Lighthouse International, 2005). By means of a small television camera with a zoom lens and a sliding reading stand on which the printed materials are placed, greatly enlarged printed material (up to 60 times the original size) can be viewed on a television monitor. Another version, the Magni-Cam, has a TV camera embedded in something that looks like a computer mouse and can roll over printed pages. Such equipment provides immediate access to all types of printed materials, such as magazines, textbooks, and photocopied handouts.

Other equipment can also increase print size. For example, overhead projectors, although they are not useful to most individuals with low vision, can be used to enlarge printed materials. Personal computers can produce large-print displays on the computers' screens, allowing persons with low vision to adjust the size and style of print to match their own visual efficiencies. Accompanying printers permit the user to select different sizes of print for hard-copy printout. These features enable teachers to prepare different versions of handouts—one version for students with visual disabilities and one for sighted classmates. Remember that most standard copy machines can also adjust print size.

Audio Input Devices

Audio input devices are equipment or technologies that enable people to hear what otherwise would be read or seen. An example is "talking ATMs." Despite much controversy nationally, Bank of America in California is making these audio-capable banking machines available (Grupé, 2000). Talking books have been available through the Library of Congress since 1934 and today can be found at most bookstores. The American Printing House for the Blind provides compressed-speech (eliminating natural pauses and accelerating speech) versions recorded on tape and CDs; these can be ordered from regional resource and materials centers. Developed for the general public, audio versions of many classics and current best-sellers offer people with visual disabilities greater access to books and print materials.

Another technique enables people with limited vision to enjoy plays, movies, television, and home videos. **Audiodescriptions** are orally presented narrations of nonverbal cues and visual information presented on the screen or stage. This system, initially developed for television by Margaret Pfanstiehl, uses the added sound track available in stereo televisions to describe aspects (such as costumes, scenes, sets, and body language) important to a fuller understanding of the story. A similar system has been devised for theaters; it uses an earphone and a tiny FM receiver. The explanations occur in the speech pauses or otherwise silent parts of the film or play. This accommodation is not so common in movie theaters, because many owners of cinema chains do not want to spend the $15,000 it takes to equip a theater, even though new systems, allowing for both captions for deaf movie-goers and audiodescriptions for blind patrons, are now available (McMahon, 2000). TV shows that have audiodescription versions are becoming more common, because the second audio track that is necessary to play the descriptions is now included on most TV sets (Descriptive Video Service [DVS], 2005).

visual input devices Assistive technology to help people with visual disabilities with their vision

closed-circuit television (CCTV) An assistive visual input technology; uses a television to increase the size of objects or print

audio input devices Assistive technology to help people with visual disabilities by changing what would otherwise need to be seen into information that is heard

audiodescriptions An assistive audio input technology; presents visual information on screen or stage via oral narrations

tactile input devices Assistive technology; allows people to use touch to gain information

Tactile Input Devices

Tactile input devices are equipment or technologies that allow people to use touch to gain information. For example, a well-known tactile system is braille, which allows people to read by feeling letters that have been translated into patterns of dots raised or embossed on a flat surface such as paper. Those people who use braille as their preferred reading method find the Perkins Brailler to be a compact and portable machine that embosses special paper with the braille code. The Perkins Brailler is inexpensive but less efficient than electronic versions that use microprocessors to store and retrieve information. For example, Braille 'n Speak functions as an organizer, notetaker, calendar, and talking clock. The new (though expensive, costing almost $6,000) braille PDA gives its users, through wireless technology, access to the Internet, a planner, speech output, and phone service.

A small braille PDA that fits in the palm of the hand and syncs with computers uses Bluetooth technology to "talk" with cell phones and the Internet. It includes a personal organizer and even produces speech output.

Personal computers with special printers transform print into braille. When a specially designed braille printer is attached to a microcomputer, standard text can be translated into braille, allowing a teacher who does not know how to use braille to produce braille copies of handouts, tests, maps, charts, and other class materials. And some new printers, such as the ones made by American Thermoform, even produce braille and print on the same page.

Another limitation of braille versions of text has also been overcome. Only a few years ago, diagrams and illustrations were omitted from braille versions because there were obstacles to producing them. Today one system, Tactile Access to Education for Visually Impaired Students (TAEVIS), uses a special type of paper, backed with plastic and coated with a heat-sensitive chemical, to produce raised versions of diagrams (Tennessean, 1999). Clearly, technology continues to improve access to the world of print for individuals with visual disabilities.

Assessment

Professionals and parents use information from assessments to decide whether a student should learn to read print or to read braille and whether the student needs a curriculum that includes orientation and mobility training. These assessments also are used to specify the level and type of education placements the child will receive, what accommodations will be provided, and which related services must be specified in the student's IEP. Such decisions determine what types of special education services a student receives, but they also have lifelong implications.

Early Identification

Early identification of visual loss is very important not only to reduce its impact on learning but also to prevent the problem from worsening (Prevent Blindness America, 2004b). For students who are very young or have multiple disabilities, other testing options are available. For example, **photoscreening** is the system for testing acuity when the individual cannot actively or reliably participate in visual assessments. Photoscreening uses a special camera to take a picture of the individual's eyes that is then examined for signs of vision problems.

Pre-Referral: Vision Screenings

Most states require that all students have a visual screening test. Such initial screenings are often conducted by trained volunteers, who then refer students who may have a vision problem for further testing. Student's visual acuity often is tested in the school nurse's office or by a pediatrician using the Snellen chart. The **Snellen chart**, originally developed by a Dutch ophthalmologist in 1862, comes in two versions and is used

photoscreening A system used to test visual acuity for those who cannot participate actively or reliably in visual assessments

Snellen chart A chart used to test visual acuity, developed in 1862

Source: Dana Summers, published 1993. Copyright 1993 Tribune Media Services. Reprinted with permisssion.

to screen people's visual acuity. One test uses the letter E placed in various positions in different sizes; the other uses alphabet letters in different sizes. For the screening of substantial numbers of people, a more efficient adaptation of the Snellen chart uses the E version projected on a television monitor placed 10 to 20 feet away from the viewer. The viewer matches a key on a computer with the direction or placement of the E on the screen, and the computer analyzes the data.

Schoolwide visual screenings can help identify students with visual disabilities and get them needed services early. Alert teachers and parents, familiar with the possible signs of a visual problem (see Table 11.4), can help identify such students even sooner and ultimately reduce the impact of the disability. A school nurse, pediatrician, or ophthalmologist should check students exhibiting one or more of these characteristics. Although this is not a requirement, each child's visual screening should include teachers' observations about classroom behaviors and performance. For example, teachers should indicate whether a particular child complains about scratchy or itchy eyes or headaches, rubs the eyes excessively, or has difficulty discriminating letters or symbols when completing classroom assignments. Such information is especially helpful when recommendations are made about placement and the types of special assistance a child should receive.

Identification: Visual Assessments

Two types of eye specialists provide diagnosis and treatment:

1. Ophthalmologists (medical doctors who specialize in eye disorders)
2. Optometrists

Ophthalmologists are doctors who conduct physical examinations of the eye, prescribe corrective lenses and medicines, prescribe drugs, and perform surgery. **Optometrists** are professionals who measure vision, prescribe corrective lenses, and also make functional recommendations. An **optician** is a specialist who fills the ophthalmologist's or optometrist's prescription for glasses or corrective lenses.

Table 11.4 • Signals of Visual Problems

Appearance of the Eyes	Problems with Schoolwork	Behavior and Movement
Eyes • Water excessively • Are red or continually inflamed • Appear crusty • Seem dull, wrinkled, or cloudy • Are swollen • Look grey or white (one or both pupils) • Are not aligned	The student has difficulty • Reading small print • Identifying details in pictures • Discriminating letters • With close work	The student • Appears clumsy • Bumps or trips over objects • Can't catch a ball, button clothes, or tie shoes • Covers an eye while reading • Tilts head • Holds object close to an eye to view it • Complains of dizziness after working on an assignment

Although parents and professionals are advocating for the use of functional definitions of visual disabilities, many states still use measures of acuity to qualify youngsters for special education services. Normal visual acuity is measured by how accurately a person can see an object or image 20 feet away. Normal vision is thus said to be 20/20. A person whose vision is measured at 20/40 can see at 20 feet what people who do not need visual correction (glasses or contact lenses) can see at 40 feet away. **Field of vision**—how wide an area can be seen—is measured in degrees. Normal field of vision is about 160 to 170 degrees horizontally (CDC, 2005). In Table 11.1 we noted that people whose visual field is restricted to no more than 20 degrees are classified as legally blind. Although states and school districts vary in the criteria they use to determine eligibility for special services, people with visual acuity measuring 20/70 to 20/200 in the better eye, with correction, are typically considered to have low vision (AFB, 2005). Acuity below 20/200 classifies an individual as legally blind.

Assessing functional vision can be complicated, imprecise, and inaccurate. Information must be gathered from multiple sources. For example, diagnosticians, the children affected, their parents, general educators, teachers of students who are blind or have low vision, school nurses, and eye specialists can all provide important information employed in the comprehensive assessment of useful vision. Another source of information is the children themselves, but you may be surprised to learn that they are often very unreliable. Many parents report that their blind children, possibly motivated by the desire to please a doctor or a diagnostician, both report and simulate a level of blindness different from what they actually possess (Erin & Corn, 1994). For example, some children indicate that they can see things they cannot: a car coming, the moon at night, or the color of an object. Decisions about visual status must be made from accurate information, and collecting that information can be quite challenging.

Evaluation: Testing Accommodations

Students with visual impairments often require accommodations during instruction. Those accommodations must be available to them when they are demonstrating their mastery of the curriculum, whether during weekly quizzes or annual state- or district-wide tests. Students who cannot access print may need help during testing situations. Personal readers are people—whether teachers, paraprofessionals, or peers—who read the directions and test items to the student. Students with low vision who can read print usually do so much more slowly than their peers without visual loss (Gompel, van Bon, & Schreuder, 2004). These students need extra time to take tests so their achievement is not masked by their not having time to read the questions. It is also significant that although students with low vision match their classmates' reading comprehension abilities, their slow reading gives them an extra disadvantage when answering multiple-choice questions. Teachers must work together to determine what is a fair amount of extended time to complete tests.

Early Intervention

Just as for students with other disabilities, preschool education is vital for those with visual disabilities. During this time, the foundations of social skills, academic success, and independence are laid. Recall that those who are congenitally blind (born blind) and those who became blind at a very early age (adventitiously blind) have little or no memory of how the world looks. These infants are not stimulated like sighted infants and have limited opportunities for learning. They do not see their mother's smile or the toys in their cribs. A good preschool program can give preschoolers with visual disabilities "the right start" so that the disadvantages this disability can cause are minimized. The teacher of a preschooler

ophthalmologist Medical doctor who specializes in eye disorders

optometrist Professional who measures vision and can prescribe corrective lenses (eyeglasses or contact lenses)

optician A person who fills either the ophthalmologist's or the optometrist's prescriptions for glasses or corrective lenses

field of vision The width of the area a person can see, measured in degrees with visual disabilities should coordinate a multidisciplinary team of specialists, including an ophthalmologist, occupational therapist, physical therapist, orientation and mobility instructor, and social worker. The preschool years provide the foundation for lifelong learning and independence. This is a time when children learn basic communication and interaction patterns, and for blind students this can be a problem area. *Tips for Effective Teaching* offers suggestions about how to facilitate the development of these important skills.

Play

Researchers are learning that play is a very important part of human development (McGaha & Farran, 2001). Through play, young children learn to socialize, interact with others, and cooperate. Via discovery and exploration, which are encouraged through play activities, young children also learn about their environment, develop motor skills, and often enhance their language skills. Because of their disability, children who are blind or have low vision play very differently from others and are also delayed about two years behind their sighted peers in the development of play skills (Hughes, Dote-Kwan, & Dolendo, 1998).

Many characteristics of their play follow individuals who are blind into adulthood: engaging in high rates of solitary play, not playing spontaneously, seeking play with adults rather than with other children, not taking conversational turns, and selecting only concrete, familiar toys (McGaha & Farran, 2001; Tröster & Brambring, 1992, 1994). Delayed play development may contribute to later difficulties in social interactions and concept formation. Sighted children often find it difficult to adjust their play to the ability levels of blind children, who prefer noisy play activities to abstract or symbolic ones (Tröster & Brambring, 1994). They often find their play styles in conflict with those of their blind peers. The quick and sometimes unpredictable movements of sighted children can disorient children with visual disabilities. Some experts are convinced that simply providing inclusive opportunities does not ensure interactions and play among sighted preschoolers and those who are blind; adult intervention may be necessary (Hughes, Dote-Kwan, & Dolendo, 1998; McGaha & Farran, 2001).

*tips for Effective Teaching

INCREASING INTERACTIONS

The goal is for natural interactions to occur at school, at home, and in the community, which requires the child to both initiate and respond to communications (Dote-Kwan, 2001).

1. Understand the child's visual functioning capabilities.
2. Identify visual features that enhance the child's visual functions (color, contrast, size).
3. Encourage the child's interest in objects, events, and people (children need to have something they are interested in talking about).
4. Learn the child's nonverbal cues indicating interest.
5. Develop a predictable and understandable system to initiate communications.
6. Add signs and nonverbal signals to enhance communications, if necessary.
7. Design many opportunities for interactions in the child's natural settings.
8. Expand the child's vocabulary and communications by repeating and modeling extensions of the child's interaction.
9. Reduce the child's reliance on adult initiations, and allow and encourage increased initiations from the child.
10. Make interactions enjoyable for both the child and the adult.

Independence

Orientation and mobility are major curriculum targets for many students with visual disabilities. Because instruction in this area needs to begin as early as possible, parents and professionals are encouraging the introduction of the long cane to children between the ages of two and six (Pogrund, Fazzi, & Schreier, 1993). Although some orientation and mobility teachers believe that young children should begin learning how to use a long cane with the adult size that they will use later in life (which would be extra long for their present size), research findings indicate that children are better off learning how to use a mobility cane that is cut to their size (Clarke, Sainato, & Ward, 1994). Sometimes called the "kiddy cane" or the Connecticut precane, this homemade version of the long cane is tailored to the size of the user, even a preschooler. It is made of rigid, white PVC pipe and is cut at midchest height. It has a red stripe at the bottom and tape across the top for a grip. Because the home is the most natural setting for infants' and toddlers' educational programs, most programs for blind infants include home-based instruction with considerable parent involvement. One of the most important lessons parents can learn is to encourage later independence. To this end, they must allow their infants and toddlers to explore the environment, even if they get the same bumps and bruises as young children without visual loss.

Teaching Students with Visual Loss

The educational needs of students with low vision differ from the needs of those who are blind. Students with low vision might require some extra tutorial assistance to learn the same number of phonetic rules as their classmates or additional time to read their history assignment. Teachers can help these students in many ways. They can make adjustments in the way they lecture and present information to students. Students who are blind might require the introduction of entirely different curriculum topics. You have already learned about orientation and mobility as an additional curriculum target, but for many of these students, additional topics must be the focus of instruction. For example, they might need to learn independent life skills so that they can manage an apartment, pay their bills, shop for food, cook their meals, and hold competitive jobs without assistance from others. Clearly, the curriculum for many students with visual loss is jam-packed full. The crucial factor is that the educational and developmental goals, and the instruction designed to meet those goals, reflect the specific needs of each individual (Spungin, 2002).

Access to the General Education Curriculum: Literacy

Today, a large percentage (about 54 percent) of students with visual disabilities spend over 79 percent of their school day in general education classrooms. Over 86 percent of students who have low vision or are blind receive their education at a neighborhood school, possibly with support from a resource specialist or itinerant teacher (U.S. Department of Education, 2005a). These students participate in the general education curriculum with their sighted classmates and, if they do not also have coexisting disabilities, perform well academically. This is reflected in their having the highest graduation rates of all high school students with disabilities. Many use aids (such as glasses or technology that enlarges type) to help them enhance their vision for accessing information from printed material, whether it be in text form or on the board. Others, even those with low vision, use their tactile senses, and some employ braille as their reading method. Some members of both groups rely on audio means for gaining information and don't use either print or braille. One of the singular characteristics of this group of learners is the wide variety of ways in which they access information, but professionals agree that literacy should be a goal for every student with a visual disability and that direct instruction in accessing print or braille is the best way to help them master reading and achieve the goal of being fully literate (Corn & Koenig, 2002; Wormsley, 2004).

Many individuals who are blind are not proficient readers, regardless what reading method they use. One obvious reason for these students' reading difficulties is their visual disabilities. Another reason is that many of these individuals have coexisting disabilities, such as learning disabilities or cerebral palsy. Students with visual disabilities who also have coexisting disabilities often benefit from learning strategies developed for students with learning disabilities (read again the Validated Practices section of Chapter 5) that emphasize boosting comprehension by skimming passages to look for the main ideas. Although some teachers might conclude that braille instruction is not appropriate for these learners, many vision experts do not agree (Dote-Kwan, Chen, & Hughes, 2001; Wormsley, 2004). They think that instructional methods need to be adjusted. They suggest that additional instructional strategies, also borrowed from the field of learning disabilities, be used so these students can master reading, whether the method used to access information be print or braille. Students learning braille, like many students without visual loss, need instruction in phonemic awareness, phonics, and sight words.

Literacy is a goal for all Americans and an expectation for all high school graduates, and braille literacy is a goal being advocated by experts for those students who find print, even enlarged print, inaccessible (Wormsley, 2004). Education professionals are suggesting that all students be exposed to a literacy-rich school environment, and the same is true for students learning braille. How does the concept of a *braille-rich environment* apply? The notion is that just as sighted learners are exposed to print—whether or not they can actually read the words yet—students learning braille should be exposed to braille everywhere in their environments as well. How can teachers help create a braille-rich environment for these students? They can seek the assistance of the vision teacher and help label the learner's immediate environment in braille: signs in the hallways, names on lockers, personal belongings, on and off light switches, bathroom doors, class schedules, and notices on bulletin boards. A braille-rich environment can be fun and inclusive for all, as students who are learning to access print also learn and respect other ways to access information.

Instructional Accommodations

Most students with visual disabilities require accommodations and assistive devices (beyond eye glasses) to access the general education curriculum and succeed at school. One important rule applies: Each individual has different needs, so different responses to those needs are necessary. In other words, there is no single answer to the question "What accommodations benefit students with visual disabilities?" Of course, some general guidelines are helpful as teachers think about how to make a real difference in their students' academic learning environments (Hagelman, 2004). Some students may need time to explore the classroom each time the classroom layout changes. Others may need extra space when working with a personal reader (someone who reads printed text to the student) or using a special lamp for more illumination. Yet other students with visual disabilities may need a seating arrangement where glare is eliminated. More suggestions about how to modify the learning environment so that classrooms are safe and maximal learning can occur are found in *Accommodating for Inclusive Environments*.

Some other minor adjustments in teaching style help all students gain more from the learning environment. One such modification is the careful use of language. For example, many of us, when speaking, use words that substitute for other words, rather than terms that concretely name their referents; we say *it, this, that,* and *there* without naming the things or locations we are discussing. For example, an adult might say, "Go get it. It's over there," instead of saying, "Please get the large book at the end of my desk." Clearly, more concrete and explicit instruction is more helpful to a blind student.

A commonly used accommodation for all students with disabilities is extended time. Many students with visual disabilities do require more time to complete assignments because it takes them more time to read. In these cases, teachers often

Accommodating for Inclusive Environments

Modifying the Learning Environment

Make the Classroom Safe

- Open or close doors fully (a half-open door can be a dangerous obstacle).
- Eliminate clutter from the room, particularly in aisles and movement paths.
- Don't leave the classroom without telling the student.

Supplement instruction

- Prepare enlarged-print or braille handouts, summarizing key points.
- Repeat orally what is written on the blackboard or overhead projector (remember that enlargements on an overhead projector are not helpful to all students with visual disabilities).
- Audio record lectures.

Adjust Seating Arrangements

- Place the student's desk near the teacher's desk, the blackboard, and the classroom door.
- Seat the student where glare is minimized.
- Allow the student to relocate depending on the type of activity.

Ask for Help

- Don't forget to ask the student about his or her preferences.
- Ask the student's parents about ways they believe their child learns best.
- Seek the assistance of a vision specialist.

set a later due date for homework or major projects, but they also insist that this extended deadline be met. Other teachers reduce or change the requirement somewhat, for instance by allowing students to make an oral report instead of a written one or assigning a 10-page paper instead of a 20-page report. Another common accommodation is the use of a computer for both in-class assignments and homework. Whatever accommodations are made, however, teachers should not lower their expectations for students with visual disabilities.

Validated Practices

As you have learned, students with visual disabilities often need modifications to both their physical and learning environments to be maximally successful. You have also learned that many of these adjustments or modifications to the classroom are not difficult to achieve; they just require some careful thought and planning. As you read this chapter's *Validated Practices,* think about how simple such adjustments are to implement and how much of a difference they make in the educational lives of students with visual loss.

We introduced the concept of universal design for learning in Chapter 2, but because of its great benefit to students with visual disabilities, we are reminding you about it here. Universal design for learning extends the principles of universal design that are outlined in the ADA law. Universal design creates accommodations to the physical environment so that buildings, parking lots, and communities are more accessible to people with disabilities. What was learned when universally designed environments became commonplace is that everyone benefits! In Chapter 2 we cited the example of "curb cuts" and how they were instituted to help people who use wheelchairs but have come to be appreciated by anyone looking for an easier way to negotiate a curb. Captioned television is another example. Originally developed to enable people who are deaf to access information and entertainment shown (and heard) on television, it is now used by everyone—

Validated Practices Classroom Modifications

What Are Classroom Modifications?

Classroom modifications for students with visual disabilities are important for them to be successful in the general education curriculum. Remember that everyone has different levels of ability, so some students need only simple modifications to the classroom and instruction, whereas others may need more intense accommodations.

Why Classroom Modifications Are Beneficial

With simple modifications beneficial to everyone, most students with visual disabilities learn well alongside their peers in the general education classroom. In these situations, students with and without visual disabilities learn from each other.

Implementing Classroom Modifications

Below is a list of simple things that teachers can do to make their classrooms more adaptable for students with visual disabilities. Vision specialists can guide the implementation of modifications to be sure that these are right for the individual child.

Chalkboards and Dry Eraser Boards

- Seat students close to the window for more natural lighting and fewer reflections off shiny surfaces impairing view of writing on the board.
- Encourage students who are blind or have low vision to use their assistive technology devices (e.g., magnifying glasses, telescopes), and create a climate where they are not embarrassed by using them.
- Before lessons, prepare enlarged-print or braille versions of what will be written on the board.
- Prior to each lesson, provide students with a copy of your lecture notes.
- Explain your notes as you write them on the board.

Classroom Demonstrations

- Avoid standing with your back to the window, because glare makes it more difficult for students to see.
- Either before or after the lesson, allow students to touch the materials.
- To avoid considerable confusion, be sure your students have all the required materials prior to the lesson.
- Provide the vision teacher early with all texts and other materials that need to be adapted.

Writing in the Classroom

- So that their writing is more visible, allow students to use bold-line paper and felt tip pens.
- Remember that your students will need to write larger so that they can read what they have written.

Homework, Tests, and Reproduced Materials

- As with all materials that need to be adapted, give homework assignments to the teacher of visually impaired students far in advance.
- When assigning a bigger project, give your students advance notice so that they will have sufficient time to gather needed materials.
- Provide text-only versions of worksheets because those with graphics are difficult to enlarge.
- Allow students with visual disabilities to take more time on assignments and tests—perhaps time and a half for students with low vision and double time for students who read braille.
- Allow your students to answer their questions on the test form, or have another student or paraprofessional record the answers the student gives orally.

Maps and Charts

- Provide desk copies of charts and maps to your students with visual disabilities.
- Use raised maps with your students with visual disabilities.

Films, Videos, and Multimedia Presentations

- Schedule an individualized session for students with visual disabilities so that they can view multimedia presentations with the vision specialist to ensure that they understand visual concepts.
- If presentations have subtitles, have someone read them to students who cannot read print.

Moving Around the School

- Be very specific when giving verbal directions.
- Secure rugs and other floor covering so students don't trip.
- Keep cupboards and closet doors closed.
- Make sure all chairs are pushed under desks.

This scientifically validated practice is a teaching method proved by systematic research efforts (Cox & Dykes, 2001; Spungin, 2002). Full citations are found in the references for this chapter.

—By Kimberly Paulsen, Vanderbilt University

people exercising in the gym, those learning English as a second language, family members who don't wish to disturb people engaged in other activities, and fans watching a sporting event at a crowded restaurant.

Universal design for learning builds upon what has been learned through the applications of universal design to the *physical* environment. The learner is not viewed as "the problem"; rather, the premise is that the *learning* environment is the barrier (Hitchcock et al., 2002). Although all students, including those with disabilities, can benefit from a learning environment that provides multiple ways to access information, students with visual disabilities definitely find that flexible means of interacting with instruction helps them surmount many of the instructional challenges they face. When text can be displayed and accessed in multiple ways, students can select the means that best suits their learning preferences. Universal design for learning uses technology to allow individuals to adjust the size of print to meet their visual requirements, to translate print into speech, or to convert print into braille. It also exploits the advances of technology to hyperlink to dictionaries so that students who need assistance with vocabulary can become independent learners and find explanations of unknown words or unfamiliar concepts. Graphics or animation can support the content by providing visual illustrations of the information being learned. Thus universal design is freeing both students and teachers from the chores of finding or developing accommodations. Think of the opportunities that will open up when not only our physical environments but also our learning environments are universally accessible.

Technology

In the Overcoming Challenges section of this chapter (see pages 409–411), you learned about many assistive devices developed specifically for people with visual loss. You learned about visual input devices using CCTV technology to enlarge the size of print. You learned about audio input devices that provide information through the auditory channel instead of the visual channel: audiodescriptions, audio versions of books, and speech-to-text translations. And, of course, you learned about tactile input devices such as equipment that helps create braille versions of text. In this section, we introduce some surprising information about one of the most common applications of technology in America today and its use among people with visual disabilities.

It seems that computers are everywhere. They are plentiful at schools, commonplace in many homes, and a requirement in most workplaces. It seems as though everyone must have access to the Internet not only to stay in touch with friends through e-mail but also to get important information, do on-line shopping, and even pay bills. Basic computer skills are a requirement for most jobs today, and it is easy to assume that everyone uses a computer. Of people without disabilities, some 57 percent report using a computer, and 51 percent say they use computers on a regular basis (Gerber, 2003). And yet, even though computers are at the heart of most assistive technologies, only 21 percent of people with visual disabilities report that they use a computer, and only 13 percent say they do so regularly. Some people with visual disabilities indicate that they feel liberated because of their computer skills, but many say computers are just too frustrating because of hidden navigational barriers and because the skills needed to use computers efficiently are hard to learn on your own.

Because of the importance of computer literacy in U.S. society and because these skills will soon be expected of nearly all those entering the workforce, instruction in the use of computers is critical. They are an important part of overcoming the challenges that disabilities present. Here, then, is another way in which teachers can make a difference in the present and future lives of their students with visual disabilities. They should integrate computer use into the curriculum.

Teachers can assign interesting and useful activities that draw on the Web to supplement content instruction. And, perhaps even more important, teachers must be certain that their students have the basic skills needed so that this technology works for them—and not the other way around.

Transition

Some young adults with visual disabilities have a difficult time adjusting to independence and the world of work. Many of these individuals do not possess the level of literacy necessary to be successful in the community or on the job. Many do not possess other skills (e.g., social interaction, job skills, self-advocacy) needed to be competitive in the workplace. When such deficiencies are coupled with bias and discrimination, the result is underemployment and a group of individuals not achieving to the level of their capabilities. With education specifically directed toward literacy, career education, and job training, this situation can be corrected.

Postsecondary Options

As you have learned, more and more students with disabilities are attending college. In fact, some 16 percent of first-year students with disabilities attending four-year colleges report having visual disabilities (Henderson, 2001). Graduating from college has a significant bearing on a person's career and earning power, but less than half of those with visual disabilities who enter college graduate. Their reasons for leaving college are usually based not on the academic demands but rather on the difficulties of living independently. Fortunately, the skills needed for successful college life can be taught either before or during the college years. Since 1969, the University of Evansville's summer school precollege program has taught students who are blind the mobility, orientation, academic, and life skills needed for college life (Evansville Association for the Blind, 2003). At that program, students learn how to negotiate a college campus, do their own laundry, live in a dormitory, and take notes during lectures. For students who have participated in the program, college is a less frightening and more successful experience. Whether or not students attend such an orientation session, some general tips about college are helpful and increase students' chances for graduation. Here are some suggestions for students with visual disabilities (HEATH Resource Center, 2001):

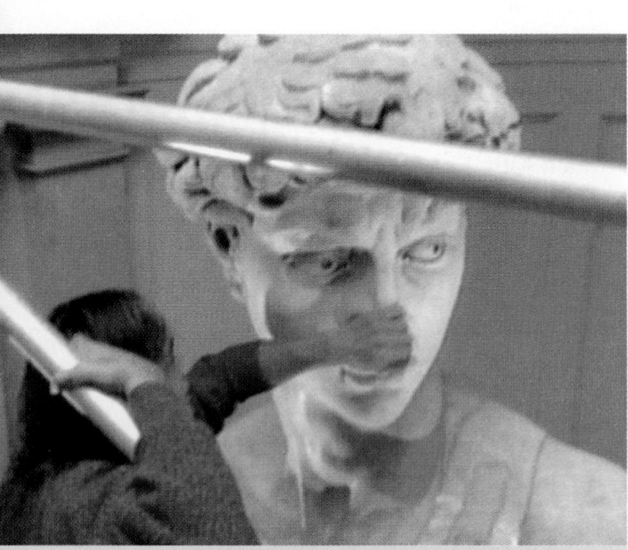

Michael Naranjo, a blind artist, is shown here "seeing" Michelangelo's famous sculpture "David" with his hands. Scaffolding around the statue was erected especially for his benefit. You can see one of Naranjo's sculptures on the cover.

- Begin the search for the "right" college program early.
- Interview, before selecting a college, the campus coordinators of services for students with disabilities as well as current students with visual disabilities.
- Register for classes as early as possible to order e-textbooks and adapt other course materials.
- Contact readers, locate assistive devices, and arrange for accommodations.
- Meet with faculty individually to explain which accommodations are effective, advise them of your unique learning needs, and explain assistive devices that you will bring to class.
- Stay in close communication with faculty.

Regardless of the approach, it is clear that students who are blind or have low vision can improve their chances for success in college and in later life by participating in programs specifically designed to develop skills needed for independence and employment.

Transition to Work

Although adults with visual disabilities hold jobs at every level (scientists, engineers, teachers, office workers, managers of business, and laborers), as a group they tend to be underemployed or unemployed at rates far beyond expectations (Oddo & Sitlington, 2002). Students who are blind or have low vision have one of the highest high school graduation rates of all students with disabilities. They also attend college at a rate close to that of their peers without disabilities. Despite these facts, only about 30 percent of recent graduates (compared to 57 percent of all students with disabilities and 69 percent of graduates without disabilities) are able to find competitive employment (Nagle, 2001). Only about half of adults with visual disabilities between the ages of 22 and 50 are working, and education is one reason why these younger workers are finding jobs more often than older individuals (AFB, 2005). Although for almost everyone else, high school and college graduation rates are associated with higher salaries, graduates with visual disabilities tend to earn only slightly more than their peers with mental retardation (Kirchner & Smith, 2005). Thus more formal education must not be the only answer to better jobs and higher salaries for these individuals (Capella-McDonnall, 2005).

Why do so many individuals who are blind have difficulty finding good jobs? This situation is hard to explain. One reason may well be bias and discrimination. Another reason may be lack of job skills and work experience. During high school, many sighted classmates hold jobs after school or during the summer. These sighted peers learn about finding and keeping jobs and also about salaries, wages, and benefits. For students who are blind, however, their high school years are focused on educational tasks, and they often spend their summers learning important skills (such as orientation and mobility) that they need for independence. Unfortunately, not having practical work experience can later put them at a disadvantage in the job market. Researchers and educators (Kirchner & Smith, 2005; Nagle, 2001; Oddo & Sitlington, 2002) suggest the following goals and ideas:

- Community employment during high school
- Internships in real work settings during high school
- College graduation
- Education of potential employers about the skills and abilities of workers with visual disabilities
- Informing employers about how the costs of special equipment can be paid by state, federal, and private programs

Access to the Community

Many adults with visual disabilities express frustration because their access to the community remains restricted. They believe their access to recreational, leisure, and cultural activities is limited. Even so, more cultural events are accessible than ever before. For example, concert programs of the New York Philharmonic, the Chamber Music Society, and the Great Performances at Lincoln Center come in different formats: standard print, enlarged print, and braille. The ADA law has helped to expand community opportunities. Museums and entertainment centers are more accessible. More and more museums are including tactile exhibits for both children and adults. And even children's theater performances are now offering "freeze frames" so young people can feel the costumes and sets of plays (Ansariyah-Grace, 2000). Although guide dogs were not allowed in zoos only a few years ago, they now join their companions visiting most sections of the animal parks. But there is considerable room for improvement. Possibly, greater public exposure will make a difference.

Considering Culture

A "Special" Child

Reynaldo Reynoso is four years old, is blind, and has just entered a regular preschool. Things aren't going well. Although Reynaldo has many abilities and skills he learned during his years in early intervention programs with an orientation and mobility specialist, he doesn't use those skills. He clings to the teacher. Whenever he is asked to do something he doesn't want to do, he has kicking and screaming tantrums.

Ms. Stein, his teacher, is very experienced with preschoolers with and without special needs and is very good at welcoming children into her class, supporting their development, and setting appropriate limits. Puzzled by Reynaldo's behavior, she called his mother and set up a meeting with her. At the meeting Ms. Stein began by describing some of Reynaldo's positive qualities and discussing the goals of the preschool program. She then asked Mrs. Reynoso how she thought Reynaldo was doing.

Mrs. Reynoso spoke glowingly about Reynaldo, commented that he "has a mind of his own," and mentioned no concerns.

Ms. Stein continued, "I do have some concerns about Reynaldo's behavior. He doesn't like to do anything independently. He relies too much on the classroom assistant or me. He wants one of us to be with him all of the time. When we move away from him or expect him to do something that we know he can do for himself, he clings to us, cries, and kicks."

Mrs. Reynoso said, "We don't worry about Reynaldo's behavior. To us, he is a gift from God, a *milagro* [miracle]. We want to be sure that he has everything he wants. Our family is very lucky to have been chosen for this special gift."

Ms. Stein wasn't sure what to say, but she knew that Reynaldo couldn't continue to behave in this way in her classroom. And she was worried about this behavior continuing when he was older and went to elementary school. She described some of his behavior more specifically, commenting on the disruption that it caused in the classroom and emphasizing the problem it presented to Reynaldo.

Mrs. Reynoso became concerned and asked what they could do to help. Ms. Stein discussed behavior management techniques that work well with preschoolers and said she would use them at school as well. She also offered to help Mrs. Reynoso implement the techniques at home. Finally, she inquired whether Mrs. Reynoso would like to meet other mothers of children with visual disabilities who share her Caribbean background. Mrs. Reynoso was eager to meet another mother, and the meeting ended with a plan in place.

Questions to Consider

1. How well do you think Ms. Stein handled this situation? What else do you think she could have done and said?
2. Mrs. Reynoso considered Reynaldo to be a milagro, a gift from God. What are some other cultural beliefs associated with individuals with disabilities?

—By Eleanor Lynch, San Diego State University and
Marci Hanson, San Francisco State University

Collaboration

Collaborative services from experts in the field of visual disabilities should be available to all students who have low vision or are blind, regardless of where they go to school. It takes many different related service providers, working together, to develop an appropriate education program for these students. The array of services they need to support their education can be substantial. For example, the district's itinerant vision teachers, as well as professionals providing outreach services from a center school (e.g., the state's school for the blind), can help general educators structure both the physical and the academic environment to ensure the success of inclusive efforts (De Mario & Caruso, 2001). They help teachers understand the best ways of positioning furniture and materials. They can also help reorganize the classroom every month so that the student with visual disabilities learns to adjust to changes in the environment. These experts can help organize the classroom's physical space so that bulky equipment and aids (optical aids, magnifiers, tape recorders) are efficiently stored, yet readily available when needed. Vision teachers help teachers and students determine how much text enlargement is necessary to provide access to printed materials, and they also offer important information about accommodations needed during instruction and assessments. As you know, students who are blind often have difficulty moving freely and independently in their environments. Orientation and mobility teachers are a valuable resource not only to help students improve freedom of movement in the classroom but also to develop follow-through activities that teachers can implement in their classrooms (Miller, 2002).

Partnerships with Families and Communities

Family members play very special roles as they help their children grow up, and this is especially true of mothers of children with visual disabilities. Their responsiveness in complying with their children's requests, repeating or rephrasing their communications, facilitating turn-taking, and giving directions and instructions contributes considerably to positive development in expressive and receptive language (Pérez-Pereira & Conti-Ramsden, 2000). As with all children, the relationships among family, school, and culture affect those with visual disabilities in many ways. Sometimes, one set of beliefs clashes with another set of beliefs, and it is important for teachers and parents to talk about them frankly. As you read this chapter's *Considering Culture* feature, you will understand the importance of developing partnerships with families, the trust that must be nurtured for partnerships to be effective, and the benefits that the efforts yield.

As part of understanding their visual differences, these students need to gain knowledge about their visual status, the cause of their vision problem, and the probability of its worsening or improving. Many of the children have great confusion about their disabilities, which is apparent in the questions they ask about their blindness. In one very interesting study, parents were asked to list questions that their children had asked about their vision (Erin & Corn, 1994). Among the frequently asked questions were the following: When would they be able to see? Would they be able to see when they got older? Why did God make them blind? Why could they not see certain things (such as rainbows)? How do their eyes look? Would anything help them see better? Are they special? Why are they different? What is it like to see? Why did they fail the vision test?

The targets for parents to address with children with visual disabilities are many. They must help their children develop many skills across a range of areas: communication, independent living, mobility, sensory development, fine and gross motor skills, cognition, and social skills. And these parents want more help from schools to learn how to teach these skills more effectively to their children (Milian, 2001). In this regard, teachers can make an important difference to parents—sometimes with a "strategy" as simple as being a good listener and providing support.

Imagine a world . . .

where everyone achieves to their fullest potential . . .

Summary

For most of us, the primary way we learn is through vision. Often, in the process of learning a new skill, we are shown how to do the task and imitate it. We gain information by watching television or reading. People with visual disabilities have a restricted ability to use their sight, which can affect how they function as independent adults. For students, the category of visual disabilities is one of the smallest. The incidence of visual disabilities increases with age. Although these students have been successfully included in general education, they do not find integration the norm when they are adults. Many have not found competitive employment and are not included in the mainstream of society. Stereotypes and old traditions impede their participation. Improvement in this area is essential and will require the concerted efforts of adults with this disability, their families, and their advocates.

Addressing the Chapter Objectives

1 How can the category of visual disabilities be divided into two functional subgroups?

The majority of causes for visual loss are unknown.

- Group students on the basis of the severity of the disability or the amount of their functional use of sight: low vision and blind.
- Group students by age of onset: congenitally blind (at birth or during infancy) and adventitiously blind (after the age of two).
- Falling in the category "legally blind" qualifies people for special tax benefits and materials.

More than half of children with visual disabilities are placed in the multiple disabilities category.

2 What are some ways to accommodate the general education setting for students with visual disabilities?

Teachers can help by

- Using commonsense teaching strategies such as advance organizers, oral summaries, printed information, and handouts of lectures
- Positioning students with low vision where they can benefit most from each instructional activity: close to the chalkboard, away from the glare of a window
- Eliminating dangerous obstacles and hazards
- Providing organization, expectations, and consequences in the physical and instructional environments

3 Why must orientation and mobility be long-term curriculum targets for many students with visual disabilities, and what specific skills must be included?

- Good orientation and mobility skills are needed for independent living, maintaining a household, personal care, transportation, mobility within the workplace, and sports/recreation.

- Orientation and mobility skills are difficult to master, taking years of instruction and practice.
- Challenges in the physical environment include escalators, elevators, public transportation, orientation to new places, and use of maps.

4 What advances in assistive technology can assist people with visual disabilities at school, in the workplace, and in independent living?

- *Visual aids:* enlarged-print displays, large-print newspapers, (CCTV) enlargements
- *Audio aids:* talking books, talking watches and clocks, audiodescriptions
- *Tactile aids:* labels for household appliances, tactile maps, braille books, text-to-braille software

5 What are the issues surrounding braille literacy and individuals who are blind?

For those who do not read print, braille is an access to it and a means of achieving literacy. But braille literacy has been declining for several reasons.

- Braille instruction is not consistently available.
- Not enough teachers are proficient in braille.
- Cognitive disabilities impede learning.

The individual needs and abilities of each individual should be matched to reading style, and appropriate instruction should be delivered.

MyLabSchool is a collection of online tools for your success in this course, your licensure exams, and your teaching career. Visit www.mylabschool.com to access the following:

- Online Study Guide
- Video cases from real classrooms
- Help with your research papers using Research Navigator
- Career Center with resources for:
  - Praxis exams and licensure preparation
  - Professional portfolio development
  - Job search and interview techniques
  - Lesson planning

Supplementary Resources

Popular Novels and Books

Mehta, V. (1989). *The stolen light.* New York: Norton.

Richards, E. (2001). *Fox River.* New York: MIRA Books.

Runyan, M., & Jenkins, S. (2001). *No finish line: My life as I see it.* New York: G. P. Putnam's Sons.

Vermeji, G. (1997). *Privileged hands: A remarkable scientific life.* New York: W.H. Freeman.

Weihenmayer, E. (2001). *Touch the top of the world: A blind man's journey to climb farther than the eye can see.* New York: Penguin Group.

Movies

***Ray* (2004). Universal**

See the *On the Screen* feature on page 394.

***Daredevil* (2003). Twentieth Century Fox**

This movie is based on a comic book that has been in publication for over 30 years. In an unusual approach, the title character is a blind lawyer by day and a superhero fighting crime by night. The idea of blind justice is the central premise behind the film, as Daredevil battles a crime syndicate led by his nemesis Kingpin.

***Scent of a Woman* (1992). Universal/MCA**

While on break from an eastern boarding school, Charlie agrees to serve as a personal assistant to an older blind man whose family is away. At first, the two—Charlie and Lt. Col Frank Slade—do not get along because of the blind man's alcoholism and abrasive personality. But as their week together proceeds, they both end up saving each other and developing a lifelong friendship. Individuals with disabilities often feel isolated and become detached from people and society, a theme developed in this film. Al Pacino won the "best actor" Oscar for his portrayal of Slade.

Professional, Parent, and Advocacy Groups

American Foundation for the Blind in New York
www.afb.org

Division of the Blind and Visually Impaired, Rehabilitation Services Administration U.S. Department of Education in Washington, DC
www.ed.gov/offices/OSERS/RSA

American Printing House for the Blind in Louisville, Kentucky: http://www.aph.org

National Federation of the Blind in Baltimore, Maryland: www.nfb.org

Division for the Visual Impairments (DVI), Council for Exceptional Children in Arlington, Virginia
www.cec.sped.org

Prevent Blindness America in Shaumberg, Illinois
www.prevent-blindness.org

Professional Standards and Licensure Tests

After reading this chapter, you should be able to link basic knowledge and skills described in the CEC Standards and INTASC Principles with information provided in this text. The table below shows some of the specific CEC Visual Impairments Knowledge and Skill Standards and INTASC Special Education Principles that can be applied to each major section of the chapter. Other standards may also be applied to this chapter. Associated General Praxis II topic areas are identified in the right column.

Major Chapter Headings	CEC Knowledge and Skill Core Standard and Associated Subcategories	INTASC Core Principle and Associated Special Education Subcategories	PRAXIS II Exam Topic
Where We've Been . . . What's on the Horizon	**1: Foundations** VI1K2 Historical foundations of education of individuals with visual impairments	**1: Subject Matter** 1.10 Special education teachers have knowledge of the range of assistive technology that supports students in the learning environment and know how to access resources related to this technology.	1: Understanding Exceptionality 2: Legal and Social Issues
Low Vision and Blindness Defined	**1: Foundations** VI1K3 Educational definitions, identification criteria, labeling issues, and incidence and prevalence figures for individuals with visual impairments	**1: Subject Matter** 1.04 All teachers have knowledge of the major principles and parameters of federal disabilities legislation.	1: Understanding Exceptionality 2: Legal and Social Issues
Characteristics	**2: Development and Characteristics of Learners** VI2K5 Psychosocial aspects of visual impairment	**2: Student Learning** 2.03 All teachers recognize that students with disabilities vary in their approaches to learning depending on factors such as the nature of their disabilities, their level of knowledge and functioning, and life experiences.	1: Understanding Exceptionality 2: Legal and Social Issues
Causes and Prevention	**2: Development and Characteristics of Learners** VI2K1 Development of the human visual system	**2: Student Learning** 2.06 Special education teachers understand how disabilities in one area can impact learning and development in other areas.	1: Understanding Exceptionality 2: Legal and Social Issues

Assessment	**8: Assessment** VI8K2 Ethical considerations, laws, and policies for assessment of individuals with visual impairments	**8: Assessment** 8.11 Special education teachers ensure that students with disabilities participate in district and statewide assessments and document on the IEP the use of accommodations or an alternate assessment when appropriate.	2: Legal and Social Issues 3: Delivery of Services to Students
Teaching Students with Visual Loss	**4: Instructional Strategies** VI4K8 Strategies for teaching basic concepts to individuals with visual impairments	**4: Instructional Strategies** 4.08 All teachers expect and support the use of assistive and instructional technologies to promote learning and independence of students with disabilities.	2: Legal and Social Issues 3: Delivery of Services to Students
Transition	**10: Collaboration** VI10K1 Strategies for assisting families and other team members in planning appropriate transitions for individuals with visual impairments	**7: Planning Instruction** 7.07 Special education teachers oversee the development of individualized transition plans to guide learners' transitions from preschool to elementary school, middle school to high school, and high school to postschool opportunities.	2: Legal and Social Issues 3: Delivery of Services to Students
Collaboration	**10: Collaboration** VI10K2 Services, networks, publications for and organizations of individuals with visual impairments	**10: Collaboration, Ethics, and Relationships** 10.08 Special education teachers include, promote, and facilitate family members as partners on parent-professional, interdisciplinary, and interagency teams.	2: Legal and Social Issues 3: Delivery of Services to Students
Partnerships with Families and Communities	**10: Collaboration** VI10S1 Help families and other team members understand the impact of a visual impairment on learning and experience	**10: Collaboration, Ethics, and Relationships** 10.04 All teachers accept families as full partners in planning appropriate instruction and services for students with disabilities and provide meaningful opportunities for them to participate as partners in their children's instructional programs in the life of the school.	2: Legal and Social Issues 3: Delivery of Services to Students

Sara Moodie is from Canada. She has many talents and interests, which are best described by her. "Currently, I am not as active in the art world as I used to be, though I still draw cartoons for my workplace newsletter. I am working two jobs right now, and my working hours take up a lot of my free time. I work in computer services, building and fixing computers, for the local hospital, and I work as a security guard in an auto parts plant. My autism has given me an edge in both jobs."

"I don't consider autism a negative thing. I believe autism is a natural and normal segment of the human developmental profile and that society needs autistic thinkers to progress and avoid stagnation. Autism does not automatically mean a life in an institution or dependence on parents for our entire lives. I have a good career, I own and drive a car, I own my own home and live independently with my many pets, and I am exactly as social as I want to be. Never underestimate an autistic person. We're capable of a lot more than even most "autism experts" can understand."

12

Autism Spectrum Disorders

The interaction of subatomic particles is much less complicated than the interaction of people.

Dick Solomon

The newest special education category is at the center of much attention and concern. One reason for worry is that in many cases the result is severe disabilities that are persistent and oftentimes resistant to treatment. A second reason for alarm is that the incidence of this disability is on the rise. **Autism spectrum disorders (ASD)**[1] is a broad term that includes five conditions characterized by limitations in three areas of development: communication, social interaction, and repetitive behaviors or interests. Autism is one of the specific diagnoses included within ASD. The other conditions, in addition to autism, that are included in the group of disabilities called ASD are Asperger syndrome, Rett syndrome, childhood disintegrative disorder, and pervasive developmental disorder—not otherwise specified.

Where We've Been . . . What's on the Horizon?

Autism was first identified in the last century. Considerable confusion has surrounded this condition and its causes since it was first recognized. Until fairly recently autism was narrowly defined, and this diagnosis was restricted to those individuals with severe disabilities. Today it is understood that, like most other disabilities, autism can range from mild to severe problems. Also, present-day experts consider autism one of a spectrum of similar disorders. To better understand today's perspective on ASD, let's review how this field emerged and the direction of its development.

Historical Context

Although autism spectrum disorders (ASD) have always been part of the human condition, their discrete identification is relatively recent. Leo Kanner (1943), a child psychiatrist at Johns Hopkins University Medical School, first described children with the condition he called "early infantile autism."

Chapter Objectives

After studying this chapter, you will be able to:

1. Understand the relationship between autism and other autism spectrum disorders (ASD).
2. Identify core characteristics of individuals within the autism spectrum.
3. List the causes of ASD.
4. Describe how environments can be structured so that individuals with ASD maximally benefit from instruction.
5. Explain why social relationships are important for people with ASD.

This chapter was contributed by Craig Kennedy and Deborah Deutsch Smith of Vanderbilt University.

[1]The term *autism spectrum disorders* is used by the National Institutes of Health, whereas other agencies, such as the Centers for Disease Control, use the term *autistic spectrum disorders*. These terms are interchangeable. We use *autism spectrum disorders* in this text.

Children with autism are often excluded from social interactions with peers.

(Independently, but almost simultaneously, Hans Asperger described a similar condition that would be named Asperger syndrome.) Kanner's use of the phrase *early infantile* reflected his belief that the condition was present at or shortly after birth (which has yet to be confirmed). Kanner borrowed the term *autism* from Eugen Bluer, a Swiss psychiatrist who had coined the term in 1911. Bluer used the term *autism* to describe patients with schizophrenia who actively withdrew into their own world. Unfortunately, the notion of voluntary withdrawal also became associated with children with autism, inviting the false idea that these children were withdrawing because parents—particularly mothers—were cold or uncaring. The effects of these mistaken ideas were devastating. Many children were removed from their families and raised in institutions (Powers, 2000). And just as tragically, effective interventions for ASD did not emerge during this time period.

In the 1960s, however, the treatment of autism changed dramatically. First, enough scientific evidence had been collected to rule out the idea that "refrigerator mothers" cause ASD. Instead, experts began to believe that ASD probably resulted from neurobiological problems with a genetic basis. Second, a number of behavioral interventions were developed that showed that autistic behaviors were very sensitive to educational interventions and could be dramatically improved. Third, parents organized their efforts and advocated for themselves and their children. Bernard Rimland, a psychologist, spearheaded this advocacy movement. He dedicated his career to studying ASD after his son was diagnosed with the condition. Rimland helped to collect and organize the information known about ASD. He also joined with other parents to form a parent advocacy group called the National Society for Autistic Children (now called the Autism Society of America). Currently, several major parent organizations advocate for the rights of children with ASD and their families. These organizations raise money for research, hoping to find a cure for ASD. The federal government has also increased funding for research to determine the causes of autism, as well as to develop both medical and behavioral/educational treatments for this condition.

autism spectrum disorders (ASD) A group of disorders with similar characteristics, including difficulties with communication, social interaction, and manneristic behaviors

Challenges That Autism Spectrum Disorders Present

Currently, ASD is very much in the public spotlight and is gaining the recognition it deserves from public officials who provide the funds to better understand and more appropriately educate individuals with ASD. Everyday we learn more about ASD. One vital source of information is people who have ASD, such as Sara Moodie, whose art and story are found at the beginning of this chapter. Probably the best-known person with autism (one condition included in ASD) is Temple Grandin. Through her books and speeches, she has enlightened us about what it is like to have autism. (For more about her, read *Temple Grandin in the Spotlight* on page 442)

Another important way that we learn more about ASD is through research. The basic science of ASD is rapidly emerging, and new findings are being announced every week about how brain development and genetics interact to produce ASD. This information will tell us much about what ASD truly is and how it develops. Perhaps these findings will lead to very early identification and to the possible amelioration of many of ASD's most devastating biological and behavioral effects. At the same time, rapid strides are being made in the development of educational supports for children, youth, and adults with ASD. Increasingly, individuals with ASD are being educated in inclusive settings, learning from the same curriculum as other children, and developing lasting friendships with them. This is an exciting time to be involved in the education of students with ASD. More than ever before, there is increased optimism about our ability to understand ASD and more effectively educate individuals with these disabilities.

Making a Difference

Surfers Healing

A "special day" is a rare experience for most parents who have children with autism. Exactly what constitutes a special day is different for each of us. However, it often is, or includes, dreaming of a day at the beach. For those who live near a coastline, a special day might even be a day atop a board, catching wave after wave.

The Paskowitz Surf Camp—based in San Clemente, California—was established in 1972 and is one of the oldest surfing schools in the United States. Izzie Paskowitz is a former surfing champion and a son of "Doc" Paskowitz, the founder of the surfing school and one of the school's surfing instructors. In 1996 he discovered that Isaiah, his son who has autism, truly enjoyed using a special tandem board for "surfing." Izzie and his wife thought that other children with autism might also enjoy catching a wave, so they invited other parents of children with autism to join them at the beach for a surfing adventure. The overall joy of the experience was truly unexpected. Parents, families, and friends hung out together at the beach. Everyone reported that they were not stigmatized or judged by others.

Inspired by this experience, Izzie established Surfers Healing, a surfing camp especially for individuals with autism. Special sessions are available every summer. And, because of generous people who donate their time, expertise, and money, campers with autism attend free. On January 23, 2004, thanks to local surfers volunteering their time and skills and to businesses and charities donating funds, Surfers Healing held a special session in Waikiki, Hawaii. What a success! With 125 kids with autism surfing and many more volunteers and family members all having the time of their lives, the beach was packed with happy people sharing a unique time together.

For more about the camp, how you might volunteer at a future camp, and for pictures of the latest events, log on at **www.surfershealing.com**

Autism Spectrum Disorders (ASD) Defined

ASD is a diverse set of five syndromes:

1 Autism
2 Asperger syndrome
3 Rett syndrome
4 Childhood disintegrative disorder (CDD)
5 Pervasive developmental disorder–not otherwise specified (PDD-NOS)

Each of the five types of ASD has specific diagnostic criteria. Thus one way to think of ASD is as an umbrella of disorders: autism and others that share a range of traits with it. Figure 12.1 illustrates ASD in this way. These conditions share similar behavioral characteristics in the areas of social interaction, verbal or nonverbal communication, and repetitive behaviors or interests. Unusual responses to sensory stimuli are also often present. The key word in the term *autism spectrum disorders* is *spectrum*, which implies similar characteristics but great variance in the actual behavioral patterns exhibited. Table 12.1 shows the IDEA '04 definition of autism and the National Institute of Mental Health definition of ASD. Individual definitions for each of the ASD conditions, as called out in the DSM-IV-TR, are found in their respective sections.

Professionals are just beginning to understand ASD, so different views of each condition, the symptoms that each presents, and their severity, are still developing. To some, the ASD umbrella represents distinctly different types of autism. Others, however, suggest that types of autism may be formed across diagnostic categories and may instead be based on level of intellectual functioning, age of onset, or number or severity of symptoms (Tanguay, Robertson, & Derrick, 1998). And, as scientists' understanding of the neurobiology and genetics of ASD develops, the underlying differences in the brains of people with various types of ASD may reveal an organizational scheme consistent with or completely different from our current behavioral definitions. As it stands now, no consensus exists among experts about what dimensions should be used to develop subtypes of ASD, although most agree that it is useful to establish such categories. Now let's examine each condition to gain a better understanding of the similarities and differences among them.

Figure 12.1 • Autism Spectrum Disorders (ASD) Umbrella

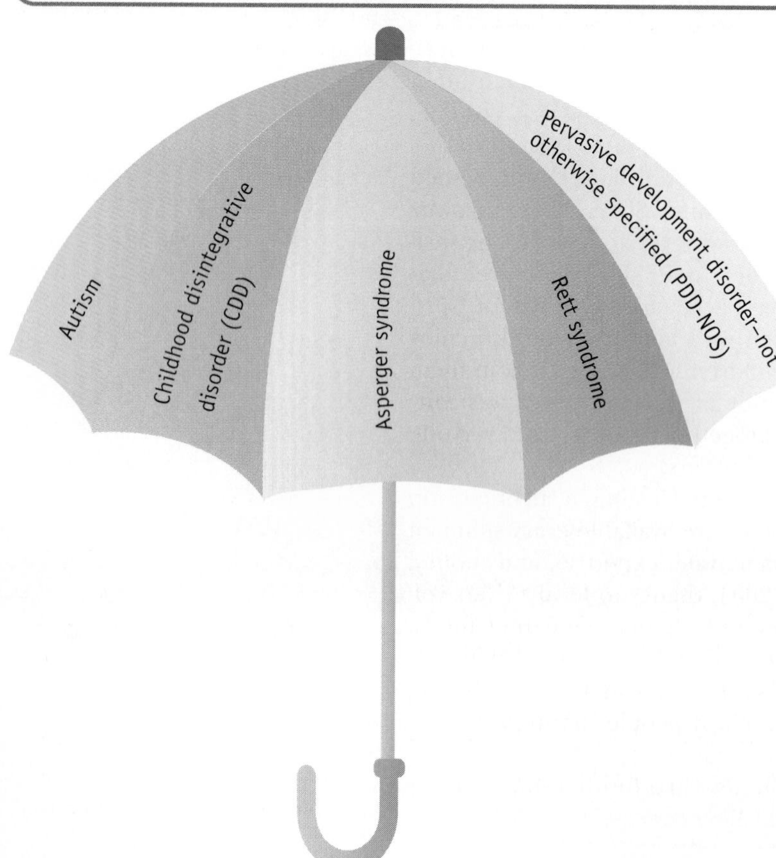

Autism

Technically, the term **autism** refers to a specific diagnosis within the ASD cluster, much like the words *sports car* identify a specific type of motor vehicle that has similarities to and differences from other automobiles. The term *autism* is often used in place of the term *ASD* to refer to

Table 12.1 • Definitions of Autism Spectrum Disorders and Autism

Source	Definition of Autism Spectrum Disorders (ASD)
National Institute of Mental Health (NIMH)[1]	Children with ASD do not follow the typical patterns of child development. In some children, hints of future problems may be apparent from birth. In most cases, the problems in communication and social skills become more noticeable as the child lags further behind other children the same age. Some other children start off well enough. Often between 12 and 36 months of age, the differences in the way they react to people and other unusual behaviors become apparent. Some parents report the change as being sudden, and that their children start to reject people, act strangely, and lose language and social skills they had previously acquired. In other cases, there is a plateau, or leveling, of progress so that the difference between the child with autism and other children the same age becomes more noticeable. ASD is defined by a certain set of behaviors that can range from the very mild to the severe.
	Definition of Autism
Office of Special Education Programs (OSEP), Federal Government[2]	*Autism* means a developmental disability significantly affecting verbal and nonverbal communication and social interaction, generally evident before age three, that adversely affects a child's educational performance. Other characteristics often associated with autism are engagement in repetitive activities and stereotyped movements, resistance to environmental change or change in daily routines, and unusual responses to sensory experiences. (i) Autism does not apply if a child's educational performance is adversely affected primarily because the child has an emotional disturbance, as defined in paragraph (c)(4) of this section. (ii) A child who manifests the characteristics of autism after age three could be identified as having autism if the criteria in paragraph (c)(1)(i) of this section are satisfied.

Sources: [1]*Autism spectrum disorders (pervasive developmental disorders).* (NIH Publication No. NIH-04-5511) (p. 2) by M. Strock, 2004, Bethesda, MD: National Institute of Mental Health.

[2]From 34 CFR Parts 300 and 303, Assistance to States for the Education of Children with Disabilities and the Early Intervention Program for Infants and Toddlers with Disabilities; Proposed Regulations (p. 309), U.S. Department of Education, 2005a, *Federal Register,* Washington, DC.

all of the disorders included under the ASD umbrella, but this is technically inaccurate. Instead, autism is one specific type of disorder within the ASD umbrella of disorders.

The IDEA '04 definition is found in Table 12.1, and the one developed by the American Psychiatric Association (APA) in its *Diagnostic and Statistical Manual of Mental Disorders* (DSM-IV-TR) is found in Table 12.2 (APA, 2000). Note that the IDEA '04 definition of autism is a general description and lacks the specificity we would need to fully appreciate the different ways in which ASD can be expressed. Now compare the IDEA '04 definition to the APA definition. According to that description, all children with autism have impairments in social skills, impairments in communication, and a restricted range of interests.

Children with autism do not communicate with other people in typical ways. Approximately 50 percent of children with autism do not talk as a way of communicating; these individuals are often labeled "nonverbal." The other 50 percent do use spoken language (i.e., are "verbal"), but much of what they say is a repetition of words they have previously heard; this speech pattern is called **echolalia** (Wetherby & Prizant, 2005). Some children with autism generate spoken language but reverse personal pronouns or have a difficult time understanding or forming semantic categories. Here's an example: a child with autism may say, "You are" rather than "I am" (as in "You are happy today"), when referring to himself or herself. Regardless of the actual verbal abilities of a particular child, all children with autism have trouble with the use of pragmatics in language. (See Chapter 4 for a

autism One of the autism spectrum disorders (ASD); ranges from low to high functioning

echolalia Repeating words, sounds, or sound patterns with no communicative intent, meaning, or understanding; this repetition may occur immediately or even days later

Table 12.2 • DSM-IV Diagnostic Criteria for Autism

A. A total of six (or more) items from (1), (2), and (3), with at least two from (1) and one each from (2) and (3):

(1) Qualitative impairment in social interaction, as manifested by at least two of the following:

(a) Marked impairment in the use of multiple nonverbal behaviors such as eye-to-eye gaze, facial expression, body postures, and gestures to regulate social interaction

(b) Failure to develop peer relationships appropriate to developmental level

(c) A lack of spontaneous seeking to share enjoyment, interests, or achievements with other people (e.g., by a lack of showing, bringing, or pointing out objects of interest)

(d) Lack of social or emotional reciprocity

(2) Qualitative impairments in communication as manifested by at least one of the following:

(a) Delay in, or total lack of, the development of spoken language (not accompanied by an attempt to compensate through alternate modes of communication such as gesture or mime)

(b) In individuals with adequate speech, marked impairment in the ability to initiate or sustain a conversation with others

(c) Stereotyped and repetitive use of language or idiosyncratic language

(d) Lack of varied, spontaneous make-believe play or social imitative play appropriate to developmental level

(3) Restricted repetitive and stereotyped patterns of behavior, interests, and activities as manifested by at least one of the following:

(a) Encompassing preoccupation with one or more stereotyped and restricted patterns of interest that is abnormal either in intensity or focus

(b) Apparently inflexible adherence to specific, nonfunctional routines or rituals

(c) Stereotyped and repetitive motor mannerisms (e.g., hand or finger flapping or twisting, or complex whole-body movements)

(d) Persistent preoccupation with parts of objects

B. Delays or abnormal functioning in at least one of the following areas, with onset prior to age 3 years: (1) social interaction, (2) language as used in social communication, or (3) symbolic or imaginative play

C. The disturbance is not better accounted for by Rett's disorder or childhood disintegrative disorder.

Source: Reprinted with permission from *Diagnostic and Statistical Manual of Mental Disorders, Fourth Edition, Text Revision,* (Copyright 2000). (p. 75). American Psychiatric Association.

review of pragmatics and language impairments.) Typically, they do not understand that communication happens between people, nor do they understand that nonverbal cues and personal perspectives are important to successful communication.

Children with autism also have problems with social interactions. They often appear to live in their own world and may not seek out the company of peers or adults. Many children with autism seem to use people as tools (Powers, 2000). For example, a child may lead an adult by the hand to the refrigerator and push the adult's hand toward the juice the child wants. In this way, the child with autism is using the adult as a means to an end. Also, children with autism do not generally initiate social interactions or engage in social turn-taking.

stereotypies Nonproductive behaviors (such as twirling, flapping hands, rocking) that an individual repeats at a high rate; commonly observed in youngsters with autism spectrum disorders; also called stereotypic behaviors

People with autism typically exhibit repetitive patterns of behavior referred to as **stereotypies** (sometimes called stereotypic behaviors), or they might have unusual or very focused interests (Lewis & Bodfish, 1998). For example, a child with autism may be interested only in spinning the wheel of a toy car or only in wiggling the string of a pull toy. In addition, some children may have rigid or set patterns of behavior. For example, one child might line up his toys in a specific way and have to follow the same routine every day. If these patterns of behavior are violated, a tantrum may result to protest the disruption. Other children may repeat the same movement over and over again. For example, a child may rapidly wave her hand in front of her eyes. An understanding of these stereotyped behaviors is only beginning to emerge, but they seem to be used primarily to produce sensory stimulation (Kennedy, 2002).

Alex Mont has unusual mathematical abilities, excelling far beyond even many of his gifted peers. However, as is true of many autistic savants, his abilities are not uniform.

Intelligence scores are not considered in the diagnosis of autism, yet most children diagnosed with autism (approximately 75 percent) also have mental retardation (Sturmey & Sevin, 1994). Thus 25 percent of people with autism have typical intelligence. This wide range of cognitive ability has resulted in people using other terms to distinguish among people with autism. *Low functioning autism* often refers to children with autism and mental retardation who are often nonverbal, whereas *high functioning autism* often refers to children who have minimal or no mental retardation and who are verbal. High functioning autism should not be confused with Asperger syndrome, a related but distinct form of ASD.

Are there subtypes of autism? As the previous discussion illustrates, the skills found in children diagnosed with autism vary greatly. Some experts think the different levels of intellectual functioning, variety in the age of onset, and differences in the number and severity of symptoms suggest subtypes of autism (Tidmarsh & Volkmar, 2003). That is, "autism" may not be one single thing but, rather, a tight clustering of highly related disorders that manifest themselves in multiple, but often similar, ways. One important implication of this, and probably one means of identifying autism subtypes, is the differential responses to interventions that children with autism often have (Gillum & Camarata, 2004). For example, some children with autism and communication deficits respond very well to spoken language intervention, but others respond better to visually oriented interventions.

One potential subtype of autism, **autistic savants**, is far more interesting to the general public than to researchers. The number of people who are autistic savants is very small—less than 1 percent of individuals diagnosed with autism—but the public is fascinated by the paradox of this group's abilities (Begley & Springen, 1996). Some, like the character Raymond in the film *Rain Man*, can instantly count the number of wooden matches that have fallen on the floor, remember the dates of important events, or recall the numbers of all of the winning lottery tickets for the past year. Others have outstanding musical or artistic abilities. But even in light of such talents, these individuals are unable to initiate or maintain conversations and often have other severe disabilities. For example, nine-year-old Alex Mont can solve complicated mathematics problems, even calculus, but has difficulties comprehending social cues. Alex also could not distinguish a horse from a cow until after he finished kindergarten. Although these incidental skills are fascinating to the observer, they are rarely functional for the individual with autism.

Asperger Syndrome

First described by Dr. Hans Asperger, **Asperger syndrome** is a collection of behavioral characteristics that are associated with problems developing adequate social skills and with restricted or unusual interests. Table 12.3 provides the DSM-IV-TR description of this type of ASD. Although the communication of people with Asperger syndrome may be peculiar, this characteristic is not due to a delay in language development. In fact, children with Asperger syndrome develop speech and language on a par with children without disabilities. Other aspects of communication, however, are problematic. Some children with Asperger syndrome understand language very literally, which can make it difficult for them to form flexible conceptual categories, understand jokes, or interpret the behavior of others (such as gestures). For these individuals, the social use of language can be a particular challenge, as can the ability to comprehend other people's feelings or emotions (Safran, 2001).

autistic savant An individual who displays many behaviors associated with autism yet also possesses discrete abilities and unusual talents

Asperger syndrome One of the autism spectrum disorders (ASD) wherein cognition is usually in the average or above-average range

Table 12.3 • DSM-IV-TR Diagnostic Criteria for Asperger Syndrome

A. Qualitative impairment in social interaction, as manifested by at least two of the following:

(1) Marked impairments in the use of multiple nonverbal behaviors such as eye-to-eye gaze, facial expression, body postures, and gestures to regulate social interaction

(2) Failure to develop peer relationships appropriate to developmental level

(3) A lack of spontaneous seeking to share enjoyment, interests, or achievements with other people (e.g., by a lack of showing, bringing, or pointing out objects of interest to other people)

(4) Lack of social or emotional reciprocity

B. Restricted repetitive and stereotyped patterns of behavior, interests, and activities, as manifested by at least one of the following:

(1) Encompassing preoccupation with one or more stereotyped and restricted patterns of interest that is abnormal either in intensity or focus

(2) Apparently inflexible adherence to specific, nonfunctional routines or rituals

(3) Stereotyped and repetitive motor mannerisms (e.g., hand or finger flapping or twisting, or complex whole-body movements)

(4) Persistent preoccupation with parts of objects

C. The disturbance causes clinically significant impairment in social, occupational, or other important areas of functioning.

D. There is no clinically significant general delay in language (e.g., single words used by age 2 years, communicative phrases used by age 3 years).

E. There is no clinically significant delay in cognitive development or in the development of age-appropriate self-help skills, adaptive behavior (other than in social interaction), and curiosity about the environment in childhood.

F. Criteria are not met for another specific pervasive developmental disorder or schizophrenia.

Source: Reprinted with permission from the *Diagnostic and Statistical Manual of Mental Disorders, Fourth Edition, Text Revision* (Copyright 2000). (p. 84). American Psychiatric Association.

Unlike individuals with autism, the majority with Asperger syndrome have normal intelligence. Children with autism are diagnosed when a language delay becomes apparent, whereas children with Asperger syndrome develop language normally. The distinction between high functioning autism and Asperger syndrome, however, may turn out to be only a matter of semantics. While today controversy exists about whether there are any meaningful differences in the behaviors or performance of people with high functioning autism and those with Asperger syndrome, future research may help scientists resolve this issue.

Rett Syndrome

Discovered more then 40 years ago by Andreas Rett, an Austrian physician, **Rett syndrome** is a genetically based condition. Table 12.4 indicates how the DSM-IV-TR describes this syndrome. Signs of Rett syndrome appear early in life, but only after a period of seemingly normal development that then stops and begins to reverse (Percy, 2001). Unlike many genetic conditions, Rett syndrome occurs only in girls. Behaviorally, it is characterized by a progressive expression of repeated, stereotypic hand wringing; lack of muscle control; and communication and social deficits. Sometimes initially misdiagnosed as autism, Rett syndrome has different

Rett syndrome One of the autism spectrum disorders (ASD); has a known genetic cause; occurs only in girls

Table 12.4 • DSM-IV-TR Diagnostic Criteria for Rett Syndrome

A. All of the following:

(1) apparently normal prenatal and perinatal development

(2) apparently normal psychomotor development through the first 5 months after birth

(3) normal head circumference at birth

B. Onset of all of the following after the period of normal development:

(1) deceleration of head growth between ages 5 and 48 months

(2) loss of previously acquired purposeful hand skills between ages 5 and 30 months with the subsequent development of stereotyped hand movements (e.g., hand-wringing or hand washing)

(3) loss of social engagement early in the course (although often social interaction develops later)

(4) appearance of poorly coordinated gait or trunk movements

(5) severely impaired expressive and receptive language development with severe psychomotor retardation

Source: Reprinted with permission from *Diagnostic and Statistical Manual of Mental Disorders, Fourth Edition, Text Revision* (Copyright 2000). (p. 77). American Psychiatric Association.

characteristics. Autism is not usually characterized by hand wringing and a progressive loss of motor skills. Children with Rett syndrome tend to have better social skills than children with autism. And whereas about half of the individuals with autism have mental retardation, most of those with Rett syndrome do. It develops progressively and results in cognitive disabilities typically more severe than those observed in people with autism.

Childhood Disintegrative Disorder (CDD)

A far rarer disorder than autism is **childhood disintegrative disorder (CDD)**. The DSM-IV-TR description of CDD is found in Table 12.5. The most distinguishing aspect of CDD is that these children develop as their peers without disabilities do until they are five or six years old, at which time a developmental regression begins. In particular, these children lose already acquired language and social skills. Eventually, their behaviors are similar to the behavior patterns of children with autism, but their long-term outcomes are far worse because the regression continues. CDD is the least well understood of the disorders under the ASD umbrella.

Pervasive Developmental Disorder–Not Otherwise Specified (PDD-NOS)

Problems in the areas of communication, social skills, and unusual behaviors (including a restricted range of interests) are the three common characteristics of ASD. Each type of ASD is different in how these behavioral profiles are expressed, but nearly all individuals with ASD exhibit all three areas of concern to some extent. However, when children do not display problems in all three areas, or when problems in all three areas are mild, a different diagnosis is made. In these cases, the disorder is identified as **pervasive developmental disorder–not otherwise specified (PDD-NOS)**. (Although the DSM-IV-TR describes PDD-NOS, it does not provide a table of its common characteristics.) The PDD part of the diagnosis signifies that characteristics very similar to those of autism, Asperger syndrome, Rett syndrome, and CDD exist but are not so clearly expressed. The NOS

childhood disintegrative disorder (CDD) One of the autism spectrum disorders (ASD); the individual has typical development until about the age of five or six

pervasive developmental disorder–not otherwise specified (PDD-NOS) One of the autism spectrum disorders (ASD); either not all three ASD characteristics (problems in communication, social interaction, and repetitive or manneristic behaviors) are present or they are mild

Table 12.5 • DSM-IV-TR Diagnostic Criteria for Childhood Disintegrative Disorder

A. Apparently normal development for at least the first 2 years after birth as manifested by the presence of age-appropriate verbal and nonverbal communication, social relationships, play, and adaptive behavior.

B. Clinically significant loss of previously acquired skills (before age 10 years) in at least two of the following areas:

(1) expressive or receptive language

(2) social skills or adaptive behavior

(3) bowel or bladder control

(4) play

(5) motor skills

C. Abnormalities of functioning in at least two of the following areas:

(1) qualitative impairment in social interaction (e.g., impairment in nonverbal behaviors, failure to develop peer relationships, lack of social or emotional reciprocity)

(2) qualitative impairments in communication (e.g., delay or lack of spoken language, inability to initiate or sustain a conversation, stereotyped and repetitive use of language, lack of varied make-believe play)

(3) restricted, repetitive, and stereotyped patterns of behavior, interests, and activities, including motor stereotypes and mannerisms

D. The disturbance is not better accounted for by another specific pervasive developmental disorder or by schizophrenia.

Source: Reprinted with permission from *Diagnostic and Statistical Manual of Mental Disorders, Fourth Edition, Text Revision* (Copyright 2000) (p. 79). American Psychiatric Association.

means that the symptoms do not match those of another condition found within the ASD umbrella. Although they share ASD characteristics, PDD-NOS is currently considered to be distinct (Walker et al., 2004).

Characteristics

Despite the heterogeneity of ASD, some general statements can be made about characteristics that people with these disorders share (see Table 12.6). ASD is a lifelong disability, and no specific physical characteristics are associated with the condition. Although identified during early childhood, ASD is present very early in development. Although ASD results in unique profiles of symptoms across individuals and conditions, it typically affects three important areas that help to define the condition (Barnhill, 2001):

1. Social interactions
2. Communication
3. Restricted range of interests or behavioral repertoires

In addition to exhibiting these three defining characteristics of ASD, and those described in the DSM-IV-TR diagnostic criteria (review the definitions found in Tables 12.2 through 12.5), individuals with ASD may be unusually sensitive to sensory input, such as loud noises or soft touches (Talay-Ongan & Wood, 2000). Some individuals with ASD have serious problems with their behavior. They might

Table 12.6 • Characteristics of Autism

Impairment in Reciprocal Social Interactions

- Normal attachments to parents, family members, or caregivers do not develop.
- Friendships with peers fail to develop.
- Cooperative or peer play is rarely observed.
- Emotions, such as affection and empathy, are rarely displayed.
- Nonverbal signals of social intent (smiling, gestures, physical contact) tend not to be used.
- Eye contact is not initiated or maintained.
- Imaginative play is seldom observed.
- The lack of social-communicative gestures and utterances is apparent during the first few months of life.
- Preferred interaction style could be characterized as "extreme isolation."
- Understanding of others' beliefs, emotions, or motivations is greatly impaired.
- Joint attention deficits (not being able to cooperate or share interest with others in the same event or activity) impair normal social reciprocation.

Poor Communication Abilities

- Functional language is not acquired fully or mastered.
- Content of language is usually unrelated to immediate environmental events.
- Utterances are stereotypic and repetitive.
- Gestures, facial expressions, and nonverbal cues are poorly understood.
- Conversations are not maintained.
- Spontaneous conversations are rarely initiated.
- Speech can be meaningless, repetitive, and echolalic.
- Many fail to use the words *I* and *yes* and have problems with pronouns in general.
- Both expressive and receptive language are extremely literal.
- Verbal turn-taking, choosing a topic, and contributing properly to a conversation are rare.

Insistence on Sameness

- Marked distress is typically experienced over trivial or minor changes in the environment.
- Aspects of daily routine can become ritualized.
- Obsessive and compulsive behavior is frequently displayed.
- The need to complete self-imposed, required actions is intense.
- Stereotypic behaviors (rocking, hand-flapping) are repeated in cycles difficult to stop.

Unusual Behavior Patterns

- Hypersensitive and/or inconsistent behaviors are the response to visual, tactile, or auditory stimulation.
- Aggression to others is common, particularly when compliance is requested.
- Self-injurious or outwardly aggressive behavior (hitting, biting, kicking, head-banging) is common and frequent.
- Extreme social fears are manifested toward strangers, crowds, unusual situations, and new environments.
- Loud sounds (barking dogs, street noises) can result in startle or fearful reactions.
- Severe sleep problems occur with frequency.
- Noncompliant behavior to requests from others results in disruption to the individual and others (tantrums).
- Self-stimulation (twirling objects, rocking) consumes a considerable amount of time and energy.
- The ability to pretend is lacking.

turn these tendencies inward and hurt themselves, inflicting **self-injury**, or they might turn such behavior outward and hurt others through what is called **aggression**. Others with ASD have trouble developing the abilities necessary to understand other people's perspectives or to predict others' behavior—both important skills for successful communication (Baron-Cohen, 2001). Here are a few more specifics. Among children with ASD

- 75 percent have a concurrent diagnosis of mental retardation
- 50 percent never develop functional speech
- 17 percent engage in self-injury or aggression
- 4 out of 5 are male
- 33 percent have epilepsy (Sturmey & Sevin, 1994)

self-injury Self-inflicted injuries (head banging, eye poking)

aggression Hostile and attacking behavior, which can include verbal communication, directed toward self, others, or the physical environment

Despite this list of "ASD characteristics," it is important to remember that people with ASD are more like people without ASD. And, as you will learn, great educational gains are made when teachers treat students with ASD as if they are capable of many of the things that students without ASD are capable. Most individuals, it seems, have the amazing capacity to rise to the level of expectations that others set for them. So, with this sage wisdom in mind, let's proceed to a discussion of how many students have ASD.

Prevalence

No precise census, or count of the number, of students with ASD has been made, so it is not possible to say exactly how many people have ASD. Since 1990, when autism became a separate special education category, states have reported to the federal government the number and percentage of these students identified and served in the public schools. Despite the national concern about the rising incidence of autism and the other four ASD conditions, this disability remains very low incidence (U.S. Department of Education 2005b). Only 0.27 percent of all students provided with special education services are identified through the IDEA '04 autism category. In the 1999–2000 school year, some 61,406 students between the ages of 6 and 17 received special education services (Newschaffer, Falb, & Gurney, 2005). Although it is not possible to chart prevalence rates of ASD across time, parents, professionals, and policymakers agree that many more children are diagnosed with autism today than were in the past (Burton, 2002).

Two sources of information are used when reporting prevalence: epidemiological studies and the data collected by states about enrollment in special education programs (National Research Council, 2001). Epidemiological studies conducted in ten countries with approximately 4 million children reveal that the incidence rate of ASD has increased from 2 to 5 children in 10,000 in the 1970s to 7.5 to 10 children in 10,000 since 1987 (Fombonne, 1999). Exact estimates vary, but data from school districts' special education programs confirm this increase. Figure 12.2 illustrates the numbers of students in California who have received special education services under the state's ASD category since 1991. As you can see, there has been a dramatic rise in the number of children with ASD receiving special education services. Three possible explanations for this increase are

1 Improved diagnostic methods

2 Use of the broader term *ASD* instead of the narrower term *autism*

3 An actual increase in the condition

Emerging evidence supports the view that improved diagnostic methods and the broadening of the term *ASD* beyond autism are responsible for much of the rapid increase in prevalence rates during the 1990s (National Research Council, 2001). This conclusion, however, is still somewhat controversial. Some experts and many parents believe that an actual increase in the number of children with ASD is occurring. However, until a definitive census criterion defines ASD, associates causes with this disability, and then counts individuals accordingly, the reason for the increased number of children diagnosed with ASD will continue to be debated. Remember, even with this increase in prevalence, ASD remains a low incidence disability. Most health care professionals and teachers are likely to have had limited opportunities to meet or work with students who have ASD.

Figure 12.2 • Prevalence Rates of ASD in California

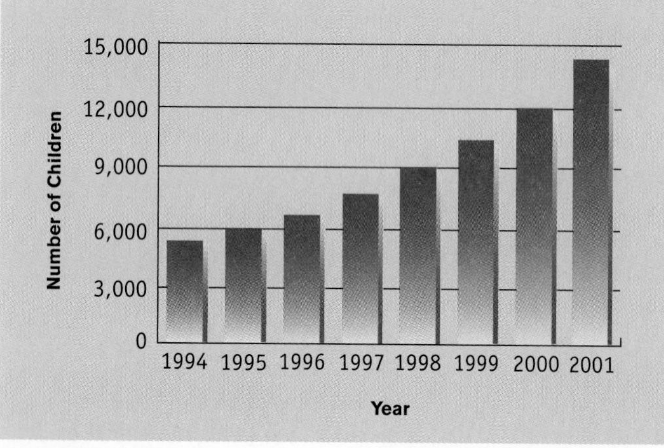

Source: From "Scant evidence for an epidemic of autism" by E. Stokstad, 2001, *Science*, 294, p. 35. Data from R. Huff, California DDS. Reprinted with permission.

Causes and Prevention

Experts have been trying to identify the causes of ASD, but no definitive answers are yet available. With no specific causes having been identified, it is impossible to develop early identification (e.g., newborn screening) or prevention strategies. This situation is frustrating to professionals who work with children with ASD, but it is most frustrating to families. Because they want to know the chances of having another child with ASD, it is important for researchers to continue their work in determining the precise genetic basis of these disorders. Despite the lack of clear information, a number of suggestions and reasonable conclusions have been made. Let's consider some of these ideas.

Causes

The process of elimination contributes to our understanding of why ASD occurs. Several suggested causes of ASD have already been ruled out. For example, autism is not the result of inadequate parenting. Ruling out this source of pathology has enabled researchers to focus on more plausible causes of ASD. This ongoing process will eventually lead to identification of the cause(s) of ASD.

Most experts agree that ASD is a neurobiological disorder that has a genetic basis. Currently, researchers know that in the brains of people with ASD, there are anomalies that involve areas used for perceptual integration, emotion, and filtering sensory information (Polleux & Lauder, 2004). In addition, researchers are making progress in identifying what is emerging as the complex genetic basis of ASD (Dykens, Suttclife, & Levitt, 2004). However, many questions remain to be answered. It is likely that in the next decade, many key findings about the nature and cause of ASD will be discovered and will assist in the early identification of and intervention for autism and other forms of ASD.

Current research is beginning to show linkages among behavioral characteristics, developmental trajectories, neurobiology, and genetics as they relate to ASD, but many myths about what causes ASD persist in the popular media. The causes suggested in recent years have included environmental toxins, gastrointestinal anomalies, vitamin deficiencies, and vaccines. Such speculation about possible causes of ASD creates dangerous situations. For example, some parents believe that the measles/mumps/rubella (MMR) vaccine causes ASD. Although there is strong evidence that *no* such link exists (Smeeth et al., 2004), some parents are withholding MMR vaccines from their children because they are concerned that the vaccine might cause a child to develop ASD. The unfortunate result of this will be an increase in cases of measles, mumps, and rubella among children who do not receive the vaccine (Cowley, Brownell, & Footes, 2000).

Prevention

Because we still have so much to learn about the causes of ASD, prevention is not currently a realistic goal. Perhaps in the future, as researchers learn more about why ASD occurs, steps can be taken to prevent children from being born with, or later developing, characteristics associated with ASD. Until then, educational interventions are our primary basis for improving symptoms associated with ASD.

Overcoming Challenges

Just as there is rampant public speculation about possible causes of ASD, there is also an ongoing stream of "cures" (Seroussi, 2000). The Internet and popular press are littered with stories—often based on a single case history—of children being "cured" using vitamins, special diets, or newly discovered medical drugs. Parents and professionals who support these alternative treatments may believe in them

Temple Grandin in the Spotlight

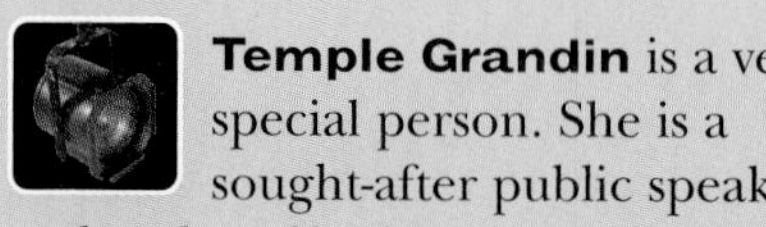

Temple Grandin is a very special person. She is a sought-after public speaker and author. She has a remarkable understanding of animals, an understanding that far surpasses most everyone else's. And she has autism. Temple Grandin helps us all because she shares insights into a disability that few others are able to express.

Most groups of people have "representatives"—leaders who speak out on others' behalf or who are appointed in some way to express the group's position. As you learned in Chapter 1, most disability advocates are people with physical disabilities. Very few, if any, individuals with autism are public figures. We don't know whether Temple Grandin's experiences with autism are similar to those of others with this condition. But the fact that she speaks openly about her life and shares insights about her disability is important. In 1996 she wrote her first autobiographical volume, *Thinking in Pictures and Other Reports of My Life with Autism.* And in 2005, by means of her latest book, *Animals in Translation: Using the Mysteries of Autism to Decode Animal Behavior,* she once again let's us see the world of autism through her eyes.

Oliver Sacks, himself a famous author, in the foreword to Ms. Grandin's 1996 book underscored the importance of the rare glimpse she offers into what it is like to have autism.

> Unprecedented because there had never before been an "inside narrative" of autism; unthinkable because it had been medical dogma for forty years or more that there was no "inside," no inner life, in the autistic, or that if there was, it would be forever denied access or expression; extraordinary because of its extreme (and strange) directness and clarity. Temple Grandin's voice came from a place which had never had a voice, never been granted real existence before—and she spoke not only for herself, but for thousands of other, often highly gifted, autistic adults in our midst. She provided a glimpse, and indeed a revelation, that there might be people, no less human than ourselves, who constructed their worlds, lived their lives, in almost unimaginably different ways. (pp. 11, 16)

Temple Grandin describes her thought processes as being very different from those of most other people:

> I think in pictures. Words are like a second language to me. I translate both spoken and written words into full-color movies, complete with sound, which run like a VCR tape in my head. When somebody speaks to me, his words are instantly translated into pictures. (p. 19)

She explains that her senses are too active:

> Overly sensitive skin can be a big problem. . . . When I was little, loud noises were also a problem, often feeling like a dentist's drill hitting a nerve. They actually caused pain. I was scared to death of balloons popping, because the sound was like an explosion in my ear. Minor noises that most people can tune out drove me to distraction. . . . My ears are like microphones picking up all sounds with equal intensity. (pp. 66–68)

By talking about her emotional differences, she makes it easier to understand various behaviors often observed in children with autism:

> Some people believe that people with autism do not have emotions. I definitely do have them, but they are more like the emotions of a child than of an adult. My childhood temper tantrums were not really expressions of emotion so much as circuit overloads. . . . When I get angry, it is like an afternoon thunderstorm; the anger is intense, but once I get over it, the emotion quickly dissipates. . . . I still have difficulty understanding and having a relationship with people whose primary motivation in life is governed by complex emotions, as my actions are guided by intellect. (pp. 87–90)

Ms. Grandin gives us guidance about how educational programs should be developed:

> My daydreams were like Technicolor movies in my head. I would also become completely absorbed in spinning a penny or studying the wood-grain pattern on my desktop. During these times, the rest of the world disappeared. . . . Autistic children will remain in their own little worlds if left to their own devices. (p. 96)
>
> [Teachers must] be able to determine whether a tantrum or other bad behavior is caused by fear or pain or [is] a learned avoidance response. Sometimes it's because of pain from sounds that hurt their ears or fear of an unexpected change in routine. . . . Autistics are afraid of the unexpected. (pp. 149–150)

Temple Grandin describes typical autistic behaviors not as an observer, but as the participant. And in doing so, she unveils some of the mystery surrounding this disability and the individuals affected.

Source: From *Thinking in Pictures and Other Reports from My Life with Autism* by Temple Grandin, copyright @1995 by Temple Grandin. Used by permission of Doubleday, a division of Random House, Inc.

and think these treatments help remediate a child's symptoms, but no scientific evidence validates these claims. Until ASD is well understood and consistently effective treatments are developed, the causes and treatments for ASD will remain the subject of considerable speculation, conjecture, and controversy.

However, it is important to remember that ASD is a significant, lifelong disability. Long-term outcomes, even for those with average intelligence, in the areas of independent living, employment, and life satisfaction are inconsistent (Sperry, 2001). Most people with ASD require comprehensive services and supports across the lifespan. In general, the more severe the form of ASD (e.g., low functioning autism or Rett syndrome), the greater the supports the individual needs. Effective services and supports require high levels of coordination and consistency. Unfortunately, because services offered by social service agencies, health care providers, and mental health systems are often fragmented, these goals are difficult to achieve.

From early in life, the skill deficits of children with ASD affect their learning, as well as their development of social relationships. They do not participate in turn-taking exchanges. This lack of reciprocal social interaction adversely affects the acquisition and use of preverbal communication (e.g., gestures), as well as the eventual acquisition of speech and language skills (Stone & Yoder, 2001). Most cultural morés are passed from generation to generation via implicit teaching that involves social interactions and observational learning. Both of these means of learning represent deficit areas for children with ASD. Most instruction at school is socially mediated and language-based, again problem areas for students with ASD. Thus the social and communication problems faced by children with ASD create a cascade of obstacles to learning and development (Carpenter, Pennington, & Rogers, 2002). In this way, ASD pervasively affects the person's entire developmental trajectory.

Assessment

Until recently, children with ASD were not diagnosed until the age of five, but now it is possible to diagnose children before the age of three (Stone, Coonrod, & Ousley, 2000). In part because of the development of new assessment tools, some children are even being identified as early as age two. For example, the *Autism Diagnostic Observation Scale (ADOS)* and the *Screening Test for Autism in Two Year Olds (STAT),* along with developmental assessments and parent reports, can help to identify very young children with ASD. Because many typically developing children are just beginning to develop spoken language at the age of two, and because the diagnostic features of ASD include language delay, both the ADOS and the STAT include measures examining other skills, such as children's ability to imitate motor movements. Apparently, children with ASD also have early deficits in motor imitation skills that can be used for diagnosis before deficits in language become apparent.

Although current assessment procedures cannot diagnose children younger than two, researchers are working to develop assessments to identify even younger children with ASD. It is likely that these efforts will be successful, because researchers can now diagnose children retrospectively when they are one year old. Julie Osterling and Gerry Dawson first made this breakthrough by examining videotapes that parents had made of their children's first birthday parties. They recognized that the children who were later diagnosed with autism behaved differently from typically developing children (Osterling & Dawson, 1994). They have identified four major differences that distinguish these children. The children later diagnosed with ASD did *not*

- Use a finger to point at an object
- Show their presents to others
- Respond to their names
- Make direct eye contact with others

As interesting as this information is, it has not yet been incorporated into an assessment instrument that can be used prospectively to diagnose one-year-old babies with ASD.

Efforts are under way to develop methods to detect ASD even before a child's first birthday. Around nine months of age, children without disabilities begin to engage in what psychologists describe as joint attention. **Joint attention** involves two people, such as a child and a parent. It occurs when first one person looks at an object and then looks at the other person, and finally when the two people simultaneously look at the object. That is, they together (or jointly) look at (or attend to) the same object. Researchers believe that joint attention is important in the development of both language and social skills (Mundy & Neal, 2001). Children with ASD do participate in joint attention episodes, but their pattern and type of participation are different from those of children without disabilities (Shienkopf et al., 2000). Why is this information important? It may help us understand more about the development of social and language skills as well as about the core characteristics of ASD. Such information might also lead to earlier identification of children with ASD. No diagnostic tools that address deficits in joint attention are currently available, but many psychologists look for a child's joint attention skills when forming their clinical impressions about him or her.

Trained psychologists who have experience in diagnosing children with ASD are needed to administer most assessment instruments used to identify ASD. One screening tool that does not require training is the *Checklist for Autism in Toddlers (CHAT)*. It was developed to help physicians spot early warning signs. Another measure, the *Childhood Autism Rating Scale (CARS)*, is widely used to confirm a diagnosis and also to monitor the child's growth over time. The CARS also describes the severity of problems that a child with ASD demonstrates.

Early Intervention

Even though children can be diagnosed with ASD before the age of three, little empirical evidence suggests which practices and programs are best for these very young children. In other words, the ability to diagnose children with ASD has outpaced the validation of effective interventions. A few practices developed for older children with ASD and other developmental disabilities have also proved effective with toddlers with ASD (Garfinkle & Kaiser, 2004). For example, the increased frequency of making choices boosts appropriate engagement and also decreases inappropriate behaviors. Similarly, the *Walden Program* is effective with preschoolers with ASD and has been adapted to serve even younger children. Others, such as the *Inclusive Program for Very Young Children with Autism*, are being developed from collective information about child development, the nature of ASD, and existing interventions that have been validated with two-year-olds with ASD.

Educational programs for three- to five-year-old children are some of the most well developed and best studied, but much is still to be learned (Handleman & Harris, 2000). For example, no one program is consistently effective, so universal recommendations about educational programming cannot be made. Also, no guidelines can suggest whether one type of program would be better than another for a particular child. Finally, few studies have measured the effectiveness of a treatment program using randomized, control group experiments, and no studies have compared the effectiveness of one program against that of another.

Although no programs have been completely validated, research has identified some key features of effective programs that make a difference in the lives of these preschoolers. These key features are apparent even across programs that differ in philosophy, theoretical background, intensity of services, and timing of instruction with peers (Dawson & Osterling, 1997; Harris & Handleman, 1994). Key elements of successful programs include

joint attention Ability to mutually interact or to share interest in events or objects

- Supportive teaching environments
- Plans for generalization
- Predictable and routine schedules
- Behavioral approaches to address problem behaviors
- Supports for program transitions
- Family involvement and support

These programs also include some common targets for instruction. For example, students with ASD profit from instruction that is clear, specific, and concrete. More important content that teachers should include in their curriculum for these preschoolers is found in *Tips for Effective Teaching*.

Even though most effective programs for young children with ASD share some features, significant differences exist across programs. (Some disagreements among the advocates of different programs have been so intense that they have had to be resolved in the courts!) Two particular programs are popular in the education of preschoolers with ASD: the *Treatment and Education of Autistic and Communication-Handicapped Children* (TEACCH) and the *Young Autism Program* (YAP). However, most programs actually use a blended, or eclectic, approach. Let's look at some highlights of these programs.

for Effective Teaching

EXPLICIT INSTRUCTION

Explicitly teach preschoolers with autism these skills

- *Attention:* by focusing on the discrete elements of the task being taught
- *Imitation:* by guiding practice and reinforcing each step of a skill copied
- *Making requests:* by insisting that the desire be expressed orally before it is fulfilled
- *Compliance:* by insisting that an adult's request be followed
- *Play with objects:* by providing opportunities to interact with interesting toys and rewarding preschoolers when they play with the toys
- *Play with others:* by arranging opportunities and toys appropriate for playing with peers and rewarding preschoolers when they do so

TEACCH

One program often used with students with autism was developed at the University of North Carolina at Chapel Hill. TEACCH is an intervention program that emphasizes the use of structured teaching (Lord & Schopler, 1994). **Structured teaching** involves adapting materials and environments to help children make sense of the world. Once new skills are acquired, children are taught to perform them more and more independently. The program relies on "start-to-finish boxes" as well as visual supports and schedules in teaching. The underlying philosophy of the program is that children with ASD are missing skills that they cannot learn but can compensate for through visual supports and other forms of structure. TEACCH is an individualized program that supports families through collaboration and training. In this program, parents become co-therapists.

The Young Autism Program (YAP)

This well-known program grew out of the work of O. Ivar Lovaas at UCLA (Lovaas, 1987). Sometimes it is simply referred to as "the Lovaas program" or, incorrectly, as ABA (which stands for applied behavior analysis[2]). YAP is an intensive (usually 40 hours per week) program that uses the principles of **behavior analysis** (e.g., positive reinforcement, extinction, and shaping) that have been developed over the previous five decades, beginning with the work of Dr. Charles B. Ferster at the Indiana University Medical Center (Ferster & DeMeyer, 1961). The goal of YAP is to teach children, one skill at a time, all the skills the child needs to be able to participate independently in all facets of daily living.

[2]Laypersons often refer to the UCLA program as "ABA therapy." This is incorrect. ABA stands for applied behavior analysis (Baer, Wolf, & Risley, 1968). ABA is the science of behavior first developed in the laboratory by experimental psychologists such as B. F. Skinner and then applied to educational and other settings. YAP and other programs for children with ASD use ABA techniques, but ABA is not synonymous with any one treatment program. Rather, it is the basis of most effective treatments for ASD.

structured teaching A feature of the instructional program TEACCH, developed for students with autism, wherein visual aids (start-to-finish boxes) are used to help students comprehend their environments

behavior analysis Research methodology using single-case designs; derived from the work of B. F. Skinner; paradigms describing human behavior in terms of events that stimulate or cause a behavior's occurrence, maintain behavior, and increase its likelihood

Blended Programs

Most programs for children with ASD are blended or use a variety of techniques. Although the theoretical bases of two popular intervention programs—TEACCH and YAP—are very different from one another, they have many similar components and use the same validated strategies. Both programs target the same skill areas: communication, social skills, toy play, attention, and motor imitation (Dawson & Osterling, 1997). Many researchers, teachers, and parents of children with ASD are more interested in effective intervention strategies than in strictly following one particularly philosophy or theory. Thus, combining or blending some elements of established programs, such as structured teaching with discrete trial teaching, is becoming the preferred approach. One example of a blended program being developed by researchers who are including successful aspects of established early interventions programs is the *Developmentally Appropriate Treatment for Autism Project* (DATA Project) at the University of Washington's Experimental Education Unit. In this program, strategies that are effective for a particular child are applied without regard to the theoretical background from which the strategy was initially developed. In other words, these clinicians use what works and assess effectiveness through program evaluation. Such types of programs use elements of a variety of procedures (such structured teaching, behavioral principles, and discrete trial training) in various combinations (Schwartz et al., 2001).

Teaching Students with ASD

Many of the basic principles that are effective in working with children with ASD also work well when incorporated into educational programs for older children, youth, and young adults with ASD (Kennedy & Horn, 2004). In particular, consistent structure, support of functional communication, instruction in social skills, and a functional and positive approach are important for school-age individuals with ASD (Scott, Clark, & Brady, 2000). When planning educational programs for students with ASD, educators must work together to develop plans for the delivery of an appropriate education for each student. Here are some questions that educators typically ask themselves during such planning sessions:

- What skills will help this student in his or her current and future settings?
- What skills will help this student be successful in inclusive settings?
- What age-appropriate and socially acceptable goals does this student need to learn?
- Are support and instruction being provided for skills the student is good at and enjoys executing?
- Is the curriculum being individualized for the student, while access to the general education curriculum is ensured?

Four areas in particular have come to the fore in recent investigations of how to effectively educate school-age learners with ASD—accessing the general education, making instructional accommodations, using validated practices, and using technology.

Accessing the General Education Curriculum

A major barrier to the academic and social inclusion of students with ASD has been difficulty accessing the general education curriculum. Traditionally, students with ASD have been taught a separate curriculum, often one that was age-inappropriate and nonfunctional. For example, in previous decades it was common to see teenagers with ASD being taught, as a primary instructional objective, to sort different colored chips into different bins. Such a curriculum was not academically challenging, nor did it facilitate the development of social skills for interacting with others. However, in the past decade, educators have shifted their focus: What students with ASD learn is being aligned with what students without disabilities learn (such as science, history, mathematics, and English/language arts). This content alignment encourages students with and without ASD to access similar general education material. It also provides a basis for common learning and social experiences (Ryndak & Alper, 2003).

Instructional Accommodations

Because there is such a large ability range for students with ASD, the general education curriculum must be adjusted to each student's strengths and needs. Making instructional accommodations enables educators to tailor the general education curriculum to the needs of students with ASD, while minimally changing the learning environment for other students. Here are a few general principles: Educators should make events predictable, they should carefully explain expectations, and they must foster a positive learning environment. Through accommodations such as those listed in *Accommodating for Inclusive Environments,* students with ASD are more easily and meaningfully included in general education classrooms.

Validated Practices

Along with accessing the general education curriculum and making instructional accommodations, most programs for students with ASD specifically include explicit instruction on social skills, as well as on reducing distracting behaviors that interfere both with learning and with successful interactions with others. As we have noted, many individuals with ASD engage in behaviors such as "hand flapping" or rocking that not only signal their disability to others but also interrupt the learning process. Such inappropriate behaviors should be reduced or eliminated. In the past, educators would have directly targeted the specific behavior of concern and sought to remove it from the student's repertoire. Today, instead of seeking only to discourage inappropriate behaviors, educators replace them with positive behaviors that are incompatible with the undesired ones. What are "incompatible" behaviors?

Accommodating for Inclusive Environments

Creating Situations Where Individuals with ASD Participate Successfully

Make Events Predictable

- Develop a schedule
- Make novel experiences predictable
- Avoid surprises
- Do not make unannounced changes
- Provide structure and a routine
- Know how well the individual handles free time

Communicate Instructions and Consequences Carefully

- Seek consistency in everyone's responses to inappropriate behavior
- Use direct statements
- Do not use slang or metaphors
- Avoid using only nonverbal cues
- Use personal pronouns carefully

Foster Positive Participation

- Provide feedback about the appropriateness of responses
- Remember to tell the individual when behavior is proper
- Arrange tasks that the person can perform
- Translate time into something tangible or visible
- Enhance verbal communications with illustrations or pictures
- Use concrete examples

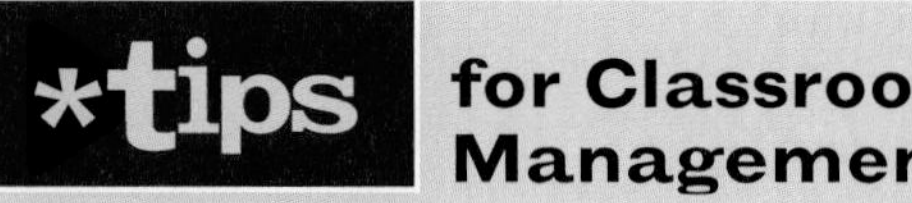

for Classroom Management

TEACH FUNCTIONALLY EQUIVALENT BEHAVIORS

Replace inappropriate behaviors with alternate ones that are productive and incompatible with the inappropriate behaviors.

1. Carefully identify the inapproporate behavior(s) in observable terms (e.g., Sean flaps his hands in the air above his head).
2. Analyze the behavior, occasions when it occurs, and events that seem to maintain it (e.g., Sean engages in this behavior when he has nothing to do, is bored, or the work is too hard. He continues his behavior until he is reminded to go back to work).
3. Determine substitute behaviors to develop (e.g., independent seatwork, reading silently, and computing math problems are substitute behaviors that Mrs. Norega, his teacher, has selected).
4. Teach and reward alternate behaviors (e.g., Mrs. Norega matches assignments with Sean's skills, has alternate work available, prompts Sean with these words: "Sean, time to go back to work," and reinforces him for completing assignments, with a color pencil).
5. Ensure consistency across all settings (e.g., using the data from her successful program, Mrs. Norega shows other teachers who work with Sean and his parents how to implement it as well).

Here's an example: Students can't be out of their seats, roaming around the classroom, if they are at their desks studying. The idea is that reinforcing behaviors that are *functionally equivalent* leaves students with useful skills (Scott, Clark, & Brady, 2000). For more about this positive and functional approach, read this chapter's *Tips for Classroom Management.*

Difficulty with social interactions is a defining characteristic of ASD, and the basis for some of these problems lies in the fact that these individuals seem unable to comprehend other people's emotions, feelings, or perspectives (Barnhill, 2001). Many of them are unable to take turns or execute "polite" behaviors without direct and systematic instruction. Deficits in these areas can lead to lifelong problems in the community and the workplace. Instruction on social skills can be embedded across a student's entire school day, or such activities can take place during specified, social skills training times. Typically, objectives include learning how to take another person's perspective, how to make and maintain friendships, and what social behaviors are appropriate in different contexts (Kennedy, 2001). Students with ASD often develop excellent job skills but have difficulty keeping jobs because of deficits in their social performance. Thus social skills instruction at school makes a difference for later successes during adulthood (Chadsey & Beyer, 2001).

Although there are many strategies for teaching social and communication skills to students with ASD, many of these strategies involve the use of visual cues or supports. In the next section, you will see how technology assists with the implementation of such visual cues and supports. Written text and pictures are effective interventions to facilitate the development of social skills (Thiemann & Goldstein, 2001). In one approach, students are shown drawings of appropriate social behaviors (e.g., how to gain someone's attention properly or how to initiate conversations) as part of an instructional routine that includes role playing, modeling, and rewards. The **picture exchange communication system (PECS)** is proving to be effective in helping students with ASD develop language and communication skills (Bondy & Frost, 2002). Read this chapter's *Validated Practices* to learn how this system enables students to use pictures to express their desires and needs to others.

Technology

People with ASD usually do not need the high-tech supports that many students with other disabilities do. Rather, the technology that is useful to these individuals revolves around two areas:

- Visual supports to help simplify and structure the environment
- Augmentative and assistive communication (AAC) to increase language use

Visual supports help simplify and structure the environment and can serve many purposes. For example, concrete objects, photographs, drawings, or words can create a schedule and cue the child about tasks to complete that day. Holding-baskets, templates, and other visual adaptations can reduce nonessential cues in the environment and draw attention to cues that are useful.

Augmentative and assistive communication devices are helpful for people with ASD because they provide them with an alternative system for communication, even though sometimes additional intervention needs to be put into place so they

picture exchange communication system (PECS) A technique wherein pictures are used to make requests; devised for individuals with autism who are nonverbal

Validated Practices The Picture Exchange Communication System (PECS)

What Is the PECS?

PECS is a method of providing communication support to nonverbal individuals. PECS uses pictures to represent categories such as clothing, toys, activities, feelings, special events, foods, body parts, and more. The pictures are computer generated or cut out of old magazines. Students begin by using single pictures and eventually form requests using complete sentences.

Why PECS Is Beneficial

Students are taught to use PECS to request items they need or want. This communication act is initiated by the student, not by you. Students ask for and receive concrete objects within real-life situations. Students have also been taught to use PECS to engage in positive peer interactions.

Implementing the PECS

A brief description of the first four initial phases follows.

Phase One: Initiating Communication

- Students are taught to request an object, rather than your asking, "What do you want?"
- Two adults (a partner and a prompter) are needed.
- Select a desired item and don't allow the student to use it for a brief time. This is so the student will "miss" the item and be motivated to ask for it.
- The communicative partner sits across from the student with the desired object: provides no verbal prompts.
- The physical prompter guides the student to give the picture to the communicative partner.
- When the student places the picture in the communicative partner's hand, she or he immediately gives the object.

Phase Two: Expanding the Use of Pictures

- The communicative partner moves, leaving the student to find the adult when requesting something.
- The items are moved farther from the student, but they must remain in sight and be easy to access.
- The number of items increase and span several categories.
- Students are required to place a picture in the adult's hand prior to receiving the item.

Phase Three: Choosing the Message Within PECS

- The main goal is to ensure that students are able to discriminate between pictures, demonstrating that they understand what they are asking for.
- Select one favorite picture (e.g., a toy) and one that the student dislikes (e.g., carrots).
- Say, "What do you want?" The student selects the picture.
- Give the selected item to the student. You will know by the student's reaction if he or she selected the correct picture.
- Add more pictures once students can discriminate between objects they like and those they dislike.
- Students exchange the picture for the desired item.

Phase Four: Introducing Sentence Structure

- Provide picture cards for I want ______; I see ______.
- I want ______ or I see ______ is placed on sentence strip.
- Students select the picture of what they want and place it on the strip. (See Figure A for an example.)
- Students give the sentence strip to you.
- You read the sentence, encouraging the student to touch each picture as you read.

Figure A • Example of a Sentence Strip

This scientifically validated practice is a teaching method proven by systematic research efforts (Bondy & Frost, 2002; Garfinkle & Scwhartz, 2001; Frost & Bondy, 1994; Schwartz, Garfinkle, & Bauer, 1998). Full citations are found with the reference for this chapter.

Source: From *Topics in autism: A picture's worth. PECS and other visual communication strategies in autism* (p. 90) by A. Bondy and L. Frost 2002, Bethesda, MD: Woodbine House. Reprinted by permission.

—By Kimberly Paulsen, Vanderbilt University

will use these devices (Garfinkel & Schwartz, 2001). (For more about AAC, review the Technology section in Chapter 4.) For example, children with ASD have been taught to sign exact English, to point to pictures, and to press a machine's button for a pre-recorded voice message of their intended communication. Only one AAC system, however, was specifically designed for children with autism, although it is also used with children who have other types of disabilities. PECS combines prompting and fading techniques to help children learn how to use the system, while at the same time teaching the basics of communication (see page 449). For example, this program teaches that communication is between people, that to be a successful communicator one needs to be persistent, and that communication is about something specific (Frost & Bondy, 1994). PECS has been validated through research and has proved to be an effective and efficient system (Charlop-Christy et al., 2002). Nearly all people with ASD learn how to use PECS, and more then half of those who master the program also develop some verbal language.

Transition

Everyone makes many transitions in life. Some of those transitions are made with excitement and others with fear or trepidation. For some of us, a move to a new city is filled with joy; the thrill of what is waiting around the next corner is uplifting. For others, transitioning to a new town is fraught with worry. Each of us is different and each situation is different. The same is true for individuals with ASD. In particular, successful transitions at two different times—moving from early intervention programs to school and leaving the shelter of school to move on to adult services—make real differences in the lives of these individuals and their families. Let's take a look at each of these milestones.

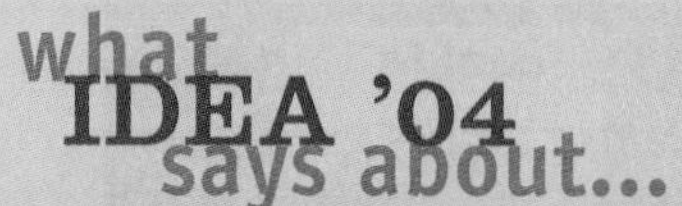

Options for Children Ages Three to Five

Federal funds to support the preschool education of students with disabilities who are beyond age three are allocated through Part B of IDEA. Part C of the law outlines the requirements for early intervention services for infants and toddlers.

Parents of children eligible for preschool services provided through Part B may choose to continue early intervention services under Part C. This continuation of Part C early intervention services:

- Must have an educational component that
  - Promotes school readiness
  - Incorporates preliteracy, language, and numeracy skills
- May continue until the child is eligible to enter kindergarten
- Must be developed and implemented jointly through the state and local school systems
- Must be approved by the parents through informed written consent

Transition to Preschool

Not all infants, toddlers, and preschoolers with disabilities, whether they have ASD or not, receive early intervention services in the same way. These programs are not guided by the same rules, regulations, or funding mechanisms. Most early-identified infants and toddlers with disabilities receive early intervention services through Part C of the IDEA '04 law. Typically, Part C services are designed to serve the family, as well as the child with the disability. Often, these services are brought to the family's home. Part B services are designed for preschoolers and students up through their high school years (for some, up to the age of 21). Services are delivered at schools: preschools, elementary schools, middle schools, and high schools. Some families find the transition from one type of service to another too difficult and ask the federal government for other options. See *What IDEA '04 Says About Options for Children Ages Three to Five.*

Transition to Services for Adults

An important part of educational programming for students with ASD is the successful transition from school-based supports to adult-focused supports (Wehman, 2000). Although many persons with ASD have skills that make them employable, their difficulty with social interactions and their need for routine often require that they receive **supported employment**. In addition, like other adults, people with ASD often want opportunities to continue their education

Table 12.7 • Transition Outcomes

Individuals know how to	Coworkers or the employer	Individuals experience social support as demonstrated by increased
• Ask for help, offer assistance, ask questions • Answer questions, respond to criticism • Interact with others socially at work • Initiate conversations appropriately • Advocate for themselves • Interpret and discriminate social cues	• Initiates social interactions with the individual • Responds to social interactions initiated by the individual • Advocates for the individual • Teaches the individual new social skills	• Happiness at work • Self-esteem • Friendship network • Support network
Personal acceptance is demonstrated by coworkers	**Individuals participate socially by interacting with coworkers**	**Individuals are accepted in the workplace as indicated by coworkers**
• Voluntarily eating lunch with the individual • Seeing the individual after work • Taking breaks with the individual • Indicating that the individual is a friend • Encouraging the individual to attend company social events	• About work upon arrival, at breaks, during lunch, several times throughout the day, and after work • On nonwork topics upon arrival, at breaks, during lunch, and after work • At company-sponsored events. • At social occasions that occur outside of work	• Indicating they like the person • Advocating for or supporting the person • Considering the person to be an acquaintance • Considering the person to be a team player • Displaying positive, general interactions • Training the person to perform work tasks better

Source: From Building consensus from transition experts on social integration outcomes and interventions by J. Chadsey-Rusch and L. W. Heal, 1995, *Exceptional Children, 62,* pp. 170–174. Adapted with permission.

after high school, but for these individuals, additional supports may be required to ensure ongoing success (Getzel & Wehman, 2004). In general, the difficulties faced by people with ASD are similar to those faced by others with severe disabilities. Transition plans are necessary, but issues such as living and working independently require ongoing support for people with ASD and their families. Transition outcomes, such as living and working in the community, become the focus of educational programming in high school and on through adulthood (see Table 12.7).

For people with ASD, life as an adult can be a challenging and rewarding part of life, just as it is for all of us. However, people with ASD may need additional supports to succeed. Many of these individuals, such as Jessy Park, are happy, successful adults, particularly when they are able to focus on their interests, preferences, and opportunities to continue to grow as individuals (Park, 2001). Jessy is an artist whose work is receiving national attention, but she is unable to live independently or interact with people comfortably enough to participate in the community without additional help from others. With these supports, she does well; without them, she often struggles to succeed. Anthony Crudale, another recognized artist with ASD, is a college graduate and a marathon runner (Raia, 2001). Although he drives a car and has a college degree, at age 24 he requires assistance to live independently and work. His mother worries that people do not understand ASD and that Anthony's inability to maintain eye contact with other people, his short verbal responses, and his inability to carry on conversations make others uncomfortable. She believes that he, and others with ASD, are excellent employees because of characteristics such as focusing on specific tasks, attention to detail, and the need to complete jobs, but that others in society need to understand the unique characteristics of people with ASD. These observations highlight the fact that for people with ASD to be successful as adults, they require understanding and support from others in their community.

supported employment
Strategy used in job training; student is placed in a paying job, receiving significant assistance and support, and the employer is helped with the compensation

Collaboration

Students with ASD must have access to the least restrictive environment (LRE), which in school contexts means general education settings and peers without disabilities (Ryndak & Alper, 2003). Sometimes this access is hard to achieve and maintain. Techniques such as adapting or modifying the school curriculum and using **peer supports** can help teachers encourage behaviors that will allow students to remain engaged in instruction provided in the general education classroom (Kennedy & Horn, 2004). Such interventions, along with adjustments and accommodations, become part of the package necessary to ensure LRE and a free appropriate public education (FAPE) to students who are challenging to teach. Interdisciplinary teams of professionals, including general and special educators and related service professionals such as behavior analysts, need to work together to identify the specific accommodations needed for each student. It is imperative that students with ASD experience typical and supported interactions with peers without disabilities. Such inclusion provides these students with appropriate role models, where they can observe how others behave and interact. Some programs, such as *Learning Experiences: An Alternative Program for Preschoolers and Parents (LEAP),* integrate children with autism into inclusive settings at the outset of treatment (Strain & Hoyson, 2000). With older students, the focus is on inclusive education and skill building in the LRE. However, it is important to remember that the following elements must be present:

- Sufficient structure
- Supports for functional communication
- Use of behavior analysis techniques
- Supports for social interactions

Partnerships with Families and Communities

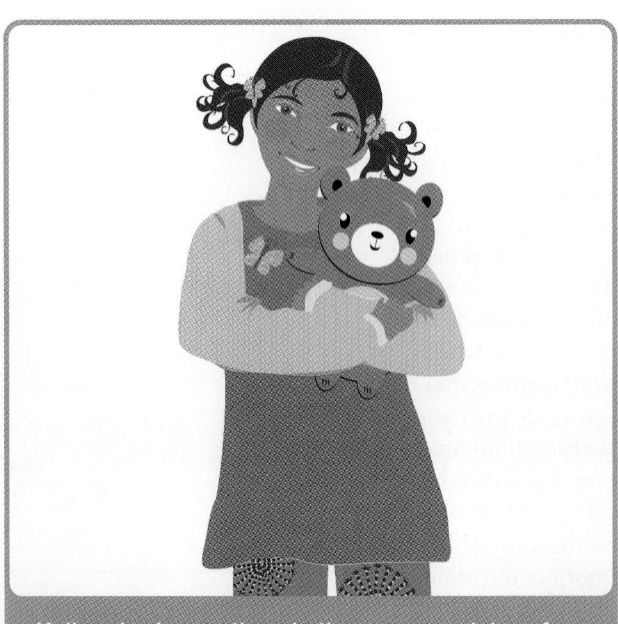

Kelly, who has autism, is the younger sister of Katani, one of the Beacon Street Girls, a popular series of books of the same name. Both autism and dyslexia are presented in this book.

Having a child with ASD is a challenge, even for the most confident parents (Powell, Hecimovic, & Christensen, 1992). Like the parent discussed in this chapter's *Considering Culture,* many parents blame themselves for not being able to solve their children's problems or help them become like other children of the same age. Clearly, the challenges presented to the entire family can seem overwhelming. Having a brother or sister with ASD can be challenging; siblings may not understand what to do when an inappropriate behavior occurs in public or when friends ask about their sibling. Children with ASD often lack independent play and leisure skills, which means that parents must spend more time providing direct care to their children. One result is that parents have less time to take care of other important activities, such as self-care and household chores.

Perhaps more frustrating for these families are the ways in which their children seem different. Some parents report difficulties connecting with or relating to their child. This experience is common with children who do not like physical affection such as hugs or who are socially avoidant. Parents who believe they are in part responsible for their children's instruction often find it very frustrating when learning is not achieved or is achieved very slowly.

Considering Culture

Being a "Better" Mother

Mariko is an intensely quiet woman who faithfully brings her child to school, attends parent meetings, and cooperates with all the teacher's recommendations. As the mother of seven-year-old Toshi, who has been diagnosed with autism, she feels that it is her primary duty to care for him. Her whole day is spent getting him ready for school, volunteering in his class, taking him to a community play group, driving him to swim lessons, and ensuring that he regularly attends therapy sessions with an SLP. She rarely talks with other parents or leaves the house other than to take Toshi to his activities. Meredith, Toshi's teacher, wishes that all of her students' parents were so cooperative and engaged with their children's education. Yet, on the other hand, she worries because Mariko appears anxious and depressed.

Meredith schedules a meeting with Mariko to discuss Toshi's progress. At the meeting Mariko bows her head as tears fill her eyes. She laments, "If I were a better mother, he would be a better boy." She relates how she feels responsible for the fact that he does not communicate like the other children and has problems in school. Her brother and sister-in-law's children who are close to Toshi's age are so lively and gifted. She only wishes that she could work harder to make Toshi more like them. Meredith is concerned for Mariko as well as for Toshi. She suggests that Mariko attend a support group for parents of children with disabilities. Mariko rejects the idea of getting together with a group of parents. Meredith then remembers a mother of another child with autism who went through her program several years ago. She feels this mother may be a good support for Mariko. Mariko agrees to meet with her if Meredith can make the arrangements.

Questions to Consider

1 Can you identify ways in which your family's cultural background and history influenced your parents' expectations and goals for you?

2 How might you identify community resources and support systems to help parents get parent-to-parent support or mental health support when needed, and how could you ensure that the providers of these services would be culturally competent and culturally responsive?

—By Eleanor Lynch, San Diego State University, and Marci Hanson, San Francisco State University

ASD is nevertheless not a readily apparent disability; these children do not typically have physical features indicating a disability. Although this may seem fortunate, many families find it a source of concern. For example, one mother was worried that on shopping trips, strangers would say "Hi" to her child, her child would ignore the stranger's greeting, and the stranger would assume that she was a bad mother because her child was rude. To prevent this from happening, the mother used signs with the child, even though the child did not understand them. The mother thought that her use of signs would cue others that her child had a disability. Another mother kept a letter from her son's pediatrician in her purse, describing her son's ASD diagnosis. Her son was nonverbal but screamed when in noisy situations or when unpredictable changes took place. This screaming had happened several times in public, resulting—more than once—in the police being called. This mother was afraid of being arrested for child abuse.

The behaviors that define the ASD umbrella make being a parent challenging. Many programs recognize these difficulties and provide supports for families. Some offer support groups and information on how to access community services such as respite care. Others help parents develop skills they need. For example, the TEACCH program in North Carolina offers an eight-week course for parents. These "teaching sessions" provide information about the nature of ASD, as well as presenting techniques whereby parents can "co-treat" their child with ASD. Regardless of the model, support from professionals, support from other parents of children with ASD, access to information, and access to high-quality comprehensive services are paramount.

peer supports Instructional strategy that facilitates social interaction and access to the general education curriculum

Imagine a world...

where every family gathering is a celebration . . .

Summary

Autism, Asperger syndrome, Rett syndrome, CCD, and PDD-NOS are the autism spectrum disorders. ASD is a complex set of conditions that have in common deficits in communication, deficits in social interaction, and repetitive behaviors or unusual interests. Early intervention is important in ASD, but current diagnostic approaches often do not identify children until age five. Most validated practices for individuals with autism rely on behavior analysis. Effective approaches share features, including sufficient structure, supports for functional communication, use of behavior analysis techniques, and supports for social interactions. These needs are lifelong for most individuals with ASD. With support, people with ASD can lead very accomplished and successful lives.

Addressing the Chapter Objectives

1 What is the relationship between autism and other autism spectrum disorders (ASD)?

- Autism is one of five types of conditions included under the umbrella of ASD.
- The five ASD conditions are autism, Asperger syndrome, Rett syndrome, CCD, and PDD-NOS.

2 What core characteristics identify individuals within the autism spectrum?

- Problems with communication
- Limited social interaction
- Repetitive behaviors or unusual interests

3 What is known about the causes of autism spectrum disorders?

- ASD is a neurobiological disorder that affects brain development and probably has some genetic basis.
- The degree to which brain development, genes, and the environment interact has yet to be determined.

4 How can learning environments be arranged so that individuals with autism spectrum disorders will maximally benefit from instruction?

- Provide sufficient structure.
- Support functional communication.
- Use behavior analysis techniques.
- Support social interactions.

5 Why are social relationships so important to people with autism spectrum disorders, particularly as they enter adulthood?

Social relationships provide social support and assistance to people with ASD. Without these supports, many people with ASD have trouble succeeding in school, at home, or in the community.

MyLabSchool is a collection of online tools for your success in this course, your licensure exams, and your teaching career. Visit **www.mylabschool.com** to access the following:

- Online Study Guide
- Video cases from real classrooms
- Help with your research papers using Research Navigator
- Career Center with resources for:
  - Praxis exams and licensure preparation
  - Professional portfolio development
  - Job search and Interview techniques
  - Lesson planning

Supplementary Resources

Popular Novels and Books

Grandin, T. (1995). *Thinking in pictures and other reports from my life with autism.* New York: Viking Books.

Grandin, T. (2005). *Animals in translation: Using the mysteries of autism to decode animal behavior.* New York: Scribner.

Haddon, M. (2003). *The curious incident of the dog in the night-time.* New York: Doubleday.

Harland, K. (2002). *A will of his own.* New York: Woodbine House.

Park, C. C. (2001). *Exiting Nirvana: A daughter's life with autism.* Boston: Little, Brown.

Peralta, S. (2002). *All about my brother.* Shawnee Mission, KS: Autism Asperger Publishing Co.

Sacks, O. (1995). *An anthropologist on Mars: Seven paradoxical tales.* New York: Random House.

Movies

House of Cards (1993). Miramax

After the death of Ruth's husband, her young daughter develops symptoms of autism. Ruth takes her daughter to a specialist in childhood autism named Jake, who employs a strictly traditional approach to therapy at his special school. However, Ruth does not accept that Jake's method is the only treatment, so she attempts to connect with her daughter to see the world through her eyes. Through further examination, Ruth and Jake realize that the little girl was not really autistic but is just coping with her father's death in a very unconventional way.

Rain Man (1989). United Artists

Charlie Babbit's father bequeaths most of his vast estate to his brother, who has a rare form of autism: Raymond is an autistic savant who has an incredible ability to remember mathematical details. In an effort to gain access to Raymond's inheritance, Charlie kidnaps him from the institution where he has lived for 30 years. Charlie's affection for Raymond grows, and he realizes that he cannot care for Raymond. This film won Oscars in the categories of best director, best original screenplay, best picture, and best actor, Dustin Hoffman for Raymond.

Parent, Professional, and Consumer Organizations and Agencies

Autism Society of America in Bethesda, Maryland **www.autism-society.org**

Autism Center, the University of Washington in Seattle: **http://departments.washington.edu/uwautism**

Cure Autism Now in Los Angeles **www.cureautismnow.org**

International Rett Syndrome Association in Clinton, Maryland: **irsa@rettsyndrome.org**

National Alliance for Autism Research in Princeton, New Jersey: **www.naar.org**

Professional Standards and Licensure Tests

After reading this chapter, you should be able to link basic knowledge and skills described in the CEC Standards and INTASC Principles with information provided in this text. The table below shows some of the specific CEC Individualized Independence Curriculums Knowledge and Skill Standards and INTASC Special Education Principles that can be applied to each major section of the chapter. Other standards may also be applied to this chapter. Associated General Praxis II topic areas are identified in the right column.

Major Chapter Headings	CEC Knowledge and Skill Core Standard and Associated Subcategories	INTASC Core Principle and Associated Special Education Subcategories	PRAXIS II Exam Topic
Where We've Been . . . What's on the Horizon	**1: Foundations** IC1K2 Historical foundations, classic studies, major contributors, major legislation, and current issues related to knowledge and practice	**1: Subject Matter** 1.01 Special education teachers have a solid understanding of the major concepts, assumptions, issues, and processes of inquiry in the subject matter that they teach.	1: Understanding Exceptionality 2: Legal and Social Issues
Autism Spectrum Disorders (ASD) Defined	**1: Foundations** IC1K1 Definitions and issues related to the identification of individuals with disabilities	**1: Subject Matter** 1:12 Special education teachers serve as a resource to others by providing information about the laws and policies that support students with disabilities and how to access additional information when needed.	2: Legal and Social Issues
Characteristics	**2: Development and Characteristics of Learners** IC2K4 Psychological and social-emotional characteristics of individuals with disabilities	**2: Student Learning** 2.07 Special education teachers seek to understand the current and evolving development and learning of individual students from a life-span perspective.	1. Understanding Exceptionality
Causes and Prevention	**2: Development and Characteristics of Learners** IC2K3 Etiologies and medical aspects of conditions affecting individuals with disabilities	**2: Student Learning** 2.08 Special education teachers seek a holistic understanding of each student's current learning and development, based on knowledge of the student's performance within a variety of settings.	1: Understanding Exceptionality 2: Legal and Social Issues

Assessment	**8: Assessment** IC8K1 Specialized terminology used in the assessment of individuals with disabilities	**8: Assessment** 8.07 Special education teachers plan and conduct assessments in the school, home, and community in order to make eligibility and placement decisions about individuals students with disabilities.	3: Delivery of Services to Students
Teaching Students with ASD	**4: Instructional Strategies** IC4S3 Use a variety of nonaversive techniques to control targeted behavior and maintain attention of individuals with disabilities	**4: Instructional Strategies** 4.09 All special education teachers have responsibility for ensuring the appropriate delivery of instruction for students with disabilities.	3: Delivery of Services to Students
Transition	**4: Instructional Strategies** IC4K4 Resources, and techniques used to transition individuals with disabilities into and out of school and postschool environments	**1: Subject Matter** 1.09 Special education teachers of students with disabilities have knowledge of services, procedures, and policies that support transition from secondary school settings to postsecondary and work settings, as well as to participation in all aspects of community life.	3: Delivery of Services to Students
Collaboration	**10: Collaboration** IC10K2 Collaborative and/or consultative role of the special education teacher in the reintegration of individuals with disabilities	**10: Collaboration, Ethics, and Relationships** 10.09 Special education teachers collaborate with families and with school and community personnel to include students with disabilities in a range of instructional environments in the school and community.	3: Delivery of Services to Students
Partnerships with Families and Communities	**10: Collaboration** IC10K1 Parent education programs and behavior management guides that address severe behavior problems and facilitation communication for individuals with disabilities	**10: Collaboration, Ethics, and Relationships** 10.10 Special education teachers understand the impact that having a child with a disability may have on family roles and functioning at different points in the life cycle of a family.	2: Legal and Social Issues 3: Delivery of Services to Students

Inner Demons. Tempra, 28 × 22 inches. © Katie Dallam. Photograph of the artist, Katie Dallam, with her painting *Monster.* Both images © Katie Dallam. Used with kind permission of the artist.

Katie Dallam's life parallels that of Maggie, the boxer played by Hillary Swank in Clint Eastwood's film *Million Dollar Baby*. Like Maggie, Katie was left with permanent disabilities that were the result of brain injuries sustained in a boxing match. Katie earned $300 for that fight, and no one (including the boxing commission) helped her with her medical bills, which approached $1 million. Although Katie entertained thoughts of suicide, she did not go down that path. After years of rehabilitation, and with the help of a very supportive family, Katie has regained much of her independence, and she now battles her demons on the paint canvas instead of the canvas of the boxing ring.

13

Very Low Incidence Disabilities

Multiple-Severe Disabilities, Deaf-Blindness, and Traumatic Brain Injury

> *"For the 50 million-plus Americans with disabilities, education will open the door to many interesting jobs and will give you choices in life. Use all the wonderful tools available to you today to get educated and help yourself. Persevere, take risks, and don't forget to give back."*

T. Alan Hurwitz

CEO/Dean of the National Technical Institute for the Deaf and vice president of Rochester Institute of Technology

In this chapter you will learn about three distinct special education categories; what they share is their very low incidence and the probability that the disability is severe. Accordingly, this chapter is organized somewhat differently from chapters that focus on only one special education category. It first outlines the history and background of severe disabilities and showcases a very special organization that makes a difference in the lives of individuals with many different low incidence disabilities. Next, separate sections explain each of these three special education categories. Then, combined discussions about topics such as assessment, instruction, transition, collaboration, and partnerships with families follow as in previous chapters. The three disabilities presented in this chapter are multiple-severe disabilities, deaf-blindness, and traumatic brain injury.

The **multiple-severe disabilities** category includes individuals with coexisting disabilities that have very serious results. **Deaf-blindness** is also a disability category wherein the individuals affected have coexisting disabilities, but in this case they specifically have problems with both vision and hearing. **Traumatic brain injury (TBI)** is the special education category through which services are offered to individuals and their families because of head injuries. In many cases these services include hospital or homebound instruction until such time as the student can return to school.

Because all three are very **low incidence disabilities**—that is, they do not occur very often—it is likely that most educators will not teach many youngsters with these conditions during their careers. This is so in part because of the severe nature of these disabilities and in part because of their relatively low prevalence. Most typically, students with these disabilities require substantial and intensive accommodations, modifications, supports, and special education services.

Chapter Objectives

After studying this chapter, you will be able to:

1. Explain the major characteristics of students with multiple-severe disabilities.
2. Describe the impact of deaf-blindness.
3. Discuss how cases of traumatic brain injury (TBI) can be prevented.
4. Explain alternate assessments and what they mean for students with low incidence disabilities.
5. List the key elements of functional behavioral assessments (FBA).

Where We've Been . . . What's on the Horizon?

Confusion has surrounded people with low incidence disabilities since the beginning of time. Their proper place in society has often been denied them, and questions of how best to educate them so they can achieve their potential and participate fully in the community continue to be raised. Individuals with severe low incidence disabilities were those most often excluded from public schools before the original passage of IDEA in 1975. (See Chapter 1 for a review of why IDEA came into existence and what protections this law offers to students with disabilities and their families.) These individuals' disabilities present major challenges to themselves, their families, the schools, and society. However, we now know—from the evidence of their participation in schools and in the community—that education makes a real difference in their results and lifts our expectations for what they can and do achieve.

Historical Context

Lessons about the remarkable achievements and community participation of people with low incidence and severe disabilities began long ago. Yet despite these success stories, society denied many of them opportunities to develop and flourish. Here's an example of an individual who surprised everyone and proves that the determination of teachers and the individuals themselves can overcome what seems insurmountable. Probably the most famous person with deaf-blindness is Helen Keller. She was a woman of many accomplishments, but none of her achievements, which included graduating from Radcliffe with honors in 1904, would have been possible without the efforts of her teacher, Anne Sullivan (Holcomb & Wood, 1989). Sullivan's "family tree" is interesting and noteworthy. Samuel Gridley Howe was the founder of the Perkins School for the Blind. Located in Boston, it was the first school in the United States for students who are blind. One of Howe's pupils was Laura Dewey Bridgman, herself a person with deaf-blindness, who talked to other people by tapping letters and using a manual alphabet. She used braille for reading. Miss Bridgman became a teacher, and one of her students, Anne Sullivan, was a girl with low vision. When Sullivan grew up, she learned of a six-year-old girl with deaf-blindness living in Alabama. Sullivan visited young Helen Keller and brought her a gift, a doll that had been given to her by Laura Bridgman. Sullivan became Helen Keller's teacher and lifelong companion. Of her disabilities, Keller said, "Blindness separates a person from things, but deafness separates him from people" (Miles, 2005, p. 6). Clearly, the case of Helen Keller is unique and remarkable. Although it is unrealistic to expect the outcomes for all individuals with low incidence disabilities to be like hers, her story serves to remind us of the importance of high expectations, hard work, intensive instruction, and meaningful supports.

Helen Keller and her teacher, Anne Sullivan, proved that people with multiple-severe disabilities, such as deaf-blindness, can achieve beyond most people's expectations.

Despite success stories like Helen Keller's, until relatively recently most children and adults with severe disabilities spent their lives in large residential institutions with little or no access to the community or chance to participate in mainstream society. This is why TASH (formerly called The Association for Persons with Severe Handicaps and now just referred to as TASH) continues to call for the closing of all institutions (TASH, 2000a). Today's situation is quite different. Many adults with severe disabilities live in apartments or group homes in the community. They hold jobs, and thanks to advances in supported employment, the number of them working in the community is expanding as well. Community based instruction helps these individuals prepare for the challenges of adult living (NICHCY, 2004a). These efforts and services are still being developed, so the outcomes for the next generations of these students will continue to improve.

As we have said, the current picture for students with multiple and exceptionally complex disabilities is very different from what it was only a few decades ago. Before IDEA was passed in 1975, many of these individuals were excluded from school and had no opportunity to benefit from a special education complete with the related services they needed. For those who did find access to education, it was often in segregated settings. And it was not until the 1960s and 1970s that researchers began to turn their attention to developing and validating instructional procedures that are effective specifically for these learners.

The special education programs and services for these students often were provided almost exclusively outside of the general education setting. The inclusive education movement has brought more and more students with disabilities to their neighborhood schools and to general education classes (U.S. Department of Education, 2005a). Today, the nation's call for accountability for educational progress includes the progress of students with disabilities. These actions have now brought the education delivered to even those with the most serious cognitive and low incidence disabilities to the forefront of national discussions (e.g., *Education Week's* report: *Special Education in an Era of Standards, Count Me In, Quality Counts,* 2004).

The situation of students with TBI is a bit different from that of their peers with other low incidence disabilities. In fact, many students with TBI received special education services long before IDEA was passed in 1975. Their education was even the topic of books describing "best practices" for them. In 1947 Strauss and Lehtinen published a groundbreaking book, *Psychopathology and Education of the Brain-Injured Child,* in which they recommended highly structured educational approaches for children who had many of the characteristics observed in today's students with TBI. Although these students received specialized services, this disability was not considered a special education category until the 1990 reauthorization of IDEA (PL 101-476). Before 1990, these students were simply counted in whatever category most closely matched their primary learning needs.

Team Hoyt has proved to all that first impressions can be misleading. We should never make assumptions about what people with disabilities can or cannot accomplish.

Challenges That Low Incidence Disabilities Present

Having more than one major disability presents unique challenges to the individual and the family. The combined effects of two disabilities create a pattern of problems different from those presented by one disability alone (NICHCY, 2004a). For example, children who are deaf and also have intellectual disabilities need teachers who are specialists in more than one area. They also need teachers who understand the special problems that this unique combination of disabilities raises.

The impact of multiple-severe disabilities is significant in so many ways. Besides the seriousness of the disability itself, unfounded assumptions about these individuals' abilities and potential can limit their educational opportunities, the expectations held for them, and ultimately their outcomes. In fact, many individuals with severe disabilities are still relegated to nursing homes and institutions, receive only minimal services, and are afforded no education. Clearly, prophecies of poor outcomes are self-fulfilling under such conditions! But when people are not limited by attitudes and perceptions, a world of possibilities opens up. Take, for example, the story of Rick Hoyt, born with cerebral palsy and multiple-severe disabilities (McNeill, 2005; Nall, 2002). Doctors told Rick's parents after his birth that there was little hope for his development or of his ever being able to communicate, but the Hoyts refused to believe them. When Rick was ten years old, Tufts University engineers designed a special communication system for him. Rick uses head movements to select letters and words, and a computer "speaks" for him, allowing him to share his wit, humor, and conversations with others. He also lives in his own apartment. Today, "Team Hoyt"—the father and son team that competes in marathons—inspire us all not to be restricted by assumptions but, rather, to seek to break all barriers.

multiple-severe disabilities Exceptionally challenging disabilities where more than one condition influences learning, independence, and the range of intensive and pervasive supports the individual and the family require; developmental disabilities

deaf-blindness A dual disability involving both vision and hearing problems

traumatic brain injury (TBI) Head injury causing reduced cognitive functioning, limited attention, and impulsivity

low incidence disabilities Disabilities the prevalence and incidence of which are very low

Making a Difference

Sprout

Anthony di Salvo

The joy and fun of getting out for a weekend adventure, taking a drive in the country, or traveling with friends to Mexico or Disney World are something we all look forward to. Unfortunately, most people with multiple-severe disabilities have few opportunities to experience such pleasures. In 1979 the Sprout Organization of New York City launched a program to provide a range of organized trips to people who have need for intensive supports. Some 25 years ago such an idea—taking people with very challenging needs on holidays without their family members—was unheard of and even unthinkable. Since Sprout's beginning, however, it has continued to expand its services. Today, Sprout serves over 1,800 people a year, providing vacations and recreational opportunities that are age-appropriate. The Sprout programs serve as models for others. Although not nearly enough exist, more travel programs are available today, across the country, for people with severe disabilities because of the example set by Sprout.

Filling any important need for people with disabilities can be all-consuming. Some might suggest that arranging and delivering many exciting traveling opportunities is sufficient. But not to Anthony di Silvo! He didn't stop with the development of a vacation program. He continued to see needs, and he continues to put his creativity to the test.

As you have learned throughout this text, people with disabilities have been marginalized in film and television. Few actors with disabilities are able to find work, and few filmmakers with disabilities are employed in the entertainment industry. The idea behind the Sprout Film Festival, initiated in 2003, was to reinforce accurate portrayals of people with disabilities, break down stereotypes, and show that people with disabilities can be serious filmmakers. The Sprout Film Festival, now an annual event, is held in New York City. Three days of showcasing outstanding films made by people with disabilities culminate in a grand awards celebration. What an exciting opportunity for so many who have had little chance to show off their skills and talents! To see folks having a great time traveling, making their own movies, or participating at annual Sprout Film Festivals, visit www.gosprout.org

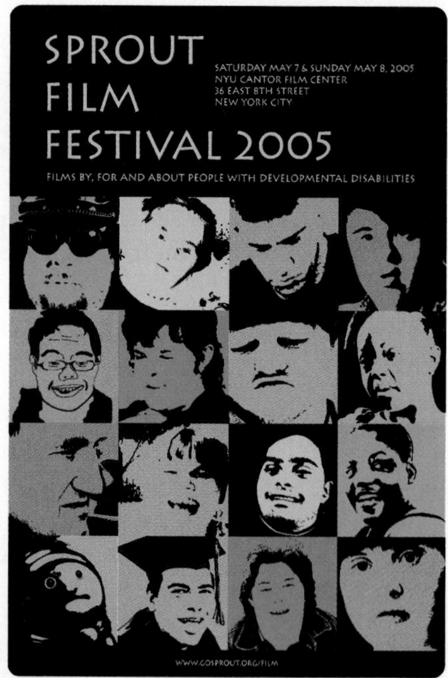

Very Low Incidence Disabilities

Although each very low incidence disability has a separate definition (see Table 13.1), they do share many things. For example, those affected must overcome many challenges to gain independence, meaningful employment, and community presence. Typically, in order for these goals to be attained, intensive and pervasive supports from a wide range of individuals and systems must be in place. These individuals tend to have fewer opportunities because of bias and restricting attitudes, but as Cheryl Richter shows us, all it takes is a little creativity and opportunities abound. As you'll learn from this chapter's *In the Spotlight* feature, people who combine compassion with creativity to turn troubling situations into opportunities can make a tremendous difference in the lives of others, particularly people with disabilities.

Table 13.1 • Definitions of Very Low Incidence Disabilities

Source	Severe Disabilities
Professional Organization[1]	Individuals of all ages, races, creeds, national origins, genders, and sexual orientation who require ongoing support in one or more major life activities in order to participate in a integrated community and enjoy a quality of life similar to that available to all individuals. Support may be required for life activities such as mobility, communication, self-care, and learning as necessary for community living, employment, and self-sufficiency.
	Developmental Disabilities
Centers for Disease Control (CDC)[2]	Developmental disabilities are a diverse group of severe chronic conditions that are due to mental and/or physical impairments. People with developmental disabilities have problems with major life activities such as language, mobility, learning, self-help, and independent living. Developmental disabilities begin anytime during development up to 22 years of age and usually last throughout a person's lifetime.
	Multiple Disabilities
Federal Government[3]	Concomitant impairments (such as mental retardation–blindness, mental retardation–orthopedic impairment, etc.), the combination of which causes such severe educational needs that they cannot be accommodated in special education programs solely for one of the impairments. The term does not include deaf-blindness (p. 311).
	Deaf-Blindness
Federal Government[3]	Deaf-blindness means concomitant hearing and visual impairments, the combination of which causes such severe communication and other developmental and learning needs that the persons cannot be appropriately educated in special education programs solely for children and youth with hearing impairments or severe disabilities, without supplementary assistance to address their education needs due to these dual, concurrent disabilities (p. 310).
National Technical Assistance Center[4]	If the deficit in hearing and vision is sufficient to require special adaptations in instruction in both the auditory and visual modes to produce maximum learning, then the person qualifies to be identified as deaf-blind and should be included in the annual census . . . a person needs, at a minimum, to have a visual acuity of 20/70 in the better eye with correction and an auditory deficit of 30 dB in the better ear.
	Traumatic Brain Injury
Federal Government[3]	Traumatic brain injury means an acquired injury to the brain caused by an external physical force, resulting in total or partial functional disability or psychosocial impairment, or both, that adversely affects a child's educational performance. The term applies to open or closed head injuries resulting in impairments in one or more areas, such as cognition; language; memory; attention; reasoning; abstract thinking; judgment; problem solving; sensory, perceptual, and motor abilities; psychosocial behavior; physical functions; information processing; and speech. The term does not apply to brain injuries that are congenital or degenerative, or to brain injuries induced by birth trauma (p. 313).

Sources: [1] *TASH resolution on the people for whom TASH advocates* (p. 1), TASH, 2000b, Baltimore, MD: Author.

[2] *Developmental Disabilities,* Centers for Disease Control (CDC), National Center on Birth Defects and Developmental Disabilities (p. 1) www.cdc.gov/cnbdd/dd/default.htm#publications, 2004.

[3] From 34 CFR Parts 300 and 303, Assistance to States for the Education of Children with Disabilities and the Early Intervention Program for Infants and Toddlers with Disabilities; Proposed Regulations (pp. 310, 311, 313), U.S. Department of Education, 2005b, *Federal Register,* Washington, DC.

[4] *Annual Deaf-Blind Census–1995* (pp. 2, 5), V. Baldwin, Monmouth, OR: Teaching Research, Western Oregon State College.

Cheryl Richter in the Spotlight

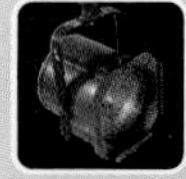

Employment opportunities for people with severe or developmental disabilities, even in "good times," are not plentiful. Although most of these individuals want to work, jobs are hard to find. There simply aren't enough opportunities. At the same time, growers and nurseries destroy high-quality plants that remain unsold. They are transported to the dump (landfill), are plowed under, or get burned or buried.

Cheryl Richter, a garden writer and photographer, put the two problems together and came up with three marvelous—and socially responsible—solutions. She knew that there would be a demand for trees, plants, flowers, and shrubs, particularly if they were free except for the cost of shipping and handling. Cheryl believed that growers and nursery owners would rather give their unwanted plants to serve a purpose, rather than having them destroyed or discarded. And she clearly understood that there was a desperate need for more employment opportunities for people with severe disabilities.

So in 2004, Cheryl and her husband Greg created a Web site to let Internet shoppers order plants to be delivered directly to them. The shipping fees benefit her workers with disabilities, who package and ship the plants that are ordered online.

To see the amazing stock that is available and to provide such jobs for those who want them, visit the Web site www.freetreesandplants.com. As they say, "How can you afford not to?"

Multiple-Severe Disabilities

IDEA '04 does not call out multiple-severe disabilities as a separate special education category, but the U.S. Department of Education does so in its regulations of IDEA '04 (U.S. Department of Education, 2005b). Neither the law nor its regulations use the term **developmental disabilities**, which is often used interchangeably with the term *multiple-severe disabilities.* The term *developmental disabilities* is used by the Centers for Disease Control (CDC) to describe severe conditions that often combine intellectual and physical problems (see Table 13.1 for CDC's definition). Regardless what term is used to describe this disability, one emphasis for these students is developing skills that promote independence and community presence (Kennedy & Horn, 2004; McDonnell, Hardman, & McDonnell, 2003). When they receive an individualized, intensive, and creative education that truly meets each person's unique learning needs, the possibilities are almost beyond imagination.

Multiple-Severe Disabilities Defined

developmental disabilities Severe disabilities that often combine intellectual and physical problems; often used interchangeably with term multiple-severe disabilities

The themes emerging from modern perspectives on the education that should be provided for individuals with severe disabilities and on goals for them to live, work, and play in community settings have moved away from previous definitions. Instead of describing individuals in terms of deficits—what they cannot do—new orientations focus on what the individual can accomplish through a variety of supports across many of life's dimensions. TASH's description of people with severe disabilities is found in Table 13.1. The definition that the federal government, in its IDEA '04 regulations, developed to define multiple disabilities also appears in Table 13.1.

Characteristics

Individuals with multiple-severe disabilities display a wide range of skills and abilities, as well as a wide range of problem areas where they need intensive instruction. According to NICHCY (2004a), this group of individuals shares some common characteristics:

- Problems transferring or generalizing learning from one situation to another, one setting to another, and one skill to another
- Limited communication abilities
- Difficulties with memory
- Need for supports for many of life's major activities (domestic, leisure, community participation, vocational)
- Need for services from many different related service providers

Compounding their problems, many individuals with multiple-severe disabilities face other challenges. Many of them experience health problems (such as seizure disorders, heart disease) or physical problems (such as cerebral palsy, vision or hearing problems) and face communication challenges. Consequently, they and their families interface with many professionals from many disciplines—all with different styles of interaction, terms and jargon, and approaches. Multiple modes of interactions can complicate an already difficult situation. But, when multidisciplinary teams of related service providers (e.g., physical therapists, assistive technology specialists, speech/language pathologists) are brought together and their expertise is orchestrated to meet the needs of each student, the outcomes are amazing.

People with multiple-severe disabilities require both intensive and sustained supports across their school years and typically across their lives. For some, these supports may well be in only one life activity, but for many of these individuals, supports are needed for access and participation in mainstream society. Supports are necessary because most individuals with multiple-severe disabilities require assistance in many adaptive areas (NICHCY, 2004a). For example, an individual with a cognitive disability might need supports to pay bills and manage a budget. If that

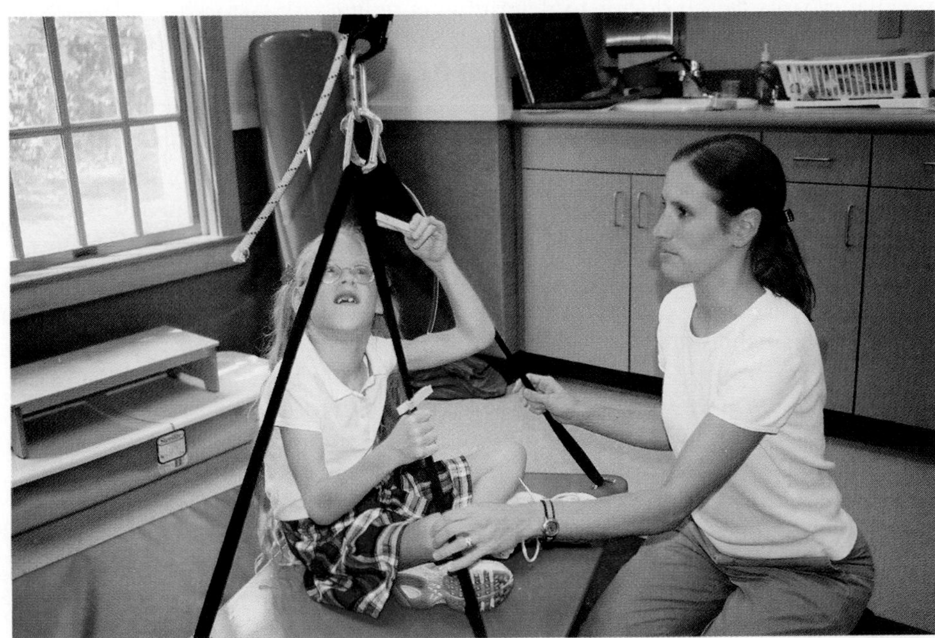

With the help of her occupational therapist, Kailyn, whom you first met in Chapter 2 (see page 55), is working to improve her fine motor skills.

individual also has a moderate hearing loss, she or he might need an assistant to facilitate communication at the doctor's office but might function at work with only natural supports from coworkers.

Prevalence

Relatively speaking, few students have multiple-severe disabilities and require intensive educational opportunities to meet their complex needs. Only 0.23 percent of American students are included in the federal special education category of multiple disabilities, representing some 132,333 students aged 6 to 21 (U.S. Department of Education, 2005b). Depending on how states include individuals in one category or another, fewer or more students can be considered as having this disability. For example, some states do not include in this category students with learning disabilities and also a hearing problem; other states do (Müller & Markowitz, 2004). Some states include in the mental retardation category students with a mild visual disability who also have substantial cognitive disabilities; other states report these students to the federal government as having multiple disabilities. Regardless, all students with severe problems are served by special education, and the overall goal for their education usually focuses on achieving independent living in the community.

Causes and Prevention

Many factors can cause disabilities. As you have learned throughout this academic term, heredity, problems during pregnancy, problems at birth, and incidents after birth can all lead to a lifelong set of challenges—sometimes even to multiple-severe disabilities. Because of advances in medical technology, many children born with multiple-severe disabilities now have long life expectancies (McDonnell, Hardman, & McDonnell, 2003). For example, increasing numbers of babies with extremely low birth weights—as low as 1,500 grams—are surviving infancy and joining the ranks of schoolchildren (March of Dimes, 2002). Many of these youngsters have multiple problems, including substantial cognitive disabilities. Although reasons for the majority of birth defects are unknown, many could have been prevented with prepregnancy visits to the doctor to determine potential risk factors (e.g., hereditary possibilities, health and lifestyle issues) and to ensure good prenatal health care during pregnancy (March of Dimes Perinatal Data Center, 2001). Universal access to health care and raised public awareness of prevention strategies help to reduce the number of children and families affected (Children's Defense Fund [CDF], 2004).

Deaf-Blindness

When you hear the word *deaf-blindness*, you probably think of people who have no vision and no hearing abilities. Although this is true for some individuals, the majority of them have some residual hearing and/or vision. In fact, according to the National Deaf-Blind Census, more of them have some functional use of their vision than have some hearing (DB-Link, 2005). Regardless, the world for children with deaf-blindness can be exceptionally restricted. For those whose hearing and vision fall into the ranges of severe or profound losses, their immediate world may well end at their fingertips (Miles, 2005).

Almost half of these students have enough residual vision to allow them to read enlarged print, see sign language, move about in their environment, and recognize friends and family (Miles, 2005). Some have sufficient hearing to understand some speech sounds or hear loud noises; some can develop speech themselves. But others have such limited vision and hearing that they profit little from either sense. In addition to their visual and hearing losses, the majority of these individuals have other disabilities, such as mental retardation, that further complicate their education. Most individuals with deaf-blindness need considerable supports for their worlds to be safe and accessible; these students' educational programs need to be carefully thought through and must be uniquely designed to ensure that each of these children meets his or her potential.

Deaf-blindness should not be minimized; it is serious and has significant effects on those involved. It definitely affects these students' education, which is often so individualized and intensive that it does not occur in the general education setting. In the United States, only 7 percent of these students (fewer than 400 nationally) attend general education classes for most of their school day—12 percent when resource rooms are included. More than a third attend specialized center or hospital schools, and almost 30 percent receive their education in separate special education classes (DB-Link, 2005).

Deaf-Blindness Defined

A separate funding base for students with deaf-blindness was initiated in 1969. This period was a time of national crisis. The rubella epidemic had caused dramatic increases in the numbers of babies with disabilities, particularly blindness, deafness, and deaf-blindness. Thus deaf-blindness was created as a special category of disabilities. The IDEA '04 definition of deaf-blindness is found in Table 13.1 on page 463. Some experts believe that the IDEA '04 definition does not assist in the accurate identification of, and the provision of appropriate services for, all children with this disability (Brown & Bates, 2005). They believe a functional definition—one that focuses on the conditions needed for optimal learning and considers the unique challenges imposed by the interplay of two sensory impairments—produces better outcomes. (A functional definition is also found in Table 13.1.) The result is inconsistent identification, services, and different indications of how many students are involved. This confusion is compounded because in addition to problems with vision and hearing, most of these youngsters have other coexisting disabilities, such as cognitive disabilities and health impairments (Miles, 2005). For these reasons, many of these youngsters are counted in the multiple disabilities category.

Characteristics

From the name of this disability, it is clear that those involved have reduced distance senses: restricted vision and hearing. However, the degree and amount of vision and hearing loss are not uniform, and the combination of these losses affects each individual differently. Increasingly, over the last 20 years, more and more individuals included in the National Deaf-Blind Census have more than one additional coexisting disability (DB-Link, 2005). Of the almost 10,000 students (ages 6 to 21) on the deaf-blind census, 60 percent also have physical disabilities, 68 percent have intellectual disabilities, and 40 percent have complex health care needs. Clearly, the multitude of the disabilities that confront this group of learners and their families and teachers has increased across time (Brown & Bates, 2005).

How serious are these students' visual and hearing disabilities? Any loss of sensory input, particularly if it cannot be corrected through optical aids (e.g., glasses or contact lenses) and assistive listening devices (e.g., hearing aids), interrupts the learning

for Effective Teaching

FOSTERING A SENSE OF BELONGING FOR STUDENTS WHO ARE DEAF-BLIND

1 Gently touch the person's nearest hand to indicate you are nearby.
2 Every time you meet the person, identify yourself, perhaps with a special sign.
3 Help classmates come to feel comfortable interacting with their deaf-blind peer.
4 Communicate directly with the deaf-blind person; don't ask someone else what the individual wants.
5 Have the individual join in class discussions.
6 Create cooperative teams for academic tasks.
7 Encourage classmates to include their peer with deaf-blindness in games during recess and free time.
8 Offer assistance only when necessary.
9 Demonstrate respect for the individual.
10 Laugh and play with all students.

process. When these disabilities occur together, the impact is even greater, affecting every aspect of the child's education—the way it is delivered, the accommodations needed, and the adjustments required (Brown & Bates, 2005).

One question that you should be asking is related to the seriousness of these youngsters' visual and hearing disabilities. You should also be wondering how these degrees of loss combine. For example, do most of these students have a mild vision loss but a profound hearing loss? Do they have little or no functional use of either sense? First, some 21 percent have low vision and another 24 percent are legally blind. From these data, one can assume that at least half of these individuals have some functional vision and can access print through their residual vision (see Chapter 11 for a review). Second, 28 percent of deaf-blind students have severe or profound deafness (DB-Link, 2005). Hence about 70 percent perceive some meaningful sounds and profit at least somewhat from amplification.

The individuals affected by deaf-blindness, their family members, and their teachers must address

- Feelings of isolation
- Problems with communication
- Problems with mobility

Let's think about how we can make a difference by in each of these problem areas.

Isolation

Feelings of isolation are a particular problem for many individuals with deaf-blindness, and this is an area that educators can and must address. The world of these individuals is restricted. It is the educator's role to expand their "world view" and connect them with other people and with their environments (Haring & Romer, 1995). Casey Cook, a deaf-blind triathlete, illustrates the connection these individuals can make (Boeck, 1998). Cook, winner of an Arete Award for Courage in Sports, has Voigte-Carnegie syndrome, which resulted in blindness and severe hearing impairments. Despite his disabilities, he races with training partners and says of himself, "I'm a regular guy. . . . I have a few physical quirks. I'm mystified why others see what I do as a big deal" (p. C3). See *Tips for Effective Teaching* for suggestions about including students with severe disabilities, and reducing their feelings of isolation, through everyone becoming more "disability sensitive."

Communication

Possibly the greatest challenge facing individuals with deaf-blindness is learning to communicate (Stremel et al., 2002). Some never learn to talk. Children with this condition are dependent on others to make language accessible to them and help them join the many adults with this disability who have achieved some level of independence. For many of these individuals, the way they approach their world is through touch (Chen, Downing, & Rodriguez-Gil, 2000–2001; Miles, 2005). Thus various forms of manual communication (e.g., sign language, body language, gestures) are their primary means to express their needs and also to learn and grow. Some of these students learn a different kind of sign language to communicate with others. **Hand over hand** is a tactile form of sign language where the signs are conveyed through touch. In this system, fingers placed in the other person's palm form the means of interaction.

hand over hand Sign language for individuals with deaf-blindness wherein signs are conveyed through touch

Mobility

Movement is important to all of us. We move to exercise, play, get from one location to another for so many purposes, and communicate our emotions. Moving freely in our environments is a natural human behavior, but for those who have significant visual losses, movement is often restricted and can even be dangerous. The components of purposeful movement—becoming aware of one's environment, changing locations, seeking protection from danger, deciding when to move—must become instructional targets for many students (Barnes & Whinnery, 2002; Whinnery & Barnes, 2002). The activities used to teach mobility skills should

- Be functional
- Be age-appropriate
- Increase independence
- Improve access to the community
- Reduce dependence and custodial care
- Promote communication, social interactions, and daily living skills

What should be clear from this discussion is that the significance of deaf-blindness and its associated problems is great. The impact on the individuals affected is substantial. The work and effort to overcome these challenges is considerable and involves teams of dedicated people, including the individuals themselves, their families, educators, and experts from many disciplines. But when services all come together to meet the specific needs of each individual student, the results are amazing!

Prevalence

According to the National Deaf-Blind Census, some 9,853 students—ages 6 to 21—were identified as having deaf-blindness and as being in special education programs during the 2003–2004 school year (DB-Link, 2005). However, for that same year, the federal government reports that only 1,667 students were included in this category across the entire nation (U.S. Department of Education, 2005a). Why might such a large discrepancy exist? The answer is that the federal government insists that states report students' disabilities in only one area, and many deaf-blind students are reported in other categories because they have so many additional problems. Many students are reported in the multiple disabilities category, some in the mental retardation category, and so on. In fact, more students with both hearing and vision problems are included in the multiple disabilities category than in the deaf-blind category. Whether we should be concerned about which category a student is counted in is questionable. What is important to understand is that relatively few students have these problems. When they do, their condition is often very serious. But with intensive services and supports, these students make remarkable progress.

Causes and Prevention

Causes associated with prematurity or with heredity are the most common known reasons for deaf-blindness (DB-Link, 2005). The role of heredity is becoming more clearly understood. In 1994, only 18 different hereditary syndromes had been associated with this disability (Heller & Kennedy, 1994). Today, almost 60 genetic causes of deaf-blindness have been identified (DB-Link, 2005).

Here's an example of one genetic reason for deaf-blindness. Usher syndrome is a hereditary cause of congenital deafness and progressive blindness, along with mental retardation. In addition to these three disabilities, many individuals with

Usher syndrome have problems with walking, balance, and other motor activities (National Institute on Deafness and Communication Disorders [NIDCD], 2003). This recessive, X-linked genetic syndrome is rare, affecting 3 out of every 100,000 people. However, its prevalence varies by locale. For example, in Louisiana some 15 to 20 percent of students with deaf-blindness have Usher syndrome, and 30 percent of all deaf individuals in three parishes (counties) have the syndrome (Melancon, 2000). By comparison, nationally only 3 percent of students with deaf-blindness have Usher syndrome. Why the concentration of Usher syndrome in Louisiana? Remember the story of the Deaf on Martha's Vineyard who came to America from Kent, England, carrying a gene for congenital deafness? The Cajuns have a similar story. When they came to Louisiana from Nova Scotia, they brought with them the gene responsible for the Usher syndrome. Because Cajun communities are small and tight-knit, the prevalence is higher in this part of the United States. This knowledge makes it possible to prevent some cases.

Deaf-blindness is associated with other conditions besides Usher syndrome (Miles, 2005). Prematurity is a common known cause; risk factors, such as poverty and limited access to health care, are now well understood. These risk factors can be reduced or eliminated with systematic national prevention programs (CDF, 2004).

Traumatic Brain Injury (TBI)

About one million children annually experience a head injury, and more than 30,000 of those injuries result in life-long disabilities (NICHCY, 2004b). Prior to the 1960s, most children whose brains were seriously damaged died soon after the trauma. Changes in emergency treatment, imaging technology, and surgical and pharmaceutical treatments now routinely save children's lives. After the medical emergencies are over, however, it often takes intensive special education services and accommodations for the problems resulting from the accident to be resolved. The Council for Exceptional Children (CEC) believes that every teacher, at some time during his or her career, will work with a student with TBI (Van Kuren, 2001).

Just as they are today, many students with TBI were educated in general education classes, receiving the same instructional strategies as their peers with learning disabilities. Like their classmates with learning disabilities, these students often exhibit memory deficits, attention problems, language impairments, and reduced academic performance. Many benefit from instructional procedures proved effective with students with learning disabilities: direct instruction, structured school days, and organized classes where expectations are clearly specified. Others, because of their head injuries, experience seizures and receive many of the same accommodations as students with epilepsy. Although specific programs for students with TBI are emerging across the nation (the Weld County TBI Task Force outside of Greeley, Colorado; the Rehabilitation Center in Austin, Texas; the Wisconsin Department of Public Instruction), most are served within existing programs for students with other disabilities.

Traumatic Brain Injury (TBI) Defined

In 1990 Congress added TBI to the list of special education categories. The IDEA '04 definition can be found in Table 13.1 on page 463. Like other disabilities, TBI ranges in severity from mild to severe (National Institute of Neurological Disorders and Stroke [NINDS], 2005). Table 13.2 lists some characteristics that are associated with TBI and some that are not. Brain injury often results in these symptoms: dizziness, headache, selective attention problems, irritability, anxiety, blurred vision, insomnia, fatigue, motor difficulties, language problems, behavior problems, or cognitive and memory problems (NICHCY, 2004b). These problems can last for a very short time

Table 13.2 • Some Features That Suggest TBI and Some That Rule It Out

Characteristically Associated with TBI	Not Characteristically Associated with TBI
Concussion, head injury	Present at birth
Shaken baby syndrome (child/infant abuse)	Internally caused brain damage (e.g., stroke, brain tumor)
Not always apparent or visible, even with brain imaging techniques	Head injury not resulting in documented change in educational performance
May or may not cause loss of consciousness	

or for years. In many cases the effects eventually disappear, but some cases of TBI result in lifelong problems. Youngsters with moderate to severe injuries often experience dramatic changes in their cognitive, language, motor, sensory, and behavioral performances (Michaud et al., 2002). Some of these students are typical learners one day, but then, after their injury, have significant disabilities. In these cases, it is also common for the individual to experience depression or withdrawal.

Characteristics

Students with TBI and their families face great emotional turmoil during the time shortly after the injury. They must adjust to changes in ability, performance, and behavior (NICHCY, 2004b). Even those with mild cases of TBI must cope with sudden changes in performance and with many (though not necessarily all) of the characteristics shown in Table 13.3. What came easily before is now filled with frustration and confusion. Attempting tasks once easy to perform may lead to repeated failure. Many youngsters with TBI tend to have uneven abilities, a fact that is confusing to the individuals and to their teachers. These students also often experience reduced stamina, seizures, headaches, hearing losses, and vision problems (Van Kuren, 2001). They get tired easily, so some receive home instruction, often for a year, before returning to school part-time. Many of these youngsters have difficulty adjusting to and accepting their newly acquired disability. Because of the frustrations of having difficulty doing tasks that used to be easy, many display behavior problems and reduced self-esteem.

Table 13.3 • Frequent Characteristics of TBI

Physical	Cognitive	Social/Emotional	Educational
Headaches	Short-term memory problems	Mood swings	Difficulty with multistep tasks
Fatigue	Long-term memory problems	Anxiety	Requires consistent schedule and routine
Muscle contractions	Attention deficits	Depression	Needs distractions reduced
Imbalance	Disorganized	Restlessness	Requires shortened assignments
Paralysis	Nonsequential thinking	Not motivated	Must have lots of opportunities for practice of new skills

Source: Adapted from *Traumatic Brain Injury* (pp. 3–6), NICHCY, 2004b, Washington, DC: National Dissemination Center for Children with Disabilities.

Prevalence

More than 100,000 children sustain brain injuries each year, and 30,000 of them have permanent disabilities (Lash & DePompie, 2002). Most of these disabilities are mild. According to the federal government, 22,509 students, ages 6 through 21, were served by special education in the 2003–2004 school year as having TBI (U.S. Department of Education, 2005a). These students represent a percentage of all students so small that it registers at 0.00 percent.

Causes and Prevention

The most common cause of TBI is car accidents, but bicycle accidents, sports accidents, and falls on the playground are also major causes of TBI (Lash & DePompie, 2002). These injuries typically occur among older children, particularly teenage boys, who are careless in the street; do not take safety precautions while bicycling, skiing, or skateboarding; engage in high-risk behaviors such as driving too fast or mixing alcohol or drugs with driving; and participate in contact sports. Less straightforward to address is the sad fact that for many young children, a very common cause of TBI is child abuse (Michaud et al., 2002). Many accidents can be prevented through commonsense measures. For example, wearing helmets when bicycling or skateboarding, not driving a car or motorcycle when using intoxicating substances, and avoiding high-risk behaviors can prevent tragic accidents.

It is obvious that appropriate medical treatment and rehabilitation are critical to preventing the devastating outcomes seen in untreated individuals. Education is also a powerful tool. To ensure responsive educational services, some states have developed interagency initiatives so that children hospitalized with TBI can be transitioned to schools in a seamless fashion (Markowitz & Linehan, 2001).

Educational Considerations for Students with Low Incidence Disabilities

You have just learned about three very low incidence disabilities. You should now understand that although they are considered separate disabilities by IDEA '04, they share many common characteristics. Many of these students have complex coexisting conditions that result in the need for exceptional and unique educational responses. Thus, although there is no single answer to how best to educate these students, we come back to the pattern established in the other chapters in this book about special education categories. But we have organized discussions for these three disabilities around issues related to these students' evaluation, education, postschool experiences, collaborative efforts, and families. Let's first turn our attention to assessment and evaluation.

Assessment

The path toward identification as having a disability is often different for those with low incidence disabilities than for those with high incidence disabilities. In many cases, these individuals are identified when they are infants or toddlers because their delays in development are obvious at birth or their disabilities are quickly identified during early childhood. Thus unless the onset of the disability occurs later—as with students who incur a head injury sometime after birth—most of these individuals are identified before they reach kindergarten or first grade. Also, for many of them the accountability systems that are used to test the effectiveness of their educational programs are different from those used for their peers with high incidence disabilities. Let's first think about early identification.

After automobile accidents, bicycle accidents are the most common cause of brain injuries. The seriousness of most of these injuries could be limited with the use of proper protection, such as helmets.

Early Identification

Because of infant identification measures such as universal hearing screening, and because of better understanding by the medical profession about issues like the long-term impact of low birth weight, babies with severe disabilities are identified earlier than ever before. The number of children and families receiving special services increased from 128,000 in 1988 to almost 270,000 in 2003 (U.S. Department of Education, 2000; 2005a). The reasons for these early and increased participation rates are the quick response of the medical and social services communities and the widespread awareness of well-documented signals for long-term serious developmental disabilities.

As you have learned throughout this book, early intervention makes a real difference in the long-term outcomes of individuals with disabilities (for example, Schweinhart, 2005; Strain & Timm, 1998). More of these children than ever are now identified early, and more families are receiving services to assist them as they learn how to interact in special ways with their baby with severe disabilities. It is these families that benefit from individualized family service plans (IFSPs) and from the services of many different professionals so that secondary disabilities and problems can be prevented or reduced in severity (McDonnell, Hardman, & McDonnell, 2003). This situation presents many opportunities for early and intensive intervention with the child and with the child's family. Unfortunately, however, the lack of highly trained personnel to work with the challenges presented by babies with multiple-severe disabilities and deaf-blindness is a barrier to systematic intervention efforts (Chen, Alsop, & Minor, 2000). If more college students select special education and its related services as a career, this challenge can be met and individuals with disabilities and their families will have the opportunities for success that they deserve.

Pre-Referral

We have noted that most students with severe disabilities are identified long before their school years. However, for many students with TBI this is not the case. And medical professionals are often slow to determine which of these youngsters have long-term problems. Even when accidents are serious, injury to the brain may go unnoticed at first. Too often, families bring their children home from the hospital not knowing that long after the broken bones are mended, the head injury could result in long-term disabilities (NINDS, 2005). Most families are unaware of the signs associated with TBI, and medical staff at the hospital may not have informed parents that their children might have long-term cognitive effects from their injuries. Sometimes it is educators who must confirm families' worst (and often unspoken) fears: "The bicycle accident several weeks ago caused more than a broken leg; it may have also caused brain injury. You better take Justin to the doctor again."

Alert teachers are the first to suspect that injuries may go far beyond broken bones or obvious bruises. They see many different characteristics that signal possible brain injury. Many of those were listed on Table 13.3 on page 471. However, before teachers actually suggest to families that their son or daughter may have additional problems, they should take responsible actions. They may seek advice from the district's school nurse. They might consult with the principal and other school officials. And most important, they need to document the student's classroom performance, comparing academic and social behaviors before and after the incident that might have resulted in brain injury. Teachers sensitive to changes in their students' performance make a genuine long-term difference because they not only bring problems more quickly to the attention of those who can help but also provide evidence that saves valuable time during the diagnostic process.

Identification

The ways in which students with multiple and coexisting disabilities are identified are as unique as the individuals themselves. Many of them are identified at birth. Doctors and hospitals' nursing staffs know well the signs that alert them to disabilities in newborns and the signals of the risk of disabilities. Also, universal screening procedures bring babies with hearing and vision problems to the attention of service providers during the critical months after birth. And for those not identified with disabilities during the first six weeks of life, alert pediatricians usually identify infants and toddlers who are not developing in typical ways. It is a very rare case for a student with multiple-severe disabilities to be first diagnosed with problems during the elementary school years. The main exceptions, of course, are those individuals whose age of onset is after their entrance to kindergarten.

The situation for students with TBI is different, but the ways in which individuals with TBI are identified will probably surprise you. As you might expect, medical professionals typically identify children with TBI. What is surprising, however, is the lateness of most diagnoses. Many children with TBI are not identified immediately after their injuries. This happens because many of these youngsters show no visible signs (cuts, bruises) of brain injury (NICHCY, 2004b). The impact of what has sometimes been called the silent epidemic may go misunderstood for months. How can this be? Think about Ryan, who was not wearing a helmet, despite his mother's warnings, and fell while skateboarding. Because he did not want to tell his mother that he was not wearing his helmet, he also did not tell her about the accident. Instead, he told his mom that he was tired and went off to his room to take a nap.

Evaluation: Alternate Assessments–The "1-Percent Kids"

As you have learned this academic term, IDEA '04 and the No Child Left Behind Act require that *all* students—those with and without disabilities—be included in the national accountability system. Not all of these students, however, need to take the standard state- or district-wide tests. The U.S. Department of Education provides guidance about alternate assessments and how they are to be implemented (Briggs, 2005; U.S. Department of Education, 2005b). The government allows each state to use **alternate assessments**—another form of testing and evaluation of learning gains for students with the most significant cognitive disabilities. Such students are given these alternate assessments on **alternate achievement standards**, which are the achievement expectations of those participating in the general education curriculum but with fewer objectives or different expectations. These assessments *must reflect* the general education curriculum (e.g., reading, math, science).

alternate assessments Means of measuring the progress of students who do not participate in the general education curriculum

alternative achievement standards Content standards applied to students with low incidence disabilities participating in the general education curriculum, but with fewer objectives or somewhat different expectations may apply

The students who participate in alternate assessments are those with very low incidence disabilities (Browder et al., 2004). They are students with multiple-severe disabilities, those who are deaf-blind, many with TBI, and a considerable number of students with mental retardation. Typically, students who use alternate assessments to document their progress are participating in alternative curricula. Therefore, their tests reflect academic skills and might also reflect functional skills that are targets of instruction and specified on the student's IEP.

How many students may participate in alternate assessments? The government allows states to get credit for proficient scores from alternate assessments in their overall reporting, as long as the number included "does not exceed 1.0 percent of *all* students in the grades assessed (about 9 percent of students with disabilities)" (Briggs, 2005, p. 28). *What IDEA '04 Says About Alternate Assessments and the "1-Percent Kids"* provides more information about these different assessment procedures. Let's first review what standardized tests with accommodations imply. Then we'll take a closer look at alternate assessments and new interpretations of what they mean and how they are to be implemented.

Most students with disabilities participate in state- and district-wide assessments by taking what are referred to as "high stakes tests" with *accommodations*. These measures are to ensure that all students receive high-quality instruction and profit from their education (Ziegler, 2002). As you'll recall from your reading of Chapter 2 and other assessment sections in this book, testing accommodations must be called out in the student's IEP, are typically those used by the student in the classroom, and may include a wide range of aids. There is great variability across states and districts about what accommodations can be made available (National Research Council, 2004; Thurlow et al., 2000). Adjustments to students' performance evaluations or testing routines might include breaks, a test scheduled at a different time, or extended time. Accommodations might reflect changes in the materials used for the test, such as enlarged-print or braille versions of the test. The presentation of the test's items may vary from that used for students without disabilities; for example, someone may read the questions to the student. Also, students may provide their answers by using a different format than everyone else: for example, they may not have to use the machine-score answer sheet.

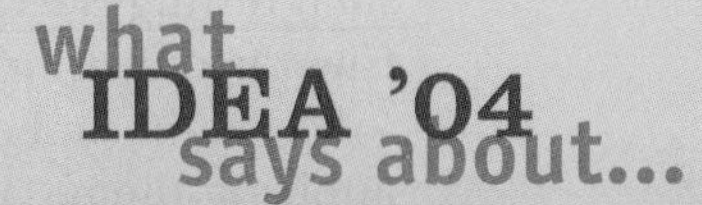

Alternate Assessments and the "1-Percent Kids"

Students with disabilities are to be included in general state- and district-wide assessments, with appropriate accommodations and modifications as necessary. Some students with disabilities who cannot participate in regular assessments may take alternate assessments. States are permitted to assess up to 1 percent of students against alternate achievement standards with alternate assessments.

IDEA stipulates that these alternate assessments must

- Be aligned with the state's challenging academic content and student achievement standards
- Measure student achievement against any alternate academic achievement standards that the state has developed

If an IEP team determines that a student should take an alternate assessment, the IEP must include

- A statement of why the child cannot participate in the regular assessment
- An explanation of why the selected alternate assessment is appropriate for the student
- A description of benchmarks, or short-term objectives, that are aligned with alternate achievement standards

Although they must reflect grade-level achievement standards, *alternate assessments* are different from accommodations (Briggs, 2005). Designed for students who can't participate in the standard grade-level assessment, they might differ in these ways

- *Format:* portfolios or different versions of achievement tests
- *Narrower range of topics or fewer objectives:* different set of expectations
- *Less complex questions:* stated more simply

These alternate assessments, however, *must* reflect grade-level achievement standards and evaluate students' progress across the elementary and high school years in reading/language arts and mathematics. By the 2007–2008 school year, these tests must also include science.

Needless to say, considerable debate and confusion surround these new requirements (*Education Weekly, 2004, January 8*). Most teachers are convinced that schools should be accountable for the progress of students with disabilities, but about 80 percent feel that no student with a disability should be held to the same standards as their general education classmates. Some 85 percent of teachers believe that special education students' scores should not be included in states' reports to the federal government. Students who fall into and slightly above the 1 percent group also have expressed concerns about participating in these assessments, even alternate versions (Johnson, 2005). They indicate that such testing is extremely stressful to them, too difficult, and a waste of their time. Clearly, only time will tell whether these standards and assessment requirements will remain or be modified as educators better understand the implications of applying them.

Early Intervention

The benefits of high-quality education for all of us cannot be overestimated. For students with low incidence disabilities, high-quality early intervention and preschool education can determine critical outcomes: the number and intensity of supports they will need as adults, their attainment of independence, their level of community presence, and their quality of life (Rafferty, Piscitelli, & Boettcher, 2003). Sometimes, families with great resources—either financial or personal—decide that they need only minimal support from early intervention teams. You will learn of one such example in *Considering Culture.* Parents and, often, extended family members are at the heart of early intervention services, making a difference in the lives of their children. This is true whether they take advantage of publicly available services or not. What is important is that infants and toddlers with extensive needs because of their disabilities receive extra help learning, growing, and getting prepared for life and their school years.

The first real difference is that more children with low incidence disabilities receive federally funded services for early intervention than any other students with special needs (U.S. Department of Education, 2000). Unlike the vast majority of students with special needs, such as those with learning disabilities, children with low incidence disabilities are identified during their first years of life. Some 20 percent of all children who receive early childhood special education programs began their school careers by the age of 6 months.

Also, more than ever before, young children with severe disabilities participate in organized preschool programs. Many of these classes are fully inclusive programs where preschoolers with and without disabilities learn and grown together (McWilliams, Wolery, & Odom, 2001). The benefits of such inclusive early intervention programs to individuals with severe disabilities are great in terms of motor development, language skills, social interaction abilities, and academics. The long-term benefits in the lives of these children and their families are inestimable.

Teaching Students with Low Incidence Disabilities

Students with very low incidence disabilities present unique sets of complex profiles to their families and their teachers. Despite being assigned to a category, each student should be considered a unique member of a diverse group of learners, all of whom exhibit different learning styles and characteristics. Accordingly, instructional programs must be designed on an individual basis to meet each student's needs. However, despite their diversity, these children often share many common goals and desired outcomes.

Access to the General Education Curriculum

Many students with very low incidence disabilities do not have access to the general education curriculum as their primary objective. Although these students may participate in general education classes, which many of them do for some period during the school day, they are typically striving to meet other curriculum targets (such as independent living). Of this group, students with TBI have the highest participa-

Considering Culture

The Family as the Mainstream

Pablo is 10 months old. He has significant disabilities that have interfered with his cognitive, motor, and physical development. When he was 5 months old, he and his family began participating in an early intervention program that included home visits, group interaction, and special services from therapists. Recently, his mother has canceled the majority of home visits and has not participated in the group program with Pablo. The program staff is concerned, and the service coordinator telephoned Mrs. Alvarado to talk with her about these changes.

In their conversation, Mrs. Alvarado said that she, her husband, and their parents had talked about the program and decided that it was no longer necessary. She said, "We know that Pablo will never be like other children, and we don't think that school is important for him. We have a large family. They all love Pablo and will always take care of him." The service coordinator listened and then talked about how important it was for Pablo to have the services that the program provided. She talked about the importance of his being with other children and the importance of other families for Mrs. Alvarado. Mrs. Alvarado was polite but firm. She said that their lives were full of medical appointments for Pablo, soccer for the older children, church, and family gatherings.

The service coordinator was stunned. She couldn't imagine that anyone would refuse services. Soon after she finished talking with Mrs. Alvarado, she called Carmelita, Pablo's home visitor. When she described the conversation, Carmelita was not surprised. She said, "The Alvarado family is large and very close. They have raised many children, and Pablo's mother is probably right. They don't need any more appointments than they already have. He is not the only child in the family, and they are very caring parents who will ask for help if they need it." She said that she would call Mrs. Alvarado to tell her how much she had enjoyed working with Pablo and meeting the family.

When Carmelita called Mrs. Alvarado, she explained that she would miss Pablo and the rest of the family but that she understood how the needs of the entire family had to come first. She then asked Mrs. Alvarado if she could stay in touch by phone "just to check in on Pablito." Mrs. Alvarado was happy not to lose touch, and Carmelita continues to provide telephone support and keep the lines of communication open between the program and the Alvarado family.

Questions to Consider

1. Although IDEA '04 mandates that states and U.S. territories provide early intervention programs and services for infants and toddlers with disabilities (ages birth to three), parents have the right to refuse services. Why do you think that this right is part of the law?
2. How do you think you would feel if a parent said that your services were not needed?

—By Eleanor Lynch, San Diego State University and Marci Hanson, San Francisco State University

tion rate in general education (U.S. Department of Education, 2005a). Of those between the ages of 6 and 11, about 38 percent attend general education classes for more than 79 percent of the school day. Students with multiple disabilities, however, have a much lower participation rate. Only about 12 percent of them learn alongside students without disabilities for more than 79 percent of the school day, and almost 70 percent of them receive less than 40 percent of their education in general education settings. These rates are even lower for students who are deaf-blind.

Although integration is clearly important and is necessary for these students to achieve adult independence, concerns about fully inclusive programs across all of the school years are emerging (Palmer et al., 2001). Some experts maintain that effective education often requires specially trained teachers who implement carefully designed instructional programs. Many techniques that have proved effective through research—such as community based instruction to learn functional skills needed for adult life—are not compatible with the instruction provided to typical learners. For example, structured class schedules, use of concrete examples, controlled teacher language, reduction or elimination of distractions, instruction in different natural settings, and rigorously applied behavioral tactics often prove effective and necessary. But students who participate in such a program have restricted assess to the general education curriculum. Although general education placements might not be appropriate at every point in these learners' educational careers, it is a serious decision to change placements or services. Multidisciplinary teams must evaluate a student's progress continually to balance the drawbacks and benefits of every educational option available. They must also work together to see that the necessary accommodations are in place to ensure successful outcomes in general education settings.

Instructional Accommodations

As you have learned throughout this book, each student with a disability requires different forms of assistance, accommodations, or modifications to the instructional program to achieve maximally. Such is very much the case with students who have very low incidence disabilities.

For many of these students, accommodations are almost a matter of common sense. For example, with some simple adjustments to and modifications in the classroom routine, students with TBI are reintegrated easily into classroom situations. If students spend only half a day at school, the teacher can schedule instruction on important academic tasks during the morning, when they are alert. Homework assignments can be abbreviated to accommodate their reduced stamina. If some students find that their balance, coordination, and ability to carry materials are more limited than before the accident, the teacher can provide another set of textbooks for home use to make life easier for them and their families. Because many of these students get confused easily, teachers should clearly specify and consistently apply classroom rules and expectations. It is also helpful to use instructional tactics that incorporate a considerable amount of drill and practice to help students remember what is being taught.

Other students, particularly those with developmental disabilities or with coexisting intellectual disabilities, require more intensive supports to participate in the general education curriculum and classroom successfully. Some of these students receive assistance from paraprofessionals (classroom aides) who provide extra instructional assistance or support behavioral intervention programs. Most often, paraprofessionals support the classroom teacher with all the students with disabilities in the class. However, in cases of the most challenging disabilities, a paraprofessional may be assigned full-time to only one student.

Validated Practices

In this section, we discuss two important practices used with students with low incidence disabilities. The first instructional practice, semantic feature analysis, helps students increase their vocabulary and enhance their ability to categorize objects. The second procedure, functional behavioral assessments, should now be familiar to you. We discussed this technique in previous chapters (see those sections in Chapters 2 and 7), but because of its value and importance we will expand on those discussions here.

Learning Organizers

Most students with severe disabilities, including TBI, need to develop functional vocabulary skills. They must not only know the words for things they need but also be able to associate objects along multiple dimensions. However, to enhance such thinking skills can take considerable effort, because these students tend not to be organized, have difficulty focusing on one task for any length of time, and often need concrete representations or structured ways to visualize information. Students with TBI tend to have learning styles similar to students with learning disabilities.

These students profit from techniques such as graphic organizers or story maps, discussed in the *Validated Practices* features of Chapters 6 and 9. Students with multiple-severe disabilities also profit from tactics that help structure learning. The technique, semantic feature analysis, described in this chapter's *Validated Practices* benefits students who need to expand their vocabulary, practice associating, and learn to connect characteristics along various dimensions. This validated practice helps students who need structure to help them organize learning.

Functional Behavioral Assessments (FBA)

FBA is a very important technique: It is required by IDEA '04, and it is a wonderful tool that helps teachers design appropriate programs for students with disabilities. This system was originally developed for students with severe disabilities, yet it is now used in the design of behavioral support for students with a full range of disabilities and types of problem behaviors (Scott et al., 2003).

Rob Horner and George Sugai have spent considerable time and energy refining the procedures employed in conducting FBAs, and they are now used nationwide (Sugai & Horner, 1999). These assessments are part of a larger system referred to as positive behavioral supports. According to Rob Horner and George Sugai (Smith, 2001), FBA is a process as well as a set of procedures designed to identify events that trigger and maintain problem behaviors. FBA is based on an extensive body of research that has demonstrated that behavior support is more likely to be effective when it is based on information derived from functional assessment that follows these basic steps

1. Operationally define the target behavior.
2. Develop a clear, observable statement of the conditions (routines and events) that set the occasion for the target behavior.
3. Identify and describe precisely the consequences that maintain the target behavior (gaining others' attention; escaping aversive situations; getting access to desirable situations, social status, or privileges).
4. Collect data to ensure that the target behavior is accurately identified, the conditions that cause the behavior's occurrence are well described, and the circumstances that maintain the behavior are correctly determined.

This method helps parents and educators better understand the relationship between what happens in the student's environment and how the student behaves (Sugai et al., 1999). One result is a list of target behaviors that require intervention (Condon & Tobin, 2001). Another result is a better idea about interventions that might be successful in improving the behavior of concern. Functional behavioral assessments also reveal what causes inappropriate or undesirable behavior to occur and why such behaviors continue. Educators often find that some unproductive behaviors occur for purposes of escape, attention, or communication. For example, for children who do not know how to ask for help, a tantrum may be a means of escaping schoolwork that is too difficult or frustrating. When such is the case, educators have found that teaching a student to engage in functionally equivalent behaviors (e.g., "Is this right?" "I need help") often replaces the disruptive behavior (Koegel et al., 1995). Thus functionally equivalent behaviors are useful skills for these students to learn.

How does functional behavioral assessment work? Functional behavioral assessments should be conducted anytime a student with a disability presents significant problem behavior that might affect eligibility, placement, or disciplinary actions and/or might represent a significant barrier to the student's education. General educators, special education teachers, and all people concerned about the student's performance should participate in the assessment (Kennedy et al., 2001). They should form a team and work together to understand how the student's behavior might be interfering with efficient learning. Simple steps to follow when

Validated Practices Semantic Feature Analysis

What Is Semantic Feature Analysis?

Semantic feature analysis (SFA) is a strategy used to increase a student's vocabulary. SFA links a student's prior knowledge with new information by showing the relationships among words from a specific topic. Students are required to complete a matrix (see Figure A) and to discuss associations among words in a category.

Why Semantic Feature Analysis Is Beneficial

Adults use about 10,000 words in their everyday conversations. Students understand and comprehend between 20,000 and 24,000 words by age 6 and more than 50,000 words by age 12 (Owens, 2001). Difficulties in content area classes (e.g., science, social studies) are common among students with a low vocabulary base. By using words and features familiar to most students, SFA helps youngsters build their vocabulary by considering how words and objects are related to each other. Discussion is essential to SFA. It increases students' participation, thus increasing their expressive language skills.

Implementing Semantic Feature Analysis

Students may have difficulty understanding the concept of SFA at first. It is important for you to model the process several times before students work independently. First, use categories familiar to the students. As students become accustomed to the strategy, more abstract categories can be added. The following seven-step process is recommended for developing and implementing SFAs.

1 *Select a Category*

- Select a familiar category.

2 *List Words*

- Down the left side of the grid, list three or four familiar words or objects related to the category.

3 *List and Add Features*

- List three or four features in a row across the top of the grid.
- Discuss features with your students, encouraging them to add more to the grid.

4 *Determine Possession*

- Guide your students through the matrix, having them determine whether each word on the left side possesses the features listed across the top.
- Students place a plus sign in the box if the word possesses the feature, a minus sign if the word does not.
- Students place a question mark in the boxes if they are unsure of the relationship.

5 *Add More Words and Features*

- Students provide additional words that fit the category.
- Students provide additional features.

6 *Complete the Grid*

- Students complete the grid by adding plus signs, minus signs, or question marks for the new words and features.

7 *Discuss the Grid*

- Students examine the grid and discuss the relationships among the words.
- You should facilitate the discussion only if the students do not recognize the relationships.

Figure A shows one SFA for use with young students. Looking at the grid, students quickly realize which vehicles have only two wheels and which vehicles can hold passengers.

Figure A

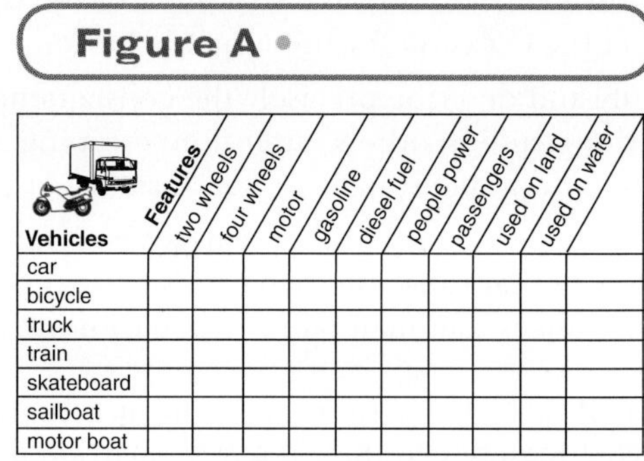

Vehicles / Features	two wheels	four wheels	motor	gasoline	diesel fuel	people power	passengers	used on land	used on water	
car										
bicycle										
truck										
train										
skateboard										
sailboat										
motor boat										

This scientifically validated practice is a teaching method proven by systematic research efforts (Bos & Anders, 1992: Owens, 2001; Pittelman et al., 1991). Full citations are found in the references for this chapter.

Source: From *Semantic Feature Analysis: Classroom Application* (p. 10) by S. D. Pittelman, J. E. Heimlich, R. L. Berglund, and M. P. French, 1991, Newark, DE: International Reading Association. Reprinted with permission.

—By Kimberly Paulsen, Vanderbilt University

for Classroom Management

TEAM-BASED FUNCTIONAL BEHAVIORAL ASSESSMENTS

Tasks	*Considerations*
Develop a team	• Represent persons who have interactions with student • Invite parents • Involve student as appropriate • At least one person on team is familiar with FBA
Define problem behavior	• All team members collaborate to define problem • Create observable and measurable definition • Define the contexts under which behavior occurs
Share data and observations	• Summarize existing data (referrals, reports, etc.) • Team members discuss their interactions with student • Discuss appropriate and inappropriate behaviors
Analyze patterns	• Consider how the environment predicts behavior • Identify predictable antecedents and consequences • Analyze both appropriate and inappropriate behavior
Hypothesize function	• Create a testable statement of behavior's function • Define when the behavior is likely to occur • Define how consequences maintain the behavior

Source: From Ensuring student success through team-based functional behavioral assessment by T. M. Scott, C. J. Liaupsin, C. M. Nelson, and K. Jolivette, 2003, *Teaching Exceptional Children, 35,* p. 17. Arlington, VA: Council for Exceptional Children. Used with permission.

conducting functional assessments are listed in *Tips for Classroom Management.* The resulting information reveals how environments should be modified so that students are successful, because that very success promotes durable reductions in problem behaviors.

Technology

The increased availability of technology in school settings and the increasing understanding of how technology can support standard instruction benefit students with disabilities, particularly those with severe problems (Buckley, 1999–2000). The federal government has made a considerable investment in technology for students with disabilities. It continues with this commitment because technology has improved outcomes for students with disabilities (OSEP, 2000). The data on which the federal government bases this conclusion indicate that technology helps these individuals

- Communicate more effectively
- Increase their levels of independence
- Control their environments
- Have greater mobility
- Gain access to information

Sound output, screen enlargements, and such assistive devices as switches, sticks, and mouse adaptations all make it easier for students with disabilities to participate in standard instruction in general education classes. Of course, one ultimate goal for technology is for it to address and compensate for disabilities, and that hope is becoming a reality (Reichle, Beukelman, & Light, 2002). Technology has opened up avenues of communication for many students who are unable to communicate with others through oral speech (Byrant & Bryant, 2003). Advances in **augmentative and alternative communication devices (AAC)**, which we also discussed in the Technology section of Chapter 4, allow for communication and participation not possible until recently (Kangas & Lloyd, 2006; Noonan & Siegel, 2003). Whether in the form of simple devices, such as communication boards, or complicated speech synthesizers that actually speak for the individual, technology now enables individuals to make their needs known, express their feelings, and interact with others (McCormick & Wegner, 2003). Like so many others, Rick Hoyt—whom you met near the beginning of this chapter—would be unable to exchange his thoughts with others if it were not for the AAC system he uses to talk through a computer. In the most straightforward systems, words and/or pictures are placed on a flat surface or in books. The student use these *communication boards* to communicate by pointing to the appropriate symbols or pictures. Symbols are customized to the individual; the words or symbols on the board reflect the specific salient features of the environments in which he or she operates. Some boards are simple homemade projects; others use quite sophisticated technology.

Other assistive devices enable students with multiple-severe disabilities to participate in classroom activities in new and important ways. For example, most students raise their hands to get their teachers' attention, to take their turn to participate, or to ask for help. Joey cannot raise his hand, but he has learned to operate a switch that turns on a light instead. He uses another switch to hear a tape-recorded story when classmates are reading silently, and other switches enable him to use a communication device (Bryant & Bryant, 2003). The teacher's job is to encourage and shape these techniques into a reliable system of communication for the student. With reliable communication, learning and social interaction can take place.

Transition

Unlike their peers without disabilities and their peers with mild disabilities, most students with very low incidence disabilities do not leave school at high school graduation. In fact, IDEA '04 provides them with the option of receiving educational services until age 21. School services focus on the transition to adulthood and on preparing for successful independent living. At whatever point they leave school (at the conclusion of high school or at the age of 21), many of these individuals are served and assisted by their state's department of vocational rehabilitation services. After school, many receive services that include supported living arrangements and supported employment. Let's consider two important transitional goals for individuals with low incidence disabilities: achieving a presence in their community and attending college.

Community Presence

One important goal of transition programs for many individuals with severe disabilities is to achieve a community presence, which includes social integration into workplace, residential, and recreational settings (Hughes, 2001; Stuart & Smith, 2002). Being able to hold a meaningful job and live independently is at the core of many education programs during the transitional years. Clearly, being employed, possessing functional life skills, and meeting the requirements of daily life (managing a budget, maintaining a household, cooking, shopping) are important to

augumentative and alternative communication devices (AAC) Such methods for communicating as communication boards, communication books, sign language, and computerized voices what is considered successful adulthood. Knowing how to make choices and advocate for preferences is also important. More programs like the ones developed by Sprout (read the Making a Difference section of this chapter again), need to be available, and people need to be prepared to take advantage of such opportunities, like sharing time with friends, skiing in Colorado, gathering at a local pub, attending a Super Bowl party, or having dinner at a restaurant.

Rick Slaughter, who contributed many photos to this book, is the director of ABLE, a recreational program for youth with disabilities. He also coaches the Music City Wheelchair Basketball Team. Here he is teaching one of "his boys" how to ski at an accessible ski resort in Colorado.

The education of many students with low incidence disabilities includes a unique component: As they get older, many participate less in the general education curriculum and more in **community based instruction (CBI)**—an approach in which instruction on functional skills occurs in real community settings. This strategy was developed because a common characteristic of many individuals with severe disabilities is their inability to *generalize* skills taught in one setting to another setting. Therefore, being able to learn and practice important skills used in adult life in real-life settings is critical to later success in living and working in the community. Some experts believe that many students with multiple-severe disabilities spend as much as 90 percent of their school day learning in community settings (NICHCY, 2001). These students then transition to supported employment with the goals of attaining job placements in competitive work rather than in sheltered employment or day activity centers, where the pay is low and the work is often artificial and menial.

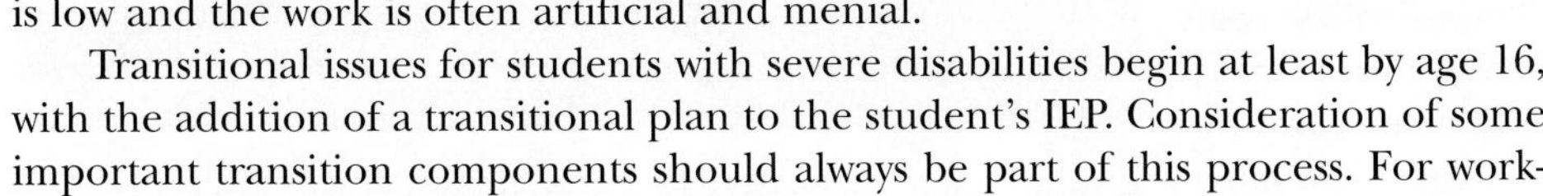

Transitional issues for students with severe disabilities begin at least by age 16, with the addition of a transitional plan to the student's IEP. Consideration of some important transition components should always be part of this process. For work-related goals and objectives, the following topics are part of the conversation (Stuart & Smith, 2002):

- Coordinating sets of activities (e.g., real work experience)
- Moving from school to postschool environments (e.g., school to work)
- Assessing the individual's specific needs
- Determining the individual's preferences and interests
- Developing employment objectives

Everyone performs better in situations where she or he has the skills necessary to succeed—but also when the tasks are of interest. For these reasons, educators are realizing the importance of the individual's preferences and interests in making effective plans for living arrangements and employment opportunities (Lohrmann-O'Rourke & Gomez, 2001; Stuart & Smith, 2002). The importance of promoting individual choice and self-determination (read again the *Validated Practices* section in Chapter 8) as a precursor to community based instruction is widely acknowledged among experts in this field. For example, careers can be developed in many different areas (e.g., landscaping, food services, office or clerical work). Not everyone enjoys each type of opportunity equally. Some of us prefer being indoors; others enjoy quiet settings; some prefer to sit rather than stand for long periods of time. Some of us prefer to live in urban areas; some want a roommate; others prefer a house to an apartment; and some of us desire proximity to churches, convenience stores, bus routes, doctors, and other resources. Decisions about these and many other factors related to success and happiness should be made with full participation of the individual involved. What is now being called "person-centered planning" is just that! It involves the individual with disabilities and the family in decisions about services needed, jobs to be supported, living arrangements, and related preferences (Holburn & Vietze, 2002). This approach is very different from

community based instruction (CBI) Teaching functional skills in the environments in which they occur

Changing Times: A Very Special Place for Very Special People

Not too many years ago the housing options for people with multiple disabilities were restrictive. Most individuals with complicated independent living needs still find themselves with limited choices. Some have to live in large institutions, nursing homes, or smaller group homes. Group homes are often built in marginal areas and sometimes far away from stores, restaurants, and community centers. Few community housing options are designed specifically for individuals who are deaf, blind, or deaf-blind or who face significant physical challenges (Charles, 2005).

Salvatore Monarca Place in Middletown, Connecticut, is different. This new apartment building has 16 one- and two-bedroom units uniquely created for people with very special living needs and supports. The complex, which is built on land donated by the city and cost over $3 million to build, is in a neighborhood where homes cost between $400,000 and $750,000. It is a few blocks from the town's center, close to shops, over 40 restaurants, and new office buildings and businesses. The only restriction is that occupants must earn less than $40,000 per year to rent an apartment in the complex. What a dream come true! Affordable housing that is both desirable in location and built with the needs of people with disabilities in mind. These lucky residents will show everyone how much of a difference carefully planned living arrangements make in the lives of people who want to be independent and have a real community presence.

Salvatore Monarca Place, a 16-unit residential facility designed specifically for individuals with hearing impairment.

the professional telling the person with a disability what he or she needs. Of course, to make choices one must *have* choices, and for many people with disabilities, the options for living arrangements are limited. But as you will see in *Changing Times,* the situation is improving (Charles, 2005).

College Participation

Students with multiple-severe disabilities, those who are deaf-blind, and those with TBI do go to college. It is a grave error to assume that they don't or can't! Think again about Helen Keller, who graduated from Radcliffe, now part of Harvard, at the turn of the last century. Consider Stephen Hawking, whose scientific theories challenge the understanding of most of us. Also, reflect on what the world would be like without their contributions.

For more students with such disabilities to participate in postsecondary education requires an increased number of supports, many of which are becoming more readily available at colleges and universities (HEATH, 2005). For example, interpreters—whether to translate ASL, signed English, finger spelling, or hand-over-hand sign language—are available to assist college students with limited hearing. Braille services and enlarged-print options are also becoming more commonplace, particularly with recent advances in technology. The same is true for notetakers and personal readers. You learned about these accommodations in Chapters 10 and 11. In Chapter 5, you learned how peer tutors can assist those students who may need additional help accessing and organizing difficult content. Regardless of the type of disability, many students profit from accommodations to the testing environment,

intervener Paraprofessional who, under the supervision of a teacher, translates sign language and helps children gain assess to information from the environment such as being allowed additional time, taking alternate forms of tests, or being able to dictate answers to another person. When the supports needed to participate and demonstrate learning mastery are in place, the benefits are enormous.

Collaboration

Multidisciplinary teams that serve students with very low incidence disabilities are composed of a wide range of professionals. Expertise is needed in so many areas that it is impossible for one or even two teachers to provide an appropriate education for these students. Clearly, collaboration among many different teachers (general educators, special education teachers, paraprofessionals, teachers of the visually impaired, teachers of the deaf), as well as multidisciplinary team members representing many different related services (assistive technology specialists, SLPs, OTs, PTs), is necessary.

As the needs of students with low incidence disabilities become better understood, new roles and services are being defined. Here are a few examples. Students who are deaf-blind often need help to access information and have meaningful linkages to the environment (Olson, 2004). Many students who are deaf receive assistance from sign language interpreters, but students who are deaf-blind require somewhat different services. A new professional role is developing. An **intervener** is a paraprofessional who works under the supervision of a teacher (Carnes & Barnard, 2003). These paraprofessionals are trained not only to translate and use sign language but also to provide instruction. An intervener understands the student's visual and auditory needs and helps students with this disability gain access to visual and auditory information, develops the use of receptive and expressive communication, and promotes social and emotional well-being. Interveners intercede and work between a child and the environment, helping the child gain access to information that others gain via vision and hearing. Interveners do more than just translating; they typically work on an individual basis with a student who is deaf-blind. Part of this new professional's role is to facilitate inclusive efforts, so here is one more member of the collaborative team working with general educators to provide FAPE in the LRE. *Accommodating for Inclusive Environments* lists some of the major activities that interveners perform to make participation in the general education classroom and access to the general education curriculum possible for students who are deaf-blind.

Kailyn takes her first independent steps with the help of her physical therapist. Free from her wheelchair or walker, Kailyn can more easily join in games and other activities with her friends. What a difference intensive physical therapy makes!

When so many professionals need to work together, some special communication problems can occur. Coordination of services and careful instructional planning are sometimes hard to accomplish. Effective teams of professionals seem to follow these six steps when addressing their concerns about target students (Snell & Janney, 2000, p. 480):

1. Identify the problem: "Identify your concern."
2. Gather information: "Watch, think, and talk."
3. Generate potential solutions: "Think and throw out ideas."
4. Evaluate potential solutions: "That sounds good" or "That won't work."
5. Implementation: "Give it a shot."
6. Evaluation: "More watch, think, and talk."

* Accommodating for Inclusive Environments

The Role of the Intervener

Interveners facilitate participation of students who are deaf-blind in the general education classroom by

1 Facilitating the access of environmental information usually gained through vision and hearing, but which is unavailable or incomplete to the individual who is deaf-blind

The intervener can

- Present information in ways that match the unique capabilities of the individual with deaf-blindness, so that he or she can detect and interpret it
- Facilitate opportunities for direct learning and the development of concepts that others learn incidentally

2 Facilitating the development and use of receptive and expressive communication skills

The intervener can

- Provide a consistently responsive environment to the individual's reactions and communicative behaviors
- Act as a bridge to facilitate communication with others

3 Developing and maintaining a trusting, interactive relationship, which can promote social and emotional well-being

The intervener can

- Increase and strengthen the individual's positive interactions with others
- Facilitate opportunities for the individual to have control through choice making, problem solving, and decision making

Source: Adapted from Alsop, L., Blaha, R., & Kloos, E. (2000). "The intervener in early intervention and educational settings for children and youth with deafblindness" (Briefing Paper). Monmouth, OR: The National Technical Assistance Consortium for Children and Young Adults Who Are Deaf-Blind. Adapted with permission.

Partnerships with Families and Communities

Particularly since the 1992 AAMR definition of mental retardation was formulated, professionals in the field of special education have been reconceptualizing programs and services for people with disabilities (Luckasson et al., 1992). Expanded in the 2002 AAMR definition, concepts related to supports emphasize the importance of helping individuals with mental retardation and their families become independent and function in the community (Luckasson et al., 2002). The focus is on the type and amount of supports that individuals need to remain in the community, living, working, and playing alongside people without disabilities. The family is one obvious source of natural support for all individuals with disabilities, particularly those with low incidence disabilities. In some cases, support requires more than commitment; it requires a wealth of personal resources and an effective system of supports that assist and sustain families.

Services and programs for individuals with low incidence disabilities must be an integral part of the community (ERIC/Clearinghouse on Disabilities and Gifted Education, 2001). The premise is that sustained family involvement in the lives of those with disabilities increases the probability of their achieving success and independence as adults in the community. For example, instead of living in an institution miles from their home communities, these individuals live in homes, apartments, and neighborhoods like everyone else. In many cases, this cannot occur without considerable support from a variety of sources. To prevent the terrible treatment that has been inflicted on many individuals with disabilities living in institutions far removed from public scrutiny, those who give family support and community support need to be aware of the signs of abuse. To some, not only is the family system the best source of support, but family members have some clear roles to fill (Dell-Orto & Power, 1997). If they choose to accept these roles, they should be considered full members of the individual's multidisciplinary team. They also can be information providers, active participants in assessment and treatment, and advocates. Individuals from the family system can extend treatment programs to all aspects of the individual's life and can assist with generalization. This network of people expresses the hopes and dreams for the achievement of goals for the family member with disabilities.

Despite the normalization movement and the growing systems of family and natural supports, professionals must realize that meeting all the needs of a child with severe disabilities is beyond the resources and capabilities of many families (Bruns, 2000). The daily physical care, medication and pain management, and round-the-clock assistance that some children require, along with financial and logistic difficulties, force some families to seek out-of-home placements for their child, particularly when fragile health compounds the child's multiple disabilities. Professionals must assist families and help to create solid systems of supports, but they must not make value judgments about the difficult decisions that families make about the care of their children. Professionals need to understand that such decisions usually are made because of a "triggering event" (such as illness of the primary caregiver), the demands of other children in the family, and the overwhelming nature of the disability.

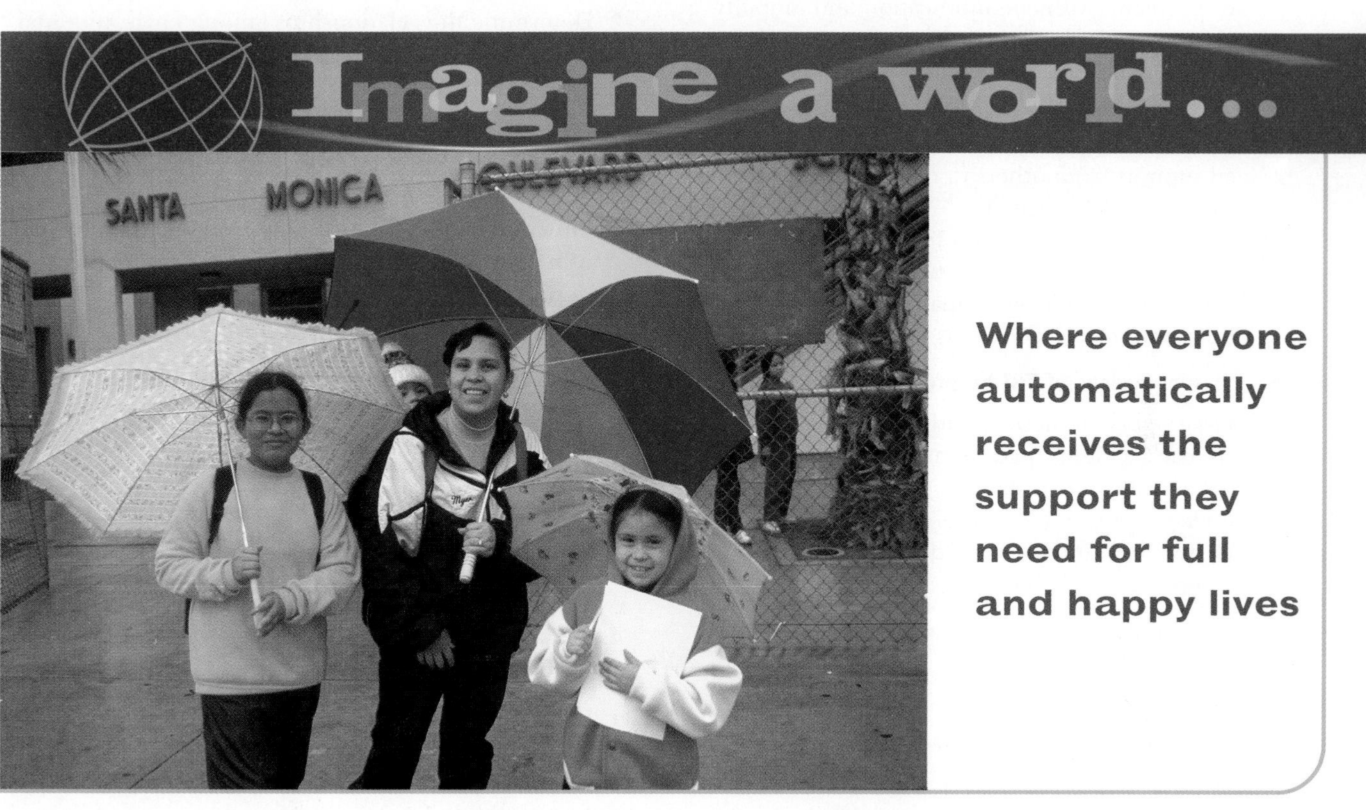

Imagine a world...
SANTA
MONICA
Where everyone automatically receives the support they need for full and happy lives

Summary

Although the size of the disability group is of little importance to the individuals or the families affected, these three special education categories all comprise very few students. Together, multiple-severe disabilities, deaf-blindness, and traumatic brain injury account for less than 1 percent of all schoolchildren. But these disabilities are often severe, affecting overall performance significantly and requiring considerable resources and intensive individualized instruction. Many of these individuals also have additional problems in cognition, language, speech, and/or motor skills. Many have mental retardation. Individuals with low incidence disabilities have complex learning needs that require the collaborative input of many experts from comprehensive multidisciplinary teams.

Addressing the Chapter Objectives

1 What are the major characteristics of children with severe-multiple disabilities?

- Difficulties with generalization (situations, settings, and skills)
- Limited communication abilities
- Poor memory
- Need for ongoing and intensive supports for many major life activities (domestic, leisure, community participation, vocational)
- Presence of at least two disabilities whose combination results in complex educational needs

2 How would you describe the impact of deaf-blindness on those affected?

People with deaf-blindness

- Live in very restricted environments
- Have problems with communication and mobility
- Require special adaptations and instruction for both vision and hearing deficits

Many people with deaf-blindness

- Develop speech and can learn to read print
- Need support from others to make their environments safe and accessible
- Often experience significant feelings of isolation
- Have additional disabilities, such as mental retardation, speech or language impairments, physical disabilities, and health problems

3 How can many cases of TBI be prevented?

- *Common causes:* domestic accidents, motorcycle accidents, car accidents, pedestrian and bicycle accidents, assaults, sports injuries, and child abuse
- *Prevention measures:* wearing protective gear (seat belts, helmets) and avoiding drugs and alcohol when operating a vehicle

4 What are alternate assessments and what do these assessments entail?

Alternate assessments

- Are a form of evaluation used to assess annually the progress of those students with the most severe disabilities
- Reflect *both* certain goals of the general education curriculum and additional instructional targets, such as those included in functional curricula
- Include accommodations as specified on students' IEPs

Only a limited number of students in each state may participate in alternative assessments—1 percent of all students, which is estimated to be about 9 percent of all students with disabilities.

Various forms of assessments are allowed:

- Different forms of standardized tests
- Items that reflect a narrower range of topics or fewer objectives
- Portfolios

Debate surrounds the "1 percent cap." Many educators and parents believe that more students should be allowed to take alternate assessments and that for some students, performance measures should not be mandated to include general education curriculum topics.

5 What are the key elements of functional behavioral assessments?

Purposes:

- Identify behaviors that require intervention.
- Determine the relationships among environmental events and the student's behaviors.
- Plan for instruction.

Components:

- Interviews with people who know the student well
- Direct observations
- Functional analysis, including studying the impact of interventions by frequently collecting observational data

Outcomes:

- Operational definition of the problem behavior(s)
- Statement of conditions that set the scene for the problem behavior
- Description of the consequences that maintain the problem behavior
- Direct data supporting the observations

mylabschool™
Where the classroom comes to life!

MyLabSchool is a collection of online tools for your success in this course, your licensure exams, and your teaching career. Visit www.mylabschool.com to access the following:

- Online Study Guide
- Video cases from real classrooms
- Help with your research papers using Research Navigator
- Career Center with resources for:
  - Praxis and licensure preparation
  - Professional portfolio development
  - Job search and interview techniques
  - Lesson planning

Supplementary Resources

Popular Novels and Books

Brown, C. (1990). *My left foot.* Dublin: Minera.
Brown, C. (1990). *Down all the days.* Dublin: Minera.
Keller, H. (1988). *The story of my life.* Mineola, NY: Dover Thrift Editions.
Nall, S. (2002). *It's only a mountain: Dick and Rick Hoyt, Men of Iron* (2nd ed.). Holland, MA: Dick Hoyt.

Movies

Inside I'm Dancing: Rory O'Shea Was Here (2004). Universal

Michael, a young man with cerebral palsy, had been living in a long-term-care facility for people with severe disabilities for a number of years. He never questioned his situation; he simply accepted his disability and his unchanging life. All that changed when brash and assertive Rory O'Shea moved into the residential facility. As a consequence of muscular dystrophy, Rory has physical control only over his head and two fingers. After some time, these two become friends. Rory's irreverence and constant challenging of authority lead them to seek independent living. Through a special program, they are able to get their own apartment, which had to be fitted for their wheelchairs and made accessible to them. They need a full-time assistant to support their independence, and one night they meet a beautiful young woman whom they both become enamored of, and they ask her to do the job. She reluctantly agrees. The film explores the lives of these two young men and the desires of people their age for independence, love, and friendship.

Regarding Henry (1991). Paramount

Henry, a high-paid lawyer, appears to have the perfect life. But then one night he goes to the corner store, and while he is buying a pack of cigarettes, a man robs the store. During the chaotic event, Henry is shot in the head. After surviving the gun wound, he has to go through a long rehabilitation and slowly recovers some memory. He realizes that he will never again be "important," as he was before the shooting, but he also remembers that his previous life was filled with deceit and infidelity. This film offers insight into the difficulty and critical importance of rehabilitation for a person with brain injury. It is also a touching look into how life can change in an instant. Henry will have cognitive disabilities for the rest of his life, but the film suggests that even such a severe situation can have a positive outcome.

The Miracle Worker (1936). United Artists

This 1936 version of the story of the early years of Helen Keller and how she developed the ability to communicate is one of many that have been made into film. At first, Helen's family had indulged her as a child out of pity because she was blind and deaf. Her family finally decides to hire a teacher, who is legally blind. After a few days of dealing with Helen's tantrums and abuse, the teacher takes Helen into seclusion to give her individual instruction—and to remove her from the counterproductive, overindulgent environment that the family had created. After a few weeks, Helen makes the cognitive connection between signs and their meanings, a breakthrough that enables her to communicate. The film vividly illustrates the frustrations of being deaf and blind, as well how difficult it is to teach a child with these sensory losses. The film ends with the triumphant moment in which Helen and the teacher are able to break through communication barriers.

Professional, Parent, and Advocacy Groups

American Association of the Deaf-Blind in Silver Springs, Maryland: www.tr.wou.edu/dblink/aadb.htm

Helen Keller National Center for Deaf-Blind Youths and Adults in Sands Point, New York www.helenkeller.org

DB-LINK: National Information Clearinghouse on Children Who Are Deaf-Blind in Monmouth, Oregon: www.tr.wosc.osshe.edu/dblink

Brain Injury Association, Inc. in Washington, DC www.biausa.org

The Association for Persons with Severe Handicaps (TASH) in Baltimore, Maryland www.tash.org

Professional Standards and Licensure Tests

After reading this chapter, you should be able to link basic knowledge and skills described in the CEC Standards and INTASC Principles with information provided in this text. The table below shows some of the specific CEC Individualized Independence Curriculums Knowledge and Skill Standards and INTASC Special Education Principles that can be applied to each major section of the chapter. Other standards may also be applied to this chapter. Associated General Praxis II topic areas are identified in the right column.

Major Chapter Headings	CEC Knowledge and Skill Core Standard and Associated Subcategories	INTASC Core Principle and Associated Special Education Subcategories	PRAXIS II Exam Topic
Where We've Been . . . What's on the Horizon	**1: Foundations** IC1K5 Laws and policies related to provision of specialized health care in educational settings	**1: Subject Matter** 1.04 All teachers have knowledge of the major principles and parameters of federal disabilities legislation.	1: Understanding Exceptionality 2: Legal and Social Issues
Multiple-Severe Disabilities Defined Deaf-Blindness Defined Traumatic Brain Injury Defined	**1: Foundations** IC1K1 Definitions and issues related to the identification of individuals with disabilities	**1: Subject Matter** 1.08 Special education teachers have knowledge of when and how to develop, structure, and implement accommodations, modifications and/or adaptations to provide access to the general curriculum for students with disabilities.	1: Understanding Exceptionality 2: Legal and Social Issues
Characteristics Multiple-Severe Disabilities Deaf-Blindness Traumatic Brain Injury	**2: Development and Characteristics of Learners** IC2K3 Etiologies and medical aspects of conditions affecting individuals with disabilities	**2: Student Learning** 2.08 Special education teachers seek a holistic understanding of each student's current learning and development, based on knowledge of the student's performance within a variety of settings.	1: Understanding Exceptionality
Causes and Prevention Multiple-Severe Disabilities Deaf-Blindness Traumatic Brain Injury	**2: Development and Characteristics of Learners** IC2K1 Etiology and diagnosis related to various theoretical approaches	**2: Student Learning** 2.04 All teachers are knowledgeable about multiple theories of learning and research-based teaching practices that support learning.	1: Understanding Exceptionality 2: Legal and Social Issues

Assessment	**8: Assessment** IC8K3 Types and importance of information concerning individuals with disabilities available from families and public agencies	**8: Assessment** 8.08 Special education teachers initiate, contact, and collaborate with other professionals throughout the identification and initial planning process.	3: Delivery of Services to Students
Teaching Students with Low Incidence Disabilities	**4: Instructional Strategies** IC4S2 Use appropriate adaptations and assistive technology for all individuals with disabilities	**4: Instructional Strategies** 4.08 All teachers expect and support the use of assistive and instructional technologies to promote learning and independence of students with disabilities.	3: Delivery of Services to Students
Transition	**4: Instructional Planning** IC7K1 Model career, vocational, and transition programs for individuals with disabilities	**7: Planning Instruction** 7.07 Special education teachers oversee the development of individualized transition plans to guide learners' transitions from preschool to elementary school, middle school to high school, and high school to postschool opportunities.	2: Legal and Social Issues 3: Delivery of Services to Students
Collaboration	**10: Collaboration** IC10S4 Collaborate with team members to plan transition to adulthood that encourages full community participation	**10: Collaboration, Ethics, and Relationships** 10.07 Special education teachers work with related services professionals to design, implement, and evaluate instructional plans for students with disabilities.	3: Delivery of Services to Students
Partnerships with Families and Communities	**10: Collaboration** IC10S5 Collaborate with families of and service providers to individuals who are chronically or terminally ill	**10: Collaboration, Ethics, and Relationships** 10.10 Special education teachers understand the impact that having a child with a disability may have on family roles and functioning at different points in the life cycle of a family.	2: Legal and Social Issues 3: Delivery of Services to Students

Annie Mae Young, *Work-clothes quilt with center medallion of corduroy strips.* 1976. Denim, corduroy, synthetic blend. 108 × 77 inches. Collection of the Tinwood Alliance. © Tinwood. Photograph of the artist: Annie Mae Young, born 1928. © Matt Arnett. Both images used with kind permission of Tinwood Ventures.

Annie Mae Young, a quiltmaker born in 1928, was descended from slaves who worked on Pettway plantation at Gee's Bend, Alabama. During the Depression, Gee's Bend was declared one of the poorest places in the United States. Because of the attention this section of Alabama received, much is known about the close community where women passed down from one generation to the next the art of quiltmaking, using bits of otherwise useless cloth to create artistic masterpieces. Annie May Young was born and raised in a log cabin. Her father farmed land he didn't own, raising cotton, corn, peas, sweet potatoes, and sorghum cane. When Annie Mae was about 13, her mother taught her to quilt using bits and pieces of old clothing. Over the many years during which she made colorful, linear quilts, old cotton clothing remained her favorite fabric. The quilt shown here was made from denim and strips of corduroy.

14

Giftedness and Talent Development

All kids deserve to learn something new every day—including the gifted.

Camilla Benbow

Dean, Peabody College, Vanderbilt University

Gifted and talented people are highly visible in American society. They are credited for advances in medicine, in technology, in business, in theater and cinema, and in the arts. The roads these individuals took to achieve their high levels of contribution to society vary, depending on their families' socioeconomic status, their own determination, and the educational opportunities available to them. **Gifted** or **talented** students have high potential to succeed at school and later in life as leaders who make unique contributions to society. Unfortunately, opportunities—particularly from the educational system—are inconsistent, and the gifts of many with high potential are lost to themselves and to the rest of us. The protections of a unique and appropriate education guaranteed to students with disabilities are not available to students who are gifted or talented. IDEA '04 does not include students considered gifted or talented, nor has any previous version of this law done so.

Chapter Objectives

After studying this chapter, you will be able to:

1. Describe the current vision of giftedness and talent development.
2. List common characteristics of giftedness, observed regardless of the definition applied.
3. Explain the factors that can inhibit giftedness and talent development.
4. Discuss reasons for the underrepresentation of some subgroups of gifted learners, and explain why educators are concerned.
5. Compare the two major approaches used in the education of gifted learners.

Where We've Been . . . What's on the Horizon?

Historians and anthropologists have long recognized that concentrations of extraordinary abilities and outstanding achievement can be observed during different periods of history. For example, the Indus civilization that flourished in northern India between 2400 and 1800 B.C. demonstrated advanced concepts of city planning and architecture. Indus cities were built on a regular grid with major streets running north and south. A drainage system served an entire city, and each home had a bathroom and toilet connected to a sewer system. During the time of the ancient Greeks, athletic prowess and excellence in the fine arts reached peak levels that are obvious in the legacies of their civilization: their philosophical writings, dramas, architecture, and sculpture. In ancient China, literary works, architecture, music, and art far surpassed the standards of other cultures. During the second century B.C., the Chinese wrote books, at first using silk for paper, on topics such as astronomy, medicine, and pharmacology. Between A.D. 300 and 750, the Teotihuacan culture in Mexico developed a sophisticated craft industry that produced figurines, pottery, and tools for export throughout the region. Almost 200 years ago, a concentration of musical prodigies (Handel, Haydn, Mozart, Chopin, Liszt) created work that will no doubt be performed forever. Today computer developers, software designers, and Internet innovators amaze us with their brilliance and technical aptitude.

Why have there been periods in history when particular talents are displayed in abundance? One answer is that periods of brilliance result from a combination of excellent early opportunities, early and continuing guidance, and instruction for the individual (Morelock & Feldman, 1997; Simonton, 1997). These features must be coupled with a major societal interest in a particular ability, opportunities to practice continually and hence to progress, close association and interaction with others of similar abilities, and strong success experiences. Certainly, individuals who demonstrate superiority in a particular area must also have innate talent, but it seems that traits valued by a culture emerge with some frequency when importance is placed on them.

Historical Context

Special education for those with exceptional abilities is not a new concept, but it has not been consistently available across time. As early as 3000 B.C., the Egyptians sent the best students (along with royalty) to court schools or assigned mentors to work with them in intensive internships to develop their special talents (Hunsaker, 1995). Confucius, a Chinese philosopher who lived around 500 B.C., proposed special education for gifted children. By A.D. 618, gifted and talented children were brought to the Chinese imperial court for special education. In Japan between 1604 and 1868, children born of the samurai nobility were given a differentiated curriculum consisting of Confucian classics, martial arts, history, moral values, calligraphy, and composition. The children of the poor, however, were taught the value of loyalty, obedience, humility, and diligence (Davis & Rimm, 2004). In West African cultures, specialized education was provided to children on the basis of the children's status, recognized characteristics, or cleverness.

In Western cultures, interest in people's innate and superior abilities was stimulated by the work of Charles Darwin and Sir Francis Galton in the middle 1800s. Charles Darwin is most famous for his theories about natural selection and the evolution of species. Before his time, no one had studied, on a broad scale, individual differences among people or issues related to intelligence and heredity (Clark, 2002). In 1869 Galton proposed his theory that genius was attributable solely to heredity and that eminence was due only to two factors: (1) an internal motivation to excel and (2) intellect. Both of these factors were thought to be genetically determined.

In the United States, our wavering commitment to the education of the gifted reflects our national philosophy about equity and social justice. During the 18th Century, many leaders of the country leaned toward the view that education was best for the elite. Thomas Jefferson, however, argued against elitism, believing that the purpose of education was to foster democracy. During the 19th Century, egalitarianism—the notion that no one should get special treatment—became popular. The egalitarian position was extreme, holding that no individual could be considered better than anyone else, regardless of innate abilities, status, or education. Gardner (1984) suggests that the concept of equal opportunity derived from the egalitarian attitude that special education for gifted children is undemocratic, elitist, unnecessary, and wasteful.

Most chroniclers of education of the gifted in the United States stress the importance of the intelligence test (Clark, 2002; Davis & Rimm, 2004). Alfred Binet developed the first one in 1905 (Binet & Simon, 1905). Although it was not originally developed to identify students who are gifted, this test nonetheless marks the beginning, in this country, of interest in such individuals. Some programs for the gifted were established as early as 1866, but real development and growth in educational services for these individuals did not come until the 1920s. Leta Hollingworth, one of the early pioneers in the field of education of the gifted, who joined the faculty at Teachers College, Columbia University, in 1916, taught the first course and wrote the first textbook in this area (Silverman, 1992). One of Hollingworth's major contributions to the field was her proposal that giftedness is affected by both heredity and environment, a concept widely held today.

gifted or **talented** Terms describing individuals with high levels of intelligence and/or creativity, outstanding abilities, and capacity for high performance

Another pioneer, Lewis Terman, began a classic, long-term follow-up study in 1925 of individuals who were gifted, both as children and as adults. This comprehensive study drew attention to gifted individuals but did not give rise to consistent "gifted education" services. The promotion of unique educational services can be linked to a specific historical event: Russia's 1957 launching of the satellite Sputnik. This launch was viewed as a risk to national security and a blow to national pride, and the United States vowed to catch up and surpass the competition. Hence federal funding was appropriated to establish programs, develop ways to identify students with high academic achievement, particularly in math and science, and conduct research to find effective methods for providing excellent educational experiences. Gifted students were now seen as a great national resource—the people who would make the United States the leader once again.

Leta Hollingworth, here working in 1938 with students at the Speyer School (the laboratory school of Teachers College of Columbia University), provided the foundation for many of the methods used today in education of the gifted.

During the late 1960s and 1970s, the nation turned its attention to the civil rights movement—to the needs of the culturally and linguistically diverse and the poor. Education of the gifted was thought to be yet another advantage showered on already privileged youth who could make it on their own. During this time, however, June Maker did attract national attention to the needs of one subgroup of gifted students: those with learning disabilities. In 1977 she first published the results of her research, shedding light on this previously ignored group of learners and stressing the importance of providing them with a truly unique educational experience (Maker, 1977, 1986).

The late 1980s saw the situation change once again, as the country took renewed interest in education of the gifted. In 1988 Congress passed the Jacob K. Javits Gifted and Talented Students Education Act. Many states also invested substantial funding in education of the gifted. However, commitment waxes and wanes, and this cycle will probably continue because of the public's continuing confusion about the vulnerability of these children, along with concerns about equity. For example, in 2005 the U.S. House of Representatives voted to include zero funding for gifted education programs, although the U.S. Senate reinstated some of the funds into the appropriations budget (National Association for Gifted Children [NAGC], 2005). Today, 19 states have no mandate for special programs for gifted students, and one state (New Hampshire) makes no mention of special services for students who are gifted or talented (Council of State Directors of Programs for the Gifted and NAGC, 2003). Only eight states have laws or regulations that provide full protections and guarantees to these students and their families, mirroring those that IDEA '04 guarantees for students with disabilities (Zirkel, 2005).

Challenges That Giftedness and Talents Present

Gifted individuals are not handicapped by any lack of ability. They can be handicapped, however, by (1) negative attitudes about them, and (2) the assumption that they do not need special services to reach their full potential and develop their talents. Let's look at each of these factors.

Gifted students are often the envy of their typical classmates (Massé & Gagné, 2002). Such attitudes can become a real source of problems, causing worry and influencing the behavior of gifted youngsters. For example, not "sticking it out" may be one reason why so many gifted students underachieve; they do not want to call attention to themselves through accelerated academic performance (Hartigan, 2005; Neumeister & Hébert, 2003). Other reasons explain these students' common pattern of underachievement. One major reason is that they are bored, finding the curriculum too slowly paced and uninteresting (Kanevsky & Keighley, 2003). And some very exceptional individuals, such as Christopher Paolini, whose story is found in this chapter's *In the Spotlight,* even find that they just don't have enough time for school.

Christopher Paolini in the Spotlight

Once upon a time, there was a little boy named Christopher who lived with his parents and his sister in a beautiful green valley in some very tall mountains. They were poor but very happy. Christopher loved to read fantasy stories about knights and wizards and dragons, and one day he decided to write a fantasy story of his own. People loved Christopher's story, so much that everyone wanted a copy. Suddenly Christopher's family wasn't so poor anymore. (Grossman, 2005, p. 69)

Christopher Paolini is clearly a prodigy. At age 15, he wrote his first novel, *Eragon*, which is in the genre of Tolkin's trilogy. First published by his family, *Eragon*—a story of a magical dragon and a young boy living in medieval times—sold over 2.5 million copies. The next book in the series, *Eldest*, was published in the fall of 2005 with a first printing of 1.5 million copies. Paolini was homeschooled but did participate in high school soccer and football. With the success of his books, he doubts that he will attend college. Why? Well, in addition to a full writing schedule, which occupies him seven days a week from breakfast to dinnertime, he is involved with the production of a movie based on his first book. Wouldn't you pass on college (at least temporarily) if you could work with John Malkovich and Jeremy Irons on the books that you'd written?

Source: From "The Real-Life Boy Wizard" by L. Grossman, August 29, 2005, *Time, 166*, p. 69. Adapted by permission.

Some education professionals and policymakers have openly argued against special programs for the gifted, stating that such programs are elitist and socially incorrect (Margolin, 1996; Sapon-Shevin, 1996). To them, education of the gifted should be merged with general education or even eliminated. Such beliefs contribute to the "reasons" why access to special services should not be guaranteed to gifted students and why their education is not included in this or any version of the IDEA law. This situation puts the field in a precarious position and results in services being inconsistently available across the nation.

Negative attitudes about education of the gifted seem to stem from myths about the field and the individuals it serves. For example, many people think that these children will thrive without special programs—that they can make it on their own. Quite sadly, this is simply untrue: Gifted individuals often do not reach their potential because their educational programs did not meet their needs (Benbow & Stanley, 1996).

Although some gifted children achieve their potential without the benefits of special education, many do not. For example, despite their academic potential, gifted males are three times more likely to drop out of school than gifted females, and overall, it is estimated that some 15 to 25 percent of gifted students leave school before finishing (Renzulli & Park, 2000). Research findings about these students' achievement also clearly support the need for special services and a differentiated educational experience for these youngsters (Cornell et al., 1995). These students' statements of "consumer satisfaction" also support such findings. Elementary, middle, and high school gifted students attending general education classes were asked whether their educational programs in general education were appropriate and were meeting their needs (Gallagher, Harradine, & Coleman, 1997). In general, here's what they had to say:

- The curriculum is not challenging.
- The instructional pace is too slow.
- Too much information already mastered is repeated.
- Few opportunities are available to study topics of personal interest or to study in more depth.
- An emphasis on mastery of facts, rather than on thinking skills, predominates.

All children need to develop the motivation to grow and expand. For many gifted children, the general education classroom alone cannot provide the challenges they require to remain motivated or to learn at an accelerated and comfortable pace.

Making a Difference

100 Black Men of America

David Dinkins

African American boys who live in challenging circumstances are particularly at risk for not achieving to their potential. They often do not have role models or mentors who can show them that success at school is the path toward success in life. These Black boys do not know Black men who have successful careers in business, industry, science, or technology. They and their families do not have associations with community leaders. Such youth often believe that college is not in their future, and they do not grasp the possibility of their becoming leaders themselves.

In 1963 David Dinkins (now a former mayor of New York City), Dr. William Hayling, Jackie Robinson (the famed baseball player), and other business and industry leaders decided to take action. They were concerned about the poor quality of life and the dismal outcomes of too many Black boys in New York City. These men formed the concept of what became 100 Black Men of America, Inc., and is now an international organization. Their idea was that if they could channel resources into youth development, providing young African American males with mentors who would also serve as role models, they might be able to make a real difference both for the community and for these individuals.

The original idea has since become a thriving, active international organization of 103 chapters comprising over 10,000 Black men: corporate executives, physicians, attorneys, entrepreneurs, entertainers, elected officials, professional athletes, educators, and other professionals. Each of these men volunteers his time and resources to mentor Black boys, helping them succeed in school, go on to college, and pursue productive careers. For more about this organization, its members, and how to join them in making a difference in the lives of so many children and youth, visit the Web site **www.100blackmen.org**

Giftedness and Talent Development Defined

What does gifted and talent development mean? Let's start answering this question by coming to an understanding of how the concepts *gifted* and *talented* have been defined and have evolved. Definitions are important because they reflect beliefs about who qualifies and what services they should receive. Across time, the definitions of giftedness have ranged from a narrow view based exclusively on cognition, reasoning, and the score a person receives on a test of intelligence, to a multidimensional view of intelligence, aptitudes, abilities, and talent development.

As early as 1925, Lewis Terman studied individuals with exceptionally high cognitive aptitude. Terman's definition reflects a narrow view of giftedness in which high intelligence is closely associated with high academic achievement. In addition to tying giftedness to a score on an IQ test, Terman also believed intelligence to be a fixed characteristic—one that people are born with and one that does not increase or decrease across time. He viewed intelligence as determined solely by heredity—as a trait inherited from one's parents. Lastly, this view of giftedness reflects many biases that were prevalent in Terman's time about women and people of underrepresented ethnic groups. He considered children gifted who scored in the highest 1 percent (having scores over 140) on an intelligence (IQ) test. Figure 14.1 illustrates how few students are included when the 1 percent cutoff score is used—and how many more "make the cut" when we include those students whose scores fall within the band created by two standard deviations from the mean. Remember that we discussed the problems with the concepts of normal distributions—the normal curve—and tests of intelligence in (Chapters 1 and 8).

Today's professional educators are much less confident than Terman was in the results of standardized tests. They now recognize that such tests can be inherently biased against individuals who are not from the dominant American culture or who have not received a strong and traditional educational foundation. Our understanding of intelligence has also changed since Terman's time. Researchers now understand that intelligence, like any other trait, is influenced by both genetics and environment (Sternberg, 2000). In other words, IQ is no longer thought of as a fixed characteristic of the individual or as signaled only by a high score on an intelligence test.

Can giftedness and talents be defined in such a way that all of the students who can benefit from gifted education are identified? Perhaps Mary Frasier, founder and director of the Torrance Center for Creative Studies, explains giftedness in the sim-

Figure 14.1 • IQ Scores Distributed Along a Normal Curve

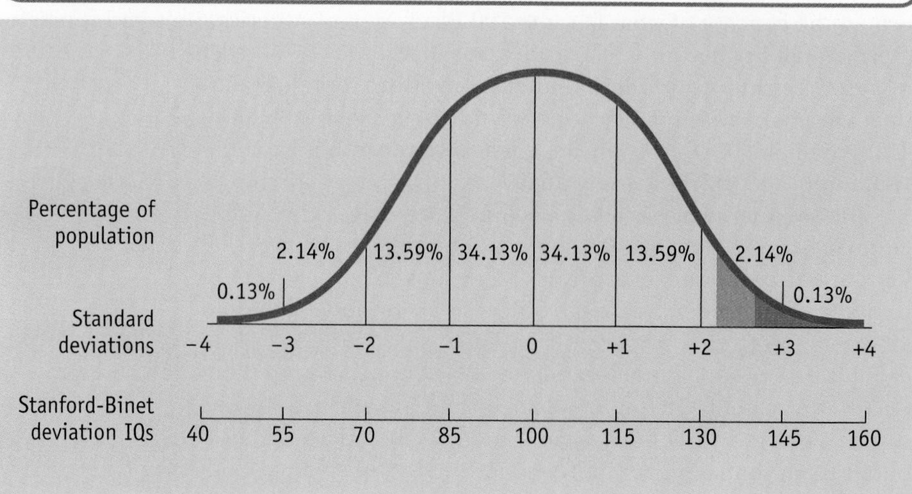

plest and most straightforward way: "I define giftedness as the potential to excel at the upper end of any talent continuum" (Frasier as cited in Grantham, 2002, p. 50).

New definitions and visions of giftedness and talents began to emerge at the end of the last century, and calls for a new consensus definition continue today (Coleman, 2004; Cramond, 2004; Gagné, 2004). Table 14.1 provides definitions commonly used to describe students who are considered gifted or talented. The "new view" of giftedness gained national prominence in 1978 with the adoption of what came to be referred to as the "Marland definition," named after Sidney Marland, the U.S. Commissioner of Education in 1972. With the passage of the Jacob K. Javits Gifted and Talented Students Education Act of 1988 (PL 100-297), a broader perspective about the concept of education of the gifted and talent development emerged, and that basic definition was retained in the 2001 passage of the NCLB law. These two definitions are the basis for the current states' definition and federal definition. The third definition shown in Table 14.1 is the present national definition of giftedness. Note that the two newer definitions do not include the word *gifted* but, rather, include the concepts of outstanding talent and capability for high performance.

Who, then, are young people who are gifted? James Gallagher, a noted expert in the area, believes that some people are born with a "neurological constitution that allows them to learn faster, remember more, process information more effectively, and generate more new and unusual ideas than their age peers" (2000, p. 6). To those who share Gallagher's view, environment can inhibit or facilitate the development of individuals' talents, but without some innate predisposition for accelerated achievement or performance, exceptional development is not possible. Not everyone agrees with Gallagher's perception of giftedness, and many think that the definition should be more inclusive. Joseph Renzulli, for example, believes that enhanced educational services should be available to as many students as possible—

Table 14.1 • Definitions of Giftedness and Talent Development

Source	Definitions of Giftedness and Talent Development
U.S. Department of Education (the Marland Definition)[1]	[T]he term "gifted and talented children" means children and, whenever applicable, youth, who are identified at the preschool, elementary, or secondary level as possessing demonstrated or potential abilities that give evidence of high performance capability in areas such as intellectual, creative, specific academic, or leadership ability or in the performing and visual arts and who by reason thereof require services or activities not ordinarily provided by the school. . . . gifted and talented will encompass a minimum of 3 to 5 percent of the school population.
Jacob K. Javits Gifted and Talented Students Education Act of 1988 (PL 100–297)[2]	Children and youth with outstanding talent perform or [who] show the potential for performing at remarkably high levels of accomplishment when compared with others of their age, experience, or environment. These children and youth exhibit high performance capability in intellectual, creative, and/or artistic areas, possess an unusual leadership capacity, or excel in specific academic fields. They require services or activities not ordinarily provided by the schools. Outstanding talents are present in children and youth from all cultural groups, across all economic strata, and in all areas of human endeavor.
Federal Government, NCLB[3]	Students, children, or youth who give evidence of high achievement capability in areas such as intellectual, creative, artistic, or leadership capacity, or in specific academic fields, and who need services or activities not ordinarily provided by the school in order to fully develop those capabilities

Sources: [1]*Education of the Gifted and Talented, Vol. 1, Report to Congress of the United States by the U.S. Commissioner of Education* by S. P. Marland, Jr., 1972. Washington, DC: U.S. Government Printing Office.

[2]*Jacob K. Javits Gifted and Talented Students Education Act*, p. 26, U.S. Department of Education, 1994. Washington, DC: U.S. Government Printing Office.

[3]*No Child Left Behind (NCLB)*, Elementary and Secondary Education Act, PL 107-110, Part A, Section 9101 (22), 2001, p. 544.

Table 14.2 • Gardner's Eight Multiple Intelligences

Intelligence	Explanation	Adult Outcomes
1. Linguistic	The ability to think in words and use language in complex ways	Lawyer, poet, public speaker, writer
2. Logical-mathematical	The ability to calculate, quantify, and hypothesize and to recognize patterns	Engineer, mathematician, scientist
3. Spatial	The capacity to think three-dimensionally	Architect, artist, pilot, surgeon
4. Body-kinesthetic	The ability to use the body and hands skillfully	Acoustic engineer, composer, musician
5. Musical	Sensitivity to rhythm, pitch, melody, and tone	Choreographer, rock climber, skilled artisan
6. Interpersonal	The ability to understand and act productively on others' actions and motivations	Actor, political leader, salesperson, teacher, therapist
7. Intrapersonal	The abiltity to understand one's own feelings and capabilities	Autobiographer, sensitive individual, good decision maker
8. Naturalist	The ingenuity to observe patterns, create classifications, and develop and understand systems	Archeologist, farmer, hunter, landscape architect

Source: From M. Kornhaber et al., *Multiple Intelligences: Best Ideas from Research to Practice.* Published by Allyn and Bacon, Boston, MA. Copyright 2004 by Pearson Education. Adapted by permission of the publisher.

to *all* who have potential to be both creative and productive, far beyond the 3 to 5 percent of students typically identified (Renzulli, 2004). Most researchers today believe that giftedness is multidimensional and that high academic aptitude or intelligence is only one facet of it.

And finally, an even broader view of giftedness prevails. In 1983 Howard Gardner, in a book entitled *Frames of Mind,* proposed a flexible and multidimensional view of intelligence and giftedness that is still hailed today as the best way to think about giftedness (Kornhaber, Fierros, & Veenema, 2004). Gardner first proposed seven dimensions of intelligence—eight dimensions are now included—and suggested that a person can be gifted in any one or more of these areas (Gardner, 1983, 1993). A summary of the eight multiple intelligences is presented in Table 14.2. The notion is that extreme potential in any of these areas, even in just one—should be developed. By studying this table, you should be able to see how some youngsters can be excluded when traditional views of giftedness are applied, resulting in their not receiving the educational services they need to develop their unique abilities and talents.

Characteristics

As with any group of people, it is unfair to generalize "group characteristics" to individual members. On the other hand, it is easier to understand a group when some commonly observed features are described. Research findings suggest some characteristics that gifted people share (Clark, 2002; Davis & Rimm, 2004). These are listed in Table 14.3.

Although gifted and talented students make up a heterogeneous group, some common characteristics are important to monitor. Despite their high levels of talents and abilities, many experts consider gifted students—particularly those who

Table 14.3 • Common Characteristics of Students Who Are Gifted

Intellectual/Academic	Social/Emotional
Reasons abstractly	Criticizes self
Conceptualizes and synthesizes	Empathizes
Manages and processes information quickly and meaningfully	Plays with older friends
Solves problems	Persists
Learns quickly	Is intense
Shows intellectual curiosity	Exhibits individualism
Has wide interests	Has strength of character
Dislikes drill and routine	Demonstrates leadership abilities
May show unevenness	Is concerned about ethical issues
Generalizes learning	Takes risks
Remembers great amounts of material	Is independent and autonomous
Displays high level of verbal ability	Is highly sensitive to others and self
Prefers learning in a quiet environment	Has mature sense of humor
Adapts to new learning situations	Is nonconforming
Applies varied reasoning and thinking skills	Uses different modes of expression
Uses nonstandard pools of information	Strives for perfection
Is highly motivated by academic tasks	Experiences great stress from failure
Focuses and concentrates on topic or idea for long periods of time	

are highly gifted—vulnerable (Brody & Benbow, 1986; Higgins & Boone, 2003; Shaywitz et al., 2001). Although gifted students in general are no more likely than typical learners to exhibit disruptive or problem behaviors in classroom settings, or to have emotional or behavioral disorders, they have acquired that reputation (Freeman, 1994). And it may be that highly gifted students do exhibit behavior patterns (e.g., hyperactivity, impulsivity) similar to those of students with learning disabilities or ADHD (Hartnett, Nelson, & Rinn, 2004; Shaywitz et al., 2001). However, gifted students complain about being bored at school, a possible explanation for misbehavior (Kanevsky & Keighley, 2003). Certainly, keeping these students engaged can be challenging for educators, particularly for those who have a class of students who exhibit a wide range of abilities and achievement levels.

Sensitivity, Perfectionism, and Intensity

Educators should also be aware of three common characteristics often seen in these youngsters: sensitivity, perfectionism, and intensity (Neumeister, 2004a&b). For example, being highly sensitive may lead some gifted and talented students to overreact to even mild criticism. This, coupled with a need for perfection, causes many of them to experience more negative reactions to what they perceive as failure (Dixon, Lapsley, & Hanchon, 2004). These tendencies may well contribute to underachievement in some gifted students—an unfortunate situation seen in about half of students with high ability (Peterson, 2000). Another characteristic, intensity, can manifest itself both socially and academically (Van Tassel-Baska, 2004). Their intensity might also explain why many of these students experience high levels of stress (Nichols & Baum, 2000). On the positive side, this characteristic causes these students to become highly focused on an activity they find fascinating, enabling them to concentrate on an intriguing idea for long periods of time and also to explore curriculum content in depth. Knowledge of these characteristics and learning styles can help the alert educator understand these students' educational needs.

Subgroups of Gifted Students

Are there subgroups of gifted students that demand special attention and considerations? The answer to this question is a resounding "Yes!" Some students who are gifted and talented are underachievers and need special intervention to help them become motivated to achieve their potential (Neumeister & Hébert, 2003). Others, students whose special abilities are not even identified because of bias and different perceptions about what constitutes giftedness, are excluded from education of the gifted. Typically, these children come from one of four subgroups:

- Females
- Culturally and linguistically diverse students
- Students with disabilities
- Students with ADHD

Females

Sally Reis says of gifted females, "So much talent and so few opportunities to develop it" (Reis, 2003, p. 154). Since the 1920s, when gifted individuals as a group came to the attention of educators, differences between males' and females' academic achievement and outcomes have been noted. For example, although many of his research associates were women who went on to highly productive academic careers, Lewis Terman included very few women in his study of gifted individuals (Rogers, 1999). During the same time period, Leta Hollingworth argued that the prevailing notion that women were intellectually inferior to men was incorrect; rather, women did not have equal opportunities to excel and realize their potential. Gender differences, particularly girls' poor achievement in math, science, and computer sciences, concern many in the field of gifted education today (Reis & Park, 2001; Shapka & Keating, 2003). Gifted girls also tend to have lower self-esteem and to lack confidence about their popularity (Kitano & Perkins, 2000). The consensus is that these differences are due to bias both at school and, later, in the workplace (Roeper, 2003).

Although the number of preschool boys and the number of preschool girls identified as gifted are about equal, the ratio of girls to boys in accelerated programs diminishes over time (Kloosterman & Suranna, 2003; Silverman, 2005). Why might this be so? Are there innate differences between the genders that cause giftedness to occur more frequently in men than in women? Innate differences have never been proved in research. Rather, are society's expectations for people and the roles they assume the crucial factors in the achievement levels of either gender? It appears that the interplay of society's and people's personal expectations contribute greatly to these differences in outcomes (Reiss, 2003; Roeper, 2003). Gifted girls and boys have different attitudes, likes and dislikes, and achievement across academic subjects. For example, boys favor science, technology, and math, whereas girls tend to favor English, writing, reading, and the arts (Reis & Park, 2001; Swiatek & Lupkowski-Shoplik, 2000). Interestingly, negative attitudes about certain academic subjects increase across the grades: More high school girls than girls in elementary school say they dislike math and science. Reports of such lack of interest in math and science are not universal, providing evidence of the importance and impact of special programs for targeted and vulnerable groups of students. In

Britain, for example, once single-sex programs for girls became available, and when that curriculum incorporated more concrete and real-life examples, girls' performance levels soared (Freeman, 2003).

Special programs can make a real difference! Girls enrolled in education of the gifted are different from girls who attend general education classes (Mendez, 2000). For example, girls in such special programs show high levels of motivation, have greater interest in seeking nontraditional careers, and tend to have more liberal attitudes about the rights and roles of women. Successful women report that it was important during their school years to have friends who valued learning and achievement (Rimm & Rimm-Kaufman, 2001). And girls who enroll in girls-only special programs in mathematics and science do better and remain more interested in these subjects than girls who don't participate in such very special programs (Freeman, 2003; Shapka & Keating, 2003). For these reasons, it is easy to conclude that special programs do make a difference in the lives of gifted females and that these programs should be more readily available.

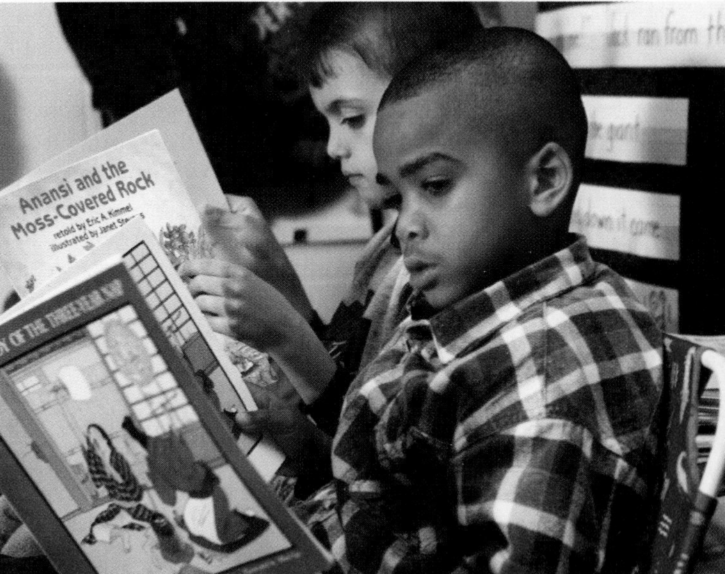

These first grade students are already demonstrating advanced reading and conceptual abilities. Teachers must be alert to continually challenge and support children with giftedness and creativity.

Culturally and Linguistically Diverse Students

Culturally and linguistically diverse students face many challenges. Three related issues are of great concern to education professionals and makers of national policy about diverse students (National Research Council, 2002; Naglieri & Ford, 2005). Diverse students

- Are overrepresented in disability categories
- Are underrepresented in gifted education programs
- Drop out of school at a high rate

African American, Native Americans, and Hispanic students participate in gifted education at rates substantially below what their percentages in the general school population would predict (Antrop-González, Vélez, & Garrett, 2003; Ford et al., 2002). National data support the public perception that Asian/Pacific Islanders are overrepresented in the education of the gifted, but this assumption is not universally true. Subgroups of Asian/Pacific Islanders vary greatly in their participation rates, and some are considerably underrepresented in gifted education (Kitano & DiJiosia, 2002). Besides raising very important concerns about equity and social justice, over- and underrepresentation result in lost potential to both the individual and society. Let's consider why disproportionate representation happens and how schools can make a difference in solving this problem.

Why do African American, Native American, Hispanic, and some Asian/Pacific Islander youngsters not participate in programs for gifted students at rates one would expect? One major reason is that individuals from these groups are at greater risk of being poor, which is clearly related to both overrepresentation in disability categories and underrepresentation in programs for gifted and talented students (National Research Council, 2002). Supporting this idea is the fact that Asian/Pacific Islander students from subgroups that are more likely to live in poverty (Samoans, Hmong) are less likely to be identified as gifted or talented (Kitano & DiJiosia, 2002). And programs are less likely to be available, possibly because some policymakers assume that giftedness and talents do not occur among this group of learners. Mary Frasier believes that "people in their heart of hearts really think that when kids are poor they cannot possibly perform at the level of kids who are advantaged" (Frasier as cited in Grantham, 2002, p. 50).

Both being poor and being a person of color are risk factors for dropping out of gifted programs or out of school (Moore III, Ford, & Milner, 2005). Almost half of gifted students who drop out are from the lowest socioeconomic levels, whereas less than 4 percent of gifted students who drop out are from the highest socioeconomic levels (Renzulli & Park, 2000). Children of poverty often do not come from families that have an education tradition, and they often do not have access to a computer at home; both of these disadvantages seem to contribute to their lack of interest in staying in school. What can turn these facts around? Students who stay in school and succeed receive highly motivating curricula, exciting instruction, and extracurricular activities delivered by caring and competent teachers (Naglieri & Ford, 2005). When it all goes right, students flourish.

A number of other reasons contribute to the disproportionately low participation of diverse students in education programs for the gifted (Bernal, 2002, 2003; Castellano, 2002, 2003; Ford et al., 2002; Harmon, 2002; Kaplan, 2001; Morris, 2002). Let's first look at some explanations advanced for these students' poor participation rates:

- Bias in traditional methods used for testing and identification
- Cultural values at variance with mainstream society and teaching methods used at school
- Barriers created by poverty
- Educators' attitudes toward, and lack of familiarity with, culturally and linguistically diverse students
- Low expectations, bias, and discrimination directed toward diverse individuals
- Limited proficiency in English
- Application of rigid definitions of giftedness and talents

Now let's consider what needs to happen for this situation to change. First, educators must become serious about bringing services to those students who are natural leaders, artistically talented, and capable (Grantham, 2003). Second, they must move beyond their dependence on standardized tests, and consider using alternative and innovative measurements—portfolio assessments, peer nominations, authentic assessments (frequent evaluations of students' classroom work), and curriculum based measurements that allow diverse students to display their talents better (Hébert & Beardsley, 2001). Applying less traditional concepts of giftedness could also result in the inclusion of more diverse learners (Brice & Brice, 2004). For instance, using Gardner's theory of multiple intelligences would allow students with talents in at least one of Gardner's intelligence areas to receive special attention (Reid et al., 2000). Clearly, we also need to broaden our search for talent to encompass more artistic and creative individuals, including those who come from rural and remote areas (Baldus, 2003; Montgomery, 2004). Teachers should consider the background and culture of their students' families. Children whose families have different cultural values, different emphasis on cognitive development, or different expectations often find the classroom situation and the teaching methods used there hostile and confusing. For example, children from cultures where working cooperatively in groups is valued may find it difficult to function well in classes where individual competition is stressed (Bernal, 2002; Kitano, 1997; Kitano & DiJiosia, 2002). Likewise, children who come from homes where being silent and reserved is encouraged are often uncomfortable in American classrooms where individuals are called on to answer questions and share private feelings.

Teachers can do even more to increase the likelihood of more diverse students succeeding at school. Donna Ford and her colleagues suggest that the books students read, if they are representative of youngsters' culture, can motivate and challenge them to learn (see *Validated Practices* on page 518 for some examples). Also, high expectations can make a difference (Harmon, 2002). For example, when teachers perceive diverse individuals as having deficits—when such students are considered "deprived" or "disadvantaged"—the result is reduced access and limited opportunities for challenging work (Ford et al., 2002). And tragically, if teachers do not expect specific youngsters to excel at school, those students may fulfill that prophecy by not working for good grades on their report cards and doing poorly on class assignments (Kitano, 1998). When the content of the curriculum and instruction is "anchored" with examples relevant to diverse students' experiences and values, they gain a sense of belonging and membership that translates into high outcomes (Ford et al., 2000).

for Effective Teaching

CREATING SUCCESS FOR GIFTED STUDENTS WITH LEARNING DISABILITIES

1. View such students as gifted first and having a disability second.
2. Provide access to an enriched curriculum in education of the gifted.
3. Allow accommodations through technology.
4. Facilitate a collaborative team approach including general educators, special educators, educators of the gifted, and related service professionals (e.g., school counselors, SLPs).
5. Find opportunities for gifted peers with learning disabilities to interact with each other.
6. Apply a curriculum that incorporates the theory of multiple intelligences.
7. Allow test accommodations.
8. Accelerate when appropriate.
9. Provide opportunities for students to talk about stress and emotional difficulties either in groups or with professionals.
10. Provide students with role models and mentors who are also gifted and have learning disabilities.

Students with Disabilities

When you think of people with disabilities who are also gifted and have developed outstanding talents, you might think of people like Stephen Hawking, Ludwig van Beethoven, Thomas Edison, Helen Keller, Franklin D. Roosevelt, Stevie Wonder, Ray Charles, Itzhak Perlman, and others. Despite their disabilities, their genius and major contributions to their respective fields have brought them considerable recognition. Remember that regardless of disability, anyone can have exceptional abilities, talents, or creativity. Never make an assumption about an individual from a casual meeting.

Clearly, society's biases about people with disabilities can overshadow individuals' strengths. Even today, teachers are less likely to refer students with disabilities than students without disabilities for identification and placement in special programs for gifted students (Gardynik & McDonald, 2005). It was in the 1970s when June Maker (1977) raised the awareness of educators about the needs of gifted learners with learning disabilities. Gifted students with learning disabilities came to be called **twice exceptional students**, a term now used for giftedness coexisting with any disabilities (Nielsen et al., 1993). Clearly, Maker's first observations about the challenges faced by students with learning disabilities who are also gifted were right. These students are at great disadvantage because of the importance of reading and writing in the general education curriculum (Cooper, Ness, & Smith, 2004). It is certainly difficult to demonstrate potential for academic excellence when accessing the curriculum in traditional ways does not come easily. But there are many ways to make a difference in these students' educational experiences (Nielsen, 2002). *Tips for Effective Teaching* provides some simple guidelines to follow. When all goes well, individual success can be stunning. Certainly Charles Schwab's story, told in Chapter 5, Making a Difference section, attests to this fact. Gifted individuals with learning disabilities have and do overcome these challenges.

Today, experts have broadened their view and refer to gifted individuals with a wide range of disabilities as being twice exceptional (Baum, 2004a&b). For example, gifted students with Asperger syndome are now being recognized (Neihart, 2000). Asperger syndome is a disorder that is considered part of the autism spectrum disorders (ASD) that you learned about in Chapter 12. The characteristics of this disorder include lack of empathy, monotonous speech patterns, social isolation, and inflexibility. And gifted students with Asperger syndrome tend to display inappropriate affective behavior, low tolerance for change, seamless speech, and inability to comprehend humor that requires social reciprocity. Regardless, many of these individuals rise to eminent positions because of their abilities to compensate for their atypical behaviors, to exhibit extraordinary intellectual powers, and to display tenacious determination.

twice-exceptional students Gifted students with disabilities

You first met Lizzy B. *In the Spotlight* in Chapter 4. Gifted students with disabilities should have all the opportunities possible so that they can make a difference in everyone's lives. When they're given a chance, the world is theirs!

Too many students with disabilities are not included in education of the gifted. A number of factors contribute to this unfortunate situation (Baum, 2004a&b, Silverman, 2005):

1. Disabilities depress IQ scores, masking potential.
2. Students are not allowed appropriate testing accommodations (e.g., assistive technology, extended time to take a test) so that they can demonstrate their talents in spite of their disabilities.
3. States' regulations for education of the gifted are not flexible.
4. Bias about some disabilities, such as cerebral palsy, overshadows the actual abilities and talents of individuals.

Successful gifted students with disabilities tend to share some common characteristics (Baum, 2004b). They often possess skills that allow them to compensate for their disabilities (Dole, 2000). After years of devising alternative ways to learn and keep up with their classmates, they typically have developed exceptional problem solving abilities as well. It is often their persistence and determination that have enabled them to succeed, even with no expert assistance.

Experts agree: Gifted students with disabilities are in desperate need of intervention (Nielsen, 2002; Robinson, 1999). The challenge here is for educators to address aspects of both their talents and their disabilities. For example, these students respond best to an instructional environment that fosters critical thinking and problem solving focused on highly interesting topics. However, direct instruction in areas in need of remediation must also be included in these students' instructional programs. Some experts suggest that students actually be taught (and encouraged) to compensate for their weaknesses (Reis, McGuire, & Neu, 2000). For example, rather than receiving instruction geared to specific content remediation, these students should be taught strategies—such as how to study more effectively and how to advocate for accommodations—that might help compensate for their learning challenges. They also should be encouraged to use a broad array of technologies (word processing, spellcheckers, calculators, database software, and other assistive devices) and other accommodations, such as audio-recorded literature for their reading assignments and tape recorders to take class notes.

Finally, it is important that these students come to understand the nature of their disabilities. Many of them, particularly those with learning disabilities, come to think of themselves as "not smart"—a belief that, if not corrected, can become a self-fulfilling prophecy (Reis, 2000). These students must be encouraged to accept their personal strengths and weakness, develop a good self-concept, and take pride in their accomplishments. For these goals to be met, support systems and intervention programs are often required. Some professionals argue that at least some of these students may require intensive instruction in separate classes for part of their educational careers, emphasizing the importance of making an array of educational alternatives available to gifted students with disabilities (Moon, Swift, & Shallenberger, 2002).

Students with ADHD

Educators are just beginning to focus their attention on students who are gifted and also have attention deficit hyperactivity disorder (ADHD) or whose giftedness signals ADHD (Chae, Kim, & Noh, 2003). These students can be confusing to educators. Possibly, for some individuals, high energy levels are confused with hyperactivity. Some students' boredom waiting for their classmates to catch up and the slow pace of traditional instruction may be misinterpreted as inattention (Hartnett, Nelson, & Rinn, 2004). Questioning authority might be seen as a characteristic of ADHD by some educators and a signal of intellectual curiosity by others. For such students, what may be most important is for them to receive a more challenging curriculum and engaging instruction.

How many of these students are there? Probably many more than teachers expect to find. Some estimate are that as many as 46 percent of those referred for ADHD may well be gifted students with ADHD (or even gifted students misidentified as having ADHD). Remember that many students with ADHD do not meet the criteria for disabilities but still should receive accommodations for their learning difficulties. However, it is difficult to identify those who are gifted, because ADHD is likely to mask intellectual giftedness. Thus most of these youngsters go unidentified (Zentall et al., 2001). Compounding the problem, many gifted students with ADHD are underachievers (Reis & McCoach, 2000). Because of their tendency to be disorganized, distractible, and impulsive, they, like their peers with ADHD, are at greater risk to fail. They are retained a year and eventually to drop out. But these problems do not have to lead to poor results. Think back to David Needleman, whose story was told in Chapter 6, *In the Spotlight* feature. The founder of the airline JetBlue attributes much of his success to his ADHD.

Prevalence

We do not know precisely how many gifted and talented students are being served by special programs, and we don't know how many would be eligible if programs were available to them. Why? Remember that education of the gifted is not mandated or funded by IDEA '04, so there is no requirement that states report these statistics to the federal government. We can, however, make some estimates.

The number of students to serve depends on what concept of giftedness is being applied. For example, if Terman's concept of giftedness were applied, only those who score in the highest 1 percent on an intelligence test would be considered gifted, and only 1 in every 100 children would qualify for special services. If we consider those who score in the highest 2 percent, then 2 in every group of 100 children qualify, and so on. Traditional identification methods used in many schools identify about 3 percent to 5 percent of the school population as gifted. More inclusive approaches (such as Renzulli's enrichment model) are popular. These approaches do not use a score from a test of intelligence as the sole means of identifying gifted students. Therefore the percentage receiving at least some special services increases to somewhere between 10 and 15 percent (Renzulli, 2004; Renzulli & Reis, 1997). Regardless of what criteria are applied to identify gifted and talented students, special programs or services for students who are gifted are not universally available, so many of these students are not even identified.

Causes and Prevention

Throughout this book we have talked about important ways to prevent disabilities. Knowing more about the causes of a disability enables researchers to pinpoint reasons for that disability's occurrence and then provide guidance about how to prevent at least some of the conditions that contribute to it. In the case of giftedness, of course, our hope is not to prevent it from occurring but, rather, to foster talents whenever we can.

Causes: Factors That Enhance or Inhibit Giftedness

Both environment and heredity play important roles in the development of the intellect. On the one hand, there seems to be a strong genetic link to superior intelligence (Silverman, 2005). The IQ scores of highly gifted children—those above

160—are like their parents' and grandparents' scores. Also, environmental factors correlate with both increased and diminished giftedness. Remember from your studies about disabilities that IQ is not a fixed characteristic in people. Early intervention programs have brought about demonstrable improvement in these scores, and these enhancements persist across time (Schweinhart, 2005). Attitudes, motivation, expectations, and values expressed in different cultures, societies, socioeconomic levels, and families influence the development of talent. (Kitano, 1997, 1998; McCoach & Siegle, 2003; Neumeister & Hébert, 2003). In other words, education does make a difference in the results of students who are gifted and talented.

Prevention

One important goal for everyone interested in youngsters who are gifted and talented is to prevent as many situations as possible that negatively affect talent development. Attitudes and opinions expressed by family, friends, TV, and print media (including textbooks) influence behavior and teach role expectations (Reis, 2003). Particularly for girls, what is deemed appropriate behavior ("Don't be too aggressive." "Girls don't do well in math.") influences their choices and may limit their ultimate achievement (Rimm & Rimm-Kaufman, 2001). The power of the peer group and of school culture is a critical element that influences all youngsters' behavior (Schroeder-Davis, 1998). For example, 66 percent of high school students say that athletes get more attention, including school-wide celebration of their accomplishments, than student scholars. "Jocks" and "partyers" are three to five times more popular than "brains." Possibly, educators should seriously reconsider the priorities that some of these celebrations reflect.

Other characteristics, in addition to intellectual and academic achievement, are influenced by attitudes, expectations, and opportunities. Some time ago, Renzulli (1978) observed that many young children are inherently creative, yet relatively few adults are. Creativity is a developed trait, related to risk taking, that affects the expression of talents (Sternberg, 2000). It is likely that the suppression of creativity begins early, during the preschool and early elementary school years. Teachers tend to favor highly intelligent students who do well academically, but they do not encourage divergent, independent, or imaginative behavior. Many educators tend to promote realism instead of imagination. For example, dolls actually "talk," expressing needs like real children. Computerized toys teach children the correct answers to arithmetic problems and the correct way to spell words. The

Creating opportunities for students to express unique talents allows individuals to feel "unfettered," and surprises abound.

qualities that educators value seem to be getting along with others, working toward a goal, and adapting for the common good. Many of these qualities are not compatible with being creative or expressing individual differences (Kirschenbaum, 1998). If creativity is not fostered, it can be lost.

Overcoming Challenges

Educators must come to understand that they may inadvertently be inhibiting creativity. However, managing divergent thinking can be a challenge to teachers who are trying to meet the needs of children with a wide range of abilities and interests. Particularly in these times of high stakes testing, the pressure to have entire classes attain a standard level of achievement can be overwhelming. Many teachers feel that just to progress through the curriculum at the required pace leaves little time for topics not listed in their state's curriculum content standards. The pressure for increased academic achievement for general education students often results in activities focused on thinking skills and creativity being eliminated from classroom instruction. Such pressures can also stifle efforts to enrich or enhance the curriculum. This is a situation that must be avoided.

Assessment

Students who are highly gifted or talented are obvious to their families and to their teachers. If special services and programs for gifted students are available in these youngsters' districts or states, most often they participate. That is, they participate unless (as in this chapter's *Considering Culture*) the family makes a conscious decision not to have a student participate. Where assessment issues come into play, a variety of alternative means for evaluation are suggested for students on the margins of qualifying for programs. As you learned in this chapter, some version of Sidney Marland's 1972 definition of giftedness is being applied across the 50 states. That definition included the assumption that somewhere between 3 and 5 percent of the school population would qualify for special services (Renzulli, 2004). Using these percentages and working with the way IQ scores are distributed along the normal curve (see Figure 14.1 again), states often use the IQ score of 130 as the cutoff point above which students are included in education of the gifted.

Early Identification

Gifted children express their uniqueness almost from birth. These infants and toddlers master developmental milestones early (Silverman, 2005). They are walking independently well before they are one year old; they are talking in complete sentences before they are two. It is common to see these babies turning pages in books by the time they are six months old and reading books before they come to school. Highly gifted youngsters are obvious to family members—and to practically everyone they meet. Surely you've noticed that rare, precocious toddler shopping with his mom!

Preschoolers who are diverse, however, are sometimes missed. New ways of finding diverse students who have superior cognitive skills are emerging (Scott & Delgado, 2005). One reason for paying special attention to this group of learners is their underrepresentation in education programs for the gifted and the importance of more of these students being included. A simple screening device that accepts all true answers from preschoolers, even if they are not on the answer sheet, may be one method. This instrument includes tasks such as picture identification, picture remembering, identifying features of items that are the same or unique,

Considering Culture

Standing Out or Fitting In

Rhonda has been playing the piano since she was three years old and composing music since she was five. Now in second grade, she is showing remarkable ability in math. Her teacher, Ms. Clark, is eager to refer her to a program for students who are gifted and talented where she thinks Rhonda's special abilities will be fostered. Ms. Clark has developed a portfolio of Rhonda's work to share with her parents. Ms. Clark plans to shown it to them at the meeting where she'll request permission for a formal assessment.

Ms. Clark began the meeting by showing Rhonda's parents her work and pointing out how advanced she was compared to others her age. She then requested their permission to allow an assessment, which is required for Rhonda to qualify for programs and services for the gifted and talented. Rhonda's father responded, speaking quietly and deliberately. "Like all of our children, Rhonda is special. She has been blessed with gifts that others do not have, but all children bring gifts to the family and to the tribe. We are pleased that she is doing so well."

The response was not what Ms. Clark expected, and she wasn't certain whether Rhonda's parents had agreed to the assessment or not, so she asked again. "So, do we have your permission for the assessment?"

Rhonda's father paused and then said, "Being with her cousins in the class is important. It would not be good for her to be moved. To be better than others or call attention to one's personal ability and achievement is not the tribal way. We care for one another, not for one *above* another."

Ms. Clark was not prepared for this response. Her first thought was to argue for the assessment and the programs and services available for students who are gifted and talented, but she paused before she spoke. In that moment of reflection, she realized that the tribe's values were an integral part of Rhonda's life, that Rhonda was happy in her class, and that she was involved in many challenging activities in school, at home, and within the tribe that fostered her talent and ability. Perhaps special services weren't the answer for Rhonda. Instead of arguing, Ms. Clark said, "Thank you for describing your values to me. There are many ways to encourage Rhonda's abilities without isolating her from her classmates, her family, and the values that are important to you. I will continue to support Rhonda's musical and mathematical abilities without violating your wishes."

Questions to Consider

1 What values were Rhonda's parents expressing in their refusal to have her assessed and placed in programs designed specifically for students who are gifted and talented?

2 If you had been in Ms. Clark's position, what do you think you would have said to Rhonda's parents?

—By Eleanor Lynch, San Diego State University and Marci Hanson, San Francisco State University

sequencing, rhyming, vocabulary, and descriptive abilities. It identifies more diverse youngsters who are gifted but might otherwise have been denied the opportunity of participating in special programs.

Pre-Referral

During the pre-referral period, teachers have an opportunity to collect important information about the abilities and performance of their students. These activities can be particularly important to those from diverse backgrounds (Bernal, 2003). Gifted students whose IQ scores are below the top 1 percent of all students stand out to their teachers but are not always identified as being gifted or talented. For these students, documentation of outstanding classroom performance should be used for both identification and referral (Brown et al., 2005). Also, community leaders, other teachers, family members, and peers can add to the documentation. When asked to nominate students for special programs, friends, extended family

Signs of giftedness appear early in life.

members, and teachers consistently recognize leadership capabilities, insightfulness, and artistic talents. Sometimes, however, because of bias inherent in standardized tests, these students' scores are too low for them to qualify for special programs. In these cases, experts agree: These students should not be excluded; rather, they should be identified through alternate means—such as portfolios documenting their academic and creative achievements, and teacher recommendations (Bernal, 2003; Castellano, 2003). Also, when the definition of *gifted* is broadened, perhaps to reflect Gardner's ideas about multiple intelligences, more diverse learners are included in special programs (Stanford, 2003). As more and more students from diverse backgrounds are included, charges of elitism and arguments for the elimination of special programs for these students will cease.

Identification

Ideas about who should be included in any group of learners define the identification process. For example, if you are looking for students who have outstanding fine motor skills, you might look for students with the neatest handwriting. Or, if you are searching for individuals who might become the best engineers, you might devise a system to identify the preschoolers most adept at creating buildings and bridges with interlocking blocks. If, however, you are looking for students whose school administrators believe should be included in special programs for students who are gifted, you are likely to create identification procedures to find the "bright achievers." This is exactly what some experts believe: The schools have defined those who are gifted as high achievers and academically able (Gagné, 2004). Of the 29 states that mandate education of the gifted and talented, 26 require documentation of intellectual giftedness and 25 require documentation of high academic achievement (Council of State Directors of Programs for the Gifted and NACG, 2003). The way to find such students is to use IQ tests, achievement tests, and grades. Because IQ scores are commonly used to identify these students, let's consider the ideas behind their design.

Although most definitions of giftedness do not include precise criteria to determine eligibility for special programs, IQ tests are probably the most common way in which students are determined to be eligible for gifted education programs

(Hunsaker, Finley, & Frank, 1997). Therefore, you should know what these IQ scores mean. Let's look at how intelligence scores are distributed. The assumption is that if measurements of intelligence were given to a large sample of people, the scores obtained would approximate a normal (bell-shaped) curve. The scores would cluster around the mean, or average, in a predictable way. Two commonly used tests of intelligence, the *Stanford-Binet Intelligence Test* and the *Wechsler Intelligence Scale for Children IV (WISC-IV)*, use the score of 100 as the mean. Each of these tests breaks scores into groups, and each group is called a standard deviation (SD). On the *Stanford-Binet*, 16 points from the mean equals one standard deviation. On the WISC-IV, 15 points from the mean equals one SD. Thus a score of 130 on the WISC-IV is two SDs from the mean. Look back at Figure 14.1, found on page 498 in this chapter. It shows a normal curve that has been divided by SDs and the percentage of the population that falls within each SD grouping. Remember, though, that this unidimensional (using a single IQ score) approach to identifying gifted students is becoming outdated as theories like Gardner's multiple intelligences are becoming more widely adopted.

Evaluation

Underachievement is of great concern to most experts in the area of gifted education (McCoach & Siegle, 2003; Neumeister & Hébert, 2003). Efforts to halt the cycle of underachievement must begin early. In this regard, the annual accountability efforts outlined in NCLB are most helpful. When gifted students' scores on state- and district-wide achievement tests are below what is expected, quick action should be taken. Teachers should seek to boost motivation and self-esteem. They should also bring additional educational services to the student. Concerted efforts to help such students truly make a difference, avoiding disengagement and the eventuality of leaving school early.

Early Intervention

Recognizing giftedness in young children is important because not responding to their educational needs early could diminish their accomplishments during later school years (Smutny, 2000). Without early identification and the delivery of special services, many gifted preschoolers feel forced to underachieve to remain on a par with their typical classmates (Mooij, 1999). Preschoolers also benefit when their parents receive services from experts in this area. For example, parents can be helped to understand better the importance of family during times of play and can learn how to capitalize on these times to build their gifted child's self-esteem, creativity, and communication skills (Strom, 2000).

Preschool teachers should be aware of differences between preschoolers who are gifted and those who are not. As we saw when we studied students with disabil-

BATIUK, Inc. North America Syndicate.

ities, early intervention with a differentiated education program, offered as soon as the child is identified, makes a tremendous difference. This is true for gifted students as well (Silverman, 2005). What characteristics are commonly observed in these children? The three-year-old who reads books, counts to 100, or plays the piano is a prime candidate. But other characteristics are also benchmarks. At a young age, gifted and talented children may express talent in art or music or may show high levels of verbal expression, curiosity, concentration, internal motivation, exceptional memory, problem solving, theoretical thinking, imagination, and enthusiasm (Harrison, 2004; Smutny, 2000). They are also able to handle complex and abstract language relationships earlier than most. They can come to understand metaphors (such as "Presidents are heads of state" and "Time flies") long before their classmates. And recent research has identified another important difference between these youngsters and their more typically learning peers: Their language skills not only develop more rapidly than those of their peers who are not gifted, they also develop differently, with their language reflecting their superior mental capacity very early (Hoh, 2005). Even at very young ages, these children are able to connect knowledge to form complex sentences, create humor, and understand and play with multiple meanings of words. They are also very motivated to use language as a tool for social interactions and to express interests and needs. Gifted preschoolers seem to function well in typical early childhood programs. However, they must be challenged so that their motivation to learn is not dulled. Researchers also caution that children should not be forced to relearn what they have already mastered (Gallagher & Gallagher, 1994). Time after time, stories are told about children who come to kindergarten already reading but, instead of being allowed to continue developing their reading skills, are forced to engage in readiness activities with classmates. For these students, instructional time might better be spent on enrichment activities, such as teaching students to classify and organize information or to think critically.

Teaching Gifted and Talented Students

A variety of educational services, varying by locale and in philosophy and orientation, are offered to gifted students. Remember that special services are inconsistently available; not every state has special programs, nor does every school district in states that do. At the very least; all gifted students should have some enhancements to their learning experiences. A **differentiated curriculum** is one in which different learning experiences are provided—experiences above and beyond those provided to typical learners through the general education curriculum (Tomlinson, 2004a&b; Van Tassel-Baska & Stambaugh, 2006). A differentiated curriculum can be achieved in many different ways: by modifying the standard curriculum's content, the learning environment, or the instruction provided (Gallagher, 2000). *Tips for Classroom Management* provides examples of ways to extend content found in the general education curriculum to create a differentiated curriculum for gifted learners. Services for students who are gifted and talented are delivered through a variety of placement options: general education classrooms, resource rooms or pullout programs, self-contained classes, and even special schools. Regardless of the method used, these key features define differentiated instruction for gifted learners:

- Problem-based learning
- Abstract thinking
- Reasoning activities
- Creative problem solving
- Content mastery
- Breadth and depth of topic
- Independent study
- Talent development

differentiated curriculum
The flexible application of curriculum targets to ensure content mastery, in-depth learning, and exploration of additional issues and themes

*tips for Classroom Management

DIFFERENTIATING THE CURRICULUM FOR GIFTED STUDENTS

General Education Assignment	Differentiated Assignment
Discuss plot, setting, and characters in the novel *The Pearl* by John Steinbeck.	Compare and contrast the plot, setting, characters, motivation, theme, and climax of *The Pearl* with *Of Mice and Men*, two novels by John Steinbeck. How would you characterize the author's style?
Charles invested $10,000 in stock in January. When he sold it in December, the price was up 10 percent from his purchase price. What was his profit on this stock?	Which would you rather choose? a. Eighty percent profit in year 1, and 50 percent loss in year 2 b. Five percent profit in year 1, and 5 percent profit in year 2 Explain your reasoning in writing, and share your thinking with the class.
Pretend you are a newscaster studying World War II. Select one of the following to complete, based on your role: a. Write a news report that outlines a significant event in the war. b. Re-create a significant event and describe how that event was critical to the outcome of the war. c. Design a flyer based on a significant event.	Using a medium of your choice (song, dance, poster, PowerPoint presentation, flowchart, etc.), illustrate the cause-and-effect relationships among the precipitating events of World War II.

Source: From *Comprehensive Curriculum for Gifted Learners* (3rd ed.; pp. 81–83), by J. Van Tassel-Baska and T. Stambaugh, 2006, Boston: Allyn and Bacon. Adapted by permission

Access to the General Education Curriculum: Acceleration

The case for students with disabilities being able to access the general education to the greatest extent their abilities allow has been well made by professionals, policymakers, and parents. However, for students who are gifted and talented, the argument has not been clearly articulated or understood until recently. Today's consensus among professionals is that gifted students must access the curriculum *at their own level* (Bernal, 2003). They must be intellectually and academically challenged, which cannot be accomplished without additional instruction or opportunities: They need opportunities beyond what is available to typical learners participating in general education classes. A simple answer to these challenges is available; it is acceleration and it just needs to be more widely adopted.

Acceleration is an option that allows students to move through the curriculum more rapidly than their peers who learn in more typical ways. Because acceleration is effective and does not require expensive special classes or programs, it is receiving considerable positive attention (Colangelo, Assouline, & Gross, 2004; Lubinski & Benbow, 1995). Acceleration can take many different forms (Van Tassel-Baska, 2004). Acceleration may be offered through options such as grade skipping, advanced placement courses, or ability groups such as honors sections.

acceleration Moving students through a curriculum or years of schooling in a shorter period of time than usual

A common form of acceleration, **grade skipping**, has students advance to a grade ahead of their classmates of the same age. Grade skipping usually happens in the early elementary years, often at or during kindergarten, when a child's giftedness is apparent because he or she can already read books, write stories, or solve mathematics problems. Grade skipping is observed with some frequency again toward the end of high school, when students skip their remaining years and enter college through early admissions programs.

Another acceleration option is available to students who qualified as gifted students and to those who are high achievers in specific areas of study. **Advanced placement (AP) courses** enable students, while in high school, to take classes for which they earn college credit. Advanced placement allows students to study course content in more depth. A side benefit is that they do not have to take these courses over again in college. Unfortunately, as you'll recall from our discussions in the Overcoming Challenges section of Chapter 3 about diverse students living in urban areas, advanced placement is less readily available to these students (Tornatzky, Pachon, & Torres, 2003).

Another approach, **ability grouping**, has students of comparable abilities working together in courses or activities in which they excel. **Honors sections** are one example of ability grouping. Advanced ability groups are easily arranged in middle school and high school, where students attend different sections of classes or where honor sections are available. For example, a ninth-grader might attend a sophomore- or junior-level mathematics class, and a high school senior might take several classes at a local college. Many high schools offer honors sections of academic courses as a form of ability grouping. The criterion for entrance into these classes is outstanding academic achievement in specific subject areas. In fact, research indicates that gifted students *need* at least some ability grouping, wherein comprehensiveness of coverage, speed and pacing of instruction, and advancement through content match their abilities (Rogers, 2002, 2003).

The benefits of acceleration are great (NAGC, 2004). It adjusts the pace of instruction, provides an appropriate challenge, avoids boredom from repetitious instruction, and reduces the time required to master curricular content. The following benefits are also cited (Colangleo, Assouline, & Gross, 2004):

1. Students can complete the traditional general education curriculum in a shorter period of time and may be able to finish high school several years early.
2. Academic material can be completed more quickly, allowing students to study related topics in more depth.
3. Research efficacy validates this approach.
4. Some students develop better self-concepts and more positive attitudes about course content and school.
5. Gifted students are not segregated from more typical learners, because although they are not placed with students of the same age, they are participating in general education programs.

Acceleration programs are also cost-effective for both schools and families. For those participating in advanced placement courses, college can be completed in a shorter time, saving families a portion of college tuition costs. By graduating a semester or a year earlier, students can spare their families (or their own debt burden if they borrow money for college expenses) anywhere from 12 to 25 percent of the costs for college. Schools do not need to spend precious resources hiring special teachers or offering special sections of courses for their few very talented students. In fact, many schools send gifted students to local colleges and universities for the specific advanced courses they need or are ready for. And now, distance education offers even more advantages. For example, Stanford University's Educational Program for Gifted Youth (EPGY) is one of many university programs that offer special online courses for high school students who want to study specific content in more depth.

grade skipping A form of acceleration; advances students to a grade ahead of their age peers

advanced placement (AP) courses High school courses that carry college credit

ability grouping Placing students with comparable achievement and skill levels in the same classes or courses

honors sections Advanced classes for students who show high achievement in specific subject areas

Instructional Accommodations: Enrichment

Many educators feel that advanced placement does not lend itself well to the elementary school. Also, for some students, grade skipping is inappropriate because they are not socially ready to join older peers for their studies. These justifications are used to support another option for education of the gifted. **Enrichment**, broadly speaking, adds topics or skills to the traditional curriculum. For example, a group of students might spend a small amount of time each week working with instructional materials that enhance creativity or critical thinking. Alternatively, enrichment might consist of studying a particular academic subject in more depth and detail. Twice exceptional students profit from enrichment activities, but they often need some additional supports to compensate for the disabilities so that their gifted abilities are not masked (Baum, 2004b).

Three of the many other examples of the enrichment approach are independent study, mentorships, and internships. As an enrichment option, **independent study** is generally used within a traditional course; a student studies topics in more depth or explores a topic that is not part of the general education curriculum. Independent study does not mean working alone but, rather, learning to be self-directed and to explore topics in which the individual has an interest. **Mentorships** pair students who have special interests with adults who have expertise in those areas or (like the volunteers of The 100 Black Men of America described in this chapter's Making a Difference section) pair students with highly successful adults who serve as role models and provide guidance to talented youngsters. Mentorships need to be carefully arranged by teachers, but the effects are often amazing. They have both an immediate and a long-term impact on the students' retention in programs for education of the gifted, as well as positively influencing college and career paths (Corwin, 2001; Grantham, 2004). The powerful relationship that often develops between a gifted youngster and his or her mentor can reverse stubborn patterns of underachievement (Hébert & Olenchak, 2000). **Internships** are working assignments that enable gifted high school students who have expressed interest in a particular career to gain experience with that profession.

The **enrichment triad/revolving-door model**, a popular enrichment approach, seeks to modify the entire educational system by allowing some 15 to 20 percent (instead of just 3 percent to 5 percent) of the school population to participate in advanced activities (Renzulli, 1999, 2004; Renzulli & Reis, 1997). Supporters of this approach maintain that it includes students with high potential for creative production and a larger pool of culturally and linguistically diverse students. How does the program work? Students "revolve" into and out of different levels of their program, which includes three types of skills categories. Here are a few examples of each type:

- *Type 1.* Enrichment activities expose the entire class of general education students to new and exciting topics of study carried out through a variety of instructional approaches (speakers, field trips, demonstrations, videotapes and films, and interest centers).
- *Type 2.* Activities encourage all students to develop their cognitive and affective abilities through their own expressive skills (writing a play, doing a pen-and-ink sketch, using equipment).
- *Type 3.* Opportunities to apply advanced investigative and creative skills are given to students who are motivated, and those who show great interest are provided with specialized instruction and activities to explore particular topics, issues, or ideas.

How can general education teachers find time in the busy school day to enrich students' curriculum? **Curriculum compacting** recaptures instructional time by reducing (or even eliminating) coverage of topics that gifted students either have already mastered or will master in a fraction of the time that their peers need. Saved

enrichment Adding topics or skills to the traditional curriculum or presenting a particular topic in more depth

independent study Allows a student to pursue and study a topic in depth on an individual basis

mentorship A program in which a student is paired with an adult in order to learn to apply knowledge in real-life situations

internship A program that places students, usually high school seniors, in job settings related to their career goals

enrichment triad/revolving-door model An inclusive model for education of the gifted wherein 15 to 20 percent of a school's students participate in activities to develop thinking skills, problem solving, and creativity

curriculum compacting Saving instructional time for enrichment activities time can then be reallocated to enrichment activities such as mentoring, independent study, internships, and/or advanced study (Stamps, 2004).

Validated Practices

Enrichment programs are offered in a variety of settings. For example, in **cluster grouping**, a teacher who specialized in education of the gifted both supports the general education teacher and provides special instruction to the top six to eight students at each grade level (VanTassel-Baska & Stambaugh, 2006). Students might be assigned independent study activities that support and extend topics that are part of the general education curriculum. Sixth-graders, studying state history in social studies, might come to a resource room (pullout program) to prepare a "Who's Who" book of key figures in their state's history. They might prepare a position paper on a current issue, such as water rights, including the historical reasons for the controversy and concluding with possible solutions to the problem. And they might enrich their studies by either being assigned or being able to select additional readings that are relevant to their individual backgrounds, heritage, and culture. Such an approach is strongly supported by Donna Ford and her colleagues and is described in this chapter's *Validated Practices*.

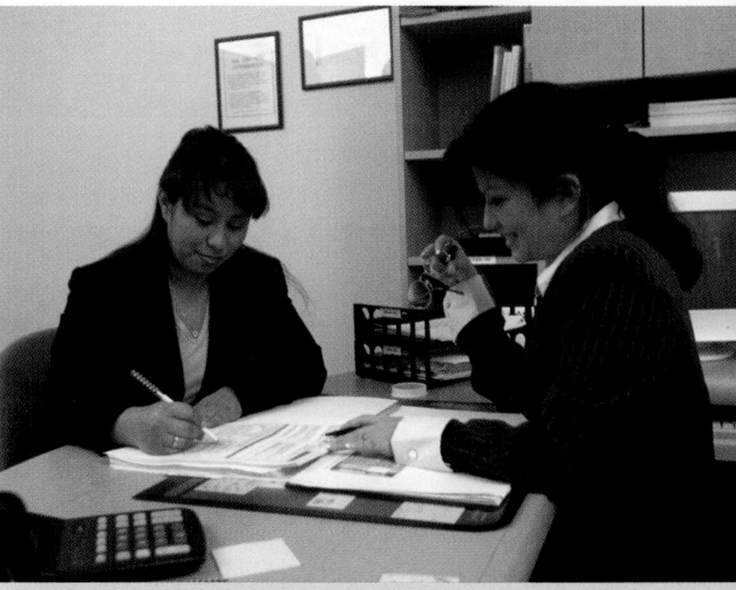

For her senior-year internship, this student has been matched with a local law firm and has been assigned to a lawyer whose specialty is medical malpractice.

The most common placement and administrative arrangements for gifted students are pullout programs (VanTassel-Baska & Stambaugh, 2006). In **pullout programs**, students leave the general education class for a portion of the school day to attend a special class, like a resource room. Such programs provide services for either several days a week or an hour or so each day. In addition to enrichment activities, some of these programs address the needs of gifted students who are exhibiting characteristics of underachievement. Here teachers address motivation and self-esteem and often provide students with strategies to self-monitor their progress with techniques such as those you learned about on pages 221–225 in Chapter 6 (McCoach & Siegle, 2003; Neumeister & Hébert, 2003). Some schools combine cluster and pullout programs, but at some schools, the special education teacher provides extra assistance both to students who are gifted and to students with disabilities. Both cluster and pullout programs rely heavily on the general education classroom for the majority of a student's education.

Some experts believe that pullout and cluster programming is an insufficient response to the education of gifted students (Bernal, 2003). Even though separate programs for these students had been thought to be unfair and inequitable, there is now a growing consensus that gifted students require more intensive instruction. Suggestions include more opportunities for acceleration, magnet schools, advanced placement courses blocked strictly for gifted students, and even separate schools or classes. Some gifted students attend special classes, and even special schools are once again growing in popularity with parents and students. Support for separate programs may be due to their unique and comprehensive elements: acceleration, enrichment, counseling, parent involvement, supplemental programs for those with special learning needs, and behavior management. Some students receive the majority of their instruction in a special class, possibly at their neighborhood school, where they are educated in a homogeneous environment in which all the other students have comparable abilities. Some advantaged youngsters receive their education at exclusive private schools. A few students attend special public schools exclusively for students who are gifted. Hunter Elementary, for instance, administered by Hunter College of the City University of New York, is a public elementary school for these students, but such schools are usually at the high

cluster grouping Pullout programs delivered by a teacher who specializes in education of the gifted

pullout programs Part-time special services outside of the general education classroom; resource rooms; the most common educational placement for gifted students

Validated Practices Bibliotherapy

What Is Bibliotherapy?

Bibliotherapy uses literature to enhance gifted students' self-awareness, persistence, and social relationships. Bibliotherapy consists of five components: identification, catharsis, insight, universalization, and action. Teachers and students identify areas of need and select a story or novel that will help them understand the problem and generate positive alternatives.

Why Bibliotherapy Is Beneficial

Bibliotherapy helps gifted students deal with issues they face (e.g., anxiety, self-image, working with others).

Moreover, the strategy will assist all students in understanding something or someone different from themselves. Students are provided with ample opportunity to discuss the issues, the solutions generated in the story, and how they can implement positive change in their own situation. These discussions occur in an environment in which students are familiar and comfortable before they apply the strategies in other situations.

Implementing Bibliotherapy

Select a book or novel you feel will assist your students with a current issue they are facing. Follow these five steps to implement bibliotherapy:

1 *Identification*

- Guide students to understanding how they are like the character in the story.

2 *Catharsis*

- As students read, help them recognize their emotions and begin to discuss them with others.
- If students do not initiate the discussion, you may need to facilitate it.

3 *Insight*

- Students make connections with the characters and the issues affecting them.
- Again, they may need some assistance from you at first.

4 *Universalization*

- Readers understand that they are not alone and their problem is not unique.
- Students realize that other individuals confront the same issues that they do.
- Students recognize what the characters have done to solve their problems.

5 *Action*

- The reader exhibits behavioral and cognitive change.
- Students positively change their thinking and behaviors to influence their actions.

An example of a Bibliotherapy and sample activities for elementary-age students using the story "The Cracked Egg" is presented in Figure A. (See Ford and Harris [1999] for an extensive annotated bibliography and activities to use with students in grades P–12, plus a list of suggested books to use with African American students who are gifted.)

Figure A • Bibliotherapy Example

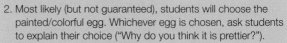

- Boil two eggs.
- Paint one of the eggs and cover it with glitter.
- Leave the other egg unpainted.

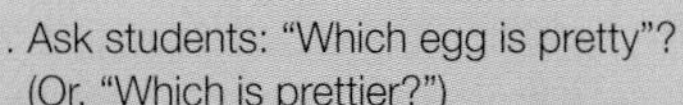

1. Ask students: "Which egg is pretty"? (Or, "Which is prettier?")
2. Most likely (but not guaranteed), students will choose the painted/colorful egg. Whichever egg is chosen, ask students to explain their choice ("Why do you think it is prettier?").
3. Ask students: "Which egg tastes better? Why?"
4. "What does the outside of the egg have to do with the inside?" "Just because it is pretty outside, does that mean it is pretty inside?"
5. Crack the eggs. Ask students to look for differences on the inside.
6. What do students see? What does this mean?
7. Ask students: "What have you learned about yourself from this activity and book?"

This scientifically validated practice is a teaching method proven by systematic research efforts (Ford, Grantham, Harris, 1996; Ford & Harris, 1999; Ford & Harris, 2000; Ford et al., 2002). Full citations are found in the references for Chapter 14.

Source: From *Multicultural Gifted Education* (p. 142) by D. Y. Ford and J. J. Harris, 1999, New York: Teachers College Press. Reprinted with permission of the publisher.

—By Kimberly Paulsen, Vanderbilt University

school level and stress special areas of education. Magnet schools often emphasize a theme, specializing in the performing arts, math, or science, and are available to students who pass qualifying exams or auditions. Finally, there are 12 public residential schools for gifted students in the nation, research has documented the social and academic benefits of such separate schools (Coleman, 2001).

Technology

Technology can be a tool, an inspiration, and a means to independent learning for all students. For gifted students, it can facilitate differentiated instruction, particularly for those who live in rural and remote areas (Belcastro, 2002; Johnson, 2000). For example, one student can work on a tutorial in chemistry or physics while a classmate is learning how to program the computer to develop an environmental monitoring and control system. Or these students can work on accelerated or enriched topics while their general education classmates' work on their own assignments. For gifted students bored by instruction paced too slowly for them or on topics they have already mastered, technology can enable them to study advanced topics more in depth. And for gifted students, technology could well be considered a functional life skill: desktop publishing, creating multimedia presentations, accessing information via the Internet, word processing, making graphics, managing databases, and building spreadsheets. The Internet offers exciting opportunities for independent study and extended learning. For example, students learning about other planets and solar systems can experience traveling through space by visiting the Web site of NASA's Jet Propulsion Laboratory (JPL). They can take a virtual tour of the wonderful art in the collection at the Louve, in Paris (in English if they enter through Google). Virtual tours of many other museums bring art and national history to students' computers. This chapter's *Accommodating for Inclusive Environments* provides only a few examples of the exciting adventures that await students who enrich their learning through the Internet.

Nearly all of us can attest to the benefits of telecommunications in our daily lives. We are now able to communicate with friends efficiently and economically through e-mail. We can find important or interesting information "on the Web." Many of you registered for this class online and use Web editions of your college textbooks as you explore topics discussed in class. The practical benefits to all students, particularly gifted students, cannot be overestimated.

Telecommunications and Internet technology enable students who live miles apart, and who may not even have met, to work together on joint projects. For example, UNICEF "assembles" students around the world to discuss important current events. Students who live in remote areas can access major library facilities and computers that have the capability to analyze complicated sets of data. They can link up to scientists who work at research laboratories to ask for help in solving a scientific or mathematical problem. Telecommunications can also provide opportunities for dialog between students and experts from all across the nation on real issues and problems. Those who live in rural areas can participate in courses not available at their home schools and can take advanced courses in math, foreign languages, science, and the arts—all without leaving their home schools (Belcastro, 2002).

Transition

Possibly because of gifted students' heightened intensity and sensitivity, the transition years can be difficult, particularly as these students affirm themselves and seek independence from their families (Higgins & Boone, 2003). As previously noted, not all gifted and talented individuals achieve to their potential, and too many become bored and disengaged during the high school years. College attendance and graduation

Accommodating for Inclusive Environments

Enriching Instruction Through the Internet

Area of Interest	Topic	Provider	Web Site
Math and Science	Math challenges	Dr. Math	http://mathforum.org
	Geology, biology, chemistry, physics, and more	Lee Summit, Missouri School District	http://its.leesummit.k12.mo.us/science.htm
	Space exploration	Jet Propulsion Labs, NASA	http://www.jpl.nasa.gov
	Weather	National Oceanic and Atmospheric Association	http://www.wrh.noaa.gov/vef/kids/kids.php
	Environmental education	EnviroLink Network	http://envirolink.org/envrioed
	Astronomy	University of Washington	http://www.astro.washington.edu
Social Studies	American government	FirstGov for Kids	http://www.kids.gov/k_history.htm
	American history	Library of Congress	http://www.loc.gov/families
	Art history	Getty	http://www.getty.edu/art
		Smithsonian	http://www.smithsonianeducation.org/students/index.html
Research Skills	How to conduct Internet research	Big 6 Associates	http://www.big6.com/kids
Connecting	World issues	UNICEF	http://www.unicef.org/voy/

are clearly linked to adult outcomes in American society, and high school achievement is related to success in college (Peterson, 2000). An unexpectedly high percentage of gifted individuals drop out of high school or college (Renzulli & Park, 2002). Regardless of these findings, longitudinal studies do support the common belief: Gifted children tend to grow up to be highly successful, accomplished adults (Benbow & Stanley, 1996; Oden, 1968; Terman, 1925; Terman & Oden, 1959).

However, good outcomes are not guaranteed for all gifted individuals. And, for those who are successful, their path is often difficult. For these reasons, experts remain concerned. Some suggest linking these students to activities beyond school, such as internships, mentorships, and community volunteerism and social learning opportunities (Higgins & Boone, 2003). And others suggest many different acceleration options to keep these students interested and challenged (Colangelo, Assouline, & Gross, 2004). In addition to the ones we have already discussed, early entrance to college is once again being suggested as a viable option (Muratori, Colangelo, & Assouline, 2003). Other options include special summer school programs and distance education courses like the ones offered by Stanford University. Its Educational Program for Gifted Youth (EPGY) not only prepares students for the challenges associated with a college education but also provides motivation to finish high school and then attend college. Educators may find that capitalizing on future college plans motivates youngsters to do well in high school so that they have better choices for college.

A subgroup of gifted students also needs special attention. Tragically, the long-term outcomes for "twice exceptional" students appear not to be as good as they should be (Winebrenner, 2003). The performance of these individuals as adults

As we have learned from the TV show "Malcolm in the Middle," giftedness expresses itself in many different ways.

tends to be more consistent with their learning disabilities than with their intellectual potential. They are more likely to complete high school than their peers with learning disabilities, but they are also more likely than their gifted peers to complete only a few semesters of college. Their earnings outcomes reflect their school completion rates; many earn close to minimum wage. To avoid this negative pattern will require intervention. Schools should consider including gifted students with learning disabilities in organized transition programs or including them in career exploration opportunities along with their gifted peers who do not have disabilities. Realistic career and college counseling should help these individuals understand their potential and select reasonable alternatives for postsecondary experiences.

Collaboration

Most gifted students attend general education classes, receive enrichment activities, and attend pullout or cluster programs for a limited portion of the school week (Van Tassel-Baska & Stambaugh, 2006). Even those students who participate in programs using the acceleration model spend most of their school day with their general education classmates. Thus gifted education teachers and general education teachers work closely together to ensure that an appropriate education is provided to gifted students. The specialist in education of the gifted helps general education teachers differentiate instruction, deliver enrichment activities, and ensure that gifted students remain challenged in their schoolwork. For example, general education teachers often need assistance when they schedule a commonly applied technique that groups gifted students with their general education classmates. **Cooperative learning** groups students of mixed abilities together in small groups (Slavin, 1990; Tomlinson, 2004a&b). However, cooperative learning may not be the best answer to the question "What teaching technique is effective for a wide range of student abilities and particularly engages the gifted learner?" Research has revealed that gifted youngsters complain that the pace of cooperative learning is too slow and repetitive and that group instruction is not challenging enough. For this strategy to be effective, teachers must present complex, problem-based, and open-ended tasks. Teachers with special expertise in education of the gifted can be most helpful in this regard. They help general education teachers ensure that gifted students are engaged without "losing" the other students because they cannot keep up.

cooperative learning Students working in small groups on the same material; mixed-ability grouping

Successful collaboration efforts do not happen by accident (Robinson, 1999). It takes considerable effort and planning. Teachers must work together to

- Define the educational problems that individual students or groups of students are facing
- Research the problem and identify "best practices" that might be effective
- Identify backup or alternative solutions
- Determine how to evaluate the solution's effectiveness (agree on criteria or level of student performance needed to retain the intervention)
- Develop a plan of action
- Decide on a meeting schedule

Of course these tasks seem self-evident, but they are not easily accomplished, particularly when teachers are working in isolation. Collaboration and partnerships with other educators, community members, and families can make a real difference in the educational lives of gifted and talented children.

Partnerships with Families and Communities

Family is just as important in the lives of young gifted and talented individuals as in those of other children. Indeed some experts in education of the gifted believe that these children's vulnerability and sensitivity often require special attention from family members (Hébert, 2001; Rimm, 2001). Supporting this belief are studies of eminent adults that clearly show how powerful the long-term influence of family is on gifted children (Hébert, 1998; Kitano, 1997, 1998). Definitive common threads run through the early lives of eminent adults. For example, regardless of the father's occupation, learning was valued for its own sake. The family was prepared to commit whatever time and resources were necessary to foster achievement and to develop talent. These families arranged for instruction, encouraged and supervised practice and study, were involved in their children's education, and developed open channels of communication between parents and children. Perhaps most important, these parents served as role models by living an achieving lifestyle.

"Sons learn about feelings by watching their fathers and other men" (Hébert, 2001). For gifted boys, learning how to deal with and express emotions is important, particularly because gifted children are often overly sensitive. Hébert (2001) suggests that fathers can develop more intense relationships with their sons by being certain that they really listen, writing them letters at times of important decisions and times of major disappointments, and also sharing time and experiences. Recall that diverse gifted students are at increased risk for underachievement and underrepresentation among those identified as gifted. Some believe that Black boys are at the greatest risk (Hébert, 1998). For these children, it is important that parents and family instill an achievement orientation and a strong belief in self by holding high and reasonable expectations while recognizing accomplishments.

Finally, parents and families also need to guide gifted children in making appropriate choices and in holding realistic expectations for themselves and others. These children seem to be more mature than others of their age, but appearances can be deceiving (Clark, 2002). One result of the combination of these characteristics can be stress unlike that experienced by their peers (Nichols & Baum, 2000). And remember that these children, just like others of their age, are not capable of making complex decisions or setting their own goals and directions. Families make a difference by maintaining open lines of communication through family meetings, talking with their children about values and how to balance life's events, and helping them determine what is important and what is not.

Imagine a world...

where anyone and everyone can make a difference

Summary

Gifted students do not have a disability that presents obstacles to their learning and participating in society. However, they can be handicapped by our social and educational systems, which can present barriers to their achieving their full potential. Gifted individuals possess unique intellectual abilities that can be developed into talents. Subgroups of learners who are gifted and talented—females, twice exceptional, diverse, and those with ADHD—need extra special attention from education professionals so they meet their potential. One challenge facing educators is to develop and put in place a consistent array of educational options that will facilitate each individual's development.

Addressing the Chapter Objectives

1 What is the current concept of giftedness and talent?

- Giftedness is construed as potential for high performance and accomplishments at the upper end of any talent continuum: intellectual, artistic, creative, academic, or leadership.
- Talent development consists of the efforts of families, teachers, peers, and mentors to help students develop their aptitudes into outstanding abilities and achievements.

2 Regardless of the definition applied, what descriptors can be used for gifted and talented individuals?

- Demonstrate high intellectual abilities
- Score well on tests of intelligence
- Learn more quickly than peers
- Apply complex thinking skills
- Achieve significantly higher than their classmates academically
- Tend to become leaders
- Are sensitive
- Tend to be perfectionists
- Are intense
- Are successful

3 What factors can inhibit giftedness and talent development?

- Heredity
- Environment: deprivation, lack of stimulation, family values, low expectations, family's low socioeconomic level

- Few educational opportunities: little availability of programs
- Bias

4 Why are educators concerned about issues related to underrepresentation of some subgroups of gifted learners?

- Diverse students do not have equal access to programs for education of the gifted.
- Fewer African American, Hispanic, and Native American children receive educational services for gifted students than would be expected from their percentage in the general student population.
- The identification process is biased and favors students from, and talents encouraged in, the dominant culture.

5 What are two approaches to education of the gifted, and how do they differ from one another?

Two approaches to gifted education:

- *Enrichment:* interdisciplinary instruction, independent study, mentorships, internships, enrichment triad/revolving-door model, curriculum compacting
- *Acceleration:* advanced placement, honors sections, ability grouping, individualized instruction

Acceleration often places gifted students in existing general education programs for older students, whereas enrichment offers gifted students unique and special programs. The most common educational arrangement is pullout programs (resource rooms).

mylabschool™ Where the classroom comes to life!

MyLabSchool is a collection of online tools for your success in this course, your licensure exams, and your teaching career. Visit www.mylabschool.com to access the following:

- Online Study Guide
- Video cases from real classrooms
- Help with your research papers using Research Navigator
- Career Center with resources for:
  - Praxis and licensure preparation
  - Professional portfolio development
  - Job search and interview techniques
  - Lesson plannning

Supplementary Resources

Popular Novels, Children's, and Adolescents' Books

Corwin, M. (2001). *And still we rise: The trials and triumphs of twelve gifted inner-city students.* New York: HarperCollins.

Fitzgerald, J. D. (1985). *The great brain.* New York: Dell.

Hawking, S. (2003). *The universe in a nutshell.* New York: Bantam.

Kanigel, R. (1991). *The man who knew infinity: A life of the genius Ramanujan.* New York: Scribner.

Paolini, C. (2005). *Eragon.* New York: Knopf.

Paolini, C. (2006). *Eldest.* New York: Knopf.

Simpson, D. E. (1995). *A matter of color.* Austin, TX: The Inspirational Pen.

Movies

Good Will Hunting (1998). Miramax

Will is an extremely gifted youth who grew up in foster homes and was abused. One day, working at M.I.T. as a janitor, he anonymously solves some Ph.D-level problems in mathematics, showcasing his intelligence. He is discovered and, because of his police record, is forced to see a psychiatrist as well as to practice math with a noted professor. After a time with the psychiatrist, Will enters into a healthy father–son relationship and eventually is able to see his potential in the world by letting old wounds heal. Even though Will is a genius, his brilliance cannot shelter him from the problems of having been raised in terrible foster homes and having experienced abuse and a fragmented childhood. Ben Affleck and Matt Damon won the Academy Award for best original screenplay with this film, and Robin Williams was named best supporting actor.

Searching for Bobby Fisher (1993). Paramount

Josh is typical child, but one day he plays a game of chess with his father, and it soon becomes apparent that Josh is a prodigy at the game. He begins to develop his talent with a traditional instructor, while also honing his skill with a hustler in the park. Josh's father becomes overly competitive, putting too much pressure on his son always to win and to make chess the focal point of his young life. Josh is able to incorporate the methods of both of his "teachers" for relieving stress and pressure.

Little Man Tate (1991). Orion

Jane directs a school for gifted children and discovers Tate, a seven-year-old boy who is exceptional in a number of fields. Tate has difficulty fitting in with other children his own age and therefore is very unhappy and depressed. Jane, herself a musical prodigy, offers Tate the opportunity to join a school that will allow him to grow both academically and socially. This film provides insight into the alienation often experienced by gifted youth. Unable to fit in with children his own age, Tate enrolls in a summer college course that challenges him academically, but his experience there demonstrates that being alienated from an age group can also lead to social isolation. Once Tate enrolls in a program for gifted children, he begins to feel comfortable with his exceptional abilities because many of his classmates come from similar situations.

Amadeus (1984). Republic Pictures

This film depicts the entire life of Wolfgang Amadeus Mozart through the eyes of an extremely jealous, substantially older contemporary, Antonio Salieri whose ability cannot be compared to that of Mozart. Salieri cannot understand why God would bless such a person with incredible talent; this obsession infuriates and torments Salieri for his entire life. Mozart's talent is legendary, and he was a true child prodigy. At 6 he was performing, at 7 he created his first sonata, and at 13 he produced his first full-length opera. His superior talent and potential for a long-lasting career ended tragically at the early age of 33.

Professional, Parent, and Advocacy Groups

Gifted Child Society in Glen Rock, New Jersey
www.gifted.org/society

National Association for Gifted Children in Washington, DC: www.nagc.org

National Office for American Mensa, Gifted Children Program in Arlington, Texas
www.us.mensa.org

The Association for the Gifted (TAG), Council for Exceptional Children in Arlington, Virginia
www.cectag.org

The Belin & Blank International Center for Gifted Education and Talent Development at The University of Iowa in Iowa City, Iowa
www.education.uiowa.edu/belinblank

National Research Center on the Gifted and Talented in Storrs, Connecticut
www.gifted.uconn.edu

Professional Standards and Licensure Tests

After reading this chapter, you should be able to link basic knowledge and skills described in the CEC Standards and INTASC Principles with information provided in this text. The table below shows some of the specific CEC Gifts and Talents Knowledge and Skill Standards and INTASC Special Education Principles that can be applied to each major section of the chapter. Other standards may also be applied to this chapter. Associated General Praxis II topic areas are identified in the right column.

Major Chapter Headings	CEC Knowledge and Skill Core Standard and Associated Subcategories	INTASC Core Principle and Associated Special Education Subcategories	PRAXIS II Exam Topic
Where We've Been . . . What's on the Horizon	**1: Foundations** GT1K2 Models, theories, and philosophies that form the basis for gifted education	**1: Subject Matter** 1.02 All teachers know which key concepts, ideas, facts, and processes in their content area students should understand at different grades and developmental levels and can appropriately structure activities that reflect the scope and sequence of the content area.	1: Understanding Exceptionality 2: Legal and Social Issues
Giftedness and Talent Development Defined	**1: Foundations** GT1K5 Issues in definition and identification of individuals with gifts and talents, including those from culturally and linguistically diverse backgrounds	**1: Subject Matter** 1.04 All teachers have knowledge of the major principles and parameters of federal disabilities legislation.	1: Understanding Exceptionality 2: Legal and Social Issues
Characteristics	**2: Development and Characteristics of Learners** GT2K5 Characteristics and effects of the cultural and environmental milieu of the child and the family	**2: Student Learning** 2.08 Special education teachers seek a holistic understanding of each student's current learning and development, based on knowledge of the student's performance within a variety of settings.	1: Understanding Exceptionality

Causes and Prevention	**2: Development and Characteristics of Learners** GT2K9 Effects of families on the development of individuals with gifts and talents	**2: Student Learning** 2.07 Special education teachers seek to understand the current and evolving development and learning of individual students from a life-span perspective.	1: Understanding Exceptionality
Assessment	**8: Assessment** GT8K4 Screening, pre-referral, referral, and identification procedures for individuals with gifts and talents	**8: Assessment** 8.09 Special education teachers are aware of and guard against over and under identification of disabilities based on cultural, ethnic, gender, and linguistic diversity.	1: Understanding Exceptionality 3: Delivery of Services to Students
Teaching Gifted and Talented Students	**4: Instructional Strategies** GT4S3 Teach individuals to use self-assessment, problem solving, and other cognitive strategies to meet their needs	**4: Instructional Strategies** 4.11 Special education teachers collaborate with general education teachers to infuse individualized goals and specialized strategies into instruction for students with disabilities.	3: Delivery of Services to Students
Transition	**4: Instructional Planning** GT5S5 Create an environment that encourages self-advocacy and increased independence	**7: Planning Instruction** 7.07 Special education teachers oversee the development of individualized transition plans to guide learners' transitions from preschool to elementary school, middle school to high school, and high school to postschool opportunities.	2: Legal and Social Issues 3: Delivery of Services to Students
Collaboration	**10: Collaboration** GT10S6 Communicate with school personnel about the characteristics and needs of individuals with gifts and talents	**10: Collaboration, Ethics, and Relationships** 10.05 All special education teachers provide leadership that enables teams to accomplish their purposes.	2: Legal and Social Issues 3: Delivery of Services to Students
Partnerships with Families and Communities	**10: Collaboration** GT10K2 Concerns of families of individuals with gifts and talents and strategies to help address these concerns	**10: Collaboration, Ethics, and Relationships** 10.09 Special education teachers collaborate with families and with school and community personnel to include students with disabilities in a range of instructional environments in the school and community.	2: Legal and Social Issues 3: Delivery of Services to Students

Glossary

A

ability grouping Placing students with comparable achievement and skill levels in the same classes or courses

absence seizures Seizures characterized by a short lapse in consciousness; petit mal seizures

academic enablers Skills and behaviors (interpersonal skills, motivation, study skills, engagement) that influence successful academic performance

acceleration Moving students through a curriculum or years of schooling in a shorter period of time than usual

accommodation The focusing process of the lens of the eye

accommodations Supports to compensate for disabilities, adjustments to assignments or tests

acquired immunodeficiency syndrome (AIDS) A usually fatal medical syndrome caused by infection from the human immunodeficiency virus (HIV)

adaptive behavior Performance of everyday life skills expected of adults

advance organizers A tactic that previews lectures and provides organizing structures to acquaint students with the content, its organization, and its importance before the lesson

advanced placement (AP) courses High school courses that carry college credit

adventitious blindness Blindness occurring after the age of two

aggression Hostile and attacking behavior, which can include verbal communication, directed toward self, others, or the physical environment

air conduction audiometry method A method to test hearing that uses pure-tone sounds generated by an audiometer

alerting devices Assistive devices for people who are deaf to make them aware of events in their environment through a loud sound or other means (e.g., flashing lights, vibrators)

alternate assessments Individualized means of measuring the progress of students who do not participate in the general education curriculum

alternative achievement standards Content standards applied to students with low incidence disabilities participating in the general education curriculum, but with fewer objectives or somewhat different expectations

Americans with Disabilities Act (ADA) Antidiscrimination legislation guaranteeing basic civil rights to people with disabilities

American Sign Language (ASL) The language of Deaf Americans that uses manual communication; a signal of Deaf culture

anorexia Intense fear of gaining weight, disturbed body image, chronic absence or refusal of appetite for food, causing severe weight loss (25 percent of body weight)

anxiety disorders Conditions causing painful uneasiness, emotional tension, or emotional confusion

array of services Constellation of special education services, personnel, and educational placements

articulation problems Abnormal production of speech sounds

Asperger syndrome One of the autism spectrum disorders (ASD) where in cognition is usually in the average or above-average range

assistance animals Animals (dogs, monkeys, guide dogs) trained to serve the individual needs of people with disabilities; service animals

assistive listening devices (ALDs) Equipment (e.g., hearing aids, audio loops, FM transmission devices) that helps improve the use of residual hearing

assistive technology (AT) Equipment (devices) or services to help compensate for an individual's disabilities

Assistive Technology Act (ATA) Law that facilitates increased accessibility through technology

associating A thinking skill; the ability to see relationships among different concepts or knowledge bases

asthma The most common, chronic health condition resulting in difficulty breathing

at risk Condition or situation making it probable that a child will develop disabilities

ataxia cerebral palsy Characterized by movement disrupted by impaired balance and depth perception

athetoid cerebral palsy Characterized by purposeless and uncontrolled involuntary movements

attention deficit hyperactivity disorder (ADHD) A condition characterized by hyperactivity, impulsivity, and inattention; included in the "other health impairments" category

attributions Explanations that individuals give themselves for their successes or failures

audiodescriptions An assistive audio input technology; presents visual information on screen or stage via oral narrations

audiogram A grid or graph used to display a person's hearing abilities

audio input devices Assistive technology to help people with visual disabilities by changing what would otherwise be seen into information that is heard

audiologist Related service provider; diagnoses hearing losses and auditory problems

audio loop A listening device that directs sound from the source directly to the listener's ear through a specially designed hearing aid

audiometer An instrument that audiologists use to measure hearing

auditory nerve The eighth cranial nerve, which carries messages from the hearing mechanisms to the brain

augumentative and alternative communication devices (AAC) Such methods for communicating as communication boards, communication books, sign language, and computerized voices; assistive technology that helps individuals communicate, including devices that actually produce speech

authentic assessments Performance measures that use work generated by the student

autism One of the autistic spectrum disorders (ASD); ranges from low to high functioning

autism spectrum disorders (ASD) A group of disorders with similar characteristics, including difficulties with communication, social interaction, and manneristic behaviors

autistic savant An individual who displays many behaviors associated with autism yet also possesses discrete abilities and unusual talents

automatic speech recognition (ASR) Technology that converts speech into text almost instantaneously

B

behavior analysis Research methodology using single-case designs; derived from the work of B. F. Skinner; paradigms describing human behavior in terms of events that stimulate or cause a behavior's occurrence, maintain behavior, and increase its likelihood

behavioral intervention plan Includes a functional assessment and procedures to prevent and intervene for behavioral infractions

bell-shaped curve Theoretical construct of the typical distribution of human traits such as intelligence; normal curve

Best Buddies A program that pairs college students with people with mental retardation to build relationships, friendships, and opportunities for supports

bilingual-bicultural approach A method of instruction for students who are deaf, combining practices of ESL and bilingual education; ASL is the native language, and reading and writing in English are taught as a second language

bilingual education Teaching in and seeking mastery of students' native language and English

bilingual paraprofessionals Classroom assistants fluent in at least two languages

blindness Degree of visual loss wherein the individual uses touch and hearing to learn and does not have functional use of sight

bone conduction audiometry method A method to test for conductive hearing loss; uses a vibrator placed on a person's forehead so that sound bypasses the outer and middle ear and goes directly to the inner ear

braille A system of reading and writing that uses dot codes embossed on paper; tactile reading; in 1824, Louis Braille created a precursor to the method used today

bulimia Chronically causing oneself to vomit or otherwise remove food to limit weight gain

C

captions Subtitles that print words spoken in film or video

cerebral palsy (CP) A neuromotor impairment; a nonprogressive disease resulting in motor difficulties associated with communication problems and mobility problems

child find A requirement of IDEA '04 to help refer and identify children and youth with disabilities

childhood disintegrative disorder (CDD) One of the autistic spectrum disorders (ASD); the individual has typical development until about the age of five or six

chunking A thinking skill; aids memory by organizing information by groups or topics

civil rights Rights that all citizens of a society are supposed to have

classifying A thinking skill; the ability to categorize items or concepts by their common characteristics

classroom English Level of English mastery required to access the general education curriculum and profit from instruction

cleft lip A congenital condition where the upper lip is not formed or connected properly to allow for correct articulation of sounds, resulting in a speech impairment

cleft palate An opening in the roof of the mouth causing too much air to pass through the nasal cavity, resulting in a speech impairment

closed captions Subtitles to a film or video that are available only to those who select the option

closed-circuit television (CCTV) An assistive visual input technology; uses a television to increase the size of objects or print

cluster grouping Pullout programs delivered by a teacher who specializes in education of the gifted

cochlea Structure that contains the organs of hearing

cochlear implant A microprocessor, surgically placed in the hearing mechanism, that replaces the cochlea so that people with sensorineural hearing loss can perceive sounds

CODA A child of a Deaf adult who may or may not have a hearing loss

code switching Using two languages in the same conversation; a sign of developing dual language proficiency

cognitive disabilities A disability characterized by impaired intellectual functioning, limited adaptive behavior, need for supports, and initial occurrence before age 18; intellectual disabilities; mental retardation

collaboration Professionals working in partnerships to provide educational services

communication Transfer of knowledge, ideas, opinions, or feelings

communication boards Low-tech assistive technology devices that display pictures or words that the individual can point to in order to communicate

communication disorders Disorders in speech, language, or hearing that impair communication

communication signals A variety of nonverbal cues that announce some immediate event, person, action, or emotion

communication symbols Voice, letters of the alphabet, or gestures used to send communication messages

communicative competence Proficiency in all aspects of communication in social and learning situations

community based instruction (CBI) Teaching functional skills in real life situations or in environments in which they are occur

comorbidity Coexisting disabilities

complex partial seizures A type of epilepsy causing a lapse in consciousness

computerized language translators Computers that provide translations of written text from one language to another

conduct disorders A psychiatric term describing externalizing, "acting-out" behaviors

conductive hearing loss Hearing impairment that is due to damage or obstruction to the outer or middle ear and that interferes with transfer of sound to the inner ear

congenital blindness Blindness present at birth or occurring during early infancy

consulting teacher Special education teacher serving as a resource to general education teachers

content An aspect of language that governs the intent and meaning of the message delivered in a communication

content enhancement strategies Methods to help students organize and remember important concepts

contextualized instruction Instruction that incorporates students' cultures, interests, and backgrounds into course content

continuum of services Each level of special education services is more restrictive, and services come in a lock-stepped sequence

conversational English Level of English mastery adequate for general communications but not necessarily for academic learning

cooperative learning Students working in small groups on the same material; mixed-ability grouping

cornea Transparent, curved part of the front of the eye

co-teaching General and special education teachers team teaching

cross-categorical special education Special education services delivered in terms of students' needs, not their identified disability; noncategorical special education

cross-cultural dissonance Mismatch that occurs when the home and school cultures are in conflict

cued speech Hand signals for "difficult to see" speech sounds; assists with speech reading

cultural pluralism All cultural groups are valued components of the society; language and traditions of each group are maintained

culturally competent Knowing and understanding the cultural standards from diverse communities

culturally diverse Being from a cultural group that is not Euro-centric or of mainstream America

culturally responsive A curriculum that includes multiple perspectives

curriculum based measurement (CBM) A system of progress monitoring; evaluates performance frequently (daily or weekly) by collecting data directly on mastery of academic subjects being taught

curriculum compacting Saving instructional time for enrichment activities

D

deaf Having profound hearing loss

Deaf culture Structures of social relationships, language (ASL), dance, theater, literature, and other cultural activities that bind the Deaf community

Deaf of Deaf Members of the Deaf community who are prelingually deaf and have at least one parent who is Deaf

deaf-blindness A dual disability involving both vision and hearing problems

decibel (dB) Unit of measure for intensity of sound

demographics Characteristics of a human population

depression A state of despair and dejected mood

developmental disabilities Severe disabilities that often combine intellectual and physical problems; often used interchangeably with term multiple-severe disabilities

dialect Words and pronunciation characteristic of a geographic region or ethnic group and different from those of standard language

differentiated curriculum The flexible application of curriculum targets to ensure content mastery, in-depth learning, and exploration of additional issues and themes

differentiated instruction Providing an individualized array of instructional interventions

digital divide Unequal availability of technology as a consequence of differences in socioeconomic status

digital hearing aids Assistive listening devices that amplify sound according to individuals' hearing profiles

dignity of risk The principle that taking ordinary risks is part of the human experience

disability Result of conditions or impairments

discrepancy formulas Calculations used to determine the gap between a student's achievement and her or his potential; used to identify students with learning disabilities

disproportionate representation Unequal proportion of group membership; either over- or underrepresentation

distance senses Senses—both hearing and vision—used to gain information; developed to guard against danger

Down syndrome Chromosomal disorder with identifiable physical characteristics, resulting in delays in physical and intellectual development

drop out To leave school before completion

due process hearing Noncourt proceeding before an impartial hearing officer, used when parents and school personnel disagree on a special education issue

dynamic assessment Assessment process used by SLPs to determine the potential effectiveness of different language interventions

dysfluencies Aspects of speech that interrupt the pattern of speech; also known as fluency problems; stuttering

E

eardrum Vibrates with the presence of sound waves and stimulates the ossicles of the middle ear; tympanic membrane

early intervening Providing explicit and intensive instruction to all struggling students to prevent the compounding of learning problems

Ebonics A learned and rule-governed dialect of nonstandard English, spoken by some African Americans

e-books Electronic versions of textbooks allowing for the application of universal design for learning

e-Buddies A program that creates e-mail friendships between people with and without mental retardation

echolalia Repeating words, sounds, or sound patterns with no communicative intent, meaning, or understanding; this repetition may occur immediately or even days later

Education for All Handicapped Children Act (EHA) Originally passed in 1975 to guarantee a free appropriate public education to all students with disabilities; Public Law (PL) 94-142

educational interpreters Related service providers for deaf students; translate or convert spoken messages to the deaf person's preferred mode of manual communication

emotional or behavioral disorders A disability characterized by behavioral or emotional responses that are very different from all norms and referent groups and have adverse effects on educational performance

emotional disturbance The term used in IDEA '04 for emotional or behavioral disorders

English language learners (ELLs) or limited English proficient (LEP) Students learning English as their second language

English as a second language (ESL) Instructing students in English until English proficiency is achieved; does not provide support in the student's native or primary language

enlarged print Adjusted size of print so individuals with low vision can read

enrichment Adding topics or skills to the traditional curriculum or presenting a particular topic in more depth

enrichment triad/revolving-door model An inclusive model for education of the gifted where in 15 to 20 percent of a school's students participate in activities to develop thinking skills, problem solving, and creativity

epilepsy or seizure disorders A tendency to experience recurrent seizures resulting in convulsions; caused by abnormal discharges of neurons in the brain

Eustachian tube Equalizes pressure on both sides of the eardrum

executive functions Higher-order cognitive functions that influence the ability to plan, self-regulate, and engage in goal-directed behavior

explicit instruction Direct teaching of the specific skills that make up the instructional target

externalizing behaviors Behaviors directed toward others (e.g., aggressive)

F

fetal alcohol effects (FAE) Congenital conditions caused by the mother's drinking alcohol during pregnancy and resulting in reduced intellectual functioning, behavior problems, and sometimes physical differences; not as severe as FAS

fetal alcohol syndrome (FAS) Congenital conditions caused by the mother's drinking alcohol during pregnancy and resulting in reduced intellectual functioning, behavior problems, and sometimes physical differences

field of vision The width of the area a person can see, measured in degrees

fluency problems Hesitations or repetitions of sounds or words that interrupt a person's flow of speech; stuttering is an example; a speech impairment

FM (frequency-modulated) transmission devices Assistive listening devices that provide oral transmissions directly from the teacher to students with hearing loss

form The rule system of language; includes phonology, morphology, and syntax

fragile X syndrome The most common inherited reason for mental retardation

free appropriate public education (FAPE) Ensures that students with disabilities receive necessary education and services without cost to the family
frequency of sound The number of vibrations per second of molecules through some medium such as air, water, or wires causing sound
functional behavioral assessment (FBA) Behavioral evaluations, interviews, observations, and environmental manipulations are conducted to determine the exact nature of problem behaviors
functional curriculum A curriculum made up of skills needed for daily living
functional skills Skills used to manage a home, cook, shop, commute, and organize personal living environments with the goal of independent living; life skills

G

generalized seizures Seizures involving the entire brain
generalized tonic–clonic seizures Grand mal seizures; the most serious type of epilepsy, resulting in convulsions and loss of consciousness
generalizing Transferring learning from particular instances to other environments, people, times, or events
generic supports Public benefits to which everyone has access
gifted Term describing individuals with high levels of intelligence and/or creativity, outstanding abilities, and capacity for high performance; talented
goal setting Determining desired behavior and the criteria that will mark its attainment
grade skipping A form of acceleration; advances students to a grade ahead of their age peers
graphic organizers Visual aids used to help students organize, understand, and remember academic content

H

hair cells The part of the cochlea that responds to different frequencies of sound and produces electrochemical signals sent on to the brain
hand over hand Sign language for individuals with deaf-blindness wherein signs are conveyed through touch
handicaps Challenges and barriers imposed by others
hard of hearing Having hearing losses that impair understanding of sounds and communication
health disabilities Chronic or acute health problems resulting in limited strength, vitality, or alertness; special health care needs; other health impairments
hearing aids Assistive listening devices that intensify sound
hertz (Hz) Unit of measure for sound frequency
heterogeneous Exhibiting great variety, such as a wide range of strengths and abilities in a group
high incidence disabilities Special education categories with the most students
high stakes testing State- and district-wide assessments to ensure all students' progress in the curriculum
high-tech devices Complex assistive technology devices that use computers or computer chips
homeless Not having a permanent home
honors sections Advanced classes for students who show high achievement in specific subject areas
human immunodeficiency virus (HIV) A microorganism that infects the immune system, impairing the body's ability to fight infections
hyperactivity Impaired ability to sit or concentrate for long periods of time

I

impulsivity Impaired ability to control one's own behavior
inattention Inability to pay attention or focus
independent study Allows a student to pursue and study a topic in depth on an individual basis
individualized education program (IEP) Management tool to identify and organize needed services
individualized family service plan (IFSP) Identifies and organizes services and resources for infants and toddlers (birth to age three) and their families
Individuals with Disabilities Education Act (IDEA) The 1990 reauthorization of PL 94-142
intellectual disabilities A disability characterized by impaired intellectual functioning, limited adaptive behavior, need for supports, and initial occurrence before age 18; cognitive disabilities; mental retardation
interim alternative educational setting (IAES) A special education placement to ensure progress toward IEP goals, assigned when a serious behavioral infraction requires removal from current placement
internalizing behaviors Behaviors directed inward (e.g., withdrawn, anxious, depressed)
internship A program that places students, usually high school seniors, in job settings related to their career goals
intervener Paraprofessional who, under the supervision of a teacher, translates sign language and helps children gain assess to information from the environment
Intervention Ladder A hierarchy of disciplinary tactics organized from the least intrusive and complex to the most intrusive and complicated
iris Colored part of the eye
itinerant Working in different locations

J

joint attention Ability to mutually interact or to share interest in events or objects
juvenile arthritis A chronic and painful muscular condition seen in children

L

language Rule-based method used for communication
language delays Slowed development of language skills; may or may not result in language impairments
language differences Emerging second language acquisition or nonstandard English
language impairments Difficulty or inability to master the various systems of rules in language, which then interferes with communication
language-sensitive environments Classrooms that encourage, foster, and support language development
learned helplessness Usually a result of repeated failure or excessive control by others; individuals become less willing to attempt tasks and less able to believe that their actions can result in success
learning disabilities (LD) A condition that causes significant learning problems, most often related to reading and writing; a disability of unexpected underachievement that is typically resistant to treatment
Learning Strategies Curriculum Instructional methods to help students read, comprehend, and study better by helping them organize and collect information strategically; a supplemental high school curriculum designed for students with learning disabilities; developed at the University of Kansas Center for Research on Learning
least restrictive environment (LRE) Educational placement with as much inclusion and integration with typical learners as possible and appropriate
legally blind A category of blindness used to qualify for federal and state benefits
lens Part of the eye, located behind the iris, that brings objects seen into focus
letter fluency Quickly reading and naming letters of the alphabet
life skills Skills used to manage a home, cook, shop, commute, and organize personal living environments with the goal of independent living; functional skills
limb deficiencies Missing or nonfunctioning arms or legs resulting in mobility problems

linguistically diverse Having a home or native language other than English

loudness An aspect of voice, referring to the intensity of the sound produced while speaking

low achievers All students who experience school failure and poor academic achievement

low incidence disabilities Special education categories with relatively few students

low-tech devices Simple assistive technology devices such as communication boards, homemade cushions, or a classroom railing

low vision Degree of visual loss wherein the individual uses sight to learn and to execute tasks, but visual disabilities interfere with daily functioning

M

manifestation determination Determines whether a student's disciplinary problems are due to her or his disability

mathematics/learning disabilities Condition where a student's learning disability is most significant in areas related to mathematics

medically fragile A term used to describe the status of individuals with health disabilities

melting pot Concept of a homogenized United States; cultural traditions and home languages are abandoned for the new American culture

mental retardation A disability characterized by impaired intellectual functioning, limited adaptive behavior, need for supports, and initial occurrence before age 18; cognitive disabilities; intellectual disabilities

mentorship A program in which a student is paired with an adult in order to learn to apply knowledge in real-life situations

mnemonics A learning strategy that promotes remembering information by associating the first letters of items in a list with a word, sentence, or picture (e.g., HOMES for the Great Lakes)

mobility The ability to travel safely and efficiently from one place to another; a topic of instruction for students who are blind

modifications Adjustments to assignments or tests that reduce the requirements

morphology Rules that govern the parts of words that form the basic elements of their meanings and structures

multicultural education Education that incorporates the cultures of all students into instruction

multidisciplinary teams Individually determined groups of professionals with different areas of expertise

multiple intelligences Multidimensional approach to intelligence inspired by Howard Gardner's theory; allowing those exceptional in any one of eight areas to be identified as gifted

multiple-severe disabilities Exceptionally challenging disabilities where more than one condition influences learning, independence, and the range of intensive and pervasive supports the individual and the family require; developmental disabilities

muscular/skeletal conditions Conditions affecting muscles or bones and resulting in limited functioning

N

natural supports Supports that occur as a natural result of family and community living

neuromotor impairments Conditions involving the nerves, muscles, and motor functioning

No Child Left Behind Act (NCLB) Reauthorization of the Elementary and Secondary Education Act mandating higher standards for both students and teachers, including an accountability system

noncategorical special education Special education services delivered in terms of students' needs, not their identified disability; cross categorical special education

nondiscriminatory testing Assessment that takes into account cultural and linguistic diversity

nonpaid supports Ordinary assistance given by friends and neighbors

normal curve Theoretical construct of the typical distribution of human traits such as intelligence; bell-shaped curve

normalization Making available ordinary patterns of life and conditions of everyday living

O

obturator A device that creates a closure between the oral and nasal cavities when the soft palate is missing or damaged; helps compensate for a cleft palate

occupational therapist (OT) A professional who directs activities that help improve muscular control and develop self-help skills; provides a special education related service

open captions Subtitles or tickers that are part of the screen image of a film or video for everyone to see

ophthalmologist Medical doctor who specializes in eye disorders

optician A person who fills either the ophthalmologist's or the optometrist's prescriptions for glasses or corrective lenses

optometrist Professional who measures vision and can prescribe corrective lenses (eyeglasses or contact lenses)

oral-only approach A method of instruction for students with hearing loss, using only oral means to communication

orientation The mental map people use to move through environments; a topic of instruction for students who are blind

orthopedic impairments The term used in IDEA '04 for physical disabilities resulting in special health care needs

ossicles Three tiny bones (hammer or malleus, anvil or incus, stirrup or stapes) in the middle ear that pass information to the cochlea

other health impairments The term used in IDEA '04 for health disabilities; special health care needs

otitis media Middle ear infection that can interrupt normal language development

otoacoustic emissions (OAEs) Low level of sound produced when the hair cells inside the inner ear vibrate

overrepresentation Too many students from a diverse group assigned to a special education category, relative to the level expected on the basis of the proportion of that diverse group in the population of students

P

paraprofessional An aide who assists and supports the special education program

partial seizures Seizures involving only part of the brain

Peer-Assisted Learning Strategies (PALS) A validated method wherein students coach each other to improve academic learning; peer tutoring for reading and mathematics

peer supports Instructional strategy that facilitates social interaction and access to the general education curriculum

peer tutoring Pairs of students teaching each other

perinatal During birth

peripheral vision The outer area of a person's visual field

personal data assistants (PDAs) Devices that allow the user to send text messages, use e-mail, and access the Web via wireless telephone systems

personal readers People who read for others

pervasive developmental disorder–not otherwise specified (PDD-NOS) One of the autistic spectrum disorders (ASD); either not all three ASD characteristics (problems in communication, social interaction, and repetitive or manneristic behaviors) are present or they are mild

petit mal seizures Seizures characterized by a short lapse in consciousness; absence seizures

phenylketonuria (PKU) Inherited condition that results in mental retardation from a build-up of toxins from foods (such as milk) containing amino acids
phonics The sounds represented by letters and letter-groups
phonological awareness Identifying, separating, or manipulating sound units of spoken language or sound-symbol relationships (letter sounds, rhyming)
phonology The rules within a language used to govern the combination of speech sounds to form words and sentences
photoscreening A system used to test visual acuity for those who cannot participate actively or reliably in visual assessments
physical disabilities Conditions related to a physical deformity or disability of the skeletal system and associated motor function; physical impairments; orthopedic impairments
physical therapist (PT) A professional who treats physical disabilities through many nonmedical means; works to improve motor skills; a special education related service provider
picture exchange communication system (PECS) A technique wherein pictures are used to make requests; devised for individuals with autism who are nonverbal
pinna Outer structure of the ear
pitch An aspect of voice; its perceived high or low sound quality
portfolio assessment Authentic assessments where students select their work for evaluation
positive behavior support A three-tiered model of support offering progressively more intensive levels of intervention
postlingually deaf Having lost the ability to hear after developing language; having acquired or adventitious deafness
postnatal After birth
postsecondary education Educational opportunities beyond high school; two-year or four-year colleges and universities
pragmatics The understanding of an object's purpose or function
preictal stage or aura Warning of an imminent seizure in the form of heightened sensory awareness
prelingually deaf Having lost the ability to hear before developing language
prenatal Before birth
pre-referral process Steps taken prior to actual referral to special education
prevalence Total number of cases at a given time
process/product debate Argument about whether perceptual training or direct (explicit) instruction is the more effective way to teach reading
progress monitoring Systematically and frequently assessing students' improvement in the skills being taught
Public Law (PL) 94-142 Originally passed in 1975 to guarantee a free appropriate public education to all students with disabilities; Education for All Handicapped Children's Act
pull-in programming Special education or related services delivered exclusively in the general education classroom
pullout programs Part-time special services outside of the general education classroom; resource rooms; the most common educational placement for gifted students
pupil Hole in the center of the iris that expands and contracts, admitting light to the eye.
pure sounds Pure-tone sound waves; used across specific frequencies to test an individual's hearing ability

Q

quality of life A subjective and individual-specific concept reflecting social relationships, personal satisfaction, employment, choice, leisure, independence, and community presence

R

reading/learning disabilities Condition where a student's learning disability is most significant in reading
real-time captioning (RTC) Practically instantaneous translations of speech into print; an accommodation for deaf students attending lectures
rear window captioning (RWC) Closed captioned used in movie theaters that projects printed words onto a clear screen on the back of the seat in front of the moviegoer
reciprocal teaching A tactic wherein teachers and students switch roles reading stories and asking questions, focusing on predicting, summarizing, questioning, and clarifying reading passages
related services Special education services from a wide range of disciplines and professions
residual hearing The amount of functional hearing a person has
residual vision The amount and degree of vision a person has functional use of despite a visual disability
resistant to treatment A defining characteristic of learning disabilities; validated methods typically applied in general education settings are not adequate to bring about sufficient learning; student requires more intensive and sustained explicit instruction
resonating system Oral and nasal cavities where speech sounds are formed
respiratory system The system of organs whose primary function is to take in oxygen and expel carbon dioxide
response to intervention (RTI) A multi-tiered pre-referral method of increasingly intensive interventions; used to identify students with learning disabilities
restricted central vision Severe limitation in peripheral vision; limitations in the width of the visual field; tunnel vision
retina Inside lining of the eye
retinopathy of prematurity (ROP) A cause of visual disabilities from prematurity and excess oxygen used to help the infant breathe but damaging to the retina
Rett syndrome One of the autistic spectrum disorders (ASD); has a known genetic cause; occurs only in girls
robotics Use of high-tech devices to perform motor skills
schizophrenia A disorder, rare in children, that includes bizarre delusions and dissociation from reality

S

school nurse A professional who assists with medical services at school; delivers health services; designs accommodations for students with special health care needs; provides a special education related service
Section 504 of the Rehabilitation Act of 1973 First law to outline the basic civil rights of people with disabilities
self-advocacy Capacity to understand, ask for, and explain one's need for accommodations; expressing one's rights and needs
self-determination Behaviors needed for independent living, which include making decisions, choosing preferences, and practicing self-advocacy
self-injury Self-inflicted injuries (head banging, eye poking)
self-instruction Self-induced statements to assist in self-regulation; self-talk
self-management Includes many techniques that the individual uses, individually or in combination, to modify her or his own behavior or academic performance
self-monitoring Keeping a record (data) of one's own performance
self-regulation Managing one's own behaviors through goal setting, time management, self-reinforcement, and other self-management techniques
self-reinforcement Awarding self-selected reinforcers or rewards to oneself contingent on meeting self-selected criteria
self-talk Self-induced statements to assist in self-regulation; self-instruction
semantics The system within a language that governs the content, intent, and

meanings of spoken and written language

sensorineural hearing loss Hearing impairment due to damage to the inner ear or the auditory nerve

sequencing A thinking skill; categorizing and putting items, facts, or ideas in order along various dimensions

service animals Animals (dogs, monkeys, guide dogs) trained to serve the individual needs of people with disabilities; assistance animals

service coordinator Case manager who oversees the implementation and evaluation of IFSPs

sheltered English Restating concepts and instructions, explicitly teaching vocabulary, using visuals and concrete examples, and relating new language skills to students' experiences to provide language support to ELLs

sickle cell anemia A hereditary blood disorder that inhibits blood flow; African Americans are most at risk for this health impairment

signed English Translation of English into a form of manual communication

simple partial seizures Seizures that cause people affected to think their environments are distorted or strange

Snellen chart A chart used to test visual acuity, developed in 1862

social competence Being able to understand social situations and respond appropriately in them

socially maladjusted A term applied to students who do not act within society's norms but are not considered to have emotional or behavioral disorders

sound intensity Loudness

spastic cerebral palsy Characterized by uncontrolled tightening or pulling of muscles

special education Individualized education and services for students with disabilities sometimes including gifted and talented students

special education categories System used in IDEA '04 to classify disabilities among students

special health care needs Chronic or acute health problems resulting in limited strength, vitality, or alterness; health disabilities; other health impairments

specialized supports Disability-specific benefits to help people with disabilities participate in the community

speech Vocal production of language

speech impairments Abnormal speech that is unintelligible, is unpleasant, or interferes with communication

speech/language pathologist (SLP) A professional who diagnoses and treats speech or language impairments; a related services provider

speech mechanisms The various parts of the body (tongue, lips, teeth, mandible, and palate) required for oral speech

speech synthesizers Assistive technology devices that create "voice"

statement of transition services Component of IEPs for students older than age 16 to assist students moving to adulthood

stay-put provision Prohibits students with disabilities from being expelled because of behavior associated with their disabilities

stereotypies Nonproductive behaviors (such as twirling, flapping hands, rocking) that an individual repeats at a high rate; commonly observed in youngsters with autism spectrum disorders; also called stereotypic behaviors

story maps Simple diagrams that help students organize and recall important elements and features of stories they have heard or read

structured teaching A feature of the instructional program TEACCH, developed for students with autism, wherein visual aids (start to finish boxes) are used to help students comprehend their environments

stuttering The lack of fluency in an individual's speech pattern, often characterized by hesitations or repetitions of sounds or words; dysfluency; a speech impairment

supported employment Strategy used in job training; student is placed in a paying job, receiving significant assistance and support, and the employer is helped with the compensation; a government program to help individuals with disabilities be successful in competitive employment situations

syntax Rules that govern word endings and the order of words in phrases and sentences

systems of supports Network of supports everyone develops to function optimally in life

T

tactile input devices Assistive technology; allows people to use touch to gain information

talented Term describing individuals with high levels of intelligence and/or creativity, outstanding abilities, and capacity for high performance; gifted

task analysis Breaking down problems and tasks into smaller, sequenced components

technology-dependent students Individuals who probably could not survive without high-tech devices (such as ventilators)

telecommunication devices Devices that provide oral information in alternative formats (e.g., captions for TV or movies)

telecommunications relay service (TRS) A telephone system, required by federal law to be available in all states, wherein an operator at a relay center converts a print-telephone message into a voice-telephone message

text telephone (TTY) A device that allows people to make and receive telephone calls by typing information instead of speaking; formerly called the telecommunication device for the deaf (TDD)

total communication approach A method of instruction for students with hearing loss, employing any and all methods of communication (oral speech, manual communication, ASL, gestures)

toxins Poisonous substances that can cause immediate or long-term harm

traumatic brain injury (TBI) Head injury causing reduced cognitive functioning, limited attention, and impulsivity

tunnel vision Severe limitation in peripheral vision; limitations in the width of the visual field; restricted central vision

twice-exceptional students Gifted students with disabilities

tympanic membrane Vibrates with the presence of sound waves and stimulates the ossicles of the middle ear; ear drum

typical learners Students and individuals without disabilities

U

underrepresentation Insufficient presence of individuals from a diverse group in a special education category; that is, their presence in smaller numbers than would be predicted on the basis of their proportion in the population of students

unexpected underachievement A defining characteristic of learning disabilities; poor school performance cannot be explained by other disabilities or limited potential

universal design Barrier-free architectural and building designs that meet the needs of everyone, including people with physical challenges

universal design for learning (UDL) typically by using technology increases access to the curriculum and instruction for all students

universal newborn hearing screening Testing of all newborns for hearing loss

universal screening Testing of everyone, particularly newborns, to determine existence or risk of disability

use An aspect of language; applying language appropriately

V

validated practices Thoroughly researched or evidence-based practices; scientifically validated instruction

vibrating system The larynx and vocal folds, which vibrate and produce the sounds and pitch of speech

visual acuity Sharpness of response to visual stimuli

visual disabilities Impairments in vision that, even with correction, affect educational performance, access to the community, and independence

visual efficiency How well a person can use sight

visual input devices Assistive technology to help people with visual disabilities with their vision

vocational rehabilitation A government service that provides training, career counseling, and job placement services

voice carry over (VCO) A text telephone allowing both voice and text

voice problem An abnormal spoken language production, characterized by unusual pitch, loudness, or quality of sounds

W

wraparound services A service delivery model in which needs are met through collaboration of many agencies and systems (education, mental health, social services, community)

References

CHAPTER 1

Introduction to Special Education Making a Difference

Aiello, B. (1976). Especially for special educators: A sense of our own history. *Exceptional Children, 42,* 244–252.

Americans with Disabilities Act of 1990, Pub. L. No. 101–336.

Artiles, A. J. (1998). The dilemma of difference: Enriching the disproportionality discourse with theory and context. *The Journal of Special Education, 32,* 32–36.

Artiles, A. J. (2003). Special education's changing identity: Paradoxes and dilemmas in views of culture and space. *Harvard Educational Review, 73,* 164–202.

Assistive Technology Act of 2004. Pub. L. No. 108–364.

Ballard, J., Ramirez, B. A., & Weintraub, F. J. (1982). *Special education in America: Its legal and governmental foundations.* Reston, VA: Council for Exceptional Children.

Bennett, V. (1997, December 18). Ill children in Kyrgyzstan used as pawns. *Los Angeles Times,* pp. A24–A25.

Biklen, D. (1985). *Achieving the complete school: Strategies for effective mainstreaming.* New York: Teachers College Press.

Bragg, L. (1997). From the mute god to the lesser god: Disability in medieval Celtic and Old Norse literature. *Disability & Society, 12,* 165–177.

Branson, J., & Miller, D. (2002). *Damned for their difference: The cultural construction of deaf people as disabled.* Washington, DC: Gallaudet University Press.

Brown, C. (1954). *My left foot.* London: Secker & Warburg.

Brown v. *Board of Education,* 347 U.S. 483 (1954).

Burlington School Committee v. *Department of Education,* 471 U.S. 359 (1985).

Carter v. *Florence County School District 4,* 950 F. 2d 156 (1991).

Cedar Rapids School District v. *Garret F.,* 106 F. 3rd 822 (8th Cir. 1997), cert. gr. 118 S. Ct. 1793 (1998), aff'd, 119 S. Ct. 992 (1999).

Center for Universal Design (2003). *Universal design in housing.* Raleigh, NC: North Carolina State University.

Cheng, L. L. (Ed.). (1995). *Integrating language and learning for inclusion: An Asian-Pacific focus.* San Diego: Singular Publishing Group.

Cheng, L. R. (1996). Beyond bilingualism: A quest for communication competence. *Topics in Language Disorders, 16,* 9–21.

Cook, B. G., & Schirmer, B. R. (2003). What is special about special education? Overview and analysis. *The Journal of Special Education, 37,* 200–205.

Danforth, S., & Rhodes, W. C. (1997). Deconstructing disability: A philosophy for inclusion. *Remedial and Special Education, 18,* 357–366.

de Bettencourt, L. U. (2002). Understanding the differences between IDEA and Section 504. *Teaching Exceptional Children, 34,* 16–23.

Deshler, D. D. (2003). A time for modern-day pioneers. *LDA Newsbriefs, 38,* 3–9, 24.

Doe v. *Withers,* 20 IDELR 422 (1993).

Dunn, C., Chambers, D., & Rabren, K. (2004). Variables affecting students' decision to drop out of school. *Remedial and Special Education, 25,* 315–323.

Dymond, S. K., & Orelove, F. P. (2001). What constitutes effective curricula for students with severe disabilities? *Exceptionality, 9,* 109–122.

Education for All Handicapped Children Act (EHA). Pub. L. No. 94–142.

Education for All Handicapped Children Act (EHA) (reauthorized). Pub. L. No. 99–457.

Elementary and Secondary Education Act. Pub. L. No. 107–110.

Erevelles, N. (1996). Disability and the dialects of difference. *Disability & Society, 11,* 519–537.

Fuchs, L. S., & Fuchs, D. (2001). Principles for the prevention and intervention of mathematics difficulties. *Learning Disabilities Research & Practice, 16,* 85–95.

Gallagher, H. G. (1994). *FDR's splendid deception* (Rev. ed.). Arlington, VA: Vandamere Press.

Garcia, E. E. (2001). *Hispanic education in the United States.* New York: Rowman & Littlefield Publishers.

Gregg, N., & Mather, N. (2002). School is fun at recess: Informal analyses of written language for students with learning disabilities. *Journal of Learning Disabilities, 35,* 7–22.

Gresham, F. (2002). Responsiveness to intervention: An alternative approach to the identification of learning disabilities. In R. Bradley, L. Danielson, & D. P. Hallahan (Eds.), *Identification of learning disabilities: Research to practice.* Mahwah, NJ: Erlbaum.

Groce, N. E. (1985). *Everyone here spoke sign language: Hereditary deafness on Martha's Vineyard.* Cambridge, MA: Harvard University Press.

Grossman, H. (1998). *Ending discrimination in special education.* Springfield, IL: Charles C Thomas.

Hardman, M. L., & Mulder, M. (2003). *Critical issues in public education: Federal reform and the impact on students with disabilities.* Conference Proceedings of the Texas Eagle Summit on Policy Issues and Teacher Preparation in Emotional and Behavioral Disorders. Dallas, TX: University of North Texas and Old Dominion University.

Harry, B. (2002). Trends and issues in serving culturally diverse families of children with disabilities. *The Journal of Special Education, 36,* 131–138, 141.

Heward, W. L. (2003). Ten faulty notions about teaching and learning that hinder the effectiveness of special education. *The Journal of Special Education, 36,* 186–205.

Hitchcock, C., & Stahl, S. (2003). Assistive technology, universal design, universal design for learning: Improved learning opportunities. *Journal of Special Educational Technology, 18,* 45–52.

Hockenbury, J. C., Kauffman, J. M., & Hallahan, D. P. (1999–2000). What is right about special education. *Exceptionality, 8,* 3–11.

Honig v. *Doe,* 484 U.S. 305, 108 S. Ct. 592 (1988).

Individuals with Disabilities Education Act. Pub. L. No. 101–476.

Individuals with Disabilities Education Act. Pub. L. No. 105–17, 111 STAT.37.

Individuals with Disabilities Education Improvement Act of 2004. Pub. L. No. 108–446. 118 STAT. 2647.

Irving Independent School District v. *Tatro,* 468 U.S. 833 (1984).

Johnson, K. (1998). Deinstitutionalization: The management of rights. *Disability & Society, 13,* 375–387.

Katsiyannis, A., & Yell, M. L. (2000). The Supreme Court and school health services: *Cedar Rapids* v. *Garret F. Exceptional Children, 66,* 317–326.

Kauffman, J. M. (1997). Caricature, science, and exceptionality. *Remedial and Special Education, 18,* 130–132.

Kauffman, J. M., & Hallahan, D. P. (2005). *Special education: What it is and why we need it.* Boston: Allyn & Bacon.

Kauffman, J. M., Landrum, T. J., Mock, D. R., Sayeski, B., & Sayeski, K. L. (2005). Diverse knowledge and skills require a diversity of instructional groups. *Remedial and Special Education, 26,* 2–6.

Kavale, K. A., & Mostert, M. P. (2003). River of ideology, islands of evidence. *Exceptionality, 11,* 191–208.

Kirk, S. (1978). The federal role in special education: Historical perspectives.*UCLA Educator, 20,* 5–11.

Kitchin, R. (1998). "Out of place," "knowing one's place": Space, power and the exclusion of disabled people. *Disability & Society, 13,* 343–356.

Kohler, P. D., & Field, S. (2003). Transition-focused education: Foundation for the future. *The Journal of Special Education, 37,* 174–183.

Kyle, S. J., Papdopoulou, E., & McLoughlin, M. J. (2004). *Accountability for all: Results from a study on accountability policies affecting students with disabilities educated in special schools and settings.* College Park, MD: The Institute for the Study of Exceptional Children, University of Maryland.

Laskas, J. M. (2003, October). Blind faith. *Ladies' Home Journal.* pp. 46, 48.

Lehr, C. A. (2004). Increasing school completion: Learning from research-based practices that work. *Improving Secondary Education and Transition Services Through Research: Research to Practice Brief, 3,* 1–4.

Longmore, P. K. (1995). The second phase: From disability rights to disability culture. *Disability Rag & Resource, 16,* 4–22

Longmore, P. (2002). *San Francisco State University: Institute on disability.* Retrieved June 21, 2002, from **http://online.sfsu.edu/~longmore**

Longmore, P. (2003). *Why I burned my book and other essays on disability.* Philadelphia: Temple University Press.

Lynch, E. W., & Hanson, M. J. (2004). *Developing cross-cultural competence: A guide for working with children and their families* (3rd ed.). Baltimore: Paul H. Brookes.

MacMillan, D. L. & Siperstein, G. N. (2002). Learning disabilities as operationally defined by schools. In R. Bradley, L. Danielson, & D. P. Hallahan (Eds.), *Identification of learning disabilities: Research to practice* (pp. 287–333). Mahwah, NJ: Erlbaum.

Martin, E. W., Martin, R., & Terman, D. L. (1996). The legislative and litigation history of special education. *Special Education for Students with Disabilities, 6,* 25–39.

McMasters, K., Fuchs, D., Fuchs, L., & Compton, D. (2000). Monitoring the academic progress of children who are unresponsive to generally effective early reading intervention. *Assessment for Effective Intervention, 27,* 23–33.

Mills v. *Board of Education of the District of Columbia,* 348 F. Supp. 866 (1972).

Müller, E., & Markowitz, J. (2004). *Disability categories: State terminology, definitions & eligibility criteria.* Washington, DC: Project Forum, National Association of State Directors of Special Education (NASDSE).

National Center for Education Statistics (NCES). (2004). Dropout rates. *NCES Fast Facts,* retrieved September 12, 2004, from **www.ed.gov**

National Center for Learning Disabilities. (2004). *No child left behind and students with learning disabilities: Ensuring full participation and equal accountability.* Retrieved September 14, 2004, from **www.ld.org/advocacy**

National Council on Disability [NCD] (2001 June 21). *The accessible future: Transmittal letter.* Washington, DC: Author.

National Organization on Disability (NOD). (2004 October 19). Barriers restrict voting by people with disabilities. Retrieved October 22, 2004, from **www.nod.org**

Nirje, B. (1985). The basis and logic of the normalization principle. *Australia and New Zealand Journal of Developmental Disabilities, 11,* 65–68.

No Child Left Behind Act of 2001. PL 107–110.

Pennsylvania Association for Retarded Children v. *Commonwealth of Pennsylvania,* 343 F. Supp. 279 (E. D. Pa., 1972).

Phyler v. *Doe,* 102 S. Ct. 2382 (1982).

Powell, B., & Dlugy, Y. (1998, December 21). Human rights: Russia's gulags for children. *Newsweek,* pp. 40–41.

Prater, M.A. (2003). Learning disabilities in children's and adolescent literature: How are characters portrayed? *Learning Disability Quarterly, 26,* 47–62.

Rehabilitation Act of 1973. Section 504, 19 U.S.C. Section 794.

Roos, P. (1970). Trends and issues in special education for the mentally retarded. *Education and Training of the Mentally Retarded, 5,* 51–61.

Rowley v. *Hendrick Hudson School District,* 458 U.S. 176 (1982).

Safford, P. L., & Safford, E. J. (1996). *A history of childhood and disability.* New York: Teachers College Press.

Safran, S. P. (1998). The first century of disability portrayal in film: An analysis of the literature. *The Journal of Special Education, 31,* 467–479.

Safran, S. P. (2000). Using movies to teach students about disabilities. *Teaching Exceptional Children, 32,* 44–47.

Smart, J. (2001). *Disability, society, and the individual.* Austin: PRO-ED.

Smith v. *Robinson,* 468 U.S. 992 (1984).

Stapleton, D. C., & Burkhauser, R. V. (Eds.). (2003). *The decline in employment of people with disabilities: A policy puzzle.* Kalamazoo, MI: W.E. Upjohn Institute for Employment Research.

Timothy W. v. *Rochester, New Hampshire, School District,* 875 F. 2d 945.

Tollestrup, B. (2003). Keeping disabilities from becoming handicaps. *The Special Edge, 16,* 16.

Torgesen, J. K. (1996). Thoughts about intervention research in learning disabilities. *Learning Disabilities, 7,* 55–58.

Treanor, R. B. (1993). *We overcame: The story of civil rights for disabled people.* Falls Church, VA: Regal Direct Publishing.

20 U.S.C. Section 1400 (b & c).

U.S. Department of Education. (2002). *Twenty-fourth annual report to Congress on the implementation of the Individuals with Disabilities Education Act.* Washington, DC: U.S. Government Printing Office.

U.S. Department of Education. (2005a). Assistance to states for the education of children with disabilities program and the early intervention program for infants and toddlers with disabilities; proposed regulations. *Federal Register,* 34, CRF Parts 300, 301, and 304.

U.S. Department of Education (2005b) *Children served under IDEA, Part B (2003),* Data Tables. **www.ideadata.org**

Utley, C. A., & Obiakor, F. (2001). Multicultural education and special education. In C. A. Utley and F. Obiakor (Eds.), *Special education, multicultural education, and school reform: Components of quality education for learners with mild disabilities* (pp. 1–29). Springfield, IL: Charles C Thomas Publisher.

Van Kuren, L. (2004). Transition—more important than ever. *Today: Exclusively for members of the Council for Exceptional Children, 10,* 1, 8, 11, 17.

Wehmeyer, M. L., Lattin, D. L., Lapp-Rincker, G., & Agran, M. (2003). Access to the general education curriculum of middle school students with mental retardation: An observational study. *Remedial and Special Education, 24,* 262–272.

West, J. (1994). *Federal implementation of the Americans with Disabilities Act, 1991–1994.* New York: Milbank Memorial Fund.

Wolfensberger, W. (1972). *The principle of normalization in human services.* Toronto: National Institute on Mental Retardation.

Wolfensberger, W. (1995). Of "normalization," lifestyles, the Special Olympics, deinstitutionalization, mainstreaming, integration, cabbages and kings. *Mental Retardation, 33,* 111–119.

Young, B. A. (2004). *Public school student, staff, and graduate counts by state: School year 2001–2002: Statistical Analysis Report: April 2004.* Washington, DC: NCES. Retrieved September 12, 2004, from **http://www.nces.ed.gov/pubs2003/snf_report03/index.asp#fig4**

Ziegler, D. (2002). *Reauthorization of the Elementary and Secondary Education Act: No Child Left Behind Act of 2001.* Arlington, VA: The Council for Exceptional Children, Public Policy Unit.

Zobrest v. *Catalina Foothills School District,* 963 F. 2d 190 (1993).

CHAPTER 2

Individualized Special Education Programs: Planning and Services

Allen, M., & Ashbaker, B. Y. (2004). Strengthening schools: Involving paraprofessionals in crisis prevention and intervention. *Intervention in School and Clinic, 39,* 139–146.

Art Institute of Chicago. (1999) *Henri de Toulouse-Lautrec.* On-line. **www.artic.edu**

Barnett, D. W., Daly, E. J., Jones, K. M., & Lentz Jr., F. E. (2004). Response to intervention: Empirically based special service decisions from single-case designs of increasing and decreasing intensity. *Journal of Special Education, 38,* 66–79.

Barnhill, G. P. (2005). Functional behavior assessment in schools. *Intervention in School and Clinic, 40,* 131–143.

Bigby, L. M. (2004). Medical and health related services: More than treating boo-boos and ouchies. *Intervention in School and Clinic, 39,* 233–235.

Bolt, S. E., & Thurlow, M. L. (2004). Five most frequently allowed testing accommodations in state policy: Synthesis of research. *Remedial and Special Education, 25,* 141–152.

Borthwick-Duffy, S. A., Palmer, D. S., & Lane, K. L. (1996). One size doesn't fit all: Full inclusion and individual differences. *Journal of Behavioral Education, 6,* 311–329.

Bradley, R., Danielson, L., & Hallahan, D. P. (Eds.). (2002). *Identification of learning disabilities: Research to practice.* Mahwah, NJ: Erlbaum.

Bremer, C. D., Clapper, A. T., Hitchock, C., Hall, T., & Kachgal, M. (2002). Universal design: A strategy to support students' access to the general education curriculum. *Information Brief: Addressing trends and developments in secondary education and transition, 1,* 1–5.

Brown, M. R., Paulsen, K., & Higgins, K. (2003). Remove environmental barriers to student learning. *Intervention in School and Clinic, 39,* 109–112.

Buehler, V. (2004). Easy as 1-2-3 IEPs. *Volta Voices, 11,* 20–23.

Cartledge, G., Kea, C. D., & Ida, D. J. (2000). Anticipating differences—celebrating strengths: Providing culturally competent services for students with serious emotional disturbance. *Teaching Exceptional Children, 32,* 30–37.

Center for Applied Special Technology (CAST). (2004a). *Universal design.* Retrieved on September 23, 2004, from **www.cast.org**

Center for Applied Special Technology (CAST). (2004b). *Teaching every student in the digital age.* Retrieved on September 23, 2004 from **www.cast.org**

Cook, B. G. (2001). A comparison of teachers' attitudes toward their included students with mild and severe disabilities. *Journal of Special Education, 34,* 203–213.

Cook, B. G., Tankersley, M., Cook, L., & Landrum, T. J. (2000). Teachers' attitudes toward their included students with disabilities. *Exceptional Children, 67,* 115–135.

Council for Exceptional Children (CEC). (1999). *IEP Team Guide.* Reston, VA: Author.

Curran, C. M., & Harris, M. B. (1996). *Uses and purposes of portfolio assessment for general and special educators.* Albuquerque: University of New Mexico.

Dabkowski, D. M. (2004). Encouraging active parent participation in IEP team meetings. *Teaching Exceptional Children, 36,* 34–39.

de Fur, S. H. (2003). IEP transition planning—from compliance to quality. *Exceptionality, 11,* 115–128.

Demchak, M. A., & Greenfield, R. G. (2003). *Transition portfolios for students with disabilities: How to help students, teachers, and families handle new settings.* Thousand Oaks, CA: Corwin Press.

Denvir, B. (1991). *Toulouse-Lautrec.* London: Thames and Hudson.

Downing, J. A. (2004). Related services for students with disabilities: Introduction to the special issue. *Intervention in School and Clinic, 39,* 195–208.

Dworetzky, B. (2004). Effective practices for involving families of children with disabilities in schools. *Newsline: The Federation of Children with Special Needs, 24,* 1, 12.

Earles-Vollrath, T. L. (2004). Mitchell Yell: IDEA 1997 and related services. *Intervention in School and Clinic, 39,* 236–239.

Elementary and Secondary Education Act. Pub. L. No. 107–110.

Elliott, S. N., Kratochwill, T. R., & McKevitt, B. C. (2001). Experimental analysis of the effects of testing accommodations on the scores of students with and without disabilities. *Journal of School Psychology, 39,* 3–24.

Etzel-Wise, D., & Mears, B. (2004). Adapted physical education and therapeutic recreation in schools. *Intervention in School and Clinic, 39,* 223–232.

Finn, Jr., C. E., Rotherham, A. J., & Hokanson, Jr., C. R. (Eds.). (2001). *Rethinking special education for a new century.* Washington, DC: Thomas B. Fordham Foundation and the Progressive Policy Institute.

Fisher, D., Frey, N., & Thousand, J. (2003). What do special educators need to know and be prepared to do for inclusive schooling to work? *Teacher Education and Special Education, 26,* 42–50.

Friend, M. (2000). Myths and misunderstandings about professional collaboration. *Remedial and Special Education, 21,* 130–132, 160.

Fuchs, L. S. & Fuchs, D. (2001). Principles for the prevention and intervention of mathematics difficulties. *Learning Disabilities Research & Practice, 16,* 85–95.

Fuchs, L. S., Fuchs, D., Eaton, S., Hamlett, C. L., & Karns, K. (2000). Supplementing teachers' judgments of mathematics test accommodations with objective data sources. *School Psychology Review, 29,* 65–85.

Fuchs, L. S., Fuchs, D., Hosp, M., & Jenkins, J. R. (2001). Oral reading fluency as an indicator of reading competence: A theoretical, empirical, and historical analysis. *Scientific Studies of Reading, 5,* 239–256.

Fuchs, L., Fuchs, D., & Powell, S. (2004). *Using CBM for Progress Monitoring.* Washington, DC: American Institutes for Research.

Haager, D., & Klingner, J. K. (2005). *Differentiating instruction in inclusive classrooms: The special educator's guide.* Boston: Allyn & Bacon.

Hall, L. J., & McGregor, J. A. (2000). A follow-up study of the peer relationships of children with disabilities in an inclusive school. *Journal of Special Education, 34,* 114–126, 153.

Hammond, H., & Ingalls, L. (2003). Teachers' attitudes toward inclusion: Survey results from elementary school teachers in three southwestern rural school districts. *Rural Special Education Quarterly, 22,* 22–30.

Hanley, G. P., Iwata, B. A., & McCord, B. E. (2003). Functional analysis of problem behavior: A review. *Journal of Applied Behavior Analysis, 36,* 147–185.

Hanson, M. J., Horn, E., Sandall, S., Beckman, P., Morgan, M., Marquart, J., Barnwell, D., & Chou, H-Y. (2001). After preschool inclusion: Children's educational pathways over the early school years. *Exceptional Children, 68,* 65–83.

Hébert, T. (2001, June). Man to man: Building channels of communication between fathers and their talented sons. *Parenting for High Potential,* pp. 18–22.

Hitchcock, C., & Stahl, S. (2003). Assistive technology, universal design, universal design for learning: Improved learning opportunities. *Journal of Special Education Technology, 18,* 45–52.

Hoffman, B., Hartley, K., & Boone, R. (2005). Reaching accessibility: Guidelines for creating and refining digital learning materials. *Intervention in School and Clinic 40,* 171–176.

Hoover, J. J., & Patton, J. R. (2004). Differentiating standards-based education for students with diverse needs. *Remedial and Special Education, 25,* 74–78.

Hughes, M. T., Valle-Riestra, D. M., & Arguelles, M. E. (2002). Experiences of Latino families with their child's special education program. *Multicultural Perspectives, 4,* 11–17.

Individuals with Disabilities Education Improvement Act of 2004. Pub. L. No. 108–446. 118 STAT. 2647.

Kamens, M. W. (2004). Learning to write IEPs: A personalized, reflective approach for preservice teachers. *Intervention in School and Clinic, 40,* 76–80.

Kern, L., Delaney, B., Clarke, S., Dunlap, G., & Childs, K. (2001). Improving the classroom behavior of students with emotional and behavioral disorders using individualized curricular modifications. *Journal of Emotional and Behavioral Disorders, 9,* 239–247.

Kravetz, J. (2005, January 7). Under new IDEA, districts no longer required to provide, maintain implants. *The Special Educator, 20,* 1, 6.

Lovitt, T. C., & Cushing, S. S. (1994). High school students rate the IEPs: Low opinions and lack of ownership. *Intervention in School and Clinic, 30,* 34–37.

Magiera, K., Smith, C., Zigmond, N., & Gebauer, K. (2005). Benefits of co-teaching in secondary mathematics classes. *Teaching Exceptional Children, 37,* 20–24.

McNamara, K., & Hollinger, C. (2003). Intervention-based assessment: Evaluation rates and eligibility findings. *Exceptional Children, 69,* 181–193.

Moody, S. W., Vaughn, S., Hughes, M. T., & Fischer, M. (2000). Reading instruction in the resource room: Set up for failure. *Exceptional Children, 66,* 305–316.

Müller, E., & Tschantz, J. (2003, April). Universal design for learning: Four state initiatives. *Quick Turn Around.* Washington, DC: National Association of State Directors of Special Education (NASDSE), Project Forum.

National Alliance of Black School Educators (NABSE), & ILIAD Project (2002). *Addressing over-representation of African American students in special education.* Arlington, VA: Council for Exceptional Children, and Washington, DC: National Alliance of Black School Educators.

National Association of School Nurses (NASN). (2004). Impact of *Cedar Rapids Community School District* v. *Garret F.* on school nursing services. *School Health Nursing Services Role in Health Care: Issue Brief.* Retrieved December 12, 2004, from **www.nasn.org**

National Center for Educational Statistics (NCES). (2002). *Condition of education: 2002.* Washington, DC: U.S. Department of Education.

National Center on Secondary Education and Transition [NCSET]. (2005). Key provisions on transition: IDEA 1997 compared to H.R. 1350 (IDEA 2004). Minneapolis: University of Minnesota. Retrieved on December 12, 2005, from **www.ncset.org**

Neal, J., Bigby, L. M., & Nicholson, R. (2004). Occupational therapy, physical therapy, and orientation and mobility services in public schools. *Intervention in School and Clinic, 39,* 218–222.

Neubert, D. A. (2003). The role of assessment in the transition to adult life process for students with disabilities. *Exceptionality, 11,* 63–75.

Nichols, P. (2000, Spring). Role of cognition and affect in a functional behavioral analysis. *Exceptional Children, 66,* 393–402.

NIMAS Development and Technical Assistance Center. (2005). *NIMAS related sections within IDEA 2004.* Wakefield, MA: CAST, Inc.

No Child Left Behind Act of 2001. PL 107–110.

Obiakor, F. W., & Ford, B. A. (2002). Educational reform and accountability: Implications for African Americans with exceptionalities. *Multiple Voices, 5,* 83–93.

Office of Special Education Programs (OSEP). (2000). *A guide to the individualized education program.* Washington, DC: U.S. Department of Education.

Palmer, D. S., Fuller, K., Arora, T., & Nelson, M. (2001). Taking sides: Parent views on inclusion for their children with severe disabilities. *Exceptional Children, 67,* 467–484.

Perruchor, H. (1962). *Toulouse-Lautrec.* New York: Collier.

Praisner, C. L. (2003). Attitudes of elementary principals toward the inclusion of students with disabilities. *Exceptional Children, 69,* 135–145.

Rubin, J. (2004, November 28). Are schools cheating poor learners? Officials say federal rules compel them to focus on pupils more likely to raise test scores. *Los Angeles Times, Education* (p. 1).

Ryan, A. L., Halsey, H. N., & Matthews, W. J. (2003). Using functional assessment to promote desirable student behavior in schools. *Teaching Exceptional Children, 35,* 8–15.

Sataline, S. (2005, January 30). A matter of principal. *The Boston Globe Magazine.*

Shippen, M. E., Simpson, R. G., & Crites, S. A. (2003). A practical guide to functional behavioral assessment. *Teaching Exceptional Children, 35,* 36–44.

Shriner, J. G., & Destefano, L. (2003). Participation and accommodation in state assessment: The role of individualized education programs. *Exceptional Children, 69,* 147–161.

Smith, R., Salend, S., & Ryan, S. (2001). Closing or opening the special education curtain. *Teaching Exceptional Children, 33,* 18–23.

Sopko, K. M. (2003). *The IEP: A synthesis of current literature since 1997.* Washington, DC: National Association of State Directors of Special Education (NASDSE), Project Forum.

Test, D. W., Mason, C., Hughes, C., Konrad, M., Neale, M., & Wood, W.M. (2004). Student involvement in individualized education program meetings. *Exceptional Children, 70,* 391–412.

The Study of Personnel Needs in Special Education (SPeNSE) (2000). *The role of paraprofessionals in special education.* Rockville, MD: Westat. Available at **www.spense.org**

Thompson, S., Lazarus, S., Clapper, A., & Thurlow, M. (2004). *Essential knowledge and skills needed by teachers to support the achievement of students with disabilities: EPRRI Issue Brief Five.* College Park, MD: The Institute for the Study of Exceptional Children and Youth, Educational Policy Reform Research Institute.

Thurlow, M. L. (1998). *Assessment: A key component of education reform.* Boston: The Federation for Children with Special Needs.

Tomlinson, C. A., Brighton, C., Hertberg, H., Callahan, C. M., Moon, T. R., Brimijoin, K., Conover, L. A, & Reynolds, T. (2003). Differentiating instruction in response to student readiness, interest, and learning profile in academically diverse classrooms: A review of the literature. *Journal for the Education of the Gifted, 27,* 119–145.

Tornatzky, L. G., Pachon, H. P., & Torres, C. (2003). *Closing achievement gaps: Improving educational outcomes for Hispanic children.* Los Angeles: The Center for Latino Educational Excellence, The Tomás Rivera Policy Institute, University of Southern California.

Trautman, M. L. (2004). Preparing and managing paraprofessionals. *Intervention in School and Clinic, 39,* 139–146.

U.S. Department of Education (2005). *Children served under IDEA, Part B (2003),* Data Tables. **www.ideadata.org**

Van Kuren, L. (2004). Transition—more important than ever. *Today: Exclusively for members of the Council for Exceptional Children, 10,* 1, 8, 11, 17.

Villa, R. A., Thousand, J. S., & Nevin, A. I. (2004). *A guide to co-teaching.* Thousand Oaks, CA: Corwin Press.

Whitbread, K. (2004, Spring). Access to the general education curriculum for ALL students. *The inclusion notebook: Problem solving in the classroom and community.* Farmington, CT: A. J. Pappanikou Center for Developmental Disabilities, University of Connecticut.

Wood, W. M., Karvonen, M., Test, D. W., Browder, D., & Algozzine, B. (2004). Promoting student self-determination skills in IEP planning. *Teaching Exceptional Children, 36,* 8–16.

Ziegler, D. (2002). *Reauthorization of the Elementary and Secondary Education Act: No Child Left Behind Act of 2001.* Arlington, VA: The Council for Exceptional Children, Public Policy Unit.

CHAPTER 3

Cultural and Linguistic Diversity

Antunez, B. (2001, July). *What legal obligations do schools have to English language learners?* ASK NCELA No. 23. Washington, DC: National Clearinghouse for English Language Acquisition and Language Instruction Educational Programs, George Washington University.

Antunez, B., & Zelasko, N. (2001, August). *What program models exist to serve English language learners?* ASK NCELA No. 22. Washington, DC: National Clearinghouse for English Language Acquisition and Language Instruction Educational Programs, George Washington University.

Artiles, A. J. (2003). Special education's changing identity: Paradoxes and dilemmas in views of culture and space. *Harvard Educational Review, 73,* 164–202.

Artiles, A. J., Harry, B., Reschly, D. J., & Chinn, P. C. (2002). Overidentification of students of color in special education: A critical overview. *Multicultural Perspectives, 4,* 3–10.

Baca, L. M. (1998). The diversity of America's schoolchildren. In R. Tharp, *Teaching alive, CD Rom.* Santa Cruz, CA: The Center for Research on Education, Diversity and Excellence, University of California, Santa Cruz.

Baca, L. M., & Cervantes, H. T. (Eds.). (2004). *The bilingual special education interface* (4th ed.). Columbus, OH: Merrill.

Banks, J. A. (2002). *An introduction to multicultural education* (3rd ed.). Boston: Allyn and Bacon.

Banks, S. (2004). Voices of tribal parents and caregivers of children with special needs. *Multiple Voices, 7,* 33–47.

Bernal, E. M. (2000). Three ways to achieve a more equitable representation of culturally and linguistically different students in GT programs. *Roeper Review, 24,* 82–88.

Brice, A., & Rosa-Lugo, L. I. (2000). Code switching: A bridge or barrier between two languages? *Multiple Voices, 4,* 1–9.

Brown v. *Board of Education,* 347 U.S. 483 (1954).

Brown, M. R., Higgins, J., Pierce, R., Hong, E., & Thoma, C. (2003). Secondary students' perceptions of school life with regard to alienation: The effects of disability, gender, and race. *Learning Disability Quarterly, 26,* 227–238.

Cartledge, G., & Loe, S. A. (2001). Cultural diversity and social skill instruction. *Exceptionality, 9,* 33–46.

Castellano, J. A., & Díaz, E. I. (Eds.). (2002). *Reaching new horizons: Gifted and talented education for culturally and linguistically diverse students.* Boston: Allyn and Bacon.

Cheng, L. L. (1996). Beyond bilingualism: A quest for communication competence. *Topics in Language Disorders, 16,* 9–21.

Cheng, L. L. (1999). Moving beyond accent: Social and cultural realities of living with many tongues. *Topics in Language Disorders, 19,* 1–10.

Cheng, L. L., & Chang, J. (1995). Asian/Pacific Islander students in need of effective services. In L. L. Cheng (Ed.), *Integrating language and learning for inclusion: An Asian-Pacific focus* (pp. 3–59). San Diego, CA: Singular Publishing Group.

Children's Defense Fund (CDF). (2001). *The state of America's children: 2001.* Washington, DC: Author.

Children's Defense Fund (CDF). (2004). *The state of America's children: 2004.* Washington, DC: Author.

Cuccaro, K. (1996). Teacher observations key in bilingual assessment. *Special Education Report, 22,* 1, 3.

Cummins, J. (1984). *Bilingualism and special education: Issues in assessment and pedagogy.* San Diego, CA: College-Hill.

Currie, J., & Thomas, D. (1995). *Does Head Start make a difference?* Santa Monica: Rand.

D'Anguilli, A., Siegel, L. S., & Maggi, S. (2004). Literacy instruction, SES, and word-reading achievement in English-Language learners and children with English as a first language: A longitudinal study. *Learning Disabilities Research & Practice, 19,* 202–213.

Davis, C., Brown, B., Bantz, J., & Manno, C. (2002). African American parents' involvement in their children's special education programs. *Multiple Voices, 5,* 13–27.

Diana v. *State Board of Education,* No. C-70-37 Rfp (N.D. Calif. 1970).

Donovan, M. Z., & Cross, C. T. (Eds.) (2002). *Minority students in special education and gifted education.* Committee on Minority Representation in Special Education. Washington, DC: National Academy Press.

Fletcher, T. V., Bos, C. S., & Johnson, L. M. (1999). Accommodating English language learners with language and learning disabilities in bilingual education classrooms. *Learning Disabilities Research & Practice, 14,* 80–91.

Ford, D. Y., Harris III, J. J., Tyson, C. A., & Trotman, M. F. (2002). Beyond deficit thinking: Providing access for gifted African American students. *Roeper Review, 24,* 52–58.

Ford, D. Y., Howard, R. C., Harris III, J. J., & Tyson, C. A. (2000). Creating culturally responsive classrooms for gifted African American students. *Journal for the Education of the Gifted, 23,* 397–427.

Furger, R. (2004 November). High school's new face. *Edutopia Magazine.* Retrieved December 27, 2004, from **www.edutopia.org**

Garcia, E. E. (2001). *Hispanic education in the United States.* New York: Rowman & Littlefield.

Gardner, H. (1983). *Frames of mind: The theory of multiple intelligences.* New York: Basic Books.

Garrett, M. T., Bellon-Harn, M. L., Torres-Rivera, E., Garrett, J. T., & Roberts, L. C. (2003). Open hands, open hearts: Working with Native youth in the schools. *Intervention in School and Clinic, 38,* 225–235.

Gersten, R., & Baker, S. (2000). *Topical summary: Practices for English language learners.* Eugene, OR: National Institute for Urban School Improvement.

Gollnick, D. M., & Chinn, P. C. (2002). *Multicultural education in a pluralistic society* (6th ed.). Columbus, OH: Merrill.

Goode, T. (2002 August). *Cultural competence.* Presentation to National Council on Disability, Cultural Diversity Committee, Washington, DC.

Grupp, L. L. (2004). Felipe's story: In response to the National Research Council report. *Multiple Voices, 7,* 1–15.

Harry, B. (1992). Restructuring the participation of African- American parents in special education. *Exceptional Children, 59,* 123–131.

Harry, B. (1994). *The disproportionate representation of minority students in special education: Theories and recommendations.* Alexandria, VA: National Association of State Directors of Special Education.

Harry, B. (2002). Trends and issues in serving culturally diverse families of children with disabilities. *The Journal of Special Education, 36,* 131–138.

Haynes, J. (2005). *Using the Internet for content based instruction.* Everything ESL.net. Retrieved January 5, 2005, from **http://www.everythingesl.net/inservices/internet_reousrces.php**

Hébert, T. P., & Beardsley, T. M. (2001). Jermaine: A critical case study of a gifted Black child living in rural poverty. *Gifted Child Quarterly, 45,* 85–103.

Henning-Stout, M. (1996). "Que Podemos Hacer?" Roles for school psychologists with Mexican and Latino migrant children and families. *School Psychology Review, 25,* 152–164.

Holman, L. J. (1997). Working effectively with Hispanic immigrant families. *Phi Delta Kappan, 78,* 647–649.

Hosp, J. L., & Reschly, D. J. (2002). Predictors of restrictiveness of placement for African-American and Caucasian students. *Exceptional Children, 68,* 225–238.

Hosp, J. L., & Reschly, D. J. (2003). Referral rates for intervention or assessment: A meta-analysis of racial differences. *The Journal of Special Education, 37,* 67–80.

Hughes, M. T., Valle-Riestra, D. M., & Arguelles, M.E. (2002). Experiences of Latino families with their child's special education program. *Multicultural Perspectives, 4,* 11–17.

Individuals with Disabilities Education Improvement Act of 2004. Pub. L. No. 108–466.

Ingersoll, R. (2001). *Teacher turnover, teacher shortages, and the organization of schools.* Seattle, WA: University of Washington, Center for the Study of Teaching and Policy.

Jairrels, V., Brazil, N., & Patton, J. R. (1999). Incorporating popular literature into the curriculum for diverse learners. *Intervention in School and Clinic, 34,* 303–306.

Johnson S., Fletcher, T., & Bos, C. (2002). Effective pedagogy for English language learners in inclusive classrooms. In A. J. Artiles & A. Ortiz (Eds.), *English language learners with special needs: Identification, placement, and instruction,* Washington, DC: Center for Applied Linguistics.

Kaufman, P., Alt, M. N., & Chapman, C.D. (2004). *Dropout rates in the United States: 2001.* (NCES 2005–046) Washington, DC: U.S. Department of Education, Institute of Education Sciences, National Center for Education Statistics (NCES).

Kea, C. D., & Utley, C. A. (1998). To teach me is to know me. *Journal of Special Education, 32,* 44–47.

Kirnhaber, M., Fierros, E., & Veenema, S. (2004). *Multiple intelligences: Best ideas from research and practice.* Boston: Allyn & Bacon.

Kishi, G. (2004a). Pihana Na Mamo: The Native Hawaiian Special Education Project. Presentation to International Council for Exceptional Children Meeting.

Kishi, G. (2004b). Pihana Na Mamo:. *Students of Hawaiian ancestry.* Honolulu, HI: The Native Hawaiian Special Education Project, Hawaii Department of Education.

Klinger, J., & Vaughn, S. (1996). Reciprocal teaching of reading comprehension strategies for students with learning disabilities who use English as a second language. *Elementary School Journal, 96,* 275–293.

Kornhaber, M., Fierros, E., & Veenema, S. (2004). *Multiple intelligences: Best ideas from research and practice.* Boston: Allyn and Bacon.

Kozleski, E. B., Sobel, D., & Taylor, S. V. (2003). Embracing and building culturally responsive practices. *Multiple Voices, 6,* 73–87.

Kozol, J. (1991). *Savage inequalities: Children in America's schools.* New York: Crown.

Kozol, J. (1995). *Amazing grace: The lives of children and the conscience of a nation.* New York: Crown.

Kraft, S. G. (2001). HHS: Full early childhood inclusion maximizes kids' potential. *Early Childhood Report, 12,* 7.

Krause, M. (1992). Testimony to the Select Senate Committee on Indian Affairs on S. 2044, *Native American Languages Act of 1991,* to assist Native Americans in assuring the survival and continuing vitality of their languages, pp. 16–18.

Larry P. v. *Riles,* Civil Action No. C-70-37 (N.D. Calif. 1971).

Lau v. *Nichols,* 414 U.S. 563 (1974).

Lee, V. E., & Burkam, D. T. (2002). *Inequality at the starting gate.* Washington, DC: Economic Policy Institute.

Lynch, E. W., & Hanson, M. J. (2004). *Developing cross-cultural competence: A guide for working with young children and their families* (3rd ed.). Baltimore: Paul H. Brookes.

Maker, C. J., Nielson, A. B., & Rogers, J. A. (1994). Giftedness, diversity and problem solving. *Teaching Exceptional Children, 27,* 4–18.

Malveaux, J. (2002). Quality preschool education pays off, long-term study says. *Early Childhood Report, 13,* 1, 4.

Markowitz, J. (Ed.). (1999). *Education of children with disabilities who are homeless.* Proceedings of Project FORUM convened April 5–7, 1999, 1–24. Alexandria, VA: NASDSE.

Martella, J. (2002). Research shows poverty as greatest indicator of student achievement. *Gaining Ground: Achieving Excellence in High Poverty Schools, 4,* 5.

McLaughlin, M. J., Pullin, D., & Artiles, A. J. (2001). Challenges for transformation of special education in the 21st century: Rethinking culture in school reform. *Journal of Special Education Leadership, 14,* 51–62.

Milian, M. (1999). Schools and family involvement: Attitudes among Latinos who have children with visual impairments. *Journal of Visual Impairment & Blindness, 93,* 277–290.

Montgomery, W. (2001). Creating culturally responsive, inclusive classrooms. *Teaching Exceptional Children 33,* 4–9.

Müller, E., & Markowitz, J. (2004, March). English language learning with disabilities. *Synthesis brief.* Arlington, VA: Project Forum, National Association of State Directors of Special Education.

National Alliance of Black School Educators (NABSE), & ILIAD Project. (2002). *Addressing over-representation of African American students in special education.* Arlington, VA: Council for Exceptional Children, and Washington, DC: National Alliance of Black School Educators.

National Center for Educational Outcomes (NCEO). (2005a). *Accommodations for LEP students/English Language Learners.* Retrieved January 3, 2005, from **http://education.umn.edu/NCEO/LEP/Accommmodations/Accom_lep.htm**

National Center for Educational Outcomes (NCEO). (2005b). *Accommodations for LEP students/English language learners.* Retrieved January 3, 2005, from **http://education.umn.edu/NCEO/LEP/Accountability/Account_lep.htm**

National Center for Educational Statistics (NCES). (2003). Bilingual education/limited English proficient students. *Fast Facts.* Retrieved January 8, 2005, from **http://nces.ed.gob/fastfacts/display.asp?id=96**

Neal, L. I., McCray, A. D., Webb-Johnson, G., & Bridgest, S. T. (2003). The effects of African American movement styles on teachers' perceptions and reactions. *The Journal of Special Education, 37,* 49–57.

Obiakor, F. E. (1994). *The eight-step multicultural approach: Learning and teaching with a smile.* Dubuque, IA: Kendall/Hunt.

Ochoa, S. H., Robles-Pina, R., Garcia, S. B., & Breunig, N. (1999). School psychologists' perspectives on referrals of language minority students. *Multiple Voices, 3,* 1–14.

Ortiz, A. A. (1997). Learning disabilities occurring concomitantly with linguistic differences. *Journal of Learning Disabilities, 30,* 321–332.

Ortiz, A. A., & Yates, J. R. (2001). A framework for serving English language learners with disabilities. *Journal of Special Education, 14,* 72–80.

Palinscar, A. S., & Brown, A. L. (1987). Reciprocal teaching of comprehension-fostering and comprehension-monitoring activities. *Cognition and Instruction, 1,* 117–175.

Parette, H. P., & Petch-Hogan, B. (2000). Approaching families: Facilitating culturally/linguistically diverse family involvement. *Teaching Exceptional Children,* 33, 4–10.

Patton, J. M., & Baytops, J. L. (1995). Identifying and transforming the potential of young gifted African Americans: A clarion call for action. In B. A. Ford, F. E. Obiakor, and J. M. Patton (Eds.), *Effective education of African American exceptional learners: New perspectives* (pp. 27–68). Austin, TX: PRO-ED.

Pew Hispanic Center. (2002, January). *Educational attainment: Better than meets the eye, but large challenges remain.* (Fact Sheet). Washington, DC: Author.

Phyler v. *Doe,* 102 S. Ct. 2382 (1982).

Potter, D. (2002, January 24–30). An extraordinary young man. *Lakota Journal, Health,* pp. C-1, C-4.

Reid, R., Casat, C. D., Norton, H. J., Anastopoulos, A. D., & Temple, E. P. (2001). Using behavior rating scales for ADHD across ethnic groups: The IOWA Conners. *Journal of Emotional and Behavioral Disorders, 9,* 210–218.

Reschly, D. J. (2002). Minority overrepresentation: The silent contributor to LD prevalence and diagnostic confusion. In R. Bradley, L. Danielson, & D. P. Hallahan (Eds.), *Identification of learning disabilities: Research to practice* (pp. 361–368). Mahwah, NJ: Erlbaum.

Rivera, D. P., & Smith, D. D. (1997). *Teaching students with learning and behavior problems.* Boston: Allyn and Bacon.

Rogers-Dulan, J. (1998). Religious connectedness among urban African American families who have a child with disabilities. *Mental Retardation, 36,* 91–103.

Rossell, C. (2004/2005). Teaching English through English. *Educational Leadership, 62,* 32–36.

Rothstein, R. (2004, May 19). Social class leaves its imprint. *Education Week,* pp. 40–41.

Ruiz, N. (1995). The social construction of ability and disability: I. Profile types of Latino children identified as language learning disabled. *Journal of Learning Disabilities, 29,* 491–502.

Salend, S. J., & Salinas, A. (2003). Language differences or learning difficulties: The work of the multidisciplinary team. *Teaching Exceptional Children, 35,* 35–43.

Santos, R., Fowler, S., Corso, R., & Bruns, D. (2000). Acceptance, acknowledgement, and adaptability: Selecting culturally and linguistically appropriate early childhood materials. *Teaching Exceptional Children, 32,* 14–22.

Schettler, R., Stein, J., Reich, F., Valenti, M., & Wallinga, D. (2000). *In harm's way: Toxic threats to child development.* Cambridge, MA: Greater Boston Physicians for Social Responsibility. **www.igc.org/psr**

Seymour, H. N., Abdulkarim, L., & Johnson, V. (1999). The Ebonics controversy: An educational and clinical dilemma. *Topics in Language Disorders, 19,* 66–77.

Shapiro, J., Monzo, L. D., Rueda, R., Gomez, J. A., & Blacher, J. (2004). Alienated advocacy: Perspectives of Latina mothers of young adults with developmental disabilities on service systems. *Mental Retardation, 42,* 37–54.

Short, D., & Echevarria, J. (2004/2005). Teacher skills to support English language learners. *Educational Leadership, 62,* 9–13.

Sileo, R. W., & Prater, M. A. (1998). Preparing professionals for partnerships with parents of students with disabilities: Textbook considerations regarding cultural diversity. *Exceptional Children, 64,* 513–528.

Sileo, T. W., Sileo, A. P., & Prater, M. A. (1996). Parent and professional partnerships in special education: Multicultural considerations. *Intervention in School and Clinic, 31,* 145–153.

Slater, R. B. (2004). The persisting racial gap in college student graduation rates. *Journal of Blacks in Higher Education, 45,* 77–85.

Suro, R. (2002). *Counting the "other Hispanics": How many Colombians, Dominicans, Ecuadorians, Guatemalans and Salvadorans are there in the United States?* Washington, DC: The Pew Hispanic Center.

Suro, R., & Passel, J. S. (2003). *The rise of the second generation: Changing patterns in Hispanic population growth.* Washington, DC: Pew Hispanic Center.

Suro, R., & Singer, A. (2002, July). Latino growth in metropolitan American: Changing patterns, new locations. *Survey Series: Census 2000.* Washington, DC: The Brookings Institution.

Taylor, O. L. (1997). *Testimony of Orlando L. Taylor on the subject of "Ebonics" to the United States Senate Committee on Appropriations Subcommittee on Labor, Health and Human Services and Education.* Washington, DC: United States Senate.

Thorp, E. K. (1997). Increasing opportunities for partnership with culturally and linguistically diverse families. *Intervention in School and Clinic, 32,* 261–269.

Thurlow, M. L., & Liu, K. K. (2001). Can "all" really mean students with disabilities who have limited English proficiency? *The Journal of Special Education, 14,* 63–71.

Thurston, L. P., & Navarrete, L. A. (2003). Rural, poverty-level mothers: A comparative study of those with and without children who have special needs. *Rural Special Education Quarterly, 22,* 15–23.

Tiedt, P. L., & Tiedt, I. M. (2002). *Multicultural teaching: A handbook of activities, information, and resources* (6th ed.). Boston: Allyn and Bacon.

Tornatzky, L. G., Pachon, H. P., & Torres, C. (2003). *Closing achievement gaps: Improving educational outcomes for Hispanic children.* Los Angeles: The Center for Latino Educational Excellence, The Tomás Rivera Policy Institute, University of Southern California.

Tyler, N. T., Lopez-Reyna, N., & Yzquierdo, Z. (2004). The relationship between cultural diversity and the special education workforce. *The Journal of Special Education, 38,* 22–38.

U.S. Department of Education (2001). *Twenty-third annual report to Congress on the implementation of the Individuals with Disabilities Education Act.* Washington, DC: U.S. Government Printing Office.

U.S. Department of Education. (2002). *Twenty-fourth annual report to Congress on the implementation of the Individuals with Disabilities Education Act.* Washington, DC: U. S. Government Printing Office.

U.S. Department of Education. (2005). Child count, December 2004. *2005 OSEP/Westat Combined Part C/B Annual Report Tables.* Retrieved from **www.ideadata.org**

Van Kuren, L. (2003). Exceptional and homeless. *Today, 9,* 1–2, 7, 13.

Voltz, D. (1998). Cultural diversity and special education teacher preparation: Critical issues confronting the field. *Teacher Education and Special Education, 21,* 63–70.

Voltz, D. (2005). Cultural influences on behavior. *Who's in charge?: Developing a comprehensive behavior management system. STAR Legacy Module.* Nashville, TN: IRIS Center for Faculty Enhancement, Peabody College, Vanderbilt University. **http://iris.peabody.vanderbilt.edu**

Vraniak, D. (1998). Developing systems of support with American Indian families of youth with disabilities. *Health Issues for Children & Youth & Their Families, 6,* 9–10.

Winzer, M. A., & Mazurek, K. (1998). *Special education in multicultural contexts.* Columbus, OH: Merrill.

Yates, J. R., Hill, J. L., & Hill, E. G. (2002). "A vision for change" but for who? A "personal" response to the National Research Council report. *DDEL News, 11,* 4–5.

Young, B. A. (2004). *Public school students, staff, and graduate counts by state: School year 2001–2002* (NCES 2003-358R). Washington, DC: U.S. Department of Education, National Center for Education Statistics.

Yzquierdo, Z. (2005). *Distinctions between language differences and language disorders.* Nashville, TN: Peabody College of Vanderbilt University, Department of Special Education.

Yzquierdo, Z., & Blalock, G. (2004). Language-appropriate assessments for determining eligibility of English language learners for special education services. *Assessment for Effective Intervention, 29,* 17–30.

Zehr, M.A. (2004, January 14). Report updates portrait of LEP students. *Education Week.* Retrieved March 15, 2005, from **www.edweek.org**

Zelasko, N., & Antunez, B. (2000). *If your child learns in two languages.* Washington, DC: National Clearinghouse for Bilingual Education, George Washington University.

Zima, B. T., Forness, S. R., Bussing, R., & Benjamin, B. (1998). Homeless children in emergency shelters: Need for prereferral intervention and potential eligibility for special education. *Behavioral Disorders, 23,* 98–110.

CHAPTER 4

Speech or Language Impairments

American Speech-Language-Hearing Association Ad Hoc Committee on Service Delivery in the Schools (1993). Definitions of communication disorders and variations, *Asha, 35,* (Suppl. 10), pp. 40–41.

American Speech-Hearing-Language Association (ASHA). (2002). *ASHA 2002 desk reference* (Vol. 3). Rockville, MD: ASHA.

American Speech-Hearing-Language Association (ASHA). (2005). *Membership trends: Highlights and trends: ASHA counts for 2004.* Retrieved April 14, 2005, from **www.asha.org**

Anderson, N. B., & Shames, G. H. (2006). *Human communication disorders: An introduction* (7th ed.). Boston: Allyn and Bacon.

Baca, L. M., & Cervantes, H. T. (Eds.). (2004). *The bilingual special education interface* (4th ed.). Columbus, OH: Merrill.

Bailey, Jr., D. B., Aytch, L. S., Odom, S. L., Symons, F., & Wolery, M. (1999). Early intervention as we know it. *Mental Retardation and Developmental Disabilities Research Reviews, 5,* 11–20.

Bakken, J. P., & Whedon, C. K. (2002). Teaching text structure to improve reading comprehension. *Intervention in School and Clinic, 37,* 229–233.

Bernthal, J. E., & Bankson, N. W. (2004). *Articulation and phonological disorders* (5th ed.). Boston: Allyn and Bacon.

Blackorby, J., Wagner, M., Cadwallader, T., Cameto, R., Levine, P., & Marder, C., with Giacaione, P. (2002). *Behind the label: The functional implications of disability.* Menlo Park, CA: SEELS Project, SRI International.

Blank, M., Rose, S. A., & Berlin, L. J. (1978). *The language of learning: The preschool years.* New York: Grune & Stratton.

Boulineau, T., Fore III, C., Hagan-Burke, S., & Burke, M. D. (2004). Use of story-mapping to increase the story-grammar text comprehension of elementary students with learning disabilities. *Learning Disability Quarterly, 27,* 105–121.

Boyle, J. R. (1996). The effects of a cognitive mapping strategy on the literal and inferential comprehension of students with mild disabilities. *Learning Disability Quarterly, 19,* 86–98.

Children's Defense Fund (CDF). (2004). *The state of America's children: 2004.* Washington, DC: Author.

Cleminshaw, H., DePompei, R., Crais, E. R., Blosser, J., Gillette, Y., & Hooper, C. R. (1996). Working with families. *ASHA, 38,* 34–45.

Conture, E. G. (2001). *Stuttering: Its nature, diagnosis, and treatment.* Boston: Allyn and Bacon.

Culatta, B., & Wiig, E. H. (2006). Language disabilities in school-age children and youth. In N. B. Anderson and G. H. Shames (Eds.), *Human communication disorders: An introduction* (7th ed, pp. 352–358). Boston: Allyn and Bacon.

Dale, P., Price, T., Bishop, D., & Plomin, R. (2003). Outcomes of early language delay, I: Predicting persistent and transient language difficulties at 3 and 4 years. *Journal of Speech and Hearing Research, 34,* 565–571.

Education of the Handicapped (1992, February 26). *Early education greatly reduces learning problems, study says.* Washington, DC: U.S. Department of Education. Author, p. 7.

Ely, R. (2005). Language and literacy in the schools. In J. B. Gleason (Ed.), *The development of language* (6th ed.). Boston: Allyn and Bacon.

Falk-Ross, F. C. (2002). *Classroom-based language and literacy intervention: A programs and case studies approach.* Boston: Allyn and Bacon.

Fletcher, J. M., Lyon, G. R., Barnes, M., Stuebing, K. K., Francis, D. J., Olson, R. K., Shaywitz, S. E., & Shaywitz, B. A. (2002). Classifications of learning disabilities: An evidence-based evaluation. In R. Bradley, L. Danielson, & D. P. Hallahan (Eds.), *Identification of learning disabilities: Research to practice* (pp. 185–250). Mahwah, NJ: Erlbaum.

Fuchs, D., & Fuchs, L. S. (2005). *Response to intervention (RTI): Preventing and identifying LD.* Nashville, TN: Vanderbilt University, video conference presentation to the New York City School System.

Gleason, J. B. (Ed.) (2005). *The development of language* (6th ed.). Boston: Allyn and Bacon.

Gregory, J. H., Campbell, J. H., Gregory, C. B., & Hill, D. G. (2003). *Stuttering therapy: Rationale and procedures.* Boston: Allyn and Bacon.

Hall, B. J., Oyer, J. J., & Haas, W. H. (2001). *Speech, language, and hearing disorders: A guide for the teacher* (3rd ed.). Boston: Allyn and Bacon.

Harwood, L., Warren, S. F., & Yoder, P. (2002). The importance of responsivity in developing contingent exchanges with beginning communicators. In J. Reichle, D. R. Beukelman, & J. C. Light, (Eds.), *Exemplary practices for beginning communicators: Implications for ACC* (pp. 59–96). Baltimore, MD: Paul H. Brookes.

Horton, S. V., Lovitt, T. C., & Bergerud, D. (1990). The effectiveness of graphic organizers for three classifications of secondary students in content area classes. *Journal of Learning Disabilities, 23,* 12–22, 29.

Hudson, J. A., & Gillam, R. B. (1997). "Oh, I remember now!" Facilitating children's long-term memory for events. *Topics in Language Disorders, 18,* 1–15.

Inspiration Software, Inc. (© 1998–2005). *Inspiration®.* Portland, OR: Author.

Inspiration Software, Inc. (© 2000–2005). *Kidspiration®.* Portland, OR: Author.

Ives, B., & Hoy, C. (2003). Graphic organizers applied to higher-level secondary mathematics. *Learning Disabilities Practice, 18,* 36–51.

Jenkins, J. R., & O'Connor, R. E. (2002) Early identification and intervention for young children with reading/learning disabilities. In R. Bradley, L. Danielson, & D. P. Hallahan (Eds.), *Identification of learning disabilities: Research to practice* (pp. 99–149). Mahwah, NJ: Erlbaum.

Justice, L. M. (2004). Creating language-rich preschool classroom environments. *Teaching Exceptional Children, 37,* 36–44.

Kangas, K. A., & Lloyd, L. L. (2006). Augmentative and alternative communication. In G. H. Shames and N. B. Anderson (Eds.), *Human communication disorders: An introduction* (7th ed., pp. 436–470). Boston: Allyn and Bacon.

Lombardo, L. A. (1999). Children score higher on tests when child care meets standards. *Early Childhood Reports, 10,* 4.

Longmore, P. K. (2003). *Why I burned my book and other essays on disability.* Philadelphia: Temple University Press.

Lovitt, T. C., and Horton, S. V. (1994). Strategies for adapting science textbooks for youth with learning disabilities. *Remedial and Special Education, 15,* 105–116.

Lyon, G. R, Fletcher, J. M., Shaywitz, S. E., Shaywitz, B. A., Torgesen, J. K., Wood, F. B., Schulte, A., & Olson, R. (2001). Rethinking learning disabilities. In C. E. Finn, A. J. Rotherham, & C. R. Hokansan (Eds.), *Rethinking special education for a new century* (pp. 259–288). Washington DC: Thomas B. Fordham Foundation and the Progressive Policy Institute.

Mastropieri, M. A., Scruggs, T. E., & Graetz, J. E. (2003). Reading comprehension instruction for secondary students: Challenges for struggling students and teachers. *Learning Disability Quarterly, 26,* 103–116.

Maugh II, T. H. (1995, August 11). Study finds folic acid cuts risk of cleft palate. *Los Angeles Times,* p. A20.

McCormick, L. (2003). Language intervention and support. In L. McCormick, D. R. Loeb, & R. L. Schiefelbusch (Eds.), *Supporting children with communication difficulties in inclusive settings: School-based language intervention.* Boston: Allyn and Bacon.

McWilliams, B. J., & Witzel, M. A. (1998). Cleft palate. In G. H. Shames, E. H. Wiig, and W. A. Secord (Eds.), *Human communication disorders: An introduction* (5th ed., pp. 438–479). Boston: Allyn and Bacon.

Moore, G. P., & Kester, D. (1953). Historical notes on speech correction in the preassociation era. *Journal of Speech and Hearing Disorders, 18,* 48–53.

Norris, J. A., & Hoffman, P. R. (2002). Phonemic awareness: A complex developmental process. *Topics in Language Disorders, 22,* 1–34.

Olswang, L. B., Coggins, T. E., & Timler, G. R. (2001). Outcome measures for school-age children with social communication problems. *Topics in Language Disorders, 21,* 50–73.

Operation Smile (2004, June 2004). Jessica Simpson joins Operation Smile. *Operation Smile: Changing lives one smile at a time* (p.1). Operation Smile: Norfolk, VA.

Owens, Jr., R. E. (2006). Development of communication, language, and speech. In N. B. Anderson and G. H. Shames (Eds.), *Human communication disorders: An introduction* (7th ed., pp. 25–58). Boston: Allyn and Bacon.

Owens, Jr., R. E., Metz, D. E., & Haas, A. (2003). *Introduction to communication disorders: A life span perspective* (2nd ed.). Boston: Allyn and Bacon.

Pan, B. A. (2005). Semantic development: Learning the meanings of words. In J. B. Gleason (Ed.), *The development of language* (6th ed.). Boston: Allyn and Bacon.

Payne, K. T., & Taylor, O. L. (2006). Multicultural influences on human communication. In N. B. Anderson and G. H. Shames (Eds.), *Human communication disorders: An introduction* (7th ed., pp. 93–125). Boston: Allyn and Bacon.

Plante, E., & Beeson, P. M. (2004). *Communication and communication disorders: A clinical introduction* (2nd ed.). Boston: Allyn and Bacon.

Ramig, P. R., & Shames, G. H. (2006). Stuttering and other disorders of fluency. In N. B. Anderson and G. H. Shames (Eds.), *Human communication disorders: An introduction* (7th ed, pp. 183–221). Boston: Allyn and Bacon.

Ratner, N. B. (2005). Atypical language development. In J. B. Gleason (Ed.), *The development of language* (6th ed.). Boston: Allyn and Bacon.

Reichle, J., Beukelman, D. R., & Light, J. C. (2002). *Exemplary practices for beginning communicators: Implications for ACC.* Baltimore: Paul H. Brookes.

Roberts, J. E., & Zeisel, S. A. (2002). *Ear infections and language development.* Washington, DC: U.S. Department of Education and American Speech-Language-Hearing Association.

Robinson, N. B. (2003). Families: The first communication partners. In L. McCormick, D. R. Loeb, & R. L. Schiefelbusch (Eds.), *Supporting children with communication difficulties in inclusive settings: School-based language intervention.* Boston: Allyn and Bacon.

Rock, M. L. (2004). Graphic organizers: Tools to build behavioral literacy and foster emotional competency. *Intervention in School and Clinic, 40,* 10–18.

Ruiz, N. (1995). The social construction of ability and disability: I. Profile types of Latino children identified as language learning disabled. *Journal of Learning Disabilities, 29,* 491–502.

Salend, S. J. (2005). *Creating inclusive classrooms: Effective and reflective practices for all students* (5th ed.). Columbus, OH: Merrill/Prentice-Hall.

Salend, S. J., & Salinas, A. (2003). Language differences or learning difficulties: The work of the multidisciplinary team. *Teaching Exceptional Children, 35,* 35–43.

Sander, E. K. (1972). When are speech sounds learned? *Journal of Speech and Hearing Disorders, 37,* 62.

Scanlon, D., Deshler, D. D., and Schumaker, J. B. (1996). Can a strategy be taught and learned in secondary inclusive classrooms? *Learning Disabilities Research and Practice, 11,* 41–57.

Small, L. H. (2005). *Fundamentals of phonetics: A practical guide for students* (2nd ed.). Boston: Allyn and Bacon.

Stuart, S., & Parette, Jr., H. P. (2001). Native Americans and augmentative and alternative communication issues. *Multiple Voices, 5,* 38–53.

Sunderland, L. C. (2004). Speech, language, and audiology services in public schools. *Intervention in School and Clinic, 39,* 209–217.

U.S. Department of Education. (2002). *Twenty-fourth annual report to Congress on the implementation of the Individuals with Disabilities Education Act.* Washington, DC: U.S. Government Printing Office.

U.S. Department of Education. (2005a). Assistance to states for the education of children with disabilities program and the early intervention program for infants and toddlers with disabilities; proposed regulations. *Federal Register,* 34, CRF Parts 300, 301, and 304.

U.S. Department of Education. (2005b). *Children served under IDEA, Part B (2003),* Data Tables. **www.ideadata.org**

Utley, C. A., & Obiakor, F. (Eds.). (2001). *Special education, multicultural education, and school reform: Components of quality education for learners with mild disabilities.* Springfield, IL: Charles C Thomas Publisher.

Van Riper, C., & Erickson, R. L. (1996). *Speech correction: An introduction to speech pathology and audiology* (9th ed.). Boston: Allyn and Bacon.

Vaughn, S., Bos, C. S., & Schumm, J. S. (2003). *Teaching exceptional, diverse, and at-risk students in the general education classroom.* Boston: Allyn and Bacon.

Wagner, M. M., D'Amico, R., Marder, C., Newman, L., & Blackorby, J. (1992). *What happens next? Trends in postschool outcomes of youth with disabilities. The second comprehensive report from the National Longitudinal Transition Study of Special Education Students.* Menlo Park, CA: SRI International.

Wetherby, A. M. (2002). Communication disorders in infants, toddlers, and preschool children. In G. H. Shames and N. B. Anderson (Eds.), *Human communication disorders: An introduction* (6th ed, pp. 186–217). Boston: Allyn and Bacon.

Wilkinson, K. M., & McIlvane, W. J. (2002). Considerations in teaching graphic symbols to beginning communicators. In J. Reichle, D. R. Beukelman, & J. C. Light, (Eds.), *Exemplary practices for beginning communicators: Implications for ACC* (pp. 273–322). Baltimore, MD: Paul H. Brookes.

CHAPTER 5

Learning Disabilities

Aaron, P. G., Phillips, S., & Larsen, S. (1988). Specific reading disability in historically famous persons. *Journal of Learning Disabilities, 21,* 523–538.

Academy of Achievement. (2005, February 5). *Craig O. McCaw.* Washington, DC: Author. Retrieved on May 5, 2005, from **www.achievement.org/autodoc**

Ahearn, E.M. (2003). *Specific learning disability: Current approaches to identification and proposals for change.* Washington, DC: National Association of State Directors of Special Education (NASDSE), Project Forum.

Anderson, N. B., & Shames, G. H. (2006). *Human communication disorders: An introduction* (7th ed.). Boston: Allyn and Bacon.

Askmen.com (2005). Charles Schwab. Retrieved May 11, 2005, from **www.askmen.com/men/business_politics/59c_charles_schwab.html**

Bender, W. (2004). *Learning disabilities: Characteristics, identification, and teaching strategies* (5th ed.). Boston: Allyn and Bacon.

Bishop, A. G. (2003). Prediction of first-grade reading achievement: A comparison of fall and winter kindergarten screenings. *Learning Disability Quarterly, 26,* 189–200.

Blair, C., & Scott, K. G. (2002). Proportion of LD placements associated with low socioeconomic status: Evidence for a gradient? *Journal of Special Education, 36,* 14–22.

Block, L. S. (2005). Getting the help you need on a college campus. *Projects.* Washington, DC: The Advocacy Institute. Retrieved May 10, 2005, from **www.advocacyinstitute.org**

Bolton, L. (1989). *Manet: The history and times of great masters.* Secaucus, NJ: Chartwell.

Boulineau, T., Fore III, C., Hagan-Burke, S., Burke, M. D. (2004). Use of story-mapping to increase the story-grammar text comprehension of elementary students with learning disabilities. *Learning Disability Quarterly, 27,* 105–121.

Bradley, R., Danielson, L., & Hallahan, D. P. (Eds.). (2002). *Identification of learning disabilities: Research to practice.* Mahwah, NJ: Erlbaum.

Branson, R. (1998). *Losing my virginity.* New York: Three Rivers Press, Random House.

Brinckerhoff, L. C. (2005, March 8). Teens with LD and/or AD/HD: Shopping for College Options. *Monthly Message.* SchwabLearning.org. San Mateo, CA: Charles and Helen Schwab Foundation.

Bryan, T. (1974). Peer popularity of learning disabled children. *Journal of Learning Disabilities, 7,* 621–625.

Bryan, T., Burstein, K., & Ergul, C. (2004). The social-emotional side of learning disabilities: A science-based presentation of the state of the art. *Learning Disability Quarterly, 27,* 45–51.

Bryan, T., & Sullivan-Burstein, K. (1998). Teacher-selected strategies for improving homework completion. *Remedial and Special Education, 19,* 263–275.

Bryant, D. P., & Bryant, B. R. (2003). *Assistive technology for people with disabilities.* Boston: Allyn and Bacon.

Bryant, D. P., Bryant, B. R., & Hammill, D. D. (2000). Characteristic behaviors of students with LD who have teacher-identified math weakness. *Journal of Learning Disabilities, 33,* 168–177, 199.

Bryant, D. P., Hartman, P., & Kim, S. A. (2003). Using explicit and strategic instruction to teach division skills to students with learning disabilities. *Exceptionality, 11,* 151–164.

Bursuck, B., Montague, M., & Vaughn, S. (2001). Homework practices that support students with disabilities. *Research Connections in Special Education, 8,* 1–5.

Bursuck, W. D., Smith, T., Munk, D., Damer, M., Mehlig, L., & Perry, J. (2004). Evaluating the impact of a prevention-based model of reading on children who are at risk. *Remedial and Special Education, 25,* 303–313.

Cannell, S. J. (1999, November 22). A writing fool. *Newsweek,* p. 79.

Carlson, C. L., Booth, J. E., Shin, M., & Canu, W. H. (2002). Parent-, teacher-, and self-rated motivational styles in ADHD subtypes. *Journal of Learning Disabilities, 35,* 103–113.

Chambers, J. G., Parrish, T., & Harr, J. J. (2002). *What are we spending on special education services in the United States, 1999–2000? Advance Report no. 1.* Washington, DC: American Institutes for Research (AIR): Special Education Expenditure Project (SEEP).

Compton, D. (2002). The relationships among phonological processing, orthographic processing, and lexical development in children with reading disabilities. *Journal of Special Education, 35,* 201–210.

Curtis, P. (2005 April 18). New typeface to help with dyslexia. *Guardian Unlimited.* London: England.

Davidson, H. P. (1934). A study of reversals in young children. *Journal of Genetic Psychology, 45,* 452–465.

Davidson, H. P. (1935). A study of the confusing letters b, d, p, and q. *Journal of Genetic Psychology, 46,* 458–468.

Decker, S. N., & Defries, J. C. (1980). Cognitive abilities in families of reading disabled children. *Journal of Learning Disabilities, 13,* 517–522.

Decker, S. N., & Defries, J. C. (1981). Cognitive ability profiles in families of reading disabled children. *Developmental Medicine and Child Neurology, 23,* 217–227.

Denton, C. A., Vaughn, S., & Fletcher, J. M. (2003). Bringing research-based practice in reading intervention to scale. *Learning Disabilities Research & Practice, 18,* 201–211.

Deshler, D. (2005). A closer look: Closing the performance gap. *StrateNotes, 13,* 1–5.

Deshler, D., & Roth, J. (2002, April). Strategic research: A summary of learning strategies and related research. *StrateNotes, 10,* 1–5.

Deshler, D. D., Schumaker, J. B., Lenz, B. K., Bulgren, J. A., Hock, M. F., Knight, J., & Ehren, B. J. (2001). Ensuring content-area learning by secondary students with learning disabilities. *Learning Disabilities Research & Practice, 16,* 96–108.

Dickinson, D. K., & McCabe, A. (2001). Bringing it all together: The multiple origins, skills, and environmental supports of early literacy. *Learning Disabilities Research & Practice, 16,* 186–202.

Dickinson, D. L., & Verbeek, R. L. (2002). Wage differentials between college graduates with and without learning disabilities. *Journal of Learning Disabilities, 35,* 175–184.

Dion, E., Morgan, P. L., Fuchs, D., & Fuchs, L. S. (2004). The promise and limitations of reading instruction in the mainstream: The need for a multilevel approach. *Exceptionality, 12,* 163–173.

Ehri, L. C., Nunes, S. R., Wilows, D. M., Schuster, B. V., Yaghoub-Zadeh, Z., & Shanahan, T. (2001). Phonemic awareness instruction helps children learn to read: Evidence from the National Reading Panel's meta-analysis. *Reading Research Quarterly, 36,* 250–287.

Elksnin, L. K., Bryant, D. P., Gartland, D., King-Sears, M., Rosenberg, M. S., Scanlon, D., Stronider, R., & Wilson, R. (2001). LD summit: Important issues for the field of learning disabilities. *Learning Disability Quarterly, 24,* 297–305.

Elksnin, L. K., & Elksnin, N. (2004). The social-emotional side of learning disabilities. *Learning Disability Quarterly, 27,* 3–8.

Elliott, S. N., Malecki, C. K., & Demaray, M. K. (2001). New directions in social skills assessment and intervention for elementary and middle school students. *Exceptionality, 9,* 19–32.

Ellis, E. S. (1986). The role of motivation and pedagogy on the generalization of cognitive strategy training. *Journal of Learning Disabilities, 19,* 66–70.

Epstein, M. H., Polloway, E. A., Buck, G. H., Bursuck, W. D., Wissinger, L. M., Whitehouse, F., & Jayanthi, M. (1997). Homework-related communication problems: Perspectives of general education teachers. *Learning Disabilities Research & Practice, 12,* 221–227.

Espin, C. A., Weissenburger, J. W., & Benson, B. J. (2004). Assessing the writing performance of students in special education. *Exceptionality, 12,* 55–66.

Finn, Jr., C. E., Rotherham, A. J., & Hokanson, Jr., C. R. (Eds.). (2001). Conclusions and principles for reform. In C. E. Finn, Jr., A. J. Rotherham, and C. R. Hokanson, Jr., (Eds.), *Rethinking special education for a new century* (pp. 259–288). Washington, DC: Thomas B. Fordham Foundation and the Progressive Policy Institute.

Frensch, N. (2005). *Read Regular®.* Retrieved May 26, 2005, from **www.readregular.com**

Friend, M., & Bursuck, W. D. (2006). *Including students with special needs: A practical guide for classroom teachers* (4th ed.). Boston: Allyn and Bacon.

Frostig, M. (1978). Five questions regarding my past and future and the past, present, and future of learning disabilities. *Journal of Learning Disabilities, 11,* 9–12.

Fuchs, D., & Fuchs, L.S. (2005, April 20). *Response to intervention (RTI): Preventing and identifying LD.* Nashville; TN: Vanderbilt University, Presentation via video conferencing for the New York City Schools.

Fuchs, D., Fuchs, L. S., Al Otaiba, S., Thompson, A., Yen, L., McMaster, K. N., Svenson, E., & Yang, N. J. (2001). K-PALS: Helping kindergarteners with reading readiness: Teachers and researchers in partnerships. *Teaching Exceptional Children, 33,* 76–80.

Fuchs, D., Fuchs, L. S., & Compton, D. L. (2004). Identifying reading disabilities by responsiveness-to-instruction: Specifying measures and criteria. *Learning Disability Quarterly, 27,* 216–229.

Fuchs, D., Fuchs, L. S., Mathes, P. G., Lipsey, M. W., & Roberts, P. H. (2002). Is "learning disabilities" just a fancy term for low achievement? A meta-analysis of reading differences between low achievers with and without the label. In R. Bradley, L. Danielson, & D. P. Hallahan (Eds.), *Identification of learning disabilities: Research to practice* (pp. 747–762). Mahwah, NJ: Erlbaum.

Fuchs, D., Fuchs, L. S., Thompson, A., Al Otaiba, S., Yen, L., Yang, N. J., Svenson, E., & Braun, M. (2002). Exploring the importance of reading programs for kindergarteners with disabilities in mainstream classrooms. *Exceptional Children, 68,* 295–311.

Fuchs, D., Mock, D., Morgan, P. L., & Young, C. L. (2003). Responsiveness-to-intervention: Definitions, evidence, and implications for the learning disabilities construct. *Learning Disabilities Research & Practice, 18,* 157–171.

Fuchs, L. (2003). Assessing intervention responsiveness: Conceptual and technical issues. *Learning Disabilities Research & Practice, 18,* 172–186.

Fuchs, L. S., & Fuchs, D. (2001). Principles for the prevention and intervention of mathematics difficulties. *Learning Disabilities Research & Practice, 16,* 85–95.

Fuchs, L., Fuchs, D., & Powell, S. (2004). *Using CBM for progress monitoring.* Washington, DC: American Institutes for Research (AIR).

Gerber, P. J., & Price, L. A. (2003). Persons with learning disabilities in the workplace: What we know so far in the Americans with Disabilities Act era. *Learning Disabilities Research & Practice, 18,* 132–136.

Goldberg, R. J., Higgins, E. L., Raskind, M. H., & Herman, K. L. (2003). Predictors of success in individuals with learning disabilities: A qualitative analysis of a 20-year longitudinal study. *Learning Disabilities Research & Practice, 18,* 222–236.

Graham, S., Harris, K. R., & Larsen, L. (2001). Prevention and intervention of writing difficulties for students with learning disabilities. *Learning Disabilities Research & Practice, 16,* 74–84.

Gresham, F. (2002). Responsiveness to intervention: An alternative approach to the identification of learning disabilities. In R. Bradley, L. Danielson, & D. P. Hallahan (Eds.), *Identification of learning disabilities: Research to practice* (pp. 467–519). Mahwah, NJ: Erlbaum.

Gresham, F. M., Sugai, G., & Horner, R. H. (2001). Interpreting outcomes of social skills training for students with high-incidence disabilities. *Exceptional Children, 67,* 331–344.

Hammill, D. D. (1990). On defining learning disabilities: An emerging consensus. *Journal of Learning Disabilities, 23,* 74–84.

Hammill, D. D. (2004). What we know about the correlates of reading. *Exceptional Children, 70,* 453–468.

Hammill, D., & Larsen, S. (1974). The effectiveness of psycholinguistic abilities. *Exceptional Children, 41,* 5–14.

Herszenhorn, D. M. (2004, October 29). Reaction time to fixing lead in schools' water is disputed. *New York Times.*

Higgins, K., Boone, R., & Williams, D. L. (2000). Evaluating educational software for special education. *Intervention in School and Clinic, 36,* 109–115.

Hosp, M. K., & Hosp, J. L. (2003). Curriculum-based measurement for reading, spelling, and math: How to do it and why. *Preventing School Failure, 48,* 10–17.

Inspiration Software, Inc. (© 1998–2005). *Inspiration®.* Portland, OR: Author.

Inspiration Software, Inc. (© 2000–2005). *Kidspiration®.* Portland, OR: Author.

IRIS Center (2005). Classroom assessment: An introduction to monitoring academic achievement in the classroom. *IRIS Module.* Nashville, TN: IRIS Center for Faculty Enhancement, Vanderbilt University. **http://iris.peabody.vanderbilt.edu**

Isaacson, S. (2004). Instruction that helps students meet state standards in writing. *Exceptionality, 12,* 39–54.

Ives, B., & Hoy, C. (2003). Graphic organizers applied to higher-level secondary mathematics. *Learning Disabilities Practice, 18,* 36–51.

Jayanthi, M., Bursuck, W., Epstein, M. H., & Polloway, E. A. (1997). Strategies for successful homework. *Teaching Exceptional Children, 30,* 4–7.

Jenkins, J. R., & O'Connor, R. E. (2002). Early identification and intervention for young children with reading/learning disabilities. In R. Bradley, L. Danielson, & D. P. Hallahan (Eds.), *Identification of learning disabilities: Research to practice* (pp. 99–149). Mahwah, NJ: Erlbaum.

Jitendra, A. K., Edwards, L. L., Sacks, G., & Jacobson, L. A. (2004). What research says about vocabulary instruction for students with learning disabilities. *Exceptional Children, 70,* 299–322.

Jones, D. (2003, November 10). Charles Schwab didn't let dyslexia stop him. *USA Today,* p. B-5.

Jordan, N. C., & Hanich, L. B. (2003). Characteristics of children with moderate mathematics deficiencies: A longitudinal perspective. *Learning Disabilities Research & Practice, 18,* 213–221.

Katims, D. S. (1994). Emergence of literacy in preschool children with disabilities. *Learning Disabilities Quarterly, 17,* 58–69.

Kavale, K. A., & Forness, S. R. (1996). Social skill deficits and learning disabilities: A meta-analysis. *Journal of Learning Disabilities, 29,* 226–237.

Kavale, K. A., & Forness, S. R. (2000). What definitions of learning disability say and don't say. *Journal of Learning Disabilities, 33,* 239–256.

Kavale, K. A., Holdnack, J. A., & Mostert, M. P. (2005). Responsiveness to intervention and the identification of specific learning disability: A critique and alternative proposal. *Learning Disability Quarterly, 28,* 2–16.

Kavale, K. A., & Mostert, M. P. (2004). Social skills interventions for individuals with learning disabilities. *Learning Disability Quarterly, 27,* 31–43.

Keogh, B. K. (1974). Optometric vision training programs for children with learning disabilities: Review of issues and research. *Journal of Learning Disabilities, 7,* 36–48.

Kihl, P., Gregersen, K., & Sterum, N. (2000). Hans Christian Andersen's spelling and syntax: Allegations of specific dyslexia are unfounded. *Journal of Learning Disabilities, 33,* 506–519.

Kirk, S. A. (1977). Specific learning disabilities. *Journal of Clinical Child Psychology, 6,* 23–26.

Kirk, S. A., McCarthy, J. J., & Kirk, W. D. (1968). *Illinois Test of Psycholinguistic Abilities (ITPA).* Champagne-Urbana, IL: University of Illinois Press.

Kuhne, M., & Wiener, J. (2000). Stability of social status of children with and without learning disabilities. *Learning Disability Quarterly, 23,* 64–75.

Leafstedt, J. M., Richards, C. R., & Gerber, M. M. (2004). Effectiveness of explicit phonological-awareness instruction for at risk English learners. *Learning Disabilities Research & Practice, 19,* 252–261.

Learning Disability Summit. (2001, November 29–30). *Consensus report.* Lawrence, KS: University of Kansas.

Le Mare, L., & de la Ronde, M. (2000). Links among social status, service delivery mode, and service delivery preference in LD, low-achieving, and normally achieving elementary-aged children. *Learning Disability Quarterly, 23,* 52–62.

Lerner, J. (1993). *Learning disabilities: Theories, diagnosis, and teaching strategies* (6th ed.). Boston: Houghton Mifflin.

Lewis, R. B. (1998). Assistive technology and learning disabilities: Today's realities and tomorrow's promises. *Journal of Learning Disabilities, 31,* 16–54.

Lissner, L. S. (2005). Choosing a college. *Projects.* Washington, DC: The Advocacy Institute. Retrieved May 10, 2005, from **www.advocacyinstitute.org**

Lyon, G. R., Fletcher, J. M., Shaywitz, S. E., Shaywitz, B. A., Torgesen, J. K., Wood, F. B., Schulte, A., & Olson, R. (2001). Rethinking learning disabilities. In C. E. Finn, Jr., A. J. Rotherham, and C. R. Hokanson, Jr., (Eds.), *Rethinking special education for a new century* (pp. 259–288). Washington, DC: Thomas B. Fordham Foundation and the Progressive Policy Institute.

MacArthur, C. A. (2000). New tools for writing: Assistive technology for students with writing difficulties. *Topics in Language Disorders, 20,* 85–100.

MacMillan, D. L., Gresham, F. M., & Bocian, K. M. (1998). Discrepancy between definitions of learning disabilities and school practices: An empirical investigation. *Journal of Learning Disabilities, 31,* 314–326.

Madaus, J. W. (2005). Navigating the college transition maze: A guide for students with learning disabilities. *Teaching Exceptional Children, 37,* 32–37.

Madaus, J. W., Ruban, L. M., Foley, R. E., & McGuire, J. M. (2003). Attributes contributing to the employment satisfaction of university graduates with learning disabilities. *Learning Disability Quarterly, 26,* 159–169.

Mastropieri, M. A., & Scruggs, T. E. (1997). What's special about special education? A cautious view toward full inclusion. *The Educational Forum, 61,* 206–211.

Mastropieri, M. A., Scruggs, T. E., Spencer, V., & Fontana, J. (2003). Promoting success in high school world history: Peer tutoring versus guided notes. *Learning Disabilities Research & Practice, 18,* 52–65.

Mathes, P. G., & Babyak, A. E. (2001). The effects of peer-assisted literacy strategies for first-grade readers with and without additional mini-skills lessons. *Learning Disabilities Research & Practice, 16,* 28–44.

Mathes, P. G., Torgesen, J. K., & Allor, J. H. (2001). The effects of peer-assisted literacy strategies for first-grade readers with and without additional computer-assisted instruction in phonological awareness. *American Educational Research Journal, 38,* 371–410.

McNamara, K., & Hollinger, C. (2003). Intervention-based assessment: Evaluation rates and eligibility findings. *Exceptional Children, 69,* 181–193.

Moody, S. W., Vaughn, S., Hughes, M. T., & Fischer, M. (2000). Reading instruction in the resource room: Set up for failure. *Exceptional Children, 66,* 305–316.

Mooney, J., & Cole, D. (2000). *Learning outside the lines.* New York: Simon & Schuster.

Mulholland, R. (2005). Woodshop, technology, and reading! *Teaching Exceptional Children, 37,* 16–19.

Mull, C., Sitlington, P. L., & Alper, S. (2001). Postsecondary education for students with learning disabilities: A synthesis of literature. *Exceptional Children, 68,* 97–118.

Müller, E., & Markowitz, J. (2004). *Disability categories: State terminology, definitions & eligibility criteria.* Alexandria, VA: National Association of State Directors of Special Education (NASDSE), Project Forum.

National Center for Educational Statistics (NCES). (2003). *Digest of education statistics tables and figures: 2003.* Washington, DC: U.S. Department of Education. Retrieved May 10, 2005, from **http://nces.ed.gov/programs/digest/d03**

National Institutes of Health, National Institute of Neurological Disorders and Stroke. (2005). "What is learning disabilities?" NINDS Learning Disabilities Information Page. Retrieved May 2, 2005, from **www.ninds.nih.gov**

Nelson, J. R., Benner, G. J., & Gonzalez, J. (2003). Learner characteristics that influence the treatment effectiveness of early literacy interventions: A meta-analytic review. *Learning Disabilities Research & Practice, 18,* 255–267.

Nowicki, E. A. (2003). A meta-analysis of the social competence of children with learning disabilities compared to classmates of low and average to high achievement. *Learning Disability Quarterly, 26,* 171–188.

Office of Special Education Programs (OSEP). (2005). Responsiveness to intervention in conjunction with learning disability determination. *TA Template on RTI.* Washington, DC: Author.

Ofiesh, N. S., Hughes, C., & Scott, S. S. (2004). Extended test time and postsecondary students with learning disabilities: A model for decision making. *Learning Disabilities Research & Practice, 19,* 57–70.

Olswang, L. B., Coggins, T. E., & Timler, G. R. (2001). Outcome measures for school-age children with social communication problems. *Topics in Language Disorders, 21,* 50–73.

Pearl, R. (1982). LD children's attributions for success and failure: A replication with a labeled LD sample. *Learning Disabilities Quarterly, 5,* 173–176.

Pullen, P. C., & Justice, L. M. (2003). Enhancing phonological awareness, print awareness, and oral language skills in preschool children. *Intervention in School and Clinic, 39,* 87–98.

Raskind, M. H., & Higgins, E. L. (1998). Assistive technology for postsecondary students with learning disabilities: An overview. *Journal of Learning Disabilities, 31,* 27–40.

Reschly, D. J. (2002). Minority overrepresentation: The silent contributor to LD prevalence and diagnostic confusion. In R. Bradley, L. Danielson, & D. P. Hallahan (Eds.). *Identification of learning disabilities: Research to practice* (pp. 361–368). Mahwah, NJ: Erlbaum.

Ring, M. M., & Reetz, L. (2000). Modification effects on attributions of middle school students with learning disabilities. *Language Disabilities Research & Practice, 15,* 34–42.

Rivera, D. P., & Smith, D. D. (1997). *Teaching students with learning and behavior problems.* Boston: Allyn and Bacon.

Robinson, C. S., Menchetti, B. M., & Torgesen, J. K. (2002). Toward a two-factor theory of one type of mathematics disabilities. *Learning Disabilities Research & Practice, 17,* 81–89.

Rovet, J. (2004). Turner syndrome: Genetic and hormonal factors contributing to a specific disability profile. *Learning Disabilities Research & Practice, 19,* 133–145.

Sáenz, L. M., Fuchs, L. S., & Fuchs, D. (2005). Peer-assisted learning strategies for English language learners with learning disabilities. *Exceptional Children, 71,* 231–247.

Savukinas, G. (2002). Community colleges and students with disabilities: Options and opportunities. *Information from HEATH.* Washington, DC: National Clearinghouse on Postsecondary Education for Individuals with Disabilities, The George Washington University HEATH Resource Center.

Schneider, P., & the Editors of Time-Life Books (1968). *The world of Manet: 1832-1883.* New York: Time-Life Books.

Schrag, J. A. (2000). Discrepancy approaches for identifying learning disabilities. *Quick Turn Around,* pp. 1–11.

Schumaker, J. B., & Deshler, D. D. (2003). Can students with LD become competent writers? *Learning Disability Quarterly, 26,* 129–141.

Sexton, M., Harris, K. R., & Graham, S. (1998). Self-regulated strategy development and the writing process: Effects on essay writing and attributions. *Exceptional Children, 64,* 295–311.

Shaw, S. (2005). College opportunities for students with learning disabilities. *Projects.* Washington, DC: The Advocacy Institute. Retrieved May 10, 2005, from **www.advocacyinstitute.org**

Shessel, I., & Reiff, H. B. (1999). Experiences of adults with learning disabilities: Positive and negative impacts and outcomes. *Learning Disability Quarterly, 22,* 305–316.

Simon, J. A. (2001). Legal issues in serving postsecondary students with disabilities. *Topics in Language Disorders, 21,* 1–16.

Sitlington, P. L. (2003). Postsecondary education: The other transition. *Exceptionality, 11,* 103–113.

Soltes, F. (2002, July 23). Making sense of "learning disabilities." *The Tennessean,* p. 4D.

Speece, D. L., Case, L. P., & Molloy, D. E. (2003). Responsiveness to general education instruction as the first gate to learning disabilities identification. *Learning Disabilities Research & Practice, 18,* 147–156.

Speece, D. L., Mills, C., Ritchey, K. D., & Hillman, E. (2003). Initial evidence that letter fluency tasks are valid indicators of early reading skill. *Journal of Special Education, 36,* 223–233.

Swanson, H. L., & Sachse-Lee, C. (2000). A meta-analysis of single-subject-design intervention research for students with LD. *Journal of Learning Disabilities, 33,* 114–136.

Swanson, H. L., Trainin, G., Necoechea, D. M., & Hammill, D. D. (2003). Rapid naming, phonological awareness, and reading: A meta-analysis of the correlation evidence. *Review of Educational Research, 73,* 407–440.

Switzky, H. N., & Schultz, G. F. (1988). Intrinsic motivation and learning performance: Implications for individual educational programming for learners with mild handicaps. *Remedial and Special Education, 9,* 7–14.

Teglasi, H., Cohn, A., & Meshbesher, N. (2004). Temperament and learning disability. *Learning Disability Quarterly, 27,* 9–20.

Terrill, M. C., Scruggs, T. E., & Mastropieri, M. A. (2004). SAT vocabulary instruction for high school students with learning disabilities. *Intervention in School and Clinic, 39,* 288–294.

Thomas, M. (2000). Albert Einstein and LD: An evaluation of the evidence. *Journal of Learning Disabilities, 33,* 149–157.

Torgesen, J. K. (2002). Empirical and theoretical support for direct diagnosis of learning disabilities by assessment of intrinsic processing weaknesses. In R. Bradley, L. Danielson, & D. P. Hallahan (Eds.), *Identification of learning disabilities: Research to practice* (pp. 565–652). Mahwah, NJ: Erlbaum.

Torgesen, J. K., & Wagner, R. K. (1998). Alternative diagnostic approaches for specific developmental reading disabilities. *Learning Disabilities Research & Practice, 13,* 220–232.

Troia, G. A., & Graham, S. (Eds.) (2004). Students who are exceptional and writing disabilities: Prevention, practice, intervention, and assessment. *Exceptionality, 12,* 1–66.

U.S. Department of Education (1991). *The thirteenth annual report to Congress on the implementation of IDEA.* Washington, DC: U.S. Government Printing Office.

U.S. Department of Education (2000). *The twenty-second annual report to Congress on the implementation of IDEA.* Washington, DC: U.S. Government Printing Office.

U.S. Department of Education. (2001). *Twenty-third annual report to Congress on the implementation of the Individuals with Disabilities Education Act.* Washington, DC: U.S. Government Printing Office.

U.S. Department of Education. (2002). *Twenty-fourth annual report to Congress on the implementation of the Individuals with Disabilities Education Act.* Washington, DC: U.S. Government Printing Office.

U.S. Department of Education (2005a). *Children served under IDEA, Part B (2003),* Data Tables. **www.ideadata.org**

U.S. Department of Education. (2005b). Assistance to states for the education of children with disabilities program and the early intervention program for infants and toddlers with disabilities; proposed regulations. *Federal Register,* 34, CRF Parts 300, 301, and 304.

U.S. Department of Education (2005c). *Number of children served under IDEA, by disability and age group (6–21), 1994 through 2003* (2003), Data Table AA9. **www.ideadata.org**

Vaughn, S. (2005). *Evidence-based reading interventions for the 2%.* OSEP 15th Annual Technical Assistance and Dissemination Conference. Washington, DC, June 8, 2005.

Vaughn, S., Elbaum, B., & Boardman, A. G. (2001). The social function of students with learning disabilities: Implications for inclusion. *Exceptionality, 9,* 47–65.

Vaughn, S., & Fuchs, L. S. (2003). Redefining learning disabilities as inadequate response to instruction: The promise and potential problems. *Learning Disabilities Research & Practice, 18,* 137–146.

Vaughn, S., Gersten, R., & Chard, D. J. (2000). The underlying message in LD intervention research: Findings from research synthesis. *Exceptional Children, 67,* 99–114.

Vaughn, S., & Linan-Thompson, S. (2004). *Research-based methods of reading instruction: Grades K–3.* Alexandria, VA: Association for Supervision and Curriculum Development.

Wiederholt, J. L. (1974). Historical perspectives on the education of the learning disabled. In L. Mann and D. Sabatino (Eds.), *The second review of special education* (pp. 103–152). Philadelphia: Journal of Special Education Press.

Wiener, J. (2004). Do peer relationships foster behavioral adjustment in children with learning disabilities? *Learning Disability Quarterly, 27,* 21–30.

Wilson, A. M., & Lesaux, N. K. (2001). Persistence of phonological processing deficits in college students with dyslexia who have age-appropriate reading skills. *Journal of Learning Disabilities, 34,* 394–400.

Wood, F. B., & Grigorenko, E. L. (2001). Emerging issues in the genetics of dyslexia: A methodological preview. *Journal of Learning Disabilities, 34,* 503–511.

CHAPTER 6

Attention Deficit Hyperactivity Disorder

American Academy of Pediatrics (2005). *ADHD—Treatment with medication.* Medical Library, retrieved March 18, 2005, from **www.medem.com**

American Psychiatric Association (APA). (2000). *Diagnostic and statistical manual of mental disorders, Fourth Edition, Text Revision* (DSM-IV®-TR). (4th ed.). Washington, DC: Author.

Austin, V. L. (2003). Pharmacological interventions for students with ADD. *Intervention in School and Clinic, 38,* 289–296.

Barkley, R. A. (1998). Attention deficit hyperactivity disorder: A handbook for diagnosis and treatment (2nd ed.). New York: Guilford.

Barkley, R. A. (2002). Consensus statement on ADHD. *European Child and Adolescent Psychiatry, 11,* 96–98.

Barkley, R. A., & Edwards, G. (1998). Diagnostic interview, behavior rating scales, and the medical examination. In R. A. Barkley (Ed.), *Attention-deficit hyperactivity disorder* (pp. 263–293). New York: Guilford.

Biederman, J., Mick, E., & Faraone, S. V. (2000). Age-dependent decline of symptoms of attention deficit hyperactivity disorder: Impact of remission definition and symptom type. *American Journal of Psychiatry, 157,* 816–818.

Bonafina, M. A., Newcorn, J. H., McKay, K. E., Koda, V. H., & Halperin, J. M. (2000). ADHD and reading disabilities: A cluster analytic approach for distinguishing subgroups. *Journal of Learning Disabilities, 33,* 297–307.

Bryan, T. (1997). Assessing the personal and social status of students with learning disabilities. *Learning Disabilities Research and Practice, 12,* 63–76.

Bussing, R., Zima, B. T., Belin, T. R., & Forness, S. R. (1998). Children who qualify for LD & SED programs: Do they differ in level of ADHD symptoms and co-morbid psychiatric conditions? *Behavioral Disorders, 23,* 85–97.

Carbone, E. (2001). Arranging the classroom with an eye (and ear) to students with ADHD. *Teaching Exceptional Children, 34,* 72–81.

Carlson, C. L., Booth, J. E., Shin, M., & Canu, W. H. (2002). Parent-, teacher-, and self-rated motivational styles in ADHD subtypes. *Journal of Learning Disabilities, 35,* 103–113.

Children and Adults with Attention-Deficit/Hyperactivity Disorder (CHADD). (2005). *The Disorder Named AD/HD—CHADD Fact Sheet 1.* Retrieved March 13, 2005, from **www.chadd.org**

Cruikshank, W. M., Bentzen, F. A., Ratzeburg, F. H., & Tannehauser, M. T. (1961). *A teaching method for brain-injured and hyperactive children.* Syracuse, NY: Syracuse University Press.

Daly, P. M., & Ranalli, P. (2003). Using countoons to teach self-monitoring skills. *Teaching Exceptional Children, 35,* 30–35.

Duhaney, L. M. G. (2003). A practical approach to managing the behaviors of students with ADD. *Intervention in School and Clinic, 38,* 267–279.

DuPaul, G. J., Barkley, R. A., & Connor, D. E. (1998). Stimulants. In R. A. Barkley (Ed.), *Attention-deficit hyperactivity disorder* (pp. 510–551). New York: Guilford.

DuPaul, G. J., Ervin, R. A., Hook, C. L., & McGoey, K. E. (1998). Peer tutoring for children with attention deficit hyperactivity disorder: Effects on classroom behavior and academic performance. *Journal of Applied Behavior Analysis, 31,* 579–592.

DuPaul, G. E., Schaughency, E. A., Weyandt, L. L., Tripp, G., Kiesner, J., Ota, K., & Stanish, Heidy. (2001). Self-report of ADHD symptoms in university students: Cross-gender and cross-national prevalence. *Journal of Learning Disabilities, 34,* 370–379.

Elliott, S. N., & Marquart, A. M. (2004). Extended time as a testing accommodation: Its effects and perceived consequences. *Exceptional Children, 70,* 349–367.

Forness, S. R., & Kavale, K. A. (2001). Are school professionals missing their best chance to help troubled kids? *Emotional & Behavioral Disorders, 1,* 80–83.

Fowler, M. (2002). *Attention-deficit/hyperactivity disorder.* Washington DC: NICHY, the National Dissemination Center for Children with Disabilities. Retrieved August 26, 2004, from **www.nichcy.org**

Fowler, M. (2004). *Attention-deficit/hyperactivity disorder: Briefing paper* (3rd ed.). Washington DC: NICHY, the National Dissemination Center for Children with Disabilities.

FTC Publishing (2003–2005). *Report Writer Interactive®.* Bloomington, IL: Author.

Fuchs, D., & Fuchs, L. S. (1998). Researchers and teachers working together to adapt instruction for diverse learnings. *Learning Disabilities Research & Practice, 13,* 126–137.

The Future of Children (2005). Special education for students with disabilities: Analysis and recommendations. *Special Education for Students with Disabilities.* Retrieved March 15, 2005, from **www.futureofchildren.org/information2827**

Gantos, J. (1998). *Joey Pigza swallowed the key.* New York: Farrar, Straus and Giroux.

Gay, G. (2002). Preparing for culturally responsive teaching. *Journal of Teacher Education, 53,* 106–116.

Gephart, H. R. (2003). Attention-deficit/hyperactivity disorder: Diagnosis and treatment through adulthood. *Primary Psychiatry, 10,* 27–28.

Getzel, E. E., McManus, S., & Briel, L. W. (2004). An effective model for college students with learning disabilities and attention deficit hyperactivity disorders. *National Center on Secondary Education and Transition (NCET): Research to Practice Brief, 3,* 1–5.

Gordon, M., & Barkley, R. A. (1998). Tests and obsersvational measures. In R. A. Barkley (Ed.), *Attention-deficit hyperactivity disorder* (pp. 294–311), New York: Guilford.

Gotsch, T. (2002, March 13). Medication issue could emerge in IDEA debate. *Special Education Report, 28,* 1–2.

Gresham, F. M., Lane, K. L., & Lambros, K. M. (2000). Comorbidity of conduct problems and ADHD: Identification of "fledgling psychopaths." *Journal of Emotional and Behavioral Disorders, 8,* 83–93.

Guyer, B. P. (Ed.) (2000). *ADHD: Achieving success in school and in life.* Boston: Allyn & Bacon.

Hallowell, E. M., & Ratey, J. J. (2005). *Delivered from distraction: Getting the most out of life with attention deficit disorder.* New York: Random House.

Hoffman, B., Hartley, K., & Boone, R. (2005). Reaching accessibility: Guidelines for creating and refining digital learning materials. *Intervention in School and Clinic, 40,* 171–176.

Honos-Webb, L. (2005). *The gift of ADHD: How to transform your child's problems into strengths.* Oakland, CA: New Harbinger Publications.

Individuals with Disabilities Education Act. Pub. L. No. 105–17, 111 STAT.37.

Individuals with Disabilities Education Improvement Act of 2004. Pub. L. No. 108-446. 118 STAT.2647.

Inspiration Software, Inc. (© 1998–2005). *Inspiration®.* Portland, OR: Author.

Inspiration Software, Inc. (© 2000–2005). *Kidspiration®.* Portland, OR: Author.

Jensen, P. S. (2000). ADHD: Advances in understanding its causes, and best treatments. *Emotional and Behavioral Disorders in Youth, 1,* 9–10, 19.

Kaplan, B. J., Crawford, S. G., Dewey, D. M., & Fisher, G. C. (2000). The I.Q.s of Children with ADHD are normally distributed. *Journal of Learning Disabilities, 33,* 425–432.

Kendall, J., Hatton, D., Beckett, Ann., & Leo, M. (2003). Children's accounts of attention-deficit/hyperactivity disorder. *Advances in Nursing Science, 26*(2), 114–130.

Keogh, B. (1971). Hyperactivity and learning disorders: Review and speculation. *Exceptional Children, 38,* 101–109.

Kephart, N. (1960). *The slow learner in the classroom.* Columbus, OH: Merrill.

Kessler, R. C., Adler, L., Ames, M., & Barkley, R. (2005). The prevalence and effects of adult attention deficit/hyperactivity disorder on work performance in a nationally representative sample of workers. *Journal of Occupational and Environmental Medicine, 47,* 565–572.

Kunzelmann, H. P., Cohen, M. A., Hulten, W. J., Martin, G. L., & Mingo, A. R. (1970). *Precision teaching: An initial training sequence.* Seattle, WA: Special Child Publications.

Mathur, S., & Smith, R. M. (2003). Collaborate with families of children with ADD. *Intervention in School and Clinic, 38,* 311–315.

Mayes, S. D., Calhoun, S. L., & Crowell, E. W. (2000). Learning disabilities and ADHD: Overlapping spectrum disorders. *Journal of Learning Disabilities, 33,* 417–424.

Merrell, K. W., & Boelter, E. (2001). An investigation of relationships between social behavior and ADHD in children and youth: Construct validity of the home and community social behavior scales. *Journal of Emotional and Behavioral Disorders, 9,* 260–269.

Mount, I. (2004). 25 most fascinating entrepreneurs: David Neeleman, JetBlue, for creating an airline fit for humans. Retrieved July 14, 2005, from **http://www.inc.com/magazine/20040401/25neeleman.html**

Müller, E., & Markowitz, J. (2004). *Disability categories: State terminology, definitions & eligibility criteria.* Alexandria, VA: National Association of State Directors of Special Education (NASDSE), Project Forum.

Murphy, K. R. (1998). Psychological counseling of adults with ADHD. In R. A. Barkley (Ed.), *Attention-deficit hyperactivity disorder* (pp. 582–591), New York: Guilford.

National Association of School Nurses (NASN). (2002a). *Controlled substances in the school setting.* Retrieved April 19, 2005, from **www.nasn.org**

National Association of School Nurses (NASN). (2002b). *School health nursing services role in health care.* Retrieved April 19, 2005, from **www.nasn.org**

National Institute of Mental Health. (2005). *Attention Deficit Hyperactivity Disorder.* Bethesda, MD: National Institutes of Health. Retrieved March 15, 2005, from **www.nimh.nih.gov**

National Institutes of Health Consensus Development Conference Statement. (2000). Diagnosis and treatment of attention-deficit/hyperactivity disorder (ADHD). *Journal of the American Academy of Child and Adolescent Psychiatry, 39,* 182–193.

Office of Special Education Programs (OSEP). (2003). *Identifying and treating attention deficit hyperactivity disorder: A resource for school and home.* Washington, DC: U.S. Department of Education, Office of Special Education and Rehabilitative Services.

Office of Special Education Programs (OSEP). (2004). *Teaching children with attention deficit hyperactivity disorder: Instructional strategies and practices.* Washington, DC: U.S. Department of Education, Office of Special Education and Rehabilitative Services.

Olmeda, R. E., Thomas, A. R., & Davis, C. P. (2003). An analysis of sociocultural factors in social skills training studies with students with attention deficit/hyperactivity disorder. *Multiple Voices, 6,* 58–72.

Pappadopulos, E., & Jensen, P. S. (2001, Spring). What school professionals, counselors, and parents need to know about medication for emotional and behavioral disorders in kids. *Emotional & Behavioral Disorders in Youth,* 35–37.

Pierce, K. (2003). Attention-deficit/hyperactivity disorder and comorbidity. *Primary Psychiatry, 10,* 69–70, 75–76.

Powell, S., & Nelson, B. (1997). Effects of choosing academic assignments on a student with attention deficit hyperactivity disorder. *Journal of Applied Behavior Analysis, 30,* 181–183.

Reason, R. (1999). ADHD: A psychological response to an evolving concept (Report of a working part of the British Psychological Society). *Journal of Learning Disabilities, 32,* 85–91.

Rehabilitation Act of 1973. Section 504, 19 U.S.C. Section 794.

Reid, R., Casat, C. D., Norton, H. J., Anastopoulos, A. D., & Temple, E. P. (2001). Using behavior rating scales for ADHD across ethnic groups: The IOWA Conners. *Journal of Emotional and Behavioral Disorders, 9,* 210–218.

Reid, R., & Lienemen, T. (2006). *Strategy instruction for children with learning disabilities: What it is and how to do it.* New York: Guilford.

Reid, R., Trout, A. L., & Schartz, M. (2005). Self-regulation interventions for children with attention deficit/hyperactivity disorder. *Exceptional Children, 71,* 361–377.

Salend, S. J., Duhaney, D., Anderson, D. J., & Gottschalk, C. (2004). Using the Internet to improve homework communication and completion. *Teaching Exceptional Children, 36,* 64–73.

Salend, S. J., Elhoweris, H., & van Garderen, D. (2003). Educational interventions for students with ADD. *Intervention in School and Clinic, 38,* 280–288.

Salend, S. J., & Rohena, E. (2003). Students with attention deficit disorders: An overview. *Intervention in School and Clinic, 38,* 259–266.

Shaw, G., & Giambra, L. (1993). Task unrelated thoughts of college students diagnosed as hyperactive in childhood. *Developmental Neuropsychology, 9,* 17–30.

Stevens, G. A., & Birch, J. W. (1957). A proposal for classification of the terminology used to describe brain-injured children. *Exceptional Children, 23,* 346–349.

Still, G. F. (1902). Some abnormal psychical conditions in children. *The Lancet, 1,* 1008–1012, 1077–1082, 1163–1168.

Strauss, A. A., & Lehtinen, L. (1947). *Psychology and education of the brain-injured child.* New York: Grune & Stratton.

U.S. Department of Education. (1999). Assistance to states for the education of children with disabilities program and the early intervention program for infants and toddlers with disabilities; proposed regulations. *Federal Register,* 34, CRF Parts 300 and 303.

U.S. Department of Education. (2002). *The twenty-fourth annual report to Congress on the implementation of IDEA.* Washington, DC: U.S. Government Printing Office.

U.S. Department of Education. (2005). Assistance to states for the education of children with disabilities program and the early intervention program for infants and toddlers with disabilities; proposed regulations. *Federal Register,* CRF Parts 300, 301, and 304.

Van Kuren, L. (2003). Technology: The great equalizer. *CEC Today, 10,* 1, 5–6, 15.

Volpe, R. J., DuPaul, G. J., Loney, J., & Salisbury, H. (1999). Alternative selection criteria for identifying children with ADHD: Observed behavior and self-reported internalizing symptoms. *Journal of Emotional and Behavioral Disorders, 7,* 103–109.

Ward, J., & Guyer, K. E. (2000). Medical management of ADHD. In B.P. Guyer (Ed.), *ADHD: Achieving success in school and life* (pp. 38–54). Boston: Allyn & Bacon.

Weyandt, L. L. (2001). *An ADHD primer.* Boston: Allyn and Bacon.

Weyandt, L. L. (2005). Executive function in children, adolescents, and adults with attention deficit hyperactivity disorder: Introduction to the special issue. *Developmental Neuropsychology, 27*(1), 1–10.

Weyandt, L. L., Iwaszuk, W., Fulton, K., Ollerton, M., Beatty, N., Fouts, H., Schepman, S., & Greenlaw, C. (2003). The internal restlessness scale: Performance of college students with and without ADHD. *Journal of Learning Disabilities, 36,* 382–389.

Willcutt, E. G., & Pennington, B. F. (2000). Cormorbidity of reading disability and attention-deficit/hyperactivity disorder: Differences by gender and subtype. *Journal of Learning Disabilities, 33,* 179–191.

Woodyard, C. (2002). JetBlue soars on CEO's creativity. Retrieved July 14, 2005, from **http://www.usatoday.com/travel/news/2002/2002-10-08-jetblue-ceo.htm**

World Health Organization (WHO). (2005). *Health and behaviours, facts and figures: Mental retardation from knowledge to action.* Retrieved March 20, 2005, from **http://w3.whosea.org/en/section1174/section1199/section/1567/section1825_8084.htm**

CHAPTER 7

Emotional or Behavioral Disorders

Adoption and Foster Care Analysis and Reporting System. (2002). *Child welfare statistics.* **www.acf.dhhs.gov/programs/cb/dis/afcars/scstats.html**

Ahearn, E. (Ed.). (1995, February). Summary of the 16th annual report to Congress on special education. *Liaison Bulletin,* pp. 1–3. Alexandria: NASDSE.

Allen, K. M., Hart, B. M., Buell, J. S., Harris, F. R., & Wolf, M. M. (1964). Effects of social reinforcement on isolated behavior of a nursery school child. *Child Development, 35,* 511–518.

Ama, S., & Caplan, E. H. (2001). The human face of foster care in America. *Focal Point, 15,* 25–26.

American Psychiatric Association. (2000). *Diagnostic and statistical manual of mental disorders,* fourth Edition, Text Revision (DSM-IV®-TR) (4th ed.). Washington, DC: Author.

Archwamety, T., & Katsiyannis, A. (2000). Academic remediation, parole violations, and recidivism rates among delinquent youth. *Remedial and Special Education, 21,* 161–170.

Armsden, G., Pecora, P. J., Payne, V. H., & Szatkiewicz, J. P. (2000). Children placed in long-term foster care: An intake profile using the child behavior checklist/4-18. *Journal of Emotional and Behavioral Disorders, 8,* 49–64.

Axelrod, S., & Hall, R. V. (1999). *Behavior modification: Basic principles.* Austin, TX: PRO-ED.

Babyak, A. E., Koorland, M., & Mathes, P. G. (2000). The effects of story mapping instruction on the reading comprehension of students with behavioral disorders. *Behavioral Disorders, 25,* 239–258.

Babyak, A. E., Luze, G. J., & Kamps, D. M. (2000). The good student game: Behavior management for diverse classrooms. *Intervention in School and Clinic, 35,* 216–223.

Barrish, H. H., Saunders, M., & Wolf. M. M. (1969). Good Behavior Game: Effects of individual contingencies for group consequences on disruptive behavior in the classroom. *Journal of Applied Behavior Analysis, 2,* 119–124.

Begley, S. (1999, May 3). Why the young kill. *Newsweek,* pp. 32–35.

Bender, W. N., & McLaughlin, P. J. (1997). Weapons violence in schools: Strategies for teachers confronting violence and hostage situations. *Intervention in School and Clinic, 32,* 211–216.

Bender, W. N., Shubert, T. H., & McLaughlin, P. J. (2001). Invisible kids: Preventing school violence by identifying kids in trouble. *Intervention in School and Clinic, 37,* 105–111.

Bower, E. M. (1960). *Early identification of emotionally disturbed children in school* (Rev. ed.). Springfield, IL: Charles C Thomas.

Bower, E. M. (1982). Defining emotional disturbance: Public policy and research. *Psychology in the Schools, 19,* 55–60.

Bower, E. M., & Lambert, N. M. (1962). *A process for in-school screening of children with emotional handicaps.* Princeton, NJ: Educational Testing Service.

Brigham, A. (1847). The moral treatment of insanity. *American Journal of Insanity, 4,* 1–15.

Brophy, F. (1981). Teacher praise: A functional analysis. *Review of Educational Research, 51,* 5–32.

Bryant, D. P., & Bryant, B. (2003). *Assistive technology for people with disabilities.* Boston: Allyn and Bacon.

Bullis, M., Walker, H. M., & Sprague, J. R. (2001). A promise unfulfilled: Social skills training with at-risk and antisocial children and youth. *Exceptionality, 9,* 67–90.

Burrell, B., Wood, S. J., Pikes, T., & Holliday, C. (2001). Student mentors and protégés learning together. *Teaching Exceptional Children, 33,* 24–29.

Cade, T., & Gunter, P. L. (2002). Teaching students with severe emotional or behavioral disorders to use a musical mnemonic technique to solve basic division calculations. *Behavioral Disorders, 27,* 208–214.

Cartledge, G., Kea, C. D., & Ida, D. J. (2000). Anticipating differences, celebrating strengths: Providing culturally competent services for students with serious emotional disturbance. *Teaching Exceptional Children, 32,* 30–37.

Cauce, A., Paradise, M., Ginzler, J., Embry, L., Morgan, C. J., Lohr, Y., & Theofelis, J. (2000). The characteristics and mental health of homeless adolescents: Age and gender differences. *Journal of Emotional and Behavioral Disorders, 8,* 230–239.

Cheney, D., & Barringer, C. (1995). Teacher competence, student diversity, and staff training for the inclusion of middle school students with emotional and behavioral disorders. *Journal of Emotional and Behavioral Disorders, 3,* 174–182.

Chesapeake Institute. (1994). *National agenda for achieving better results for children and youth with serious emotional disturbance.* Washington, DC: U.S. Department of Education, Office of Special Education Programs.

Chicago Youth Centers. (2005). *Success stories!* Retrieved March 19, 2005, from **http://www.chicagoyouthcenters.org/programs/index.html**

Children's Defense Fund (CDF). (2001). *The state of America's children.* Washington, DC: Children's Defense Fund.

Children's Defense Fund (CDF). (2004). *The state of America's children.* Washington, DC: Children's Defense Fund.

Cochran, L., Feng, H., Cartledge, G., & Hamilton, S. (1993). The effects of cross-age tutoring on the academic achievement, social behaviors, and self-perceptions of low-achieving African-American males with behavioral disorders. *Behavioral Disorders, 18,* 292–302.

Committee for Children. (2001). *Steps to respect: A special issue on bullying prevention program.* Seattle, WA: Author.

Costenbader, V., & Buntaine, R. (1999). Diagnostic discrimination between social maladjustment and emotional disturbance. *Journal of Emotional and Behavioral Disorders, 7,* 2–10.

Cruz, L., & Cullinan, D. (2001). Awarding points, using levels to help children improve behavior. *Teaching Exceptional Children, 33,* 16–23.

Dawson, L., Venn, M. L., & Gunter, P. L. (2000). The effects of teacher versus computer reading models. *Behavioral Disorders, 25,* 105–113.

Day, D. M., & Hunt, A. C. (1996). A multivariate assessment of a risk model for juvenile delinquency with an "under 12 offender" sample. *Journal of Emotional and Behavioral Disorders, 4,* 66–72.

Deutsch, A. (1949). *The mentally ill in America: A history of their care and treatment from colonial times* (2nd ed.). New York: Columbia University Press.

Deveres, L. (1999a). Social skills training aids students in life's lessons. *The Special Educator, 15,* 1, 8–9.

Deveres, L. (1999b). *A primer on functional behavioral assessments.* Horsham, PA: LRP Publications.

Duckworth, S., Smith-Rex, S., Okey, S., Brookshire, M., Rawlinson, D., Rawlinson, R., Castillo, S., & Little, J. (2001). Wraparound services for young schoolchildren with emotional and behavioral disorders. *Teaching Exceptional Children, 33,* 54–60.

Eber, L., Smith, C. R., Sugai, G., & Scott, T. M. (2002). Wraparound and positive behavioral supports in the schools. *Journal of Emotional and Behavioral Disorders, 10,* 171–180.

Edens, J. F., & Otto, R. K. (1997). Prevalence of mental disorders among youth in the juvenile justice system. *Focal Point, 11,* 1, 6–7.

Englert, C. S., Tarrant, K. L., & Mariage, T. V. (1992). Defining and redefining instructional practice in special education. Perspectives on good teaching. *Teacher Education and Special Education, 15,* 62–86.

Espin, C. A., & Yell, M. L. (1994). Critical indicators of effective teaching for preservice teachers: Relationships between teaching behaviors and ratings of effectiveness. *Teacher Education and Special Education, 17,* 154–169.

Falk, K. B., & Wehby, J. H. (2001). The effects of peer-assisted learning strategies on the beginning reading skills of young children with emotional or behavioral disorders. *Behavioral Disorders, 26,* 344–359.

Feil, E. G., Walker, H. M., & Severson, H. H. (1995). The early screening project for young children with behavior problems. *Journal of Emotional and Behavioral Disorders, 3,* 194–202.

Forness, S. R., & Kavale, K. A. (2001). Are school professionals missing their best chance to help troubled kids? *Emotional and Behavioral Disorders, 1,* 80–83.

Forness, S. R., & Knitzer, J. (1992). A new proposed definition and terminology to replace "serious emotional disturbance" in IDEA. *School Psychology Review, 21,* 12–20.

Franca, V. M., Kerr, M. M., Reitz, A. L., & Lambert, D. (1990). Peer tutoring among behaviorally disordered students: Academic and social benefits to tutor and tutee. *Education and Treatment of Children, 3,* 109–128.

Frey, K. S., Hirschstein, M. K., & Guzzo, B. A. (2000). Second step: Preventing aggression by promoting social competence. *Journal of Emotional and Behavioral Disorders, 8,* 102–112.

Fuchs, D., & Fuchs, L. S. (1994). Inclusive schools movement and the radicalization of special education reform. *Exceptional Children, 60,* 294–309.

Furlong, M., & Morrison, G. (2000). The school in school violence: Definitions and facts. *Journal of Emotional and Behavioral Disorders, 8,* 71–82.

Gable, R. A., Hendrickson, J. M., Young, C. C., Shores, R. E., & Stowitschek, J. J. (1983). A comparison of teacher approval and disapproval statements across categories of exceptionality. *Journal of Special Education Technology, 6,* 15–22.

Greenbaum, P. E., Dedrick, R. F., Friedman, R. M., Kutash, K., Brown, E. C., and Lardierh, S. P. (1996). National Adolescent and Child Treatment Study (NACTS): Outcomes for children with serious emotional and behavioral disturbance. *Journal of Emotional and Behavioral Disorders, 4,* 130–146.

Gresham, F. M. (2002). Social skills assessment and instruction for students with emotional and behavioral disorders. In K. L. Lane, F. M. Gresham, and T. E. O'Shaughnessy (Eds.), *Interventions for children with or at risk for emotional and behavioral disorders* (pp. 242–258). Boston: Allyn & Bacon.

Gresham, F. M., Lane, K. L., MacMillan, D. L., & Bocian, K. M. (1999). Social and academic profiles of externalizing and internalizing groups: Risk factors for emotional and behavioral disorders. *Behavioral Disorders, 24,* 231–245.

Griller-Clark, H. (2001). Transition services for youth in the juvenile justice system. *Focal Point, 15,* 23–25.

Hall, R. V., Lund, D., & Jackson, D. (1968). Effects of teacher attention on study behavior. *Journal of Applied Behavior Analysis, 1,* 315–322.

Hallahan, D. P., & Kauffman, J. M. (2006). *Exceptional children: Introduction to special education* (10th ed.). Boston: Allyn and Bacon.

Haring, N. J., & Phillips, E. L. (1962). *Educating emotionally disturbed children.* New York: McGraw-Hill.

Harper, G. F., Mallette, B., Meheady, L., Bentley, A. E., & Moore, J. (1995). Retention and treatment failure in classwide peer tutoring: Implications for further research. *Journal of Behavioral Education, 5,* 399–414.

Hartwig, E., & Ruesch, G. (1998). *Discipline in the schools.* Horsham, PA: LRP Publications.

Hawkins, J. D., Catalano, R. F., Kosterman, R., Abbott, R., & Hill, K. G. (1999). Preventing adolescent health-risk behaviors by strengthening protection during childhood. *Archives of Pediatrics & Adolescent Medicine, 1153,* 226–234.

Hoagwood, K. (2001a). Surgeon general's conference on children's mental health sets out a national action agenda. *Emotional and Behavioral Disorders in Youth, 1,* 33–34, 40–44.

Hoagwood, K. (2001b). Evidence-based practice in children's mental health services: What do we know? Why aren't we putting it to use? *Emotional and Behavioral Disorders in Youth, 1,* 84–87, 90.

Horner, R. H., Sugai, G., Lewis-Palmer, T., & Todd, A. W. (2001). Teaching school-wide behavioral expectations. *Emotional and Behavioral Expectations, 1,* 77–79, 93–95.

Hosp, J. L., & Reschly, D. J. (2002). Predictors of restrictiveness of placement for African-American and Caucasian students. *Exceptional Children, 68,* 225–238.

Hunter, L. (2001). The value of school-based mental health programs. *Emotional and Behavioral Disorders in Youth, 1,* 27–28, 46.

Hunter, L., & Chopra, V. (2001). Two proactive primary prevention program models that work in schools. *Emotional and Behavioral Disorders in Youth, 1,* 57–58, 71.

IDEA Practices. (2002). *Youth with disabilities in the juvenile justice system.* Retrieved July 17, 2002, from **www.ideapractices.org**

Jolivette, K., Stichter, J. P., Nelson, C. M., Scott, T. M., & Liauspin, C. (2000, August). *Improving post-school outcomes for students with emotional and behavioral disorders.* Reston, VA: ERIC/OSEP Digest (ERIC Document Reproduction Service No. EDO-EC-00-6).

Kamps, D., Kravits, T., Stolze, J., & Swaggart, B. (1999). Prevention strategies for at-risk students and students with EBD in urban elementary schools. *Journal of Emotional and Behavioral Disorders, 7,* 178–188.

Kanner, L. (1957). *Child Psychiatry.* Springfield, IL: Charles C Thomas.

Kauffman, J. M. (1999). How we prevent the prevention of emotional and behavioral disorders. *Exceptional Children, 65,* 448–468.

Kauffman, J. M. (2005). *Characteristics of behavioral disorders of children and youth* (8th ed.). Columbus, OH: Merrill.

Kern, L., Delaney, B., Clarke, S., Dunlap, G., & Childs, K. (2001). Improving the classroom behavior of students with emotional and behavioral disorders using individualized curricular modifications. *Journal of Emotional and Behavioral Disorders, 9,* 239–247.

Lane, K. L. (1999). Young students at risk for antisocial behavior: The utility of academic and social skills interventions. *Journal of Emotional and Behavioral Disorders, 7,* 211–223.

Lane, K. L. (2003). Identifying young students at risk for antisocial behavior: The utility of "teachers as tests." *Behavioral Disorders, 28,* 360–389.

Lane, K. L. (2004). Academic instruction and tutoring interventions for students with emotional/behavioral disorders: 1990 to present. In R. B. Rutherford, M. M. Quinn, and. S. R. Mathur (Eds.), *Handbook of research in emotional and behavioral disorders* (pp. 462–486). New York: Guilford.

Lane, K. L., & Beebe-Frankenberger, M. E. (2004). *School-based interventions: The tools you need to succeed.* Boston, MA: Allyn and Bacon

Lane, K. L., Gresham, F. M., & O'Shaughnessy, T. (2002). Identifying, assessing and intervening with children with or at-risk for behavior disorders: A look to the future. In K. L. Lane, F. M. Gresham, and T. E. O'Shaughnessy (Eds.), *Interventions for children with or at risk for emotional and behavioral disorders* (pp. 317–326). Boston: Allyn and Bacon.

Lane, K. L., Mahdavi, J. N., & Borthwick-Duffy, S. A. (2003). Teacher perceptions of the prereferral intervention process: A call for assistance with school-based interventions. *Preventing School Failure, 47,* 148–155.

Lane, K. L., O'Shaughnessy, T. E., Lambros, K. M., Gresham, F. M., & Beebe-Frankenberger, M. E. (2001). The efficacy of phonological awareness training with first-grade students who have behavioral problems and reading difficulties. *Journal of Emotional and Behavioral Disorders, 9,* 219–231.

Lane, K. L., & Wehby, J. (2002). Addressing antisocial behavior in the schools: A call for action. *Academic Exchange Quarterly, 6,* 4–9.

Lane, K. L., Wehby, J. H., Little, M. A., & Cooley, C. (2005a). Academic, social, and behavioral profiles of students educated in self-contained classrooms and self-contained schools: Part I—Are they more alike than different? *Behavioral Disorders, 30,* 349–361.

Lane, K. L., Wehby, J. H., Little, M. A., & Cooley, C. (2005b). Students educated in self-contained classes and self-contained schools: Part II —How do they progress over time? *Behavioral Disorders, 30,* 363–374.

Lane, K. L., Wehby, J., Menzies, H. M., Doukas, G. L., Munton, S. M., & Gregg, R. M. (2003). Social skills instruction for students at risk for antisocial behavior: The effects of small-group instruction. *Behavioral Disorders, 28,* 229–248.

Lane, K. L., Wehby, J. H., Menzies, H. M., Gregg, R. M., Doukas, G. L., & Munton, S. M. (2002). Early literacy instruction for first-grade students at-risk for antisocial behavior. *Education and Treatment of Children, 25,* 438–458.

Lee, Y. Y., Sugai, G., & Horner, R. H. (1999). Using an instructional intervention to reduce problem and off-task behaviors. *Journal of Positive Behavior Interventions, 1,* 195–204.

Lewis, T. J., & Sugai, G. (1999). Effective behavior support: A systems approach to proactive schoolwide management. *Exceptional Children, 31,* 1–24.

Little, L. (2002, Winter). In preschool classrooms: Linking research to practice. *Early Developments,* pp. 7–9.

Lohrmann-O'Rourke, S., & Zirkel, P. A. (1998). The case law on aversive interventions for students with disabilities. *Exceptional Children, 65,* 101–123.

Lucent Technologies (1999). *Reinventing today's classrooms with wireless technology.* Bell Labs Innovations. **www.wavelan. com/educational**

Maag, J. W. (2000). Managing resistance. *Intervention in Schools and Clinics, 35,* 131–140.

Maag, J. W. (2001). Rewarded by punishment: Reflections on the disuse of positive reinforcement in schools. *Exceptional Children, 67,* 173–186.

MacMillan, D. L., Gresham, F., & Forness, S. (1996). Full inclusion: An empirical perspective. *Behavioral Disorders, 21,* 145–159.

Manley, R. S., Rickson, H., & Standeven, B. (2000). Children and adolescents with eating disorders: Strategies for teachers and school counselors. *Intervention in School and Clinic, 35,* 228–231.

Mattison, R. E., Hooper, S. R., & Glassberg, L. A. (2002). Three-year course of learning disorders in special education students classified as behavioral disorder. *Journal of the American Academy of Child & Adolescent Psychiatry, 41,* 1454–1461.

McConaughy, S. H., & Wadsworth, M. E. (2000). Life history reports of young adults previously referred for mental health services. *Journal of Emotional and Behavioral Disorders, 8,* 202–215.

McLane, K. (1997). School-wide behavioral management systems. *Research Connections in Special Education, 1,* 1–5.

McLaughlin, T. F. (1992). Effects of written feedback in reading on behaviorally disordered students. *Journal of Educational Research, 85,* 312–315.

Miller-Johnson, S., Coie, J. E., Maumary-Gremaud, A., Lockman, J., & Terry, R. (1999). Relationship between childhood peer rejection and aggression and adolescent delinquency severity and type among African-American youth. *Journal of Emotional and Behavioral Disorders, 7,* 137–146.

Myles, B. S., & Simpson, R. L. (1998). Aggression and violence by school-age children and youth: Understanding the aggression cycle and prevention/intervention strategies. *Intervention in School and Clinic, 33,* 259–264.

National Alliance of Black School Educators [NABSE] & ILIAD Project. (2002). *Addressing over-representation of African American students in special education.* Arlington, VA: Council for Exceptional Children, and Washington, DC: National Alliance of Black School Educators.

National Center on Education, Disability, and Juvenile Justice. (2002). *Monograph series on education, disability, and juvenile justice.* Retrieved July 13, 2002, from **www.edjj.org/monographs/index.html**

National Center for Educational Statistics (NCES). (2005). *Quick tables and figures.* **www.nces.ed.gov/quicktables**

National Research Council (2002). *Minority students in special education and gifted education.* Committee on Minority Representation in Special Education. M. Suzanne Donovan and Christoper T. Cross, editors. Washington, DC: National Academy Press.

Nelson, J. R., Benner, G. J., Lane, K., & Smith, B. W. (2004). An investigation of the academic achievement of K–12 students with emotional and behavioral disorders in public school settings. *Exceptional Children, 71,* 59–73.

Nelson, J. R., Crabtree, M., Marchand-Martella, N., & Martella, R. (1996). Teaching good behavior in the whole school. *Teaching Exceptional Children, 30,* 4–9.

Nelson, J. R., Johnson, A., & Marchand-Martella, N. (1996). Effects of direct instruction, cooperative learning, and independent learning practices on the classroom behavior of students with behavioral disorders: A comparative analysis. *Journal of Emotional and Behavioral Disorders, 4,* 53–62.

Newcomer, P. L. (1993). *Understanding and teaching emotionally disturbed children and adolescents* (2nd ed.). Austin, TX: PRO-ED.

Nichols, P. (2000). Role of cognition and affect in a functional behavioral analysis. *Exceptional Children, 66,* 393–402.

O'Dell, K., Alba, L., Lehman, C., Mayer, J., & Hein, M. (2001). Powerhouse: Empowering young adults as they transition from foster care. *Focal Point, 15,* 27–28.

O'Leary, K. D., & Becker, W. C. (1969). The effects of intensity of a teacher's reprimands on children's behavior. *Journal of School Psychology, 7,* 8–11.

Olweus, D. (2000). *Bullying prevention program.* Boulder, CO: Center for the Study and Prevention of Violence.

Pancheri, C., & Prater, M. A. (1999). What teachers and parents should know about Ritalin. *Teaching Exceptional Children, 31,* 20–26.

Pappadopulos, E., & Jensen, P. S. (2001). What school professionals, counselors, and parents need to know about medication for emotional and behavioral disorders in kids. *Emotional and Behavioral Disorders in Youth, 1,* 35–37.

Reid, J. B., & Patterson, G. R. (1991). Early prevention and intervention with conduct problems: A social interactional model for the integration of research and practice. In G. Stoner, M. R. Shinn, & H. M. Walker (Eds.), *Interventions for achievement and behavior problems* (pp. 715–740). Silver Spring, MD: NASP.

Rivera, D. P., & Smith, D. D. (1997). *Teaching students with learning and behavior problems* (3rd ed.). Boston: Allyn and Bacon.

Rosenberg, M. S., & Jackman, L. A. (1997). Addressing student and staff behavior: The PAR model. *The Fourth R, 79,* 1–12.

Rosenberg, M. S., & Jackman, L. A. (2002). *Development, implementation, and sustainability of comprehensive school-wide behavior management systems.* Baltimore, MD: Johns Hopkins University. Manuscript submitted for publication.

Rosenshine, B. (1995). Advances in research on instruction. *The Journal of Educational Research, 88,* 262–268.

Rudo, Z. H., Powell, D. S., & Dunlap, G. (1998). The effects of violence in the home on children's emotional, behavioral, and social functioning: A review of the literature. *Journal of Emotional and Behavioral Disorders, 6,* 94–113.

Schoenwald, S. K., & Hoagwood, K. (2001). Effectiveness and dissemination in research: Their mutual roles in improving mental health services for children and adolescents. *Emotional and Behavioral Disorders in Youth, 2,* 3–4, 18–20.

Scott, T. M., & Shearer-Lingo, A. (2002). The effects of reading fluency instruction on the academic and behavioral success of middle school students in a self-contained EBD classroom. *Preventing School Failure, 46,* 167–173.

Sinclair, E. (1998). Head Start children at risk: Relationship of prenatal drug exposure to identification of special needs and subsequent special education kindergarten placement. *Behavioral Disorders, 23,* 125–133.

Sinclair, M. F., Christenson, S. L., Evelo, D. L., & Hurley, C. M. (1998). Dropout prevention for youth with disabilities: Efficacy of a sustained school engagement procedure. *Exceptional Children, 65,* 7–21.

Smith, D. D. (1984). *Effective discipline.* Austin, TX: PRO-ED.

Smith, D. D., & Rivera, D. P. (1993). *Effective discipline* (2nd ed.). Austin, TX: PRO-ED.

Special Education Elementary Longitudinal Study (SEELS; 1999). *Existing instrument analysis.* Retrieved on August 22, 2005 from **http://seels.net/infoproduct.htm**

Special Education Elementary Longitudinal Study. (2004). *Info and reports.* **www.seels.net/infoproduct.htm**

Strain, P. S., Steele, P., Ellis, R., & Timm, M. (1982). Long-term effects of oppositional child treatment with mothers as therapists and therapist trainers. *Journal of Applied Behavior Analysis, 15,* 163–169.

Strain, P. S., & Timm, M. A. (1998). *The early childhood intervention study.* Nashville, TN: Regional Intervention Project (RIP). Unpublished paper.

Strain, P. S., & Timm, M. A. (1999). *Preliminary results from the early childhood intervention study.* Nashville, TN: Regional Intervention Project (RIP). Unpublished paper.

Sutherland, K. S. (2000). Promoting positive interactions between teachers and students with emotional/behavioral disorders. *Preventing School Failure, 44,* 110–115.

Sutherland, K. S., & Wehby, J. H. (2001). The effects of self-evaluation on teaching behaviors in classrooms for students with emotional and behavioral disorders. *Journal of Special Education, 35,* 161–171.

Sutherland, K. S., Wehby, J. H., & Copeland, S. R. (2000). Effect of varying rates of behavior-specific praise on the on task behavior of students with EBD. *Journal of Emotional and Behavioral Disorders, 8,* 2–8, 26.

Sutherland, K. S., Wehby, J. H., & Yoder, P. J. (2001). An examination of the relation between teacher praise and students' with emotional/behavioral disorders opportunities to respond to academic requests. *Journal of Emotional and Behavioral Disorders, 10,* 5–14.

Talbott, E., & Thiede, K. (1999). Pathways to antisocial behavior among adolescent girls. *Journal of Emotional and Behavioral Disorders, 7,* 31–39.

Test, D. W., Karvonen, M., Wood, W. M., Browder, D., & Algozzine, B. (2000). Choosing a self-determination curriculum. *Teaching Exceptional Children, 33,* 48–54.

Tobin, T. J., & Sugai, G. M. (1999). Using sixth-grade school records to predict school violence, chronic discipline problems, and high school outcomes. *Journal of Emotional and Behavioral Disorders, 7,* 40–53.

Tobin, T., Sugai, G., & Colvin, G. (1996). Patterns in middle school discipline records. *Journal of Emotional and Behavioral Disorders, 4,* 82–94.

Tolan, P., Gorman-Smith, D., & Henry, D. (2001). New study to focus on efficacy of "whole school" prevention approaches. *Emotional and Behavioral Disorders in Youth, 2,* 5–6, 22–23.

Townsend, B. L. (2000). The disproportionate discipline of African American learners: Reducing school suspensions and expulsions. *Exceptional Children, 66,* 381–391.

Umbreit, J., Lane, K. L., & Dejud, C. (2004). Improving classroom behavior by modifying task difficulty: The effects of increasing the difficulty of too-easy tasks. *Journal of Positive Behavior Interventions, 6,* 13–20.

U.S. Department of Education. (1999). Assistance to states for the education of children with disabilities program and the early intervention program for infants and toddlers with disabilities; proposed regulations. *Federal Register,* 34, CRF Parts 300, 301, and 304.

U.S. Department of Education (2001). *The twenty-third annual report to Congress on the implementation of IDEA.* Washington, DC: U.S. Government Printing Office.

U.S. Department of Education. (2005a). Assistance to states for the education of children with disabilities program and the early intervention program for infants and toddlers with disabilities; proposed regulations. *Federal Register,* 34, CRF Parts 300, 301, and 304.

U.S. Department of Education (2005b). *Children served under IDEA, Part B (2003),* Data Tables. **www.ideadata.org**

Wagner, M., Cameto, R., & Newman, L. (2003). *Youth with disabilities: A changing population: A report of findings from the National Longitudinal Transition Study (NLTS) and the National Longitudinal Transition Study-2 (NLTS2).* Menlo Park, CA: SRI International.

Wagner, M., Marder, C., Blackorby, J., Cameto, R., Newman, L., & Levine, P. (2003). *The achievements of youth with disabilities during secondary school.* Menlo Park, CA: SRI International.

Walker, H. M., & Gresham, F. M. (1997). Making schools safer and violence-free. *Intervention in School and Clinic, 32,* 199–204.

Walker, H. M., Kavanagh, K., Stiller, B., Golly, A., Severson, H. H., & Feil, E. G. (1998). First step to success: An early intervention approach for preventing school antisocial behavior. *Journal of Emotional and Behavioral Disorders, 6,* 66–80.

Walker, H. M., Ramsey, E., & Gresham, F. M. (2004). *Antisocial behavior in school: Evidence-based practices* (2nd ed.). Belmont, CA: Wadsworth.

Walker, H. M., & Severson, H. H. (1992). *Systematic screening for behavior disorders* (SSBD): User's guide and technical manual. Longmont, CO: Sopris West.

Walker, H. M., & Sprague, J. (1999). The path to school failure, delinquency, and violence: Causal factors and potential solutions. *Intervention in School and Clinic, 35,* 67–73.

Walker, H. M., & Sprague, J. R. (2000). Intervention strategies for diverting at-risk children and youth from destructive outcomes. *Emotional and Behavioral Disorders in Youth, 1,* 5–8.

Walker, H. M., & Sylvester, R. (1994). Where is school along the path to prison? *The Frontline, 1,* 3–6.

Wehby, J. H., Symons, F. J., Canale, J. A., & Go, F. J. (1998). Teaching practices in classrooms for students with emotional and behavioral disorders: Discrepancies between recommendations and observations. *Behavioral Disorders, 24,* 51–56.

Wehby, J. H., Symons, F., & Shores, R. E. (1995). A descriptive analysis of aggressive behavior in classrooms for students with emotional and behavioral disorders. *Behavioral Disorders, 20,* 87–105.

Wehmeyer, M. L., Palmer, S. B., Agran, M., Mithaug, D. E., & Martin, J. E. (2000). Promoting causal agency: Self-determined learning model of instruction. *Exceptional Children, 66,* 439–453.

Witt, J. C., Elliott, S. N., Gresham, F. M., & Kramer, J. J. (1988). *Assessment of special children: Tests and the problem-solving process.* Glenview, IL: Scott, Foresman.

Zametkin, A. J., & Earnst, M. (1999). Problems in the management of attention-deficit-hyperactivity disorder. *New England Journal of Medicine, 340,* 40–46.

Zirkel, P. (1999). How to determine eligibility of students with problem behaviors. *The Special Educator, 17,* 1, 7–8.

CHAPTER 8

Mental Retardation

Abbeduto, L., Seltzer, M. M., Shattuck, P., Krauss, M. W., Orsmond, G., & Murphy, M. M. (2004). Psychological well-being and coping in mothers of youths with autism, Down syndrome, or fragile X syndrome. *American Journal on Mental Retardation, 109,* 237–254.

Alber, S. R., & Heward, W. L. (1997). Recruit it or lose it! Training students to recruit positive teacher attention. *Intervention in School and Clinic, 32,* 275–282.

Alexander, G. R., & Slay, M. (2002). Prematurity at birth: Trends, racial disparities, and epidemiology. *Mental Retardation and Developmental Disabilities Research Reviews, 8,* 215–220.

Allen, M. C. (2002). Preterm outcomes research: A critical component of neonatal intensive care. *Mental Retardation and Developmental Disabilities Research Reviews, 8,* 221–233.

American Association on Mental Retardation [AAMR]. (2002). *Mental retardation: Definition, classification, and systems of support* (10th ed.). Washington, DC: AAMR.

Amiel-Tison, C., Allen, M. C., Lebrun, F., & Rogowski, J. (2002). Macropremies: Underpriviledged newborns. *Mental Retardation and Developmental Disabilities Research Reviews, 8,* 281–292.

Arc, The (2001). *Preventing mental retardation: A guide to the causes of mental retardation and strategies for prevention.* Silver Spring, MD: Author.

Arc, The (2005, May). Causes and prevention of mental retardation. *Frequently Asked Questions.* Retrieved June 17, 2005, from **www.thearc.org**

Artiles, A. J., Harry, B., Reschly, D. J., & Chinn, P. C. (2002). Over-identification of students of color in special education: A critical overview. *Multicultural Perspectives, 4,* 3–10.

Ayllon, T., & Azrin, N. H. (1964). Reinforcement and instructions with mental patients. *Journal of Experimental Analysis of Behavior, 7,* 327–331.

Ayllon, T., & Azrin, N. H. (1968). Reinforcer sampling: A technique for increasing the behavior of mental patients. *Journal of Applied Behavior Analysis, 1,* 13–20.

Bauer, C. R. (1999). Perinatal effects of prenatal drug exposure: Neonatal aspects. *Clinics in Perinatology, 26,* 87–106.

Beach Center on Families and Disability. (1995a). Dads feel left out. *Families and Disability Newsletter, 6,* 4.

Beach Center on Families and Disability. (1995b). How to involve fathers more with their children with special needs. *Families and Disability Newsletter, 6,* 5–6.

Beach Center on Disability. (2002a). *Introduction to our research.* Retrieved July 4, 2002, from **www.beachcenter.org**

Beach Center on Disability. (2002b). *Fathers.* Retrieved July 4, 2002, from **www.beachcenter.org**

Belser, R. C., & Sudhalter, V. (2001). Conversational characteristics of children with fragile X syndrome: Repetitive speech. *American Journal on Mental Retardation, 106,* 28–38.

Birnbrauer, J. S., Wolf, M. M., Kidder, J. D., & Tague, C. E. (1965). Classroom behavior of retarded pupils with token reinforcement. *Journal of Experimental Child Psychology, 2,* 219–235.

Briggs, K. (2005). *Alternate achievement standards for students with the most significant cognitive disabilities: Non-regulatory guidance.* Washington, DC: U.S. Department of Education.

Brolin, D. (2002). *Life centered career education, a competency based approach* (5th ed.). Arlington, VA: Council for Exceptional Children.

Browder, D. M., Flowers, C., Ahlgrim-Delzell, L., Karvonen, M., Spooner, F., & Algozzine, R. (2004). The alignment of alternate assessment content with academic and functional curricula. *The Journal of Special Education, 37,* 211–223.

Browder, D. M., Spooner, F., Algozzine, R., Ahlgrim-Delzell, L., Flowers, C., & Karvonen, M. (2003). What we know and need to know about alternate assessment. *Exceptional Children, 70,* 45–61.

Browder, D. M., & Xin, Y. P. (1998). A meta-analysis and review of sight word research and its implications for teaching functional reading to individuals with moderate and severe disabilities. *The Journal of Special Education, 32,* 130–153.

Bryant, B. R., Taylor, R. L., & Rivera, D. P. (1996). *Assessment of adaptive areas (AAA): Examiner's manual.* Austin, TX: PRO-ED.

Butterworth, J., Hagner, D., Helm, D. T., & Whelley, T. A. (2000). Workplace culture, social interactions, and supports for transition-age young adults. *Mental Retardation, 38,* 342–353.

Centers for Disease Control (CDC). (2004a). Fetal alcohol syndrome. *Fast Facts.* Retrieved June 17, 2005, from **www.cdc.gov**

Centers for Disease Control (CDC). (2004b, May 7). Spina bifida and anaencephaly before and after folic acid mandate—United States, 1995–1996 and 1999–2000. *MMWR Weekly.* Retrieved June 17, 2005, from **www.cdc.gov**

Chadsey, J., & Beyer, S. (2001). Social relationships in the workplace. *Mental Retardation and Developmental Disabilities Research Reviews, 7,* 128–133.

Chapman, R. S., & Hesketh, L. J. (2000). Behavioral phenotype of individuals with Down syndrome. *Mental Retardation and Developmental Disabilities Research Reviews, 6,* 84–95.

Children's Defense Fund (CDF). (2001). *The state of America's children: 2001.* Washington, DC: Author.

Children's Defense Fund (CDF). (2004). *The state of America's children: 2004.* Washington, DC: Author.

Colins, B. C., & Stinson, D. M. (1994–1995). Teaching generalized reading of product warning labels to adolescents with mental disabilities through the use of key words. *Exceptionality, 5,* 163–181.

Cone, A. A. (2001). Self-reported training needs and training issues of advisors to self-advocacy groups for people with mental retardation. *Mental Retardation, 39,* 1–10.

Conley, R. W. (2003). Supported employment in Maryland: Successes and issues. *Mental Retardation, 41,* 237–249.

Copeland, S. R., Hughes, C., Agran, M., Wehmeyer, M. L., & Fowler, S. E. (2002). An intervention package to support high school students with mental retardation in general education classrooms. *American Journal on Mental Retardation, 107,* 32–45.

Craft, M. A., Alber, S. R., & Heward, W. L. (1998). Teaching elementary students with developmental disabilities to recruit teacher attention in a general education classroom: Effects on teacher praise and academic productivity. *Journal of Applied Behavior Analysis, 31,* 399–415.

Crawford, D. C., Acuna, J. M., & Sherman, S. L. (2001). FMR1 and fragile X syndrome: Human genome epidemiology review. *Genetics in Medicine, 3,* 359–371.

Cummins, R. A. (2001). Living with support in the community: Predictors of satisfaction with life. *Mental Retardation and Developmental Disabilities, 7,* 99–104.

Davern, L. (2004). School-to-home notebooks: What parents have to say. *Teaching Exceptional Children, 36,* 22–27.

Davis, S., & Davis, L. A. (2003). Fetal alcohol syndrome. *Frequently Asked Questions.* Retrieved June 18, 2005, from **www.thearc.org**

Demark, J. L., Feldman, M. A., & Holden, J. J. A. (2003). Behavioral relationship between autism and fragile X syndrome. *American Journal on Mental Retardation, 108,* 314–326.

e-Buddies. (2005). Retrieved July 3, 2005, from **www.ebuddies.org**

Edgerton, R. B. (1996). A longitudinal-ethnographic research perspective on quality of life. In R. L. Schalock (Ed.), *Quality of life: Conceptualization and measurement* (pp. 83–90). Washington, DC: American Association on Mental Retardation.

Eisensmith, R. C., Kuzmin, A. I., & Krougliak, V. A. (1999). Prospects for treatment of phenylketonuria by gene therapy. *Mental Retardation and Developmental Disabilities Research Reviews, 5,* 150–154.

Elks, M. A. (2005). Visual indictment: A contextual analysis of the Kallikak family photographs. *Mental Retardation, 43,* 268–280.

Emerson, E., Robertson, J., Gregory, N., Hatton, C., Kessissoglou, S., Hallam, A., Järbrink, K., Knapp, M., Netten, A., & Walsh, P. N. (2001). Quality and costs of supported living residences and group homes in the United Kingdom. *American Journal on Mental Retardation, 106,* 401–415.

Finlay, W. M. L., & Lyons, E. (2005). Rejecting the label: A social constuctionist analysis. *Mental Retardation, 43,* 120–134.

Ford, D. Y., Harris III, J. J., Tyson, C. A., & Trotman, M. F. (2002). Beyond deficit thinking: Providing access for gifted African American students. *Roeper Review, 24,* 52–58.

Foucart-Walter, E., & Rosenbergy, P. (1987). *The painted cat: The cat in Western painting from the fifteenth to the twentieth century.* New York: Rizzoli.

Gelf, S. (1995). The beast in man: Degenerationism and mental retardation, 1900–1920. *Mental Retardation, 33,* 1–9.

Grigal, M., Neubert, D. A., Moon, M. S., & Graham, S. (2003). Self-determination for students with disabilities: Views of parents and teachers. *Exceptional Children, 70,* 97–112.

Guralnick, M. J. (1998). Effectiveness of early intervention for vulnerable children: A developmental perspective. *American Journal on Mental Retardation, 102,* 319–345.

Hannah, M. E., & Midlarsky, E. (1999). Competence and adjustment of siblings of children with mental retardation. *American Journal on Mental Retardation, 104,* 22–37.

Hannah, M. E., & Midlarsky, E. (2005). Helping by siblings of children with mental retardation. *American Journal on Mental Retardation, 110,* 87–99.

Hatton, D. D., Wheeler, A. C., Skinner, M. L., Bailey, D. B., Sullivan, K. M., Roberts, J. E., Mirrett, P., & Clark, R. D. (2003). Adaptive behavior in children with fragile X syndrome. *American Journal on Mental Retardation, 108,* 373–390.

Holburn, S., Jacobson, J. W., Schwartz, A. A., Flory, M. J., & Vietze, P. M. (2004). The Willowbrook futures project: A longitudinal analysis of person-centered planning. *American Journal on Mental Retardation, 109,* 63–76.

Holburn, S., & Vietze, P. M. (2002). *Person-centered planning.* Baltimore: Paul H. Brookes.

Hosp, J. L. & Reschly, D. J. (2002). Predictors of restrictiveness of placement for African-American and Caucasian students. *Exceptional Children, 68,* 225–238.

Hosp, J. L. & Reschly, D. J. (2003). Referral rates for intervention or assessment: A meta-analysis of racial differences. *The Journal of Special Education, 37,* 67–80.

Hughes, C. (2001). Transition to adulthood: Supporting young adults to access social, employment, and civic pursuits. *Mental Retardation and Developmental Disabilities Research Reviews, 7,* 84–90.

Itard, J. M. G. (1806). Wild boy of Aveyron. (G. Humphrey and M. Humphrey, translators). (1962). Englewood Cliffs, NJ: Prentice-Hall. Originally published in Paris by Gouyon (1801).

Johnson, G., Johnson, R. L., & Jefferson-Aker, C. R. (2001). HIV/AIDS prevention: Effective instructional strategies for adolescents with mild mental retardation. *Teaching Exceptional Children, 33,* 28–32.

Johnson, L. (2005). First, do no harm: An argument against mandatory high-stakes testing for students with intellectual disabilities. *Mental Retardation, 43,* 292–298.

Kennedy, C. H. (2001). Social interaction interventions for youth with severe disabilities should emphasize interdependence. *Mental Retardation and Developmental Disabilities Research Review, 7,* 122–127.

Kennedy, M., & Lewin, L. (2002). *Fact sheet: Summary of self-determination.* From the Center of Human Policy, Syracuse University. Retrieved July 3, 2002, from **http://soeweb.syr.edu/thechp**

Keogh, B. K., Bernheimer, L. P., & Guthrie, D. (2004). Children with developmental delays twenty years later: Where are they? How are they? *American Journal of Mental Retardation, 109,* 219–230.

Kohler, P. D. & Field, S. (2003). Transition-focused education: Foundation for the future. *Journal of Special Education, 37,* 174–183.

Kraemer, B. R., McIntyre, L. L., & Blacher, J. (2003). Quality of life for young adults with mental retardation during transition. *Mental Retardation, 41,* 250–262.

Lakin, K. C., Braddock, D., & Smith, G. (2004a). States' initial response to the President's New Freedom Initiative: Slowest rates of deinstitutionalization in 30 years. *Mental Retardation, 42,* 490–493.

Lakin, K. C., Braddock, D., & Smith, G. (2004b). Trends and milestones. *Mental Retardation, 42,* 490–493.

Lent, J. R., & McLean, B. M. (1976). The trainable retarded: The technology of teaching. In N. G. Haring and R. L. Schiefelbush (Eds.), *Teaching special children* (pp. 197–223). New York: McGraw-Hill.

Luckasson, R., Borthwick-Duffy, S., Buntinx, W. H. E., Coulter, D. L., Craig, E. M., Reeve, A., Schalock, R. L., Snell, M. E., Spitalnik, D. M., Spreat, S., & Tassé, M. J. (2002). *Definition of mental retardation.* Washington, DC: American Association on Mental Retardation (AAMR).

Luckasson, R., Coulter, D. L., Polloway, E. A., Reis, S., Schalock, R. L., Snell, M. E., Spitalnik, D. M., & Stark, J. A. (1992). *Mental retardation: Definition, classification, and systems of supports.* Washington, DC: American Association on Mental Retardation (AAMR).

MacMillan, D. L., Gresham, F. M., & Bocian, K. M. (1998). Discrepancy between definitions of learning disabilities and school practices: An empirical investigation. *Journal of Learning Disabilities, 31,* 314–326.

Mank, D., Cioffi, A., & Yovanoff, P. (2003). Supported employment outcomes across a decade: Is there evidence of improvement in the quality of implementation? *Mental Retardation, 41,* 188–197.

Manuel, J., & Little, L. (2002). A model of inclusion. *Early developments, 6,* 14–18.

McComb, D. (2003). If not self-determination, then what? *Mental Retardation, 41,* 290–298.

McDonnell, J. J., Hardman, M. L., & McDonnell, A. P. (2003). *Introduction to persons with moderate and severe disabilities: Educational and social issues* (2nd ed.). Boston: Allyn and Bacon.

Mechling, L. C., Gast, D. L., & Langone, J. (2002). Computer-based video instruction to teach persons with moderate intellectual disabilities to read grocery aisle signs and locate terms. *Journal of Special Education, 35,* 224–240.

Moore, C. L., Harley, D. A., & Gamble, D. (2004). Ex-post-facto analysis of competitive employment outcomes for individuals with mental retardation: National perspective. *Mental Retardation, 42,* 253–262.

Moore, D. G. (2001). Reassessing emotion recognition performance in people with mental retardation: A review. *American Journal on Mental Retardation, 106,* 481–502.

Moseley, C., & Nerney, T. (2000, November/December). Emerging best practices in self-determination. *AAMR News and Notes, 13,* 4–5.

Müller, E., & Markowitz, J. (2004). *Disability categories: State terminology, definitions & eligibility criteria.* Alexandria, VA: National Association of State Directors of Special Education (NASDSE), Project Forum.

National Alliance of Black School Educators (NABSE), & ILIAD Project. (2002). *Addressing over-representation of African American students in special education.* Arlington, VA: Council for Exceptional Children, and Washington, DC: National Alliance of Black School Educators.

National Center for Educational Outcomes (NCEO). (2005, February 10). Alternate assessments for students with disabilities. *Special Topic Area.* Retrieved June 17, 2005, from **http://education.unm.edu/nceo**

National Down Syndrome Society (NDSS). (2005). *Questions and answers about Down syndrome.* Retrieved June 19, 2005, from **www.ndss.org**

National Research Council. (2002). *Minority students in special education and gifted education.* Committee on Minority Representation in Special Education. M. Suzanne Donovan and Christoper T. Cross, editors. Washington, DC: National Academy Press.

Neal, L. I., McCray, A. D., Webb-Johnson, G., & Bridgest, S. T. (2003). The effects of African American movement styles on teachers' perceptions and reactions. *The Journal of Special Education, 37,* 49–57.

Nirje, B. (1969). The normalization principle and its human management implications. In R. Kugel & W. Wolfensberger (Eds.), *Changing patterns in residential services for the mentally retarded* (pp. 179–195). Washington, DC: President's Committee on Mental Retardation.

Nirje, B. (1976). The normalization principle. In R. B. Kugel & A. Shearer (Eds.), *Changing patterns in residential services for the mentally retarded* (Rev. ed., pp. 231–240). Washington, DC: President's Committee on Mental Retardation.

Office of Special Education Programs [OSEP]. (2000). Applying positive behavioral support in schools. *Twenty-second annual report to Congress on the implementation of the Individuals with Disabilities Education Act* (pp. III-7 through III-31). Washington, DC: U.S. Department of Education.

Oswald, D. P., Coutinho, M. J., Best, A. M., & Nguyen, N. (2001). Impact of sociodemographic characteristics on the identification rates of minority students as having mental retardation. *Mental Retardation, 39,* 351–367.

PACER. (2002, May). *Parent brief.* Minneapolis, MN: PACER Center, Inc.

Perry, J., & Felce, D. (2005). Factors associated with outcome in community group homes. *American Journal on Mental Retardation, 110,* 121–135.

Perske, R. (1972). The dignity of risk. In W. Wolfensberger (Ed.), *The principle of normalization in human services* (pp. 194–200). Toronto: National Institute on Mental Retardation.

Philofsky, A., Hepburn, S. L., Hayes, A., Hagerman, R., & Rogers, S. J. (2004). Linguistic and cognitive functioning and autism symptoms in young children with fragile X syndrome. *American Journal on Mental Retardation, 109,* 208–218.

Polloway, E. A. (1997). Developmental principles of the Luckasson et al. (1992) AAMR definition of mental retardation: A retrospective. *Education and Training in Mental Retardation and Developmental Disabilities, 32,* 174–178.

Repetto, J. B. (2003). Transition to living. *Exceptionality, 11,* 77–87.

Roberts, C. D., Stough, L. M., & Parrish, L. H. (2002). The role of genetic counseling in the elective termination of pregnancies involving fetuses with disabilities. *Journal of Special Education, 36,* 48–55.

Roberts, J. E., Schaaf, J. M., Skinner, M., Wheeler, A., Hooper, S., Hatton, D. D., & Bailey, Jr., D. B. (2005). Academic skills of boys with fragile X syndrome: Profiles and predictors. *American Journal on Mental Retardation, 110,* 107–120.

Roizen, N. J. (2001). Down syndrome: Progress in research. *Mental Retardation and Developmental Disabilities Research Reviews, 7,* 38–44.

Ruth, G. (2005, February/March). No books, no problem. *Edutopia,* 22–23.

Salend, S. J., Duhaney, D., Anderson, D. J., & Gottschalk, C. (2004). Using the Internet to improve homework communication and completion. *Teaching Exceptional Children, 36,* 64–73.

Schettler, R., Stein, J., Reich, F., Valenti, M., & Wallinga, D. (2000). *In harm's way: Toxic threats to child development.* Cambridge, MA: Greater Boston Physicians for Social Responsibility from **www.igc.org/psr**

Schweinhart, L. J. (2005). *The High/Scope Perry Preschool study through age 40: Summary, conclusions, and frequently asked questions.* Ypsilanti, MI: High/Scope Educational Research Foundation. Retrieved June 17, 2005, from **www.highscope.org**

Seltzer, M. M., & Krauss, M. W. (2001). Quality of life of adults with mental retardation/developmental disabilities who live with the family. *Mental Retardation and Developmental Research Reviews, 7,* 105–114.

Shriver, M. (2001). *What's wrong with Timmy?* Boston: Warner Books and Little, Brown, and Company, AOL Time Warner Companies.

Stancliff, R. (2001). Living with support in the community: Predictors of choice and self-determination. *Mental Retardation and Developmental Disabilities Research Reviews, 7,* 91–98.

Sudhalter, V., & Belser, R. C. (2001). Conversational characteristics of children with fragile X syndrome: Tangential language. *American Journal on Mental Retardation, 106,* 389–400.

Tassé, M. H., Schalock, R., Thompson, J. R., & Wehmeyer, M. (2005). *Guidelines for interviewing people with disabilities: Supports intensity scale.* Washington, DC: American Association on Mental Retardation.

Tindal, G., McDonald, M., Tedesco, M., Glasgow, A., Almond, P., Crawford, L., & Hollenbeck, K. (2003). Alternate assessments in reading and math: Development and validation for students with significant disabilities. *Exceptional Children, 69,* 481–494.

U.S. Department of Education. (2001). *Twenty-third annual report to Congress on the implementation of the Individuals with Disabilities Education Act.* Washington, DC: U. S. Government Printing Office.

U.S. Department of Education. (2005a). Assistance to states for the education of children with disabilities program and the early intervention program for infants and toddlers with disabilities; proposed regulations. *Federal Register,* 34, CRF Parts 300, 301, and 304.

U.S. Department of Education. (2005b). *Children served under IDEA, Part B (2003),* Data Table. **www.ideadata.org**

U.S. Senate Appropriations Committee. (2004, September 15). *Senate Appropriations Committee report on the Labor/HHS/Education bill.* Washington, DC: U.S. Senate.

Wehmeyer, M. L., & Metzler, C. A. (1995). How self-determined are people with mental retardation? The national consumer survey. *Mental Retardation, 33,* 111–119.

Winzer, M. A. (1993). *The history of special education: From isolation to integration.* Washington, DC: Gallaudet University Press.

Wolery, M., Ault, M. J., & Doyle, P. M. (1992). *Teaching students with moderate to severe disabilities: Use of response prompting strategies.* New York: Longman.

Wolfensberger, W. (1972). *The principle of normalization in human services.* Toronto: National Institute on Mental Retardation.

Wolfensberger, W. (2002). Social role valorization and, or versus, "empowerment." *Mental Retardation, 40,* 252–258.

Ye, X., Mitchell, M., Newman, K., & Batshaw, M. L. (2001). Prospects for prenatal gene therapy in disorders causing mental retardation. *Mental Retardation and Developmental Disabilities Research Reviews, 7,* 65–72.

Youth Record. (1995, August 15). *Child abuse leads to lower IQ and body responsiveness,* p. 1. Author.

CHAPTER 9

Physical or Health Disabilities

Arthritis Foundation of America (AFA). (2005). *School success.* Retrieved July 7, 2005, from **www.arthritis.org/resources/school_success.asp**

Asthma Foundation (2005). *Asthma facts and figures.* Retrieved July 7, 2005, from **www.aafa.org/display.cfm**

Barnes, S. B., & Whitney, K. W. (2002). Effects of functional mobility skills training for young students with physical disabilities. *Exceptional Children, 68,* 313–324.

Bryant, D. P., & Bryant, B. R. (2003). *Assistive technology for people with disabilities.* Boston: Allyn and Bacon.

Carnine, D., Silbert, J., and Kame'enui, E. J. (1997). *Direct instruction reading* (3rd ed.). Columbus, OH: Merrill.

Centers for Disease Control. (2005a). *HIV/AIDS among youth.* Fact Sheets. Retrieved July 7, 2005, from **www.cdc.gov/hiv/pubs/facts/youth.htm**

Centers for Disease Control. (2005b, March). *Poliomyelitis.* Retrieved July 11, 2005, from **www.cdc.gov**

Children's Defense Fund. (CDF). (2004). *The state of America's children: 2004.* Washington, DC: Author.

CNN. (2004, October 29). *Dog saves woman's life by calling 911.* Retrieved April 24, 2005, from **www.cnn.com**

Coster, W. J., & Haltiwanger, J. T. (2004). Social-behavioral skills of elementary students with physical disabilities included in general education classrooms. *Remedial and Special Education, 25,* 95–103.

Delta Society. (2005a). *Basic information about service dogs.* Retrieved July 14, 2005, from **www.deltasociety.org**

Delta Society. (2005b). *Service dog etiquette.* Retrieved July 14, 2005, from **www.deltasociety.org**

Dolch, E. W. (1948). *Helping handicapped children in school.* Champaign, IL: Garrard Press.

Eberle, L. (1922). The maimed, the halt and the race. *Hospital Social Service, 6,* 59–63. Reprinted in R. H. Bremner (Ed.), (1970), *Children and youth in America, A documentary history: Vol. II, 1866–1932* (pp. 1026–1928). Cambridge, MA: Harvard University Press.

Edens, R. M., Murdick, N. L., & Gartin, B. C. (2003). Preventing infection in the classroom: The use of universal precautions. *Teaching Exceptional Children, 35,* 62–66.

Elliot, J. L., Erickson, R. N., Thurlow, M. L., & Shriner, J. G. (2000). State-level accountability for the performance of students with disabilities: Five years of change? *Journal of Special Education, 34,* 39–47.

Elliott, S. N. (2003). *Academic enablers and the development of academically competent students.* Unpublished manuscript: Madison, WI: Wisconsin Center for Education Research, University of Wisconsin Madison.

Elliott, S. N., DiPerna, J. C., Mroch, A., & Lang, S. C. (2004). Prevalence and patterns of academic enabling behaviors: An analysis of teachers' and students' ratings for a national sample of students. *School Psychology Review, 33,* 297–304.

Emory University School of Medicine. (2003). *Sickle cell disease.* The Sickle Cell Information Center. Retrieved July 8, 2005, from **www.scinfo.org**

Emory University School of Medicine. (2005). *Sickle cell information for teachers, students, and employers.* The Sickle Cell Information Center. Retrieved July 8, 2005, from **www.scinfo.org**

Epilepsy Foundation of America (EFA). (2005a). Managing seizures at school. Retrieved July 7, 2005, from **www.efa.org/answerplace/teachers/managing.cfm**

Epilepsy Foundation of America (EFA). (2005b). *Epilepsy and seizure statistics.* Retrieved July 7, 2005, from **www.efa.org/answerplace/statistics.cfm**

Fowler, G. L. (1982). Developing comprehension skills in primary students through the use of story frames. *Reading Teacher, 36,* 176–179.

Frayer, D. W., Horton, W. A., Macchiarelli, R., & Mussi, M. (1987). Dwarfism in an adolescent from the Italian late Upper Palaeolithic. *Nature, 330,* 60–61.

Gibson, D., Haeberli, F. B., Glover, R. A., & Witter, E. A. (2005). The use of recommended and provided testing accommodations. *Assessment for Effective Instruction* (in press).

Guthrie, P. (2001, October 26). "Gentler" treatment for sickle cell hailed. *Atlanta Journal Constitution.* Retrieved July 6, 2002, from **www.emory.edu/PEDS/SICKLE/bonemarr.htm**

Heller, K. W., Forney, P. E., Alberto, P. A., Schwartzman, M. N., & Goeckel, T. (2000). *Meeting physical and health needs of children with disabilities: Teaching student participation and management.* Pacific Grove, CA: Wadsworth: Brooks/Cole.

Helman, S. W. (2002, May 28). A disabled student's battle could aid others' struggles. *Boston Globe,* pp. B1–2.

Henderson, C. (2001). *College freshmen with disabilities: A biennial statistical profile.* Washington, DC: HEATH Resource Center, American Council on Education.

Horgan, P. (1994). *The artifice of blue light: Henriette Wyeth.*

Idol, L. (1987). Group story mapping: A comprehension strategy for both skilled and unskilled readers. *Journal of Learning Disabilities, 20,* 196–205.

Kennedy, C., & Horn, E. (2004). *Including students with severe disabilities.* Boston: Allyn and Bacon.

Küpper, L. (2005). Resources within the medical and healthcare community. *NICHCY eNews Foundations.* Retrieved July 14, 2005, from **www.nichcy.org/enews/foundations**

La Vor, M. L. (1976). Federal legislation for exceptional persons: A history. In F. J. Weintraub, A. Abeson, J. Ballard, & M. L. La Vor (Eds.), *Public policy and the education of exceptional children* (pp. 96–111). Reston, VA: Council for Exceptional Children.

Longmore, P. (2003). *Why I burned my book and other essays on disability.* Philadelphia: Temple University Press.

Maddox, S. (Ed.). (1987). *Spinal network: The total resource for the wheelchair community.* Boulder, CO: Author.

McDonnell, J. J., Hardman, M. L., & McDonnell, A. P. (2003). *Introduction to persons with moderate and severe disabilities: Educational and social issues* (2nd ed.). Boston: Allyn and Bacon.

National Association of School Nurses (NASN). (2002). Asthma management in the school setting. *Issue Brief: School health nursing services role in health care.* Retrieved July 11, 2005, from **www.nasn.org**

National Human Genome Research Institute of the National Institutes of Health. (2005). *Learning about sickle cell disease.* Retrieved July 6, 2005, from **www.genome.gov**

National Institute of Allergy and Infectious Diseases. (2004 July). *HIV infections in infants and children.* Retrieved July 7, 2005, from **www.niaid.nih.gov/factsheets/hivchildren.htm**

National Institute of Environmental Health Sciences (NIEHS). (2005). *Asthma and the environment.* Hot topics packs. Retrieved July 10, 2005, from **www.niehs.nih.gov/outreach/education/Resources/HTasthma.cfm**

Niebling, B. C., & Elliott, S. N. (2005). Testing accommodations and inclusive assessment. *Assessment for Effective Instruction* (in press).

Owens, R. E., Metz, D. E., & Haas, A. (2003). *Introduction to communication disorders: A life span perspective* (2nd ed.). Boston: Allyn & Bacon.

Scheerenberger, R. C. (1983). *A history of mental retardation.* Baltimore, MD: Paul H. Brookes.

Schwartz, J. (2005, April 5). Apartment house lifts barriers for the disabled. *New York Times—Health.* Retrieved April 5, 2005, from **www.NYTimes.com**

Shaw, B. (1995, May/June). Ed Roberts: 1939–1995. *Disability Rag,* p. 25.

Shriner, J. G., & DeStefano, L. (2003). Participation and accommodation in state assessment: The role of individualized education programs. *Exceptional Children, 69,* 147–161.

Smart, J. (2001). *Disability, society, and the individual.* Austin, TX: PRO-ED.

Smith, B. (2005). NICHCY connections . . . to weighing information for what it's worth. Retrieved July 11, 2005, from **www.nichcy.org**

Stone, K. G. (1995, March 19). Disability rights pioneer inspired his community. *Albuquerque Journal,* p. C6.

Thompson, S. J., Quenemoen, R. F., Thurlow, M. L., & Ysseldyke, J. E. (2001). *Alternative assessments for students with disabilities.* Thousand Oaks, CA: Corwin Press.

Thurlow, M. L., House, A. L., Scott, D. L., & Ysseldyke, J. E. (2000). Students with disabilities in large-scale assessments: State participation and accommodation policies. *Journal of Special Education, 34,* 154–163.

United Cerebral Palsy Association (UCP). (2001). *Cerebral palsy—Facts and figures.* Retrieved July 7, 2005, from **www.ucp.org**

U.S. Department of Education. (2002). *Twenty-fourth annual report to Congress on the implementation of the Individuals with Disabilities Education Act.* Washington, DC: U. S. Government Printing Office.

U.S. Department of Education. (2005a). Assistance to states for the education of children with disabilities program and the early intervention program for infants and toddlers with disabilities; proposed regulations. *Federal Register,* 34, CRF Parts 300, 301, and 304.

U.S. Department of Education. (2005b). *Children served under IDEA, Part B (2003),* Data Tables. **www.ideadata.org**

Williams, J. P. (1998). Improving the comprehension of disabled readers. *Annals of Dyslexia, 48,* 213–238.

Williams, J. P., Brown, L. G., Silverstein, A. K., and deCani, J. S. (1994). An instructional program in comprehension of narrative themes for adolescents with learning disabilities. *Learning Disability Quarterly, 17,* 205–221.

CHAPTER 10

Deaf and Hard of Hearing

Adams, M. E. (1929). 1865–1935: A few memories of Alexander Graham Bell. *American Annals of the Deaf, 74,* 467–479.

Alby, J. F. (1962, Spring). The educational philosophy of Thomas Hopkins Gallaudet. *Buff and Blue,* 17–23.

American Council on Education, HEATH Resource Center (ACE HEATH). (2005). *Students who are deaf or hard of hearing in postsecondary education.* Washington, DC: Author.

American Speech-Language-Hearing Association (ASHA). (2005a). *Causes of hearing loss in children.* Retrieved July 23, 2005, from **www.asha.org/public/hearing/disorders/causes.htm**

American Speech-Language-Hearing Association (ASHA). (2005b). *Status of state universal newborn and infant hearing screening legislation and laws.* Retrieved July 23, 2005, from **www.asha.org/about/legislation-advocacy/state/issues/overview.htm**

Anderson, G. B., & Miller, K. R. (2004/2005). Appreciating diversity through stories about the lives of Deaf people of color. *American Annals of the Deaf, 149,* 375–383.

Antia, S. D., & Kreimeyer, K. H. (2001). The role of interpreters in inclusive classrooms. *American Annals of the Deaf, 146,* 355–365.

Bauman, N. (2004, November). *Hair cell regeneration—Looking beyond the hype.* Retrieved from July 23, 2005, **www.hearinglosshelp.com**

Bergeson, T. R., Pisoni, D. B., & Davis, R. A. O. (2003). A longitudinal study of audiovisual speech perception by children with hearing loss who have cochlear implants. *The Volta Review, 103,* 347–370.

Blade, R. (1994, October 31). Sign language is beautiful, close-knit Deaf community says. *Albuquerque Tribune,* p. A5.

Blue Cross of California. (2004). Semi-implantable middle ear hearing aids as a treatment of hearing loss. *Medical Policy.* Retrieved from **http://medpolicy.bluecrossca.com/policies/medicine/semi_implantable_hearing_aids.html**

Bowe, F. G. (2002). Enhancing reading ability to prevent students from becoming "low-functioning deaf" as adults. *American Annals of the Deaf, 147,* 22–27.

Branson, J., & Miller, D. (2002). *Damned for their difference: The cultural construction of deaf people as disabled.* Washington, DC: Gallaudet University Press.

Byrnes, L. J., & Sigafoos, J. (2001). A "consumer" survey of educational provision for deaf and hard of hearing students. *American Annals of the Deaf, 146,* 409–419.

Calderon, R., & Greenberg, M. T. (1999). Stress and coping in hearing mothers of children with hearing loss: Factors affecting mother and child adjustment. *American Annals of the Deaf, 144,* 7–23.

Campbell, C. D. (1999). The central asylum for the instruction of the deaf and dumb, Canajoharie, New York, 1823–1835. *American Annals of the Deaf, 144,* 365–372.

Carroll, C. (2002). *Thomas Hopkins Gallaudet: A father, a son, and a university.* Laurent Clerc National Deaf Education Center, Gallaudet University. Retrieved July 30, 2005 from *Info to Go* at **www.gallaudet.edu**

Chin, S. B., & Kaiser, C. L., (2002). Measurement of articulation in pediatric users of cochlear implants. *The Volta Review, 102,* 145–156.

Cone-Wesson, B. (2003). Electrophysiologic assessment of hearing in infants: Compound nerve action potential, auditory brainstem response, and auditory steady state response. *The Volta Review, 103,* 253–279.

Cuculick, J. A., & Kelly, R. R. (2003). Relating Deaf students' reading and language scores at college entry to their degree completion rates. *American Annals of the Deaf, 148,* 279–286.

Davey, M. (2005, March 21). As town for Deaf takes shape, debate on isolation re-emerges. *New York Times, National Desk.* Retrieved on July 23, 2005.

Davis, C. (2001, July/August). Automatic speech recognition and access: 20 years, 20 months, or tomorrow? *Hearing Loss,* 11–14.

DiSarno, N. J., Schowalter, M., and Grassa, P. (2002). Classroom amplification to enhance student performance. *Teaching Exceptional Children, 34,* 20–26.

Drasgow, E. (1998). American Sign Language as a pathway to linguistic competence. *Exceptional Children, 64,* 329–342.

Easterbrooks, S. (1999). Improving practices for students with hearing impairments. *Exceptional Children, 65,* 537–554.

Easterbrooks, S. R., & Baker, S. (2002). *Language learning in children who are deaf and hard of hearing: Multiple pathways.* Boston: Allyn and Bacon.

Evans, C. J. (2004). Literacy development in deaf students: Case studies in bilingual teaching and learning. *American Annals of the Deaf, 149,* 17–27.

Fiedler, B. C. (2001). Considering placement and educational approaches for students who are deaf and hard of hearing. *Teaching Exceptional Children, 34,* 54–59.

Fletcher, R. (1994). On deaf culture and cultures. *Border Walking, 2,* 2.

Gallaudet Research Institute. (1998). *Regional and national summary report of data from the 1997–1998 annual survey of deaf and hard-of-hearing children and youth.* Washington, DC: GRI, Gallaudet University.

Gallaudet Research Institute. (2005). *Regional and national summary report of data from the 2003–2004 annual survey of deaf and hard-of-hearing children and youth.* Washington, DC: GRI, Gallaudet University.

Gannon, J. R. (1989). *The week the world heard Gallaudet.* Washington, DC: Gallaudet University Press.

Goldberg, B. (1995). Families facing choices: Options for parents of children who are deaf or hard of hearing. *ASHA, 37,* 38–45.

Goldin-Meadow, S., & Mayberry, R. I. (2001). How do profoundly deaf children learn to read? *Learning Disabilities Research & Practice, 16,* 222–229.

Gordon-Langbein, A. L., & Metzinger, M. (2000). Technology in the classroom to maximize listening and learning. *Volta Voices, 7,* 10–13.

Groce, N. E. (1985). *Everyone here spoke sign language: Hereditary deafness on Martha's Vineyard.* Cambridge, MA: Harvard University Press.

Haller, A. K., & Montgomery, J. K. (2004). Noise-induced hearing loss in children: What educators need to know. *Teaching Exceptional Children, 36,* 22–27.

Halligan, P. (2003). "Turn on the Lights" with an FM system. *Volta Voices, 10,* 20–21.

Harrington, M. (2003). Hard of hearing students in the public schools: Should we be concerned? *Volta Voices, 11,* 18–22.

HearingLoss.org (2005, January). *Facts on hearing loss.* Retrieved July 24, 2005, from **www.shhh.org**

Hignett, S. (1983). *Brett from Bloomsbury to New Mexico: A biography.* New York: Franklin Watts.

Hoover, B. M. (2000). Hearing aid fitting in infants. *The Volta Review, 102,* 57–73.

Huebner, M. (2002). Hearing loss: A challenge not a restriction. *Hearing Loss, 23,* 7–9.

Jensema, C. J., Danturthi, S., & Burch, R. (2000). Time spent viewing captions on television programs. *American Annals of the Deaf, 145,* 464–468.

Johnson, K. C., & Winter, M. E. (2003). Audiologic assessment of infants and toddlers. *The Volta Review, 103,* 221–251.

Johnson, R. C. (2001–2002). High stakes testing and deaf students: Comments from readers. *Research at Gallaudet,* 1.

Kaderavek, J. N., and Pakulski, L. A. (2002). Minimal hearing loss is not minimal. *Teaching Exceptional Children, 34,* 14–19.

Kageleiry, J. (2002, February). *The island that spoke by hand.* Martha's Vineyard Chamber of Commerce. Retrieved February 25, 2002, from **www.mvy.com/spokehand.htm**

Kelly, R. R., Albertini, J. A., & Shannon, N. B. (2001). Deaf college students' reading comprehension and strategy use. *American Annals of the Deaf, 146,* 385–400.

King, S., DeCaro, J. J., Karchmer, M. A., & Cole, K. (2001). *College and career programs for deaf* (11th ed.). Washington, DC: Gallaudet University.

Kirk, K. I., Miyamoto, R. T., Ying, E. A., Perdew, A. E., & Zuganelis, H. (2002). Cochlear implantation in young children: Effects of age at implantation and communication mode. *The Volta Review, 102,* 127–144.

Kramlinger, J. (1996). Making noise in a silent world: A profile of the deaf college experience. *Volta Voices, 3,* 20–21.

Lane, H. (1995). Construction of deafness. *Disability & Society, 10,* 171–187.

Laurent Clerc National Deaf Education Center (2002). Some facts about otitis media. *Info to Go.* Gallaudet University. Retrieved July 23, 2005, from **http://clerccenter.gallaudet.edu**

Laurent Clerc National Deaf Education Center (2005). *The history of Kendall Demonstration Elementary School.* Retrieved July 25, 2005, from **http://clerccenter.gallaudet.edu**

Linehan, P. (2000). Educational interpreters for students who are deaf and hard of hearing. *Quick Turn Around.* Alexandria, VA: Project Forum, National Association for State Directors of Special Education.

Lowenbraun, S. (1995). Hearing impairment. In E. L. Meyen and T. M. Skrtic (Eds.), *Exceptional children and youth: An introduction* (4th ed. pp. 453–486). Denver, CO: Love.

Luetke-Stahlman, B. (1999). *Language across the curriculum: When students are deaf or hard of hearing.* Hillsboro, OR: Butte Publications.

Magnuson, M. (2000). Infants with congenital deafness: On the importance of early sign language acquisition. *American Annals of the Deaf, 145,* 6–14.

Marschark, M. (1993). *Psychological development of deaf children.* New York: Oxford University Press.

Marschark, M. (2001). *Language development in children who are deaf: A research synthesis.* Alexandria, VA: Project Forum, National Association of State Directors of Special Education (NASDSE).

Moores, D. F. (2001). *Educating the deaf: Psychology, principles, and practices* (5th ed.). Boston: Houghton Mifflin.

Moores, D. R., Jatho, J., & Dunn, C. (2001). Families with deaf members: American Annals of the Deaf, 1996 to 2000. *American Annals of the Deaf, 146,* 245–250.

Most, T. (2003). The use of repair strategies: Bilingual deaf children using sign and spoken language. *American Annals of the Deaf, 148,* 308–314.

Most, T., Weisel, A., & Lev-Matezky, A. (1996). Speech intelligibility and the evaluation of personal qualities by experienced and inexperienced listeners. *The Volta Review, 98,* 181–190.

National Center for Hearing Assessment and Management (NCHAM). (2005). *Universal Newborn Hearing Screening Fact Sheet.* Logan, UT: Utah State University. Retrieved July 28, 2005, from **www.infanthearing.org**

National Dissemination Center for Children with Disabilities (NICHCY). (2004, January). *Deafness and hearing loss: Fact Sheet 3.*

National Institute on Deafness and Other Communication Disorders (NIDCD). (2000). *American Sign Language.* Retrieved July 24, 2005, from **www.nidcd.nih.gov**

National Institute on Deafness and Other Communication Disorders (NIDCD). (2002a). *Noise-induced hearing loss.* Retrieved July 24, 2005, from **www.nidcd.nih.gov**

National Institute on Deafness and Other Communication Disorders (NIDCD). (2002b). *Cochlear implants.* Retrieved July 24, 2005, from **www.nidcd.nih.gov**

Nikolaraizi, M., & Makri, M. (2004/2005). Deaf and hearing individuals' beliefs about the capabilities of deaf people. *American Annals of the Deaf, 149,* 404–414.

Nittrouer, S., & Burton, L. R. (2003). The role of early language experience in the development of speech perception and language processing abilities in children with hearing loss. *The Volta Review, 103,* 5–57.

Northern, J. L., & Downs, M. P. (1984). *Hearing in children.* Baltimore, MD: Williams & Wilkins.

Owens, Jr., R. E., Metz, D. E., & Haas, A. (2003). *Introduction to communication disorders: A life span perspective* (2nd ed.). Boston: Allyn and Bacon.

Roffé, S. (2000). Cued speech: Another option. *Volta Voices, 7,* 13.

Ross, M. (2002, March/April). Developments in research and technology. *Hearing Loss,* 32–36.

Ross, M., & Levitt, H. (2000). Developments in research and technology: Otoacoustic emissions. *Volta Voices, 7,* 30–31.

Schroedel, J. G., & Geyer, J. J. (2000). Long-term career attainments of deaf and hard of hearing college graduates: Results from a 15-year follow-up study. *American Annals of Deaf, 145,* 303–314.

Sheridan, M. (2001). *Inner lives of deaf children: Interviews & analysis.* Washington, DC: Gallaudet University Press.

Silcon Chalk (2004). *Teaching and learning.* Retrieved on January 22, 2005, from **www.silicon-chalk.com**

Smaldino, J. (2004). Barriers to listening and learning in the classroom. *Volta Voices, 11,* 24–25.

Soloman, A. (1994, August 28). Defiantly deaf. *New York Times Magazine,* pp. 38–45, 64–68.

Sorkin, D. L. (2002). Cochlear implant candidacy and outcomes: 2002 update. *Hearing loss, 23,* 12–14, 15–17.

Steffan, R. C., (2004). Navigating the difficult waters of the No Child Left Behind Act of 2001: What it means for education of the Deaf. *American Annals of the Deaf, 149,* 46–50.

Stinson, M. S., Elliot, L. B., McKee, B. G., & Francis, P. G. (2001). Accessibility in the classroom: The pros and cons of C-Print. *Volta Voices, 8,* 16–19.

Sussman, K. D., Duncan, J., Estabrooks, W., Hulme, J., Moog, J. S., & Robbins, A. M. (2004). The option of spoken communication. *2004 summit on deafness proccedings: Spoken language options in the 21st Century: Predicting future trends in deafness.* Washington, DC: Alexander Graham Bell Association for the Deaf and Hard of Hearing.

Svirsky, M. A., Chin, S. B., Miyamoto, R. T., Soan, R. B., & Caldwell, M. D. (2002). Speech intelligibility of profoundly deaf pediatric hearing aid users. *The Volta Review, 102,* 175–198.

Sweetow, R. W., & Luckett, E. (2001). Selecting the "best" hearing aids for yourself or child. *Volta Voices, 8,* 18–21.

Szalay, J. (2005, March 26). Our town: A home for the Deaf. *New York Times, Editorial Desk.* Retrieved on July 23, 2005.

Tharpe, A. M. (2004, November 18). *Even minimal, undetected hearing loss hurts academic performance.* Presentation at the American Speech-Language-Hearing Association (ASHA) National Convention, Pennsylvania Convention Center.

Trychin, S. (2001, November/December). Why don't people who need hearing aids get them? *Hearing Loss,* 21–23.

Uffen, E. (2005, April 12). AAAS session explores cochlear hair cell regeneration: Research shows promise, limitations for treatment. *The ASHA Leader,* 1, 20–21.

U.S. Department of Education. (2005a). Assistance to states for the education of children with disabilities program and the early intervention program for infants and toddlers with disabilities; proposed regulations. *Federal Register,* 34, CRF Parts 300, 301, and 304.

U.S. Department of Education. (2005b). *Children served under IDEA, Part B (2003),* Data Tables. **www.ideadata.org**

Vanderhoff, M. (2003). Genetic researchers take first step toward hair cell regeneration. *Volta Voices, 10,* 22.

Vanderhoff, M., & Lakins, L. (2003). High-tech homes: The new wave in visual alert systems. *Volta Voices, 10,* 8, 11, 25.

Wagner, H. (2002, August 29). New middle-ear hearing device gives hope to people with moderate to severe hearing loss. *Ohio State Research.* Retrieved on July 23, 2005, from **http://researchnews.osu.edu/archive/midear1.htm**

Williams, C. B., & Finnegan, M. (2003). From myth to reality: Sound information for teachers about students who are deaf. *Teaching Exceptional Children, 35,* 40–45.

Yarnell, B. J., & Schery, T. (2003, November). *Kids with cochlear implants: Supporting inclusive education.* Presentation made to the American Speech-Language-Hearing Association (ASHA), Chicago.

Yoshinaga-Itano, C. Y., & Apuzzo, M. L. (1998). Identification of hearing loss after age 18 months is not early enough. *American Annals of the Deaf, 143,* 380–387.

Yoshinaga-Itano, C., & Sedey, A. (2000). Early speech development in children who are deaf or hard of hearing: Interrelationships with language and hearing. *The Volta Review, 100,* 181–211.

Zazove, P., Meador, H. E., Derry, H. A., Gorenflo, D. W., & Saunders, E. W. (2004). Deaf persons and computer use. *American Annals of the Deaf, 148,* 376–384.

CHAPTER 11

Low Vision and Blindness

American Association of Retired Persons (AARP). (2002). *Gold violin: Thoughtfully designed products for seniors.* Retrieved June, 16, 2002, from **www.goldviolin.com**

American Foundation for the Blind (AFB). (2002). *Statistics and sources for professionals.* Retrieved September 14, 2002, from **www.afb.org**

American Foundation for the Blind. (2005). *Statistics and sources for professionals.* Retrieved August 7, 2005, from **www.afb.org**

American Printing House for the Blind. (1992). *Annual report.* Louisville, KY: Author.

Ansariyah-Grace, T. (2000, August 6). Touched by arts. *The Tennessean,* p. 1F–2F.

Associated Press (2002, June 1). Blind bicyclists to ride the Trace to Keller's home. *The Tennessean,* Local News section, p. B1.

Bailey, I. L., Lueck, A. H., Greer, R. B., Tuan, K. M., Bailey, V. M., & Dornbusch, H. G. (2003). Understanding the relationships between print size and reading in low vision. *Journal of Low Vision and Blindness, 97,* 325–333.

Barraga, N. C. (1964). *Increased visual behavior in low vision children.* New York: American Foundation for the Blind.

Barraga, N. C., & Collins, M. E. (1979). Development of efficiency in visual functioning: Rationale for a comprehensive program. *Journal of Visual Impairment and Blindness, 73,* 121–126.

Buhrow, M. M., Hartshorne, T. S., & Bradley-Johnson, S. (1998). Parents' and teachers' ratings of the social skills of elementary-age students who are blind. *Journal of Visual Impairment and Blindness, 92,* 503–511.

Cappella-McDonnall, M. (2005). Predictors of competitive employment for blind and visually impaired consumers of vocational rehabilitation services. *Journal of Visual Impairment and Blindness, 99,* 303–315.

Centers for Disease Control (CDC). (2005). *Vision impairment.* Atlanta: National Center on Birth Defects and Developmental Disabilities. Retrieved August 7, 2005, from **www.cdc.gov/ncbddd/dd/ddvi.htm**

Clarke, K. L., Sainato, D. M., & Ward, M. E. (1994). Travel performance of preschoolers: The effects of mobility training with a long cane versus a precane. *Journal of Visual Impairment and Blindness, 88,* 19–30.

Corn, A. L. (1989). Instruction in the use of vision for children and adults with low vision: A proposed program model. *RE:view, 21,* 26–38.

Corn, A., & Koenig, A. J. (2002). Literacy for students with low vision: A framework for delivering instruction. *Journal of Visual Impairments and Blindness, 96,* 305–321.

Cox, P., & Dykes, M. (2001). Effective classroom adaptations for students with visual impairments. *Teaching Exceptional Children, 33,* 68–74.

De Mario, N., & Caruso, M. (2001). The expansion of outreach services for specialized schools for students with visual impairments. *Journal of Visual Impairment and Blindness, 95,* 488–491.

Descriptive Video Service (DVS). (2005). *Descriptive video service.* Logan, UT: Utah State Library for the Blind and Disabled. Retrieved August 10, 2005, from **http://blindlibrary.utah.gov/descriptive_video**

Dote-Kwan, J., Chen, D., & Hughes M. (2001). A national survey of service providers who work with young children with visual impairments. *Journal of Visual Impairment and Blindness, 95,* 325–337.

Duzak, W. (2002, June 3). Young cyclists who are blind ride the Trace. *The Tennessean, DAVIDSON,* p. 12B.

Erin, J. N., & Corn, A. L. (1994). A survey of children's first understanding of being visually impaired. *Journal of Visual Impairment and Blindness, 88,* 132–139.

Evansville Association for the Blind. (2003). *Summer college program.* Retrieved August 10, 2005, from **http://eab.evansville.edu/college.htm**

Eye of the Pacific. (2005). *Electronic aids.* Retrieved August 11, 2005, from **www.eyeofthepacific.org/electronic%20aids.htm**

Frank, J. (2000). Requests by persons with visual impairment for large-print accommodation. *Journal of Visual Impairment and Blindness, 94,* 716–719.

Fruchterman, J. R. (2003). In the palm of your hand: A vision of the future of technology for people with visual impairments. *Journal of Visual Impairment and Blindness, 97,* 585–591.

Gerber, E. (2003). The benefits of and barriers to computer use for individuals who are visually impaired. *Journal of Visual Impairment and Blindness, 97,* 536–550.

Gompel, M., van Bon, W. H. J., & Schreuder, R. (2004). Reading by children with low vision. *Journal of Visual Impairment and Blindness, 98,* 77–89.

Grupé, B. (Ed.). (2000). *Report on Disability Programs, 23,* 41–48.

Hagelman, E. (2004). Design your classroom to aid students with low vision, blindness. *Inclusive Education Programs, 11,* 3.

Hatton, D. (2001). Model registry of early childhood visual impairment: First-year results. *Journal of Visual Impairment and Blindness, 95,* 418–433.

HEATH Resource Center. (2001). *Students who are blind or visually impaired in postsecondary education.* Washington, DC: George Washington University. Retrieved August 7, 2005, from **www.heath.gwu.edu**

Heller, K. W., Alberto, P. A., Forney, P. E., & Schwartzman, M. N. (1996). *Understanding physical, sensory, and health impairments.* Pacific Grove, CA: Brooks/Cole.

Henderson, C. (2001). *College freshmen with disabilities: A biennial statistical profile.* Washington, DC: HEATH Resource Center, American Council on Education.

Hill, E. W. (1986). Orientation and mobility. In G. R. Scholl (Ed.), *Foundations of education for blind and visually handicapped children and youth: Theory and practice* (pp. 315–340). New York: American Foundation for the Blind.

Hitchcock, C., Meyer, A., Rose, D., & Jackson, R. (2002). Providing new access to the general curriculum: Universal design for learning. *Teaching Exceptional Children, 35,* 8–17.

Hughes, M., Dote-Kwan, J., & Dolendo, J. (1998). A close look at the cognitive play of preschoolers with visual impairments in the home. *Exceptional Children, 64,* 451–462.

Jindal-Snape, D. (2005). Use of feedback from sighted peers in promoting social interaction skills. *Journal of Visual Impairment and Blindness, 99,* 403–412.

Kirchner, C., & Smith, B. (2005). Transition to what? Education and employment outcomes for visually impaired youths after high school. *Journal of Visual Impairment and Blindness, 99,* 499–503.

Koenig, A., & Holbrook, M. (2000). Ensuring high-quality instruction for students in braille literacy programs. *Journal of Visual Impairment and Blindness, 94,* 677–694.

Levin, A. V. (1996). Common visual problems in classrooms. In R. H. A. Haslam & P. J. Valletutti (Eds.), *Medical problems in the classroom: The teacher's role in diagnosis and management* (pp. 161–180). Austin, TX: PRO-ED.

Lighthouse International. (2005). *Lighthouse catalog.* New York: The Lighthouse Store.

Loots, G., Devisé, I., & Sermijn, J. (2003). The interaction between mothers and their visually impaired infants: An intersubjective developmental perspective. *Journal of Visual Impairment and Blindness, 97,* 403–417.

Lueck, A. H., Bailey, I. L., Greer, R. B., Tuan, K. M., Bailey, V. M., & Dornbusch, H. G. (2003). Exploring print-size requirements and reading for students with low vision. *Journal of Low Vision and Blindness, 97,* 335–355.

MacCuspie, P. A. (1992). The social acceptance and interaction of visually impaired children in integrated settings. In S. Z. Sacks, L. S. Kekelis, and R. J. Gaylord-Ross (Eds.), *The development of social skills by blind and visually impaired students* (pp. 83–102). New York: American Foundation for the Blind.

McGaha, C., & Farran, D. (2001). Interaction in an inclusive classroom: The effects of visual status and setting. *Journal of Visual Impairment and Blindness, 95,* 80–94.

McHugh, E., & Lieberman, L. (2003). The impact of developmental factors on stereotypic rocking of children with visual impairments. *Journal of Visual Impairment and Blindness, 97,* 453–474.

McMahon, P. (2000, February 4). Hearing-impaired wage fight in theaters. *USA Today,* p. 3A.

Milian, M. (2001). School's efforts to involve Latino families of students with visual impairments. *Journal of Visual Impairment and Blindness, 95,* 389–402.

Miller, J. (2002). The role of orientation and mobility instructors and rehabilitation teachers in enhancing employment opportunities for persons who are visually impaired. *Journal of Visual Impairment and Blindness, 96,* 852–855.

Mogk, L., & Goodrich, G. (2004). The history and future of low vision services in the United States. *Journal of Visual Impairment and Blindness, 98,* 585–600.

Nagle, K. (2001). Transition to employment and community life for youths with visual impairments: Current status and future directions. *Journal of Visual Impairment and Blindness, 95,* 725–738.

Oddo, N. S., & Sitlington, P. L. (2002). What does the future hold? A follow-up study of graduates of a residential school program. *Journal of Visual Impairment and Blindness, 96,* 842–851.

Peréz-Pereira, M., & Conti-Ramsden, G. (2001). The use of directives in verbal interactions between blind children and their mothers. *Journal of Visual Impairment and Blindness, 95,* 133–149.

Pogrund, R. L., Fazzi, D. L., & Schreier, E. M. (1993). Development of a preschool "Kiddy Cane." *Journal of Visual Impairment and Blindness, 86,* 52–54.

Prevent Blindness America (2004a). *Your child's sight.* Retrieved August 7, 2005, from **www.preventblindness.org**

Prevent Blindness America (2004b). *Children's vision screening.* Retrieved August 7, 2005, from **www.preventblindness.org**

Prevent Blindness America (2005a). *New CDC study confirms significant number of children are not receiving proper vision care.* Retrieved August 7, 2005, from **www.preventblindness.org**

Prevent Blindness America (2005b). *New study proves effectiveness of vision screenings in children.* Retrieved August 7, 2005, from **www.preventblindness.org**

Randall, K. (2005). *Uncommon vision: Blind student focuses on her goal to become elementary school teacher.* Austin, TX: University of Texas-Austin, Office of Public Affairs, College of Education. Retrieved August 5, 2005, from **www.utexas.edu/features/2005/wolf**

Rettig, M. (1994). The play of young children with visual impairments: Characteristics and interventions. *Journal of Visual Impairment and Blindness, 88,* 410–420.

Runyan, M., & Jenkins, S. (2001). *No finish line: My life as I see it.* New York: G. P. Putnam's Sons.

Sacks, S. Z., & Rosen, S. (1994). Visual impairment. In N. G. Haring, L. McCormick, & T. G. Haring (Eds.), *Exceptional children and youth* (6th ed., pp. 403–446). Columbus, OH: Merrill.

Shapiro, D. R., Moffett, A., Lieberman, L., & Dummer, G. M. (2005). *Journal of Visual Impairment and Blindness, 99,* 15–25.

Sherman, A. (1994). *Wasting America's future: The Children's Defense Fund on the cost of child poverty.* Boston: Beacon Press.

Sinatra, A. (2002, August 4). Use of braille declines. Retrieved August 4, 2002, from **www.ABCNEWS.com**.

Spungin, S. (Ed.). (2002). *When you have a visually impaired student in your classroom: A guide for teachers.* New York: American Foundation for the Blind.

The Tennessean (1999, February 16). Net lets blind "see" diagrams, p. A4.

Trent, S. D., & Truan, M. B. (1997). Speed, accuracy, and comprehension of adolescent braille readers in a specialized school. *Journal of Visual Impairment and Blindness, 91,* 494–500.

Tröster, H., & Brambring, M. (1992). Early social-emotional development in blind infants. *Child: Care, Health and Development, 18,* 421–432.

Tröster, H., & Brambring, M. (1994). The play behavior and play materials of blind and sighted infants and preschoolers. *Journal of Visual Impairment and Blindness, 88,* 421–432.

Tuttle, D. W., & Ferrell, K. A. (1995). Visually impaired. In E. L. Meyen and T. M. Skrtic (Eds.), *Exceptional children and youth: An introduction* (4th ed., pp. 487–531). Denver, CO: Love.

U.S. Department of Education. (2005a). *Children served under IDEA, Part B (2003),* Data Tables. **www.ideadata.org**

U.S. Department of Education. (2005b). Assistance to states for the education of children with disabilities program and the early intervention program for infants and toddlers with disabilities; proposed regulations. *Federal Register,* 34, CRF Parts 300, 301, and 304.

Weihenmayer, E. (2001). *Touch the top of the world.* New York: Dutton, the Penguin Group.

Wetzel, R., & Knowlton, M. (2000). A comparison of print and braille reading rates on three reading tasks. *Journal of Visual Impairment and Blindness, 94,* 146–154.

Wilkinson, M. E., & Trantham, C. S. (2004). Characteristics of children evaluated at a pediatric low vision clinic: 1981–2003. *Journal of Low Vision and Blindness, 98,* 693–702.

Wormsley, D. P. (2004). *Braille literacy: A functional approach.* New York: AFB Press.

CHAPTER 12

Autism Spectrum Disorders

American Psychiatric Association (APA). (2000). *Diagnostic and statistical manual of mental disorders, Fourth Edition Text Revision* (DSM-IV®-TR) (4th ed.). Washington, DC: Author.

Baer, D. M., Wolf, M. M., & Risley, T. R. (1968). Some current dimensions of applied behavior analysis. *Journal of Applied Behavior Analysis, 1,* 91–97.

Barnhill, G. P. (2001). What is Asperger syndrome? *Intervention in School and Clinic, 36,* 259–265.

Baron-Cohen, S. (2001). Theory of mind and autism: A review. In G. Lavaine Masters (Ed.), *International review of research in mental retardation.* New York: Academic Press.

Baron-Cohen, S., Cox, A., Baird, G., Swettenham, J., Nightingale, N., Morgan, K., Drew, A., & Charman, T. (1996). Psychological markers in the detection of autism in infancy in a large population. *The British Journal of Psychiatry, 168,* 158–163.

Begley, S., & Springen, K. (1996, May 13). Life in a parallel world: A bold new approach to the mystery of autism. *Newsweek,* p. 70.

Bondy, A., & Frost, L. (2002). *Topics in autism: A picture's worth. PECS and other visual communication strategies in autism.* Bethesda, MD: Woodbine House.

Burton, D. (2002, April 18). *The autism epidemic: Is the NIH and CDC response adequate?* Committee on Government Reform, Opening Statement, U.S. Congress.

Carpenter, J., Pennington, B. E., & Rogers, S. T. (2002). Interrelations among social-cognitive skills in young children with autism. *Journal of Autism and Developmental Disorders, 32,* 91–106.

Chadsey, J., & Beyer, S. (2001). Social relationships in the workplace. *Mental Retardation and Developmental Disabilities Research Reviews, 7,* 128–133.

Charlop-Christy, M. H., Carpenter, M., Le, L., LeBlanc, L. A., & Kellet, K. (2002). Using the picture exchange communication system (PECS) with children with autism: Assessment of PECS acquisition, speech, social-communicative behavior, and problem behavior. *Journal of Applied Behavior Analysis, 35,* 213–231.

Cowley, G., Brownell, G., & Footes, D. (2000, July 31). Parents wonder: Is it safe to vaccinate? *Newsweek,* p. 52.

Dawson, G., & Osterling, J. (1997). Early intervention in autism. In M. J. Guralnick, (Ed.), *The effectiveness of early intervention.* Baltimore, MD: Paul H. Brookes.

Dykens, E. M., Sutcliffe J. S., & Levitt, P. (2004). Autism and 15q11–q13 disorders: Behavioral, genetic, and pathophysiological issues. *Mental Retardation and Developmental Disabilities Research Reviews, 10,* 284–291.

Ferster, C. B., & DeMyer, M. K. (1961). The development of performances in autistic children in an automatically controlled environment. *Journal of Chronic Diseases, 13,* 312–345.

Fombonne, E. (1999). *Epidemiological findings on autism and related developmental disorders.* Paper presented at the First Workshop of the Committee on Educational Interventions for Children with Autism, National Research Council, Washington, DC.

Frost, L. A., & Bondy, A. S. (1994). *The picture exchange communication system training manual.* Cherry Hill, NJ: Pyramid Educational Consultants, Inc.

Garfinkle, A., & Kaiser, A. P. (2004). Communication. In C. H. Kennedy & E. Horn (Eds.), *Including students with severe disabilities.* Boston: Allyn and Bacon.

Garfinkle, A. N., & Schwartz, I. S., (2001). "Hey! I'm talking to you": A naturalistic procedure to teach preschool children to use their AAC systems with peers. In M. Ostorsky & S. Sandall (Eds.), *Young Exceptional Children Monograph Series: Teaching strategies No. 3.* Longmont, CO: Sporis West.

Getzel, M., & Wehman, P. (2004). *Going to college: Expanding opportunities for people with disabilities.* Baltimore, MD: Paul H. Brookes.

Gillum, H., & Camarata, S. (2004). Importance of treatment efficacy research on language comprehension in MR/DD research. *Mental Retardation and Developmental Disabilities Research Reviews, 10,* 201–207.

Handleman, J. S., & Harris, S. L. (2000). *Preschool education programs for children with autism.* Austin, TX: PRO-ED.

Harris, S. L., & Handleman, J. S. (1994). *Preschool education programs for children with autism.* Austin, TX: PRO-ED.

Hoyson, M., Jamieson, B., & Strain, P. (1984). Individualized group instruction of normally developing and autistic-like children: The LEAP curriculum model. *Journal of the Division of Early Childhood, 1,* 151–171.

Kanner, L. (1943). Autistic disturbances of affective contact. *Nervous Child, 2,* 217–250.

Kennedy, C. H. (2001). Social interaction interventions for youth with severe disabilities should emphasize interdependence. *Mental Retardation and Developmental Disabilities Research Reviews, 7,* 122–127.

Kennedy, C. H. (2002). The evolution of stereotypy into self-injury. In S. Schroeder, M. L. Oster-Granite, & T. Thompson (Eds.), *Self-injurious behavior: Gene–brain–behavior relationships* (pp. 133–143). Washington, DC: American Psychological Association.

Kennedy, C. H., & Horn, E. (2004). *Including students with severe disabilities.* Boston: Allyn and Bacon.

Lewis, M. H., & Bodfish, J. W. (1998). Repetitive behavior disorders in autism. *Mental Retardation and Developmental Disabilities Research Reviews, 4,* 80–89.

Lord, C., Rutte, R. M., Goode, S., Heemsbergen, J., Jordan, H., Mawhood, L., & Schopler, E. (1989). Autism diagnostic observation schedule: A standardized observation of communicative and social behavior. *Journal of Autism and Developmental Disorders, 19,* 185–212.

Lord, C., & Schopler, E. (1994). TEACCH services for preschool children. In S. Harris & J. Handleman (Eds.), *Preschool education programs for children with autism.* Austin, TX: PRO-ED.

Lovaas, O. I. (1987). Behavioral treatment and normal educational and intellectual functioning in young autistic children. *Journal of Consulting and Clinical Psychology, 55,* 3–9.

Lovaas, O. I. (1993). The development of a treatment-research project for developmentally disabled and autistic children. *Journal of Applied Behavior Analysis, 26,* 617–630.

Mundy, P., & Neal, A. R. (2001). Neural plasticity, joint attention, and transactional social-orienting model of autism. In L. M. Glidden (Ed.), *International review of research in mental retardation: Autism,* (Vol. 23; pp. 139–168). San Diego: Academic Press.

National Research Council. (2001). *Educating children with autism.* Washington, DC: National Academy Press.

Newschaffer, C. J., Falb, M. D., & Gurney, J. G. (2005). National autism prevalence trends from United States special education data. *Pediatrics, 115,* 277–282.

Osterling, J., & Dawson, G. (1994). Early recognition of children with autism: A study of first birthday home videotapes. *Journal of Autism and Developmental Disorders, 24,* 247–257.

Park, C. C. (2001). *Exiting Nirvana: Daughter's life with autism.* Boston: Little, Brown.

Percy, A. K. (2001). Rett syndrome: Clinical correlates of the newly discovered gene. *Brain Development, 23,* Suppl 1, S202–205.

Polleux, F., & Lauder, J. M. (2004). Toward a developmental neurobiology of autism. *Mental Retardation and Developmental Disabilities Research Reviews, 10,* 303–317.

Powell, T. H., Hecimovic, A., & L. Christensen. (1992). Meeting the unique needs of families. In D. E. Befkell (Ed.), *Autism: Identification, education and treatment.* Hillsdale, NJ: Erlbaum.

Powers, M. D. (2000). What is autism? In M. D. Powers (Ed.), *Children with autism: A parent's guide.* Bethesda, MD: Woodbine House.

Raia, J. (2001, June 18). Autism doesn't slow this marathoner. *Los Angeles Times,* p. D7.

Ryndak, D., & Alper, S. (2003). *Curriculum and instruction for students with significant disabilities in inclusive settings* (2nd ed.). Boston: Allyn and Bacon.

Safran, S. P. (2001). Asperger syndrome: The emerging challenge to special education. *Exceptional Children, 67,* 151–160.

Schopler, E., Reicheler, J., DeVeillis, R. F., & Daly, K. (1980). Toward objective classification of childhood autism: Childhood Autism Rating Scale (CARS). *Journal of Autism and Developmental Disorders, 10,* 91–103.

Schwartz, I. S., Boulware, G. L., McBride, B. J., & Sandall, S. R. (2001). Functional assessment strategies for young children with autism. *Focus on Autism and Other Developmental Disabilities, 16,* 222–227.

Schwartz, I. S., Garfinkle, A. N., & Bauer, J. (1998). The picture exchange communication system: Communicative outcomes for young children with disabilities. *Topics in Early Childhood Special Education, 18,* 144–159.

Scott, J., Clark, C., & Brady, M. (2000). *Students with autism: Characteristics and instructional programming.* San Diego, CA: Singular Publishing Group.

Seroussi, K. (2000). *Unraveling the mysteries of autism and pervasive developmental disorder: A mother's story of research and recovery.* New York: Simon and Schuster.

Shienkopf, S. J., Mundy, P., Oller, D. K., & Steffens, M. (2000). Vocal atypicality of preverbal autistic children. *Journal of Autism and Developmental Disabilities, 30,* 345–354.

Smeeth, L., Cook, C., Fombonne, E., Heavey, L., Rodrigues, L. C., Smith, P. G., & Hall, A. J. (2004). MMR vaccination and pervasive developmental disorders: A case-control study. *Lancet, 364,* 963–969.

Sperry, V. W. (2001). *Fragile success: Ten autistic children, childhood to adulthood.* Baltimore, MD: Paul H. Brookes.

Stone, W. L., Coonrod, E. E., & Ousley, O. Y. (2000). Brief report: Screening tool for autism in two-year-olds (STAT): Development and preliminary data. *Journal of Autism and Developmental Disorders, 30,* 607–612.

Stone, W. L., & Yoder, P. J. (2001). Predicting spoken language level in children with autism spectrum disorders. *Autism, 5,* 341–361.

Strain, P. S., & Hoyson, M. (2000). The need for longitudinal, intensive social skill intervention: LEAP follow-up outcomes for children with autism. *Topics in Early Childhood Special Education, 20,* 116–122.

Sturmey, P., & Sevin, J. A. (1994). Defining and assessing autism. In J. L. Matson (Ed.), *Autism in children and adults: Etiology, assessment, and intervention* (pp. 13–36). Pacific Grove, CA: Brooks/Cole.

Talay-Ongan, A., & Wood, K. (2000). Unusual sensory sensitivities in autism: A possible crossroads. *International Journal of Disability, Development and Education, 47,* 201–212.

Tanguay, P. E., Robertson, J., & Derrick, A. (1998). A dimensional classification of autism spectrum disorder by social communication domains. *Journal of the American Academy of Child and Adolescent Psychiatry, 37,* 271–277.

Thiemann, K. S., & Goldstein, H. (2001). Social stories, written text cues, and video feedback: Effects on social communication of children with autism. *Journal of Applied Behavior Analysis, 34,* 425–446.

Tidmarsh, L., & Volkmar, F. R. (2003). Diagnosis and epidemiology of autism spectrum disorders. *Canadian Journal of Psychiatry, 48,* 517–525.

U.S. Department of Education. (2005a). Assistance to states for the education of children with disabilities program and the early intervention program for infants and toddlers with disabilities; proposed regulations. *Federal Register,* 64 (48), CFR Parts 300 and 303.

U.S. Department of Education. (2005b). *Children served under IDEA, Part B (2003),* Data Tables. **www.ideadata.org**

Walker, D. R., Thompson, A., Zwaigenbaum, L., Goldberg, J., Bryson, S. E., Mahoney, W. J., Strawbridge, C. P., & Szatmari, P. (2004). Specifying PDD-NOS: A comparison of PDD-NOS, Asperger syndrome, and autism. *Journal of the American Academy of Child and Adolescent Psychiatry, 43,* 172–180.

Wehman, P. (2000). *Life beyond the classroom: Transition strategies for young people with disabilities* (3rd ed.). Baltimore, MD: Paul H. Brookes.

Wetherby, A. M., & Prizant, B. M. (2005). Enhancing language and communication development in autism spectrum disorders: Assessment and intervention guidelines. In D. Zager (Ed.), *Autism spectrum disorders: Identification, education, and treatment* (3rd ed., pp. 327–365). Mahwah, NJ: Erlbaum.

CHAPTER 13

Very Low Incidence Disabilities

Baldwin, V. (1995). *Annual Deaf-Blind Census.* Monmouth, OR: Teaching Research, Western Oregon State College.

Barnes, S. B., & Whinnery, K. W. (2002). Effects of functional mobility skills training for young students with physical disabilities. *Exceptional Children, 68,* 313–324.

Boeck, S. (1998, November 4). Blind, deaf triathelete honored. USA *Today Sports Section,* p. C3.

Bos, C., & Anders, P. L. (1992). Using interactive teaching and learning strategies to promote text comprehension and content learning for students with learning disabilities. *International Journal of Disability, Development and Education, 39,* 225–238.

Briggs, K. (2005). *Alternate achievement standards for students with the most significant cognitive disabilities: Non-regulatory guidance.* Washington, DC: U.S. Department of Education.

Browder, D., Flowers, C., Ahlgrim-Delzell, L., Karvonen, M., Spooner, F., & Algozzine, R. (2004). The alignment of alternate assessment content with academic and functional curricula. *The Journal of Special Education, 37,* 211–223.

Brown, D., & Bates, E. (2005). A personal view of changes in the deaf-blind population, philosophy, and needs. *Deaf-Blind Perspectives, 12,* 1–5.

Bruns, D. A. (2000). Leaving home at an early age: Parents' decisions about out-of-home placement for young children with complex medical needs. *Mental Retardation, 38,* 50–60.

Bryant, D. P., & Bryant, B. R. (2003). *Assistive technology for people with disabilities.* Boston: Allyn and Bacon.

Buckley, W. L. (1999–2000). Computers in our classrooms. *Deaf-Blind Perspectives, 7,* 1–7.

Carnes, S., & Barnard, S. (2003). Oregon deafblind project intervener training program. *Deaf-Blind Perspectives, 10,* 1–3.

Centers for Disease Control (CDC), National Center on Birth Defects and Developmental Disabilities. (2004). *Developmental Disabilities,* 1–4. Retrieved August 7, 2005, from **www.cdc.gov/cnbdd/dd/default.htm#publications**

Charles, E. (2005, May 15). Apartments for a special clientele. *New York Times,* In the Region, Connecticut. Retrieved May 15, 2005, from **www.NewYorkTimes.com**

Chen, D., Alsop, L., & Minor, L. (2000). Lessons from project PLAI in California and Utah: Implications for early intervention services to infants who are deaf-blind and their families. *Deaf-Blind Perspectives, 7,* 1–4.

Chen, D., Downing, J., & Rodriguez-Gil, G. (2000–2001). Tactile learning strategies for children who are deaf-blind: Concerns and considerations from Project SALUTE. *Deaf-Blind Perspectives, 8,* 1–6.

Children's Defense Fund (CDF). (2004). *The state of America's children: 2004.* Washington, DC: Author.

Condon, K. A., & Tobin, T. J. (2001). Using electronic and other new ways to help students improve their behavior: Functional behavioral assessment at work. *Teaching Exceptional Children, 34,* 44–51.

DB-Link (2005). *National deaf-blind census.* Monmouth, OR: DB Link, National Technical Assistance Consortium for Children and Youth Who Are Deaf-Blind. Teaching Research, Western Oregon University. Retrieved August 14, 2005, from **www.tr.wou.edu/ntac/census.htm**

Dell-Orto, A. E., & Power, P. W. (1997). *Head injury and the family: A life and living perspective.* Boca Raton, FL: GR/St. Lucie Press.

Education Weekly. (2004, January 8). Special education in an era of standards, count me in, quality counts. *Education Week, 23,* 1–154.

ERIC Clearinghouse on Disabilities and Gifted Education. (2001). *Educating exceptional children: A statistical profile.* Arlington, VA: The Council for Exceptional Children.

Haring, N. G., & Romer, L. T. (Eds.). (1995). *Welcoming students who are deaf-blind into typical classrooms: Facilitating school participation, learning, and friendships.* Baltimore, MD: Paul H. Brookes.

HEATH. (2005). *Students who are deaf or hard of hearing in postsecondary education.* Washington, DC: American Council on Education (ACE), HEATH Resource Center. Retrieved August 25, 2005, from **www.heath-resource-center.org**

Heller, K. W., & Kennedy, C. (1994). *Etiologies and characteristics of deaf-blindness.* Monmouth, OR: Teaching Research Publications.

Holburn, S., & Vietze, P. M. (2002). *Person-centered planning.* Baltimore, MD: Paul H. Brookes.

Holcomb, M., & Wood, S. (1989). *Deaf woman: A parade through the decades.* Berkeley, CA: DawnSignPress.

Hughes, C. (2001). Transition to adulthood: Supporting young adults to access social, employment, and civic pursuits. *Mental Retardation and Developmental Disabilities Research Reviews, 7,* 84–90.

Johnson, L. (2005). First, do no harm: An argument against mandatory high-stakes testing for students with intellectual disabilities. *Mental Retardation, 43,* 292–298.

Kangas, K. A., & Lloyd, L. L. (2006). Augmentative and alternative communication. In N. B. Anderson and G. H. Shames (Eds.), *Human communication disorders: An introduction* (7th ed.) (pp. 436–470). Boston: Allyn and Bacon.

Kennedy, C. H., & Horn, E. (2004). *Including students with severe disabilities.* Boston: Allyn and Bacon.

Kennedy, C. H., Long, T., Jolivette, K., Cox, J., Tang, J. C., & Thompson, T. (2001). Facilitating general education participation for students with behavior problems by linking positive behavior supports and person-centered planning. *Journal of Emotional and Behavioral Disorders, 9,* 161–171.

Koegel, R. L., Koegel, L. K., Frea, W. D., & Smith, A. E. (1995). Emerging interventions of children with autism: Longitudinal and lifestyle implications. In R. L. Koegel and L. K. Koegel (Eds.), *Teaching children with autism: Strategies for initiating positive interactions and improving learning opportunities.* Baltimore, MD: Paul H. Brookes.

Lash, M., & DePompei, R. (2002). *Kids corner.* Available from the Brain Injury Association of America. Retrieved August 31, 2002, from **www.biausa.org/children.htm**

Lohrmann-O'Rourke, S., & Gomez, O. (2001). Integrating preference assessment within the transition process to create meaningful school-to-life outcomes. *Exceptionality, 9,* 157–174.

Luckasson, R., Borthwick-Duffy, S., Buntinx, W. H. E., Coulter, D. L., Craig, E. M., Reeve, A., Schalock, R. L., Snell, M. E., Spitalnik, D. M., Spreat, S., & Tassé, M. J. (2002). *Definition of mental retardation.* Washington, DC: American Association on Mental Retardation (AAMR).

Luckasson, R., Coulter, D. L., Polloway, E. A., Reis, S., Schalock, R. L., Snell, M. E., Spitalnik, D. M., & Stark, J. A. (1992). *Mental retardation: Definition, classification, and systems of supports.* Washington, DC: American Association on Mental Retardation (AAMR).

March of Dimes. (2002). *Health library: Infant health statistics.* Retrieved September 1, 2002, from **www.modimes.org/HealthLibrary/344_1361.htm**

March of Dimes Perinatal Data Center. (2001). *Maternal, infant, and child health in the United States, 2001.* Retrieved August 31, 2002, from **www.modimes.org/HealthLibrary/334_598.htm**

Markowitz, J., & Linehan, P. (2001, January). *Quick turn around: Traumatic brain injury.* Washington, DC: Project Forum at NASDSE.

McCormick, L., & Wegner, J. (2003). Supporting augmentative communication. In L. McCormick, D. F. Loeb, and R. L. Shiefelbusch (Eds.), *Supporting children with communication difficulties in inclusive settings: School-based language intervention* (pp. 435–460). Boston: Allyn and Bacon.

McDonnell, J. J., Hardman, M. L., & McDonnell, A. P. (2003). *Introduction to persons with moderate and severe disabilities: Educational and social issues* (2nd ed.). Boston: Allyn and Bacon.

McNeill, J. (2005, August 17). Famed father–son "Team Hoyt" to compete at marathon of the Palm Beaches. *Running Cool.* Retrieved August 25, 2005, from **www.coolrunning.com/engine/3/3_4/famed-fatherson-team-hoyt.shtml**

McWilliams, R. A., Wolery, M., & Odom, S. L. (2001). Instructional perspectives in inclusive preschool classrooms. In M. J. Guralnick (Ed.), *Early childhood inclusion: Focus on change* (pp. 503–530). Baltimore, MD: Paul H. Brookes.

Melancon, F. (2000). A group for students with Usher syndrome in South Louisiana. *Deaf-Blind Perspectives, 8,* 1–3.

Michaud, L. J., Semel-Concepcion, J., Duhaime, A-C., & Lazar, M.F. (2002). Traumatic brain injury. In M. L. Batshaw (Ed.), *Children with disabilities* (5th ed.). Baltimore, MD: Paul H. Brookes.

Miles, B. (2005, January). *Overview on deaf-blindness.* Retrieved August 29, 2005, from **www.dblink.org/lib/overview.htm**

Müller, E., & Markowitz, J. (2004). *Disability categories: State terminology, definitions & eligibility criteria.* Washington, DC: Project Forum, National Association of State Directors of Special Education (NASDSE).

Nall, S. (2002). *It's only a mountain: Dick and Rick Hoyt, men of iron* (2nd ed.). Holland, MA: Dick Hoyt.

National Institute on Deafness and Other Communication Disorders (NIDCD). (2003). *Usher syndrome.* Washington, DC: National Institutes of Health. Retrieved September 2, 2005, from **www.nidcd.nih.gov/health/hearing/usher.asp**

National Institute of Neurological Disorders and Stroke. (2005). *NINDS traumatic brain injury information page.* Washington, DC: National Institutes of Health. Retrieved September 2, 2005, from **www.ninds.nih.gov/disorders/tbi/tbi.htm**

National Research Council. (2004). *Keeping score for all: The effects of inclusion and accommodation policies on large-scale educational assessments.* Washington, DC: The National Academies Press.

NICHCY. (2001). *Severe and/or multiple disabilities.* Washington, DC: National Information Center for Children and Youth with Disabilities.

NICHCY. (2004a). *Severe and/or multiple disabilities.* Fact Sheet 10. Washington, DC: National Dissemination Center for Children with Disabilities. Retrieved August 30, 2005, from **www.nichcy.org**

NICHCY. (2004b). *Traumatic brain injury.* Fact Sheet 18. Washington, DC: National Dissemination Center for Children with Disabilities. Retrieved August 31, 2005, from **www.nichcy.org**

Noonan, M. J., & Siegel, E. B. (2003). Special needs of students with severe disabilities or autism. In L. McCormick, D. F. Loeb, and R. L. Shiefelbusch (Eds.), *Supporting children with communication difficulties in inclusive settings: School-based language intervention* (pp. 409–434). Boston: Allyn and Bacon.

Office of Special Education Programs (OSEP). (2000). Applying positive behavioral support in schools. *Twenty-second annual report to Congress on the implementation of the Individuals with Disabilities Education Act* (pp. III-7 through III-31). Washington, DC: U.S. Department of Education.

Olson, J. (2004). Intervenor training. *Deaf-Blind Perspectives, 12,* 1–5.

Owens, Jr., R. E. (2001). *Language disorders: A functional approach to assessment and intervention* (5th ed.). Columbus, OH: Merrill.

Palmer, D. S., Fuller, K., Arora, T., & Nelson, M. (2001). Taking sides: Parent views on inclusion for their children with severe disabilities. *Exceptional Children, 67,* 467–484.

Pittleman, S. D., Heimlich, J. E., Berglund, R. L., & French, M. P. (1991). *Semantic feature analysis: Classroom applications.* Newark, DE: International Reading Association.

Rafferty, Y., Piscitelli, V., & Boettcher, C. (2003). The impact of inclusion on language development and social competence among preschoolers with disabilities. *Exceptional Children, 69,* 467–479.

Reichle, J., Beukelman, D. R., & Light, J. C. (2002). *Exemplary practices for beginning communicators: Implications for ACC.* Baltimore, MD: Paul H. Brookes.

Schweinhart, L. J. (2005). *The High/Scope Perry Preschool study through age 40: Summary, conclusions, and frequently asked questions.* Ypsilanti, MI: High/Scope Educational Research Foundation. Retrieved June 17, 2005, from **www.highscope.org**

Scott, T. M., Liaupsin, C. J., Nelson, C. M., & Jolivette, K. (2003). Ensuring student success through team-based functional behavioral assessment. *Teaching Exceptional Children, 35,* 16–21.

Smith, D. D. (2001). *Introduction to special education: Teaching in an age of opportunity.* Boston: Allyn and Bacon.

Snell, M. E., & Janney, R. E. (2000). Teachers' problem-solving about children with moderate and severe disabilities in elementary classrooms. *Exceptional Children, 66,* 472–490.

Strain, P. S., & Timm, M. A. (1998). *The early childhood intervention study.* Nashville, TN: Regional Intervention Project (RIP). Unpublished paper.

Strauss, A., & Lehtinen, L. (1947). *Psychopathology and education of the brain-injured child.* New York: Grune & Stratton.

Stremel, K., Bixler, B., Morgan, S., & Layton, K. (2002). *Communication fact sheets for parents.* Monmouth, OR: National Technical Assistance Consortium for Children and Young Adults Who Are Deaf-Blind (NTAC).

Stuart, C. H., & Smith, S. W. (2002). Transition planning for students with severe disabilities: Policy implications for the classroom. *Intervention in School and Clinic, 37,* 234–236.

Sugai, G., & Horner, R. H. (1999). Discipline and behavior support: Preferred procedures and practices. *Effective School Practices, 17,* 10–22.

Sugai, G., Horner, R. H., Dunlap, G., Hieneman, M., Lewis, T. J., Nelson, C. M., Scott, T., Liaupsin, C., Sailor, W., Turnbull, A. P., Turnbull, R. H., Wickham, D., Ruef, M., & Wilcox, B. (1999, December). *Applying positive behavioral support and functional behavioral assessment in schools.* Washington, DC: OSEP Center on Positive Behavioral Interventions and Support.

TASH. (2000a). *TASH resolution on deinstitutionalization.* Baltimore, MD: Author. Resolution originally adopted October 1979; revised November 1999 and March 2000. Available at **www.tash.org/resolutions/res02deinstitut.htm**

TASH. (2000b). *TASH resolution on the people for whom TASH advocates.* Baltimore, MD: Author. Definition originally adopted April 1975; revised December 1985 and March 2000. Available at **www.tash.org/resolutions/R21PEOPL.html**

Thurlow, M. L., House, A. L., Scott, D. L., & Ysseldyke, J. E. (2000). Students with disabilities in large-scale assessments: State participation and accommodation policies. *Journal of Special Education, 34,* 154–163.

U.S. Department of Education (2000). *Characteristics of children and families entering early intervention (pp. IV-1 through IV-13). Twenty-second annual report to Congress on the implementation of the Individuals with Disabilities Education Act.* Washington, DC: U. S. Government Printing Office.

U.S. Department of Education. (2005a). *Children served under IDEA, Part B (2003),* Data Tables. **www.ideadata.org**

U.S. Department of Education. (2005b). Assistance to states for the education of children with disabilities program and the early intervention program for infants and toddlers with disabilities; proposed regulations. *Federal Register,* 34, CRF Parts 300, 301, and 304.

Van Kuren, L. (2001). Traumatic brain injury—the silent epidemic. *CEC Today, 7,* 1, 5, 15.

Whinnery, K. W., & Barnes, S. B. (2002). Mobility training using the MOVE curriculum: A parent's view. *Teaching Exceptional Children, 34,* 44–50.

Ziegler, D. (2002). *Reauthorization of the Elementary and Secondary Education Act: No Child Left Behind Act of 2001.* Arlington, VA: The Council for Exceptional Children, Public Policy Unit.

CHAPTER 14

Giftedness and Talent Development

Antrop-González, R., Vélez, W., & Garrett, R. (2003). Challenging the academic (mis)categorization of urban youth: Building a case for Puerto Rican high achievers. *Multiple Voices, 7,* 16–32.

Baldus, C. (2003). Gifted education in rural schools. In J. A. Castellano (Ed.), *Special populations in gifted education: Working with diverse gifted learners* (pp. 163–176). Boston: Allyn and Bacon.

Baum, S. (Ed.) (2004a). *Twice exceptional and special populations of gifted students.* Thousand Oaks, CA: Corwin Press and the National Association for Gifted Children.

Baum, S. (2004b). Introduction to twice-exceptional and special populations of gifted students. In S. Baum (Ed.), *Twice exceptional and special populations of gifted students.* Thousand Oaks, CA: Corwin Press and the National Association for Gifted Children.

Belcastro, F. P. (2002). Electronic technology and its use with rural gifted students. *Roeper Review, 25,* 14–16.

Benbow, C. P., & Stanley, J. C. (1996). Inequity in equity: How "equity" can lead to inequity for high-potential students. *Psychology, Public Policy, and Law, 2,* 249–292.

Bernal, E. (2002). Three ways to achieve a more equitable representation of culturally and linguistically different students in gt programs. *Roeper Review, 24,* 82–88.

Bernal, E. M. (2003). To no longer educate the gifted: Programming for gifted students beyond the era of inclusionism. *Gifted Child Quarterly, 47,* 183–191.

Binet, A., & Simon, T. (1905). Méthodes nouvelles pour le diagnostic du niveau intellectual des anormaux. *L'Année psychologique, 11,* 191–336.

Brice, A., & Brice, R. (2004). Identifying Hispanic gifted children: A screening. *Rural Special Education Quarterly, 23,* 8–15.

Brody, L. E., & Benbow, C. P. (1986). Social and emotional adjustment of adolescents extremely talented in verbal or mathematical reasoning. *Journal of Youth and Adolescence, 15,* 1–18.

Brown, S. W., Renzulli, J. S., Gubbins, E. G., Siegle, D., Zhang, W., & Chen, C-H. (2005). Assumptions underlying the identification of gifted and talented students. *Gifted Child Quarterly, 49,* 68–79.

Castellano, J. A. (2002). Renavigating the waters: The identification and assessment of culturally and linguistically diverse students for gifted and talented education. In J. A. Castellano and E. I. Díaz (Eds.). *Reaching new horizons: Gifted and talented education for culturally and linguistically diverse students* (pp. 94–116). Boston: Allyn and Bacon.

Castellano, J. A. (Ed.) (2003). *Special populations in gifted education: Working with diverse gifted learners.* Boston: Allyn and Bacon.

Chae, P. K., Kim, J-H, & Noh, K-S. (2003). Diagnosis of ADHD among gifted children in relation to KEDI-WISC and T.O.V.A performance. *Gifted Child Quarterly, 47,* 192–201.

Clark, B. (2002). *Growing up gifted: Developing the potential of children at home and school* (6th ed). Upper Saddle River, NJ: Prentice-Hall.

Colangelo, N., Assouline, S., & Gross, M. (2004). *A nation deceived: How schools hold back America's brightest students* (Vol. 1). Iowa City: University of Iowa.

Coleman, L. J. (2001). A "rag quilt": Social relationships among students in a special high school. *Gifted Child Quarterly, 45,* 164–173.

Coleman, L. J. (2004). Is consensus on a definition in the field possible, desirable, necessary? *Roeper Review, 27,* 10–11.

Cooper, E. E., Ness, M., & Smith, M. (2004). A case study of a child with dyslexia and spatial-temporal gifts. *Gifted Child Quarterly, 48,* 83–94.

Cornell, D. G., Delcourt, M. A. B., Goldberg, M. D., & Bland, L. C. (1995). Achievement and self-concept of minority students in elementary school gifted programs. *Journal for the Education of the Gifted, 18,* 189–209.

Corwin, M. (2001). *And still we rise: The trials and triumphs of twelve gifted inner-city students.* New York: HarperCollins.

Council of State Directors of Programs for the Gifted and National Association of Gifted Children (NACG). (2003). *State of the states: Gifted and talented education report 2001–2002.* Washington, DC: National Association for Gifted Children.

Cramond, B. (2004). Can we, should we, need we agree on a definition of giftedness? *Roeper Review, 27,* 15–16.

Davis, G. A., & Rimm, S. B. (2004). *Education of the gifted and talented* (6th ed.). Boston: Allyn and Bacon.

Dixon, F. A., Lapsley, D. K., & Hanchon, T. A. (2004). An empirical typology of perfectionism in gifted adolescents. *Gifted Child Quarterly, 48,* 95–106.

Dole, S. (2000). The implication of the risk and resilience literature for gifted students with learning disabilities. *Roeper Review, 23,* 91–96.

Ford, D. Y., Grantham, T. C., & Harris, J. J. (1996). Multicultural gifted education: A wakeup call to the profession. *Roper Review, 19,* 72–78.

Ford, D. Y., & Harris, J. J. (1999). *Multicultural gifted education.* New York: Teachers College Press.

Ford, D. Y., & Harris, J. J. (2000). A framework for infusing multicultural curriculum into gifted education. *Roper Review, 23,* 4–10.

Ford, D., Harris III, J., Tyson, C., & Trotman, T. (2002). Beyond deficit thinking: Providing access for gifted African American students. *Roeper Review, 24,* 52–58.

Ford, D. Y., Howard, T. C., Hattis, J. J., & Tyson, C. A. (2000). Creating culturally responsive classrooms for gifted African American students. *Journal of Education of the Gifted, 23,* 397–427.

Freeman, J. (1994). Some emotional aspects of being gifted. *Journal for the Education of the Gifted, 17,* 180–197.

Freeman, J. (2003). Gender differences in gifted achievement in Britain and the U.S. *Gifted Child Quarterly, 47,* 202–211.

Gagné, F. (2004). An imperative, but, alas, improbable consensus. *Roeper Review, 27,* 12–14.

Gallagher, J. J. (2000). Unthinkable thoughts: Education of gifted students. *Gifted Child Quarterly, 44,* 5–12.

Gallagher, J. J., & Gallagher, S. A. (1994). *Teaching the gifted child* (4th ed.). Boston: Allyn and Bacon.

Gallagher, J., Harradine, C. C., & Coleman, M. R. (1997). Gifted students in the classroom: Challenge or boredom? Gifted students' views on their schooling. *Roeper Review, 19,* 132–136.

Gardner, H. (1983). *Frames of mind: Theory of multiple intelligences.* New York: Basic Books.

Gardner, H. (1993). *Multiple intelligences: The theory in practice.* New York: Basic Books.

Gardner, J. W. (1984). *Excellence: Can we be equal and excellent too?* (Rev. ed.). New York: Norton.

Gardynik, U. M., & McDonald, L. (2005). Implications of risk and resilience in the life of the individual who is gifted/learning disabled. *Roeper Review, 27,* 206–214.

Grantham, T. C. (2002). Underrepresentation in gifted education: How did we get here and what needs to change? *Roeper Review, 24,* 50–51.

Grantham, T. C. (2003). Increasing Black student enrollment in gifted programs: An exploration of the Pulaski County Special School District's advocacy efforts. *Gifted Child Quarterly, 47,* 46–65.

Grantham, T. C. (2004). Multicultural mentoring to increase Black male representation in gifted programs. *Gifted Child Quarterly, 48,* 232–245.

Grossman, L. (2005). The real-life boy wizard. *Time Magazine, 166,* 69.

Harmon, D. (2002). They won't teach me: The voices of gifted African American inner-city students. *Roeper Review, 24,* 68–75.

Harrison, C. (2004). Giftedness in early childhood: The search for complexity and connection. *Roeper Review, 26,* 78–84.

Hartigan, T. (2005, March 6). Young + brilliant blessed + cursed. *Boston Globe Magazine,* p. 34.

Hartnett, D. N., Nelson, J. M., & Rinn, A. N. (2004). Gifted or ADHD? The possibilities of misdiagnosis. *Roeper Review, 26,* 73–76.

Hébert, T. P. (1998). Gifted Black males in an urban high school: Factors that influence achievement and underachievement. *Journal for the Education of the Gifted, 21,* 385–414.

Hébert, T. P. (2001, June). Man to man: Building channels of communication between fathers and their talented sons. *Parenting for High Potential,* pp. 18–22.

Hébert, T. P, & Beardsley, T. (2001). Jermaine: A critical case study of a gifted Black child living in rural poverty. *Gifted Child Quarterly, 45,* 85–103.

Hébert, T. P., & Olenchak, F. R. (2000). Mentors for gifted underachieving males: Developing potential and realizing promises. *Gifted Child Quarterly, 44,* 196–207.

Higgins, K., & Boone, R. (2003). Beyond the boundaries of school: Transition considerations in gifted education. *Intervention in School and Clinic, 38,* 138–144.

Hoh, P-S. (2005). The linguistic advantage of the intellectually gifted child: An empirical study of spontaneous speech. *Roeper Review, 27,* 178–185.

Hunsaker, S. L. (1995). The gifted metaphor from the perspective of traditional civilizations. *Journal for the Education of the Gifted, 18,* 255–268.

Hunsaker, S. L., Finley, V. S., & Frank, E. L. (1997). An analysis of teacher nominations and student performance in gifted programs. *Gifted Child Quarterly, 41,* 19–24.

Jacob K. Javits Gifted and Talented Students Education Act of 1988 (PL 100-297).

Johnson, D. T. (2000). Teaching mathematics to gifted students in mixed-ability classrooms. *ERIC Digest,* E594. Reston, VA: ERIC Clearinghouse on Disabilities and Gifted Education, the Council for Exceptional Children.

Kanevsky, L., & Keighley, T. (2003). To produce or not to produce? Understanding boredom and the honor in underachievement. *Roeper Review, 26,* 20–28.

Kaplan, S. (2001). Building bridges: Teaching gifted emergent English-language learners. *Teaching for High Potential, 3,* 1–2.

Kirschenbaum, R. J. (1998). The creativity classification systems: An assessment theory. *Roeper Review, 21,* 20–26.

Kitano, M. K. (1997). Gifted Asian American women. *Journal for the Education of the Gifted, 21,* 3–37.

Kitano, M. K. (1998). Gifted Latina women. *Journal for the Education of the Gifted, 21,* 131–159.

Kitano, M., & DiJiosia, M. (2002). Are Asian and Pacific Americans overrepresented in programs for the gifted? *Roeper Review, 24,* 76–80.

Kitano, M., & Perkins, C. (2000). Gifted European American women. *Journal for the Education of the Gifted, 23,* 287–313.

Kloosterman, V., & Suranna, K. (2003). Gifted and talented females: The struggle for recognition. In J. A. Castellano (Ed.), *Special populations in gifted education: Working with diverse gifted learners.* Boston: Allyn and Bacon.

Kornhaber, M., Fierros, E., & Veenema, S. (2004). *Multiple intelligences: Best ideas from research to practice.* Boston: Allyn and Bacon.

Lubinski, D., & Benbow, C. P. (1995). Optimal development of talent: Respond educationally to individual differences in personality. *The Educational Forum, 59,* 381–392.

Maker, C. J. (1977). *Providing programs for the gifted handicapped.* Reston, VA: Council for Exceptional Children.

Maker, C. J. (1986). Education of the gifted: Significant trends. In R. J. Morris and B. Blatt (Eds.), *Special education: Research and trends* (pp. 190–221). New York: Pergamon.

Margolin, L. (1996). A pedagogy of privilege. *Journal for the Education of the Gifted, 19,* 164–180.

Marland, S. P., Jr. (1972). *Education of the gifted and talented. Vol. 1. Report to Congress of the United States by the U.S. Commissioner of Education.* Washington, DC: U.S. Government Printing Office.

Massé, L., & Gagné, F. (2002). Gifts and talents as sources of envy in high school settings. *Gifted Child Quarterly, 46,* 15–29.

McCoach, D. B., & Siegle, D. (2003). Factors that differentiate underachieving gifted students from high-achieving gifted students. *Gifted Child Quarterly, 47,* 144–154.

Mendez, L. (2000). Gender roles and achievement-related choices: A comparison of early adolescent girls in gifted and general education programs. *Journal for the Education of the Gifted, 24,* 149–169.

Montgomery, D. (2004). Broadening perspectives to meet the needs of gifted learners in rural schools. *Rural Special Education Quarterly, 23,* 3–7.

Mooij, T. (1999). Integrating gifted children into kindergarten by improving educational processes. *Gifted Child Quarterly, 43,* 63–74.

Moon, S., Swift, M., & Shallenberger, A. (2002). Perceptions of a self-contained class for fourth- and fifth-grade students with high to extreme levels of intellectual giftedness. *Gifted Child Quarterly, 46,* 64–79.

Moore III, J. L., Ford, D. Y., & Milner, H. R. (2005). Recruitment is not enough: Retaining African American students in gifted education. *Gifted Child Quarterly, 49,* 51–67.

Morelock, M. J., & Feldman, D. H. (1997). High IQ children, extreme precocity, and savant syndrome. In N. Colangelo and G. A. Davis (Eds.), *Handbook of gifted education* (2nd ed., pp. 439–459). Boston: Allyn and Bacon.

Morris, J. (2002). African American students and gifted education: The politics of race and culture. *Roeper Review, 24,* 59–62.

Muratori, M., Colangelo, N., & Assouline, S. (2003). Early-entrance students: Impressions of their first semester of college. *Gifted Child Quarterly, 47,* 219–238.

Naglieri, J. A., & Ford, D. Y. (2005). Increasing minority children's participation in gifted classes using the NNAT: A response to Lohman. *Gifted Child Quarterly, 49,* 29–36.

National Association for Gifted Children (NAGC). (2004). *Position Paper: Acceleration.* Retrieved September 8, 2005, from **www.nagc.org/policy/pp_acceleration.html**

National Association for Gifted Children (NAGC). (2005). *Funding for the Javits program in fiscal year 2006.* Retrieved September 6, 2005, from **www.nagc.org/policy/javits/javits_funding_FY2006.html**

National Research Council. (2002). *Minority students in special education and gifted education. Committee on Minority Representation in Special Education.* M. Suzanne Donovan and Christoper T. Cross, editors. Washington, DC: National Academy Press.

Neihart, M. (2000). Gifted children with Asperger's syndrome. *Gifted Child Quarterly, 44,* 222–230.

Neumeister, K. L. S. (2004a). Interpreting successes and failures: The influence of perfectionism on perspective. *Journal for the Education of the Gifted, 27,* 311–335.

Neumeister, K. L. S. (2004b). Understanding the relationship between perfectionism and achievement motivation in gifted college students. *Gifted Child Quarterly, 48,* 219–231.

Neumeister, K. L. S., & Hébert, T. P. (2003). Underachievement versus selective achievement: Delving deeper and discovering the difference. *Journal for the Education of the Gifted, 26,* 221–238.

Nichols, H. J., & Baum, S. (2000, December). High achievers: Keys to helping youngsters with stress reduction. *Parenting for High Potential,* pp. 9–12.

Nielsen, M. E. (2002). Gifted students with learning disabilities: Recommendations for identification and programming. *Exceptionality, 10,* 93–111.

Nielsen, M. E., Higgins, L. D., Hammond. A. E., & Williams, R. A. (1993). Gifted children with disabilities: The twice-exceptional child project. *Gifted Child Today, 16,* 9–12.

No Child Left Behind Act of 2001. PL 107–110. Reauthorization of the *Elementary and Secondary Education Act.*

Oden, M. H. (1968). The fulfillment of promise: 40-year follow-up of the Terman gifted group. *Genetic Psychology Monographs, 77,* 3–93.

Peterson, J. (2000). A follow-up study of one group of achievers and underachievers four years after high school graduation. *Roeper Review, 22,* 217–224.

Reid, C., Romanoff, B., Algozzine, B., & Udall, A. (2000). An evaluation of alternative screening procedures. *Journal for the Education of the Gifted, 23,* 378–396.

Reis, S. (2000, March). Overcoming barriers to girls' talent development. *Parenting for High Potential,* pp. 18–21.

Reis, S. (2003). Gifted girls, twenty-five years later: Hopes realized and new challenges found. *Roeper Review, 25,* 154–157.

Reis, S., & McCoach, D. B. (2000). The underachievement of gifted students: What do we know and where do we go? *Gifted Child Quarterly, 44,* 152–170.

Reis, S. M., McGuire, J. M., & Neu, T. W. (2000). Compensation strategies used by high-ability students with learning disabilities who succeed in college. *Gifted Child Quarterly, 44,* 123–134.

Reis, S., & Park, S. (2001). Gender differences in high-achieving students in math and science. *Journal for the Education of the Gifted, 25,* 52–73.

Renzulli, J. (1978). What makes giftedness? Reexamining a definition. *Phi Delta Kappan, 60,* 180–184, 261.

Renzulli, J. S. (1999). A rising tide lifts all ships: Developing the gifts and talents of all students. *Phi Delta Kappan, 80,* 104–111.

Renzulli, J. S. (2004). The myth: The gifted constitute 3–5% of the population. In J. S. Renzulli (Ed.), *Identification of students for gifted and talented programs.* Thousand Oaks, CA: Corwin Press and the National Association for Gifted Children.

Renzulli, J. S. & Park, S. (2000). Gifted dropouts: The who and the why. *Gifted Child Quarterly, 44,* 261–271.

Renzulli, J. S., & Park, S. (2002). *Giftedness and high school dropouts: Personal, family, and school-related factors.* (RM02168) Storrs, CT: the National Research Center on the Gifted and Talented, University of Connecticut.

Renzulli, J. S., & Reis, S. M. (1997). The schoolwide enrichment model: New directions for developing high-end learning. In N. Colangelo and G. A. Davis (Eds.), *Handbook of gifted education* (2nd ed., pp. 136–154). Boston: Allyn and Bacon.

Rimm, S. (2001, December). Parents as role models and mentors. *Parenting for High Potential,* pp. 14–15, 27.

Rimm, S., & Rimm-Kaufman, S. (2001). *How Jane won: 55 successful women share how they grew from ordinary girls to extraordinary women.* New York: Crown Publishers.

Robinson, S. M. (1999). Meeting the needs of students who are gifted and have learning disabilities. *Intervention in School and Clinic, 34,* 195–204.

Roeper, A. (2003). The young gifted girl: A contemporary view. *Roeper Review, 25,* 151–153.

Rogers, K. B. (1999). The lifelong productivity of the female researchers in Terman's genetic studies of genius longitudinal study. *Gifted Child Quarterly, 43,* 150–169.

Rogers, K. B. (2002). Grouping the gifted and talented: Questions and answers. *Roeper Review, 24,* 102–107.

Rogers, K. B. (2003). *Reforming gifted education: How parents and teachers can match the program to the child.* Scottsdale, AZ: Great Potential Press.

Roid, G. H. (2003). *Stanford-Binet Intelligence Scales* (5th ed.). Itasca, IL: Riverside.

Sapon-Shevin, M. (1996). Beyond gifted education: Building a shared agenda for school reform. *Journal for the Education of the Gifted, 19,* 192–214.

Schroeder-Davis, S. (1998). Parenting high achievers: Swimming upstream against the cultural current. *Parenting for High Potential,* pp. 8–10.

Schweinhart, L. J. (2005). *The High/Scope Perry Preschool study through age 40: Summary, conclusions, and frequently asked questions.* Ypsilanti, MI: High/Scope Educational Research Foundation. Retrieved June 17, 2005, from **www.highscope.org**

Scott, M. S., & Delgado, C. F. (2005). Identifying cognitively gifted minority students in preschool. *Gifted Child Quarterly, 49,* 199–210.

Shapka, J. D., & Keating, D. P. (2003). Effects of a girls-only curriculum during adolescence: Performance, persistence, and engagement in mathematics and science. *American Educational Research Journal, 40,* 929–960.

Shaywitz, S. E., Holahan, J. M., Fletcher, J. M., Freudenheim, D. A., Makuch, R. W., & Shaywitz, B. A. (2001). Heterogeneity within the gifted: Higher IQ boys exhibit behaviors resembling boys with learning disabilities. *Gifted Child Quarterly, 45,* 16–23.

Silverman, L. (1992). Leta Stetter Hollingworth: Champion of the psychology of women and gifted children. *Journal of Educational Psychology, 84,* 20–27.

Silverman, L. (2005). *What we have learned about gifted children.* Denver, CO: Gifted Development Center. Retrieved August 8, 2005, from **www.gifteddevelopment.com**

Simonton, D. K. (1997). When giftedness becomes genius: How does talent achieve eminence? In N. Colangelo and G. A. Davis (Eds.), *Handbook of gifted education* (2nd ed., pp. 335–349). Boston: Allyn and Bacon.

Slavin, R. E. (1990). Ability grouping, cooperative learning and the gifted. *Journal for the Education of the Gifted, 14,* 3–8.

Smutny, J. F. (2000, May). Teaching young gifted children in the regular classroom. (Report No. E595-EDO-EC-00-4). *ERIC Digest,* Reston, VA: The Council for Exceptional Children.

Stamps, L. S., (2004). The effectiveness of curriculum compacting in first grade classrooms. *Roeper Review, 27,* 31–41.

Stanford, P. (2003). Multiple intelligence in every classroom. *Intervention in School and Clinic, 39,* 80–85.

Sternberg, R. J. (2000). Patterns of giftedness: A triarchic analysis. *Roeper Review, 22,* 231–235.

Strom, R. D. (2000, March). Too busy to play? *Parenting for High Potential,* pp. 18–22.

Swiatek, M., & Lupkowski-Shoplik, A. (2000). Gender differences in academic attitudes among gifted elementary school students. *Journal for the Education of the Gifted, 23,* 360–377.

Terman, L. (1925). *Genetic studies of genius* (Vol. 1). Stanford, CA: Stanford University Press.

Terman, L. M., & Oden, M. H. (1959). *The gifted group at midlife.* Stanford, CA: Stanford University Press.

Tomlinson, C. A. (2004a). Introduction to differentiation for gifted and talented students. In C. A. Tomlinson (Ed.), *Differentiation for gifted and talented students.* Thousand Oaks, CA: Corwin Press and the National Association for Gifted Children.

Tomlinson, C. A. (Ed.). (2004b). *Differentiation for gifted and talented students.* Thousand Oaks, CA: Corwin Press and the National Association for Gifted Children.

Tornatzky, L. G., Pachon, H. P., & Torres, C. (2003). *Closing achievement gaps: Improving educational outcomes for Hispanic children.* Los Angeles: The Center for Latino Educational Excellence, The Tomás Rivera Policy Institute, University of Southern California.

Van Tassel-Baska, J. (2004). *The acceleration of gifted students' programs and curricula.* Waco, TX: Fastback Series, Prufrock Press.

Van Tassel-Baska, J., & Stambaugh, T. (2006). *Comprehensive curriculum for gifted learners* (3rd ed.). Boston: Allyn and Bacon.

Williams, P. E., Weiss, L. G., & Rolfhus, E. (2003). *Wechsler Intelligence Scale for Children IV (WISC-IV),* San Antonio, TX: Harcourt/Psychcorp.

Winebrenner, S. (2003). Teaching strategies for twice-exceptional students. *Intervention in School and Clinic, 38.* 131–137.

Zentall, S., Moon, S., Hall, A., & Grskovic, J. A. (2001). Learning and motivational characteristics of boys with AD/HD and/or giftedness. *Exceptional Children, 67,* 499–519.

Zirkel, P.A. (2005). State laws for gifted education: An overview of the legislation and regulations. *Roeper Review, 27,* 228–232.

Name Index

Subject Index

Note: Page numbers followed by the letters *f* or *t* represent figures and tables, respectively

B

D

E

F

G

H

W

X

Y